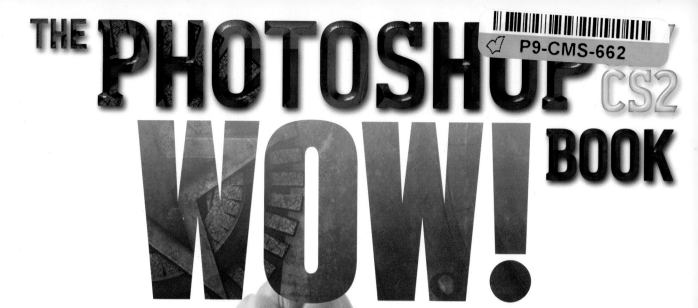

THE PHOTOSHOP CS2 WOW! BOOK

LINNEA DAYTON   **CRISTEN GILLESPIE**

Peachpit Press

The Photoshop CS/CS2 Wow! Book

Linnea Dayton & Cristen Gillespie

Wow! Series Editor: Linnea Dayton

Peachpit Press
1249 Eighth Street
Berkeley, CA 94710
(510) 524-2178
(510) 524-2221 (fax)

Find us on the Web at www.peachpit.com

To report errors, please send a note to errata@peachpit.com

Peachpit Press is a division of Pearson Education.

ISBN 0-321-21345-9

0 9 8 7 6 5 4 3 2 1

Printed and bound in the United States of America

MICHAL KORALEWSKI

Acknowledgments

Although for the first time in the 14-year history of this book Jack Davis's name is missing from the cover, evidence of Jack's larger-than-life talent, no-nonsense methodology, and generous collaboration are still found throughout the book and on the DVD-ROM. Like the previous ones, this edition would not have been possible without him.

We've had a great deal of support from others as well — photographers, designers, illustrators, and fine artists who have so generously allowed us to include their work and reveal their secrets. The "Artists & Photographers" appendix lists their names and tells where in the book their work can be found. Special thanks go to Donal Jolley, who designed and produced the cover for this edition, as well as some fantastic tutorial examples and "Gallery" images.

We appreciate the support of Adobe Systems, Inc., who allowed us to participate in the Photoshop beta program for authors. Our thanks also go to Stephanie Robie of PhotoSpin.com, Olga Zorina at iStockphoto, Inc., and Stephen French of Corbis Images, who let us include photos from their collections as essential parts of our tutorials.

We thank a stellar group of writers and illustrators who know and love Photoshop: Steven Gordon, for searching out and writing about new pieces for our Gallery sections; Victor von Salza, for researching and writing about Photoshop's relationship to other programs in the Adobe Creative Suite collections; Tim Plumer, for organizing and drafting the introduction to the "Web & Animation" chapter; Jan Kabili for providing the "Creating Remote Rollovers" section; and John Odam, Frankie Frey, and K & L Designs (Kelly Williamson and Lisa Schornack) for creating new artwork for our tutorials.

We thank Rod Golden of Adobe Systems, Heidi Jonk-Sommer, Jay Payne, and Garen Checkley, each of whom "beta-tested" some of our step-by-step tutorials.

And many thanks, as always, to Jonathan Parker, an absolutely essential part of the team, who once again made room in his design studio's schedule — much more room than he bargained for! — to do the production and prepress for this edition.

We'd like to thank our friends and colleagues at Peachpit Press, who have now supported us through 10 editions of *The Photoshop Wow! Book*. In particular, we thank publisher Nancy Ruenzel, associate publisher Keasley Jones, and editors Cary Norsworthy and Victor Gavenda for their continuing support; editor Becky Morgan, new to the project with this edition; design director Charlene Charles-Will, production experts Hilal Sala, Mimi Vitetta, Lupe Edgar, and Connie Jeung-Mills for getting the book to press; and media producer Eric Geoffroy for checking and engineering the DVD-ROM. Thanks also to freelancers Whitney Walker and Haig MacGregor for copyediting and proofreading. And much appreciation to Joy Dean Lee for preparing the index.

Over the course of this project, the day-in and day-out support of our families and friends — and *their* families and *their* friends — has been remarkable, and we feel extraordinarily lucky.

Finally, heartfelt thanks to those readers of previous editions who have let us know that *The Photoshop Wow! Book* has inspired as well as educated them, and to those who have just quietly used and appreciated it. Thanks also for pointing out where we could improve the book so all of us can continue to get the most "Wow!" from our favorite tool — Photoshop.

— *Linnea Dayton & Cristen Gillespie*

To Cristen Gillespie, Don Jolley, Jonathan Parker, and Rod Deutschmann. Your talent, enthusiasm, and perseverance are awe-inspiring.

— *Linnea*

To my kids, Kate and Adam, for being supportive through it all. I am eternally grateful.

— *Cristen*

Contents

On the Wow DVD-ROM

PS CS-CS2 Wow Presets • Wow Project Files • Wow Goodies

WELCOME TO
THE PHOTOSHOP CS/CS2 WOW! BOOK

ADOBE PHOTOSHOP (WITH IMAGEREADY) is one of the most powerful visual design and production tools ever to appear on the desktop. For print, for the web, or for anywhere else where photos or graphics appear, Photoshop is the standard for professional design, production, and organization. Adobe has now included Photoshop and ImageReady in its combined set, or "suite," of image-processing, graphics, page layout, and web software — first **Adobe Creative Suite** and now **Adobe Creative Suite 2**. The Photoshop-and-ImageReady duo is also still available as a separate product. Many of the most important changes in the Creative Suite and Creative Suite 2 versions are introduced in "What's New?" starting on page 6. (For brevity, we often refer to Photoshop CS and CS2 as simply "CS" and "CS2.")

The aim of *The Photoshop CS/CS2 Wow! Book* is to provide the kind of inspirational examples and practical "nuts-and-bolts" info that will help you maximize the performance of Photoshop and ImageReady and boost your own creativity with them. Its goal is to help you produce work that's better and faster, and easier to change or repurpose if you need to later. The book provides version-accurate instructions for both CS and CS2, and if you're still using version CS, the book will give you a look at what's to be gained from an upgrade.

PICTURE THIS . . .

You're the designer in charge of the annual report, and your client just handed you a (let's face it) boring photo or graphic that has to be included, "but give it some punch!" Or you're the photographer who shot the product, but now the client wants you to change the lighting, add something that wasn't there, "and make it sing!" Maybe you have to get an animated banner up on the company web site by Monday, update the online catalog by Tuesday, and "put in some of those remote rollovers."

Need a raft? A bigger boat? To get your sea legs before you set sail on Photoshop's ocean, take a look at the first four chapters. They provide a crash course in how Photoshop thinks.

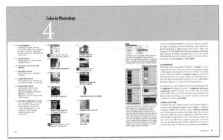

In the chapter introductions, learn the basics of how Photoshop works.

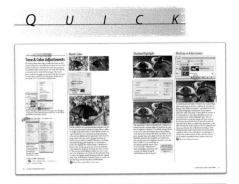

Each "Quick" section, such as the nine-page "Quick Tone & Color Adjustments" in Chapter 5, provides a short introduction and then several easy-to-grasp solutions. Many of the examples are supplied as layered files on the Wow DVD-ROM so you can learn by deconstructing them.

For more complex techniques, or to find out the "why" behind each step of the instructions, try the longer tutorials. Each one starts with an overview of the technique.

Or your doting Aunt Mary just handed you a precious but severely damaged family portrait — "You're good with the computer, dear. . ."

So Photoshop is launched and looking at you from your computer screen — a virtual *ocean* of tools, palettes, menu choices, and creative possibilities. Rest assured that you don't have to navigate the entire ocean to get the professional results you want. If you understand *a few Photoshop basics*, you'll have enough of a vessel under you to cruise off to any of the fabulous creative destinations in this book and beyond.

Like Photoshop itself, this book is an ideal tool for:

- **Photographers,** who need faster, easier ways to do the retouching, resizing, cropping, and basic color correction of their daily production work.

- Print-oriented **designers, illustrators,** and **fine artists,** whose professional horizons have been broadened by Photoshop and by the advances in digital photography.

- **Information architects** who are forging ahead, designing and creating on-screen imagery for the web and other interactive digital delivery systems.

Beyond that, *The Photoshop CS/CS2 Wow! Book,* along with its Wow DVD-ROM, supports creative people of all kinds who want to use the Photoshop-ImageReady laboratory for synthesizing textures, patterns, and all kinds of visual effects — from subtle to flamboyant — that can be applied to photos, graphics, type, or video. And it helps you automate many of these tasks — from routine production to complex special effects.

ANCHORS AWEIGH!

If you're new to Photoshop, you'll benefit from learning the "basics" in Chapters 1 through 4 of this book. Even if you're an old salt, already experienced with Photoshop, you might want to at least *skim* the first four chapters, just to see if there's anything helpful that you might not have encountered before.

With or without the basics under your belt, choose any technique in the book and sail forth confidently. The directions you need to get where you're going will be supplied in the step-by-step directions for the technique, though we recommend that you occasionally put into port for provisions by reading the few opening pages of the chapter you're working in.

EXERCISING

Each "Exercising" tutorial explores an especially useful part of the Photoshop interface, to familiarize you with its stunning capabilities.

ANATOMY OF

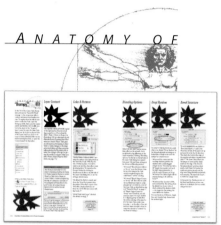

Each "Anatomy" section explores some kind of Photoshop construction. For instance, "Anatomy of 'Bumpy'" on page 522 analyzes the important components of a Layer Style that simulates a rusted-metal surface texture.

"Is It 'Real'? Or Is It Photoshop?" sections relate Photoshop to more traditional approaches to art and photography. And in "Secrets of the Universe Revealed" sections, look for novel approaches to using Photoshop.

Throughout the book, pointers like this one▼ and their **"Find Out More"** boxes will direct you if you want more information about something basic. But they're designed to be easy to ignore if you've mastered the basics and don't want to be interrupted.

FIND OUT MORE

▼ What is the Adobe Creative Suite?
page 6

If there's a deadline pressing, or if you simply want a *short* excursion into Photoshop, take a look at the techniques in the new **"Quick" sections**, where even beginners can get great results really quickly. On the other hand, when you have more time and you want to delve deeper, the longer **step-by-step tutorials** and the new **"Exercising"** and **"Anatomy" sections** are designed to help you explore some of the most useful, sometimes nearly hidden, gems in Photoshop, and to learn to "think like Photoshop," to become an expert at analyzing each Photoshop challenge that comes your way, and building the file you need to meet it.

You can also find **tips** throughout the book, like the one below, with the gray title bar on top. (The title bar is blue for tips that relate to Photoshop CS2 only.) The tips are nuggets of information that relate to the text nearby, but each one also stands on its own. You can quickly pick up a lot of useful information simply by flipping through the book and reading the tips.

You'll find a different kind of insight in **"Secrets of the Universe Revealed"** and **"Is It 'Real'? Or Is It Photoshop?"** New in this edition of the book, these "sidebars" provide the discoveries, some of them a bit off the beaten track, of other Photoshop users, who have been kind enough to share them with us.

Each chapter ends with a **"Gallery"** of inspirational real-world examples of outstanding work by Photoshop professionals. Extensive captions are packed with useful information about how the artwork was produced.

"SCRUBBING"

In Photoshop CS and CS2, you can change the value in many of the labeled fields in palettes and dialog boxes simply by clicking on the name of the field and "scrubbing" left or right. To change the value 10 times faster, hold down the Shift key as you scrub. Holding down the Ctrl/⌘ key while hovering the cursor directly over a numeric input box will also bring up the scrubber.

"Gallery" pages display the artwork large, and show how the artists arrived at their inspiring results.

At the very back of the book, you'll find **"Appendix" sections,** with visual examples of the wealth of goodies found in Photoshop itself or on the Wow DVD-ROM that comes with this book, along with tips and instructions for putting them to work. "Appendix D" lists artists and photographers whose work appears in the book.

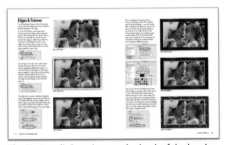

The "Appendix" sections at the back of the book serve as catalogs of the Adobe filters, as well as the Wow Layer Styles and other goodies from the Wow DVD-ROM that comes with this book. In addition, "Appendix D" has contact information for all the artists and photographers whose work appears in the book.

DON'T MISS THE WOW DVD-ROM!

The Wow DVD-ROM has **"before" and "after" files** for the step-by-step techniques, as well as finished files for the "Quick," "Exercising," and "Anatomy" sections, so you can compare as you build or deconstruct the projects in the book.

The DVD-ROM also holds the **Wow presets and Actions:**

- **Styles** that instantly transform photos, graphics, type, and web buttons with effects from subtle to spectacular
- **Tools** crafted especially for painting, image-editing, and cropping
- **Patterns** and **Gradients** to use as fills or layers or to incorporate into your own Styles
- **Actions** that automate many of the creative and production techniques covered in the book

BON VOYAGE!

This book will get you started "thinking like Photoshop" and using the tools if you're new at it, and it will give you some new insight and ideas if you're an old hand. Try out the tips, techniques, Styles, and Actions, and use them to set forth fearlessly toward your own Photoshop destinations.

The Wow Layer Styles, Tool Presets, Gradients, Patterns and Actions are designed to make your work easier — not to mention more spectacular. You'll find complete sets in the PS CS-CS2 Wow Presets folder on the Wow DVD-ROM, and individual presets in some of the tutorial sections in the Wow Project Files folder.

In the Wow Goodies folder on the DVD-ROM, you'll find the **Wow Shortcuts.pdf** file of useful time-and-effort-savers, to view on-screen or print out for reference.

INSTALLING WOW STYLES, PATTERNS, TOOLS & OTHER PRESETS

In Photoshop CS and CS2, installing presets couldn't be easier: **Drag the Wow Presets folder** from the Wow DVD-ROM **into the Presets folder** within your installed Adobe Photoshop CS or CS2 folder **A**. Now whenever you launch Photoshop, the program will find the Wow presets and automatically load them into the menus of the palettes and dialog boxes where they can be used.

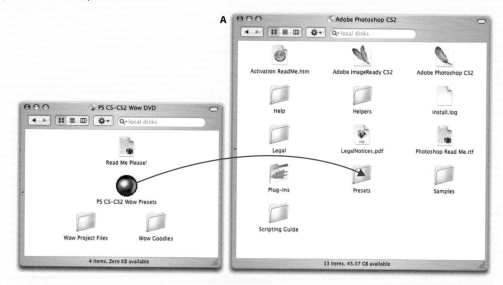

Unfortunately, **ImageReady** can't find presets unless they are inside the appropriate labeled folders inside Photoshop's main Presets folder. So, for the sake of ImageReady, carry out one more step in installing the **Wow Styles** presets, which are the only Wow presets you'll also use in ImageReady: Once the Wow Presets folder has been dragged into Photoshop's Presets folder, open Photoshop's Presets folder, and then open the Wow Presets folder and **drag the Wow Styles folder into Photoshop's Styles folder B**.

WHAT'S NEW IN PHOTOSHOP CS/CS2?

With Photoshop CS2 Adobe has provided several premade custom **Workspaces**, including one that highlights the new features of CS2. When you choose Window > Workspace > What's New, the new CS2 commands are highlighted in the menus so it's easy to see what's changed.

NOW PART OF ADOBE'S CREATIVE SUITE of print and web programs, versions CS and CS2 of Photoshop include some important new features, as well as impressive improvements to old ones. This section introduces some of the most important changes.

THE CREATIVE SUITE

The **Creative Suite** is Adobe's new approach to designing and selling its software tools. For both the CS and CS2 versions, the **Standard** edition of the Suite includes Photoshop (with ImageReady), Illustrator, InDesign, and Version Cue, which is software that can be used to track and control a project as it passes through various stages on its way to completion. The **Premium** package includes all of these as well as Acrobat Professional and GoLive. Also in each box are free Open Type fonts (in both CS and CS2). Both CS2 packages include Bridge, an improved standalone version of Photoshop CS's File Browser. Although Photoshop CS was sold separately from the rest of the Suite, and so is CS2, the full package offers ways to work with the applications together that are worth noting because they save time and effort. Briefly, here's what they offer:

- When you use Photoshop to design for the web, **moving into GoLive** (Adobe's aggregation tool for assembling web pages) gives you some advantages. Since no web browser can render a Photoshop file directly, the files must be converted to a web-ready format such as GIF or JPEG. GoLive, however, can accept a Photoshop file directly and automatically make the conversion. If you need to make a change later, all you do is open the Photoshop file, make the change, and save the file. GoLive does the rest of the work, re-creating the necessary GIF or JPEG.

- For print, Photoshop and **InDesign** now work together essentially the same way as Photoshop and GoLive do for the web. InDesign can handle native Photoshop (.psd) files,

InDesign's Links palette lists all the Photoshop files used in the InDesign file. Clicking the name of a linked image and then clicking the Edit Original button ✐ at the bottom of the palette opens the file in Photoshop. There you can edit and save it, with an automatic update to the InDesign file. Lance Hidy used this feature in creating a set of "save the date" stamps (page 148).

LANCE HIDY

as well as the TIFF and EPS formats accepted by other page layout applications.

- Photoshop and **Illustrator** were initially designed to create very different kinds of graphics, but they've grown in their shared capabilities over the years. With CS/CS2, as with each earlier upgrade, it's easier to move "live" artwork from one program into the other.

- Here are three ways Photoshop CS/CS2 users can take advantage of the interaction with **Acrobat Professional** or the free **Adobe Reader**: You can create a file in Photoshop that can be opened, viewed, and printed by people who don't have Photoshop; this can make it much easier to gather comments about the file in a proofing process. Even better, you can add electronic "sticky notes" to the file that will be visible in Acrobat or Reader. And if the recipients own Acrobat (not just the free Reader), they can even add sticky notes in response, saving paper and time. Beyond this, you can collect several Photoshop files into a multi-page PDF document, or even a self-running on-screen **PDF Presentation** "slide show," complete with a variety of transitions between slides.

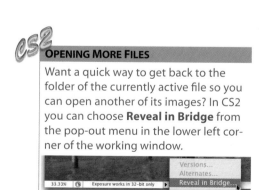

With Adobe Creative Suite 2 you can now paste Illustrator artwork into Photoshop as a "Smart Object." Smart Objects are introduced on page 8.

IMPROVEMENTS TO FILE MANAGEMENT & WORKFLOW
Photoshop has new and improved ways to manage the myriad files that Photoshop users accumulate, so we can be more creative and more efficient.

- A number of improvements, such as high-quality previews and drag-and-drop reordering make the **File Browser** (in CS) and **Bridge** (in CS2) more efficient.

OPENING MORE FILES

Want a quick way to get back to the folder of the currently active file so you can open another of its images? In CS2 you can choose **Reveal in Bridge** from the pop-out menu in the lower left corner of the working window.

PHOTOS: PETER CARLISLE

For easy access, a permanent button on the Options bar will launch the File Browser (in CS) or Bridge (in CS2). Both File Browser (shown here) and Bridge allow drag-and-drop reordering of images and batch renaming. See page 128 for more about these two interfaces for opening and managing files. Bridge has more viewing options than File Browser, including the chance to customize and save workspaces.

The **Edit History Log** is useful for recording data, such as settings for filters that aren't otherwise kept as part of the file. You can choose how much detail to record (see page 28), and you can view the History Log (as shown here) by choosing File > File Info and clicking on History.

In Photoshop CS and CS2 a 16-bit image can be a full-featured Photoshop file, with multiple layers, type, shapes, and painting with brushes. But the file can get very large and Photoshop's response time slow. For tips on conserving memory and scratch disk space for 16-bit files as well as CS2's new 32-bit mode by using History, see "Memory Economy in 16-Bit Mode" on page 217.

Choosing Edit > Keyboard Shortcuts opens a dialog box for creating and saving your own sets of shortcuts. In Photoshop CS2, the Keyboard Shortcuts dialog is nested with one for hiding or highlighting menu items from the program's main menus or from the menus of the individual palettes. **Note:** In this book Photoshop's *default* shortcuts are used in step-by-step instructions.

- In both CS and CS2, more kinds of *metadata* (information about the origin and processing of an image) can be recorded and used. You can add to the **File Info** panels to store extra information of your choice with the file. And you can track in detail all changes made to an image by using the new **Edit History Log**, which can help you remember how you created a particular Photoshop result. This Log is also useful if you need to document your editing process for client or legal requirements. You'll find more about the Edit History Log on page 28.

- With Photoshop able to handle **huge documents** (up to 300,000 pixels square) and files in **16-bit color**, you can now use most of Photoshop's tools and commands on these extra-capacity file formats. Photoshop CS2, with its new 32-bit features, can address more than 2 gigabytes of RAM in order to handle large files easily. Learn about the new Large Document (**.psb**) format on page 118 and about 32-bit files on page 157.

- As the latest addition to customizing your Photoshop workspaces, you can now make your own **custom keyboard shortcut**s for tools and menu and palette commands. CS2 even lets you customize the menus themselves. As features have been added to the program and menus have grown longer, you can now choose Edit > Menus to hide some menu items or highlight others. Workspaces can be saved with palette locations, keyboard shortcut sets, and customized menus. You can also create and save your own **document presets**, with size, color space, and background preference, so you can choose them when you start a Photoshop document with the File > New command.

- In Photoshop CS2, **Smart Objects** provide a way to resize, reshape, and make certain other changes to artwork as many times as needed without deterioration. Smart Objects can be created in Photoshop from one layer or several, or they can be imported from Adobe Illustrator. A Smart Object acts like a file within a file. It maintains a link back to the original artwork that it was made from, and updating the original artwork automatically updates the Smart Object and any copies of it that you may have made within your Photoshop file. Page 39 provides an introduction to Smart Objects.

- The new File > Scripts > **Image Processor** command in Photoshop CS2 is designed to convert several files at once

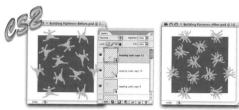

A Smart Object protects its contents from deterioration due to repeated transforming. And if you repeat an element by using several instances of a Smart Object (as shown here), you can simply replace one element to replace them all.

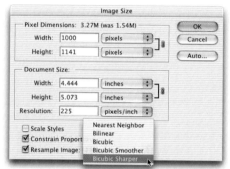

If you use the Image > **Image Size** command to resample an image (scaling it up or down in a way that changes the number of pixels), you can choose **Bicubic Smoother** (for enlarging) or **Bicubic Sharper** (for reducing) to preserve image quality. A **Scale Styles** option in the Image Size dialog box now lets you choose either to scale all the special effects (such as drop shadows, glows, and strokes) along with the file, or scale the image but leave the effects settings as they are.

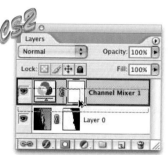

In CS2 you can simply drag a layer mask thumbnail to move the mask to a different layer, or Alt/Option-drag to copy it. Here the mask from Layer 0 is Alt/Option-dragged to replace the empty mask on the Channel Mixer Adjustment layer, in order to limit the Channel Mixer so it affects the building but not the sky.

to PSD, JPG, or TIF. Its dialog box lets you choose which files or folder to process and where to place them after processing. You can resize them if you like, and even run an Action of your choice on all the files as they are converted. CS2 also has a new **Script Events Manager** (File > Scripts > Script Events Manager) that you can set to run a script or an Action whenever a particular event happens, such as Open, Save, or Export.

• Go ahead — put as many photos as you can fit on your flatbed scanner and scan them all at once. File > Automate > **Crop and Straighten Photos** will automatically find each photo in the scan, copy it into its own document, and straighten it if necessary. Simply make sure to leave some white space around each image when you scan, so Photoshop can "see" the images separately. Page 92 shows an example.

• In the past, standard advice to Photoshop users has been not to scale an image file larger, because of the loss of quality that can occur as Photoshop invents the new pixels needed to make the image bigger. Instead, we were advised to rescan the original if a larger file was needed. It's still good advice, but with digital photos there's no film to rescan. As digital photography's popularity grows by leaps and bounds, Photoshop provides a new "scaling up" option: **Bicubic Smoother** is designed to do a better job of *enlarging*. Likewise, **Bicubic Sharper** helps prevent an image from getting "soft" as you *reduce* its size.

ESSENTIAL SHORTCUTS

Photoshop CS2 now has keyboard shortcuts for the often-used Image Size and Canvas Size commands:

• **Alt-Ctrl-I** (Windows) or **Option-⌘-I** (Mac) for **Image > Image Size**

• **Alt-Ctrl-C** (Windows) or **Option-⌘-C** (Mac) for **Image > Canvas Size**

TAKE TWO

With the Bicubic Smoother and Bicubic Sharper options, Photoshop CS/CS2 does a better job of *resampling* (changing the size of an image by changing the number of pixels that make it up) than previous versions did. Still, when you photograph, if you know you'll need to use an image at both a large *and* a small size, or as a full shot *and* a close-up, it's a good idea to take the photo twice — once as the full shot and once zoomed in close. The results you get with the camera may be noticeably better than resampling, even with the best resampling setting.

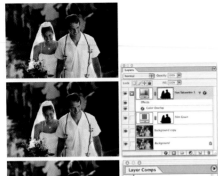

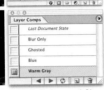

Layer comps are different "views" of a layered file. Use the Layer Comps palette to create, store, and recall the different versions. See "Focusing Attention on the Subject" starting on page 285 for an example.

When you open a frame from a video in Photoshop, it can look out of proportion (left). But in CS/CS2 if you choose Image > Pixel Aspect Ratio and select the format used for the video, Photoshop will show how the image will look (right) when you convert it for print or for the web, as described in the "Video" section of Chapter 3.

In Photoshop CS2, you can design a template file — a "reusable" layout that can automatically "swap in" images or text. Photoshop CS doesn't have this ability, but you can take advantage of the fact that ImageReady CS does. Chapter 9 has an example.

- Photoshop CS2 offers new ways to work with layers. In the CS2 Layers palette you can **target more than one layer** at a time and manipulate or link all the targeted layers at once. After Shift-clicking or Ctrl-clicking several layers in the palette, Shift-click on the "Create a new group" button (labeled "Create a set" in CS) to put them all in a set, or click the "Link layers" button ⊷ at the bottom of the Layers palette. This button, along with the ⊷ icon that appears to the right of the name of a linked layer, replaces the Links column that was part of earlier versions of the palette.

- If your files tend to have lots of layers, You'll like the **Select > Similar** command. Use it to select all the Shape layers or type layers, for instance, without having to scroll through the Layers palette looking for them. Likewise you can choose **Select Linked Layers** from the Layers palette's own menu.

- In CS2 you can also move a mask from one layer to another by dragging its thumbnail, or copy the mask by Alt/Option-dragging.

- In both CS and CS2 you can make a **hierarchy of *layer sets*** (now ***groups*** in CS2)**,** collecting sequences of related layers of a composite image into folders in the Layers palette and then nesting several of these folders within another folder for tighter organization and control.

- With the new **layer comps** in both Photoshop and ImageReady, you can capture several different configurations of a document, with different layers and effects visible or hidden. This makes it quicker and easier than before to review options with a client, customize your work for different markets, or cycle through a progression of images for an animation. You can use your layer comps to spin off separate files by choosing File > Scripts > **Layer Comps To Files**. Or incorporate them into a PDF for review by choosing File > Scripts > **PDF from Layer Comps**. If you import a Photoshop file with layer comps into InDesign CS2, you can choose which one of the comps you want expressed on the page.

- For those who work in **video**, Photoshop CS/CS2 makes it easier to design for nonsquare video pixels, or to convert between them and the square pixels of digital images. CS2 also allows you to send a video preview to a connected device, such as a video monitor.

- In CS, ImageReady lets you set up a file with layers (either images or text) defined as variable data. The file becomes a **template** that holds both the persistent (unchanging) parts of the layout and the **variables**. In CS2, as part of the

Photoshop CS2 has its own Animation palette, so it's possible to complete an Animation project without jumping to ImageReady. The animation projects in Chapter 10 are described step-by-step for both CS and CS2.

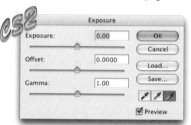

Using Camera Raw (shown here) with the File Browser (in CS) or Bridge (in CS2), you can make corrections to one of a series of photos and then apply the same corrections to other images. For more about Camera Raw, see page 102.

Exposure dialog image

The Image > Adjustments > Exposure command is designed for the new ultra-high-resolution (32 Bits/Channel) files that CS2 can handle. It's one of the only commands for adjusting tone and color in these images.

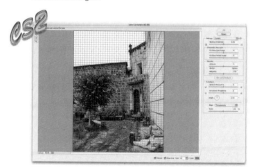

CS2's Filter > Distort > Lens Correction can fix barreling or pincushioning (bulging or "pinching" in the center), unintended perspective distortion, or a crooked horizon.

integration of ImageReady into Photoshop, templates and variables have been added to Photoshop as well. "Building a Template with Masks & Variables" in Chapter 9 tells how to set up a template so you can quickly swap out images and text to customize or "personalize" content — for instance, for web banners, catalogs, ads placed in different publications, or a series of postcards or school photo packages.

- Another step in integrating ImageReady features is the addition of the **Animation palette** to Photoshop CS2. Open it by choosing Window > Animation.

ESPECIALLY FOR PHOTOGRAPHERS

Some of photographers' favorite camera features have now been reproduced in Photoshop so you can apply them *after* you take the picture. Many of the new additions are designed as "one-stop" solutions, with a single "mega-dialog box," a virtual studio that has all the adjustments you need to meet a particular challenge:

- **Camera Raw**, previously a plug-in but now integrated into Photoshop (File > Open > Format: Camera Raw), lets you work with images in a camera's original "raw" format, *before* the camera's software processed them with settings that compensate for lighting, exposure, and so on. For an increasing selection of digital cameras, you can use Camera Raw to correct mistakes or even "relight" the photo shoot. The version of Camera Raw that comes with CS2 can do even more. It has color samplers, crop and straighten tools, and a Curves panel, as well as a new Synchronize panel that lets you apply corrections to more than one image at a time when you select multiple files in Bridge. A file opened and edited in Camera Raw can be included in a Photoshop file as a Smart Object (described on page 8). This means you can resize or make other "nondestructive" changes to the image as a Smart Object and still have the option of going all the way back to the original raw image data, if needed, to adjust exposure, color, or other qualities. See page 102 for more on Camera Raw.

- Designed for files in Photoshop CS2's new 32 Bits/Channel format, the **Exposure** command in CS2 lets you balance shadows, midtones, and highlights within the image.

- The **Lens Correction** filter in CS2 (Filter > Distort > Lens Correction) gives photographers a single dialog box for correcting many common distortion problems. See it in action in "Compensating for Camera-Related Distortion" on page 279.

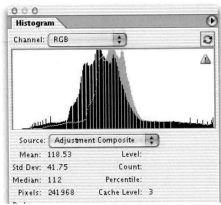

Added with Photoshop CS, the Histogram palette can be kept open as you work to help you analyze the tonal values in your image. With the Source set to **Adjustment Composite** as you try out an adjustment, it gives you a "live" preview of the tonal distribution (the vivid graph) compared to the pre-adjustment condition (the pale graph).

PAUL K. DAYTON, JR.

Photo Filter layers can warm a photo or cool it (as shown here) or produce a unique tint effect, as shown on page 204 in "Quick Tint Effects."

GAGE DAYTON

Here the Image > Adjustments > Shadow/Highlight command at its default settings lightens the subject while still maintaining the "bright sun and shade" character of the image.

- The **Histogram** (Window > Histogram) is now a "live" monitor of tone and color in your image. You can open it and view its graphs to help make an initial assessment of a photo, and then keep it open on-screen as you make adjustments, previewing your changes to see their effect on highlights, shadows, and overall contrast *before* you commit to the changes. You'll find examples of its use throughout this book.

- Many of the color filters that professional photographers have traditionally attached to the lenses of their cameras are now built into Photoshop, so you can apply them after you shoot the photo. Because these new **Photo Filters** are Adjustment layers, you can keep your options open to change the tinting later. You can see Photo Filter layers at work in "Quick Tone & Color Adjustments" on page 266 and in "Quick Tint Effects" on page 200.

- With the **Shadow/Highlight** command you can automatically adjust over- and underexposed areas in photos. It offers an "instant fix" for many images in which the subject is underexposed, or for images with a dark foreground and blown-out sky. It can also be good for bringing out shadow detail, as in "Bringing Out Detail" on page 321.

- Improvements to photo-retouching tools include a Use All Layers/Sample All Layers option for the **Healing Brush** ✐. This means that you can seamlessly remove unwanted blemishes from a photo, keeping the changes on a separate layer so you can partially mask them or change their opacity independently of the rest of the image. In CS2 the **Spot Healing Brush** ✐ (which also offers Sample All Layers) automatically samples from a nearby area. Nested with the Spot Healing Brush in CS2 is a new quick **Red-Eye** tool ⌖. The photo retouching tools play a role in "Quick Coverups" on page 317, "Softening a Portrait" starting on page 307, and "Quick Cosmetic Changes" on page 311.

- A new and improved method for sharpening images, **Smart Sharpen** in CS2, has a **Lens** option specifically designed to correct the blur in photos shot slightly out-of-focus, as well as a **Motion** option for the blur that happens with "camera shake" or when the subject moves.

- In CS2 the **Reduce Noise** filter can help eliminate digital noise or film grain in a photo without blurring the subject. Reduction of noise can be overall, or on a channel-by-channel basis. So, for instance, the typically noisier Blue channel can be filtered separately.

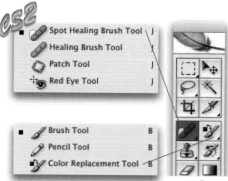

In Photoshop CS2 the Spot Healing Brush and the Red Eye tool have been added to the Tools palette, sharing a position with the Healing Brush and Patch tool. The Color Replacement tool, which used to be in this grouping, has been moved right to share a spot with the Brush and Pencil, and its icon has changed.

Choosing Image > Adjustments > Match Color opens a dialog box where you can specify the image or selection you want to change and the one you want to match. The Image Options sliders let you modify the automatic match to suit your eye.

So far, a shallow depth of field is harder to achieve with most digital cameras than with most film cameras. But Photoshop's Lens Blur "one-stop" dialog box lets you protect the subject and blur the background (left) more "camera-realistically" than the Gaussian Blur filter can (right). Lens Blur can even simulate the way highlights in out-of-focus areas take on the shape of the camera's iris, and its Noise feature can put back the "grain" that its blurring takes away.

- **High Dynamic Range (HDR)** photographs store more tone and color distinctions than can possibly be reproduced in a print or on a screen display. The advantage of having this extra info in a single file is that it's all there for you to choose from, depending on what you want to emphasize in the photo and which display or print process you want to use. So far HDR has been used mainly by movie makers for special effects and by 3D artists who need to better simulate real-world lighting for proper texturing. In CS2 Photoshop takes its first step into the world of HDR with Automate > Merge to HDR. This command creates a single HDR file from two or more 8-bit or 16-bit photos that are identical except for being exposed from 1 to 2 EV (exposure value) steps apart. Only a few of CS2's commands work with a 32-bit file, but converting HDR to 16-bit or 8-bit files allows several special options for compressing the extended HDR tonal range to fit into the smaller bit depths. Sunny skies can be blue without underexposed foregrounds, and daytime interior shots no longer have to have windows covered to avoid blown-out highlights. For those who have other programs that can handle HDR, Photoshop CS2 can save the unconverted HDR file to several special formats, as well as to Photoshop (PSD) and Large Document Format (PSB).

- You can now design custom **Picture Package** layouts (File > Automate > Picture Package) to print several copies of a photo (or more than one photo) on a page. Modify an existing layout or create your own.

- A **new Web Photo Gallery template** includes a feedback mechanism so photographers can quickly create a way for clients to select and comment on photos. See "Making a Web Photo Gallery" in Chapter 10 for more. CS2 has added more new Web Photo Gallery templates, including Flash galleries.

OTHER NEW FEATURES

Photoshop has some great new ways for designers to work with **photos**, **type**, and hard-edged **graphics**:

- The **Match Color** command lets you apply the color and luminance of one image to another with a great deal of user control. It can help integrate a transplanted subject (perhaps isolated with the Extract command) into its new background (as in "Swapping a Background" on page 628). It can also adjust the color and lighting of an image to match others in a series of related images (page 266). Or use it to adjust color in the components of a panorama, before you use the

ORIGINAL PHOTO: PAUL K. DAYTON, JR.

The Average filter can get you off to a great start in restoring faded color photos, such as this scan of a 1940s color transparency shown on the left. The simple three-step process of restoring the image to the version on the right is described on page 271.

The Filter Gallery lets you experiment with two or more filters interactively, adjusting any or all settings and changing the order of application. Find examples in "'Framing' with Masks" in Chapter 5.

With Vanishing Point you can automatically match the perspective of an image as you paint, clone, and paste in elements.

new **File** > **Automate** > **Photomerge** command to put them together as in "'Photomerging' a Panorama" (page 604).

- The **Color Replacement tool** (in CS, or in CS2) lets you "paint" a color change, replacing the color under the cursor with a color of your choice. With the right settings, you can limit the change to hue, saturation, or luminosity.

- The **Lens Blur** filter (Filter > Blur > Lens Blur) provides a more "camera-realistic" way to reduce depth of field in a photo than Photoshop has offered before. "Exercising Lens Blur" on page 291 shows what this new feature can do.

- Three more new blurs have been added in CS2: **Box Blur**, for special effects; **Shape Blur**, for shaping pin-point lights or creating a camera-motion type of blur on a subject or background; and **Surface Blur**, for creating a soft-focus glow or softening detail in a portrait, as shown on page 315.

- The **Average** filter (Filter > Blur > Average) can be useful for correcting color casts in old faded photos and other images that don't respond well to other methods, as shown in the two Average examples on page 271.

- The **Liquify** "megafilter" (for "hand-painting" distortions to an image) has been improved. Options for reconstructing and masking have been expanded. In CS the Show Backdrop command has more options than before for viewing the "Liquified" layer in conjunction with the other layers in the image file, and in CS2 these options have been improved further. You'll find an example on page 615.

- The **Fibers** filter (Filter > Render > Fibers) is useful for creating textures and patterns, as shown on pages 559 and 560.

- The **Filter Gallery** shows thumbnail examples of what many of Photoshop's special-effects filters do and shows bigger previews than before for most of these filters. More important, the Filter Gallery lets you combine filters interactively, previewing the *combination* of two or more filters at different settings before you commit to the changes.

- CS2's big new megafilter is **Vanishing Point**. After creating a grid that follows the perspective in an image, you can clone to add or remove elements, transform them, even add new elements or paint — all in the perspective of the grid. It's fairly easy to translate the grid to follow any other plane in the image at right angles to the first grid, so you can move objects in all three dimensions — from a side surface of a box to the top surface, for instance, or from one wall of a room to another. You can see Vanishing Point in action in "Exercising Vanishing Point" on page 588.

DONAL JOLLEY

Chapter 7, "Type & Vector Graphics," has several examples of setting type on a path, including the special case of two settings on the same circle (page 452).

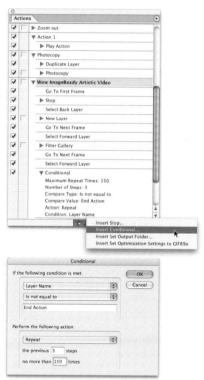

In ImageReady's Actions palette menu you can choose to insert a conditional step. In this example from "Creating an Action to Animate a Video" (page 134), a condition is set to repeat filtering and frame-advancing steps until a layer named "End Action" is encountered.

- Photoshop CS added the significant ability to set **type on (or within) a path**. These new features are demonstrated in Chapter 7. The only new type feature in CS2 is that the Font menu shows the word "Sample" set in the font, next to its name, so you can see the face before you choose it.

WHAT'S NEW IN IMAGEREADY?

Photoshop's workflow improvements extend beyond the program itself and into its tighter integration with ImageReady. Here are some of the important improvements in CS and CS2:

- It's now easier and less confusing to jump back and forth between Photoshop and ImageReady.

- It's easier to work with the components of a file: Besides the new layer comps (mentioned earlier), ImageReady also has **slice sets**. Also, even in version CS, you can select and move several layers at once, you can drag-copy a mask from one layer to another, and you can also export layers as a series of separate files.

- ImageReady can export files in the industry-standard **SWF (Flash) format**, and it's now easier to move artwork from ImageReady to Flash.

- **Tables** have been improved, for nesting and for generating designs that can "flex" to fit in a browser window.

- **Remote rollovers** now allow cursor action in one part of a web page to trigger a change in the graphics elsewhere.

- The **templates**, **variables**, and **data sets** that appear in Photoshop CS2 are already present in ImageReady CS.

- The "**Insert a step**" button at the bottom of ImageReady's Actions palette lets you use conditional logic within ImageReady Actions. For instance, you can tell the program to check characteristics of the file and then, based on what it finds, either continue, skip steps, or stop the Action. Some of the characteristics it can evaluate are aspect ratio, dimensions, and name of the file or layer, or the layer type (such as pixel, text, or Adjustment). You can take advantage of conditional Actions for your Photoshop files by jumping to ImageReady.

These and other ImageReady CS/CS2 features are presented more extensively in the introduction and step-by-step projects in Chapter 10. *Wow!*

Fundamentals of Photoshop

1

Photoshop's Layers palette shows how the elements of an image file stack up. Layers are important in almost every aspect of Photoshop work, as you'll see in the techniques throughout the book. The different kinds of layers and how they relate to one another are explored in "Anatomy of a Photoshop File" on page 37.

On-screen a gray-and-white checkerboard pattern represents transparent areas of the image file, so you can see where the pixels are and what parts of the visible layers are transparent.

THIS CHAPTER IS AN OVERVIEW of how Photoshop works — how the program organizes information when you create or edit an image, how you interact with the program, and what it takes to keep Photoshop sailing happily along.

HOW PHOTOSHOP THINKS

Back when Photoshop was born (late in the 20th Century), the answer to the question "What is a Photoshop file?" was a lot simpler than it is now. It was a digital picture made up of a monolayer of *picture elements*, or *pixels* for short — tiny square dots of color, like microscopic tiles in a really precise mosaic. Today the program is a lot more powerful, and most Photoshop files are more complex.

Layers, Masks, Modes & Styles

You can think of a typical Photoshop file as a stack of **layers**, kind of like an open-face sandwich. The image that you see on-screen or in print is what you would see if you looked down at the sandwich from directly above. The Layers palette — an example is shown at the left — is a dynamic "diagram" of the stack.

Several different kinds of layers can comprise the stack:

- There can be a **Background** at the bottom of the stack, completely filled with pixels.

- Like the *Background*, **regular layers** can also hold pixels. But *unlike* the *Background*, these layers can also have areas that are completely or partly transparent, so that any pixels from the layers underneath can show through.

- **Adjustment layers** don't contribute any pixels to the image at all. Instead, they store instructions that change the color or tone of the pixels in layers below.

- **Type layers** hold — you guessed it — type, in a "live," or *dynamic*, form that can be edited if you need to change the

A smooth-edged vector mask and a filtered, rough-edged layer mask work together to shape the graphic for this logo. A Layer Style adds dimension and surface texture. You'll find this example on page 517.

Organizing layers isn't the only thing layer sets/groups are good for. Even a single layer can benefit from being in a set/group because it provides a way to add another mask, independent of any on the layer itself, as in this composition from page 611.

spelling of the words or the spacing of the characters or the font or color or any other characteristics of the type.

- **Fill layers** and **Shape layers** are also dynamic. Instead of including *pixels* of color, they include *instructions* for what color (solid, gradient, or pattern) the layer should hold. They also include *masks* (described below) that determine where the color is revealed. For Fill and Shape layers, you can instantly change the color that's revealed by the masks.

- A **Smart Object**, new in Photoshop CS2, is a "package" of elements, like a file within a file. Smart Objects can be created entirely in Photoshop, pasted from Adobe Illustrator, or placed in Photoshop from another program.

Each kind of Photoshop layer, except the *Background,* can include two kinds of **masks** — a pixel-based **layer mask** and an instruction-based **vector mask**. Each mask can hide part of the layer so it lets the layers below show through. Other ways to control how a layer blends into the image are its **opacity** (how transparent it is), its **blend mode** (how its colors combine with the rest of the image), and its other **blending options** (which of its tones or colors may be excluded from blending at all).

All layers, again with the exception of the *Background,* can also include a **Layer Style**. A Style is a "kit" of instructions for creating special effects like shadows, glows, and bevels, or for simulating materials with characteristics like translucency, shine, color, and pattern. "Exercising Layer Styles" on page 44 shows how versatile and efficient Layer Styles can be.

Besides the basic "stacking order" of layers and their masks, the Layers palette provides various ways of relating layers to one another. Layers can be grouped in **"folders"** (called *sets* in CS, *groups* in CS2). In the Layers palette, folders can be closed to make the palette more compact. By adding a mask to a folder, you mask all the layers in the set. Sets and also **linked** layers can be moved and scaled all together.

Pixels or Instructions?

In the "layer sandwich" of the Photoshop file, the difference between the **pixel-based elements** and the **instruction-based elements** is an important one. We might think of the pixel-based layers as, for example, the bread, lettuce, and tomatoes put together in the sandwich. Then we could think of the instruction-based elements as little notes that say "put some mustard here between the tomato and cheese, but on the left side only" or "put Swiss cheese here, or cheddar if you want."

Instruction-based elements don't have any tiny mosaic squares — only instructions. Magically, in a Photoshop "sandwich" the computer translates the instructions and pixels into an on-screen "preview" that shows us what the complete result will be like.

Most Photoshop files rely heavily on pixel-based elements, usually scanned images or digital photos. In a layered Photoshop file, the *Background,* if there is one, is pixel-based. So are the regular layers with image material on them, and so are layer masks. For pixel-based elements, Photoshop has to work with and perhaps change the position and color of each pixel in the mosaic grid — potentially *billions* of pixels or even more.

Pixel-based elements can suffer from rounding errors. Here's an example of how that works. If you rotate a pixel-based image 90°, Photoshop can handle that with no problem. Each square pixel just changes position and turns onto another edge, and Photoshop notes the new grid positions now that the image has been turned on its side. If, however, you rotate the image some number of degrees that isn't a multiple of 90, there isn't a direct correspondence between the old pixels and the new ones. Photoshop will do its best to make the new image look the same as it did before the rotation, but the program is going to have to do some *interpolation* of the color information, as it averages the colors of the tilted pixels that fall on each square of the grid. Rotating is just one example of changes that lead to interpolation. Each time interpolation happens, the image gets a little more different from what it was originally.

On the other hand, for instruction-based elements and operations, Photoshop just thinks in terms of math formulas. For shapes, color or tonal changes, and overall opacity, for example, Photoshop can simply change a few numbers to change the instructions, without having to process and reprocess all those pixels. One advantage of using instructions instead of pixels

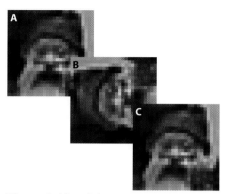

When a pixel-based element is rotated in 90° steps (or multiples of 90°), only the positions of the perfectly square pixels change, and the image is not degraded. This "dramatic re-enactment" shows a very tiny detail (27 by 27 pixels) from the photo on page 203 **A** rotated 90° to the left **B**, and then rotated 90° back to the right **C**.

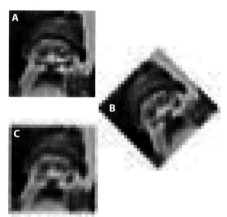

Other changes, such as scaling or non-90°-angle rotations, can change the image. Applied one by one, each transformation can take it farther from its original form. When the elf **A** is rotated 45° to the left **B**, Photoshop has to interpolate, or *resample,* the tilted pixels, averaging colors to create pixels that fit into its straight-up-and-down grid. When the element is rotated 45° back to the right, more color-averaging occurs, and the "softening" of the image is obvious **C**.

BASIC PHOTOSHOP LINGO

People use a number of terms that relate to pixels and instructions in Photoshop:

• *Raster* and *bitmap* are often used to describe **pixel-based** information.

• On the other hand, terms that refer to **instruction-based** elements or functions include *vector* or *vector-based, path,* and *object. Type* that's "live" (still able to be edited as type) is also in the instruction-based category.

• To *rasterize* means to convert instructions into pixels.

An instruction-based element like this Shape layer is only translated into dots of ink or pixels of color when it's printed on the page or displayed on the screen. It can be rotated or scaled many times without the cumulative wear and tear that happens to a pixel-based element. This Shape layer (rasterized here at 24 by 24 pixels each time) was rotated 45° to the left and back twice, but it didn't get progressively "softer" as a pixel-based element would. We've enlarged it here to show the pixels.

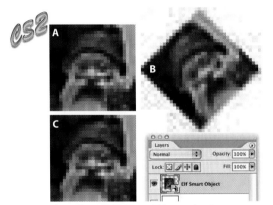

Photoshop CS2's Smart Object technology can protect pixel-based elements from damage due to repeated rotating, scaling and some other forms of distortion. Here we turned the elf from page 19 into a Smart Object **A** (Layer > Smart Objects > Group into New Smart Object) and rotated it 45° left **B**; Photoshop still had to interpolate because of the tilt. But when we rotated it 45° back **C**, there was no further damage (compare to page 19) because the Smart Object could go back to the original image data and apply the combined rotations left and right into one instruction, which left the elf as it was, rather than carrying out one transformation and then the other.

If you're working in Photoshop CS and you open a CS2 file that includes a Smart Object, you'll see this dialog box. If you click "OK," Photoshop CS will maintain the layers in the file, converting the Smart Object into a single pixel-based layer.

wherever possible is that it's a lot easier and "cleaner" to change things if you change your mind. In the Photoshop sandwich, you can decrease the mustard to half a tablespoonful or swap mayonnaise for mustard, or trim the cheese to the edges of the bread. If these elements had already been locked into the "sandwich" in *pixel* form, it would be a lot messier to "revise" the sandwich without leaving telltale traces behind, just as it would be to take off the mustard or restore the trimmed-away edges of the cheese. Changing the *instructions* is a clean operation that doesn't leave behind a residue or make us wish later that we hadn't cut something off. The instructions can be changed right up until the "sandwich is served" — in other words until the layered file is translated into a monolayer of pixels to be printed on paper or viewed on a web page. "Anatomy of a Photoshop File" on page 37 explores the components that can make up a file.

Photoshop CS2's new **Smart Object** layers provide a way to scale or reshape pixel-based elements without subjecting them to rounding errors. That's because a Smart Object layer "remembers" its original content from when it was made, along with the instructions for each transformation (scaling, reshaping, or rotating) that has been done to it since. Each time a Smart Object is scaled or reshaped, it goes back and uses that original information and combines all the transformation instructions into a single change, to arrive at its new form. So you can scale or reshape a Smart Object layer several times, each time building on the previous transformations, without degrading the image more with each change.

Channels & Paths

At the same time that Photoshop is keeping track of an image as layers in a stack, it also thinks about file content in another way — as *color channels*. If we imagine the layers as the stacked sandwich components, then we might think of the color channels as the nutrients in the food — proteins, carbohydrates,

HANG ONTO THOSE LAYERS!

For maximum flexibility, so you can make changes in the future, keep your Photoshop files in layered form. If you need a flattened (single-layer) file to put into a page layout or web program, you can make a duplicate file (Image > Duplicate) and flatten it (Layer > Flatten Image) and save this *flattened*, or *Background*-only duplicate. (In versions CS and CS2, you can use layered Photoshop files directly, without flattening, in Adobe InDesign or Adobe GoLive, the page layout and web components of the Creative Suite and Creative Suite 2.)

Alpha channels are listed at the bottom of the Channels palette, opened by choosing Window > Channels. They aren't really related to the color channels that appear above them. Instead alpha channels mainly store masks that can be activated to select different areas of the image. The layer mask of the currently active layer is a "transient" resident in the Channels palette, appearing only as long as that particular layer is active. Its name appears in italic.

The Paths palette stores vector-based outlines. The *Work Path* is the path that's currently being drawn and hasn't been saved yet. The vector mask of the currently active layer also appears in the Paths palette. Because the vector mask and the *Work Path* are transient, their names appear in italic.

ORIGINAL PHOTO: PHOTOSPIN.COM

Photo Filters Combined.psd is an example of a file that includes layer comps. By clicking the ▶ button at the bottom of the Layer Comps palette, you can cycle through different views of the file, saved to show different Photo Filter tint effects. (The "how-to" for the tinting is on page 204; making layer comps is covered in "Focusing Attention on the Subject" on page 285.)

fats, and vitamins and minerals. Same sandwich, but a different way of analyzing its content, and one that's also important for the way Photoshop works. There's much more about color channels in Chapter 4, "Color in Photoshop."

In addition to the layers (with masks and Styles) and the color channels, Photoshop files can also have:

- **Alpha channels**, which are pixel-based masks you can store permanently in the Channels palette
- **Paths**, which are instruction-based outlines or curves that are listed in the Paths palette when you add them
- **Layer comps**, which are different views of a Photoshop file, each one recording what layers were visible and what Styles and masks were in effect at the time the comp was added to the Layer Comps palette.

WORKING WITH PHOTOSHOP

On the next three pages is a "tour" of some of the important parts of Photoshop's interface. (ImageReady's toolbox is shown at the beginning of Chapter 10, and its unique palettes are explored in the techniques in that chapter. As you work with Photoshop's user interface — operating its tools and making choices from its menus, palettes, and dialog boxes — you'll find that versions CS and CS2 allow you to customize this interface to suit your needs more than ever before.

To help you manage all of its palettes, commands, and tools, Photoshop has built-in keyboard shortcuts for choosing tools and carrying out commands quickly, by pressing a few keys rather than moving the cursor around the working window. The Edit > **Keyboard Shortcuts** command lets you add your own shortcuts to saved sets. You can customize workspaces in CS to save your palettes the way you want them arranged on your desktop for particular tasks. In CS2 you can further customize your workspaces by changing menus, to hide commands you seldom use or add color to commands that you want to stand out. In both CS and CS2, you can save and load your own workspaces by choosing Window > Workspace. *Note:* Even if you customize your menus by hiding some commands, the hidden menu items will still be available for Photoshop to use if you run an Action (a prerecorded "mini-program")▼ that calls for those commands.

Continued on page 25

FIND OUT MORE

▼ Automating with Actions **page 110**

PHOTOSHOP'S WORKING WINDOW

Here's one way to set up a 1024 x 768-pixel screen with most of the palettes handy. Palettes that you want "at the ready" but that you don't use all the time (here the Swatches, Styles, Actions, and History palettes) can be stored in the "well" at the right end of the Options bar. Palettes that you want to keep open can be "nested" together, like the Layers, Channels, and Paths palettes shown here. Palettes can also be "docked" so they can be opened, closed, and moved together. In both CS and CS2 (shown here) you can save Workspaces that you've set up for a particular task or job, and in CS2 you can even customize the main menu and palette menus.

Photoshop's **Options bar** offers the choices appropriate for the tool or command that's active. On the right end of the bar is a button for opening File Browser (CS) or Bridge (CS2).

Palettes can be "nested" (stacked behind one another) by dragging the title tab of one palette onto the body of another. To bring a palette to the front of the nest, just click on its title tab.

If your monitor is big enough so the **palette well** appears at the right end of the Options bar, you can drag palettes into the well for compact storage with quick access. Open them by clicking their title tabs; they will close as soon as you click in the working window.

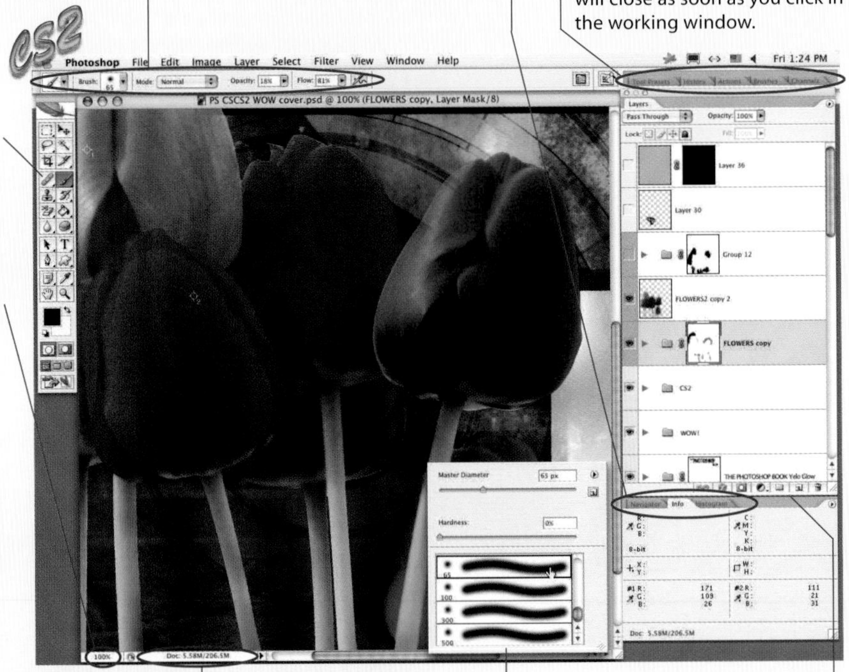

New tools added to Photoshop's **Tools palette** include the Color Replacement tool in CS and the Red Eye tool and Spot Healing Brush in CS2.

Working at **100% gives you the most accurate view.** If you have to work smaller in order to see enough of your image, choose 50%, 25%, or some other division of 100 by a factor of 2. Likewise, when you zoom up for a close view, use exact multiples of 100%, such as 200%. The "zoom" box in the lower left corner is "live" — you can type in a percentage.

This **pop-up menu** lets you view file sizes, color profile, efficiency (how often Photoshop runs out of RAM and has to use scratch disk space), and other factors. In Document Sizes mode (shown here) it shows the current open size of the file with all its layers and channels (right) and the size it would be if flattened to one layer with alpha channels removed. In CS2 this menu offers a Reveal In Bridge option, so you can easily open another file from the same folder or location.

Right-click/Ctrl-click on almost anything to open a **context-sensitive menu** of choices that are specific to the tool you're using (here the Brush) or the spot you've clicked.

Palettes can by "docked" (attached "head to toe") by dragging the title tab of one onto the bottom edge of another. Docked palettes have a single open/close button and a single expand/collapse button at the top.

PHOTOSHOP'S TOOLS PALETTE

In Photoshop's Tools palette, the smaller fly-out panels name the tools and present the keyboard shortcuts for toggling between tools that share a space. The CS Tools palette is shown here.

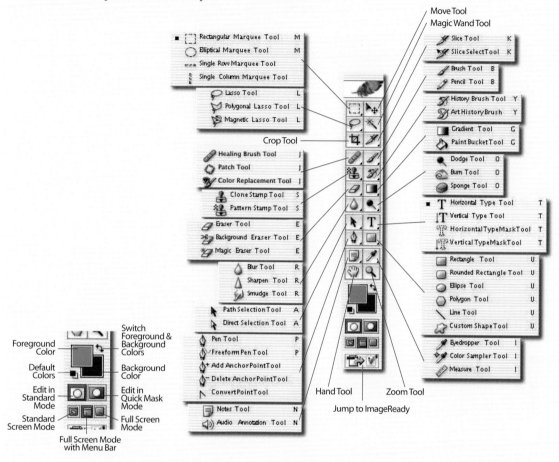

Rectangular Marquee Tool — M
Elliptical Marquee Tool — M
Single Row Marquee Tool
Single Column Marquee Tool

Lasso Tool — L
Polygonal Lasso Tool — L
Magnetic Lasso Tool — L

Crop Tool

Healing Brush Tool — J
Patch Tool — J
Color Replacement Tool — J

Clone Stamp Tool — S
Pattern Stamp Tool — S

Eraser Tool — E
Background Eraser Tool — E
Magic Eraser Tool — E

Blur Tool — R
Sharpen Tool — R
Smudge Tool — R

Path Selection Tool — A
Direct Selection Tool — A

Pen Tool — P
Freeform Pen Tool — P
Add Anchor Point Tool
Delete Anchor Point Tool
Convert Point Tool

Notes Tool — N
Audio Annotation Tool — N

Move Tool
Magic Wand Tool

Slice Tool — K
Slice Select Tool — K

Brush Tool — B
Pencil Tool — B

History Brush Tool — Y
Art History Brush — Y

Gradient Tool — G
Paint Bucket Tool — G

Dodge Tool — O
Burn Tool — O
Sponge Tool — O

Horizontal Type Tool — T
Vertical Type Tool — T
Horizontal Type Mask Tool — T
Vertical Type Mask Tool — T

Rectangle Tool — U
Rounded Rectangle Tool — U
Ellipse Tool — U
Polygon Tool — U
Line Tool — U
Custom Shape Tool — U

Eyedropper Tool — I
Color Sampler Tool — I
Measure Tool — I

Hand Tool   Zoom Tool

Jump to ImageReady

Foreground Color
Default Colors
Edit in Standard Mode
Standard Screen Mode

Switch Foreground & Background Colors
Background Color
Edit in Quick Mask Mode
Full Screen Mode

Full Screen Mode with Menu Bar

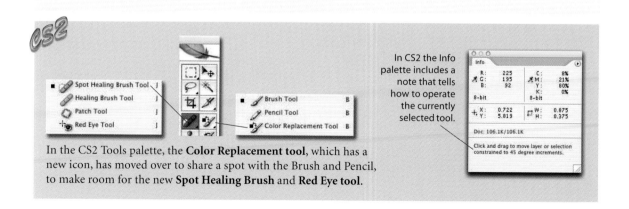

Spot Healing Brush Tool — J
Healing Brush Tool — J
Patch Tool — J
Red Eye Tool — J

Brush Tool — B
Pencil Tool — B
Color Replacement Tool — B

In CS2 the Info palette includes a note that tells how to operate the currently selected tool.

Info

R: 225   C: 8%
G: 195   M: 21%
B: 92   Y: 80%
            K: 0%
8-bit   8-bit

X: 0.722   W: 0.875
Y: 5.819   H: 0.375

Doc: 106.1K/106.1K

Click and drag to move layer or selection constrained to 45 degree increments.

In the CS2 Tools palette, the **Color Replacement tool**, which has a new icon, has moved over to share a spot with the Brush and Pencil, to make room for the new **Spot Healing Brush** and **Red Eye tool**.

OPTIONS BAR, MENUS, DIALOG BOXES, AND PALETTES

Photoshop's **Options bar**, which appears at the top of the working window by default, has buttons and entry fields for making choices for operating the current tool or command. Photoshop's **menus**, **dialog boxes**, and **palettes** offer a wide variety of options.

Near its right end, the Options bar has a button for opening the **File Browser (CS)** or **Bridge (CS2)** for managing files.

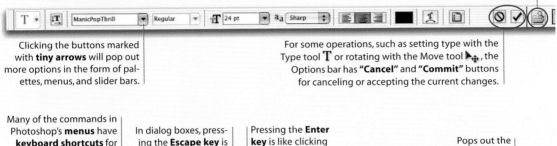

Clicking the buttons marked with **tiny arrows** will pop out more options in the form of palettes, menus, and slider bars.

For some operations, such as setting type with the Type tool T or rotating with the Move tool, the Options bar has **"Cancel"** and **"Commit"** buttons for canceling or accepting the current changes.

Many of the commands in Photoshop's **menus** have **keyboard shortcuts** for quick application.

In dialog boxes, pressing the **Escape key** is like clicking **"Cancel."**

Pressing the **Enter key** is like clicking **"OK."**

Title tab

Pops out the **palette's menu**

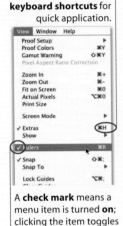

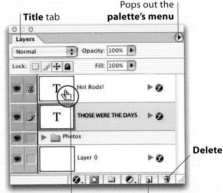

A **check mark** means a menu item is turned **on**; clicking the item toggles it off or on.

Holding down the **Alt/Option key** changes the "Cancel" button to **"Reset,"** to restore the default or previous settings.

Ctrl/⌘-click on almost any palette thumbnail to load it as a selection.

Delete

The **"Create new. . ."** button at the bottom of a palette makes a new layer, channel, or whatever the palette houses.

CS2 In Photoshop CS2, the Options bar provides access to the new **Bridge** application, which replaces the File Browser. Menus can be customized, and some new filter dialog boxes have **Settings** and **Save** options. Among the palettes, the **Layers palette** has undergone the most significant changes.

You can **target more than one layer** at a time by Shift-clicking or Ctrl/⌘-clicking their thumbnails.

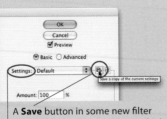

In CS2 the **Assign Profile** and **Convert to Profile** commands have moved to the Edit menu. New to the Mac, **Color Settings** is also in the Edit menu.

A **Save** button in some new filter dialogs lets you save settings, which you can then load by choosing from the **Settings** menu.

Linking of layers is now controlled with the **"Link layers"** button at the bottom of the Layers palette, and individual link icons appear to the right of layer names.

Changing the view (displayed in the file's title bar and editable in the lower left corner of the working window) doesn't change your image file — it just changes your on-screen view of it.

• When you view an image at **100%**, it doesn't mean you're seeing it at the dimensions it will print. It means that every pixel in the image file is represented by 1 pixel on-screen.

• **Higher percentages** mean that more than 1 screen pixel is being used to represent 1 pixel of the image file. For instance, at 200% each pixel in the image file is represented by a 2 x 2-pixel block on-screen.

• **Lower percentages** mean just the opposite: 1 on-screen pixel represents more than 1 image pixel. For instance, at 50% each pixel on-screen represents a 2 x 2 block of pixels in the image file.

The views at 100% (top), 50%, and 25% look much smoother and are more accurate for on-screen editing than odd settings like 33.3%, 66.7%, or the 104% view shown here (bottom). Odd views can give you the impression that your image has been somehow corrupted, when in fact it's fine.

WORKING SMART

Every accomplished Photoshop user has a particular way of working with the program to produce the highest-quality artwork. The Photoshop Wow! approach has always emphasized working quickly and with as much flexibility as possible, in case you want to make changes later. Here are some pointers that can help.

Working with Several Files at Once

In Photoshop CS and CS2 it's easier than ever to access files, more than one at a time if you like. For instance, **File Browser** in Photoshop CS and its update, the separate **Bridge** application in the Creative Suite 2, lets you see thumbnails and automatically process several files at once. File Browser and Bridge are covered in Chapter 3.

Another new CS2 feature is the option to open and save files through the **Adobe Dialog**, where you can view thumbnails, as shown on page 26. The Open, Import, Place, Export, Save, and Save As commands all offer this option.

The **Automate** and **Scripts** commands in the File menu for CS and CS2 include some useful automated production tasks. You can run **Actions** ("macros" that carry out a prerecorded series of operations) on **batches** of files. You can also export several **different files** from the individual layers or layer comps of a single file. This means you can build several versions of a composition in one file, efficiently using the elements the versions have in common, and then use this assemblage to generate several different files. You'll find more about automation in Chapter 3.

If you're running Photoshop on a Mac, for convenience you may want to replace the standard one-button mouse with a two-button variety so you can right-click instead of having to reach for the Control (Ctrl) key for many of the important Photoshop functions.

Choosing Edit > Preferences > General (Windows) or Photoshop > Preferences > General (Mac) and turning on **Show Tool Tips** can be very helpful in navigating Photoshop's streamlined but complex interface. If you pause the cursor over almost anything in the interface, a note will pop up to tell you what you're looking at.

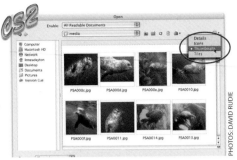

If you click the "Use Adobe dialog" button in the Open or Save As dialog box, you have the option of viewing thumbnails of your files. Clicking the "View" button in the upper right corner of the Adobe dialog and choosing the Tiles option shows file data as well as a small preview.

PHOTOS: DAVID RUDIE

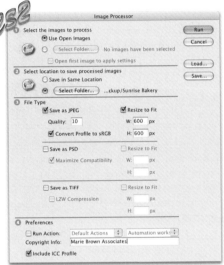

File > Scripts > Image Processor can be used to save several files at once in the same format with the same copyright information. If you choose to save files in more than one format, they will be saved in separate folders named by format. If you choose to add copyright information, the information you specify will be added to the Copyright Notice line of the File Info and a © will appear before the name in the title bar of the working window when the file is opened.

Look for "Beyond the Basic Shortcuts" (the **Wow Shortcuts.pdf** file) in the **Wow Goodies** folder on the Wow DVD-ROM. It's a collection of useful Photoshop CS and CS2 shortcuts.

The **Image Processor** in CS2 (File > Scripts > Image Processor) is ideal for saving a batch of files in one of the commonly used file formats (or more than one format), even at a particular size; you can even run an Action as part of the processing.

Learning Keyboard Shortcuts

Whether you invent your own keyboard shortcuts using the Edit > Keyboard Shortcuts command or simply use the built-in shortcuts Adobe supplies, knowing the keys that access Photoshop's tools and the menu commands you use most (both for the main menus and the palette menus) can really save time. On the Wow DVD-ROM that comes with this book you'll find the **Wow Shortcuts.pdf** file, a collection of the shortcuts we find most useful beyond those for choosing tools. The file is designed to be viewed on-screen or printed out as a reference.

Managing Presets

Photoshop gives you tremendous freedom to make your own tools and effects — brush tips, specialized tools, Layer Styles, patterns, gradients, swatches of colors, and more. As you take advantage of this potential, you can save your creations as **presets**, so you won't have to reinvent them when you want to use them again later. To save presets permanently, they need to be included in named sets and the sets have to be saved. Directions for using the Preset Manager for saving Layers Styles can be found in the "Saving Styles" tip on page 47. The process is the same for the other kinds of presets as well: First you use the "Create new. . ." option to add your new preset to the currently active set (see "The 'Make One' Button" below). Then you can choose Edit > Preset Manager, choose the appropriate Preset Type in the Preset Manager dialog box, and save a new set.

THE "MAKE ONE" BUTTON

In a pop-out palette such as the one for editing brushes or any of the ones for choosing patterns, the "Create a new. . ." button ⬚ lets you name the current element and add it as a new preset. This gives you a way to keep a brush tip you've changed, for example, or create a Pattern preset from a Pattern Overlay that's included in a Style.

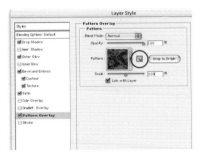

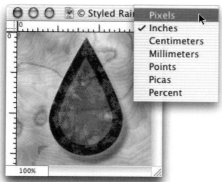

You can change the ruler units by right/Ctrl-clicking on one of the rulers.

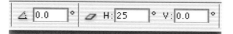

Double-click on a ruler to open the Units & Rulers section of the Preferences dialog box, so you can see or change the Column Width or Gutter. Photoshop can use Column Width as a unit of measure for creating a new file or resizing an image.

Smart Guides can be useful for lining up elements "by eye." A Smart Guide appears when the center, top, bottom, or a side of an element lines up with the center or an edge of another element. Here Smart Guides are used to align elements in a pattern tile (page 41).

The Options bar for the Transform commands reflects any changes you make by manipulating the center point or handles of the Transform box. Or you can enter numbers for the parameters you want to change, such as the rotation angle and horizontal or vertical skew, in the part of the Options bar shown here.

Taking Advantage of Precision Tools

Photoshop is equipped for precision. You can toggle the **rulers** on and off by typing **Ctrl/⌘-R**, and change the ruler units by right/Ctrl-clicking on a ruler to open a context-sensitive menu of units. Double-clicking on a ruler opens the Units & Rulers section of the Preferences dialog box, where you can see and reset the column size.

You can also create **Guides** simply by dragging from either the top or the side ruler, and set up a custom **Grid** by choosing Edit > Preferences > Guides, Grid & Slices (Windows) or Photoshop > Preferences > Guides, Grid & Slices (Mac). You can toggle visibility on and off for these Guides (**Ctrl/⌘-'**) and Grid (**Ctrl-Alt-' or ⌘-Option-'**), and make them "magnetic" by choosing the Snap options in the View menu. (For more information about Guides and Grid, see the "Drawing on the Grid" tip on page 435 and "Exercising Drawing Tools" on page 456.)

Photoshop CS2 has acquired **Smart Guides**, which in version CS are found only in ImageReady. You can turn on these transient guidelines by choosing **View > Show > Smart Guides**. Then, as long as **Extras** is turned on in the View menu, these handy "outriggers" will appear as you reposition a layer with the Move tool ▸⊕ to show you when the edges or center of the element you're moving is precisely aligned with the edges or centers of other elements in the file, such as shapes, slices, and the content of transparent layers.

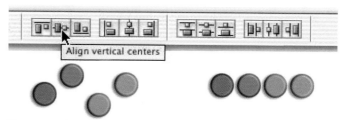

The same options provided in Photoshop's Align Linked and Distribute Linked commands from the Layer menu are also provided as buttons in the Options bar when the Move tool ▸⊕ is chosen. They let you line up or evenly space the contents of several layers. In Photoshop CS you can align them by clicking a layer thumbnail in the Layers palette, then clicking in the Links column next to the 👁 in each of the other layers to link them, and finally choosing Layer > Align Linked and selecting the type of alignment you want, or clicking the appropriate alignment button, as shown above. The elements will be aligned according to your choice (right). In CS2 it's even easier. Simply Ctrl/⌘-click or Shift-click the layers whose content you want to align, and then choose the command or click the button.

You can set options for logging the editing history of your work by choosing Edit > Preferences > General (Windows) or Photoshop > Preferences > General (Mac). The **Sessions Only** option logs every time you launch Photoshop or open or close a file. **Concise** makes a log that's similar to the information tracked by the History palette (described on page 32). And **Detailed** logs the really detailed sort of information that's collected when you record an Action (as described on page 112).

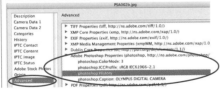

The **Options bar for the Transform and Free Transform commands** allows you to enter precise specifications for angles and distances. (See "Transforming & Warping" on page 71.)

When the **Move** tool is selected, the **Distribute Linked** and **Align Linked** commands from the Layer menu automatically accomplish even spacing and alignment of elements.

Recording What You Do

Any time you make changes that you think you might someday want to apply to other images, record the process using the Actions palette. Recording doesn't take extra time or RAM, and it may very well produce a useful "macro." Actions work better for recording some processes than for others. For instance, brush strokes with painting and toning tools are not recorded. To get a start on recording and applying Actions, see "Automating with Actions" in Chapter 3.

Using the Edit History Log

Another way to record what you're doing is to use the **Edit History Log**. Unlike an Action, this log doesn't let you replay what you've done, but it can keep a record (in text form) of everything done to the file; you can choose the level of detail you want to record by selecting from the Edit Log Items menu in the General Preferences dialog box. Unlike the History palette (described on page 32), when the file is closed the Edit History Log persists as part of the metadata (information about the file, such as camera settings, copyright, and so on). It continues when the file is reopened, and it goes along if you duplicate the file or save a copy. The log can be helpful if there's no other way to recall what you've done to a file — filter settings you used but weren't able to save, for instance, or that Levels adjustment you made directly from the menu instead of using an

When a Layer Style is applied to a layer and then the layer's content is changed, the Style automatically conforms to the new content, as shown here. The font was changed for the "Hot Rods" type layer, and the wording was changed for the other type layer.

With an Adjustment layer you can explore tone and color options as we did to recover this antique sepiatone (page 269). In the Layers palette simply double-click the layer's thumbnail to open the dialog box so you can make changes. Or change the blend mode or Opacity of the layer.

Adjustment layer. You can go back and read through the text in the log by choosing File > File Info and clicking on History.

If you choose to save the log as a separate file (the Text File or the Both option in the General Preferences dialog), the log is preserved even if you don't save the file. So if you're experimenting and close the file without saving, then decide you want to know the color or filter setting you used in the experiment, you can open the file with a text-editing program and read it.

Maintaining Flexibility

Keeping your options open is an important part of developing a Photoshop file. By planning ahead and using instruction-based methods such as Layer Styles and Adjustment layers, you can build flexibility into your files, making your work easier and your workflow more efficient.

Using Layer Styles. Applying special-effects treatments by means of a Layer Style gives you tremendous flexibility. First, you can make repeated changes to the effects themselves without degrading the image. Second, you can apply the Style to one or more other layers in the same file or even in other files. And third, you can even change the contents of the layers you've applied them to and the effects will automatically and instantly "rewrap" themselves to fit the new contents. For a demonstration of the flexibility of Layer Styles, see page 44. To learn how to put Layer Styles to work, see "Working with Layer Styles" on page 490 and the sections that follow in Chapter 8, especially the "Anatomy" sections.

Working with Adjustment layers. If you apply color and tone corrections with Adjustment layers instead of menu commands, it's easy to readjust without starting over or degrading the original image by changing your changes. Adjustment layers also let you save settings from dialog boxes that don't include a "Save" button, such as Color Balance (see "Color Adjustment Options" starting on page 165 and "Working with Adjustment Layers" starting on page 248).

Protecting pixels. You can achieve some of the benefits of using instruction-based elements, even if you're working with pixel-based images, by making use of **Camera Raw** (in both CS and CS2) and **Smart Objects** (in CS2). If your image file is a photo in a camera's raw format, Photoshop will automatically open it in Camera Raw, where you can make a variety of

Keeping image edits or stages of a painting on separate layers allows flexibility — you can modify the way your changes interact with the developing image. Rather than use the Dodge and Burn tools, which are tricky to use and can't work on a separate layer, we used a "dodge and burn" layer to lighten the area under the eyes. We could then experiment with reducing the layer's Opacity to adjust the change to taste. The technique is described on page 316.

MAKING A MERGED COPY

Say you've built a layered file and now you want to apply a change to the entire image. One way to do it is to make a layer at the top of the layer stack that's a "merged" copy of everything visible in your file. Then, because it's a single layer, you can easily modify it, experimenting freely, since you still have all the separate layers below it in the layer stack.

Here's how to make a merged copy:

In CS, **hold down Ctrl-Shift-Alt** (Windows) or **⌘-Shift-Option** (Mac) and type **N** then **E**. (The "N" combination makes a new empty layer without opening the New Layer dialog, and the "E" combination turns the empty layer into a merged copy of all that's visible.)

The same process works in CS2, but you can also shorten it. Skip the "N" part and simply type **Ctrl-Shift-Alt-E** or **⌘-Shift-Option-E** to create a new merged layer.

tone and color adjustments interactively and then apply these changes in one operation before opening the file in Photoshop. And you can always get back to the original raw data in the file. Smart Objects can provide a similar kind of protection from "pixel fatigue."

Saving selections as you work. When you use the selection tools or commands to make a complex selection (see page 55), save the selection periodically by making it into an alpha channel (Select > Save Selection). Be sure to save the selection one last time when it's finished, so you can reselect exactly the same area if you need to later.

Making a "repairs" or "painting" layer. If you're using the Sharpen/Blur/Smudge tool, or the Clone Stamp, Healing Brush, or Spot Healing Brush to make repairs to an image, you can add the repairs to a separate, transparent top layer, making sure that Use All Layers/Sample All Layers is selected in the tool's Options bar ("Softening a Portrait" on page 307 shows examples). With a repairs layer the sharpening, blurring, smudging, healing, or stamping strokes will sample from a composite of all layers, but you can keep the repairs isolated so the new work doesn't actually get mixed into the image. If you want to undo or modify part of your repair work, you can erase, or select and delete, that part from the repairs layer, leaving the rest of the repairs intact. You can also change the opacity or blend mode▼ of the layer to change its contribution to the image. A related approach can be used for applying the Dust & Scratches filter to remove blemishes from a photo, as shown in "Fixing a Problem Photo" on page 302.

FIND OUT MORE

▼ Blend modes
page 173

Using a separate layer is also a practical approach for adding brush strokes to a painting without risking the work you've already done. When you're sure you like the new brush strokes, you can merge them with the layer below (Ctrl/⌘-E), then add another new layer and experiment with more strokes.

Duplicating a layer. Sometimes you may want to make changes to a particular layer but you also want an "escape hatch" to get back to the previous version if the changes don't work out. Or you might want the flexibility of combining the changed version with the original. In that case, copy the layer (Ctrl/⌘-J) and work on the copy.

Here we started with a scan of line art (top left), duplicated the layer (Ctrl/⌘-J), and then applied the Spatter filter to the new layer (top right). We changed this new layer's Opacity to 75% and its blend mode to Screen. In Screen mode, the black "spatters" had no effect; only the light spots were combined with the original black artwork.

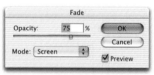

The Spatter filter result shown above can also be achieved by filtering the original layer and then using the Edit > Fade command to reduce the Opacity and change the blend mode. The difference is that it's easier to adjust the two-layer version later if you like.

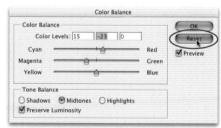

In a dialog box like Color Balance, where there are a number of settings that can be adjusted, use Ctrl/⌘-Z to undo the last slider setting or typed entry. To restore the starting values for all sliders in the box, hold down the Alt/Option key to change the "Cancel" button to a "Reset" button.

RECOVERING FROM MISTAKES

Even if you use Layer Styles, Adjustment layers, Smart Objects, and other procedural methods to give yourself as much flexibility as possible for making changes later, if you're at all adventurous, you're going to do something in Photoshop that you want to undo. Luckily, Photoshop has you covered — with enough options so you can feel free to experiment.

Undoing

Photoshop's **Ctrl/⌘-Z** (for Edit > **Undo**) will undo your last operation, and the History palette can be set up to let you go much further back. You can either click one of the states in the palette (for more, see "The History Palette" later in this section) or use **Ctrl/⌘-Shift-Z** (or Edit > Step Backward) to backtrack through your most recent changes. The History States setting (Edit > Preferences > General in Windows, or Photoshop > Preferences > General on the Mac) determines how many steps you can undo. You can also **use "Undo" inside a dialog box** that has more than one entry box or slider, pressing **Ctrl/⌘-Z** to undo the last setting you changed.

Resetting a Dialog Box

In any dialog box that lets you enter at least one value and that has a "Cancel" button, holding down the **Alt/Option** key changes the "Cancel" button to the **"Reset"** button; clicking this button leaves the box open but returns all the settings to the state they were when you first opened the box.

Fading

Immediately after you apply a filter, a color adjustment command, or a painting stroke — before you do anything else — you can use the Edit > **Fade** command to reduce the effect or change the blend mode.

Reverting

The File > **Revert** command takes the file back to its condition the last time it was saved. You can also revert to any stage you've saved as a Snapshot in the History palette, as described next. The Revert command can be undone (Ctrl/⌘-Z) if you change your mind.

Using the History Palette

The History palette (Window > History) is a kind of interactive "chain of events" that lets you go back to an earlier state of your file. The palette "remembers" the most recent **states**, or

The History palette and Fill command can be used to restore part of a previous version of the image. This method was used here to focus attention on the face: First the image was blurred and the face area was selected with a feathered Elliptical Marquee ◯. Then the original sharp version of the image (the Open state) was designated as the source, and Edit > Fill was used with History chosen to fill the selected area. The feathering of the selection allowed a seamless blend of the sharp and blurred versions of the image.▼

PHOTO: BEVERLY GOWARD

FIND OUT MORE

▼ Selecting & feathering **page 56**

steps, of your current work session — the work you've done since opening the file — and allows you to undo state by state.

More than just a step, a History **Snapshot** is a stored version of the file. You can make a Snapshot by Alt/Option-clicking the "Create new snapshot" button 🔳 at the bottom of the History palette. Typically, it's a good idea to make a **"Merged Layers" Snapshot rather than a layered one** (see "History Trouble" on the next page).

Stepping back. You can go back to a previous stage of the file by clicking on the thumbnail for a state or Snapshot in the History palette. Another way to restore part of an earlier version of an image is to choose the History Brush 🖌 and then click in the column to the left of the thumbnail for the state or Snapshot you want to use as a source, and paint. Or click to set the source and use the Edit > Fill command.

In practice, the History palette's "memory" can be quite limited. In order to keep from tying up too much RAM, by default the palette retains only the last 20 steps. You can increase the number of steps, but this increases the amount of RAM used

HISTORY

The History palette stores step-by-step **states** at the bottom, recording everything you do to the file. **Snapshots**, made when you choose to preserve the file at a particular stage of development, are stored at the top of the palette. The History Brush icon 🖌 in the **source column** means that the state or Snapshot next to the icon will be the source for any tool or command that can use History.

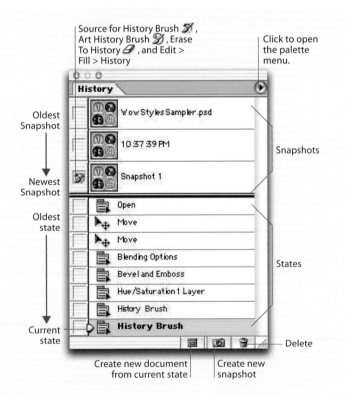

Source for History Brush 🖌, Art History Brush 🖌, Erase To History ⌫, and Edit > Fill > History

Click to open the palette menu.

Oldest Snapshot

Newest Snapshot

Oldest state

Current state

Snapshots

States

Create new document from current state

Create new snapshot

Delete

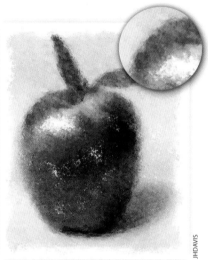

Besides providing multiple undo's, History can serve as a source for painting with the Art History Brush. This tool generates brush strokes that automatically follow the color and contrast contours in an image, using a Snapshot or state from the History palette as a source. With carefully chosen settings, you can produce a pleasing Art History Brush "painting." The lower apple was painted with a Wow Art History Brush preset that simulates pastels. You can see more Art History examples on page 396 and in "Art History Lessons" on page 388.

and potentially slows down all Photoshop operations. (To change the number of states History retains, choose Edit > Preferences > General in Windows, or Photoshop > Preferences > General on the Mac.) One approach to working with History efficiently is to limit the number of states to 20 or fewer and duplicate any current state that you think you might want to refer back to by clicking on that state in the History palette and choosing File > Save As > Save: As a Copy; it will be saved as a closed file so it won't occupy RAM.

Setting History options. If you click the History palette's ⊙ button to pop out the palette menu and choose History Options, you can set History to create a new Snapshot as soon as you open a file (the **Automatically Create First Snapshot** option is turned on by default) and whenever you save the file as you work (the **Automatically Create New Snapshot When Saving** option automatically names the Snapshot with the time you saved the file). With **Allow Non-Linear History** you can also go back to an earlier state of the file (by clicking its thumbnail in the palette) and make changes at that point, without throwing away all the states since then. The **Show New Snapshot Dialog by Default** option automatically opens the New

HISTORY TROUBLE

If you make a Snapshot from the Full Document rather than from Merged Layers, you can run into trouble later if you've added any layers in the meantime. If you try to paint on one of your new layers with the History Brush or Art History Brush from the Full-Document Snapshot, you'll see a warning:

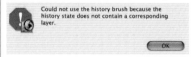

And if you try to use the Eraser tool or the Fill command, the History option will be dimmed and unavailable.

You can **avoid** this problem by choosing Merged Layers when you make a Snapshot:

But if you've already made a Full-Document Snapshot and you get the "Could not use..." message or find the History option dimmed for the Eraser or Fill, there's a way to **remedy** the situation: Click on your Full-Document Snapshot's thumbnail to activate it, then take another Snapshot — merged this time — and then drag the old one to the trash at the bottom of the palette if you no longer need it for anything.

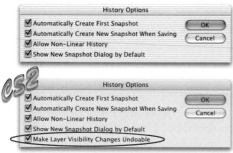

The settings in the History Options dialog box determine how the History palette operates. New in CS2 is the option to Make Layer Visibility Changes Undoable.

HOLDING ONTO HISTORY

History "evaporates" when you close a file, which means that you can no longer use its states for multiple Undo's and you can't work from any Snapshots you've previously made. With a little planning and effort, though, you can hold onto the Snapshots:

Before you close the file, in the History palette drag a Snapshot's thumbnail to the "Create new document from current state" button 🗒 at the bottom of the palette.

Repeat this process for any of the other Snapshots you want to preserve. Close and save all the new files before you quit. When you're ready to work on the image again, open the file itself, along with all the duplicates you made. Drag the initial Snapshot from each duplicate's History palette into the original file. The dragged Snapshots will be added to the current History palette.

Snapshot box when you click the 🖼 button at the bottom of the palette, so you're always offered the chance to name the Snapshot and choose "From: Merged Layers" if you like.

Ordinarily, making a layer visible or invisible by clicking in the 👁 column of the Layers palette is not recorded as a state in the History palette. However, in CS2 if you turn on the **Make Layer Visibility Changes Undoable** option, History records a state whenever you turn a layer's visibility off or on.

History disappears when you close the file, so the current states and any Snapshots you've made won't be there when you open the file again. But if you want to save Snapshots from one work session for use in the next, see the "Holding Onto History" tip at the left.

KEEPING PHOTOSHOP HAPPY

Photoshop files tend to be large — the number of layers is limited only by your computer's capacity to keep track of them. And a great deal of information has to be stored to record the color of each of the thousands or billions of pixels that can make up an image. Simply opening a file, which brings that information into the computer's working memory, or RAM, can take quite a bit of computer processing. And applying a special effect can involve complicated calculations for evaluating and changing the color of every pixel in the image. Here are some suggestions for making sure Photoshop has what it needs to do all this work efficiently.

Add RAM

The system requirements that Adobe lists for Photoshop CS and CS2, including 256 MB of RAM, can be considered minimums. The faster your computer is and the more RAM it has, the faster Photoshop will work and the more you'll enjoy using it.

Use a Bigger Scratch Disk

If Photoshop doesn't have enough room to handle a file entirely in RAM, it can use hard disk space to extend its memory — that's *virtual memory*, or in Photoshop parlance *scratch disk*. In that case, two factors become important. The first is how much empty hard disk space you should keep clear for Photohop's use, beyond the 280 MB (Windows) or 320 MB (Mac) required for running Photoshop. You'll want at least as much space as you have RAM *plus* at least five times the size of any file you might work on.

In **Scratch Sizes** mode the box near the lower left corner of the working window shows roughly how much RAM is available for Photoshop to use (right) and how much memory is currently tied up by all open Photoshop files plus the clipboard, Snapshot, and so on (left). If the left-hand figure is higher, Photoshop is using virtual memory.

Would more RAM help? You can watch the **Efficiency** indicator to see how much Photoshop is using RAM alone, rather than swapping data with the scratch disk. A value near 100% means the scratch disk isn't being used much, so adding more RAM probably wouldn't improve performance. A value less than about 75% means that assigning more RAM would probably help.

In Photoshop CS2 the Scratch Sizes and Efficiency options are accessed by clicking the arrow and choosing Show from the menu.

The second factor is the transfer rate of the disk drive, or the speed at which data can be read off the disk. Consider dedicating an entire fast multi-gigabyte hard disk drive as a scratch disk. Disk space is relatively cheap these days, and this will give Photoshop plenty of "elbow room." Second best would be to dedicate a multi-gigabyte partition of a hard disk as the scratch disk. Either way, because you won't be storing anything on it permanently, the drive or partition won't become *fragmented*, with the free space broken up into small pieces, and you won't have to run a defragmenting program periodically to put the pieces back together in the larger blocks of space that Photoshop needs to run in top-notch form.

Free Up RAM

If you find that Photoshop is slowing down or that its efficiency is consistently well below 100% (see "Efficiency Indicators" at the left), there are some things you can do to free up RAM or to operate Photoshop in ways that don't require as much memory.

Close other programs. Even if you aren't doing anything with them at the moment, open applications can tie up RAM. To make more available for Photoshop, close other programs.

Reduce the number of presets. Loading a file of Layer Styles, color Gradients, Brushes, or other presets can use a significant amount of RAM and scratch disk. Keeping presets organized so they're easy to find and load, but loading only those you need at the time, can reduce the drain on RAM. "Installing Wow Styles, Patterns, Tools & Other Presets" on page 5 tells how to make presets accessible in the menus of appropriate palettes so you can easily choose them.

Purge. As Photoshop works, it accumulates a lot more things in RAM than just what it needs to carry out the command you've given it most recently. In the *clipboard* it remembers the last thing you copied or cut from a file, and in *History* it remembers a certain number of your most recent steps in working with a file, as described in "Using the History Palette" on page 31). Since you can have more than one file open at a time in Photoshop and the program keeps track of the History for every open file, all that remembering can tie up quite a bit of memory. There are certain commands that Photoshop can carry out only in RAM, not by using the scratch disk, so it's good strategy to release RAM by clearing out a large clipboard selection or purging History that you no longer need. If you choose

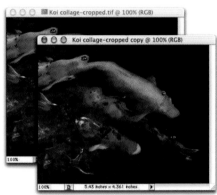

When you copy a file by using the Image > Duplicate command or the History palette's "Create a new document from current state" button 🔲, the new file is named but not saved. As soon as you duplicate a file, it's a good idea to choose File > Save (Ctrl/⌘-S) so you can rename and permanently save the document.

Edit > Purge, any choices that aren't grayed out indicate that something is stored and can be purged. When you Purge Histories, the states (step-by-step changes) will be deleted, but the Snapshots you've made will remain.

Use "low-overhead" alternatives for copying. If RAM is limited, there are several ways you can "copy and paste" without using the clipboard and tying up RAM:

- **To duplicate a targeted layer (or a selected area of it) as another layer in the same file**, press Ctrl/⌘-J (for Layer > New > Layer via Copy). ▼

FIND OUT MORE

▼ Making selections
page 55

- **To duplicate a selected area to another open file**, drag and drop the selection with the Move tool ▸⊕ from the one document's working window to the other. To center the selection in the new file, press and hold the Shift key as you drag.

- **To duplicate a layer, channel, or Snapshot from one file to another**, drag it from the Layers, Channels, or History palette of the source file into the working window of the file you want to add it to.

- **To copy an entire image as a new file**, either with all layers intact or merged into a single layer, choose Image > Duplicate.

GETTING SOME PRACTICE

To familiarize yourself with some of the options available for constructing a flexible Photoshop file, try the "Anatomy" section and the two "Exercising" sections that follow. Then enjoy the "Gallery" of inspirational artwork, starting on page 48 and demonstrating a variety of Photoshop approaches. 🖋

A Photoshop File

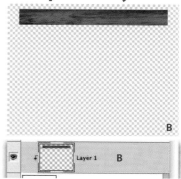

The picture we see when we look at a Photoshop file in print or on-screen is often a combination of elements. The Layers palette provides one way to look at the makeup of the file and also to access its individual components.

Here we use the finished file for "Adding Type to an Image" from Chapter 9 as an example of how the components found in a typical Photoshop file are represented in the Layers palette.

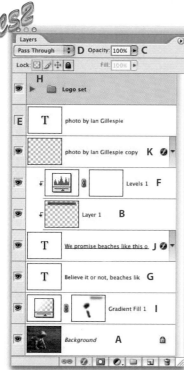

The three layers that make up the logo in the lower right corner have been collected in a layer set/group (shown at the top of the palette) to keep the parts together and help make the Layers palette more compact.

Background

A ***Background*** **A** is a pixel-based layer without the potential for transparency or for having a Layer Style applied. Locked in place, it can't be moved, rotated, or scaled. Scans and digital photos typically consist of a *Background* only. A *Background* can be given the potential for transparency by double-clicking its name. Not every layered Photoshop file has a *Background,* but if it's present, it's the bottom layer in the stack.

Transparent Layers

Regular pixel-based layers that aren't a *Background* have the potential for **transparency**, which Photoshop represents on-screen as a gray checkerboard pattern. This layer **B** holds a copy of a part of the *Background*; here it has been made part of a clipping group (as described on page 38). Besides parts of images, transparent layers can also hold pixels applied with Photoshop's painting, drawing, and image-editing tools.

Opacity, Blend Mode & Visibility

For any layer other than the *Background,* you can adjust **Opacity** and **Fill opacity C** (the difference is explained on page 577), and also change the **blend mode D** (how the colors in a layer interact with the rest of the image). Opacity and blend mode can be changed repeatedly without damage to the layer. You can also turn off a layer's visibility completely by clicking its 👁 icon, as shown in **E** at the left.

We promise beaches like this one.

Believe it or not, beaches like this still exist. Where the waves are gentle, the sand is soft, and marine life is everywhere in abundance.

For a vacation in unsurpassed natural beauty with wonders that never cease, come to La Playa Island Resorts. You'll find us on the Web at www.laplaya.com.

1.800.555.2323

Adjustment Layers

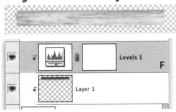

An **Adjustment layer** is instruction-based. It contributes to the image by changing the tone or color of layers below it in the stack. For instance, the role of the Levels Adjustment layer in this file **F** is to lighten the image in the layer just below it. An Adjustment layer has a built-in mask, ready to be edited to target the effect of the layer (see "Masks," at the right). The dialog box for the adjustment can be reopened at any time and the adjustment changed, so it's a very flexible way to change tone and color. Each kind of adjustment layer (Levels, Curves, Invert, and so on) is identified in the Layers palette by a specific symbol, although a generic symbol ⊘ is used if the file is much wider than it is tall.

Type Layers

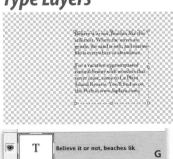

A **type layer,** represented by a "T" symbol in the Layers palette, holds "live" (editable) type. So, for instance, if we wanted to change the wording of the text in this layer **G**, we could select and edit the type; we could also change the type's font, size, or other characteristics, or reshape the area it fills.

Shape & Fill Layers

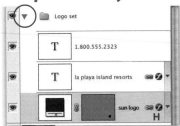

Shape and **Fill layers** are instruction-based. They tell what solid color, gradient, or pattern should be applied to the layer; these instructions can be changed without disturbing any pixels. A built-in mask controls where the color, gradient, or pattern is revealed. In this file the sun logo in the lower right corner is a shape layer **H**, and a Gradient Fill layer (shown below) is used to lighten the right side of the image to make the block of type easier to read.

Masks

With a mask you can hide part of a layer without actually removing that part, so you can easily bring back the hidden component if you want to, just by changing the mask. Each layer (except *Background*) can have two masks — a pixel-based layer mask and an instruction-based vector mask. The **layer mask** on the Gradient Fill layer **I** protects the face, hand, and an area behind the headline from being lightened by the white ramp that makes a background for the paragraph type. The **vector mask** on the shape layer (shown at the top of the column) defines the shape of the logo; a vector mask can be scaled and rotated without any "softening" of its crisp edges.

Clipping Groups

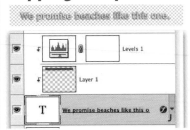

A **clipping group** is a construction that uses a clipping layer as a kind of mask for the layers above. For instance, a clipping group is used in this file to "fill" the headline type with an image **J**. The type is the clipping layer; it masks, or "clips," both the image layer and the Adjustment layer, allowing them to show only within the "footprint" created by the type. Like layer masks and vector masks, clipping groups are "nondestructive." (Page 70 has more about clipping groups.)

Layer Styles

A Layer Style can supply color, texture, dimension, and lighting for any layer except a *Background*. "Exercising Layer Styles" on page 44 is an introduction to working with Layer Styles. In the Layers palette a Style is represented by the ⓕ symbol on the layer. You can open a list to view the components of the Style, or close the list to make the Layers palette more compact, by clicking the tiny triangle ▼ next to the ⓕ. In this image Layer Styles provide drop shadows for the headline type and the logo elements, and a Style also supplies the "carved" look for the photo credit **K**.

Smart Objects

New in Photoshop CS2, a **Smart Object** is like a file within a file. Once you make a Smart Object (or import one from Adobe Illustrator or Camera Raw), you can carry it along as a "package" in your larger file, treating it as a single layer — you can scale, distort, or warp the entire "package," copy it, apply a Layer Style to it, or integrate it into the file with masks, Adjustment layers, clipping groups, and so on.

You can also open the package — by double-clicking its thumbnail in the Layers palette. This opens the Smart Object as a separate file (launching Illustrator or Camera Raw if necessary) so you can get back inside the package and edit its contents as you would any Photoshop (or Illustrator or Camera Raw) file. When you save the edited file, the changes are automatically carried through to the larger file.

Here are some of the reasons Smart Objects are so useful:

- A Smart Object **protects pixel-based contents** from deteriorating if you repeatedly scale, rotate, or otherwise transform them (as explained on page 20). For instance, you can copy a Smart Object, scale and rotate the copy, make another copy from that one and scale and rotate some more, and so on, with no more deterioration than a single scale-and-rotate operation would cause.

- If your larger file includes several copies (or *instances*) of a Smart Object, **you can edit all the instances of a Smart Object at the same time**, simply by opening, editing, and saving just one of them.

- With a Smart Object and instances, **file size is smaller** than with standard layer copies, since the Smart Objects *refer to* the original rather than actually duplicating it in the file.

- You can **"spin off" one or more instances** into a new Smart Object, which breaks the updating link. You can then change just the instances in the *new* Smart Object, without changing the other instances, or vice versa.

YOU CAN FIND THE FILES

in  > Wow Project Files > Chapter 1 > Exercising Smart Objects:

- Exercising SO-Before.psd (to start)
- Dancers.psd (for step 5)
- Exercising SO-After.psd (to compare)

THIS SECTION INTRODUCES the mechanics of working with Smart Objects by using them to build and then modify a pattern tile. Whether or not you're an avid user of patterns, the exercise will show you the potential of Smart Objects and provide some important tips about their use.

First you'll make and arrange several copies of a Smart Object to create the pattern used on the wall in the illustration above. Then you'll convert the pattern tile to a new pattern (used here for the dress) by editing the Smart Object to substitute a dancing couple for the leaping lady and then creating a new Smart Object to substitute "JOY" for some instances of the dancing couple. At the end of the process, you'll have a working knowledge of Smart Objects, as well as a file you can use to generate your own patterns if you like. If you'd like to know more about options for editing Smart Object–based patterns, see the "Gallery" on page 572.

1 Setting up the File

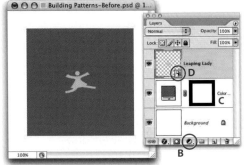

To start the pattern tile, we made a new file (File > New) 300 pixels square **A**, which was slightly larger than the tile we wanted to design. To make the tile base, we Shift-dragged with the Rectangular Marquee tool ⬚ to make a square selection,▼ leaving space at the edges of the document so our pattern elements could extend outside the tile. With the selection active, we clicked the "Create new fill or adjustment layer" button ⊘ at the bottom of the Layers palette **B** and added a Solid Color Fill layer **C** by choosing Solid Color from the menu, and picking a color.

In a separate layer we added the graphic element for the pattern — a rasterized version of a character from the Pedestria font (from MVBFonts.com). This completed the **Exercising SO-Before.psd** file; open it to follow along, or create your own similarly structured file.

In the Layers palette, target your pattern element layer by clicking its thumbnail. Turn it into a Smart Object by choosing Layer > Smart Objects > **Group Into New Smart Object**. In the Layers palette, a little notch in the thumbnail for the layer will show that the layer is now a Smart Object **D**. Creating this "file within a file" will protect the graphic from deteriorating as we transform copies of it (in step 3). The Smart Object also sets the stage for changing the entire pattern by changing a single layer (in steps 5 and 6).

FIND OUT MORE

▼ Making selections
page 55

2 Making & Copying a Smart Object

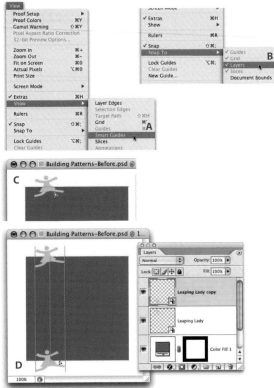

Photoshop CS2's other "smart" technology, **Smart Guides**, will make it easy to align graphics "on the fly" so they cross the edges of the tile seamlessly, to help hide our pattern's "repeat." Choose View > Show, and turn on Smart Guides **A**; also in the View menu, turn on Snap, then choose **Snap To** and turn on **Layers B**.

Choose the Move tool ▶⊕ and drag your pattern element so it overlaps the top edge of the tile. When the element is centered on the edge, you'll see a Smart Guide running through the center of it **C**.

The next step is to arrange a perfectly paired element on the opposite edge of the tile, so any overhang on the top is balanced on the bottom. This will make a seamless transition from tile to tile when you define the pattern in step 4. Duplicate the Smart Object layer (type Ctrl/⌘-J) to make a copy; the copy is tied to the original so that if *either* Smart Object is opened, edited, and saved, *both* Smart Objects will be updated with the changes. With the Move tool ▶⊕, hold down the Shift key, and in the working window drag the copy down to the bottom edge of the tile **D**. The Shift key will keep the copy aligned with the original, and a "snap" will let you know when the copy is centered on the edge.

3 Making More "Instances"

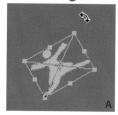

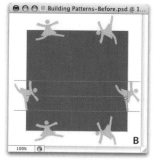

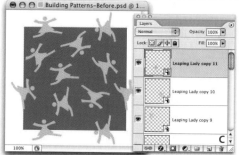

To make other edge-crossing pairs, first make another copy of the Smart Object: With either Smart Object layer targeted, type Ctrl/⌘-J again. For variety, tilt the new element (type Ctrl/⌘-T, move the cursor outside the Transform box until it turns into a curved, double-headed arrow, and drag to rotate; then press the Enter key) **A**. With the Move tool ▶₊, drag this transformed element to an edge; again rely on the Smart Guides and the "snap" to center the element on the edge. Make the second half of the pair (Ctrl/⌘-J) and Shift-drag until it's centered on the opposite edge.

(Once an edge pair is aligned, you can move the pair around, as long as you move both elements together: Click on the thumbnail for one element in the Layers palette, then Ctrl/⌘-click the other's thumbnail and use the Move tool ▶₊ in the working window to drag them into position.)

Make any additional edge elements you want **B**. Then go back to the View menu and turn off Smart Guides and Snap To > Layer, so they don't interfere as you fill in the rest of the tile. Duplicate the current Smart Object again (Ctrl/⌘-J), and drag this copy to a position fully inside the tile. Rotate the element. Then repeat the process (duplicate, drag, and transform) until you have as many elements as you want on your tile **C**. Because they were produced as copies of the original Smart Object layer, all the Smart Object instances are tied — editing any one will change all of them.

4 Defining a Pattern

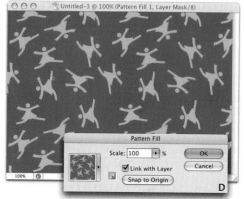

With your pattern elements arranged on the tile, define your first pattern: Make a selection by Ctrl/⌘-clicking on the layer mask thumbnail for the Fill layer in the Layers palette **A**. Then choose Edit > Define Pattern **B**, name the pattern, and click "OK" **C**.

To try out your new pattern, make a new file (File > New) more than twice the dimensions of the tile. Add a Pattern Fill layer by clicking the "Create new fill or adjustment layer" button ⬤, choosing Pattern. In the Pattern Fill dialog, choose your new pattern **D** (it will be the last swatch in the pop-out palette); finally, click "OK."

Examine the pattern fill in your new file. If you see any misalignment in the pattern (where two halves of one element don't match up exactly) or if you want to change the spacing of the elements, go back to the tile-development file and adjust alignment of the appropriate elements. You can also move any edge pairs or single internal elements to improve spacing in the pattern if you need to. Then select the pattern square again (by Ctrl/⌘-clicking its mask thumbnail) and choose Edit > Define Pattern to make a new version.

5 Editing a Smart Object

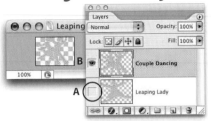

Now the *real* fun begins. The possibilities for variations on your pattern tile are endless. Experiment as described on this page and the next, and use the Edit > Define Pattern command when you've developed a tile you want to save.

Because we built the pattern using copies of a Smart Object, we can simply change one element to change them all. Double-click any of the Smart Object thumbnails in the Layers palette (or choose Layer > Smart Objects > Edit Contents). When the file-within-a-file opens, change the graphics by turning off visibility for the existing graphics layer (click its 👁 in the Layers palette **A**) and adding new graphics or type on a new layer. *Note:* **Make your replacement element no taller and no wider than the original element;** *scale it proportionately if necessary*▼ (otherwise it will be cropped in your pattern tile; see "Understanding the Package" on page 43). To follow along with this example, open the **Dancers.psd** file (another rasterized character from the Pedestria font) and use the Move tool ▶₊ to drag and position it **B**.

Save the Smart Object file (Ctrl/⌘-S). Then click in the window of your tile-development file to make it the active file; you'll see that the new character is substituted everywhere the Smart Object occurs, complete with the previously applied rotations **C**.

> **FIND OUT MORE**
> ▼ Transforming
> **page 71**

6 Creating a New Smart Object

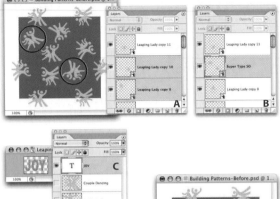

It's also possible to break the updating ties between instances of a Smart Object, so that changing one of them *doesn't* change all the others. This is done by creating a new Smart Object. In the Layers palette for your tile-development file, target the elements you want to change by clicking on the thumbnail for one of them and Ctrl/⌘-clicking the other thumbnails. (If you choose an element that crosses an edge, select its paired element also.) We targeted two internal elements **A**.

Then choose Layer > Smart Objects > **Group Into New Smart Object.** This brand-new "super" Smart Object **B** remembers any transforming you've done to the Smart Objects it contains (in this case rotating them to different angles). But you can now change the graphics in your new super Smart Object *without changing the other graphics in the file.*

In the Layers palette double-click the thumbnail for your super Smart Object. When the file opens, double-click one of its component Smart Objects, and change the graphics; we added a type layer with the word "JOY" in the Arial Black font in orange **C**. Save the file (Ctrl/⌘-S) to update your super Smart Object **D**. And finally, save the super Smart Object (Ctrl/⌘-S) to update the tile-development file **E**.

7 Applying Styles to Smart Objects

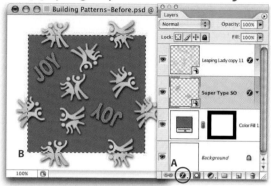

A Smart Object provides a way to apply a Layer Style to several layers at once. The **Exercising SO-After.psd** file includes the nested Smart Objects (from step 6) and the Layer Styles described next.

With the super Smart Object for "JOY" targeted in the Layers palette of the tile-development file (as shown above), we added a Drop Shadow effect — we clicked the "Add a layer style" button ✿ at the bottom of the Layers palette **A**, chose Drop Shadow from the pop-out list, and adjusted the Distance (offset), Size (softness), and Angle (where the light seems to come from) to create the kind of Drop Shadow we wanted. We saved the edited super Smart Object (Ctrl/⌘-S), which updated the tile-development file.

An efficient way to then add the same Drop Shadow to the dancing couples was to first turn them into another super Smart Object by targeting their layers in the Layers palette and choosing Layer > Smart Objects > Group Into New Smart Object, then copying the Drop Shadow for the "JOY" super Smart Object and pasting it onto the new Smart Object layer, so the shadows matched. ▼

To recolor one of the individual dancing-couple Smart Objects nested within this new super Smart Object, we double-clicked the thumbnail for one of them, then clicked the ✿ at the bottom of the Layers palette and added a Gradient Overlay effect. When we saved the edited Smart Object file, all the dancing couples in the new super Smart Object file were updated. And when we saved the super Smart Object file, the tile-development file was updated.

Now we selected the tile **B** and defined another pattern (as in step 4), and applied our two patterns to our illustration, shown on page 39. The "Gallery" on page 572 details the process of applying patterns.

FIND OUT MORE

▼ Working with Layer Styles
page 44

UNDERSTANDING THE PACKAGE

We can think of a Smart Object as consisting of two distinct parts — a *package* and its *contents.*

- The **contents** are the graphics, type, or photo material that you put into the Smart Object (by targeting layers in the Layers palette and choosing Layer > Smart Objects > Group into New Smart Object), or that you import from Camera Raw or Illustrator.

- The **package** is essentially a bounding box — the smallest rectangle that's big enough to surround the nontransparent contents of a Smart Object.

The green (nontransparent) area is the **contents.** The **"package"** is the smallest rectangle that will hold the contents.

Once a Smart Object is created, Photoshop lets you change the *contents* (for instance, by choosing Layer > Smart Objects > Edit Contents). When you save the edited Smart Object file, the larger "parent" file it resides in is updated with the changes.

But the Smart Object's *package,* or bounding box, is permanently "locked" at the size and shape it was when you first set up the Smart Object. This means that if you edit the Smart Object in a way that makes the new contents bigger than the original contents, the new contents will automatically be cropped to fit within the original package unless you scale the contents down (Ctrl/⌘-T and Shift-drag on a corner handle). Even if, instead of scaling, you were to enlarge the "canvas" of the Smart Object to accommodate the larger contents, the contents would nevertheless be scaled (often disproportionately) to fit within the original package when the parent file was updated.

If you anticipate needing to edit a Smart Object, you may be able to avoid cropping or scaling by making your original Smart Object big enough so the package can accommodate any likely edits. For instance, in Photoshop you can include a rectangle on a "placeholder" layer (with its visibility turned off) to hold some space for later changes. In an Illustrator Smart Object, include a no-stroke, no-fill rectangle larger than the artwork.

Layer Styles

With Photoshop's Layer Styles you can instantly turn flat type and graphics into glowing, textured dimensional objects, or add elegant styling to photos. From simple drop shadows to translucency to colorful bumpy surfaces, the possibilities are virtually unlimited. These three pages will give you an idea of the range of what Styles can do, and inspire you to make them part of your own Photoshop toolkit if you haven't already. There's more about how Styles are constructed and how to modify them or design your own in Chapter 8 and in "'Styling' a Photo" on page 196.

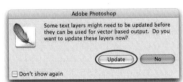

Adobe Photoshop

Some text layers might need to be updated before they can be used for vector based output. Do you want to update these layers now?

Update   No

☐ Don't show again

Because the Hot Rods files include live type, we've chosen faces that most people have (Arial Black and Trebuchet). If you see a warning when you open a Hot Rods file, you may have a slightly different version of one or more of the fonts. We suggest you click "Update" and ignore any small differences in how your file looks.

YOU'LL FIND THE FILES

in 🔵 > Wow Project Files > Chapter 1 > Exercising Styles:
- Hot Rods-Before.psd (to start)
- Hot Rods-Asphalt.psd (to compare at step 2)
- Hot Rods-Antique.psd (to compare at step 5)
- Hot Rods-Buttons.psd (to use at step 7)
- Wow Exercising Styles.asl (a Styles preset file)

1 Preparing the File

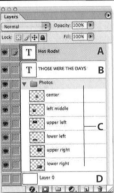

TO START, open the **Hot Rods-Before.psd** file and take a look at the Layers palette. Because there can be only one Layer Style per layer, for maximum flexibility each element is on a separate layer. To tidy up the Layers palette, we clicked the "Create a new set/group" button 🗋 at the bottom of the palette and dragged the photo layers' thumbnails into the folder thumbnail this created.

The *Background* is the only kind of layer than can't accept a Style, so we turned it into a standard layer by Alt/Option-double-clicking its thumbnail. (Here Layer 0's visibility has been toggled off by clicking its 👁 icon.)

2 Applying Styles

To add the **Wow Exercising Styles** to the Styles palette, choose Load Styles from the Styles palette's menu, opened by clicking the ⊙ button in the upper right corner of the palette. Target each layer in turn by clicking its thumbnail in the Layers palette, and apply a Style to it by clicking a thumbnail in the Styles palette.

A Wow Hot Rod (a Bevel and Emboss effect shapes the metal letters)
B Wow Red Letter* (the coloring comes from the combination of a Color Overlay and a Pattern Overlay)
C Wow Edge Glow (the Style consists of a Drop Shadow in a light color and Screen mode)
D Wow Asphalt* (the bumpy surface comes from Texture in the Bevel and Emboss effect)

"STYLING" SEVERAL LAYERS

Applying a Style from the Styles palette to several layers at once works differently in Photoshop CS than in CS2. **In CS:**

1 To link the layers, target one of them in the Layers palette; then, for all the other layers, click in the Links column to the left of the thumbnails. The 🔗 icon shows that a layer is linked to the targeted layer.

2 Apply a Style to one of the linked layers by clicking in the Styles palette.

3 Copy the Style you applied, by right-clicking (Windows) or Ctrl-clicking (Mac) on the 🎯 that appears next to the layer's name and choosing Copy Layer Style from the context-sensitive menu.

4 To paste the Style, right/Ctrl-click to the right of the name of a linked layer and choose Paste Layer Style to Linked.

In CS2's Layers palette, you can simply Shift-click or Ctrl/⌘-click the names of the layers you want to "style," and then click the Style in the Styles palette.

If the layers are in a group, it's even easier. In the Layers palette, click the group's folder icon 📁 and then click the Style in the Styles palette.

3 Scaling a Style

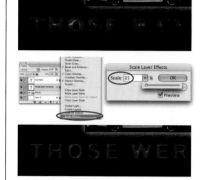

Whenever you apply a preset Layer Style, the first thing to do is to check the scale. If the Style was designed at a different resolution or for a larger or smaller element, it may look entirely different than it was designed to look until you resize it. This is the case with the **Wow Red Letter** Style on the lower line of type in this file.

You can scale all the effects in a Style together easily, by right-clicking (Windows) or Ctrl-clicking (Mac) on the 🎯 icon next to the name of the "styled" layer in the Layers palette and choosing Scale Effects from the context-sensitive menu when it opens. Use the slider, or type an entry, or hold down the Ctrl/⌘ key and "scrub" (drag left or right) over the number field. Scaling the **Wow Red Letter** Style to 25% brings out the bevel and pulls the drop shadow under the type.

* MEANS TEXTURE

In the Styles palette, an asterisk in the name of a Wow Style means that a pixel-based texture or pattern is used in this Style, so care should be taken when scaling it. Such a pattern or texture may look pixelated if you scale it up too much. And it can look fuzzy when it's scaled down, especially to a percentage other than 50% or 25%.

4 Instant Style Changes

A Layer Style can be changed instantly. With the layer targeted in the Layers palette, you can either assign a different Style by clicking in the Styles palette as we did here, or scale an entire Style to change its look as described at the left, or change any component effect.▼

A Wow Brass Edge (a Bevel and Emboss effect shapes the metal letters)

B Wow Brass Edge scaled to 50% to fit the smaller type

C Wow Antique (the Style tints the photos with a brown Color Overlay)

D Wow Painted Brick* (the same pattern used as a Pattern Overlay to define the bricks is also used as the Texture in Bevel and Emboss to create the dimensional effect)

Note: For a layer styled with **Wow Painted Brick** it's possible to keep the dimensional brick surface but remove the bevel from the edges of the layer, so the wall looks like it extends beyond the edges of the image. The "Pattern, Texture & Bevel" tip in Appendix B tells how to do this.

FIND OUT MORE

▼ Layer Style components **page 494**

5 Changing Content

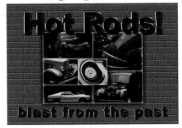

If you change the content of a layer, as we did here for both the large and the small type, the Style instantly conforms to the new content.

To change the font for the entire top line of type, target its layer in the Layers palette and choose the Type tool. Then, *without clicking in the working window*, change the Font in the Options bar to Arial Black.

To change the wording for the small type, in the Layers palette double-click the **T** thumbnail for the layer to select all the type, and in the Options bar choose the Arial Black font (or a similar bold face) and type the new wording.

COPYING & PASTING A STYLE

A Style from one layer can be copied and pasted to another layer, either in the same file or a different one. This can be especially handy if you've built a Style or changed one you applied from the Styles palette but you haven't yet given the new version a name and saved it.

1 In the Layers palette, right/Ctrl-click on the 🄵 for the layer that has the Style you want to copy. In the menu that opens, choose **Copy Layer Style**.

2 Then for the layer where you want to apply the Style, right/Ctrl-click to the right of the layer's name, and choose **Paste Layer Style** from the menu.

6 Scaling a "Styled" File

If you want to resize a scaled file, first duplicate it so you can keep the original: Choose Image > Duplicate. In the new file choose Image > Image Size. Make sure all three boxes in the lower left corner are checked, including Scale Styles. Then in the Pixel Dimensions section at the top of the box, type in a new Width or Height, whichever is the more important dimension (we used 600 pixels for Width) and click "OK."

DRAG & DROP

If you want **to copy a single effect,** such as a Drop Shadow or Outer Glow, from a "styled" layer to another layer, you can do it by dragging and dropping: In CS, with the list of effects for the layer open in the Layers palette, drag the name of the effect you want to copy onto the name of the layer you want to apply it to. In CS2, you'll need to hold down the Alt/Option key as you drag, because simply dragging *moves* the effect rather than copying it.

You can **copy all the effects** by dragging (or Alt/Option-dragging) the Effects line instead of an individual effect.

Note: Dragging and dropping **does not copy the layer's Opacity, Fill opacity, or other Blending Options** — only the *effects.* To copy these characteristics *and* the effects, use Copy Layer Style and Paste Layer Style, as described in "Copying & Pasting a Style" at the left.

7 Rollover Styles

In ImageReady, with one click in the Styles palette, you can apply combined Rollover Styles, which change when you move the cursor over a button or click on it.▼ Open the **Hot Rods-Buttons.psd** file in ImageReady **A**; this is the scaled-down file from step 6 at the left, to which we've added button labels and buttons with combined Rollover Styles.

We applied the **Wow Antique Stoplight** Rollover Style to all of the buttons. To demonstrate the rollover effect, click the Preview Document tool 👆 in the Tools palette **B**; then move the cursor over a button to trigger the Over Style **C**, and click to see the Down Style.

Like other Styles, Rollover Styles conform to the layer content, so it's easy to transform the button shape **D** while keeping the Style intact.▼ Automatic layer-based slicing in ImageReady ensures that the active area of the button conforms to the current button shape.

FIND OUT MORE

▼ Rollover Styles
page 690
▼ Transforming
page 71

Every Layer Style "remembers" its "design resolution" — the resolution (pixels per inch, or ppi) of the file in which it was originally created. Most of the Styles on the Wow DVD-ROM were designed in files at 225 ppi for printing; the exceptions are the Wow-Button Styles, which were designed at 72 ppi for use on-screen.

Whenever you apply a Style to a file whose resolution is different than the Style's design resolution, Photoshop automatically scales the Style, This scaling can make the Style look out of proportion. And if the Style includes a texture or pattern, it can also degrade the pattern.

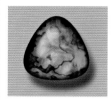  

Wow-Gibson Opal Style, (designed at 225 ppi) applied to a file whose resolution is 225 ppi

Wow-Gibson Opal Style applied to a file whose resolution is 72 ppi

To avoid unwanted automatic scaling, before you apply the Style, temporarily and nondestructively change your file to the Style's design resolution by taking these three steps:

1 To temporarily and nondestructively change a file's resolution to 225 ppi, for instance, choose Image > **Image Size** and **make sure Resample Image is turned off**. **Note the file's Resolution.** Then **change the Resolution** to 225 ppi to match the Style's "design resolution," and click "OK" to close the Image Size dialog box.

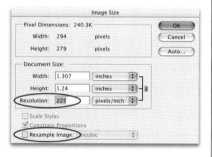

2 Now in the Layers palette click the thumbnail for the layer where you want to apply the Style, and click a thumbnail in the Styles palette to apply the Style.

3 Finally, you can nondestructively **change the file's resolution back to what it was**: Choose Image > Image Size, make sure Resample Image is still turned off, and type in the original resolution that you noted in step 1. **Nothing about the appearance of the Style will change.**

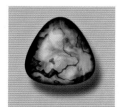

Before the **Wow-Gibson Opal** Style was applied to a 72 ppi file, the file's resolution was temporarily changed to 225 ppi (as in step 1 above). Afterwards the resolution was changed back (as in step 3).

Whenever you modify a Layer Style or create a new one, it's a good idea to name the new Style and save it as part of a set of presets so it's easy to find and use again later.

To add the Style that's on a layer to the current Styles palette, target the "styled" layer in the Layers palette and click the "Create new style" button at the bottom of the Styles palette; name the Style, and click "OK."

To save the Style permanently as part of a presets file so you can always load it and use it later, first add it to the Styles palette as described above. Then open the Styles palette's menu (click the ⊙ button) and choose Preset Manager; the Preset Manager will open to its Styles section.

To save a set with just a few of the current Styles, Shift-click or Ctrl/⌘-click those few Styles and click the "Save Set" button. But if you want to *save* more Styles than you want to *exclude*, it's faster to Shift-click or Ctrl/⌘-click on the few you *don't* want to save and click the "Delete" button. Then select all of the remaining Styles (Ctrl/⌘-A) and click "Save Set." Name the set, choose where to save it, and click "Save."

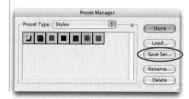

For his publisher, Haddad's Fine Arts, illustrator **Michael L. Kungl** created *Retro Tea, Deco Tea,* and *Espresso Fresco* in a style that combined the hard edges and gradients of Art Deco with the earthy and loose textures of natural media. Kungl began each poster as a pencil sketch and then moved the artmaking process to Adobe Illustrator, to Photoshop, to Corel Painter, and back to Photoshop. In Illustrator he drew the hard-edged curves that he then quickly converted into alpha channels in Photoshop. He saved the files in Photoshop (.psd) format and opened them in Painter. There he used the alpha-channels as "friskets" for masking, to control the color and textures as he applied them to several layers with Painter's outstanding brushes and gradient fills. Finally, he saved the layered files (again in PSD format) and returned them to Photoshop to make color adjustments and to convert the files to CMYK for printing. The process is described in more detail on page 484.

BLEND MODE COMPATIBILITY

While Photoshop and Painter share many layer blend modes, each program also includes unique modes that won't "travel" when files are opened in the other program. This may require combining some layers to preserve the color relationships before moving from one application to the other.

For his award-winning ***Man Walking with a Newspaper,*** **Mark Wainer** turned his photo (shown at the right) into a painterly image. For this particular piece, he cropped the sides to remove distracting elements, filtered the image, and made a series of transformations. After filtering as described for *Night Walk* on page 407, he widened parts of the image to balance the elements and to regain the width lost in cropping. He selected individual doors and other objects and transformed them, balancing the elements and widening the image to the proportions he wanted without distorting the man.▼ He used the Clone Stamp 🔧 and Healing Brush 🩹 to rearrange or modify some of the image elements including walls, doors, and stairs.▼ He used his Edge Burn Action, described on page 117 and provided on the Wow DVD-ROM, to subtly darken the edges of the image.

Wainer's finished images, hyper-real yet stylized and painterly, represent his visual impressions of the scenes as they were or as they could have been. They are printed at 24 x 32 inches or larger on coated watercolor paper with archival inks.

FIND OUT MORE

▼ Transforming **page 71**

▼ Using the Clone Stamp **page 253**

▼ Using the Healing Brush **page 315**

For **Donal Jolley's** title illustration for a magazine article, "***The Beauty of Your Thorns***," isolating the rose so it could be silhouetted began with the photography. Jolley ordered roses, chose one, and held it up against the bright sky at the angle he wanted to photograph. Aiming his digital camera at a wall close by sharing the same lighting as the rose, he set the exposure. When he then took the photo of the rose, the sky was "blown out" to a very light blue, which would make it easy to silhouette the subject.

Jolley opened the file in Photoshop and in the Layers palette double-clicked on the *Background* thumbnail to turn the *Background* into a layer that could include transparency. Then it was easy to use Select > Color Range to select the sky.▼ He added a layer mask based on the selection by Alt/Option-clicking the "Add layer mask" button ◻ at the bottom of the Layers palette. He cleaned up the layer mask▼ and then loaded the mask as a selection (by Ctrl/⌘-clicking its thumbnail in the Layers palette). He inverted the selection (Ctrl/⌘-Shift-I), targeted the layer itself rather than the mask, and pressed the Delete key to remove the sky pixels, so they wouldn't contaminate the blurring he would do next.

He composed the Illustration using two copies of the rose layer, the lower one sharp and the upper one blurred in Overlay mode and with the layer mask removed to show the blur. He also incorporated several copies of a paint drip he had scanned and isolated, a background image he had created earlier, and two photos of textured surfaces. To combine all these images, he created layer masks and used different blend modes.▼

FIND OUT MORE

▼ Using Select > Color Range **page 57**

▼ Working with layer masks **page 68**

▼ Using blend modes to combine images **page 173**

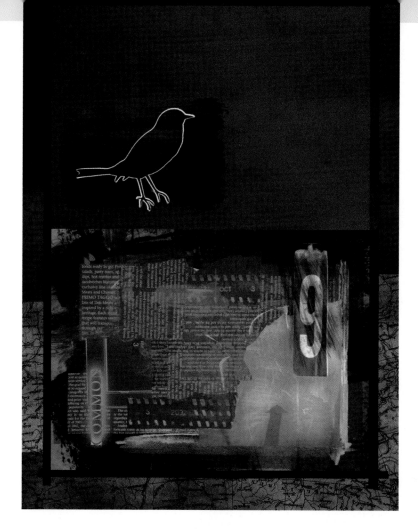

Alicia Buelow mixed many images and techniques in developing *No. 9, The Escape.* After scanning a photo of concrete to use as a background, she created the top section of the central rectangle by selecting an area with the Rectangular Marquee ⬚ and colorizing it with Image > Adjustment > Hue/Saturation (she made sure to turn on the Colorize option in the dialog box).

She made the bottom section of the inner rectangle using traditional collage methods, pasting paper scrap on illustration board. Then she scanned the result, opened the scan in Photoshop, and reversed the color (Ctrl/⌘-I), making a negative, before colorizing it with Hue/Saturation in the same way she had done the top.

Buelow painted a wide stroke with a dry brush using black ink on watercolor paper. She scanned the stroke and opened it in Photoshop, copied it (Ctrl/⌘-C), and pasted it into the working file (Crl/⌘-V), using the Move tool ▶⊕ to position this new layer and putting it in Multiply mode.

She used the Pen tool ◊ to draw the bird outline, then used this path to create a "calligraphic" outline of the bird. The method she used, along with another way of creating an outline from a path, is described in "Alicia Buelow Applies Different Strokes" on page 80.

The dark "taped" border was created by selecting a strip of the concrete texture with the Rectangular Marquee ⬚ and copying the strip to a new layer (Ctrl/⌘-J). Once she had positioned the strip with the Move tool ▶⊕, Buelow put the layer in Color Burn mode at 75% Opacity. She repeated the process of copying, positioning, and blending to make the other three sides of the frame.

To complete the background, she colorized it gold and layered over it a 19th-century map that she had scanned from *The Complete Encyclopedia of Illustration* by J. G. Heck, a book of copyright-free images. She put the map layer in Color Burn mode at 60% Opacity.

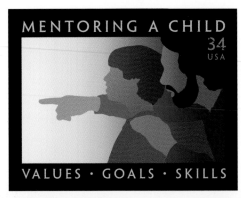

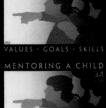

To be considered to design a stamp for the U. S. Postal Service, **Lance Hidy** reduced several of his hard-edge, solid-color poster designs to stamp size, arranged them on a page, complete with fake perforations, and then printed this "portfolio" and sent it to Derry Noyes, an art director for the Postal Service. The result was the commission for the ***Mentoring stamp*** and later the ***Special Olympics commemorative***. (The portfolio assembly method is described for the Society of Printers calendar stamps, shown on page 148.)

Hidy's illustration techniques combine traditional methods with Photoshop and Adobe Illustrator. When he had decided upon the gesture he wanted to capture for the mentoring stamp, he shot several rolls of color print film, asking the models to make adjustments and shifting his camera angle slightly between shots. "For me, photography is more than a reference," says Hidy. "I have come to think of my art *as* photography. True, I manipulate the photograph by flattening the shapes and eliminating details, but the essence of the photograph is still there."

Reviewing the prints from the photo shoot, he chose one that was almost exactly what he wanted in terms of content and composition **A**. Hidy scanned the print and lightened it in Photoshop with a Levels adjustment, printed the lighter version on a desktop inkjet, and outlined the shapes with a technical pen. He scanned the traced print, eliminated the photo to leave only the line

work **B**, and used Photoshop's selecting and filling tools to develop the scanned file into his stamp design. For an early draft he used solid-color fills everywhere except in the background, which he filled with a custom white-to-yellow-to-violet gradient that introduced light to symbolize the child's future **C**.

After filling the shapes, he selected the black line work. He could then use the active selection to contain the color as he refined the edges, using the Pencil ✎ to slightly expand one or both shapes where two colors met.

In the final version of the stamp (shown on the facing page) Hidy reinforced the effect of the implied light source by adding gradients to all shapes except the boy's shirt, whose vivid hue emits a light of its own. He completed the stamp design by adding type in the Adobe Penumbra typeface, which he had designed.

Using an Adobe Illustrator template that the Postal Service had provided, Hidy also set type for the pane (the sheet of stamps), confining the type to the selvedges, outside the block of stamps **D**. He submitted files for the pane and the stamp, and the Postal Service assembled them for printing. The same process was used later for the Special Olympics stamp.

You can find details of Hidy's method for translating photos to illustrations on page 412. His approach to composition and color is described in *Designing the Mentoring Stamp,* to be published by Kat Ran Press, **www.katranpress.com**.

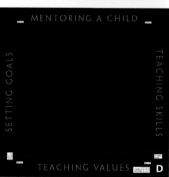

Essential Photoshop Skills

2

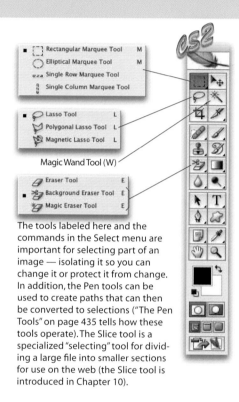

The tools labeled here and the commands in the Select menu are important for selecting part of an image — isolating it so you can change it or protect it from change. In addition, the Pen tools can be used to create paths that can then be converted to selections ("The Pen Tools" on page 435 tells how these tools operate). The Slice tool is a specialized "selecting" tool for dividing a large file into smaller sections for use on the web (the Slice tool is introduced in Chapter 10).

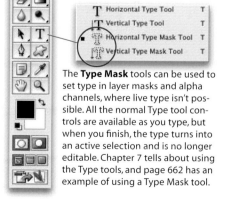

The **Type Mask** tools can be used to set type in layer masks and alpha channels, where live type isn't possible. All the normal Type tool controls are available as you type, but when you finish, the type turns into an active selection and is no longer editable. Chapter 7 tells about using the Type tools, and page 662 has an example of using a Type Mask tool.

THERE ARE CERTAIN KINDS OF OPERATIONS you'll need in almost any Photoshop project you work on. Some of these — selecting, masking, blending, and transforming — are covered next. Other Photoshop essentials are covered in Chapter 3 (input, file management, and output) and Chapter 4 (working with color and contrast).

MAKING SELECTIONS

For most of Photoshop's tools and commands, you have to tell the program which part of the image you want to affect. You start this by targeting a layer or its mask, simply by clicking on its thumbnail in the Layers palette. In Photoshop CS2 you can target more than one layer at a time, although not all tools or commands will work on more than one layer at once. To limit changes even more, you can *select* part of a targeted layer or mask. Knowing the ins and outs of making, cleaning up, storing, and recalling selections is at the heart of successful image editing and compositing.

Selections of pixel-based layers and masks can be made with commands from the **Select menu**, with the **Extract command** from the Filter menu, with **selection tools**, or by modifying one of the file's **color channels** — for instance, the Red, Green, or Blue Channel of an RGB image — and turning it into a selection.

Some tools and commands make selections **procedurally** — by using information like color or brightness that's intrinsic to the image. With others, you draw a selection boundary **by hand**. Procedural methods are often faster and more accurate. Sometimes the best way to select is to use one selection method to start and then add to or subtract from the selection with another tool or command. "Modifying Selections" on page 65 tells how to accomplish these changes.

Before there were layers and masks in Photoshop, feathering was especially important. A feathered edge can help to make a "seamless" change when part of an image is selected, modified, and then released back into its original unmodified surroundings. Feathering extends the selection outward but at reduced opacity so that some of the surrounding image is included. At the same time the opacity of the image is also reduced for a distance *inside* the selection border. It's the Feather Radius that determines how far this transition extends.

• With the Lasso and Marquee tools, you can **feather a selection as you make it**: Enter a Feather setting in the Options bar and then make the selection.

• If you forget to set the Feather ahead of time, or if the selection method you used didn't have a Feather option, you can **feather the selection boundary after you've made it**: With the selection active choose Select > Feather and set the Feather Radius.

Feathering can involve some guesswork and trial-and-error, because you need to pick a number for the Feather Radius without being able to see how soft the edge will be. Another approach is to make an unfeathered, or only slightly feathered, selection, then convert it to a layer mask, and blur the edges of the mask, previewing as you experiment, until you get exactly the softness you want. For more about this method, see "Softening a Mask" on page 79.

The edges of a selection can be abrupt and "stairstepped" (each pixel is either fully selected or not selected at all); **antialiased** (sharp with just a little transparency in the edge pixels to make the edge smooth), or **feathered** (soft-edges with obvious partial transparency).

An **active selection** is represented on-screen by a pulsating dashed border. If you click outside the selection boundary with a selection tool, the pulsating dashes disappear — and the selection is gone. In many cases if you act quickly, you can **recover a lost selection** by choosing **Select > Reselect** before you make another selection. But a more permanent way to preserve a selection is to store it. You can save it as an **alpha channel** (as described on page 67). Or a selected area can be turned into a **layer** of its own or a **layer mask**, which limits how much of a particular layer is hidden or revealed.

To make a selection that's partly sharp-edged and partly feathered, set the Feather in the Options bar and make the feathered selection first; then set the Feather to 0 and add the unfeathered selection by holding down the Shift key as you select. (If, instead, you make the sharp-edged selection first and then the feathered, the feather softens the junction of the two selections.)

The feathered selection was made first; then the sharp-edged selection was added.

Each of the selection tools and commands has its own advantages and disadvantages. To decide which tool or command to use, you need to analyze the area you want to select. Is it organic or geometric? Is it fairly uniform in color, or is it multicolored? Does it contrast with its background or blend into it, or do some parts of it contrast and others blend in? Then you can choose the tool, command, or combination of techniques that will do the job. The three sections that follow — "Selecting by Color," "Selecting by Shape," and "Selecting by Shape *and* Color" — tell how to choose and use selection methods.

SELECTING BY COLOR

Cleanly silhouetting a subject by color can help you grab elements such as a purple flower among pink ones, or a brown dog on a green lawn. Selecting by color is a *procedural* method that uses the image's hue, saturation, or brightness information to define the selection. To make a selection of all the pixels

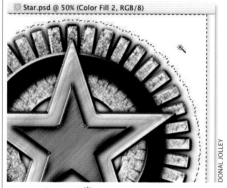
of a similar color, Photoshop has the **Magic Wand** tool ✎ and the **Select > Color Range** command. A selection can also be developed from one of the **color channels**.

The Magic Wand ✎

Using the **Magic Wand** is a quick and easy way to select one uniformly colored area or a small number of similarly colored areas in an image where there are other spots of the same color but you don't want to select them all. Just click the Magic Wand on a pixel of the color you want to select. By default the Wand is in **Contiguous** mode, so it selects the pixel you clicked and all similarly colored pixels for as far as that color continues without interruption. You can use the Wand to **select *all* pixels of the same color** in the entire image by clicking the check box to turn off the Contiguous option in the Options bar. You can add to the Magic Wand selection by Shift-clicking.

To specify how broad a range of color the Magic Wand should include in a selection, set the **Tolerance** value in the Options bar to a number between 0 and 255. The lower the number, the smaller the range of colors. **To control whether the selection is based on the color of only a single layer or of all visible layers** combined, turn **Use/Sample All Layers** off or on in the Options bar. By default, Magic Wand selections are **antialiased**, or smooth-edged, but you can turn that option off if you like.

The Magic Wand's "cousin," the **Magic Eraser** ✎, does the same kind of selecting as the wand, except that the process is destructive — it erases everything it "selects."

Select > Color Range

The Color Range command is more complex than the Magic Wand, but in some cases it offers more control of what's selected, and it **shows the extent of the selection more clearly**. By default, the little preview window in the Color Range dialog box shows a grayscale image of the selection. White areas are selected; gray areas are partially selected, and black indicates areas that are completely outside the selection. With its many levels of gray, this picture is much more informative than the pulsating border you see when you use the Magic Wand.

The **Fuzziness** setting in the Color Range dialog box is like the Magic Wand's Tolerance setting, but it's easier to work with, since the entire range is spread out on a slider scale and the preview window instantly shows the effect of changing it. Keeping the setting above 16 will usually prevent jagged edges in the completed selection.

A

B

C

D

E

Use the **Select > Color Range** command in its **Sampled Colors** mode (the default) to select a broad expanse of closely related colors. Here the challenge was to add drama to the sky without having to make a manual selection in a photo with a subtle gradation at the hazy horizon and complex shapes (the palms) that had to be excluded **A**. The Color Range eyedropper was dragged across the sky to select a range of blues. Then the Alt/Option key was held down and the eyedropper was clicked on the colors we wanted to exclude. Fuzziness was adjusted between 15 and 30 — a good range for Fuzziness in general — to antialias the selection around the palms and "feather" the horizon area **B**. With the selection active, we clicked the "Create new fill or adjustment layer" button ⬤ at the bottom of the Layers palette and chose Gradient for the type of Fill. We chose a gradient **C** and a layer mask for the new Gradient Fill layer was automatically made from the active selection. We chose Hard Light for the new layer's blend mode **D**, which added the color ramp while retaining some of the subtle cloud structure from the original sky **E**.

The **Select** field at the top of the Color Range dialog box lets you choose the color selection criteria. **To select based on colors you sample from the image,** choose **Sampled Colors,** then choose the dialog box's leftmost Eyedropper tool and click on the image. The selection extends throughout the image as if you had clicked with the Magic Wand with Contiguous turned off. (What's visible to the Color Range sampling function is the same thing that's visible to you on-screen. If you want Color Range to ignore the contribution of some layers, turn off their visibility by clicking their 👁 icons in the Layers palette.) **To extend or reduce the range of colors in the current selection,** click or drag with the + or – Eyedropper to add new colors or to subtract colors. Or click or drag with the plain Eyedropper, with Shift (to add) or Alt/Option (to subtract). You can also expand or contract the selection by adjusting the Fuzziness, but pixels whose colors are at the extremes of the selected color range are only partially selected ("fuzzy").

To select a family of colors instead of sampling color, choose from the color ranges in the dialog box's "Select" menu. The color families are predefined — you can't change the Fuzziness or use the Eyedroppers to expand or shrink these ranges. **To select only the light, medium, or dark colors,** choose Highlights, Midtones, or Shadows. Again, there's no opportunity to make adjustments to the range.

The **Invert** box provides a way **to select a multicolored subject on a plain background:** Use the Color Range eyedropper to select the background, and then click the Invert box to reverse the selection.

Color Channels

A color channel can be a good starting point for a selection. Often one of the color channels (Red, Green, or Blue in an RGB file, for instance) shows much better contrast between a subject and its surroundings than the other channels do. Look for a channel where the subject is very light and the surrounding area very dark, or vice versa. Then copy that channel to make an alpha channel by dragging the color channel's name to the "Create new channel" button ⬛ at the bottom of the Channels palette. You can apply the Image > Adjustments > Levels command to increase the contrast even more. ▼ Finally, load the alpha channel as a selection by Ctrl/⌘-clicking on the channel's name in the Channels palette. (This technique is illustrated on the facing page.)

FIND OUT MORE

▼ Levels **page 165**

To start a mask to select the surgeon, we found that the Red channel showed good contrast between the subject and the background (above). So we duplicated it to make an alpha channel (below).

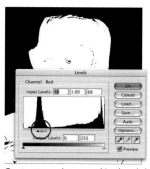

Contrast was increased in the alpha channel by adjusting the Input Levels (Image > Adjustments > Levels). The Brush ✎, sometimes in Airbrush mode, was used to touch up the alpha channel with black and white paint, getting rid of unwanted gray pixels.

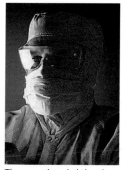

The completed alpha channel was loaded as a selection, and Image > Adjustments > Variations was used to change the overall color and lighting.

SELECTING BY SHAPE

If the subject you want to select is not distinctly different in tone or color from its surroundings, outlining its shape by hand may be the best way to select it. In that case the Marquees, Shapes, Lassos, and Pens are the tools to choose from.

Selecting Geometric or Custom Shapes

To "frame" a selection, you can use the Rectangular or Elliptical Marquee tool, as explained next, or use one of the Shape tools to draw a more complex outline. The Marquees offer a variety of options for selecting:

- The default mode for the Marquee tools ⬚ ◯ is to position the cursor where you want one "corner" of the selection to be and then drag diagonally to form the selection boundary. But many times you have better control of exactly what you select if you draw the selection from the center out. **To draw a selection outward from the center,** press and hold the **Alt/Option** key at any time while you're dragging the Marquee.

- **To select a square or circular area,** constrain the Rectangular or Elliptical Marquee by holding down the **Shift** key as you drag.

- **To make a selection of a particular width-to-height ratio,** choose **Constrained Aspect Ratio** for the Style in the Options bar and set the ratio. Now the Marquee will make selections of those proportions.

- **To make a selection of a specific size,** choose **Fixed Size** for the Style and enter the Width and Height measurements in pixels (adding "px" to the number), inches (add "in"), or centimeters (add "cm").

For a vignette effect with a soft (feathered) border, use the Rectangular or Elliptical Marquee, or use a Shape tool, convert the path to a selection, and choose Select > Feather.

To select an area that has a complex outline and shares colors with its surroundings so it's hard to select by color, the Lasso tool 𝒫 may be the best option.

Beginning a selection with either the Lasso 𝒫 or the Polygonal Lasso ⩔ and then adding the Alt/Option key lets you switch between dragging the Lasso in its freeform mode and clicking it as the Polygonal Lasso.

With the Alt/Option key held down, you can drag the Lasso 𝒫 outside the boundaries of the image, to make sure your selection doesn't miss any pixels at the edges.

In addition to the Marquees, the vector-based **Shape tools** offer many more preformed shapes, both geometric and custom, that you can use for selecting. First drag to draw the shape (the same Alt/Option and Shift modifiers apply as for the Marquees) and then convert the path you've drawn to a selection by Ctrl/⌘-clicking its thumbnail in the Layers palette or in the Paths palette.▼

Selecting Irregular Shapes

To select a multicolored subject, especially if it shares colors with its surroundings so that you can't select by color, you may need to "hand-draw" the selection border with a Lasso or Pen tool. If the element you want to select has smooth, curved edges, use a Pen.▼ If the boundary is complex with detailed "ins and outs," try a Lasso:

- For **very detailed edges,** drag the standard **Lasso** 𝒫.

- For fairly smooth edges, clicking a **series of short line segments with the Polygonal Lasso** ⩔ is often easier and more accurate than trying to trace the edge by dragging the Lasso. Holding down the **Shift key** as you use the **Polygonal Lasso** restricts its movement to **vertical, horizontal,** or **45° diagonal.**

- Holding down the **Alt/Option key** lets you **operate the tool as either** the Lasso 𝒫 or the Polygonal Lasso ⩔, switching back and forth between them simply by dragging 𝒫 or clicking ⩔.

There are other advantages to holding down the Alt/Option key: First, it **keeps the selection from closing up** if you accidentally let go of the mouse button before you've finished selecting. Second, if you make a mistake, you can **"unravel" the selection boundary** you're drawing, repeatedly pressing the Delete key while you also hold down Alt/Option until you get back to the "good part." And if you want **to make sure your Lasso selection extends all the way to the edges** of the image without missing any pixels, you can hold down Alt/Option and click or drag the tool outside the image. Finally, you can even switch between these two tools and the Magnetic Lasso ⩔, described next and demonstrated in step 2 of "Focusing Attention on the Subject" on page 285.

FIND OUT MORE

▼ Working with Shape tools
page 433

▼ Working with Pens
page 435

The Magnetic Lasso's 🖈 Options bar, most of which is shown above, includes the four buttons characteristic of the Options bar for all selection tools. There you can specify whether the selection you are about to make will be (left to right) a new selection, an addition to the current selection, a subtraction from it, or the intersection.

EASIER SELECTING

No matter what selection method you use, selecting can be made easier if you exaggerate the color or tone contrast between the area you want to select and its surroundings before you try to make the selection. For instance, a Levels Adjustment layer can be added above the image layer to make color differences more obvious than they were in the original. Then you may be able to select by color, or at least have a better view of an area you're selecting by hand. After the selection is made, the Adjustment layer can be deleted, or its visibility 👁 can be turned off.

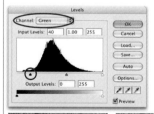

This image was lightened overall by moving the Levels dialog's gamma slider, to make the colors more obvious than they were in the shadows.

In this example, the Levels adjustment was made to the Green channel only, to increase the color difference between the leaves and the rock; see page 545 for details.

SELECTING BY SHAPE *AND* COLOR

Some of Photoshop's selecting tools are designed to let you take advantage of distinct color differences where they exist, but then also select by hand in areas where this contrast breaks down. These tools include the Magnetic Lasso 🖈 and Magnetic Pen 🖈, the Background Eraser 🖌, and the Extract command. The Background Eraser and Extract command are "destructive" selection methods. That is, they remove rather than just isolate the pixels they select.

The Magnetic Lasso 🖈

To operate the Magnetic Lasso 🖈, you click the center of the circular cursor somewhere on the edge you want to trace and then "float" the cursor along, moving the mouse or stylus without pressing its button. The tool automatically follows the edge. Parameters that can be set in the Options bar include **Width, Frequency, Edge Contrast,** and **Feather,** and if you have a graphics tablet, you can turn on the **Stylus Pressure** option.

Here are some pointers for using the Magnetic Lasso 🖈:

- If you're tracing a **well-defined edge**, use a large Width and move the tool quickly. **To increase the contrast at the edge**, and thus make the tool easier to operate, you can use a temporary Adjustment layer as described in the "Easier Selecting" tip at the left. **If there are distinct edges nearby**, use a small Width and keep the cursor carefully centered on the edge you're tracing. **If the edge is soft** with little contrast, use a smaller Width and trace carefully. **Where there is no contrast** for the Magnetic Lasso to follow, you can operate the tool like the Polygonal Lasso, clicking from point to point. **Or hold down the Alt/Option key to have access to all three Lassos**, switching between the Magnetic Lasso (by floating), the Polygonal Lasso (by clicking), and the Lasso (by dragging).

- As for most other tools whose cursor size can vary, you can use the left and right **bracket keys** — [and] — to change the Width as you operate the Lasso, as described below, or

TWO-HANDED SELECTION

When you use the Magnetic Lasso 🖈 (or Magnetic Pen), you can decrease or increase the Width by pressing the bracket keys: [and]. This means you can **shrink or enlarge the tool's footprint** with one hand **while you operate the tool** with the other hand, tailoring its size to the nature of the edge as you work.

The Protect Foreground Color option for the Background Eraser  makes this a very powerful selection tool. It lets you sample a color that you want to protect from being erased, even though that color falls within the range of colors you're erasing. For instance, it's used here to protect the mannikin (top) as the multi-tone gray of the background is erased.

use a graphics tablet and turn on **Stylus Pressure**. With increasing pressure the Width becomes smaller.

- Increase the **Frequency** to put down more fastening points, which determine how far back the selection border will "unravel" each time you press the Delete key.

- The **Edge Contrast** determines how much contrast the tool should be looking for in finding the edge. Increase the Edge Contrast setting if the subject contrasts strongly with its surroundings. Use a low setting for a low-contrast edge.

The Background Eraser

The Background Eraser tool, which shares a spot with the other Erasers in the Tools palette, erases the pixels you drag it over, leaving transparency instead. The "+" in the center of the tool's cursor is the "hot spot," and the circle around it defines the tool's "reconnaissance area." When you click, the Background Eraser samples the color under the hot spot. And as you drag the tool, it evaluates the color of pixels within the reconnaissance area, to see which ones should be erased. Which pixels get erased depends on how you customize the settings in the Options bar.

Tolerance affects the range of colors to be erased. With a setting of **0**, pixels of only a **single color** are erased — the specific color under the hot spot when you click. **At higher Tolerance** settings the tool erases a **broader range of colors**.

Sampling controls how the "hot spot" is used in choosing the color to erase:

- Choose **Once to erase only the color that's under the hot spot when you first push the button down** on your mouse or stylus. When you push the button down, the Background Eraser will choose the color to erase. It will erase this color as you drag, until you release the mouse button. When you

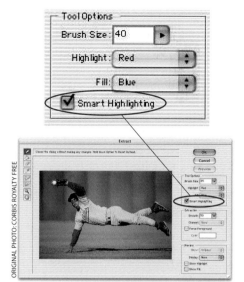

ORIGINAL PHOTO: CORBIS ROYALTY FREE

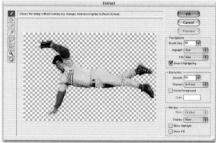

The **Extract** command is ideal for isolating a subject with fairly distinct edges from a background without distinct edges that could confuse the filter. The automated aspects of this filter can save painstaking hand-tracing. When using Extract, make sure to take advantage of **Smart Highlighting**, which operates the filter's Edge Highlighter tool magnetically, to help you follow the edge of the element you want to select. The **Cleanup** and **Edge Touchup** tools can improve the edge of an extracted image before you leave the Extract dialog box.

push the button down again, it will sample again, choosing the new color that's now under the hot spot.

- **To set a single specific color or color family to be erased,** regardless of when you press and release the mouse button, choose **Background Swatch** and click the Background square in the Tools palette; then either specify a color in the Color Picker or click in your image to sample a color.

- **Continuous** sampling repeatedly updates the color to be erased, so the tool erases every color you drag the hot spot over, unless it's protected (see below).

For the **Limits**, you can choose Discontiguous, Contiguous, or Find Edges.

- **To erase any occurrence of the color anywhere within the circular cursor** as it moves along, choose **Discontiguous**.

- To erase **only pixels whose color continues uninterrupted** from the hot spot, choose **Contiguous**.

- **Find Edges** is like Contiguous, but it pays special attention to **preserving sharp edges**.

What really sets the Background Eraser apart from other selecting tools, both destructive and nondestructive, is the **Protect Foreground Color** option in the Options bar. It lets you sample and protect any one color at a time as you erase. This is useful for preserving an element that's within the range of the colors you want to erase — even if you drag the cursor over it, the color won't be erased.

The Extract Filter

The Extract command (located in the Filter menu) isolates a part of an image by erasing all other pixels on that layer, leaving transparency in their place. Choosing Filter > Extract opens a dialog box that lets you set the stage for Photoshop to do its "intelligent masking." The Extract interface can be confusing, but one fairly direct way to proceed is outlined below. (For a step-by-step tutorial and tips on using Extract, work through the example in "Swapping a Background" on page 628.)

1 With the **Edge Highlighter** tool ✎, set the Brush Size in the Tool Options section. Choose a size that's big enough so you can easily drag it around the edge of the area you want to isolate (the subject) without veering off the edge. But keep in mind that anything the Edge Highlighter paints is fair

COREL KNOCKOUT 2

Corel KnockOut 2 is an image extraction and masking plug-in that goes beyond the selecting capabilities of Photoshop's Extract command. The KnockOut 2 program excels at silhouetting subjects with difficult edges, like a photo of fine wisps of hair or a glass or anything else that you can't successfully Extract. You can switch to a hand-selecting mode in areas where that works better, and use multiple undo's and redo's to go back to different stages of your work.

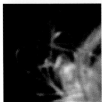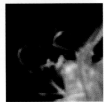

In Corel KnockOut 2 you define what's definitely inside and what's definitely outside the part of the image you want to isolate, and the program very successfully deals with the "border area" in between. It provides tools for identifying and selecting complex color transitions and soft edges such as shadows, and touch-up tools for perfecting the edges after the selection is made. On the left above is a Corel KnockOut selection, with a Photoshop Extract selection on the right for comparison.

TOLERANCE VALUES

The Tolerance for the Magic Wand ✺ also controls the range of Select > Similar and Select > Grow. If there is a lot of color variation and contrast in the original selection, you may not get exactly the results you expect when you choose Grow or Similar. If so, you can try again by undoing the Grow or Similar function (Ctrl/⌘-Z), resetting the Tolerance lower, and choosing Grow or Similar again.

game for Extract to make fully or partially transparent. When you come to an area of high edge contrast, trace the edge "magnetically" by switching to **Smart Highlighting** (by clicking the check box in the Tool Options section of the Extract dialog box, or by holding down the Ctrl/⌘ key). When contrast gets low again, turn off Smart Highlighting.

2 Continue to drag the Highlighter around the edge until you've outlined the entire subject. If the area you want to select extends to the edge of the image, you can draw just to the edge — you don't have to drag around the border. You can use the bracket keys as described in "Two-Handed Selection" on page 61 to change the tool's footprint as you drag.

3 In order to be able to preview your "extraction," choose Extract's own **Fill** tool 🖌 to click inside the highlight-bordered subject area. Then click the **"Preview"** button to see the extracted subject. You can zoom in for a closer look at the edge with Extract's own **Zoom** tool 🔍. To check the quality of the edge, you can change the preview's background color by choosing from the pop-out **Show** list in the Preview section of the dialog box. You can also toggle the view to compare the extracted subject with the original by choosing from the **View** settings.

If you don't like what the Preview shows you about the edge quality, you have several choices for making corrections:

- If the Extract process has left **problems at the edge** — extra pixels outside the edge, or semitransparency where the subject's edge should be solid — use the **Cleanup tool** 🖌 **to erase excess** material from the edge, or use the **Cleanup tool with Alt/Option held down to restore** edge material. Use the **Edge Touchup tool** 🖌 **to consolidate and remove "pixel debris"** at the edge. As you touch up the extraction, keep in mind that **it's better to leave too much material at the edge than not enough** (you can remove any excess later, but it won't be easy to restore any missing material once you leave the Extract dialog box).

- If the edge looks so sloppy that you want **to start over** completely, hold down the Alt/Option key to change the "Cancel" button to **"Reset,"** click the button, enter a **new Brush Size,** and start again.

- If the edge itself looks good but there are areas completely inside the edge that need to be eliminated — such as **small**

The **Transform Selection** command is great for angling and skewing selections. Here it's used in the process of shaping a shadow for the lipstick, which was already isolated on a transparent layer. With a new layer added below the lipstick layer to hold the shadow, we Ctrl/⌘-clicked the lipstick layer's thumbnail to load its outline as a selection. Then we chose Select > Transform Selection. Ctrl/⌘-dragging the top center handle down and to the right allowed us to lay the selection down where we wanted the shadow. Then we Ctrl/⌘-dragged the top left corner handle to the right to distort the selection so it got narrower as it receded into the distance. Pressing the Enter key accepted these changes. We filled the selection with gray, dropped the selection (Ctrl/⌘-D), and blurred the layer.

The Options bar for selection tools includes four buttons for specifying whether the selection you are about to make will be (left to right) a new selection, an addition to the current selection, a subtraction from it, or the intersection.

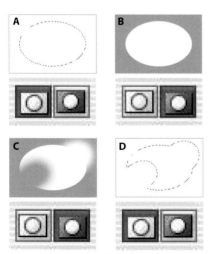

Making a selection in Standard mode **A**, converting to Quick Mask mode **B**, changing the selection mask by adding to the mask with black paint and removing from the mask with white paint **C**, and turning the altered mask back into a selection **D**

patches of sky showing through the leaves of a tree you've selected — you don't need to highlight the edge of each patch. Instead, click "OK" to close the Extract dialog box and then use the **Background Eraser**.

MODIFYING SELECTIONS

Photoshop allows you to change a selection boundary while it's still active. When you've completed a selection boundary:

- To **move the boundary** without moving any pixels, drag inside the selection with any selection tool.

- To **skew**, **scale**, **distort**, or **flip the selection boundary**, choose Select > Transform Selection. Then right/Ctrl-click to bring up a menu where you can choose the kind of transformation you want to make. Drag or Shift-drag the handles of the Transform frame, and press Enter (or double-click inside the frame) to complete the transformation.▼

- To **invert the selection**, changing the selected area to unselected and vice versa, type Ctrl/⌘-Shift-I or choose Select > Inverse.

- To make an **addition to**, **subtraction from**, or **intersection with** the current selection, click one of the buttons at the left end of the selection tool's Options bar, and then make the new selection. (See also "Fingers & Thumbnails" on page 67.)

- To **expand** a selection outward, so it will pick up more pixels at the edge, use **Select > Modify > Expand**. To **contract** a selection inward, shrinking it, choose **Select > Modify > Contract**.

- To **add all pixels in the image that are similar in color** to the pixels in the current selection, choose **Select > Similar**.

- To **add pixels that are similar in color *and adjacent* to the current selection**, you can choose **Select > Grow**. Each time you use the command, the range of colors selected gets larger.

Using Quick Mask

By making a selection and then clicking the Quick Mask button ▣ (on the right side near the bottom of the toolbox), you can view the active selection as a clear area in a mask that you can then modify with Photoshop's painting tools and filters. In Quick Mask mode you can see both image and mask, so you can do some fairly subtle editing. As you edit, Quick Mask remains stable, preserving the selection while you work on it. When you've finished modifying the mask, you can turn it back

Pixelated edges on a mask such as a selection stored in an alpha channel **A** can be cleaned up by blurring **B** and then using Image > Adjustments > Brightness/Contrast to sharpen up the edge. First adjust the Contrast to reduce the blur to an antialiasing effect **C**. Then move the Brightness slider to the right to enlarge the white part of the mask (so it will make a larger selection) **D** or to the left to shrink it **E**.

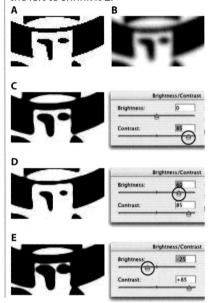

into a selection boundary by clicking the Standard mode button ▣ (to the left of the Quick Mask button).

Cleaning Up Selected Areas

Although masking (coming up on page 68) provides more options than removing a subject from its original background, sometimes, despite your best efforts, you may find yourself with an isolated element with a tinge of the original background visible around the edge. To get rid of this unwanted "fringe," you can use the commands of the **Layer > Matting** submenu. The Matting commands include **Remove White Matte** (for replacing white with transparency in the edge pixels of an element selected from a white background), **Remove Black Matte** (for replacing black with transparency in the edge pixels of an element selected from a black background), and **Defringe** (for dealing with obvious "edging" in an element selected from a multicolor background; an example is shown at the left below). Note that these commands work only *after* the selected material has been separated from its surrounding pixels and put on a transparent layer of its own.

Another option is to **trim away the fringe**. Make a selection based on the layer's content outline (also called its *transparency mask*) by Ctrl/⌘-clicking the layer's thumbnail in the Layers palette. Next choose the Select > Modify > Contract command to shrink the selection. Then type Ctrl/⌘-Shift-I to invert the selection and press the Delete key to remove the fringe; or you can **trim nondestructively** by Ctrl/⌘-clicking the layer thumbnail and then clicking the "Add a layer mask" button ▣ at the bottom of the palette. "Swapping a Background" on page 628 has other pointers for fitting a selected and silhouetted subject into a new background.

Sometimes you don't notice a "fringe" of background pixels surrounding a silhouetted subject until you've layered it on top of a new background (left). But it isn't too late to remove it. Choose Layer > Matting > Defringe before you merge the layer with the composite. The Defringe command pushes color from the inside of the selection outward to replace the edge pixels, thus eliminating the fringe.

To smooth out rough areas in a selection, choose Select > Modify > Smooth and set a degree of "rounding." The Smooth command is also useful for "absorbing" tiny unselected "holes" into the larger selection surrounding them.

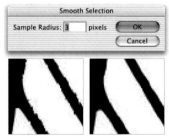

Shown here are close-ups of alpha channels made from the same selection, without smoothing (left) and with a 3-pixel Smooth Radius (right).

The Reselect command can sometimes recover your last selection after you've deselected.

ROB HAGIERA

In creating the trees for *Seeds of Internet Growth*, Rob Magiera worked on a black background in Alias Maya, knowing he could use Photoshop's Remove Black Matting command to remove all remaining traces of black when he isolated each tree and brought it into his Photoshop composition. Page 568 has more about creating this image.

Page 568 has more about creating this image.

FINGERS & THUMBNAILS

To load a path, channel, layer mask, or a layer's content outline (its transparency mask) as a selection — either a new selection or in combination with an existing one — just hold down Ctrl/⌘ and the other modifier keys listed below and click the appropriate thumbnail in the Paths, Channels, or Layers palette. The cursor changes to show what you are about to do:

- To load the item as a new selection, **Ctrl/⌘-click** on its thumbnail.
- To add to the current selection, **Ctrl/⌘-Shift-click** the thumbnail.
- To subtract from the current selection, **Ctrl-Alt-click** (Windows) or **⌘-Option-click** (Mac) on the thumbnail.
- To create a selection that is the intersection of the current selection and the item, **Ctrl-Shift-Alt-click** (Windows) or **⌘-Shift-Option-click** (Mac) on the thumbnail.

SAVING & LOADING SELECTIONS

After you've invested the time and effort to make a selection, it makes sense to preserve it so you can load it back into the image if you need to later. You can store selections as alpha channels. When a selection is stored in an alpha channel, white shows areas that can be recalled as an active selection, black areas won't be selected, and gray areas will be partially selected, proportionally to the lightness of the gray.

To make an alpha channel from an active selection (pulsating border), choose Select > Save Selection, choose New Channel, and click "OK." Or in the Channels palette (opened by choosing Window > Channels) simply click the "Save selection as channel" button ⬛ at the bottom of the palette.

To make an active selection from an alpha channel, Ctrl/⌘-click on the alpha channel's thumbnail in the Channels palette. Another option is to choose Select > Load Selection, and in the Load Selection dialog box, choose the document and channel you want to load. With this command you can load an alpha channel from any open document that has the same pixel dimensions as the one you're working on.

ALPHA CHANNEL EFFICIENCY

Why do the same job twice? If you're going to need to select adjacent areas of an image, store your first selection in an alpha channel. Then you can make the second selection quite rough and subtract the more detailed first selection from it to form a matching edge.

In this "hand-tinting" project we saved the skin selection **A** in an alpha channel **B**. Then we could make a rough selection of the dress, without tracing the neck or arm **C**. We Ctrl-Alt-clicked (Windows) or ⌘-Option-clicked (Mac) the alpha channel in the Channels palette to subtract it from the rough selection so we could color the dress **D**.

Here are two tips that make it easier to edit layer masks or alpha channels:

• For a Quick Mask–like view with a transparent red overlay that represents the mask, in the Channels palette, target the thumbnail of the alpha channel (or the layer mask for the active layer). Make sure its visibility is turned on (click to the left of the thumbnail to turn on the 👁), and then click the tilde key ~, and edit. Clicking ~ again shows the mask alone.

ORIGINAL PHOTO: PHOTOSPIN.COM

• To switch quickly between black paint and white for adding to or subtracting from the red mask, set the Foreground and Background colors to black and white (type D, then X if needed) and then just tap the B and E keys to switch between the Brush (to paint with black) and the Eraser (to paint with white). With this method you can set separate brush tips, Opacity, and Flow in the Options bar for the two tools.

MASKING

Each layer in a Photoshop file, except a *Background* at the bottom of the stack, can have two kinds of "masks" for hiding or revealing parts of the layer. These masks are invaluable because they hide without permanently changing the content of the layer. Instead of erasing or cutting away part of an image, you can leave it intact but block it with a **layer mask** or a **vector mask**. Masks are often used to combine images, but they're equally useful for combining two different versions of the same image, or for targeting a tone or color adjustment layer to a particular area. There are some important differences between layer masks and vector masks. ("Quick Masking & Blending" on page 75 will quickly get you up to speed on using masks.)

Layer Masks

A **layer mask** is a pixel-based, grayscale mask that can have up to 256 shades of gray, from white to black. Where the mask is white, it's transparent, and it allows the image or adjustment on its layer to show through and contribute to the composite. Where the mask is black, it's opaque, and the corresponding portion of the image is blocked (masked out). Gray areas are partly transparent — the lighter the gray, the more transparent — and the corresponding pixels in the layer's image (or adjustment) make a semitransparent (or partial) contribution to the composite. You can **create a layer mask by clicking the "Add layer mask" button** ⬚ at the bottom of the Layers palette. If there's a selection active when you add a layer mask, the selected area becomes the white (revealing) area of the mask; or if you Alt/Option-click the ⬚ button, the reverse mask is produced and the selected area becomes the black (hiding) area of the mask.

One way to mask an element inside part of an existing image is to use the **Paste Into** command: Select and copy (Ctrl/⌘-C) the element you want to paste, then activate the layer you want to paste into (by clicking its name in the Layers palette). Make a selection of the area where you want to paste, and choose Edit > Paste Into. The pasted element will come in as a new layer, complete with a layer mask that lets it show only within the area you selected.

If you hold down the Alt/Option key as you choose Paste Into, the effect will be to **Paste Behind** instead. Keyboard shortcuts are **Ctrl/⌘-Shift-V** for **Paste Into** and **Ctrl-Alt-Shift-V** (Windows) or **⌘-Option-Shift-V** (Mac) for Paste Behind.

Typically, when you add a layer mask, the image and mask are linked, so moving or transforming the image moves or transforms the mask, too. But when you use Paste Into (as shown here) or Paste Behind, the mask and image are unlinked by default. That way you can move the image around, resize it, or make other transformations and still keep the mask in the right position.

To make changes to a layer mask, click the mask thumbnail. An outline around the thumbnail will show that the mask is active. You'll still be viewing the image rather than the mask, but any painting, filtering, or other changes you make will affect the mask, not the layer.

To make a *layer mask* visible instead of the image, Alt/Option-click the mask thumbnail. Alt/Option-click again to make the image visible again.

To see and edit the outline of a *vector mask* at the same time you're viewing the layer *or* the layer mask, click the thumbnail for the vector mask. An outline appears around the thumbnail and the path appears on-screen. You can then change the path with the Shape or Pen tools or with one of the Transform commands. Click the thumbnail again to turn off the outline.

To turn a layer mask or vector mask off temporarily so it has no effect, Shift-click the mask thumbnail. An "X" on the thumbnail shows that the mask is turned off. Shift-click again to turn it back on.

Vector Masks

As the name implies, a **vector mask** is vector-based. It's resolution-independent so it can be resized, rotated, skewed, and otherwise transformed repeatedly without the deterioration. And it creates a smooth outline when the file is output to a PostScript printer, regardless of the resolution (pixels per inch) of the file. However, since it's vector-based, it has crisp edges and doesn't have the capacity for softness or partial transparency in the parts of the layer it reveals. You can **create a "reveal all" vector mask by holding down the Ctrl/⌘ key and clicking the** 🔲 at the bottom of the Layers palette (the Ctrl/⌘ key turns it into the "Add vector mask" button); or if the layer already has a layer mask, the button changes automatically, and you don't need the Ctrl/⌘ key. For a "hide all" mask, add the Alt/Option key. If a path is active when you add the mask, the mask will reveal the area inside the path, unless you use the Alt/Option key to hide it instead.

By default, a mask on a layer that has a Style applied to it **A** will help define the shape the Style conforms to. Edges created by the mask are treated with any edge effects that are part of the Style. For instance, if the Style includes a Bevel and Emboss effect, the edges created by the mask will also be beveled **B**. If you want to avoid this **C**, change your Blending Options settings for the "styled" layer: Open the Blending Options section of the Layer Style dialog (Ctrl/⌘-click on the image thumbnail for the layer, or choose Layer > Layer Style > Blending Options). Then, in the Advanced Blending section, click the appropriate check box to exempt the mask edges from the Style: For a layer mask, turn on "Layer Mask Hides Effects"; for a vector mask, turn on "Vector Mask Hides Effects."

 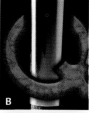 

With the Layer Mask Hides Effects option turned off **A** the Bevel and Emboss effect in the Layer Style on the "Q" layer follows the edges of the mask, which interferes with the illusion of the brush passing through the "Q." With the Layer Mask Hides Effects option turned on **B**, the illusion is preserved.

A clipping group provides a way to mask a photo or painting inside live type, leaving open the option of changing the font or editing the text.

MAKING & RELEASING "CLIPS"

To create a clipping group comprised of the active layer and the layer below it, in CS press **Ctrl/⌘-G**. If there is already a clipping group below, the active layer is added to it. **Ctrl/⌘-Shift-G** releases the active layer from the clipping group, along with any other layers above it in the group.

In CS2 the keyboard shortcut for making or releasing a clipping group is a toggle — **Ctrl-Alt-G** (Windows) or **⌘-Option-G** (Mac).

Clipping Groups

Another nondestructive compositing element, a **clipping group**, is a group of layers, the bottom layer of which acts as a mask. The outline of the bottom layer — including pixels and masks — "clips" all the other layers in the group so only the parts that fall within the outline can contribute to the image.

You can make a clipping group by Alt/Option-clicking on the borderline between the names of two layers in the Layers palette. The lower layer becomes the **clipping mask**, and its name is now underlined in the palette. The other layer is clipped; its thumbnails are indented, and a down-pointing arrow points to the clipping layer below. To add more clipped layers to the group, you can just work your way up the Layers palette, Alt/Option-clicking more borderlines. (To be members of a clipping group, layers have to be together in the stack. You can't add one, skip one, add the next, and so on.)

A clipping group can also be set up (or added to) when a layer is first added to the stack. To do this, check the Group With Previous Layer/Use Previous Layer to Create Clipping Mask box in the New Layer dialog box.

BLENDING

A layer's Blending Options include its Opacity, its Fill opacity, and several other options that can be set in the Advanced Blending and **"Blend If"** sections of the Layer Styles dialog box. In the "Blend If" section you can control how the pixels of the active layer (called "This Layer") and the image underneath (called "Underlying Layer") will combine in the composite. (The term "Underlaying Layer" is a bit deceptive. It actually refers to the *entire underlying image*, whether it's only a single layer or a composite of layers.)

The sliders of the **"Underlying Layer"** bar (shown on the facing page) define what range of colors in the underlying image are available to be affected by the active layer. So, for instance, if you wanted only the medium-to-dark pixels to be affected, you would move the white "Underlying Layer" slider inward so the lightest tones are outside the range and thus can't be affected.

The sliders of the **"This Layer"** bar determine what range of colors in the active layer will be allowed to contribute to the composite image. So, for instance, if you want only the dark colors of the active layer to contribute, move the white slider for "This Layer" inward so the light colors are outside the range.

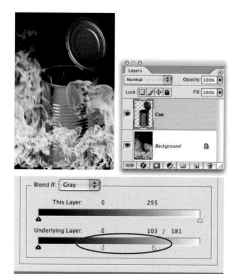

Using the "Blend If" sliders can be an important step in developing a composite. Here the pixels of the can layer are hidden where they overlap the light pixels in the flame image. Each slider can be split (by Alt/Option-dragging) to make a smooth transition. Here splitting the white slider smooths the blend of the flames and the can. The Blending Options process for compositing is described in "'Blend If' Tonality" on page 76 and other examples in "Quick Masking & Blending."

"AUTO TRANSFORM"

In Photoshop CS2, turning on **Show Transform Controls** in the Move tool's ▸₊ Options bar automatically brings up the Transform frame for the active layer whenever the Move tool is chosen in the Tools palette. This means you can Transform without choosing from the Edit menu or even typing Ctrl/⌘-T. As soon as you start any transformation, the Transform Options bar appears, and right/Ctrl-clicking opens the menu of transforming commands.

Holding down the Alt/Option key as you drag a slider will allow you to split the slider. This lets you smooth the transition by defining a range of colors that are only partially visible. If the "Blend If" sliders are new to you, the examples in "Quick Masking & Blending" starting on page 75 will quickly make you comfortable with this valuable tool.

TRANSFORMING & WARPING

To scale, rotate, skew, distort, create perspective, warp, or flip a selected element, you can choose **Transform** or **Free Transform** from the Edit menu to open the Transform frame, or use the Ctrl/⌘-T keyboard shortcut. Transformations can be carried out "freehand" by dragging on the handles of the Transform box or with numeric precision by typing numbers into the appropriate fields in the Options bar. (The distort and perspective options aren't available for live type or for Smart Objects.)

In CS2 the Edit > Transform command offers a new option: Warp. In some ways this command, which is used with pixel-based and vector-based layers and masks, is like the type-warping feature available in both CS and CS2, ▼ but in other ways it's different. Like type warp, CS2's Warp command has premade warping styles available through a menu in the Options bar. But unlike type warp, the Warp command has a Custom warping mesh that you can reshape by hand. Another difference is that the Warp command doesn't remain live as the type warp does. Once you press the Enter/Return key (or click the "Commit transform" button ✔ in the Options bar), the transformation is finished, like any of the other transformations available in the Edit menu.

Often you'll want to carry out more than one transformation at a time — scaling and then skewing or warping, for instance. You can right-click (Windows) or Ctrl-click (Mac) inside the Transform box to open a context-sensitive menu to switch the kind of transformation, working back and forth between the different transformations until you get exactly what you want. Finally, press the Enter key (or double-click inside the frame) to complete the transforming "session." Only when the session ends does Photoshop "redraw" the image to include all the transformations you've made.

In Photoshop CS2 the new "megafilters" Vanishing Point (demonstrated on page 588) and Lens Correction (pages 276 through 283) do specialized forms of transforming.

FIND OUT MORE

▼ Warping type
page 486

As with the Transform commands, the redrawing is done only at the end of the session, when you click "OK" to close the filter dialog.

After you've completed a Transform session, you can repeat the transformation on the same element by using the Edit >

TRANSFORM OPTIONS

Choosing the Transform or Free Transform command brings up a Transform frame whose handles you can move to scale, rotate, skew, or distort the content of a layer. Instead of using the handles, you can set parameters in the Options bar.

The **Transform** Options bar offers a way to enter precise position, scale, and skew factors, and angle of rotation. It also has a "Commit" button ✔ (the Return/Enter key is the shortcut) and a "Cancel" button ⊘ (the Escape key is the shortcut).

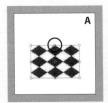

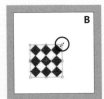

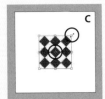

Once the Transform frame is on-screen, **dragging any handle will resize** the layer contents **A**. **Shift-dragging** a corner handle will keep the image in proportion as you scale it **B**. Adding the **Alt/Option key**, with the Shift key as shown here, or without it — scales from the center point **C**.

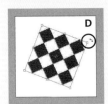

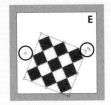

If you move the cursor outside the Transform frame, the cursor will become a **double-headed curved arrow**, and dragging will **rotate** the image **D**. To change the center of rotation, before you rotate, drag the center point icon to a new position **E**.

To **Skew, Distort** by moving a single corner, or transform in **Perspective**, first choose one of those options from the Transform menu **F** (right/Ctrl-clicking opens it), or use a keyboard shortcut.

With **Skew** chosen, dragging a **side handle** tilts the frame, keeping sides parallel **G**. Dragging a corner handle allows you to skew, scale, and even flip in the same move **H**.

With **Distort** chosen, you can move a single corner independently **I**, or drag a side handle to skew scale, and flip. The shortcut for performing Skew or Distort transformations is to hold down the **Ctrl/⌘** key as you drag.

With **Perspective** chosen, moving one corner causes an equal but opposite move in its horizontal or vertical mate **J**. The keyboard shortcut for Perspective is to hold down **Ctrl-Alt-Shift** (Windows) or **⌘-Option-Shift** (Mac) and drag a corner handle.

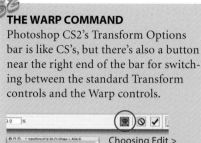

THE WARP COMMAND

Photoshop CS2's Transform Options bar is like CS's, but there's also a button near the right end of the bar for switching between the standard Transform controls and the Warp controls.

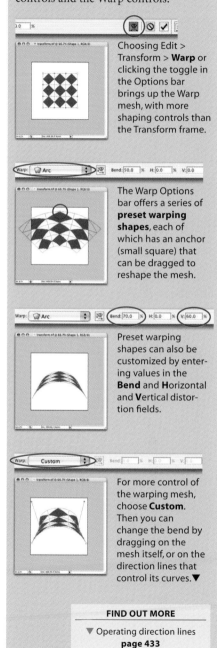

Choosing Edit > Transform > **Warp** or clicking the toggle in the Options bar brings up the Warp mesh, with more shaping controls than the Transform frame.

The Warp Options bar offers a series of **preset warping shapes**, each of which has an anchor (small square) that can be dragged to reshape the mesh.

Preset warping shapes can also be customized by entering values in the **Bend** and **H**orizontal and **V**ertical distortion fields.

For more control of the warping mesh, choose **Custom**. Then you can change the bend by dragging on the mesh itself, or on the direction lines that control its curves.▼

FIND OUT MORE

▼ Operating direction lines
page 433

Transform > Again command or pressing Ctrl/⌘-Shift-T. Or make a duplicate and transform it by also holding down the Alt/Option key in addition when you transform again.

UNDERSTANDING RESAMPLING

As explained in Chapter 1 (page 19), each time you transform a pixel-based element, you risk degrading the image a bit, making details a little softer or less distinct. This happens because of *resampling:* Additional pixels are "filled in" if the transformation made the element bigger, or the colors of adjacent pixels are averaged and assigned to fewer pixels if the element got smaller, or tilted pixels have to be remapped to the square pixel grid when an element is rotated. So rather than making a series of separate transformations, each time pressing the Enter key and starting another one, do all the transforming operations you can in a single session, so the image is redrawn only once. In CS2 you can switch back and forth between the Transform frame and the new warping mesh (as shown at the left), so you can do both in a single transforming session. For vector elements such as Shapes and type and for CS2's new Smart Objects, transforming causes no degradation (see page 20), but it's still more efficient to do all the transformations that you can in the same session.

SIZING UP OR SIZING DOWN

Regardless of how well you plan, there are likely to be times when you need to make an entire file smaller (*resample down*) or make it bigger (*resample up*). You might resample down because you have more information than you need for printing and you want to reduce the bulk of the file. You might resample up if the original you scanned isn't available to be scanned again at the resolution you need for the screen frequency or display size you want, because the original is no longer available. Or your original may have been a digital photo, and there's no way to go back and reshoot the picture.

To resample, you can use the **Image Size dialog box** as shown on the next page, or use the Resize Image Wizard/Assistant (choose **Help** > **Resize Image**). The Help command leads you through the process by asking a series of questions, but it doesn't give you as much "hands-on" control as the Image Size dialog (shown on the next page). If you use the Image Size dialog box, make sure that **Constrain Proportions** is checked (so the image stays in proportion as it's resized). The **Resample Image** box should also be checked.

SIZING FOR COLUMNS

If you're sizing images for a publication whose column width you know, choose Edit/Photoshop > Preferences > Units & Rulers and enter the column and gutter widths. Then when you size an image in the Image Size dialog box, you can choose Columns as the unit of Width and set the number of columns wide that you want the image to be. If you specify more than one column, the calculation automatically takes the gutter measure into account.

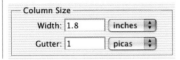

- From the Resample Image menu, **choose Bicubic Smoother for enlarging** (resampling up). The **Bicubic Sharper** option is designed **for reducing the size** (sampling down).

- **To change the size at which the image will print,** in the Document Size section, enter a new value in the Height or Width field. The other dimension will change automatically, the Resolution will stay the same, and so the file size will change.

- **To keep the print dimensions the same but change the resolution,** in the Document Size section, set Height and Width units to anything but pixels. Then enter a new value in the Resolution field. The size at which the image will print will stay the same but file size will change with the change in resolution. *Wow!*

THE IMAGE SIZE DIALOG BOX

Choosing Image > Image Size opens the Image Size dialog box, where you can see and change the dimensions and resolution of the file.▼

In the **Resolution** field you can set the number of pixels per inch (or centimeter) that you need for output.

When you resize a file, turn on the **Scale Styles** option if you want to scale effects such as drop shadows, bevels, and glows along with the file. Leaving Scale Styles unchecked will make these effects look relatively bigger or smaller after the file is scaled down or up.

When **Constrain Proportions** is checked, changing **Width** or **Height** automatically changes the other dimension, to keep the original proportions.

If **Resample Image** is checked, changing Width, Height, or Resolution will change the file's Pixel Dimensions, causing resampling. **Uncheck the Resample Image box** if you want to change Width, Height, or Resolution but you want the other two settings to compensate for the change without changing the number of pixels in the file, and thus without resampling.

In the **Pixel Dimensions** section, you can see or change the Width and Height of the document in pixels or as a percent of the size you started with. You can also see the size of the flattened file these dimensions will produce. (Not included in these numbers are any parts of layers that extend beyond the document bounds, or any alpha channels.)

If the **Resample Image** box is checked, you can choose from a menu of resampling options. **Bicubic Smoother** was designed for resampling up (making the file larger), and **Bicubic Sharper** was designed for resampling down (making the file smaller).

Clicking the **"Auto"** button opens the **Auto Resolution** dialog box, where you can enter the printing line screen and choose Good or Best to prepare the image for print. The Good option produces a smaller file but the Best option may produce a better print.

The link icon 🔗 is a reminder that **Constrain Proportions** is turned on.

FIND OUT MORE

▼ Pixel dimensions or Resolution required for output **page 94**

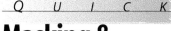

Masking & Blending

Whether you work in Photoshop CS or CS2, layer masks, Blending Options, and clipping groups provide a variety of options for blending images, as shown by the examples on these five pages. Files for some of the examples are provided on the Wow DVD-ROM so you can experiment or "dissect" them.

A blend of two photos can be quite seamless and convincing if one of the images is fairly amorphous and fluid, such as a photo of clouds, fire, ocean surf, or vegetation at a distance. But masking and blending techniques are also excellent for seamlessly blending two versions of the same image (filtered and original, for example) or for targeting a tone or color change to part of an image.

Throughout the book you'll find examples of carefully made selections, turned into masks. But the examples on the next five pages show that in many situations you can do a fine job of blending *without* painstaking selection, using a quickly made mask, or the premade silhouette that comes with many stock photos, or a quick Blending Options adjustment.

Most of the Layers palettes shown here are from Photoshop CS2, although the blending works exactly the same way in CS.

FIND OUT MORE

▼ Using the Gradient tool ■ **page 160**
▼ Using the Brush tool ✦ **page 362**

YOU'LL FIND THE FILES
in (wow) > Wow Project Files > Chapter 2 > Quick Masking and Blending

Gradient Mask

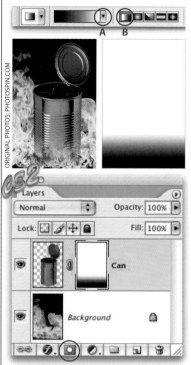

TO FADE the bottom of the can into the flames while keeping both originals intact, add a layer mask (by targeting the "Can" layer and clicking the "Add layer mask" button ▣) and fill the mask with a black-to-white gradient. To draw the gradient, choose the Gradient tool ■, and in the Options bar, click the little arrow to the right of the gradient sample **A** and choose the "Black, White" gradient (it's the third one in the default set that comes with Photoshop); make sure the Linear option is chosen **B**. Then be sure the mask is targeted (click its thumbnail in the Layers palette). Hold down the Shift key so the gradient will be drawn straight up as you drag from a point just above the bottom edge of the can to the point where you want the can to completely emerge from the flames.▼

Painted Mask

BY HAND-PAINTING a layer mask you can precisely control how the two images are blended. Target the "Can" layer and add a layer mask by clicking the ▣ button, then choose the Brush tool ✦ and in the Options bar choose Photoshop's soft 100-pixel brush tip; we left the Opacity for the Brush at 100%. (The Opacity needed will vary with the images and the kind of blend you want.)▼

In the Layers palette make sure the layer mask is targeted (click its thumbnail) and set the Foreground color to black (typing X once or twice will do it). To help in painting the mask, reduce the Opacity for the "Can" layer to about 60% so you can see through the can to the flames you want to reveal. After painting the mask, restore the layer's Opacity to 100%.

 **Can and Flames-Before.psd**

Blurred Mask

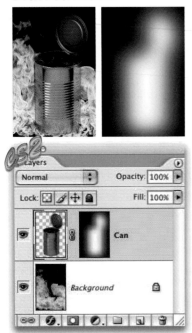

TO MAKE A LAYER MASK that fades a silhouetted subject at its edges, in the **Can and Flames-Before.psd** file start by Ctrl/⌘-clicking on the subject's thumbnail in the Layers palette; this creates a selection based on the silhouette. Then click the "Add layer mask" button ⬛ at the bottom of the palette to make a mask that reveals the selected area and hides the rest of the layer (you won't see any difference in your image at this point, since the rest of the layer is transparent and so there's nothing to hide). Now blur the mask: Choose Filter > Blur > Gaussian Blur and increase the Radius as you watch the image; we used a Radius of 70 pixels. The can's reflective surface plays a part in the end result of this blend. A more general, nonreflective example is shown at the right.

Blurred & Painted

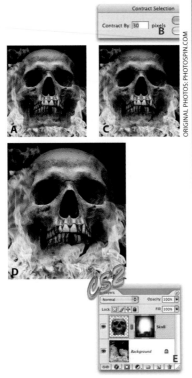

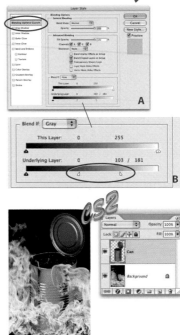

IF YOU USE THE METHOD shown at the left, the edge becomes partly transparent, but it can still be clearly seen **A**. Here are two approaches to making the edge less distinct:

- Undo the masking you've done (drag the layer mask thumbnail to the "Delete" button 🗑 at the bottom of the Layers palette and click "Delete" in the Caution box that appears). Then Ctrl/⌘-click the subject's thumbnail again to load the selection. This time choose Select > Modify > Contract to make the selection smaller all around; we used a "Contract By" value of 30 pixels **B**. Blur the mask as before **C**.

- Paint the edges of the mask with black (as on page 75) **D**, **E**; we used the Brush 🖌 with a soft 100-pixel tip and Opacity set to 50%.

 **Skull and Flames.psd**

"Blend If" Tonality

ORIGINAL PHOTOS: PHOTOSPIN.COM

STARTING with **Can and Flames-Before.psd**, double-click the thumbnail for the "Can" layer in the Layers palette to open the Blending Options section of the Layer Style dialog box **A**. In the "Blend If" area, adjust the sliders (as described next) to blend the layers based on their tonality.▼

Here we set up the "Blend If" sliders **B** so the "Can" layer would *not* cover up the light colors in the *Background*. Any colors lighter than the tone set by the white slider for "Underlying Layer" will show through from the *Background*. Separating the two sliders (by holding down the Alt/Option key as you drag) makes the tones between the two brightness values show through partially for a smooth blend. Any tones darker than that set by the left half will be totally hidden by the layer above.

Notice that the Layers palette shows no evidence of any work you do in the "Blend If" section.

FIND OUT MORE

▼ Using the "Blend If" sliders **page 70**

76 CHAPTER 2: ESSENTIAL PHOTOSHOP SKILLS

"Blend If" & Mask

ADJUSTING THE "BLEND IF" sliders (as in "'Blend If' Tonality" on page 76) can be combined with a layer mask (such as the one from "Gradient Mask" on page 75). Notice that the Layers palette looks the same as the one in "Gradient Mask," since "Blend If" changes don't show up in the palette.

Mode & Mask

WHEN THESE TWO IMAGES are layered, putting the "Lightning" layer in Screen mode removes the black, since black has no effect in Screen mode.▼ Reducing the layer's Opacity will tone down the lightning a bit, and a painted layer mask hides the otherwise obvious edges of the "Lightning" layer; we used the Brush 🖌 with a soft 100-pixel brush tip at 100% Opacity with the Airbrush option turned on in the Options bar.

FIND OUT MORE

▼ Using blend modes **page 175**
▼ Using the "Blend If" sliders **page 70**

Mode, Mask & "Blend If"

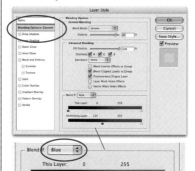

TO PUT THE LIGHTNING at the top of the rocks, or behind them, you can use the "Blend If" sliders for the Blue channel.▼ Open the Blending Options section of the Layer Style dialog box by double-clicking at the right side of the layer's entry in the Layers palette. Then choose Blue (instead of the default Gray) from the "Blend If" menu. Dragging to the right on the black point for the "Underlying Layer" slider makes the lightning disappear from areas that contain almost no blue, such as the reddish-brown rock (the black end of the bar represents colors with no blue component). Again, working with the "Blend If" sliders makes no change to the Layers palette.

Lightning Landscape.psd

Masking a Filter

TO PROTECT part of an image from a change, first duplicate the original to a new layer (Ctrl/⌘-J). Then apply the change to the upper layer (we used the Radial Blur filter in Zoom mode, with the zoom centered on the biker's head). Add a layer mask to the changed layer (click the ◻ button at the bottom of the Layers palette). For this example, choose the Gradient tool ▦ and choose the Radial style in the Options bar. Use the "Black, White" gradient, dragging outward from the center of the area you want to protect. To show other parts of the original (sharper) image, such as the sign and the biker's hands, paint the mask with black (as in "Painted Mask," page 75).

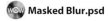 **Masked Blur.psd**

Filtering a Mask

A LAYER MASK treated with a filter can artistically frame one image against another. For such a custom-edged vignette treatment, you can make a selection (we used the Rectangular Marquee [⬚]), turn it into a layer mask, and then blur the mask to create some gray at its edges and run a filter on the mask. See page 260 for the technique and pages 264 and 265 for filter ideas.

Here we filled the *Background* with the **Wow-Weave 03** pattern, first clicking the *Background* thumbnail in the Layers palette to target it, then selecting all (Ctrl/⌘-A), and finally choosing Edit > Fill > Pattern and choosing from the pop-out palette.

FIND OUT MORE

▼ Using Adjustment layers
page 165

Masking an Adjustment

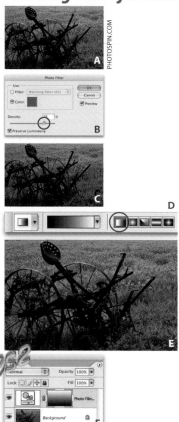

ADJUSTMENT LAYERS, which make changes in tone and color, have their own built-in layer masks. So you can set up your adjustment and then mask it to target the effect, leaving some areas of your image "unadjusted."▼ Starting with a photo of antique farm equipment **A**, we clicked the "Create new fill or adjustment layer" button ◖ at the bottom of the Layers palette and chose Photo Filter; in the Photo Filter dialog **B** we clicked the color square and chose a red, increased the Density to 75% for stronger color, and clicked "OK" to tint the photo **C**. Then we faded the tint by Shift-dragging up with the Gradient tool ▦ using a "Black, White" Linear gradient **D**, **E**, **F**.

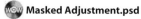 **Masked Adjustment.psd**

SOFTENING A MASK

A slightly soft edge on an Adjustment layer's mask can prevent an artificially sharp transition between a recolored background and the original subject (as shown here) or vice versa. This helps the subject look "at home" in its surroundings. Christine Zalewski, whose work appears in the "Gallery" sections of Chapters 4 and 5 and in "Protecting with a Layer Mask" on page 201, sometimes develops a layer mask from one of the color channels.▼ Then she chooses Filter > Blur > Gaussian Blur and experiments with the Radius until she sees a transition in the image that's still just a bit "sharper" than she wants. She can then re-run the filter (Ctrl/⌘-F) repeatedly to make small changes in the mask edge as she watches the image until she sees the result she's aiming for.

CHRISTINE ZALEWSKI

FIND OUT MORE

▼ Developing selections from channels
page 58
▼ Creating a layer set/group **page 583**
▼ Aligning layers **page 636**
▼ Using Layer Styles **page 44**

Masking a Set/Group

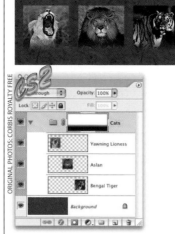

ORIGINAL PHOTOS: CORBIS ROYALTY FREE

TO MASK SEVERAL LAYERS at once, you can collect them together and then apply a layer mask to the entire collection. The collection is called a *layer set* in Photoshop CS and a *group* in CS2, and the symbol in the Layers palette is a folder icon 📁.▼

Here we aligned three image layers▼ and grouped them in a folder. Then we used the masking method described in "Gradient Mask" on page 75 to fade all the images at their bottom edges.

DOUBLE MASKING

When a set/group is masked, the mask works on all layers within it. That means you use an individual layer mask to reveal or hide parts of any layer in the set/group, and also apply a mask that affects all the layers.

Using a Clipping Group

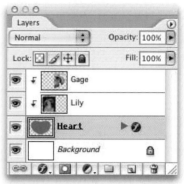

YOU CAN USE THE CONTENT of one layer to mask other layers above it by forming a clipping group. Using a clipping group instead of a layer mask allows you to combine images in more complex ways. For instance, with a clipping group you can mask more than one image in a single shape *and* apply a Layer Style, such as the dark Inner Glow used here, to the shape. The Style applies to the enclosed images.▼ With a layer set/group (as in "Masking a Set/Group" at the left), you can't do this because a set/group won't accept a Layer Style.

Another advantage of using a clipping group is that you can combine the blend mode and Opacity of the clipped and clipping layers in interesting ways.

Alicia Buelow Applies Different Strokes

GIVE DESIGNER ALICIA BUELOW a shape to work with and she and Photoshop can turn it into exactly the kind of outline she wants in an image — sharp or soft, glowing or calligraphic. Here we look at some of the methods she employs.

For her *Songbirds* illustration for *Audubon* magazine, a detail of which is shown here, Alicia outlined each bird in white and added a bright circle around it. She made the white outline by selecting the bird, adding a new layer, and stroking the selection with the Foreground color, white in this case (Edit > Stroke); then she moved the outline layer up and to the left with the Move tool.

She added the bright circle on another layer, drawing a circular selection by Shift-dragging with the Elliptical Marquee ⬭, feathering the selection (Select > Feather) before stroking it (Edit > Stroke).

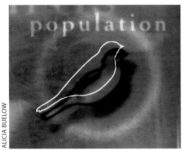

The interactions between the outline and the underlying composite were created with the blend modes assigned to the layers and with masking.

In *From Far Away She Looked Like Jesus,* Alicia kept the distinct lines of the cube framework she had imported from Adobe Illustrator, but also added a glow around them with an Outer Glow effect, adjusting the Spread and Size to get just the intensity and diffusion she wanted. She used a layer mask to hide parts of the cube, thus bringing the arm from the image beneath inside the frame. A detail is shown here; see page 566 for the full image and more about how she composed it.

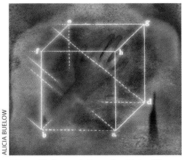

A Layer Style consisting of an Outer Glow effect in Overlay mode was applied to the line work.

Here's a method for making a "calligraphic" outline like the one used for the bird in *No. 9, The Escape,* shown on page 51 (a detail is shown at the right). Alicia started by outlining the bird with the Pen tool ✑. Then with white as the Foreground color (typing D, then X does it), she added a new layer to her file (Ctrl/⌘-Shift-N), and made a white-filled silhouette based on the path by clicking the "Fill path with Foreground color" button ● at the bottom of the Paths palette.

Next, to add a layer mask that completely hid the silhouette, she Ctrl/⌘-clicked the silhouette layer's thumbnail in the Layers palette to load the layer's transparency mask as a selection. She made the selection a little smaller, so the mask she would make from it would allow an outline of the bird to show (Select > Modify > Contract). Then Alt/Option-clicking the "Add a layer mask" button ▣ at the bottom of the palette created a mask that hid most of the bird. She "unlinked" this mask from the silhouette (by clicking to turn off the 🔗 icon between their thumbnails), so she could move the mask by dragging in the image with the Move tool without disturbing the white-filled bird. The result was an irregular outline of the bird.

Turning off the link between the mask and the layer content allows you to transform the mask independently. (The silhouette thumbnail is shown here in red instead of white to make it easier for you to see.)

Hands reaching into and out of the image to support a mutually held object illustrate **Web Services,** the Internet services and applications that allow remote users to share resources. **Rob Magiera** started in Alias Maya, a 3D software program, where he created the hands and central object. He constructed a patterned line for the outer rings in Adobe Illustrator, opened the file in Photoshop, and saved it as a TIFF for import into Maya. Magiera created a texture in Photoshop that conveyed the idea of "data," imported it into Maya, and applied it to the central object. He rendered each form as a separate file so that he could add special effects and masks to combine them in Photoshop. Maya automatically generated an alpha channel to each file during rendering, which Magiera could load as a selection in Photoshop in order to delete the background (this process is described on page 568).

After Magiera had opened the rendered files in Photoshop and dragged and dropped each one into his working file, he added layer masks (by clicking the "Create a layer mask" button ◨ at the bottom of the Layers palette) and painted them with black to make some elements appear to be partly in front of and partly behind others.

To make the glow of the outer rings, Magiera duplicated the layer with the rings (Ctrl/⌘-J), blurred the copy (Filter > Blur > Gaussian Blur), and set the blurred layer's blend mode to Screen.▼

To unify the image, he then scaled up a copy of the texture he had used for the central object (by pressing Ctrl/⌘-T for Edit > Free Transform and dragging a corner handle) and layered it over the image. To confine the texture to the outer edges of the illustration, he added a layer mask and filled it with a black-to-white radial gradient.▼

To complete the dimensional "atmosphere," Magiera filled a layer with a pattern of blue vertical stripes (Edit > Fill > Pattern) that he then blurred. After reducing Opacity and adding a layer mask, he customized a large airbrush▼ and painted the mask with black to block out the stripes in the center and corners.

FIND OUT MORE

▼ Blend modes **page 175**

▼ Masking with gradients **page 191**

▼ Creating brushes **page 363**

Rainforest Butterflies is the final set in the *Nature of Australia* series of stamps issued by Australia Post. Over the life of the series, **Wayne Rankin** has designed all of its stamps, using the format he introduced in 1996.

For the rainforest environment backgrounds, Rankin combined photos from several sources, using the Move tool ▶⊕ to drag them into the composite file he had set up for each stamp. He then used layer masks to blend them together. For the background of the large $2 stamp, for instance, Rankin used three photos of the Daintree Rainforest. He started with the largest of the three photos **A** and then filled in the extra width in his stamp format by copying a

selection from the right side of this image to a new layer (Ctrl/⌘-J) and using the Move tool ▶⊕ to slide the new layer over to the left. In the final composition the tree with buttresses **B** would hide the top part of this copy, and the waterfall image **C** would hide the lower right side of the original, so there would be no obviously repeating elements.

ALIGNING IMAGE LAYERS

When you need to see how the layer you're working on lines up with the image underneath, temporarily reduce the upper layer's Opacity using the slider in the Layers palette. Once the layer is in place and any masks are painted, restore the Opacity to 100%.

While he worked, Rankin clicked 👁 icons to toggle on and off the visibility for layers that held the vignette edges, the color-filled rectangle for the denomination of the stamp, the type elements, and the layout of the stamp outline. The type and outline had been created in Adobe Illustrator and rasterized into Photoshop as separate layers so Rankin could develop his design in relation to these standard elements.

To blend the images together, he added a layer mask to each of the image layers except the bottom one, by clicking (or Alt/Option-clicking) to make a white-filled "reveal all" (or a black-filled "hide-all") mask. Working on the layer masks, he used the Brush tool 🖌 to paint, or made selections and filled them with white or black and then modified them by painting soft edges, watching the composite as the masks blended the images. Rankin added Adjustment layers (such as Curves) with painted masks to direct their tone and color changes where they were needed for a seamless blend.▼

To isolate the butterflies **D**, **E** from their backgrounds so he could drag them into the composite, Rankin started by inspecting the channels.

Clicking on a channel's thumbnail in the Channels palette makes that channel alone visible and active, so that any Photoshop operations will affect that channel only.

For each butterfly photo he chose the channel with the best definition of the edge between butterfly and background and duplicated it as an alpha channel by dragging its thumbnail in the Channels palette to the "Create new channel" button 🔲 at the bottom of the palette. Then he used various Image > Adjustments commands▼ to enhance the edge definition. In the example shown below **F**, Levels and Invert were used. By turning on the 👁 icon for the RGB entry in the Channels palette, Rankin could see both the image itself and the alpha channel (as a translucent red mask) at the same time **G**. Then the Brush tool 🖌 could be used with white or black paint to erase the red over the white spots in the wings or solidify the red over the background **H**, until the alpha

channel showed a white butterfly on a black background **I**, indicating that the entire butterfly with all of its details had been successfully isolated from its background. Ctrl/⌘-clicking this channel's thumbnail loaded the light areas of the channel as a selection, and the selected butterfly could then be dragged with the Move tool ▶⊕ into the composite file to make its own transparent layer **J**. Rankin invoked the Edit > Free Transform command (Ctrl/⌘-T) to scale each butterfly layer and rotate it into place.▼

For final output, visibility for the type and outline layers was turned off **K** before the flattened file was made (Image > Duplicate > Duplicate Merged Layers Only). The final layout, with live type, was assembled in Illustrator.

© PETER WALTON

© LIK HOTSTOCK

© LIK HOTSTOCK

© STANLEY BREEDON

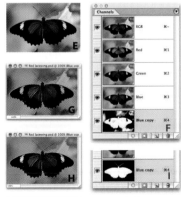

AUSTRALIA POST 2004. REPRODUCED WITH PERMISSION OF AUSTRALIA POST.

FIND OUT MORE

▼ Using Adjustment layers **page 165**

▼ Transforming **page 71**

Cristen Gillespie's *Fireworks Celebration* blends two images (shown at the right) using a layer mask made with Photoshop's Transparent Stripes gradient. First Gillespie adjusted each image separately, keeping in mind that the two would later need to work together. She used Image > Adjustments > Shadow/Highlight on both images — to reduce the blown highlights in the Fireworks and to lighten the Capitol Building where the fireworks would "light it up."▼

To better define the streaks in the Fireworks image, Gillespie copied the layer (Ctrl/⌘-J) and placed it in Soft Light mode at a lowered Opacity. She masked out the increased contrast in the highlights by using Select > Color Range > Highlights and checking Invert, so that she could see the black mask developing in the Color Range dialog box **A**. When she clicked "OK" to close the Color Range box and then clicked on the "Add a layer

mask" button ▣ at the bottom of the Layers palette, the Color Range selection automatically became a mask to protect the highlights from the Soft Light change.

The next step was to neutralize and match the black in both backgrounds. For this, Gillespie used the Info palette, a Color Sampler, and a Selective Color adjustment together **B**, **C**. First she placed a Color Sampler ⚲ on a solid black area of the background of each image. In the Info Palette, she clicked on the triangle beside the Eyedropper ⚲ icon and chose CMYK from the pop-up menu. Working first with the Fireworks image, she added a Selective Color Adjustment layer by clicking the "Create new fill or adjustment layer" button ◐ at the bottom of the Layers palette and choosing from the pop-up list. She chose Blacks from the "Colors:" menu in the Selective Color dialog and adjusted the sliders for a neutral Black until she could see in the Info palette that Magenta and Yellow

PHOTOSPIN.COM

PHOTOSPIN.COM

were equal, with Cyan about 10 points higher. (A higher percentage of Cyan is needed to balance Magenta and Yellow and make the black neutral.) She jotted down the final CMYK readouts from the Info Palette; she would need them later for the Capitol image. Then she chose Reds for the "Colors:" and increased the amount of Cyan and Black to intensify the reds in the fireworks. After clicking "OK," she repeated the process with a Selective Color Adjustment layer added to the Capitol image and adjusted the sliders for Blacks until the readouts in the Info palette matched the numbers she had written down from the Fireworks image.

Finally, Gillespie used CS2's Filter > Distort > Lens Correction on the Capitol to correct the vertical tilt **D**.▼

She saved the layered files and duplicated each (Image > Duplicate > Duplicate Merged Layers Only), and then dragged the Fireworks image on top of the Capitol image. She added a layer mask to the Fireworks image,

chose the Transparent Stripes gradient, and dragged with the Gradient tool ⬛ horizontally.▼ (With this gradient, the width of the bars is determined by how far you drag with the Gradient tool, so a very short drag produces very thin bars, with a wide black area on one side and a wide white area on the other; a long drag, on the other hand, makes wide bars across the entire mask.) In the Layers palette she clicked on the link icon 🔗 between the layer mask and image thumbnail to unlink the two, then dragged in the image window to move the layer mask until the bars revealed the dome. Next she targeted the image itself (by clicking its thumbnail) and dragged until the fireworks were centered over the dome. She clicked between the thumbnail and mask again to relink them so she couldn't accidentally move one without the other.

To blend the two images so the fireworks would seem to come from inside the dome, she targeted the

gradient-filled layer mask and used Filter > Blur > Gaussian Blur, increasing the amount until the Preview showed the sharp edges of the mask had disappeared. She then chose Image > Adjustments > Brightness/Contrast. To further lighten the bars on the layer mask, allowing more of the Capitol dome to show through the mask, she moved the Brightness slider to the right. She then "softened" the edges of the bars somewhat for smoother transitions by moving the Contrast slider slightly to the left. She added a Levels Adjustment layer ◑ above the Capitol building, which was now too light in the center, and moved the gamma slider for Input Levels to the right to darken the midtones. To target the darkening to the center of the building, she inverted the Level's layer's built-in mask to make it black (Ctrl/⌘-I) and then painted with white on the mask using a large, soft brush at low opacity **E**. When she was satisfied with the blend, she dragged with the Crop tool ⛶ to crop the image.▼

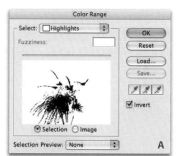

A

B

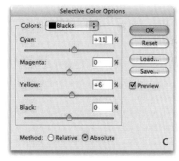

C

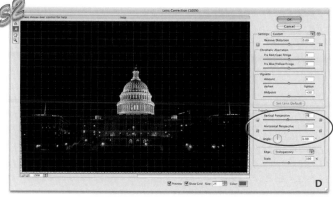

D

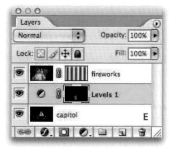

E

The organic geometry of lines and colors that emerges in the images of **Laurie Grace's** *Intrusions* series comes from the interaction of repeated instances of a photo or painting, arranged in a grid and flipped, with several copies layered together and combined by changing the blend modes of the layers.▼ For *Intrusion 2*, shown here, Grace made a new Photoshop file (File > New, with the default

choices of RGB Color for the Color Mode and White for the Background Contents) and used the Move tool ▶⊕ to drag-and-drop a grayscale version of a photo of a dog **A** into the new file. She aligned the photo with the upper right corner, and scaled it down (Ctrl/⌘-T brings up the Transform frame, and Shift-dragging a corner handle of the frame inward will shrink the image, keeping its original proportions).▼

Grace made a duplicate of most of this imported image, right beside the original **B**. One way to do that is to drag with the Rectangular Marquee ⬚ to select the part of the image you want and then Ctrl-Alt-drag (Windows) or

FIND OUT MORE

▼ Blend modes **page 174**

▼ Transforming **page 71**

▲ Adding a drop shadow **page 498**

⌘-Option-drag (Mac) sideways to make a duplicate of the selected part of the image; adding the Shift key after starting to drag keeps the motion horizontal so the copy stays aligned with the original and the two together form a rectangular unit.

Next Grace selected and repeated her entire two-image unit in the same way, to make a four-image unit, and then selected and repeated the four-image unit to complete a row of eight. She selected the row of eight and repeated the row four times, moving each copy down, to complete her grid of images **C**.

She duplicated the layer of images (Ctrl/⌘-J), and then flipped this new layer (Edit > Transform > Flip Horizontal) **D**. When she put this layer in Difference mode (by choosing from the blend mode

menu in the upper left corner of the Layers palette), the grids of dog images interacted to become something entirely different **E**.

Adding a blue-filled layer, also in Difference mode, turned the black in her composite blue, and colored the white with the opposite color, an orange **F**; page 211 has more about this color interaction.

Next Grace layered another grid of images made from selections from the same original photo **G**, making this grid a little smaller than the other layers **H**. She put the new layer in Soft Light mode **I** and added a drop shadow, which can be seen in the final montage on the facing page.▼ Finally she added an enlarged copy of a detail made from the grid of **E**. She put the layer in Normal mode and added a drop shadow.

THE KEYS MAKE THE DIFFERENCE

When a selection is active, the result you get when you drag depends on what keys you're holding down:

- Dragging while any selection tool is chosen, without any helper keys, will reposition the selection boundary only — no pixels are moved.

- If you hold down the Ctrl/⌘ key and drag, the selection tool turns into the Move tool ▶⊕ temporarily, and the pixels are moved along with the selection boundary, leaving a hole behind.

- If you hold down both Ctrl/⌘ and Alt/Option and drag, you make a *copy* of the selected area on the same layer.

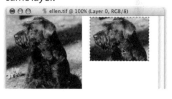

- To make a copy on a separate layer so you can move it without making a change to the original layer, and still keep the original layer intact, type Ctrl/⌘-J, and then hold down the Ctrl/⌘ key to turn the selection tool into the Move tool ▶⊕ temporarily so you can drag the copy.

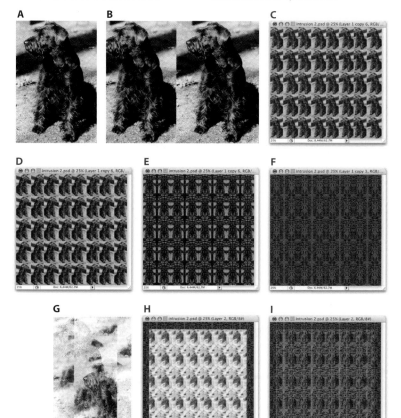

A   **B**   **C**

D   **E**   **F**

G   **H**   **I**

Getting In, Going Fast & Getting Out

3

THIS CHAPTER COVERS the best ways to get images into and out of Photoshop. It also has some hints for organizing your files so you can find them when you want them, and suggests ways to shift some of your work to Photoshop's Actions and other automation skills.

Looking first at input, or acquiring images, the quality of the images you put into Photoshop can have a big impact on the quality of the output. It will also affect the amount of work you'll need to do in Photoshop. As a rule of thumb, it's a good idea to collect more information in your input file than you think you will need for output — billions of colors instead of millions in an RGB scan or a digital camera photo, for instance, or twice the resolution (pixels/inch) you need for final output for scanned line art. With more color depth and higher resolution, you can get smoother color transitions and clearer edges. Even when you ultimately reduce the number of colors or the resolution, the image or line art will look better than if you had started with less information.

SCANNING

With a flatbed scanner, you can capture photographic prints, drawings and paintings, and even some three-dimensional objects, as files you can work with in Photoshop. The more *color depth* your scanner offers — that is, the more colors it can distinguish — the more shadow and highlight detail it will be able to record. You and Photoshop can use this extra information to help make finer color and tone adjustments.

While many new flatbed scanners now come with adapters for scanning slides or film negatives, if you have a lot of slides or negatives that you want to scan, a dedicated film scanner is worth considering. Prices have fallen dramatically over the past

SCANNING IN 3D

By placing small objects on a flatbed scanner, you may be able to capture their dimensionality. One or more sides of an object may show, depending on where on the bed you place it. The farther off-center you move the object (toward an edge or corner of the scan bed), the more the depth of its sides will show.

few years, while the quality and resolution of the scans can now rival drum scanning from a professional shop.

The model you choose for a film scanner depends partly upon the film format you need to scan. Not all film scanners can handle medium format or APS in addition to 35mm, but some can. A few film scanners also have an attachment for feeding entire rolls of negative film.

Another input option is to have your film scanned by a photo service and delivered on CD-ROM, in which case the quality of the scan will depend on the optical and mechanical precision of the scanner and the skill of the person operating it.

Setting Up a Scan

Scanners let you **_prescan_** your image so you can identify the area you want to scan. Then, as described on these next two pages, you can specify the dimensions and color mode you want for your scanned image, and enter a scan resolution. The goal is to collect all the information you need for the way you want to use the file in Photoshop, without collecting an inconveniently large amount.

SETTING UP A SCAN

Your scanning software's interface has the input fields you need to tell the scanner how much information to collect.

For a color scan, set the scan to capture as many colors as possible. Your scanner's software may offer "Millions" or "Billions" of colors, or in this case "True Color," the definition of which is controlled by Preference settings.

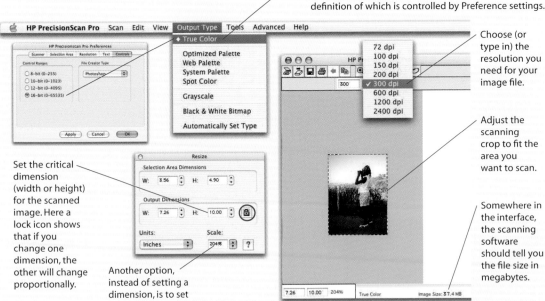

Choose (or type in) the resolution you need for your image file.

Adjust the scanning crop to fit the area you want to scan.

Somewhere in the interface, the scanning software should tell you the file size in megabytes.

Set the critical dimension (width or height) for the scanned image. Here a lock icon shows that if you change one dimension, the other will change proportionally.

Another option, instead of setting a dimension, is to set a scale factor.

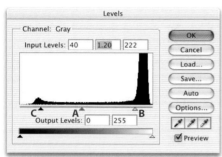

TOMMY YUNE

Scanning line art in Grayscale mode produces smooth lines and allows the "ink" to be lightened or darkened with a Levels adjustment. After adding a Levels Adjustment layer or choosing Image > Adjustments > Levels, move the gamma (gray, midpoint) slider for Input Levels **A** to the left to thin the lines, or to the right to thicken them. Use the Input Levels white point slider **B** to brighten a gray background to white, and the black point slider **C** to darken the ink.

Setting the dimensions of the scan. When your scanner shows you a preview of your image, use the scanning software's cropping tool to identify the area you want to scan. Then tell the scanner whether you want your scanned image to be the same dimensions as the original or some other size. Most scanners will let you set a new height or width, and then will automatically adjust the other dimension. Or you can set the new dimensions as a percentage of the original size.

Setting the color mode of the scan. Color mode also affects file size.▼ For example, a full-color scan records at least three times as much information as a grayscale scan (one with black and white and 254 shades of gray in between). Here are some criteria for choosing the color mode for scanning:

- **For color images,** even if you plan to convert them to "black-and-white" (Grayscale) for output,▼ scan in full color. Your scanner may call this, its best color mode, "millions of colors," "billions of colors" (for 16 Bits/Channel mode), or "true color."

- **Grayscale images,** such as black-and-white photos, often turn out better if you scan in color and then convert to Grayscale mode in Photoshop.

- **Black-and-white line art** usually has smoother, more consistent lines if it's scanned in Grayscale mode and then perfected with a Levels adjustment in Photoshop.▼

Setting the scan resolution. Scanner software typically asks for the scan resolution you want as *pixels per inch (ppi)* or *dots per inch (dpi)*. To figure out the scan resolution you need in order to print the image on a press, you can multiply the print resolution (number of lines per inch, or lpi, in the halftone screen that the printer will use) by 1.5 to 2. The 1.5 multiplier (for example, 1.5 ppi/lpi x 150 lpi = 225 ppi for the file) works well for photos of natural scenery without stark geometric patterns, sharp color boundaries, or ultra-fine details (most of the images in this book, including the cover, fit in this category). For photos of manmade structures, which tend to have straight lines and sharp color breaks, or for close-up "beauty" photography with details like fine eyelashes, a multiplier of 2 is a safer choice (typically 2 ppi/lpi x 150 lpi = 300 ppi for the file). A multiplier greater than 2 increases the file size without making the picture look significantly better.

FIND OUT MORE

▼ Color modes **page 151**

▼ Converting from color to grayscale **page 212**

▼ Levels adjustments **page 165**

When you scan an image that was printed on a press, the halftone screen pattern used for printing can interact with the scanner's sampling scheme to produce an unwanted *moiré* (interference pattern). Many desktop and other scanners have built-in *descreening* algorithms for eliminating the moiré. *Note:* Most printed material is copyright-protected. You can find information about U.S. copyright law and fair use at **www.copyright.gov.**

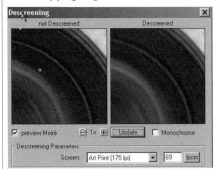

Many scanners come with software designed to eliminate the moiré pattern that can develop when printed material is scanned and the halftone screen from printing interacts with the scanner's sampling pattern. Shown here is the descreening interface from LaserSoft's SilverFast AI, a scanning program that can be purchased separately for many scanners. SilverFast SE, the "lite" version of the software, is bundled with some scanners and can also be bought separately for supported scanners.

Note: The difference in file size between a file that's 1.5 and 2 times the line screen is almost double, which is a lot of extra weight to carry around if you don't really need it.

Inkjet printers may use dpi or ppi to indicate their print-quality resolutions, or they may only use words like "Good" and "Best." For files that will be printed on an inkjet, scanning at a resolution between 225 and 300 ppi and choosing "Best" in the printer setup dialog will come close to photo-quality prints on most recent inkjets. Fine-art inkjet printers typically require 200 to 400 dpi, for a print whose resolution (as viewed with our eyes or through a loupe) looks much higher. If you will be sending a file out to be printed on a high-quality commercial inkjet, ask the printer what resolution or file size will be needed for the size and kind of print you want.

Double-checking

Once you've chosen image size, color mode, and resolution, your scanner will tell you how big (in megabytes, MB) the file will be when your image is scanned. As a check, the chart on page 94 shows some typical files sizes and print dimensions.

If you put several photos side-by-side on your flatbed scanner, with a little space in between, Photoshop will separate the images into individual files, straightening them in the process, when you choose File > Automate > Crop and Straighten Photos.

Four photos were scanned at once (left), and the Crop and Straighten Photos command was run to separate them, producing four files with the same name, followed by the word "copy" and a sequence number.

William White Conquers "Pepper Grain"

DESIGNER WILLIAM WHITE needed a solution for the "pepper grain" he encounters when making large prints from scans of Fuji transparency film. "Unlike traditional darkroom enlargements, these high-resolution dry scans are often peppered with tiny black specks," William says. "No matter how well you clean your slide before you scan, the 'pepper' is always there. That's because it isn't dirt, but a result of how light from the scanner interacts with particles in the film base." Here's his quick fix:

You can experiment with the **Pepper Grain.psd** file provided on the Wow DVD-ROM. Look in Wow Goodies > Pepper Grain.

1 Start with a thoroughly cleaned slide, and make sure to set your scanning software so it doesn't sharpen the image. Open the RGB scan in Photoshop. Duplicate the file (Image > Duplicate) so you have one copy to work on and one untouched original as a spare.

WILLIAM WHITE

As shown in this detail of the image above it, tiny black specks pepper this 4000-pixel/inch scan of a painted wooden bell tower photographed in 2002 with 35mm Velvia transparency film.

2 Choose Filter > Sharpen > Unsharp Mask. "The goal here is not only to sharpen the image," says William, "but also to bring the pepper grain into biting sharp relief." Set the Threshold at 0 and the Radius at 1, and adjust the Amount slider until the pepper is sharp. Then, to avoid oversharpening and degrading the image, adjust the Threshold up until the sharpening of the film grain goes away but the pepper stays sharp.

Sharpening the pepper grain turns it into something the Dust & Scratches filter can eliminate.

3 Now duplicate the image to a new layer and choose Filter > Noise > Dust & Scratches. With the Threshold set at 0, set the Radius to 1, or if the pepper grain remains largely unaffected, to 2. At this point don't worry about the fact that film grain and image details are blurring. Move the Threshold slider to the right just until the pepper grain reappears; in the process you'll restore the film grain. Then move the slider to the left until the pepper grain just disappears again. Finally, in the top left corner of the Layers palette, choose Lighten for the blend mode. In this mode the pepper grain will be gone, but the image will be left sharp.

The Dust & Scratches filter, applied to a duplicate layer in Lighten mode, hides the pepper grain without blurring the image.

A high-quality digital camera can capture an image with enough detail for successful enlargement.

JHDAVIS

DIGITAL CAMERAS

Digital cameras bypass film and record images directly as digital files. Many come with USB or FireWire connections for downloading images directly to your computer's hard drive or importing them into Photoshop as if the camera itself were a hard drive. To save the camera's battery life, inexpensive card readers (USB and FireWire) are available for all types of camera storage media.

Compared to Film

Besides eliminating the scanning step, digital photography has two major advantages over film. The first is the instant feedback you get from seeing the picture as soon as you take it, or even *before* you take it, with an accurate preview of the framing and lighting. The second advantage is "reusable film." The value of these features can't be overstated. They encourage experimentation and let you know right away if you've captured the right shot or if you should try again. Failed images can be erased immediately to make room for more successful ones.

Comparing digital cameras to film cameras, the *dynamic range* (the ability to capture many levels of brightness) is now close

MEGAPIXELS, MEGABYTES & PRINT SIZE

This chart is an enlargement guide for images from digital cameras (at their rated megapixel size) and scans of various file sizes (in megabytes). Or you can read the chart from the other direction — choose the print size you want and the printing method you plan to use, and see how big a file you will need. The numbers in the chart are conservative — for a given enlargement size, you will have plenty of resolution at the number of megapixels, megabytes, or pixel dimensions listed, without enlarging the image in Photoshop.

			Enlargement Size (to the nearest half-inch)		
Megapixels	Megabytes	Pixel Dimensions	Inkjet Printer (300 ppi)*	Halftone Press (133 lpi)**	Poster/Billboard (72 ppi)***
2	5.5	1600 x 1200	5" x 4"	6" x 4.5"	22" x 16.5"
3	9	2048 x 1536	7" x 5"	7.5" x 6"	28.5" x 21"
4	11.1	2272 x 1705	7.5" x 5.5"	8.5" x 6.5"	31.5" x 23.5"
5	14.4	2592 x 1944	8.5" x 6.5"	10" x 7"	36" x 27"
6	18	3072 x 2048	10" x 7"	11.5" x 7.5"	42.5" x 28.5"
8	22.9	3264 x 2448	11" x 8"	12" x 9"	45" x 34"
11	31.4	4064 x 2704	13.5" x 9"	15" x 10"	56.5" x 37.5"

*   Inkjet printers produce high-quality prints between 225 and 300 pixels/inch.

**   Halftone printing requires 1.5 to 2 pixels per inch for every line per inch in the halftone screen. For these enlargements, at 133 lpi, the ratio of ppi to lpi is high (2 ppi to 1 lpi); for the same enlargements at 150 lpi, the ratio is 1.77 to 1; at 175 lpi, the ratio is 1.52 to 1.

***   Billboards may require less resolution. Posters benefit from higher resolutions at closer viewing distances.

Besides the size and format of the photos it can take, some qualities that owners of digital cameras find useful are a **camera size** that's convenient to carry and has enough of its controls available on the body **A**; an **LCD screen that swivels** so you can preview shots at odd angles **B**; a **tethered lens cap C**; a **transformer** for plugging the camera itself into the wall to recharge the (standard-size) batteries **D**; and the availability of an **adapter** for attaching filters (such as the infrared filter shown here) **E**. A separate **card reader** that accepts one **F** or more formats **G** of camera media makes it easier to transfer images to the computer, and if your LCD screen is not a swivel model that can be closed up and so is constantly exposed, replaceable cut-to-size LCD **screen protectors** will help keep it from getting scratched **H**.

to slide film in good digital cameras. The size to which you can enlarge the photo (see the chart on the facing page) may be a limitation, though less so now that you can enlarge an image in Photoshop with the Bicubic Smoother option.▼ Digital files often have more noise at high speeds (ISO 200 and up) than film has grain. While digital cameras are getting faster, most are still slower to respond than most new film cameras. Prefocusing and panning, two film photography techniques for capturing action, are tricky at best for many digital cameras. Apertures (lens openings) are not in the same relationship to the "film" plane as in film cameras, which means you can't use depth of field as creatively, keeping the subject in focus and blurring the background.▼ Aperture sizes in fixed-lens digital cameras usually lack the range of good film camera lenses, and shutter speeds are often neither as fast nor as slow as the extremes of the average 35mm camera. This limits stop-action photography or shooting in very bright or dim lighting.

FIND OUT MORE

▼ Enlarging an image **page 73**

▼ Simulating a shallow depth of field in Photoshop **page 291**

Shopping for a Digital Camera

If you're thinking about getting your first digital camera, or upgrading, it can be helpful to make a list of your own priorities before you begin shopping — just so you don't succumb to "feature lust" and get sidetracked by features you'll seldom use. To prioritize, think about what type of photography you're most interested in. (Keep in mind, though, that once you start using a digital, your horizons are likely to broaden.) Following is a brief list of features to consider when trying to find a digital camera that fits your budget:

- **Megapixels.** The chart on the facing page shows that the more megapixels, the bigger the print you can make without having to enlarge the file in Photoshop. If you need to crop an image, having too few megapixels in the original photo can spoil the results.

- **Size and shape.** Be sure to handle various styles and try out the controls to see which camera suits you. A **very compact** camera fits in a shirt pocket, but few camera controls can be on the body, and they may be awkwardly placed. Features are sometimes limited, and changing settings can mean scrolling through a number of menus. **Medium-sized** cameras, bigger and slightly heavier, often have a comfortable camera grip and more controls on the body, and they have room for more features. **SLR-type** bodies and full digital **SLRs** (*single-lens reflex* cameras, with interchangeable lenses

One advantage of an LCD preview screen that flips out and swivels is that you can put the camera under things — such as live, growing flowers — and shoot without looking through the viewfinder. This was how Katrin Eismann shot *Poppy Underbelly*.

VERY LOW-COST DIGITAL CAMERAS

The image quality that can be achieved with low-cost digital cameras is not as good as film. But if an image is to be extensively manipulated for a photo-illustration, or reproduced at a small size, or used only at a fairly low resolution — for instance, for placement on a web page — the convenience of having the "photo" instantly available may outweigh the quality difference. Even when a photographer wants the resolution or tone and color qualities of traditional film, a low-resolution digital camera can be used to set up the shot, while the film camera waits until the photographer has practiced on the subject, set up proper lighting, if necessary, and made all the basic adjustments to the scene.

and the ability to view directly through the lens without waiting for the camera to project the image on an LCD screen) are bigger and bulkier, though they still may be small and lightweight compared to many film SLRs. They often have far more controls on the body and more features.

- **Viewfinders.** The **LCD screens** on digital cameras come in various styles and sizes. Some LCDs tilt and swivel, making it easier to take pictures at unusual angles, to be less obtrusive doing "street" photography, or simply to reduce glare on the screen.

On a real SLR, the mirror that allows direct viewing through the lens has to flip out of the way at the last instant as you take the picture. For this reason the LCD on a digital SLR can only be used for accessing menus and reviewing images after they've been taken, not for previewing them. On other cameras, though, they show you exactly what you will get, before you take the picture. Some LCDs have features to assist viewing in very dim or bright conditions, and some can be fitted with a hood to shield the screen from bright light.

Many cameras also have an **optical viewfinder**. It provides a continuous live view of the subject, but it usually shows less of the image than is being captured (sometimes a *lot* less) and can be partially blocked by a zoom lens. However, an optical viewfinder coupled with a short lag time (with the LCD turned off) between pressing the shutter and recording the image is important for action photography.

Some digital cameras have an SLR-type **electronic viewfinder** (EVF) instead of an optical viewfinder. These generally show more of the image and don't suffer from screen glare, but like LCDs they have some lag in viewing.

While you won't want to compromise on how many pixels you need, how comfortable the camera is to hold, or how well the viewfinder works for you, the features list of user-set functions (along with the price, of course) is what separates cameras within your now narrowed range. As a Photoshop user, you may find that some of the image-processing features offered by the more expensive cameras are not essential, as Photoshop can take care of problems with color casts, contrast, saturation, and even exposure to some degree. But you will want to consider features like file formats recorded, lens capabilities (such as aperture range, shutter speeds, optical zoom, metering modes, and focusing options), and placement of controls. Except for file formats, these are the same features you would examine when buying a film camera.

One advantage of a camera that can save files in a camera's 16 Bits/Channel "raw" format is that you can quickly and easily adjust color and lighting before taking the file into Photoshop for further work. It's likely that you can open the raw files with Photoshop's Camera Raw plug-in (the CS version is shown here; see how Camera Raw works on page 102). But even if the latest version of Camera Raw doesn't yet support the raw format for your particular digital camera, you can still open and adjust the raw files with the camera manufacturer's own software before you bring the files into Photoshop.

SMART SHOPPING

The quality-to-price ratio of digital cameras continues to improve, quickly and dramatically. As new models come out, keep your eye out for a really good deal on a just-superseded model that has the features you want. Or you may even find a camera with features you aspire to grow into that's suddenly within your price range.

- **File formats.**▼ Most camera makers don't implement **JPEG** compression schemes as well as Photoshop does, and JPEG can produce image defects. But two or three JPEG options (roughly Fine and Normal) are plenty for those occasions when storage space is at a premium.

Not all cameras offer **TIFF**, the only uncompressed image format supported by camera makers. If the only other option is JPEG, consider buying more or bigger storage cards (most new cameras support up to 1 gigabyte) and using TIFF whenever possible.

Some cameras support their manufacturer's own *raw* format, which will have its own file suffix (.CRW, .NEF and .MRW for Canon, Nikon, and Minolta are some examples). For Photoshop users, this raw format is the most versatile. The first advantage is that the raw files can be color-rich, with more potential for detail that Photoshop's 16 Bits/Channel mode offers.▼ The second advantage is that each image is stored in two separate parts: image data (the light information the camera collects) and the camera settings (the processing instructions, based on how you have the camera set). When you view a raw file in Photoshop's Camera Raw dialog box▼ or with the camera manufacturer's own software, you'll see the image as if the camera's settings had been applied to the image data, but you can quickly and easily apply alternate settings without changing the raw data and without throwing away the original settings. This means you can get back to the raw data again later if you like and try different settings. Often a camera's raw format is compressed and is faster to save than TIFF.

- **Metering and focusing.** If you plan to do your metering by pointing the camera at the subject, **center-weighted metering** is adequate only for evenly lit scenes and for flash photography. **Matrix**, or **Pattern**, **metering** is better for averaging light and dark areas in a scene. The addition of **spot metering** allows you to meter to a specific subject in high-contrast lighting conditions. The more metering options you have, the easier it will be to handle any kind of lighting.

Some cameras offer various **program modes**, such as portrait, landscape, sports, and night scenes to set an optimal aperture and shutter speed for you, based on the camera's metering system. Several cameras offer more options to let you take control, including aperture and

FIND OUT MORE

▼ File formats described **page 118**

▼ 16 Bits/Channel mode **page 156**

▼ Using Camera Raw **page 102**

A digital camera takes the White Balance setting into account when processing the image data to make the picture. These photos were taken under incandescent light at night without a flash. For the one at the top, the White Balance was set to Tungsten, so the camera corrected the image to "ignore" the yellow in the light. The bottom image shows what happens if the White Balance is set for Daylight.

CS2 SHOOTING FOR HDR

Here are some pointers for taking a series of exposures of the same image for Photoshop CS2's new Merge to HDR command: ▼

• Take at least three shots at different exposures, from 0.5 to 1 EV step apart. If the scene has a very large dynamic range — from very bright to very dark — take more. If you end up with more than you need, you can omit the extras from the Merge process.

• To keep the depth of field constant and avoid noise or vignetting, vary the shutter speed only, not the f/stop (aperture) or the ISO (receptor sensitivity).

• Make sure nothing moves in the scene, and stabilize the camera; a tripod is a good solution.

• Keep the lighting constant, using no flash or the same flash setting for all photos.

shutter priority modes, white balance, saturation and contrast controls, manual exposure, exposure lock, and bracketing.

White balance is the digital camera equivalent of changing your film to suit the lighting. You've probably seen the orange- or green-tinged skin typical of tungsten or fluorescent lighting shot with daylight-balanced film. Unless you want the color cast for creative reasons, you can choose to have the camera adjust the "white" values to make the image look like it was taken in normal daylight. Some cameras will even "program" a custom correction if you shoot a white target in the scene first.

Saturation and *contrast* controls are also like changing the type of film — for instance, you might want more vivid colors for landscapes and less so for portraits.

With *autobracketing*, all you need to do is select what to alter (exposure or saturation, for instance), and the camera typically will set up three shots — at normal, overexposed (or oversaturated), and underexposed (or undersaturated). Exposure bracketing is especially useful if lighting conditions are extreme and might fool the meter into over- or underexposing (for photographing a big black dog or a sunset, for instance).

Photoshop CS2 can merge several exposures of the same shot into a single high-dynamic-range (HDR) file. ▼ To take advantage of the extra highlight and shadow detail this offers, you'll need a camera that can autobracket in steps of at least 0.5 EV (larger than the typical 0.33 EV steps), or that offers aperture priority or manual mode so that you can do your own exposure bracketing.

Focus options range from *autofocus* to *focus lock* (on a subject that can be off-center), to *continuous focus* (on moving subjects). Many cameras also provide *autofocus assist*, which is a beam of light that the autofocusing system can use to continue to work in dim light.

• **Zoom.** If it's important to you to have a camera that can zoom in on a subject, the criterion to pay attention to is the **optical zoom** capability. **Digital zoom** does one of two things, neither of which is true lens zooming. In some cases a cropped version of the image is recorded; there is no loss of quality but no real advantage over using Photoshop for cropping. In other situations the camera's software enlarges the picture, but not as well as you can do it in Photoshop CS or CS2.

FIND OUT MORE

▼ Merging to HDR
page 157

While bracketing is often used for exposure, with some digital cameras you can also bracket other image characteristics. These three shots resulted from bracketing saturation with a Minolta Dimage A1 camera.

COOLING A "HOT" FLASH

If you find that your built-in flash is too bright for a particular situation, and you don't have easy-to-use software control of its brightness, try this: Cut a small rectangle of single- or double-ply toilet paper just big enough to cover and slightly overlap the flash. Moisten one edge and stick it onto the camera so it hangs down in front of the flash unit.

- **Flash.** Most cameras come with a small built-in flash unit that works in **Auto** mode, has **red-eye reduction** (which it needs because the flash is typically mounted very close to the lens, where the subject is likely to be looking)▼, and can be turned off. Some also offer **fill flash** and **slow**, or **rear**, **sync** for taking long exposures in low ambient light while freezing the subject in sharp focus. These flashes work only over short distances and rarely work well with wide-angle lenses, which span a wider field of view (to the right and left) than our normal vision and much wider than the beam of a small flash unit. Some cameras offer a **hot shoe** for attaching a bigger, more flexible flash system. If you think you'll want that option, be sure to check that the camera will work with all the features of these expensive flash units.

FIND OUT MORE

▼ Dealing with red-eye **page 313**

- **Macro.** If you plan to take photos of small objects at close range, a close-up, or *macro*, capability can be important. Pay attention to the range of focus. If there aren't several inches between the minimum and maximum focusing distances, your macro photography will be limited. Macro settings that engage only at the wide-angle setting can also be limiting, since there might not be enough magnification for the subject until you're so close that perspective is distorted. Check also to see if the camera can be equipped with a flash unit designed for macro mode — good lighting at close range can be difficult, and the built-in flash may not work at all.

Other features that are nice to have and that may be worth considering include:

- Long-lasting, rechargeable battery systems, the option to use batteries that are easy to find in most stores, and the ability to set the camera to turn off automatically if it's inactive for a period of time;

- Adapters or lens threads for filters and other lens accessories, such as macro, telephoto, and wide-angle lenses;

- Image stabilization, which allows you to hand-hold the camera with a longer zoom or in low-light conditions;

- Weather resistance;

- Diopter adjustments on viewfinders so people who wear glasses for normal distance correction can still see if they take off their glasses to keep them from bumping into the viewfinder.

Digital Infrared

FOR MANY YEARS, INFRARED-SENSITIVE black-and-white film, shot with a very dense filter, has produced results that are spectacular, evocative, and always a bit of a surprise. The photographer can't preview the photo because the near infrared wavelengths the film records are just beyond what we can see. Digital cameras vary in their ability to record infrared, but if they are infrared-capable (see "Checking for IR Capability" at the right), they offer certain advantages over film cameras. First, except in the case of a digital SLR, the LCD preview can give you an idea of how the shot will look before you take it. Second, you can see your results immediately after you take the picture. And finally, you can shoot infrared in color as well as black-and-white.

"Real" (mostly) The digital infrared examples on these two pages are mostly "real" — that is, the special effects were created primarily in the camera — with just a little help from Photoshop. We hope they'll inspire you to experiment.

To block the visible light so it doesn't overwhelm the infrared, you'll need an infrared filter. The filter that works best will depend on your camera and your own personal preferences. Some infrared filters are black and pass no visible light. The Hoya R72 filter, which is less expensive than some others, passes near infrared and some deep red light also.

If you can't mount a filter directly on your camera, you may be able to buy a conversion lens adapter (or tube adapter) designed for that purpose. For most infrared photography, you'll need a long exposure to pick up enough infrared "light" to make an image. So unless you want a blurred motion effect, you'll need a way to steady the camera; a tripod is one solution. Also, before you shoot, you'll want to make sure your flash is turned off.

The "real" part For the example below, photographer and Photoshop instructor Rod Deutschmann shot a color image **A** with a Canon PowerShot S45 in Program mode at 1/1000s at f/7.1. Next, for comparison, he turned on the black-and-white effect and shot image **B** at the same exposure.

With the black-and-white effect still turned on, for image **C** Rod attached his infrared filter, switched to the camera's Manual mode, and watched the LCD monitor as he adjusted the exposure to 0.5s at f/3.2. To hold the camera still for the long exposure, he set it on a custom beanbag.

ROD DEUTSCHMANN

Compared to a color **A** or black-and-white photo **B**, in infrared photographs (**C** and **D**), green leaves generally look white and luminous because of the way they reflect and refract infrared energy. Skies often look black because the infrared is absorbed, or sometimes they look silvery, depending on what's in the air. Shadow patterns are often different than in a standard photograph, and water surfaces tend to appear smoother and less reflective.

The Photoshop part Digital black-and-white infrared images are often low in contrast. One way to fix that is to add a Levels Adjustment layer in Photoshop by clicking the "Create new fill or adjustment layer" button ⊘ at the bottom of the Layers palette and choosing Levels. In the Levels dialog box, Rod moved the black point and white point Input Levels sliders inward to adjust contrast **D** (facing page). ▼

Infrared in color Digital infrared in color opens up a whole new world of possibilities. When infrared images are shot without turning on the camera's black-and-white effect, a magenta/red range is a typical result, though the color varies with the combination of camera, filter, and "lighting." For the image below, Alexis Marie Deutschmann photographed the building at noon with a Nikon D100 camera (0.25s at f/4) fitted with an infrared filter; she enhanced the contrast with a Levels adjustment in Photoshop.

Experimenting Inspired by the Deutschmanns' infrared work, we tried some experiments of our own (shown at the right). Shot in color in Auto mode with a Canon PowerShot G5, our snapshot of the duck pond looked quite ordinary **A**. Our infrared version **B**, taken after we added a Hoya R72 filter and set the exposure at 0.8s at f/2.0, was somewhat soft and grainy, like many infrared photos taken with film.

We made a Levels adjustment for contrast, moving the white and black point Input Levels sliders inward **C**. To warm up our duck pond dreamscape, we could have used any of several adjustments to shift from magenta to a yellow-orange color scheme **D**. Choosing to add a Channel Mixer layer, we clicked the ⊘ button at the bottom of the Layers palette and picked Channel Mixer from the menu. In the Channel Mixer dialog box we reduced the Blue channel's contribution **E** by choosing Blue from the Output Channel menu and moving the Blue slider from +100 down to +38. To brighten the image, we boosted the Red and Green channels by adding a little Green to the Red channel and vice versa. ▼

A

B

C

D

If you don't stabilize the camera, or if you intentionally move it by shooting from a moving vehicle, for instance, digital infrared in color can produce a striking new look.

FIND OUT MORE

▼ Using Levels **page 165**

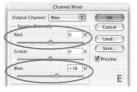

E

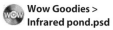

**Wow Goodies >
Infrared pond.psd**

CAMERA RAW

Photoshop's amazing Camera Raw import filter is a powerful incentive in itself to switch from film to digital photography. Once you try it, you'll be hooked.

A digital camera does a lot of sophisticated data processing, based on the camera settings you've chosen, to get from the light it collects (raw data) to the image it displays on its LCD monitor or downloads to your computer as a JPEG or TIFF file. For a growing number of digital cameras, Photoshop's Camera Raw plug-in lets you step right in and get your hands on that conversion process. Camera Raw automatically intercepts digital cameras' raw-format files when you open them in Photoshop. And what you can do with this hefty dialog box is impossible in the world of film. It would be like sending your

CAMERA RAW IN CS

Photoshop's Help file offers a thorough explanation of what all the settings in the powerful Camera Raw interface do. Here's a brief introduction.

Camera Raw's **Adjust** panel lets you control several aspects of the color and contrast. Most notable is the **White Balance** menu, which lets you make big changes to get close to the lighting you want for your image. The **Temperature** slider can then be used for finer adjustments. These two controls let you get your hands on the lighting and "film" characteristics in a direct way that you won't find inside Photoshop.

In the **Detail** panel you can sharpen the image (or just the preview, depending on how your Camera Raw Preferences are set). You can also reduce noise, both digital "grain" (with the **Luminance Smoothing** slider) and color artifacts (with the **Color Noise Reduction** slider), which can occur because of low light or a high ISO setting.

If you continually get images in the Camera Raw window that look different than you expect based on what your camera shows you, the **Calibrate** panel can help you develop and save a profile to adjust the preview for files from that camera.

Camera Raw's tools include the **Zoom**, **Hand**, and **White Balance**, which is operated by clicking on a point that should be neutral in color.

The settings at the bottom of the Camera Raw interface tell Photoshop how you want it to handle the file when you click "OK" to close the Camera Raw dialog and open the file in Photoshop. All of these things can also be changed once you're in Photoshop, but you may want to get a head start. You can change from the camera's color **Space** to your working color space. You can also avoid dealing with the extra bulk of a 16 Bits/Channel file by changing the **Depth** to 8 Bits. If you change the **Size** (pixel dimensions), the image will be resampled when it opens (the + or – following the dimensions shows which). An increase or decrease in **Resolution** won't cause resampling; it will simply make the image's print dimensions smaller or larger.

On the **Lens** panel you can fix chromatic aberration (separation of the colors in an image at high-contrast edges). Here you can also lighten the vignetting (dark edges) that often occurs with wide-angle lenses.

Original

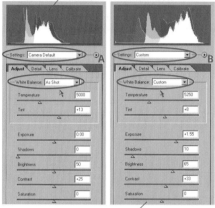

Adjusted

When this photo (the original is at the top) was taken with a Minolta Dimage A1 digital camera, the light from the white clouds fooled the camera into using a fast shutter speed ($\frac{1}{3200}$ sec) and a small aperture (f/9), which resulted in an underexposed image. Because the camera was set to record in raw format, when the file was opened in Photoshop CS, it was intercepted by Camera Raw **A**. In the Adjust panel, White Balance, Temperature, and other controls could be changed **B** and quickly viewed. Clicking the dialog box's "OK" button opened the file in Photoshop.

film back to be processed another way, or redoing exactly the same photo shoot but with a different type of film or lighting. And it's quick and easy.

Recall that a digital camera's raw-format file has two separate parts — (1) the image information that comes through the lens and is recorded (raw data) and (2) the camera settings at the time the picture was taken (recorded as processing instructions). Camera Raw acts on the camera settings. As you experiment with its menus and sliders, Camera Raw shows you an on-screen preview, but it doesn't actually process the image until you click the "OK" button to go beyond Camera Raw and into Photoshop.

Working with raw files in Camera Raw offers some huge advantages over opening a file directly into Photoshop. For one thing, you can work quickly and painlessly with large files in 16 Bits/Channel mode, preserving all their extra color depth

CAMERA RAW & THE FILE BROWSER

Like Camera Raw, the File Browser (in CS) works with previews and with instructions stored with the file. This makes the two a great combination for getting a lot of work done in a hurry! If you need to make the same correction to several raw-format images, you can automate the process with the File Browser:

1 Open your first raw file, make the adjustments you want in the Camera Raw dialog box and click "OK."

2 In Photoshop, open the File Browser (click the button on the Options bar). In the File Browser window, select the thumbnails of the other images you want to treat with the Camera Raw settings you just applied.

3 Open the File Browser's Automate menu (or right/Ctrl-click on one of the selected images) and choose **Apply Camera Raw Settings**.

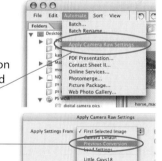

4 When the dialog box opens, choose **Previous Conversion** and click the "Update" button.

(Notice that you also have other interesting options, such as using one of the selected files as the basis for your changes, or going back to the Camera Defaults, or loading settings you've saved in a sidecar file. And if you want to customize the settings for this batch even further, you can click the "Advanced" button to access all the Camera Raw settings, though without a preview.)

CAMERA RAW IMPROVEMENTS IN CS2

Camera Raw in Photoshop CS2 has several new time- and work-saving features. Some of the most useful are the ability to open several files at once from Bridge (see "Camera Raw & Bridge" on the next page); to do more routine editing tasks, such as Crop, Straighten, and adjust Curves; and to place Color Samplers to monitor changes as you edit.▼ You can now quickly save copies of your images in several other formats, without taking the time to open them in Photoshop first.

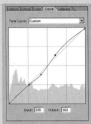

The tools, including the new **Color Sampler**, **Crop** tool, and **Straighten** tool, have been collected in the upper left corner.

The new **Crop** tool crops freely (Normal) or to a specified ratio or to Custom dimensions you set (Ratio, Pixels, Inches, or Cm).▼

Toggle **Preview** on and off if you want to compare previous settings with a new adjustment.

Toggle **Shadows** or **Highlights** on to get a warning color if your image has shadows that are too dark or blown highlights (as shown here). Or toggle them off if the warning color interferes with viewing.

The new **Curve** panel operates like Photoshop's Curves adjustment,▼ except that it has three presets — Linear (like Photoshop's Curves default), Medium, and Strong Contrast. Adjusting any of these automatically creates a Custom Curve.

Some or all of the changes you make in a Camera Raw session can be saved by clicking the ⊙ button and choosing **Save Settings Subset** from the menu (the options are shown in the tip below).

In CS2 by default Camera Raw opens with a number of **Auto** settings based on image data, designed to give you a head start in processing the photo. This feature can be toggled off and on in the ⊙ menu.

Size now shows both pixel dimensions and megapixels in the image, or in the crop if the Crop tool is in action. (The table on page 94 shows how big you can print an image based on its megapixel size.)

"Save" now allows you to convert and save your image as JPG, TIF, DNG (Adobe's new digital negative format), or PSD▼ without opening it in Photoshop.

"Done" saves the settings to the file but doesn't open the file in Photoshop.

FIND OUT MORE

▼ Using Color Samplers **page 162**

▼ Cropping **page 244**

▼ Using Curves **page 166**

▼ File formats **page 118**

CAMERA RAW & BRIDGE

If you use images shot in a camera's raw format, you'll find that one of the most useful new features in CS2 is the ability to select several images in Bridge▼ and open them in Camera Raw — **Ctrl/⌘-R** is the shortcut. They open in Camera Raw's new **Synchronize panel**, allowing you to choose one thumbnail and make any changes you want in Camera Raw. Then select the other images that you want to share these settings, click the "Synchronize" button, choose which Camera Raw settings you want these images to share, as shown below, and click "OK." You can then open any or all of these images for further editing in Photoshop, or save them with their new settings without opening them.

Another option for working with raw files in Bridge is to copy Camera Raw settings and paste them to one or more other raw files, or return to the Camera Default or Previous Conversion, all in Bridge, without going through the Camera Raw interface. In Bridge when you choose Edit > Apply Camera Raw Settings > **Copy Camera Raw Settings**, the same list of options shown above appears, so you can choose which settings to copy (or instead of using the Edit menu, you can **right/Ctrl-click** on the image and choose from a context-sensitive menu). Then Ctrl/⌘-click or Shift-click to select the files you want to paste these settings to, and paste via Edit or the context-sensitive menu.

and detail without slowing the processing of the image with each change. The more you can do in Camera Raw, the less "heavy lifting" you'll need to do in Photoshop.

For another thing, you gain tremendous power from Camera Raw's ability to change the *white balance,* which is the digital camera equivalent of changing your film to suit the lighting (or changing the lighting itself). For instance, if you meant to capture the warm yellow light of a cozy interior but the camera's automatic white balance didn't take that into consideration, you can put back the yellow and restore the mood. Or if you just want to experiment with color options for an art print, you can do that, too. Camera Raw follows the raw-format protocol of keeping the settings separate from the pixels. No matter what you do to the file in Photoshop, you can't "save over" the file, since Photoshop itself can't save in raw camera formats. So you can go back to the original data and, if you like, the original camera settings — weeks, months, or even years later.

By default, your Camera Raw settings are stored in an Adobe Camera Raw Database file on your computer, and they're associated with file content, not with the file's name or where the file is stored. Even if you rename or move the raw-format file, the next time you open it, Camera Raw will bring it up with your most recent settings, and it will also offer the choice of using the original camera settings.

You can also save the Camera Raw settings as a separate *sidecar* (**.xmp**) file in the same folder as the image, so you can send it along with the raw-format file wherever it goes (to storage on a CD or to a collaborator in a project). Once you have the settings you like, click the ⊙ button (to the right of the Settings menu in the Camera Raw dialog) and choose Export Settings. You can load the settings (by clicking the ⊙ button to the right of Settings in the Camera Raw dialog and navigating to the .xmp file you want)

FIND OUT MORE

▼ Using Bridge
page 109

▼ Merge to HDR
page 157

CAMERA RAW & HDR

If you take a series of exposures in order to use CS2's Merge to HDR,▼ results will be more reliable if you set all the exposure-related parameters (Exposure, Shadows, Brightness, and Contrast) to 0. You can still adjust color, as long as you keep the adjustments constant for the entire set of images. The Synchronize panel in Bridge (see the description at the left) is a great way to ensure this, and to open all your images, ready to merge to HDR.

Cher Threinen-Pendarvis used Photoshop with a Wacom Intuos tablet and a laptop computer to draw sketches (top two) for her *Alps Study* on location, then completed the painting on her desktop computer, also with the Intuos. To optimize Photoshop's performance while working on location and the "natural media" feel of the painting tools, she painted on a single layer and purged History often.

and apply them to other files — maybe other photos you shot at the same time, under the same lighting conditions, or other images destined for the same series of art prints.

If you want a particular set of Camera Raw settings to appear in the Settings menu, choose Save Settings from the ⊙ menu, give it a name that will remind you of its content, and put it in the default Settings folder.

STOCK PHOTOGRAPHY

In addition to the images you scan yourself or capture with a digital camera, there's a wealth of stock images, patterns, textures, and illustrations available on CD-ROM and downloadable from the web, with a variety of arrangements for use and payment. As an alternative to per-image fees, some stock photo sources offer subscriptions that allow you to pay in advance for a number of images at a reduced rate and then download files as you need them.

Sources of stock photos include those that provided some of the images used in this book — PhotoSpin.com, Corbis Royalty Free, iStockphoto, and PhotoDisc. In CS2 Adobe has also made it very easy to buy from their Adobe Stock Photos source (www.adobe.com/products/creativesuite/adobestockphotos). With an internet connection and CS2 you can click on the Favorites tab in Bridge and choose Adobe Stock Photos to go directly to the web site to browse, download comping versions of images, and buy. Another great source is Stock.XCHNG (www.sxc.hu), self-described as "a friendly community of photography addicts who generously offer their works to the public free of charge." Stock.XCHNG photos, many by professional photographers, are offered free, with few or no restrictions beyond prohibitions on reselling them as a collection or using them in "hate" materials or adult entertainment; some require attribution to and notification of the photographer.

PRESSURE-SENSITIVE TABLETS

For imitating traditional art media such as the paintbrush, pencil, airbrush, or charcoal, a pressure-sensitive graphics tablet with stylus — for example, any of those in Wacom's Intuos or less expensive Graphire line — has a more familiar feel than a mouse and also provides much better control. Photoshop's painting tools (see Chapter 6) are "wired" to take advantage of pressure sensitivity for controlling brush size, how thick or thin the paint is and how fast it flows, how much paint the brush can hold, and how much the color of the paint varies.

ACQUIRING IMAGES FROM PDF'S

In Photoshop CS you can open individual images embedded in a PDF document. Choosing **File > Import > PDF Image** and choosing a PDF file opens the PDF Image Import dialog box. There you can choose which image(s) to import, as shown below. Another PDF Import function (File > Automate > Multipage PDF to PSD) lets you separate the individual pages and save them as named and numbered PSD files, which you can then open in Photoshop. Like the File > Open command, which can open one page of a multipage PDF at a time, this command can result in files that include transparency, so they may not look exactly as you would expect from looking at the PDF pages. In CS2 the PDF-opening functions have been reassigned from File > Import to File > Open, or to the new Bridge program (see page 109). With one PDF file targeted in **Bridge**, choose **File > Open With > Adobe Photoshop CS2** to bring up the Import PDF dialog. Here you can choose Image or Page, then click to identify the image or page you want to open (or Ctrl/⌘-click or Shift-click for more than one) and click "OK."

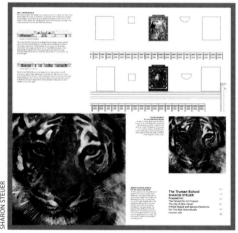

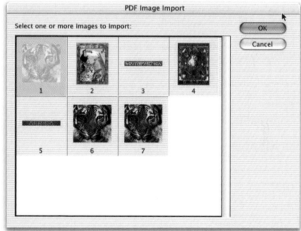

In Photoshop CS, when the File > Import > PDF Image command is used to access the images in a PDF, a dialog box opens where you can choose the image(s) you want to open. (In CS2, choose File > Open, or from Bridge, File > Open With > Adobe Photoshop CS2 to bring up the PDF Image Import dialog.) Included in the thumbnails are all pixel-based images that were on the page when the PDF was made, even hidden images. Here is a PDF made from Sharon Steuer's proposal for mural installations at the Truman School (shown at the left). When Photoshop CS's Import > PDF Image command was used with this file, all the pixel-based images showed up in the PDF Import Images dialog box (right), including a hidden version of the tiger that Steuer had covered with a more vivid one.

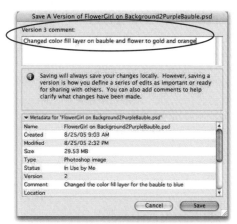

Choosing File > Save a Version to save a file to an existing Version Cue project allows you to add comments that will appear with the preview in Bridge in its Alternates and Versions view, opened by choosing View > As Alternates and Versions, in Bridge's main menu.

MULTIPLE METADATA

If you have more than one file selected in the main File Browser/Bridge panel (which you can do by Shift-clicking or Ctrl/⌘-clicking thumbnails), the Metadata panel displays any metadata that's common to all of them.

MANAGING FILES

The Adobe Creative Suite and Creative Suite 2 offer Photoshop users some great options for tracking, viewing, sorting, and automatically processing files. The main players are File Browser (in CS), Bridge (in CS2), and Version Cue (in both versions). Descriptions follow, and you can learn more in "Exercising File Browser/Bridge" on page 128.

Version Cue

Version Cue is designed to keep track of component files as a project develops. Even if you don't have Version Cue installed on your own computer, you might find yourself working with it on a network. Though it's designed for work groups, individual users may find that it makes project management more efficient.

Once a Version Cue project has been opened and a source file has been copied into it, if you open that file within the project, Version Cue automatically opens a **working copy** for you to edit. You can s**ave** the working copy to your hard drive without affecting the project's **master** file. When you're ready to add your edits to the project, choosing **File > Save a Version** (instead of File > Save) from Photoshop will save a new version to the project, along with any comments you want to include about the changes you made. You can always go back to an earlier version by **promoting** that version to make it the current one.

New to CS2 is the additional ability to alter a file and save an edited file as an **Alternate,** rather than as another version (use File > Save As with the new Adobe dialog, which you can open from the standard Save As dialog by clicking the "Use Adobe Dialog" button). In the Adobe dialog, give the file a new name and check the Save as Alternate box at the bottom of the dialog. Then, in InDesign for example, you or your colleague can place one of the alternate files in the InDesign file, and later, using the Links palette, choose from all the Alternates, making it easy to preview and try out different concepts based on the same file.

Also new to CS2 is the ability to view and manage your project files from within Bridge. When you use Bridge to move files from their source locations into your project, the files are automatically copied and you won't accidentally alter the originals.

Adobe's web site has pointers for using Version Cue, at **www.adobe.com/products/creativesuite/versioncue.html.**

A simple and quick but really worthwhile task you can do with File Browser (in CS) or Bridge (in CS2) is to reorient your images and store their orientation in the folder with the files, so that whenever you open a folder of files in File Browser or Bridge, each one appears vertically or horizontally, the way you want to see it:

1 Ctrl/⌘-click the thumbnails of any images you want to reorient the same direction, and click the button for "Rotate Clockwise" or "Rotate Counter-Clockwise" to turn them 90°.

2 Target and rotate thumbnails for any other files that need a different rotation.

3 When all the files are correctly oriented and you've done any other File Browser/Bridge organizing you want — adding keywords, flagging, ranking, sorting, and so on — choose File > Export Cache (in File Browser), or Tools > Cache > Export Cache (in Bridge). This stores the cache containing your File Browser work inside the folder with the images.

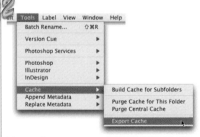

Now when you copy the folder — for instance, if you burn it onto a CD-ROM — the cache goes with it. When you open the folder in File Browser or Bridge again, the thumbnails appear instantly, oriented correctly. And when you take the time to open the files in Photoshop, the File Browser/Bridge rotation instructions will be carried out, and the images will open in the right orientation.

File Browser (CS)

File Browser was designed to be a customizable "digital lightbox" for viewing and sorting files. When you choose File > Browse or click the Toggle File Browser button 🗐 on the Options bar, the File Browser window opens up. Here you can choose a folder in the Folders panel, view its contents as a series of thumbnails in the main panel, choose a thumbnail, and view information (metadata) about the file's origin; you can even add a caption or copyright data. You can tag a file as flagged or unflagged, then rank it, and assign keywords. When you want to find the file again, you can search with as many as 13 different criteria, including whether or not it's flagged, what its rank is, what's in the metadata (such as file type or date of origin), and keywords.

As a slide sorter, one of the File Browser's most valuable functions is to pick out a set of files to use with one of Photoshop's automated processes, such as making a panorama, a contact sheet, or a web gallery, or opening in Camera Raw. "Exercising File Browser/Bridge" on page 128 runs through some of File Browser's useful features.

Bridge (CS2)

In CS2 the organizing, browsing, and searching functions seen in File Browser have been improved and housed in a separate program — Bridge — that works not only with Photoshop but with other applications as well. Bridge gives you more viewing options than File Browser did. You can change thumbnail size on the fly, scaling the previews up so you can see more detail, or scaling them down so you can see a greater number of them on the screen at once. The flagging and rating system has been changed to color-coded labeling and a "star" system (you can rate images using one to five stars).

In addition to the Thumbnails and Details options available for viewing in File Browser, Bridge's View menu offers a Compact view (a smaller window with thumbnails only, no Folders, Metadata, or Keywords), the Filmstrip option (with one large image and a strip of smaller thumbnails), Versions and Alternates (which works with Version Cue), and Slide Show (showing one large image at a time, with the option to rate, rotate, and label each one as you view it). Using keyboard shortcuts in Slide Show, you can view individual images or turn through the pages of a multipage PDF created in Acrobat.

The Window menu allows you to save any combination of Bridge options as a custom workspace (Window > Workspace

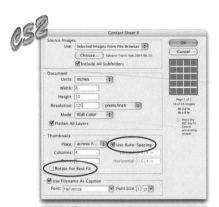

Photos: Peter Carlisle

Photoshop's **Contact Sheet II** command produces a sheet of thumbnails to your specifications. Even with the Rotate For Best Fit option turned off as shown here, the CS/CS2 version of Contact Sheet makes better use of the space for vertical images than previous versions did; with this option turned on, all images are mounted in the same orientation to optimize space. Choosing the Use Auto-Spacing option puts the images as close together as practical, making them as large as possible given the numbers of Columns and Rows you specify.

Actions provide a way to automate effects that are more complex than applying a single filter or Layer Style. Find examples of Wow Actions for painting on page 398 and for special effects on page 551.

> Save Workspace) so that you can load it for use later (again via Bridge's Window > Workspace menu)

Beyond organizing your files and running Photoshop's automated functions, Bridge can also coordinate color management among the programs of the Creative Suite, so that all of the programs are set up to use the same color space.▼

FIND OUT MORE

▼ Bridge & color management
page 180

File Browser (through its Automate menu) and Bridge (through Tools > Photoshop) provide a gateway to Photoshop's Contact Sheet, Photomerge, and other automated operations. You can use File Browser/Bridge to sort out the files you want to use, and then go directly into the automated Photoshop routine of your choice.

AUTOMATING

Automation is built into Photoshop and ImageReady in all kinds of ways. Many filters and Layer Styles essentially automate complex dimensional or tone-and-color effects. Two menus — File > Automate and File > Scripts — offer several options for automating.▼ And the Actions palette is one of the most useful automation tools found in Photoshop or ImageReady.

FIND OUT MORE

▼ **Some useful automation commands:**

Cropping & straightening photos from a scan **page 92**

Making a Picture Package
page 668

Making a Web Photo Gallery
page 691

Piecing together a panorama
page 604

ACTIONS

The Actions palette offers a way to **record** a whole series of Photoshop (or ImageReady) operations and **play them back** in order, on a single file or a whole batch. An Action can be a great way to automate routine production tasks that you find yourself repeating often, or just to record your creative process as you work out some phenomenal Photoshop treatment, so you have an operational record of what you did.

In a nutshell the process of creating and using an Action is this: You open a file of the kind you want to operate on, turn on Photoshop's (or ImageReady's) recording apparatus, carry out the operations you want to record, and stop recording. Then you can play back the Action on another file whenever you want to. "Creating an Action To Animate a Video Clip" on page 134

Continued on page 112

THE ACTIONS PALETTE

Actions are listed in **sets** in the Actions palette. The control strip at the bottom has buttons for recording and playing Actions, while the palette's ⊙ menu offers most of the commands you need for editing, controlling playback, saving and loading Actions, and assigning keyboard shortcuts. Each Action is made up of a series of recorded **steps**, and each Action is part of a set, even if the set includes only one Action.

A **black check mark** next to the name of a **set**, an **Action**, or an individual **step** shows that it's active and will play if you click or Ctrl/⌘-click on its name and click the "Play" button ▶ at the bottom of the palette.

A **red check mark** alerts you to the fact that **some steps** in a set or an Action are **currently not active** and won't play.

A **black modal control icon next to an Action or set** means there will be a stop at *every* step that involves a dialog box or an Enter/Return option.

A **red modal control icon next to an Action or set** means there is *at least one* stop-and-wait-for-input step included.

A **black modal control icon next to a step** indicates that this step will stop and wait for input via a dialog box or the Enter/Return key.

If **no check mark** appears, that particular set, Action, or step is **currently turned off** and will not be carried out if you try to play it.

Stop: Click to stop recording or playing.

Record: Click to begin recording. When the button is red, recording is in progress.

Play: Click to run a selected Action or to play from a selected step onward. **Ctrl/⌘-click** to play only the selected step and then stop.

Click to **expand or close the listing**.

Action **set**
Action
Step

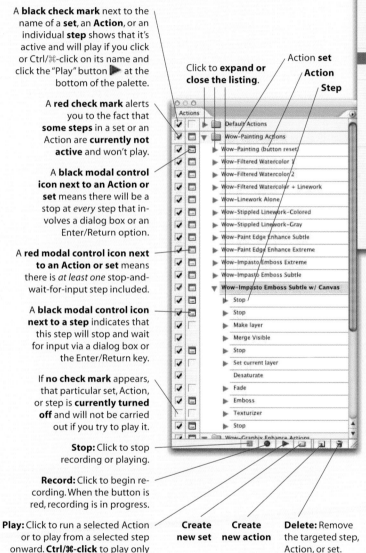

Create new set **Create new action** **Delete:** Remove the targeted step, Action, or set.

Dock to Palette Well
Button Mode

New Action...
New Set...
Duplicate
Delete
Play

Start Recording
Record Again...
Insert Menu Item...
Insert Stop...
Insert Path

Action Options...
Playback Options...

Clear All Actions
Reset Actions
Load Actions...
Replace Actions...
Save Actions...

Commands
Frames
Image Effects
Production
Sample Actions
Text Effects
Textures
Video Actions

If you put the Actions palette in **Button mode** (as shown here), you can use a multicolumn layout that takes up less space per button: Simply drag the lower right corner to widen the palette to two or more columns; the individual buttons will get narrower. To toggle back to **List mode**, choose Button Mode again from the palette menu. Also, you can color-code Actions, making it easier to find and play them again. **Color coding** an Action can be done in the New Action dialog box when an Action is recorded, or by choosing Action Options from the Actions palette's menu.

There are some things that are worth including at the beginning of almost any Action you record:

- As soon as you start recording, **make a copy of the file's "pre-Action" state** with the Image > Duplicate command, so you have a way to recover your original if you don't like the "actioned" result.

- For some Photoshop operations the file has to be in a certain mode. For instance, the Lighting Effects filter runs only on RGB Color files. If your Action requires that the file be in a specific mode, record choosing the **File > Automate > Conditional Mode Change** command.

Turning on all the Source Mode options and setting the Target Mode to RGB Color ensures that the Conditional Mode Change command will convert a file in any other color mode to RGB Color.

- Whenever your Action creates a new layer or channel, make sure to give it a **unique name** rather than leaving it at the default "Layer 1" or "Alpha 1," for instance. That way you'll avoid problems that can arise from running your Action on a file that already has a "Layer 1" or "Alpha 1."

- Unless you keep your Desktop extremely well-organized and consistent, **avoid** including steps that load from **specific locations**. If the file the Action is looking for has been moved or renamed, it won't be found. And, of course, an Action that relies on specific locations often won't be useful to others.

leads you step-by-step through the process of recording an Action.

Actions are listed by name in the Actions palette, where they are grouped in **sets**, with each set indicated by a folder icon 📁. Sets make it possible to assemble "toolkits" of Actions for particular jobs, and you can include the same Action in several different sets.

To run an Action on more than one file at a time, use the File > Automate > **Batch** command, or incorporate the Action in an Image Processor or Script Events Manager routine (described on pages 116 and 118). Or turn an Action into a ***Droplet***, a "stand-alone" macro with its own icon that sits on the Desktop and runs the Action on any files whose icons are dragged onto it, as described on page 115. You can also **save**, **load**, and **edit** Actions.

Recording an Action

To record an Action so you'll be able to apply the whole series of steps again, start by opening a file like the ones you want the Action to work on. Then do one of the following:

- **To record your Action as the first in a brand-new set,** click the "Create new set" button 📁 at the bottom of the Actions palette, name the set, and click "OK." Then click the "Create new action" button 🔲 next to it, name the Action, and click "Record." Start performing operations, tailoring your choices within the limitations of "actionable" operations, as described in "What's 'Actionable'" on page 113.

- **To record your Action as part of an existing set,** do as described above, except skip the "Create new set" step and start with the 🔲 button instead, choosing from the Set menu in the New Action dialog box before you click "Record."

The "Record" button ⬤ at the bottom of the Actions palette will stay red (indicating that recording is in progress) until you press the "Stop" button ⬛ to end the recording session.

Choices from the Actions palette itself are among the things that can be recorded in an Action. That means you can nest an existing Action within the one you're currently recording. Here's how: As you record, click in the Actions palette to target the Action you want to include, then press the "Play" button ▶. This Action will be added as a step in the one you're recording. Being able to nest Actions means that you can easily run several nested Actions with one application of the File > Automate > Batch command or with File > Scripts > Image Processor.

There are a few dialog box and palette settings that are recorded *only if they are changed* from an existing setting. Examples are the Layer Properties, Color Settings, and Preferences dialogs. So if you want to record current settings, you have to *change to other settings before recording* so you can then record the process of *changing* to the desired settings. As a check, after you've recorded the use of a dialog box or palette, you can tell which settings have been recorded by expanding the Actions palette's listing for the recorded step to see what it includes.

In an Action the effect of a **toggle command** like Snap To Guides or Show/Hide Guides will depend on the state of the file when the Action plays the command. In other words, even though the command you recorded when you made the Action was Show Guides, if guidelines are already showing when the Action plays the Show Guides command, it will *Hide Guides* instead.

In ImageReady, Actions operate somewhat differently than in Photoshop. ImageReady doesn't organize Actions in sets, but it has these added advantages:

- You can insert **Conditional steps**, to be carried out or skipped, depending on whether certain conditions are met.

- In Photoshop, using the Edit > Undo command **(Ctrl/⌘-Z)** immediately after running an Action will undo *only the last step* of the Action. In ImageReady, the *entire Action* is undone.

- **Droplets** made in ImageReady **can be edited**, just as Actions can. Double-click the Droplet icon to start the process. (For more detail, in ImageReady, choose Help > ImageReady Help, click on "Search," and type "editing Droplets.")

What's "Actionable"

Many of Photoshop's **commands** and **tool operations** are "actionable" — they are recorded as part of an Action as you carry out the command or use the tool. Also recorded are choices made in the **Layers, Channels, Paths,** and **History palettes,** as well as the **Actions palette** itself (see the "Nesting Actions" tip on page 112).

For other commands and operations that can't be recorded directly, there are workarounds.

- **Paths drawn "by hand" with the Pen tools ✎ ✐ won't be recorded as you draw them,** but you can include a path as part of an Action by drawing the path, saving it in the Paths palette with a unique name,▼ then selecting the path in the Paths palette, clicking the Actions palette's ⊙ button to open the palette menu, and choosing the **Insert Path** command. When the Action is played on another file, the original path will be added to the new file's Paths palette as the *Work Path*, and further commands in the Action can use that path.

FIND OUT MORE

▼ Working with paths **page 432**

- **The strokes of brush-based tools aren't recorded.** These are strokes made with the Brush ✏, Pencil ✐, Healing Brush ✐, Spot Healing Brush ✐, Clone Stamp ♣, Pattern Stamp ♣, Erasers ✐✐✐, Smudge ✎, Sharpen △, Blur ○, Dodge ✎, Burn ✎, and Sponge ●. Instead you can insert a pause, complete with directions for what to do during the pause, so the user can stop and do the necessary work with these tools. To put a pause in the Action, choose the **Insert Stop** command from the Actions palette's menu ⊙, as described on page 114.

- Some of the choices made in the **Options bar**, **palettes**, and **dialog boxes** are recorded, and others are not. (To tell which choices are recorded, watch the Actions palette as you record to see whether your choice adds a step to the Action.) Again, you can include the **Insert Stop** command for a choice that isn't recorded, with directions so the person playing the Action can make the appropriate settings.

- Commands that affect the "working environment" rather than an individual file — such as those in the Window menu and many in the View menu — won't be recorded directly as you carry them out. Instead this kind of command has to be recorded by choosing **Insert Menu Item** from the Actions palette's menu ⊙. Then choose the command, or type the command's name into the Insert Menu Item dialog box.

When you choose Insert Stop from the Actions palette's pop-out menu so that your Action will stop running and display a message or give the user a chance for input, you have the opportunity to "Allow Continue." If you check this box, the message that's displayed when the Action stops will include a "Continue" button to make it easier to continue the Action if the user doesn't need to do anything.

The Playback Options command from the Actions palette's pop-out menu can be used to make Actions run speedily (Accelerated, the default) or one step at a time so you can see the result of each step before the Action continues (good for diagnosing a problematic Action) or with a defined pause. By default, an Action will pause to finish playing any audio annotation recorded as part of an Action before the Action continues, but you can turn off this option. (Both text and audio annotations, added with the Annotation tools are recordable.)

Note: When you use Insert Menu Item, *the inserted command won't be carried out during the recording session.* So if you need a nonrecordable command to be carried out in order for the rest of the Action to be recorded correctly, you'll have to both **carry out the operation in its nonrecordable form** (to do the job in the file you're recording from) *and* **use the Insert Menu Item command** (to get the operation recorded so that it will be carried out when the Action is played).

• Of course, your Action will work only if the **conditions of the file** you're working on will allow it to work. For instance, if your Action includes a step to add a layer mask, that won't happen if the layer that's active when that step is played is the *Background* layer, which can't have a mask. So you have to be sure that you include in the Action all the steps necessary to prepare the file for each step of the Action to work — or choose **Insert Stop** from the palette's menu ⊙, and type a message that explains the requirements so the user can pause and get the file ready. Select the **Allow Continue** option if you want the user to be able to proceed with the Action without doing anything more than reading the message. Leave the Allow Continue box unchecked anytime that some input is *required* before the Action can proceed. When you've finished making entries in the Record Stop dialog box, click "OK."

Playing an Action

Once you've recorded an Action or loaded an Action that was recorded by someone else (see "Saving & Loading Actions" on page 116), you have several playback options:

• **To run an entire Action (or even a series of nested Actions),** click its name in the Actions palette and click the "Play" button ▶ at the bottom of the palette.

• **To play an Action from a specific step** forward — for instance, if you've encountered a Stop and completed the work necessary for continuing — simply click the "Play" button ▶. (The next step will have been targeted automatically, and the Action will play from there.)

• **To play a single step** of an Action, click on that step to select it, and then **Ctrl/⌘-click** the "Play" button ▶.

Automating Actions

To run an Action on a whole batch of files, put the files into a folder and use the File > Automate > **Batch** command. Or create a standalone **Droplet,** an application made from the Action,

In either CS or CS2, if you click on the name of an Action in the Actions palette's list mode and then choose the File > Automate > Create Droplet command, the Create Droplet dialog box opens, where you can choose how your processed documents will be named. Here the word "-sharp" and the file extension are added to the document name for files processed by a Smart Sharpen Droplet so it's easy to tell, just from the name, that the file has been sharpened.

When you click "OK" in the Create Droplet box, the Action is exported as a standalone macro. You can run the Action saved in the Droplet by dragging a file or folder icon onto the Droplet icon.

by choosing File > Automate > **Create Droplet**. In the Batch or Create Droplet dialog box, choose the Action you want to play. In designating a Destination for the files after they've been treated with the Action, if you choose "Save and Close," the old files will be overwritten by the altered ones. If you choose to save the files to a designated Folder, you have tremendous flexibility in naming them. You can choose from the pop-up File Naming lists, or type in your own choices. This makes it possible, for instance, to create a numbered or lettered series of files with the same basic name.

Once you've made a Droplet, you can drag a file or a folder of files onto the Droplet's icon on the Desktop to launch Photoshop (if necessary), run the Action on the file(s), and save the results in the folder you chose.

The process of running Actions can also be automated through the File > Scripts menu with the Image Processor command or with Script Events Manager, as described on page 116.

Editing Actions

If you want to modify an Action or set you've recorded or loaded, here are some easy methods. Start by expanding the list of steps in the Action by clicking the ▶ to the left of the Action's (or set's) name in the Actions palette, so you can see all the steps.

- **To remove a step** (or even an entire Action or set), drag it to the "Delete" button 🗑 at the bottom of the palette.

- **To insert a new step** (or steps) in an Action, click the step you want the new step to come after. Then click the "Record" button ●, record the new step, and click "Stop" ■.

- **To change the order of steps,** drag their names up or down to new positions in the list of steps for the Action.

- **To duplicate a step,** hold down the Alt/Option key and drag the step's name to the point where you want the copy.

- **To change settings** for a step that involves a dialog box, double-click the step in the expanded listing to open the dialog, then enter new settings, and click "OK."

- To make the Action **pause within a step** so the user can change the settings in a dialog box, click in the **modal control column** just to the left of the step's name. A **modal control icon** ▦ will appear in the column to show that the Action will pause with the dialog box open. Clicking again in this column toggles the pause function off.

The modal control works not only for dialog boxes but also for operations that require pressing the Enter/Return key (or double-clicking) to accept the current settings, such as using the Free Transform command or the Crop tool.

- **To temporarily disable a step** so it isn't carried out when you play an Action, click the check mark in the farthest left column of the Actions palette. Click in this column again to bring back the check mark and re-enable the step. (This also works for disabling or re-enabling an Action without permanently removing it from the set.)

Saving & Loading Actions

A new or changed Action set can (and should!) be permanently saved. You can do this by clicking on the set's name in the Actions palette, then clicking the ⊙ button in the top right corner of the palette, and choosing Save Actions. (If you don't want to replace the old version, give the new one a new name.)

You can load any saved Actions set as an *addition* to the current palette (choose **Load Actions** from the palette's pop-out menu), or you can load it *instead of* the current palette (choose **Replace Actions**). ***Note:*** Before you replace Actions, make sure you've saved the current set so you'll be able to retrieve it again.

SCRIPTS

Another source of automation in Photoshop CS/CS2 is the File > Scripts menu. Even if you don't care to do your own script-writing, you're likely to find the Scripts provided with CS, and especially CS2, worth exploring. Both versions have scripts to export all the layers or layer comps in a file as a series of separate files. CS2 also has Image Processor and Script Events Manager.

Image Processor (CS2)

If you want to save a group of files in a particular format, at a particular size, or after performing the same set of operations on each file, Image Processor can speed up the process. Open the dialog box (File > Scripts > Image Processor), choose the folder or open files you want to process, and choose the file formats (TIFF, PSD, or JPEG) and sizes you need. Choose to add copyright data if you like, or run an Action of your choice. If this process is one you use often, save your Image Processor settings to load and use again. You can also run Image Processor through Bridge.

Among the choices provided in the Script Events Manager's Script menu is the Display Camera Maker.jsx script. Perhaps you work with images from two or three different digital cameras, and you don't want to have to scroll through the metadata every time you open an image to know which camera was used to shoot the photo. In the Script Events Manager you can choose Open Document as the Event, and Display Camera Maker.jsx as the Script (top). Now whenever you open a file, a popup alert will tell you what digital camera took the picture, or if no camera data could be found for the image.

Continued on page 118

Mark Wainer Works the Percentages

WE GET SO USED TO THINKING of image dimensions in pixels, inches, or cm that it's easy to forget about the Percent option. But Mark Wainer finds this choice ideal for recording certain Actions. Using percentages, Mark developed an Action that adds an Adjustment layer to subtly vignette his completed painterly images. Many images can benefit from subtly darkening the edges to draw the viewer's attention into the center of the image. In a traditional darkroom this is called "burning the edges."

 You'll find **Mark Wainer's Edge Burn.atn** Action for subtle vignetting on the Wow DVD-ROM in the Wow Goodies folder. Use it "as is," or use his technique to record a similar Action of your own, customized for the file sizes and kind of vignetting you want.

For his **"Edge Burn"** Action, Mark started by opening one of his large-format painterly images (like the one on page 49) and turning on the rulers (Ctrl/⌘-R). Then he set the ruler units to percentages; to do that, you can right-click (Windows) or Ctrl-click (Mac) on either of the rulers and choose Percent.

Mark opened the Actions palette (Window > Actions) and clicked the "Create a new action" button ▣ at the bottom of the palette. In the New Action dialog, he entered a name and clicked the "Record" button ●. Now his operations would be recorded as an Action.

He knew from experience that for his large images he liked the subtle vignette effect he got with about a "10%" edge and a 35-pixel Feather. So he chose the Rectangular Marquee tool [ ], set the Feather in the Options bar, and dragged from a point near 10%, 10% in the upper left corner of his image to a point near 90%, 90% at the lower right. *Because he had set the ruler units to Percent,* his Action recorded the percentages rather than pixels or inches. This would make it possible to use the Action with files with a range of dimensions, and in either horizontal or vertical format. (For images very much larger or smaller than the 81

MB files Mark uses, the selecting step would be recorded with a larger or smaller Feather setting.)

Mark reversed the selection (Select > Inverse) so the edges were selected and added a Levels Adjustment layer (by clicking the ◐ button at the bottom of the Layers palette and choosing from the menu). When he moved the middle Input Levels slider to .93 for a darkening effect and clicked "OK" to close the Levels dialog box, the active edge selection became a mask that restricted the darkening to the edges only. In the Layers palette Mark changed the Adjustment layer's blend mode to Luminosity so it would darken without

causing a color shift, named the layer "edge burn," and clicked the "Stop playing/recording" button ▣ at the bottom of the Actions palette to finish recording.

After running an "Edge Burn" Action to create subtle vignetting, Mark can run the Action again for a stronger effect or reduce the "burn" in areas such as the sky, where it may be too strong for the subtle effect he wants. To reduce the effect, he paints on the Adjustment layer's mask with the Brush tool 🖌 using black paint and a large, relatively soft Brush tool preset he created. (For his 81 MB images the diameter of the brush tip is set to 700 pixels, and the Hardness is set at 50%.)

MARK WAINER

Before (left) and after running Mark Wainer's "Edge Burn Action" to subtly darken the edges

The Photoshop Format Options dialog box appears when you save a file in PSD format. If you know that you always want to include the composite, you can avoid having the dialog box appear: Choose Preferences > File Handling (from the Edit menu in Windows, the Photoshop menu on the Mac) and choose from the Maximize Compatibility pop-up menu.

A COMPOSITE SHORTCUT

One good reason to choose Maximize Compatibility in the Photoshop Format Options box in order to save a composite with your Photoshop (PSD) files is that it can allow you to open a file *even if you don't have enough memory or scratch disk space to open the layered version.*

You can open just the composite version of the file by holding down the Alt and Shift keys (Windows) or Option-Shift (Mac) as you open the file. It will open with the composite as the *Background*, and any notes that have been added to the file will also be present.

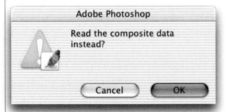

Be careful in CS, though! If you open the composite and then Save without giving the file a new name, with no warning at all the composite will permanently replace the layered version, which could be a disaster! In CS2 this risk has been reduced. The Save command is unavailable, and choosing File > Save As gives you the usual warning about replacing the existing file.

Script Events Manager (CS2)

The Script Events Manager in CS2 could be called the Script and Action Events Manager. With this command you can set up Photoshop to invoke a Script (or an Action) of your choice whenever the *event* you specify happens. An event can be the startup of Photoshop, or opening, creating, or saving a file, for instance.

FILE FORMATS

Photoshop CS/CS2 can open and save files in dozens of different formats. The format to choose from Photoshop's wealth of options depends on how you want to use the file. Here are some suggestions.

Photoshop (PSD) Format

Photoshop (PSD) is a very conservative and flexible format that can make it easy to change or repurpose a file later. It preserves all the layers, masks, channels, paths, live type, Layer Styles, and annotations added with the Notes tool 📝 or Audio Annotation tool 🔊. Whenever you plan to open and work on a file in Photoshop again, the PSD format is an ideal way to save it.

By default, when you save in PSD format, you can save with or without the composite, as shown at the left. Saving **without the composite** makes the file size smaller. But if you save **with the composite**, the image can be displayed in programs that accept Photoshop files but don't necessarily support all the features of Photoshop CS/CS2 — programs like earlier versions of Photoshop, as well as InDesign CS and Illustrator CS, which need the composite in order to work with 16 Bits/Channel PSD files. Another good reason to opt for PSD is that Adobe recommends **PSD with "Maximize compatibility"** turned on as the format that will give you the most flexibility for use in future versions of Photoshop.

Very Large Files

If you need to create an image that's bigger than the 2 gigabyte limit that PSD and other file formats allow, you can use Large Document Format (PSB), which supports documents up to 300,000 by 300,000 pixels and also supports CS2's 32 Bits/Channel mode. Like PSD, it preserves all the layers, channels, paths, live type, Layer Styles, and annotations you can create in Photoshop. By default in CS, Large Document Format doesn't appear in the menu of options in the Save As dialog box (it does in CS2). But you can add it to CS by choosing Preferences > File Handling (via the Edit menu in Windows or the Photoshop

If a PSD file from Photoshop CS/CS2 is opened in an earlier version of Photoshop, the earlier version does the best job it can with any new CS/CS2 features, or it offers a choice. For instance:

- If the Photoshop CS/CS2 file includes a layer in the Hard Mix blend mode (new in CS), Photoshop 7 lets you open either the composite (showing the result of using Hard Mix) or the layered file but with the Hard Mix layer in Normal mode.

- If the Photoshop CS/CS2 file includes type on a path, Photoshop 7 will open the file, and the type will appear in position, as if it were on the path. But the path isn't really there, and any attempt to edit the text will make the "shaping" go away and the type become normal point type.

- For a layered 16 Bits/Channel file, Photoshop 7 opens the composite, if there is one.

You can see a complete list of which features were introduced in versions 4, 5, 6, 7, and CS/CS2 by choosing Help > Photoshop Help, then clicking <u>Search</u> typing "Photoshop format (PSD)," and clicking the "Search" button.

Caution: If a Photoshop CS/CS2 file is opened in an earlier version of the program *and then resaved in that earlier version,* the file will lose any features that aren't supported by that version.

menu on the Mac) and checking the Enable Large Document Format check box. ***Note:*** PSB files can be opened in Photoshop CS and CS2 only, not in earlier versions.

Formats for Page Layout Programs & Output Services

Photoshop (PSD) files can be placed directly into **Adobe InDesign CS/CS2** with transparency maintained. This means that a silhouetted or partly transparent element will let the InDesign page show through.

For page layout programs that don't support PSD files, the formats of choice are TIFF, Photoshop EPS, and Photoshop DCS 2.0. **Photoshop EPS** files can include clipping paths, to silhouette the image so it appears without a background or a block of white space around it. **TIFF** files can use lossless compression, making the file smaller for storage and transport without degrading the image at all, and they can also include clipping paths. Because not all programs support all TIFF and EPS features, it's a good idea to check your page layout program or ask your imagesetting or printing service to find out what formats and features they accept or prefer.

For files that include **spot colors** (custom inks that are used instead of or along with the standard CMYK printing inks), PSD format works with InDesign CS/CS2. For QuarkXPress or earlier versions of InDesign, save spot-color files in the Photoshop EPS, PDF, or DCS 2.0 format. Again, check your page layout program or ask your output service for the format of choice.

PDF for Communicating with Others

When you need a file format that's **readable by others who may not have Photoshop, Photoshop PDF** is a very flexible choice. All that's needed to display the image and to read any notations you may have added with Photoshop's Notes tool 📝 is the free Adobe Reader software.

When you choose File > Save As > Photoshop PDF and click the "Save" button, the PDF Options dialog box offers the option to Include Vector Data, which retains paths and type as vector information rather than converting them to pixels. Then, if your file includes live type, you can make a choice about how to handle it:

- Choosing **Embed Fonts** ensures that type will be displayed as you designed it, whether or not the font exists on the system where the PDF is viewed.

One way to export a file from Photoshop with transparency is to choose Help > Export Transparent Image and follow the directions.

- If embedding fonts makes the file too large, you can preserve crisp type edges by choosing **Use Outlines for Text.** You preserve the look of the type but lose its editability.

- If **neither option** is chosen, the type will be live text, but it may not look exactly as you designed it, since the PDF-viewing software will substitute fonts if the ones you used aren't present on the system where the file is being viewed.

In addition to saving a single file in PDF format, you can create a slide show using the PDF format to show multiple Photoshop images, one after the other with a choice of transitions, on a darkened screen. Use File > Automate > **PDF Presentation**. In CS2 you can include a PDF Presentation within a Bridge slide show. If you open a folder in Bridge and choose View > Slide Show, any PDF Presentation in the folder will be displayed as part of the Bridge slide show, though without any transition effects between slides. Page 133 tells about Bridge slide shows.

Formats for Compact Storage & Transfer

Some file formats are more compact than others. When file size is important, the format you use to compress your file will depend on how you want to use that file:

- For maximum flexibility, keeping layers and other Photoshop features intact, use PSD, TIFF, or PDF.

- For on-screen viewing and printing, use JPEG (described next) or PDF.

- To send via email for on-screen viewing only, use JPEG, but first reduce the file's size (see "Preparing an Image for Emailing" on the facing page).

- For display on the web, use JPEG or GIF, as described in "Choosing a File Format for Static Web Graphics" on page 682.

The **JPEG** format is the default format for many digital cameras and it can be great for embedding or attaching to an email as a quick way to let someone look at an image. JPEG is popular because it can be so compact, but its file compression can be "lossy" — that is, it throws away some color detail information in the process of reducing the file's bulk. The File > Save As > JPEG command gives you 12 choices for degree of compression. In general, the more you increase compression to decrease file size, the more you reduce image quality. JPEG was designed to start its compression by throwing away the kinds of color detail data that would be lost in the printing process anyway. So a high-quality JPEG file may not show a loss of quality when the file is printed.

By default, when the File > Save As command makes a JPEG file, it includes an icon and thumbnails, which add to the file size. You can reduce file size somewhat by choosing Preferences (the shortcut is Ctrl/⌘-K) > File Handling and setting the Image Previews option to Ask When Saving, so you can choose not to include these extras.

PREPARING AN IMAGE FOR EMAILING

When you want to make an image file smaller so you can send it as an email attachment, choosing the right file format is only part of the solution. Before you even address the file format question, you can save on file size by making a flattened, low-res version of the file. Suppose, for example, you want to email a copy of a 7.5-by-9.25-inch book cover illustration for someone to look at on-screen. Your original file is composed of several layers and designed at an appropriate resolution for printing, say 225 pixels per inch. Our layered example file in PSD format started out at 82.7 MB. Let's look at what happens to the closed file size (since the closed size is what's important for transport) as we make the file smaller:

1 We can **start by making a single-layer copy** (Image > Duplicate > Duplicate Merged Layers Only) so the full-size, full-resolution layered file will be preserved separately as we reduce the copy. Saved in PSD format, our closed single-layer example file is 8.4 MB.

2 Using the copy, we **reduce the resolution to 72 ppi** for viewing on the screen (choose Image > Image Size, make sure Resample Image is turned on in the Image Size dialog box, change the Resolution setting to 72, and click "OK"). The closed size is now 1 MB.

3 Now we can put the 72 ppi file in JPEG format (File > Save As > JPEG, using a Quality setting of 10), to produce a 284 KB file.

Every file is different, and the savings varies according to the file structure, image content, and degree of compression. For our particular test image, if we had made our JPEG after step 1 — before reducing the resolution of the file — the result would have been a 1 MB file, more than three times as "bulky" as the file we ended up with, and potentially less convenient because of its large display size.

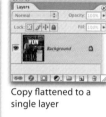

Copy flattened to a single layer

Reducing the resolution to 72 ppi

Original multi-layer file

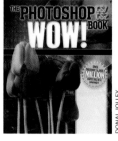

Saving as a high-quality JPEG

Ready to email at 284K, the file will appear on-screen at its 7.5-by-9.25-inch size.

DONAL JOLLEY

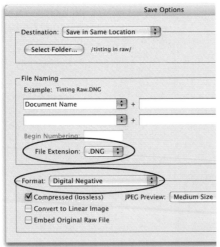

Adobe's new Digital Negative (DNG) is designed to be adopted by camera manufacturers as the standard format for raw photos. You can save in DNG format from the version of Camera Raw that comes with Photoshop CS2.

The **JPEG 2000** format produces fewer artifacts than standard JPEG, especially in areas of solid color; it also has a lossless compression option that produces no artifacts at all. Other advantages are that it supports transparency and 16-bit images, and it's the only JPEG that can include the Edit History Log.▼ However, this better JPEG option requires that the JPEG2000 plug-in (which comes with Photoshop CS and CS2) be installed before JPEG 2000 files can be created or viewed. Unfortunately JPEG 2000 isn't yet supported by most web browsers.

File Formats for 16 & 32 Bits/Channel

Photoshop offers seven file formats that support 16 Bits/Channel mode. Photoshop (PSD), Large Document Format (PSB), Photoshop PDF, and TIFF formats preserve all the layers, channels, paths, live type, Layer Styles, and annotations that Photoshop supports. Cineon (CIN), PNG, and Photoshop RAW are specialized formats that don't support layers, and therefore 16 Bits/Channel images are saved flattened; to find out more see Help > Photoshop Help.

Photoshop CS2's 32 Bits/Channel images can be saved in PSB, as well as PSD, TIFF, HDR, and PBM (portable bitmap, a format widely used for transferring files between programs).

Digital Negative Format for Camera Raw files

New in CS2 is Adobe's **Digital Negative (DNG)** format, a format for archiving any camera's raw files. (Recall that raw formats store photos in two parts, as the raw data recorded by the camera's sensors and the *metadata* that describes the camera settings to be used to produce an image from the raw data.) Adobe hopes to establish DNG as a standard that will be used instead of an ever increasing number of camera makers' proprietary formats. DNG is one of the formats that you can save directly from Camera Raw▼ (along with TIFF, JPEG, and PSD), without opening the file in Photoshop. If you save in DNG format, it's a good idea to also keep the original file in the camera's own raw format, just in case the original metadata from the camera includes something that isn't supported in DNG.

VIDEO

Making movies isn't the highly specialized, exclusively expensive endeavor that it used to be. Camcorders are small and relatively inexpensive. Stock video footage is readily available. DVD burners are becoming standard equipment with new computers, and

FIND OUT MORE

▼Edit History Log
page 28

▼Camera Raw
page 102

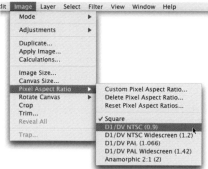

When you open a frame from a video in Photoshop, it can look out-of-proportion (top) until you tell Photoshop what format the video file is (center); in addition to the video formats shown here for CS, version CS2 offers D4/D16 Standard (0.95), HDV Anamorphic (1.333), and D4/D16 Anamorphic (1.9). Then Photoshop automatically converts the on-screen display (bottom) so you can preview how it will look when you actually convert it to standard square-pixel format for print or for the web (as described on page 138).

video-editing programs (also called *nonlinear editing systems*) now range from professional to home-use. Whether you're editing a commercial for broadcast television or fixing up footage of your travels for a DVD movie, Photoshop CS/CS2 makes it much easier than before.

Pixel Aspect Ratio

Video for analog TV can be digitally encoded in a number of different file formats. Most of these formats use nonsquare pixels to encode the image, and then it's decoded for the TV screen so it looks normal rather than squashed. Photoshop has always been a square-pixel program. But now Photoshop CS/C2 is a virtuoso at managing the oblong pixels of many video formats along with its own standard square-pixel format, so that what you see on your computer screen is what you will get when the image appears on TV. You can now:

- Take a frame from a video and turn it into a still image for print or the web; Photoshop can quickly convert the video aspect ratio to the square-pixel ratio used in print and on the computer screen.

- Create a video file with nonsquare pixels while getting a "normal" square-pixel view of the image in Photoshop as you work.

- Import video frames, use Photoshop's superb image-editing abilities to enhance them, and then save the frames in video format again.

To get a feel for these video capabilities of Photoshop, try the "Exercising Video" sections, starting on page 138. These sections include tips for working with pixel aspect ratio, de-interlacing (getting rid of the horizontal scan lines that make up a video image), resizing Photoshop images for video, and vice versa.

Photoshop CS2 has an additional new feature for video under File > Export. If you have a video camera or monitor and a FireWire link, you can plug your camera or monitor in via the FireWire cable and choose File > Export > Video Preview. This opens a dialog box where you set up the options for your camera or monitor. Once this is done, you can select File > Export > Send Video Preview to Device to update your view of your Photoshop file on your camera or monitor.

Designing for Video

Apart from the nonsquare pixel aspect ratio, when you design for video in Photoshop, you can work with all of Photoshop's features, including multiple layers, live type, Shapes, masks, and

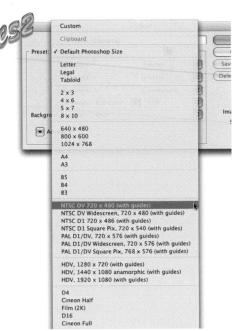

Custom
Clipboard

Preset: ✓ Default Photoshop Size

Letter
Legal
Tabloid

2 x 3
4 x 6
5 x 7
8 x 10

640 x 480
800 x 600
1024 x 768

A4
A3

B5
B4
B3

NTSC DV 720 x 480 (with guides)
NTSC DV Widescreen, 720 x 480 (with guides)
NTSC D1 720 x 486 (with guides)
NTSC D1 Square Pix, 720 x 540 (with guides)
PAL D1/DV, 720 x 576 (with guides)
PAL D1/DV Widescreen, 720 x 576 (with guides)
PAL D1/DV Square Pix, 768 x 576 (with guides)

HDV, 1280 x 720 (with guides)
HDV, 1440 x 1080 anamorphic (with guides)
HDV, 1920 x 1080 (with guides)

D4
Cineon Half
Film (2K)
D16
Cineon Full

Photoshop CS offers a variety of formats for designing for broadcast video. CS2 offers an additional HDV format (1440 x 1080) and several film formats, seen below the video formats in the New dialog box's Preset menu.

When you start a new Photoshop file to design an image for video (File > New), it comes with guides that define the action-safe and title-safe areas, as shown in this example from "Exercising Video: From Photoshop to Video" on page 141.

Layer Styles. But it's good to be aware of the differences between designing for video and designing for print or for the web.

Broadcast standards. To produce a video-ready file, you need to know which broadcast standard your video has to adhere to. There are several, with variations on each. The most commonly used broadcast standards are NTSC (the North American standard), PAL (the primary format in Europe, Japan, Australia, and New Zealand), SECAM (the French standard), and now HDTV (or HDV), which is still evolving. This broadcast standard information is used in choosing the appropriate Preset in the New dialog box when you start a video file in Photoshop.

"Safe" areas. When you start a new file in a video format, Photoshop provides guides for keeping type and important parts of the image within "safe" areas of the TV frame, so they won't be cropped out or distorted at the edges, as described in "Respecting the Guides," a tip on page 141).

Flicker. Horizontal lines thinner than 2 pixels can show an unwanted flicker when displayed. Fine serifs on type will have the same problem. You may need to make graphics and type more "robust" than you would for print or for the web, or limit yourself to sans serif type.

Contrast & color. Color for video goes through a conversion process when it's broadcast that doesn't allow the kind of precision that we ask of print media. For example, analog video reserves pure black for special keying purposes, and bright whites can cause the signal to "bleed" into the audio track. A file with sharp contrast, such as you might find in a heavily sharpened image, can benefit from a small amount of blur (try Filter > Blur > Motion Blur at an Angle of 0°). Blurring can add enough intermediate tones to reduce the tendency of the image to vibrate when broadcast, or even to generate audible noise.

To keep black-and-white contrast within a safe range, you can use the very conservative standard of a black no lower than 16 and a white no higher than 235, which you can achieve by adding a Levels Adjustment layer (click the "Create a new fill or adjustment layer" button ◐ at the bottom of the Layers palette, and use the Output Levels sliders in the Levels dialog box to "dial in" those values). Or, if you want to try for blacker blacks and whiter whites, you can investigate the limits for the specific broadcast standard you're working with and use those settings.

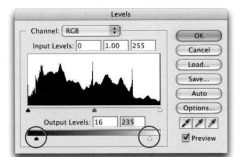

Sharp contrast can be problematic in video. The Output Levels sliders of a Levels Adjustment layer can be moved inward as shown here to bring contrast (and sometimes color) into a video-safe range. The standard of no color darker than 16 or lighter than 235 (shown here) is a conservative one. For a particular broadcast standard, you may be able to use a broader range. And don't worry too much about Photoshop showing you a washed-out image; the TV monitor will restore much of the contrast.

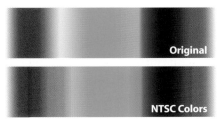

Photoshop's Filter > Video > NTSC Colors command "subdues" certain colors to prevent color from "bleeding" across the scan lines of broadcast TV.

Highly saturated (intense) colors can also be problematic for TV broadcast; a bright red shirt, for instance, can "bleed" outside the boundaries of the clothing and onto the background. The Levels Adjustment layer recommended in the previous paragraph may be enough to bring the color into the color range of your broadcast format. If not, there are at least three options for bringing your Photoshop file's color into line:

- Photoshop's **Filter > Video > NTSC Colors** command reduces saturated colors to broadcast-safe colors. Keep in mind that if your destination is PAL or SECAM, and even some versions of NTSC, this NTSC filter may be too conservative, dulling the color more than you need to for broadcast.

- You can convert your file from your normal working RGB color space to the appropriate profile for your broadcast standard by choosing **Image > Mode > Convert To Profile** and selecting the appropriate destination color space.

- You can keep the file in your working RGB color space, save it with that profile, and make the conversion to "broadcast color" in your **video-editing program**.

Alpha-channel masking. Alpha channels can play a special role in video. A single alpha channel, sometimes called a *track matte*, can be used to mask an entire sequence of frames. For example, an alpha channel containing type shapes can restrict the movie to playing within the type, while a background image sits below all that.

Saving Your File for Video

To save your video document, you need to know which file formats will work with your video-editing software. Some programs, among them Adobe Premiere Pro, can read layered Photoshop (PSD) files, but will ask you which layer you want to import; you can import layers one at a time or import a merged version of the file. Adobe After Effects can import native PSD files as layered compositions, even preserving live type layers. But while After Effects does work with video, it's for animating and compositing, and it isn't, strictly speaking, a nonlinear editing system. Some other programs can take only a flattened file, with a *Background* alone.

Layer Styles. Even if your video editor can read layered Photoshop files, Layer Styles ▼ will need to be *rasterized* (turned into pixels) before you save the file. You can do that in the Layers palette, as follows: Right/Ctrl-click the 🌀 to

FIND OUT MORE
▼ Using Layer Styles
page 44

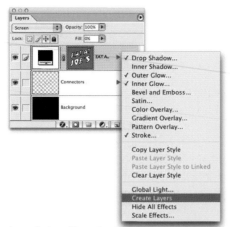

Layer Styles will need to be rasterized (turned into a series of pixel-based layers) before a Photoshop file is saved for video. Save your PSD file with Layer Styles intact, and then make a duplicate file (Image > Duplicate) and rasterize the styles (Layer > Layer Style > Create Layers). Merging the resulting layers simplifies the file, as required by some video editors.

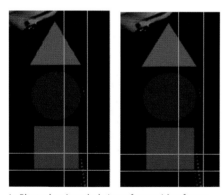

In Photoshop's scaled view of your video frame (with pixel aspect ratio corrected), you can draw a circle by holding down the Shift key and dragging with the Ellipse tool ⬭, and it will look like a circle (left). In the unscaled view, it will look stretched (right). But either way, when it's displayed on TV, it will be decoded as a circle, and that's how the audience will see it.

the right of the name of the styled layer and choose Create Layers from the context-sensitive menu that pops up. Photoshop will generate the extra pixel-based layers it needs above and below the original "styled" layer. To combine all the new layers with the original:

- In CS, link the originally styled layer with all the new layers that this command creates (except the shadow layer if your video editor permits one) by clicking in the box next to the 👁 for each new layer; then choose Layer > Merge Linked (Ctrl/⌘-E).
- In CS2, click the topmost of the layers and Shift-click the bottom one to select all of them; then choose Layer > Merge Layers (Ctrl/⌘-E).

SAVE THAT COMPOSITE!

Some video editors, including Adobe Premiere Pro, can import a single-layer version from a layered Photoshop file, as long as you've included a composite when you saved the layered file in Photoshop. To include the composite, turn on the "Maximize compatibility" option in the warning box that appears when you save a layered Photoshop file.

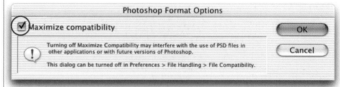

For maximum compatibility with your video-editing software, save the composite along with the layered Photoshop file.

"Roundtrip" Video Editing

You may want to export a single frame or a series of frames from your video-editing program, then use Photoshop's superb image-editing tools to enhance them, and finally return the frame(s) to your video editor. There are a number of ways to bring video frames into Photoshop and export them back out again, including exporting the frames of the video as individual files from your video editor, processing and resaving the files in Photoshop, and then assembling them again in your video-editing software. For a "round trip" like this, you won't want to *convert* the video frames to a square-pixel aspect ratio, but you may want Photoshop to correct the *preview*, so you can avoid the "stretched" look while you're working on the frames. A critical aspect of a video-to-Photoshop-to-video process like this is knowing what Photoshop-compatible formats your video editor can use to export a frame or a series of frames, and what file

To create an animated crossfaded introduction for a video clip, a QuickTime video clip was imported into ImageReady, and each frame was treated with the Chalk & Charcoal filter. The filtered clip was then exported again as a QuickTime video. The process, automated with an Action, is described in "Creating an Action To Animate a Video Clip" on page 134.

ORIGINAL VIDEO: JOHN ODAM

formats it can accept on the return trip. For a series of frames, you'll also need to know what naming conventions to follow in order to make the transition work right. Look for that information in your video editor's Help resource.

QuickTime, Photoshop, and ImageReady. QuickTime (**.mov**) is a common digital video format. Photoshop can't open these files, but ImageReady can. When ImageReady opens a .mov file, it opens as a layered document with each frame on a layer. You can work with the document there, taking advantage of ImageReady's Actions with Conditional steps to automate the process of applying the same treatment to each frame. Then save the edited file back to QuickTime format.

Learning More
Using Photoshop in conjunction with video-editing software is a fairly deep subject, and complex because of the differences between video-editing programs. In addition to your video editor's Help, you may need a resource such as Richard Harrington's *Photoshop CS for Nonlinear Editors*. It gives practical advice about which kinds of tasks to tackle in the video editor and which can be better done in Photoshop, and it catalogs the file formats and Photoshop features — layers, Layer Styles, and alpha channels, for instance — that can be successfully ported to the various video-editing programs.

Richard Harrington's *Photoshop CS for Nonlinear Editors* provides a broad range of helpful information and examples for using Photoshop along with several widely used video-editing programs.

File Browser/Bridge

The File Browser in Photoshop CS and Bridge in CS2 address a challenge that Photoshop users face all the time — how to sort and store their images so they can work with them easily and find them again later. Both the File Browser plug-in and the standalone Bridge application can sort files and assign search criteria, as well as carrying out some basic file operations. File Browser/Bridge also provides a practical entrée into some of Photoshop's automated functions, such as Photomerge.▼

For this brief exercise we've provided a folder of images like those downloaded from a digital camera. Use our files, or follow along with your own folder of files. As you work, you'll notice other intriguing menu items to explore on your own.

Note: Throughout this exercise, **the menu choices are all made within the File Browser/Bridge**, and not from Photoshop's main menu.

YOU'LL FIND THE FILES
in  > Wow Project Files > Chapter 3 > Wow Browser-Bridge

FIND OUT MORE
▼ Using Photomerge
page 580

NO "UNDO"

File Browser and Bridge work directly on the files that reside on your hard drive or removable media. So, for instance, if you rename or move a batch of files on a hard drive, there's no Undo command that will restore their earlier names or locations.

KEYBOARD SHORTCUTS

You can open File Browser/Bridge from the keyboard:

• In Photoshop CS press Ctrl/⌘-Shift-O (the letter "o") to open the File Browser plug-in.

• In Photoshop CS2 press Ctrl-Alt-O (Windows) or ⌘-Option-O (Mac) to open the Bridge application.

1 Taking a Look Around

PHOTOS: ANAIKA DAYTON

With Photoshop open, click the "Toggle File Browser"/ "Go to Bridge" button at the right end of the Options bar **A**. You can also open File Browser/Bridge from Photoshop's main menu (File > Browse) or with a keyboard shortcut (see the tip at the left). Use File Browser/Bridge's drop-down menu at the top of the window to navigate to the **Wow-Browse** folder. A thumbnail will be generated for each image — for a folder with a large number of files, this can take some time, but it creates a cache of information that allows File Browser/Bridge to work faster when you return to the folder in the future.

By default, File Browser/Bridge opens with an arrangement of panels on the left and image thumbnails in order alphabetically and numerically in the content window on the right **B**. In File Browser, folders appear after files; in Bridge, files and folders are intermixed. In addition to the default **Thumbnails** layout, the View menu offers a **Details** layout (with metadata, or file information, displayed along with the thumbnails) **C**. Other options available from the View menu in Bridge (but not in File Browser) are **Compact Mode** (the panels on the left disappear to save screen space), **Slide Show** (see page 133), **Versions and Alternates** (see page 108), and **Filmstrip** (one large preview with a strip of thumbnails on the right or below) **D**; click the "Switch filmstrip orientation" button to change the strip's location.

2 Customizing the Interface

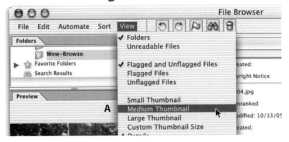

If you tried other views in step 1, use the View menu to return to a Thumbnails view:

- In File Browser choose View and choose Small, Medium, or Large Thumbnails **A**. Or set a size of your own by choosing Edit > Preferences, setting the Custom Thumbnail Size, and clicking "OK," and then choosing View > Custom Thumbnail Size.

- In Bridge choose View > As Thumbnails. To change the size, simply drag the slider at the bottom of the window to resize thumbnails on the fly **B**.

Now reach right in and start rearranging the interface. You can change the relative sizes of the panels on the left by dragging up or down on the borders between them, or change the width of all of the panels by dragging on their righthand border. Try it. You can also minimize a panel by double-clicking its tab (double-click again to expand it), and you can drag a tab to another tab to nest the first panel behind the other one:

- Double-click on a panel's tab to minimize it, and then drag to nest it with a different set of panels.

- In Bridge you can show or hide panels via the View menu. To make the Preview window easily accessible, choose View > Preview Panel. To expand or minimize it, double-click its tab. Drag it to the Folders tab to nest it.

Notice that the Metadata and Keywords panels are nested by default, or that in Bridge the Folders panel is nested with Favorites (a customizable "short list" of files).

3 Renaming (File Browser)

Often files downloaded from a digital camera or from a stock photo service on the web have names that read like serial numbers, and you may want to rename them with the name of the project or batch they're from. Here's a way to rename an entire folder of files all at once in File Browser (see page 130 for Bridge): First select them all (Ctrl/⌘-A, or Edit > Select All). From the Automate menu, select **Batch Rename**.

If it's possible to write to the folder you're in, the Batch Rename dialog will allow you to rename the files to the same folder. Otherwise, in File Browser "Move to new folder" will be checked **A**. With the "Move" option checked, click the "Choose" button below it and navigate to the folder where you want to store the renamed files; or make a new folder by clicking the "New Folder" button in the "Choose a destination folder" dialog box, typing a name for the folder (to follow our example, type **"Wow Files"**), and clicking "Create."

Back in the Batch Rename dialog, assign the batch name: In the first of the six File Naming fields, type the name (we used "Sumatra") **B**. Then tab to the next field and choose an option; to follow along with our example, choose "2 Digit Serial Number" to add a numbering scheme to the batch **C**. (Since you could be adding files to an existing serially numbered batch, File Browser offers the choice of a starting number for your files; we left it at the default "1.") Then tab again and choose "extension" **D** so the file format will be included in the file name.

Click "OK" and File Browser performs its magic. When renaming is complete, you can use the Folders panel to find the folder of renamed files. If you created a new folder and you don't see it in the directory, use the panel's menu ⊙ or press the F5 key to refresh the view **E**.

3 Copying & Renaming (Bridge)

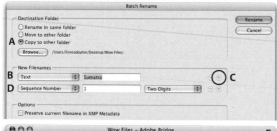

In Bridge you can rename an entire folder of files all at once, at the same time copying them to a new location: First select them all (Ctrl/⌘-A, or Edit > Select All). From Bridge's Tools menu, select **Batch Rename**.

If it's possible to write to the folder you're working in, the Batch Rename dialog box will offer you the option of saving the renamed files to the same folder. You can also "Copy to other folder" **A**. There's a third option — "Move to other folder" to rename and move the selected files to a different folder instead of making copies. With the "Copy" option checked, click the "Browse" button below it and navigate to the folder where you want to store the renamed files; or make a new folder by clicking the "New Folder" button in the "Choose a destination folder" dialog box, typing a name for the folder (we used **"Wow Files"**), and clicking "Open."

To assign the batch name, in the first of the **New Filenames** menus, choose an option; to follow our example, choose Text from the dropdown menu **B** and type in the name "Sumatra." Then click the "+" button **C** to add a new dropdown menu and choose an option; to follow along with our example using a two-digit numbering scheme, choose Sequence Number **D**, leave the starting number at the default "1," and choose Two Digits from the menu on the right. (Bridge offers the choice of a starting number other than "1" for your files, so you can add files to an existing serially numbered batch.)

Click "Rename" and Bridge performs its magic. When renaming and copying are complete, you can use the Folders panel to find the folder of renamed files. If you created a new folder and you don't see it in the directory, use the panel's ⊙ menu or press the F5 key to refresh the view **E**.

4 "Rough" Sorting (File Browser)

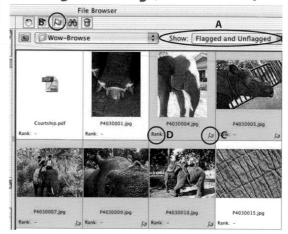

In Photoshop CS the File Browser has two ways to tag files for "rough" sorting within the folder — *flagging* and *ranking* — in addition to the more specific custom ranking (as described in "Custom Sorting" on page 131) and the Keywords and Metadata you can add (in step 6).

Flagging is a way to mark some images in a folder so it's easy to sort them out from the others. (If you look at the upper right corner of the File Browser window, you'll see the Show menu **A**, which offers Flagged and Unflagged options for viewing.) For instance, if you have 300 images in a folder but want to consider only 20 of them for inclusion in the project you're working on, you can flag these 20. Try flagging — target 5 thumbnails by Ctrl/⌘-clicking or Shift-clicking (for contiguous files), and click on the "Flag File" button ⚑ at the top of the window **B**. A flag will appear in the lower right corner **C**. (If you wanted to "unflag" some of these images, you would target their thumbnails and click on the ⚑ button again.) Now if you choose Flagged in the Show menu, only the flagged files will appear in the window.

Ranking provides another sorting mechanism. If you don't see the word "Rank" in the lower left corners of your Flagged thumbnails **D**, choose View > Show Rank. Now you can rank a file by clicking just to the right of the "Rank:" label and typing a letter or number. To give more than one file the same rank, Ctrl/⌘-click or Shift-click to target their thumbnails, then right/Ctrl-click to bring up a context-sensitive menu; choose Rank, type a letter or number in the Rank File dialog box, and click "OK"; we assigned an "A" rank to two of our flagged files, and a "B" rank to two others. Now you can use the Sort > Rank command to order the files; the A's will be first, followed by the B's, followed by the unranked.

4 "Rough" Sorting (Bridge)

Instead of File Browser's Flagged and Unflagged categories, Bridge has **Labeled** and **Unlabeled**, with the option of five different Label colors. For instance, if you have 300 images in a folder but want to consider only 20 of them for inclusion in the project you're working on, you can label these 20, differentiating them further with label colors that show their sources or what parts of the project they will be used for. In addition, Bridge allows **Ratings** of one to five stars — great for indicating relative importance or preference. (Labeling and rating are two Bridge functions that can be "undone" with Ctrl/⌘-Z.)

Labeling can be accomplished by choosing a color from the Label menu, or by using a keyboard shortcut (Ctrl/⌘ plus a number between 6 and 9). Try labeling — target five thumbnails by Ctrl/⌘-clicking or Shift-clicking (for contiguous files), and type Ctrl/⌘-6 (for Red); then target two more and type Ctrl/⌘-8 (for Green).

Rating can be done by targeting a file or files, then choosing from the Label menu, or clicking one of the five dots in a file's color Label bar, or using an easy-to-remember keyboard shortcut (Ctrl/⌘ plus the number of stars, between 1 and 5). To follow along with our example, target three of the Red-labeled files and rate them at four stars; then target one and rate it at two stars, and target another and rate it at one star.

You can limit which files are displayed by clicking the tiny triangle next to "Unfiltered" or "Filtered" in the top right corner of the file and choosing from the menu, or use a keyboard shortcut. Sorting (changing the order) can be done by choosing View > Sort and choosing a sorting routine. The Sort shown above was done By Label.

5 Custom Sorting

A

B

In addition to flagging and ranking in File Browser or labeling and rating in Bridge, both of these file managers offer a **Custom Sort** option. To exercise it, you simply drag one thumbnail to the position before or after another thumbnail, waiting until a dark line appears to indicate that the thumbnail you're moving will be inserted there **A**. To follow along with our example, rearrange the files as shown above. In preparation for a Slide Show in Bridge (coming up on page 133), we put all the elephant photos first, and then the rhino images, including the PDF file **B**.

When you do a custom sort, it will be remembered until you replace it by moving thumbnails around again. You can recall your most recent custom sort by choosing Sort > Custom in File Browser or View > Sort > Manually in Bridge.

DELETING KEYWORDS

There are two different kinds of keyword deletion:

- To delete a keyword from a Keywords set, click on it in the Keywords panel and click the "Delete Keyword" button 🗑 at the bottom of the panel. (The deleted keyword stays in the metadata of any files you've already added to it.)

- To delete a keyword from a file, target the file and click the ✔ in front of the word in the Keywords panel. The keyword is removed from the file's metadata, but it remains in the Keywords panel so you can still apply it to other files.

6 Adding Keywords

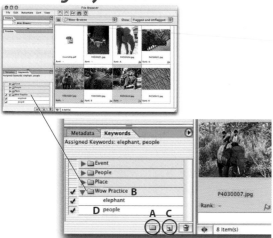

Keywords provide a way to store information about the content of an image, which can help us find that specific image more easily later. Deselect all images by clicking on a blank spot in the thumbnail panel, and click on the Keywords tab. You can see that File Browser/Bridge has already created sets, or categories, with keywords in them. We'll add our own category. At the bottom of the Keywords panel **A** click on the "New Keyword Set" button ▢. By default a new set is added at the top of the list, with the same name as the one right below it — but highlighted so it's ready for you to type a new name. If you're following along with our example, type "Wow Practice" and hit Enter/Return. File Browser/Bridge will automatically alphabetize your new set with the others **B**. To create a new keyword in the set, click on your new set to highlight it, click the "New Keyword" button ▢ at the bottom of the panel **C**, and then type "elephant."

In the Thumbnails panel, target the four photos related to elephants, and then click in the box to the left of the keyword you just added, or double-click the keyword itself. A checkmark ✔ next to the **keyword** shows that it has been added to the targeted file. A "–" next to the **set** name tells you that at least one keyword from that set has been added; a ✔ means all keywords in the set have been added. Add another keyword — "people" **D** and assign it to the two photos that show people, as shown above. If you now click on the Metadata tab and expand the IPTC list, you should see the keywords you added to the files.

MOVING KEYWORDS

If you forget to highlight the set you want a new keyword to be in, don't worry — keywords can be moved. After adding it, simply drag the keyword to the name of the set you want it in.

7 Searching for Files

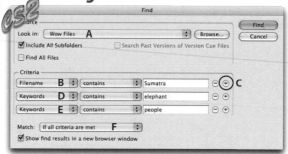

You can search for files using as many as 13 criteria, which can really cut the time spent looking for a file. To search:

- In File Browser, choose File > Search or click the "Search" button 🔍 at the top of the window.
- In Bridge choose Edit > Find (or use Ctrl/⌘-F).

When the Search/Find dialog box opens, you can click "Browse" to find the folder you want to search. We'll search for images of people riding elephants from our photos of Sumatra. Make sure the "Look in" field lists the folder you want to search, or a folder that contains this folder. Restricting "Look in" to a single folder makes the search go more quickly, but often the reason you're searching is that you don't know where the images you're seeking are stored, so you may want to set up a broader search (With "Include All Subfolders," you can search an entire hard drive if you have the patience to wait it out.) For this simple example, "Look in" your **Wow Files** folder (from step 3) **A**.

In the first of the Criteria lines, select the file name choice **B**, then press the Tab key and choose "contains," then tab again and type "Sumatra." ("Contains" is a safer choice than "is," even if you think you remember precisely.) Click the "+" button **C**. In the next row select "Keywords" "contains" and type "elephant" **D**; then click the "+" button, and in the next line choose "Keywords" "contains" and type "people" **E**. (While you're in this dialog, take a look at the other Criteria options available in this versatile search tool.) In Bridge, make sure that "Match" is set to "if all criteria are met" **F**. You can also choose to open a new Bridge window to show the results of your search, rather than replacing the contents of the current window. Click the dialog's "Search"/"Find" button. You should see thumbnails for the two photos of people riding an elephant.

If a File Browser/Bridge search doesn't produce the results you expected, or is too broad and returns too many files, try again (in File Browser click the "Search" button 🔍; in Bridge type Ctrl/⌘-F). The Search/Find dialog will open exactly as you left it, and you can make changes and search again.

8 Running a Slide Show

Bridge's **Slide Show** mode can be a great way to review or sort the files in a folder, either with a client or coworker or on your own. Slide Show mode shows each image by itself in the content window. To demonstrate this, choose View > Slide Show. Once you're in Slide Show mode, typing **H** will show or hide a list (shown above) of all the keyboard commands you can use to run or pause the show, change the view, or label and rate an image as it appears on the screen:

- To scale the slides to fit the window, type **D** until you see "Scale to Fit."

- To show the images only, without names, labels, or ratings, type **C** until you see "Caption:Off."

- Automate the slide show by pressing the **spacebar** to start or pause the show. To change the amount of time each image is on the screen, type **S** to increase the time by 1 second, Shift-S to decrease it.

- For direct control of the pacing of the slides, instead of the spacebar use the right arrow key ➡️ to advance from one slide to the next, or the left arrow ⬅️ to move backwards (see also "Nested Slide Shows" at the right).

WORKSPACES

In Bridge you can choose from several Workspaces that come with the program (Window > Workspace), or save a Workspace that you've customized (Window > Workspace > Save Workspace) so that it will appear in the Window > Workspace menu and you can load it again later.

9 Nesting Slide Shows

PDF Presentation is one of the file formats that Bridge can display. In most of Bridge's viewing modes only the initial slide in the PDF Presentation appears. But in Slide Show mode you have the additional option of looking at all the images in the Presentation. This means you can create a "branching" slide show that allows you to either show the first slide of a PDF Presentation and then go on to the next file in the folder, or to run through some or all of the slides within the PDF Presentation itself before going on.

As Bridge works through the files in the current folder, when it comes to a PDF Presentation, the arrow keys (➡️ and ⬅️), or simply allowing the slide show to run automatically, will move from page to page within the Presentation. But if you use Ctrl/⌘ along with the arrow, the slide show will skip any remaining pages in the PDF and display the next file.

Try this demonstration. In the **Wow Files** folder (from step 3) the **Sumatra08.pdf** file is a PDF Presentation of four slides. (If you didn't create a Wow-Files folder, you can use the original Wow-Browse folder from the Wow DVD, where the PDF Presentation file is **Courtship.pdf**). Choose View > Slide Show, type **C** until you see the **"Caption:Compact"** or **"Caption:Full"** option so you can see the file names, and then press the ➡️ key repeatedly to display the files in the Bridge layout one after the other. When you come to the **.pdf** file, pressing the ➡️ key will move to the second slide in the PDF Presentation, and pressing it two more times will show the third and then the fourth slide, as shown above. To see the other option, use the ⬅️ key to go back to the slide before the PDF Presentation. Then press the ➡️ key to move to the PDF Presentation as before, but this time press Ctrl/⌘- ➡️, and Bridge will skip over the other slides in the PDF Presentation and go on to the next file.

Note: When you run a PDF Presentation from Bridge, the slide show will run without any special transitions you may have built into it.

ORIGINAL VIDEO: JOHN ODAM

Creating an Action To Animate a Video Clip

YOU'LL FIND THE FILES
in ⊙ > Wow Project Files > Chapter 3 > Creating an Action:
  • Video Clip-Before.mov (to start)
  • Video Clip-After.mov (to compare)
  • Wow ImageReady Artistic Video.isa (to compare)

OPEN THESE IMAGEREADY PALETTES
from the Window menu:
  • Layers • Actions • Animation

OVERVIEW
Open a **.mov** file in ImageReady • Add a "marker" layer • Record an Action to filter each frame, including a Conditional step to stop the Action when the marker layer is encountered • Preview and export the altered file

RECORDING AN ACTION WORKS BASICALLY THE SAME WAY in Photoshop and ImageReady. But for this particular Action — adding a special-effects treatment to every frame of a video clip — ImageReady has some great extra features. ImageReady has the same versatile Filter Gallery that Photoshop has. Combine that with a few features Photoshop *doesn't* have — like the ability to open and export QuickTime movies and to record Conditional steps in an Action — and you have a terrific tool for applying a custom treatment to an entire video clip.

Videographer John Odam wanted an animation to crossfade as an introduction to his original video. So he exported a clip from Adobe Premiere in QuickTime (**.mov**) format, and we went to work in ImageReady to automate the process of applying one of Photoshop's Sketch filters to all of its frames. We used a 4-second clip (about 120 frames) at full size (720 x 480 pixels). To follow along with the Action-recording process, you can use any QuickTime movie clip you have, or use a reduced version of Odam's clip, provided on the Wow DVD-ROM.

1 Starting the Action. In ImageReady open your QuickTime movie (File > Open). In the Open Movie dialog box, you can choose the entire clip (use "From Beginning to End") **1a**. Or use the slider at the bottom of the window to scroll to the beginning of the section you want to change, then hold down the Shift key and continue to drag the scroll box to the end of the

1a

The Open Movie dialog box lets you open the entire video clip (as shown here) or Shift-drag the slider below the image to preview and open just part of the clip.

1b

Starting to record a new Action

1c

To start the Action, we want the first frame and the bottom layer to be active.

2a

Creating the "End Action" layer

USING KEYBOARD SHORTCUTS IN ACTIONS

In either Photoshop or ImageReady, when you record an Action step that involves navigating up or down the Layers palette rather than targeting a specific layer, it's important to use a keyboard shortcut, rather than clicking on a layer thumbnail. If you don't use a keyboard shortcut, the layer name will be recorded as part of the Action, and when you play that step back, the Action will be looking for a particular named layer instead of simply moving up or down the stack.

desired section. Click "OK" and wait for the file to open. (The pixel aspect ratio of the clip makes the images look like they're stretched horizontally. We won't worry about this, since we'll be exporting the filtered clip to the same video format. But if you did need to "square up" the file, "Exercising Video: From Video to Web or Print" on page 138 tells how to do it.)

In the Actions palette (Window > Actions) click the "Create new action" button ▣ at the bottom of the palette, and in the New Action dialog box, enter a name and click the "Record" button **1b**.

QuickTime movies open with the first frame and bottom layer active and all other layers hidden, which is the state we want for running this Action **1c**. But it's a good idea to include "setup" steps in the Action itself, to get back to this starting state in case you've changed something in the file before you get around to running the Action. To target the **first frame,** press Shift-Alt/Option-← on the keyboard. Then target the **bottom layer** by pressing Shift-Alt/Option-[(this is the opening square bracket key).

2 Setting up for a Conditional step. We want the Action to change every frame and thus every layer, regardless of how many frames might be in the clip, and then we want the Action to stop running — rather than looping on, *re-*changing every frame *ad infinitum.* We can make sure the Action stops by inserting a layer with a unique name and then using a Conditional step that tells ImageReady to continue to run the Action on layer after layer until it encounters a layer with that particular name.

As you continue to record, open the New Layer dialog box by pressing Shift-Ctrl-N (Windows) or Shift-⌘-N (Mac). Type in the name "End Action," and click "OK." This puts an empty layer just above the bottom layer **2a** and records this addition as part of the Action **2b**.

2b

The Action records the step of adding the "End Action" layer.

3a

Applying the Chalk & Charcoal filter (The settings are for Odam's full-size video clip. You may prefer other settings for the reduced clip or for another .mov file.)

3b

The final Filter Gallery settings are recorded in the Action.

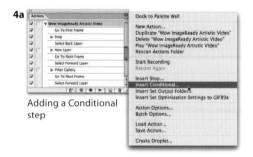

4a

Adding a Conditional step

3 Filtering. We'll set up the Action to target the next layer up, apply the artistic effect we want, and then continue to work up the layer stack, applying the effect. After the top layer, we want the Action to loop back to the bottom layer and then finally, when it encounters the "End Action" layer, delete this layer and stop. Click the Animation palette's "Select next frame" button ▐▶ to select the next frame. This makes the next layer up *visible;* and pressing Alt/Option-⟧ (closing bracket) makes it the *active* layer.

Now open the Filter Gallery (choose Filter > Filter Gallery) and begin experimenting. Choose a filter by clicking its sample thumbnail in the Filter Gallery's middle panel, or choose from the alphabetical pop-up list of filters in the right panel **3a**. We tried Charcoal and Chalk & Charcoal (from the Sketch set) and Colored Pencil, Neon Glow, and Palette Knife (from Artistic). We settled on Chalk & Charcoal. Experiment with any filters and settings you'd like to try — only your final setting will be recorded in the Action **3b**, not any experimenting that you did beforehand.

4 Putting in the Conditional step. Move to the next frame of the clip by clicking the ▐▶ again. To target the associated layer so the Filter Gallery can act on it, once again press Alt/Option-⟧. Before running the filter on this layer, set up the Conditional step by clicking the ⊙ button in the upper right corner of the Actions palette and choosing Insert Conditional from the fly-out menu **4a**. In the Conditional dialog box **4b**, set the conditions so the Action will check the name of the current layer, and if it doesn't find "End Action," it will repeat the three-step sequence that applies the Filter Gallery, advances to the next frame, and targets the next layer. For the "no more than" limit, choose a number that's larger than the longest clip you'll want to run the Action on (we used 150). Click "OK."

5 Finishing the Action. When the Action finally encounters the "End Action" layer, it will stop repeating the three steps and go on to the next steps of the Action. To add those next steps, click on the "End Action" layer's name in the Layers palette (in this case you *do* want to pick the layer by name; the "Name Your Layers & Channels" tip on page 135 tells why) and then Alt/Option-click the "Delete" button 🗑 to remove this temporary layer. Now the Action is complete and you can stop recording (click the "Stop playing/recording" button ■ at the bottom of the Actions palette) **5**.

6 Running the Action. To test the Action, choose File > Revert, and in the Open Movie dialog box choose the entire clip

4b

Setting the conditions for repeating the three filtering and frame-advancing steps, limiting the repetition to no more than 150 times

5

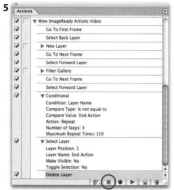

The last two steps of the Action will delete the "End Action" layer after all frames of the clip have been filtered. After you record these steps, stop the recording.

6

Playing the Action

7a

Previewing the animation in ImageReady

7b

Playing the animation in QuickTime Player

or a section you want to filter (if it's a long clip, you may want to test the Action first on a small section, to see how your effect looks when it's in motion). Then click on the name of your new Action in the Actions palette and click the "Play" button ▶ at the bottom of the palette **6**. Three frames from the Action-filtered file are shown at the top of page 134.

7 Exporting the clip. After running the Action, you can preview a slow version of the filtered movie in ImageReady: At the bottom of the Animation palette, click the "Play" button ▶ **7a**. Then, if the result looks promising, export the file (File > Export > Original Document, choosing QuickTime Movie for the format and giving the new file a different name). In the Compression Settings dialog box, choose an appropriate compression scheme and click "OK" (we used Odam's original DV/DVCPRO-NTSC format, but you may want to use the default Photo-JPEG if you started with **Video Clip-Before.psd**, just to keep the "After" file small). Now you can open the filtered movie in QuickTime and play it **7b**. (QuickTime Player for Mac or Windows can be downloaded free of charge: **www.apple.com**.)

Crossfading. Happy with the filtered result, Odam imported the QuickTime clip back into Adobe Premiere and set up the crossfade, as shown below.

Adapting the Action. You can play your Action on any QuickTime movie that's "no more than" the frame limit you set in the Conditional dialog box (at step 4). To change the limit, simply double-click on the Conditional step in the Actions palette. In the Conditional dialog box, change the "no more than" setting and click "OK." Your modified Action is ready to play.

Or for a different effect, duplicate your Action by dragging its name in the Actions palette to the 🔲 button at the bottom of the palette. Then double-click the Filter Gallery step in this new Action and change the settings; click "OK" to close the filter Gallery, and save the edited Action. *Wow*

Shown here in Adobe Premiere are the starting (filtered) frame (left), a frame from halfway through the crossfade transition (center), and a frame after the crossfade is complete (that is, a frame of the original unaltered video).

Video: From Video to Web or Print

If you want to select a single video frame and repurpose it for the web or for print, simply save the frame in your video-editing software in one of the many file formats that Photoshop can open, such as the .tif format we used for the **Video to PS-Before.tif** file in this exercise. (You can see a list of formats Photoshop can open by choosing File > Open and clicking to open the Enable menu.)

YOU'LL FIND THE FILES

in 〈wow〉 > Wow Project Files > Chapter 3 > Exercising Video > Video to PS:

  • Video to PS-Before.tif (to start)

  • Video to PS-After.tif (to compare)

PIXEL ASPECT RATIO WARNING

Photoshop's View > Pixel Aspect Ratio Correction command lets you toggle between a pixel-for-pixel view and a view that's scaled so it looks on your square-pixel computer screen as it will when it appears on TV. By default, whenever you turn on Pixel Aspect Ratio Correction, a warning box will pop up to let you know that while the corrected view shows the right proportions, the scaling may show artifacts; for details of edge quality, for instance, the uncorrected view will be more accurate.

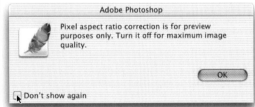

Once you've absorbed this warning, you may want to click the "Don't show again" check box so its popping up doesn't become annoying.

1 Opening the Video Frame

VIDEO: JOHN ODAM

Open the video frame (**Video to PS-Before.tif,** shown at the top) in Photoshop (File > Open). Photoshop assumes that an image has square pixels unless you tell it otherwise. So a non-square-pixel image will look out-of-proportion when you open it. To correct the on-screen view, let Photoshop know that this image was *not* created as a square-pixel document — choose **Image** > **Pixel Aspect Ratio** and choose the aspect ratio that's built into your video frame, such as D1/DV NTSC (0.9) for the image above.

MISSING ASPECT RATIO?

If you open a video file in Photoshop and its aspect ratio isn't among those listed in the Image > Pixel Aspect Ratio menu, you can create a custom setting (Image > Pixel Aspect Ratio > Custom Pixel Aspect Ratio). If you simply don't know the aspect ratio of your video frame, try the different default options or create a custom aspect ratio, experimenting until you find one that makes the image look right on your computer screen.

2 The Corrected View

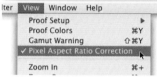

When you choose an aspect ratio, Photoshop will scale the on-screen display so the image appears on your computer screen with the same height-width proportions as it would on TV (top). The "scaled" label in the title bar tells you that you're now looking at the corrected view.

The toggle for switching between the corrected (scaled) view and the uncorrected view is the **View** > **Pixel Aspect Ratio Correction**. This is automatically turned on (to the corrected view) when you tell Photoshop, as you just did, that your image is a non-square-pixel file.

TWO VIEWS AT ONCE

To see both the uncorrected and corrected views of your file on-screen at once, choose Window > Arrange > New Window for. . . , and turn on View > Pixel Aspect Ratio Correction for one window and turn it off for the other.

3 Converting the File

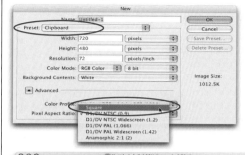

Once your video file is open in Photoshop and you can see what it really looks like because of the Pixel Aspect Ratio Correction, you still need to actually *convert* the image to the square pixels you need for the web or for print. So far, you've only corrected Photoshop's computer-screen *view*; you haven't changed the pixel shape in the file.

You can create the square-pixel image you need by simply copying the video image to the clipboard and pasting it into a new square-pixel file, as follows: Select all (Ctrl/⌘-A) and copy (Ctrl/⌘-C). Then start a new file (File > New). Photoshop assumes that you want to create a file the right size to hold the clipboard contents — good assumption! At the bottom of the **New** dialog, you'll see that Photoshop also assumes you want the file to be the same Pixel Aspect Ratio as the clipboard contents — a reasonable assumption, but not the one you want this time. Choose **Square** instead. Click "OK" to close the dialog box, and then paste the clipboard contents into the new file (Ctrl/⌘-V).

You'll notice extra white space along some edges of the image in your new square-pixel document. How much space and which edges will depend on the aspect ratio of the video file you started with. We'll get rid of the extra space shortly (in step 5).

4 De-Interlacing

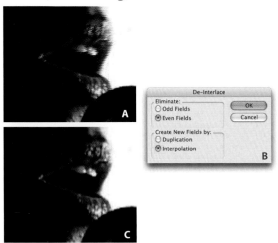

For smooth motion and to keep images crisp and flicker-free on analog TV, video frames are typically *interlaced* **A**, or separated into two *fields* per frame. Each field consists of half the horizontal *scan lines* the TV uses to display the image; one field has the odd-numbered lines, the other the even-numbered ones. For print or web purposes, you'll want to get rid of any visible interlacing. Photoshop's De-Interlace filter can do the job, and now is a great time to do it, *before* you make any changes to the file —such as resizing, smoothing, or sharpening — that will disrupt the interlacing and "confuse" the filter. Choose Filter > Video > De-Interlace. The filter smooths the image by eliminating either the odd-numbered or even-numbered rows of pixels. To fill in, you can choose whether to simply double the remaining lines, or interpolate between them **B**. You may need to try one group of settings, then undo and try others until you see which ones work best for your image; we used the settings shown above **C**.

"SIZING UP" FOR PRINT

If you need to make your converted video image file bigger for printing, use Image > Image Size with Resample Image turned on and Bicubic Smoother chosen. After scaling up, the image may be soft enough that the Unsharp Mask filter isn't enough to bring out detail before the sharpening becomes too much for the rest of the image. In that case, try one of the techniques in "Quick Ways To Bring Out Detail," starting on page 326.

---

5 Trimming, Resizing & Sharpening

To remove the extra white space at the edges of your image (from step 3), choose Image > Trim, set the "Based On" option to "Top Left Pixel Color," turn on all of the "Trim Away" options, and click "OK."

To make the image the right size for your web or print purposes, use the Image > Image Size command, with Constrain Proportions and Resample Image turned on. We sized our image to a Width of 3 inches at 300 pixels/inch; we liked the look of the enlargement we got when we chose Bicubic Smoother from the pop-up Resample menu. Click "OK" to complete the resizing.

De-interlacing and resizing can soften the image, so sharpening will probably be needed.▼ You may also need to boost color and contrast. To keep TV images from "vibrating," contrast is often reduced for broadcast video. And to keep colors from "bleeding," vivid colors may be toned down. So you may want to add a Levels Adjustment layer to boost color and contrast when you repurpose a video image for the web or for print.▼

If your output process requires a flattened image, save the layered file in PSD format and then make a flat copy (Image > Duplicate > Merged Layers Only) and save it in the format needed.

FIND OUT MORE

▼ Sharpening **page 326**
▼ Using Levels **page 250**

Video: From Photoshop to Video

If you want to create a file in video format from a standard square-pixel Photoshop file, the first step is to create a new file for the video frame, using the correct size and pixel aspect ratio. Then you'll move the layer(s) you need from your standard Photoshop file into this new video file, add any new material you want, and save the video file.

YOU'LL FIND THE FILES

in 🅦 > Wow Project Files > Chapter 3 > Exercising Video > PS to Video:

- PS to Video-Before.psd (to start)
- PS to Video-After.psd (to compare)

RESPECTING THE GUIDES

When you create a new video-format file, Photoshop provides two sets of guides. The outer guides set the limits for the *action-safe* area of a TV screen, and the inner guides define the *title-safe* area. Some TVs can't show all of a standard video frame, so the outer guides are provided to help you keep important detail within the action-safe area. Furthermore, on some TVs the signal becomes increasingly distorted at the edges of the screen, so the title-safe area ensures that text will remain clear and readable. In newer TVs there's less edge loss and distortion. For a home-use video, you may not lose anything if you choose to ignore the guides, but if you're working for a client, the default is to respect the guides.

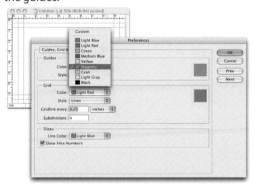

If the Guides won't show up well enough against the image you want to develop, choose Edit > Preferences (in Windows) or Photoshop > Preferences (on the Mac) and choose Guides, Grid & Slices, and choose a different color for Guides.

1 Starting a Video-Format Document

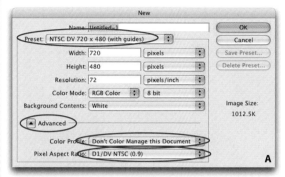

action-safe guides
title-safe guides

To start the video-format document, choose File > New. In the New dialog box, you'll find a pop-up Preset menu that includes several standard video formats. For our example, we chose NTSC DV 720 x 480 (with guides) **A**.

Looking at the bottom of the dialog box, if the Advanced section isn't already open, click on its toggle button so that you can see that Photoshop has already chosen the Pixel Aspect Ratio that matches the Preset you chose — in this case D1/DV NTSC (0.9). For the Color Profile, choose "Don't Color Manage this Document."▼ If you needed to, you could limit the color for TV later, as described in "Contrast and color" on page 124. Click "OK"; if a warning box pops up, click "OK" again.

The blank document you have just opened **B** will have two sets of guides (if you don't see them, choose View > Show > Guides). The "Respecting the Guides" tip at the left explains why they are there. Notice also that the "scaled" label appears in the title bar, to let you know that your on-screen preview will be "normalized" to the familiar square-pixel view, even though the file will be saved with the non-square pixels of the file format you chose.

FIND OUT MORE

▼ Color Management
page 179

2 Importing an Image

To convert an image for your new video document, open the source image file **A**, in this case **PS to Video-Before.psd**. Choose the Move tool ▸⊹ , put the cursor in the working window of this source file and drag the image into the window of the video document **B**. Photoshop will automatically change the pixel aspect ratio of the imported material. If your source file is in CMYK or some other color mode, or is a 16-Bits/Channel file, Photoshop will also automatically convert the elements you transfer to the modes you need (RGB and 8-Bits/Channel),▼as shown in the title bar of the video document.

MOVING MORE THAN ONE LAYER

If you want to add more than one layer from a source file to your video document, target one of the layers by clicking its thumbnail in the Layers palette. Then link any other layers you want to add.▼Choose the Move tool ▸⊹ and drag or Shift-drag the targeted element *from the working window* into the working window of your new video document. The linked layers will be duplicated in the video file. *Note:* Dragging-and-dropping *from the Layers palette* (instead of the working window) brings only the layer you drag, *not* any layers that may be linked to it.

3 Scaling the Image

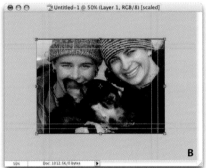

Photoshop doesn't automatically resize the image to fit the video file. Since our source image is bigger than the new video document, we'll need to scale it to fit. Type Ctrl/⌘-T (for Edit > Free Transform). If you can't see all four corner handles of the Transform frame in your working window, press Ctrl/⌘-0 (that's zero) to expand the window to show the entire Transform frame **A**. Once you can see the entire Transform frame, Shift-drag on a corner handle of the frame to resize the image to fit **B**.▼ Our image will scale to fit exactly, but if it didn't, you could drag the image around until it was framed the way you wanted it within the "safe" areas indicated by the guides. When you're satisfied with the size and position, double-click inside the Transform frame to complete the transformation, or press the Enter key.

FIND OUT MORE

▼ Color modes **page 151**
▼ Linking layers **page 582**
▼ Transforming **page 71**

PRE-SCALING

If you know that your Photoshop source file is a lot bigger than the video file you're constructing, it may be easier to duplicate the image file (Image > Duplicate) and reduce the duplicate (Image > Image Size with Resample Image turned on and Bicubic Sharper chosen) before you import it into the video file — rather than transforming it once it's imported.

4 Working on the Video File

You can toggle off the View > Pixel Aspect Ratio Correction command to see the unscaled view of the video file; then toggle it back on. Or to see both views at once, open a second window for the document (Window > Arrange > New Window for. . .), and toggle its View.

Now you can add to the image if you like, within the limits of your video format.▼ As you work, Photoshop will show you the result correctly in either view. For instance, if you hold down the Shift key and drag with the Ellipse tool to draw a circle,▼ it will look circular in the "scaled" window but oblong in the one that isn't scaled.

5 Saving the File

There are two things to do before you save a video document: First, for future use, save the file in PSD format with any layers intact. Second, check your video-editing software to find out which file formats it can work with (and which features within a file format; for instance, it may accept .tif files, but not with layers). Photoshop CS/CS2 has all the major file formats covered,▼and some of the obscure ones as well, so you should be able to find one that will work. To be conservative, you can merge your imported image and any additions you've made with the *Background* (Layer > Merge Visible). This will also trim away any of your imported image that extends outside the limits of the video format.

At this point you could make sure the color is within the gamut of the video format you are using (see "Contrast and color" on page 124), or leave the file in your working RGB profile, as we did, and make the change in your video editor.

To save the file, choose File > Save As, choose a format your video editor can use, and click the "Save" button. If you save in .psd format, be sure to choose the "Maximize compatibility" option when it's offered.

FIND OUT MORE

▼ Designing for video
page 123
▼ Using Shape tools
page 433
▼ File formats for broadcast
page 124

SHARON STEUER

In developing her digital paintings, **Sharon Steuer** layers her changes, so that in repainting some parts of the image, she doesn't destroy what's underneath. ***Louis Armstrong*** was painted in Grayscale mode, using a Wacom Intuos tablet and Photoshop's Brush and Eraser tools, with and without the Airbrush option turned on in the Options bar. Steuer set up the controls so stylus pressure controlled only opacity (stylus options can be set in the various "Control:" entries in the Brushes palette).▼ Before she flattened it for printing, the final portrait was a stack of three layers (shown at the left) — with the main portrait in the middle, some elements showing through from an earlier version on a layer below, and loose strokes applied to the background and clothing on a top layer.

The image at the right shows how Steuer simulated the installation of another version of this painting. She took a digital snapshot of the room, then used the Polygonal Lasso to select the wall area. With this selection active, she went to the painting file and selected all and copied. Back in the room file she chose Edit > Paste Into, which added the painting as a layer with a layer mask that hid it except in the selected area. The mask stayed in place as she adjusted the position of the painting with the Move tool and used Edit >Transform > Perspective.▼ Then she selected the piano, targeted the layer mask on the painting layer by clicking its thumbnail in the Layers palette, and filled the selection with black so the painting would appear to be behind the piano.

FIND OUT MORE

▼ Brush controls **page 361**

▼ Transforming **page 71**

Wendy Grossman relies on Photoshop as part of the process when she paints her *Rosebud Studios custom furniture*. Starting with a piece of furniture, she develops an idea for a composition, then looks for visual reference, such as a photo of a cow, rooster, or sunflower, a deck of playing cards, or a pair of dice. After scanning the images and objects, Grossman uses the Move tool to drag and drop the images into a new file sized to fit the area she will paint on the furniture. She scales each layer (pressing Ctrl/⌘-T and dragging a corner handle of the Transform frame) and moves the element into place in the layout (by dragging inside the Transform frame) before pressing the Enter key to complete the transform. Because she will use the file as a reference for handpainting rather than as a final printed piece, she doesn't have to be too concerned about image quality deteriorating as the elements are enlarged.

Grossman makes any color changes needed before printing the composited image. For example, she uses Image > Adjustments > Hue/Saturation to modify colors in selected areas of the image, sometimes altering the colors of one element so it better harmonizes with other elements.

Finally she prints the layout. The print serves two purposes: She uses it with carbon paper to transfer outlines of the major elements onto the furniture piece, and it also serves as a color and detail reference while she paints the design with oils or acrylics.

When **Donal Jolley** photo-graphed the model for ***Red-Striped Couch***, he didn't hesitate to use a fast shutter speed and a low ISO setting (100), to capture a sharp image with little noise. Because he knew he could adjust the exposure as much as two f-stops later in Camera Raw, he could concentrate on getting the pose and the angle exactly as he wanted them.

Viewing his photo shoot in Adobe Bridge, Jolley chose an image **A** and double-clicked its thumbnail. It was automatically recognized as a raw image and opened in Camera Raw. There the Auto settings instantly adjusted color and tone, making corrections based on the data in the raw file itself **B**. Camera Raw is fast, and because its many controls work interactively, the adjustment routine is fluid.

Jolley altered the Shadows and Brightness settings slightly, increasing the contrast **C**. When he had the color and lighting set, he clicked the "Open" button to open the file in Photoshop, where he saved it in the native PSD format.

> Open the **Red Couch Detail.psd** file (in the Wow Goodies folder) to see how the layers, masks, and blend modes interact.

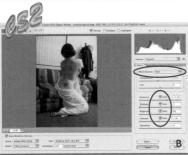

A B C D

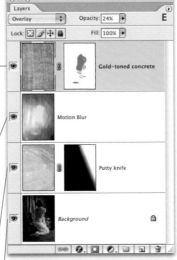

Layers

Overlay   Opacity: 24%   E

Lock: Fill: 100%

Gold-toned concrete

Motion Blur

Putty knife

Background

Jolley opened the file in Corel Painter and used the Tracing Paper feature to view the image as he blocked in the figure, couch, and floor and created the drapery and the wall. With his reference photo on the screen next to his developing painting, he sampled color as he worked to add detail. When he had finished painting **D**, he saved the file and opened it in Photoshop again.

To build up a "lacquer finish," Jolley drew from his "texture library," adding three texture layers, as shown in the final Layers palette **E**.

The first texture layer was a photo of an old putty knife, which Jolley desaturated (Image > Adjustments > Desaturate) and lightened (Image > Adjustments > Levels, moving the Output Levels black point slider inward to lighten and reduce contrast). He changed the layer's blend mode to Overlay▼ and added a layer mask,

using the Gradient tool [ ] to create a divided mask that restricts the layer's contribution to the upper right corner of the image.▼

The middle texture layer was a photo of a concrete garage floor, blurred (Filter > Blur > Motion Blur at 90° at a high Distance setting to make long vertical streaks). He put the layer in Overlay mode and reduced the Opacity to 34%, using the more pronounced streaking that the Motion Blur filter creates at the "front" and "back" edges of the blur to add a slight vignetting effect at the top and bottom edges of the painting. Using the Brush tool [ ] with a soft brush tip, a low Opacity setting, and the Airbrush option, Jolley painted the motion-blurred layer with white. This protected the figure from the texture (as a layer mask would have); with the layer in Overlay mode, it had the added advantage of brightening the skin tones.

The top texture layer started as a shot of Jolley's concrete driveway, which he tinted (Image > Adjustments > Hue/Saturation, moving the Hue slider). In Overlay mode and with Opacity reduced to 24%, the light olive-gold layer completed the surface texture of the painting as it lightened and warmed the image overall. Jolley added a layer mask and airbrushed it with gray paint to mostly eliminate the texture from the torso.▼

FIND OUT MORE

▼ Blend modes **page 176**

▼ Gradient masks **page 191**

▼ Painting layer masks **page 75**

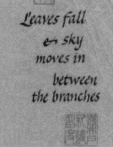

PILGRIMAGE
ERIC CARLE MUSEUM OF
PICTURE BOOK ART · LISA
BASKIN · KAT RAN PRESS
20 SEPTEMBER 2003

GAY WALKER
ON LLOYD REYNOLDS
OREGON CALLIGRAPHER
1 OCTOBER 2003

CHAZ MAVIYANE-DAVIES
DWIGGINS LECTURE
BOSTON PUBLIC LIBRARY
20 NOVEMBER 2003

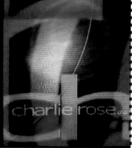

RUFFIN, ROGERS, & STARR
PAPYRUS TO PRINT TO
PIXEL AT WELLESLEY
3 DECEMBER 2003

PAUL PARISI
ON-DEMAND PRINTING
AT ACME BOOKBINDING
7 JANUARY 2004

CHRIS PULLMAN
WHY DOES TV
LOOK THAT WAY?
4 FEBRUARY 2004

LUCY BARTHOLOMAY
DESIGNING THE
BOSTON GLOBE
3 MARCH 2004

MARTINO MARDERSTEIG
FINE PRINTING AT THE
STAMPERIA VALDONEGA
7 APRIL 2004

CHIP COAKLEY
THE HISTORY OF
HARVARD DIPLOMAS
5 MAY 2004

To announce a series of meetings of the Society of Printers of Boston, **Lance Hidy** developed a sheet of *"save-the-date" stamps*, using Photoshop to create the artwork for the individual stamps. Two of the stamps (in the top right corner and bottom center) included artwork provided by the presenters. Hidy assembled most of the others from scans of pieces in his own collection. For "Papyrus to Print to Pixel at Wellesley" he applied the Mosaic filter (Filter > Pixelate > Mosaic, adjusting the Cell Size to get the result he wanted) and then used Image > Adjustments > Hue/Saturation, moving the Hue slider to the right to shift the color palette toward yellow **A**.

Using a Sony CyberShot 4.1 digital camera, he photographed a *Boston Globe* newspaper in his backyard. He used the same camera, this time with its setting for shooting a TV screen, to photograph the *Charlie Rose* graphics, which he then blurred slightly to soften the TV scan lines without completely removing them **B**.

Once he had developed the individual stamp images, he placed them in InDesign **C**, where he could rotate them as needed and crop them inside the frames he had created to lay out the sheet of stamps. In the process of developing the "stamps," he could easily make changes to the individual Photoshop files by clicking on the name of the file in InDesign's Links

palette **D** and then clicking the "Edit Original" button ✏ at the bottom of the palette to reopen the file in Photoshop. After the changes were made, InDesign automatically updated the layout to include the latest version. From InDesign Hidy exported PDFs for proofing and made final adjustments.

He printed the sheets two-up on his Epson Stylus Photo 2200 printer with pigmented inks said to resist fading for 75 years. He perforated the sheets, three at a time, on an antique Latham Machinery Company pin perforator machine borrowed from the collection of the Museum of Printing in North Andover, Massachusetts.

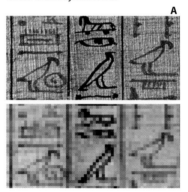

A

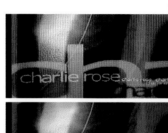

B

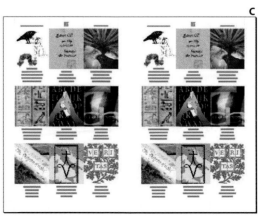

C

D

Color in Photoshop

4

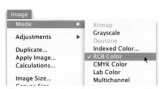

If certain choices in the Image > Mode menu are "grayed out" (unavailable), it's because those modes aren't directly accessible from the mode the file is in currently. For instance, to get to Bitmap or Duotone mode, you have to go through Grayscale.

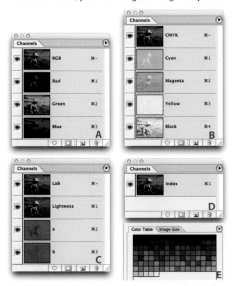

In all color modes the first listing in the Channels palette represents the combined channels. In some modes, such as RGB Color **A** and CMYK Color **B**, the palette shows the primary colors. In Lab Color mode **C** the palette shows the Lightness (gray) channel and two channels that supply the other color ingredients. In Indexed Color mode (in which the color palette is reduced to 256 or fewer colors), a single "channel" appears in the Channels palette **D**; the colors are stored in the Color Table **E**, which can be accessed through File > Save for Web or Image > Mode > Color Table.

COLOR IS VITALLY IMPORTANT to the way we express ourselves in images and graphics, and Photoshop has a powerful set of features dedicated to supporting us as we choose, apply, and change colors. This chapter introduces these features, and you'll find examples of their use throughout the book. But to work efficiently with color in Photoshop, you have to know a certain amount about **color modes** and **color depth**.

COLOR MODES

Photoshop uses several different systems, or **modes**, of color representation, all of which can be chosen through the Image > Mode menu, as shown at the left. In some of the color modes (such as RGB and CMYK) the *primary colors* are the basics from which all other colors can be mixed, and Photoshop stores the color data for each of the primary colors in a *color channel*. These channels are shown in the Channels palette.

In other modes, color is defined not in terms of primaries but as **brightness** (in Grayscale mode) or **brightness with color components** added (as in Lab Color mode). And in Indexed Color mode, color is not broken down into its elements at all, but is delivered instead as a limited number of specific "swatches" stored in a **color table**.

Creative Color: RGB

Computer monitors, digital cameras, and scanners display or record colors by mixing the primary colors of light — red, green, and blue, or **RGB**. When all three of these *additive primaries* are at full intensity, the result is white light; when all are turned off, black results. The various brightnesses of the three colors mix visually to make all the colors of the RGB spectrum. Unless your work in Photoshop requires a particular color mode for some specialized purpose, RGB is usually the best mode for creative work, since it offers the most function and flexibility,

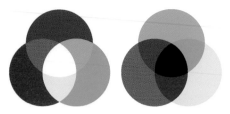

In an additive color model (represented by the illustration on the left) red, green, and blue light combine on-screen to make white light. In subtractive color (on the right) cyan, magenta, and yellow inks combine to make a dark, nearly black color.

FILTERING CMYK FILES

Some of Photoshop's most artistic and spectacular filters don't work in CMYK mode. But you may be able to get the effect you want on a CMYK file anyway. Try filtering the color channels one by one: Click on a single channel's name in the Channels palette, run the filter (choose it from the Filter menu), then click another channel, rerun the filter (Ctrl/⌘-F), and so on.

Photoshop's Save For Web dialog box or ImageReady's Optimize palette (shown here) has more options for reducing the number of colors in an image than the Image > Mode > Indexed Color command offers.

and a broader *gamut*, or range of colors, than most other modes. All of Photoshop's tools and commands work in this mode, whereas other modes have a more limited set.

Within the RGB mode, as in other modes, there can be many different *color spaces*, or subsets of the overall gamut, that different scanners, digital cameras, and monitors can reproduce. Photoshop can use ICC *profiles*, which are descriptions of these color spaces, in its color management system. ("Color Management," starting on page 179, tells more about profiles.)

Printed Color: CMYK

CMYK, or *four-color process*, is the type of commercial printing most often used for reproducing photos, illustrations, and other works. The CMYK primaries (called *subtractive primaries*) are cyan, magenta, and yellow, with black added to intensify the dark colors and details. Adding black makes dark colors look crisper than darkening with a heavier mix of cyan, magenta, and yellow. Darkening with black also requires less ink; this can be important because there's an upper limit to the amount of ink a press can apply before the ink will no longer adhere to the paper cleanly.

Web Color: Indexed (for GIF)

The process of assigning 256 or fewer specified colors to represent the millions of colors in a full-color image is called *indexing*. Since color reduction is most often done in the preparation of Web graphics, indexing is usually done in Photoshop's Save For Web dialog box or in ImageReady's Optimize palette, which offer more options than the Image > Mode > Indexed Color command. For **Indexed Color** you can choose from **Perceptual**, **Selective**, and **Adaptive** palettes, each of which uses different criteria to choose the colors (anywhere from 2 to 256) that best represent the color in the currently active image. In ImageReady you can use a **Local** palette (one based only on the current image) or a **Master** palette (based on a group of images and stored so the same colors can be used for all of them).

The **Color Table** choice at the bottom of the Image > Mode menu lets you view and edit the colors used in an Indexed Color image. You can also name and save the colors in the Color Table, and load colors from previously saved Color Tables and Swatches files.▼

FIND OUT MORE

▼ Swatches palette
page 158

Lab Color

Photoshop's **Lab Color** mode breaks color into a brightness component and two hue-saturation components. Because its gamut is large enough to include both the CMYK and the RGB gamuts, Lab Color mode serves as an intermediate step when Photoshop converts from RGB to CMYK. Working on the "L" (or lightness) channel of a Lab file is an easy way to modify the light/dark information in the image without affecting hue and saturation, or sometimes to reduce noise when converting from color to black-and-white (see page 213). Conversely, working on the "a" and "b" channels is a good way to alter color dramatically without affecting tonal range.

With a Channel Mixer Adjustment layer you can control the contribution of each color channel to a monochrome version of the image.

HSB COLOR

There's one approach to color classification that you won't find in the Image > Mode menu but that's very important in Photoshop. The **HSB** system (Hue, Saturation, and Brightness) is found in Photoshop's tools for choosing, evaluating, and adjusting colors. Look for it, for instance, in the Color Picker, the Info palette, and the Hue/Saturation Adjustment layer.

Hue is the quality we mean when we call a color by name, such as red, yellow, or blue. In Photoshop it's expressed in degrees, as a position on the color wheel.

Saturation refers to whether the color is intense or grayish (neutral).

Brightness is a measure of a color's lightness or darkness.

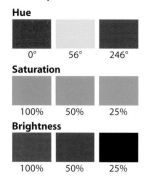

Grayscale

An image in **Grayscale** mode, such as a black-and-white photo, includes only brightness values, no data for the hue or saturation characteristic of color images. For the best reproduction of a color photo in black-and-white, you can get more control and flexibility by using a Channel Mixer Adjustment layer before converting from color to gray with the Image > Mode > Grayscale command. "From Color to Black & White" on page 212 covers several ways to convert.

Duotone

With two colors of ink (or even one color of ink applied in two passes through the printing press) it's possible to get more tones (or shades) than you could get with a single pass of a single ink, and thus you can deliver more of the detail in your image

Photoshop's Duotone mode provides curves that store information for printing a grayscale image in one to four ink colors. The program comes with several sets of preset duotone, tritone, and quadtone curves to load. Or you can shape the curves yourself.

Photoshop's Presets > Duotones folder includes settings for tritones and quadtones as well as duotones. Or you can specify your own colors. By drastically reshaping curves as in this quadtone, you can make different colors predominate in highlights, midtones, and shadows. This quadtone incorporates a custom color, available because it was used elsewhere in the color publication.

onto the printed page. As an example, adding a second color in the highlights increases the number of tones available for representing the lightest tones in an image. Besides extending tonal range, the second color can "warm" or "cool" a black-and-white image, tinting it slightly toward red or blue, for example. Or the second color may be used for dramatic effect or to visually tie a photo into a series of images or to other design elements.

In Photoshop's Duotone mode, a set of *curves* determines how the grayscale information will be represented in each of the ink colors. Will the second color in the duotone be emphasized in the shadows but omitted from the highlights? Will it be used to color the midtones?

Photoshop's Duotone mode also includes tritone and quadtone options, for producing printing plates for three or four ink colors. A Duotone image is stored as a grayscale file and a set of curves that will act on that grayscale information to produce the printing plates, as shown in the "Duotones" technique on page 192.

OVERPRINT COLORS

The Overprint Colors button in the Duotone dialog box lets you adjust the on-screen display of your duotone to look more like it will when it's printed with custom inks. To do this you need a printed sample that shows your custom inks overprinted solid. Clicking any of the color squares in the Overprint Colors dialog box opens the Color Picker so you can change the display of that color mixture to match your printed sample. The settings in the Overprint Colors dialog box are reflected in the color bar at the bottom of the Duotone Options dialog box. For color accuracy, you need to have a calibrated monitor (see "Calibrating & Characterizing Your Monitor" on page 181).

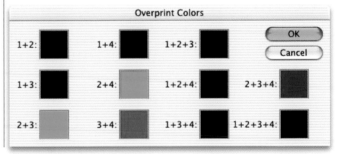

Spot colors can be added at full strength or as tints overlaid on a photo. See page 229.

8 BITS? 16 BITS? 24 BITS? 32 BITS?

The terminology used for color depth, or **bit depth**, has evolved as monitors, scanners, and digital cameras have become more capable. Here are some of the most commonly used terms and what they mean:

8-bit color has 256 (or 2^8) levels of brightness for each primary color. So for Grayscale mode there are 256 shades of gray, including black and white. In RGB color there are 256 x 256 x 256 = more than 16 million possible colors. (Previously, the term "8-bit color" was used to describe color on monitors that could display only 256 colors, or the maximum number of colors in an Indexed Color palette.)

16-bit color has more than 65,000 (or 2^{16}) levels of brightness for each primary color. That's 65,000+ grays in Grayscale, and billions of colors in RGB mode.

24-bit color is an older term, which is still sometimes used to mean the same as 8-bit RGB (8 bits per channel x 3 channels = 24 bits).

32-bit color has been introduced in Photoshop CS2. With specially taken photos converted to HDR (High Dynamic Range) format, you can take advantage of the (currently limited) editing ability in CS2's 32 Bits/Channel mode.

Bitmap

Like Grayscale, Bitmap mode uses only brightness data, no hue or saturation. But in Bitmap mode a pixel is either fully OFF or fully ON, producing a gamut of two "colors" — black and white, with no grays in between. Bitmap mode can be effective as an artistic style or for creating graphics for single-color displays.

Multichannel

Multichannel is a *subtractive* color mode, so if you convert an RGB file, the Multichannel document has cyan, magenta, and yellow channels. If you delete one or more of the channels from a color image (either CMYK or RGB), its color mode automatically becomes Multichannel, consisting of the remaining primaries.

Spot Color

You won't find a Spot Color mode in the Image > Mode menu, but **spot colors**, also called **custom colors**, can be added to files in any color mode except Bitmap. Spot colors are often special color mixes formulated to a particular system such as the Pantone Matching System.

In Photoshop you can add spot colors by clicking the Channels palette's ⊙ button and choosing New Spot Channel. A spot color channel is a good choice when an absolute color standard has to be met for printing a corporate color or logo — the custom ink is premixed to the standard, so the printed color always looks the same. Spot colors are also used to print colors that are outside the CMYK printing gamut, such as certain oranges or blues, fluorescents, or metallics, or to apply a clear varnish. "Adding Spot Color" on page 229 shows how to apply spot color.

COLOR DEPTH

Besides the color mode, the Image > Mode menu also shows the color depth, or **bit depth** — how many bits per pixel Photoshop is using to store the color data in each color channel of a file. The more bits available for this storage, the more color and tone distinctions an image can include.

8 Bits/ Channel

The standard for color in Photoshop, for print and for the screen, is still 8 Bits/Channel, which offers millions of colors and tones. All of Photoshop's functions work in 8 Bits/Channel mode.

JHDAVIS

A file acquired in 16 Bits/Channel mode — such as a Raw file from a digital camera or this scanned photo from "Memory Economy in 16-Bit Mode" on page 217 — includes a wealth of extra color information compared to an 8 Bits/Channel file. Adjusting color in 16-bit mode and then converting the file to 8 Bits/Channel for output can produce a deeper, richer-looking image than if you were to convert to 8-bit mode first and then make the color adjustments. Most of Photoshop CS's core functions — including layers, masks, Adjustment layers, and important filters such as Gaussian Blur and Unsharp Mask — are available in 16-bit mode. In CS2 even more functions and filters are available.

In Photoshop CS (left) many of the filters that might be important to run on information-rich files are available in 16 Bits/Channel mode. In CS2 more filters now have "16 -bit compatibility," including new filters such as the new Blur and Sharpen options, as well as the Liquify and the new Vanishing Point "megafilters." The filter samples in Appendix A of this book indicate which filters work in 16 Bits/Channel mode.

16 Bits/ Channel

When it comes to working in the 16 Bits/Channel mode, Photoshop CS and CS2 are miles ahead of previous versions, which allowed no layers, worked with few filters, and couldn't even copy and paste. Photoshop can now use layers (including Adjustment layers), masks, and Layer Styles, and perform most of its operations in files with more than 8 Bits/Channel. If you have a scanned image or a digital photo captured with more than 8 bits per channel of color information (as in the "billions of colors" option offered by some scanners, you can open it in Photoshop in 16 Bits/Channel mode and make tone and color adjustments using this extra information.

Why is the ability to edit in 16 Bits/Channel mode so important that all of Photoshop's core functions now work there? It's because the information in a 16 Bits/Channel image has the potential range of more than 65,000 variations for each primary color. (For comparison, an 8 Bits/Channel image is limited to 256 variations per channel.)

The wealth of extra image information in 16 Bits/Channel mode provides some very practical payoffs. First, it's much easier to coax good-looking shadow and highlight detail from an image, in whatever part of the tonal range is troublesome, because you have many more tones to work with. If you've ever tried to bring out detail in an underexposed photo in 8 Bits/Channel mode, you know the challenge. With 16 Bits/Channel you have 256 possible tonal steps for every one step you have in 8 Bits/Channel mode. Second, color transitions are smoother with billions of potential color combinations. And third, because you have a potential 65,000+ shades of gray instead of just 256, you can also get a better monochrome result when you convert an image from color to Grayscale in 16 Bits/Channel mode.

So why would you ever work in 8 Bits/Channel mode? One reason is that 16 Bits/Channel files are twice as large as 8-bit ones, and if you start with a relatively large file and begin adding layers, at some point work can get painfully slow. Although there are ways to reduce the amount of RAM and scratch disk used while working in 16 Bits/Channel mode,▼ when work gets too slow, it's probably time to reduce the file to 8 Bits/Channel mode. Also, many photos start out as 8-bit files and have to end up as 8-bit files for printing. And although theoretically you can get better results with color adjustments

FIND OUT MORE

▼ Memory economy in 16 Bits/Channel mode **page 217**

LOREN HAURY

Photoshop CS2's 32-bit color and HDR (high dynamic range) format can provide a good start for combining several exposures of the same image, without selecting or masking. To demonstrate the use of HDR, we've borrowed three exposures taken by Loren Haury. To create a seamless blend, weighting the highlights from one exposure, the shadow detail from another, and the midtones from a third, the first step is to open the images (File > Automate > Merge to HDR) **A**. After browsing to find the files you want and then clicking "OK" to merge them, you can save the file with all its combined exposure data intact by leaving the Bit Depth set at the default 32 Bits/Channel and clicking "OK" **B**. Then, to make a copy of the file in 16 or 8 Bits/Channel mode for further editing (preserving the 32-bit version as well), choose Image > Duplicate and click "OK." Choose 8 or 16 Bits/Channel from the Image > Mode menu, and when the HDR Conversion dialog opens, choose a Method and make adjustments. Here we show an adjustment made with the Local Adaptation Method **C, D**. The image is ready for dodging and burning, color correction, and a final curves adjustment without any cutting and pasting. You can see Haury's final composite of the three exposures, masterfully combined in Photoshop CS without HDR, on page 352.

if you convert to 16 Bits/Channel temporarily to make the adjustments and then switch back, the increase in color detail may very well be imperceptible when the image is printed.

32 Bits/ Channel

High Dynamic Range (HDR, or 32-bit) files allow even finer distinctions in color and tone than 16-bit. Since HDR allows a bigger dynamic range (or number of tones between pure white and pure black) than most cameras can capture or than any printer or monitor can achieve, you might wonder why you would want to work with this bigger file format. The reason is that with all that information available, you can pick and choose where in the image you want to expand the dynamic range, without losing printable or displayable tones in other areas. In a way, the ability to use the extra information in a 32-bit image when you convert it to 16-bit or 8-bit mimics the eye's ability to accommodate to different light levels in the shadows and bright areas of a scene, seeing detail in both.

Photographers can use Photoshop CS2's Merge to HDR command (from the File > Automate menu) to blend together several 8-bit or 16-bit exposures of the same scene in a more automatic way than the masking and blending techniques used with earlier versions of Photoshop. With HDR, for example, you can combine photos of the interior of a room exposed for the sunny window, the deepest shadows, and lighting in between. (There are some restrictions on how the photos must be taken and combined.▼) To further edit the image — you may still need to add a "dodge and burn" layer, for instance — or to display or print the file, you'll need to convert your image to 16 or 8 Bits/Channel. The HDR Conversion dialog box lets you try out different methods of compressing the dynamic range, comparing them to find the solution you like best.

 SAVE IN 32-BIT MODE!

When you convert an HDR file to an 8-bit or a 16-bit file, some of the original data is necessarily "thrown away" in the compression process and can't be recovered later. But saving the HDR file in 32 Bits/Channel mode first and then converting a *copy* of it allows you to keep all the data intact, so you can come back to the saved HDR file as many times as you like, make another copy, and alter exposure for different parts of the image, producing a different result each time.

FIND OUT MORE

▼ Taking photos for merging to HDR **page 98**

Right/Ctrl-clicking with the Eyedropper tool 🖋 opens a context-sensitive menu that lets you choose the sample size. You can also copy a color's hexadecimal code to the clipboard — for instance, COLOR="#B80505" — so it can be inserted into an HTML document.

Point Sample
3 by 3 Average
5 by 5 Average
Copy Color as HTML

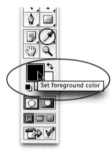

Click the Foreground or Background color swatch in the Tools palette to open the Color Picker. Or click with the Eyedropper tool 🖋 to pick a new Foreground color. Alt/Option-click to choose a new Background color.

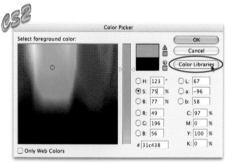

Photoshop's Color Picker lets you simply click a color you choose by eye. Or you can enter numeric values to mix colors in the RGB, CMYK, Lab, or HSB model. Click one of the round buttons to switch between color models. Clicking the "Custom" button (CS) or the "Color Libraries" button (CS2, shown here) lets you choose from several custom color-matching systems. Near the bottom of the dialog box is the hexadecimal code for the current color, which you can copy and paste into an HTML document.

FOREGROUND/BACKGROUND

To restore the Default Foreground and Background colors (black and white), type **D**. To e**X**change the Foreground and Background colors, type **X**.

CHOOSING OR SPECIFYING COLORS

The **Foreground and Background color squares** in the Tools palette in Photoshop and ImageReady show what color you'll get when you paint on any layer (the Foreground color) or erase on the *Background* layer (the Background color). Black and white are the default colors, but you can choose new colors simply by clicking on one of the two squares to open the **Color Picker** and then clicking on a color or "mixing" one by specifying components. Or sample with the **Eyedropper** tool 🖋 to set a new Foreground color by clicking on a color in any open Photoshop document; Alt/Option-click to sample a new Background color.

Other tools for choosing color include the two color palettes (Color and Swatches), which can be opened from the Window menu. The **Color palette**, with its different modes and sliders, is ideal for mixing colors scientifically (by typing in numbers), or in a painterly fashion (by mixing the colors with the sliders), or visually (by sampling from the Color Bar at the bottom of the palette).

SAMPLING COLOR FROM ANYWHERE

See a color you like in an icon on your desktop? Or in a document that's open in another program? Clicking with the Eyedropper cursor 🖋 in any open Photoshop document samples color where you click. But if you then *drag outside the document, you can sample color from anywhere.*

CHANGING THE COLOR BAR

Instead of choosing from the palette menu, you can **right/Ctrl-click** on the Color palette's color bar to display the bar for a different color mode. Or Shift-click repeatedly on the bar to step through the options.

By default, the **Swatches** palette shows a set of 125 color samples. You can click a swatch to make it the Foreground color or Alt/Option-click to select a Background color. You can add to this scrollable palette by sampling a new Foreground color and clicking the Create New Swatch button at the bottom of the palette. Or you can add an entire set of colors by choosing from the palette's fly-out menu. From this menu you can also save a custom set of Swatches or load one.

QUICK, ANONYMOUS SWATCHES

If you want to add a sampled color to the Swatches palette but you don't care about naming it, press Alt/Option as you click in the empty area at the bottom of the palette.

Certain tools have their own colors, which can be changed without changing the overall Foreground and Background colors. For instance, for the drawing tools (Pens and Shapes), color can be set in the Options bar, and for the Type tools in the Options bar or the Character palette.

The Color palette has a color bar to sample from. The color mode of the bar can be changed by clicking the palette's ⊙ button and choosing from the palette menu. The four color bar choices are RGB Spectrum **A**, CMYK Spectrum **B**, Grayscale Ramp **C**, and Current Colors (Foreground To Background) **D**. You can also choose to make the sliders or color bar Web-safe.

In CS2's Swatches palette you can Save Swatches for Exchange, to save the palette in a form that can also be used in Adobe Illustrator and InDesign. This can be a big time- and work-saver and helps ensure that colors are consistent and available to everyone who works on a project.

Three kinds of Fill layers offer the advantage of easy experimentation and changes, as described in "Adding Type to an Image" on page 596.

APPLYING COLOR

In Photoshop, color can be applied with the **painting and filling tools**; these are covered in Chapter 6, "Painting." You can also apply color with the **Edit > Fill command**, or with a Fill layer or a Shape layer, or with the effects in a Layer Style (page 196 has a step-by-step example).

Fill & Shape Layers

Add a **Fill layer** by clicking the "Create a new fill or adjustment layer" button ⊘ at the bottom of the Layers palette and choosing a type of fill — Solid Color (for the current Foreground color), Pattern, or Gradient. The color in a Fill layer is shaped by its built-in layer mask that hides or reveals parts of the color layer. A **Shape** layer provides the same kind of color-filled layer,

---

"FILL" SHORTCUTS

Try these keyboard shortcuts for the Edit > Fill command:

- To fill an entire pixel-based layer (or a selected area of it) with the **Foreground color**, press **Alt-Backspace** (Windows) or **Option-Delete** (Mac).

- **Ctrl-Backspace** or **⌘-Delete** fills with the **Background** color.

- To fill only those parts of a layer or selection where there is already color (in other words, **leave transparent areas clear** and replace color in partially transparent areas without leaving a "fringe" of the old color leftover at the edges, add the **Shift** key to the shortcuts above. Adding the Shift key has the same effect as locking transparency for the layer by clicking the ▣ button near the top of the Layers palette.

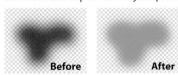

Before   **After**

Using Shift-Alt-Backspace (Windows) or Shift-Option-Delete (Mac) for a clean fill with the Foreground color.

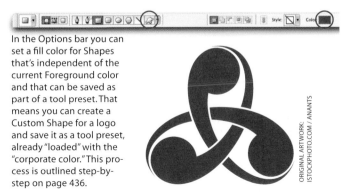

In the Options bar you can set a fill color for Shapes that's independent of the current Foreground color and that can be saved as part of a tool preset. That means you can create a Custom Shape for a logo and save it as a tool preset, already "loaded" with the "corporate color." This process is outlined step-by-step on page 436.

ORIGINAL ARTWORK: ISTOCKPHOTO.COM / ANANTS

JHDAVIS

This photo's color comes mainly from a Color Overlay effect in a Layer Style, so it's easy to change the hue or the degree to which the tint replaces the original color (see page 196 for the technique).

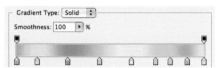

Wow-Gradient 09 is a Solid gradient without transparency. (You'll find samples of all the Wow Gradients on page 187).

Wow-Gradient 06 is a Solid gradient with transparency built in.

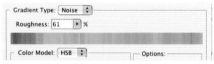

Wow-Gradient 25 is a Noise gradient.

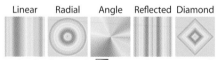

In the Gradient tool's Options bar or in any of the gradient-related dialog boxes, you can choose the type of gradient.

A Linear gradient's orientation is set by the direction you drag the Gradient tool ◼ or the Angle you set in a gradient-related dialog box.

To change the span of the color transitions, change the drag distance for the Gradient tool or the Scale in a dialog box.

but the built-in mask is a vector-based *layer clipping path.* Shape layers are covered in Chapter 7. Both Fill layers and Shape layers are flexible — you can change the color simply by clicking the layer's thumbnail in the Layers palette and choosing a new color.

Still another way to apply color is with a **Layer Style**, that portable combination of effects you can save and apply to other elements and in other files. Layer Styles are introduced on page 44 and are used in step-by-step techniques throughout the book, but especially in Chapter 8.

Gradients

In Photoshop a gradient is a sequence of transitions from color to color. Some gradients include changes in transparency as well as color. Gradients are supplied as presets that you can choose and apply, or modify to make new ones using the Gradient Editor, shown on the facing page. When you design a Solid gradient, you control all the color and opacity changes. On the other hand, if you create a Noise gradient,▼ Photoshop puts colors together somewhat randomly, but within limits you define. To apply a gradient you can use the Gradient tool ◼, a Fill or Adjustment layer, or a Layer Style.

The Gradient tool ◼. The original Gradient tool ◼ is a hands-on, direct approach — you simply drag the cursor where you want to apply the color blend. There are five kinds of gradients you can apply with the Gradient tool — Linear, Radial, Angle, Reflected, and Diamond. For the Linear gradient you drag across the span where you want the gradient to go, from where you want it to start to where you want it to stop. For the other four kinds of gradients, you drag outward from where you want the center to be. The Gradient tool lays down pixels of color. There are other more flexible ways to apply gradients (these "instruction-based" methods are described next), but for creating a graduated layer mask, the Gradient tool is ideal.

Gradient Fill. A Gradient Fill layer can apply the same five types of gradients as the Gradient tool. But using a Fill makes editing easier — at any time after you've set it up, you can double-click its thumbnail in the Layers palette to reopen its dialog box and change the gradient or choose another. To add a Gradient Fill layer, click the "Create new fill or adjustment Layer" button ● at the bottom of the Layers palette and choose Gradient.

FIND OUT MORE

▼ Noise gradients
pages 189 & 190

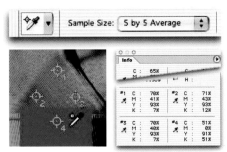

You can establish as many as four stationary samplers with the Color Sampler tool. These samplers feed color information to the Info palette. Color samplers let you pinpoint important areas of an image and watch how their color composition changes as you make adjustments to tone and color. The same Sample Size (set in the Options bar) is shared by the Eyedropper tool; changing the setting for either tool will also change it for the other, and for the eyedroppers in the Levels, Curves, and Exposure dialog boxes.

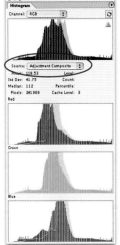

E.A.M. VISSER

Before **After**

The **Histogram** provides a wealth of information about how colors and tones are distributed in an image, and, as shown here, how their distribution will be changed by a color adjustment. The intense colors show the distribution after the adjustment; paler colors show the preadjustment condition.

on a point to remove it. "Bringing Out Detail" on page 321 uses Color Samplers.

Histogram Palette

Photoshop's Histogram palette shows how colors and tones are distributed in your image. The histogram, familiar from the Levels dialog box, now has a home of its own — a palette that you can leave open so you can preview what will happen as you make changes to the image. Open the palette by choosing **Window** > **Histogram**. Then enlarge the palette to show the individual color channels (along with the composite histogram) by clicking the ⊙ button in the upper right corner of the palette and choosing Show All Channels from the fly-out menu. The Histogram offers a range of helpful viewing options:

- Choose **Show Color Channels in Color** from the palette's ⊙ menu to show the individual graphs in color.

- Choose **Colors** from the palette's Channel menu to show colors in the *composite* histogram.

- When you activate an Adjustment layer or a Filter dialog box that includes a Preview option, choose **Adjustment Composite** to see both "before" and "after" versions of the histograms.

When you use the Histogram palette, clicking on the ⚠ when it appears will make sure the Histogram displays the most complete and accurate information.

Color Views

In the View menu you'll find three commands that relate to color. These commands let you "soft proof" your image on-screen, previewing it as closely as possible to the way it will look when it's output. Accurate soft proofing only works if you have accurate profiles for your monitor and for the device on which the image will be displayed or printed. Before you can see an on-screen proof, you need to specify the output you want to proof by choosing **View** > **Proof Setup**. You can choose to see the Working CMYK, which uses the CMYK specifications in the Color Settings dialog box, or choose to preview how the color will look when viewed in the standard RGB Macintosh or Windows color space. Choose View > Proof Setup > Custom to open the Proof Setup dialog box and load the profile for a specific output device, such as your desktop printer. Here you can select Simulate Paper White (duller than on-screen white). Or choose Simulate Ink Black to view the grayer "black"

Photoshop's out-of-gamut warning lets you know if a color in an RGB file might not print as you expect in the CMYK color space you've chosen with View > Proof Setup:

- In the **Info palette**, the warning shows up as exclamation points beside the CMYK values, which represent the closest printable color mix to the specified RGB color.

- In the **Color Picker** and **Color palette** the warning is a caution sign with a swatch of the nearest CMYK match. Clicking the swatch changes the chosen color to the printable match **A**.

Note: The out-of-gamut warning is conservative — some "out-of-gamut" colors may actually print fine.

The "not Web safe" warning (for colors outside the 216-color Web palette) is a small cube **B**. Clicking the accompanying swatch chooses the Web-safe color.

of your target printer. (These options are not available for all printers.)

The **View > Proof Colors** command is the toggle for turning the soft proof on and off. Unlike choosing Image > Mode > CMYK Color to convert the file from RGB to CMYK, the Proof Colors option doesn't actually convert the file — it just gives you a preview — so you don't lose the RGB color information as you would if you converted it. Opening a second view of your RGB file (Window > Arrange > New Window for. . .) and then choosing View > Proof Colors lets you keep Proof Colors turned on in one window and turned off in the other.

The **Gamut Warning**, also chosen from the View menu, identifies the colors in your RGB image that may be outside the printable or viewable color range that you've chosen with the Proof Setup command.

Press **Ctrl/⌘-Y** (for View > Proof Colors) to toggle your view back and forth between your working color space and the color space chosen with the View > Proof Setup command.

To change the warning color for the View > Gamut Warning command from flat gray to a color that contrasts better with your image, choose Preferences > Transparency & Gamut (from the Edit/Photoshop menu), click the Color swatch at the bottom of the dialog box, and choose a new color.

Photoshop offers on-screen "proofing" of files through the View > Proof Colors command, to show what will happen when the file is converted from the RGB Color mode as displayed by your monitor to another RGB color space or to CMYK printing colors. You can open one window for your working color space and a second one to use for proofing, like the smaller window at the right. If View > Gamut Warning is turned on (as it was for the proofing window here), the view will show flat gray (or a user-selectable color such as the lime green we've chosen here) for colors that may change when the file is converted.

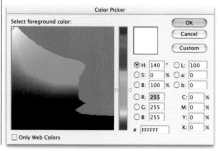
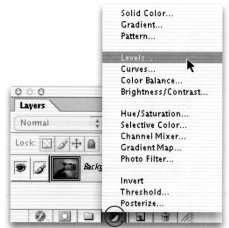
ADJUSTING COLOR

Photoshop's powerful tools for adjusting tone and color are found in the Tools palette, the Image > Adjustments menu, and the list of Adjustment layers that pops up if you click the "Create a new fill or adjustment layer" button ⊘ at the bottom of the Layers palette. For some of these adjustments, you can target your color changes to specific color families or to a particular brightness range — highlights, midtones, or shadows. "Color Adjustment Options" (below) points out the special advantages of each type of adjustment.

Adjustments Commands & Adjustment Layers

When you can, it's generally better to use an *Adjustment layer* rather than the corresponding *command* from the Image > Adjustments menu. An Adjustment layer doesn't change the pixels of the image themselves. It adds little or nothing to the file size, has a built-in layer mask for targeting the adjustment, and can easily be changed later if needed. It can modify all layers below it in the layer stack, or can be restricted to one layer or a few layers. However, some of the commands in the Image > Adjustments menu don't exist as Adjustment layers. For Adjustments commands, which *do* change the pixels, it's best to protect your work up to that point by merging the visible layers into a new layer or by making a duplicate of the entire image file and *then* applying the command to the copy.

Color Adjustment Options

One of the most challenging things about making color adjustments in Photoshop is deciding which is the right tool for the job. The short descriptions that follow point out the special talents of each of the commands found in the Image > Adjustments menu and in Adjustment layers, with references to where in the book you can find more information. In addition, "Quick Tone & Color Adjustments" on page 266 provides some practical suggestions for using Adjustment layers for "quick fixes" to improve photos.

Levels. The Levels dialog box is excellent for **overall tone (and sometimes color) adjustment**. Using the **Input Levels** sliders, you can **increase contrast** (by moving the black and white sliders in) or make the image lighter or darker overall but still keep black black and white white (by moving the gray midpoint slider). You can lighten or darken all the tones in the image (including black and white) and reduce contrast (by moving the Output Levels sliders). You can pick the black point (any tones darker than this will become black) with the Set Black

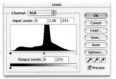

The **Levels** dialog opens to show the Histogram and two sets of black and white sliders, for increasing or decreasing contrast, and a gray slider for changing overall tone.

The **Auto Levels** command makes the same adjustment as clicking the **"Auto"** button in the Levels or Curves dialog box.

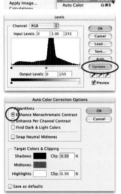

Auto Contrast (shown here) and Auto Color have corresponding choices in the Auto Color Correction Options dialog box, opened by clicking the **"Options" button** in the Levels or Curves dialog box.

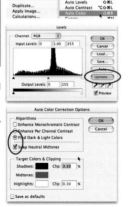

The equivalent of the **Auto Color** command is achieved in the Auto Color Correction Options dialog box by choosing **Find Dark & Light Colors** and turning on **Snap Neutral Midtones**.

Point eyedropper and the white point (any tones lighter than this will become white) with the Set White Point dropper. You can also neutralize color with the Set Gray Point eyedropper. There are many examples of using Levels throughout this book, but especially in Chapter 5, "Enhancing Photos."

Curves. The Curves dialog box is great for **adjusting specific tonal ranges** in your image without making the image lighter or darker overall. For instance, you can lighten shadow tones to bring out detail as shown on the facing page. Curves can also be used for special color effects such as solarization or to create the look of iridescence.

Auto Levels, Auto Contrast & Auto Color. These three commands from the Image > Adjustments menu can also be found (under slightly different names) in the Levels and Curves dialog boxes. You can see examples of how they work in "Quick Tone & Color Adjustments" starting on page 266.

- **Auto Levels** can be a "one-button fix" for color and tone problems in an image, or at least a starting point; in the Levels or Curves dialog box, it's available by clicking the **"Auto" button**.

- **Auto Contrast** preserves the overall color relationships while making highlights lighter and shadows darker; in the Levels or Curves dialog box, you can get the same result by clicking the **"Options" button** and selecting **Enhance Monochromatic Contrast**.

- **Auto Color** neutralizes any near-neutral midtones and increases contrast. You can achieve the same result in the Levels or Curves dialog box by clicking the "Options" button and then selecting **Find Dark & Light Colors** and turning on **Snap Neutral Midtones**.

Color Balance. Color Balance lets you **change the colors of the highlights, midtones, and shadows separately**, although there's some overlap in the ranges. To get rid of a color cast,

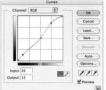

Making a slightly "M"-shaped Curves adjustment can bring out shadow detail and boost highlight tones. While the dialog box is open and the Preview is turned on, the Histogram palette, with Adjustment Composite chosen as the Source, shows the distribution of tones before (gray) and after the adjustment.

Katrin Eismann started with a desaturated photo (top) and then tinted it with a Color Balance Adjustment layer, making the highlight tones orange and the shadows blue-green to produce the tinted image shown here and on page 207.

you simply find the slider that controls the color you have too much of (such as Red) and drag toward the opposite end of the line (Cyan). It can also be useful for tinting an image, as shown below at the left.

Brightness/Contrast. Brightness/Contrast works well for hardening or softening the edges of masks, as described in "Cleaning Up Masks" on page 66, but it **isn't the best tool to use on images**. It has a restricted set of controls that lighten or darken an image overall when Brightness is changed, or reduce detail when you adjust Contrast. This can compromise color and tonal range.

Hue/Saturation. The Hue/Saturation dialog box is **packed with options**. First, it gives you separate control of hue (shifting color around the color wheel); saturation (making a color more intense or more neutral, or grayish); and lightness (pushing the color closer to black or white). You can change color overall or target any of the six color "families" independently (Reds, Yellow, Greens, Blues, Cyans, or Magentas). You can even expand or reduce the range of colors in the family, and control how sudden or gradual the transition is between the colors that are affected and those that aren't. You'll find examples of general and targeted Hue/Saturation changes in "Quick Tone & Color Adjustments" starting on page 273. With Hue/Saturation you can also tint the image with a single color by checking the **Colorize box**, as shown below and in "Quick Tint Effects," on page 201.

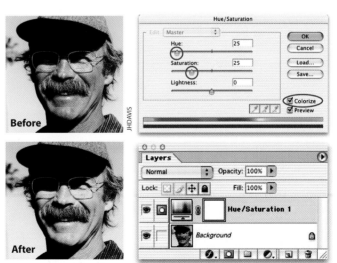

A brown monotone effect is created by using a Hue/Saturation Adjustment layer with the Colorize option chosen. To produce the brown, the Hue slider is set to an orange color and Saturation is reduced.

Before | **After**

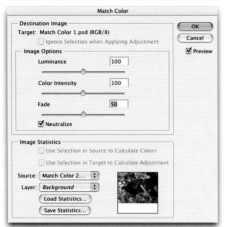

The new Match Color command can help bring images in a series into "color agreement." The photo above was matched to others in a series. The image used for the match is shown in the Match Color dialog box above (see page 266).

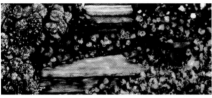

SUSAN THOMPSON

Selective Color can be a great way to make separate color adjustments to individual color families — making the reds yellower but the blues bluer, for instance. In this detail from *Summer in Arcata,* we see some of the adjustments Susan Thompson made in the Selective Color Options dialog box (see page 234 for more).

Desaturate. The Desaturate command is one way to "remove" color, producing a grayscale look but leaving the *capacity* for color, so it can be added back. You can do the same thing better with the Saturation slider in a Hue/Saturation Adjustment layer or, better yet, with the Channel Mixer; these choices give you much greater control (see page 212).

Match Color. The Match Color command lets you modify the color of an image, or a selected part of the image, to **match the color of another image**. For the image you're changing or the one you're matching it to, you can base the color match on the entire image, or pick out a particular area that has the colors you want Photoshop to consider. It can be useful for matching a number of images in a series or matching the parts of a panorama before using Photomerge. You can find examples in "Quick Tone & Color Adjustments" on page 266 and "'Photomerging' a Panorama" on page 604. Match Color **isn't available as an Adjustment layer**.

Replace Color. In the Replace Color dialog box you can make a selection based on sampled color and then change the hue, saturation, or lightness, all in one operation. But Replace Color doesn't provide flexibility for making changes later — there's no way to save the selection so you can bring it back, and Replace Color **can't be applied as an Adjustment layer**.

Selective Color. Selective Color is designed for adding or subtracting specific percentages of cyan, magenta, yellow, and black inks. You can target the changes to any of the six color families (Reds, Yellow, Greens, Blues, Cyans, or Magentas) as well as Black, White, or Neutrals. It can be ideal for **making adjustments to a CMYK file based on a color proof** that shows that you aren't getting the target color you want. If the printer says you need to add a certain percentage of one of the primary ink

Using Channel Mixer to convert a color image to monochrome gives you what seems like an infinite number of options for how the colors are "translated" to black-and-white.

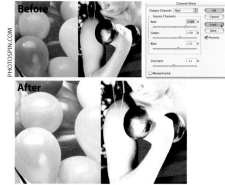

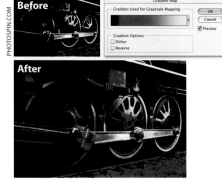

Adobe supplies a number of Channel Mixer presets for color images, such as the **RGB Pastels.cha** preset used here. Examples can be found on page 206.

A Gradient Map Adjustment layer replaces different levels of gray with several colors (see page 208).

To apply a Photo Filter Adjustment layer to an RGB file without changing the exposure or contrast, leave the Preserve Luminosity box checked. The Density slider controls the strength of the tint, simulating the different densities of filters available for camera lenses.

colors, you can do it with Selective Color. But Selective Color can also be very useful for adjusting color in RGB mode, especially if you're used to thinking in terms of inks.

Channel Mixer. The Channel Mixer lets you adjust color in an image by **adding to or subtracting from the individual color channels**. It's also excellent for converting a color image to black-and-white (you'll find examples in "From Color to Black & White," which starts on page 212).

Gradient Map. The Gradient Map adjustment **replaces the tones of an image with the colors of a gradient** you choose. It offers flexibility for trying out a variety of creative color solutions simply by clicking to choose a different gradient, or by clicking the gradient bar to open the Gradient Editor, where you can change colors. You can **invert the order** in which the original tones are remapped to the gradient's colors by clicking the "Reverse" box. Examples of Gradient Map can be found in "Quick Tint Effects" on page 208, and you'll find more about gradients in "Exercising Gradients" on page 188.

Photo Filter. The Photo Filter Adjustment layer **simulates the effect of colored filters on a camera lens**. Photo Filter works the same way whether you choose Filter or Color in the dialog box, but the Filter option gives you a list of choices that correspond to common lens filters, such as Warming and Cooling filters. You can see more Photo Filter adjustments in action in "Quick Tone & Color Adjustments" on page 272. Photo Filter can also be effective for subtle tinting, as shown in "Quick Tint Effects" on page 204.

Shadow/Highlight. The Shadow/Highlight adjustment is designed to bring out detail in underexposed or overexposed areas of an image, by brightening the shadows and adding density in the highlights. At its default settings, which are designed for

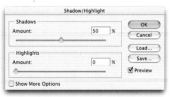

At its default settings, the Shadow/Highlight command can be a great "one-click fix" for a photo with faces in shadow (see page 267).

SHADOW/HIGHLIGHT

The Shadow/Highlight command has separate controls for lightening shadows and darkening highlights. For each pixel, Shadow/Highlight decides whether to treat it as a shadow, a highlight, or neither. Then it determines how much to brighten it (if it's a shadow pixel) or darken it (if it's a highlight pixel). Three sliders for Shadows and three for Highlights work together to achieve the final result.

Tonal Width determines how dark or how light a pixel has to be in order to be considered shadow or highlight. A higher Tonal Width puts more pixels into the shadow or highlight category. At the default 50% for Tonal Width, anything darker than 50% gray is considered a shadow pixel and anything lighter is considered a highlight pixel. But read on, it's just a bit more complicated than that.

Instead of just using the value of each pixel to determine if it falls within the Tonal Width for shadows or highlights, the Shadow/Highlight command compares each pixel to the average of the pixels in its "neighborhood." The **Radius** determines how big this neighborhood is — that is, how far around each pixel the Shadow/Highlight command looks when it figures this average. So, for instance, since most shadow pixels have other dark pixels in the immediate neighborhood, the smaller the Radius, the darker this average will be, and the more likely it is that the pixel will be considered to be within the Tonal Width for Shadows and will be brightened. As the Radius gets bigger, the neighborhood includes more lighter pixels, so the average is lighter, and it's less likely that the pixel will fall within the Tonal Width for Shadows, with the result that it won't be brightened.

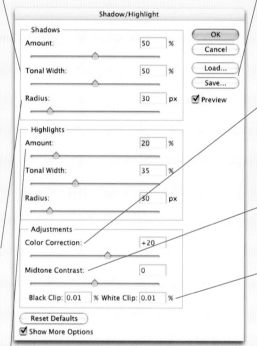

The **"Save"** and **"Load"** buttons allow you to save and reuse settings for specific problems, such as backlighting (the default settings are actually designed for this), overflashing, bright sun, and deep shade.

The **Color Correction** slider increases saturation (or decreases it with a negative setting) in areas that Shadow/Highlight has brightened or darkened. (Grayscale images have a Brightness slider here instead.)

The **Midtone Contrast** slider can be used to fix contrast in the midtones, without having to use a separate Curves adjustment.

Black Clip and **White Clip** work the same as in the Curves and Levels dialog boxes. By increasing the percentages, you push more of the 256 tones to full black or full white, increasing contrast. But pushing too many tones to the extremes causes a loss of detail in shadows and highlights and can even cause posterization (stepped tones rather than smooth transitions) as there are fewer remaining values between the extremes.

Once the Tonal Width and Radius settings have determined that a pixel is shadow or highlight, the **Amount** setting comes into play. Amount determines how much a shadow pixel will be brightened or a highlight pixel darkened. The darkest (or lightest) pixels within the Tonal Width are brightened (or darkened) the most. The higher the Amount setting, the greater the lightening or darkening effect at the extremes and the faster the effect falls off as the midtones are approached. With a lower setting, the effect at the extremes is less and the fall-off is slower.

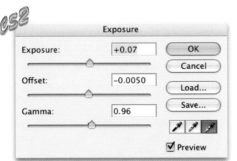

In Photoshop CS2's Exposure dialog box, moving the Exposure slider to the right increases brightness throughout the image but affects the shadow areas more slowly than the highlights. Moving the Offset slider to the left darkens the shadows faster than the highlights. The Gamma slider affects the midtones faster than the extreme darks and lights, lightening them if you move it to the right, darkening them if you move it left.

We duplicated the masked Hue/Saturation Adjustment layer that had been added to adjust the color of the sky. Then we inverted the mask and changed the Hue/Saturation settings to adjust cloud color.

CORBIS ROYALTY FREE

In Normal mode, an Invert Adjustment layer produces a negative of both color and luminosity. In Luminosity mode, tonality is inverted but color is not.

photos with backlit subjects, it acts on a wide range of shadow tones but not on highlights, as shown on page 169. Clicking the "Show More Options" button opens up the dialog box as shown in the illustration on page 170 so you can control how Shadow/Highlight decides what pixels are "dark" or "light," and how much it brightens or darkens them. Shadow/Highlight **doesn't exist as an Adjustment layer**.

Exposure. The Exposure adjustment in Photoshop CS2 is for adjusting images in the new 32 Bits/Channel mode. It's one of the few adjustments available for 32-bit files, standing in for Levels, Curves, and other adjustments. There are three sliders in the Exposure dialog box. Moving any slider to the right brightens the image, and moving it left darkens the image, but each slider behaves a little differently, affecting some parts of the tonal range more than others. You can also use Image > Adjustments > Exposure in 8-bit and 16-bit images, but you may find that Levels and Curves give you smoother, more direct control of the color and tone in these modes.

Invert. The Invert adjustment **changes colors and tones to their opposites**. Besides creating a "negative" look, it can be very useful for making an "opposite" layer mask, such as the ones shown at the left, which are used to apply different Hue/Saturation adjustments to the foreground and background of an image. You can use the Invert command to make a background mask from a foreground mask, or vice versa. (If you're working on a layer mask, you'll have to use the Invert command or keyboard shortcut [Ctrl/⌘-I] rather than an Invert Adjustment layer, since Adjustment layers work on the layer content itself, not on the mask.)

Equalize. The Equalize command can be good for seeing when a soft edge has been flattened because it was cropped too close. Equalize **exaggerates the contrast between pixels that are close in color** so you can see where stray specks or soft edges are. (To prevent cropping a soft edge too close in the first place, use the Image > Trim command, demonstrated on page 245.)

Before

After

The Equalize command is helpful for seeing if the edge of a soft shadow has been trimmed away, or for finding small specks on what's supposed to be a solid-color background.

Move the slider in the Threshold dialog box to control which tones become black and which become white.

Posterizing can help simplify images for the Web, for artistic effect, or for turning a photo into a painting, as shown on page 394.

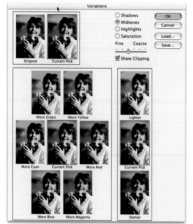

It can't be applied as an Adjustment layer, but experimenting with Variations can help you figure out what kind of color adjustment is needed.

Threshold. The Threshold command **converts each pixel in an image to either black or white.** A slider in the Threshold dialog box lets you control where in the tonal range of the image the black/white divide occurs. It can be useful for creating single-color treatments of photos or for simulating line drawings.

Posterize. The Posterize adjustment **simplifies an image by reducing the number of colors** (or tones in a grayscale image). It can provide a good start for reducing the palette of an image for the Web, to reduce file size and thus download time. Sometimes you get fewer and bigger blocks of color if you blur the image slightly before you Posterize (Filter > Blur > Gaussian Blur or Filter > Noise > Despeckle).

Variations. The Variations command has a dual appeal: It can handle a **wide array of color adjustments** — hue, saturation, and lightness, each controlled independently for highlights, midtones, and shadows; and you can **preview several different options at once** so you can choose between them. (You can see Variations in operation in "Quick Tone & Color Adjustments" on page 274.) Experimenting with Variations may suggest color adjustments that hadn't occurred to you. For instance, you may be thinking that an image needs more red, but the Variations window may show you that increasing magenta would do a better job of achieving the color you want. A major drawback to Variations is that it **can't be applied as an Adjustment layer.**

The Color Replacement Tool

With the new Color Replacement tool (in CS or in CS2) you can **brush on a color change just where you want it** without losing light-dark detail. The tool applies the color that's currently showing in the Foreground color swatch. In the Options bar you can control the tool's **Sampling** process — whether it chooses the color to be replaced the first time you click in the image and then replaces only that color, or whether it continuously samples as you drag it, or whether it replaces only a pre-chosen color. The **Tolerance** setting determines how wide a range of color is replaced. The **Mode** determines what qualities of color will change as you paint — hue or saturation or both, or luminosity. And the Limits setting helps control how widespread the change is.

Toning Tools

The toning tools — Dodge and Burn — are designed to change brightness and contrast, and thus detail, with indepen-

Before

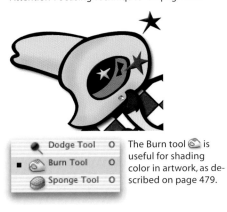

After

CORBIS ROYALTY FREE

With the Color Replacement tool ✔, you can paint a color change while preserving shading details, as the tool's Limits settings help you "stay inside the lines." In CS2 the Color Replacement tool (with its new icon ✔) has been moved to share a spot with the History and Art History brushes, since it's more similar to these tools than to the Healing Brush, and the move makes room for the new Spot Healing Brush and Red Eye tools. You'll find an example of using this tool in "Quick Attention-Focusing Techniques" on page 294.

Dodge Tool	O	
Burn Tool	O	The Burn tool 🖐 is useful for shading color in artwork, as described on page 479.
Sponge Tool	O	

CYCLING BLEND MODES

With a layer targeted in the Layers palette, pressing **Shift-+** will change the blend mode to the next one down in the list; pressing **Shift-hyphen** changes to the next one up. This shortcut also works for any tool with a blend mode list in its Options bar.

dent control in the highlights, shadows, and midtones. The other tool that shares the same spot on the palette — Sponge ⬤ — increases or decreases saturation. With all their powerful variables, the toning tools can be difficult to control for correcting exposure problems (see page 329 for a more flexible method for pinpoint control of contrast, brightness, and detail). But they can be very useful for **highlighting and shading flat-color artwork**.

Blend Modes

Blend modes control how the colors in a new layer, or in paint, interact with the existing image. They are powerful for **combining images**, or combining different versions of a single image (filtered and unfiltered, for instance). Even layering an identical copy of an image over the original and applying a different blend mode to the copy can have useful results for improving color and contrast.

The blend modes are available as a pop-up menu in the Layers palette, in the Options bar for the painting tools, and in several of Photoshop's dialog boxes. In the menu the blend modes are organized in groups. The blend modes in any group are related in the way they affect color, and the modes in most groups share the same "neutral" color (actually a neutral tone — black, white, or 50% gray) that will have no effect when applied in those modes.

BLEND MODE MENU

A blend mode can be applied by targeting a layer in the Layers palette and then choosing from a pop-up menu. Blend modes are grouped in this menu according to a common effect, and in some cases a shared neutral color. If black is the neutral color, white has the strongest effect, and vice versa. If 50% gray is neutral, the effect is strongest for both black and white.

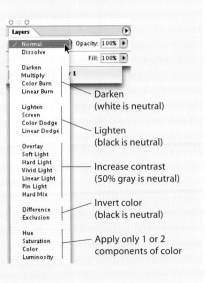

Darken (white is neutral)

Lighten (black is neutral)

Increase contrast (50% gray is neutral)

Invert color (black is neutral)

Apply only 1 or 2 components of color

Layered graphics

An image layered over itself

Modes that blend only if Opacity is reduced

Normal

Dissolve (75% Opacity)

Modes that darken (white is neutral)

Darken

Multiply

Color Burn

Linear Burn

Following are descriptions of the individual blend modes and their groups, with suggestions for how they can be useful. Examples to the left of the descriptions show how the modes blend two different images, as well as an image layered over itself. Blending was done with files in RGB mode and with the overlying layer at 100% Opacity, except in the case of Dissolve mode. The *blend color* is the color that's applied in the blend mode, the *base color* is the original color in the image, and the *result color* is the combined color after blending.

At full opacity, the first two modes in the menu don't really blend at all. They simply **cover up** what's underneath. It's when Opacity is reduced that the difference between the two becomes apparent. (With other blend modes, reducing the Opacity of the overlying layer or the paint reduces the contribution of the blend color to the result.)

Normal. A layer or paint at 100% Opacity in Normal mode covers up the layers below it. As Opacity is reduced in Normal mode, the layer or paint becomes partly transparent, allowing the color below to show through.

Dissolve. At full opacity, Dissolve mode is just like Normal. But reducing the Opacity setting makes a dither (randomized dot) pattern, instead of making the layer or paint partly transparent. In the dither, some pixels become completely transparent (they disappear) and the others remain at full opacity. **The lower the Opacity setting, the more pixels disappear.**

The next four blend modes **darken**, but in some cases only where the blend color is dark. White is the neutral color for these modes — that is, white has no effect on the image below.

Darken. Darken mode compares each pixel in the overlying layer (or the paint) and the pixel underneath, channel by channel. That is, it compares the Red channels of both, the Blue channels, and the Green channels, **chooses the darker channel component** in each case, and uses these components to "mix" the result color. Darken has no effect when an image is blended with itself.

Multiply. The effect of Multiply mode is like putting two 35 mm slides together in the same slide projector slot and projecting them. Where both of the slides have color, the projected color is darker than either. White paint, or any white on the overlying layer, is like the clear part of a slide, having no effect on the image below. Multiply mode is good for **applying**

For some blend modes, there's a noticeable difference in the effect you get in RGB Color and in CMYK Color.

To preserve the look you've achieved with blend modes in RGB when you convert to CMYK, duplicate the file (Image > Duplicate) and flatten this copy (Layer > Flatten Image), and *then* convert the flat file (Image > Mode > CMYK).

Modes that lighten (black is neutral)

Lighten

Screen

Color Dodge

Linear Dodge

shadows without completely eliminating the color of the shaded areas in the layers underneath, and for layering line work over color or vice versa, as in "Watercolor Over Ink" on page 370. Multiply mode can also be helpful for increasing the density of a badly faded photo, as in "Quick Tone & Color Adjustments" on page 270.

Color Burn. Working channel by channel, Color Burn **intensifies the color** of the image underneath as it darkens. The darker the blend color, the greater the effect it has on the image below. Because of this, when you blend an image with a duplicate of itself, the composite changes only slightly in the light colors and highlights, but it begins to darken dramatically as values approach the midtones. This makes Color Burn a good blend mode to use at very low Opacity settings if, for example, you want to give pale lips in a portrait more color and definition, without "blowing out" the highlights. You'll find an example in "Quick Cosmetic Changes" on page 312.

Linear Burn. Linear Burn darkens what's underneath by decreasing the brightness component. Linear Burn can be useful for adding definition to, say, a washed-out sky with clouds. The darker edges of the clouds will be darkened more with Linear Burn than with Multiply, giving them a more three-dimensional appearance. With Linear Burn, **color is not as intensified (saturated) as it is with Color Burn**.

The next four blend modes **lighten**, but in some cases only where the overlying layer or paint is light. Black is the neutral color for these modes — that is, black has no effect on the image below.

Lighten. Like Darken mode, Lighten **compares pixels in the paint or overlying layer and the image underneath, channel by channel**; it chooses the lighter component for each channel to make the result color. Unlike Screen mode (below), Lighten will have no effect if you try to blend an image with itself. Like Darken, Lighten mode can be useful in achieving subtle blends and natural-looking textures.

Screen. The "partner" of Multiply mode, Screen is like projecting two slides from separate slide projectors onto the same spot on the wall, or like overlapping colored spotlights. The result is to lighten the composite. Screen mode is good for **applying highlights to an image**, or for lightening a too dark image by blending it with itself.

Overlay

Soft Light

Hard Light

Vivid Light

Linear Light

Pin Light

Hard Mix

Color Dodge. Color Dodge **lightens and makes colors more vivid.** Light colors are lightened a lot more than dark colors, so there is more contrast than with Screen mode. At low Opacity, Color Dodge can add sparkle to the eyes in portraits by both intensifying the color and increasing the contrast. You can find an example in "Quick Cosmetic Changes" on page 312.

Linear Dodge. Linear Burn's "partner" Linear Dodge increases brightness. It **lightens the lightest colors more intensely than Screen mode does, but acts more evenly than Color Dodge.**

The next seven blend modes **increase contrast** in various ways. For these modes, 50% gray has no effect.

Overlay, Soft Light & Hard Light. Overlay, Soft Light, and Hard Light provide three different complex combinations of Multiply and Screen. All three increase contrast. Of the three, **Soft Light** has the least effect on deep shadows and bright highlights, **Hard Light** affects these extremes the most, and **Overlay** is intermediate. A 50%-gray-filled layer in Overlay or Soft Light mode can be an easy and flexible substitute for the **Dodge and Burn** tools. By painting the layer with white or black at low opacity, you can dodge out or burn in areas to balance the lighting and make the image look "sharper." Page 329 has an example.

Vivid Light. Vivid Light mode **burns and dodges on a channel-by-channel basis.** The farther the overlying color is from 50%, the more it increases contrast.

Linear Light. Linear Light is similar to Vivid Light, but it doesn't increase contrast as much at the extremes. As a result, Linear Light can produce a more **subdued, gradual change in contrast.** At full or close-to-full Opacity settings, both Vivid Light and Linear Light are great for modern-looking intense blends of image layers.

Pin Light. Pin Light is a complex combination of Lighten and Darken. Like these modes it compares the blend and base colors channel by channel. For each channel, if the blend color is lighter, it lightens the base color to produce the result channel, and if the blend color is darker, it darkens the base color. The closer the blend color is to 50% brightness in a particular channel, the less effect it will have in that channel. Like Lighten and Darken modes, Pin Light has no effect when an image is blended with itself (as shown at the left). But it offers some fairly subdued alternatives for blending image layers or as a blend mode used in Layer Styles.

Color-inverting modes (black is neutral)

Difference

Exclusion

Modes that apply color attributes

Hue

Saturation

Color

Luminosity

Hard Mix. This blend mode (added in Photoshop CS) applies the Threshold filter to each channel in an image. The result of blending one image layer with another (or itself) at 100% Opacity is to **posterize** the resulting image, though with a different set of colors than a Posterize Adjustment layer would produce. In a very different application, used at low Opacity settings, applying a duplicated image layer in Hard Mix mode increases contrast evenly over the range from shadows through midtones to highlights. The other contrast-enhancing modes tend to affect shadows and highlights more than midtones.

For the next two modes, **black is neutral**, having no effect, and **white inverts the color underneath**, producing its opposite. Besides having some very practical applications, these modes are also good for creating special effects.

Difference. Difference mode does complex calculations to compare the overlying color and the color underneath. If there is **no difference in pixel color, black results.** Where the colors are different, Difference produces intense, and sometimes surprising, colors. Since this mode will show any difference between two images, it's useful for aligning parts of an image that's too large for the flatbed scanner or that's torn. It's also useful for seeing what's different after you apply an adjustment or a filter — copy the image to another layer, apply the change to the copy, and put the changed layer in Difference mode.

Exclusion. In Exclusion mode, as in Difference mode, black produces no effect and white produces the opposite color. At high Opacity settings, Exclusion mode can be used to blend an image with itself to produce results like Filter > Stylize > Solarize (shown in Appendix A) but lighter and more muted. **At very low Opacity settings, a duplicate layer in Exclusion mode will reduce contrast and saturation.**

The last four modes **apply one or two of the three color attributes** (**hue, saturation,** and **brightness,** or **luminosity**). There is no neutral blend color. Hue, Saturation, and Luminosity modes each apply only one of the three color attributes of the blend color. Color mode applies two out of three (hue and saturation). When two copies of the same image are layered, none of these modes produces a change.

Hue. Hue mode is good for **shifting color without changing how intense or neutral the color is, or how light or dark.** Hue mode has no effect if the base color is black, white, or gray, because these "colors" have no hue to change.

The blend mode for painting, filtering, or a color adjustment applied through the Image > Adjustments menu can be changed using the Fade command. For instance, if you sharpen an image (Filter > Sharpen > Unsharp Mask) and find that the sharpening has created an unwanted increase in color contrast, you can change the blend mode to Luminosity to leave the overall sharpening of the details intact but eliminate the color problem.

The Edit > Fade command is available only immediately after you paint, filter, or adjust.

Instead of stacking a duplicate of an image on top of the original and using the top layer's blend mode to combine the two, you can get exactly the same result by using an "empty" Adjustment layer. The advantage is that while the duplicate image layer doubles the file size, the Adjustment layer doesn't increase file size at all.

In this example, a Levels layer was added by clicking the "Create new fill or adjustment layer" button at the bottom of the Layers palette, choosing Levels, and clicking "OK" to close the Levels dialog box without making any changes. Then the blend mode for this Levels layer was set to Hard Mix, creating the same change as a copy of the layer in Hard Mix (see page 177).

Saturation. In Saturation mode, **the saturation of the blend color becomes the saturation of the result color.** Neutral blend colors make the underlying colors neutral, and more intense blend colors boost the intensity of colors underneath, in each case without changing their hue or how light or dark they are. Saturation mode has no effect on underlying black or white.

Color. In Color mode, the **hue and saturation of the overlying color replace those of the underlying color,** but the light-dark detail remains. Underlying black and white are not changed.

Luminosity. Luminosity is the mode to use if you want **to transfer only the light-and-dark information** from a texture, graphic, or grayscale image onto an image underneath. It can also be useful in sharpening — duplicate the image layer, apply the Unsharp Mask filter, and then put the sharpened layer in Luminosity mode, to eliminate color shifts the filter might have produced.

Three more modes occur only in special situations. They have **no neutral colors**.

Behind. Behind mode is offered with the painting and filling tools and the Edit > Fill command. It allows color to be applied only to transparent (or partly transparent) areas of a layer. Any opaque pixels are protected.

Clear. In Clear mode, a painting tool or the Fill command acts like an eraser, replacing color with transparency.

Pass Through. Pass Through is the default mode for layer sets (called *groups* in CS2),▼ allowing each individual layer in the set to keep its own blend mode when it acts on the layers below the set. If you choose any other blend mode for the set (Normal is a common choice), it's as if the layers of the set (with their individual blend modes) had been merged to form a single layer and then the set's blend mode had been applied to that layer. Switching to Normal instead of Pass Through can keep the effect of an Adjustment layer "local," within the set only. Pass Through is available only for layer sets/groups.

FIND OUT MORE

▼ Layer sets/ groups **page 583**

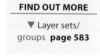

Pass Through mode allows the blend modes of the individual layers within a set/group to be passed through to affect layers below. If you change the blend mode of a layer set/ group to Normal, as shown here, any Adjustment layers inside it will affect only the other elements inside.

GETTING CONSISTENT COLOR

There are several fundamental factors that make on-screen and printed color look different from each other. First of all, monitor color, because it's lit up, looks brighter than printed color. Second, because the *gamut,* or range of colors that can be displayed or printed, is different for RGB than for CMYK, not all the colors that can be displayed on-screen can be printed, and vice versa. Third, when you convert RGB colors to CMYK for printing, you're moving from a three-color to a four-color system in which black can partially substitute for mixes of the other three colors (cyan, magenta, and yellow). Because of this fourth "primary color," there are many ways to represent a particular RGB color in the CMYK system, and because of the way ink pigments interact, the results of all these ways can look slightly different from each other. Finally, variations in printing methods, paper, and ink also affect the color in the final printed product.

Color Management

As if the differences between on-screen and printed color weren't enough, there are also differences in the way various scanners and digital cameras record colors and the way various monitors display them. Different kinds of input and display devices operate in different *color spaces,* or subsets of the full range of RGB color. To compensate for the variability in color spaces, Photoshop offers a color management system to translate color accurately between devices and printing processes. The **Color Settings** dialog box (Shift-Ctrl/⌘-K) is where you can choose how to configure Photoshop to produce consistent color from input to output.

In a perfect world — one in which every component of every computer graphics system was calibrated to a universal benchmark, stayed consistent over time, and had a known *ICC profile* — the color-management system built into Photoshop could work perfectly. (An ICC profile is a component's color characteristics according to an international standard designed to help reproduce colors accurately.) In such a world, color would stay consistent no matter what device or graphics program was used to display or print Photoshop documents. Unfortunately, the world isn't perfect yet in this regard.

Some Photoshop users, especially designers or photographers working alone who **don't share their Photoshop files as they're creating them,** prefer to choose the "Off" options in the Color

The **gamut,** or range of colors that can be displayed or printed, varies for different RGB working spaces. For instance, the sRGB space that Adobe recommends as part of the Web Graphics Defaults Settings in the Color Settings dialog box is smaller than the Adobe RGB (1998) color space recommended for Photoshop files destined for print. The Wide Gamut RGB color space, available at the bottom of the pop-out list of RGB options in the Color Settings dialog box, is bigger still. (In Photoshop CS click the Advanced check box in the Color Settings dialog to see the expanded list that includes Wide Gamut RGB and others; in CS2 click the "More Options" button.)

Wide Gamut RGB

Adobe RGB (1998)

sRGB

If you want to know more about color management, *Real World Color Management* by Bruce Fraser, Chris Murphy, and Fred Bunting is a good resource.

Through Bridge, which is part of the Adobe Creative Suite 2, you can coordinate Color Settings so that all the programs in the Suite use the same settings. Shown here is part of the expanded list of color space choices.

The ColorVision Spyder (shown here, www.colorvision.com), GretagMacbeth's Eye-One Display 2 (www.i1color.com) and MonacoOPTIX (www.xritephoto.com/product) are relatively low-cost hardware-software devices that attach to your screen and calibrate and characterize your monitor, producing an ICC-compatible profile that can be used in Photoshop's Color Settings dialog.

You can use Mac OS X's built-in Display Calibrator Assistant to walk you through the process of creating a color profile for your monitor.

Management Policies section of the Color Settings dialog box. This choice avoids any complications that might arise because the file was passed from or to another graphics program that doesn't include the same color management functions, such as many Web page applications, HTML editors, or video-editing programs. But by also **turning *on* the Embed Color Profile option** when a file is saved (File > Save As), you can still include information about the color space you were using when the file was developed, in case it's useful for the next person in the workflow — or to jog your own memory later on.

On the other hand, if your workflow involves passing files from one system to another for different stages of the creative process, it may be worthwhile to implement a color management system within the work group and to share the profiles. Setting up and using the color management system will involve searching out or creating the ICC profile for each scanner, digital camera, monitor, and output device (with various settings for different resolution and paper settings); and keeping each component in the workflow calibrated so the ICC profile is meaningful for that component.

In Photoshop CS2 you can synchronize color settings for all the Adobe Creative Suite applications. First open Bridge (you can do this by clicking the "Go to Bridge" button 🔲 near the right end of Photoshop's Options bar). In Bridge choose Edit > Creative Suite Color Settings. In the Suite Color Settings dialog box (shown at the left), choose from the short list, or choose from more options made available by clicking the "Show Expanded List of Color Settings Files" check box or the "Show Saved Color Settings Files" button, and make a choice. Finally, click the "Apply" button.

Your "Color Environment"

To get consistent color, it's important to keep not only your monitor but also your viewing environment constant, because changes in lighting conditions can change your perception of colors. Here are some ways to keep environmental color conditions from interfering with your on-screen color work:

- Position the room's light source above and in back of the monitor, and keep it dimmed and constant.

- If your room lighting is controlled by a rheostat, mark the knob and the base plate so you can always restore the lighting to the same level.

- The wall behind you should be neutral in color, with no bright posters or other images.

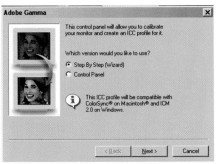

In the Adobe Gamma Wizard dialog box (Windows), choosing the Step By Step option and then clicking the "Next" button starts the process of calibrating your monitor and creating an ICC-compliant profile.

In the first Adobe Gamma Wizard screen, enter a name for the monitor profile you'll be producing with Adobe Gamma.

After the Wizard has led you through the calibration process, click the "Finish" button and give the profile the same name as you did in the first screen, described above.

Profiling services such as ColorValet offer target files you can print and send in, and the service then creates profiles for you.

- Wear neutral colors when doing color-critical work, to minimize color reflection from your clothes onto the screen.
- Use a neutral Desktop color (medium gray works well), with no bright colors or distracting pictures.

Calibrating & Characterizing Your Monitor

In order for your computer monitor to show you consistent color — so a file displayed on the screen today looks the same as it did last week and as it will next week — the monitor has to be calibrated periodically to bring it into compliance with the standards it was designed to meet. Some monitors come with special calibration software. If yours didn't, you may want to try a hardware-software combination package that either actually adjusts your monitor or tells you which settings need correcting so you can manually adjust it before the software then creates a profile that describes how your monitor is currently representing color. That way, the color management system can accurately translate color between your monitor and various input and output devices.

In Windows, another possibility for calibration is to use the **Adobe Gamma** control panel that comes with Photoshop to do a simplified calibration, and build an ICC profile. On the Mac, you can use the **display calibrator** interface that opens when you choose System Preferences from the Apple menu, click on Displays, and then click on the Color tab and the "Calibrate" button. These utilities use the factory calibration settings to calibrate the monitor and then build a profile for your particular device.

"Color-Managing" Your Local Workflow

Once your monitor is calibrated and its profile has been built, consistent color management requires that other devices in your workflow — such as your scanner and desktop color printer used for proofing — also be calibrated, or at least have ICC-compliant profiles, so color can be accurately translated from one device to the next. Your scanner or printer (and the paper you use) may vary from the profile created by the manufacturers of your equipment, and there may not be an easy way to bring the equipment into compliance with the profile. A better solution is to generate custom profiles for the specific scanner and printer you own. One option is a profiling service such as ColorValet (**www.chromix.com/colorvalet**), which offers a money-back guarantee.

If you turn on the "Ask When Opening" option for Missing Profiles in the Color Settings dialog box, as shown on the facing page, Photoshop will ask what you want to do when you open a file that has no color profile embedded. If you aren't sure of the profile used to create the file, the conservative path is to choose "Leave as is (don't color manage)" and then use the Image > Mode > Assign Profile command.

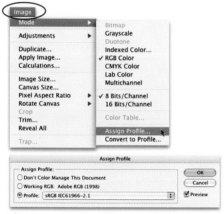

There's an advantage to using the Assign Profile command from the Image > Mode menu in CS or the Edit menu in CS2 (see below) rather than assigning a profile in the Missing Profile box when you first open the file: Using the command lets you preview the change in the file's appearance before you commit to the profile assignment.

In Photoshop CS2 the Assign Profile and Convert to Profile commands have been moved from the Image menu, where it was in version CS, to the Edit menu, just below Color Settings.

Color Settings

The Color Settings dialog box is opened in Photoshop CS by choosing Preferences > Color Settings, from the Edit menu in Windows or the Photoshop menu on the Mac. In CS2 choose Edit > Color Settings for either platform. (The Ctrl/⌘-Shift-K shortcut works in both CS and CS2.)

There, in the Settings section, you can choose one of the predefined color management options for producing consistent color in the most widely used on-screen and print workflows. Each setting can be used "as is" or you can modify it. Adobe recommends that you leave all the "Ask When Opening" options turned on, so that you will be alerted whenever you open a file that has no embedded profile or that has a profile that doesn't match the working color space in your Color Settings dialog box.

Assigning or Converting a Profile

Let's suppose that you open an RGB file with no color profile embedded — the person who created it may not have chosen to embed a profile, or the image may have come from a scanner or digital camera that can't embed profile information — so your system can't know how to display the color that the originating device intended. If you've turned on the Ask When Opening option for Missing Profiles, as shown on the facing page, the Missing Profile dialog box will open, as shown at the left. Here are some options:

- If you have a pretty good idea of the working space the file originated in (your friend always works in Apple RGB, for instance, or the type of camera was most likely sRGB), you can choose the **"Assign profile"** option. This may change the file's appearance on your monitor, but it won't change the color data in the file.

- More risky is to choose to convert the file to your working color space with **"Assign working RGB."** The on-screen appearance of the colors will be the same as if you chose "Leave as is (don't color manage)," but the color data in the file will be altered as if the file had been produced on your system to look the way it does on the screen.

- If you don't know what the originating working space was, **the most conservative choice is "Leave as is (don't color manage)."** Although the data will be interpreted for the display as if it came from your working space (as with "Assign working RGB"), no data will be altered, and you now have the option to assign a profile through the Image > Mode >

COLOR SETTINGS

In Photoshop CS the Color Settings dialog box is opened by choosing Preferences > Color Settings (in Windows it's in the Edit menu; on MacOSX it's in the Photoshop menu). In Photoshop CS2 choose Edit > Color Settings. With the Advanced Mode box checked, the Color Settings dialog offers a broad array of options for managing color. The choices you make here will affect the result you get when you choose Gamut Warning or Proof Colors from the View menu.

Clicking the **Advanced Mode** check box in CS or the "More Options" button in CS2 allows you to create or load profiles other than those listed in the pop-out Working Spaces menus. To do this, choose Custom or click the "Load" button.

Adobe recommends starting with the Settings that best describe the output process that will be used to produce your images — typically, **Web Graphics Defaults** or regional **Prepress Defaults.** Then you can change individual Working Spaces settings to match your actual workflow. For instance, you can change the CMYK working space according to custom CMYK Setup settings provided by the printer who will be producing a specific job. The printer may also provide Custom Dot Gain settings for a black-only or spot color printing job. As soon as you change any settings in the Color Settings dialog box, the Settings entry changes to **Custom,** as shown here.

With the **"Save"** button you can save different Color Settings preferences to accommodate different job requirements, and then **"Load"** them as you need them.

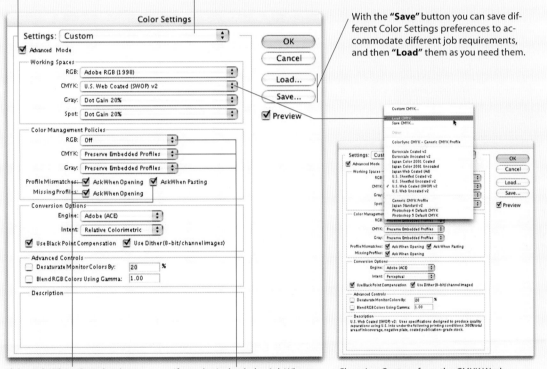

If the **Ask When Opening** boxes are checked, as Adobe recommends, you are offered the opportunity to override the Color Management Policies whenever you open a file or paste an element whose profile doesn't match the current working space.

If you don't check the Ask When Opening boxes, your choice of **Color Management Policies** will determine what happens if you open a file that doesn't have an embedded profile or whose profile isn't the same as the current working space.

Choosing **Custom** from the CMYK Work Spaces menu opens the CMYK Setup dialog box, where you can choose Separation Options. (Instead of choosing Custom, you can choose **Load CMYK** to load a CMYK profile — for instance, one supplied by the printer who will be producing a specific job.)

Assign Profile command (or Edit > Assign Profile in CS2), which lets you preview your choice — something the Missing Profile dialog can't do.

Even if you can't guess what working space the file originated in, you may be able to save yourself some work in Photoshop by using the Assign Profile command, to see how different profiles will affect your on-screen display of the file. If you can find a profile that improves the way the image looks on your screen, you can then choose Image > Mode > Convert to Profile (or Edit > Convert to Profile in CS2) to convert the file to your working RGB space if you want to do further work on the file. Using the Convert to Profile command changes the actual color data in the file. With the profile converted, you do whatever work is necessary to complete the file, and then embed your working profile when you save the file and pass it on. The next person to get the file won't have to do any detective work to assign a profile, because you will have already assigned it by embedding it in the file.

Making RGB-to-CMYK Conversions

If you're preparing an image for print, unless you use a desktop printer or a photo emulsion printer that actually prints using an RGB color space, the image will eventually need to be turned into CMYK ink colors. This can be done at any of several different stages in the development of the image:

- You can choose CMYK Color mode when you first create a new Photoshop file (File > New > Mode: CMYK Color) or in some cases during the scanning operation.

- If you start in RGB, you can choose Photoshop's Image > Mode > CMYK Color at any point in the development of an image to convert from the RGB working space to the CMYK working space chosen in Photoshop's Color Settings dialog box. Or you can choose Image > Mode > Convert to Profile to choose a CMYK separation, to match a profile your press operator gave you, for instance. But once you make the conversion, you can't regain the original RGB color by choosing Image > Mode > RGB Color. Instead, if you don't like the result, you may be able to undo (Ctrl/⌘-Z), or go back to a previous state or Snapshot from the History palette made before the conversion,▼ or choose File > Revert to go back to the last saved version of the file.

- You can keep the file in RGB Color mode until it reaches a page layout program or color separation utility (for the press).

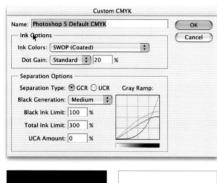

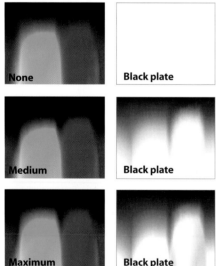

The parameters for converting RGB to CMYK color can be customized in the Custom CMYK dialog box (top). There are several options for Black Generation, which controls how much of the dark colors is contributed by black ink and how much is contributed by a mix of cyan, magenta, and yellow. Shown here are results of converting from RGB to CMYK color using each of three different Black Generation settings in the CMYK Setup dialog box.

FIND OUT MORE

▼ Using the History palette **page 31**

Before

After

Typically, for desktop printing, your printer's driver will convert your RGB document into the CMYK inks it uses.

How do you decide which one of these options is best for converting from RGB to CMYK? Here are some tips to help you choose when to convert:

- **The single advantage of working in CMYK from the beginning** is that it prevents last-minute color shifts, since it keeps the image within the printing gamut during the entire development process. But there's a risk — if you're working in CMYK mode and your printing specifications change (a different paper may be chosen for the job, for instance), the CMYK working space you chose may no longer apply.

- Working in RGB and putting off the CMYK conversion until the last possible moment allows more freedom, so you can get just the color you want on-screen and then work with Photoshop's Hue/Saturation, Selective Color, Levels, or Curves adjustments to tweak out-of-gamut colors to get CMYK alternatives that are as close as possible to your original colors.

- Another very significant advantage of working in RGB is that some of Photoshop's finest functions (for example, the Auto Color, Match Color, and Shadow/Highlight commands) don't work in CMYK in version CS. Shadow/Highlight *does* work in CMYK in CS2, but the new Exposure command doesn't. Also, half the filters in the Filter menu (including Vanishing Point and Lens Correction in CS2) don't work in CMYK.

- With Photoshop's Proof Color and Gamut Warning available, it makes sense to work in RGB, preview CMYK in a second window, and do the actual RGB-to-CMYK conversion at the end of the process. Or work in just one window and toggle between RGB and CMYK previews as needed (Ctrl/⌘-Y).

- You may be able to bow out of the conversion process altogether for many jobs. The commercial printer you work with may have a separation utility, "tweaked" to do an excellent job of converting RGB to CMYK for the particular printing environment. If that's the case, this method may save you some time and angst (although there may be an additional charge) if you carefully check the printer's proofs.

At whatever point you make the conversion, the specifications in Photoshop's Color Settings dialog box and the profiles that support those settings will affect the final result. 🖌

Sharon Steuer Channels William Randolph Hearst

FACED WITH THE CHALLENGE OF "RESTORING" a 1937 newspaper clipping that had been glued to a board and matted with an equally pulpy and acidic stock, artist and author Sharon Steuer scanned the clipping and began the search for a color channel that was clean enough to use as a starting point for redeeming the discolored document. She had to go beyond Red, Green, and Blue, but she found the channel she needed.

> **FIND OUT MORE**
> ▼ Converting from RGB to CMYK
> **page 184**
> ▼ Working with Color Settings
> **page 183**

1 The clipping was an article about the successful defense of the *New York American,* a Hearst newspaper, in a libel suit.

In the RGB scan, William Randolph Hearst's hand-written congratulations to the lawyer didn't look too bad, but the glue had streaked the clipping itself, and in some places the type showed through from the back of the page.

2 Sharon viewed the individual Red, Green, and Blue channels of the scan, looking for a relatively clean starting point for her restoration, but to no avail. She made a copy of the file to experiment with (Image > Duplicate).

The Red, Green, and Blue channels all showed the dark stains.

3 Next Sharon converted the duplicate to CMYK mode,▼ to see if she could generate a better channel. The results you get when you translate an image from RGB to CMYK depend on what CMYK Working Space and Intent you use. (Some Intent settings preserve as many of the original colors as possible. Others try to preserve the *relationship between colors,* even if it means changing more colors.)▼ By turning on Advanced Mode in the Color Settings dialog box, Sharon could set a Working Space and Intent combination, click "OK," make the conversion (Image > Mode > CMYK Color), and check the result. Then she could undo the mode change (Ctrl/⌘-Z), try other settings, and convert again, repeating the process until she found a clean channel.

Using US Web Coated (SWOP) v2 for the CMYK Working Space and Perceptual for the Intent in the Color Settings box produced a Cyan channel with little streaking.

4 Sharon made a new CMYK file from the Cyan channel. One way to do this is to click the channel's name in the Channels palette to make it the only channel visible, then select all (Ctrl/⌘-A) and copy (Ctrl/⌘-C). Start a new file (Ctrl/⌘-N, choosing RGB or CMYK Color for Mode in the New File dialog box, and click "OK"), then paste (Ctrl/⌘-V). Sharon added a Levels Adjustment layer, working with the Input Levels sliders for the individual Cyan, Magenta, and Yellow channels to improve contrast and add a tint. She stacked up several copies of the Levels layer in Multiply mode to darken the type. To fix particular problem areas, she added other Levels layers, using blend modes and layer masks.

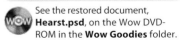

See the restored document, **Hearst.psd**, on the Wow DVD-ROM in the **Wow Goodies** folder.

Gradients

Photoshop's versatile gradients are introduced on pages 160 and 161. To supplement that introduction, these five pages have examples of gradients in use, with files for dissecting or re-creating the gradients.

You can apply a gradient with the **Gradient tool** ▭ (via the Tools palette **A**), as part of a **Layer Style** (via the "Add a layer style" button *f* at the bottom of the Layers palette **B**), or with a **Gradient Fill** or **Gradient Map** layer (via the "Create new fill or adjustment layer" button ◑ **C**).

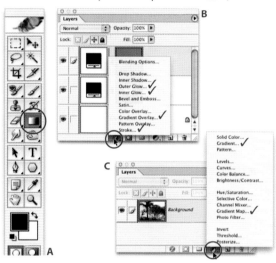

Some of the examples in this section use **Wow-Gradients**, supplied on the Wow DVD-ROM that comes with this book. If you loaded them along with the other Wow presets ▼, you can add them to any palette of gradient swatches in Photoshop by clicking the palette's ◉ button and choosing them from the menu that pops out. If you haven't already loaded them, and therefore they don't show up in the pop-out menu, you may want to simply load the gradients you need for this "Exercising" section — choose Load Gradients in the pop-out menu and navigate to the **Wow-Exercise.grd** file, located as described below.

YOU'LL FIND THE FILES
in 🔴 > Wow Project Files > Chapter 4 > Exercising Gradients

Wow Gradients

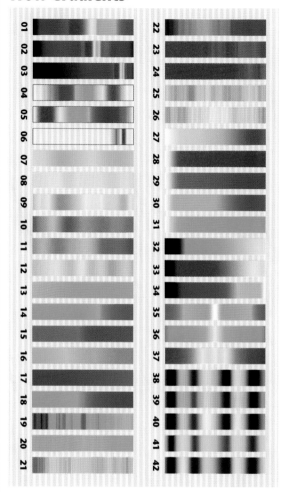

ONCE YOU'VE LOADED THE WOW GRADIENTS, ▼ they become available anywhere in Photoshop that the Gradient swatches palette appears — in the Options bar for the Gradient tool, the dialog boxes for Gradient Fill and Gradient Map layers and for Layer Styles, and in the Preset Manager.

Most of the Wow Gradients are of the **Solid** type, but **Wow Gradients 19 through 26** are **Noise** gradients. **Wow Gradients 4 through 6** have **transparency** built in.

FIND OUT MORE
▼ Loading the Wow presets **page 5**

Orienting a Gradient Fill

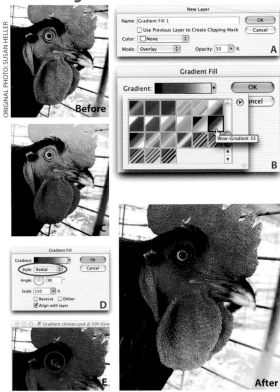

ORIGINAL PHOTO: SUSAN HELLER

Before

After

IN ANY OF THE GRADIENT-RELATED DIALOG BOXES, you can change a gradient's geometry, its orientation, and its scale. To demonstrate, start with a "black-and-white" image in RGB mode and add color by applying Wow-Gradient 33 in a Gradient Fill layer: Alt/Option-click the ⊘ button and choose Gradient; using the Alt/Option key opens the New Layer dialog box **A**, where you can set the Mode and Opacity for the new layer. Try Overlay for the Mode so the gradient will tint the image and increase contrast, and reduce the Opacity to 50% to set the intensity of the color; then click "OK."

In the Gradient Fill dialog, click the tiny triangle to the right of the gradient preview bar to open the palette of Gradient swatches **B**. Double-click the **Wow-Gradient 33** swatch — the first click chooses the gradient **C** and the second closes the palette. Change the Style to **Radial**, and "reach into" the working window for the image (your cursor will turn into the Move tool ▶⊕) and **drag the gradient** to center it on the eye **D**, **E**. This will leave the lower right corner of the image without color, but you can increase the **Scale** to spread the color.

 **Chicken Gradient.psd, Wow-Exercise.grd**

Changing the Color Transitions

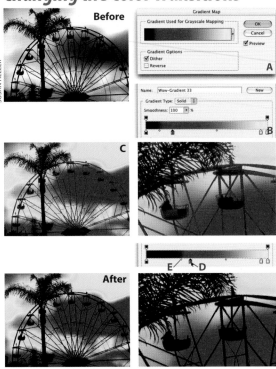

SUSAN HELLER

Before

After

A GRADIENT MAP, with a gradient whose colors progress from dark to light (such as **Wow-Gradient 32**, **33**, or **34**), can add color to your image and still maintain some of the photo's original tonality. Here we start with an image with very little color — though you can use a more colorful one if you like. Add a brilliant sunset: Click the "Create new fill or adjustment layer" button ⊘ at the bottom of the Layers palette and choose Gradient Map. In the Gradient Map dialog box **A** choose a gradient — open the palette and double-click the **Wow-Gradient 33** swatch (the same way as in the Gradient Fill dialog for the example at the left). Open the **Gradient Editor** by clicking the gradient preview bar in the Gradient Map dialog and inspect the Gradient Editor's expanded gradient preview bar **B**, **C**. To improve the silhouetting by taking the red "bloom" off the people and gondolas, "remap" the red so it doesn't tint the darker tones: Drag the **Color stop** for the red color to the right, farther from the black stop, just until the red-orange-yellow balance begins to change too much, and then drag the stop back slightly **D**. To shift more of the dark shades from red to black, without affecting the red-orange-yellow balance, drag the black-red midpoint diamond to the right **E**.

 **Sunset Gradient.psd, Wow-Exercise.grd**

Layering Gradient Overlays

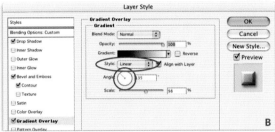

USED IN A LAYER STYLE AS A GRADIENT OVERLAY, a gradient can add surface color, or simply lighting. Here we've applied a Linear gradient to the layer that holds the front surface of a logo, and the same gradient, repositioned, to the black circle that makes the recessed areas. To see how the **Gradient Overlay** is set up, in the Layers palette double-click the Gradient Overlay entry in the Effects list under "The Best. . ." layer's thumbnail **A**. In the Gradient Overlay panel of the Layer Style dialog box, the "Black, White" gradient we used appears in the gradient preview bar **B**. As you can see, we used the **Linear** geometry. We dragged the **Angle** control to adjust the angle of the lighting, and then reached into the working window and dragged the gradient into position to light the surface.

In the Layers palette we copied the Gradient Overlay to the "Circle Base" layer. In Photoshop CS this can be done by dragging the Gradient Overlay entry in the Effects list for the "donor" layer ("The Best. . ." layer in this case) onto the thumbnail for the "recipient" layer (the "Circle Base" layer here). In CS2, you would Alt/Option-drag, since dragging alone would simply *move* the effect to the new layer rather than duplicating it. After copying the Gradient Overlay to "Circle Base," we opened the Layer Style dialog to the Gradient Overlay panel and dragged in the image to move the gradient up so a different part of it colored the "Circle Base," to complement the lighting of "The Best. . ." layer.

Logo Gradient.psd

Noise Gradients

TO ENHANCE A STREAKED METAL LOOK, we used **Noise gradients** in the Gradient Overlay effects applied to these two stars **A**. To see the first gradient, in the Layers palette double-click on Gradient Overlay in the list of Effects for the "small star" layer **B**. When the Layer Style dialog box opens to the Gradient Overlay panel, click on the gradient preview bar to open the Gradient Editor **C**. For a Noise gradient, the ranges you set by moving the sliders on the Color Model bars will determine the "outside" limits of the colors that *can* appear in the gradient, but the gradient will often include a much narrower range of colors. Working with the **HSB Color Model**, we moved the **Saturation** slider all the way to the left to remove all color to get a gradient of grays. With Saturation at 0, the **Hue** range is unimportant. We set a fairly broad **Brightness** range. Setting **Roughness** at 50% made streaks that are distinct but not too sharply defined. (A high Roughness setting makes a gradient with more and sharper color bands. At lower Roughness settings there are fewer bands and smoother transitions.) We also turned on the **Restrict Colors** option, so the gradient wouldn't include any colors too saturated to be printed with CMYK inks.

To see the Noise gradient for the large star, double-click its Gradient Overlay entry in the Layers palette as you did for the small star. This gradient uses exactly the same settings as the other one. But we made and saved a different gradient by clicking the **Randomize** button repeatedly until Photoshop generated the alternate version we wanted.

Star Gradients.psd

Shape Burst Gradients

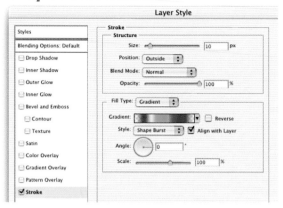

JHDAVIS

THE **STROKE**, one of the effects in Photoshop's Layer Styles, offers some exciting options — especially when you choose Gradient for the **Fill Type**. Like the Gradient found elsewhere in the program, this one offers the usual Linear, Radial, Angle, Reflected, and Diamond options. But it also offers **Shape Burst**. The Shape Burst is like a Radial gradient that conforms to the shape of the element instead of spreading out from a single center point. Here we've applied a **Shape Burst Gradient Stroke** effect using **Wow-Gradient 05**, with Position set to **Outside** for an inline/outline effect. You can find other examples of Shape Burst gradients in "'Outlining' with Neon" on page 455.

 Shape Burst Gradient.psd, Wow-Exercise.grd

"'Outlining' with Neon" on page 455.

SAMPLING FROM THE GRADIENT

When you **double-click a Color stop** in the Gradient Editor, you have the usual options for choosing a color — you can choose from the Color Picker or sample color by clicking in the Swatches palette or the working window for any open Photoshop file. Instead of double clicking, you can **single-click to sample from the gradient preview bar** itself. This makes it easy to repeat a color you've already used in the gradient.

GRADIENTS & TRANSPARENCY

You can build transparency into a gradient by using **Opacity stops** in the Gradient Editor.

Wow-Gradient 06 has transparency built-in with Opacity stops set in the Gradient Editor dialog box.

This built-in transparency is treated differently in the different methods of applying the gradient:

• For the **Gradient tool**, you can use the built-in transparency or not, simply by clicking the Transparency check box in the Options bar.

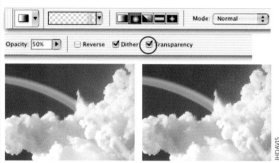

Here the **Wow-Gradient 06** rainbow gradient with transparency built-in is applied with the Gradient tool at 50% Opacity in Screen mode (set in the Options bar). For the example at the left, the Transparency option is turned on. With Transparency turned off (the example on right), the "outside" colors of the gradient extend to fill the transparent areas.

JHDAVIS

• The **Gradient Fill layer** and the **Gradient effects** that use gradients in a Layer Style have no transparency controls. Whatever transparency is built into the gradient is expressed.

• The **Gradient Map** ignores transparency, using only the information provided by the Color stops.

Wow-Gradient 06

NOISE GRADIENTS & TRANSPARENCY

To add transparency to a **Noise gradient**, you *can* introduce random variations in opacity with the **Add Transparency** check box in the lower right corner of the Gradient Editor dialog box. But if you've generated a Noise gradient that you like, random transparency will probably introduce more variability than you want to cope with. To control the transparency of your Noise gradient, it's often more effective to use a layer mask when you apply it.

Masked Gradients

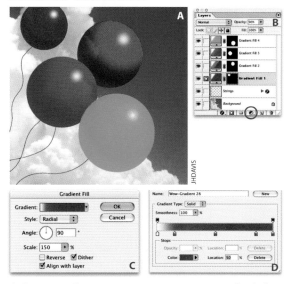

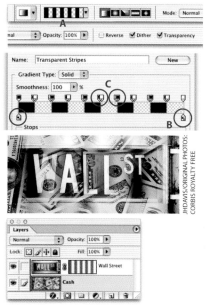

A GRADIENT FILL LAYER CAN INCLUDE A MASK that helps to shape the gradient. Our balloon image **A** includes a layer for each of the four balloons **B**. For each balloon layer we dragged with the Elliptical Marquee tool ◯ to set the size and shape of the balloon; then with the selection active, we clicked the "Create new fill or adjustment layer" button ◑ at the bottom of the Layers palette, and chose Gradient from the list. When the Gradient Fill dialog box opened **C**, we chose Radial for the gradient Style and chose a gradient by clicking the tiny triangle to open the palette of swatches and clicking on one of the **Wow-Gradients 27** through **31**. We positioned the highlight by dragging inside the working window. We experimented with the **Scale** setting to control the shading on the balloons, and then clicked "OK" to close the dialog box. To make the balloons translucent, we adjusted Opacity for each layer.

The Wow-Gradients used in this image are more complex than a simple white-to-color blend. You can see this by double-clicking on one of the Gradient Fill layer thumbnails, then clicking on the gradient preview bar in the Gradient Fill dialog box to open the Gradient Editor **D**. In order to make a sharp highlight for each gradient, the Color stops for the transition from white to a light version of the color are close together, to make this transition more abrupt than the other color changes. Also, a shadow tone is inserted near the right end of the gradient to create the rounding of the balloons.

 **Balloon Gradients.psd, Wow-Exercise.grd**

Gradient-Filled Masks

HERE WE USE A GRADIENT in a layer mask to combine two images. After dragging the "Wall Street" image into the "Cash" file, we clicked the "Add layer mask" button ▣ at the bottom of the Layers palette to add a "reveal all" mask. Then in the Tools palette we chose the Gradient tool ▬ and made sure black was the Foreground color (typing D or X accomplishes this). We clicked the little triangle next to the gradient preview bar in the Options bar, and chose Adobe's **Transparent Stripes** gradient. As you can see if you click the preview bar itself **A** to open the Gradient Editor, this gradient has only two Color stops **B**; the checkerboard pattern indicates that both stops use the current Foreground color. Above the gradient preview bar, pairs of full-opacity (100%) and full-transparency (0%) stops create the stripes **C**. The abrupt changes from Foreground to clear happen because the 100% stop for each side of each stripe is very close to the 0% stop for the clear space next to it.

When we dragged the cursor across the image, the black stripes were added to the mask. We chose Filter > Blur > Gaussian Blur (Radius 20) to blur the mask, softening the transitions. By then choosing Image > Adjustments > Brightness/Contrast, we could experiment with Brightness (to control the density of the mask overall) and Contrast (to control the sharpness of the transitions) while we watched the composite image change; we settled on Brightness 30 and Contrast –10.

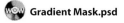 **Gradient Mask.psd**

Duotones

OPEN THESE PALETTES
from the Window menu:
- Layers · Channels

OVERVIEW
Convert a color file to Grayscale mode
and then to Duotone mode • Choose a
custom color to use with black for making
duotones • Adjust the Duotone curves
• Save the file

FOR MANY two-color design projects, the two inks are black and a custom color added for headings, rules, and other accents. With the second color available, Photoshop's Duotone mode can either add an obvious color accent to a photo or subtly but effectively extend the range of tones the printing press can produce. Here we start with a subtle use of the second color and move on to more colorful tints. For a project printed with CMYK process inks, as this book was, you may want to use Duotone mode to develop a tint, and then convert to CMYK for printing. For other approaches to tinting an image, see "Quick Tint Effects" (page 196) and " 'Styling' a Photo" (page 200).

1 Converting to Duotone mode. Photoshop's Duotone mode lets you control how each of your two ink colors is printed across the range of tones in your image. This is done through the curves for Ink 1 and Ink 2 in the Duotone Options dialog box. To set up your Duotone, if your image is in color **1a**, con-

PAUL DAYTON

1a The original color photo

1b

The photo is converted to Grayscale and a Curves Adjustment layer is added.

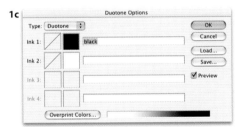

1c

Choosing Image > Mode > Duotone opens the Duotone Options box, where you can choose Duotone for a two-color treatment. Clicking the "Load" button lets you open preset Duotone curves. Alternatively, clicking the Ink 2 color square opens a dialog box where you can choose a color to build your own Duotone settings.

2a

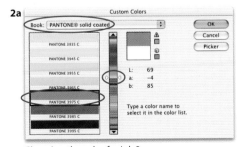

Choosing the color for Ink 2

vert it to Grayscale, ▼ because the only way to Duotone mode is through Grayscale; a Photoshop Duotone is actually a Grayscale image with special printing instructions stored with it. We converted the file by choosing Image > Mode > Grayscale and then added a Curves Adjustment layer and clicked the "Auto" button in the Curves dialog box to improve contrast **1b**.

Now convert your Grayscale file to Duotone mode (Image > Mode > Duotone). Duotone is a completely nondestructive coloring process. The pixels of the Grayscale image aren't changed when you adjust the ink curves. So you can fearlessly experiment with the settings to get the coloring you like. (If you were to open the Histogram, by choosing Window > Histogram, and watch it as you experimented with Duotone Options, you'd notice that although the on-screen preview of how the image will print might change dramatically as you worked, the Histogram itself wouldn't change.)

In the Duotone Options dialog box **1c**, choose Duotone from the Type menu. You can then set up your the curves for your two colors, as described in step 2 below, or click the "Load" button and choose one of the Duotone color sets that Adobe supplies in the Duotones folder inside Photoshop's Presets folder, or choose the **Wow Warming.ado** preset supplied for this technique.

2 Warming up the photo. To make your own set of Duotone curves as we did, leave Ink 1 set to black. When you click the color square for Ink 2, the Custom Colors dialog box will open. (If the Color Picker opens instead, click its "Custom"/"Color Libraries" button.) In the Custom Colors dialog box, choose a color system from the Book menu **2a**; we chose Pantone® Solid Coated (the default), then moved the slider on the vertical bar to a gold range and clicked on the Pantone 3975 C swatch, to warm the photo and extend the printable range of tones. Click "OK" to get back to the Duotone Options dialog box.

Once you've chosen the Ink colors, click the curve box to the left of one of the color squares in Duotone Options to open the Duotone Curve dialog. Clicking and dragging to change the curve will modify the color treatment, and you can watch the image change as you adjust the curves. The bar at the bottom of the Duotone Options dialog box shows how the ink colors will mix over the range of tones.

On the Duotone Curve, the horizontal axis represents the tones in the image, from highlights on the left to 100% shadows on the right. The vertical axis represents the

FIND OUT MORE

▼ Converting from color to grayscale
page 212

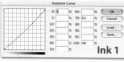

2b

With these settings, the gold tint barely shows in the image and in the Overprint preview bar at the bottom of the Duotone Options dialog box.

3a

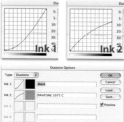

Lowering the black curve and raising the curve for Ink 2 makes the color more obvious in the image and in the Overprint preview bar at the bottom of the Duotone Options box.

tint of ink, from none at the bottom to 100% coverage at the top. So a point on the graph determines what tint of the ink will be printed for any particular tone. You control the tinting either by clicking on the curve to make a new point (the point will always snap to a vertical line) or by typing the tint you want into any of the 13 fields for tone percentage.

For a subtle use of color to expand the number of tones available for midtones and shadows, we set the curve to add Ink 2 slowly, building to only 10% coverage in the light midtones and then to 60% coverage in the darkest shadows. We reduced the amount of black (Ink 1) in the midtones just slightly by changing the 70% value to 65%. Click "OK" to return to Duotone Options **2b**. (If you want to save Duotone Options settings as a preset so you can load them again later, click the "Save" button. And if you close the Duotone Options dialog box, you can reopen it at any time by again choosing Image > Mode > Duotone.)

3 Adding a tint. Now modify the curves to try a setting that allows Ink 2 to come through as a distinct tint. Or load the **Wow Gold Tint.ado** settings; here the contribution of the black ink is reduced, especially in the highlights and light midtones by pulling the curve down to a 5% tint at the 20% point in the tonal range. Reducing the black in this way allows more of the gold to show when we increase the contribution of the Pantone 3975 by pulling the middle of the curve up. You can now see the gold in the image and also in the color bar at the bottom of the Duotone Options box **3a**.

To produce a surrealistic tinted look, try an oscillating curve for Ink 2. Here we modified the Ink 1 curve to remove black from the highlights, and we drew the Ink 2 curve to add gold in the lightest tones and in various other parts of the tonal range **3b**.

To try a different tint, click the Ink 2 color square and choose another color **3c**. If you know the number of the Pantone color you want to try, you can just quickly type the number to bring up the swatch; we chose Pantone 368 C.

Preparing to print. To convert the Duotone for printing in process inks, as we did for these pages, choose Image > Mode > CMYK Color. If the image will be used in a page layout file, save the CMYK file in a compatible format, such as TIFF (File > Save As).

If your Duotone will be printed with a custom color, two important things to discuss with your printer are which plate

3b

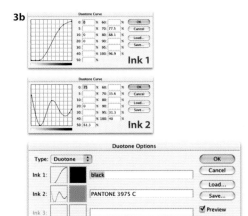

These Ink curves produce the effect in the image at the top of page 192. Set them up "by hand" or click the "Load" button in the Duotone Options box and choose **Wow Duotone FX.ado**.

3c

Once a custom color has been chosen, clicking its color square in the Duotone Options dialog box opens the Custom Colors box directly. The Ink 2 color is changed to Pantone 368 C by typing 368 quickly. (If you hesitate, the Custom Colors box thinks you've started over.)

(black or color) will be printed first and whether you or the prepress operator will take responsibility for setting the screen angles. Often the color ink is printed first, to keep it from interfering with the black where the halftone dots overlap, regardless of how opaque the color ink is. Generally, pastel colors (which contain opaque white), dark shades (which contain black) and metallics are more opaque. For screen angles, consult your prepress operator or refer to Adobe's suggestions in the "Printing duotones" and "Selecting halftone screen attributes" sections of Photoshop Help from the Help menu.

If your Duotone file will be placed in a page layout program for two-color printing, when you save the Duotone (File > Save As), Adobe recommends using Photoshop EPS or Photoshop PDF format. (If you add a spot color channel to your Duotone, however, Adobe recommends converting the file to Multichannel mode and saving in Photoshop DCS 2.0 format.)

VIEWING THE PLATES OF A DUOTONE

In Duotone mode you can't see the individual color plates that will be used for printing. But you *can* look at them if you follow these steps: Open the Channels palette (Window > Channels). If you want to see the plates in color, choose Preferences > Display & Cursors > Color Channels In Color (from the Edit menu in Windows or the Photoshop menu on the Mac). Then choose Image > Mode > Multichannel. View each channel alone by clicking to toggle off and on the 👁 icons to the left of the thumbnails in the Channels palette. You can even view both plates side-by-side by opening a second view of the image (Window > Arrange > New Window for. . .) and turning on the 👁 for a different channel in each window.

Whether you're viewing in one window or two, don't try to edit the file in Multichannel mode; you won't be able to get back to Duotone mode with the edits intact. After you've looked at the plates, Undo (Ctrl/⌘-Z) or use Edit > Step Backward to go back to Duotone mode.

Multichannel mode has a channel for each color.

Viewing the black plate in Multichannel mode

Viewing the color plate in Multichannel mode

"Styling" a Photo

YOU'LL FIND THE FILES

in > Wow Project Files > Chapter 4 > Styling a Photo:
- Styling-Before.psd (to start)
- Styling-After.psd (to compare)
- Wow-Canvas Background.pat (a Pattern preset)

OPEN THESE PALETTES

from the Window menu:
- Tools • Layers

OVERVIEW

Convert the *Background* to a standard layer • Build a custom sepiatone Layer Style • Expand the canvas so the Drop Shadow will show • Experiment with changes to make a custom cyanotype • Trim away extra white space at the edges

JHDAVIS

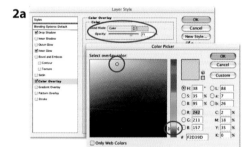

Start with an image in RGB Color mode, with the *Background* converted to a regular layer.

Clicking the 🅕 at the bottom of the Layers palette and choosing Color Overlay opens the Layer Style dialog box, where you can click the swatch to open the Color Picker. Because the Color Overlay will be in the Color blend mode, the luminosity of the color (how high up the color square you click) is not important.

AN EASY AND FLEXIBLE WAY TO TINT AN IMAGE is to use the Color Overlay component of a Layer Style. By using Color Overlay, you can get a traditional sepiatone or cyanotype look — or develop a Style that allows some of the original color to come through, as shown above. Because the tint is stored in a Style, you can incorporate other effects (such as a glow, a border, a drop shadow, or even a textured finish), creating a combination that you can then instantly apply to other photos.

1 Preparing the photo. Whether you start with a black-and-white or a color image, your file will need the *potential* for color so you can add the tint. If your file is in Grayscale mode, convert it to color (Image > Mode > RGB Color).

A *Background* can't accept a Layer Style. So if the Layers palette shows that your image consists of a *Background*, turn it into a regular layer by simply Alt/Option-double-clicking on the *Background* name **1**.

2 Adding a tint. At the bottom of the Layers palette, click the "Add a layer style" button 🅕 and choose **Color Overlay** from its menu. When the Layer Style dialog box opens to the Color Overlay panel, set the Blend Mode to **Color**. With this setting, the Style you create will control the color of the photo, but without covering up the light-and-dark picture information. Click the color swatch in the Color Overlay section to open the Color Picker. Use the vertical spectrum slider to choose a color family (orange is good if a sepiatone is your goal), and then click in the large color square to choose a color **2a**. Click "OK" to close the Color Picker **2b**, but keep the Layer Style box open.

2b

The image with a sepia Color Overlay effect at 100% Opacity

3

The Opacity of the Color Overlay effect is reduced to 60% in the Color Overlay section of the Layer Style dialog box.

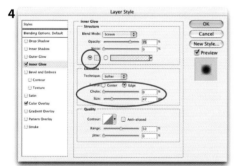

4

The light edge is made with an Inner Glow. In Screen mode, light colors have a stronger lightening effect. A Choke setting of 0% makes a soft glow.

3 Restoring some of the original color. You can reduce the brown tint effect by lowering the **Opacity** in the Color Overlay section of the Layer Style dialog. If you started with a color image, this will allow some of the original color to show **3**.

4 Adding an edge effect. While you're in the Layer Style dialog box, you can add a soft edge or a drop shadow to your sepia-tone. In the list of effects on the left side of the box, click **Inner Glow** (the name, not the check box) to open that panel. Click the color swatch and choose a pale brown. For our other Inner Glow parameters, we used the settings shown in figure **4**. The **Size** setting determines how far the glow extends inward from the edge. A low **Choke** setting makes a glow that softly fades; a higher Choke setting makes a denser, more "solid" edge.

5 Adding a drop shadow. To add a shadow that extends outward from the edge of the image, click on **Drop Shadow** in the list of effects; for starters try the default Multiply and 75% Opacity, a Size of 17 pixels, and a Distance of 0 pixels **5a**.

You'll see a small thumbnail preview of the shadow in the Layer Style dialog box, but don't expect to see the shadow in your image. Since a Drop Shadow extends outward from the edge of the layer, the shadow won't show up in your image unless you enlarge the image Canvas to make space for it. Here's how you can make some room: First click "OK" to close the Layer Style dialog. Then choose Image > Canvas Size. Click the Relative box and change the units for either Width or Height to percentage (the other will change to match). Then type in the percentages you want to add to Width and to Height; we used 10% for both, which we estimated would be more than enough room to accommodate the drop shadow. (Don't worry about expanding the Canvas too much, because you can easily trim off the excess; step 7 tells how.) Click "OK" to close the Canvas Size dialog box **5b**.

5a

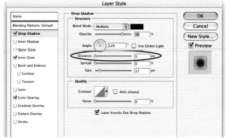

The Distance setting controls the Drop Shadow's offset. The direction of the offset is controlled by the Angle setting. But regardless of the Angle, a Distance of 0 makes the shadow extend evenly around the edge.

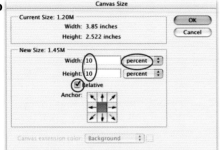

5b

Expanding the canvas with the Image > Canvas Size command, to allow room for the Drop Shadow to show. The default Anchor setting — expansion from the center — puts equal space (5% of the Height) on top and bottom and on the left and right (5% of the Width). Options for choosing a Canvas extension color are grayed out (unavailable) when you add Canvas to a file that has no *Background* layer.

5c

The Layers palette shows the "styled" photo and the white-filled backing layer.

6a

For a cyanotype effect, in the Color Overlay section we chose a blue color and increased Opacity to 90%. We also changed the color for the Inner Glow and increased its Size to 86 pixels.

Adding a layer of white below the image will give you a better look at the shadow: At the bottom of the Layers palette, Ctrl/⌘-click the "Create a new layer" button ⬓ (adding the Ctrl/⌘ key puts the new layer *below* the current one). Then fill the new layer with white (Edit > Fill > White is one way to do it) **5c**. Our result is shown at the top of page 196.

Once you develop a Layer Style, you can add it to the Styles palette so it's easy to apply it to other photos, and you can save it permanently with the Preset Manager.▼

6 Trying other options. To experiment, duplicate the "styled" layer by clicking its thumbnail in the Layers palette and typing Ctrl/⌘-J; then click the ☻ for the old layer (otherwise you'll see a double-intensity drop shadow). In the list of effects under your new layer, double-click the Drop Shadow, Inner Glow, or Color Overlay listing to open the Layer Style dialog to the panel where you can adjust the settings for this effect. Try developing a modified cyanotype look, for instance, by choosing a blue color for the **Color Overlay** and increasing the Opacity to 90%. Try also changing the color for the **Inner Glow** to a light blue and increasing its Size (we used 86 pixels) **6a**.

We didn't change the Drop Shadow setting. But if you wanted to increase the Size, you might need to enlarge the canvas more to accommodate it.

While the Layer Style dialog box is open, try adding a surface finish to the photo: Click **Pattern Overlay** in the list of effects on the left side of the box to open the Pattern Overlay panel. Click the tiny arrow to the right of the Pattern swatch to open the Patterns palette; then click the ⊙ button to open the palette's menu **6b**. If you've installed the Wow Patterns presets,▼ you'll see the **Wow-Media Patterns** listed as a choice; click on it. In the warning box that appears, click "Append" to add these patterns at the bottom of the palette or "OK" to replace the current patterns with the Wow-Media presets, and then click the **Wow-Canvas Background** thumbnail. On the other hand, if you don't see Wow-Media Patterns in the menu, you can choose Load Patterns from the menu and navigate to the **Wow-Canvas Background.pat** file supplied with the files for this section, load it, and click its thumbnail.

You can regulate the effect of the pattern by changing the Opacity, Scale, or Blend Mode. We changed the Blend Mode to Multiply **6c**. You can toggle an effect off and on

FIND OUT MORE
▼ Saving Layer Styles
page 47
▼ Installing Wow
presets **page 5**

6b

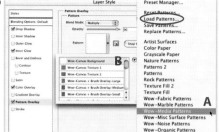

If you've already installed the Wow Patterns presets, choose Wow-Media Patterns **A** and then click on Wow-Canvas Background **B**. Alternatively, you can choose Load Patterns and load **Wow-Canvas Background.pat**, a presets file that contains a single pattern.

6c

A Pattern Overlay effect can be used to simulate a subtle texture on the surface of the print (bottom).

by clicking the check mark next to its name in the Layer Style dialog box or by clicking the 👁 column to the left of its name in the Layers palette.

7 Trimming the edges. Trimming off extra white space at the edges of an image can make it easier to work with if you plan to place it in a page layout, for instance. To remove the extra space from this image, choose Image > Trim. In the Trim dialog box, for the "Based On" option choose Top Left Pixel Color (you could also use Bottom Right Pixel Color in this case). Make sure all four "Trim Away" options are turned on. Then click "OK" **7**. All pure white around the edges will be trimmed away, but none of the shadow will be clipped, because the shadow is different than pure white and the Trim function will stop as soon as it encounters it. This ensures that you won't get an unnatural-looking flat edge on the shadow.

Other effects for photos. For other tinting techniques, see "Quick Tint Effects" on page 200. For more edge treatments, see "Framing with Masks" on page 260 and "Filtered Frames" on page 264. Appendix B shows printed examples of the tints, edges, frames, and other Wow Styles designed especially for photos; these are provided on the Wow DVD-ROM. *Wow!*

7

The Image > Trim command provides a safe way to trim away extra space at the edges of an image without clipping a soft-edged effect such as a drop shadow or glow. ***Note:*** If you set up the Trim dialog box and click "OK" and nothing is trimmed away, it could mean that your drop shadow extends to or beyond the edge of the image. To avoid a sharp edge on the shadow, add more Canvas (as in step 5b) and choose Image > Trim again.

Tint Effects

"Hand-Tinting a Black & White Photo" on page 338 takes you step-by-step through a process that imitates traditional photo-tinting with brushes and inks. But when you don't need a hand-painted look for your tinting, the simpler techniques shown on the next 10 pages can produce great results quickly. Some start with a color image, while others start with a "black-and-white." But in order to color a black-and-white, the file has to be in a color mode. Most of the techniques use RGB Color, although one (on page 209) relies on working in the color channels of a CMYK or Spot Color file.

To convert a Grayscale image to color so you can add a tint, choose Image > Mode > RGB Color.

Many tinting techniques start with clicking the "Create new fill or adjustment layer" button ⊘.

For a tinting treatment that includes custom edges, a drop shadow, or even a surface texture, see "Styling a Photo" on page 196 and check out the Wow Styles for photos, provided on the Wow DVD-ROM and shown in Appendix B.

YOU'LL FIND FILES FOR MOST OF THESE EFFECTS
in ⊚ > Chapter 4 > Quick Tint Effects

OPEN THESE PALETTES
from the Window menu:
• Tools • Layers

TINTING A SERIES

Once you've used an Adjustment layer to achieve a tint effect you like for one image, you can apply the same effect to a whole series by dragging and dropping your Adjustment layer from the Layers palette to the working window of other open images.

Tinting with a Solid Color Fill Layer

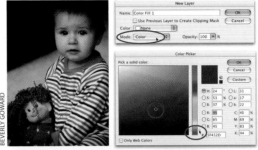

A SOLID COLOR FILL LAYER gives you several tinting options. To start, hold down the Alt/Option key as you click the "Create new fill or adjustment layer" button ⊘ at the bottom of the Layers palette and choose Solid Color from the top of its menu. In the New Layer dialog box, which opens because you used the Alt/Option key, choose Color for the Mode (in the default Normal mode, the Solid Color would simply cover up the image); click "OK." When the Color Picker opens, watch the tint effect in your image as you experiment by moving the slider up or down the spectrum bar to pick a hue and then clicking in the large color square; click "OK" to close the Color Picker.

In the Layers palette you can vary the tint effect by choosing a different blend mode from the menu near the upper left corner of the palette. While Color mode tints all the colors or tones in the photo except pure black and white, Hue mode leaves neutrals (black, white, *and grays*) untinted. (A layer in Hue mode will have no effect on a black-and-white photo.)

⊚ **Solid Color Fill.psd**

Colorizing with Hue/Saturation

A HUE/SATURATION ADJUSTMENT LAYER produces a tint effect that's a little different than a Solid Color Fill layer. To add the tinting layer, click the "Create new fill or adjustment layer" button ◖ at the bottom of the Layers palette and choose Hue/Saturation from its menu. In the Hue/Saturation dialog box, first click the Colorize check box. Black and white will remain black and white, but colors and grays will be tinted. Experiment by moving the Hue and Saturation sliders until you like the color and intensity of the tint; click "OK" to close the dialog box. For the sake of comparison, we used the same Hue here (a value of 24 in the Hue field) as we did for "Tinting with a Solid Color Fill Layer" on the facing page.

TAKE THE PHOTO IN COLOR

Many digital cameras offer a Sepia setting that records the image in sepiatone rather than full color. With the variety of tinting methods available in Photoshop, it makes sense to keep your options open by shooting in full color and then converting to sepiatone using a Solid Color Fill, Hue/Saturation, or Photo Filter layer.

Protecting with a Layer Mask

Colorized · Masked

A · **B**

Colorized · Masked

A · **B**

CHRISTINE ZALEWSKI

ADJUSTMENT LAYERS, such as the Hue/Saturation layers Christine Zalewski used to create two very different backgrounds for this image, have built-in layer masks that can be used to protect parts of the image from change. Zalewski added an Adjustment layer (by clicking the "Create new fill or adjustment layer" button ◖ at the bottom of the palette and choosing from its menu). In the dialog box she made the color changes she wanted **A**, and then clicked "OK" to close the box. To protect the flower from the color change, she painted the Hue/Saturation layer's mask with a soft Brush ✐ and black paint **B**. The edges and some internal areas of Zalewski's masks are soft enough so the flower picks up a little of the background tint, to make it "at home" in its changed surroundings.

Partial Desaturation

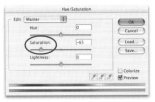

Before

After

SOMETIMES JUST "TURNING DOWN" THE COLOR in a photo, without actually colorizing it, can produce the "tinted black-and-white" look you want. For this image toning down the bright colors "antiques" the image a bit and also makes the related shapes and curves more apparent. To partially desaturate this image, add a Hue/Saturation Adjustment layer by clicking the "Create a new fill or adjustment layer" button ⬤ at the bottom of the Layers palette, choosing Hue/Saturation from its menu, and partially desaturating the image by moving the Saturation slider to the left, as shown above. The Colorize box is left unchecked.

 **Partial Desaturation.psd**

Changing the Tint

Recolored

WITH A HUE/SATURATION LAYER in place, either for colorizing or for partially desaturating an image, you can experiment further with the color. Start with the tint effect from "Partial Desaturation" at the left. In the Layers palette double-click the thumbnail for the Hue/Saturation layer to reopen the Hue/Saturation dialog box. Then move the Hue slider, changing the tint to recolor the image.

"TITRATING" THE COLOR

With an Adjustment layer you can tweak the color even after clicking "OK" to close the dialog box. Simply use the Opacity slider for the layer to restore some of the "pre-adjustment" color.

Channel Mixer at Partial Strength

WHEN WE USED A PARTIAL DESATURATION as shown on page 202 to "tint" this photo of dolls in a shop window **A**, we got a somewhat "muddy" result **B**. For better control of the conversion, we changed the Hue/Saturation layer to a Channel Mixer layer by choosing Layer > Change Layer Content > Channel Mixer layer. (Using this menu command was simply quicker than deleting the Hue/Saturation layer and then adding a Channel Mixer layer.)

In the Channel Mixer dialog, we found that clicking the check box to turn on Monochrome and using the default 100% Red channel gave us a brighter image. But we got a better result when we dragged the Green slider to the right to add some of the Green channel to bring out details in the faces and then dragged the Blue slider to the left to take away some of the extra brightness this caused **C**. ▼ After clicking "OK" to close the Channel Mixer, we reduced this layer's Opacity to 80% **D** to accomplish the tinting by letting some of the original color show through **E**.

FIND OUT MORE

▼ Using a Monochrome Channel Mixer **page 213**

Differential Tinting

IF YOU'D LIKE SOME PARTS of your image to be tinted more intensely than others, you can use an Adjustment layer's built-in mask to restore some of the color. Starting with the tinted image at the left, target the Channel Mixer layer by clicking its thumbnail in the Layers palette. Then choose the Brush tool ✎ and also choose black for the Foreground color (by tapping the X key once or twice, until the Foreground color swatch in the Tools palette is black). In the Options bar choose a soft brush tip and set the Opacity low **A**; we used one of Photoshop's default brushes (Airbrush Soft Round 100). Then paint loosely over the doll in the middle. This darkens the mask in this area **B**, protecting this part of the image from the Channel Mixer's effect, to restore even more of the doll's color than the layer's reduced Opacity has done.

 **Channel Mixer Tint.psd**

Tinting with a Photo Filter

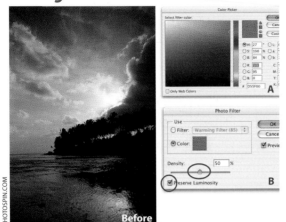

Before

Tinted

PHOTOSHOP'S PHOTO FILTER Adjustment layers simulate the effect of taking a photo with the equivalent traditional color filter mounted on the camera lens. To add a Photo Filter, click the "Create new fill or adjustment layer" button ⬤ at the bottom of the Layers palette and choose Photo Filter. In the Photo Filter dialog box both options — Filter and Color — apply color in exactly the same way. The difference between the two options is that Filter offers a menu of the traditional color filters used on camera lenses, while Color opens the Color Picker so you can choose your own tint. For the tint shown here, choose Color and pick a red-orange from the Color Picker **A**. Increase the Density to 50% for a stronger tint than you would get with the traditional 25% **B**, leave Preserve Luminosity turned on (so the filter won't darken the image), and click "OK" to close the dialog box.

 **Photo Filter Tint.psd**

Combining Photo Filters

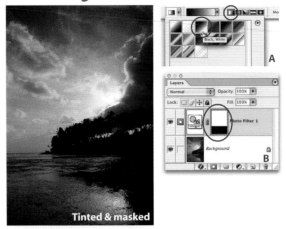

Tinted & masked

"Double-tinted"

YOU CAN COMBINE PHOTO FILTER LAYERS to get the effect of a dual filter, or two graduated filters mounted together on the camera lens. Starting with the tinted image file from "Tinting with a Photo Filter" at the left, use the Photo Filter's built-in layer mask to limit the color to the sky: Choose the Gradient tool ▭. In the Options bar click the tiny arrow to the right of the gradient swatch; from the palette that opens, choose the "Black, White" gradient and make sure the Linear Gradient style is chosen **A**. Now move the cursor just below the horizon in the image, hold down the Shift key, and drag upward a very short distance across the horizon. This will create a mask that's white on top and black on the bottom, allowing the orange tint to show only at the top **B**. To add the second tint, duplicate the Photo Filter layer (Ctrl/⌘-J), invert the mask (Ctrl/⌘-I) **C**, and double-click the new layer's Photo Filter thumbnail to open the Photo Filter dialog; click the color swatch and choose a purple.

 Photo Filters Combined.psd

Using Three Photo Filters

"Triple-tinted"

WANT TO TRY A THIRD FILTER? To add a glow centered at the level of the sun, start with the dual-tinted image file from "Combining Photo Filters" on the previous page. Duplicate your second Photo Filter layer (Ctrl/⌘-J). Then change the layer mask on this new layer: In the Gradient tool's Options bar, with the "Black, White" gradient still chosen, click the "Reflected Gradient" button for the gradient style **A**; also click the Reverse box so the gradient you're about to draw will go from white to black. Hold down the Shift key again and drag upward from just below the level of the sun in the image to the point where you want the red-orange sky tint you applied earlier to be at full strength. With the new mask now in place **B**, double-click the Photo Filter thumbnail and choose the color and density for this third tint; we clicked the Filter button and chose Deep Yellow from the list, leaving the density at 50%.

With three tinting filters in place, you now have all kinds of options if you want to experiment further:

• You can double-click the thumbnail for any one of them and change its color or density.

• You can also control color density with the Opacity slider for any of the Photo Filter layers.

• You can redirect a tint by painting the Photo Filter's layer mask with the Brush tool ✏ and a soft brush tip. Or redraw its gradient with the Gradient tool ▨. Or stretch its mask: Click the 🔗 to its left so you can transform it independently of the image. Then type Ctrl/⌘-T and drag a top or bottom handle up or down beyond the top or bottom edge of the image. Double-click inside the box to complete the transformation.

3 Photo Filters Combined.psd

Tinting with Camera Raw

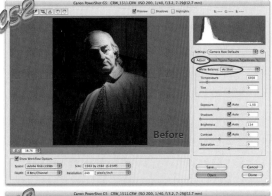

Before

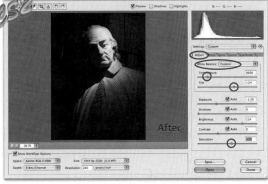

After

FOR DIGITAL PHOTOS CAPTURED in a camera's Raw format, you can do your tinting in Camera Raw. In either CS or CS2 (shown here), choose File > Open or double-click the image thumbnail in File Browser or Bridge to open the file in the Camera Raw interface. Tinting can be done in the Adjust panel. You may want to do other corrections to the file at the same time. ▼ To tint, you can change the Temperature to warm or cool the image. Then use the Tint slider to arrive at the hue you want and the Saturation slider to control color intensity. For more control over the tint, use the sliders in the Calibrate panel; we reduced the Blue Saturation to neutralize blue in the background.

One way to save the tint settings with the file is to click the palette menu button ⊙ near the top right corner of the Camera Raw interface, choose Save Settings, rename the settings if you like, navigate to where the Raw image file is stored, and click the "Save" button. These settings can now be restored anytime you reopen the Raw file, or even applied to other Raw files: Simply click the ⊙ button, choose Load Settings, navigate to the saved .xmp file and load it, and choose Custom for the White Balance.

> **FIND OUT MORE**
> ▼ Using Camera Raw
> **page 102**

Tinting Raw.CRW

Channel Mixer Pastels

Before — **A**

100% Opacity — **B**

50% Opacity — **C**

PHOTOS: PHOTOSPIN.COM

BESIDES BEING USED TO CONVERT a color image to black-and-white, Photoshop's Channel Mixer can generate some interesting color tint effects. Open an RGB image and add a Channel Mixer Adjustment layer by clicking the ⬤ button at the bottom of the Layers palette and choosing Channel Mixer from its menu.

In the Channel Mixer dialog, click the "Load" button and find and load the **RGB Pastels.cha** preset (it's on a CD-ROM that comes with the Adobe Photoshop application, in Goodies > Photoshop CS or CS2 > Channel Mixer Presets > Special Effects). Looking at the sliders in the Channel Mixer dialog box **A**, notice that the Red channel now includes all the brightness information it originally contained (Red 100%) plus the brightness information from the Green channel at half strength (Green 50%) and the brightness information from the Blue channel at 31% strength (Blue 31%). If you choose Green and then Blue from the Output Channel menu at the top of the Channel Mixer box, you'll see that the brightness values in these channels are similarly boosted. The overall effect is to lighten all the colors, producing pastels. The Constant is set at −11% to counteract some of the lightening by slightly darkening the image overall.

Experiment with the Channel Mixer layer's Opacity **B**, **C** to get the effect you want.

 **Channel Mixer Pastels.psd**

Other Channel Mixer Tints

Special Effects: RGB
Blacklight.cha

Special Effects: RGB Burnt
Foliage.cha

Special Effects: RGB Easter
colors.cha

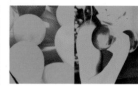
Special Effects: RGB Holiday
Wrap.cha

Special Effects: RGB Over
Saturate.cha

Special Effects: Yellows&Blues
(RGB or CMYK).cha

Special Effects: Sepiatone
subtle color.cha

Special Effects: Sepiatone
subtle color2.cha

Special Effects: Sepiatone
subtle color3.cha

Grayscale: Grayscale
Yellows.cha

SHOWN ABOVE are some more of the Channel Mixer presets that Adobe provides in the Goodies folder that comes with Photoshop. Like any other Adjustment layers, they can be applied at reduced Opacity, as shown for **RGB Pastels.cha** at the left, or masked to direct the tinting, using the technique described in "Differential Tinting" on page 203.

Tinting with Color Balance

Before

After

A

B

A COLOR BALANCE ADJUSTMENT LAYER can tint a black-and-white photo by pushing the highlights in one color direction and the shadows in another. To tint this photo in RGB Color mode, Katrin Eismann used a Color Balance Adjustment layer as follows: She clicked the "Create new fill or adjustment layer" button ⬤ at the bottom of the Layers palette and chose Color Balance from its menu. In the Color Balance dialog box, she left the Midtones as they were, with no adjustment. She clicked the button for the Shadows and adjusted the sliders to add Cyan and Blue, for a blue-green tint **A**. For the Highlights she added Red and Yellow for an orange tint **B**.

MERGE BEFORE CONVERTING

An Adjustment layer can have different effects in an RGB file, where color is based on colors of light, than it does in a CMYK file, where color is based on inks. To keep your color adjustments from changing when you convert an RGB file to CMYK, make a copy that merges any Adjustment layers with the image (Image > Duplicate > Duplicate Merged Layers Only) and then convert this copy to CMYK.

Merged before converting

Converted without merging

Changing the Color Balance

IN A COLOR BALANCE ADJUSTMENT, the ranges for Highlights, Midtones, and Shadows overlap, so changing any or all of these three ranges won't produce abrupt color breaks. Christine Zalewski sometimes uses a Color Balance Adjustment layer to generate several different color editions of her *Botanical Portraits*, shown on pages 236 and 354. In this image **A** the "dark" tones of the background are actually midtones, as the Histogram shows (Window > Histogram) **B**. To change the background color, Zalewski clicked the "Create new fill or adjustment layer" button ⬤ at the bottom of the Layers palette and chose Color Balance from its menu **C**. In the Color Balance dialog box, she adjusted the Midtones sliders to add blue-green and thus neutralize the rosy background **D**. Much smaller adjustments (also toward blue-green) were made to the Highlights, where most of the flower's colors are found, and to the few pixels in the Shadows. In another version of the image, Zalewski used a stronger Midtones adjustment to push the background toward purple **E**.

Overlaying a Gradient Fill Layer

Before

After

A

B

C

A COLOR GRADIENT can add dramatic or subtle tinting. To add color to an image by applying a Gradient Fill layer, click the "Create new fill or adjustment layer" button ◔ at the bottom of the Layers palette and choose Gradient from the top section of its menu. In the Gradient Fill dialog box, click the tiny arrow to the right of the gradient swatch and choose a gradient **A**; we double-clicked Adobe's **Blue, Yellow, Blue** gradient swatch and used the default Angle (90° vertical) and default gradient Style (Linear). The gradient will completely cover up the image, but you can fix that next with the blend mode controls for the layer, so you can go ahead and click "OK" to close the Gradient Fill dialog.

In the Layers palette **B** experiment with the Opacity of the Gradient layer and try various blend modes from the menu in the upper left corner; we found that the Overlay mode and 50% Opacity seemed to bring out the cyclist best, both tinting the image and improving contrast. But we wanted to make some adjustments to the gradient.

To adjust the gradient in a Gradient Fill layer, in the Layers palette double-click the layer's thumbnail for the layer to reopen the Gradient Fill dialog box. There you can scale the gradient; we set Scale to 115%, effectively enlarging the yellow section. With the dialog box open, you can also adjust the gradient's position by "reaching into" the working window and dragging; we dragged the gradient up a little.

 **Gradient Fill Layer.psd**

Using a Gradient Map Layer

Before

Normal mode

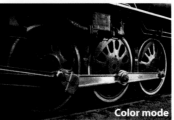

Color mode

A GRADIENT MAP ADJUSTMENT LAYER lets you recolor an image by "remapping" the brightness values to the colors of a gradient of your choice. If you use a gradient that goes from a dark color on the left through a bright color to a light color on the right, you can roughly maintain the lights and darks of your image as you add the color, especially if you put the Gradient Map layer in Color mode, which changes the color but lets the original tonal values of the image come through.

To add a Gradient Map layer that doesn't cover up the image, Alt/Option-click the "Create new fill or adjustment layer" button ◔ at the bottom of the Layers palette and choose Gradient Map from its menu. Because you used the Alt/Option key, the New Layer dialog box will open, where you can choose Color for the Mode and then click "OK" to open the Gradient Map dialog box.

In the Gradient Map dialog, click the tiny triangle to the right of the gradient swatch and choose a gradient (to use a Wow Gradient▼ we clicked the ⊙ button to open the menu of Gradient presets and chose Wow Gradients; then we clicked the swatch for **Wow-Gradient 33**). Click "OK" to close the box.

FIND OUT MORE

▼ Installing the Wow Gradients
page 5

 **Gradient Map.psd**

Tinting a "Photo Graphic"

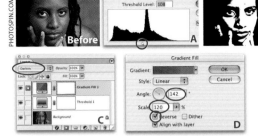

THIS TINTING TECHNIQUE starts with reducing a photo to black and white pixels only — no color and no grays. To do that, add a Threshold Adjustment layer by clicking the "Create new fill or adjustment layer" button ⬤ at the bottom of the Layers palette and choosing from its menu. In the Threshold dialog box move the slider to balance the black and white to taste **A**, **B**.

Next add a Gradient Fill layer in a way that will let you color the white areas while leaving the black intact: Alt/Option-click the ⬤ button and choose Gradient for the type of layer. When the New Layer dialog box opens, choose Darken for the Mode and click "OK" **C**. (Or choose Lighten instead of Darken to tint the black instead of the white.)

When the Gradient Fill dialog box opens, click the tiny downward arrow to the right of the Gradient swatch and choose a gradient (to use a Wow Gradient, we clicked the ⊙ button to open the palette menu, chose Wow-Gradients, and then double-clicked on **Wow-Gradient 15**).▼ In the Gradient Fill dialog box, experiment with the Angle, the Scale, and the Reverse option. We settled on 142° for the Angle and 120% for the Scale, with Reverse turned on **D**; with the Gradient Fill dialog box open we dragged in the working window to reposition the gradient and clicked "OK" to close the dialog box.

FIND OUT MORE

▼ Installing the Wow Gradients
page 5

 Photo Graphic.psd

"Painting" in the Ink Channels

IN CMYK COLOR MODE (and Spot Color also) the thumbnails in the Channels palette represent ink colors; the black shows where each ink will print, and white represents the absence of ink. A quick tinting technique involves painting loosely with black in the individual channels to apply tints of the ink colors. Here we started with a "black-and-white" in RGB color mode and converted the file to CMYK (Image > Mode > CMYK Color).

The first step is to duplicate the image to a new layer (Ctrl/⌘-J) so you can tint a copy and still protect the original **A**. Then choose the Brush tool 🖌 and in the Options bar choose a large soft brush tip and lower the Opacity of the paint to less than 10%. In the Channels palette (Window > Channels) target one of the color channels (we clicked the thumbnail for the Yellow channel) **B**. So you'll be able to see the color developing as you work, click in the 👁 column for the composite CMYK at the top of the palette. With black as the Foreground color (tapping the X key once or twice will make it so), paint quick strokes on the face, hair, and background.

Then paint the other channels. We targeted the Magenta channel (Ctrl/⌘-2), reduced the Brush tool's Opacity even more in the Options bar (because magenta is a stronger color), and again painted with black; we chose a smaller brush tip for the lips. For the Cyan channel (Ctrl/⌘-1), we used the small brush tip and increased Opacity to paint the eyes, then went back to a larger brush and lower Opacity for the hair and background.

 Painting Channels.psd

Patch Tool Tinting

Before

After

WE STUMBLED UPON THIS TINTING approach while experimenting with the Patch tool ⬦. For a "black-and-white" image in RGB Color mode, it produces a subtle glow at high-contrast edges.

First use the entire image to make a pattern by choosing Edit > Define Pattern **A**. Then add a new layer (Ctrl/⌘-Shift-N, or click the 🗔 button at the bottom of the Layers palette). Fill the new layer with the color you want for the tint. (One way to choose the color is to choose Edit > Fill > Color and choose from the Color Picker.)

Next choose the Patch tool ⬦. The Patch requires an active selection, but the selection doesn't have to be made with the tool itself, so simply select all (Ctrl/⌘-A). In the Patch tool's Options bar click the Pattern swatch (to the right of the "Use Pattern" button) to open a palette of the currently available patterns **B**. Navigate to the bottom of the palette to find your newly defined pattern, and click on it. Then click the "Use Pattern" button and have a cup of tea while Photoshop works on "Healing" to blend the color and the image.

 **Patch Tool Tinting.psd**

Patch Tool Vignettes

Before

After

THE PATCH TOOL TINTING METHOD can be used to blend a brightly colored image into a color background for a dreamy pastel look. Here we start with a detail from a photo of flowers at a market stall. As in "Patch Tool Tinting" at the left, define the image as a pattern (Edit > Define Pattern), add a new layer 🗔, and fill the layer with the color you want for the background. Make a selection (we used the Ellipse Tool ◯, holding down the Shift and Alt/Option keys and dragging outward from the center of the circular area we wanted to vignette; we dragged inside the selection boundary to adjust the position of the circle) **A**. Feather the selection so the image will have a soft edge (we chose Select > Feather and used 20 pixels for the Feather Radius).

Now choose the Patch tool ⬦, click the pattern swatch in the Options bar, and choose your new pattern from the bottom of the palette of available patterns **B**. Click the "Use Pattern" button and wait patiently for the "Healing" to be completed.

 **Patch Tool Vignettes.psd**

Laurie Grace and Don Jolley Garner Complements

Complementary colors (opposites on the color wheel) contrast with each other. Artists and designers know that complements used side-by-side can be vibrant and exciting when the colors are intense, and still pleasing to the eye if they are more neutral. Here Laurie Grace and Don Jolley let us in on two different "instant" Photoshop methods for finding a complement for any color.

FIND OUT MORE

▼ Finding the center
page 571

In developing one of the images for her *Intrusions* series, Laurie replaced the black and white in her background montage with teal and its reddish-brown complement. Here's how she did it.

Laurie created a new layer above the black-and-white graphics by clicking the "Create a new layer" button 🔲 at the bottom of the Layers palette. Then she chose a color (one way is to click the Foreground square in the Tools palette to open the Color Picker, use the vertical spectrum slider to choose a color family, and click in the large color square to choose a precise color). Laurie filled the new layer with this color (press Alt-Backspace [Windows] or Option-Delete [Mac]) and then simply put the layer in Difference mode, using the blend mode menu in the upper left corner of the Layers palette. She now had her original color (over the black area) and its complement (over the white). *Note:* With this method, if your original color is dark or light, the complement will be the opposite tonality. Both colors will be equally saturated — that is, equally intense or neutral.

In developing a fictitious book cover, Don experimented with a mathematical approach, using a masked Hue/Saturation Adjustment layer to find a complementary color. Jolley set up vertical and horizontal Guides through the center of his background illustration.▼ Then he used the guides as he dragged with the Rectangular Marquee ⌷ tool to select the upper left quadrant, then Shift-dragged to add the lower right to the selection.

With his selection active, he clicked the "Create new fill or adjustment layer" button ◕ at the bottom of the Layers palette and chose Hue/Saturation from its menu. In the Hue/Saturation dialog box he moved the Hue slider all the way left (a value of –180; moving the slider right to 180 would have done the same thing). Since there are 360 degrees in a circle, shifting the Hue *half* that number of degrees shifts the color halfway around the color wheel to the complement. The active selection created a mask for the Adjustment layer that restricted the color change to the selected quadrants.

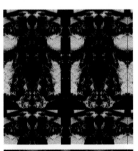

Laurie Grace created the black-and-white background for an image from her *Intrusions* series and then colored it with a teal-blue-filled layer in Difference mode (a detail is shown here). The other steps in the process of creating the image are described in the "Gallery" on page 86.

Starting with his gold-tinted background composition, Don Jolley experimented with complements using a Hue/Saturation Adjustment layer to add a contrasting color. (Continuing to experiment with colors as the cover developed, Jolley later decided on a different color solution that he liked better, which can be seen on page 664.)

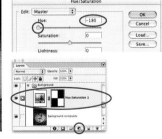

From Color to Black & White

YOU'LL FIND THE FILES

in 🔵 > Wow Project Files > Chapter 4 > Black-and-White:
- Direct Convert-Before.psd (for step 1)
- Desaturate-Before.psd (for step 2)
- Channel Mixer-Before.psd (for step 3)
- Mixed Mixers (for step 4)

OPEN THESE PALETTES

from the Window menu:
- Tools • Channels • Layers

OVERVIEW

Try one of the simple grayscale conversion methods — direct conversion, Lab conversion, or desaturation • Use Channel Mixer if the simple methods are unsuccessful • Use masking of a Channel Mixer layer to combine conversion options

1

A simple direct conversion with Image > Mode > Grayscale may work for an RGB image like this flower **A**, whose impact, even in color, depends largely on light-dark contrast. After conversion **B**, we made an Auto Levels adjustment to whiten the petals **C**.▼

FIND OUT MORE

▼ Using Auto Levels
page 166

OF PHOTOSHOP'S MANY WAYS to convert a color image to black-and-white, the method you choose will depend on the characteristics of your RGB original and whether you simply want to optimize the image for the best black-and-white reproduction, or whether you're aiming for a particular photographic effect. In either case, you may want to do some fine-tuning after you make the initial conversion. Our photo of the mannequin with parasol was converted from color to black-and-white using a combination of Channel Mixer Adjustment layers, an invaluable approach for an image that has a complex mix of tone and color relationships. But before we get into that process, let's look at some simpler methods that work well for converting certain kinds of images.

1 Making a "straight conversion." Direct conversion is done simply by choosing Image > Mode > Grayscale. This method can work well for an RGB image that shows good detail and contrast. When Photoshop makes the conversion, it relies quite heavily on the information in the Green channel, where detail contrast is often strongest, and it gives little weight to the Blue channel, which is the channel most likely to show noise. The converted image can be fined-tuned with Levels or Curves if needed **1**. We added a Levels Adjustment layer by clicking the "Create new fill or adjustment layer" button ◑ at the bottom of the Layers palette and clicked the "Auto" button to improve contrast.

2a

A direct grayscale conversion loses the visual contrast between the flowers and the leaves.

2b

Choosing Image > Adjustments > Desaturate (left) and *then* Image > Mode > Grayscale produces better contrast.

2c

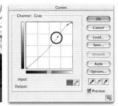

We Ctrl/⌘-clicked in the image to make a point on the curve as shown, then clicked on the curve to make another point higher up and dragged this new point upward.

2d

The desaturated and converted image after applying the Curves adjustment (For a dynamic and exciting approach to desaturating, don't miss "Russell Preston Brown Sees in Black & White!" on page 216)

RGB TO LAB TO GRAYSCALE

If the photo you start with shows color noise or grain, or if you simply want to try a slightly different look, try choosing Image > Mode > Lab Color. Then in the Channels palette, drag the thumbnails for the two color channels to the "Delete" button 🗑 at the bottom of the palette. With just the Lightness channel left (now called Alpha 1), the file is in Multi-channel mode; choose Image > Mode > Grayscale to finish converting.

The RGB image **A** was converted to Lab color. Then the two color channels were dragged to the 🗑 button and the file was converted to Grayscale **C**. The direct RGB-to-Grayscale conversion **B** is shown for comparison.

2 Desaturating. If the success of the original color image depends not on light-dark contrast but on color difference, a direct Grayscale conversion alone may not be a great success **2a**. But using Image > Adjustments > Desaturate before converting may help **2b**, and it's so quick it's worth a try.

After converting with Image > Mode > Grayscale we added a Curves Adjustment layer by clicking the ⬤ button at the bottom of the Layers palette and choosing Curves. In the Curves dialog box you can "peg" (lock) the parts of the curve that you want to remain the same, and then make adjustments to other tonal ranges. We wanted to make the flower petals lighter but preserve their markings, so we Ctrl/⌘-clicked on one of these gray markings to create a point on the Curves diagram **2c**. When we then dragged up on a higher point to brighten the highlights, our original anchor point preserved the markings **2d**.

3 Mixing channels. Sometimes one of the color channels of an RGB image is a good starting point for conversion to black-and-white. You may be able to see this just by looking at the thumbnails in the Channels palette. You can make the thumbnails larger by clicking the palette's ⓑ button, choosing Palette Options when the menu opens, then choosing the largest thumbnail in the Channels Palette Options dialog. If your single-channel images are displayed in color, you can switch to a grayscale display by choosing Preferences (Ctrl/⌘-K) > Display & Cursors and clicking the check box to turn off "Color Channels in Color." For this vase of flowers we took a closer look by clicking in the 👁 column of the Channels palette so we could view each channel alone as a grayscale image **3a**.

When you've chosen a channel to start with (we chose Green) — or even if no channel seems like a good option by itself —

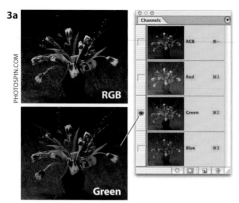

3a

PHOTOSPIN.COM

RGB

Green

Turning off visibility 👁 for the other channels of an RGB image allows you to view the channels one at a time.

3b

We used the Green channel component to maintain the contrast in the two-color parrot tulips, adding a little Red to lighten the vase and subtracting Blue to counteract some of the increase in brightness.

3c

Using the Red channel at 100% or more simulates the effect of shooting with a red filter over the lens — the red parts of the tulips are bright, and the red vase is lightened.

add a Channel Mixer Adjustment layer by clicking the 🌗 button at the bottom of the Layers palette and choosing Channel Mixer. In the Channel Mixer dialog box, you can set up for a conversion to black-and-white by clicking the **Monochrome** check box; also make sure the Preview box is checked. Now set up a starting point for your conversion to black-and-white:

- If, as described above, you found a channel that looked like a good place to start, move the slider for that channel to 100% and the other two color sliders to 0%. For our vase of flowers, we set Green at 100% to start.

- If none of the channels alone looked particularly promising, you might try starting with 30% Red, 60% Green, and 10% Blue, a "mix" that's close to the one Photoshop uses when it makes a direct conversion to black-and-white with Image > Mode > Grayscale.

Next move the Red, Green, and Blue sliders to experiment with different contributions from each channel. Moving a slider to a more positive value brightens the image in areas where that color predominates. A negative value adds the negative version of that channel to the mix. So, for instance, if you want to brighten a sky that's blue in the original color image, increase the value for Blue; conversely, a negative Blue value will darken the sky. Since Blue often holds more noise or grain than the other channels, you may want to use it sparingly (small positive or negative numbers). For instance, a small negative value for Blue can often be helpful for balancing any extra brightness you create by mixing the Red and Green channels to a total greater than 100%. For our vase of flowers we reduced Green slightly (to 98%), added 12% Red, and subtracted a little Blue (−2%) **3b**. For a different interpretation of the flowers, we started with the Red channel, increasing it above 100%, and then used a negative setting for Green to balance the overall tone of the image **3c**.

When you have a mix that you like, save the layered file (File > Save), make a flattened duplicate (Image > Duplicate > Duplicate Merged Layers Only), and convert your copy to black-and-white (Image > Mode > Grayscale).

4 Mixing Channel Mixers. For our mannequin photo we tried in turn a direct conversion (as in step 1) and a desaturation and then conversion (as in step 2). Neither approach produced the tonality we wanted **4a**, so we decided to try the Channel Mixer. As you'll see, we found that one Channel Mixer adjustment worked well for the mannequin but a different mix

4a

Neither direct conversion (Image > Mode > Grayscale) nor desaturation (Image > Adjustments > Desaturate) produced a black-and-white version we liked.

4b

When we balanced the sliders in the Channel Mixer to get the best tone and contrast for the mannequin, the parasol was a little light.

4c

With the total of the Channel Mixer sliders at 100%, the conversion for the parasol was slightly dark. But we could blend this dark version with the light version below it, next.

4d

We painted the mask for the bottom Channel Mixer layer to partially expose the parasol and the hat to the upper Channel Mixer layer. The result is shown at the top of page 212.

worked better for the parasol. So we used two Channel Mixer Adjustment layers, targeting their effects with a layer mask.

Looking at the three color channels, we decided to try a mix of the Red channel (for brightness) and the Green (for skin toning and detail). Add a Channel Mixer layer (using the ⬤ button as in step 3), and click the Monochrome check box. Experiment with the sliders; we settled on equal parts of Red and Green (+64%) with a slightly negative Blue setting (−4%) to counteract some of the added brightness, which gave us a result we liked for the mannequin (the most complicated part of the photo to convert) and the background **4b**. Click "OK" to close the dialog box. To avoid confusion, give the Channel Mixer layer a descriptive name (double-click its name in the Layers palette and type "Mannequin," for instance).

In our black-and-white conversion the parasol was a little light, but we could address that with another Channel Mixer layer, optimized for the parasol. First turn off visibility for the "Mannequin" Channel Mixer (click its ⬤) to bring back the color for the second Channel Mixer to work on. Add the second Channel Mixer layer above the first by clicking the ⬤ button at the bottom of the palette, and choosing Channel Mixer; turn on the Monochrome option. As you adjust the sliders, concentrate on the parasol and keep the total of the three sliders right at 100% if you can (you'll see why in a minute); we found that +16% Red, +84% Green, and 0% Blue gave us a good start **4c**. Click "OK" to close the dialog, and name the layer "Parasol."

To blend the effects of the two Channel Mixers, turn on visibility for "Mannequin" again. If you toggle visibility for "Parasol" on and off, you'll see that at this point "Parasol" has no effect. That's because (a) what's below is already monochromatic, and (b) the 100% mix in "Parasol" keeps it from brightening or darkening what's below, as it would if the total were more or less than 100%. To allow the "Parasol" Channel Mixer to work on the parasol, target "Mannequin" by clicking its thumbnail in the Layers palette. Choose the Brush tool ✏ and in the Options bar click the tiny triangle to the right of the Brush footprint and choose a soft brush tip. Lower the Opacity to 50% or less to make it easier to control the buildup of paint. With black as the Foreground color (typing D or X will make it so), paint the layer mask to partially block the "Mannequin" layer's effect on the parasol and partially expose it to the "Parasol" Channel Mixer **4d**. To finish, we used smaller brush tips to mask parts of the hat. We made a flattened copy of the file and converted to Grayscale mode, as in step 3. *Wow!*

Russell Preston Brown Sees in Black & White!

IF YOU CAN "THINK IN CHANNELS" and you know where you want to go with your conversion from color to black-and-white, the Channel Mixer is a powerful tool. There are also quicker, easier ways of converting, such as the "one size fits all" direct-conversion method (Image > Mode > Grayscale). Both of these methods and others are described in "From Color to Black & White" on page 212. The problem is that when you try a "one size fits all" method, you can tell whether your quick fix looks *good enough,* but you don't know whether there might be something *better* out there. "But wait — there's more!" says Photoshop guru Russell Brown, who has developed a conversion method that's almost as quick and easy as the two simple methods *and* offers more options *and* is really fun. Here's our adaptation of his approach:

You can experiment with the **Black-and-White.psd** file in the Wow Goodies folder on the Wow DVD-ROM. Look for Russell's complete "Seeing in Black-and-White" and "Dr. Brown's RAW Photo Styler," a related technique used with Camera Raw, at **www.russellbrown.com.**

1 Start with a color image in RGB mode. Here we've picked one that's tricky to "translate" to black-and-white. A big part of the appeal is the color difference between the blue paint and the red. But the red on the brightly lit seats of the boat is lighter than the blue interior, which is in shadow, while the red in shadow on the outside of the boat is darker than the adjacent blue.

ORIGINAL PHOTO: JHDAVIS

Whether we try a direct Grayscale conversion (shown here) or use the Image > Adjust > Desaturate command, much of the photo's impact is lost.

2 What Russell shows us is that we can quickly preview many different conversion options by stacking two Hue/Saturation Adjustment layers above the image: At the bottom of the Layers palette, click the "Create new fill or adjustment layer" button ● and choose Hue/Saturation from its menu. In the Hue/Saturation dialog box push the Saturation slider all the way to the left and click "OK." This turns the image into a "black-and-white."

The first of the Hue/Saturation layers removes the color.

3 In the Layers palette, click on the thumbnail for the color image layer (the *Background* in our file) and hold down the Alt/Option key as you add another Hue/Saturation layer *between* the color original and the "conversion" layer you just added. In the New Layer dialog box (which opens because you held down Alt/Option) choose Color for the mode and click "OK." When the Hue/Saturation dialog box opens, experiment with the Hue slider, for a spectacular "live audition" of different conversions. Set the Hue slider at the option you like best and click "OK."

With a middle Hue/Saturation layer in Color mode, you can change the color that the top layer "sees" and converts to black-and-white.

We chose the Hue setting above (–120) as the best option. Now the image was ready for direct conversion (Image > Mode > Grayscale) and fine-tuning with a Levels or Curves adjustment if needed.

Memory Economy in 16-Bit Mode

YOU'LL FIND THE FILES
in 🔵 > Wow Project Files > Chapter 4 > RAM Economy:
- Memory Economy-Before.psd (to start)
- Memory Economy-After.psd (to compare)

OPEN THESE PALETTES
from the Window menu:
- Tools • History

OVERVIEW

Adjust overall tone and color • To target an adjustment to a specific area, make a change overall, then make a History Snapshot, undo the overall change, and use the History Brush 🖌 to paint the change back in the spots where you want it • Apply the High Pass filter, make a Snapshot, undo the filter, and paint it back in Overlay mode

1a

The original 16-bit image

WHENEVER YOU CAN ACQUIRE a file in 16-Bits/Channel mode — as a scan or as a raw file from a digital camera — it pays to do as much work in 16-bit mode as you can. The wealth of extra information in the file can produce a deeper and richer-looking image, which you can then convert to 8 Bits/Channel mode for output. In both versions, CS and CS2, all the core Photoshop functions — including layers, masks, and Adjustment layers — can be used in 16-bit mode. All the filters that might be important to run in an information-rich file are also available (some of the most important are in the Blur and Sharpen menus). So in many cases, you can work with your 16-bit files just as you would with 8-bit images.

The downside to working with a file in 16 Bits/Channel mode is the amount of RAM and scratch disk required to support extra layers. The RAM economies of working with Adjustment layers and layer masks don't seem to apply to 16-bit files the way they do

1b

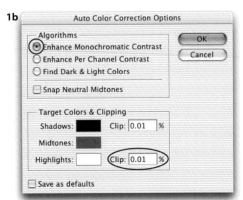

In the Auto Color Correction Options dialog, we selected a new Algorithm and reduced the amount of Shadows and Highlights clipping.

1c

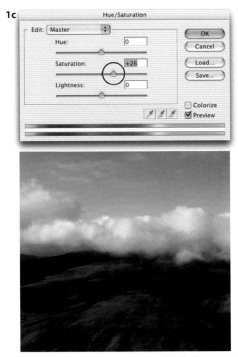

After our Levels and Hue/Saturation global adjustments

to 8-bit files. Sixteen-bit files are twice the size of 8-bit images to begin with, and adding a single layer in a 16-bit file can more than double your RAM usage (even though it may not have as drastic an effect on the size of the saved image). Even with faster machines with ever-increasing amounts of RAM and bigger hard drives, there may be times when you need to conserve memory more than you need the flexibility of a layered file, especially if you work with very large 16-bit images. For such occasions, here's a way you can adjust color and contrast without carrying the extra weight of Adjustment layers or layer masks, but still taking advantage of blend modes. It involves using only the *Background* layer and Photoshop's History Brush ✍ and History palette. This lets you save spare RAM for other tasks that really require layers, such as compositing images or adding Shape and Text layers.

1 Making global adjustments. Start by opening your file and saving it under a new name (File > Save As) so you can leave the original untouched while you work on a copy **1a**. The next step is to make sure you have a full range of tones in your image, from black to white. A quick way to do this is to choose Image > Adjustments > Curves (or Image > Adjustments > Levels) and click the "Auto" button, which instantly converts the darkest and lightest tones in your image to full black and white. Next click the "Options" button. When the Auto Color Correction Options dialog box opens **1b**, it's worth taking a few extra seconds to try all three Algorithms at the top of the box, as well as toggling the Snap Neutral Midtones option on and off. Each setting produces a different result, and you can choose the one you prefer. For our photo, we clicked the "Enhance Monochromatic Contrast" button, so that a color shift did *not* occur as part of the automatic contrast adjustment. Then we reduced the percentages of Shadows and Highlights Clip, to maintain more detail in those tonal ranges.▼

FIND OUT MORE

▼ Using Auto Color Correction Options **page 166**

After the Auto corrections, we also slightly increased the overall color saturation by choosing Image > Adjustments > Hue/Saturation and moving the Saturation slider to the right **1c**.

2 Targeting adjustments. Next you can use the History Brush to target different types of adjustments to specific areas, without having to select an area with the Lasso or Pen tool. We wanted to darken (or burn) the clouds and sky, and lighten (or dodge) the foreground landscape. We started by choosing Image > Adjustments > Curves, and when the dialog box opened we Ctrl/⌘-clicked with the cursor on a light gray area of our clouds to automatically set a control point for that specific highlight tone on the

2a

Curves diagonal line. Then we tapped on the ↓ key on the keyboard, an alternative to dragging the point downward, to darken the image until we had the desired amount of detail in the clouds **2a**. (You don't need to worry that other parts of the image are also darkened during this procedure; the next step will bring back that tonality.)

With your adjustment made, move to the History palette and Alt/Option-click the "Create new snapshot" button ▣ at the bottom of the palette; give the Snapshot a descriptive name when the New Snapshot dialog appears **2b**. The Snapshot will temporarily save the current state of the Curves-adjusted image so you can use it with the History Brush. Once the new Snapshot appears in the top section of the History palette, you can Undo the Curves adjustment (Ctrl/⌘-Z), knowing that it will still be available via the History Brush.

Targeting and darkening the tones in the highlights using Curves

2b

Making a History Snapshot of the darkening "Burn-Curves" adjustment

Next click in the column to the left of the new Snapshot's thumbnail to set this state of the document as the source for painting with the History Brush ⤬. Select the History Brush in the Tools palette, and choose a large (300 pixels) soft brush in the Options bar (click the tiny arrow to the right of the Brush footprint and choose from the palette that pops up). Then click and drag to apply the darkening Curves adjustment just where you want it; we painted across the clouds and sky **2c**.

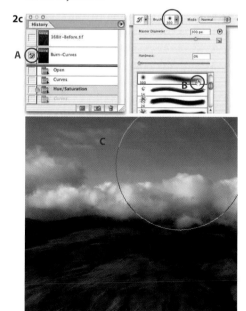
2c

We used the same five-step procedure (adjustment, make a Snapshot, Undo, set the new Snapshot as the source, and paint with the History Brush) to perform a targeted Curves *lightening* adjustment to the foreground of our photo as well **2d**.

The "Burn-Curves" Snapshot was set as the source for the History Brush **A**, a soft round brush tip was chosen **B**, and the Snapshot was applied to some areas **C**.

2d

Another Snapshot was made, this time of a "dodge" Curves adjustment. It was set as the source for the History Brush **A** and used to lighten some areas of the foreground **B**.

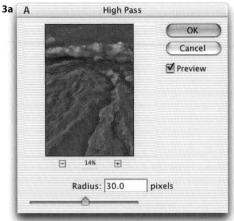

3a

We ran the High Pass Filter on our photo **A**, took one final Snapshot, designated it as the source for painting with the History Brush **B**, and used the Undo command.

3b

To apply just the light and dark attributes of the High Pass filter Snapshot to the image overall, we changed the blend mode of the History Brush to Overlay and set the Opacity to 50% and the brush size to 1000 (by clicking the tiny triangle to the right of the Brush footprint and using the Maximum Diameter slider in the palette that pops out). Then just one continuous stroke of the large brush applied the filter's effects.

Photoshop CS2's new 32-bit mode uses even more RAM than 16-bit. Of the Image > Adjustments commands, Channel Mixer, Photo Filter, and Exposure work in 32 Bits/Channel mode. Because the History Brush is one of the few tools that operate in this high-information mode, it's possible to alter the image overall using one of the three Adjustments commands that take full advantage of the high dynamic range, then make a Snapshot, undo, and step back to the Snapshot to paint in the changes, just as described here for 16-bit images. Making selective changes to the file in this way is useful for files destined for use in other programs, and it can also make it easier to get a pleasing conversion if your goal is to take the file to 8- or 16-bit in Photoshop later on.

3 High Pass filtering. In 16-bit mode, the same History Brush technique can also be used with filters, such as High Pass, found under Filter > Other. At higher settings (here we used 30), this filter can almost instantly increase contrast in areas of color change, which is what our image needed. We followed basically the same procedure as outlined in step 2, except instead of adjusting Curves, we ran the High Pass filter **3a**, then we took the Snapshot, typed Ctrl/⌘-Z to Undo, and set the new Snapshot as the source for the History Brush. For the High Pass filter to work its contrast-adjusting magic, the light areas of the filtered image have to lighten and the dark areas darken, while the midtones do nothing. You can make this happen by using the Overlay blend mode, one of the modes in which 50% gray has no effect. We set the Mode in the Options bar for the History Brush to Overlay **3b**. By choosing a large hard-edged brush at 50% opacity, we could drag the History Brush over the entire image in one stroke, applying the instant edge-enhancement effects of the filter everywhere at half-strength. We then used a smaller, softer brush, with even less Opacity, to build up the filter's effect in specific areas.

Note: In both CS and CS2 the Edit > Fade command works in 16-bit mode. So for overall edge enhancement you can apply the High Pass filter and then, instead of using a Snapshot and the History Brush, use the Edit > Fade command to reduce Opacity and change the blend mode to Overlay. However, if you want the precise control needed to build up the effect in specific areas, the History Brush method described above is the way to go. (The High Pass filter and the Edit > Fade High Pass command are available for 32-bit files in CS2, but Overlay mode is not.)

Controlled Recoloring

YOU'LL FIND THE FILES
in (wow) > Wow Project Files > Chapter 4 >
Controlled Recoloring:
  • Red Shirt-Before.psd (to start)
  • Green Shirt-After.psd (to compare)
  • Yellow Shirt-After.psd (to compare)

OPEN THESE PALETTES
from the Window menu:
  • Tools • Layers • Channels • Info

OVERVIEW
Add a swatch of your custom color
• Select the element you want to recolor
CMYK : Add a Solid Color Fill layer in Hue
mode in your custom color • Adjust
luminosity and saturation if necessary
until the color matches the swatch
Lab: Convert to Lab Color • Add Color
Samplers • Add a Curves layer and adjust
to match colors "by the numbers"

For many Photoshop print applications it makes sense
to work in RGB color, then make a duplicate file in CMYK mode
at the end when you need to save the image for printing. But if
your goal is to match a particular custom color — for a clothing catalog, for example — it works better to tackle the project
in CMYK from the beginning. That way the swatch you're trying to match is a stable target — one that you can check with a
process color chart and that won't have a chance to change during an RGB-to-CMYK conversion.

Another option that can often produce better results with less
work is to go from CMYK to Lab Color for the color changes
and then back to CMYK for printing. Lab Color is the most
versatile mode for changing colors because it makes it so easy
to control luminosity (lightness or darkness) independently of
hue and saturation. For this project we'll first change the shirt
color from red to green in CMYK Color mode. **CMYK works
well for colors that are about equal in intensity (lightness and
saturation), even if they are very different in hue.** Then we'll
start with the red shirt again, this time changing it to yellow
using Lab Color. **Lab Color works much better than other
color modes when there's a marked difference in saturation
or tone between the original and the new color.** For this kind

1a

Making a selection for
the swatch

1b

Clicking the ⊘ button
to add a Solid Color
Fill layer

1c

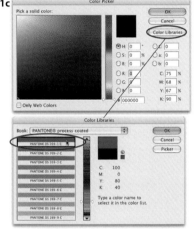

Choosing the color for the swatch layer

1d

The custom swatch in
place

2a

The background was selected
with the Magic Wand ✳ and
the selection was inverted.

---

of color change, the Lab Color process is so much easier and
more successful than trying to work in CMYK or RGB that it's
well worth the venture into a less familiar color space!

THE GREEN SHIRT (WORKING IN CMYK MODE)

1 Making an on-screen swatch. Open the photo you want
to recolor; in the **Red Shirt.psd** file we wanted to change the
color of the sweatshirt to a custom green. Duplicate the file
(Image > Duplicate) and then close the original; this way you
know you won't lose your original file no matter what you do.
If the file isn't yet in CMYK mode, choose Edit > Color Settings and *pick the color setting given to you by the printer.* Then
choose Image > Mode > CMYK Color. For this project we'll
suppose we received the CMYK file from the client.

Use a Fill layer to make a color swatch for comparison, as follows: Make a selection in the size you want the swatch in an
area that's neither heavily shaded nor strongly highlighted; we
used the Rectangular Marquee ⬚ **1a**. Then click the "Create
new fill or adjustment layer" button ⊘ at the bottom of the
Layers palette and choose **Solid Color 1b**. When the Color
Picker opens, choose the color you want to match; we needed
to match Pantone Process 269-1, so
we clicked on the "Color Libraries"
button **1c**, chose "PANTONE® process coated" from the Book menu,
scrolled to 269-1 and clicked it,
then clicked "OK" to finish adding
the Fill layer **1d**.

> **ENTERING COLOR CODES**
>
> With the Color Libraries
> dialog open, to choose a
> Pantone color without
> having to scroll the color
> list, quickly type the
> number for that color.

2 Selecting the element to recolor. Next select the item you
want to recolor. ▼ There's a selection for the shirt stored as an
alpha channel in the **Red Shirt.psd** file; we made it as described
next and as adjusted in step 4, but you can shortcut the process
if you like by simply Ctrl/⌘-clicking the thumbnail for the
"Shirt" channel in the Channels palette to load it as a selection.

Because our subject was silhouetted against white, we could
use the Magic Wand ✳ to begin selecting; with Anti-alias, Contiguous, and Use/Sample All Layers turned on in the Options
bar and Feather set to 0, we clicked once on the white background. With the background selected, we
could reverse the selection (Ctrl/⌘-Shift-I)
to select the boy **2a**. Then we subtracted
everything but the shirt from the active

> **FIND OUT MORE**
>
> ▼ Choosing a selection
> method **page 56**

2b

Using the Magnetic Lasso ⚟ in "Subtract from selection" mode

2c

Removing the area below the shirt from the selection

2d

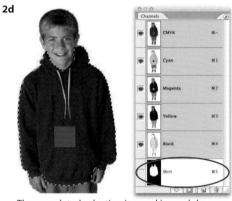

The completed selection is saved in an alpha channel.

3a

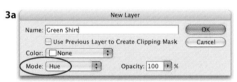

Adding a Solid Color Fill layer in Hue mode to color the shirt

3b

At this point the shirt is darker than the swatch. The ties have not changed because the Fill layer is in Hue mode, which doesn't add color to neutrals.

selection: Using the Magnetic Lasso ⚟ with mode set to "Subtract from selection" ⬚ in the Options bar, we clicked in the white background on the left near the boy's wrist. We could "float" the cursor along the bottom edges of the sleeves and shirt-front without pressing the mouse button; the tool had no trouble automatically following the clear edges of the shirt in most areas **2b**, and where it couldn't, we clicked from point to point to operate it like the Polygonal Lasso ⚟. When we had traced across to the other sleeve, we could enclose the hands, legs, and feet with a few clicks and close the selection by clicking back on the starting point **2c**; this removed from the selection everything below the shirt. We stored the developing selection in an alpha channel at this point so we wouldn't have to build it again if we made a mistake (Select > Save Selection),▼ and repeated the "subtracting" process for the neck and head, then saved the selection to the same channel again **2d**.

3 Recoloring in CMYK. With the selection active and the image layer targeted (by clicking its thumbnail in the Layers palette), add another Solid Color Fill layer in your custom color as in step 1, but this time hold down the Alt/Option key as you click the ⬤ button and choose Solid Color. The New Layer dialog box will open **3a**, where you can name the layer and choose the blend mode — Hue — and then click "OK." Choose the same custom color as in step 1 **3b**.

4 Checking the mask. At this point it will be easy to see whether your mask is a perfect fit. In this example, if you see red at the edges of the green shirt, or if you see green extending beyond the shirt, click the mask thumbnail for the custom color layer in the Layers palette and adjust the mask **4**.▼

5 Adjusting for reflected color. When the edges are clean and anti-aliased, adjust any reflected color. In this image the red of the shirt is reflected on the neck. Choose the Brush tool ✎, set a low Opacity in the Options bar, and click the tiny triangle to the right of the Brush footprint to open the Brush Preset picker; choose a brush tip large enough for half the brush size to cover that part of the neck where the red sweatshirt has reflected its color onto the skin; we chose the 9-pixel round brush, and set its Hardness at 50%, and Opacity at 10%. With white as the Foreground color (type X if necessary to choose white), we centered the brush on the neck edge and painted along it until the red was muted **5**.

FIND OUT MORE

▼ Saving selections
page 67

▼ Cleaning up masks
page 66

4

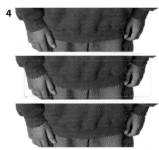

A thin red line at the bottom edges of the shirt (top) showed that the mask needed adjusting. We loaded the mask for the "Green Shirt" layer as a selection and nudged it down slightly with the ↓ key (center). Then Alt/Option-Shift-dragging with the Rectangular Marquee [ ] selected the intersection of the shirt selection and the rectangle (bottom), and we filled this selection with white.

5

The mask is painted to neutralize the red reflection on the neck.

6a

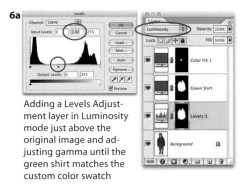

Adding a Levels Adjustment layer in Luminosity mode just above the original image and adjusting gamma until the green shirt matches the custom color swatch

6b

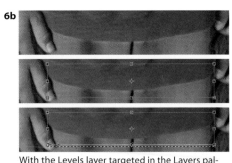

With the Levels layer targeted in the Layers palette as in figure 6a, we selected the bottom of the shirt, pressed Ctrl/⌘-T (for Edit > Free Transform) and dragged the bottom handle of the Transform frame up "just a hair" to shrink the Levels layer's mask and eliminate the light streak.

6 "Tweaking" the recoloring. Now compare your custom color swatch to the new color of the element you selected (the shirt). If the original color and your custom color are close in intensity — that is, about equally light or dark and equally saturated, even if they are opposite hues — the recoloring may be complete now. But if your recolored element is just a little lighter or darker than the swatch (as ours was; refer to **3b**), you'll need to make a change to the luminance. To fix the problem with the green of the shirt being too dark, we used Levels to retroactively adjust the luminance of the underlying shirt: We loaded the shirt selection by Ctrl/⌘-clicking the thumbnail for its mask in the Fill layer. Then we clicked on the *Background* thumbnail in the Layers palette so the Adjustment layer we were about to add would come in just above the *Background* and thus would act on the original photo only. We Alt/Option-clicked the ● button and chose Levels, putting the new layer in Luminosity mode so that it would adjust only brightness when we changed its settings. In the Input Levels section of the dialog box, we dragged the center (gray, gamma) slider to the left to lighten the shirt **6a** and clicked "OK." We now had a light streak at the bottom of the shirt — the mask for the shirt, as altered in step 4, needed to be changed again for the Levels layer; we shortened it **6b**. The results are shown at the top of page 221.

If, after lightening or darkening, your recolored element still looks just a little "hotter" (more saturated) or duller (less saturated) than your swatch, you can add a masked Hue/Saturation Adjustment layer in Saturation mode below the swatch layer and adjust the Saturation slider. *Note:* "Tweaking" the color with a Saturation adjustment works well only for minor changes; with larger changes it may be hard to keep neutral highlights and shadows from picking up color. If your recoloring requires fairly big changes in tone or changes in saturation, the Lab Color method is likely to work better.

THE YELLOW SHIRT (WORKING IN LAB COLOR MODE)

For making a color change, Lab Color mode excels at preserving smooth transitions of color and shading. Lab is a huge space, encompassing more colors than any monitor can display or any press can print. But the feature that makes Lab especially useful for a drastic color change is that it lends itself so well to controlling luminosity separately from hue and saturation. You can make big changes in color (from a dark red to a light yellow, for instance) while maintaining detail in the shadows and highlights, and keeping neutral colors neutral.

1 The Pantone 309-6
swatch added to
Red Shirt.psd

2 Converting from
CMYK to Lab
Color mode

3a

Finding the Lab numbers for Pantone 369-6

Although you can try using the "matching by eye" method we used for CMYK, there's an advantage to "doing it by the num-bers" in Lab — you can count on a stable color match, no mat-ter what inks are used to print the piece or what light it's viewed under (see "When To Do It by the Numbers" on page 228). And in Lab mode it's really easy to use the numbers.

1 Making a swatch. Open the photo you want to recolor; again we started with the **Red Shirt-Before.psd** file. Follow step 1 for "The Green Shirt" (starting on page 222) to duplicate the file for safekeeping and make a swatch of the custom color **1**; our custom yellow was Pantone process color 309-6.

2 Converting to Lab Color. To convert the image from CMYK to Lab Color, choose Image > Mode > Lab Color **2**. Choose "Don't flatten" in the warning box that opens — the layers of this file are image layers in Normal mode, and this causes no problem in the conversion, despite the warning.

Since the Lab color space was designed to encompass all the colors of RGB and CMYK color spaces and then some, you won't need to worry about losing image data in the conversion to Lab. And since you'll be working in a very limited range of prescribed colors, you won't generate any colors that might cause a difference between your Lab image and the CMYK space when you convert back to CMYK.

3 Finding the Lab numbers. To gain the advantages of an exact match "by the numbers" as we're doing here, you need to know the Lab composition for your custom color. In the Lay-ers palette, double-click on the thumbnail for the swatch layer to open the Color Libraries dialog, and click the "Picker" but-ton to open the Color Picker. Read the "L," "a," and "b" values and make a note of them **3a** — for our yellow "L" is 94, "a" is −8, and "b" is 43.

Before going further, a brief explanation of what Lab numbers represent might help **3b**. In Lab Color mode, **"L" values (for Luminosity)** range from 0 to 100, with 100 being white. The "a" and "b" components each represent an axis with opposite colors at the ends. The **"a" continuum is from Green to Ma-genta,** and the **"b" axis goes from Blue to Yellow**. The **"warm" colors Magenta and Yellow are denoted by positive numbers;** the **"cool" colors Green and Blue are negative numbers**. The full range of "a" and "b" values is from −128 to +127. But most of the colors in the CMYK gamut have values between −80 and +80. As you proceed along each axis from one color extreme to its opposite, you pass through the point where the opposites

3b

L

0   100

a

−   0   +

b

−   0   +

In Lab Color mode a color is described by a Lightness value between 0 and 100 and by positive or negative values for the "a" and "b" color channels.

3c

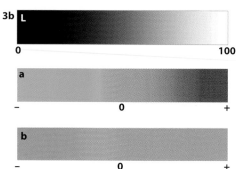

Sample Size: 3 by 3 Average

Setting up the Color Sampler tool

3d

Color Samplers are added to mark a spot on the shirt and one on the tie, so the same two spots can be sampled repeatedly for adjusting Curves.

4a

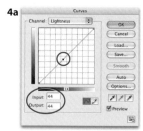

When the Curves dialog box opens to the Lightness curve, Ctrl/⌘-click on the spot on the red shirt that's marked by Color Sampler #1; this adds a point to mark this color on the Lightness curve. Since you haven't changed the curve yet, the Input and Output values are the same. (If your Curves grid shows only four rows and columns, Alt/Option-clicking the grid shows 10 columns.)

cancel each other out; this point, **zero (0) on the "a" or "b" axis, is neutral** (colorless — white, black, or gray, depending on whether the "L" value is 100, 0, or in between).

To look at some examples of Lab numbers, choose the Color Sampler tool (it shares a space in the Tools palette with the Eyedropper); in the Options bar's Sample Size menu **3c** choose "3 by 3 Average" or "5 by 5 Average" (to get a typical color sample), not "Point Sample," which could pick up color from an errant pixel. Click on a "flat color" area of the red shirt to place one Sampler there; then click on one of the ties to place a second Sampler in this neutral area **3d**. If we click on the *Background* thumbnail in the Layers palette and look in the Info palette at the numbers for the red shirt (Color Sampler #1), we see that the "L" value is 44, slightly darker than the middle tone (your value may differ if you place your Sampler in a slightly different place). The "a" channel (53) is quite positive, which means the color has a strong Magenta component. The "b" value is also quite positive (37), or quite Yellow, but somewhat less than Magenta, the two channels making the sweatshirt an intense red. To make the sweatshirt yellow to match our Pantone 309-6 swatch, we need to make the Luminosity value much lighter (94, from page 225), the "a" channel somewhat Green (−8) and the "b" channel even more Yellow (43). The gray ties (Color Sampler #2) are nearly neutral in color ("a" is 0 and "b" is 1), but the Luminosity is darker than white (83). Our client's yellow sweatshirts have near-white ties, so this will need to be lightened.

4 Using Curves in Lab. To make the color change, we'll use a Curves Adjustment layer. In order to restrict your color change to the sweatshirt, in the Channels palette Ctrl/⌘-click on the "Shirt" channel to load the premade selection. Then click on the "Create new fill or adjustment layer" button at the bottom of the Layers palette and choose Curves. Move your cursor over to the marker for Color Sampler #1 on the red shirt and Ctrl/⌘-click on it to set a point on the Lightness curve **4a**. If the bottom gradient has black on the left and white on the right as ours does, the Curves you are about to make will match ours, with darker values (lower numbers) on the left and bottom and lighter values (higher numbers) on the right and top. If you are set up the opposite way, either click on the triangles in the center of the horizontal gradient to switch the orientation, or note that your curves from here on will be opposite of ours. Now, for the anchor point you set on the Lightness curve, keep the Input number the same but change the Output value to 94; an easy way to do this is to type 94 into the Output field **4b**. Notice that the ties have also lightened, which is fine.

4b

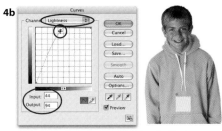

Typing "94" (the Lightness value for Pantone 309-6) into the Output field lightens the shirt and the ties.

4c

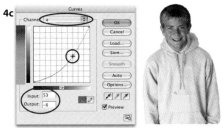

Moving the anchor point downward lowers the "a" curve to remove magenta from the shirt color.

4d

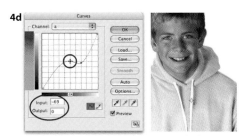

Adding a second point for the ties and adjusting it to keep the ties neutral

4e

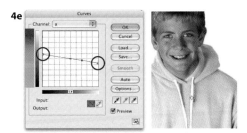

Moving the end points to straighten the "a" curve maintains a smooth color transition from the intense to the neutral colors. In this instance, it took a green tinge out of the shadows.

To change the Output value of an anchor point in Curves, while keeping the Input value the same:

- If you know the precise Output value you want, type it into the Output field.

- If you don't know exactly what Output value you're aiming for, use the ↑ or ↓ arrow key to nudge the value up or down (add the Shift key for bigger moves).

Next choose "a" from the Curves dialog's Channel menu. Set the anchor point as you did for the "Lightness" channel, and change the Output number to –8, which we noted as the "a" component of our custom color **4c**. This change has moved the ties away from neutral. Set another anchor point, for the ties, by clicking on the spot marked by Color Sampler #2, and change the Output value to 0 (neutral, since we don't want a magenta or green cast) **4d**. Since straight lines in the Curves dialog are best for maintaining the relationships between colors, drag the ends of the "a" curve to straighten the line **4e**.

Already we can see that the sweatshirt is yellow, but we need it to be Pantone 309-6 yellow. Select the "b" channel in the Curves dialog's Channel menu, set an anchor point for the shirt, and change the "b" Output value to 43 (more Yellow). Again set the anchor point for the ties and adjust to near neutral (we tapped the ↑ key to change the Output value to 2) **4f**.

With the color change complete — we can compare "by eye" using the swatch and also "by the numbers" in the Info palette. Check the highlights and shadows. We felt the shadows were too deep for this light, soft yellow. Fortunately, in Lab we can lighten the shadows without disturbing the color at all. We returned to the "L" channel and moved the black point anchor (bottom left in our setup) straight up using the ↑ key until the shadows lightened enough to look more realistic to us **4g**.

5 Checking the mask. Check the masking as in step 4 in "The Green Shirt" (page 223). The grommets and ties had lost detail. We painted the mask with black to restore the grommets. We selected the ties by clicking one with the Magic Wand ✳ (Tolerance 32, Contiguous and Anti-alias on) and Shift-clicking the other, then filled the selection with light gray **5**.

Saving and converting. To keep your Lab Color file in case further changes are required, save the file in PSD format while you're still in Lab mode. Then turn off visibility for the swatch layer (by clicking its ☻ icon in the Layers palette) and choose Image > Duplicate, turning on the Duplicate Merged Layers

4f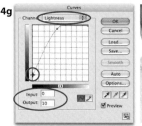

For the "b" curve we added a point for Color Sampler #1 and increased its Output value from 37 to 43. We added a point for Color Sampler #2 and changed its Output value from 1 to 2. We moved the endpoints to straighten the line. Our "b" curve was now steeper than it had been before we started. A steep color channel curve in Lab improves color definition.

4g

In the Lightness channel, moving the black point anchor straight up made the shadows lighter.

5

Painting the mask with black restores the grommets. The ties are selected and filled (Edit > Fill, Use: Black at 10% Opacity).

LEARNING ABOUT LAB COLOR

Lab is a powerful color mode to work in, and it doesn't take long to get comfortable there if you have a good guide to get you started. For more about using Lab, including how it can sometimes help you avoid the time-consuming work of making selections to target your color changes, we recommend Dan Margulis's latest bestseller, ***Photoshop LAB Color: The Canyon Conundrum and Other Adventures in the Most Powerful Colorspace*** (Peachpit Press).

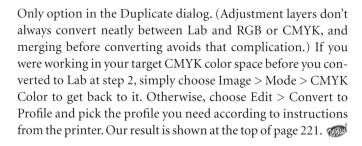

Only option in the Duplicate dialog. (Adjustment layers don't always convert neatly between Lab and RGB or CMYK, and merging before converting avoids that complication.) If you were working in your target CMYK color space before you converted to Lab at step 2, simply choose Image > Mode > CMYK Color to get back to it. Otherwise, choose Edit > Convert to Profile and pick the profile you need according to instructions from the printer. Our result is shown at the top of page 221.

WHEN TO DO IT BY THE NUMBERS

When your goal is to match a particular CMYK process color, much of the "art" of the match is in choosing the right area to compare to your custom color — a well-lit area, not shadowed but also not blown out. This can be difficult in a photo of clothing, with folds, drapes, or a pronounced weave, or in an image of a shiny car or bicycle. Since choosing the right area is subjective — there's no practical way around it — we might as well avoid color composition numbers altogether and do the entire process by eye, right? This is the method in "The Green Shirt" starting on page 222, and for many projects, this is a great way to go.

However, an argument can be made for moving into Lab Color mode and matching the numbers, as in "The Yellow Shirt," starting on page 224, even when the color change isn't terribly drastic and could be made by eye in CMYK. An example would be if the item whose color you're changing has to match something that appears near it on the printed page. Here's why: There are many ways to formulate the "same" color using CMYK inks.▼ This means that the color you arrive at by eye may have a slightly different CMYK composition than the one you're trying to match, even though it looks the same to you. The difference on-screen is so small that you don't see it, especially given the tonal variations in cloth or metal.

> **FIND OUT MORE**
> ▼ CMYK colors
> **page 184**

Printed on the page, the difference from the color standard may not be noticeable either, although the risk is higher if the standard color is printed somewhere else on the page. To add to the risk, some CMYK inks look different under different lighting conditions. If the color you arrive at "by eye" has a different CMYK composition than the "same" color that appears nearby, differences in the ink proportions could become apparent under different lighting conditions. For instance, a change in lighting may make a bigger change in how the cyan ink looks than it does in the magenta, so that if the two "matched" colors contain different proportions of cyan and magenta, they will become *more* different from each other when the lighting is changed. But if the color formulas for the two instances of the color on the page are exactly the same, when viewed under fluorescent light versus daylight, both instances will make exactly the same shift and will still match.

Adding Spot Color

OVERVIEW
Prepare a Grayscale or color image
• Create knockouts in the image where
you want custom colors to print at full
intensity without overprinting the image
• Create a spot color channel for each
custom color you want to include • To
overprint a tint of spot color, select the
area and in the spot color channel fill it
with Black at reduced opacity • Prepare a
comp from the on-screen preview
• Consult your printer and make any
necessary changes

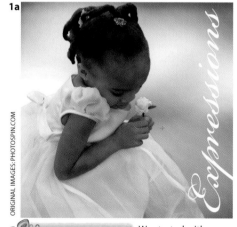

1a

ORIGINAL IMAGES: PHOTOSPIN.COM

We started with an
assembled grayscale
background image
and added the logo-
type as a Shape layer.

CUSTOM COLOR — OR *SPOT COLOR* — can be a great option
when you need to exactly match a standard branding color or
to prepare a file for screen printing a T-shirt or a poster. It's the
way to go when you want a fluorescent or metallic accent, or
that brilliant hue or solid pastel that you can't reliably achieve
with process inks. In the past, designers sometimes used spot
color to keep printing costs down; it was often less expensive
to print with black and a custom color (or two colors) than to
print in full color with CMYK process inks. Today, because of
the cost of specialty inks and because of changes in printing
and proofing processes, using black and a spot color may actually be more expensive than printing in full color. Of course, if
a project already includes spot color, you can use it to enhance
your illustrations without adding to the printing cost.

Thinking the project through. For a hang-tag for a clothing
company (shown above), we would add the brand's colors to a
black-and-white image. (You can use a similar approach for
adding spot color to a full-color image.) The two inks from the
Pantone Solid Coated series (Pantone 708, a pink, and Pantone
266, a blue-violet) would be used as spot tints in the photo
itself. In those areas the inks would print at partial intensity (a
screen tint), to color the black-and-white image.

In addition, the logotype would appear in Pantone 266 with a
white glow around it, and we would use Pantone 708 for a band

1b

We added a white Outer Glow to the Shape layer.

2a
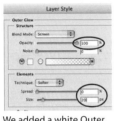

Adding a "reveal all" layer mask to the background image layer

2b

Setting options for the Gradient tool

2c

With the layer mask targeted, we dragged the Gradient tool from right to left across the logotype.

at the edge of the tag. Knockouts (white areas free of black ink) would be made in the grayscale image for the logotype and the edge, and the spot inks would print at full strength. We would also need knockouts anywhere custom-color elements overlapped each other, so the colors wouldn't overprint. For instance, the pink would be knocked out where the purple logotype overlapped the pink gradient.

1 Preparing the artwork. Create your background image. For the **Spot Color-Before.psd** file, we used the Extract filter▼ to silhouette a color photo of the child. We added an abstract background, then used the Channel Mixer to "translate" the image to black-and-white before choosing Image > Mode > Grayscale▼ The type was set in the Bickham Script font, then converted to a Shape layer (Layer > Type > Convert To Shape) and rotated to vertical (Edit > Transform Path > Rotate 90° CCW) **1a**. To create the white glow around the logotype, we clicked the "Add a layer style" button 🅯 at the bottom of the Layers palette, chose Outer Glow, and set up the Glow **1b**.▼

2 Creating knockouts in the grayscale image. The white Shape layer will automatically knock out the grayscale image to create white space for the custom-color logotype. To create the knockout for the pink edge of the tag, target the photo layer and add a "reveal all" layer mask by clicking the "Add layer mask" button ▣ at the bottom of the Layers palette **2a**. Then choose the Gradient tool ▣ and in the Options bar **2b** choose the Black, White Gradient (by default it's the third swatch in the pop-out Gradient picker that opens when you click the tiny triangle to the right of the gradient bar).

To make a transition on the mask from black (to hide the image and create the knockout for the edge) to white (where you want the image to show), click the layer mask's thumbnail in the Layers palette to target it. Then position the cursor approximately on the (vertical) baseline of the type (the point where you want the solid pink to begin to fade away), and Shift-drag to the left, stopping at about the top of the letter "s" **2c**, **2d**.

3 Creating the first spot color channel. You now have white or transparency in your image everywhere the solid custom inks will print at full strength, and also in the glow, where no ink will print. You can use these knockouts to build the spot color channels. First we made the channel for the purple logotype: Load the logotype as a selection by

FIND OUT MORE

▼ The Extract filter **page 63**

▼ Converting to grayscale **page 212**

▼ Adding Glow effects **page 498**

2d

The soft-edged black band in the layer mask clears the edge for the Pantone 708 ink. On-screen, the gray checkerboard represents transparency.

3a

The logotype is loaded as a selection by Ctrl/⌘-clicking the thumbnail for the Shape layer in the Layers palette.

3b

With the selection active, a custom color channel is added to the file.

3c

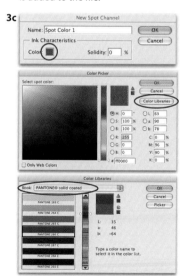

After you click the color swatch (top) and the "Color Libraries" button (middle) and choose the PANTONE® solid coated series of colors, quickly type a number code (we used 266) to choose that color for the new Spot channel.

Ctrl/⌘-clicking the logotype layer's thumbnail in the Layers palette **3a**. With the selection active, choose New Spot Channel from the pop-out menu ⊙ at the upper right corner of the Channels palette **3b**. Choose a custom color by clicking the swatch in the New Spot Channel dialog box to open the Color Picker, then clicking the "Color Libraries" button and choosing a color (we chose the PANTONE® Solid Coated series and Pantone 266) **3c**; click "OK" to close the Color Picker. In the New Spot Channel dialog box you can set the Solidity; we left it at 0 since the printer told us this ink was quite transparent, allowing other inks to show through it **3d** (see the "Previewing Spot Colors" tip on page 232). Click "OK" to close the New Spot Channel dialog box. Since there was an active selection when you chose New Spot Channel, its shape was used in making the channel, and the selection filled with black. Black in a Spot Color channel represents where the custom ink will print at 100% coverage.

4 Tinting some areas of the spot color channel. With both the Gray and Pantone 266 channels now visible and the Pantone 266 channel targeted in the Channels palette, select the area you want to tint; we used the Lasso ♀ to select the scalloped hair clip **4a.**▼ Add the tint to the spot channel by choosing Edit > Fill > Use:Black and adjusting the Opacity setting; we used 40% Opacity and clicked "OK." We used a combination of tools to select the second clip and filled it with 40% Black also **4b**.

FIND OUT MORE

▼ Selection methods
page 55

5 Adding the second spot color channel. For the Pantone 708 (pink) channel, we would need to put down the ink for the

3d

With the selection active, a custom color channel is added to the file.

4a

With the spot color channel still active, we used the Lasso ♀ to select one clip (top left), holding down the Shift key to add the second part of the clip. Filling the selection with Black at 50% Opacity tinted the clip with 50% Pantone 266.

4b

Selecting   After filling

For the second clip (right) we clicked with the Elliptical Marquee ◯ in the center of one large bead, starting to drag and then pressing Shift (to select a perfect circle) and Alt/Option (to center the selection on the starting point). To add the second bead, we held down the Shift key, began to drag from the center of the bead, then released the Shift key momentarily and pressed Shift and Alt/Option again to finish the second circular selection as shown above. We then used the Lasso ◯ (with the Shift key) to add other parts of the clip to the selection before filling with a 40% tint.

5a

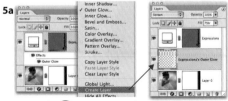

Using the context-sensitive menu for the logotype layer (left), to separate the Outer Glow (right) and make it available for selecting

edge panel but cut out the area where the logotype and its glow overlapped the panel; that way the purple ink for the type wouldn't have to overprint the pink of the edge, and the white glow would remain white. To do this we could load the edge as a selection, and then subtract the logotype and its glow, and fill the remaining selection with black in a new Spot channel.

The glow is currently an effect in a Layer Style. If you Ctrl/⌘-click the logotype layer's thumbnail in the Layers palette, the logotype will be loaded as a selection, but without the glow; we saw this in step 3. To turn the glow into pixels so its thumbnail *can* be Ctrl/⌘-clicked to load it as a selection, choose Layer > Layer Style > Create Layer **5a**.

Now create a selection for the second Spot channel: Ctrl/⌘-click the layer mask thumbnail for the photo layer to load it as a selection, and then invert (Ctrl/⌘-Shift-I) to select the edge **5b**. Then depress the Alt/Option key as you Ctrl/⌘-click on the logotype layer, and continue holding Alt/Option down as you Ctrl/⌘-click on the glow layer (the added Alt/Option key will subtract the logotype and then the glow from the edge selection). Now when you choose New Spot Channel and set up the new pink channel (Pantone 708), it will automatically include a knockout for the logotype and glow **5c**.

To tint the rose, zoom in and select it (we used the Lasso ◯). Fill the selection with a tint; we used a 40% tint here, using the same method as for the clips in step 4 (Edit > Fill, using Black at 40% Opacity) **5d**.

6 Proofing. A reliable way to produce a comp for your client or as a guide for the printer is to use the screen-capture function

5b   **5c**

   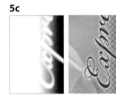

With the layer mask targeted (as in figure 2a), make a selection based on the layer mask (left), then subtract the logotype (center) and the glow (right).

A detail of the Pantone 708 channel, viewed alone (left) and with the other channels

5d

Selecting and filling the rose with a 40% tint in the Pantone 708 channel

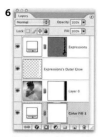

6

Before making this screen capture as a comp for the printer, we added a Solid Color Fill layer below the image layer by using the "Create new fill or adjustment layer" button ⬤ at the bottom of the Layers palette and then dragging this new layer's thumbnail down below the image layer (if your image is a *Background*, you'll first need to turn it into a regular layer by double-clicking its name in the Layers palette).

7a

With the layer mask targeted, we selected and stretched the black edge to hide more of the background image so the pink would print cleanly.

7b

We viewed the Gray and the Pantone 708 channels, targeted the Pantone 708 channel, and used the Eraser ⬦ to lighten the tint in the darkest and lightest areas of the rose, to bring out the petals. In the Eraser's Options bar we chose the Brush option, picked a small soft brush tip, and set the Opacity to 15%.

built into your System software to capture your on-screen preview **6**:

- On a Windows-based system, press **Alt-Print Screen** to copy the active window to the clipboard. In Photoshop create a new file (File > New) and paste (Ctrl-V).

- On a Mac, press ⌘-**Shift-4** and drag to highlight the area you want to capture. The file will be saved to your Desktop as "Picture *number*" using the lowest number not already in use in another Picture file name.

7 Tweaking the file. Once your custom-color Photoshop file is set up and you've produced a comp, your printer may be able to help you improve the result. We showed our screen-capture comp and our Photoshop file to the printer, who suggested that we "push" the black ink farther back from the edge, to get a "cleaner" fade for the pink. We targeted the layer mask for the photo layer and used the Rectangular Marquee ⬚ to select an area from the edge inward beyond the fade. Then we pressed Ctrl/⌘-T (for Edit > Free Transform) and dragged the left side handle of the Transform frame to the left to expand the knockout for the edge **7a**.

Another suggestion was to partially erase some of the pink rose, "to let the black ink 'shape' the flower." Working on the Pantone 708 (pink) channel, we used the Eraser ⬦ with a low Opacity setting and a small, soft brush tip to take away some of the pink in the darkest and lightest areas of the rose **7b**.

Printing. When a comp has been approved, the file can be output directly from Photoshop. Or to place it in a page layout program, save a copy of the file in Photoshop DCS 2.0 format; turn on the As a Copy and Spot Colors options, but turn off the Alpha Channels and Layers options. Ask your printer for advice on the other settings. 🖉

PREVIEWING OPAQUE INKS

In a Grayscale file with Spot channels added, Photoshop's on-screen preview attempts to show how the printed piece will look if the inks are laid down in the order they appear in the Channels palette — that is, if the black ink in the top channel prints first, then the ink in the next channel down, and so on. To preview the effect of laying down a spot color before the black, you'll need to convert the file from Grayscale to Multichannel (Image > Mode > Multichannel), so you can freely drag Spot channel thumbnails above the Black ink channel.

When you want to preview an opaque metallic ink (for instance, Pantone 8062) that will print before the other inks, convert from Grayscale to Multichannel mode and reorder the channels. A screen capture of the preview shows how the inks should knock out or overprint.

Susan Thompson begins her impressionistic images by shooting the photos with a vintage 1970s Polaroid SX-70 camera, which uses film with the dye encapsulated under a protective sheet of clear mylar. The next step is to massage the unhardened emulsion with chopsticks and wooden hors d'oeuvres picks, carving lines and swirls and mixing the colors, as shown at the left. (Thompson begins altering the film about 15 minutes after the image appears, and the dyes typically remain pliable for about two hours, as long as the photo is kept warm.)

Thompson scans the photo into Photoshop and duplicates it to a new layer (Ctrl/⌘-J) to protect the original (shown at the left). She chooses View > Actual Pixels to get the most accurate view, and scrolls through the image, removing spots and scratches with the Healing Brush 🩹 and Clone Stamp 🔖. For **Summer in Arcata** she also used the Sponge 🧽 with Saturate Mode chosen in the Options bar to boost color in the hydrangeas and nasturtiums.▼

FIND OUT MORE

▼ Using the Healing Brush **page 310**
Clone Stamp **page 253**
& Sponge tool **page 173**

To transform the color of the scanned and edited photo, Thompson adds a number of Adjustment layers on which she makes changes globally or to selected areas of the image. Working on a calibrated monitor, she experiments in the Adjustment layer dialogs until she sees the colors she wants.

To improve color and contrast globally in **Summer in Arcata,** she added a **Curves Adjustment layer** (by clicking the ⬤ button at the bottom of the Layers palette and choosing Curves). In the Curves dialog box, she selected each of the color channels in turn and dragged the endpoints of the curve inward horizontally (as shown below for the Red channel). The result of adjusting all three curves was similar to (but more precise than) clicking the Curves dialog's "Auto" button, which enhances the color and contrast by adjusting each color channel separately. For the overall RGB curve, Thompson Ctrl/⌘-clicked in the image on shadow tones that she wanted to fine-tune; each click added a point to the curve, which she could then drag up slightly to lighten the targeted tones. To keep the highlights from getting too light in the process, she added another point near the top of the Curve and dragged down slightly.

Thompson also typically uses **Selective Color Adjustment layers** (⬤) to deepen or shift the color of specific color families throughout the image. She starts by choosing Neutrals from the Colors menu at the top of the dialog, so the changes she makes next will affect primarily the neutral (near gray) colors. As shown below, she warmed the grays in *Summer in Arcata* by removing a little blue (moving the Cyan and Magenta sliders to the left) and adding Yellow, and also added a small amount of Black. Then she went on to the other color families, making the Greens more intense, for example, by reducing the opposite component (Magenta), as shown below.

After making global changes, Thompson hones selected areas of the image with masked Adjustment layers. In this image she brightened the door with a Selective Color layer and neutralized the gray steps with a Hue/Saturation layer. She often creates the masked Adjustment layers by using the Lasso tool ◯ to select the area she wants to adjust, with the tool's Feather set to 0 pixels in the Options bar. With her selection active, she adds an Adjustment layer (⬤). The selected area automatically becomes the white area in the Adjustment layer's built-in mask,

revealing the changes she makes in the Adjustment layer's dialog box. Thompson then blurs the mask to soften the edge between the black and white areas (by choosing Filter > Blur > Gaussian Blur). This smooths the transition between the areas affected and unaffected by the adjustment. Thompson prefers the finer control of creating a hard-edged mask and then blurring the edges as she changes the Radius in the Gaussian Blur dialog box and previews changes on-screen, rather than trying blindly to pick the right Feather setting when she first makes the selection.

To complete her images, Thompson often uses Nik filters (www.niksoftware.com). For *Summer in Arcata,* first she added a new composite layer at the top of the stack; this can be done by holding down Shift-Ctrl-Alt (Windows) or Shift-⌘-Option (Mac) and typing N, then E. (In CS2 you can skip the N.) Photoshop automatically copied all visible artwork to the new layer. She ran the Sunshine and Skylight filters from the nik Color Efex Pro series, and then duplicated the filtered image to a new layer (Ctrl/⌘-J) and ran a sharpening filter from the nik Sharpener Pro series.

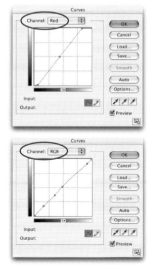

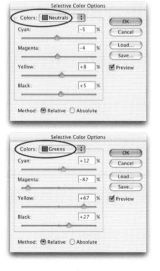

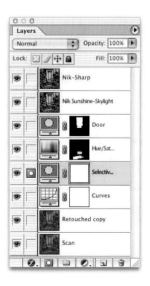

This glowing ***Botanical Portrait*** by **Christine Zalewski** started with her original photo of the flower **A**, which she duplicated to another layer (Ctrl/⌘-J) to keep the original safe. To straighten the stem and remove the leaves at the bottom of the duplicate but still maintain the photo's original proportions, she used the Rectangular Marquee ⌷ to make a selection the full width of the photo, extending from just below the upper leaves to just above the bend in the stem at the bottom of the image. Then she used the Edit > Free Transform command to stretch this section of the image to the bottom of the canvas (this technique, useful for extending the background of a photo, is described step-by-step in "Adding Type to an Image" on page 597).

After using the Healing Brush ⌷ to retouch a few spots,▼ she sharpened the transformed duplicate slightly.▼ Then she made a rough selection of the flower. With this selection active, she added a layer mask that hid the selected area by Alt/Option-clicking the "Add a layer mask" button ⌷ at the bottom of the Layers palette. She used the Brush tool ⌷ and black and white paint to clean up the mask.▼

Clicking the duplicate layer's image thumbnail in the Layers palette to target the image again instead of the mask, she added noise to the layer (Filter > Noise > Add Noise, Gaussian, Monochromatic) **B**. The "noisy" layer increased the visual contrast between the noise-textured background and the smooth flower showing through from the image underneath. For the noisy layer Zalewski chose the Darken blend mode from the pop-up list at the top of the Layers palette, so the noise would add texture rather than sparkle.

SUBTLE CAMOUFLAGE

If you need to slightly stretch part of an image that has an obvious "grain," a small amount of noise added to the entire image after stretching can help hide the difference in the grain between the stretched and unstretched areas.

To make the flower glow, Zalewski made another duplicate of the image and dragged it up to the top of the stack in the Layers palette. She blurred this image (Filter > Blur > Gaussian Blur) **C** and changed its blend mode to Overlay **D.** (Creating a glow by applying a blurred layer in Screen, Lighten, or one of the contrast blend modes, such as Overlay, is described step-by-step in "Softening the Focus" on page 334.)

Using a series of Curves Adjustment layers, similar to those described for ***Anemone*** on page 354, Zalewski lightened the image and made the flower more luminous **E**. Next she added a Hue/Saturation Adjustment layer; in the Hue/Saturation dialog box she made a minor adjustment to the Hue slider to make the image pinker and moved the Saturation slider to the right slightly to increase color intensity. As one last color adjustment, she added a Selective Color Adjustment layer; in the Selective Color dialog box she chose Reds from the Colors menu, and made the Yellow value slightly negative to remove yellow from the reds without affecting other colors in the image, producing the final portrait on the facing page.

SUBTLE HUE/SATURATION

A Hue/Saturation Adjustment layer can be ideal for subtle color changes. To avoid obvious digital artifacts in the color, it's a good idea to keep changes relatively small when you work with the Hue and Saturation sliders. For adjusting brightness, an additional Curves or Levels layer gives you more control of the change than does the Lightness slider in the Hue/Saturation dialog box.

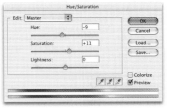

FIND OUT MORE

▼ Using the Healing Brush ⌷
  page 310

▼ Sharpening an image **page 255**

▼ Selecting & making masks **page 55**

A　B　C　D　E

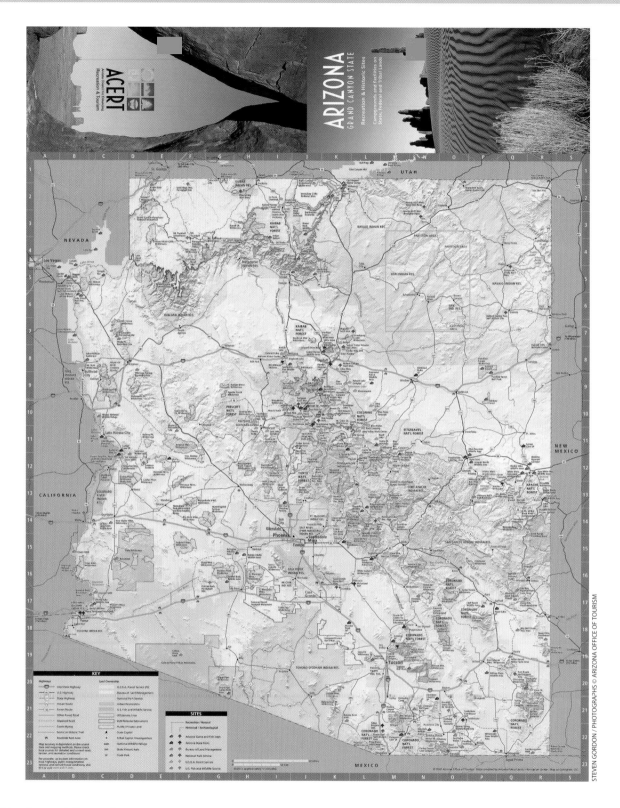

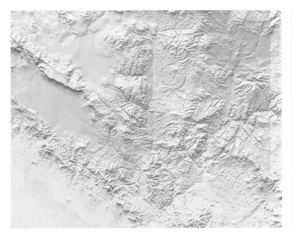

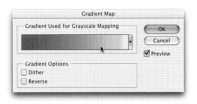

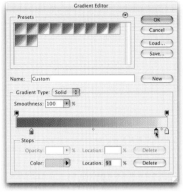

For the ***Arizona Recreation and Historical Sites*** map, cartographer **Steven Gordon** built a terrain image with colors signifying the federal agencies and tribal nations that own public land in Arizona. He began the terrain image in Natural Scene Designer, software that imports real geographic-elevation data, lets you set the sun angle and other parameters, and turns the data into an image (**www.naturalgfx.com**). After opening the resulting RGB TIFF in Photoshop, he converted the image to gray tones in a CMYK file (Image > Mode > Grayscale, then Image > Mode > CMYK) so he could color it using the CMYK specifications in government publication guidelines for map colors representing federal agency lands.

To prepare for coloring, Gordon placed Illustrator files (File > Place) that he had created earlier from geographic data for each class of public land, using MAPublisher plug-ins (**www.avenza.com**). He chose Gradient Map Adjustment layers for coloring the map because each gradient could maintain the unique color for a class of public land while allowing natural variations of color in the terrain shadows and highlights. To start building the adjustment layers, Gordon made a selection from each layer of the placed Illustrator artwork by Ctrl/⌘-clicking the layer's thumbnail in

the Layers palette. Then he clicked the ⊘ button at the bottom of the Layers palette and selected Gradient Map from the pop-up menu. This automatically created an Adjustment layer in the palette, masked to color the selected area, and displayed the Gradient Map dialog box, where Gordon clicked "OK" to finish creating the Adjustment layer.

Once all Adjustment layers had been created, Gordon made an additional mask for coloring the areas that surround the public lands. To do this, he held down the Shift key as he Ctrl/⌘-clicked the thumbnails of all of the placed Illustrator artwork layers; then he inverted the selection (Select > Inverse) and clicked the ⊘ button again to add another Gradient Map Adjustment layer, masked for this surrounding area. Finally, he deleted each of the Illustrator artwork layers by dragging its thumbnail to the 🗑 button at the bottom of the Layers palette.

Now he was ready to begin coloring each Adjustment layer. He double-clicked a Gradient Map thumbnail in the Layers palette to reopen the Gradient Map dialog box, where he made sure that the Preview box was checked and then clicked on the gradient preview bar to open the Gradient Editor.

He wanted the gradient to start with a dark brown color for terrain shadows, then progress into the distinctive color chosen for the particular class of public land, and end with a pale tint of that color for the highlights. To do this, he clicked below the gradient preview bar to create a third color stop in the gradient. Then he double-clicked each of the three Color stops in turn to open the Color Picker, where he entered numbers to mix the colors he needed. By sliding the Color stops, Gordon could preview the gradient's effect on the terrain image. When he was satisfied, he typed a name into the Name field of the Gradient Editor and then clicked the "New" button to add the gradient to the current palette of Presets. He finished by clicking the Gradient Editor's "OK" button and then clicking the Gradient Map box's "OK" button.

Gordon followed much the same procedure to create the Gradient Map Adjustment layers for the remaining public land areas. When he completed the terrain image, he saved a flattened copy of the file as a TIFF and placed it in Illustrator, where he added type, symbols, and linework to complete the map.

JHDAVIS / MODEL: LATISHA TOLBERT / AGENCY: ANDERSON PHOTOGRAPHICS.COM

To draw viewers' attention to the model's eyes in the *Portrait* above, **Jack Davis** started with his original photo **A** and did a quick "dodge and burn" treatment to increase the contrast between the background and the hair, and to lighten the area around the eyes **B**. First he added a layer by Alt/Option-clicking the "Create a new layer" button at the bottom of the Layers palette. Because of the Alt/Option key, the New Layer dialog box opened, where he could choose Overlay as the Mode and turn on the "Fill with Overlay-neutral color (50% Gray)" option. (Use Soft Light mode instead of Overlay if you want to affect mostly the midtones.)

Because it was in Overlay mode, the new 50% gray–filled layer made no change in the image until Davis started painting on the layer with a large, soft-edged Brush . Using black or white paint and with a low Opacity setting in the Options bar, he could quickly darken or lighten the image where he wanted, without worrying about permanently changing the image itself on the layer below. ▼

Next he experimented with reducing the image to monochrome **C**. He added a Channel Mixer Adjustment layer by clicking the "Create new fill or adjustment layer" button at the bottom of the Layers palette and choosing from the pop-up menu. In

the Channel Mixer dialog box he chose Monochrome and balanced the mix of Red, Green, and Blue channels to control the look of the black-and-white version of the image. ▼

Finally, he took advantage of the Channel Mixer layer's built-in mask to restore color to the eyes and hair. In the Layers palette he clicked the layer's mask thumbnail to activate it and painted with light gray **D** to partially bring back the color.

FIND OUT MORE

▼ Using a "dodge & burn" layer
page 329

▼ Using Channel Mixer
page 213

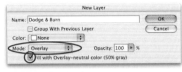

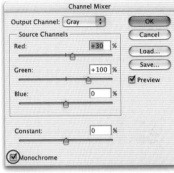

A

B

C

D

DODGING & BURNING ON GRAY

A quick and effective way to "dodge and burn" a photo is to add a layer in Overlay mode (or sometimes Soft Light, if you want changes primarily in the midtones) and paint it with black and white using a soft Brush at low Opacity. Because 50% gray is neutral (transparent) in these blend modes, the result will be the same whether you paint on an empty transparent layer or a 50% gray–filled one. But it can be easier to see what you're doing if you use a gray-filled layer. Temporarily switching the blend mode from Overlay to Normal will let you see where you've painted, which can help you decide where to paint next. With the neutral gray background, it's easier to see your lighter and darker strokes than it is if the layer is transparent.

Enhancing Photos

5

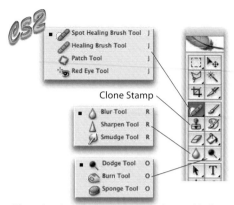

Clone Stamp

Photoshop's retouching tools have been added to and improved in versions CS and CS2. The Healing Brush , which automatically blends the edges of its repairs with the surroundings, now has a Use All Layers/Sample All Layers option, as do the Clone Stamp and Spot Healing Brush, so you can keep your repairs on a separate layer and mask them or change their opacity if needed. The Spot Healing Brush automatically samples from the area surrounding the brush tip, without the need to designate a source. The Blur, Sharpen, Dodge, Burn, and Sponge tools, while sometimes useful for a quick touchup, can be tricky to use with photos. Often you can get better results with a filter applied to a masked duplicate image, or with a "dodge-and-burn" layer, as described in the "Retouching Photos" section on pages 253 through 256.

The new Red Eye tool was designed especially to quickly repair that particular flash artifact (see page 313).

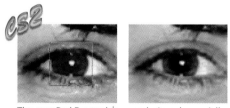

Using the Rectangular Marquee and the Image > Crop command trims away edges without resampling the photo. Your file's dimensions are reduced, but its resolution stays the same.

PHOTOSHOP HAS A WEALTH OF TECHNIQUES for enhancing photos — from emulating traditional camera and darkroom techniques such as soft focus and vignettes, to retouching and hand-tinting. But much of the day-to-day production work done with Photoshop involves simply trying to get the best possible reproduction of a photo — a crisp and clear print or on-screen image, with the fullest possible range of accurate tone and color. Many photos will need cropping, and some will need correction for camera lens distortion or for the digital noise typical of photos taken in low-light conditions. Many can also benefit from overall ("global") adjustments to tonality and color, selective ("local") touch-up, and sharpening to repair any "softness" introduced in the scan or the fixing process.

If the photo you start with was taken in a camera's raw format, you can adjust color and contrast, sharpen, and reduce noise in the Camera Raw interface, before the photo is actually opened in Photoshop.▼ In the version of Camera Raw that comes with Photoshop CS2, you can also crop and straighten raw photos.

If your photo is in 16 Bits/Channel mode,▼ you can now add regular layers and Adjustment layers and use blend modes — you have nearly the full range of capabilities for adjusting tone and color that you have in 8 Bits/Channel mode. Image files in 16 Bits/Channel mode are large, however, so a method for economizing by working with a single layer is described in "Memory Economy in 16-Bit Mode" on page 217.

If your photo is in the 32 Bits/Channel mode offered by Photoshop CS2,▼ you can still crop and adjust exposure,▼ taking advantage of the extra color and tone information in the file before you convert it to 16 Bits or 8 Bits for further work or output.

CROPPING

Cropping a photo is often done to improve composition, to remove something distracting in the background, or to reduce the work involved in repairing a damaged photo. As usual, Photoshop provides several ways to do the job:

- Make a selection of the area you want to keep and then choose **Image > Crop**;
- Choose **Image > Trim** and make choices in the Trim dialog box.

FIND OUT MORE

▼ Camera Raw
page 102

▼ 16 Bits/Channel
mode **page 156**

▼ 32 Bits/Channel
mode **page 157**

▼ The Exposure
command **page 171**

To allow a soft or decorative edge on a crop made with the Rectangular Marquee ⬚, you can make the rectangular selection, create a layer mask from it, and modify the mask with filters, as in "'Framing' with Masks" on page 260.

Using the Trim command is a good way to avoid abruptly cutting off the outer part of a soft edge.

To keep the relationship between the height and width of your cropped image the same as it was in the original, choose the Crop tool ⬚ and click the "Front Image" button in the Options bar **A**; to crop without resampling, delete the value in the Resolution field **B**, and drag with the Crop tool to reframe the photo **C**.

- Or choose the **Crop tool** ⬚ and make choices in the tool's Options bar.

The Crop Command

The advantage of the first method — **Image > Crop** — is that it's very **simple and straightforward**. If you make your selection with the Rectangular Marquee ⬚ and choose Image > Crop, the image is trimmed to the pulsating selection border. If you make the selection with any other method, the image will be cropped to the smallest rectangle that can completely contain the selection, including any antialiasing or feathering *inside* the selection boundary, *but not including any feathering outside the border or any exterior effects applied by a Layer Style*, such as a Drop Shadow, Outer Bevel, or Outer Glow.▼ **To change the size or proportions of the crop** after you've made the selection but before choosing Image > Crop, choose Select > Transform Selection, adjust the size of the selection, and double-click to complete the transformation.

FIND OUT MORE

▼ Working with Layer Styles **page 44**

The Trim Command

The **Trim** method is ideal for **cropping images with soft edges**, to get them to their smallest possible size without accidentally clipping off part of the soft edge. To crop with the Trim command, choose **Image > Trim** and then choose the options you want in the Trim dialog box. You can choose to trim away any or all of the four edges of the image. The trim will be based on "cutting off" pixels from the edge inward, and it can be set to trim transparent pixels (you have to turn off visibility for any background layers before using this option), or pixels that are the same color as the top left or bottom right pixel.

The Crop Tool

Using the **Crop tool** ⬚ also has advantages in some cropping situations. Once you drag the tool across your image to define the area you want to keep:

- **It's easy to adjust the size or proportions of the cropping frame** simply by dragging on a corner handle. To keep the ratio of height to width constant as you change size, Shift-drag on a handle.

- **You can change the orientation of an image** as you crop it by dragging around just outside a corner handle to rotate the frame. This function lets you **straighten a crooked scan**, **level the horizon** in an image that was taken at a tilt, **or simply reframe an image in a different orientation**.

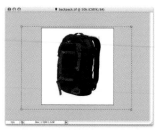

K & L DESIGNS / ORIGINAL PHOTOS: JEFF LANCASTER

Dragging the Crop tool 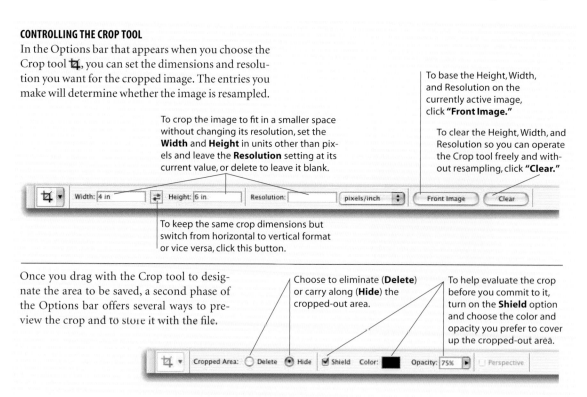 outward beyond the edges of the image (top) added more canvas for building a still life.

- **It's possible to crop *and* resize** the image in a single step by setting the Height, Width, and Resolution values you want for the cropped image in the Options bar before you drag to make the crop. (If you set the Height and Width in pixels, there's no need to set Resolution.) ***Note:*** A disadvantage of using the Crop tool is that it's possible to *unintentionally* resample an image as you crop it. To avoid this, make sure that in the Options bar either the dimension fields or the Resolution field are empty, and the dimensions are not set in pixels.

- **To maintain the original aspect ratio of your photo** (so it isn't apparent whether the image was framed in the camera when it was shot or whether it was cropped afterwards), before you crop, click the "Front Image" button in the Options bar. This sets the Crop tool to the Height, Width, and Resolution of the original image. If you want to maintain the aspect ratio, but don't want to resample the image, select and delete the value in the Resolution field before you drag with the Crop tool.

- **You can enlarge** the "canvas" around your image, with full control of how much is added at each edge of the photo.

CONTROLLING THE CROP TOOL

In the Options bar that appears when you choose the Crop tool ⬚, you can set the dimensions and resolution you want for the cropped image. The entries you make will determine whether the image is resampled.

To base the Height, Width, and Resolution on the currently active image, click **"Front Image."**

To crop the image to fit in a smaller space without changing its resolution, set the **Width** and **Height** in units other than pixels and leave the **Resolution** setting at its current value, or delete to leave it blank.

To clear the Height, Width, and Resolution so you can operate the Crop tool freely and without resampling, click **"Clear."**

To keep the same crop dimensions but switch from horizontal to vertical format or vice versa, click this button.

Once you drag with the Crop tool to designate the area to be saved, a second phase of the Options bar offers several ways to preview the crop and to store it with the file.

Choose to eliminate (**Delete**) or carry along (**Hide**) the cropped-out area.

To help evaluate the crop before you commit to it, turn on the **Shield** option and choose the color and opacity you prefer to cover up the cropped-out area.

Correcting distortion with Photoshop CS2's Filter > Distort > Lens Correction often leaves "empty" areas at the edges of an image. The Lens Correction interface has its own cropping function, allowing you to enlarge the image from the center until transparent edges are "pushed" outside the frame (see page 283). Or you can exit the Lens Correction interface and use one of Photoshop's standard cropping methods.

First make more space in the working window for expanding the crop (drag outward on the working window's lower right corner, or type Ctrl-Alt-hyphen in Windows or ⌘-Option-hyphen on the Mac). Then use the Crop tool ⊞ to drag across the entire image. And finally, drag a corner handle of the cropping frame outward to the proportions you want for the enlarged canvas (Shift-drag to maintain proportionality, Alt/Option-drag to enlarge the crop from the center, or combine these keys to do both at once).

Once you drag to frame the crop, the Crop tool's Options bar changes. You can now choose to **Shield** the cropped-out portion with the color and Opacity you choose, and move the Crop box around until you have the crop you want. If your image isn't flattened — that is, if it doesn't consist of a *Background* alone, with no other layers — you can also choose whether to **Delete** the area you're about to crop out or **Hide** it (keeping the cropped-out edge areas outside the image frame but still available). Hiding allows flexibility — you can later decide to change the "framing" of the image. And it can be useful in animation — the cropped image defines the size of the "stage" area, and the frames of the animation can be created by dragging the image across the stage with the Move tool ▶⊹ in small steps, and capturing each move as a frame. But hiding may also cause trouble, as described in the "Caution: 'Hidden' Crop" tip at the left. To complete the cropping operation, click the ✔ button in the Options bar to "commit" the crop, or click the ⊘ button to cancel it (double-clicking and pressing the Escape key are the respective shortcuts).

CORRECTING FOR CAMERA DISTORTION

Photoshop CS2's **Lens Correction** (Filter > Distort > Lens Correction) provides an interface designed specifically for correcting camera-related distortion of both geometry and color that can happen when a photo is taken. In CS you can use a combination of Transform commands, Distort filters, and Gaussian Blur to accomplish similar corrections. "Compensating for

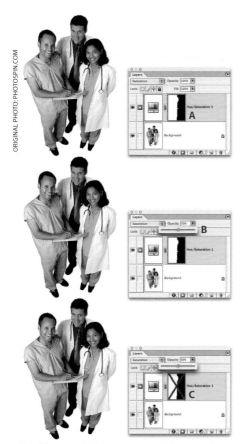

For this example from page 298, adding an Adjustment layer provided more flexibility than using a command from the Image > Adjustments menu would have. For example, we could paint a layer mask to restrict the adjustment **A**. It was also easy to go back later and reduce the layer's Opacity to only partially desaturate the two men **B**. And we could turn off visibility for the layer mask (by Shift-clicking its thumbnail) so the adjustment applied to the entire photo **C**.

STACKING ORDER

When you use more than one Adjustment layer to correct the contrast, exposure, or color in an image, it's as if you had applied the corrections in order: The lower the Adjustment layer is in the stack, the earlier its correction was made.

Camera-Related Distortion" on page 279 works through an example in both CS and CS2, and "Exercising Lens Correction" on page 276 examines how the Lens Correction filter works.

ADJUSTING TONE & COLOR

Once your image is cropped, you'll often want to make tone and color changes to the entire image or to selected areas. You can apply these changes either by choosing commands from the **Image** > **Adjustments** submenu or by adding an **Adjustment layer**. As you work with tone and color adjustments, remember that for your final image to match the preview that your screen shows you, your monitor and output system need to be calibrated and matched, as described in "Getting Consistent Color" in Chapter 4.

Working with Adjustment Layers

Because they provide so much flexibility, **it's almost always worthwhile to use an Adjustment layer** rather than choosing the same command from the Image menu. With the adjustment in a separate layer that's maintained in the file, you can later change the settings for the adjustment itself, or change its strength by reducing the layer's Opacity. You can also target the adjustment to a particular area using the built-in layer mask.▼ Or target a particular tonal range or color family with the "Blend If" sliders.▼

FIND OUT MORE

▼ Using layer masks
  page 75

▼ Using Blending
  Options **page 76**

You add an Adjustment layer by clicking the "Create new fill or adjustment layer" button ◑ at the bottom of the Layers palette and choosing the type of adjustment you want from the pop-out menu. You'll find many examples of using Adjustment layers in this chapter and throughout the book. Look on page 266 for a "how-to catalog" of examples of tone and color corrections, many of which were accomplished with Adjustment layers.

The Histogram

In Photoshop CS/CS2 the **Histogram** (which was previously available only when the Levels dialog box was open) now has its own palette and can sit open on-screen so that you can monitor tone and color changes "live" while you make adjustments. The Histogram's graph shows what proportion of the image's pixels (indicated by the relative height of each vertical bar) is in each of 256 tones or *luminance values* (spread along the horizontal axis, from black on the left to white on the right). The darkest pixels in the image are represented by the leftmost

When you try out changes in a dialog box with a Preview option, the Histogram shows the distribution of tones before (lighter graph) and after the proposed change. If you're using an Adjustment layer, set the Histogram's Source to Adjustment Composite.

Spaces in the Histogram indicate that the tonal range you've set holds more potential tones than are expressed in the image. (Using the "Auto" button avoids gaps because tones in each of the color channels are adjusted separately, but for the same reason, it can cause a color shift.)

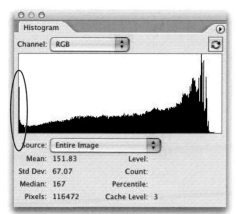

When an adjustment causes a peak to build up at either end of the Histogram, it indicates that highlight or shadow detail is being lost as the lightest or darkest tones are pushed to white or black.

vertical bar of the histogram; the lightest pixels are represented by the bar at the right end.

The distribution of tones in the Histogram for an unadjusted photo often just reinforces what you can already see by looking at the image. If the graph doesn't extend all the way to the left edge of the frame, it means there are no fully black pixels; if it doesn't extend all the way to the right, there are no fully white pixels. Often you'll want to increase the contrast in that case, but there may be times when you prefer a limited range of tones. The Histogram can't answer preference questions — it simply reflects the state of the image.

For an image that's dark overall, the Histogram shows more of its pixels on the left side of the graph than on the right. A light image shows more pixels on the right. Your photo may be under- or overexposed and you may want to correct for this. Or the image may simply be dark or light because of its content and may not need correction.

If you expand the Histogram palette to look at the distribution of tones in each of the color channels for the image, it may help you identify a color cast and see what to do to correct it.

The Histogram can be very helpful in monitoring changes in contrast (tonal range) or shadow and highlight detail as you make adjustments. For any tone or color dialog box that has a Preview option (such as Curves, Hue/Saturation, Color Balance, and many others), the Histogram can compare the "before" version of the image with what will be the "after" version if you make the adjustment that's currently set up in the dialog box. As you make color and tone adjustments, if either end of the Histogram builds up as you adjust tone and color, it can mean that you're losing detail in the highlights or shadows as contrast increases and more of the lightest or darkest tones are pushed to white or black. If one of the colors in the expanded Histogram shifts farther left or right than the others, a color cast may be developing (or diminishing). ▼

FIND OUT MORE

▼ Using the Histogram **page 163**

Adjusting Overall Contrast & Exposure

In an image with highlights and shadows, you'll often want to get the broadest range of tones possible by lightening the lightest tones in the image to the lightest printable "white," and darkening the darkest area to the darkest printable "black," and thus spreading the in-between tones over a greater range of brightness.

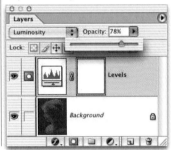

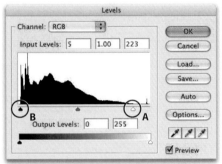

When you move the white Input Levels slider inward **A**, you're telling Photoshop that you want all pixels lighter than this value to become white. Likewise, moving the black point slider inward **B** says that you want all pixels darker than this value to be black.

Auto adjustments. The Levels and Curves dialog boxes both have **"Auto"** and **"Options"** buttons for automated corrections to tone and color. "Color Adjustment Options" starting on page 165 tells how they work, and "Quick Tone & Color Adjustments" starting on page 266 includes several step-by-step examples of applying and adapting these "instant fixes." If an "Auto" adjustment to Levels or Curves doesn't work, you can undo it (by holding down Alt/Option to turn the "Cancel" button into "Reset," and clicking it); then try adjusting "by hand" instead, as described next.

Adjusting Levels or Curves by hand. You can set the black point, white point, midtones, and neutral color by hand in the Levels or Curves dialog box. We'll cover both dialog boxes together, so it's easy to see how their settings correspond. When you adjust Levels or Curves, be sure the Preview option is turned on in the dialog box so you can see the effect of your changes in the image. Turning on Preview also allows the Histogram palette to show "before" and "after" versions of the tone distribution.

1 The first step is to expand the range of tones in the image.

Using Levels. Like the Histogram palette, the Levels dialog graphs the distribution of tones. To improve contrast, in the Levels box drag the **black point** slider and the **white point** slider for Input Levels to a point just a little inside where the graph's bars start at the left and right ends of the graph, respectively. As you watch the changes in the Histogram palette, contrast will be at its (technical) optimum when the graph indicates that there are some white and some black pixels. But stop your contrast adjustment before the black and white bars get disproportionately taller, because that will mean you're losing shadow or highlight detail as dark and light pixels get pushed all the way to black or white.

Sometimes you can identify a narrow "hump" at the extreme left or right end of the histogram that may come from extraneous very dark or very light pixels. In that case you may get better results by dragging the black or white point slider inward to a position just barely inside the hump.

Using Curves. The "curve" in the Curves dialog box represents the relationship of tones before and after you make adjustments. It starts out as a straight line, until you add points and move them to reshape the line into a curve. With the Curves dialog set up so the dark ends of the tone bars are at the bottom and left, you can increase contrast by

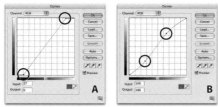

Moving the endpoints of the graph straight inward in the Curves dialog box **A** produces a result like moving the black and white Input Levels sliders inward in the Levels dialog. By allowing you to make an S-shaped curve **B**, the Curves dialog offers more control of what happens to the darkest and lightest tones than Levels does (see page 332).

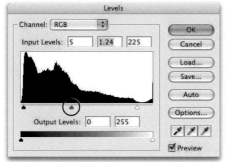

Dragging the gamma Input Levels slider in the Levels dialog box lightens or darkens the image overall without changing the black or white points.

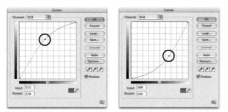

Dragging the middle of the Curve up or down will lighten or darken the image. Because you can also drag left or right, you have more control of overall tonal adjustments when you use Curves than when you use the gamma slider in Levels.

moving the black corner point horizontally along the axis until the bars in the Histogram palette reach the far left end; move the white point horizontally along its axis until the Histogram palette shows bars at the far right end, being careful not to overdo it, as described earlier for Levels.

2 Once you've made the Levels or Curves adjustments in step 1, you'll have a full range of tones from black to white. But the photo may still be too dark overall (underexposed) or too light overall (overexposed).

In the Levels dialog, you can remedy this by moving the gray (gamma, middle) Input Levels slider to lighten or darken the image overall.

In the Curves dialog, the same correction can be made by dragging the middle of the curve. To lighten the image, drag up. To darken the image, drag down. An advantage of Curves over Levels is that you can "bow" the curve downward or upward to control which part is steep and which is shallow. Where the curve is steep, the tones are being stretched farther from each other, increasing the contrast between them. This contrast can create sharpness and an illusion of detail because the eye is attuned to finding edges, and the increased contrast can help us see the edges. Conversely, where the curve is shallow, the number of tonal steps is reduced, decreasing contrast and sharpness.

3 Even with contrast and overall exposure adjusted, there may be an unwanted color cast in the image. **To attempt to correct a color cast,** choose the gray eyedropper in the Levels or Curves dialog (the Set Gray Point dropper) and click it on a color in the image that should be a neutral middletone gray, with no color. Page 270 shows an example. (If you can't find a spot that works, see "Removing a Persistent Color Cast" below, or try one of the Average methods on page 271.)

Correcting Particular Exposure Problems

Once the overall contrast and exposure are adjusted, it's time to address exposure problems in particular tonal ranges or particular areas of the image.

Assessing and adjusting with Curves. You can **adjust particular parts of the tonal range** using the **Curves** dialog box; for instance, you can bring out shadow detail without affecting other parts of the range, or increase contrast in the midtones. If you move the cursor out of the Curves dialog box, it turns into an eyedropper. Clicking on a particular value in the

An "S" Curves adjustment increases contrast in the midtones. See page 332 for the step-by-step process.

A modified "M" Curves adjustment can also be used to increase contrast. See page 332.

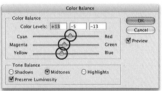

One way to remove a color cast is by adding the opposite of what you have too much of. Here a greenish-blue cast from light coming through the tent was removed by adding red, yellow, and a little magenta to the midtones.

image shows the position of that tone on the curve, or **Ctrl/⌘-clicking automatically adds the point to the curve**. Once you've identified the part of the tonal range you want to affect, you can anchor the curve in other areas, where you don't want the contrast to change, by clicking to set points on the unaltered part of the curve. Then you can lighten or darken your targeted part of the tonal range by dragging a point to reshape that area of the curve. Examples of two useful adjustments — an "M" adjustment and an "S" adjustment — are described step-by-step on page 332. *Note:* If you move points to create more extreme curves than a "gentle M" or "S," you can run into trouble. Anything more than a subtle move can cause solarizing of the image (inversion of some tones) or posterizing (obviously reducing the number of colors).

Removing a Persistent Color Cast

If the image still seems to have color problems after you've expanded the tonal range, corrected for exposure, and tried the Set Gray Point eyedropper in the Levels or Curves dialog box, you can try a Hue/Saturation or Color Balance Adjustment layer (you'll find examples in "Quick Tone & Color Adjustments," starting on page 266). Keeping the Histogram palette open allows you to watch for changes in contrast or loss of highlight or shadow detail as you work.

- **To make the same overall color shift** in highlights, midtones, and shadows all at once, you can use **Hue/Saturation:** With the Preview box checked, drag the Hue slider. At the bottom of the dialog box, the top spectrum bar shows the "before" state, and the bottom bar shows how colors have shifted in the "after" state.

- **To target color shifts to the highlights, midtones, or shadows individually,** use **Color Balance**. In the Color Balance dialog box, click to choose which of the three tonal ranges you want to change, then drag the sliders to add the opposite of what your image has too much of. For instance, if it shows a blue cast in the highlights, click the Highlights button and move the Blue/Yellow slider toward the Yellow end.

Targeting Color Changes

Some images may require a targeted color change rather than an overall adjustment. **To change one particular color or family of colors,** pick the appropriate color family from the Edit menu at the top of the **Hue/Saturation** dialog box, then use the dialog box's eyedropper to click in your image to target a

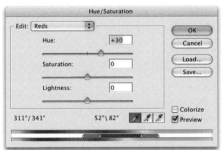

The family of colors you want to target — for instance, oranges — may not be listed as a choice in the Edit menu of the Hue/Saturation dialog. In that case just choose one of the color families next to it on a standard color wheel — Yellows or Reds in the case of orange. Then click or drag the "+" dropper in the image to expand the range of targeted colors. Use the "–" dropper to remove colors (such as reds that aren't "orangey") from the range. To make a more gradual transition between the colors that will change and those that won't, drag the small white triangles outward to enlarge the light gray "fuzziness" bars, or drag inward to make sharper transitions.

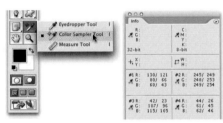

In the Info palette for an RGB file, higher "after" numbers overall for Color Samplers indicate lightening, and lower numbers indicate darkening (just the opposite is true for a CMYK file). A disproportionate increase in one or more of the component colors indicates that color is shifting.

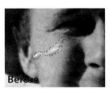

The Patch tool, which automatically blends the edges of its repairs, is great for repairing scratches and tears in photos (see page 317). It doesn't have a Use All Layers option, so it's a good idea to use it on a duplicate layer.

particular color within that range. You can expand the range (shown by the dark gray bar that appears between the spectrum bars) as described at the left. Pages 273 and 274 have several step-by-step examples of Hue/Saturation adjustments.

Just as the Histogram palette can be useful for monitoring overall changes in tone and color, **Color Samplers** provide a great way to monitor changes in specific areas. You can use the Color Sampler tool, which shares a spot in the tools palette with the Eyedropper, to place up to four Samplers, and then read the data in the Info palette. ▼

FIND OUT MORE

▼ Color Sampler tool
page 162

RETOUCHING PHOTOS

With Photoshop's retouching tools (shown on page 244) you can "hand-paint" repairs to an image. If you use these tools directly on an image, it can be difficult to go back later and correct a several-stroke mistake. Here are some ways to do retouching so you don't risk damaging the original image if you make a mistake, and so individual corrections can be easily identified so you can remove or repair them. You'll find step-by-step examples of using the retouching tools in "Quick Coverups" on page 317 and in "Quick Cosmetic Changes" on page 311.

• One quick way **to remove dust and small scratches** is to duplicate the image in a layer above and run the Dust & Scratches filter on this layer. Then add a black-filled layer mask to hide the entire filtered image, and finally paint the mask with white where you need the filtered image to hide the blemishes. This method is described step-by-step in "Fixing a Problem Photo" on page 302. You can also use Dust & Scratches as a "pretreatment" before using the **Healing Brush**, as described in "Healing Brush in Pattern Mode" on page 318.

• **To remove larger blemishes or to cover up a distracting element in the background of a photo,** use the **Patch Tool** or **Clone Stamp**. The Clone Stamp can work on a transparent "repairs" layer above the image if you first set the tool to Use All Layers/Sample All Layers in the Options bar. The Clone Stamp works especially well in Non-aligned mode with a medium-soft brush tip. Alt/Option-click to pick up neighboring image detail, and click to deposit it over the area you want to hide. Since the repairs are on a separate layer, you can change your fixes at any time.

The Healing Brush ✎ can be set to "heal" by using a pattern, rather than by sampling color and texture from an image. This makes it possible to quickly remove fine lines such as telephone wires against the sky by using the Dust & Scratches filter on a copy of the image, and then using this blurred copy as the Pattern for the Healing Brush. See "Quick Coverups" on page 318 for the method.

It's easier to control targeted changes in tone and color control with a "dodge-and-burn" layer in Overlay or Soft Light mode than with the Dodge and Burn tools.

Photoshop CS2's Vanishing Point filter▼ has its own Stamp tool ⊕ that works according to the grid you set up for your image. Here this tool is being used to clone leaf litter and grass from near the bottom of the image to hide distracting elements near the top.

FIND OUT MORE

▼ Using Vanishing
Point **pages 357 & 588**

The **Patch tool** ◌ works on the current layer only, unlike the tools that can sample from all visible layers and make repairs on a separate, empty layer. For more flexibility, before you use the Patch tool, duplicate the layer that needs fixing (Ctrl/⌘-J will do this), and work on this copy, leaving the original layer intact. The Patch tool uses the same edge-blending and tone-matching technology as the Healing Brush, but it can work by selecting the area to be repaired and then replacing it with other image material. It's good for camouflaging large scratches or tears in a photo, and it can be used to duplicate selected material to other areas of an image, blending it with the surroundings. (If the material you need to use for the repair is in the foreground of your image, and the repair itself needs to be done in the background, you can automatically shrink the repair material proportionally by using the Stamp tool that you'll find inside the Vanishing Point filter's interface.)▼

- **To increase the contrast, brightness, or detail of particular areas of an image,** add a layer above your image, putting this new layer in Overlay or Soft Light mode and filling it with 50% gray, which is neutral (invisible) in these modes. Then work on this layer by using black paint (to dodge), white paint (to burn), or shades of gray, with a soft Brush ✎ with or without Airbrush mode ✎ turned on in the Options bar; set Pressure or Opacity very low. (If oversaturation occurs in Overlay mode, try changing the blend mode of this gray-filled "Dodge & Burn" layer to Soft Light.) This dodge-and-burn method is shown on page 329 and is also demonstrated in step 6 of "'Photomerging' a Panorama" on page 608. *Note:* The Dodge tool ✎ and Burn tool ◌ can also target adjustments to contrast, brightness, and detail. But using these tools can be slow and a bit confusing. First, you have to contend with three different Range options for each tool (Highlights, Midtones, or Shadows) set in the Options bar. And second, when you hand-paint with the tools, you don't really know that you've reached the optimal result until you've overshot it and gone too far; then you have to undo and redo until you get it right. Also, you can't isolate your changes on a separate "repairs" layer. So it often works better to use the "dodge and burn layer" method, described above.

- **To increase or decrease color saturation of certain areas in an image,** add a Hue/Saturation Adjustment layer and make a Saturation adjustment that cures the particular problem — for the moment, ignore what happens to the rest of the image. Fill the Adjustment layer's built-in mask with

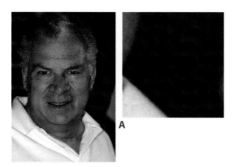

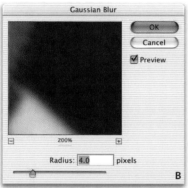

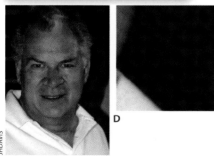

In an image with obvious digital noise **A**, you can even out the color by duplicating the image to a new layer (Ctrl/⌘-J) and running the Gaussian Blur filter just enough to get rid of the "clumps" of colored noise **B**. Then set the blend mode of this layer to Color **C**. Your "after" image will be cleaner, with less noticeable noise **D**. In Photoshop CS2, the new Reduce Noise filter also addresses this problem.

black, which will completely mask the Saturation change. Finally, use a soft Brush 🖌, with or without the Airbrush function 🖌 turned on in the Options bar, to paint with white in the problem areas; the lightened areas of the mask will allow the saturation changes to come through. *Note:* The Sponge tool 🖌 can also be used for saturating or desaturating, but it can be difficult to make the saturation changes you want without also changing contrast or affecting more of the image than you intended. So using a masked Hue/Saturation layer often works better than using the Sponge. Also, the Sponge can't be used on a separate "repairs" layer.

NOISE REDUCTION

The **Gaussian Blur** filter and the new Reduce Noise filter in Photoshop CS2 are effective for evening out the fine-grained color irregularities (**noise**) in a digital photograph, particularly one that has had dramatic tone and color adjustments. Either of these methods can also be useful for fixing a color fringe (chromatic aberration). An example of the Gaussian Blur technique is shown at the left, and another example, addressed with Gaussian Blur in Photoshop CS and **Reduce Noise** in CS2, can be found in step 3 of "Bringing Out Detail" on page 323.

SHARPENING

Running the **Unsharp Mask** filter or the **Smart Sharpen** filter in Photoshop CS2 almost always improves a scanned photo. Likewise, transforming or resizing an image can also "soften" it, so that sharpening is helpful, although the Bicubic Sharper option available in the Resample Image menu in CS/CS2's Image Size dialog box may provide enough sharpening in some cases. ▼ You can find step-by-step examples of sharpening, both with the sharpening filters and with other methods, in "Quick Ways To Bring Out Detail" on page 326. Usually sharpening is the last thing that should be done to an image before it's prepared for the press, because otherwise the synthetic effects of sharpening can be magnified in other image-editing processes, such as increasing the color saturation.

FIND OUT MORE

▼ Using the Image Size dialog box
page 74

To sharpen particular parts of the image, add a duplicate layer, Sharpen this layer with the appropriate filter (Filter > Sharpen > Unsharp Mask or Smart Sharpen). Add a black-filled layer mask and use the Brush 🖌 and white paint. You can also target sharpening to particular tonal ranges using the "Blend If" sliders

SHARPENING LUMINOSITY

Sharpening can cause changes in color as the contrast is increased. The more intense the sharpening, the greater the changes. To minimize color changes, apply the Unsharp Mask or Smart Sharpen filter and then choose Edit > Fade and change the blend mode of the applied filter to Luminosity. Another approach is to duplicate the image to another layer (Ctrl/⌘-J) before you sharpen it, sharpen the copy, and put this layer in Luminosity mode.

To silhouette the children, we moved the black point slider for Input Levels inward to hide the detail in their clothes. The "Blend If" sliders were used to restrict the darkening to the darkest colors.▼

Silhouetting a subject with a clipping path allows it to be exported without its background, so you can layer it with other elements in your page layout program.

or the built-in controls in the Smart Sharpen interface; see page 327.

REPURPOSING PHOTOS

There are times when a photograph is *almost* what you want to use in a project, but not quite — the camera has stopped the motion just as the photographer intended, but now you want to emphasize the energy in the shot; the photographer didn't notice (or couldn't control) distracting detail in the background, and it's generalized so you can't crop or successfully retouch it out; the lighting doesn't work for the way you want to use the photo. Here are some ideas for those kinds of photos:

- **To hide unwanted detail in a dark subject against a bright background,** apply a Levels Adjustment layer, moving the black point slider for Input Levels to the right as far as necessary to silhouette the subject or at least remove the unwanted foreground detail. Depending on the image, you may need to select the subject before making the adjustment, or use the "Blend If" sliders to restrict the Levels adjustment to the darkest tones,▼ or even paint over lighter areas of the darkened subject with black.

- **To suppress unwanted detail in a background,** select the background and blur it as described in "Focusing Attention on the Subject" on page 285 and in some of the examples in "Quick Attention-Focusing Techniques," starting on page 294. "Exercising Lens Blur" on page 291 shows several other ways to alter depth of field with the Lens Blur filter.

- **To remove a background altogether,** duplicate your image file (so you have a copy), and then select the background and delete it. (If your image consists of a *Background*, you'll have to convert it to a regular layer before deleting: Double-click the *Background* entry in the Layers palette.) To **be able to export a subject** for use in a page layout program without its background, you can use a clipping path, as described on page 444.

ADDING DEPTH

Sharpening can help add depth and form. Sharpen the areas of the image that extend toward the viewer and leave unsharpened (or even blur) the areas that are farther away.

After François Guérin painted a still life of fruit in Corel Painter (left), he opened the file in Photoshop and continued to "paint" with the Sharpen tool △, to sharpen the parts of the pear nearest the viewer (right).

FIND OUT MORE

▼ Using the "Blend If" sliders **page 70**

To emphasize the energy in this karate match, a copy of the original high-speed photo was treated with Filter > Blur > Motion Blur and dragged beneath the original. A black-filled layer mask was added to the sharp original layer and was painted with white to sharpen parts of the athlete on the left. The Motion Blur filter blurs in both directions along the axis you choose, so the sharp image and mask were then dragged with the Move tool ▶♣ to line up with the right edge of the blurred athlete.

- To **replace the background with a different image,** remove the background, and then copy-and-paste or drag-and-drop the new background into the subject file, or vice versa. "Swapping a Background" on page 628 includes pointers for selecting the subject and for making it at home in the new background.

- Some of the Blur filters (Motion Blur and Radial Blur) can put the **energy and motion** of a scene back into a stop-action photo, as shown at the left, below, and on page 77.

- For **special artistic effects,** try one of the filters found in the **Artistic, Brush Strokes,** or **Sketch** submenus of the Filter

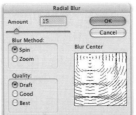

Before a Spin blur was applied to enhance the motion of the swing (Filter > Blur > Radial Blur), extra height was added by expanding the canvas with the Crop tool 🔲 (as described on page 246) so the blur center could be defined above the image, where the chain is fastened. With the blurred layer underneath the masked sharp layer (as described for the images at the left), the photo was then recropped to remove the extra canvas.

The Unsharp Mask filter can be used with extreme settings for special color effects. Here the settings were Amount 500, Radius 50, Threshold 50. (Images with large expanses of very light colors, such as sky, are usually not good candidates.)

menu. Many of the Sketch filters use the Foreground and Background colors to create their effects, so you can choose the colors before you run them. Another approach is to **oversharpen** with the Unsharp Mask filter. Appendix A shows examples of these and the other Photoshop filters, and step 4 of "Framing with Masks" on page 260 tells how to combine filters using the Filter Gallery.

- **To simplify and stylize an image,** use a filter such as **Cutout** (Filter > Artistic > Cutout) to create a posterized effect. You can choose the number of colors or shades of gray you want to use, and you can also control the smoothness and fidelity of the color breaks. The Cutout filter produces smoother, cleaner edges and more color control than you can get with the Posterize command or with a Posterize Adjustment layer. Or try Filter > Blur > **Smart Blur**.

The Cutout filter (Filter > Artistic > Cutout) translates an image into patches of color. Here we used Number of Levels 8, Edge Simplicity 5, and Edge Fidelity 2.

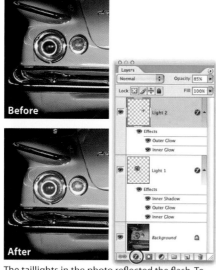

Before

After

The taillights in the photo reflected the flash. To brighten them up even more, we selected each one in turn with the Elliptical Marquee ◯ and copied it to a new layer (Ctrl/⌘-J). Then we clicked the 🄵 at the bottom of the Layers palette to add a Layer Style consisting of an Inner Glow (set to Center so the light would spread outward from the center rather than inward from the edge) and an Outer Glow. For the larger light we also used a red Inner Shadow in Screen mode as an additional component of the glow.

 Valiant.psd

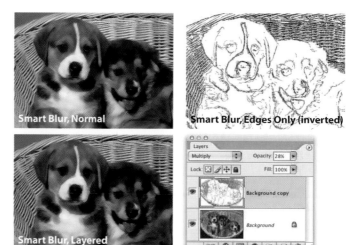

Here we duplicated the image layer and then used Filter > Blur > Smart Blur with Radius 10, Threshold 30, Quality High, and Mode Normal on the *Background*. Smart Blur was then applied to the copy in the filter's Edges Only mode, and the filtered copy was inverted to make a black-on-white image (Ctrl/⌘-I). The blend mode of this layer was changed to Multiply to make the white disappear, and layer Opacity was reduced to blend the lines with the color.

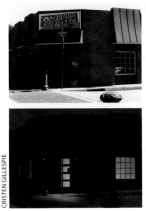

One treatment with the Lighting Effects filter lit the windows. Another created the two lamps beside the door and the light spilling out onto the walls and pavement. Page 344 tells how it was done.

CRISTEN GILLESPIE

- **To change the lighting in a photo,** you can add light with a **Layer Style** using one or both of the Glow effects (as shown on the facing page). Or try the **Lighting Effects** filter (Filter > Render > Lighting Effects; its dialog box is shown below). Lighting Effects can spotlight an area of an image to focus attention there (page 301). Or use it to darken a corner of a scene to add mystery. Unify several fairly different images in a printed or online publication by applying the same lighting scheme to all of them. Or even turn day into night, as shown at the left. *Wow!*

LIGHTING EFFECTS

The **Lighting Effects filter** can be used as a miniature lighting studio, working on an entire layer or a part you've selected. You can set up both ambient lighting and individual light sources. Ambient light is diffuse, nondirectional light that's uniform throughout the image, like daylight on an overcast day. And it may have an inherent color, like daylight underwater. The ambient light will affect the density and color of "shadow" areas that are unlit by any individual light sources you set up.

The three varieties of individual light sources are **Omni**directional, which sends a glow in all directions, like a light bulb in a table lamp; a **Spotlight**, which is directional and focused, making a pool of light like a real spotlight; and **Directional**, which has a definite direction but is too far away to be focused, like bright sunlight or moonlight.

To save a lighting scheme so you can apply it to another layer or file later, click the "Save" button and name the style. Your new style will be added to the Style menu.

To control the direction, size, and shape of a Spotlight, drag one of the four handles on its ellipse. To change the angle only, Ctrl/⌘-drag a handle. To change the shape only, Shift-drag a handle.

To move a light source, drag its center point. **To duplicate a light source,** Alt/Option-drag its center point.

To add an individual light source, drag the light bulb icon into the Preview area.

To turn a light source off temporarily, click to turn off the "On" check mark.

To remove a light, drag its center point to the 🗑 icon below the Preview area.

To set the color for an individual light or ambient light, click the appropriate color swatch and choose a color.

The **Properties** section controls the ambient lighting and other overall properties of the environment.

The more positive the **Ambience** setting, the stronger the ambient light will be relative to the individual light sources set in the top sections of the dialog box, so the less pronounced will be the shadows produced by those lights.

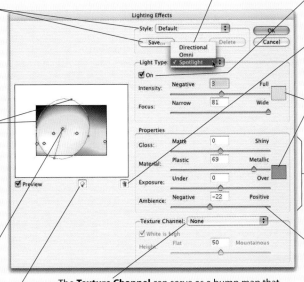

The **Texture Channel** can serve as a bump map that interacts with the light sources for an image, tricking the eye into perceiving dimension or texture. The Texture Channel list includes all of the color channels (including any Spot colors) and alpha channels (if any) in the file, as well as the transparency mask and layer mask of the layer you're working on.

"Framing" with Masks

YOU'LL FIND THE FILES
in 🅦 > Wow Project Files > Chapter 5 > Framing with Masks:
- Framing-Before.psd (to start)
- Framing-After.psd (to compare)

OPEN THESE PALETTES
from the Window menu:
- Tools • Layers • Channels

OVERVIEW
Create a layer mask to "crop" the image to be framed • Blur the mask • Add a black-filled backing layer • Filter the edges of the mask, combining effects

1a

The original image

1b

The *Background* is changed to a regular layer, and a layer mask is made from a rectangular selection.

IT'S EASY TO CREATE CUSTOM EDGE TREATMENTS for photos, starting with a layer mask that defines the area you want to frame, then blurring the black-and-white mask to create soft edges that blend the photo into the page. As shown above, you can also create a well-defined dark edge for the image within the soft vignetting.

1 Creating the layer mask. Open **Framing-Before.psd** or a photo of your own **1a**. If your image consists of a *Background* layer, give it the option for transparency so it can have a layer mask: In the Layers palette, double-click the *Background* label. In the New Layer dialog box, name the layer if you'd like, and click "OK"; we named ours "Image & mask."

To add the layer mask, first choose the Rectangular Marquee tool 🔲 and drag to select the part of the image you want to frame; be sure to leave room at the edge for the soft vignetting you'll create in step 2. The border on our 800-pixel-wide image was about 65 pixels all around. Turn your selection into a layer mask by clicking the "Add layer mask" button 🔲 at the bottom of the Layers palette **1b**.

> **AVOIDING HARD EDGES**
>
> To avoid having soft edges extend so far that the edge of the document cuts them off abruptly, a good rule of thumb is to make your edge at least 1.5 times as wide as the Gaussian Blur setting you plan to use. Since the Gaussian Blur setting is in pixels, to gauge your edges, make the rulers visible (Ctrl/⌘-R) and then right-click (Windows) or Ctrl-click (Mac) on a ruler and choose Pixels.

2

A white background is added and the mask is blurred, with a Gaussian Blur Radius of 20 pixels for our approximately 65-pixel-wide borders.

3

A layer was added with a black-filled rectangle the same size as the original frame selection. This clearly defines the frame without eliminating the soft edges.

4a

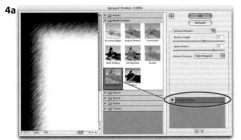

Targeting the layer mask and choosing Filter > Brush Strokes > Sprayed Strokes opens the Filter Gallery to the controls for this filter, with a preview on the left side of the box. Stroke Length was set at 12, Spray Radius at 20, and Stroke Direction at Right Diagonal.

Before you soften the mask in the next step, store the frame shape for safekeeping: In the Channels palette drag the *Layer Mask* name to the "Create new channel" button ▣ at the bottom of the palette.

2 Softening the edges. Adding a white-filled layer below the image layer will give you a better look at the frame edges as you develop them: To create and name a new layer *below* the current one, Ctrl-Alt-click (Windows) or ⌘-Option-click (Mac) the "Create a new layer" button ▣ at the bottom of the Layers palette. Then fill the new layer with white (type D for "default colors" and then Ctrl/⌘-Delete to fill with the Background color).

To soften the edges, click the layer mask's thumbnail in the Layers palette and choose Filter > Blur > Gaussian Blur. Experiment with the Radius setting until the image has the soft-edged fade-to-white effect you want. We used a setting of 20 pixels **2**.

3 Adding black to define the frame. For a well-defined frame in combination with the soft edge treatment **3**, you can add a black backing layer that shows through the softened edge of the masked image: In the Layers palette, create another new layer, immediately below the masked photo. Then activate the same selection you used to make the mask (if you haven't made a selection since creating the mask, you can choose Select > Reselect or use its shortcut, Ctrl/⌘-Shift-D; otherwise, in the Channels palette Ctrl/⌘-click the alpha channel you made in step 1). Fill the selection with black, the Foreground color **3**, by pressing Alt/Option-Delete, and then deselect (Ctrl/⌘-D).

To soften the transition between sharp frame and soft edge, you can blur the black layer slightly. We used a Gaussian Blur with a Radius of 2 pixels for the result at the top of page 260.

4 Filtering the edges. Now to experiment with some custom edge effects. In the Layers palette, click on the mask thumbnail in the "Image & mask" layer. Then make a choice from the Filter menu; we chose Filter > Brush Strokes > Sprayed Strokes. This opens the Filter Gallery dialog box, with an initial "layer" for Sprayed Strokes already created **4a**. Filtering will change the edge of the mask, which will change the "frame." Click "OK" to close the Filter Gallery and see the result **4b**.

To try a different filter instead, first undo the Filter Gallery (Ctrl/⌘-Z). Then apply the Filter Gallery again by choosing the first item in the Filter menu or pressing Ctrl-Alt-F (Windows) or

4b

Here the Sprayed Strokes filter alone has been applied to the mask, using the settings in Figure 4a ; visibility for the black layer is turned off by clicking its 👁 in the Layers palette.

4c

The Filter Gallery lets you combine some of Photoshop's filters. Clicking 🔲 duplicates the filter "layer" you've been working with, and you can then replace this copy by choosing a different filter. Here Mosaic Tiles was applied (Tile Size 10, Grout Width 2, Lighten Grout 10); then a Glass "layer" was added (Distortion 2, Smoothness 5, Texture: Tiny Lens, Scaling 100%). Several other examples of Filter Gallery combinations are shown on pages 264 and 265.

⌘-Option-F (Mac) to open the last filter dialog used, in this case the Filter Gallery, so you can make changes. Now you can click on a sample thumbnail in the center section of the Filter Gallery, or choose from the pop-up alphabetical list (under the "Cancel" button). To keep the effect you have but also add another, click the "New effect layer" button 🔲 near the bottom right corner of the dialog box, and then choose another filter. Paint Daubs, Rough Pastels, and Stamp produce interesting interactions with Sprayed Strokes. (You can see these combinations and others in "Quick Filtered Frames," page 264.)

A big advantage of the Filter Gallery is that you can work interactively to combine filters **4c**. To experiment, you can click any filter in the stack in the bottom right corner of the Gallery and

SAVE THAT FILTER COMBO!

The Filter Gallery doesn't have a "Save" button, but it's easy to capture your filter combinations so you can apply them again. Develop the combination you like, and click "OK" to apply it. Then click Ctrl/⌘-Z to undo the Filter Gallery. In the Actions palette, click the "Create new action" button 🔲, and in the dialog box, name the Action and click "Record." Press Ctrl/⌘-F (to apply the previous Filter Gallery settings); then press the "Stop playing/recording" button ⬛ at the bottom of the Actions palette. Your Action has captured the settings for all the effects in the Filter Gallery.

FIND OUT MORE

▼ Saving and playing Actions
pages 116 & 114

OUTSIDE THE GALLERY

Using the masking and layering techniques described in "'Framing' with Filters," you can also get some great framing effects with filters that aren't included in the Filter Gallery. The process involves making a layer mask for the image, blurring the mask's edges, applying a filter to modify the blurred part of the mask, and then applying another filter to modify it further. Try a swirling edge (Filter > Distort > Twirl with a high Angle setting). Or, as shown here, get a confetti effect with Filter > Pixelate > Color Halftone (default settings), followed by Filter > Pixelate > Crystallize (Cell Size 10).

5a

The Texturizer filter is applied to the mask (Texture Canvas, Scaling 125%, Relief 10, Light Top); visibility for the black layer is turned off.

5b

To reduce (but not completely eliminate) the texture in the image area, visibility for the "Image & mask" layer is turned on but its Opacity is reduced to 70%; this allows the "White background" layer to show through only a little.

change its settings, or drag a filter up or down in the stack, effectively changing the order in which the filters are applied. To completely remove the effect of one of the filters in the stack, click on its name and then click the 🗑 button.

5 Trying an "all over" filter. To try a different approach, first remove the filter effect by undoing your last step (Ctrl/⌘-Z). In the Layers palette duplicate the "Image & mask" layer (Ctrl/⌘-J), so you can work on the new layer and still have the original "Image & mask" layer with its blurred mask intact. Turn off visibility for the original "Image & mask" layer by clicking its 👁. Then click on the new layer's mask thumbnail to make the mask active.

Now try a filter that affects the white area of the mask as well as the blurred gray, such as one of the Texture filters; we chose Filter > Texture > Texturizer. This "texturized" both the image and the "frame" **5a**. We liked the edge, but we wanted to remove most of the texture from the image itself. So we turned on visibility 👁 for the "Image & mask" layer and worked with its Opacity **5b**. Its image shows through the "holes" created by the mask on the filtered layer and smooths the photo.

Experimenting. With a filtered mask, a blurred mask, a black backing, and a white background, you can try out a wealth of framing possibilities, just by turning on and off visibility for different layers as you test a variety of filters. The next two pages show other examples of filtered edge treatments. 🖌️

IMAGE SWAPPING

Once you have a framing file set up, it's easy to experiment with the same frame and another image of similar size: Start by targeting the image-and-mask layer and then drag-and-drop your new image into the file. Press Ctrl/⌘-G in CS or in CS2 press Ctrl-Alt-G (Windows) or ⌘-Option-G (Mac) to make a clipping group of the new image layer and the masked layer below.

ORIGINAL PHOTO: CORBIS ROYALTY FREE

Filtered Frames

The examples on these two pages were made by running filters on a blurred layer mask in an 800-pixel-wide image, framed as in the "'Framing' with Masks" technique on page 260. White and black were used as the Foreground and Background colors when the filters were run.

Each of the images at the top of these pages was made by applying a single filter. Each of the images at the bottom was made with two filters:

- For the two-filter images on this page, one filter was chosen from the Filter menu and applied, and then the other, since both weren't available in the Filter Gallery.

- For the examples on the facing page we chose Filter > Filter Gallery, clicked the "New effect layer" button ⬒ (near the bottom right corner of the dialog box), and chose from the alphabetical pop-up menu (near the top of the right side of the box). We adjusted the settings, then clicked the ⬒ button again, picked another filter from the list, and chose its settings.

YOU'LL FIND THE FILE

in ⬤ > Wow Project Files > Chapter 5 > Filtered Frames

The examples on these pages were made with the mask targeted, and the visibility of the black backing layer turned off. Turn on the backing layer's visibility to see another set of options.

Halftone Pixelate > Color Halftone (Max. Radius 5, all Screen Angles 45)

Sketch Sketch > Graphic Pen (Stroke Length 15, Light/Dark Balance 25, Stroke Direction: Right Diagonal)

Twirl-Mild Distort > Twirl (Angle 400°)

Twirl-Strong Distort > Twirl (Angle, 999°)

Confetti-Crisp Pixelate > Color Halftone (default settings); then Pixelate > Crystallize (Cell Size 10)

Confetti-Soft Brush Strokes > Spatter (Spray Radius 25, Smoothness 5) then Pixelate > Crystallize (Cell Size 10)

Comb Edges Distort > Wave (Sine, Generators 5, Wavelength Min. 10 Max.11, Amplitude Min. 5 Max. 6, Scales 100); then Blur > Lens Blur > Alt/Option-click "Reset" (default)

Zigzag-Soft Distort > Ripple (Amount 250, Size: Large); then Noise > Median (Radius 15)

Grainy Texture > Grain (Intensity 85, Contrast 75, Grain Type: Enlarged)

Ripples Distort > Ocean Ripple (Ripple Size 1; Ripple Magnitude 12)

Spatter-Soft Brush Strokes > Spatter (Spray Radius 15, Smoothness 5)

Border-Stepped Pixelate > Mosaic (Cell Size 25)

Mosaic-Organic Pixelate > Crystallize (Cell Size 25)

Water Paper Sketch > Water Paper (Fiber Length 50; Brightness 60, Contrast 75)

Dithered Filter Gallery > Smudge Stick (Str. Length 1, Highlight Area 15, Intensity 10) on the bottom; Grain (Intensity 25, Contrast 50, Grain Type: Speckle) on top

Splash Filter Gallery > Spatter (Spray Radius 15, Smoothness 5) on the bottom; Paint Daubs (Brush Size 10, Sharpness 10, Brush Type: Sparkle) on top

Border-Inline Filter Gallery > Stamp (Light/Dark Balance 25, Smoothness 5) on the bottom; Chrome (Detail 1, Smoothness 10) on top

Cut-out Filter Gallery > Ocean Ripple (Ripple Size 7, Ripple Magnitude 15) on the bottom; Stamp (Light/Dark Balance 25, Smoothness 5) on top

Glass Filter Gallery > Glass (Distortion 5, Smoothness 5, Texture: Frosted, Scaling 85) on the bottom ; Sumi-e (Stroke Width 10, Stroke Pressure 5, Contrast 0) on top

Reflections Filter Gallery > Glass (Distortion 10, Smoothness 5, Texture: Frosted, Scaling 100) on the bottom; Sumi-e (Stroke Width 10, Stroke Pressure 5, Contrast 30) on top

Tone & Color Adjustments

Photoshop offers many ways to make a less-than-perfect photo look good or a good photo look great. In most cases you'll be looking for a solution that saves time, produces top-quality results, and leaves you with a file that's flexible, in case you need to make further changes. The "quick fixes" on these nine pages are presented with that in mind. In some cases a quick fix may not get you all the way to your goal, but it can provide a big head start.

Most of the adjustments on these nine pages are available by clicking the "Create new fill or adjustment layer" button ⬤ at the bottom of the Layers palette.

Others, such as Match Color, Shadow/Highlight, and Variations are available only through the Image > Adjustments menu.

YOU'LL FIND THE FILES
in 🔵 > Wow Project Files > Chapter 5 > Quick Tone and Color

Match Color

IMAGES TAKEN at the same general time and place can differ in color and contrast because they were taken at different angles to the light source, or with different camera settings. The **Match Color** command can help bring these color and tone differences into agreement. Open both the image whose color you want to change **A** and the one whose color you want to match **B**. Working on the image that needs changing, first duplicate it to a new layer to protect the original; then choose Image > Adjustments > Match Color. In the pop-up **Source** menu in the Match Color dialog box, designate the image you want to match **C**. You can now use the sliders to adjust the color: **Luminance** for brightness; **Color Intensity** for saturation; **Fade** to reduce the change overall, blending it with the original color. Turn on **Neutralize** if needed to remove a color cast. For this image we used only Fade and Neutralize **D**.

 Match Color 1.psd & **Match Color 2.psd**

Shadow/Highlight

A

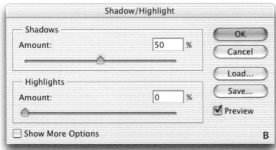

B

C

THE REMARKABLE SHADOW/HIGHLIGHT COMMAND can increase or reduce contrast where it's needed at the same time it brightens or darkens.▼ Its default settings (shown above) can so often do wonders that it's almost always worth trying on an image with shadow problems. In this photo the girls' faces are in shadow **A**. Since the **Shadow/ Highlight** correction isn't available as an Adjustment layer, our first step was to duplicate the photo to another layer (Ctrl/⌘-J) so we would have an untouched original in reserve. Then we chose Image > Adjustments > Shadow/Highlight and clicked "OK" to accept the default settings **B**, which brightened up the image **C**.

FIND OUT MORE

▼ Using the Shadow/
Highlight command
page 169

Masking an Adjustment

JHDAVIS

TO INVESTIGATE ANOTHER OPTION for the Shadow/High-light-treated image at the left — lighting up the girls but keeping other shaded areas dark — we created a **mask** for the Shadow/Highlight-treated layer: We Alt/Option-clicked the "Add a layer mask" button 🔲 at the bottom of the Layers palette to add a black-filled layer mask that completely hid the Shadow/Highlight layer. Then we chose the Brush tool ✐, picked a large, soft brush tip from the Options bar and took about 20 seconds to paint the mask with white where we wanted the adjustment to take effect.▼ Because the mask's edges are soft, the adjusted areas blend smoothly into the unaltered surroundings. Shift-clicking the layer mask's thumbnail in the Layers pal-ette toggled the effect of the mask off and on, allowing us to compare the masked version of the correction (shown above) with the unmasked version (shown at the left).

🎯 **Masking an Adjustment.psd**

FIND OUT MORE

▼ Painting a layer
mask **page 75**

Auto Levels or Curves

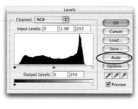

SIMPLY APPLYING AN "AUTO" CORRECTION often markedly improves the overall color and contrast of a photo. To do this, click the "Create new fill or adjustment layer" button ◑ at the bottom of the Layers palette and choose a Levels or Curves Adjustment layer from the pop-up list.▼ In the dialog box, click the "**Auto**" button. (You can also use Auto by choosing Image > Adjustments > Auto Levels. But, as always, the Adjustment layer allows more flexibility for later changes.)

FIND OUT MORE

▼ Using Levels or Curves **page 250**

 Auto.psd

Auto Options

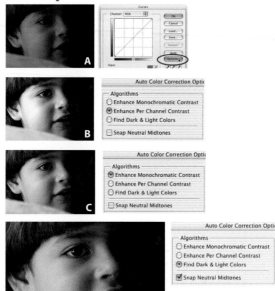

IN THE LEVELS OR CURVES DIALOG BOX — whether you apply it with an Adjustment layer or via Image > Adjustments — if you click the "Options" button instead of "Auto," Photoshop applies the Auto adjustment (described at the left) but also opens another dialog box with more choices. When you have an image that needs color and contrast adjustment **A**, it's easy to click through the three options and try them out, with and without Snap Neutral Midtones. The default **Enhance Per Channel Contrast** option is what you get when you click the "Auto" button **B**. Because it balances contrast for each color channel independently, this option can remove (or sometimes add, as in this case) an unwanted color cast. The **Enhance Monochromatic Contrast** option balances contrast without changing color balance **C**. It applies the same correction as choosing Image > Adjustments > Auto Contrast. The bottom choice, **Find Dark & Light Colors**, with **Snap Neutral Midtones** turned on **D**, produces the same result as choosing Image > Adjustments > Auto Color. (Snap Neutral Midtones brings any close-to-neutral midtones in the newly adjusted image to true neutral, with equal parts of the primary colors.)

 **Auto Options.psd**

Selecting & Auto

AN AUTO OR OPTIONS CORRECTION often works better if you first **select** the area that's most important for Photoshop to "look at" when it adjusts the contrast. For instance, in this photo **A**, we clicked the "Options" button in the Levels dialog box and chose Enhance Monochromatic Contrast with Snap Neutral Midtones. But the result was too dark because Photoshop found pure white in the border areas and used that to set the white point for the entire image **B**. So we clicked the "Cancel" button and dragged with the Rectangular Marquee tool ⬚ to make a selection that stopped short of the border. *Then* we added the Levels Adjustment layer; only the area inside the selection was used in the adjustment, and the result was much better **C**. Making a selection also creates a mask for the Adjustment layer, but to extend the adjustment to the entire image, you can delete the mask (drag its thumbnail to the Layers palette's 🗑 button).

 **Selecting-Auto.psd**

Auto & Luminosity

WITH AN ADJUSTMENT LAYER, you aren't limited to "full-strength" (100% Opacity) or to Normal mode. For this sepiatone **A**, the Auto correction improved the contrast but removed the color **B**. We clicked the "Options" button in the Levels dialog box and tried Enhance Monochromatic Contrast; this made the color too intense **C**. The Find Dark & Light Colors option also overcorrected the color. So we went back to the default **Enhance Per Channel Contrast** and closed the dialog boxes. We changed the blend mode of the Levels layer to **Luminosity** and reduced the Opacity to maintain some of the color **D**.

 Auto-Luminosity.psd

Levels/Curves & Multiply

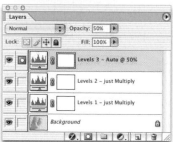

TO RESTORE DENSITY to a photo that's severely "washed out" because it's overexposed or faded **A**, add a Levels Adjustment layer in **Multiply** mode (by Alt/Option-clicking the "Create new fill or adjustment layer" button ⊘ at the bottom of the Layers palette and choosing Levels from the pop-up list). In the New Layer dialog box, choose Multiply for the mode and click "OK." When the Levels dialog box opens, click "OK" without making any adjustment. If this "blank" Levels layer in Multiply mode hasn't improved the range of tones enough **B**, you can duplicate it (by pressing Ctrl/⌘-J) **C**. If the image still lacks contrast, try adding a Levels Adjustment layer in Normal mode to apply Levels either manually or by using the "Auto" button as we did here. Adjust Opacity of this top layer if needed **D**.

 Levels-Multiply.psd

Set Gray Point

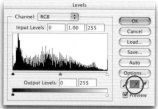

PAUL K. DAYTON, JR.

THE SET GRAY POINT EYEDROPPER, which is found in both the Levels and the Curves dialog boxes, can be useful for correcting a color cast like the one in this discolored transparency. By clicking the dropper on the image, you tell Photoshop that the pixel you've clicked on is supposed to be a neutral gray, and Photoshop makes an overall adjustment to the color balance of the image to make that happen. Here clicking on the gray rock fixed the color. If you don't get the change you want on your first try, click on another spot that might be neutral. Of course, if your image doesn't include anything that should be neutral gray, this method won't work, because you'll actually be adding a color cast each time you try to force some color to neutral. In that case you might try the Average method on the facing page, or take the time to adjust Color Balance.▼

 Set Gray Point.psd

FIND OUT MORE

▼ Adjusting Color
Balance **page 252**

Average Filter

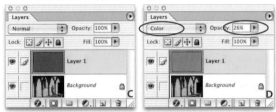

IF YOU TRY THE "SET GRAY POINT" METHOD on an image (as described on the facing page) but the color just switches wildly from one tint to another, Photoshop's **Average** filter is worth a try. To repurpose this image **A**, we wanted to remove some of the golden glow. We duplicated the photo to a new layer (Ctrl/⌘-J) and chose Filter > Blur > Average **B**. The filter "averaged" the duplicate layer to a solid orangish-tan **C**. We then inverted the color (Image > Adjustments > Invert, or Ctrl/⌘-I), which changed the tan to its opposite blue. By applying this opposite in Color mode **D** (or Hue mode for a slightly different effect), you can adjust Opacity to get the more neutral coloring that you want. We reduced the Opacity of the layer until we had the neutralizing effect we wanted at 26% **E**.

🔵 **Average Filter.psd**

Average & Auto

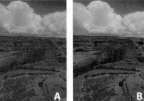

USING THE AVERAGE FILTER can also be a good place to start in recovering a badly discolored photo. We opened this scan of a color transparency from the 1940s **A**, duplicated it to a new layer (Ctrl/⌘-J), and chose Filter > Blur > **Average** (the same as for the image at the left). The Average filter turned the duplicate layer a solid pink. We then inverted the color (Image > Adjustments > Invert, or Ctrl/⌘-I), which changed the pink to its opposite greenish blue. We changed the blend mode of this layer to Color and adjusted the layer's Opacity to balance the color as closely as possible to what we wanted **B**. Now that we had more realistic color to work with, we could add a Levels Adjustment layer **C** and click the "**Auto**" button as the next step in the rescue **D**.

🔵 **Average-Auto.psd**

Warming

A

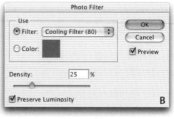

Photo Filter

Use
◉ Filter: Warming Filter (85)
○ Color: [   ]

OK
Cancel
☑ Preview

Density: 25 %

☑ Preserve Luminosity

B

C

TRADITIONALLY, photographers have used warming filters on their camera lenses to absorb the excess blue and achieve warmer tones when shooting outside in the shade or with an electronic flash — or just to "warm up" the color in a photo, especially a portrait. You can get similar results with Photoshop's Warming "filter layers." To warm this photo **A**, we clicked the ⬤ button at the bottom of the Layers palette and chose **Photo Filter**. Then we chose **Warming Filter** (85) from the Filter menu in the Photo Filter dialog box **B** and clicked "OK" **C**.▼

 Warming.psd

Cooling

A

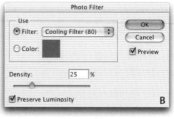

Photo Filter

Use
◉ Filter: Cooling Filter (80)
○ Color: [   ]

OK
Cancel
☑ Preview

Density: 25 %

☑ Preserve Luminosity

B

C

TO INCREASE THE COOL FEELING of a seascape or a snow scene, for instance **A**, you can use one of the Cooling "filter layers." Here we clicked the ⬤ button at the bottom of the Layers palette, chose **Photo Filter** from the pop-up list, and chose **Cooling Filter (80) B**, **C**. For all the Photo Filters, the default Density of 25% mimics the effect of the most widely used traditional filters, but you can adjust it to suit your image.▼ Photoshop CS2 has added Warming Filter LBA and Cooling Filter LBB to the Photo Filter list.

 Cooling.psd

> **FIND OUT MORE**
>
> ▼ Using Photo Filter
> **page 204**

Color Balance

B

C

PAUL K. DAYTON, JR.

A **COLOR BALANCE** ADJUSTMENT LAYER (click the ⬤ button and choose) can target a color change to the highlights, midtones, or shadows separately. You simply add the opposite of the color you have too much of. This RGB image showed a yellow cast in the highlights **A**. To remove the yellow, the Highlights option was chosen in the Color Balance dialog box and the Yellow-Blue slider was moved toward Blue. To bring back a little warmth, the Cyan-Red slider was moved slightly toward Red **B**, **C**. We kept Preserve Luminosity checked to ensure we altered only the color and not the tonal values.

 Color Balance.psd

Hue/Saturation

A   B

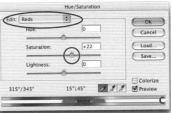

C

D

PAUL K. DAYTON, JR.

SOME IMAGES JUST NEED A SATURATION BOOST to restore color — either generally or in a specific range of colors. For this image **A**, we added a Hue/Saturation Adjustment layer by clicking the ⬤ button and choosing from the list. In the Hue/Saturation dialog, we moved the **Saturation** slider slightly to the right to generally brighten up the color **B**. Then, to emphasize the overalls, tricycle, and flowers, we chose the **Reds** color family from the Edit menu and boosted its **Saturation** separately as well **C**, **D**.

🄦 Hue-Saturation.psd

Boosting CMYK

AN RGB IMAGE whose colors look intense and lively can sometimes lose its punch when converted to **CMYK** mode for printing **A**. In that case a subtle change applied in a Hue/Saturation Adjustment layer may help restore some of the vibrancy of the color overall, or of a particular color range. Here we clicked the ● button, chose Hue/Saturation, and increased the **Saturation** overall (with the default Master chosen in the dialog box's Edit menu) **B, C**.

🔵 **Boosting CMYK.psd**

Variations

THE VARIATIONS COMMAND has the dual appeal of being able to handle a wide array of color adjustments — hue, saturation, and lightness controlled independently for highlights, midtones, and shadows — and letting you preview several different options at once. You can set **Variations** to make finer adjustments, and you can turn on the Show Clipping function, to alert you so you won't produce colors that may be outside the color gamut you're working in. As with some of the other tone and color commands, a major drawback is that Variations can't be applied as an Adjustment layer — only by choosing from the Image > Adjustments menu — so it's important to duplicate the image before using Variations. When you click "OK," all your color and tone adjustments will be applied at once, and you can't go back later and "undo" the individual changes. For more flexibility later, you might prefer to use Variations to get a sense of the kinds of adjustments needed, and then make those changes with separate Adjustment layers, such as Color Balance and Hue/Saturation.

🔵 **Variations-Before.psd**

Deeanne Edwards Coaxes a Little More from the Ocean

TO GET HER VIBRANT UNDERWATER SHOTS (see page 410), Deeanne Edwards often works under less-than-ideal conditions — it's dark, it's cold, it's wet, time is limited, and her subjects — and even the background — are often in constant motion. Sometimes she's nearly "shooting blind" until her strobes light up the scene as she takes the photo, and reshooting often isn't an option. On the way to getting the best images possible, she uses some quick fixes that can be equally helpful to land-based photographers.

FIND OUT MORE

▼ Using Shadow/Highlight **page 169**
▼ Sharpening **page 326**
▼ Dodging & burning **page 329**

When photographing in kelp beds, Deeanne often uses strobe lighting to balance the ambient exposure. She used a Nikon N90 in a Nexus housing with two Nikonos SB105 strobes to take these photos off San Clemente Island, California. For additional fill lighting after the fact, Photoshop's Shadow/Highlight command (Image > Adjustments > Shadow/Highlight) comes in handy. Simply applying the command and clicking "OK" in the Shadow/Highlight dialog box, even without touching the sliders, improves the evenness of the light.▼

In this close-up portrait of a Sheephead fish, shot with a 60 mm lens and Kodak 100VS film, the tip of the lip seemed to be cropped out of the image. But Deeanne found that simply taking the slide out of the mount and rescanning reclaimed the missing millimeters.

The photos of the fish in the kelp were taken with a 24 mm lens and Fuji Sensia film. Shown on the left are the original scans of the slides. On the right, the default settings of Shadow/Highlight bring out detail in the shadows that adds texture and dimension.

The lip lost in the original scan (top) was recovered by removing the slide mount and scanning again (center). Sharpening (Filter > Sharpen > Unsharp Mask)▼ and a small amount of dodging and burning▼ to lighten the snout and reduce the glare in the eye completed the portrait (bottom).

Lens Correction

"Compensating for Camera-Related Distortion" on page 279 shows Photoshop CS2's new **Lens Correction** filter at work on a real-world photo challenge. Here we try out the controls inside the Lens Correction dialog box, just to learn the mechanics of this "megafilter," using a grid image to show the kinds of distortions that are Lens Correction's stock in trade.

The Lens Correction filter (**Filter > Distort > Lens Correction**) fixes lens-related distortions: **barreling** (bulging outward from the center) and **pincushioning** (pinching in toward the center); **vignetting** (darkening around the edges); and **chromatic aberration** (color fringing at high-contrast edges).

Lens Correction also addresses **perspective** and **angle** distortions that happen because of how the camera was aimed — for instance, accidentally holding the camera at an angle (creating a tilted horizon), or photographing a tall building from the ground (so the top of the building looks narrower than the bottom).

Lens Correction has a **grid** to help you evaluate and correct distortion. You can resize the grid (in the **Size** box at the bottom of the dialog box) and move the grid around with the filter's Move Grid tool to align it with parts of your image. There are tools for zooming and panning. And the filter has a **preview** you can turn off and on to compare the "before" version of your image to its current state.

Here we'll use Lens Correction to both *create* and correct distortion of a square grid figure, in order to see how the filter's adjustments work.

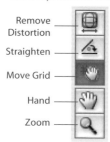

Remove Distortion — Straighten — Move Grid — Hand — Zoom

The toolbox in the upper left corner of the Lens Correction dialog box has three tools for adjusting the interface (Move Grid, Hand, and Zoom) and two others for applying the filter's adjustments (Remove Distortion and Straighten).

YOU'LL FIND THE FILE
in (wow) > Wow Project Files > Chapter 5 > Lens Correction

Barrel & Pincushion

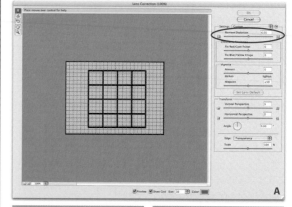

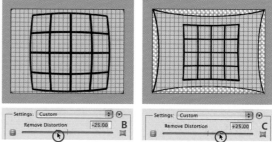

A

B   C

TO BEGIN EXPERIMENTING with Lens Correction, open the **Lens Correx Demo.psd** file in Photoshop CS2 and choose Filter > Distort > Lens Correction **A**. The **Remove Distortion** slider, at the top of the column of Lens Correction controls, counteracts the barreling (bulging) that can happen in wide-angle photos especially, and the opposite effect — pincushioning (pinching) — more often seen in telephoto shots.

Make sure **Show Grid** is turned on (at the bottom of the Lens Correction dialog) to give you some straight vertical and horizontal guides. Start by creating the kind of barreling you might see in a photo taken with a wide-angle lens by moving the Remove Distortion slider left, toward the icon **B**; we used a setting of –25. Then correct this distortion by moving the slider in the other direction until it counteracts the barreling. If you move the slider farther, you'll start to see pincushioning **C**. Before going on, return to a "barrel" condition at –25, as shown in **B**.

Chromatic Aberration

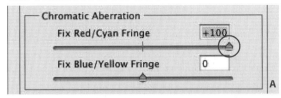

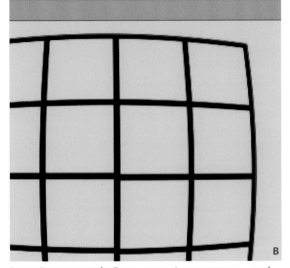

LENS CORRECTION'S **CHROMATIC ABERRATION** controls **A** are designed to eliminate (or at least reduce) the color fringe that can occur at high-contrast edges, especially in photos taken with digital cameras. Lens Correction's **"Fix"** sliders adjust the sizes of the color channels relative to one another to get rid of the color edging.

Again we can demonstrate these controls by using them to create the kind of distortion they're designed to fix. To get a clearer view of the chromatic aberration, you may want to turn off Lens Correction's grid by clicking the check box for Show Grid. Move the Fix Red/Cyan slider to the right to +100. If you zoom in — you can use Lens Correction's 🔍 tool or the Ctrl/⌘-+(plus) shortcut — and look at the color fringes that develop along the black edges of the figure **B**, you'll see that the fringe effect is stronger the farther from the center of the image you go. Return the "Fix" slider to 0.

In reality, getting rid of chromatic aberration can be tricky. Page 283 has a real-world example of using this control, and "Bringing Out Detail" on page 321 gives other solutions to the problem of color fringing.

Vignette

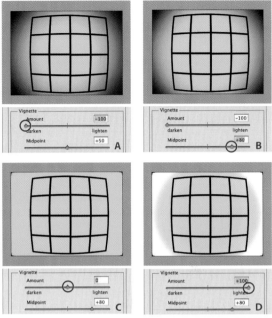

LENS CORRECTION CAN REMOVE unwanted vignetting (darkening of corners and edges), which can be characteristic of some lenses at particular f-stop settings and focal lengths; lens shades can also cause vignetting. Besides correcting a photo, you can also use the two **Vignette** sliders to purposely *add* vignetting to help direct the viewer's attention to the lighter center of the image, or to create a viewed-through-the-lens effect. The **Amount** slider determines how dark or light the vignette is. The **Midpoint** slider determines how sharply or gradually the vignette or vignette removal happens.

To create a vignette, move the Amount slider toward the "darken" end; try setting it at –100 **A**. Then experiment with the Midpoint **B**. Finally, to correct for this vignetting as if it were a lens artifact, move the Amount slider toward "lighten." Because we created this vignetting, returning the Amount setting to 0 corrects it **C**. If the camera had created the vignette, of course, the setting would need to be a positive number to lighten the edges and corners. Pushing the slider even farther to the right creates a "negative vignette," brightening the corners and edges **D**.

Because Lens Correction was designed to adjust for camera artifacts, the Vignette effect or correction is always focused at the center of the image. For another vignette method that gives you more control of the position of the highlighted area, see page 349.

Before going on, remove the barreling and the vignette.

Transform

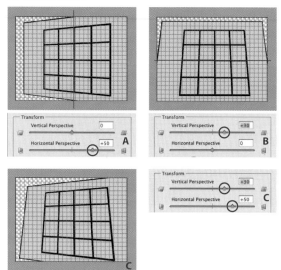

LENS CORRECTION'S **PERSPECTIVE** CONTROLS can help if a plane that should be facing you appears to be slanted away instead. You'll want to **turn the grid back on** for this adjustment. With the barrel and vignette removed and the grid turned on, let's investigate the two perspective sliders in Lens Correction's Transform section. The **Horizontal Perspective** slider pivots the image around a vertical axis, like a door revolving on a center pole, with one side moving closer to the viewer and the other side moving farther away **A**. The **Vertical Perspective** slider does the same kind of thing, except the imaginary pole runs crosswise (the axis of rotation is horizontal) **B**. With both kinds of perspective distortion going on in a photo **C**, not to mention barreling or pincushioning and angle distortion, you may need to work back and forth between the sliders.

THE LENS CORRECTION TOOLS

The **Remove Distortion tool** 🔲 corrects barreling if you drag it inward toward the center of the image; drag it outward from the center to correct pincushioning. Since it can be hard to control the tool well enough to make very small changes, you may prefer the finer control of the sliders or input fields.

The **Straighten tool** 📐 is a hand-operated angle correction. Dragging it along an element that should be horizontal or vertical and then releasing the mouse button rotates the image. Small changes may be difficult, and for some reason, we find that the Straighten tool's changes aren't consistently reflected in the Angle number box.

Angle

IF THE PHOTOGRAPHER was holding the camera with the left side a little lower than the right, or vice versa, the Angle control can fix that. Often a very small correction is all that's needed, so "scrubbing" (short drags) over the word "Angle" can work well, or click in the number field and tap the ↑ and ↓ keys (hold down the Shift key as you tap for 10-times-bigger increments).

Edge & Scale

CHANGES MADE by your barrel, pincushion, Perspective, and Angle corrections can leave empty space at the edges of the image. Lens Correction gives you four ways to deal with the space: You can leave it transparent (the default **Transparency** option for the **Edge** setting), extend the pixels at the edges to fill the space (**Edge Extension**), or in an 8 Bits/Channel image fill it with black (**Background Color**). Or you can use the **Scale** slider to enlarge the image from the center until no space remains at the edges; when you click "OK" to close the dialog box, the image will be cropped. (Other cropping methods, outside the Lens Correction dialog, give you more control,▼ but for a centered crop, Scale has the advantage of quickly and automatically cropping to the original aspect ratio of the photo.)

FIND OUT MORE

▼ Cropping **page 244**

INSTANT BORDER

To add a proportional black border around any 8-bit image, choose Filter > Distort > **Lens Correction**. Set the **Scale** slider at less than 100% and choose **Background Color** for Edge. If you record an Action for adding the border, you can then apply it to an entire folder of images by choosing File > Scripts > Image Processor or File > Automate > Batch.

E. A. M. VISSER

Compensating for Camera-Related Distortion

OPEN THIS PALETTE
from the Window menu:
   • Layers

OVERVIEW
Open the Lens Correction interface
• Adjust the grid to fit the image • Pivot
and tilt to correct awkward angles
• Reduce barrel or pincushion effects
• Reduce chromatic aberration

1

The original photo shows a complex mix of rustic stonework, modern masonry, angled planes, and different kinds of camera-related distortion. Our goal is to arrive at a more "comfortable" view.

PHOTOSHOP CS2'S LENS CORRECTION FILTER was designed as a "one-stop" solution for correcting much of the camera-related distortion that can happen when a photo is taken. In CS you can use the Transform commands and the Spherize filter to accomplish similar results. But Lens Correction's all-in-one approach and its better accuracy, not to mention its customizable grid, may make it worthwhile to upgrade.

Before you begin, you might want to check out the mechanics of Lens Correction on page 276. Like so many of Photoshop's amazing operations, Lens Correction is firmly based in science and engineering, but using it is an art. As you follow along with this example, matching the numbers we came up with (or trying other settings), keep in mind that part of the beauty of Lens Correction is that you can work back and forth among its controls, adjusting the corrections interactively until you have a pleasing combination — there isn't necessarily one "right answer." When you finally click "OK" to leave the dialog box, all the changes are applied at once, with only one resampling of the image, leaving it crisper than if you had made the changes separately.

At the end of each of steps 3 through 7, you'll find a description of how to approach the adjustments in Photoshop CS,

2a

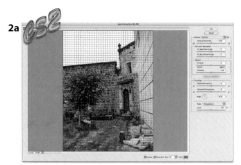

The Lens Correction dialog box itself, the grid, and the Preview magnification can all be resized to suit any level of precision required. ("Fit in View" resizes the image to fit in the Preview if you resize the dialog box smaller than full-screen.)

2b

Fit in View is the default opening view; in this case the magnification is 80.6%. Click on the number box in the lower left corner to pop up a list of magnifications to choose from, or click the "+" or "−" button. Actual Pixels gives an accurate view of details.

2c

Click on the **Color swatch** to bring up the Color Picker, and select a color that contrasts with your image. Then change the grid size (as described next) so you have enough grid lines for easy comparison with horizontal and vertical elements in your image, but not so many that they interfere with seeing the photo. For **Size**, use the pop-out slider, or drag-select the number and type a new one, or position the cursor over the word "Size" and scrub (make a series of short drags).

without Lens Correction. Even if you have CS2, you may find these short tutorials on the Transform command and Spherize filter interesting.

1 Analyzing distortion. To start, open the **Camera Distortion-Before.psd** file or a file of your own (see "Saving a Closed Copy" at the left). For our obviously distorted photo **1**, we can't completely rely on perfectly straight edges to guide us, but we can pick a few horizontals and verticals that were probably reasonably straight and use Lens Correction's grid to guide us in making corrections. Because the stones in the back wall were probably about the same size on each side of the wall, we can conclude that the camera lens and the angle at which the photographer held the camera caused much of the slant in the roofline, and the image will look better if we place this wall directly opposite our viewpoint, aiming to make its roofline horizontal. These corrections will make a big change to all the other angles in the image, so we'll tackle them first.

The wall on the right side, with its more obvious geometry, is a good place to check for barrel or pincushion distortion, and we see barreling. We can also see bright colors along some high-contrast edges, especially on the left edge of the tower, which indicates that we'll need to correct for chromatic aberration. Although we'll want to crop the image for composition as shown in the "after" image at the top of page 279, we'll do the Lens Correction work first, since the filter is designed to work on images as they come from the camera rather than after cropping.

2 Setting up Lens Correction. From Photoshop's main menu choose Filter > Distort > Lens Correction. By default Lens Correction opens with the image set to "Fit in View" **2a**, and a neutral gray grid with Size set to 16. (This is one of the few filters in Photoshop that does not automatically retain the last-used settings, but always opens with default settings.)

The first thing to do is to choose a magnification for viewing your image. Actual Pixels (100% magnification) will give you an accurate pixel-for-pixel view **2b**. Then choose a grid color that contrasts with the image and a size that makes it easy to compare horizontal and vertical lines in the image with the lines of the grid **2c**.

As we work, we'll use the Move Grid tool 🖐 by dragging to line up the grid with the elements we're trying to straighten, often zooming in (Ctrl/⌘-+) and panning with the Hand tool ✋ to

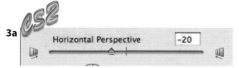

3a

Pivoting the wall by changing the Horizontal Perspective

3b

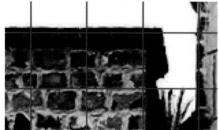

Straightening the horizon

3c

After pivoting the viewpoint and straightening the back wall roofline

4a

The back wall appears to bow upward, indicating barreling.

get a better look. Using the Move Grid tool, put some of the grid lines on or next to the vertical lines of the wall on the right, the roofline, or the right end of a line of mortar between rows of building blocks.

3 Pivoting the image and adjusting for camera tilt. We can begin our correction with what appears to be the largest correction we'll want to make; it may make other adjustments easier. In this case, swinging the back wall around to face us and making the roofline horizontally straight looks like it's going to alter the image more than any other correction.

In Photoshop CS2's Lens Correction dialog box, begin by moving the Horizontal Perspective slider to the left to swing the wall **3a**. This pivots the image around a vertical axis, moving the left side of the wall closer to us. With very little to guide us in this adjustment, we can "eyeball" our correction as we play with the slider until the blocks on the left and right sides of the wall seem to be the same size; we settled on a setting of −20. This corrects much of the roofline slant, but it looks like the camera might have been tilted a little to the right when the photo was taken. (To better see the change, readjust the size of the grid and use the Move Grid tool 🖐 as needed.)

To adjust for the tilt, highlight the number box to the right of the Angle diagram and use the ⬆ or ⬇ arrow keys (with Shift for greater increments) until most of the important vertical and horizontal lines closely follow the grid. If you prefer to use a mouse, "scrubbing" over the word "Angle" can be equally precise (move the cursor into position over the word and when the scrubber icon appears, make short, quick drags for slight changes). We finally settled on 357.40 for the Angle **3b**. The screen preview at "Fit in View" magnification shows how far we've come toward fixing the image **3c**. (You can compare your current version with the "before" image by clicking the Preview checkbox at the bottom of the dialog box to toggle the preview off and on.)

To correct horizontal perspective and angle in Photoshop CS, without the Lens Correction filter, you can choose Edit > Transform > Perspective, drag the lower right corner of the working window down and out to make some room outside the image, and drag the upper left corner of the Transform box up until the sizes of the stones at the top of the wall on the left and right sides seem to match; we found a match when "H" was set at about 128% in the Options bar. Then, without closing the

4b

Scrubbing to remove distortion

4c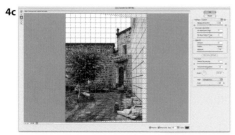

After the Remove Distortion adjustment to diminish barreling

5a

Matching the grid size to the tower window, we moved the Vertical Perspective slider until the top and bottom of the straight vertical elements were parallel with the lines of the grid.

5b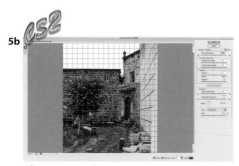

After correcting for barrel distortion and vertical tilt. The corrections have distorted the image from its rectangular shape, leaving transparency at the right edge.

Transform box, choose Edit > Transform > Rotate and with the curved cursor just outside a corner handle of the Transform frame, drag clockwise to straighten the roofline; even while the Transform box is open, you can add a horizontal guideline by making the rulers visible (Ctrl/⌘-R) and dragging a Guide down from the top ruler. When we stopped rotating, the angle field in the Options bar showed 11.5°. Since correcting barreling is the next step in this image, and it can't be done with the Transform command, close the Transform box (press the Enter key).

4 Correcting for barreling. With the horizontal perspective and the angle adjusted, our image now clearly shows the barreling in the back wall's roofline as it curves up from the left, as well as in the newer wall on the right **4a**. In CS2 we can concentrate on the roofline as we scrub the Remove Distortion slider with short drags to the right until the roofline no longer bulges upward in the middle. An amount of +6 reduced the barrel effect without disturbing our other corrections **4b**, **4c**.

To reduce the barreling in Photoshop CS, choose Filter > Distort > Spherize and set the Amount to 0 to start. Use the "–" button in the dialog box to zoom out enough to get a good view of the roofline of the wall and move the Amount slider left until the roofline no longer bulges upward; we found that a setting of –5 worked well. Then click "OK" to close the dialog box.

5 Adjusting vertical perspective. The tower and the high wall on the right appear to narrow or lean as they go up. In CS2, to straighten these elements, start by carefully moving and resizing the grid so the grid lines match a vertical element you can use as a benchmark; we set our grid to match the width of the tower window. We then moved the Vertical Perspective slider slightly to the left (–6) to straighten the edges of the window, watching our earlier corrections to see that they weren't disturbed by this correction **5a**, **5b**.

To adjust vertical perspective in Photoshop CS, choose Edit > Transform > Perspective and once again drag the lower right corner of the working window down and out to make some room outside the image. Then drag the upper left corner of the Transform frame to the left until elements such as the edges of the window and door and the lines in the righthand wall are vertical. For comparison, you can drag a vertical Guide onto the image from the ruler at the left edge of the window. Press the Enter key to close the Transform box.

6a

A fringe of color is visible at several spots on the tower.

6b

Adjusting the Fix Red/Cyan Fringe slider to +15 reduces the color fringing.

7 *CS2*

Edge: Transparency

Scale _____ 116 %

Experimenting with using Lens Correction's Scale to crop the image. A Scale setting of 116% (shown above) was the smallest enlargement that eliminated transparency from the edges. We decided to leave the Scale set at 100% instead, click "OK," and use Photoshop's Crop tool ⛏. The result is shown at the top of page 279.

FIND OUT MORE

▼ Cropping **page 244**

6 Subduing the color "fringe." Some photos show a "bloom," or fringe, of color along edges of high contrast. This *chromatic aberration* can come from a combination of factors, such as the way the lens bends the different wavelengths (colors) that make up white light and the way the color sensors in a digital camera respond to bright light. In CS2 the Lens Correction filter can often help remove these color outlines, if not completely, at least enough so they aren't obvious when the photo is printed. In this photo, the tower is dark against a white sky. By zooming in, we can see the color fringing **6a**. As you move the Fix Red/Cyan Fringe slider to the right, notice that some bands of color become more neutral **6b**, but if we move it farther, more bands pop out someplace else. In many pictures you can reduce the fringe to the point where you don't see it when you view the image at print size; we settled on a setting of +15, which reduces the color fringe on the edges of the tower somewhat without creating a noticeable fringe in other places. If the color fringe is still too obvious after you use the "Fix" sliders, you can try neutralizing it with other Photoshop methods after you leave the Lens Correction dialog box. For instance, other approaches to fixing chromatic aberration for both CS and CS2 can be found in step 3 of "Bringing Out Detail" on page 323.

7 Cropping the image. The Edge and Scale features in the Lens Correction dialog box are there to help if your corrections have distorted the normal rectangular shape of the image, as our corrections have. The default Edge setting is Transparency, with the Scale slider at 100%. By increasing the Scale, you can enlarge the image to fill the frame, without any transparency at the edges, while maintaining the original photo width-to-height ratio **7**. Like the other adjustments in the Lens Correction dialog box, Scale works from the center, so if you want a crop that's centered differently, or one that doesn't necessarily maintain the original width-to-height ratio, you can leave the Scale at 100% as we did, click "OK" to close the dialog box, and do the cropping outside, as described next.

There are several ways to crop the image in CS, or in CS2 without using Lens Correction. ▼ We chose the Crop tool ⛏ and pressed the "Clear" button in the Options bar so we wouldn't resample the image in the process. We dragged the Crop tool to frame the image. Then with Shield turned on and Perspective turned off in the Options bar, we could drag the handles of the Crop frame to resize the frame and drag inside the frame to move it; pressing the Enter key completed the crop. The result is shown at the top of page 279. *Wow!*

Using a Spin Blur

ON THIS PAGE ARE TWO SPIN BLUR EXAMPLES. One was done entirely in the camera as a way to avoid problems arising from a low-light environment. The other was applied in Photoshop after the photo was taken, in order to put the action back into a stop-action photo.

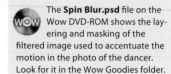

The **Spin Blur.psd** file on the Wow DVD-ROM shows the layering and masking of the filtered image used to accentuate the motion in the photo of the dancer. Look for it in the Wow Goodies folder.

"Real" (mostly). The image was cropped, so the "sharp center" is now off-center, higher than it was when the photo was taken.

© KATRIN EISMANN

Photoshop (mostly). Some of the motion we see results from strobe lighting used for the original photo.

ORIGINAL PHOTO: CORBIS ROYALTY FREE

"Real": Visiting Lisbon's Coach Museum, which doesn't allow flash photos, photographer Katrin Eismann decided to take control of the blur instead of trying to avoid it. Using a high ISO setting (800) for the low-light environment, she still needed an exposure of a half-second to capture enough light. Rather than fight the wobble that would be almost inevitable on a long handheld exposure, she rotated the camera while shooting, starting the movement first and then pushing the shutter button. Turning the camera smoothly creates a blur that's most extreme at the outside edges of the photo. The center of the lens doesn't move at all, so the middle part of the image is relatively sharp. "To shoot like that you have to shoot a lot," says Katrin, "and have some luck on your side!" If you crop the image later in Photoshop, the "sharp center" doesn't have to be the actual center of the final image.

Photoshop: Photoshop's Radial Blur filter seemed promising for accentuating the swirl in this photo of a dancer in motion. So that we could later combine the filtered and unfiltered versions of the image, we first duplicated the photo to a new layer (Ctrl/⌘-J). Then we chose Filter > Blur > Radial Blur to open the Radial Blur dialog box. ▼ We chose the Spin option for the Blur Method and dragged the spin center slightly to the right in the Blur Center diagram, to a position corresponding to the dancer's left hip (the place where the skirt fabric seemed to be anchored and thus where the spinning motion would be centered). Since the Radial Blur dialog box has no Preview option, we set the Quality to Draft for a quick result, tried an Amount setting, and clicked "OK." To try another setting, we pressed Ctrl/⌘-Z to undo the filter, then applied the filter again (Ctrl-Alt-F in Windows, ⌘-Option-F on Mac), changing the Amount setting, until we got the motion we wanted, with Amount set to 10. After one final "undo" we reapplied the filter with Quality set to Best and clicked "OK."

Throughout the blurring process, we had ignored the blur everywhere but in the skirt because we knew we could clear it later with a layer mask, which we now added by Alt/Option-clicking the "Add layer mask" button 🔲 at the bottom of the Layers palette. The mask was black because we had used Alt/Option when we clicked, so it hid the blurred image entirely. To add spin to the skirt, all we had to do was paint the mask with a soft Brush 🖌 with white as the Foreground color in the areas where we wanted the blur to show, varying the Opacity setting in the Options bar when needed. ▼ If the white painting revealed too much of the filtered image, we could paint with black on the mask to hide it again.

FIND OUT MORE

▼ Using Radial Blur **page 257**
▼ Painting layer masks **page 75**

Focusing Attention on the Subject

YOU'LL FIND THE FILES
in ⊙ > Wow Project Files > Chapter 5 > Focusing Attention:
  • Focusing Attention-Before.psd (to start)
  • Wow-Noise Patterns.pat
  • Focusing Attention-After.psd (to compare)

OPEN THESE PALETTES
from the Window menu:
  • Tools • Layers • Channels • Layer Comps

OVERVIEW
Select the subject • Blur the background with Lens Blur • Restore film grain • Make a layer comp • Try desaturating and tinting effects on the background, making a layer comp of each treatment • Compare treatments with a Layer Comp "slide show"

A POPULAR EFFECT IN PRINT, FILM, AND VIDEO is to emphasize the subject of an image by *de*-emphasizing the background. This effect can be used to make the subject stand out, to simplify the background for overprinting type, or to tie an image to others in a series. Three approaches often used to achieve this effect are:

• **Blurring the background** while keeping the subject in focus. **In the camera** you can achieve this shallow depth of field by zooming in or getting close to the subject, and opening up the iris (setting the f-stop low). **In Photoshop** you can blur the background by applying the new Lens Blur filter, which is more efficient and more sophisticated than the Gaussian Blur filter we once used. Any film grain or digital-camera noise will be lost with the blurring, but you can restore it in order to make the blurred areas match the sharp ones.

• **Removing color from the background**, so the subject "pops"

• **Tinting the background** with a contrasting color

In many cases one or two of these techniques will do the job nicely. Here we'll explore all three.

1a

The original photo

1b

The image is duplicated to a new layer.

2a

The Magnetic Lasso 🪄 can automatically follow a distinct edge. If necessary, you can click to anchor the selection border in a spot where the edge is ambiguous. Before you begin, be sure to set the Feather to 0 in the Options bar.

2b

In areas where the Magnetic Lasso can't follow the edge, you can hold down the Alt/Option key and drag to use the Lasso 🔗.

CARLA GILBERT

1 Deciding on an approach. Choose a color photo of your own or open **Focusing Attention-Before.psd 1a**. For this outdoor wedding photo taken in the late afternoon, we wanted to keep the sense of the wedding guests' presence, but increase the emphasis on the bride and groom. We decided to try blurring the background first and then desaturating and tinting.

> ### DEFINING THE FOREGROUND
>
> If you want to keep a foreground subject in focus while blurring only the background, it's much easier to produce a photorealistic result if the subject extends off the bottom of the picture, as if the photo was taken close-up. It may even be worth cropping the image to achieve this if necessary. Otherwise, it can require some tricky masking to ensure that everything else in the image that's at the same distance as the subject is in focus, and that elements closer to or farther away from the camera are out of focus by the right amount. ▼

Before you start experimenting, it's a good idea to duplicate the image as a new layer (one way is to press Ctrl/⌘-J, short for Layer > New > Layer Via Copy) **1b**. As always, duplicating the image gives you an untouched original for safekeeping.

2 Selecting the subject. With the new layer active, select the subject using the appropriate Photoshop tools or commands. ▼ For the **Focusing Attention-Before.psd** file, you can either make and store your own selection (the method we used is described next), or go on to step 3, using the selection we've already stored in the file as the "background" channel.

To make the initial selection for this image we used the Magnetic Lasso, Lasso, and Polygonal Lasso in combination, which you can do by choosing the Magnetic Lasso and then using the Alt/Option key to switch to the other tools. First we chose the Magnetic Lasso 🪄 from the Tools palette and made sure Feather was set to 0 in the Options bar. We clicked once on the edge of the veil to start the selection, and "floated" the cursor around the subject without depressing the mouse button, letting it draw the selection border automatically as long as it could successfully follow the contrast at the edges **2a**. Occasionally we clicked to anchor the selection border in place.

When the Magnetic Lasso couldn't follow the edge of what we wanted to select because the edge wasn't distinct enough, we switched temporarily to the hand-operated Lasso 🔗 by holding down the Alt/Option key and the mouse button and dragging **2b**.

> **FIND OUT MORE**
>
> ▼ Masking for Lens Blur
> **pages 292 & 293**
>
> ▼ Choosing a selection method
> **page 56**

2c

Clicking with the Alt/Option key held down switches the tool to the Polygonal Lasso ⌘. Clicking on the "window frame" directly below the last point in the selection, then clicking on the frame again below the left edge of the subject before continuing the selection will ensure that the selection boundary won't miss any pixels along the bottom edge of the image.

2d

Touching up the selection in Quick Mask mode with Quick Mask Options set to the defaults (To open the dialog box and check the settings, double-click the Quick Mask button ⬚ in the Tools palette.)

2e

The inverted selection is stored in an alpha channel so it can be loaded and used with the Lens Blur filter later.

At the bottom edge, we Alt/Option-clicked as if extending the selection onto the frame of the working window to ensure that the bottom edge of the image would be selected **2c**.

When the selection boundary was complete, we clicked the "Edit in Quick Mask Mode" button ⬚ near the bottom of the Tools palette and used the Brush tool ✎ for touch-up, painting with white where we wanted to erase the red mask to include an area in the selection of the subject, and painting with black where we wanted to exclude something, leaving it as part of the background **2d**. Then we clicked the "Edit in Standard Mode" button ⬚ to turn the mask back into the "marching ants" selection border. Because we actually wanted to be able to select the background — not the couple — for blurring and coloring, we inverted the selection (Select > Inverse, or Ctrl/⌘-Shift-I) before choosing Select > Save Selection to save it as an alpha channel **2e**.

3 Blurring the background. With the duplicate layer still active, choose Filter > Blur > Lens Blur and set the parameters in the Lens Blur dialog box **3**; you can press Ctrl/⌘-+ and Ctrl/⌘-hyphen as needed to change the magnification of the preview as you work. We Alt/Option-clicked the Cancel/Reset button and then set the parameters as follows:

- In the **Depth Map** section we chose the "background" channel as the **Source**. We set the **Blur Focal Distance** at 0 (minimum brightness, or black) to tell the filter that areas of the photo corresponding to the black areas of the channel (0 brightness) should be fully protected from the blur. Since the mask was strictly black (for the subject) and white (for the background), the subject would be kept in sharp focus and the background would be blurred uniformly, right up to the edge of the subject. There wouldn't be a gradual transition.

- In the **Iris** section we adjusted the **Radius** to 18 to produce a blur amount that we liked. The Shape, Blade Curvature, and Rotation were left at the defaults.

- The **Specular Highlights** section of the dialog box has controls that imitate what a camera does to out-of-focus highlights, shaping and brightening them. We didn't want to increase the brightness of the highlights in the image (the sunlight on the ground and the guests, for example), since they would compete with the subject. In the Specular Highlights section, we left the **Threshold** at the default 255, which meant that only pixels with a brightness of 255 (white) would

3

The "background" channel is chosen as the Source for the Depth Map, and parameters are set in the Lens Blur dialog box. Specular Highlights and Noise settings are left at their default "off" settings.

4a

Creating a "Film Grain" layer in Overlay mode

4b

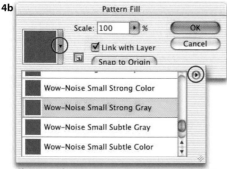

Choosing the Wow-Noise Small Strong Gray pattern for the "Film Grain" Pattern Fill layer

4c

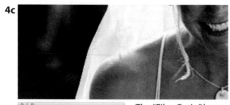

The "Film Grain" layer at 80% Opacity in Overlay mode

be brightened (an impossibility, so no pixels would be brightened). We also left the **Brightness** value at 0, which meant that any pixels chosen for brightening would be brightened by a zero amount, in other words not at all. Actually, either of these settings would have worked alone to prevent the highlights from being brightened.

- Our photo has a pronounced grain; the bride and groom had requested that the photographer not use a flash, so she was shooting with a high-speed film in the late afternoon shadows. We experimented with the Lens Blur's **Noise** section, which is designed to add back the grain (film or digital) that blurring takes away; a setting of 15 Gaussian produced a pretty good result in this 1200-pixel wide version of the image, but we decided to set the **Amount** at 0 and restore the grain with a Pattern Fill layer instead, as described next. This would give us greater control and flexibility than applying the noise with Lens Blur.

With our options set, we clicked "OK" to close the dialog box.

4 Restoring film grain. To create a Pattern Fill layer that will add grain to the background only, first select the background; you can do it this way: In the Channels palette, Ctrl/⌘-click the "background" channel's thumbnail to load the channel as a selection. So that you will be able to compare the added grain with the original, in your working window, zoom to a 100% or 200% view of an area that includes both blurred and sharp parts of the image (Ctrl/⌘-+ or Ctrl/⌘-hyphen to zoom in or out).

Next Alt/Option-click the "Create new fill or adjustment layer" button ⊘ at the bottom of the Layers palette, and choose Pattern from the pop-up list. In the New Layer dialog box (which opens because of the Alt/Option modifier), choose Overlay for the mode, so the noise pattern you choose will add texture rather than completely covering up the background **4a**. Name the layer if you like (we called ours "Film Grain") and click "OK."

When the Pattern Fill dialog box opens **4b**, click the tiny arrow next to the pattern swatch to open the scrollable list of patterns. If you haven't yet loaded the Wow Pattern presets,▼ they won't appear in the list. In that case you can click the ⊙ button at the right of the list and choose Load Patterns. All of the Wow patterns are located in the Wow Presets folder on the Wow DVD-ROM; the **Wow-Noise Patterns.pat** file is also provided separately in the folder of files for this exercise.

FIND OUT MORE

▼ Loading Wow Presets **page 5**

5

With the Wow-Noise patterns loaded, try different patterns until you find the one that best matches the size, distribution, and color of the grain in the image; we chose Wow-Noise Small Strong Gray. If needed, adjust the Scale slider to match the grain; we left the Scale at 100%. Now you can experiment with the Opacity and even the blend mode of the Pattern layer; we left the layer in Overlay mode and set the Opacity at 80% **4c**.

5 Making a layer comp. Even for simple projects, descriptively named layer comps can help you look at design options. Make a "snapshot" of the current state of the Layers palette by clicking the "Create New Layer Comp" button ⬛ at the bottom of the Layer Comps palette **5**. Your new layer comp captures the position, visibility, opacity, blend mode, and Layer Style (if any) for each layer and remembers these settings even if you change them in the file later. (This and other layer comps will be used for a quick and easy "slide show" of options in step 8.)

A layer comp, named "Blur Only," is made from the current state of the image, with blurred background and restored film grain.

> **LAYER COMPS FOREVER — ALMOST**
>
> Unlike Photoshop's History snapshots, layer comps live on when a file is closed. They are preserved with the file, so they will still be there in the Layer Comps palette when you open the file again.
>
> Layer comps are also automatically carried along when you duplicate your file (Image > Duplicate), *but not if you choose the "Duplicate Merged Layers Only" option in the Duplicate Image dialog box.* Merging the layers eliminates information that Photoshop needs to maintain the comps.

6 "Ghosting" the background. By adding a Hue/Saturation Adjustment layer, you can desaturate the color of the background and also make it lighter or darker as needed: Select the background (one way is to Ctrl/⌘-click the "Film Grain" layer's mask thumbnail in the Layers palette). Click the "Create new fill or adjustment layer" button ⬤ at the bottom of the Layers palette and choose Hue/Saturation from the list. The selection creates a mask in the Adjustment layer that protects the subject, so when you make changes in the Hue/Saturation dialog box, only the background will change.

6

Decrease Saturation by moving the slider to the left; we used a setting of –70. Move the Lightness slider in the direction that boosts the contrast between background and subject **6**; we darkened the background, using a setting of –20. Click "OK," and then make another layer comp by clicking the ⬛ button at the bottom of the Layer Comps palette; we named the new Comp "Ghosted."

Using a Hue/Saturation Adjustment layer to remove color from the background and darken it

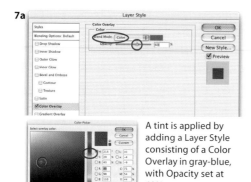

7a

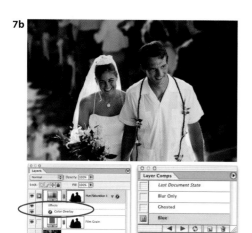

A tint is applied by adding a Layer Style consisting of a Color Overlay in gray-blue, with Opacity set at 60%.

7b

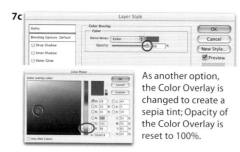

After the Layer Style is applied, another layer comp is made.

7c

As another option, the Color Overlay is changed to create a sepia tint; Opacity of the Color Overlay is reset to 100%.

8

In the Layer Comps palette, click to the left of a comp's name to display that state of the file. You can step through the comps by clicking the ▶ button.

7 Adding a tint. One way to tint the background would be to change the settings in the Hue/Saturation Adjustment layer. (This approach is shown in "Quick Attention-Focusing Techniques" on page 294.) But a layer comp *doesn't freeze image content.* If you were to change the settings in the Hue/Saturation Adjustment layer, this would also change the existing "Ghosted" comp, which includes that Adjustment layer. To change color *without* changing the existing comp, you can use a Layer Style.

Add a Style to the Hue/Saturation layer by clicking the ● button at the bottom of the Layers palette and choosing Color Overlay. The existing layer mask for the Hue/Saturation layer will limit the Color Overlay effect to the background. In the Layer Style dialog box, choose Color for the Color Overlay's Blend Mode, and then click the color swatch and choose a color **7a**. We chose a gray-blue and experimented with the Color Overlay's Opacity, deciding on 60%. Click "OK" when you have a tint you like. At this point make another layer comp to protect this tint option; we named our new Comp "Blue" **7b**.

You can now change the Color Overlay to try other tinting options, without affecting existing comps. In the Layers palette, double-click the "Color Overlay" entry below the Hue/Saturation layer to open the Layer Style dialog box. Click the color swatch to change the color (we chose a gray-brown), and adjust the Opacity if you like **7c**. Click "OK" to close the Layer Style box, and then make another comp; we named our comp "Warm Gray." Make more Style changes and comps if you like.

8 "Playing back" the Layer Comps. Now you can compare the options you stored as layer comps. In the Layer Comps palette, click in the column to the left of the name of any Comp you want to display **8**. Or click the "Apply Next Selected Layer Comp" button ▶ repeatedly to advance through the Comps. Each click will restore the Layers palette to its state when the corresponding comp was made. You can reverse the order of display by clicking the ◀ button. We chose to print the "Warm Gray" comp (it's shown at the top of page 285). 🎨

SELECTIVE SLIDE SHOWS

By default, repeatedly clicking the "Apply Next Selected Layer Comp" button ▶ at the bottom of the Layer Comps palette provides a "slide show" by advancing through *all* the comps in the palette. If you want to show only *some* of the Comps instead, Shift-click or Ctrl/⌘-click the ones you want in your slide show and then start clicking the ▶ button.

EXERCISING

Lens Blur

Traditionally, photographers have used a shallow depth of field to blur a distracting environment while keeping the subject sharp. Many digital cameras can't shorten depth of field as well as a comparable film camera might. But Photoshop's Lens Blur filter can help "after the fact." It can quite realistically simulate a shallow depth of field, even shaping highlights in the background into out-of-focus points of light. Proceed through the examples on these three pages for an introduction to tapping the power of Lens Blur.

If your goal is a realistic simulation, here are some things to keep in mind about a shallow depth of field:

- To take a photo with a shallow depth of focus, the photographer often sets the lens wide open (a low f-stop produces a shorter in-focus span) and gets close to the subject, either actually or through the use of a telephoto lens. So close-ups are good candidates for Lens Blur.

- With a shortened depth of field, the span that's in focus is about one-third in front of the in-focus subject and about two-thirds behind it.

- An extremely blurry foreground, whether it looks "camera-realistic" or not, can be distracting.

An easy way to work with Lens Blur is to use a grayscale mask stored in an alpha channel. By default, black in the channel tells Lens Blur to keep the corresponding parts of the image in sharp focus. Areas that correspond to white parts of the channel will be the most out-of-focus (you can switch to the opposite by clicking the Invert check box in the Lens Blur dialog). The more gradually the mask goes from black to white, through intermediate shades of gray, the more gradual the change in focus will be.

PRESERVING THE ORIGINAL

To keep your options open, duplicate your image to a new layer (Ctrl/⌘-J) so you can run the Lens Blur filter on a copy and preserve the original. Another advantage of the second layer is that you can reduce its Opacity to blend the filtered and original versions for a less pronounced effect.

YOU CAN FIND THE FILES

in (wow) > Wow Project Files > Chapter 5 > Exercising Lens Blur

FIND OUT MORE

▼ Making an alpha channel from a selection **page 67**

Foreground Subject

A CREDIBLE BLUR is easiest to manage if the subject of the photo is the closest thing to the viewer, extending off one edge of the photo, typically the bottom. That way there's an obvious gap between the in-focus plane, where the subject is, and the out-of-focus background, and you don't need to craft the transition between what's blurred and what isn't. "Focusing Attention on the Subject" on page 285 is an example, going step-by-step through isolating the subject, putting the background out of focus with Lens Blur, and adding noise to match the photo's original grain. Another instance that doesn't require a fall-off in focus is a photo whose subject is in mid-air, such as the butterfly above **A**.

To put the background out of focus, you'll need a sharp mask for the subject. **Lens Blur Butterfly.psd** has a mask already stored in an alpha channel (Alpha 1), which you can see if you open the Channels palette (Window > Channels) **B**.▼ To create or enhance a background blur, choose Filter > Blur > Lens Blur **C**; restore the filter's default settings by Alt/Option-clicking the "Cancel" button. Then experiment with the **Radius** slider to set the amount of blur; the **Iris** and **Specular Highlights** settings control the character of the out-of-focus highlights.

 Lens Blur Butterfly.psd

Focus Fall-off

TO KEEP ONLY *PART* of the subject in focus, such as part of the face in this portrait **A**, the alpha channel mask used with the Lens Blur filter needs to show a gradual transition. You can paint such a mask by viewing both image and alpha channel together as you paint the channel: With the Channels palette open, add an alpha channel by clicking the "Create new channel" button ▣ at the bottom of the Channels palette. With your black channel visible, turn on visibility for the image as well (tap the tilde key ▣); you'll see the image, completely covered with a color overlay that represents the alpha channel mask. For our portrait, we changed the mask color to green (by double-clicking the alpha channel's thumbnail, clicking the Color swatch, and choosing a new color) **B**. We would use the green to represent the out-of-focus areas.

We painted the alpha channel using the Brush tool ✐ with white paint and a soft brush tip and 50% Opacity chosen in the Options bar **C**, to clear the mask in the area of sharp focus and partly clear it to make the transition from sharp to blurred **D**.▼

With the mask painted, we targeted the image (Ctrl/⌘-~) and turned off visibility for the alpha channel (clicking its ◉ in the Channels palette). We chose Filter > Blur > Lens Blur; we chose **Alpha 1** as the **Source**, but because the mask was white where we wanted the image to remain sharp, we turned on the **Invert** option. Then we moved the **Radius** slider to get the degree of blurring we wanted (we used a setting of 30), and clicked "OK" **E**. The effect seemed stronger than we wanted, so we reduced it. One way is to choose Image > Fade Lens Blur and reduce the Opacity.▼

Lens Blur Portrait.psd

Midground Subject

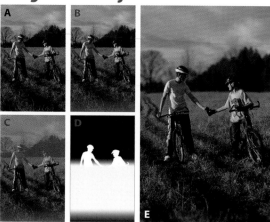

FOR AN IN-FOCUS SUBJECT that *isn't* at the front of the image — the bike riders here **A** — the surface where that sharp subject stands will also need to be in-focus, but it will go out of focus both in front and behind. We started an alpha channel to use with Lens Blur (clicking ▣ at the bottom of the Channels palette) and also turned on visibility for the image (tap ▣). To establish the "in focus" zone on the grass, we chose the Gradient tool ▣ and in the Options bar chose the **Black, White** gradient, **Normal** mode, **Linear** style, and the **Reverse** option **B** (to start our gradient with white). To mask the foreground, we held down the Shift key (to keep the gradient vertical) as we dragged the Gradient tool from where we wanted the front edge of the in-focus zone, down to where we wanted the maximum blur to start. To mask the background, we chose **Darken** for the Gradient tool's Mode in the Options bar to protect the existing gradient. Then we Shift-dragged from where we wanted the back of the sharp zone to be, upward to where the image was as out-of-focus as it was going to get; to maintain the illusion, the gradient had to end on the grassy surface rather than extending into the vertical trees at the horizon **C**.

Now all that was left was to "unmask" any part of the subject that extended above the clear area and into the mask; we used the Brush ✐ with a fairly hard brush tip (Hardness 80%) and high Opacity to paint with white. Tapping ▣, we could toggle to a mask-only view **D**.

We targeted the image (Ctrl/⌘-~), chose Filter > Blur > Lens Blur and Alt/Option-clicked the "Cancel" button to reset. We turned on the **Invert** option, and adjusted the **Radius** (we used 8 for this small image) **E**.

FIND OUT MORE

▼ Painting a mask **page 75**
▼ Using the Fade command **page 31**

Lens Blur Bikes.psd

Masking Other Elements

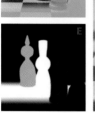

IF YOUR SUBJECT isn't the only thing that "stands up" in your photo, adding a convincing Lens Blur may require a more complex mask. In our photo of chess pieces **A**, we wanted to focus on the bishop, with the rook, knight, and king out-of-focus and the queen in the transition zone.

We added an alpha channel and used the Gradient tool ▭ to create the "in-focus" zone as in "Midground Subject" on the facing page **B**. We also added the bishop to the mask **C**, using the Pen tool ◊ to trace it,▼ then clicking the "Load path as selection" button ● at the bottom of the Paths palette, and filling it with white — typing X once or twice makes black the Foreground color and Alt-Backspace (Windows) or Option-Delete (Mac) fills the selection. The knight was standing in the out-of-focus foreground, so it needed to be masked to match the black out-of-focus areas of the channel. We used the Pen tool ◊ to select the part of the knight that intruded into the in-focus area and in the alpha channel filled the selection with black (type X and delete).

Next we selected the rook, and with the alpha channel still targeted, we used the Eyedropper tool ✐ to sample the mask next to its base; we filled the selection with this sampled dark gray Foreground color. We repeated the selecting, sampling, and filling for the queen, using a lighter gray sampled from where she stands in the transition zone. The Alpha 1 channel of the **Lens Blur Chess.psd** file holds the resulting mask **D** (viewed alone in **E**).

Now we chose Filter > Blur > Lens Blur, turned on the **Invert** option, set the **Radius** (we used 25), and clicked "OK" to complete the effect **F**.

 **Lens Blur Chess.psd**

Flat Subject

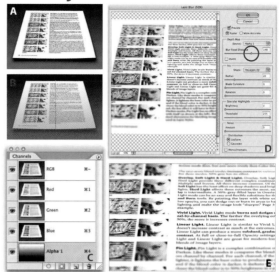

IF THE SUBJECT ITSELF RECEDES into the distance — like the page above **A** — it's really easy to put the band of sharp focus where you want it to be. To establish the focus on our page, we added an alpha channel (clicking the ▣ button at the bottom of the Channels palette) and turned on visibility for the image also (tapping ~). We chose the Gradient tool ▭, and in the Options bar chose the **Black, White** gradient, **Normal** mode, and **Linear** style. Holding down the Shift key, we dragged from the top edge of the page in the image to its bottom edge to establish a gradient **B**, **C**.

We targeted the image again (Ctrl/⌘-~) and chose Filter > Blur > Lens Blur, then chose our **Alpha 1** channel for the **Source**, with **Invert turned off**. In the working window, we clicked where we wanted sharp focus, on the words "**Vivid Light**" near the middle of the page; the **Blur Focal Distance** slider moved automatically **D**, and the rest of the image went out of focus gradually both in front of and behind the point we had clicked. We could easily experiment, changing the focus by clicking at a different point. When you click, the gray in the gradient-filled alpha channel that corresponds to the point you've clicked becomes the in-focus tone, and all the lighter or darker shades in the gradient become progressively out-of-focus. Each time you click, you set a new "in-focus" gray. By changing the **Radius**, you can change the maximum blurring. We chose 20 for the Radius, returned to the original in-focus point, and clicked "OK."

 Lens Blur Page.psd

FIND OUT MORE

▼ Operating the Pen tool ◊ **page 435**

Attention-Focusing Techniques

"Focusing Attention on the Subject" on page 285 tells how to select a subject and blur or tint the background, building in flexibility with layer comps. It's a good method to use when you want to isolate the subject with a precise selection, and when you or your clients want to see options. But there are less elaborate ways to use color, background-blurring, or other techniques to direct viewers' attention within a photo. Since many of these methods don't require making a careful selection of the subject, they can greatly reduce your work time. It pays to start by analyzing your photo and your goal and "thinking like Photoshop," to see if a quick method will do the job:

- Can you get the desired result without having to precisely select the subject? Most of the examples on these eight pages don't require a precise selection.

- Is the area around the subject fairly neutral in color? If so, some of the "ghosting" methods can be quick and successful (see pages 296 and 300).

- Can you isolate the subject with a rectangular selection? One of the "stripping" methods may do the trick (pages 297 through 299).

- Is the subject a portrait with a fairly busy outdoor background, with green plants and blue sky? If so, the "Channel Mixer Trick" on page 299 could be worth a try.

YOU'LL FIND THE FILES
in **wow** > Wow Project Files > Chapter 5 > Quick Attention-Focusing

Cropping

CORBIS ROYALTY FREE

CROPPING IS AN OBVIOUS WAY to help focus attention on a subject, by trimming off distracting elements or simply by allowing the subject to occupy a bigger fraction of the image space. After duplicating the photo **A** (Image > Duplicate), we chose the Crop tool ⊟ because it would make it easy to look at different cropping options by hiding the cropped-out parts of the image as we experimented with the cropping frame. In the Options bar we clicked the "Clear" button **B** to ensure that we wouldn't accidentally resize the file in the process of cropping it. We dragged diagonally in the image to make a cropping rectangle for the boy and his breakfast. We dragged inside the cropping box to move it around and dragged on its handles to change its size and shape, then pressed the Enter key to complete the crop **C**.

Framing with Focus

Before

After

PHOTOSPIN.COM

A QUICK AND EASY WAY to focus attention on one particular area of a photo starts with duplicating the image to a new layer (Ctrl/⌘-J) and then selecting the area with the Rectangular Marquee tool ⬚. Copy the selected area to make a new layer (Ctrl/⌘-J), and then blur the original image on the layer below. Here we blurred the "Background copy" layer by choosing Filter > Blur > Gaussian Blur; a Radius setting of 1.0 worked well to slightly blur this low-resolution image.

To further emphasize the separation between the sharp and blurred regions, add a "dark glow" around the sharp area using a Layer Style: Click the "Add a layer style" button 🟢 at the bottom of the Layers palette, and choose Drop Shadow from the pop-up list of effects. In the Layer Style dialog box, change the Drop Shadow's Distance setting to 0 pixels, which will put the shadow directly under the subject rather than offsetting it.

 **Framing with Focus.psd**

Masking a Blur

E.A.M. VISSER

THERE'S ANOTHER EASY WAY to keep the subject in sharp focus and create a stylized out-of-focus effect to subdue background detail, especially if you want to imply or enhance motion. Layer a blurred version of the image over the sharp original and then add a layer mask, to let the sharp subject show through. Here we started by duplicating the image **A** to a new layer (Ctrl/⌘-J) and then applying a Zoom blur to the new layer: Choose Filter > Blur > Radial Blur; click the "Zoom" button, move the Blur Center so it matches the location of your subject **B**, and set the Amount of blur you want (we used 10); click "OK."

Add a layer mask (click the 🔲 button at the bottom of the Layers palette). Then choose the Gradient tool ▬ and in the Options bar choose the black-to-white gradient and click the "Radial Gradient" button **C**. Center the cursor over the subject, and drag outward, stopping where you want the blur to be fully in effect **D**.

 Masking a Blur.psd

Vignetted "Ghosting"

Before

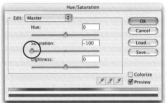

After

COLOR IS COMPELLING, so the subject stands out if you leave it in color and turn the rest of the image black-and-white. To spotlight one of the rafters in this photo, we chose the Elliptical Marquee tool ◯ and set the Feather in the Options bar (we tried a setting of 10 pixels). Then we dragged the cursor in the image to select the rafter, and inverted the selection (Ctrl/⌘-Shift-I) to select everything but the rafter. We added a Hue/Saturation Adjustment layer by clicking the "Create new fill or adjustment layer" button ⬤ at the bottom of the Layers palette and choosing Hue/Saturation from the pop-up list. We moved the Saturation slider all the way to the left to remove all color and clicked "OK." Our inverted selection became a mask that protected the color of the rafter. In the Layers palette we experimented with the Hue/Saturation layer's Opacity, returning some of the color to the image by setting Opacity at 85%. (See page 79 for another option for softening the edges of a mask.)

 **Vignetted Ghosting.psd**

Painted "Ghosting"

Before

After

FOR THIS PHOTO WE WANTED MORE than a simple geometric vignette like the one at the left, in order to spotlight the daughter. Thinking that a loosely painted mask would do the trick, we added a Hue/Saturation Adjustment layer by clicking the ⬤ button at the bottom of the Layers palette; we chose Hue/Saturation, and in the Hue/Saturation dialog box we moved the Saturation slider all the way to the left to remove all color, and then clicked "OK."

Next we chose the Brush tool 🖌 and picked a large, soft brush tip from the pop-up Brush Preset picker in the Options bar. We painted the Adjustment layer's mask with black to restore the girl's color. (This photo's neutral background makes it ideal for this technique; you don't have to be precise in painting.) We reduced the size of the brush tip and lowered the Opacity in the Options bar, then painted with white to remove color that had spilled over onto the mother's hand.

 Painted Ghosting.psd

Isolating a Strip

Before

After

PHOTOSPIN.COM

SOMETIMES A SIMPLE "STRIP SELECTION" can do a great job of highlighting one person in a group shot or one area of a street scene. Here we used the Rectangular Marquee ⌞⌟ to select a strip that included the woman we wanted to spotlight. We reversed the selection so everything outside the strip was selected (Select > Inverse). With this selection active, we clicked the "Create new fill or adjustment layer" button ◐ at the bottom of the Layers palette and chose Hue/Saturation. Moving the Saturation slider all the way to the left turned the rest of the photo black-and-white. When we clicked "OK," we could see that our selection had created a mask for the Adjustment layer that protected only the selected strip.

 **Isolating a Strip.psd**

Stripping a Color

Before

CORBIS ROYALTY FREE

After

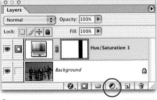

IN AN IMAGE WITH A RELATIVELY MONOCHROMATIC background, you may be able to preserve the background color when you desaturate. As in "Isolating a Strip" at the left, we made a strip selection of the one passenger, inverted the selection, and added a Hue/Saturation Adjustment layer. However, in the Hue/Saturation dialog box we chose Reds from the pop-up Edit menu, and *then* moved the Saturation slider to the left. This removed the red in the skin tones and clothing of the passengers who weren't protected by the mask, without affecting the blue background. If you want to remove the traces of color in the passengers' hair, in the Layers palette double-click the thumbnail for the Hue/Saturation layer to reopen the dialog box. Choose Yellows from the Edit menu, and move the Saturation slider left; repeat for Magentas.

 Stripping a Color.psd

Modifying a Strip

PHOTOSPIN.COM

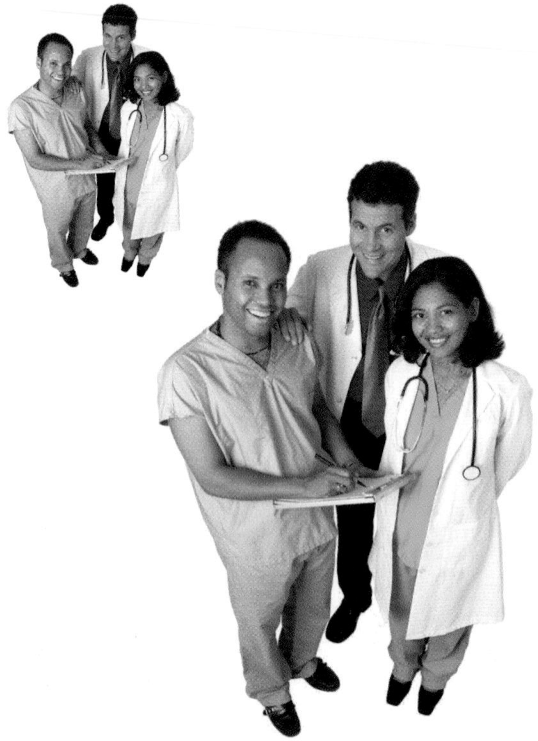

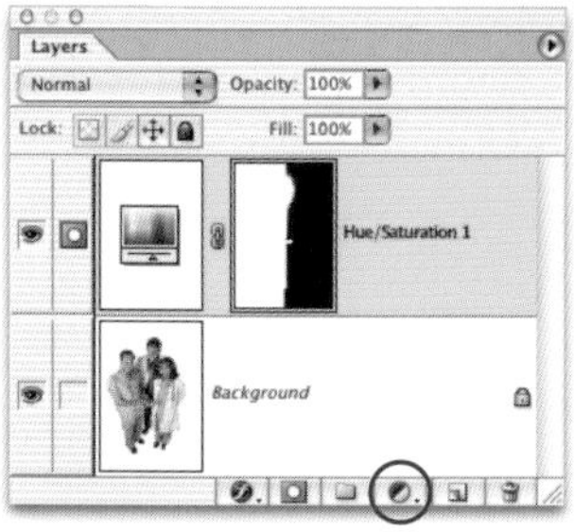

A STRIP SELECTION can be an effective way to start isolating a subject, even if you know it won't do the job completely. Here we used the Rectangular Marquee [ ] to make a strip selection of the woman. We reversed the selection (Ctrl/⌘-Shift-I), clicked the ◐ button at the bottom of the Layers palette, and added a Hue/Saturation layer, moving the Saturation slider all the way to the left. Then, because the man in back was dressed in nearly neutral colors, it was a simple matter to use the Brush tool to paint the mask with white where his head and the other man's clipboard were included in the strip of color, and to paint a vertical stroke along the left edge of the strip, to soften the transition between almost neutral and fully neutral.

Modifying a Strip.psd

Stripping a Silhouette

CORBIS ROYALTY FREE

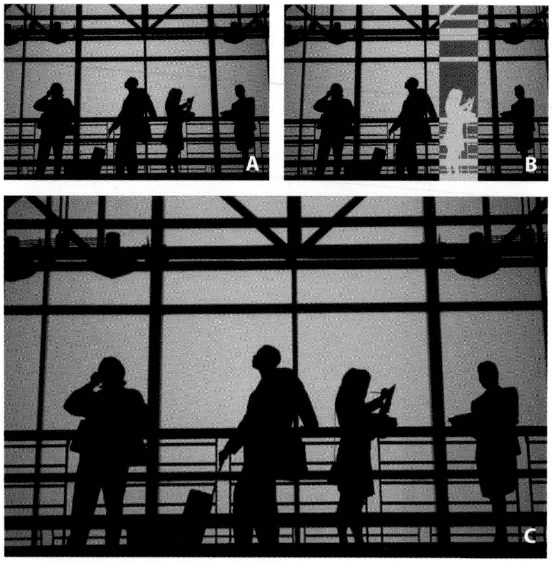

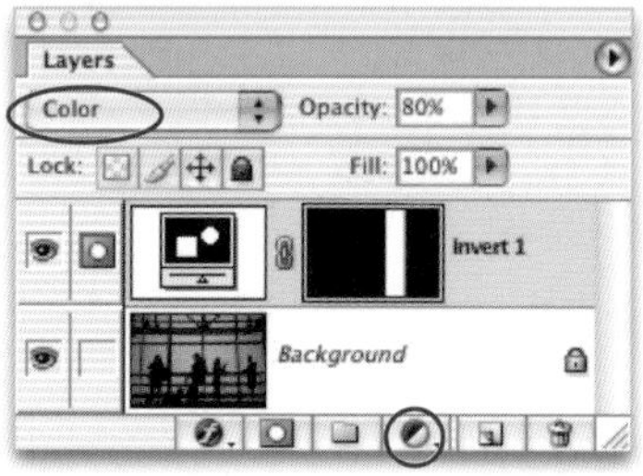

IF YOU START WITH AN IMAGE in which several subjects are silhouetted **A**, you can target a single member of the group by reversing the color in a strip around that subject. We used the Rectangular Marquee [ ] to make a strip selection of one of the figures. Then we clicked the "Create a new fill or adjustment layer" button ◐ at the bottom of the Layers palette, and chose Invert. This added an Invert Adjustment layer that made a color negative of the strip **B**. By changing the blend mode for the Invert layer to Color,▼ we could keep the silhouette black **C**. (For some silhouetted images, it may work better to keep the subject in its original background and instead change the color of the rest of the image. In that case, reverse the selection — Ctrl/⌘-Shift-I — before adding the Invert Adjustment layer.)

Stripping a Silhouette.psd

FIND OUT MORE

▼ Blend modes **page 177**

Soft-Edged Stripping

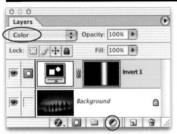

ANOTHER APPROACH FOR A SILHOUETTE **A** is to start with a strip selection, add the Invert layer, and then edit the mask. In an illustration for an article about birth order, we used the Rectangular Marquee ⌞⌝ to select the oldest child. Then we clicked the "Create new fill or adjustment layer" button ◑ at the bottom of the Layers palette, added an Invert Adjustment layer, and put the layer in Color mode **B**. We chose Filter > Blur > Gaussian Blur and, with the Preview box checked, we watched the image as we experimented with the Radius, to soften the mask edges and blur the color transition; we settled on a setting of 15 pixels for this 640-pixel-wide image **C**.

 Soft-Edged Stripping.psd

FIND OUT MORE

▼ Blend modes
page 174

A Channel Mixer Trick

IN AN RGB IMAGE **A**, people's skin tones typically include much more red than blue or green, a fact we can sometimes use to "pop" the subject with very little work. We clicked the "Create new fill or adjustment layer" button ◑ at the bottom of the Layers palette and added a Channel Mixer Adjustment layer. In the Channel Mixer dialog box, we left the default settings for the Source Channels (100% Red, 0% Green, and 0% Blue) and clicked the Monochrome check box **B**. This told the Channel Mixer to use the Red channel as the black-and-white version of the image **C**; we clicked "OK." In the Layers palette we changed the blend mode for the Channel Mixer layer to Darken, ▼ so the monochrome treatment would show up only where it was *darker* than the original. Reds and very light colors remained in color **D**.

 Channel Mixer Trick.psd

"Ghosting" & Tinting

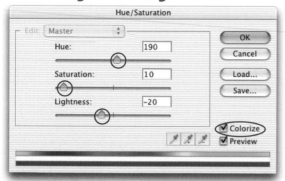

WHETHER YOU HAVE TO MAKE A DETAILED SELECTION, as shown here, or use one of the masking or stripping techniques on the previous pages, the Hue/Saturation dialog box can provide "one-stop shopping" to desaturate, darken, and tint the surroundings. Starting with the cropped photo from page 294, we selected the subject, reversed the selection (Ctrl/⌘-Shift-I), and then clicked the "Create new fill or adjustment layer" button ⊘ at the bottom of the Layers palette and added a Hue/Saturation Adjustment layer. In the Hue/Saturation dialog box, we clicked the Colorize check box (to apply a tint) and moved the three sliders, adjusting the color and tone to contrast with the subject, until we got the balance we liked.

Adding a Dark "Halo"

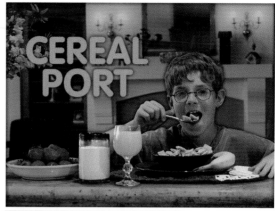

IF YOU MAKE A PRECISE SELECTION of your subject, and then ghost and tint it (as at the left), but you want even more emphasis, try adding a "dark glow" by applying a Layer Style to the Hue/Saturation layer. When you apply a Style, by default any edge effects in the Style follow the edges of the mask. The Hue/Saturation layer's mask is for the *surroundings,* not the subject. So to put the dark glow *around* the subject, we can't use a Drop Shadow effect, which would spread the shadow effect onto the subject. Instead, use the Inner Shadow: Click the "Add a layer style" button ⊘ at the bottom of the Layers palette and choose Inner Shadow from the list of effects. Set the Distance at 0 so the shadow won't be displaced off-center. Increase the Size to spread the shadow out from the edge; increase the Choke to make the shadow denser.

Any type or graphics you add can have a matching dark glow. Add a Layer Style, but this time choose Drop Shadow from the pop-out list of effects. Again set the Distance to 0; match the Size you used for the Inner Shadow, and match the Spread to the Choke value you used.

 **Ghost-Tint-Halo.psd**

Replacing with Red

CORBIS ROYALTY FREE

Before

After

OUR EYES ARE ATTRACTED TO RED, even in small patches. In this photo we first duplicated the image to a new layer (Ctrl/⌘-J) so we would have an untouched original in reserve. We zoomed to a close-up view (press Ctrl/⌘-+ to zoom in), then clicked the Foreground color square in the Tools palette, chose a red in the Color Picker, and clicked "OK." We chose the Color Replacement tool (🖌 in CS or 🖌 in CS2; the keyboard shortcut is J). We set parameters in the Options bar: With Mode set to Color, the tool would change the hue and saturation of the boy's shirt as we painted, but the original lights and darks would remain. Sampling was set to Continuous, and Tolerance was set to 30% to start. The Limits option was set to Find Edges so the green of the shirt would help limit the color change. As the cursor moved, the tool replaced the color under the crosshairs, and any close shades and tones within the tool's footprint, with red. We reduced brush tip size and Tolerance as needed to work on small areas of green in this low-resolution image.

 **Replacing with Red.psd**

Spotlighting

GAREN CHECKLEY

Before

After

ONE WAY TO GUIDE THE VIEWER'S EYE is to enhance the center of attention with a spotlight. This method works well for photos that show many people or lots of activity, that can also stand to be darkened overall so the spotlighted area stands out. For this photo we used the Lighting Effects filter to create the spotlight and then "separated" the resulting lighting from the image so we could manipulate it. We started by choosing Filter > Render > Lighting Effects. The Lighting Effects filter's preview is small — it was hard to see exactly what was going on as we changed the settings. But we modified the Default Spotlight to produce lighting that we knew would be more extreme than we wanted: We dragged the spotlight's handles in the preview to make the lighted area smaller, more vertical, and lit from the top, and we changed the Ambience setting to 28, then clicked "OK" to close the box.

"Moving" the spotlight to a separate layer would make it easier to manipulate. Before we did anything else, we typed Ctrl/⌘-Z to undo the effects of the filter. Then we added a new layer to hold the spotlight by Alt/Option-clicking the "Create a new layer" button ◑ at the bottom of the Layers palette. In the New Layer dialog box we chose Overlay for the Mode and clicked the check box for "Fill with Overlay-neutral color (50% gray)." All we had to do to re-create our spotlight on this layer was to type Ctrl/⌘-F to rerun the last filter. Now we could experiment with the blend mode▼ and Opacity of the new layer; we decided on Overlay mode at 40% Opacity.

 **Spotlighting.psd**

FIND OUT MORE

▼ Blend modes
page 176

Fixing a Problem Photo

YOU'LL FIND THE FILES
in **wow** > Wow Project Files > Chapter 5 >
Fixing a Problem Photo:
- Problem Fix-Before.psd (to start)
- Problem Fix-After.psd (to compare)

OPEN THESE PALETTES
from the Window menu:
- Tools • Layers

OVERVIEW
Blur a copy of the image with the Dust &
Scratches filter • Apply a "hide all" mask
to the blurred layer • To hide blemishes,
dab the mask with white or fill selected
areas with white • Clean up blemishes
too large or too small for the Dust &
Scratches settings with the Healing
Brush 🩹, Spot Healing Brush 🩹, and
Clone Stamp 🖌 • Adjust contrast and
remove the color cast

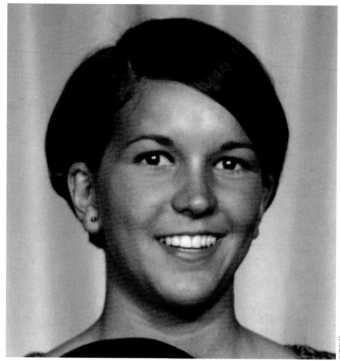

JHDAVIS

WHEN YOU NEED TO FIX A "PROBLEM PHOTO," the built-in power and speed of Photoshop filters and Adjustment layers can make global changes such as eliminating dust and scratches and adjusting color and tonality. But you also want the "human touch" to direct these "automatic" changes so they do precisely what you want. The image above shows the "after" version of a scanned color slide from the 1960s. The following technique removed almost all of the million bits of "junk" from our original (shown at the left) in about three minutes! And when the entire problem-fixing process was complete — including cosmetic changes and tone and color corrections — the original image remained untouched on the *Background* layer and the various changes were on their own layers, where they could easily be modified if necessary. This retouching method can be successfully applied to all kinds of images. It works on relatively soft portraits like this one, on detailed landscapes, and on photos that show distinct edges.

1 Analyzing your photo. Start by identifying your photo's worst problem, so you can tackle it first. Specific challenges vary from image to image, but many old photos show the problems seen in this scan **1**. The most obvious flaw was the dark junk scattered all over the image, caused by dust on the slide or deterioration of the emulsion. Another problem was the faded color.

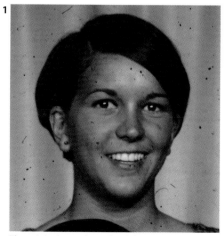

The original scan from the slide

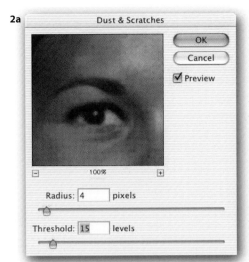

The Dust & Scratches filter is run on the duplicate layer. Setting the Radius at 4 and the Threshold at 15 eliminates almost all the spots and scratches in the image but retains the film grain.

2b

A black-filled layer mask is added to the filtered layer. Note that the layer has been given a meaningful name (by double-clicking the name and typing to edit it).

2c

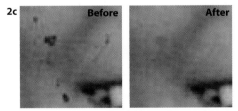

Defects are removed by dabbing white on the layer mask. The largest spots and the finest scratches will need more work.

2 Eliminating dust and scratches. To quickly get rid of dust or scratches, start by copying your original image to another layer (Ctrl/⌘-J). Next filter this copy to hide all (or almost all) of the junk, as follows: Choose Filter > Noise > Dust & Scratches. The Dust & Scratches filter looks for spots that differ from their surroundings in color or brightness; then it blurs the surrounding color into the spots to eliminate them.

To control the blurring, in the Dust & Scratches dialog box, first move the sliders all the way to the left — to 1 for the Radius, and to 0 for Threshold. Then slowly move the Radius slider to the right to make all (or most) of the problem spots disappear. If your photo has some really big spots, it may be better to leave them partly visible and fix them another way later, because a Radius setting high enough to hide them completely may blur the image too much to be useful. When you reach the Radius setting that hides the spots, you'll find that you've also eliminated any inherent noise or film grain. To restore the grain, leave the Radius slider where it is and move the Threshold slider to the right until the spots just begin to reappear; then "back off" by moving the Threshold slider just slightly to the left until the spots are gone again **2a**. What you've just done by increasing the Threshold is to make the filter "smarter" so that it blurs away only those spots that are *very* different from their surroundings. It ignores small color differences such as those due to film grain.

Although the spots are gone and the grain is restored, you'll find that a lot of the important image detail has also been eliminated. That's because the Dust & Scratches filter can't tell the difference between a scratch and an eyelash, or a dust speck and the catchlight in an eye. To solve that problem, you can use a layer mask to hide the filtered image and then "paint it back" only where you need it to hide the blemishes: Make a mask to hide the new filtered layer completely by Alt/Option-clicking the "Add a layer mask" button 🔲 at the bottom of the Layers palette **2b**. The spots will be visible again, and the palette should now show that the black-filled mask is targeted. The Tools palette should show that white is the Foreground color — it's the default when a mask is active. If not, it can be restored by typing D (for "Default colors") or X (for "eXchange colors").

Choose the Brush tool 🖌, and in the Options bar click the brush tip thumbnail immediately to the right of the "Brush:" label to open the Brush Preset picker; choose a soft-edged brush that's about the size of the specks you need to hide. Set the Mode to Normal and Opacity to 100%. In detailed areas such as the face

2d

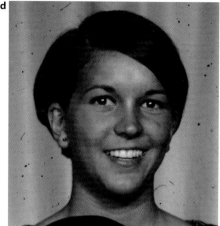

After removing the specks from the face by painting white onto the black-filled layer mask

2e

To remove the specks from the drape in the background, this area of the layer mask is selected and filled with white.

in this image, dab with the brush where you see specks **2c**. The dabs will make white "holes" in the mask, allowing the filtered image to cover the spots in those areas **2d**.

Eliminating specks in large areas that have little detail can be done all at once by selecting these areas and filling them with white on the mask: Choose the Lasso ⌒ and in the Options bar set its Feather (we used a 3-pixel feather); surround the area you want to fill; then Alt/Option-Delete to fill the selected area of the mask with white, the current Foreground color **2e**, **2f**.

3 Clean-up and cosmetic changes. The next step is to hide the remaining specks and scratches that were either too large or too small to be fixed by the Dust & Scratches layer, such as the large spot on the cheek and the fine scratches on the face and the right side of the background. For these changes, it's best to add a "repair" layer above the filtered layer, where you can make your "hand-painted" alterations. This protects the image from painting mistakes and also makes it easy to make changes to your repairs later if you need to. Start by adding another layer (click the "Create a new layer" button ▣ at the bottom of the Layers palette) **3a**.

Both the Healing Brush 🖊 and the Spot Healing Brush 🖊 in Photoshop CS2 will work on a separate layer. With the Healing Brush, you sample a "source" area to use for the repair and then click on the spot to hide it. With the Spot Healing Brush the sampling is done automatically from the surrounding area

SELECTING TO THE EDGES

An easy way to make sure that a feathered Lasso selection extends all the way to the edges of an image and doesn't leave a "halo" of partly selected pixels at the margin is to hold down the Alt/Option key and drag *beyond* the edges. This works whether or not your working window shows extra space outside the canvas, but it's easier to see what you're doing if you have this extra space. By default, pressing Ctrl-Alt-hyphen (Windows) or ⌘-Option-hyphen (Mac) shrinks the image without changing the window size. Another way to increase the space outside the canvas is to drag the lower right corner of the window frame outward.

2f

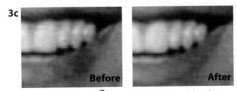

After filling the selected area of the layer mask with white

3a

A separate "repair" layer is added to hold repairs made with the Healing Brush 🖊, Spot Healing Brush 🩹, and Clone Stamp 🖳.

3b

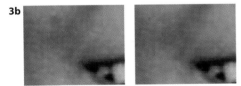

The Healing Brush 🖊 is used in Lighten mode, with Use All Layers/Sample All Layers turned on, to hide remaining dark spots and scratches.

3c

Before   After

The Clone Stamp 🖳 is used to repair a blotchy area on the lip, mostly with dabs and short strokes, with low opacity and frequent sampling (by Alt/Option-clicking), and with Aligned turned off.

when you click on the spot. Sometimes this makes healing easier — it's quicker because you don't have to click on a source. Other times this tool will select from an area you *don't* want to use; in that case, use the Healing Brush instead.

Choose the Healing Brush 🖊 or Spot Healing Brush 🩹 if appropriate. (The Spot Healing Brush may work well now that the widespread spots have been removed by the Dust & Scratches process so that the tool won't be likely to automatically sample a blemish rather than an appropriate area.) In the Options bar click the brush footprint to the right of the "Brush:" label and set Hardness at 100% (the tool itself will take care of blending the edges). Set the Mode to Lighten (for dark spots, or to Darken for light spots), and make sure Use All Layers/Sample All Layers is turned on. In this mode the Healing Brush or Spot Healing Brush applies the correction to the targeted repair layer, but it "sees" the composite image formed by the layers below and uses all that information to work its blending magic for a seamless repair. We used the Healing Brush to fix the large spots and thin scratches on the face and background **3b**, holding down the Alt/Option key and clicking in an area near the flaw to sample an appropriate "source" area with the desired color and texture, and then painting over the flaw.

To fix problems that are more diffuse and complex than spots and scratches, such as the discoloration on the lips, the Clone Stamp 🖳 may work better than the Healing Brush or Spot Healing Brush because it gives you more direct control of the repair process, especially for blemishes that don't show strong contrast with their surroundings. To use the Clone Stamp for cosmetic repairs, in the Options bar set the Opacity low and make sure the Use All Layers/Sample All Layers option is turned on. To start the repairs, hold down the Alt/Option key and click to sample an appropriate source area. Then paint over the flaw **3c**.

4 Adjusting contrast and removing a color cast. A quick way to try an overall correction to color and contrast is with a Levels Adjustment layer: At the bottom of the Layers palette, click the "Create new fill or adjustment layer" button 🔘 and choose Levels **4a**. For this image it didn't work to use one of the Auto corrections, described in "Quick Tone & Color Adjustments" on page 266; the subtle detail that shapes the individual teeth, for example, was lost as they went to a bright but flat white. If you try an "Auto" approach and it doesn't work, cancel it in the Levels dialog box by holding down the

4a

A Levels Adjustment layer is added so that overall tone and color can be corrected.

4b

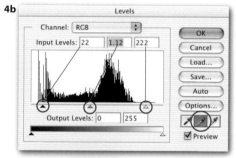

Moving the Input Levels sliders improved the overall contrast, and the Set Gray Point eyedropper helped remove the color cast. The final corrected image is shown at the top of page 302.

4c

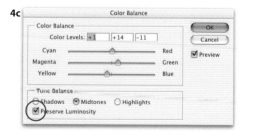

The Set Gray Point method neutralized the color cast in our image, but if it doesn't work for yours, try a Color Balance Adjustment layer. In an RGB image, leaving Preserve Luminosity turned on keeps your color adjustments from changing the overall brightness and contrast of the image. Placing Color Samplers and monitoring their readouts in the Info palette can help you check neutrality. To get a result very similar to the one shown at the top of page 302, we used the Color Levels shown here for Midtones, made no changes to the Highlights, and used Color Levels settings of –6, 0, 0 for Shadows.

Alt/Option key to turn the "Cancel" button into the "Reset" button, and clicking it to restore the original contrast in the file. Then move the black-point and white-point Input Levels sliders inward and the gamma (gray) slider left, experimenting until the tonality looks right **4b**, but don't close the dialog box yet.

To get rid of the color cast, click on the center eyedropper button in the Levels box (the Set Gray Point control) and click in the image to sample an area that should be a neutral gray; we clicked on the background, thinking that it was probably a neutral gray before the color of the image faded. If your first try doesn't fix the color cast, "hunt and peck" your way around until you hit upon the right gray tone to remove the cast. This "quick fix" often works well for color casts due to scanner malfunction, erroneous white balance settings in the camera (like what may happen when shooting under fluorescent lighting), or fading in old photos. If the Set Gray Point dropper doesn't solve the problem for your particular image (because a neutral gray can't be found), type Ctrl/⌘-Z to undo the Set Gray Point operation. Then, with or without the color cast corrected, click "OK" to close the Levels dialog box.

If you still need to correct a color cast, try this: Click the ⊘ button at the bottom of the Layers palette and add a Color Balance Adjustment layer. In the Color Balance dialog, adjust the Midtones: Look to see what color is too prominent in the midtones of the image, find the slider bar for that color, and move the slider in the opposite direction to balance the color cast **4c**. (It may be helpful to click with the Color Sampler tool to add monitoring points in the image. The readouts in the Info palette will tell you what's happening to the color composition as you adjust the Color Balance sliders; the more similar the values for R, G, and B, the more neutral the color.) Repeat the balancing process for Highlights and Shadows as needed. *wow!*

Softening a Portrait

YOU'LL FIND THE FILES

in  > Wow Project Files > Chapter 5 > Softening a Portrait:
- Soft Portrait-Before (to start)
- Soft Portrait-After (to compare)

OPEN THIS PALETTE

from the Window menu:
- Tools • Layers

OVERVIEW

Apply the Dust & Scratches filter to a duplicate layer • Reduce Opacity of the filtered layer to blend it with the original image for a more natural look • Add a layer mask to protect certain features from blurring • Use the Healing Brush to lighten sharp shadow lines

The original photo did a great job of capturing the smile, but the flash created some shiny spots on the face and distracting shadow lines on the neck.

ORIGINAL PHOTO: JHDAVIS

WHEN YOUR AIM IS TO SOFTEN or smooth the skin overall, the Dust & Scratches filter can be ideal, since you can set it to smooth fine wrinkles and conceal small spots while still showing the subtle skin texture that keeps the image looking real. If you run the filter on a copy of the photo, you can then blend the smoothed version and the sharp original to get a really natural-looking result. For blemishes or shadow lines that need more fixing, try the Healing Brush, again blending the result if needed.

In CS2 you have a new option for smoothing skin — the new Surface Blur filter. It produces a different kind of result than Dust & Scratches, but again you can smooth the skin without losing its character or creating a heavily "made up" look. Its use is described in the "Smoothing Skin with Surface Blur" tip on page 309.

1 Adding a layer to filter. Open the **Soft Portrait-Before.psd** file **1** or a photo of your own. To preserve the original image, duplicate it to a new working layer; to be able to name the new layer at the same time you add it, press Alt-Ctrl-J on Windows or Option-⌘-J on the Mac.

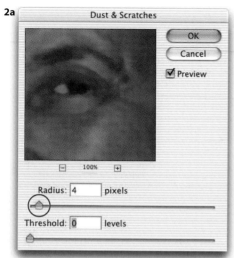

2a

Setting the Dust & Scratches filter's Radius to 4 softens the skin, tones down hot spots, and hides blemishes.

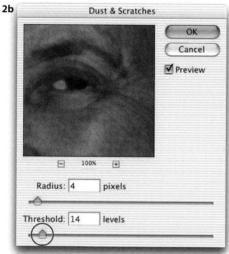

2b

Setting the Threshold to 14 restores the "fine-grained" skin texture and to some degree the "laugh lines."

2 Smoothing with Dust & Scratches. In retouching a portrait, you can use Dust & Scratches to do quite a bit of smoothing of the skin (by raising the Radius) and still get a result that doesn't look heavily retouched (by raising the Threshold enough to protect the small-scale texture, such as pores, from blurring). The viewer's impression? "If these tiny pores are visible, the rest of the skin must really be as smooth as it looks."

To smooth the skin, choose Filter > Noise > Dust & Scratches. Set the Radius and Threshold as low as possible to start with. Then increase the Radius until the spots and wrinkles disappear, at least to the maximum extent you might want them to. We settled on a Radius setting of 4, which smoothed away dark spots and toned down "hot spots" by blurring surrounding color into them **2a**. (Don't worry at this point if important details such as highlights in the eyes, teeth, or hair are lost. We'll fix these things with masking in step 3. Also, for now, ignore bigger features such as the shadow lines on the neck. If we were to set the Radius high enough to hide them, the rest of the image would be blurred too much. We'll soften them in step 3 also.)

To bring back the skin's pores and the noise of the original photo, raise the Threshold until the blemishes you've hidden just begin to reappear. Then lower the Threshold a little, until they disappear again. We ended up with a Threshold setting of 14. At this setting the "laugh lines" were softened but still present, contributing to the smile **2b**.

3 Combining the filtered layer with the original. In the Layers palette, experiment by lowering the Opacity of the filtered layer while you look at the skin, until you get just the right blend between smoothing and character.

We decided that 80% Opacity for the Dust & Scratches layer revealed the laugh lines just the right amount **3a**. The next step was to blend the two layers together, using a layer mask and a soft-edged brush to paint on the mask. Any time you add a layer mask, you have a choice to make: Use a black mask that completely hides the layer and paint with white to reveal parts of it? Or use a white mask and paint with black? We decided to start with a black-filled mask that would hide the filtered image so we could look at the sharp original photo and see exactly where we wanted to paint with white to soften the skin.

To add a black-filled mask for the Dust & Scratches layer, Alt/Option-click the Layers palette's "Add layer mask" button ⬛. (Clicking ⬛ without the helper key makes a white mask.) To

3a

Reducing the Opacity of the filtered layer creates a pleasing and believable amount of smoothing of the skin.

3b

Adding a layer mask to control the smoothing

FIND OUT MORE

▼ Choosing & sizing
brush tips
page 363

bring back the smoothing, choose the Brush tool ✐ with a fairly large soft-edged brush tip (we used 35 pixels) and white paint.▼ (With a mask active, typing D or X makes white the Foreground color). Paint the mask in the areas you want to soften. You can reduce the Opacity setting in the Options bar to further control how much the Brush reveals or hides. If you accidentally paint over sharp details that you want to keep, switch to a smaller brush tip and set the Foreground color to black (type X), and then paint the mask to restore them **3b**.

CS2 SMOOTHING SKIN WITH SURFACE BLUR

The Surface Blur filter works by detecting edges — areas of strong contrast or color difference — and protecting these edges while it blurs the smaller, less contrasty details, or texture. It can be useful for smoothing skin while preserving facial features. And you can do this without losing the highlights in the eyes, teeth, and hair. On the other hand, it doesn't allow you to preserve the finest detail while smoothing slightly larger marks.

Blurring is a color-averaging process. When you choose Filter > Blur > Surface Blur, the Surface Blur dialog box opens. The Radius slider controls how widely Photoshop looks when it computes an average color for each pixel; so the bigger the Radius, the more blurred things become. The Threshold slider determines how similar adjacent pixels have to be in order *not* to be considered an edge; the higher you set the Threshold, the fewer "edges" Photoshop will see and the more blurring will occur. In using the Surface Blur filter "cosmetically," the trick is to balance the Radius and Threshold settings so that facial features and some skin detail are preserved, but small differences such as pores, fine wrinkles, and color inconsistencies are smoothed.

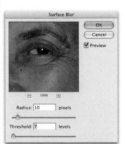

We found that a Radius of 10 and a Threshold of 7 gave us a slightly more "made-up" look than we wanted, but we knew we could control that with the layer's Opacity slider, so we clicked "OK."

In the Layers palette we reduced the Opacity of the Surface Blur layer to remove just enough of the "makeup" for the look we wanted. Remaining were some overbright highlights and dark spots that we would hide with the Spot Healing Brush ✐ on a separate layer.

4a

We set the Mode to Luminosity and turned on "Aligned" and "Use All Layers."

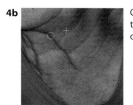

4b Getting ready to use the Healing Brush 🩹 on the first shadow line

4c

The healing strokes after adjusting Opacity and masking. The masked strokes on the two healing layers are shown alone at top right. (We also tried the Spot Healing Brush as an option. Like the Healing Brush, it was used on a separate layer in Luminosity mode with Sample All Layers turned on. For the right-hand shadow it worked quickly and well. For the left-hand shadow, we found that we preferred the Healing Brush's ability to direct the sampling to the right of the shadow.)

4 Softening shadow lines. To soften the dark shadow lines below the chin, choose the Healing Brush tool 🩹 and Alt/Option-click the "Create a new layer" button ⬛ at the bottom of the Layers palette, naming the layer as you create it.

In the Options bar for the Healing Brush **4a:**

- Choose a **hard-edged brush tip** that's just a bit wider than the mark you want to cover.

- In this image the darkly shadowed skin is the same *color* as the more brightly lit skin around it — it's just the *brightness* (or luminosity) that needs adjusting. So we can set the **Mode** to **Luminosity**. With this setting the Healing Brush will repair the dark lines without changing the color.

- Make sure **Sampled** is chosen so the healing texture will be picked up from the image.

- Turn on **Use All Layers** (**Sample All Layers** in CS2) so the Healing Brush can sample from the composite image and paint on the new empty layer.

- Turn on the **Aligned** option. That way, each time you start a stroke, the Healing Brush will sample from a spot parallel to your stroke, rather than starting again from the exact spot you originally sampled.

When the Options are set, move the cursor to a point near the top of the right-hand shadow line, and Alt/Option-click and release to set the starting point for sampling. Then move the cursor onto the shadow line itself **4b** and use short strokes to "paint over" the line. In CS2 you can switch to the Spot Healing Brush 🩹 for efficiency if you like (using the same Options bar settings as for the Healing Brush) — you won't have to sample because the tool does it automatically; if the automatic sampling picks up a tone that doesn't work, undo (Ctrl/⌘-Z) and switch back to the Healing Brush.

Now add another new layer (Alt/Option-click the ⬛ button) and use the Healing Brush on the other shadow. Although the shirt and skin are very different in *color,* they're not so different in *luminosity,* so with Luminosity (instead of Normal) chosen in the Options bar, the nearby shirt color is less likely to be "smeared" by the Healing Brush. To blend the Healing Brush strokes into the photo, adjust the Opacity of each healing layer and add a mask to "fade" parts of the marks **4c** as in step 2. 🎨

Cosmetic Changes

The process of improving a photo usually works best if you start with overall tone and color corrections▼ and *then* proceed to specific retouching tasks, such as meeting the "cosmetic challenges" covered on the next five pages. In most of the fixes, we've kept the correction separate from the original image. That way, if you need to correct the correction, you won't run the risk of degrading the original image by working and reworking it. Some of Photoshop's image-fixing tools, such as the Healing Brush, can make their corrections on a separate, transparent layer above the photo. For tools that don't offer this option, you can duplicate the image (or part of it) and work on the duplicate. Then, for even more flexibility, you can change the blend mode, lower the Opacity, or add a layer mask, for a rich variety of options in "mixing" the changed copy with the original.

LOADING THE WOW-IMAGE FIX BRUSHES

Some of the "Quick Cosmetic Changes" involve **Wow Image Fix Brushes** from the **Wow DVD-ROM.** "Installing Wow Styles, Patterns, Tools & Other Presets" on page 5 tells how to load the **Wow Image Fix Brushes** along with all the other Wow presets. Or load them from the Wow DVD-ROM by navigating to Wow Project Files > Chapter 5 > Quick Cosmetic Changes, then double-clicking the icon for **Wow Image Fix Brushes.tpl.**

BRUSH SIZE

You can use the bracket keys to resize brush tips. Typing ❘] ❘ enlarges the brush tip; typing ❘ [❘ makes it smaller.

YOU'LL FIND THE FILES

in  > Wow Project Files > Chapter 5 > Quick Cosmetic Changes

---

FIND OUT MORE

▼ Tone & color adjustment **page 248**

Whitening Teeth

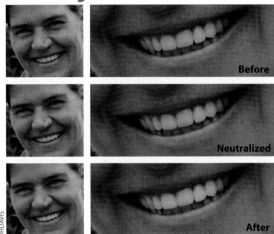

Before

Neutralized

After

JHDAVIS

A QUICK AND EASY WAY to whiten teeth or eyes is to first use the **Wow-White Teeth Neutralize** brush to take the color out of any stains, and then use the **Wow-White Teeth Brighten** brush to brighten the teeth overall. If you haven't yet loaded the **Wow Tool Presets**, follow the instructions on page 5. Or load them from the Wow DVD-ROM, as described at the left.

Copy the entire image to a new layer (Ctrl/⌘-J), or make a loose selection of the mouth (with the Lasso ◯, for instance) and copy the selected area (Ctrl/⌘-J).

Choose the Brush tool ✐. At the far left end of the Options bar, click the ✐ to open the Tool Preset picker, and double-click the **Wow-White Teeth-Neutralize** brush (the first click targets the preset, and the second click closes the palette). The Options bar shows that the brush has a soft tip. The Mode is set to Color, to neutralize the stains without changing surface detail. Opacity is set low so the neutralizing won't happen too fast to control. The Airbrush feature ✎ is chosen so the brush will keep working as you hold it in one place. The white color setting is built into the brush.

Resize the brush tip as needed (see "Brush Size" at the left). Avoiding the gums and lips, dab the teeth to remove stains. Copy this layer to a new layer above (Ctrl/⌘-J).

Next choose the **Wow-White Teeth-Brighten** preset. Brush over the teeth to whiten them. In the Layers palette, you can check the whitening by toggling the white-teeth layer's visibility on and off (click the layer's ◉ icon). If the whitening seems too dramatic, lower the layer's Opacity (in the upper right corner of the Layers palette).

🔘 **White Teeth.psd**

Adding Color to Lips

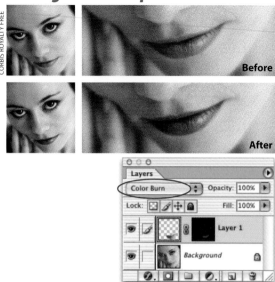

Before

After

TO GIVE PALE LIPS a bit more color and definition without blowing out the highlights, try blending a copy of the lips in Color Burn mode at low Opacity. The lips will change only slightly in the light tones and highlights, but the midtones will darken fairly dramatically.

Copy the image to a new layer (Ctrl/⌘-J), or make a loose selection of the lips and a little of the area around them (we used the Lasso tool ⌿) and make a new layer from the selected area (Ctrl/⌘-J). In the upper left corner of the Layers palette, choose Color Burn from the pop-up list of blend modes. Then add a black-filled ("hide all") layer mask by Alt/Option-clicking the "Add a layer mask" button ◙ at the bottom of the Layers palette. (Adding the Alt/Option key is what makes the mask black.)

Then choose the Brush tool ⌿ and white paint (with a mask active, typing D (for "default") makes white the Foreground color). In the Brush tool's Options bar set the Mode to Normal and set the Opacity low (we used 25%). Click the "Brush:" footprint and choose a soft brush at a size small enough to maneuver within the lip area. Now paint (you'll be painting the mask) to reveal the intensified color of the lips. If the color isn't intense enough, paint over the lips again to "thin" the mask. If it's too intense, lower the Color Burn layer's Opacity in the top right corner of the Layers palette. Or switch to black paint (typing X will make black the Foreground color), lower the Brush tool's Opacity even more (in the Options bar), and paint the mask where you want to reduce the effect.

Brightening Eyes

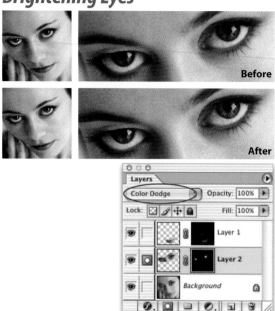

Before

After

TO ADD SPARKLE TO EYES, try Color Dodge mode. When a copy of the eyes in Color Dodge mode is combined with the original, light colors are lightened more than dark colors. If you select and duplicate only the iris and pupil of the eyes, for instance, Color Dodge will lighten the color while enhancing the contrast, giving the eyes more sparkle.

Duplicate the image, or just the eyes, to a new layer, as described for the lips (at the left). Here we started with the file with the lips already colored. We targeted the original image by clicking on the *Background* thumbnail in the Layers palette, and then we selected the eyes and surrounding area with the Lasso tool ⌿ and duplicated them to a new layer (Ctrl/⌘-J).

Just as for the lips at the left, add a black-filled (hide all) layer mask to the new layer by Alt/Option-clicking the ◙ button at the bottom of the Layers palette. In the upper left corner of the palette, choose Color Dodge from the pop-up list of blend modes.

Paint the mask, using the Brush tool and white paint to reveal the eyes, the same as for the lips, except that you'll need to set the Opacity in the Brush tool's Options bar higher (we used 80%). If the highlights in the eyes were "burned out" in the process, you can calm them down by dabbing the mask with black; we did this with 40% Opacity set in the Options bar.

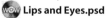 **Lips and Eyes.psd**

Fixing "Red-Eye"

Before **Neutralized** **Darkened**

TO GET RID OF "RED-EYE," you can use one or more of the **Wow-Red Eye** presets. Install the **Wow Image Fix Brushes** as described on page 5. Or load them from the Wow DVD-ROM as described on page 311.

Duplicate your image to a new layer, and choose the Brush tool. Then at the left end of the Options bar click the button to open the Tool Preset picker, and double-click on **Wow-Red Eye Neutralize**. Type `]` or `[` to make the brush the appropriate size to paint away the red in the pupil (and the iris if necessary). If you have to remove red from the iris, restore color with one of the **Wow-Red Eye Replace** brushes; you can match the color of the iris by Alt/Option-clicking where iris color is still present. If the pupil needs darkening, use the **Wow-Red Eye Darken** preset.

 Red-Eye.psd

ABOUT RED-EYE

Red-eye happens because the subject, with pupils open wide in order to see better in the dim surroundings, is looking directly at the flash when the camera takes the photo. This happens with many compact cameras, both film and digital, because the flash unit is very near the lens. When subjects "look at the camera," they're also looking right at the flash. The retina at the back of the eye, with its rich blood supply, is lit up by the light coming through the wide-open pupil.

Cameras with red-eye reduction solve this problem by "pre-flashing." The eyes respond to this early light, so when the real flash goes off, the pupils are small. Less light gets to the retina, and less retina is exposed to the camera. Thus, no red-eye.

Red-eye reduction has its price, though. The pupils look as if it were broad daylight instead of a low-light ambience. Also, the "pre-flash" forces the subject to pose longer, pretty much eliminating any natural facial expression. So there are times when you may prefer to *turn off* red-eye reduction, take the photo, and fix up any red-eye in Photoshop. Or you may be able to avoid red-eye by using an offset flash, or by having the subject look somewhere other than straight at the camera.

CS2 Using the Red Eye Tool

A

B **C** **D**

PHOTOSHOP CS2'S RED EYE TOOL is designed to take care of the red-eye problem in one quick click. You may find that using the neutralizing and darkening approach with the Wow-Image Fix Brushes in "Fixing 'Red-Eye'" at the left gives you more precise control of the result (not as much of the eye goes black, and you can build up to the darkness you want rather than trying, undoing, and trying again). But because the Red Eye tool is so quick and easy to use, and to undo, it's worth a try for quick fixes.

To fix red-eye with the Red Eye tool, choose the tool and Shift-drag diagonally to make a square that surrounds the red plus a little margin outside it **A**; then release the mouse button **B**. Defining a square in this way, instead of just clicking, seems to do a consistently better job of keeping the black from "blooming" outside the pupil and iris, or shifting off-center. If you don't get results that you like on the first try, undo (Ctrl/⌘-Z), change the Pupil and Darken Amount settings in the Options bar, and try again. For **B** we used the default settings of 50% and 50%. Lowering these settings reduces the extent and density of the black (here we used 1% and 1%) **C**; increasing them (100% and 100%) has the opposite result **D**.

USING TWO VIEWS

Repairing "red-eye" is one of those tasks that demands zooming in to see what's going on. Whenever you're working at a zoomed-in view, it's a good idea to have another window open where you can see how your improvements look in the context of the image overall. To open a second window, choose **Window > Arrange > New Window for. . .**, and then set the magnification (you might try View > Print Size, or type Ctrl/⌘-hyphen until you reach 25%). Now you can work in one window and view your changes in both.

Fixing "Eyeshine"

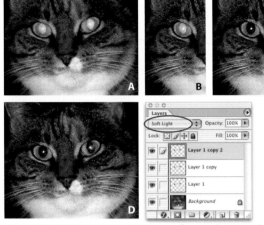

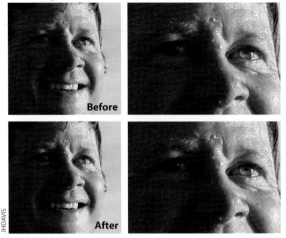

Taking the Heat Out

Before

After

THE EQUIVALENT OF RED-EYE in cats, dogs, and some other animals is "eyeshine" **A** that comes from an extra reflective membrane in the eye. The first step in removing eyeshine is the same as fixing red-eye — neutralize the color with the **Wow-Red Eye Neutralize** brush on page 313 **B**.

Because the pupil is so light, to darken it would take several applications with the **Wow-Red Eye Darken** brush, and the dark tint could build up unevenly where brush strokes overlap. Here's another way to darken the pupils: Add an empty layer by clicking the "Create a new layer" button ☐ at the bottom of the Layer palette. Reset the Foreground color to black (type D), and choose the Brush tool. In the Options bar, click the "Brush:" footprint; set the Hardness at 0 and use Master Diameter to adjust the cursor to a size that's comfortable for painting the pupils. In the Options bar, set the Mode to Normal and the Opacity to 100% and turn off the Airbrush option (✐ is the toggle). Working on the new transparent layer, paint over the eyes, applying black paint so the pupils are solid black, with the soft edge of the brush strokes extending just beyond. When you can see that the black is solid, with soft edges, change the layer's blend mode from Normal to Soft Light (in the upper left corner of the Layers palette). To build the density, duplicate the layer several times (Ctrl/⌘-J), until the pupils are darker than you want. We used a total of three layers of painted eyes **C**.

Now refine the restoration by working on the top copy. For instance, we applied Filter > Blur > Gaussian Blur to help the changed pupils blend in with the rest of the eye **D**. Though we didn't, you can also lower the top layer's Opacity or add a layer mask and paint it with black to selectively reduce the effect.

 Eyeshine.psd

TO TAKE THE HEAT OUT of sunburn or other generalized skin redness, you can use a soft, low-opacity Brush in Hue mode to reduce the red. The **Wow-Red Skin Neutralize** preset is such a brush. To use it, install the **Wow CS-Image Fix Brushes** as described on page 5. Or load them from the Wow DVD-ROM as described on page 311.

Copy your entire image to a new layer above the original (Ctrl/⌘-J), or make a selection (with the Lasso ♺, for instance) and copy it (Ctrl/⌘-J). Choose the Brush tool ✐, then at the left end of the Options bar click the ✐ button to open the Tool Preset picker, and double-click on the **Wow-Red Skin Neutralize** preset. A look at the Options bar shows that this brush works in Hue mode, so when you paint, it will change the hue of the skin but the detail and shading won't be covered up. The brush uses a soft tip and a low Opacity (set in the Options bar) so the hue change will be gradual and easy to control. Now brush the image to take the red out. If the color that's built into the brush isn't right for your image, Alt/Option-click on your photo to sample the desired skin color.

 Red Out.psd

Removing Spots

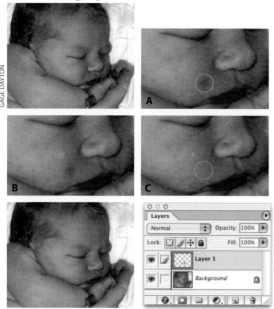

GAGE DAYTON

THE HEALING BRUSH AND SPOT HEALING BRUSH are almost magical for removing spots and blemishes. Start by opening your image and adding a new layer for the repairs (click the "Add a new layer" button ▣ at the bottom of the Layers palette). Choose the Healing Brush 🖊 or Spot Healing Brush 🩹, and in the Options bar, make sure the Use All Layers/Sample All Layers option is turned on (use the check box). Set the Mode to Normal.

Move the cursor to the first spot you want to fix, and type [or] to shrink or enlarge the cursor until it comfortably surrounds the spot **A**. Then:

- In CS, move the cursor to a nearby area that looks the way you want the spot area to look when it's fixed **B**. Hold down the Alt/Option key and click to sample. Now release the Alt/Option key and move the cursor back to the blemish and click to make the magical repair **C**.

- In CS2, if the area immediately around the spot has the tone and color you want for the repair, simply click the spot with the Spot Healing Brush 🩹. Otherwise, use the Healing Brush.

- For the smaller spots in this image in CS, we used the Healing Brush, making sure "Aligned" was turned on in the Options bar. Once we had sampled immediately above the first small spot, we could simply click each of the other spots and the Healing Brush (with "Aligned" on) would automatically sample near it to make the fix.

Removing Spots.psd

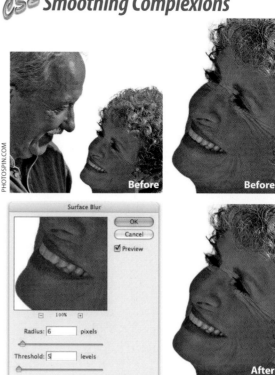

PHOTOSPIN.COM

THE SURFACE BLUR FILTER, new in Photoshop CS2, preserves high-contrast edges while blurring detail. It looks at differences in color and brightness and "decides," based on your settings, whether the difference qualifies for being blurred and if so, how much to blur it. The Radius setting controls the extent of the blur (the higher the setting, the more extensive the blur) and the Threshold setting controls what level of detail is subject to blurring. With a low Threshold setting, only the finest details are blurred; with higher settings, higher-contrast differences are blurred also.

To use Surface Blur for cosmetic purposes, as shown above, first duplicate the layer (Ctrl/⌘-J) to protect the original. Then choose Filter > Blur > Surface Blur. Adjust Radius and Threshold, watching the areas you want to smooth and the areas you want to keep sharp, until you see the result you want. For this image a Radius of 6 and a Threshold of 5 act together to slightly smooth out the man's skin color, without making him look made up. These settings also smooth the woman's skin slightly and get rid of the noise that results from her being in the shade. Notice that hair and other details remain sharp.

Smoothing.psd

Lightening Under the Eyes

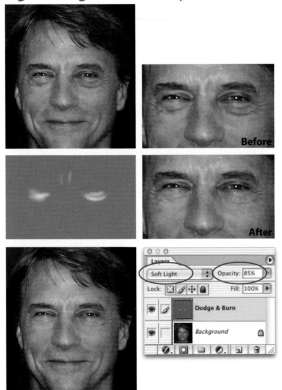

Before

After

DARK OR PUFFY AREAS UNDER THE EYES can be lightened up with a "Dodge & Burn" layer. Open your image and Alt/Option-click the "Add a new layer" button ▣ at the bottom of the Layers palette. When the New Layer dialog box opens, choose Soft Light for the Mode, click the check box for "Fill with Soft Light-neutral color 50% Gray," and click "OK." The gray will be invisible in Soft Light mode.

Start by typing D, then X to make white the Foreground color. Choose the Brush tool ✎. In the Options bar click the "Brush:" footprint and set the Hardness at 0, for a soft brush; set a Master Diameter appropriate for the area you want to fix; for this small image, we started at 18 px and would later use the [key to reduce the brush as small as 6 px for finer lines. Reading left to right on the Options bar, the Mode should be Normal, since Soft Light is already set as the blend mode for the layer; set Opacity low (we used 10%); and turn off the Airbrush feature so the white won't build up too fast. Now brush over the areas you want to lighten. Make the maximum correction you think you will want, and then experiment with the layer's Opacity in the upper right corner of the Layers palette to get just the right amount of lightening.

 **Under Eyes.psd**

Dodge & Burn Collagen

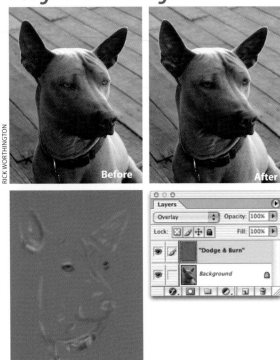

Before

After

RICK WORTHINGTON

PROMINENCES ON A FACE typically catch the light, and consequently they also shade the areas below them. With a little more contrast than was used in "Lightening Under the Eyes" at the left, you can create a dodge-and-burn layer to "sculpt" the features of a face by adding fairly concentrated light and shadow. Here we created the "Dodge & Burn" layer in Overlay mode (Alt/Option-click ▣); in the New Layer dialog box we turned on "Fill with Overlay-neutral color 50% Gray" and clicked "OK." In Overlay mode, light and dark tones lighten and darken more intensely than in Soft Light mode. We painted on this layer with white to create a ridge above each eye, and with black to create shaded areas on the eyelids and below the eyes. We did similar sculpting with white to soften the muzzle and the neck, and used white again to enhance the backlighting of the ears.

 Makeover.psd

Coverups

Photoshop's retouching tools are used in projects throughout this chapter. But on these three pages we tackle two retouching challenges — repairing an old, worn photo and removing wires from a sky. The goal is to be able to analyze each problem and choose the approach that will do the job efficiently, using a combination of retouching tools (Patch, Healing Brush, Spot Healing Brush, and Clone Stamp) and filters.

MONA DAYTON

JHDAVIS

YOU'LL FIND THE FILES

in (wow) > Wow Project Files > Chapter 5 > Quick Coverups

FIND OUT MORE

▼ Making selections **page 55**

1 Preparing to Patch

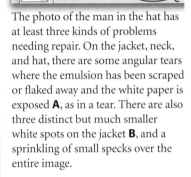

The photo of the man in the hat has at least three kinds of problems needing repair. On the jacket, neck, and hat, there are some angular tears where the emulsion has been scraped or flaked away and the white paper is exposed **A**, as in a tear. There are also three distinct but much smaller white spots on the jacket **B**, and a sprinkling of small specks over the entire image.

To start with the biggest problem — the angular tears, choose the **Patch** tool ⬦, which is really good at this kind of repair. Choose **Source** in the Options bar **C**, so you can start by selecting the *source of the problem*. The Patch tool doesn't have a Use/ Sample All Layers option; it has to work on the layer with the image that needs repair, rather than on a separate transparent layer designed to hold repairs only. So duplicate the image to a new layer to work on (Ctrl/⌘-J), preserving the original underneath in case you need to go back to it.

(wow) **Quick Coverup 1.psd**

SELECTING FOR PATCHING

With the Patch tool ⬦ you aren't limited to selecting with the Patch itself. You can make your selection with another tool or command, or a combination, ▼ and then choose the Patch; make sure the Options bar for the Patch is set the way you want it, move the cursor inside the selection boundary, and drag.

2 Patching

The **Patch** tool ⬦ can be operated like the Lasso ○ (by dragging to "draw" the selection boundary free-hand) or like the Polygonal Lasso ▷ (by Alt/Option-clicking to construct the boundary from straight segments). Use the Patch to select one of the tears; we began with the large "three-arm" one on the jacket, Alt/ Option-clicking around it **A**. With the selection made, move the cursor inside the selection boundary and drag to an area that has the right texture to fill in the tear; we dragged up until all the white had disappeared from the original selection **B**. Releasing the mouse button completes the patch **C**. We used the same technique for the tears on the neck, cheek, and hat, typing Ctrl/⌘-D to deselect when we were finished with the last repair.

3 Spot Healing

A

B

C

D

For the three smaller spots we decided to use the Healing Brush and Spot Healing Brush, which would be quicker than selecting and repairing them with the Patch tool. Both tools have a Use/Sample All Layers option so you can isolate repairs on a separate layer. Add a new layer for the repairs (click the ⊡ button at the bottom of the Layers palette) **A**. Photoshop CS2's **Spot Healing Brush** 🖌 is ideal for hiding a spot that's completely surrounded by fairly uniform material that can be drawn in to cover it up. The white mark just under the collar is such a spot. Choose the Spot Healing Brush (if you're working in CS, you can simply use the Healing Brush method described at the right). Put the cursor over the spot, open the Brush Preset picker by right/Ctrl-clicking **B**, and adjust the Diameter to make the brush tip just a little bigger than the spot **C**; then click once to make the repair **D**.

4 Healing Brush

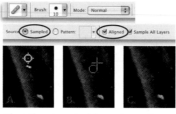

The other two sizable spots on the jacket have a range of tones around them; so using the Spot Healing Brush is likely to pull highlighted material into a shadow area. The **Healing Brush** 🖌 works better in a case like this because you control where it samples from. Choose the Healing Brush, and in the Options bar set it to **Sample** and turn on **Aligned**. For each spot, right/Ctrl-click near the spot (as described at the left for the Spot Healing Brush), and make the brush tip just a little bigger than the spot. Then Alt/Option-click on a similarly shaded area nearby (we chose an area just above the spot) **A**, release the Alt/Option key, and click or drag to paint over the spot **B**; release the mouse button to complete the healing **C**.

5 Dust & Scratches

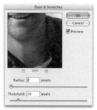

Use the **Dust & Scratches** filter for the hundreds of tiny spots. First make a composite layer for the filter to work on: Hold down Ctrl-Alt-Shift (Windows) or ⌘-Option-Shift (Mac) and type N, then E. Choose Filter > Noise > Dust & Scratches and adjust the Amount (to hide the specks) and Threshold (to retain the grain of the emulsion); for this small image (640 by 838 pixels) we used Radius 2 pixels and Threshold 20 levels).▼

1 Making a Pattern for the Healing Brush

A

B

C

With or without clouds, the tonal changes across a sky can make it hard to seamlessly "clone" over a mark that spans any distance. However, the **Healing Brush** 🖌, when used with the **Dust & Scratches** and **Add Noise** filters, makes it easy to remove wires. This approach uses the Healing Brush in **Pattern** mode.

Start by duplicating the image to a new layer (Ctrl/⌘-J). Because the wires are relatively fine, like scratches, start by choosing Filter > Noise > Dust & Scratches **A**. We blurred the image enough (Radius 9 pixels) to eliminate even the thick wires; we set the Threshold at 6 to keep the wires hidden but bring back the "grain" of the image and clicked "OK" to close the dialog box.

With the wires eliminated in the blurred duplicate image, the next step is to define this duplicate as a pattern by choosing Edit > **Define Pattern**. Now turn off visibility for the blurred layer (by clicking its 👁 in the Layers palette **B**) so you can see the wires, and add a new empty layer for making repairs (click the ⊡ button at the bottom of the palette) **C**.

🔵 **Quick Coverup 2.psd**

FIND OUT MORE

▼ Dust & Scratches **page 303**

2 Healing with Pattern *CS2*

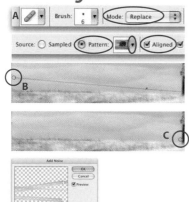

Now choose the **Healing Brush** 🖌. In the Options bar **A**, choose **Pattern** as the Source. Also choose **Replace** as the tool's Mode (this will prevent the "smearing" that can happen when you work with the Healing Brush in Normal mode near contrasting elements, such as the tree and pole in this image). And turn on the **Aligned** option. Right/Ctrl-click near a thin wire and make the brush tip a little bigger than the thin wire; we used 6 pixels. Then it's a simple matter of clicking to start a stroke at one end of a wire **B** and Shift-clicking at the other end of the wire to paint a straight stroke between the two points **C** (for sagging wires, of course, you could drag the cursor instead of Shift-clicking). Continue the click-then-Shift-click routine to cover all the wires; enlarge the brush tip if needed for the thicker ones.

When all the wires are hidden, choose Filter > Noise > **Add Noise** to restore the grain to the repairs layer **D**; we adjusted the filter settings, checking the result in the working window, until the repairs matched the grain in the photo at Amount 2%, Gaussian.

3 Spot-Healing

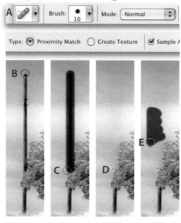

To remove the pole, CS2's **Spot Healing Brush** can do most of the job. (If you're working in CS, or find it frustrating to get the Spot Healing Brush in exactly the right starting spot, the Clone Stamp, described in "Cloning" at the right, also works.)

Because the Spot Healing Brush pulls image material from its surroundings to fill in the spot, it's important to start the stroke in a place (and drag in a direction) that pulls sky in to hide the pole. Choose Normal in the tool's Options bar **A** and choose a brush size a little bigger than the width of what you want to cover (the pole in this case; we used 10 pixels). Position the cursor so it encompasses some sky above and on both sides of the pole **B**; then drag downward **C** to pull in sky to replace the pole; we held down the Shift key to move the cursor in a straight line down the pole to the leaves, where we stopped. As you drag the cursor down, the new sky you're creating will contribute to covering up the next part of the pole. Release the mouse button to see the repair **D**.

Zoom in and out to check your work in several views. If you see any telltale edges or smudges, you can take care of them by crisscrossing the area with the Spot Healing Brush **E**.

4 Cloning

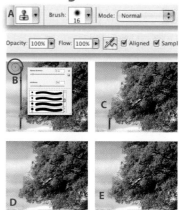

The **Clone Stamp** 🔖 (instead of the Spot Healing Brush) can be used to remove the pole. For the top of the pole, we turned on the Aligned feature in the Options bar **A**, so the Clone Stamp would always pick up sky just to the left of where the cursor was, even if we had to restart the stroke; we also turned on Use/Sample All Layers so we could continue to work on our repairs layer. We got good results with a brush tip about twice the diameter of the pole (16 pixels) with Hardness set at 30% **B**; this was soft enough to blend the edges of the cloned material. (In CS2, choosing Photoshop > Preferences > Display & Cursors and turning on Full Size Brush Tip lets you see the full diameter of the tip, including soft edges, as shown above.) We Alt/Option-clicked to sample sky close to the pole, but not close enough for the Clone Stamp to sample the pole itself. We moved the cursor onto the pole and dragged down, stopping when we came to the tree leaves **C**.

For the bottom of the pole, with the Clone Stamp set to Aligned (as described above), we Alt/Option-clicked the sky to the left of the pole, then moved the cursor over and dragged down over the pole to cover it **D**. Finally we Alt/Option clicked to sample some sparse leaves and "dabbed" them over the pole **E**.

Rod Deutschmann Lets His Fingers Do the Blocking

"I TELL MY STUDENTS to get their photos as close to perfect as they can *before* they take them into Photoshop," says photo editor Rod Deutschmann. Here's his closer-to-perfect solution for shooting into the sun.

The lighthouse, fence, and shadows were too good for Rod to pass up, even though it meant pointing his Nikon D100 directly into the sun. Rod took a shot, knowing he would get a lens flare, and a quick look at the captured image confirmed it, as shown below. The bright rays of light in the flare were interesting but too strong, the red-fringed green patch over the shadow interfered with the composition, and it would be really difficult to fix all this in Photoshop. So he took the photo again, this time holding his hand in front of the camera to block the sun, swapping a nearly impossible challenge for one that would be easy to address: Patch or replace the sky in Photoshop.

Opening the image in Photoshop, Rod first manufactured a "sky patch" to hide the hand. Here's one way to do it: Add a new empty layer above the image

The lens flare from shooting into the sun (left) was more than Rod Deutschmann wanted to tackle in Photoshop. So he re-shot the photo with a different problem (right) that would be easy to fix.

(Ctrl/⌘-Shift-N). Then choose the Gradient tool ▭, hold down the Alt/Option key to turn it into the Eyedropper 🖊 temporarily, and click the sky at the top of the image to sample this blue as the Foreground color. Typing X swaps Foreground and Background colors, and Alt/Option-clicking again, this time in the sky near the tips

 of the fingers, picks up the second color needed for the sky gradient.

In the Options bar click the tiny arrow to the right of the gradient swatch and click on the "Foreground to Background" option (the first choice in the palette).

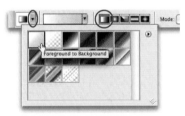

Holding down the Shift key and dragging up from the level of the fingertips to the top of the image, fill the layer with the sky gradient. To reveal the image again, Alt/Option-click the "Add a layer mask" button ▣ at the bottom of the Layers palette to make a "hide all" (black) mask. Now all that's left is to choose the Brush tool 🖌, pick a soft brush tip in the Options bar, and paint the mask with white to reveal the manufactured sky and

hide the hand. Rod used a lower Opacity setting in the Options bar to add some streaks of white to the mask to help blend the real sky with the manufactured one.

(If the sky is hard to "patch" — because of telephone wires or tree branches, for example — consider selecting the entire sky area▼ and using that selection to make the layer mask that reveals the sky gradient.)

FIND OUT MORE

▼ Selection methods
page 55

ROD DEUTSCHMANN

The black mask on the gradient layer is painted with white to patch the sky seamlessly.

Bringing Out Detail

1a

RICK WORTHINGTON

Original photo

PHOTOSHOP OFFERS MANY WAYS to bring out detail in an image. The goal is always to do the job efficiently and preserve the maximum opportunity for making changes later. Our approach to this image is to first correct the "digital noise" and chromatic aberration that can interfere with detail, and then work with the Shadow/Highlight command. Finally we soften a harsh shadow without blurring details in the wall it falls on. (Check out "Quick Ways To Bring Out Detail," starting on page 326, for different approaches for other situations.)

1 Analyzing the photo. This digital photo **1a** has a full range of tones, from black to white, as the Histogram shows **1b.** The light-dark balance in the image is striking, but we wanted to bring out detail in the shaded wall to illustrate an article in an archeology publication. Our plan was to lighten the recessed area and increase contrast there if needed, and to tone down the bright highlights elsewhere in the image.

2 Setting up to monitor the changes. To find the darkest and lightest parts of the image so you can keep track of what's

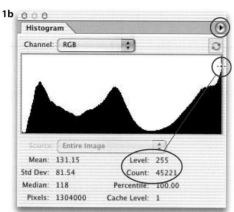

1b

To open a menu where you can choose Expanded View, click the ▶ button in the upper right corner of the Histogram palette. Moving the cursor across the Histogram gives you the number of pixels at each brightness level.

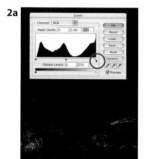

2a

To see where the lightest pixels in the image are located, open the Levels dialog box and hold down the Alt/Option key as you press and hold (or drag) the white point slider for Input Levels.

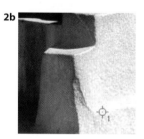

2b

With the Levels box open, Shift-clicking in the image places a Color Sampler. You can set up to four stationary Samplers whose readouts appear in the Info palette.

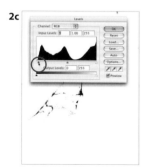

2c

Finding the darkest pixels by Alt/Option-dragging on the black point slider for Input Levels in the Levels dialog box

happening to them as you make adjustments, you can use the Levels dialog in Threshold mode. Click the "Create new fill or adjustment layer" button ● at the bottom of the Layers palette and choose Levels to open the dialog box. To see the lightest pixels in the image, hold down the Alt/Option key as you put the cursor on the white point slider for Input Levels and press the mouse button **2a**. Note where the brightest areas are and choose one of these areas as a place to monitor changes.

To place a Color Sampler to monitor your color changes, hold down the Shift key (the cursor turns into the Color Sampler tool ✎) and click in the light area; now you'll be able to watch the readout in the Info palette to see how your adjustments are affecting color at this location **2b**. (Once you've placed a Color Sampler, you can Ctrl/⌘-drag to move it if you want to.)

To find the darkest spots in the image, this time Alt/Option-press the *black point* slider for Input Levels. If no dark pixels appear, slowly drag the slider inward toward the center of the bar until dark areas show up **2c**. Choose a location and Shift-click to place another Color Sampler.

Since Photoshop allows up to four Color Samplers, you can place two more in areas of interest **2d**. Once the Samplers are placed, close the Levels box without making any changes to the image, by clicking the "Cancel" button.

2d

In both CS and CS2 you can set four Color Samplers whose readouts appear in the Info palette. (Your Info readings may differ from these, since your Samplers may be placed a little differently.)

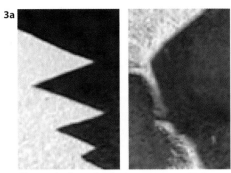

3a

Chromatic aberration in the camera results in color "fringe" at some high-contrast edges.

3b

Digital color noise is evident in some shaded areas.

3c

Making a duplicate layer. As you add layers to your file, you can rename them by double-clicking the name in the Layers palette and typing.

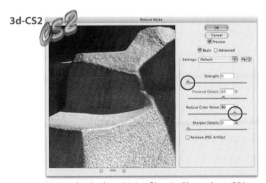

3d-CS2

Using the Reduce Noise filter in Photoshop CS2 to remove digital color noise

3 Removing color fringe and color noise. Before you adjust tonality in an image, it's a good idea to correct any problems that might be made worse by your coming adjustments. Zoom to 100% view (Ctrl/⌘-0) or higher (Ctrl/⌘-+) and look along high-contrast edges. In this photo you'll see a soft reddish fringe along the diagonal shadow on the vertical wall at the left and sharper fringing color in several places along shadows on the steps and on the upper right side of the image **3a**. This fringe results from *chromatic aberration*, a separating of colors that can happen in the camera at high-contrast edges within the image. Also notice the digital noise (a sort of pixel color confetti) in some of the shaded areas **3b**.

Photoshop CS2's Lens Correction filter includes sliders for correcting chromatic aberration.▼ With Lens Correction, it's sometimes hard to remove the color fringe without having it pop up somewhere else in the image; we found this to be the case for this photo. (In both CS and CS2, chromatic aberration correction is also available in Camera Raw for digital photos taken in a camera's raw format, which this one wasn't.) In both CS2 and CS we can eliminate the fringe and the color noise in this photo with a single fix. Start by duplicating the image to a new layer (Ctrl/⌘-J) to protect the original **3c**. Then:

FIND OUT MORE

▼ Using the Lens Correction filter
page 276

- In CS2 choose Filter > Noise > Reduce Noise to open the new Reduce Noise dialog box **3d**. This filter addresses both color noise and luminosity noise (light/dark variation). For this image, light-dark variation is important to the texture of the rock, so we don't want to remove it. Set the **Strength**, which controls luminosity noise, to 0, or no effect; setting Strength to 0 dims the **Preserve Details** option, since this option works with Strength.

Next experiment with the **Reduce Color Noise** slider until the color noise and color fringe just barely disappear. Keep the setting as low as you can and still eliminate the color noise. Since reducing noise can soften the image, the **Sharpen Details** setting is designed to restore sharpness. But because there are many other ways to sharpen, and sharpening is often best done as the last step in correcting an image, set Sharpen Details at 0.

Turning on **Remove JPEG Artifact** didn't improve this image, so we left its box unchecked.

If you're working in CS2, go on to step 4.

3d-CS

Reducing color noise in Photoshop CS. A duplicate image layer is added and put in Color mode. As you increase the Amount setting in the Gaussian Blur dialog box, in the working window you can see the color noise and chromatic aberration disappear. With the duplicate layer in Color mode, areas of near-neutral color can tolerate a fairly high blur setting if necessary.

4a

In Photoshop CS (shown here) it's necessary to make a merged copy of the original and the blurred version for Shadow/Highlight to work on. In CS2 the noise reduction was done in a single layer, so you can simply duplicate that layer for Shadow/Highlight to work on.

• In Photoshop CS, which doesn't have the Reduce Noise filter, you can use a blurred copy of the image in Color mode to smooth out the color while the image underneath maintains the luminosity, which preserves detail in the image. To be able to preview the effect of your blurring (coming next), first put your duplicate layer in Color mode (choose Color from the menu in the upper left of the Layers palette) **3d**. Then choose Filter > Blur > Gaussian Blur. In the Gaussian Blur dialog box, make sure the Preview box is checked. Watch the image *in the working window* (rather than in the Gaussian Blur dialog) as you increase the **Radius** until the color noise is eliminated; we used 5.0 pixels. (The preview window inside the dialog box shows how the blurred layer would look in Normal mode, so you can ignore it — except for the sake of interest.) Click "OK" to close the dialog box.

4 Lighting up the back wall. The Shadow/Highlight command can bring detail out of the darkness. Since Shadow/Highlight can't be applied as an Adjustment layer, the next step is to make a copy of your noise-reduced image so you can apply Shadow/Highlight to it and still preserve the noise-reduced image in case you want to get back to it at some point.

• In Photoshop CS2 simply press Ctrl/⌘-J.

• In Photoshop CS, since the image is a composite of the original and the blurred layer in Color mode, you'll need to make a merged copy: Hold down Ctrl-Alt-Shift (Windows) or ⌘-Option-Shift (Mac) as you type N (for a new empty layer) and then E (to turn the new layer into a merged copy) **4a**.

Apply the Shadow/Highlight command to the duplicate layer by choosing Image > Adjustments > Shadow/Highlight. (As you experiment in the Shadow/Highlight dialog, watch the Histogram and the Color Sampler values in the Info palette.)

In the Shadow/Highlight dialog box, the default 50% **Shadow Amount lightens** the back wall **4b**. Click the **Show More Options** check box and adjust the **Shadow Tonal Width** slider; we used a setting of 30 to restrict the lightening effect to the shadows. The default 50% Shadow Tonal Width affects all pixels darker than 50% brightness; reducing the Tonal Width setting below 50% partially protects the midtones in the shaded steps. Adjusting the **Radius** to 35 restored some contrast.

In the **Highlight** section of the dialog box, we used settings of **Amount** 10%, **Tonal Width** 10%, and **Radius** 30 pixels to tone down the lightest highlights.

4b

The two different ways of reducing the noise in CS and CS2 produce slightly different results. We found that leaving the Shadow Amount at the default setting of 50% worked well to lighten the shadows in our CS2 file (shown here); in the CS version 45% seemed to work better.

4c

In both CS and CS2 the Histogram shows two versions of the tonal distribution while the Shadow/Highlight dialog box is open. As long as you have Shadow/Highlight's Preview box checked, the "current" (black) distribution responds as you adjust the Shadow/Highlight settings. Comparing the "before" (gray) version with the current distribution, we can see that the shadow and midtone peaks are not as distinctly separate now that the brightness of many pixels in the recessed area has been increased. Also, the "pile-up" of the lightest pixels has been spread over more tonal values.

4d

In both CS and CS2 the Info palette shows the changed readouts for the Color Samplers.

Adjusting **Midtone Contrast** to +10 protects the large steps in the middle of the image from being lightened too much and adds depth and dimension to the lightened back wall. Click "OK" to close the dialog box.

The Histogram reflects the changes in shadows and midtones, and also shows that the brightest highlights have been toned down a bit **4c**. Likewise, comparing the Color Sampler readings in the Info palette with their initial values (from step 2) shows that the lightest highlights (Sampler #1) are not quite as bright as before, the shadows have been made quite a bit lighter (Samplers #2 and #3), and the dark midtones (Sampler #4) have also been lightened a little, but not as much as the shadows **4d**.

5 Softening the "flash shadow." Now that the back wall is lighter, the sharp shadow created by the flash is more obvious by contrast **5a**. To soften the shadow without losing detail in the wall, start by adding a new layer for the "shadow repair" you're about to make. Put this layer in Darken mode (from the Layers palette's menu of blend modes). Now choose the Blur tool ◊. In the Options bar choose a brush tip (we used the "Soft Round 13 pixels" tip), set the Strength (we used 100%) and turn on the Use All Layers option (CS) (it's Sample All Layers in CS2). "Paint" along the outer edge of the shadow; the new layer will now hold a blurred version of the edge. The blurring has made some pixels lighter and some darker. But with the layer in Darken mode, only the darker pixels will contribute, spreading and softening the shadow edge without creating a light halo **5b**.

BLURRING IN A STRAIGHT LINE

The Blur tool ◊, like any other tool that uses brush tips, can be operated in a straight line. Click at the point where you want to start the straight stroke, then move the cursor to the point where you want to end the stroke and Shift-click.

5a

The sharp shadow caused by the flash

5b

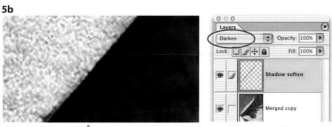

Using the Blur tool ◊ on a separate layer in Darken mode softens the edge of the shadow slightly.

Ways To Bring Out Detail

"BRINGING OUT DETAIL" on page 321 uses a combination of methods to bring out detail that's "hidden" in an image. Here are some other methods — quick and easy — for enhancing small differences in color and tone:

- Using a filter, such as **Unsharp Mask**, **Smart Sharpen**, or **High Pass**, that identifies "color edges" in the image and increases the contrast between the two sides of the edge

- Layering a copy of the image above the original and applying one of the **"contrast" blend modes** chosen from the menu at the top left corner of the Layers palette (Overlay mode, for example)

- Making a **Shadow/Highlight adjustment** or quickly painting a **"dodge and burn" layer** in a contrast blend mode to increase contrast in the shadow tones and highlights

- Adding a Curves Adjustment layer, with an **S-shaped or M-shaped curve**

Whatever methods you try, it pays to keep the duplicated, adjusted, or filtered image in a separate layer above the original, so you'll have the maximum range of options for fine-tuning your "detail boost":

- You can **compare various "contrast" blend modes** for your duplicate.

- **To reduce the effect** of your duplicate layer, you can simply lower its Opacity in the Layers palette to blend it with the original.

- **To target your changes** to a particular place in the image, paint a layer mask to reveal the enhancement in the areas where you want it and to hide it elsewhere.

- If you've arrived at a way to enhance certain details perfectly, but you want **to protect some tones or colors** from change, try the "Blend If" sliders in the Blending Options panel of the Layer Style dialog box.

For any image, you aren't limited to one way of bringing out detail or one way of targeting the effect. The "mix and match" possibilities are endless.

YOU'LL FIND THE FILES FOR MOST EXAMPLES
in ⦿ > Wow Project Files > Chapter 5 > Quick Detail

Sharpening with Unsharp Mask

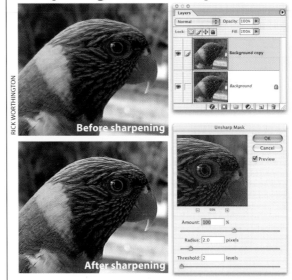

RICK WORTHINGTON

Before sharpening

After sharpening

WHEN THE SUCCESS OF THE IMAGE depends on increasing contrast in the details, the Unsharp Mask filter can be a good option. For the digital photo above we started by duplicating the image to a new layer (one way is to drag the layer thumbnail to the "Create new layer" button ⬚ at the bottom of the Layers palette; another option is to type Ctrl/⌘-J). Then we chose Filter > Sharpen > Unsharp Mask and set the parameters in the Unsharp Mask dialog box. A practical approach is to start with the Threshold set at 0 temporarily (Threshold controls how different the colors at an edge have to be for the filter to recognize it as a color edge and sharpen it; 0 means that *all* differences are seen as edges). Then adjust the Amount (how much the contrast at a color edge is enhanced by the filter) and the Radius (how far in from the color edge the increased contrast will extend) until the important details are as sharp as you want. Next raise the Threshold as high as you can without losing the sharpening of this detail. Raising the Threshold keeps the filter from sharpening very small differences in tone or color such as grain or noise.

⦿ **Detail-Unsharp Mask.psd**

EVALUATING SHARPENING

Too much sharpening can give a photo an artificial look. You don't want to overdo it, but if you're preparing an image for the printed page, keep in mind that sharpening tends to look much "stronger" on-screen than it will when the image is printed at a much higher resolution on a press.

 **Using Smart Sharpen**

RICK WORTHINGTON

Before Smart Sharpen

A

B

After Smart Sharpen

PHOTOSHOP CS2'S NEW SHARPENING FILTER — Smart Sharpen — can produce a more realistic "sharp focus" result than you could get in earlier versions of Photoshop. Like Unsharp Mask (on the facing page), Smart Sharpen looks for color edges and sharpens them, but it tends to produce less "halo" at the edges. You can choose to have the filter counteract a Gaussian Blur (which is the calculation method the Unsharp Mask filter uses); a Lens Blur (a better choice if the image was shot a little out of focus), or Motion Blur (the one to try for "camera shake" or if the subject moved). With the Advanced setting turned on, you can protect the Shadows or Highlights from sharpening, which can also contribute to a more realistic result.

To bring out detail in this photo, we duplicated the image to a new layer (Ctrl/⌘-J) and chose Filter > Sharpen > Smart Sharpen. We got the sharpening we wanted with settings of Strength 100%, Radius 1.9 px, and Remove Lens Blur **A**. With the Advanced option chosen, we could experiment to fade the oversharp "bright white" look in Highlight areas (Amount 15%, Tonal Width 80%, Radius 1) and to fade the sharpening in Shadow areas slightly (Amount 4%, Tonal Width 20%, Radius 5) **B**.

 **Detail-Smart Sharpen.psd**

One of the advantages of the Smart Sharpen filter in Photoshop CS2 is that you can use the Advanced mode to protect highlights from being sharpened to the point where the contrast gives them a "brittle" look. You can also reduce the sharpening effect in shadow areas, where sharp detail typically isn't visible to the human eye or recorded by the camera. But if you're working with Unsharp Mask rather than Smart Sharpen (maybe because you're working in Photoshop CS, where Smart Sharpen doesn't exist), here's a method you can use to protect the shadows or highlights from sharpening too much:

1 Duplicate your image to a new layer (Ctrl/⌘-J).

2 Run the Unsharp Mask filter on this new layer (Filter > Sharpen > Unsharp Mask).

After sharpening with the Unsharp Mask filter (Amount 200%, Radius 1, Threshold 4)

3 Open the Blending Options panel of the Layer Style dialog box (one way to do this is to choose it from the Layers palette's ▶ menu).

4 While you're looking at highlights in your sharpened image, in the "Blend If" section at the bottom of the Blending Options panel, drag the white point of the "This Layer" slider toward the middle of the slider. You'll see a reduction in sharp white highlights.

Reducing "brittle" highlights

5 For a smooth transition between the sharpened and unsharpened areas, hold down the Alt/Option key and drag the right half of the white point back toward the end of the slider.

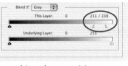

Smoothing the transition

6 To return some of the softness to the darkest areas of the image, adjust the black point of the "This Layer" slider in a similar way (drag it inward, hold down Alt/Option, and drag the left half back toward the left end).

High Pass in a "Contrast" Mode

Before

After

PHOTOSHOP'S HIGH PASS FILTER SUBDUES color and contrast in non-edge areas, but preserves the contrast in "edge" areas, where colors abut. When you apply this effect in one of the "contrast" blend modes (Overlay and those right below it in the pop-up blend modes list in the top left corner of the Layers palette), you have a powerful tool for sharpening detail.

The first step is to duplicate your image to a new layer (Ctrl/⌘-J). Then set up this layer so you'll be able to see the effect of High Pass on your image as you experiment with the filter's settings: In the Layers palette, change the blend mode for the duplicate layer to Overlay **A**. Now apply the filter by choosing Filter > Other > High Pass, and experiment with the Radius setting **B**. In the square preview inside the High Pass dialog box, you'll see how the filter is pushing the image toward medium gray except at color edges. In the image window you'll see the combined effect of the filter and the blend mode.

Once you set up a High Pass layer in Overlay mode, it can be worthwhile to experiment with some of the other blend modes in the "contrast" group — especially Soft Light, Hard Light, and even Vivid Light, as shown at the right.

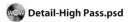 **Detail-High Pass.psd**

Protecting with a Layer Mask

Vivid Light before masking

After masking

IF YOU LIKE THE OVERALL RESULT of a detail enhancement you've made, but you don't like what it does in specific areas of the image, you can simply use a layer mask with some quick strokes of black paint to hide the effect in those areas. For instance, starting with the finished example from "High Pass in a 'Contrast' Mode" (at the left) and putting the filtered layer in Vivid Light mode emphasizes detail in the flower and butterfly even more than Overlay does, but *without* "popping" the detail in the more neutral brick wall. Vivid Light works on a *channel-by-channel basis*, so it tends to "burn" or intensify already bright colors, but it has less effect on neutral colors. It also has less effect on neutral midtones than on highlights or shadows. But Vivid Light can create "halos" at some color edges; you can see them around some of the petals in the top image above.

To remove the halos, with the filtered layer active, click the "Add a layer mask" button at the bottom of the Layers palette to add a white (reveal all) mask. Then choose the Brush in the Tools palette. Set the Foreground color to black (with the mask targeted in the Layers palette, if black isn't the Foreground color, type X). In the Options bar reduce the Opacity (we used about 30%) and choose a soft brush tip from the Brush Preset picker that pops out when you click the brush footprint icon. Now paint where you want to reduce or hide the halo effect (you'll be painting the mask).

Using Shadow Highlight

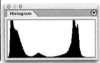

Before

After

THE SHADOW/HIGHLIGHT COMMAND can bring out detail by adding contrast where detail is washed out by bright lighting or subdued by shading. For this photo, the Histogram (opened by choosing Window > Histogram) showed a peak in the shadows, suggesting that spreading out the darker tones might bring out detail in the terrain. We chose Image > Adjustments > Shadow/Highlight and clicked the check box for "Show more options." We left most of the settings at their defaults, changing only the Amount and Tonal Width in the Shadows section at the top of the box. The default 50% Tonal Width treats anything darker than 50% gray as a shadow and therefore lightens it. This setting meant losing some of the detail in the clouds, since they were dark enough to fall in the Shadow range. To avoid the loss, we reduced the Tonal Width so that only the darkest 34% of the tonal range would be changed. We experimented with the Amount until we got the result we liked best at 45%. The Histogram showed the resulting redistribution of shadow tones.

 **Detail-Shadow Highlight.psd**

Adding a "Dodge & Burn" Layer

Before

"Dodge & Burn" layer

After

WITH A "DODGE AND BURN" LAYER it's easy to increase contrast in exactly the light and dark areas where you want it, toning down or brightening up the detail. To try it, open the image file and Alt/Option-click the "Create a new layer" button ▣ at the bottom of the Layers palette. When the New Layer dialog box opens, set the mode to Overlay, click the check box for "Fill with Overlay Neutral 50% gray" and click "OK." Your image won't look any different on-screen since 50% gray is neutral (invisible) in Overlay mode. But now you can paint black and white onto this layer with a soft Brush ✐ (with or without the Airbrush option turned on in the Options bar) with Opacity and Flow set low. This builds up the paint slowly enough so you can control it as you bring out the detail you want.

 Detail-Dodge and Burn.psd

MANAGING A DODGE & BURN LAYER

As you paint a "dodge and burn" layer in Overlay mode, if your image starts to look oversaturated — that is, the colors become too intense — try changing the blend mode of this layer to Soft Light.

Duplicating in a "Contrast" Mode

ANAIKA DAYTON

SOFT LIGHT IS A BLEND MODE that enhances contrast mainly in the midtones. Besides bringing out detail, it also tends to increase color intensity. So it works well for images like this one that are concentrated in the midtones and have unsaturated colors that can benefit from a color boost. (If you work with images that are colorful, it's easy to push colors out of the printable gamut with Soft Light, so you run the risk that the color differences you see on screen may disappear when the image is printed.)

To try out the effect of Soft Light, simply duplicate your image to a new layer (Ctrl/⌘-J) or add an "empty" Levels Adjustment layer as we did (the method and rationale are described in the "'Lightweight Copies' of Image Layers" tip below). Change the blend mode for the added layer to Soft Light by choosing it from the pop-up menu in the upper left corner of the Layers palette.

 Detail-Soft Light.psd

"LIGHTWEIGHT COPIES" OF IMAGE LAYERS

You can get the same effect as you would by duplicating your image to a new layer and changing its blend mode — but without increasing the file size the way a second image layer would. The trick is to use an "empty" Adjustment layer. Simply click the "Create new fill or adjustment layer" button ◐ at the bottom of the Layers palette and choose Levels (actually, any of the choices from the "Levels" grouping in the pop-up menu will work). When the dialog box opens, just click "OK" to close it without making any changes. In the Layers palette change the blend mode for this new layer. An added advantage of this method is that if you make a change to the image itself, you won't have to remake the "copy."

Reducing Opacity

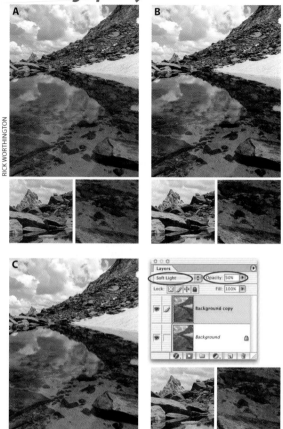

RICK WORTHINGTON

SOMETIMES A DUPLICATE LAYER or an Adjustment layer produces the right *kind* of effect, but the result is just too strong overall. To reduce the effect of the filter, blend mode, or adjustment, you can simply reduce the Opacity of the added layer, reducing its contribution to the blended image.

Our goal for this image was to bring out detail in the rocks, both above the water and under it. In the original photo **A** the colors were quite neutral and the tones we wanted to enhance were midtones, so we decided to use a duplicate image layer in Soft Light mode **B**, as described in "Duplicating in a 'Contrast' Mode" at the left. The midtone detail was improved, but the greens were more saturated than we wanted. And even though Soft Light works mainly on midtones, it had also affected the deeply shaded areas and the light snow and sky, so we had lost detail in both of these ranges. Setting the Soft Light layer's Opacity to about 50% produced a result we liked better **C**.

 **Detail-Opacity.psd**

Protecting Tones with "Blend If"

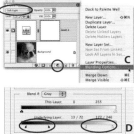 

FOR THIS PORTRAIT **A**, an "empty" Levels Adjustment layer in Soft Light mode (as described in "Duplicating in a 'Contrast' Mode" on page 330) did exactly what we wanted for the brown hair, increasing contrast in the midtones to add richness by enhancing color detail **B**. But in an image that starts out with a full tonal range, as this one did, Soft Light can also muddy the shadows or blow out detail in the highlights. Here the darkest and lightest parts of the dog's coat had lost some of their detail. In a situation like this, the "Blend If" sliders in the Layer Style dialog box can often help.

With the Soft Light layer targeted in the Layers palette, we opened the Blending Options section of the Layer Style dialog box by choosing Blending Options from the Layers palette's fly-out menu **C** (for an Adjustment layer, you can't use the shortcut of double-clicking the layer thumbnail as you can for an image layer, because this would open the dialog box for the adjustment instead of the Layer Style box). Moving the black point for "Underlying Layer" to the right **D** lightened the shadows, because the dark tones of the image — the tones represented to the left of the black point — were now protected from the Soft Light layer. To make a smooth transition from the protected tones to the exposed tones, you can split the black point by holding down the Alt/Option key and dragging the left half of the slider back to the left. A similar adjustment to the white point protects the light tones of the dog's coat **E**.

 Detail-Blending Options 1.psd

Because the Linear Light blend mode intensifies colors as it increases contrast, it can be great for bringing out detail in the sky — whether it's light blue with clouds (the sky will get bluer) or a sunset or sunrise (the colors will get more intense). The effect can be just what's needed for the sky itself or, as in the image below, for its reflection on land, snow, or water.

To try out Linear Light, add a Levels Adjustment layer with no changes: Click the "Create new fill or adjustment layer" button ⊘ at the bottom of the Layers palette, choose Levels, and click "OK" without making any changes. You'll see that the addition of the "empty" Adjustment layer has no effect on the image. Then put this new Adjustment layer in Linear Light mode by clicking the blend mode menu in the upper left corner of the Layers palette and choosing Linear Light from the group of "contrast" modes. For most images, the result will be a lot stronger than you want, as shown immediately below.

Reduce the Linear Light effect by using the Opacity slider near the top right corner of the palette.

For our mountain image, an Opacity of 35% cut through the haze to bring out the detail and color as the photographer remembered it, without losing the soft mistiness of the scene.

 Detail-Linear Light.psd

Using an "S-Curve"

AN "S-CURVE" ADJUSTMENT can improve an image (or part of an image) with little contrast in the midtones and no very light or very dark tones, such as the hay field in this photo **A**. To bring out detail in the rolled hay, we clicked the "Create new fill or adjustment layer" button ◉ at the bottom of the Layers palette **B** and chose Curves from the pop-up menu. In the Curves dialog box **C**, we clicked the midpoint on the line to anchor it in place, since we didn't want to lighten or darken the midtones overall. Then we clicked the three-quarter-tone point and dragged down a little; and finally we clicked the quarter-tone point and dragged up a little to complete the "S." In tonal ranges where the curve was now steeper (closer to vertical), contrast had been increased. And conversely, where the curve was flatter (closer to horizontal), contrast was reduced. The S-curve brought out detail by pushing some of the midtones into the high and low tonal ranges **D**.

Notice that the Curves adjustment that brought out detail in the hay also changed the sky, the trees, and the hills. If you don't like these changes, you can use a loosely painted layer mask to hide the adjustment in these areas, as described in "Protecting with a Layer Mask" on page 328.

 **Detail-S Curve.psd**

Using an "M-Curve"

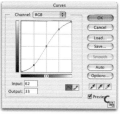

IF YOU WANT TO BRING OUT DETAIL in the midtones in an image that also has some very dark tones **A**, a slightly M-shaped Curves adjustment is more likely to be useful than is an S-curve. To bring out the carving on the stone in the image above, we added a Curves Adjustment layer by using the ◉ button as described at the left. Once the Curves dialog box was open, we moved the cursor into the image window and dragged it around the face of the carved stone **B**. By watching the movement of the little circle that appeared on the diagonal line in the Curves dialog box **C**, we could see that most of the rock face — both the carving and the surface — had tones in the upper midtone range. To bring out detail, we wanted to increase contrast in these tones, and we could do that by making the curve steeper here. We started by dragging the midpoint down and to the right to darken the stone a little overall. Then we clicked near the upper end of the curve and moved this new point to the left and up a little, making the curve steeper between the midpoint and this point and creating the first "hump" of the "M." We completed the "M" by clicking near the lower end of the curve and again dragging up and to the left to lift the curve here **D**. This restored the shadow detail **E** that had been "flattened" when we moved the midpoint. Clicking "OK" completed the adjustment.

 **Detail-M Curve.psd**

Targeting with a Layer Mask

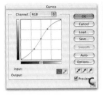

CHRISTINE ZALEWSKI

TO TARGET A DETAIL-ENHANCING EFFECT to just one area of your image, you can add a "hide all" layer mask to the enhanced layer and then paint it with white to reveal the effect. Christine Zalewski often targets the effect of the S-shaped Curves she uses to enhance detail in her botanical portraits (see page 354). In the magnolia shown here, she targeted the changes to the center structure of the flower, to help draw the viewer's eye there. Starting with an original photo **A**, she finished most of her preparation **B**, and then applied a Curves Adjustment layer with an S-shaped curve ("Using an S-Curve" on the facing page describes how to do this). She adjusted the curve **C** until the flower's center had the "punch" she wanted **D**. Then she filled the Adjustment layer's built-in mask with black to completely hide the Curves effect (if black is the Foreground color, this can be done by typing Alt/Option-Delete; or if black is the Background color, by typing Ctrl/⌘-Delete). Zalewski chose the Brush tool 🖌; in the Options bar she picked a large soft brush tip from the Brush Preset picker, which pops out when you click the brush footprint icon, and lowered the Opacity setting. She made white the Foreground color (type X if necessary) and painted the mask with white over the center of the flower **E**, **F**.

Protecting Colors with "Blend If"

E. A. M. VISSER

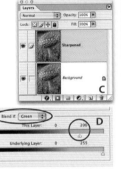

THE "BLEND IF" SLIDERS in the Layer Style dialog box can protect certain tonal ranges, as seen in the tip on page 327 and in "Protecting Tones with 'Blend If'" on page 331. But these sliders can sometimes be helpful for protecting certain *colors* also. In the small photo of the toadstool above **A**, a duplicate layer had been sharpened with Unsharp Mask (Amount 200, Radius 2, Threshold 1) **B**, **C**. At these settings the sharpening emphasized detail in the red and white cap, but it also increased contrast in the surrounding grass, enough so that it was a little distracting. Because the grass and the toadstool cap were so different in color, we thought we might be able to use the Green "Blend If" sliders to take some of the contrast out of the green grass without reducing the sharpening very much in the cap.

We clicked the ⊙ button in the upper right corner of the Layers palette and chose Blending Options from the fly-out menu. In the "Blend If" section of the Blending Options panel, we chose Green from the pop-up "Blend If" menu so we could make changes to the Green channel only. Working with the "This Layer" slider, we moved the "white" point at the bright green end of the bar to the left. This reduced the contrast in the grass much faster than it reduced sharpening in the mushroom cap. We settled on a setting of 200 **D**, **E**.

 Detail-Blending Options 2.psd

Softening the Focus

YOU'LL FIND THE FILES
in **WOW** > Wow Project Files > Chapter 5 >
Soft Focus:
  • Soft Focus-Before.psd (to start)
  • Soft Focus-After.psd (to compare)

OPEN THESE PALETTES
from the Window menu:
  • Tools • Layers • Layer Comps

OVERVIEW
Blend a blurred copy with a sharp
original • Control the effect by changing
Opacity and blend mode, or limiting the
tonal range in which the two versions
can interact • Mask the blurred layer to
further limit the effect

SINCE THE END OF THE 19TH CENTURY, photographers have
been using soft-focus and haze effects to impart an appealing,
romantic quality to their images. Often the goal is to create a
diffuse glow around the highlights in the photo, or to soften
the appearance of skin or hair. **In the camera** this can be done
by smearing a clear gel on a neutral-density filter in front of
the lens or by breathing on the filter to fog it. **In Photoshop**
you can use the Gaussian Blur filter and a skillful blending of
the blurred image with the sharp original, experimenting with
Opacity, blend mode, tonal restrictions, and masking. And with
the Layer Comps palette you can easily record your successful
blending experiments as you work, and then very quickly compare them to choose the one you like best.

1 Duplicating the image on a new layer. Open the **Soft
Focus-Before.psd** file or an image of your own, and copy it to
a new layer — a quick way to do this is to press Ctrl/⌘-J, the
shortcut for Layer > New > Layer Via Copy **1**.

1

The original photo is duplicated to a second layer.

CORBIS ROYALTY FREE

2

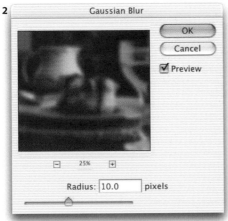

The top copy of the photo is blurred.

2 Blurring the duplicate layer. To start the "haze," choose Filter > Blur > Gaussian Blur **2**. The Radius setting will determine the amount of halo or softening you can achieve; we used a Radius of 10 pixels for our 1000-pixel-wide image.

3 Adjusting blend mode and Opacity. To turn the blur into a romantic glow, choose Lighten from the pop-up menu of modes at the top left of the Layers palette **3a**. Also try Screen mode **3b**. Both of these modes allow the light pixels of the blurred image to lighten the pixels underneath, while the dark pixels in the blurred image have little or no effect. In the blended image, this limits most of the softening to the highlights, leaving some of the sharp detail in the midtones and shadows.

Notice that Lighten doesn't "blow out" the highlights or lighten the midtones as much as Screen does. In Screen mode all pixels in the top layer are used to lighten the pixels underneath, with the lightest ones lightening the most. As a result, the entire blended image, except the darkest areas, gets significantly lighter. ▼

4 Making layer comps. Before you experiment further, make layer comps for both the Lighten and Screen options so you can compare them to other options later: With the mode for the blurred layer set to Lighten in the Layers palette, turn your attention to the Layer Comps palette and click the "Create New Layer Comp" button ▣ at the bottom of the palette. In the New Layer Comp dialog box, make sure the "Appearance (Layer Style)" option is turned on **4a**. (You'll be experimenting with Opacity and blend mode, both of which are recorded in layer comps if you have the Appearance option turned on.) Name

3a

The blur is turned into "atmosphere" by putting the top layer in Lighten mode.

3b

Putting the top layer in Screen mode lightens and brightens the photo even more.

FIND OUT MORE

▼ Lighten & Screen modes **page 175**

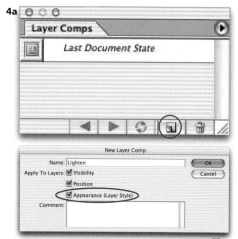

Clicking the "Create New Layer Comp" button ⊡ opens the New Layer Comp dialog box. To record the Opacity and blend mode in the Layer Comp, the "Appearance (Layer Style)" option is turned on.

Clicking "OK" in the New Layer Comp dialog box records the comp in the Layer Comps palette.

Another layer comp, named to reflect the blend mode of the blurred layer, is added to the list in the Layer Comps palette.

Reducing the Opacity of the blurred layer in Screen mode produces a gentler glow.

your comp "Lighten," and click "OK" **4b**. Then change the blend mode to Screen and make another comp, naming it "Screen" **4c**.

Now experiment with the Opacity and with more blend modes, making layer comps for the results you like. We found that 60% Opacity in Screen mode produced a result we wanted to save **4d**, so we made another comp. Overlay mode at 60% Opacity **4e** and also Soft Light at 60% **4f** added drama to the image — results we also saved as comps.

5 Blending based on tone. Of our experiments, we thought Screen mode looked the most promising, if we could adjust the blending to get the full glow of Screen in the highlights but still keep the dark parts dark. Try this: In the Layers palette double-click the image thumbnail for the blurred layer to open the Layer Style dialog box. In the General Blending section of the Layer Style box, set the Blend Mode to Screen and the Opacity to 80%. In the "Blend If: Gray" section, hold down the Alt/ Option key and on the "This Layer" bar, drag the right half-triangle of the black slider to the right **5a**. (The Alt/Option key lets you split the slider.) The slider bar represents the full tonal range, from black to white. The tones to the right of the slider you moved (the lighter tones) will contribute their full effect to the composite. The tones between the two halves of the black slider (the darker tones) will contribute partially, with any tones beyond the dark end of this range not contributing at all. By mostly eliminating the contribution of the darkest pixels of the blurred layer, you soften the image overall but at the same

4e

Putting the blurred layer in Overlay mode at 60% Opacity brightens the light areas and darkens the dark parts of the image.

APPEARANCE (LAYER STYLE)

With the "Appearance (Layer Style)" option turned on in the New Layer Comp dialog box, the layer comp will record everything that can be set in the Layer Style dialog box. That includes Blend Mode and Opacity, even if you actually set them in the Layers palette.

4f

Soft Light mode at 60% Opacity also exaggerates lights and darks, but with less contrast than Overlay mode.

5a

By splitting the "This Layer" black slider, you can control how the dark tones in the blurred image contribute to the composite. Besides providing the Advanced Blending options, this section of the Layer Style dialog box also allows you to reset the Blend Mode and Opacity.

5b

The "This Layer" settings limit the effect of the blurred layer mainly to the highlights and light midtones.

6

In the Layer Comps palette, clicking the "Apply Next Selected Layer Comp" button advances through the stack.

time maintain the detail contributed by the darker tones in the original sharp image. Splitting the slider makes a smooth transition, preventing a sharp break between where the blurred image contributes and where it doesn't **5b**. Try different "Blend If" settings. Whenever you get a result you like, click "OK" and then make a new layer comp. Because the Appearance option is turned on in the New Layer Comp dialog box, the layer comp will record the settings in the Layer Style box.

6 Choosing a comp. Now we can use the Layer Comps palette to choose from the options we saved as we experimented **6**. To advance through the comps, click the "Apply Next Selected Layer Comp" button ▶ at the bottom of the palette, stopping at the one you like best. We chose "Screen 80% Adv Blend."

> **SELECTING COMPS**
>
> To review some, but not all, of the layer comps you've made, first Ctrl/⌘-click on the names of the comps you want to look at. Then click the "Apply Next Selected Layer Comp" button ▶ to advance through the selected comps.

7 Masking the effect. Now, with a quickly and loosely painted layer mask, we can direct the "romance" to just the areas of the image where we want it. Add a layer mask by clicking the "Add layer mask" button ◨ at the bottom of the Layers palette. Choose the Brush tool and a large, soft round brush. Make black the Foreground color (with the mask active, if black isn't already the Foreground color, typing D or X will do the trick). In the Options bar set the Brush's Opacity low (we used 15%) and paint the mask with black in the areas where you want to reduce the glow. If you overdo it, switch to white paint (type X to switch), set an even lower Opacity in the Options bar, and paint over your strokes. To emphasize the pastries, we partially masked the effect on the glass, pitcher, and spoon **7**. (If you cycle through your layer comps now, all will show the masking.) ◗

7

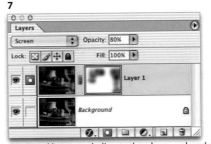

A painted layer mask directs the glow — already controlled with blend mode, Opacity, and Advanced Blending — to highlight the pastries. The resulting image is shown at the top of page 334.

Hand-Tinting a Black & White Photo

YOU'LL FIND THE FILES

in 🌀 > Wow Project Files > Chapter 5 > Hand-Tinting:

- Hand-Tint-Before.psd (to start)
- Wow Tints.aco (a Swatches preset)
- Hand-Tint-After.psd (to compare)

OPEN THESE PALETTES

from the Window menu:

- Tools • Layers • Swatches

OVERVIEW

Start with a black-and-white image in RGB Color mode • Paint a separate layer in Color mode for each color and adjust its Opacity • Organize layers in sets/groups • Create a "dodge-and-burn" layer

1a The original RGB scan file was duplicated so we could store one copy for safekeeping as we worked on the other copy.

1b

After color is neutralized, tonality adjusted, and damage repaired, this is **Hand-Tint-Before.psd**.

FROM THE EARLIEST DAYS OF PHOTOGRAPHY, artists hand-tinted black-and-white photos with a variety of paints and dyes. Today the look is back, in a variety of styles. In Photoshop, using a separate layer in Color mode for each tint gives a great deal of flexibility in controlling how each color interacts with the black-and-white image. You can make the tinting process quite detailed, as we did for the face of this portrait, or keep it simple and loose, as we did for the dress and background. (For a variety of other tinting methods that don't involve hand-painting, be sure to check out "Quick Tint Effects" on page 200.)

1 Preparing the photo. The process starts with a "black-and-white" photo that has the potential for color. If your photo is a Grayscale file, start by converting it to RGB (Image > Mode > RGB Color). The photo's appearance won't change, but it will now be "tintable." If your photo is a color file to start with **1a**, the most controlled way to neutralize the color in preparation for tinting is to use the Channel Mixer, but there are alternative quick conversion methods also.▼

FIND OUT MORE

▼ Converting color to black-and-white **pages 212 & 216**

In tinting a black-and-white photo, when you paint a layer whose blend mode has been set to Color, it can be hard to predict exactly how a particular color will interact with the range of grays in a layer below it. Here we applied a fully saturated spectrum gradient to a transparent layer in Color mode over a layer that holds a full range of tones from black to white.

You can see that the tints don't affect black or white at all. Also, the tints are most intense in the midtones, but the tonal range that accepts the most tint varies from color to color. Notice that if something is very light gray, you won't be able to tint it bright red with this method. And if something is dark gray, you won't be able to successfully tint it yellow.

A gradient on a layer in Color mode tints the grays on the layer below.

2 Wow Tints appears in the Swatches palette's menu if the Wow presets have already been loaded. Otherwise, choose Load Swatches, higher up in the menu, to add it to the current palette.

To get a full range of grays to tint, use Photoshop's Shadow/Highlight command or a Levels or Curves adjustment if needed.▼ Do any clean-up that's necessary, using the Healing Brush, Spot Healing Brush, Patch, or other tools **1b**.▼

2 Setting up your colors. Choose a few colors to use in the tinting process. We chose 10 colors and isolated them in the Swatches palette, as described in "Collecting Your Colors" below. If you want to use the same colors we used, load the **Wow Tints.aco** file (a Swatches palette) by clicking the Swatches palette's ⊙ button and choosing from the list at the bottom of the pop-up menu **2**. If you haven't yet loaded the Wow Presets,▼ this palette won't appear in the list. In that case, choose Load Swatches and navigate to the **Wow Tints.aco** file (see "You'll Find the Files" on page 338) to add it to the palette.

COLLECTING YOUR COLORS

To make a limited set of colors easy to pick out as you work, store them together at the end of the Swatches palette: For each color, click on its swatch in the palette (or otherwise make it the Foreground color). Move the cursor to the empty space at the end of the palette, where it will turn into a Paint Bucket. Click to "pour" the Foreground color to make a new swatch.

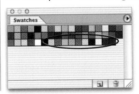

We sampled or mixed the colors we would use for "Hand-Tinting a Black & White Photo" and poured them as 10 swatches at the end of the **Wow Tints** palette, following the black swatch. **Wow Tints** includes a variety of skin, hair, and eye colors and accents, as well as environmental colors useful for tinting.

COLOR NAMES

To see the Swatches palette as a list of names and swatches rather than as swatches alone, click the palette's ⊙ button and choose Small List.

3 Setting up layers and brushes. To maintain flexibility in our tinting, we will add a new layer for each tint — sometimes more than one layer per tint so we can use a color differently in different parts of the image. Start by adding a layer above your image by clicking the "Create a new layer" button ⬛ at the bottom of the Layers palette. When the layer appears in the palette, choose Color from the palette's pop-up menu of blend modes **3a**. Putting the tinting layers in Color mode will maintain the original luminosity (darks and lights) of the image as we add the tints. That way we won't end up with any opaque-looking patches of color.

FIND OUT MORE

▼ Adjusting tonal range **page 249**

▼ Repairing photos **page 253**

▼ Loading the Wow Presets **page 5**

3a A new layer is added and put in Color mode.

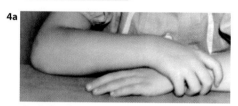

3b A soft brush tip is chosen for the Brush tool. Opacity and Flow are set at 100%. The size is set at 100 pixels, which seems like a comfortable size to use on the girl's arm.

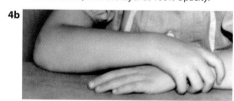

4a

The first stroke, with the layer at 100% Opacity.

4b

Reducing the layer's Opacity to 75% produces a pleasing tint.

4c

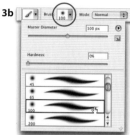

The color on the "Basic Skin" layer, erased over the eyes and teeth. (The painted color is shown at the left, alone and at 100% Opacity.)

Choose the Brush ✏ from the Tools palette. From the pop-up Brush Preset picker in the Options bar **3b**, pick a soft-edged brush tip, choosing a size that fits within the area you want to color first. Set the Opacity and Flow at 100%. At full Opacity and Flow, you can apply the color evenly, without developing streaks if you overlap your strokes.

Our approach for each color will be to test it at full opacity (maximum tint) by painting one stroke, then reduce the layer's Opacity until we get the degree of tint we want, and then continue to paint. That first stroke can be a little startling because the color is sometimes intense, but once the layer Opacity is adjusted so the color looks right, the painting process feels quite natural and goes quickly. To reduce color intensity in spots, we can use the Eraser ✐, with its mode set to Brush in the Options bar and its Opacity reduced quite low so it takes away a little of the tint at a time.

4 Starting with skin tones. To begin painting with the Brush ✏ on your Color layer, click on a color in the Swatches palette and make one stroke; we started on the girl's arm with the "Light Skin" color **4a**. Then adjust the layer's Opacity in the Layers palette until the tint looks the way you want it; we reduced the layer's Opacity to 75% **4b**. (If you can't get the tint you want by adjusting Opacity, choose a different color from the Swatches palette. Or click the Foreground square in the Tools palette and choose another color in the Color Picker; when you get a color you like, save it in the Swatches palette by clicking in the empty space after the last color.)

As you paint, you can use the bracket keys ([and]) to make the brush tip smaller or larger. Don't worry about perfect edges — in traditional hand-tinting, the dyes weren't applied perfectly either. We painted the girl's arms and face, making no attempt to avoid her eyes and mouth. With the Eraser ✐ set in Brush mode at a low Opacity, we used a small, soft brush tip to erase any spill of skin color into other areas. We erased the eyes but not the lashes or brows, and erased the teeth but not the lips. The color in the lips serves as a base for later coloring.

At this point, in the Layers palette we double-clicked on our tinting layer's name and typed in "Basic Skin" so we could easily identify the layer later if we wanted to make changes **4c**.

5 Painting accents. The next step is to accent the places where the shape of the face catches the light. Add a new layer in Color mode, choose "Light Skin Accents" for the color, and make the

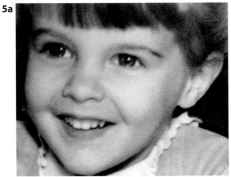

5a

The "Light Skin Accents" color is applied on a new layer in Color mode at 20% Opacity. (The painted accents are shown at the left, alone and at 100% Opacity.)

5b

The same "Light Skin Accents" color is used for the "Lips" and "Gums" layers, with layer Opacity set to 20% for "Lips" and 35% for "Gums."

5c   **5d**

The "Light Brown Hair" color is applied to the "Basic Hair" layer (shown here alone), with layer Opacity left at 100%.

Highlights are added with strokes of "Hair Highlights 1" and "Hair Highlights 2" on another layer. The layer is shown here alone at 100% Opacity, but in the file its Opacity was reduced to 15%.

Brush smaller. Try a single stroke on the cheek, and adjust the layer's Opacity until the color is right; we settled on 20%. Then continue to paint the cheeks, chin, tip of the nose, and over the brow. With a very small Brush, place a dab of color at each corner of the eyes, and stroke along the edges of the lower eyelids **5a**. If you like, accent her hands and arms.

You may want to make a separate layer in Color mode for the lips, and one for the gums. For light-skinned people, natural lips and gums are usually the same color as the skin accents, but darker **5b**. For dark-skinned people, you may want to use cooler skin tones (with more blue in them) for the lips and gums than you used for the cheeks.

Continue adding layers for hair, irises, whites of the eyes, and teeth. For the base layer of hair color, we simply picked a color that looked right for the lightest values and left the layer Opacity at 100% **5c**. Hair painted with just one color can look artificial, so we added another layer, and painted a few streaks of two accent colors. Setting the layer's blend mode at Normal and reducing the Opacity to 15% produced the result we liked **5d**.

We tinted the irises of the eyes blue. We also tinted the whites of the eyes and the teeth. In a tinted photo even a faint hint of color is more natural-looking than the original gray **5e**.

6 Organizing the layers. When we had finished painting the girl, we linked all the painted layers and placed them in a layer set (called a group in CS2), so that we could change the overall color intensity later, simply by changing the Opacity of the set/group itself, without changing the color balance of the related parts. To make a layer set in CS, in the Layers palette target one

5e

The irises are tinted with the "Blue Eyes" color (layer Opacity at 25%), and the warm "White-Eyes & Teeth" color takes the gray out of the eyes (10% layer Opacity) and teeth (20%).

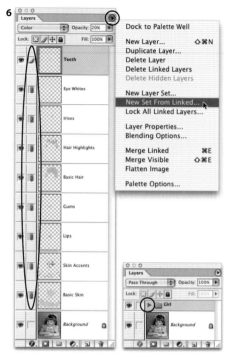

6

The layers are linked and a "Girl" layer set is made. To expand the set to show thumbnails to get access to the individual layers, the layer set can be opened by clicking the ▶ button to the left of its folder thumbnail.

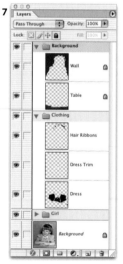

7

The "Table" and "Wall" layers were tinted with two browns, the last two swatches we had stored at the end of the Wow Tints in the Swatches palette. Layers for the clothing are collected in a layer set, and another set/group called "Background" is created for the "Wall" and "Table" layers.

of the painted layers by clicking on its thumbnail; then click in the column to the left of the thumbnail for each of the other painted layers. Finally, click the Layers palette's ▶ button and choose New Set From Linked **6**. In CS2, simply click the top layer you want to use in the group, then Shift-click the bottom layer, and Shift-click the "Create a new group" button 🗀 at the bottom of the palette.

7 Completing the tinting. Finish painting the parts of the image that you want to color. We painted the dress, hair ribbons, and trim on separate layers, and made them into another layer set/group. For the dress, we used the same blue as for the eyes with layer Opacity at 45%. We painted right over the trim, tinting it a very pale blue; we could have left it this way to indicate translucency in the collar's fabric, or reflection from the dress, but instead we used a small Eraser ⬭ to erase it. We also used the Eraser (at lower Opacity) to remove some of the color from the shadows, where it was too intense. We added another Color layer and painted the trim with "Pale Yellow," adjusting layer Opacity to 25%. We painted the hair ribbons with the same color as the dress, but put the layer in Overlay mode so the increased contrast would simulate the shine of the satin; Opacity was set at 50%. We painted the table and the wall on separate layers also, organizing them in another layer set/group **7**.

8 Final touches. To balance tone and color in the final image, you can add a "dodge and burn" layer as follows: With the top layer of your file targeted in the Layers palette, Alt/Option-click the 🔲 button at the bottom of the palette. In the New Layer dialog box, choose Overlay for the Mode and click the check box for "Fill with Overlay-neutral color (50% gray)" and then click "OK." Now use the Brush with a large, soft brush tip and a low Opacity setting to paint with black where you want to darken the image and increase color density, and with white where you want to lighten it **8**.

Trying other options. With each color on a separate layer and with layers grouped in sets, you have a tremendous amount of flexibility. The two images on the facing page show the effect of starting with the file from step 8 and making some of the following changes:

- You can change the color intensity by adjusting the Opacity of single layers or of an entire layer set.

- Change the blend mode of some or all layers. Use Overlay to add shine or brilliance. Or try changing the blend mode

8

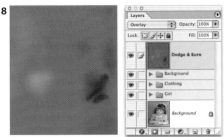

A quickly painted "dodge and burn" layer at the top of the stack is used to balance the lighting in the image. It slightly darkens the face and sleeve on the right side of the photo, which intensifies their color, and lightens the sleeve on the left. The result is shown at the top of page 338.

for some or all layer sets from Pass Through (the default, which simply "passes through" the modes of the individual layers in the set) to Soft Light, for a pale tint effect.

- You can change a single color by adding a Hue/Saturation Adjustment layer, "clipped" to the layer you want to change. For instance, to adjust the color of the "Wall" you can target this layer in the Layers palette, then choose Hue/Saturation from the list, and in the New Layer dialog box, click the check box for "Use Previous Layer to Create Clipping Mask." Clicking "OK" adds a layer that affects only the "Wall" layer immediately below it. By adjusting the Hue and Saturation sliders, with or without the Colorize option turned on, you can change the color of the wall. *Wow!*

Starting with the tinted photo from step 8 (shown at the top of page 338), we changed the blend mode of the "Clothing" and "Background" layer sets/groups to Soft Light and reduced the Opacity of the "Girl" layer set/group to 70%.

Starting with the tinted photo at the top of page 338, we added a Hue/Saturation Adjustment layer above the "Wall" layer to change the color of the background. To show that the adjustment is limited to the "Wall" layer, the name of the clipping layer is underlined and the Adjustment layer's thumbnail is indented.

Cristen Gillespie Turns Day into Night

STARTING WITH HER ONLY PHOTO of the Portofino Cafe, taken in daylight, Cristen Gillespie set out to create a stylized nighttime image. Photoshop's Lighting Effects filter provided everything she needed.▼

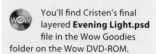

You'll find Cristen's final layered **Evening Light.psd** file in the Wow Goodies folder on the Wow DVD-ROM.

To preserve her original photo, Cristen duplicated it to a new layer (Ctrl/⌘-J). Then she chose Filter > Render > Lighting Effects, with **Light Type turned off** and a **blue Ambient lighting** set to darken the copy overall.

Since Ambient lighting is designed to work with lights set in the top part of the Lighting Effects box, even a positive Ambience setting (+25 in this case) will darken the image if no other light is turned "On."

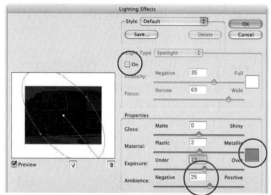

To light the windows, Cristen added a new empty layer by clicking the "Create a new layer" button 🔲 at the bottom of the Layers palette. She selected the windows with the Polygon Lasso 🔽, using the Shift key to add each window to the selection and using Alt/Option to remove the stop sign and the plant from the selection. She then filled her selection with white on the new layer. After deselecting, she used the Lighting Effects filter again, this time with a warm yellow Omni light turned on, positioned up and to the right of the door to represent a light inside the building.

An Omni light radiates the same distance in every direction. The dialog box showed the light falling on surfaces in between the windows, but since that area of the "Windows" layer was transparent, the light actually colored only the windows themselves.

FIND OUT MORE

▼ Working in the Lighting Effects dialog box **page 259**

To light the lamps beside the door and to create the light spilling from the windows, Cristen first made a layer with a composite of the developing image (holding down Ctrl-Alt-Shift in Windows, ⌘-Option-Shift on the Mac and typing N, then E). She ran the Lighting Effects filter on the composite layer, adding two Spotlights for the wall lamps, one for the door, and one for each of the three windows.

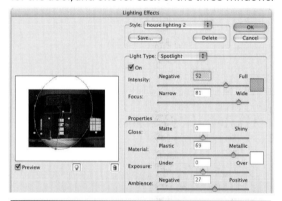

With more light than she needed, Cristen could now add a hide-all layer mask (by Alt/Option-clicking the "Add layer mask" button at the bottom of the Layers palette) and paint the mask with white. Using the Brush tool with a hard round brush tip at full opacity (chosen in the Options bar), she clicked to add the lamps by the door. Then, with a larger, softer brush tip and lower Opacity, she painted the mask to reveal as much of the layer as she wanted for the light spilling from the interior. To finalize the image, she reduced the Opacity of the "Windows" layer to 70%, which allowed some of the interior detail to show, and adjusted the Opacity of the "Spilling Light" layer, settling on 90%.

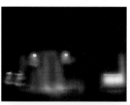

In painting the mask, if too much white allowed too much light to show, "repairs" could be made by switching to black paint, lowering the Opacity in the Options bar, and painting over the white.

Cristen used Spotlights to provide more light than she needed, spilling out from the wall lamps and windows.

The finished nightime image

Spectacular Lens Flare

TRADITIONALLY, LENS FLARE is produced when light "bounces around," reflecting off surfaces inside a camera lens. The glaring light that becomes part of the photo as a result is often unwanted. With film cameras, other than single-lens reflex cameras (SLRs), lens flare damage is apparent only after the film is developed and the image ruined. With an SLR, either film or digital, lens flare can be previewed through the viewfinder, and thus can be avoided — or captured as a dramatic enhancement to the scene, conveying a sense of intense sunlight or adding an intriguing design element to the photo. In digital cameras other than SLRs, lens flare shows up on the LCD preview screens so it's quite easy to incorporate it into a digital shot intentionally. And, of course, if you want to add lens flare after the fact, there's Photoshop!

REAL OR SURREAL?

Photoshop's Lens Flare filter can be a great source of glows and rays of light for special effects.

Real: Lens flare is likely to happen "in camera" when a very bright light source is part of the scene being photographed, or is just outside the frame of the photo. It's likely to happen when no hood is used to shade the camera lens, and when the lens is fairly wide open (a low f-stop value).

RICK WORTHINGTON

The arc of pentagonal reflections in this lens flare becomes one more "line" leading to the hiker crossing the bridge in this photo (top). In a cropped version of the image, the flare is a counterpoint to the silhouetted figure and balances the deep shadows on the left side of the image.

Photoshop: Photoshop's Filter > Render > Lens Flare can be used as shown here to simulate a glare and the resulting inside-the-lens reflections, adding interest to a photo.

PHOTOSPIN.COM

The preview in the Lens Flare dialog box lets you watch what happens as you experiment with the type of lens and the Brightness and position of the light source.

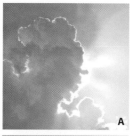

A

B

C

To add drama to his original late-afternoon photo of clouds **A** to create ***Tampa God Rays***, **Jack Davis** added a Levels Adjustment layer. In the Levels dialog box, he clicked the "Auto" button, which expanded the tonal range in the image from full white to full black **B**.

Next he targeted the *Background* by clicking its thumbnail in the Layers palette, duplicated it (Ctrl/⌘-J), and dragged the copy's thumbnail up to the top of the palette so it was above the Levels Adjustment. To add to the feeling of dimension and space, he turned this layer into a "dodging and burning" treatment by choosing Filter > Other > High Pass. He used settings that left the filtered layer mostly medium gray, with the edges of clouds and rays emphasized by darker gray on one side and lighter gray or white on the other **C**.

Changing the blend mode of the filtered layer to Overlay, one of the contrast-enhancing blend modes, made the medium gray in the layer disappear, since 50% gray is neutral, or transparent, in these modes.▼ The lighter and darker grays, however, acted to increase the contrast where Davis wanted it most — around existing shapes and areas of contrast, to make the light and shadows more dramatic.

FIND OUT MORE

▼ Contrast blend modes **page 176**

SETTING THE BLEND MODE FIRST

When you plan to filter a layer and combine it with your image by changing its blend mode, consider changing the blend mode *before* you apply the filter. That way — at least for filters that have a Preview option (such as High Pass) — you can see the effect on the image as you experiment with filter settings.

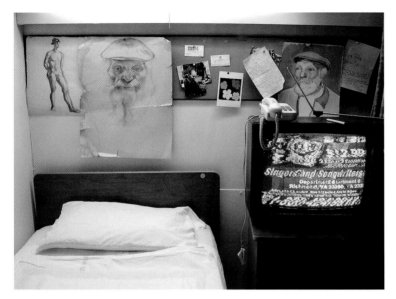

Katrin Eismann wanted just a hint of color for her series of photos of the day-to-day life of a talented resident at a Greenwich Village senior citizens' home. Working in relatively low light and avoiding a flash, she took the photos with a Nikon E990 in Program mode, in which the camera calculates the best shutter and aperture settings to get a crisp picture. By using low ISO speed settings (100 to 200) Eismann forced the camera to use a wide-open aperture, reducing depth of field, and a long exposure time, which captured the motion of the hands as a blur.

Working on one of her photos, Eismann used a Channel Mixer Adjustment layer to tone down the color in the images **A**. The Monochrome mix,

made up of 35% Red channel information and 70% Green channel, lightened the image slightly as well as desaturating it.▼ Reducing the Opacity of this Channel Mixer layer to 50% restored part of the color. Once she had a Channel Mixer layer that produced the effect she wanted, Eismann dragged and dropped it into the other files in the series.

In the two photos on the facing page, Eismann duplicated the Channel Mixer layer and experimented with changing the blend mode of the duplicate from Normal to one of the contrast-boosting modes,▼ settling on Soft Light as the best option for bringing out detail in the woman's hair, the man's hands, and other areas **B**.

For these two images she also used a Photoshop version of a classic photo

darkroom technique — "burning down" areas of less importance, to make the visual-interest areas brighter by contrast, so they draw the viewer's eye. To burn the left edge of the top photo and the right edge of the bottom one, she added a transparent layer, put it in Soft Light mode, and used the Gradient tool ▨ to "sweep in" the darkness she wanted: In the Options bar she chose a black-to-transparent Linear Gradient. Then she clicked near the edge of the image, and dragged inward to the point where she wanted the burning to end. She repeated this sweeping motion from various points on the edge and finally reduced the layer's Opacity to create the effect she wanted.

For the image of the bedroom (the original is shown small above), she used a Curves Adjustment layer to lighten and brighten it overall before desaturating with the Channel Mixer layer. In the Channel Mixer layer, she selected the TV screen and filled the selection with black, to protect that area from desaturation **C**.

FIND OUT MORE

▼ Using Channel Mixer **page 213**

▼ Blend modes **page 176**

Alexis Marie Deutschmann took the original photo for *Point Loma Harbor* with a Nikon D100 camera, setting the exposure for the blue water and using a graduated neutral-density filter to reduce the brightness of the sky **A**.

She then used Photoshop to apply Curves and Hue/Saturation adjustments to brighten the image and bring out the color. She used blend modes, Opacity adjustment, and a layer mask to mix three versions of the image, directing the increased contrast and color where she wanted them, as follows.

Deutschmann opened her image in Photoshop and duplicated it to another layer (Ctrl/⌘-J). She applied

Image > Adjustments > Curves to this duplicate layer to increase contrast **B**.▼ Then she chose Screen from the Layers palette's blend mode menu to limit the increase in contrast to the highlights and lighter midtones.▼ This protected the shadows and dark midtones from losing detail. Also in the Layers palette, she reduced the Opacity for the Screen layer to 60% to prevent blowing out the highlights **C**.

Targeting the *Background* again by clicking its thumbnail in the Layers palette, Deutschmann duplicated the image again (Ctrl/⌘-J) and dragged the new copy up the palette to the top of the layer stack. To intensify color in this third layer, she chose

Image > Adjustments > Hue/Saturation and moved the Saturation slider to the right **D**. She chose Saturation as the blend mode for this layer to avoid affecting brightness **E**. She also added a layer mask (by clicking the ▣ button at the bottom of the Layers palette) and used the Brush tool 🖌 and black paint to protect parts of the image from the saturation boost **F**.▼

FIND OUT MORE
▼ Using Curves **page 250**
▼ Blend modes **page 175**
▼ Painting a mask **page 75**

A

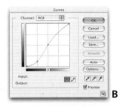
B

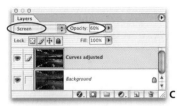
C

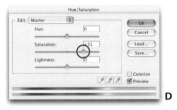
D

E

F

Cliff *Dwelling* by **Loren Haury** is actually a composite of three photos, identical except for the exposure time. Using his Olympus C-50 on a tripod, Haury set up the exposure for the first photo **A**. Then he took two more shots, using the camera's aperture priority setting so the shutter speed was the only parameter that changed. He took one

VARY THE TIME

When you take several exposures with the idea of combining them in a single image to get detail in both highlights and shadows, keep the aperture (f/stop) and ISO constant to keep depth of field and "grain" the same for all the shots. To change the exposure, change the shutter speed.

shot at +2 on the camera's exposure meter **B** and the second at −2 on the meter **C**.

Haury used the Lasso ◯ to roughly select slightly larger areas than he needed from the over- and underexposed photos, and copied and pasted these pieces into the file of the correctly exposed photo **D**. There he reduced the Opacity of the pasted layers to about 50% and dragged with the Move tool ▶⊕ to align them with the *Background* image. He raised the Opacity again until he had the right blend of exposures, then used the Eraser ⬙ with a soft brush tip and low Opacity to partially erase the edges of the pasted elements ▼ to blend them seamlessly with the main image **E**. (Another way to combine the exposures would be to Shift-

drag the overexposed and underexposed versions into the file with the correct exposure. Shift-dragging would center the imported images in the file, and thus perfectly align them with the *Background*, since all three are exactly the same size. A "hide all" layer mask added to each of the imported layers and painted with white would reveal parts of the imported photos. This masking method is described for Haury's "dodging and burning" step, in the next paragraph. It's a "nondestructive" approach — the entire overexposed or underexposed image is still intact on the layer, and if you decide you'd like to change the layer's contribution to the image later, it's easy — just modify the mask. The trade-off is that full masked layers produce a "bulkier" file. For *Cliff Dwelling*, for instance, the file would have been more than twice the size of Haury's cut-and-pasted version.

Once he had assembled the pieces, Haury made a merged duplicate (Image > Duplicate > Duplicate Merged Layers Only) and went to work "dodging and burning." First he lightened the ceiling area as follows: He duplicated the image as a new layer (Ctrl/⌘-J for Layer > New > Layer Via Copy), and put the new layer in Screen mode using the menu in the upper left corner of the Layers palette. Then he added a "hide all" layer mask by Alt/Option-clicking the "Add layer mask" button 🔲 at the bottom of the palette. He painted the black mask with the Brush 🖌, using a soft brush tip and white paint to reveal the image only where he wanted to lighten the composite **F**.▼

He once again made a merged duplicate of the file, duplicated the image to a new layer, and added a black mask. But this time he put the layer in Multiply mode and painted the mask with white where he wanted to *darken* the image **G**, **H**.

To finish the image, Haury made adjustments to bring back the color of the scene the way he remembered it. He used Image > Adjustments > Hue/Saturation to reduce Saturation to neutralize the color slightly. He added a Color Balance Adjustment layer (by clicking the "Create a new fill or adjustment layer" button 🖤 at the bottom of the Layers palette) and added Cyan and Yellow to the Midtones and Shadows to balance the red. He clicked the 🖤 button again and this time added a Curves Adjustment layer **I**, setting up an "S" curve to increase contrast in the midtones▼ to arrive at the result on the facing page.

EV 0

EV +2

EV –2

Combined

Dodged & burned

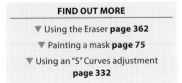

FIND OUT MORE

▼ Using the Eraser **page 362**

▼ Painting a mask **page 75**

▼ Using an "S" Curves adjustment
page 332

For each of her **Botanical Portraits**, **Christine Zalewski** captures the personality and "attitude" of her plant subject in a digital photo and then uses Photoshop to enhance the color and contrast. She starts by duplicating her original digital photograph to a new layer (Ctrl⌘-J) and sharpening this copy **A**, preserving the original in the *Background* for safe-keeping within the file. For **Anemone**, shown here, she followed the sharpening with a series of Adjustment layers that turned the image into a sepia-tone and pulled out detail over a broad range of tones.

First she added a Channel Mixer layer **B** by clicking the "Create new fill or adjustment layer" button ⦸ at the bottom of the Layers palette and choosing from the pop-up menu. She chose the Monochrome option in the

Channel Mixer dialog box, set the sliders for the conversion to black-and-white, ▼ and clicked "OK." Then she painted this Adjustment layer's built-in layer mask; she used the Brush tool ✎ with a soft brush tip and reduced Opacity in the Options bar to hide the Channel Mixer effect and bring back color in the lightest areas of the flower petals. The masking was not for the sake of the color itself, since she was making a sepia-tone, but to protect the lightest areas of the petals from going to pure white when she lightened the image next.

Zalewski added another Adjustment layer **C**, this time choosing Curves, and made a modified "S-curve" adjustment that both lightened the image overall and "stretched" the range of the darker midtones and shadows to bring out detail in the leaves. ▼ Where this adjustment darkened the

leaves too much, she protected them by painting on the Curves layer's built-in mask.

She created the sepia-tone effect by adding a Hue/Saturation Adjustment layer **D**. In the Hue/Saturation dialog box she clicked the Colorize option, adjusted the Hue, and set the Saturation low.

Three more Curves layers, their adjustments targeted to various parts of the image, completed the portrait. Zalewski put the Curves layer for the center of the flower **E** in Luminosity mode so she could get the increased contrast from its S-curve without the increased color intensity that Normal mode produced. The Curves layer for the petals was another "S" that darkened the targeted area overall and "stretched" the range of the midtones and highlights.

A

B

C

D

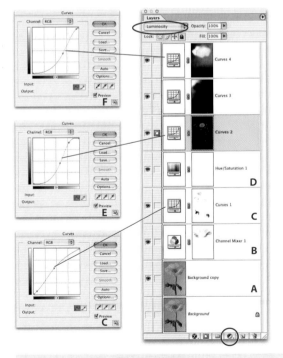

F

E

C

D

C

B

A

FIND OUT MORE

▼ Using Channel Mixer **page 213**

▼ Using an "S-curve" adjustment to bring out detail **page 332**

To create **Grandma's Cherries, Susan Thompson** started with a Polaroid SX-70 photo (left) and manipulated the still-wet emulsion, building impressionistic swirls and hand-rendered textures, as shown at the left; the process is described for *Summer in Arcata* on page 234. After opening a scan of the Polaroid in Photoshop, Thompson duplicated the image to a new layer (Ctrl/⌘-J), where she could fix imperfections with the Healing Brush 🩹 and Clone Stamp 🛆 without working directly on the original scan. She added a Hue/Saturation Adjustment layer (by clicking the ◑ button at the bottom of the Layers palette and choosing from the pop-up list). In the Hue/Saturation dialog she chose the Reds from the Edit pop-up menu and watched the warming changes in the image as she shifted the Hue slightly toward yellow and increased Saturation and Lightness. Before closing the Hue/Saturation dialog, she also shifted and boosted the color for the Yellows and Greens.

Thompson made local color changes using a Selective Color Adjustment layer with a layer mask (as described on page 235) to get the result above.

LILY DAYTON

For ***Afternoon in the Park,* Marie Brown** duplicated Lily Dayton's photo **A** to a new layer and then chose Filter > Vanishing Point.▼ She clicked with Vanishing Point's Create Plane tool ⊞ to establish the four corners of a grid that she thought would provide the right perspective for cloning grass and leaves from the foreground to cover distractions in the background **B**. After adjusting the grid with the Edit Plane tool ▶, she alternately Alt/Option-clicked with the Stamp tool ♣ to sample near the bottom of the image and then clicked to cover up the more distant elements she wanted to hide. As she worked, Vanishing Point's dynamic "loaded"

brush tip showed how the cloning material would shrink to fit into the image as she moved it to the area she wanted to cover **C**.

A CLONING PREVIEW

Unlike the cursor for Photoshop's Clone Stamp tool ♣, the equivalent Stamp tool cursor inside CS2's Vanishing Point interface lets you see the cloned material, including the hardness of the edge, before you click or drag to "paint" with it. There may be instances when you want to take advantage of this "preview," even when your retouching task needs no perspective correction.

FIND OUT MORE

▼ Working with Vanishing Point **page 588**

Painting

6

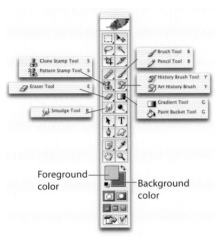

Photoshop's tools for stroking with paint and pattern are the Brush ✏, Pencil ✏, Eraser ⬲, and Smudge ✺. The cloning tools that are most useful for painting are the Pattern Stamp ⬚ (in Impressionist mode) and the Art History Brush ✺. For restoring an earlier version of an "overworked" area of a painting, the History Brush ✺ can also be helpful. The filling tools — Paint Bucket ⬠ and Gradient ⬛ — "pour" color into a selected area.

Two hand-operated painting tools — the Brush ✏ and the Smudge ✺, respectively — were used to add color to a scanned ink sketch and to "run" the ink. A detail is shown here, and the technique is presented step-by-step in "Watercolor Over Ink" on page 370.

PHOTOSHOP'S POWERFUL ART-MAKING TOOLS can simulate all kinds of painting media and techniques, remarkably realistically. With them you can even create some new and different combinations that would be difficult or impossible with traditional media. In putting pixels onto your digital canvas, Photoshop's painting tools run the gamut from freehand stroking (you control exactly where each stroke is painted) to fully automated cloning (Photoshop turns an entire image into a "painting" for you), with lots of intermediate options that give you varying degrees of control over the strokes.

PAINTING IN PHOTOSHOP

There are at least four great ways to stroke "paint" onto "canvas" in Photoshop:

- You can start with a blank canvas or a scanned photo or drawing and "hand paint" with the Brush tool ✏. You'll find an example in "Watercolor Over Ink" on page 370.

- Or reproduce an existing image by hand-painting with the Smudge tool ✺, as described in "Painting 'Wet on Wet'" on page 376.

- The Impressionist option for the Pattern Stamp tool ⬚ is an excellent way to "clone" a photograph into a natural-media masterpiece, as described in "Pattern Stamp Watercolors" on page 384.

- Or you can use the Art History Brush ✺ to automate the process of turning a photo into a painting, as in "Art History Lessons" on page 388.

The next 10 pages cover the basics of the painting and cloning tools, including what goes into making a custom brush tip or painting tool; using the filling tools; applying filters to create a painterly look without actually putting down strokes; and enhancing your paintings with "post-processing" techniques. References to step-by-step techniques later in the chapter tell where you can learn more.

INSTANT BRUSHES PALETTE

With a painting or cloning tool chosen, right-clicking (Windows) or Ctrl-clicking (Mac) anywhere within your working window automatically calls up a Brush Preset picker, so you can choose a new brush tip without making a trip to the Options bar or Brushes palette.

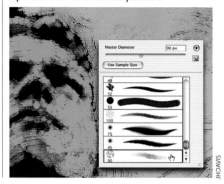

Photoshop also has tools for technical drawing — less painterly but very precise, and resolution-independent for smooth scaling. ▼

THE PAINTING TOOLS

The hand-operated painting tools are the **Brush** ✎, **Pencil** ✎, **Eraser** ✐, and **Smudge** ✐. Each one behaves in its own unique way. Many of the characteristics of the painting tools can be set in the Options bar — for instance, blend mode, paint opacity, paint flow, and airbrush behavior. (For fine-tuning brush size, shape, or behavior, or for creating your own elaborate media brushes, you'll need to dive into the Brushes palette.) "Brush Control Options" on the facing page shows the Brush tool's Options bar and the Brushes palette.

The Wow presets for the painting and cloning tools incorporate many of the characteristics that can be built into custom painting tools. "Exercising Wow Painting Tools" on page 395 shows how to use these presets.

IF PAINTING DOESN'T WORK

If you try to paint on a Shape layer or Type layer, or on a layer whose visibility is turned off, you won't be able to. Photoshop will open a warning that tells you why not, and what to do about it. But there are at least two situations in which painting doesn't work but Photoshop doesn't let you know why:

- It may be because there's an **invisible active selection** — invisible either because you've zoomed in on your painting and the selected area is now outside the working window, or because you've pressed Ctrl/⌘-H to temporarily hide the "marching ants" selection border. Pressing Ctrl/⌘-D "drops" (or releases) the selection.

- The layer you're trying to paint may be protected because the layer's **transparency or pixels are locked** (you can tell by looking at the check boxes for the Lock icons at the top of the Layers palette).

A FEW WORDS ABOUT TERMINOLOGY

There's a bit of overlap in the terminology Photoshop uses for its painting tools and palettes. You might want to open Photoshop and explore the interface as you read this:

First, the **Brush tool** ✎ (it used to be called the Paintbrush) can be chosen in the Tools palette, or by typing B.

Once you choose the Brush, or any other painting or cloning tool, you can change its **brush tip** by choosing from the **Brush Preset picker**, which can be found in two places — in the Options bar (as shown at the right) and in the standalone **Brushes palette** (Window > Brushes).

"Brush tip" is our term, not Photoshop's. Photoshop calls them **"brushes."** So the **Brush Preset picker** and the **Brushes palette** have to do with **brush tips**, or **brushes in the generic sense**, rather than with the Brush tool ✎ itself.

Tool presets are ready-made versions of specific tools. A tool preset for the Brush tool ✎, for instance, has not only a brush tip but also a built-in blend mode, stroke opacity and flow, and sometimes even color. Tool presets are available in the **Tool Preset picker**, in the Options bar (as shown here at the right) and in the standalone **Tool Presets palette** (Window > Tool Presets).

BRUSH CONTROL OPTIONS

The **Options bar** offers a few controls for modifying how painting and cloning tools perform. The standalone **Brushes palette**, with its seven panels of controls and five additional on/off toggles, offers many more options. The Brush tool's Options bar and three panels of the expanded Brushes palette are shown below.

Click to open the **Tool Preset picker** (not shown).

Click to pop out the **Brush Preset picker** as shown.

Set the **blend mode** for the paint.

Set the **maximum paint coverage**.

Click to open the **Brushes palette**; three of the palette's panels are shown below.

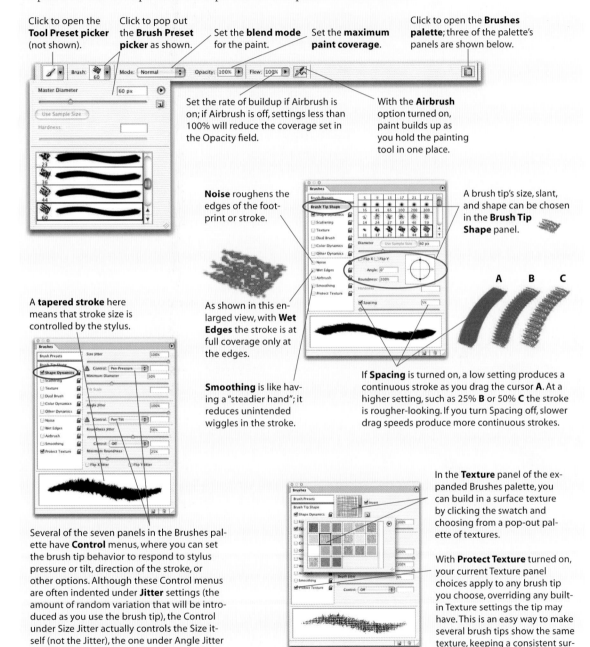

Set the rate of buildup if Airbrush is on; if Airbrush is off, settings less than 100% will reduce the coverage set in the Opacity field.

With the **Airbrush** option turned on, paint builds up as you hold the painting tool in one place.

Noise roughens the edges of the footprint or stroke.

A brush tip's size, slant, and shape can be chosen in the **Brush Tip Shape** panel.

A **tapered stroke** here means that stroke size is controlled by the stylus.

As shown in this enlarged view, with **Wet Edges** the stroke is at full coverage only at the edges.

Smoothing is like having a "steadier hand"; it reduces unintended wiggles in the stroke.

If **Spacing** is turned on, a low setting produces a continuous stroke as you drag the cursor **A**. At a higher setting, such as 25% **B** or 50% **C** the stroke is rougher-looking. If you turn Spacing off, slower drag speeds produce more continuous strokes.

Several of the seven panels in the Brushes palette have **Control** menus, where you can set the brush tip behavior to respond to stylus pressure or tilt, direction of the stroke, or other options. Although these Control menus are often indented under **Jitter** settings (the amount of random variation that will be introduced as you use the brush tip), the Control under Size Jitter actually controls the Size itself (not the Jitter), the one under Angle Jitter controls the Angle itself, and so on.

In the **Texture** panel of the expanded Brushes palette, you can build in a surface texture by clicking the swatch and choosing from a pop-out palette of textures.

With **Protect Texture** turned on, your current Texture panel choices apply to any brush tip you choose, overriding any built-in Texture settings the tip may have. This is an easy way to make several brush tips show the same texture, keeping a consistent surface for the painting.

With Photoshop's painting tools, you can get some interesting results by choosing the **Fade** option for several of the **Control** settings in the standalone Brushes palette. For example, by setting some of the Control settings in the Shape Dynamics, Color Dynamics, and Other Dynamics panels to Fade, with a different numbers of steps for each, you can shrink the brush size, fade to transparency, and change the color (from the Foreground to the Background color) all at different rates, within a single brush stroke.

Both of these strokes were made with the Brush tool. For the lefthand stroke we set the Size, the Foreground-to-Background shift, and the Opacity all to Fade in 40 steps. For the right-hand stroke, we faded Size in 40 steps, but changed the color shift to fade in 15 steps and the Opacity to fade in 30 steps. The Jitter settings (such as the Opacity and Flow Jitter settings shown in the dialog box here) create variation in the stroke.

Brush

By default the **Brush** lays down a smooth-edged (antialiased) stroke of color as you drag. If you click without dragging, it leaves a single footprint of the brush tip shape. Many of Photoshop's Brush tool presets depart from the default hard-but-smooth-edged setting and are soft, so that the stroke is solid in the center but more transparent at the edges. This is controlled by the Hardness setting. The Brush tool's **Opacity** setting (in the Options bar) controls paint coverage; the higher the setting, the more opaque the paint can be. The **Flow** setting (also in the Options bar) modifies the Opacity setting, reducing coverage if Flow is set at anything less than 100%.

No matter how long you hold the Brush cursor in one place, the color doesn't build up or spread out — *unless* the **Airbrush** option on the Brush tool's Options bar is turned on. With the Airbrush, the longer you keep the cursor in one spot, the more the paint builds up. With the Airbrush on and high Flow settings, the paint flows quickly, building up until it reaches the full Opacity setting. With low Flow settings, the paint will build up to the same Opacity setting if you hold the cursor in place long enough, but it builds up more slowly. The Airbrush setting is a toggle, so clicking the button again turns off the Airbrush option.

Pencil

The **Pencil** operates like the Brush, but the stroke edges are pixelated — they can't be soft or even smooth (antialiased) as the Brush's can. With the Pencil, Photoshop doesn't have to do the continuous calculations required for softness or antialiasing, so there's no delay between when you move the cursor and when the stroke appears on the screen. For this reason the Pencil can seem like the most "natural" of all the tools for doing quick sketches. Pixelation can be seen in the "stairstepping" of curved or slanted edges of a Pencil stroke, but if your sketch is done at high resolution, or if the sketch is just for reference and won't show in the final artwork, the Pencil can be ideal.

Eraser

The **Eraser** removes pixels or changes their color. By default it leaves behind (erases to) the **Background color** if you're working on a *Background* layer. On other layers it erases to **transparency**. It can operate like a **Brush**, **Airbrush**, or **Pencil**, depending on what you choose from the Mode menu in the Options bar. Another Mode choice is **Block**. (Block was the only mode the Eraser had in early versions of Photoshop. It isn't as

For working on a fairly small drawing, the performance difference between the Pencil  and the Brush  with a simple brush tip is less obvious than it used to be when computers were slower. Cher Threinen-Pendarvis used the Brush tool with the "Hard Round 5 pixels" tip, gray "paint," and a Wacom Intuos pressure-sensitive tablet to make a sketch to use as a guide for painting *Two Ducks*, shown on page 394.

The Smudge tool 💧 can automatically sample color from a reference photo as you paint, as shown in "Painting 'Wet on Wet'" on page 376. A detail of the reference photo is shown here at the top, with the same detail at an early stage of the painting shown below it.

useful as other modes, though it can be helpful for removing color along a straight horizontal or vertical edge.)

The **Erase To History** choice in the Options bar lets you erase back to a previous stage of your painting. (See "Two History Brushes" on page 366 for more.)

HISTORY "ON-OFF": SWITCH

Holding down the Alt/Option key while brushing, toggles the Eraser in and out of Erase To History mode.

Smudge 💧

The **Smudge** tool 💧 smears color as you drag it. If Finger Painting is turned on in the Options bar, the smear starts with the Foreground color. Otherwise, each stroke starts by sampling the color under the cursor, and the Smudge smears with that color. If the brush tip is big enough to pick up more than one color, the Smudge tool applies streaks of the sampled colors. The higher the **Strength** setting in the Options bar, the farther the Smudge tool will smear each new color it encounters. At 100% Strength the Smudge applies only the first color(s) it samples. At lower percentages the first color fades out and new ones are picked up and smeared as the cursor encounters them. At any Opacity setting other than 100% the smearing process can be tediously slow. But at 100% it can be very effective for moving around pixels with a "painterly" result, as demonstrated in "Painting 'Wet on Wet'" on page 376.

CHOOSING, EDITING & CREATING BRUSH TIPS & TOOLS

Before you start working with and customizing the painting tools, be sure you've looked at the tip "A Few Words About Terminology" on page 360. The term *brush* is used in several ways in Photoshop, which can be confusing unless you get it sorted out early. Then read the "Brush Tips" and "Tool Presets" sections here.

Brush Tips

The brush tips for the painting and cloning tools are all made available through the **Brush Preset picker**. Whenever you choose a tool that uses a brush tip, the Brush Preset picker, with its controls for brush tip size and hardness, can be opened by clicking the **"Brush:"** icon (second from the left) in the Options bar. The Brush Preset picker can also be found in the standalone **Brushes palette** (Window > Brushes). The Brushes palette, which offers a wealth of additional options, can be opened by clicking the "Toggle the brushes palette" button 🔲 near the right end of the Options bar.

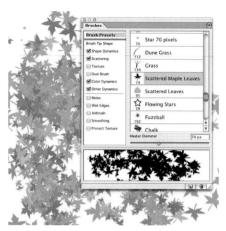

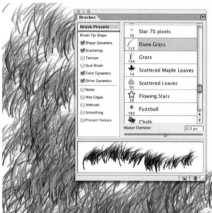

By experimenting with your selection of Fore-ground and Background colors in the Tools pal-ette and with the settings in the Color Dynamics panel of the expanded Brushes palette, you can achieve amazing instant illustrations with the brush tips that ship with Photoshop. For the Scat-tered Maple Leaves preset (top, from Photoshop's default set of brush tips), we went into the Color Dynamics panel of the Brushes palette and set the Foreground/Background Jitter amount to 100% to "give the brush permission" to randomly vary the color within the whole range between our Foreground yellow and Background orange. For the Dune Grass preset (also from the default set), the built-in Foreground/Background Jitter was already 100%, so all we had to do was to choose two shades of green for the Foreground and Background colors.

To **choose a brush tip** from those that are currently loaded and available to Photoshop, you can open either version of the **Brush Preset picker** and click on the brush tip you want.

To **modify a brush tip and add the modified version to the Brush Preset picker**, first choose the brush tip as described above. Then change any settings you want, either in the Brush Preset picker (size, hardness, or roundness) or in the Brushes palette (with more options). Then click the ⊡ button (or click the ⊙ button and choose New Brush Preset) to open the Brush Name dialog box; enter a name and click "OK." Your new brush tip will be added as the last one in the Brush Preset picker.

To **build your own custom brush tip**, construct your brush's footprint, then use the Rectangular Marquee [] to surround this footprint, and choose **Edit > Define Brush**. Your new brush tip will be added at the end of the Brush Preset picker. "Quick Brush Tips" on page 381 runs through the process of creating and saving brush tips and Brush tool presets.

If your Brush Preset picker gets cumbersome because it has so many brush tips, you can **delete brush tips** one by one by Alt/Option-clicking on the ones you want to remove.

Any brush tip you've added to the Brush Preset picker can be permanently saved, so you can load it again later. To add it to the current set of brush tips, click the ⊙ button on either version of the picker and either choose Save Brushes or choose Preset Manager and choose Brushes as the Preset Type. ▼

FIND OUT MORE

▼ Using the Preset Manager **page 47**

Any brush tip you add to or remove from one version of the Brush Preset picker, is also added to or removed from the others. Once it's in the Picker, you can choose it for any tool that uses brush tips. So that you won't permanently lose brush tips you've added or deleted, Photoshop will always ask whether you want to save the modified set before it lets you replace them by loading a different set.

CYCLING THROUGH BRUSHES

As you paint, you can cycle through the brush tips without in-terrupting your painting to go to the Brush Preset picker:

• Use the > (period) key to cycle forward through the picker.

• Use the < (comma) key to cycle backwards through the picker.

• Shift-> chooses the last (bottom) brush tip, and Shift-< chooses the first (top) brush tip.

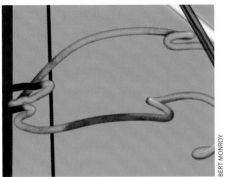

BERT MONROY

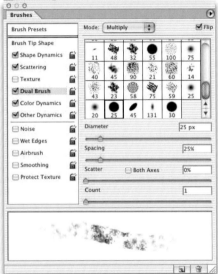

Bert Monroy uses the Dual Brush option in the Brushes palette to create brush tips for applying "urban grime" to the neon tubing in his paintings. After creating a "grunge" brush tip, he turns it into a Dual Brush: He clicks on Dual Brush and chooses a hard round brush tip, setting its diameter to match the brush tip he used for defining the neon tubing in the first place. This confines the grunge within the diameter (for more, see "Bert Monroy Does Neon" on page 397).

USING A TABLET & STYLUS

Using a pressure-sensitive tablet and stylus provides better control of painted strokes, not to mention putting them down faster. If you use a tablet such as the Wacom Intuos, take some time to explore the many settings available for customizing brush-tip behavior.

Within each category of Brushes palette settings (listed below) is a **Control** option. **Pen Pressure**, **Pen Tilt**, and **Stylus Wheel** controls are available for:

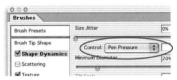

- **Shape Dynamics** – Size, Angle and Roundness of the brush tip
- **Scattering** – Count (how many footprints) and Scattering (how widely distributed)
- **Texture** – Minimum Depth
- **Color Dynamics** – change from Foreground to Background color
- **Other Dynamics** – Opacity and Flow

In the driver software for the stylus itself, you may also want to:

- Set the **top rocker button** on the side of the stylus to act as **Alt/Option**-click so you can easily sample color as you paint.
- Set the **bottom rocker button** to act as the **right-click/Ctrl-click** for bringing up context-sensitive menus.
- Set the **end button** to be the **Eraser**, so you can turn the stylus upside-down and erase as you would with a traditional pencil.

Eraser   Alt/Option-click
Right/Ctrl-click

Both flowers were painted with the Brush tool 🖌 and a Soft Round brush tip, with Hardness adjusted to 25% and spacing to about 30%. For the one on the left (painted with the mouse) we changed the brush tip size often using the bracket keys — [and] . For the one on the right (painted with a tablet and stylus), brush tip size was changed only once, to paint the center; otherwise the stroke width was regulated by Pen Pressure. The biggest difference, though, was that painting with the stylus was much quicker and more natural than controlling the mouse.

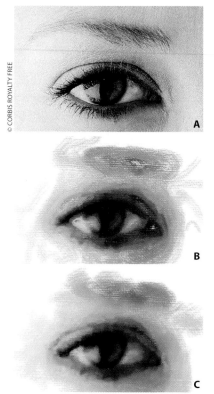

A

B

C

Starting with the same source image **A** and the same brush tip, the Art History Brush 🖌 generates different results depending on the settings in the Options bar. If you change the Style setting from Tight Long **B** to Tight Short **C**, the automated brushing process more closely follows the contours of the source image — good for images with a lot of detail that you want to maintain.

TWO HISTORY BRUSHES

The **Erase To History** option for the Eraser tool 🖌 gives you an easy way to keep two different "History brushes" ready to paint: You can choose a different brush tip for each of the two tools and quickly switch back and forth between them by using the keyboard shortcuts:

E for the Eraser 🖌

Y for the History Brush 🖌

Both brushes will use the same History Snapshot or state for the source.

Tool Presets

Besides brush tip presets, there are more complex *tool presets* for individual painting tools, such as the Brush and Smudge. These are made available in the **Tool Preset picker**, which can be opened by clicking the tool icon at the left end of a tool's Options bar (shown on page 361), or by choosing Window > Tool Presets. By default, the palette shows only the presets for the current tool, but the palette menu offers the option of enlarging it to show all the other tool presets currently loaded in Photoshop as well. The presets for the painting tools include not only a brush tip but also other characteristics set for the tool. For instance, for the Brush tool it can include blend Mode, Opacity, Flow, and even color.

THE ARTISTS' CLONING TOOLS

Photoshop's cloning tools provide a way of reproducing part of the current image, or another image, or a previous stage in the development of the current image. The cloning tools that are of most interest for digital painting are the Art History Brush 🖌 and the Pattern Stamp 🖼 in its Impressionist mode. Many of the choices in the Options bar for the cloning tools are the same as for the painting tools. Other options are specific to the individual tools, as described next.

Pattern Stamp 🖼

With the **Impressionist** option chosen in the Options bar, you can use the Pattern Stamp 🖼 to convert a photo to a "handpainted" work of art. This tool applies brushlike smears of color based on the colors in the original image. The trick to using the Pattern Stamp is to make a "pattern" of your entire image, so the tool can use it as a resource as you lay down each brush stroke. The technique is demonstrated in "Pattern Stamp Watercolors" on page 384, and "Exercising Wow Painting Tools" on page 395 also includes examples.

Art History Brush 🖌

The **Art History Brush** 🖌 is an automated painting tool that lays down a batch of strokes with a single click. The strokes automatically follow the edges of color or contrast in the source chosen in the History palette (Window > Show History). To choose a source, you click in the column to the left of either a Snapshot (one of the versions of the file shown at the top of the palette) or a state (one of the recent steps listed in the lower part of the palette). ▼

FIND OUT MORE

▼ Using the History palette **page 31**

Although their illustration styles are quite different, both Lance Hidy and Steve Conley use solid-color and gradient fills to color their artwork. You can see more of Hidy's work on pages 52 and 412, and more of Conley's in the Chapter 10 "Gallery."

Success with the Art History Brush depends on controlling the tool's automation. This is done partly by choosing the **Style** and **Area** settings in the Options bar to control how long the automated strokes are, how closely they follow the color in the image, and how many strokes are laid down with each click. The **Tolerance** setting controls how different from the source image the current version has to be in order for the Art History Brush to be allowed to paint on it. This means you can preserve some of your recently painted details that are not very different from the History you're painting from, while painting other areas. But for most painting, it works well to leave the Tolerance set at the default setting of 0, so that the Art History Brush can paint over any existing strokes.

With the Art History Brush it's helpful to be able to see the original image as you paint over it, because where you click determines which of the color edges in the source will be given the most weight in determining the shape and color of the strokes that are laid down. "Art History Lessons" starting on page 388 provides step-by-step instructions for taming this tool so the results look "painterly" rather than simply "processed." "Exercising Wow Painting Tools" on page 395 includes examples of using the Art History Brush with the Wow presets that come with the book, which were designed to produce results that look like artists' media on canvas or paper.

History Brush

As the backward-pointing arrow in its icon suggests, the **History Brush** can use a previous version of your image, without painterly effect, as a source, restoring former colors and details stroke-by-stroke. Especially if you plan ahead and save History Snapshots as you paint, this can be a great way to recover if you overwork a part of your painting. Choosing a History source is the same as for the Art History Brush (page 366).

THE FILLING TOOLS

Photoshop's filling tools, the **Paint Bucket** and **Gradient** tools, were originally the only means of applying solid fills or color gradations to a layer or a selected area. In recent versions of the program they've been largely superseded by the Solid Color, Pattern, and Gradient Fill layers, and by the Color, Pattern, and Gradient Overlay effects in Layer Styles. But the original "click-and-fill" tools still have a certain hands-on appeal.

To change the color of a filled area, in the Layers palette, lock the transparency for the layer you want to change. Then refill with the Paint Bucket 🪣 or Gradient ▭. Or choose the Edit > Fill command. Any partial transparency will be maintained, and none of the original color will be left behind.

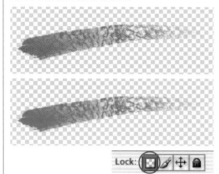

Before (top) and after refilling with transparency locked. No residue of the first color remains.

The Rainbow was "painted" onto this photo with the Gradient tool ▭. The technique is described in "Exercising Gradients" on page 187.

The Smart Blur filter can be used to give an image a painted, cartoonlike look, as on page 258.

Paint Bucket 🪣

The **Paint Bucket** 🪣 can apply a solid color or a pattern. It fills areas that are chosen by sampling the color where you click — either the composite color of all layers (if **All Layers** is turned on in the Options bar) or of only the layer that's active when the tool is used. The **Tolerance** setting determines how closely other pixels have to match the sampled color before they'll be replaced. With the **Contiguous** box checked, clicking with the Paint Bucket replaces pixels that are the same color as *and continuous with* the pixel that you click with the tool's hot spot. With Contiguous turned *off*, all pixels of the sampled color throughout the entire layer or selection will be replaced with the color applied by the Paint Bucket. The edges of the fill can be **Anti-aliased** or not.

Gradient ▭

The **Gradient** tool ▭ fills an entire layer or a selected area with a color gradation. The center and direction of the gradient is controlled by where you drag the tool. In the Options bar you can choose a preset color blend and specify what type of gradient geometry you want — **Linear**, **Radial**, **Angle**, **Reflected**, or **Diamond**. You can also choose whether to **Reverse** the order of the colors, whether to **Dither** (jumbling the pixels slightly at the color transitions to prevent the gradient from appearing as distinct bands of color when it's printed), and whether to take advantage of any **Transparency** that's built into the gradient or simply ignore any built-in transparency and use opaque colors. "Exercising Gradients" on page 187 shows several ways to set up and apply gradients.

Other Fill Options

Besides the Gradient and Paint Bucket tools and the Edit > Fill command, there are two other ways to apply fills:

- You can add a **Fill layer** by choosing from the top of the list when you click the Create New Fill/Adjustment Layer button at the bottom of the Layers palette. Depending on which kind of Fill layer you choose, the entire layer is assigned a

The **Magic Eraser** 🪄, which shares a space in the toolbox with the Eraser, is like a Paint Bucket that "pours" clear transparency instead of color. Like the Paint Bucket, it can "fill" Contiguous or noncontiguous color areas and have Anti-aliased edges or not. It can base its fill region on the composite color or on the color in just one layer.

DEEANNE EDWARDS

Detail of a print made by posterizing an image with the Cutout filter (center) and then outlining with the Posterize Edges filter (bottom) (see page 410 for more about the process)

Some of the Actions on the Wow DVD-ROM are designed to apply painterly treatments to photos (see page 398).

color, pattern, or gradient. The layer includes a layer mask you can modify to control where the fill shows up.

- Still another way to fill an area is to use a Color, Pattern, or Gradient **Overlay effect** as part of a **Layer Style**. This makes it easier to control how the Fill interacts with other effects in the Style, such as glows, drop shadows, and bevels. The Overlay effects are introduced in "Anatomy of a Layer Style" in Chapter 8 and are used in techniques throughout the book.

"PAINTING" WITH FILTERS & ACTIONS

Some of Photoshop's filters (and other filters developed especially to simulate art media in Photoshop) can be useful for stylizing images as artwork. Choosing Filter > **Filter Gallery** opens up several sets of Photoshop filters especially designed for this purpose, such as the **Artistic**, **Brush Strokes**, and **Sketch** sets. Try using these filters as a starting point, combining them in the Filter Gallery, adding painted details, or combining a filtered image with the original. The **Smart Blur** filter can also be useful. You'll find examples of the Photoshop filter effects, along with tips on using them, in "Appendix A: Filter Demos."

For painterly treatments more complex than filter combinations alone, recording an **Action** provides a way to save a process as you develop it, so you can easily apply it to other images. "Quick 'Painting' with Wow Actions" starting on page 398 provides examples of "painterly" effects you can achieve with Actions supplied on the Wow DVD-ROM.

"POST-PROCESSING" A PAINTING

Once you've created a painting, whether from scratch or with some degree of automation, you may want to add an enhancing layer to emphasize the pooling of pigment or the texture of brush strokes or canvas. Applied with the right blend modes, the **Photocopy** and **Find Edges** filters can be useful for darkening the edges of painted areas in watercolors (as shown on pages 387 and 402). The **Emboss** filter can be helpful in thickening the paint for an impasto effect (page 379). And a texture-filled layer can add canvas or paper texture, or complement the texture that's built into the brushes used in the painting (page 373). Some of these techniques have been automated in the Wow-Paint Enhance Actions; you can find demonstrations starting on page 398.

Watercolor Over Ink

YOU'LL FIND THE FILES

in (wow) > Wow Project Files > Chapter 6 > Watercolor Over Ink:

- Watercolor-Before.psd (to start)
- Wow-BT Watercolor.tpl (a tool presets file)
- Wow-Texture 01.asl (a Style presets file)
- Watercolor-After.psd (to compare)

OPEN THESE PALETTES

from the Window menu:

- Tools • Layers • Brushes • Styles

OVERVIEW

Scan a drawing • Put the scan layer in Multiply mode over a white-filled layer • Paint with the Brush tool 🖌 and Wow BT-Watercolor brushes, with colors on separate layers between the background and the scan • Adjust paint colors to taste • Add paper texture and a background wash • Use the Smudge tool 👆 to "run" the "ink" in the drawing

A QUICK ILLUSTRATION STYLE that simulates watercolor over an ink drawing can start with a hand-drawn sketch, as in this case, or with line art created in Illustrator or Photoshop, or with clip art. Like most other artists' media in Photoshop, watercolor is much more flexible and forgiving than the traditional materials. For one thing, you can warp time, separating parts of the process that would occur simultaneously in the traditional medium, or changing the order of the steps in building a painting. You can apply the paint, feeling the watercolors flowing onto the paper, and *then* decide how much you want the ink to run. And you can choose the color for your background wash *after* the foreground colors are in place. For this example, Frankie Frey started with a scan of an original felt-tip pen drawing, and painted with the **Wow-BT Watercolor** presets for the Brush tool. When she had finished painting, the colors were brightened, the ink was smeared where the watery paint had touched it, and a background wash was added.

1 Preparing the drawing. Scan a drawing and do any cleanup work that's necessary ▼, or place or open a clip-art or drawing file **1a**. To develop the painting, this method puts the line work layer on top (so the colors won't obscure it) and in Multiply mode (so the white background is transparent and won't obscure the colors) with the paint on layers beneath it. A "paper" layer is added below the paint layers, and below that, we can keep a spare copy of the cleaned-up drawing **1b**.

FIND OUT MORE

▼ Scanning and cleaning up line art
page 91

1a

The grayscale scan was opened in Photoshop and converted to color (Image > Mode > RGB Color).

1b

As the painting develops, a copy of the drawing is in Multiply mode above the transparent painting layers. A Solid Fill "paper" layer hides a spare copy of the drawing.

USING THE WOW WATERCOLOR PRESETS

You can make a brush larger or smaller by clicking the **"Brush:" button** in the Options bar and resetting the Master Diameter, or by pressing the **bracket keys** as you paint — *]* to enlarge and *[* to shrink. With a pressure-sensitive tablet, applying more **pressure** will enlarge the stroke.

To control the amount of paint, in the Options bar reduce the **Opacity** to decrease the maximum amount of color that can be applied in a stroke; decrease the **Flow** to slow down the rate at which the color builds up to the maximum Opacity. Flow and Opacity for these brushes also increase with stylus pressure.

For **overlapping strokes** whose edges show, make a stroke and release the mouse button (or lift the stylus), and then depress the mouse button or stylus and stroke again.

For a **continuous wash** — to build up color without internal stroke marks — use one continuous stroke, rather than starting and stopping.

Results vary with the **colors** used (light colors tend to show texture less) and with **painting style** (if you paint quickly, you might want to set the Flow higher than if you paint slowly).

To start, duplicate the drawing layer (press Ctrl/⌘-J). Add a white "paper" layer between the new layer and the original by clicking on the *Background* thumbnail in the Layers palette and clicking the "Create a new fill or adjustment layer" button ⬤ at the bottom of the Layers palette, choose Solid Color from the pop-up list, and choose white in the Color Picker; click "OK" to close the Picker.

To leave the ink black but make the white in the top drawing layer appear transparent, so the colors you add next will show through it, click on the top layer's thumbnail to target it, and then choose Multiply from the pop-up list of blend modes in the upper left corner of the Layers palette. Add a transparent layer below this drawing layer to hold the first of the paint (Ctrl/⌘-click the "Create a new layer" button ▣ at the bottom of the palette; the Ctrl/⌘ key will make the new Adjustment layer come in *below* the target layer instead of above it).

2 Painting. Now choose the Brush tool ✐ from the Tools palette. At the left end of the Options bar, click the Tool Preset picker and double-click one of the **Wow-BT Watercolor** presets from the pop-up palette; Frey started with **Medium 2a.** (If you haven't yet loaded the **Wow-Art Media Brushes** presets, the **Wow-BT Watercolor** presets won't appear in the list of tools to choose▼; you can load just the **Wow-BT Watercolor** tools you need for this project by clicking the ⊙ button in the top right corner of the menu, choosing Load Tool Presets, and locating the **Wow BT-Watercolor.tpl** file on the Wow DVD-ROM, in Wow Project Files > Chapter 6 > Watercolor Over Ink.)

FIND OUT MORE

▼ Loading the Wow presets **page 5**

Like traditional watercolor brushes, the **Wow-BT Watercolor** presets are designed to let color flow onto the paper as you hold the brush in one spot, and to build color as you stroke over previously applied paint, as well as simulating the pigment buildup at the edges of wet strokes. The interaction with the paper texture is built into the brushes, so the texture will appear as you paint. Choose a color (one way is to click the Foreground swatch in the Tools palette and use the Color Picker) and begin painting loosely, modifying the brush as needed, keeping in mind the painting tips in "Using the Wow Watercolor Presets" at the left. For maximum flexibility, add a new layer for each new color.

For this painting Frey started with the **Wow-BT Watercolor-Medium** preset, making it slightly smaller and reducing the Opacity and Flow in the Options bar to make the color thinner

2a

Choosing the medium-size **Wow-BT Watercolor** Brush from the Tool Preset picker

2b

Reducing the Opacity in the Options bar (to about 50%) while keeping the Flow high (100%), Frey could paint smoothly, building color by layering strokes, as in the pink flower on the left. With Flow reduced (25%) and Opacity high (100%), the paint pools, and the texture is more obvious, as in the flower on the right.

2c

For the watering can and the plaid on the couch, Frey reduced Opacity in the Options bar somewhat (75%), keeping the Flow low (25%); she painted the blue stripes on one layer and the pink stripes on a layer above.

and to control the buildup **2b**. As she painted, she switched to other sizes of Wow-BT Watercolor brushes, modified the Opacity and Flow, and added more layers **2c, 2d**. With elements on different layers, you can make the paint more transparent by reducing a layer's Opacity. Or, to make the paint denser, duplicate the layer (Ctrl/⌘-J) and adjust the Opacity of this extra layer to get the color density you want. Where strokes of different colors overlap, you can load your brush with the mixed color as described in "Sampling Color" below.

SAMPLING COLOR

For the painting and filling tools — Brush, Pencil, Paint Bucket, and Gradient — holding down the **Alt/Option key toggles to the Eyedropper** tool so you can sample color, changing the Foreground color by clicking. You can also add the **Caps Lock** key to toggle the precise cursor on or off for sampling. The area sampled — Point Sample (a single pixel), 3 by 3 Average, or 5 by 5 Average — is determined by the current Sample Size setting in the Options bar for the actual Eyedropper tool.

3 Collecting layers. To reduce the working file size, you can combine some layers. Where colors overlap (as in the plaid on the sofa), it's a good idea to keep the layers separate so you can control the colors independently in case you want to make changes. But where elements don't overlap, you can combine them, because if you need to change something later, you'll be able to isolate each element with a selection. To combine layers:

• In CS, target one of the layers in the Layers palette, and for the others click in the column to the right of the 👁 to link

2d

For the clothing, she used a medium Opacity (around 50%) and a low Flow (25% or less).

3

To reduce working file size, layers whose elements don't overlap are linked in preparation for merging into a single layer in Photoshop CS. In CS2 you can target several layers at once, without linking, and then merge them. Renaming the layers helps keep track of the elements of the painting (double-click the name and then type a new one).

4

Before (top) and after brightening the colors with a masked Hue/Saturation Adjustment layer.

5

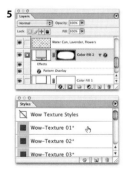

A masked Solid Color layer creates a background wash. The **Wow-Texture 01*** Layer Style applies a texture similar to the one in the Wow-BT Watercolor Brush presets.

them. Then merge them (choose Layer > Merge Linked, or press Ctrl/⌘-E) **3**.

- In CS2, target all of the layers you want to combine by clicking the thumbnail of one of them in the Layers palette and then Shift-clicking or Ctrl/⌘-clicking to target the others as well. (Shift-click to target all layers between what's already targeted and the layer you click; Ctrl/⌘-click to target additional layers one by one. Shift-click and Ctrl/⌘-click are toggles; so using them on targeted layers releases the layers from targeting.)

4 Brightening up the color. Frey targeted the top paint layer (just below the ink drawing layer) by clicking its thumbnail in the Layers palette, and then added a Hue/Saturation Adjustment layer by clicking the ⦿ button at the bottom of the palette and choosing Hue/Saturation. In the Hue/Saturation dialog box she moved the Saturation slider to the right (to +30) and clicked "OK." Then, since the shirt now seemed too bright, she chose one of Photoshop's default soft brush tips (from the palette of brush tips that pops up when you click the "Brush:" button in the Options bar) to paint the Hue/Saturation layer's built-in mask with black to hide the effect in the shirt area **4**. (When a mask is active, you can make black the Foreground color by typing D for "Default" and then X for "eXchange.")

5 Adding a background wash. To put in a background wash of color, add another Solid Color layer: In the Layers palette, target the white layer near the bottom of the layer stack. To add a Solid Color layer above it, click the ⦿ button, and choose Solid Color; choose a light, fairly neutral color from the Color Picker and click "OK." (This color will "fill in" all white areas; if you want to leave some areas white, you can mask them as described below.) Now add paper texture to match the texture in the brush strokes on the paint layers: In the Styles palette, click the ⊙ button in the upper right corner of the palette, choose **Wow-Texture Styles** from the list, and then click on **Wow-Texture 01*** in the palette **5**. (If you haven't yet loaded the Wow presets,▼ the **Wow-Texture Styles** won't appear in the list. To load just the texture you need for this painting, you can choose Load Styles and navigate to **Wow Texture 01.asl**, located in the folder with the other files for this project.)

This is similar to the pattern that's built into the **Wow-BT Watercolor** brushes and will match the painted strokes. To give the wash a soft, irregular shape, we chose the 100-pixel

FIND OUT MORE

▼ Loading the Wow Presets **page 5**

soft tip from the "Brush:" pop-up and painted the built-in mask on the Solid Color layer with black at the edges.

6 "Running" the ink. To create the "bleed" for the water-soluble ink, in the Layers palette click on the "Background copy" layer's thumbnail to target the layer. Then choose the Smudge tool and choose a soft brush tip from the "Brush:" list; we chose the 17-pixel soft brush and reduced its Strength to about 50% in the Options bar. Make sure the "Use All Layers" and "Finger Painting" options are turned *off*. To make it easier to "bleed" a wider segment of the line with a single stroke, you can flatten the brush: In the Brushes palette, click on "Brush Tip Shape" in the list on the left and in the shape diagram, drag down on the top handle to a Roundness of about 50% **6a**.

In the painting, look for an area where the paint touches or crosses the line work. Touch the cursor to the line and drag downward to "run" the ink. If you start *on* the line rather than *above* it, the ink will bleed but the line itself will remain. If you start above the line and drag down through it, the line will be smeared away. If the result of your first "running" experiment is too strong or not strong enough, undo (Ctrl/⌘-Z); then adjust the Strength, brush tip size, or brush roundness, and try again. Run the ink at other points on the line work as well **6b**.

Even after the painting is complete, there are many ways to experiment with changes. **To increase the density of the line work,** in the Layers palette, unlock the *Background* by double-clicking its name and clicking "OK"; then drag it to the top of the stack, put it in Multiply mode, and adjust layer Opacity to taste. You can **paint details** on additional transparent layers. Or **change the paper or the wash** by double-clicking the Solid Color layer's thumbnail in the Layers palette and choosing a new color.

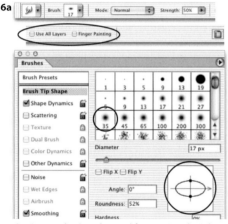

Setting up the Smudge tool for running the ink

6b

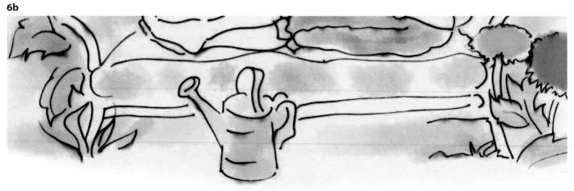

Dragging downward on the line work creates the impression of blurred ink.
The completed painting is shown at the top of page 370.

Cher Threinen-Pendarvis Picks Some Winners

"IF YOU TAKE A PEEK inside the Brushes preset libraries that ship with Photoshop, you'll discover some real gems," says Cher Threinen-Pendarvis, author of *The Photoshop and Painter Artist Tablet Book,* which we recommend if you're serious about painting with the computer. Here Cher shows us some of her favorite native Photoshop brushes. To paint these sample strokes, she used the Brush tool 🖌 and a Wacom Intuos tablet. "You won't get this kind of performance with a mouse," says Cher.

For more tips from Cher on painting in Photoshop, check out the excerpt from *The Photoshop and Painter Artist Tablet Book: Creative Techniques for Digital Painting* (Artist Tablet Book.pdf) in the Wow Goodies folder on the Wow DVD-ROM.

For sketching, the "Hard Round 5 pixels" preset is located right in the Photoshop default Brushes presets. It's nice for varying the thickness of line work, and it responds quickly, keeping up with the motion of the brush.

"Hard Round 5 pixels" in its default Normal mode

The "#2 Pencil" is from Photoshop's Dry Media brushes (see the tip below). For the sample strokes below, medium gray simulates graphite. This brush is useful for methodical drawing, but its complex controls (such as the Dual Brush setting) can make its performance lag if you want to sketch quickly.

"#2 Pencil" in its default Normal mode

To work in watercolor, the "Watercolor Loaded Wet Flat Tip" preset, one of the default brush presets, is useful for calligraphic line work, such as painting details in foliage, or flow lines on water. It's a Dual Brush, so it doesn't have the quickest performance, but it produces great strokes when you're painting methodically.

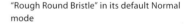

"Watercolor Loaded Wet Flat Tip" in its default Normal mode

To simulate the transparent look of conventional watercolor, try changing the blend mode of the "Watercolor Loaded Wet Flat Tip" to Multiply in the Options bar.

"Watercolor Loaded Wet Flat Tip" using Multiply mode

The "Rough Round Bristle" (in Photoshop's default brush set) is fun to paint with because it applies different values of the Foreground color. It's useful for laying in large areas of paint, and for adding texture over existing paint. The streaked bristle effect results from the Color Burn mode that's built into its Dual Brush settings.

"Rough Round Bristle" in its default Normal mode

If you want to paint semi-transparent washes, change the blend mode from Normal to Multiply in the Options bar.

"Rough Round Bristle" using Multiply mode

You can simulate the look of pastel or chalk with the "Pastel Medium Tip" preset from the Dry Media Brushes (see the tip at the left). With this expressive brush, you can achieve a subtle layering of color and texture.

"Pastel Medium Tip" in its default Normal mode

LOADING AN ALTERNATE BRUSH LIBRARY

To load a different set of Brushes presets — such as Dry Media, one of the libraries that's installed with Photoshop — click the brush footprint on the Options bar and then click the ▶ in the upper right corner of the pop-out palette, and choose from the list. When the dialog box appears, clicking "OK" replaces the current presets with the set you chose; this keeps the list shorter and more manageable than if you choose "Append." (If you've added or modified brushes in the default set, you'll be warned to save the set before you replace it.)

JH DAVIS

Painting "Wet on Wet"

YOU'LL FIND THE FILES

in 🔵 > Wow Project Files > Chapter 6 > Wet Paint:
- Wet Paint-Before.psd (to start)
- Wow-Wet Paint.pat (a Pattern presets file)
- Wet Paint-After.psd (to compare)

OPEN THESE PALETTES

from the Window menu:
- Tools • Layers • Brushes

OVERVIEW

Adjust color and crop • Add a noise pattern layer in Overlay mode, a "ground" canvas layer, and an empty layer for painting • Paint with the Smudge tool 👋 • Add an embossed copy of the painting in Overlay mode • Add more brush texture with a Pattern Fill layer

WHEN PAINTERS WORK "WET ON WET" in oils or acrylics, their brushes pick up color from previous strokes, and the colors mix. Wet-on-wet painting tends to be informal and quick, as the artist seeks to capture the light in a landscape painted on-site. The paint stays wet during the painting process, and in order to keep the colors pure, it has to be put on thick. Photoshop's Smudge tool will be a responsive "brush," and the painting experience can be spontaneous, as long as you have a powerful enough computer and you work with the Smudge tool *at 100% Strength*; lower Strength settings require the computer to do even more calculation, and the painting will lag behind your brush strokes. A pressure-sensitive tablet and stylus also make the process more like traditional painting, giving the strokes more personality as the pressure you apply to the stylus scales each stroke on the fly.

1 Preparing an image for painting. Choose an image and adjust the color and crop to taste, or open **Wet Paint Before.psd 1a**. To variegate the "paint" so your brush strokes will show bristle marks, add a Pattern Fill layer with one of the **Wow-Noise Patterns** presets (as described in the next paragraph). We used the **Wow-Noise Small Strong Gray** preset as the pattern, but others, such as the Wow-Reticulation (from the Wow-Media Patterns presets) also work well; or if your image has a lot of small-scale color variability, you may not need to add to it.

1a

The original photo

1b

Alt/Option-clicking the "Create new fill or adjustment layer" button ⊘ opens a menu, where you can choose Pattern.

1c

Putting the Pattern Fill layer in Overlay mode

1d

The **Wow-Noise Small Strong Gray** pattern is chosen as the Pattern Fill.

1e

Before (left) and after adding **Wow-Noise Small Strong Gray** in the Pattern Fill layer in Overlay mode

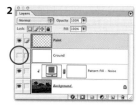

2

The canvas (or "ground") and paint layers added to the file, with the ground layer's visibility turned off during painting

To add a pattern-filled layer to introduce color variability, Alt/Option-click the "Create new fill or adjustment layer" button ⊘ at the bottom of the Layers palette and choose Pattern from the pop-up list **1b** (the Alt/Option key will cause the New Layer dialog box to open as the layer is added). In the New Layer dialog **1c** choose Overlay for the Mode (you can also turn on the "Use Previous Layer to Create Clipping Mask" option; with the way the painting will be structured, grouping won't affect your painting, but it can help to visually organize the Layers palette).

When you click "OK" in the New Layer dialog, the Pattern Fill dialog will open **1d**. Click the tiny triangle next to the pattern swatch to open the palette of patterns. Then click the palette's ⊙ button and choose the **Wow-Noise Patterns** from the pop-up menu. (If you haven't yet loaded the Wow presets ▼, the Wow-Noise Patterns won't appear in the menu. To load just the patterns associated with this painting technique — several Noise patterns to choose from and some impasto patterns for step 6 — you can choose Load Styles and navigate to **Wow-Wet Paint Noise.pat** (in Wow Project Files > Chapter 6 > Wet Paint). Then choose **Wow-Noise Small Strong Gray** (or another noise pattern) from the palette **1e**.

> **VIEWING PATTERN NAMES**
>
> If you don't see names in the Patterns palette — only swatches — you can display the names also by clicking the ⊙ button in the upper right corner of the palette and choosing Small List.

> **FIND OUT MORE**
>
> ▼ Loading the Wow presets **page 5**

2 Preparing the canvas and paint layers. At the bottom of the Layers palette, click the "Create a new layer" button ⬚ and fill this new layer with the color you want for your canvas. For example, open the Swatches palette (Window > Swatches), and click white as we did, or black, or a color that contrasts with the colors in your image; then press Alt/Option-Delete to fill the layer. We renamed the layer by double-clicking on its name in the Layers palette and typing "Ground."

Click the ⬚ button again. Leave this new layer empty. It will hold the brush strokes you paint. Turn off visibility for the "Ground" layer by clicking its ◉ icon at the left edge of the Layers palette **2**. (If you didn't do this, the Smudge tool, which you'll be using to paint, would sample the canvas color instead of the image-and-noise composite underneath; you'll make the canvas visible again later.)

3 Setting up to paint. Choose the Smudge tool 👆 from the Tools palette. In the Options bar leave Normal as the Mode, set

3a

Setting the options for the Smudge tool

3b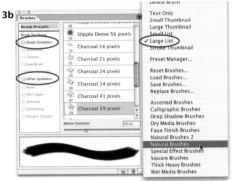

The Charcoal brushes are found in the Natural Media set that comes with Photoshop.

4a

A detail of the painting in progress. With visibility for the "Ground" layer turned off (top), it's hard to tell where there are gaps in the paint, since the original image shows through from below. With the "Ground" layer's visibility turned on, it's easy to see where the gaps are.

the Strength at 100%, and turn *on* the Use All Layers/Sample All Layers option **3a**; this will let you paint on the transparent top layer, but sample color from all the visible layers below. Also make sure that "Finger Painting" is turned *off*. In the expanded Brushes palette (by default, pressing F5 opens it), make some changes **3b**: In the list at the left, click **"Shape Dynamics"** — the name, not the check box — to open that section of the palette. If you have a pressure-sensitive tablet and stylus, for the top **"Control:"** option (it controls **Size**) choose **Pen Pressure** (strokes will get bigger as you apply more pressure); if you don't have a tablet, you can choose Off. Next, in the list at the left, click on "Other Dynamics" and for the bottom "Control:" (for **Strength**) choose **Pen Pressure** (the paint smear will be more dense with more pressure); again, if you don't have a tablet, choose Off. Click the ⓘ button in the upper right corner of the palette, and choose a set of brushes to use; we chose the **Natural Brushes**. A Caution box will open. If you click the "Append" button, this set of brush tips will be added to the current menu of brush tips; if you click "OK," they will instead replace the current brush tips.

4 Painting. Now choose a fairly large brush tip from the Natural Brushes; we chose **Charcoal 59 pixels**. Check "Tips for Painting with the Smudge Tool" below, and then drag with the Smudge tool to paint. As you paint, turn on the "Ground" layer's

---

TIPS FOR PAINTING WITH THE SMUDGE TOOL

• To make the best use of the color and shapes in the source image, **keep your strokes short** so that you sample color frequently.

• To add detail, **switch to smaller brushes** in the set you've chosen.

• As you apply strokes, you may find it easier to make more natural gestural movements if you **flip or rotate the canvas** (Image > Rotate Canvas > Flip Canvas Horizontal or Flip Canvas Vertical; or Image > Rotate Canvas > 90° CW or 90° CCW). This flips or rotates the entire image — all layers at once. And because the changes are in multiples of 90°, the image won't be degraded.

• If you add noise with a Pattern Fill layer in Overlay mode in order to make bristle marks (see step 1 on page 376), the variation in color created by the noise shows up very well in the midtones. But it doesn't show up in the lightest or darkest areas of the image. You can fix this if you temporarily **change the Pattern Fill layer's blend mode** to Multiply when you paint highlights or Screen for the shadows, and also reduce the Pattern Fill layer's Opacity. When you finish the very light or dark areas, be sure to return to Overlay mode and raise the Opacity again.

4b

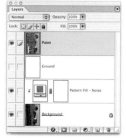

Roughing-in the fence, with the canvas rotated to make stroking easier. The detail is shown here with visibility of the "Ground" layer turned off (left) and turned on.

4c

The blend mode for the "Pattern Fill-Noise" layer was temporarily changed to Screen to introduce color variation in the dark slats of the fence. The detail is shown here with visibility of the "Ground" layer turned off (left) and turned on.

4d

To fill the intentional gaps in the painting, we used the Brush to apply accent colors to the "Ground" layer. A detail of the layer is shown here, viewed alone.

visibility from time to time by clicking in its 👁 column. This hides the original image and noise so you can check the progress of your painting **4a**, **4b**, **4c**. To liven up the painting, you can intentionally leave unpainted gaps between your strokes and then add contrasting color, as follows: Click the "Ground" layer's thumbnail in the Layers palette to target the layer and turn on its visibility. Choose your first accent color (for instance, by clicking the Foreground color swatch in the Tools palette and choosing from the Color Picker). Looking at both "Ground" and paint layers as you paint on "Ground," you can quickly use the Brush tool on the "Ground" layer to "fill the holes" in your painting **4d**, **4e**.

5 Adding an "impasto" effect. You can make your paint look like it was thickly applied (using an impasto technique) by making a copy of your finished painting and using it to "emboss" your brush strokes, as follows: Target the paint layer (click on its thumbnail in the Layers palette) and add a new combined copy above it by using these four-fingered keyboard shortcuts — hold down Ctrl-Shift-Alt (Windows) or ⌘-Shift-Option (Mac) as you type first N (to add a layer) and then E (to turn the new layer into a merged copy); in CS2 you can skip the N if you like.

Change the new layer's blend mode to Overlay and desaturate the layer (Image > Adjustments > Desaturate). Then run the

4e

With all layers visible, the painted ground fills gaps in the painting.

5a

Embossing a combined, desaturated copy of the image

Emboss filter (Filter > Stylize > Emboss) **5a**. In Overlay mode the 50% gray in the layer will become invisible, and the darker and lighter tones of the embossing will "raise" the brush strokes, giving them an impasto look **5b**. Even after you close the Emboss dialog, you can experiment with the look. Try adjusting the Opacity of the layer or changing the blend mode to Soft Light.

6 Enhancing the impasto. To further fool the eye, you can experiment with adding more hand-painted strokes. Create another Pattern Fill layer in Overlay mode (as in step 1), but this time leave the "Use Previous Layer to Create Clipping Mask" option unchecked and fill with one of the **Wow-Canvas + Brush Overlay** patterns, which are seamlessly repeating patterns made from scans of real brush strokes on real canvas; we used **Wow-Canvas + Brush Overlay-Medium 6a**. (You can choose from the **Wow-Wet Paint** patterns from step 1, or load **Wow-Media Pattern**s.)▼ In the Layers palette, experiment with the Opacity slider for the Layer to get the degree of texture you like.

FIND OUT MORE

▼ Loading the Wow presets **page 5**

If you don't like the way some of the strokes in the pattern fall on your image, just paint with black on the mask for the new Fill layer, using the same kind of brush used for your image **6b**. (When a mask is active, you can make black the Foreground color by typing D for "Default" and then X for "eXchange.") *Wow*

A close-up of the painting, with the embossed "Impasto" layer in Overlay mode at 100% Opacity

6a

6b

A Pattern Fill layer of thickly painted strokes (a detail is shown here alone) is added in Overlay mode, to provide more brush detail.

A detail of the finished painting that appears at the top of page 376. The Pattern Fill layer in Overlay mode adds texture. Its built-in mask is painted with black to hide the brush strokes in some areas.

Q U I C K

Brush Tips

Can't find the perfect brush for the job? Here's a method for making your own very simple brush tip and using it to make a Brush tool ✐ preset. For more variation in the stroke, experiment with the Jitter settings in the various Brushes palette panels as you design the brush tip (steps 1–4). And if you have a pressure-sensitive tablet, try building in some Control settings that can take advantage of the stylus.

MAKING SEVERAL SIZES

When you make a brush tip, consider making a "matched set" in two or three sizes. Even if you don't need them now, having a complete set may come in handy in the future.

It's easy to enlarge or shrink a single brush tip as you paint (in the Brush Preset picker or with the bracket keys). But when you do that, not only do you change the footprint size (which is what you want to happen), but if you enlarge the brush tip quite a bit, it can begin to look pixelated, and if you shrink it a lot, it can lose its bristle detail.

It's easier to make three sizes of related brush tips all at once than to make one and then try to match it in a different size later.

1 Making a Footprint

To start a brush from scratch, open a new Photoshop file with the default white *Background.* Choose the Brush tool ✐ and one of the **soft round brush tip** presets (click the icon next to "Brush" in the Options bar to open the Brush Preset picker; we used the 65-pixel tip). Also in the Options bar set the Mode to **Dissolve**. As you'll see when you click in the working window, Dissolve mode turns the soft, semitransparent brush tip into a scattering of dots. These will become the bristles of your new brush tip. Click the Foreground color square in the Tools palette and click on a dark gray. Then click once in the working window. Repeat the process for as many sizes of brush tips as you want to make; we made additional footprints with the 21-pixel tip and the 45-pixel tip.

2 Editing the Tip

"Soften" the footprint (Filter > Blur > **Gaussian Blur**; we used a Radius of 0.5). To reshape the footprint, **remove some of the bristles** with the Eraser ✐ — in the Options bar choose Brush for the Mode and choose a small brush tip (you can pop out the Brush Preset picker from the Eraser's Options bar). Try varying the Hardness and Opacity settings for the Eraser to vary the type of basic footprint you're making.

3 Capturing the Tip

Drag-select the brush footprint with the Rectangular Marquee tool ⬚. Then choose Edit > **Define Brush Preset**. In the Brush Name dialog box, give your creation a name. The new brush tip will be added as the last one in the Brush Preset picker. **Deselect** (Ctrl/⌘-D).

Now if you **choose a painting tool**, such as the Brush ✐, you can **access your new brush tip** from the Options bar or the Brush Presets panel of the Brushes palette, or by right/Ctrl-clicking in the working window. Click on its thumbnail to choose it. **Choose a color** (one way is to click the Foreground swatch in the Tools palette and use the Color Picker). Change the Mode in the Options bar back to **Normal**, and paint to **test the stroke**.

4 Refining the Stroke

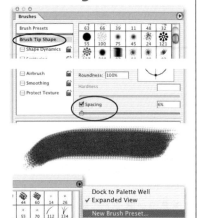

If the stroke isn't as smooth or brushlike as you want, open the Brushes palette (one way is to click the "Toggle the **Brushes palette**" button 🔲 on the Options bar). Click **Brush Tip Shape** in the list on the left side of the palette. For a smoother stroke, **lower the Spacing** setting, but keep in mind that the lower the setting, the slower the brush will operate. This can cause a delay between when you paint the stroke and when it appears on-screen, which interferes with the "natural media" feel of painting. We settled on a setting of 6%.

To save the modified spacing as part of the brush tip, click the palette's ▶ button and choose **New Brush Preset** from the menu, give the preset a new name, and click "OK."

Now that you have one variation of your basic footprint, you might like to try some of the other panels in the Brushes palette. Rather than starting a new brush tip from scratch, vary the **Angle** and **Roundness** (in Brush Tip Shape) for a more calligraphic brush, or experiment with **Color Dynamics** or the **Airbrush** toggle. Be sure to save any result you like as a New Brush Preset.

MAKING A "PICTURE" BRUSH

Photoshop's brush tips aren't limited to imitating traditional painting tools. You can make a custom tip that lays down multiples of a symbol or picture instead of a continuous painting stroke.

Photoshop's Scattered Maple Leaves brush tip distributes its symbols according to the settings in the **Scattering** panel of the Brushes palette. Size Jitter, Angle Jitter, and Roundness **Jitter** settings in the **Shape Dynamics** panel create the variation in size, orientation, and shape. **Hue Jitter** in the **Color Dynamics** panel creates the color variation. See page 364 for more.

For a "dotted line" brush, we used the Brush tool 🖌 and a hard round brush tip chosen from the Brush Preset picker. In the Brush Tip Shape panel of the Brushes palette we set **Spacing** to 200%. We painted on a new layer and applied **Wow-Gold** from the **Wow-Metal Styles** to the layer.▼

To paint a trail of arrowheads, we used Photoshop's **Custom Shape** tool 🐾, first clicking the "Fill pixels" button in the Options bar, to make a mark on the *Background*. We drag-selected the mark with the Rectangular Marquee [ ] and chose Edit > Define Brush. In the Brushes palette we set Spacing at 120%, and in the **Shape Dynamics** panel we chose **Direction** for **Angle Control** so the arrows would follow the stroke. We painted on a new layer and applied **Wow-Clear Red** from the **Wow-Plastic Styles.**

FIND OUT MORE

▼ Using Layer Styles
page 44

5 Adding Texture

With built-in texture the stroke reveals the surface of the "canvas." Click on the word **Texture** in the Brushes palette's list of panels, and click the pattern swatch to open the palette of pattern choices. Click the ▶ button to access more pattern sets. We chose **Wow-Media Patterns** to replace the current patterns, and chose the **Wow-Canvas Texture 02** texture from the palette. (If you haven't yet loaded the Wow presets,▼ you won't see the Wow-Media Patterns in the palette's list of choices.)

Paint a stroke with the texture you've added. Then experiment in the Texture panel with the **Scale**, the "**Texture Each Tip**" toggle, and the **Mode** and **Depth** settings; we used a Scale of 50%, with "Texture Each Tip" turned off, Subtract for the Mode, and Depth set at 30%.

FIND OUT MORE

▼ Loading the Wow
presets **page 5**

A CUSTOM SWATCHES PALETTE

To save a customized palette of colors — perhaps for a series of related paintings or illustrations — open the Swatches palette (Window > Swatches) and clear out the colors you don't want: Hold down the Alt/Option key to bring up the Scissors cursor, and click on each unwanted swatch to remove it.

To add a swatch, choose a color:

- Choose the Eyedropper tool 🖊 and sample a color from any open Photoshop file.
- Or click the Foreground swatch in the Tools palette and choose from the Color Picker.
- Or use the Color palette (Window > Color) to mix a color with the sliders or sample from the spectrum bar.

After choosing a color, add it to the Swatches by moving the cursor into the empty space beyond the last swatch in the palette (the cursor will turn into a Paint Bucket 🪣). "Pour" a new swatch by clicking (or Alt/Option-clicking to skip the swatch-naming dialog box).

When you've added all the colors you want, save the custom Swatches palette: Click the ⊙ button to open the palette menu and choose Save Swatches.

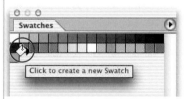

Cher Threinen-Pendarvis started with Photoshop's default Swatches palette and deleted all swatches except black, white, and several grays. To build her custom palette, she sampled from a color-enhanced photo reference (see page 394).

6 Saving Brush Tips

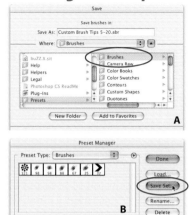

A

B

To permanently save a brush tip as part of a set (or library) of brush tips that you can choose and reload later, you have two options:

- **To save a set of all** of the brush tips currently in the Brush Preset picker, choose Save Brushes from the Brushes palette's menu, name the set, navigate to the location where you want to save it, and click "Save." (Saving the set in Photoshop's Brushes folder **A** will ensure that its name appears in the Brushes palette menu, which makes the brush tips easy to find and load later.)

- **To save only some** of the brush tips currently in the Brushes palette, choose Brush Presets from the list on the left of the Brushes palette, then click the palette's ⊙ button and choose Preset Manager from the menu. In the Preset Manager dialog **B** (shown above), Shift-select or Ctrl/⌘-select any brush tips you want to save as part of the set, and click Save Set; give the set a name, and click "OK." (To save time, if you want to save more brush tips from the current set than you want to delete, you can select the few you want to delete, click the "Delete" button, and then Select All (Ctrl/⌘-A) and click "Save Set."

7 Saving Tool Presets

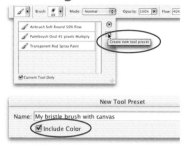

A *Tool preset* for a painting or cloning tool can include not only a brush tip but also the characteristics of the particular tool. As an example, we can save the brush tip we built in steps 1 through 5 in a Brush tool 🖊 preset.

With the Brush tool chosen, make choices in the Options bar for the default Mode, Opacity, and Flow, and set the Airbrush toggle 🖌 on or off, testing the stroke as you experiment. We reduced the Flow to 40% to show the bristle marks and turned on the Airbrush feature so paint could build up.

When you have a tool you want to save, click the icon at the far left end of the Options bar to open the **Tool Preset picker**, as shown above. Click the "Create new tool preset" button 🔲 and give the preset a name; if you want to "preload" your Brush with the Foreground color, use the check box to turn on that feature (Background color will also be included if your brush tip uses Foreground/Background Jitter). When you click the "OK" button, the new preset will appear in the Tool Preset picker, alphabetically by name. To save a set of custom tools permanently, use the **Preset Manager** as in step 6, choosing Tools instead of Brushes.

Open a copy of an image and try out other tools that use brush tips. If you find that your new brush tip makes an interesting Clone Stamp 🖌 or Eraser 🧹, for example, save it as a preset for that tool also.

JHDAVIS

Pattern Stamp Watercolors

TO TURN A FAVORITE PHOTO into a believable watercolor, try
the Pattern Stamp tool 🖏. One of two cloning tools, the Pattern Stamp provides more control than the other cloner, the
Art History Brush. With the Pattern Stamp you paint stroke-by-stroke, pulling color, but not detail, from the source image.

1 Preparing the photo. Choose the photo you want to turn
into a painting — use **Pattern Stamp-Before.psd** from the Wow
DVD or use an RGB photo file of your own **1a**. If you're starting with a photo of your own, here are some changes you might
want to make:

- If you want bright colors in your painting, exaggerate the color
  and contrast in your photo. For instance, choose Image >
  Adjustments > Hue/Saturation and increase Saturation.

- If you want your painting to have an "unfinished edges" look,
  add a white border: Type D for "default colors" to make white
  the Background color. Then choose Image > Canvas Size
  (in CS2 there's a keyboard shortcut — Ctrl-Alt-C in Windows, or ⌘-Option-C on the Mac) and increase the Height
  and Width **1b**.

2 Loading "paint" into the brush. To make the photo the
source for painting with the Pattern Stamp, define the entire
exaggerated image as a Pattern by choosing Edit > Define Pattern. In the Pattern Name dialog box, type in a name and click
"OK" **2a**.

1a

The original "before" image

1b

The prepared image with exaggerated colors and white border. This is **Pattern Stamp-Before.psd.**

2a

In the Pattern Name dialog box, type in a name and click "OK."

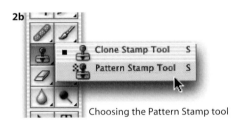

2b

Choosing the Pattern Stamp tool

2c

"Loading" the Pattern Stamp tool with the pattern

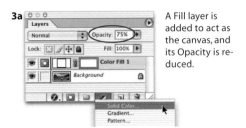

3a

A Fill layer is added to act as the canvas, and its Opacity is reduced.

Now set up this new Pattern as the cloning source for the painting: Choose the Pattern Stamp ⬚ from the Tools palette (it shares a space with the Clone Stamp ⬚) **2b**. In the Pattern Stamp's Options bar, click the little arrow to the right of the Pattern swatch to open the palette of samples; then find your new pattern's thumbnail at the end of the palette and click it. Also in the Options bar, make sure the Aligned and Impressionist options are checked **2c**.

3 Making a "canvas" (or painting surface) layer. This step will add a surface layer above your image to make a foundation for your painting and to serve as a visual barrier between the photo and the painting layer, so you'll be able to see your brush strokes clearly as your painting develops. One way to add the canvas layer is to click the "Create new fill or adjustment layer" button ⬚ at the bottom of the Layers palette, then choose Solid Color and click on white in the Color Picker. When the new layer appears in the Layers palette, reduce its Opacity **3a** so you can see the photo through it **3b**.

FILL LAYER EFFICIENCY

When you need a solid-color layer, one reason to use a Fill Layer rather than a regular transparent layer filled with color is that a Fill Layer doesn't increase file size or occupy RAM.

4 Preparing a paint layer and painting. Click the "Create a new layer" button ⬚ at the bottom of the Layers palette to add a transparent layer for painting. Then, with the Pattern Stamp ⬚ still chosen, at the left end of the Options bar, click the Tool Preset picker **4a** and double-click one of the **Wow-PS Watercolor presets** ("PS" stands for "Pattern Stamp"); we started with the **Medium** version of the tool. If you haven't yet loaded the **Wow-Pattern Stamp** presets, ▼ the **Wow-PS Watercolor** presets

3b

With the canvas layer's Opacity reduced, the photo is visible as a reference for painting.

FIND OUT MORE

▼ Loading the Wow presets **page 5**

4a Choosing a **Wow-PS Watercolor** preset to start the painting

4b

The painting in progress, shown with the Solid Color layer's Opacity set at 75% (top) and at 100%

5a

The Pattern Stamp painting is completed.

won't appear in the list of tools to choose; you can load just the **Wow-PS Watercolor** tools you need for this project by clicking the ⊙ button in the top right corner of the Picker, choosing Load Tool Presets, and navigating to the **Wow PS-Watercolor.tpl** file on the Wow DVD-ROM (in Wow Project Files > Chapter 6 > Pattern Stamp Watercolors).

Begin painting, keeping these pointers in mind:

- In general, start with a larger brush tip and then paint with smaller ones as you add finer details.

- Make brush strokes that follow the color and shape contours of the original. Just as in a real watercolor, don't let colors touch, or the details will blur as the "paint" colors run together. If you need to keep some of the edges "crisp," paint that section on a separate layer.

> **VARYING THE BRUSH SIZE**
>
> A pressure-sensitive tablet with a stylus definitely gives you a better feel and more options for controlling a brush than if you use a mouse. But even with a mouse, you can vary the size of the brush tip. Keep your fingers on the keyboard's bracket keys and toggle the brush size up (tap `]`) or down (tap `[`).

- To imitate a single-color watercolor wash, use one continuous stroke over an area, rather than starting and stopping.

- If paint builds up too much, so the paper texture doesn't show as much as you'd like, try reducing the Flow in the Pattern Stamp's Options bar.

From time to time, temporarily increase the Opacity of the Solid Color layer back to 100% to hide the original image completely so you can see how the painting is developing **4b**.

5 Enhancing the painting. When the painting is complete **5a**, you may want to try one of these techniques to further enhance the natural media effect:

- To increase the density of the color, target the paint layer by clicking its thumbnail in the Layers palette, and then duplicate it (Ctrl/⌘-J) **5b**. This extra layer will build up any strokes that are partially transparent, so it's especially effective for watercolor paintings. If the color is now too strong, you can reduce the Opacity of this top layer. When you have the color intensity you want, you can merge the two paint layers together as we did (with the top paint layer targeted, press Ctrl/⌘-E.)

- You can make the paper texture more apparent by applying the **Wow-Texture 01*** Style to the paint layer **5c**. This Style

5b

Duplicating the paint layer increases the density of the paint.

5c

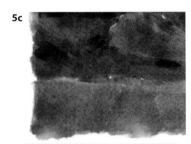

The **Wow-Texture 01*** Layer Style is applied to the merged paint layer. The Style uses Overlay mode to apply the same canvas pattern that's built into the **Wow-PS Watercolor** brushes. In Overlay mode the 50% gray in the pattern has no effect. But the lighter and darker grays lighten and darken the paint to create the canvas pattern. (To see the pattern that's at work here, in the Layers palette double-click the Pattern Overlay entry for your merged paint layer.)

uses the same tiling watercolor paper pattern that's built into the custom **Wow-PS Watercolor-Medium** tool preset (and all the other Wow Watercolor presets — it's a matched set!). To apply the Style, target the paint layer in the Layers palette; in the Styles palette click the ⊙ button in the top right corner, choose **Wow-Texture Styles** from the fly-out menu, and click on the **Wow-Texture 01*** Style in the palette. If you haven't yet loaded the **Wow-Texture Styles,** they won't be available in the Styles palette; you can load them now,▼ or you can load just the **Wow-Texture 01*** **Style** that you need for this project by clicking the ⊙ button, choosing Load Styles, and navigating to the **Wow-Texture 01.asl** file on the Wow DVD-ROM (in Wow Project Files > Chapter 6 > Pattern Stamp Painting).

FIND OUT MORE

▼ Loading the Wow presets **page 5**

• Make the edges of the colors darker and more distinct by running the Photocopy filter on a merged copy of the file. One way to make a merged copy is to target the top layer in the Layers palette, and then hold down Ctrl-Shift-Alt (Windows) or ⌘-Shift-Option (Mac) and type N, then E (in CS2 you can skip the N); we double-clicked the new layer's name and typed in a more descriptive label for the changes we were about to make. Be sure the Foreground and Background colors are set to black and white (press D). Then choose Filter > Sketch > Photocopy; adjust the settings (we set Detail at 24 and Darkness at 1) and click "OK" **5d**. In the blend mode list in the upper left corner of the Layers palette, choose Color Burn **5e**.

5d

After the two paint layers are merged, a merged copy of the entire image is made and the Photocopy filter is run on this layer.

5e

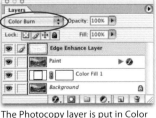

The Photocopy layer is put in Color Burn mode to make the paint pool at the edges of the colors.

JHDAVIS

Art History Lessons

YOU'LL FIND THE FILES
in 🅦 > Wow Project Files > Chapter 6 >
Art History Lessons:
   • Art History-Before.psd (to start)
   • Wow Chalk.tpl (a tool presets file)
   • Art History-After.psd (to compare)

OPEN THESE PALETTES
from the Window menu:
   • Tools • Layers • History

OVERVIEW
Take a History Snapshot • Add a "paper" layer and a transparent layer to hold the paint • Use the Art History Brush 🖌 to paint from the Snapshot, adjusting stroke size and shape • Add details with the Brush 🖌 • Add a Photocopy layer

PHOTOSHOP'S ART HISTORY BRUSH 🖌 "looks at" an image and lays down strokes — several with each click of the mouse — to reproduce that image as a painting. Depending on the choices you make in the Options bar, the result can be wildly abstract to fairly photorealistic. With carefully chosen settings, you can turn a photo into a "hand-crafted" painting or drawing — especially if you add detailing with other painting tools.

1 Preparing the photo. Open the **Art History-Before.psd** file from the Wow DVD-ROM **1a**, or use a photo of your own, saved under a new name (File > Save As) to protect the original image. Retouch the image if it needs it, removing anything you don't want in your painting. We removed the power lines and pole. ▼

FIND OUT MORE

▼ Covering up un-
wanted elements
page 318

Adjust the photo's color and contrast to the colors you want to see in your painting. We exaggerated the color by choosing Image > Adjustments > Hue/Saturation and increasing the Saturation setting to +47.

1a

Original photo, 1000 pixels wide

JHDAVIS

1b

Power lines removed, saturation boosted, and brown "paper" edge added before taking the History Snapshot

2a

Making a merged Snapshot

2b

Designating the new Snapshot as the source for painting

The plan for this "chalk sketch" was to start with "colored paper," which would provide contrast around the edges of the image and in the small spaces between chalk marks. We dragged with the Rectangular Marquee tool 🔲 to select most of the picture, leaving the outer edges unselected, and then chose Select > Inverse to switch the selection to the edges. With the Eyedropper tool 🖋 we clicked on the tree trunk, sampling a dark brown as the Foreground color, and used it to fill the selection (Alt/Opt-Delete fills with the Foreground color) **1b**. Then we deselected the border area (Ctrl/⌘-D) to get ready for the next step.

2 Setting up the History source. Once your starting image looks the way you want it to, take a merged Snapshot of the photo: On the History palette, click the ⊙ in the upper right corner to open the palette menu, and choose New Snapshot. In the New Snapshot dialog box choose Merged Layers **2a**; you can also type in a name for the Snapshot; then click "OK."

When the new Snapshot's thumbnail appears in the top section of the History palette, click in the box to the left of it to make it the source for the painting you'll be doing later **2b**.

3 Setting up the paper and chalk layers. To give yourself maximum control and flexibility, you can set up a "Paper" layer filled with the color you want for your background and another separate layer to paint on. Begin in the Layers palette by Alt/Option-clicking the "Create a new layer" 🔲 button, naming the layer "Paper," and clicking "OK." Then press Alt/Option-Delete to fill the layer with the same Foreground color you used to fill the outer-edges selection in step 1b. In order to place your strokes intelligently, you'll need to be able to see through your "Paper" layer to the image below; so at the top of the Layers palette, reduce the Opacity (we used 75%). Finally, make another new layer above the "Paper" layer for holding the first

3
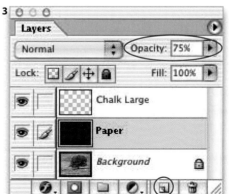

A contrasting "Paper" layer at 75% Opacity allows a view of the image beneath. The "Chalk Large" layer is added to start the painting.

4a In the Tools palette the Art History Brush shares a space with the History Brush.

4b Once you've loaded the Wow-Chalk presets, you can choose Wow-AH Chalk-Large in the Tool Presets picker.

4c Wow-AH Chalk-Large paints with Tight Short strokes in a small Area.

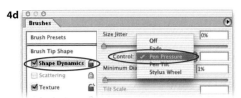

4d For a stylus and tablet, in the Shape Dynamics section of the Brushes palette, set the top Control (it controls size) to Pen Pressure.

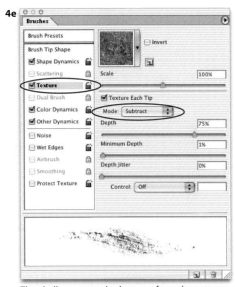

4e The chalk-on-paper look comes from the pattern in Subtract mode used as a Texture in the Wow Chalk presets.

of the chalk **3**. We named the layer "Chalk Large," since we'd be using the **Wow-AH Chalk-Large** preset.

4 Choosing and operating brushes. Next choose the Art History Brush 🖌 from the Tools palette **4a**, and pop out the Tool Preset picker by clicking the 🖌 button at the left end of the Options bar. Click the Tool Preset picker's ⊙ button to pop out a menu, and choose **Wow-Art History Brushes** if it's available, and choose **Wow-AH Chalk-Large** as shown in **4b**. If you haven't loaded the Wow presets,▼ an alternative is to choose Load Tool Presets; navigate to the **Wow Chalk.tpl** file (supplied with the files for this project) and click the "Load" button; from the new presets added to the picker, choose the **Wow-AH Chalk-Large** as shown in **4b**, and examine its settings in the Options bar:

- The blend **Mode** is set to Normal. Later, for detail strokes, you may want to change it to Lighten or Darken to add more dramatic highlights and shadows.

- **Opacity** is set at 100% so strokes will be opaque.

- The **Style** is set to Tight Short **4c**. The Style controls how closely the strokes follow the color contours in the source image (Tight or Loose) and also the length and shape of the strokes.

STYLE SETTINGS FOR THE ART HISTORY BRUSH

To imitate a painting technique with the Art History Brush 🖌, you might use Tight Long strokes for roughing in color and then switch to Tight Short later to paint details. But for an expressive chalk sketch style, it works well to use the Tight Short setting from the beginning. Applied overall, styles other than Tight Long, Tight Medium, and Tight Short can produce something that looks much more mechanical than a hand-painted effect.

- The **Area** is set at 20 pixels **4c**, which will work well for this 1000-pixel-wide image. At this small Area setting, each click of the Art History Brush will generate only a few quick, short strokes. The smaller the setting, the more closely the strokes will follow the cursor as you move it, and the less delay there will be before the strokes appear on the screen.

- **Tolerance** is set at 0%, which lets you freely paint over strokes you've applied before.

- If you use a **pressure-sensitive tablet** for painting, which we highly recommend, you can set its stylus controls in the expanded Brushes palette, which pops out if you click the 🗐 button at the right end of the Options bar.▼ On the left side of

FIND OUT MORE

▼ Loading the Wow presets **page 5**

▼ Setting controls for a pressure-sensitive tablet **page 365**

When you use the Art History Brush 🖌:

- There are at least three ways to operate the tool — you can click, hold, or drag: **Click** each time you want to apply a series of strokes. Or **hold** down the mouse button (or stylus) and watch the strokes pile up until you have the result you want. **Drag** the brush to set down several sets of strokes.

- In general, use **Tight** strokes (set in the Style section of the Options bar), for the reasons explained in the "Style Settings for the Art History Brush" tip on page 390.

- It's helpful to "anchor" your strokes by clicking the cursor in an area of color or contrast that has a clear edge, so the strokes will follow the detail that you want to emphasize.

- Each time you change the settings in the Options bar, try a quick experiment — click once with the cursor to see if you like the results. If not, undo (Ctrl/⌘-Z), change the settings, and try again.

5a

On the "Chalk Large" layer many "roughing in" strokes are laid down with the Wow-AH Chalk-Large preset. The "Paper" layer's reduced Opacity allows the original image to be seen, to help with placement of the "anchoring" strokes.

the Brushes palette, click on **Shape Dynamics** and in the Control menu nearest the top of the panel, choose **Pen Pressure 4d**. With this setting, heavier pressure will produce both a larger brush tip and longer strokes.

- With the Brushes palette open as described above, you can prowl around in the settings to discover what makes the Wow Chalk presets work. You might be especially interested in the **Texture** option (click on it on the left side of the Brushes palette) **4e**. Notice that a coarse pattern called "Wow-Watercolor Texture" has been loaded, and its Mode has been set to Subtract. The rough pattern was made by fine-tuning a scan of real watercolor paper. Combined with the Subtract setting, this pattern gives the tool its "dry medium over rough surface" look.

5 Painting. At this point, double-check the History palette to make sure the 🖌 icon appears to the left of the Snapshot you created in step 2. Before you start painting, take a look at "Art History Brush Tips" at the left. Keeping these pointers in mind will help you get good results.

As you begin painting, start with the Wow-AH Chalk-Large and paint loosely all over to rough in color **5a**. With a pressure-sensitive stylus, you can use heavy pressure for large, long strokes. Now and then, check to see how your painting is progressing: Activate the "Paper" layer (by clicking its thumbnail in the Layers palette) and restore the Opacity to 100%, to completely hide the original photo; after you've had a look, set the Opacity back to 75% or so.

Next, for maximum flexibility in case you later change your mind about some of the strokes you're about to add, click the thumbnail for your top layer and make a new layer above it (Alt/Option-click the 🔲 button) before you choose the Wow-AH Chalk-Medium (a smaller Art History Brush preset) from the Tool Preset Picker, as in step 4. Use this tool to add detail

5b

5b. With a stylus, use less pressure for finer, shorter strokes.

For still finer detail, at the top of the stack add another new layer (🔲) and paint with Wow-AH

Wow–AH Chalk-Medium adds finer strokes.

5c

The Wow–AH Chalk-Small preset brings out more detail with smaller strokes.

5d

Highlights and other details are hand-painted on a separate layer with a Wow-BT Chalk preset for the Brush tool. (These details are shown alone at the top on the right to distinguish the strokes from earlier painting.)

Chalk-Small **5c**. For almost photorealistic detail (many small brush strokes that follow the History Snapshot faithfully), let the stylus tip just "feather touch" — almost float above — the tablet.

Don't forget to do some hand-detailing with the regular Brush tool 🖊 on still another layer **5d**, for fine-tuning that can't be finessed with the automated Art History Brush. To unify the artwork, choose the Brush in the Tools palette, and in the Tool Preset picker choose the Wow-BT Chalk-Small or Wow-BT Chalk-X Small ("BT" stands for "Brush Tool") to get the same "dry medium over rough surface" look as the Wow-AH Chalk presets.

When you've finished painting, restore the Opacity of the "Paper" layer to 100% to completely hide the original photo so you can check your painting. If you want to make changes, activate the appropriate "Chalk" layer, then choose the preset you used on that layer, and paint more strokes. Use the Eraser tool 🩹 if you need to remove strokes.

When you've finalized the painting layers, you can leave them separate or combine them (as we did). We linked and then merged the "Chalk" layers. The process is a little different in CS and CS2:

• In CS in the Layers palette activate the top "Chalk" layer and then link all the other "Chalk" layers to it by dragging down the column under the active layer's 🖊 icon; the 🔗 icon shows which layers are linked; then choose Layer > Merge Linked.

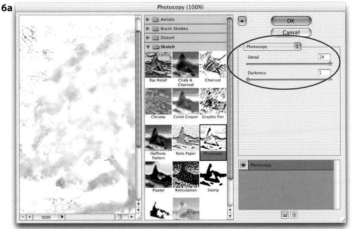

6a

To exaggerate detail, a composite of the layered image is added at the top of the layer stack and the Photocopy filter is applied to this new layer.

6b

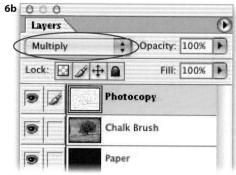

The blend mode of the "Photocopy" layer is changed to Multiply.

6c

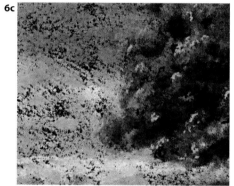

The Photocopy filter "thickens" the painted strokes.

6d

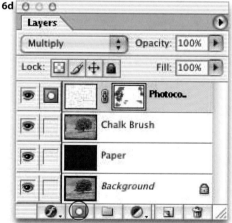

A layer mask can be used to remove the filter effect from areas where it isn't wanted.

- In CS2, click the top "Chalk" layer and Shift-click the bottom "Chalk" layer to select them all; then press Ctr/⌘-E (for Layer > Merge Layers).

Our result was a single painted layer, "Chalk Brush," taking its name from the topmost of the merged layers.

6 Enhancing the painting. Running the Photocopy filter on a "composite" of your painting and combining the filtered image with the painting underneath will bring out texture and detail. To make a composite layer, first make sure the top layer of your file is targeted by clicking its thumbnail in the Layers palette. Then add a new layer and magically turn it into a composite, as follows: In CS, hold down Ctrl-Shift-Alt (Windows) or ⌘-Shift-Option (Mac) and type N, then E. In CS2 you can skip the N, because the helper keys plus E creates the new layer *and* makes a merged copy. (Conveniently, though, if you automatically type the old N and E sequence, it still works.) You can rename the layer by double-clicking on its name in the Layers palette and typing in "Photocopy."

Before you run the Photocopy filter on the new composite layer, set the Foreground and Background colors to black and white (typing D will restore these default colors). Then choose Filter > Sketch > Photocopy, setting the Detail high (we used 24) and the Darkness low (we used 1), and click "OK" **6a**. After running the filter, in the Layers palette choose Multiply as the blend mode for this "Photocopy" layer so only its dark parts will contribute to the image **6b**. This will exaggerate the contrast and detail **6c**.

For this painting, the Photocopy texturing made some of the brown "paper" spots quite prominent, especially in the sky to the left of the tree — they seemed to compete with the tree for attention. To "tone down" these areas we added a layer mask to the Photocopy layer by clicking the ▣ button at the bottom of the Layers palette and then painted the new mask with the Brush tool with a soft, round tip▼ and black paint in the areas where we wanted to remove the added texture **6d**. (The final result is shown at the top of page 388).

Experimenting. Once you get the feel of creating with the Wow-AH Chalk presets, try the other Wow-AH presets▼ for media effects ranging from Oils and Sponge to Stipple and Watercolors. *Wow*

FIND OUT MORE

▼ Choosing a brush tip **page 363**

▼ Examples of other Wow presets for the Art History Brush **page 396**

Cher Threinen-Pendarvis Extracts Color & Form

WHEN CHER THREINEN-PENDARVIS PAINTS, whether with traditional paints and brushes, with Corel Painter, or with Photoshop, she often uses her own photos for reference. Here she lets us in on some of the nifty ways photo reference can help with creating a color palette and refining the composition for a still life, techniques that succeed whether you're painting "by hand" with the Brush tool, as Cher did here, or using the more "automated" Art History Brush or Pattern Stamp.

FIND OUT MORE
▼ Creating a custom
Swatches palette
page 383
▼ Creating custom
brushes **page 381**

1 For her *Two Ducks* painting (shown at lower right), Cher set up the toys in her studio, facing away from each other to create a kind of tension in the composition. She lit the scene, took the photo, scanned it, and made several copies. The first, unedited, would serve as a reference for sketching the composition. "Even if you choose not to reproduce all the detail," says Cher, "a photo reference with good contrast and detail can inspire the painting process and give you more choices."

2 Cher "tweaked" each of the other copies of the photo to get ideas for the color and to simplify the forms for the painting. Anticipating using the same palette of bright colors for other illustrations in the series, she used the Eyedropper tool 🖊 to sample colors from her tweaked reference photos. She "mixed" other colors by clicking the Foreground color square so she could make choices in the Color Picker. She stored her colors in a custom Swatches palette.▼

A Levels Adjustment layer with the Input Levels end-points moved close to the center helped define the simple forms of the ducks.

A Posterize Adjustment layer (here set to 5 Levels) further simplified the forms of the ducks and their environment.

A Hue/Saturation Adjustment layer, with Saturation boosted to +75, provided a source for sampling some of the colors for a custom palette.

The unedited scan was used as a reference for sketching. With a white *Background* below it, Cher could turn visibility for the photo layer on for tracing and off for assessing the progress of the sketch.

CHER THREINEN-PENDARVIS

The finished gouache-like illustration, inspired by the flat color approaches used in poster design in the 1930s and '40s and the brightly colored pop art of the '50s, was painted with simple, hard-edged oval brushes, which Cher designed to paint smoothly and to vary the stroke as she turned the stylus of her Wacom Intuos tablet.▼

EXERCISING
Wow Painting Tools

The **Wow-Tools** (in the PS Wow Presets folder on the DVD-ROM that comes with this book) include presets for three painting tools — the Brush ✐, Art History Brush ✍, and Pattern Stamp ▒. ▼ They share brush tip settings, so you can start a painting with the automated Art History Brush or Pattern Stamp and then hand-paint the finishing details with a small Brush. These Wow painting tools simulate chalk, dry brush, oil, pastel, sponge, stipple, and watercolor. Strokes for the seven kinds of Wow-Brush Tool presets (shown below) have pressure sensitivity built in. Strokes painted with mouse (top) and stylus are shown for comparison. Presets for each medium come in several sizes, just as traditional brushes do.

All of the Wow painting tool presets have surface texture built in, either to emphasize the character of the paint or to reveal the paper or canvas as the paint interacts with it. The **Wow-Grain & Texture Styles** (shown in Appendix B) and **"Quick 'Painting' with Wow Actions"** (see page 398) are designed to emphasize paper or canvas texture, or to add to the paint — either the thick strokes of impasto or the pooling or clumping of watercolor pigment.

The layered file for "Wow Brush Tool Presets" at the right is provided on the Wow DVD-ROM so you can examine its structure. Its *Background* is the original photo, used for the experiments with the **Wow-Art History Brush** and **Wow-Pattern Stamp** presets shown on page 396.

FIND OUT MORE

▼ Loading the Wow presets **page 5**

Wow-BT Chalk   Wow-BT Dry Brush   Wow-BT Oil

Wow-BT Pastel   Wow-BT Sponge   Wow-BT Stipple

Wow-BT Watercolor

YOU CAN FIND THE FILE
in 🅦 > Wow Project Files > Chapter 6 > Exercising Wow Painting

Wow Brush Tool Presets

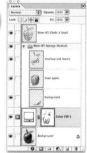

THE SEVEN KINDS OF **WOW-ART MEDIA BRUSHES** presets are for Photoshop's Brush tool ✐ ("BT" stands for "Brush tool"). With these tools you lay down strokes one by one, as you would with traditional artists' media.

One way to use these tools is to start with the original photo **A** and add a "canvas" layer above it (click the "Create new fill or adjustment layer" button ◑ at the bottom of the Layers palette, choose Solid Color, and pick the color you want for your canvas; we used white). Then add an empty layer for painting (click the "Create a new layer" button ⬚ at the bottom of the palette). Temporarily turn off visibility for the canvas layer by clicking its 👁 icon so you can sample color from the photo (Alt/Option-click with the Brush), building a custom Swatches palette if you like. ▼ Make the canvas partially transparent for a "tracing paper" effect by toggling the 👁 on again and reducing the layer's Opacity. Rough-in the image with the largest brush tip that makes sense for your particular photo (here we used **Wow-BT Sponge-Medium**); restore the canvas layer to full opacity periodically to check your painting **B**. Add more layers for parts of the image you'd like to be able to control separately, such as the background or the smaller strokes applied here with **Wow-BT Chalk-X Small C**. For the finished painting, you can leave the canvas layer at full Opacity or reduce its Opacity to allow the original photo to contribute somewhat; or paint its layer mask with black or gray **D** to partially reveal the photo. ▼

FIND OUT MORE

▼ Making a custom Swatches palette **page 383**
Painting layer masks **page 75**

🅦 **Wow Brush Painting.psd**

Wow Pattern Stamp Presets

Wow-PS Watercolor +
Wow-Texture 01*

Wow-PS Oil + Wow-
Texture 03*

Wow-PS Dry Brush +
Wow-Texture 02*

Wow-PS Chalk + Wow-
Texture 07*

WITH THE **WOW-PATTERN STAMP** PRESETS (they have "PS" in their names), you hand-paint each cloning stroke with the Pattern Stamp tool 🗿. The PS presets have the same brush tips as the corresponding Wow-Brush Tool presets on page 388, and the Impressionist mode (important for "clone painting") is included in the tool preset.

The samples above were painted using the techniques described in "Pattern Stamp Watercolors" on page 384. (Also, "Using the Wow Watercolor Presets," a tip on page 371, has pointers specifically for watercolor painting that apply to the Pattern Stamp as well as the Brush tool.) Using the method in "Pattern Stamp Watercolors," we defined the original photo as a pattern, and set up each sample's file with a "canvas" layer like the one described for "Wow Brush Tool Presets" and with several painting layers that we added and then combined.

After painting we applied one of the **Wow-Texture Styles** to the combined paint layer by clicking the layer's thumbnail in the Layers palette, clicking the "Add a layer style" button 🅕 at the bottom of the palette, and choosing the Style from the Wow-Texture Styles presets we had previously loaded.▼ (Examples of all of the Wow-Texture Styles can be seen in Appendix B.)

FIND OUT MORE

▼ Loading the Wow presets **page 5**

Wow Art History Brush Presets

Wow-AH Watercolor +
Wow-Texture 01*

Wow-AH Oil + Wow-
Texture 02*

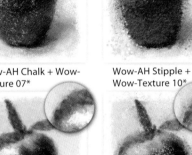

Wow-AH Chalk + Wow-
Texture 07*

Wow-AH Stipple +
Wow-Texture 10*

Wow-AH Pastel +
Wow-Texture 01*

Wow-AH Sponge +
Wow-Texture 09*

THE **WOW-ART HISTORY BRUSH** PRESETS (with "AH" in their names) are set up to apply strokes that automatically follow the contrast and color features of the source image. Because the Art History Brush 🖌 lays down several strokes at once, it clones much faster than the Pattern Stamp, but the automation makes creative control of the Art History Brush more difficult. ("Art History Brush Tips" on page 391 has pointers for controlling the tool.)

We painted the samples above using the techniques described in "Art History Lessons" on page 388. Files were set up with a "canvas" layer like the one described for "Wow Brush Tool Presets," and with several painting layers that we then combined and "styled" with one of the **Wow-Texture Styles** as described at the left.

Bert Monroy Does Neon

MASTER OF PHOTOREALISM BERT MONROY takes neon signage way beyond the "Quick Neon Type" shown on page 454 and the hand-crafted tubes of "Crafting a Neon Glow" on page 546. Here's how he does it.

You can read more about neon and other master-fully photorealistic techniques in Bert's *Commercial Photoshop with Bert Monroy* (New Riders).

Bert builds his neon tubes for street scenes such as **Spenger's,** shown on page 404, by first drawing a path with the Pen tool ✎ and then stroking it several times with the Brush ✏, adding a new layer for each kind of stroke.▼ Typically, he lays the strokes down in this order, from bottom to top:

• Using a soft round brush tip, he paints an outer glow, usually in white or a lightened version of the color of the background behind the neon.

• The tube itself is painted in three layers. He starts with a relatively intense color, painted with a hard, round brush tip, then applies a lighter, narrower version with a softer brush, and finally an even thinner white stroke, also with a soft brush.

• For the neon light that reflects off the sign base, he duplicates the layer that has the colorful stroke that defines the neon tubing and blurs the new layer (Filter > Blur > Gaussian Blur). In the Layers palette he puts this new layer in Hard Light mode and drags its thumbnail in the Layers palette to a position below the tubing but above the sign base. He uses the Move tool ▸⊕ to offset it behind the neon.

Using this "layer sandwich" approach, he can bring down the Fill Opacity of the individual colors or erase color at key spots as he builds up dimension and lighting for the tubes.

Bert has developed a set of custom "grunge" presets for the

Brush tool ✏, for adding "a light touch of urban grime." Working in the various panels of the Brushes palette,▼ he incorporates Jitter in the Size, Scatter, and Angle settings for the brush tips he builds. He also uses this palette's Dual Brush option to mask the grunge inside a hard, round brush tip, adjusted to the same size as the brush he used to define the tubes. When he uses a grunge brush to stroke a path, the grunge marks build up somewhat randomly along the tubes because of the Jitter settings, but the Dual Brush keeps them from extending beyond the edges of the neon tubes.

FIND OUT MORE

▼ Drawing & stroking paths **pages 435 & 439**
▼ Using the Brushes palette **page 361**

Duplicating the layer with the red stroke that defined the neon tube, Bert blurred the duplicate and put it in Hard Light mode. He offset this colored reflection, reduced the layer's opacity, and added the hand-detailing he's famous for.

To add the black masking on the tubes shown here, Bert loaded the tube outline as a selection by Ctrl/⌘-clicking in the Layers palette on the thumbnail for the layer with the hard-edged bright green stroke. He added a new layer and used the Brush ✏ with black paint and Eraser ⌫ to make the worn black material.

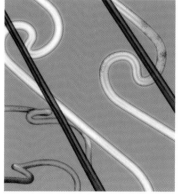

For the white neon, Bert used a soft stroke of light blue for the outer glow, a hard-edged stroke of darker blue to define the tube, and a lighter blue and white for the interior. To capture the wear and tear on the tubes, he partially erased the white and light blue layers and added grime with one of his "grunge" brushes.

"Painting" with Wow Actions

On the **Wow DVD-ROM** that comes with this book you'll find several Actions▼ that apply "painterly" treatments to photos, and several more that are designed to enhance paintings, whether done on the computer or painted in traditional media and photographed or scanned. Try out any of these Wow "miniprograms" and see what happens.

Open the Actions palette (Window > Actions). If you've loaded the Wow Actions click the palette's ⊙ button and choose the **Wow-Photo Enhance** set from the bottom of the palette's menu to add it to the palette. Do the same for the **Wow-Paint Enhance** set. If you *haven't* yet loaded the Wow Actions, you might want to do that now;▼ or simply click the Actions palette's ⊙ button, choose Load Actions, and load the **Wow-Painting.atn** file provided with the files for this section.

To run an Action, click its name in the Actions palette and click the "Play selection" button ▶ at the bottom of the palette. (If your Actions palette is set to Button Mode in the palette's menu, simply click the Action's button to start running it.) **As the Action runs, it's important to read** the directions in any "Stop" message, and then click the "Continue" button in the dialog box.

YOU'LL FIND THE FILES
in 🔵 > Wow Project Files > Chapter 6 > Wow Paint Actions

FIND OUT MORE
▼ Working with Actions **page 110**
▼ Loading Wow presets **page 5**

Wow-Filtered Watercolor

Original photo

Wow-Watercolor 1

Wow-Watercolor 2

Wow-Watercolor + Linework (Threshold 215)

TRY THE **WOW-WATERCOLOR** ACTIONS to set the style for a series of Illustrations or even to "save" a poorly taken photo.

Watercolor Actions.psd

Wow- Linework

Original photo

Wow-Linework Alone (Threshold 248)

Wow-Stippled Linework-Colored Anti-aliased (Threshold 130)

Wow-Stippled Linework-Gray (Threshold 130)

THE **WOW-LINEWORK** ACTIONS work especially well on photos with simple, easy-to-recognize forms. Each of these Actions includes a Stop so you can choose the setting for the Threshold command that determines how dense the lines or stippling will be. Each of the **Wow-Linework** Actions produces two linework layers — one with and one without antialiasing.

Linework Actions.psd

ADDING A SIGNATURE

If you have a standard brush-stroke signature that you like to use on your digital paintings, you can store it as a Custom Shape preset.▼ When you finish a painting, just use the Custom Shape tool 🖉 to add it. In an "impasto" painting, where you want to emphasize the brush strokes by embossing, be sure to add the signature, then make any coloring or opacity changes you want to its layer, and merge it with the painting (press Ctrl/⌘-E for Layer > Merge Down) *before* you create the impasto layer.▼

FIND OUT MORE
▼ Making a custom Shape preset **page 436**
▼ Adding an impasto layer **page 379**

Combining Effects

Wow-Linework Alone (Threshold 243) over original

CREATIVE POSSIBILITIES INCREASE as you layer one **Wow-Linework** treatment over another or over the original photo. Each of the Wow-Linework Actions protects the original image by creating a duplicate layer or a separate file to work on, leaving the original intact. If the Action creates a separate file, you can combine treatments (or treatment and original) by Shift-dragging the processed layer from one file into the other file. (Using the Shift key centers the imported image over the same-size original, thereby aligning the two perfectly.) Then in the Layers palette, change the blend mode or Opacity of the imported layer.

Here we ran the **Wow-Linework Alone** Action. Since this Action creates a new layer for the linework rather than an entirely new file, when the Action was finished running, all we had to do to combine the antialiased linework with the original was to change the linework layer's blend mode to Multiply and turn off visibility for the other linework layer by clicking its 👁.

Wow-Paint Enhance

Original Art History Brush painting

Wow-Paint Edge Enhance Subtle

Wow-Paint Edge Enhance Extreme

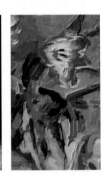 

Wow-Impasto Emboss Extreme

Wow-Impasto Emboss Subtle

Wow-Impasto Emboss Subtle w/Canvas

FOR THESE EXAMPLES the **Wow-Paint Enhance** Actions were run with their default settings on a painting done with the Art History Brush ✍, using the method in "Art History Lessons" (page 388) through step 5. If you find that the Action creates a darkening or embossing effect that's too strong, you can reduce it by lowering the Opacity of the enhancing layer.

The two **Wow-Paint Edge Enhance** Actions apply effects that are especially good for watercolors, like those in "Pattern Stamp Watercolors," step 5 on page 386, and in this chapter's "Gallery" on page 402.

🌀 **Paint-Enhancing Actions.psd**

Turpentine or Photoshop?

PAINTER DAREN BADER HAS TRANSLATED his painting techniques from oils and acrylics to Photoshop, but he hasn't put away his traditional brushes. Although for Daren, there's still nothing quite like holding a one-of-a-kind finished oil painting in his hands, he also enjoys the advantages that digital brushwork offers.

When he works on the computer, Daren prefers to display his developing painting either at its final printed dimensions (for small images) or at the largest size he can fit on-screen and still see the entire painting. He avoids zooming in, so he doesn't get lost in the details and end up painting with more precision than suits the style. He looks forward to the day when digital paintings are routinely displayed illuminated, just as they appear when the artist is painting them. In the meantime, you can see small versions of Daren's work illuminated at www.darenbader.com.

Sometimes a combination of traditional painting and Photoshop techniques is the best way to get the job done. When a painted book cover illustration needed revisions, the client emailed Daren a scan of the painting he had submitted; Daren opened the scan in Photoshop and made the required changes, then emailed it back. This eliminated the time that would have been spent sending the painting by courier both ways, not to mention the drying time for the paint.

Daren Bader's *Forest Rangers* was painted with traditional artists' tools and materials — in oils, directly over a pencil sketch on a treated cold press board.

Viking was painted entirely in Photoshop, as described on page 408.

This cover illustration for R. A. Salvatore's book *Paths of Darkness* was started in oils, then scanned and finished in Photoshop, which made the work go much faster. Daren modified Photoshop's Chalk brushes so his digital strokes would match the traditional ones.

For ***Moorea Canoe***, **Jack Davis** started by creating a rough collage from his photos of the landscape, canoe, and clouds. He used Image > Adjustments > Hue/Saturation to intensify the colors, as shown in this detail **A**, and made the brightened image into a Pattern (Edit > Define Pattern). This Pattern would become the source for the cloned painting when Davis used the Pattern Stamp tool 🖌 and its Impressionist setting, chosen in the Options bar.

Working as described in "Pattern Stamp Watercolors" on page 384, Davis added a transparent layer and began painting, following the contours of the original collage below **B**.

To create the illusion of a watercolor over an ink sketch, Davis duplicated the composite layer and used Filter > Stylize > Find Edges, followed by Image > Adjustments > Threshold to create the "ink" **C**. He blended this duplicated layer with the completed painting layer below it by setting its blend mode to Multiply **D**.

Davis then applied a Layer Style with a Pattern Overlay of "salt stain" (**Wow-Texture 09***; see Appendix B) to the finished paint layer, which you see in the final painting, and enhanced the details of the painting, using the Photocopy filter (see page 387).

> The **Wow-Linework Alone** Action (Wow Presets > Wow-Photoshop Actions > **Wow-Paint Enhance Actions.atn**) creates an "ink drawing" from a photo, as shown in **C** above.

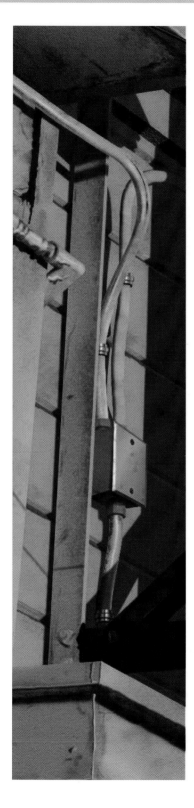

Bert Monroy painted *Spenger's* partly from his memory of how the scene looked on the day he was inspired to paint it, and partly from a photo reference shot later with a digital camera. The photo provided specific details, while the viewing angle and the sunset color came from his earlier impression.

Monroy now paints almost entirely within Photoshop, since it has almost all the "construction tools" he could previously find only in Adobe Illustrator. He now relies on Illustrator only to "blend" from one line or shape to another to create intermediate steps, or to create shapes by cutting and joining paths, which can be done more simply in Illustrator. For this painting, he used Illustrator to create the shiny clips that hold the electrical wiring to the wooden wall (shown in this detail). He drew and duplicated ovals, and cut them to make arcs, which he could then join to make fillable shapes). Monroy copied the finished Illustrator elements into the clipboard in Illustrator, and then in Photoshop pasted them into his painting by choosing Edit > Paste > Paste As: Paths. The pasted paths appeared as the temporary *Work Path* in Photoshop's Paths palette. Monroy double-clicked the *Work Path* label to make the pasted paths into a permanent, named path. With the new path chosen in the Paths palette, he used the Direct Selection tool to click in the working window on the particular subpath he wanted to fill; he loaded the subpath as a selection (by clicking the "Load path as a selection" button at the bottom of the Paths palette), and used the Gradient tool to fill it.

A master of photorealistic lighting and surface textures, Monroy uses Layer Styles minimally. He "hand-crafts" his neon, for instance, as described on page 397. Also, for the cover of the electrical box (shown here), the perspective required that the beveled edge appear wider at the bottom of the box than at the top. So rather than using a Layer Style, which would have created a uniform bevel, he constructed the face of the bevel with the Pen tool, then added a new layer and clicked the "Fill path with foreground color" button at the bottom of the Paths palette to fill the path with the Foreground color, which he had set to orange. Then he chose the Brush tool and a soft tip and yellow paint and clicked the Paths palette's "Stroke path with brush" button to stroke the path. Monroy completed the bevel color by clicking the button to load the path as a selection so it would act as a "frisket," protecting the other areas from the white paint he applied with a soft-tipped Brush.

Monroy did use a Layer Style to make the paint drips on the sign and building (seen on the cornice near the bottom of this detail). For each group of drips he added a layer and painted each drip with the Brush tool and a hard-edged round tip, often starting at the top of the drip with fairly heavy pressure on his Wacom Intuos stylus, and easing up as he painted, to narrow the drip at the bottom. He made the drips disappear by reducing the layer's Fill Opacity to 0% using the slider on the Layers palette. Then he clicked the at the bottom of the palette and chose "Bevel and Emboss." In the Layer Style dialog box he set up the bevel he wanted, assigning an Outer Bevel and watching the drips take shape in the main window as he experimented with the settings. He turned off "Use Global Light" so he could control the lighting for each layer of drips independently of the others. When Monroy saw the result he wanted, he clicked "OK" to close the dialog. By reducing Fill Opacity to 0% he had made the "dripping" process more efficient (he didn't have to sample color from the image to paint the drips because the color would disappear anyway). And he had made the drips more realistic (with only the shadow and highlight defining them, the drips appeared to be weathered and lighted in the same way as their surroundings).

Mark Wainer creates limited-edition prints of his painterly street scenes and landscapes, developed from his own original photography. His goal is to simulate natural media so well that his images don't easily reveal their computer heritage. Shown here is *Night Walk*.

Wainer begins by converting his raw digital images and upsizing them to 29 MB,▼ or by scanning his 35-mm film to a 27 MB file **A**. Then he makes initial adjustments to tone and color,▼ duplicates the adjusted image to a new layer (Ctrl/⌘-J), and posterizes the color in this layer by applying the Simplifier One filter **B**, which is included in the buZZ plug-ins sets (www.Fo2PiX.com).

In the Layers palette Wainer reduces the Opacity of the filtered layer to bring back as much of the original detail as he wants **C**. He sometimes applies a layer mask at this point to control the amount of detail in different areas of the image. He then makes a merged copy of the layered image (Image > Duplicate, choosing Duplicate Merged Layers Only) and

enlarges this copy to 81MB, the size required for his limited-edition prints.

Next Wainer "sharpens" the image, making edges more distinct, by using Dry Brush (Filter > Artistic > Dry Brush), which he applies more than once if necessary. For some images, he further sharpens edges by duplicating the image on a new layer and applying the High Pass filter (Filter > Other > High Pass), then changing the blend mode of the layer to Soft Light, which increases contrast in the midtones especially **D**.▼

At this point he often does extensive retouching, selecting some elements and moving or transforming them, and then using the Clone Stamp 🖳, Patch tool ⬙, or Healing Brush 🖊 "to cover my tracks," he says. For *Night Walk* he cropped the image at the top and bottom▼ and stretched it wider.▼ He typically makes selections to isolate areas for tone and color adjustments. For instance, to blend the altered walking figure seamlessly into the *Night Walk* scene, he made such a selection with a feathered Lasso ⬭▼ and added a Curves Adjustment layer (by clicking on the ⬤ button at the

bottom of the Layers palette and choosing from the pop-up list). The selection became a mask that limited the Curves adjustment to the area he wanted to change **E**. The Select > Color Range command is also useful for isolating areas like the sky in *Night Walk*.

FIND OUT MORE

▼ Enlarging an image **page 73**

▼ Adjusting tone & color **page 165**

▼ Blend modes **page 176**

▼ Cropping **page 244**

▼ Transforming **page 71**

▼ Selection methods **page 55**

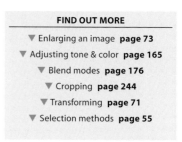

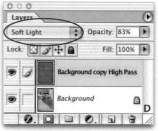

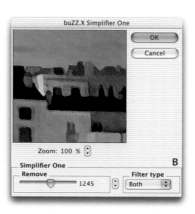

Daren Bader starts his digital paintings, such as *Viking* (above), by making a pencil sketch and scanning it. Then he starts a new file at the size and resolution he needs for the final painting. With the scan file also open in Photoshop, he drags-and-drops the scan into the new file to serve as a reference. He enlarges the scan to fit, using Edit > Free Transform and Shift-dragging a corner handle of the Transform box to keep the drawing in proportion. If necessary, he uses Image > Adjustments >

Brightness/Contrast to get sharp black line work using the method described in "Cleaning Up Masks," page 66. Then he puts the scan layer in Multiply mode, which makes the white appear clear, so he can see both the line work and the painting he will be doing on layers below.

Bader adds one transparent layer at a time, painting on it with the Brush tool 🖌 with "chalky" brush tips like the default Chalk brushes shown at the right. He sets his controls so the stylus pressure he applies on his

Wacom Intuos tablet controls Opacity and Size of the strokes.

DAREN BADER / © KOSMOS GAMES

DAREN BADER / © KOSMOS GAMES

DAREN BADER / © KOSMOS GAMES

Daren Bader often starts a new illustration by sampling color from a previous one. He then mixes more colors by using the Brush tool to overlay low-opacity strokes of color on top of existing color, Alt/Option-clicking to sample from the color this produces.

He starts by roughing in color and then adds detail, checking his progress by clicking the 👁 icon to turn visibility on and off for the layer he's currently painting. When he's pleased with his progress on a layer, he merges it into the earlier work (Ctrl/⌘-E, for Layer > Merge Down). On the other hand, if he finds that the painting on the most recent layer has taken off in a direction he doesn't like, it's easy to delete it (by dragging it to the "Delete layer" button 🗑 at the bottom of the Layers palette). "I sometimes have the same epiphany when I'm working with oils or acrylics," says Bader, "but with paint, it's harder to fix," because repainting can "muddy" the colors. In Photoshop, he can dodge and burn, so repainted colors don't lose saturation.▼

To keep brush performance high so his painting flows freely, Bader reduces file size by merging layers as he works. Eventually he paints on and merges the scanned sketch, but not before he duplicates the original sketch layer (Ctrl/⌘-J) for safekeeping, hiding it by turning off its visibility.

Bader keeps the entire image in view on-screen as he works. He zooms in only when he needs to add detail to draw attention to something, as shown below in a detail from *Helitos* (above left), one of a series of 32 illustrations Bader was commissioned to paint for a deck of cards for a fantasy game.

FIT ON-SCREEN

To size an image so it will fit, as large as it can, on your computer screen, press Ctrl/⌘-0 (that's the number zero).

For this series Bader was given a template for the card layout that showed the location and dimensions of the text boxes. He dragged this layer into each file and put it in Multiply mode so he could see the live and dead space as he developed his illustration.

To draw the first of the tattoos, seen here in *Kabukat* (above center) and *Silentosol* as well as *Helitos,* he set up a separate layer and used the Pencil tool so he could draw quickly. Then he blurred the layer a little to smooth the edges (Filter > Blur > Gaussian Blur). He worked out the blend mode and Opacity for the tattoo layer that made a perfect blend of the tattoo's color with the shading on the skin (Hard Light at 83%). He could then drag-and-drop an existing tattoo layer into a new illustration file, select the contents of the layer (Ctrl/⌘-A), and press the Delete key to remove the old tattoo. Finally he painted a new tattoo on this layer with the blend mode and opacity already set up.

FIND OUT MORE

▼ Dodging & burning
page 329

DEEANNE EDWARDS

F or her *Marine Life Impressions,* which are artistically re-created in Photoshop from her underwater photos, **Deeanne Edwards** starts by "cleaning up any messy, confusing background." To do this she often selects and darkens the background as she did for *Moray Eel, Baja California, Mexico* (the original is shown below), or she selects and blurs it.▼ Edwards then uses a combination of filters to posterize the image, simplifying it to a few colors, and to add "ink" lines. She finds that the Cutout, Dry Brush, Ink Outlines, and Poster Edges filters work especially well to get the graphic effect she wants. Any of the filters she uses can be applied by choosing Filter > Filter Gallery, then clicking the "New effect layer" button ⬛ in the bottom right corner of the Filter Gallery dialog box, and choosing from the pop-up alphabetical list of filters (located below the "Cancel" button). To arrive at the combination used for the portraits shown here she applied the Cutout filter first, then clicked the ⬛ button again and chose Poster Edges. With the two "effects layers" listed at the bottom right corner of the dialog box, she could click the name of either one and change its settings, working with the two filters interactively to arrive at the settings she wanted for each photo, as shown above right.

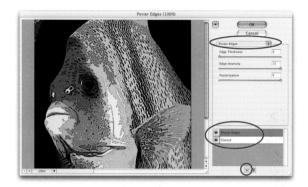

FIND OUT MORE

▼ "Subduing" a background **page 285**

A BIGGER PREVIEW

Clicking the ⬛ button at the top of the Filter Gallery dialog box toggles the sample thumbnails of filter effects on (so you can choose a filter by clicking one) or off (so you have more room for the preview).

FILTER "QUICK START"

When you use a filter treatment to turn photos into graphics, each image may require slightly different settings. But once you work out a filter treatment you like in the Filter Gallery, it's easy to save a "starting point" for other images by recording an Action: Use the Filter Gallery to set up filters to get a result you like for one of your images; then click "OK" to close the Filter Gallery. Undo the Filter Gallery effects (pressing Ctrl/⌘-Z, for Edit > Undo Filter Gallery, removes all the effects you applied with the Filter Gallery). Now open the Actions palette (Window > Actions) and click the "Create new action" button ⬛ at the bottom of the palette **A**; in the New Action dialog box, name the Action and click the "Record" button. From Photoshop's main Filter menu, choose the "Filter Gallery" entry *at the very top of the menu*, which applies your most recent Filter Gallery settings. Back in the Actions palette, click to the left of the Filter Gallery entry **B** to add the "Toggle dialog box on/off" icon ⬛; next click the "Stop playing/recording" button ⬛ at the bottom of the palette **C**. Now if you open another image, then click the name of your Action in the Actions palette **D**, and click the "Play selection" button ▶ **E**, the Filter Gallery will apply the recorded changes and leave the dialog box open so you can "tweak" the settings for your new image.

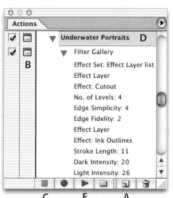

Lance Hidy's *Tree Climbers* is one of several illustrations he created for the fourth edition of Laura Berk's *Child Development* text-book, published by Allyn & Bacon. Starting with the metaphor suggested by art director Elaine Ober, Hidy photographed several young models climbing a spectacular magnolia tree. Then he turned to Photoshop. The Layers palette below shows the "anatomy" of the file he built.

He started by scanning the photo and using it as a template for making a selection of the tree.▼ He refined the selection in Quick Mask mode,▼ and saved it in an alpha channel using Select > Save Selection.

Hidy added an empty layer for the background of his illustration and used the Gradient tool ▯ to fill it with color.▼ He added another gradient-filled layer for the tree and then used the stored selection to create a mask for this gradient. (To add a layer mask based on an alpha channel, first Ctrl/⌘-click the thumbnail of the alpha channel in the Channels palette. Then target a layer in the Layers palette and click the "Add a layer mask" button ▣ at the bottom of the palette; this

makes a mask that reveals only the selected area of the layer.) Where the tree and background were too similar in tone, Hidy used the Burn tool on the tree layer to increase the tonal distinction **A**.

He colored the climbers on a layer of their own by selecting with the Lasso ⌐ with the Anti-aliased feature *turned off* in the Options bar. Once a selection was made, he used the Paint Bucket tool ⌐ to fill these areas; he set Tolerance to 0, turned on Contiguous, and turned off both Antialiased and All Layers. Once an area was filled with color, Hidy could select the adjacent area without being precise about any edges that were shared by the two areas **B**. Because he was using the Paint Bucket ⌐ with Contiguous turned on, the color was limited by both the active selection and the color of any adjacent already colored areas.

For his solid-color fills, such as those used for the children and clothing in these illustrations, Hidy avoids antialiasing. He works with hard edges in this way so that if he wants to change the colors he can click once with the Magic Wand ⌐ (with

Tolerance at 0, Contiguous turned on, and Anti-aliased turned off) and once with the Paint Bucket ⌐ to make the adjustment, without leaving any edge pixels just partially recolored. (For another approach to experimenting with solid colors, gradients, and even patterns without risking partially recolored edge pixels, see the "Advantages of Fill Layers" tip at the right.)

Without antialiasing, the edges look pixelated, or stairstepped, if you zoom in for a close look. However, the pixels aren't obvious in the printed illustrations. That's because for illustrations that will be printed by the standard CMYK halftoning process, Hidy works at full finished size, at a resolution approximately twice the halftone screen resolution that will be used for printing, so it's the halftone screen rather than the pixels that determines the smoothness of the printed edges.▼

Hidy used a layer mask, again made from the stored tree selection, to mask out parts of the climbers where the tree branches passed in front of them. (For a mask that *hides* the selected area instead of revealing it, Alt/Option-click the "Add a layer mask button 🔲.)

ADVANTAGES OF FILL LAYERS

Depending on how you like to work in Photoshop, Fill layers may be perfect for trying out a range of options in developing artwork with solid colors, gradients, or patterns. First select the area you want to fill, and then add a Solid Color, Gradient, or Pattern Fill layer by clicking the "Create new fill or adjustment layer" button 🔲 at the bottom of the Layers palette and choosing from the top of the pop-out list.

Here are some advantages of using a Fill layer for coloring rather than filling an area on a regular layer:

• To make changes, you can open the appropriate dialog box (or the Color Picker in the case of a Solid Color fill) simply by double-clicking the Fill layer's thumbnail in the Layers palette; then choose a new color, gradient, or pattern. And you can simply **drag in the working window to reposition a gradient or pattern** without leaving any unfilled space at the edges.

• If you decide to change the fill type — from a solid color to a gradient, for instance — just choose **Layer > Change Layer Content** and choose the other kind of layer.

• Once you finalize your choice of a fill, if you want to use a tool or filter that only works on a pixel-based layer, choose **Layer > Rasterize > Fill Content.** (After rasterizing, the layer no longer has its special Fill layer properties, of course.)

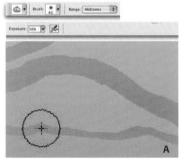

Using the Burn tool ⌐ to increase contrast between the tree and the background

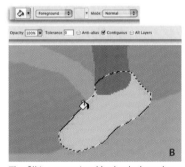

The fill is constrained by both the selection and the adjacent brown of the leg.

PREVENTING BANDING

To prevent color banding, the Options bar for the Gradient tool 🔲 and the dialog box for a Gradient Fill layer offer a Dither option that adds a little "noise" to the gradient, to prevent obvious "steps" in the gradation.

FIND OUT MORE

▼ Making selections **page 55**
▼ Using Quick Mask **page 65**
▼ Designing & using gradients **page 160**
▼ Resolution for print **page 91**

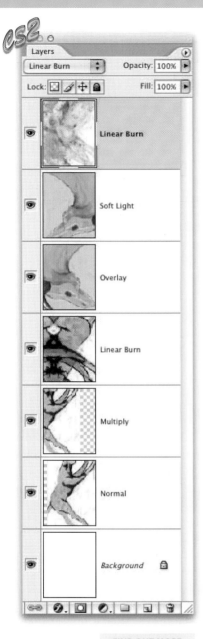

Layers

Linear Burn   Opacity: 100%

Lock: 🔲 ✏ ✛ 🔒   Fill: 100%

Linear Burn

Soft Light

Overlay

Linear Burn

Multiply

Normal

Background 🔒

FIND OUT MORE

▼ Transforming
page 71
▼ Tinting with Color
Balance **page 207**

I n the Layers palette at the left, we've renamed the layers to show the blend mode used for each layer in **Laurie Grace's *Intrusion 38***. This image is from the same series as the photo-based *Intrusion 2* on page 86, but in the painting-based *Intrusion 38* the role played by symmetry is much more subtle, and the composite retains the gesture of the strokes and the blended color of the art media.

Grace started a new file with a white *Background,* to define the size she wanted for the final image. From there her process was a fluid, experimental one of arranging, scaling, duplicating, flipping, and merging layers, all the while experimenting with blend modes.

She copied and pasted a dog from a scanned watercolor **A** and scaled it,▼ until it was "cropped" in a way she liked for a design element.

The second layer was a copy of the first (Ctrl/⌘-J), dragged to one side with the Move tool ▶₊ and put in Multiply mode (set in the upper left corner of the Layers palette), so the combination of the two layers **B** repeated the lines of the dog element.

The third layer is composed of two more copies of the dog, one flipped horizontally (Edit > Transform > Flip Horizontal) and dragged to the side to form a symmetrical combination of shapes. With the upper of the two layers active, the two were merged (Ctrl/⌘-E), and the merged element flipped vertically and offset to one side, then scaled, and tinted▼ **C**. In Linear Burn mode this layer both darkens and intensifies color.

The next two layers in the stack are from a scanned oil pastel drawing **D**. Like the dog, this imported element is larger than the frame of the document, and Grace flipped one of the copies and then offset the two a little differently. Applying one layer in Overlay mode and the other in Soft Light increased contrast and lightened the developing image **E**.

The last layer **F** was another combination of two copies of the dog image, with one copy flipped vertically this time, merged with a scan from another painting.

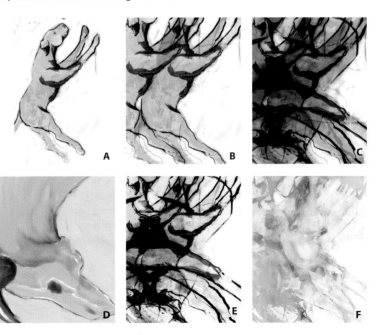

A

B

C

D

E

F

Type & Vector Graphics

7

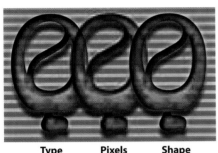

Type   **Pixels**   **Shape**

Photoshop's type and vector-based graphics are resolution-independent. When output on a PostScript output device such as the one used to make printing plates for this book, they can produce smooth outlines, no matter what the native resolution of the image file. In this demo illustration the resolution of the file was set very low at 38 pixels/inch, to produce exaggerated pixelation in the image. The file was saved in Photoshop EPS format and vector data was included. In print the outlines of the type and the vector-based Shape layer are smooth. Layer Styles, which provide the coloring and translucency for these "Q's", also conform to these smooth edges. But the pixel-based pattern built into the Style is coarse, produced at the file's native 38 pixels/inch.

PHOTOSHOP HAS AN IMPRESSIVE ARRAY of vector-based type and drawing capabilities. They rival some of the best features of PostScript drawing and page-layout programs such as Adobe Illustrator, Adobe InDesign, and QuarkXPress. Vector-based type and graphics can be scaled, rotated, and otherwise manipulated without any "softening" or deterioration of edges. With Photoshop you can produce:

- **Type** (with spell-checking and advanced formatting controls) that can now be set **on** or **inside a** *path* (defined below) and that can remain "live," editable, and crisp-edged all the way to the output device

- **Paths,** which are resolution-independent curves or outlines that aren't associated with any particular layer in a file, but that can be stored and activated for making selections, for serving as a baseline or an enclosure for type, or for silhouetting when a file is output

- **Vector masks** for sharp-edged silhouetting of individual layers or layer sets/ groups▼

FIND OUT MORE

▼ Masks **page 68**

- Vector-based **Shape layers,** which are layers of solid color, each with a vector mask that controls where the color is revealed.

Vector-based type and graphics are efficient (you can easily reshape them) and economical (they add less to file size than pixel-based layers do). This chapter tells how to use Photoshop's "vector power." It also suggests when it's better to rely on dedicated PostScript-based illustration or page-layout programs instead, and how to move your work smoothly between these programs and Photoshop.

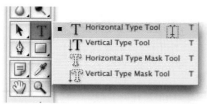

Although there are four Type tools, most type is set with the Horizontal Type tool. In most instances it's more efficient to use the "live" Type tools and make any necessary masks from the type, than to use the Type Mask tools.

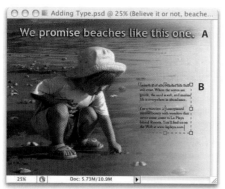

In Photoshop CS/CS2, you can use a path as a baseline for type. Center-aligned type (shown here) spreads out in both directions from the point where you first click on the path.

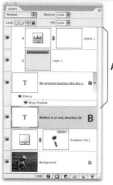

The type in a live type layer can be "filled" with an image and still maintain its editability. This is done with a clipping group **A**, as in this developing layout from "Adding Type to an Image" (page 596). The headline was set as point type, but the body copy was set as paragraph type to fit within a defined space **B**.

TYPE

Photoshop uses the same powerful type engine that's found in InDesign, including access to the special features of Open Type (fonts that use a single font file for both Windows and Mac and that provide advanced typographic controls such as automatic substitution of special characters, or *glyphs*, for ligatures). Now that in versions CS and CS2 you can set type on or inside a path, you can often do all the typesetting you need for an image-based single-page document right in Photoshop.

Under most conditions, you can maintain type as "live" (editable) and still be able to control its color, opacity, special effects, and how it blends with other layers in the file. For instance, you can add special effects with Layer Styles and Warp effects. And images can be masked inside of type by using a clipping group with the type as the base layer.

Photoshop has four **Type tools**, as shown at the left, but for most jobs the **Horizontal Type tool** (the default **T** in the Tools palette) is the one to use. When we refer to "the Type tool," that's the one we mean. The **Vertical Type tool** works like the Horizontal one, but by default it stacks the characters in a column instead of stringing them out horizontally.

Starting Out

To cover the basics of type, we'll start with a quick "executive summary" of working with type, and then move on to specific type controls. It's rare to set type perfectly on the first try, so we'll then cover how to put type exactly where you want it to be, including fitting it to the space available and repositioning it slightly. Because type-on-a-path requires specialized ways of working with type, it's treated separately, starting on page 424. Next we'll take a quick look at how to come back and edit type later. And finally, we'll look at scaling type judiciously or warping it for special effects.

Here's a quick summary of how to work with type:

- All you need to do **to add your first type** to a Photoshop file is to choose the Type tool **T**, click or drag in the working window, and begin typing. If you **click** (rather than drag) the type will be ***point type*** — it will continue in a single line unless you tell it to start a new one ("Multi-Line Point Type" on page 419 tells how to do this). If you **drag** with the Type tool instead of clicking, Photoshop will set up a rectangular bounding box, and when you type, the text will automatically "wrap" to start a new line each time it encounters the

Type-inside-a-path is a special kind of paragraph type. When a closed path is active and you move the Type tool's cursor inside the path, it becomes the type-inside-a-path cursor shown here. Any typing you do now will be paragraph type that uses the path as a bounding box,. This makes it possible to constrain the type inside spaces that aren't necessarily rectangular.

MULTI-LINE POINT TYPE

To set type on several lines, without being constrained by the bounding box that comes with paragraph type, you can use point type. Start a **new paragraph** with the **Enter/Return** key, or a **new line** with **Shift-Enter/Return**.

• A **new line** is simply that. The cursor moves into position to start another line of type, using the current alignment, (left, right, or center, set in the Options bar or Paragraph palette) and leading (space between lines, set in the Character palette).

• A **new paragraph** also starts a new line, but in addition to the current alignment and leading, there may be additional space before the new paragraph, or the first line of the new paragraph may have different indenting than other lines in the text. These paragraph characteristics are established in the Paragraph palette.

edge of the bounding box; this automatically wrapping text is called **paragraph type**.

Point type is ideal for headlines and labels. It also works well for several lines of type when you want to control exactly where the lines break or you don't want to be constrained by operating within a bounding box (for instance, in the example on page 427 from Steven Gordon's *Seasons*). **Paragraph type** is great for fitting type within a set space, because you can establish the bounding box first to exactly fit the space available, and then type into it.

• **Type specifications** — such as **font**, **size**, **alignment**, and a number of **spacing** characteristics — are set in the Options bar, Character palette, and Paragraph palette, shown on pages 422 and 423). You can set the specifications as soon as you choose the Type tool — before you click or drag to begin

THE SCOPE OF YOUR SETTINGS

The settings you choose in the Options bar or in the Character or Paragraph palette can be applied to selected characters, to a whole type layer, or even to more than one layer. In each case, you start by targeting the type layer (clicking once on its name in the Layers palette). Then:

• **To affect just *new* type** that you will add to your type layer, choose the Type tool T and click to put the insertion point where you want it. Choose your settings, and type.

• **To change just *some* of the existing type** on a layer, choose the Type tool T and select the type you want to change — by drag-selecting, for example. Then change the settings.

• **To change *all* of the type on a layer**, choose the Type tool T, and *without clicking in the working window,* change the settings.

• **To change several type layers at once**, in Photoshop CS link the other type layers to the one you've targeted (by clicking in the Links column next to the 👁 icon of each of the other type layers). Then choose the Type tool T, hold down the Shift key,

and *without clicking in the working window,* choose your settings. In CS2 you can simply Shift-click or Ctrl/⌘-click the other type layers in the Layers palette to select them (as shown at the left), choose the Type tool, and choose your settings.

Using the color swatch in the Type tool's Options bar, you can change the color of type without changing the Foreground color in the Tools palette.

"UNDOING" TYPE

When you make a mistake (or change your mind) while working in a type layer:

- **To stay in** the type layer but undo your last typing efforts or your last change in the Options bar or palettes, use Undo (Ctrl/⌘-Z).

- **To get out** of the type layer and undo all changes you've made in your current session (since you entered the type layer), press the "Cancel any current edits" button ⃠, or use the keyboard equivalent — the Escape key.

CLICKETY-CLICK

You can accomplish many type-selecting tasks simply by clicking the mouse button:

- A **single click positions the cursor**.

- **Double-click selects the word**, defined by a space or punctuation mark.

- **Triple-click selects the line** of type.

- **Quadruple-click selects the paragraph** (a paragraph is defined when the Enter/Return key is pressed to start a new line).

- **Quintuple-click** (that's five!) **selects the entire text block**.

typing — or you can type first and *then* set the specs. "The Scope of Your Settings" on page 419 tells how to apply type specs to just *some* of the type on a layer or to *all* of it.

With paragraph type, there are more options for type specifications than there are for point type. These include **justification** (the ability to make both sides of the text block straight with the edges of the text box), **hyphenation** (whether and how words are broken at the end of a line in order to make the text fit within the box), **hanging punctuation** (punctuation marks such as quotes and commas can extend slightly outside the edges of the text block for better visual balance and alignment), and access to many more sophisticated controls with **Adobe Composer** (there's more about these controls on page 422).

- Whether you set point type or paragraph type, Photoshop will set up a **type layer**, where the type is isolated from other elements in the file, so it can be manipulated separately and it can remain "live" for editing later. When you've finished typing and you're ready **to get out of the type layer** and go on to something else, the quickest way is to type Ctrl-Enter (Windows) or ⌘-Return (Mac), or simply choose a new tool or target a layer you want to work on (by clicking its thumbnail in the Layers palette, for instance). This will automatically "commit," or keep, your type.

- **To come back and edit your type later,** choose the appropriate Type tool, click once on your type layer's name in the Layers palette, and you're in! You can start selecting text and making changes as described in "Going Back To Edit Type" on page 426.

- When you want **to start another, separate type layer** in a file that already has type in it, a foolproof way to start a *new* type layer rather than accidentally clicking into an existing one is to choose a Type tool (**T** or ⌶**T**) and then **hold down the Shift key** when you click or drag (for point or paragraph type). (If you Shift-drag for paragraph type, the bounding box will be perfectly square *unless you release the Shift key after you start dragging,* freeing up the tool's operation so you can define any rectangular box for the type.)

Type Controls

Once you select a Type tool, all of Photoshop's **type controls** can be found on the Options bar, including access to the **Character palette** (for type controls on a character-by-character basis) and the **Paragraph palette** (for controls such as paragraph indents and extra space before and after paragraphs). "Type

Lorem ipsum dolor sit amet, consectetuer

Dragging a handle of the dotted-line text box for paragraph type will resize the box. (Note the hanging punctuation used here, an option chosen in the Paragraph palette's fly-out menu.

Roses are red and violets are blue. Sugar is sweet and so are you.

Roses are red and violets are blue. Sugar is sweet and so are you.

Whether paragraph type or type-inside-a-path is left-, right-, or center-aligned, it will start as close as it can to the top of the text box or closed path. If this creates an awkward break (top), you can move the type down by typing Enter/Return and then "scrubbing" the icon for "Add space before paragraph" in the Paragraph palette.

Options" on pages 422 and 423 shows these controls and tells what they do. "Exercising Type Layers" on page 447 covers kerning and other character-level controls, as well as keyboard shortcuts that can be used to speed up your work.

Making Type Fit

To fit point type or paragraph type into the space available, you can change its overall size by selecting all (Ctrl/⌘-A) and "scrubbing" the font size setting in the Options bar to quickly and dynamically experiment with changes (see "Wonderful Scrubbers" at the left). For other type-fitting settings, such as tracking (changing the letterspacing overall), open the Character palette by clicking the ▣ button in the Options bar, and use the scrubbers there. Except as a last resort, avoid type-fitting by changing settings in the Character palette that actually distort the type itself, such as the height or width of the characters ("Avoiding Type Distortion" on page 427 gives the reasoning behind this advice.)

Paragraph type offers more options for fitting type, one of which is enlarging the text bounding box. If you type more text than will fit in the text box you defined by dragging with the Type tool, Photoshop will "hold" the extra text and put an "x" in the lower right handle of the text box to alert you that there's more text stored. Dragging on any handle will reshape the box. As you enlarge the text box, the stored text appears inside it. In many cases, however, you might not have the option of stretching the bounding box, because the text area may be limited. "Type-Fitting" on page 602 offers several more suggestions for fitting paragraph type, and a logical order in which to apply them.

Fitting type that has been set **inside a path** works the same way as fitting paragraph type in general — you can grab a handle and drag to make more room so the additional type can appear, reshaping the path in the process.

Fitting **type-on-a-path** is covered on page 425.

Moving or Tilting Type

To move your entire setting of point type, paragraph type, or type-inside-a-path, make sure the type layer is targeted (click its thumbnail in the Layers palette) and that a Type tool is chosen (**T** or **⊥T**). Then click inside the type, hold down the Ctrl/⌘ key so the cursor becomes an arrowhead, rather than an I-beam, and drag. To tilt the type, again hold down the Ctrl/⌘ key, move the cursor outside one of the handles of the bounding box until

continued on page 424

TYPE OPTIONS

Photoshop's sophisticated controls for creating and editing text with the Type tool are spread among the Options bar, the Character and Paragraph palettes, and several dialog boxes. The Options bar offers **font**, **size**, and **alignment** choices. More extensive options are offered in the Character and Paragraph palettes (see below and on the facing page).

Clicking the **"Create warped text"** button opens a dialog box that lets you fit type inside one of 15 preset envelopes that you can choose from its Style menu and then modify.

The **"Toggle the character and paragraph palettes"** button opens the Character and Paragraph palettes.

The Type tool's **Options bar** offers the opportunity to set type **horizontally** or **vertically**, with a button that toggles between the Type tools.

Three **alignment options** are available in the Options bar for the Type and Type Mask tools.

Click the **color swatch** (here or in the Character palette) to set Type color independently of the Foreground color in the Tools palette.

The default Sharp **antialiasing** is a good option for most type; Crisp is a little less sharp. For small on-screen type, it may be better to choose Strong (to make the type heavier) or Smooth (to smooth it), or even None (when jagged edges are preferable to blurry edges, or if significant extra file size is added by the colors required for antialiasing).

The **"Cancel any current edits"** and **"Commit any current edits"** buttons are added to the Options bar as soon as you click with the Type tool in the working window. Clicking the "Cancel" button is equivalent to pressing Escape on the keyboard; it gets you out of typesetting without including any changes you've made in the current typing or editing session. The "Commit" button is equivalent to pressing Ctrl/⌘-Enter to accept the changes and exit typesetting.

Many of the options in the **Paragraph palette** (such as indents and spacing between paragraphs) are available only for paragraph type and type-inside-a-path. But the **"Justify All"** button can also be useful for spacing type on a path (see page 426).

Roman Hanging Punctuation (shown here in the bottom paragraph) lets opening or closing punctuation such as quotation marks, hyphens, and commas extend just beyond the limits of the text box. Since these marks are small, the type can look "indented" if they are aligned and justified with the bigger characters (as shown in the top paragraph).

"What she did," he said to his long-time friend.

"Yeah, I know," said his friend, putting his drink on the table.

In the **Justification** dialog box, acceptable ranges are set for the spacing in justified text. You can control letter and word spacing, and even the horizontal scaling of type. You can also specify what multiple of type size to use for **Auto leading**, which is chosen in the Character dialog box.

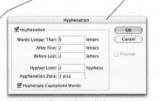

In the **Hyphenation** dialog you can choose whether to automatically hyphenate standard text and capitalized words. You can specify how many letters of a hyphenated word can be alone on a line, how many lines in sequence can end in hyphens (**Hyphen Limit**), and how far from the right margin a word can start and still be eligible to be hyphenated (**Hyphenation Zone**; this applies only to type that isn't justified and when the Single-line Composer is used).

The difference between **Single-line Composer** and **Every-line Composer** is clear in the paragraphs below. **Single-line** attempts to fix unattractive spacing by choosing the best spacing option for each line separately. It adjusts word spacing first, then hyphenation (if it's allowed, which it wasn't in this case), then letterspacing, with compressed spacing being preferable to expanded spacing. **Every-line Composer** can change spacing in the entire paragraph, if necessary, to solve a spacing problem in any one line. Keeping the spacing even throughout the paragraph is given the highest priority, which often makes it a better choice than Single-line.

Single-line

Pellentesque laoreet ligula sit amet eros. In neque mauris, sodales in, pharetra vel, condimentum sit amet, massa. Aenean lacinia ligula sit amet.

Every-line

Pellentesque laoreet ligula sit amet eros. In neque mauris, sodales in, pharetra vel, condimentum sit amet, massa. Aenean lacinia ligula sit amet.

The **Character palette** lets you **kern**, **track**, **adjust the baseline**, and set other type specifications character by character.

The **language** you choose determines which dictionary Photoshop relies on when you choose Edit > Check Spelling.

You can turn off **Fractional Widths** to ensure that characters set in small sizes for on-screen display don't run together.

With **System Layout** turned on you can see how your text will appear in an interface design displayed with your operating system's default text display. Turning on System Layout automatically sets antialiasing to None in the Options bar.

You can select a word or series of words that you don't want to break at the end of a line (**No Break**).

The **Reset Character** command quickly returns text formatting on the targeted layer to the program default. Part of the default is for the Foreground color to control the text color. If your Foreground color is green, for instance, Reset Character will make your text color green. Note that paragraph characteristics, such as justification, are not restored to the default with Reset Character but with the Reset Paragraph command in the Paragraph palette.

The **Change Text Orientation** option lets you switch between type set vertically and horizontally. **Standard Vertical Roman Alignment** stacks characters one above the other (**A**, below); turning it off gives a result like setting type horizontally and then rotating the entire setting 90° clockwise (**B**, below).

Dock to Palette Well
Change Text Orientation
✓ Standard Vertical Roman Alignment

OpenType ▶
✓ Standard Ligatures
  Contextual Alternates
✓ Discretionary Ligatures
  Swash
✓ Oldstyle
  Stylistic Alternates
  Titling Alternates
  Ornaments
✓ Ordinals
✓ Fractions

Faux Bold
Faux Italic
All Caps
Small Caps
Superscript
Subscript

Underline
Strikethrough

✓ Fractional Widths
System Layout

No Break

Reset Character

VERTICAL TEXT **B**

VERTICAL TEXT **A**

Not all **Open Type** fonts contain alternate or additional glyphs (characters). Although an Open Type font can include as many as 65,000 glyphs, many contain only the standard 256 characters they had in their PostScript or True Type format. To access any alternates in an Open Type font, simply choose from the fly-out menu. If any item on the list is grayed out, the current font doesn't contain that alternate.

Most of the styles in this part of the menu (also found as icons at the bottom of the Character palette) are generated by Photoshop rather than being part of the font. **Small Caps** will either use the small caps included with the font or generate them if the designer didn't include them.

LOREM IPSUM dolor sit amet, consectetuer ~~adipiscing~~ elit.

Type that has **Faux Bold** applied can't be converted to Shapes or paths. But Faux Bold and **Faux Italic** can be useful when you plan to use Layer Styles or filters, rasterizing the type in the finished image. For most fonts that include real Bold and Italic styles, the Faux Bold and Faux Italic look different from these.

On the 3rd Tuesday of this month, the meeting of the Guard committee was held at 17548 Banyon Street. They agreed to fulfill their contract to keep Platform 9 3/4 a secret.

On the 3rd Tuesday of this month, the meeting of the Guard committee was held at 17548 Banyon Street. They agreed to fulfill their contract to keep Platform 9¾ a secret.

LOREM IPSUM DOLOR SIT AMET,   CONSECTETUER

Lorem ipsum dolor sit amet,   consectetuer

Bold   **Faux Bold**

Italic   *Faux Italic*

To draw a path for type-on-a-path, you can use the Pen ◊ or one of the Shape tools, with the Paths option chosen in the Options bar.

When the type-on-a-path cursor appears, any typing you do will follow the path.

When this cursor appears, you can Ctrl/⌘-drag the beginning marker of type-on-a-path to reset the starting point and move the type along the path.

When this cursor appears, you can drag the end marker to reset the ending point and move the type along the path.

For center-aligned type, you can move the center point to move the type. One of the two end markers will also move.

The text overflow marker shows that there's more type being held. Move the marker outward from the type to reveal the extra.

you get the curved-arrow cursor, and drag to rotate. *Caution:* With the Ctrl/⌘ key held down, **dragging a *handle*** of the solid-line bounding box will distort the type itself along with the bounding box (see "Avoiding Type Distortion on page 427).

Type-on-a-Path

Type-on-a-path is point type that uses a path as its baseline, rather than simply setting up horizontally (or vertically if you use the Vertical Type tool ⬇T). The path can be open (with two ends) or closed (continuous, with no loose ends). To keep the type easy to read, it's usually best to use paths and shapes that are gently curved and fairly simple.

To set type on a path, you can activate an existing path (by clicking its thumbnail in the Paths palette), or activate a Shape layer (by clicking its thumbnail in the Layers palette). Or draw a new path: For a **hand-drawn path**, select the Pen tool ◊, in the Options bar click on the "Paths" button ▦, and begin drawing. For a **preset path (or shape)**, select any of the Shape tools (pressing Shift-U toggles through them); in the Options bar click on the "Paths" button ▦, and then draw your shape.▼

FIND OUT MORE

▼ Using drawing tools **page 430**

Once you have a path, set your type specifications in the Options bar, including alignment. Then move the cursor onto the path until you see the angled path mark through it ⅄ and click on the path — click where you want to **start your left-aligned type**, or where you want to **end your right-aligned type**, or where you want to **center your center-aligned type**.

When you click to begin putting type on a path, be patient. Photoshop may take a little while to display the flashing insertion cursor. A new type layer will be formed and will appear in the Layers palette. Along with the insertion cursor, two **end markers** — "x" and "o" — will appear on the path to mark the extremes of where the type can go. Photoshop does its best to put these points where you want them:

- For **left-aligned**, the "x" is where you click and the "o" is at the end of the path.
- For **right-aligned**, the "o" is where you clicked and the "x" is at the beginning of the path.
- **Center-aligned** is more interesting. First, you get an additional marker — a diamond (◊) to mark the center. Then, whichever end of the path is closer to where you clicked

When you use a Shape layer as a path for type, a new type layer is added and the separate Shape layer is also retained. To set type along opposite sides of a closed path, it's often more convenient to set the type on two different layers, as shown here. The title type was set with the Horizontal Type tool and a negative baseline shift (set in the Character palette) to put the type below the path. The author's name was added with the Vertical Type tool.

CONTROLLING TYPE-ON-A-PATH

Especially on a closed path, it can be hard to figure out what's happening as you Ctrl/⌘-drag the Type cursor over an end marker and the type starts to disappear or flip around. This series of pictures may help you "decode" what's happening and fix it.

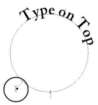

On a closed path the end markers overlap, so it's important to pay close attention to which marker you've selected.

Splitting the end markers by dragging in the correct direction moves the type along the path.

If you accidentally cross the end markers over each other, the type will flip and may partly disappear. But you can fix it by dragging back again.

If you drag the cursor perpendicular, across the path, the type flips upside down and backwards. Drag back across the path to right the type.

gets one of the end markers; the other end marker goes an *equal distance on the other side* of where you clicked — it has to, because otherwise your type wouldn't be centered around your center point.

When you start to type, the characters will start at the appropriate marker. If you type more than will fit between the end markers, Photoshop will "hold" the extra, and a "+" inside the "o" end marker will show that there's more text waiting. At any time you can move any of the markers to change the span the type can cover: With the Type tool active, click somewhere in the type (anywhere — it doesn't matter where you put the insertion point for this). Then hold down the Ctrl/⌘ key and "hover" the cursor over the marker until the cursor turns into an I-beam with one or two thick arrows — ⫯, ⫯, or ⫯; then drag in one direction or the other to move the marker along the path. A couple of warnings here:

- First, if Photoshop thinks that you're dragging the thick-arrowed cursor *perpendicular* to the path rather than along it (even though you may not think so), the type will jump to the other side of the path and flip upside down and backwards. To fix this, simply hover over a marker again to get the thick-arrowed cursor and drag back across to the other side of the path.

- Second, if at some point you change alignment by making another choice from the Options bar or Paragraph palette, *the end markers won't automatically move.* In many cases, you'll want to move them, as just described above, to work with the new alignment.

Fitting type-on-a-path. To adjust the size or tracking of type-on-a-path, you can use the same methods described for point, paragraph, and "in-path" type on page 421. But with type-on-a-path you also have another type-fitting option. If you click the ▣ button in the Options bar to open the Paragraph palette, you'll find that, way over on the right side, the "Justify all" button is active, which isn't true for other point type. If you click this button, Photoshop will spread your type from one end marker of the type-on-a-path to the other. If the text consists of a single word (no spaces between the letters), Photoshop increases letter spacing to spread out the characters. But if the text is more than one word, the type is justified by increasing the space *between* words. For more control, see the "Spreading Type Along a Path" tip on page 426.

When you set type along a path that has strong curves or angles, the type will almost always need *tracking* (adjusting space overall) or *kerning* (adjusting space between a pair of letters). Watch out for special type features that may interfere with these spacing adjustments.

The "Th" pair didn't respond to tracking or kerning (left) because the Ligatures option was selected in the Character palette's menu. When this option was toggled off, tracking and kerning worked (right).

To spread type evenly from one end marker of the type-on-a-path to the other, type the entire text string as a single word — that is, with no spaces between words **A**. Choose the "Justify All" alignment option from the Paragraph palette **B**. To insert the spaces between words but still keep the type spread out, click where a space should go, and in the Character palette set the kerning to a large positive value **C**, using additional kerning or tracking where needed.

To make more space for type along the path, you can move one or both end markers, as described earlier. Or tweak the path itself by choosing the Direct Selection tool and dragging one of the path's control points or segments.▼ (While you have the Direct Selection tool active, the thick-arrowed cursors will also be available. This means you don't have to switch to the Type tool to move the markers, but it also means you should be ready to deal with flipped type, as described on page 425.)

FIND OUT MORE

▼ Editing paths
page 437

Moving or tilting type on a path. Besides sliding type along its path, you can also move the whole path and the type along with it, or you can slide the type to reposition it along the path. To move or tilt the path, use basically the same method as described for moving point type (page 421) — with the Type tool active, hold down the Ctrl/⌘ key, move the cursor far enough from a marker so it becomes an arrowhead rather than an I-beam, and drag.

Going Back To Edit Type

If you've moved on to something else and then find that you need to come back and make changes to the type you set earlier, simply click once on the type layer's name in the Layers palette, and choose the Type tool **T**. Now:

- **To change all the type on the layer,** *don't click or drag anywhere*. Without a cursor in the type, simply make changes to settings in the Options bar or Character and Paragraph palettes.

- **To target your changes to specific characters or to refit, move, or tilt the type,** *first click in the type to get the insertion point, or drag to select some type*, and then make your changes.

When the Type tool **T** is chosen and a type layer is targeted, the Check Spelling command is available in the Edit menu. It's a good idea to leave the **"Check all layers" option turned on** in the "Check Spelling" dialog box. Otherwise, Photoshop checks spelling only on the targeted layer. The setting is a persistent preference, and there's no warning if you haven't checked *all* your layers.

Because live type is vector-based, resizing won't affect the edge quality. But it *can* affect the type's aesthetics. That's why, unless you're going for a special distortion effect, it's important to get the size and spacing close to what you want using the settings in the Options bar and Character palette, rather than depending on transforming the type itself. Big changes in type size require adjustment in the spacing relationships between characters in order to look good; proportions that look good small don't necessarily look good big, and vice versa. Also drastically scaling a block of type horizontally or vertically to make it fit a certain space can differentially distort the thick and thin strokes, ruining the proportions designed into the characters.

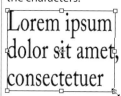

With the Type tool **T** chosen and the Ctrl/⌘ key held down, a solid-line box appears around the type, and dragging on any handle of the solid box resizes the type as well as the box.

Steven Gordon set four lines of left-justified point type with tight leading (little space between lines) and then used a Twist warp to make it flow (see the completed work on page 486).

If you have a lot of text, you may want to use Edit > **Find and Replace** to help you locate a misspelled company name, for instance; but don't expect a full-featured search-and-replace dialog box such as those in InDesign or Microsoft Word.

Resizing or Reshaping Type

We've covered the process of reshaping a text box or a path in "Making Type Fit" and "Type on a Path." It's also possible to resize or distort the type itself by using one of the Transform commands or the Warp Text function.

Transforming. Any time there's an insertion point in the type, all the point or paragraph type on a type layer can be **scaled**, **skewed**, **rotated**, or **flipped** by holding down the Ctrl/⌘ key as you make changes using the handles on the bounding box around the type. **Transforming the type is an all-or-none process** — you can't select and transform just *some* of the type on a layer. If you transform type on or inside a path, the path is transformed along with it. To make other changes to the path — adding or deleting points or reshaping the curve — use the path-editing tools nested with the Pen tool ◊.▼

FIND OUT MORE

▼ Editing paths
page 437

If you start to Ctrl/⌘-drag on a handle and *then* add the **Shift key**, the change will be **constrained** — with a corner handle, proportionality will be maintained; for other handles, the drag will be constrained to vertical or horizontal motion. If you're using the curved double-arrow cursor for rotation, the turning will be constrained to 15° steps.

Warping type. Any type can be reshaped using the **Warp Text** function, which bends, stretches, and otherwise distorts type to fit within an "envelope." When a type layer is active, the Warp Text dialog box can be opened by clicking the "Create warped text" button ⤳ on the Type tool's Options bar, or by choosing Layer > Type > Warp Text. In the Warp Text dialog box you can choose a type of envelope from the Style list, and then set parameters for bending and distorting.

- The **Style** shows you the general shape of the envelope — for instance, an Arc.
- The **Bend** controls the *degree* to which the type is distorted into that shape. For instance, is it a shallow arc (a low setting) or a more pronounced arc (a higher setting)?
- And the **Horizontal** and **Vertical Distortion** settings control where the effect is centered — left or right, up or down.

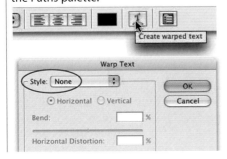

Photoshop rarely does anything "destructive" without warning you first. If you try to run a filter on a type layer, it will ask if you really want to rasterize the type.

The **warping stays "live,"** so you can come back later, choose Warp Text again, and reshape the existing envelope, or even pick a new envelope style.

Like rotating, skewing, or scaling, **warping is applied to the entire type layer**; you can't select and warp individual characters. Nor is there any way to reshape the envelope as you could a path, editing the outline point-by-point. For more sophisticated warping effects, try a drawing program such as Adobe Illustrator, or in CS2 convert the type (see "When To Convert Type," below).

Saving Type

For greatest flexibility, save any files that include type in **Photoshop PSD** format. If you save in **Photoshop PDF** format, preserving the Layers and choosing Include Vector Data and also Embed Fonts, it's possible to open the file with Adobe Reader with the resolution-independent type outlines intact and the type accessible for copying as text, even if the fonts you used aren't present on the system where the file is opened. You can also reopen the PDF in Photoshop if you ever need to edit the type further. The **Photoshop EPS** format, with the Include Vector Data option turned on when you save, can retain the vector information for the printer, but the type can't be edited — either outside of Photoshop or inside if the file is reopened, because it will have become a flattened, single-layer file, without type layers.

When To Convert Type

Keeping Photoshop type "live" and editable as long as possible provides a great deal of flexibility. And with clipping groups, Layer Styles, and the ability to save in PDF and EPS formats, you rarely have to rasterize the type or even convert it to a Shape layer for output. However, there are some exceptions:

- **To run a filter** on type, the type layer has to be rasterized first (turned into a pixel-based layer). Photoshop asks your permission (as shown at the left) and then does this for you.

- **To edit the shape or tilt** of individual characters in a type block, you can first convert the type to a Shape layer (Layer > Type > Convert to Shape) and then select and manipulate the individual character outlines, using the Direct Selection tool ▸ or the tools nested with the Pen tool ◊.▼

FIND OUT MORE

▼ Editing paths
page 437

kick

Live type can mask an image and can accept a Layer Style. But to rotate individual characters or edit a character's shape, first convert the type to a Shape layer (Layer > Type > Convert to Shape). Then use the Edit > Transform Path command and the path-editing tools, as we did here to rotate each letter separately and to extend the leg of the "K" by Shift-selecting its control points and moving them.

When warping or transforming doesn't do exactly what you want, you can convert type to a Shape layer and transform it. "Carving" this type into the sand is described on page 602.

- Although you can transform live type,▼ the Distort and Perspective functions, which give you more reshaping control, aren't available. **To access the full set of Transform functions**, convert the type layer to a Shape layer (Layer > Type > Convert to Shape) and transform it (Edit > Transform > Distort or Perspective). In Photoshop CS2, once you've converted the type, you can also choose Edit > Transform > Warp to be able to reshape the virtual envelope that encloses the type.▼

FIND OUT MORE

▼ Transforming
page 71

▼ Using Edit >
Transform > Warp
page 71

- If your type has **to exactly match** a Shape version of the same type, or a rasterized version (in a Spot Color channel or a mask, for instance), it's safer to convert your live type to a Shape layer. That's because even slight variations in the name or tracking values of the font on the system where the file is output can cause a mismatch between the live type and the channel or mask. You'll find an example of using type with spot color in "Adding Spot Color" on page 229.

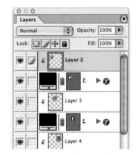

Because he set each letter of his type on a separate layer, John Odam could have left the type live as he tilted some letters and masked a photo inside each one. But to ensure that his book cover design would print correctly, regardless of the fonts included on the output system, he converted the type to Shape layers. Designing the cover is described on page 482.

When all kerning, tracking, and other adjusting is complete, converting display type to Shape layers avoids font complications (see page 451).

Illustrator has more "styles" of type on a path than Photoshop's one kind. When you save an Illustrator file in Photoshop (PSD) format, all of the type on a path is preserved. Both the type and the path can be edited in Photoshop, and the type keeps its orientation to the path, so the file can serve as an editable source for alternative approaches to type-on-a-path.

 Path Type.psd

- **To be sure that a file with display type will open and print as expected**, whether or not the font is present on the next system that handles the file, you can convert the type to Shape layers (Layer > Type > Convert to Shape). The type retains its smooth outlines, but without font complications.

Moving Type Between Illustrator & Photoshop

Adobe Illustrator CS/CS2 and Adobe InDesign CS/CS2 and QuarkXPress have additional text facilities — such as the ability to define Character and Paragraph styles — that make certain projects easier to do in these programs than in Photoshop alone. For complex, text-intensive single-page layout projects, such as menus or book jackets, it often makes sense to place your Photoshop artwork in Illustrator (or InDesign or Quark-XPress) and add the type there.

In other cases — if you want to add a Photoshop Layer Style to the type, for instance, or incorporate the type into an image — you may want to create type in Illustrator and bring it into Photoshop. In order for an Illustrator CS/CS2 text object to be exported as an editable text layer (that is, not be rasterized when the file is opened in Photoshop), you have to remove any strokes or character-level transparency applied to the text before you save the file. Then choose File > Export and save in Photoshop (PSD) format with "Preserve Text Editability" checked.

For point type and paragraph type (called *text* in Illustrator), you can also copy the type to the clipboard in Illustrator and then start a Type layer with point or paragraph type in Photoshop, and paste. Some characteristics, such as font and color, will be preserved in the live type, but others, such as Graphic Style, are lost.

DRAWING

Compared to painting, which is pixel-based, vector drawing has the advantage of being resolution-independent. When vector graphics are printed on a Postscript-based device, their smooth lines are retained regardless of the resolution of the file. This makes Photoshop's vector-based drawing tools — the Pens and Shapes — ideal for creating sharp, smooth-edged graphics.

Starting Out

There are three essential choices to make each time you start drawing in Photoshop:

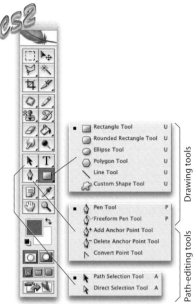

Photoshop's tools for drawing and editing vector-based graphics include the Shape tools, Pen tools, and path-editing tools; some of the path-editing tools share a Tools palette space with the Pens.

When any Shape or Pen tool is chosen, the Options bar includes buttons for all of the Shapes and Pens. To switch tools, just click your choice in the Options bar.

1 **Which drawing tool do you want to use?** Choose one of the Pen or Shape tools nested in the Tools palette — use a **Pen** to create your own shape from scratch; use a **Shape** tool to start with a preset shape.

2 **What kind of element do you want to make?** Using the "mode of operation" buttons at the left end of any drawing tool's Options bar, you can choose to make a **Shape layer** or a "bare-wire" **Path** (no layer, just a wire-frame outline that can be stored in the Paths palette). Paths can be used to make a selection, a baseline for type, or a filled or stroked element on a pixel-based layer. A third choice (for Shape tools only) is to step outside the realm of vector art and draw an area filled with **pixels** on an existing regular (transparent) layer or on the *Background*.

   Note: **The "mode of operation" setting persists** from the last time you used a Pen or Shape. In your eagerness to begin drawing after choosing a tool, it's easy to forget to check this setting. But it's worth getting into the habit. It's disappointing — not to mention time-consuming — to expect to make a Shape layer, do your drawing, and then find that you've accidentally created a *Work Path* instead. You can turn a path into a Shape layer (as described in the "Convertibility" tip on page 438), but it isn't instantaneous.

3 **Do you want to start a new** Shape layer or path, **or modify the currently targeted one?** This choice is made by clicking one of the buttons near the right end of the Options bar (see "Combining Options for Drawing Tools" on page 432.

Besides these options, you can also choose to incorporate a Layer Style or a different color as you draw (see "Style & Color Options for Drawing Tools," on page 432).

DRAWING TOOL MODES OF OPERATION

The **Shape** and **Pen** tools have the modes of operation shown here for originating vector graphics or modifying the currently targeted graphics.

For all Pens and Shapes, the **Paths** option produces a resolution-independent path. The path is stored in the Paths palette (see page 432), where it can be activated to create a Shape layer, a baseline for type, or a filled or stroked area on a pixel-based layer.

For all Pen and Shape tools, the **Shape layers** option creates a color layer with a vector mask that defines exactly where this color is revealed and where it's hidden.

Fill pixels (for Shape tools but not Pens) is a quick way to draw pixel-based graphics that you can filter or paint immediately; but these graphics aren't resolution-independent. When the *Background* or a regular (transparent) layer is active and this option is chosen, you can set the blend Mode and Opacity for the fill; you can also choose whether the edges will be antialiased (smooth) or not (pixelated).

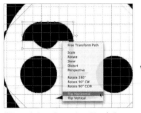

"Exercising Drawing Tools" on page 456 is a quick vector drawing and editing tutorial. Other tutorials on drawing and editing paths can be found by choosing Help > Photoshop Help, expanding the list of topics under "Drawing," and clicking one of the links.

In addition to the choices common to all vector drawing tools, each tool has its own additional options — for instance, the number of sides produced when you draw with the Polygon tool. "Options for Specific Drawing Tools" on page 434 tells about these choices.

Path Terminology

Paths, Shape layers, and vector masks can all be described by the more generic term *paths*. A *path* is made up of *path segments* that stretch between *anchor points*. An anchor point can be a smooth point (where the curve continues smoothly through the point) or a corner point (which makes a corner or cusp where the path abruptly changes direction).

COMBINING OPTIONS FOR DRAWING TOOLS

To start a Shape layer or path, use the "New" button. Then you can use any of the other buttons to add to it or subtract from it; or choose to start another one by clicking the "New" button again.

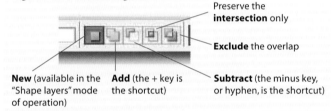

Preserve the **intersection** only

Exclude the overlap

New (available in the "Shape layers" mode of operation)

Add (the + key is the shortcut)

Subtract (the minus key, or hyphen, is the shortcut)

To add to or subtract from a Shape layer, the mask for the layer has to be targeted in the Layers palette. To do this, click once or twice on the mask thumbnail; a double border will show that the mask is active.

STYLE & COLOR OPTIONS FOR DRAWING TOOLS

When you draw a Shape layer, you can add a Layer Style or color as you draw; or change the Style or color after drawing. You can also save a drawing tool preset that includes a built-in Style and color (see page 436).

You can choose a **Layer Style** from the pop-out **Style picker**, rather than opening the Styles palette.

The **Color** of Shape layers can be controlled independently of the Foreground color by clicking this swatch and choosing a color.

When this button is **darkened** (as shown), any changes to the Style or color will be applied to the **currently active Shape layer**. When the button is **light**, the Style and color won't be applied until you draw the **next Shape layer**. To set a Style or color for the next Shape layer without changing the current layer, click the button until it's light, and then make Style and color choices.

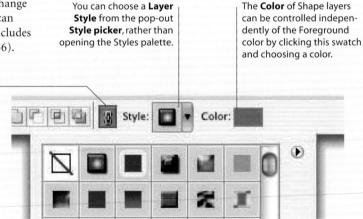

PATH PARTS

The paths produced by the Pen and Shape tools in Photoshop are defined by *anchor points* (which can be *smooth points* or *corner points*) and *direction lines*.

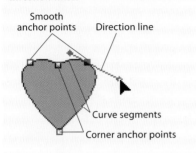

A component path can be selected and manipulated independently of other components in the path.

SAVING THE WORK PATH

The current *Work Path* will be eliminated if you click in an empty area of the Paths palette and then start to draw again. To avoid accidentally eliminating the *Work Path,* double-click its name in the Paths palette to open the Save Path dialog box.

How each segment bends between its two anchor points is determined by one or two *direction lines*, which are "levers" located at the anchor points. The amount of tension a direction line puts on the wirelike segment it controls is what determines how steep or flat the curve of the segment is; the tension can be changed by adjusting the lever. The **direction line for a smooth point** operates as a continuous rod that pivots around the smooth point. Moving one end of the direction line also moves the other in the opposite direction, controlling both segments of the curve that come into the point and maintaining the smoothness of the curve. A **corner point's two direction lines** are moved independently of each other, so you have separate control of the two segments coming into the point.

A path can include more than one *component path*, or subpath. A component path is produced when you end one series of segments and then start a separate one without starting a new Shape layer, vector mask, or path.

The Paths Palette

The Paths palette provides everything that's needed for storing, filling, and stroking paths; converting selections to paths and vice versa; and making clipping paths for exporting silhouetted areas.

The Shape Tools

The shape tools — Rectangle ▢, rounded Rectangle ▢, Ellipse ⬭, Polygon ⬠, Line ╲, and custom Shape ⬧ — are all nested in a single space in the Tools palette, as shown on page 431. The Shape tools are operated by dragging. By default, you drag from corner to corner of your shape. For many of the tools, though, you have the option of drawing the shape outward from

continued on page 435

THE PATHS PALETTE

Each entry in the Paths palette represents a **path**, which may include **component paths**. A path can be designated as a **clipping path** to export a subject without a background.

When you start drawing in Paths mode, a **Work Path** is created in the Paths palette.

If a **Shape layer** is currently active, its **vector mask** is listed in the Paths palette.

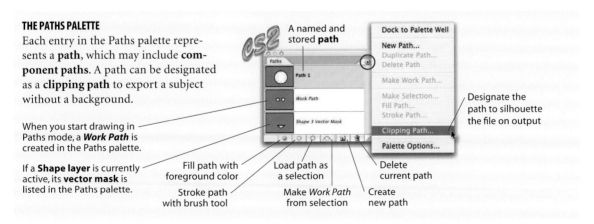

A named and stored **path**

Designate the path to silhouette the file on output

Fill path with foreground color

Stroke path with brush tool

Load path as a selection

Make *Work Path* from selection

Delete current path

Create new path

OPTIONS FOR SPECIFIC DRAWING TOOLS

In addition to the Options bar settings available for all the Shape or Pen tools, each specific tool has its own options, available in the bar itself or in the "Geometry options" palette that opens when you click the ▼ button to the right of the tool buttons. If you set a Layer Style or a color in the Options bar, it will appear as you draw.

The only option in the palette for the **Pen** tool ✎ is **Rubber Band**, which lets you "preview" the next segment of the path as you draw, before you click to set an anchor point.

The palette for the **Freeform Pen** ✐ lets you set the **Curve Fit** (to determine how closely the path will follow the movement of the cursor). In the Freeform Pen's Options bar you can also access the **Magnetic Pen** ✐ (see page 437).

The **Polygon** tool ⬡ can draw both **polygons** and **stars**, with the number of sides or arms specified in the **Sides** field. Without a specific **Radius** setting, size is determined by how far you drag. Unlike the other shapes, the Polygon is always drawn from the center; it has a fixed width-to-height proportion, and the direction you drag controls the orientation of the figure. You can choose **Smooth Corners** or sharp (as here), and for a **star**, you can choose how much to **indent** the sides and whether the indents are **Smooth** (as here) or sharp.

Custom arrowheads can be applied to either or both ends of a line as you draw it with the **Line** tool ╲. **Width**, **Length**, and **Concavity** are set as percentages of the line's **Weight**. A negative Concavity stretches the base of the arrowhead away from the tip, as in the two arrows above on the right. The arrow on the far left was made by clicking with the Line tool to place the starting arrowhead and then dragging *toward* the tip rather than away from it.

For the **Rectangle** ▢ and **Rounded Rectangle** ▢ (shown here), you can constrain the shape to a **Square**; the **Ellipse** ◯ can be constrained to a **Circle**. You can choose **Fixed Size** or a **Proportional** relationship between Width and Height, rather than controlling this by dragging. You can also choose to draw from the **Center** outward. For the Rounded Rectangle, you can set the **Radius** of the round corners as well.

For the **Custom Shape** tool 🎨 you can choose the shape you want to draw from the **Custom Shape picker** (above) with shapes that have been stored as presets; this palette is opened by clicking the ▼ button to the right of the Shape thumbnail in the Options bar. Using the "Geometry options" pop-out palette (left), you can choose to constrain the shape to its original **Defined Size** or **Proportions**, specify a **Fixed Size**, and draw from the **Center**.

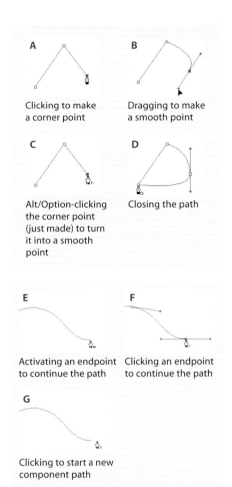

A Clicking to make a corner point

B Dragging to make a smooth point

C Alt/Option-clicking the corner point (just made) to turn it into a smooth point

D Closing the path

E Activating an endpoint to continue the path

F Clicking an endpoint to continue the path

G Clicking to start a new component path

DRAWING ON THE GRID

If you choose View > Show > Grid and View > Snap To > Grid, you can make the Pen tool ✒ follow the Grid as you draw a path, mapping anchor points and direction points to the Grid points to draw symmetrical curves and shapes.

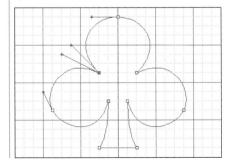

its center. Other options are described in "Options for Specific Drawing Tools" on the facing page.

CYCLING CUSTOM SHAPES

As they can with so many palettes, the bracket keys can cycle through the Custom Shape tools in the Options bar. Press `]` for the next Custom Shape in the palette or `[` for the previous one. Adding the Shift key cycles to the end or beginning of the palette.

The Pen Tools

With the tools in the Pen family, you can create your own paths by clicking and dragging.

Operating the Pen ✒**.** With the Pen tool itself (as shown at the left):

A **To set a corner point,** for a corner or a cusp (where the path abruptly changes direction), just click.

B **To place a smooth (curve) point,** click where you want to put the point, and then shape the curve by dragging in the direction you want the next segment of the curve to go.

C **To change the anchor point you just made from a smooth point to a corner point, or vice versa,** hold down the Alt/Option key and click the point. Then release the key and proceed to set the next point.

D **To close the path,** move the cursor close to the starting point and click when you see a little circle next to the cursor ✒₀.

There are three other tiny symbols that can appear next to the Pen tool's cursor to signal what will happen if you click:

E **Continue the path** from the nearby selected point ✒.

F If no point is selected, **select the nearby point and continue the path** ✒.

G **Start a new component path** in the currently active path ✒ₓ.

Operating the Freeform Pen. With the **Freeform Pen** ✒, dragging creates a curve as if you were drawing with a pencil; anchor points are placed automatically. As with the Pen, you can choose **Auto Add/Delete** in the Options bar. In the Options bar's pop-out palette, you can also set the **Curve Fit** (between 0.5 and 10 pixels), which determines how closely the path will follow your movement of the cursor. With lower settings the curve will follow more closely, placing more anchor points. The

continued on page 437

Graphics that are often used in a particular color or Layer Style can be stored in a way that lets you draw them with the Style and color already in place. This can be ideal for a logo in a corporate color, a digital signature for photos or artwork, or any other graphics that you might want to incorporate into Photoshop files. Here's how you can do that.

1 Once you've created a **Shape layer** with your graphics, you can add it to the Shapes that can be drawn with the Custom Shape tool: Target the layer's **vector mask** in the Layers palette and choose **Edit > Define Custom Shape** ("Defining & Saving" on page 459 has an example).

When the Custom Shape preset is defined, it will be stored as a black graphic, even if it already has a Layer Style or color applied. But it *is* possible to store Style and color with the graphic if you then go on to define your shape as a *Tool preset*:

2 Choose the **Custom Shape** tool , click on the **"Shape layers"** mode of operation near the left end of the Options bar **A**, and in the **Custom Shape picker** click on your stored shape to choose it **B**. Add the Style and color you want (one way is to use the **Style picker C** and **Color swatch D** in the Options bar). Scale the Style if needed. ▼

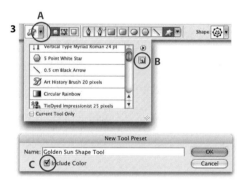

> **FIND OUT MORE**
> ▼ Scaling Styles
>   **page 45**

3 **At the left end of the Options bar**, click the ▼ button **A** to open the **Tool Preset picker**. When it opens, click the "Create new tool preset" button ▦ **B**. In the New Tool Preset dialog box, name the tool, make sure the **Include Color** box is checked **C**, and click "OK."

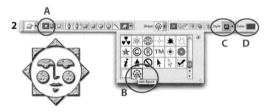

4 Choose **Edit > Preset Manager**, and in the Preset Manager dialog box, choose **Tools** (*not* Custom Shapes) from the menu of Preset Types **A**. In the array of tools, click on your new tool **B** and then Shift-click or Ctrl/⌘-click to add any other tools that you want to include in the set with it. Click the "Save Set" button **C**. In the Save dialog box **D**, name the set and click the "Save" button; then click the "Done" button to close the Preset Manager dialog. A Tool presets file will be created with your new tool and any others you specified.

Now your set will be available to load from the menu of the Tool Preset picker; click the ⊙ button and choose Load Tool Presets. If you saved your preset file (from step 4) in the Tools folder that was created when you installed Photoshop, the set will appear in the list at the bottom of the Tool Preset picker's ⊙ menu. (If you didn't store it in the Tools folder but you want it in the list, find Presets > Tools inside your Adobe Photoshop folder and move your new set into the Tools folder.)

MAKING A PERSPECTIVE GRID

Though it won't have the precision or "snap to" properties of Photoshop's native grid, in CS2 you can make a *perspective grid* to use as a guide for drawing. In your file, add a new empty layer (Ctrl/⌘-Shift-N) or duplicate the white-filled *Background* (Ctrl/⌘-J), as we did here. Then choose Filter > Vanishing Point and set up the perspective grid(s) you want.▼

FIND OUT MORE

▼ Using Vanishing Point **page 588**

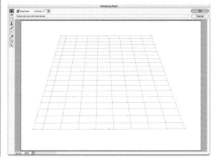

Now if you hold down the Alt/Option key as you click "OK" to leave Vanishing Point, your grid will appear on the layer you added. To use the guide for drawing on another layer, change the layer's blend mode or Opacity to suit, and

zoom in if you like. After drawing, you can go back into the Vanishing Point interface to paint or paste in perspective.

STOPPING

To end an open path you're drawing with the Pen ✎, hold down the Ctrl/⌘ key and click somewhere off the path. For the Magnetic Pen ✐ press the Enter/Return key.

tiny symbols in figures **E**, **F**, and **G** on page 435 also appear when you use the Freeform Pen to continue a path.

The **Magnetic** choice in the Freeform Pen's Options bar turns this tool into the Magnetic Pen ✐, which was designed to create a path by automatically following color and contrast differences in an image. To operate the Magnetic Pen, you click the cursor somewhere on the edge you want to trace and then "float" the cursor along, moving the mouse or stylus without pressing its button. To control the Magnetic Pen, you can set Curve Fit as you can for the Freeform Pen. You can also set the **Width** (the area where the tool looks for the edge as you float the cursor along), the **Contrast** (how much difference the tool looks for when deciding whether a change in color constitutes an "edge"), and the **Frequency** (the distance between "fastening points," which "tack down" the curve as you draw it, to determine how far back the path will "unravel" if you press the Delete key). The Magnetic Pen is tricky to use, and in real-world projects you may find it more efficient to use the Pen and Freeform Pen as described in "Tracing Edges" below.

Tracing Edges

Used together, the Pen ✎ and Freeform Pen ✐ can be especially useful for tracing edges from photo reference, especially when your goal is nicely shaped details rather than a perfectly faithful outline. You can toggle between the Pen ✎ and Freeform Pen ✐ by typing Shift-P. To make a path by tracing an element with some smooth and some detailed edges, use the Pen for the smooth edges, then type Shift-P and continue with the Freeform Pen, dragging to follow the edge. When you come to a smooth section again, type Shift-P to toggle back to the Pen. Follow the edges as carefully as you like, but rather than adjust each anchor point and segment as you draw, finish the path and then zoom in (Ctrl/⌘-+) to find areas that need fixing, and use the techniques in "Editing Shapes & Paths" (below) to quickly make adjustments.

EDITING SHAPES & PATHS

With Photoshop's path-editing tools you can edit the outlines already created with the drawing tools. Some of the editing tools are nested with the Pen tools:

A Click on a path segment with the **Add Anchor Point** tool ✎⁺ to add a point for more control in reshaping a path.

B Click on an anchor point with the **Delete Anchor Point** ✎⁻ tool to reduce the complexity of a path.

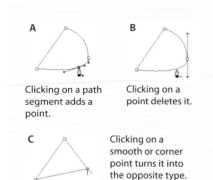

A Clicking on a path segment adds a point.

B Clicking on a point deletes it.

C Clicking on a smooth or corner point turns it into the opposite type.

C Click or drag on an anchor point with the **Convert Point** tool ⊳ to change it from a smooth point to a corner point or vice versa.

Two other path-editing tools — the Path Selection tool ▶ and the Direct Selection tool ▶ — share a space above the Pens.

To work on path segments, use the **Direct Selection tool** ▶:

- **To reposition an anchor point or a straight path segment**, drag it with the ▶.

- **To make a curved path segment steeper or flatter**, use the ▶ to drag the center of the segment.

- Another way **to reshape a curved path segment** is to click with the ▶ on an anchor point and **drag one or both ends of its direction line(s)**. Or **to convert the anchor point** from a corner to a smooth point or vice versa **and reshape the curve, Alt/Option-drag** a direction-line endpoint with the ▶.

To work on an entire path or component path, rather than a path segment, use the **Path Selection tool** ▶:

- **To move a path or component path**, drag it with the ▶.

- **To duplicate a path or component path**, click it with the ▶ once or twice (until the anchor points show), hold down the Alt/Option key, and drag. (Shift-click or drag to select more than one component of a path.)

- **To invert the nature of a Shape layer** so the solid area becomes a "hole" and vice versa, activate the vector mask component of the Shape layer (by clicking its mask thumbnail in the Layers palette once or twice, until the double border appears around it). Then, in the working window, use the ▶ to click the particular component path you want to invert, and click the Add ▫ or Subtract ▫ button on the Options bar (shown on page 432).

- **To combine closed component paths** into a single

Use the Path Selection tool ▸ to move, duplicate, or combine paths or component paths; to change a Shape layer from a shape on a transparent background to a "hole" in a solid background, or vice versa; or to align or distribute component paths.

Use the Move tool ▸⊕ to align or distribute Shape layers with one another or with other layers.

To use Smart Guides to align paths, Shape layers, and other elements, choose View > Show > Smart Guides. For the Smart Guides to show up, the Extras option in the View menu must also be turned on.

PATTERNED SHAPES

To make a pattern-based (or gradient-based) Shape layer, create the Shape layer with a Pen or Shape tool and then choose Layer > Change Layer Content > Pattern (or Gradient).

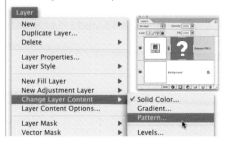

component path or a single path, you should first make sure the positive and negative attributes for all the component paths are set the way you want them. To reset these attributes, click a component path with the ▸ and then click the appropriate button in the Options bar — Add ▣, Subtract ▣, Intersect ▣, or Exclude ▣. When the attributes are set correctly, select the component paths you want to combine permanently, and click the Options bar's "Combine" button.

ALIGNING PATHS & SHAPE LAYERS

Photoshop's precise alignment capabilities can be applied to paths and Shape layers:

- **To align component paths or distribute them evenly,** Shift-click them with the Path Selection tool ▸ and click an Align or Distribute button in the Options bar.

- **To align or distribute Shape layers** with one another, target one by clicking its thumbnail in the Layers palette. Then target the others: In Photoshop CS link each of the other layers you want to align by clicking the Links column to the right of the 👁 to link it to the targeted layer. In CS2, you can simply Shift-click or Ctrl/⌘-click to target additional layers. With the layers linked or multitargeted, choose the Move tool ▸⊕ and click one of the alignment buttons in the Options bar.

In Photoshop CS2 you can also align elements "on the fly" by using the Smart Guides. If you choose View > Show > Smart Guides to turn on this option, guidelines will appear whenever the centers or edges of elements line up with one another.

TRANSFORMING PATHS

When a path or Shape layer is targeted, the Edit > Free Transform command becomes Edit > Free Transform Path. Choosing this command (or using its shortcut, Ctrl/⌘-T) gives you a Transform box, and you can scale, distort, or move the targeted path, component path, or path segment.▼

FIND OUT MORE

▼ Transforming
page 71

STROKING & FILLING PATHS

Photoshop offers a wide range of options for **filling** and **stroking** paths. A path can be filled or stroked with pixels on a *Background*, a **regular (transparent) layer,** or a **layer mask**; these layers and masks are the only ones that will accept a pixel-based

FILL OPTIONS

A single path can produce a variety of different fill effects, depending on which options are chosen in the Fill Path dialog box. Open the dialog by Alt/Option-clicking the leftmost button ● at the bottom of the Paths palette, and choose a fill, blend mode, opacity, and amount of feather.

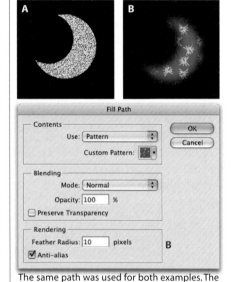

The same path was used for both examples. The path was filled with the Foreground Color in Dissolve mode **A** and with a pattern in Normal mode with a feathered edge **B**.

fill or stroke. With the layer or mask targeted, target the path you want by clicking its thumbnail in the Paths palette. (If you want to fill or stroke *some* components of a path but not all, click or Shift-click them in the working window with the Path Selection tool.) Then:

- **To simply fill with the Foreground color,** click the "Fill path with Foreground color" button ● at the bottom of the Paths palette.

- **To fill with a color you choose** (independent of the Foreground color) **or with a pattern,** Alt/Option-click the ● button to open the Fill Path dialog box, where you can choose a fill color or a pattern; you can also specify the blend Mode and Opacity for the fill, and even a Feather setting to soften the edges of the filled area.

- **To stroke a path with the Foreground color,** in the Tools palette click on the painting or toning tool you want to stroke with, set its characteristics in the Options bar, and click the "Stroke path with brush" button ○ at the bottom of the Paths palette. (If the current tool isn't a painting or toning tool, the stroke will be made with the current settings for the Brush tool ✎ or with the current settings for the last painting tool you selected in this work session.)

- **To choose from a menu of all the tools that can stroke a path,** open the Stroke Path dialog box by Alt/Option-clicking the Stroke Path button ○. The tool you choose will use its most recent settings to make the stroke; you won't be able to see or change its settings once the Stroke Path dialog is open.

LAYERING STROKES

You can stroke and restroke a path with different tools, brush sizes, or colors to layer the "paint."

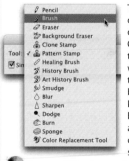

The Stroke Path dialog box, opened by Alt/Option clicking the "Stroke path with brush" button ○ at the bottom of the Paths palette, has a menu of all the tools that can be used to stroke a path.

Layered Strokes.psd

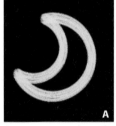

On a transparent layer the moon path was stroked with the Brush tool using a Flat Bristle brush tip (from Adobe's Thick Heavy Brush presets) with Diameter reduced to 60 px, Roundness reduced to 40%, Size control set to Off instead of Pen Pressure, and Noise turned on **A**. Then on another layer it was stroked with the Crosshatch 4 brush tip from Adobe's Assorted Brushes presets, with Diameter at 60 px, Spacing at 180% to separate the "stars," and Angle Jitter at 10% **B**. Layer Styles were added to the two layers **C**.

With the Simulate Pressure option turned on in the Stroke Path dialog, any Pen Pressure controls built into the brush tip you're using will be expressed. The stroke will be applied as if Pen Pressure started out low, increased, and then tapered off to low again.

STROKING OR FILLING A SHAPE LAYER

If a path is part of a Shape layer, it can't be filled or stroked with pixels as described on page 440. Its fill can be changed by using the Color swatch in the Shape tools' Options bar or by changing layer content (see "Patterned Shapes" on page 439). But another quick and easy way to apply a fill or stroke to a Shape layer is to use a Layer Style. The Color Overlay, Gradient Overlay, and Pattern Overlay effects can be used for fill, and the Texture component of the Bevel and Emboss effect can add surface texture. The Stroke effect in a Layer Style can be used for outlining the shape. Fills and strokes assigned as part of a Layer Style can be changed easily, and many are resolution-independent so they can be enlarged without deterioration in quality. Layer Styles are covered extensively in Chapter 8.

K & L DESIGNS

Filters and textures can be used to "soften" vector graphics (see page 467).

"SOFTENING" VECTOR ART

Beyond stroking and filling paths, there are other methods of adding texture and more complex color to vector art. "Coloring Clip Art" on page 474 adds color, shading, and dimension to black-and-white art, and "Organic Graphics" and "Quick Filter Effects" starting on page 467 suggest ways of using Photoshop's filters to stylize flat-color artwork.

USING PHOTOSHOP WITH ADOBE ILLUSTRATOR

Photoshop can exchange graphics and type with Adobe Illustrator, which is bundled with it in the Creative Suite and Creative Suite 2. (Type exchange was covered earlier in the chapter page 430.)

Illustrator's Unique Drawing Abilities

Despite all of Photoshop's typographic, vector-drawing, and layout tools, Illustrator is better at some vector-drawing tasks than Photoshop is. If you have Illustrator, here are some capabilities you might like to know about. If you don't have it, this section may help you decide whether you need it:

- Illustrator's **Spiral** tool — with control over the number of turns, the radius, and the decay rate — gives you more kinds of spirals than you get with Photoshop's Custom Shape spiral.

- If you hold down the Alt/Option key, Illustrator's **Star** tool can automatically draw stars with arms whose edges are aligned. You can control the number of arms as you draw or control the depth of the indent on the fly (after you start drawing, hold down the Ctrl/⌘ key).

- The two **Grid** tools (Rectangular and Polar) are great for quickly drawing the precisely aligned paths for these forms.

- When you need a series of related shapes or an intermediate between two shapes, the **Blend** tool or command can morph one vector path or shape into another, with the number of in-between shapes you specify.

Here are a few of the many styles of stars and spirals easily created with Illustrator's interactive Star and Spiral tools.

The two stars on the right have arms whose edges are not aligned — these stars are easy to draw in Photoshop with the Polygon tool ⬡ in Star mode (see below). The star on the left has arms whose edges *are* aligned, which can be done automatically in Illustrator. In Photoshop you can align the edges of the arms if you know the right "Indent Sides By" value, but this number changes with the number of sides on the star. (For a five-pointed star, the magic number is 50%.)

This star was drawn with Photoshop's Polygon tool ⬡ with the Star and Smooth Indents options chosen. Illustrator doesn't have an equivalent option.

Illustrator's Object > Blend command was used to create the three intermediate shapes between the star and the circle. A blend can be made with a specified number of steps (as this one was) or a specified distance between steps. The example on the bottom was created from a star with no fill. For the one at the top, the star had the same green fill as the circle but with the fill's Opacity set to 0%.

- Vector- or pixel-based artwork can be **warped** using interactive tools and dialogs similar to those of Photoshop's Liquify filter or Warp Text options, and CS2's Edit > Transform > Warp command, which works with Shape layers and paths.

- Use the **3D Effects** dialog to revolve, rotate, or extrude any vector path into a 3D object. Then apply any artwork produced in Photoshop or Illustrator onto the 3D object. In CS2 using Photoshop's Warp command to apply the artwork may be easier than doing the job in Illustrator.

- Use vector **Art brushes** to mimic watercolors, charcoal, or calligraphic pens. Or use **Pattern brushes** to quickly create complex lines and borders.

- The **Symbol Sprayer tool** can "spray" symbols (vector or pixel artwork from Photoshop or Illustrator) onto the canvas. You can then interactively manipulate their size, shape, distribution, color, and transparency.

- In Illustrator you have more options for **aligning individual points** of shapes and paths, making it easier, for instance, to create a symmetrically zigzagging path.

- **Type** is generally easier to manipulate in Illustrator.

- In Illustrator CS2, the **Live Trace** command automatically traces images as vector graphics, with interactive controls for simplifying an image for tracing.

- Illustrator CS2's **Live Paint** makes working with vector graphics much more like working with traditional artists' drawing and coloring tools. Live Paint treats all paths as if they were on a single flat surface, dividing the surface into areas that can be filled with color. When the paths are edited, the color adapts to the reshaped areas.

Moving Artwork Between Photoshop & Illustrator

In some cases, type and vector artwork can be transferred between Photoshop and Illustrator with font information or paths intact. In other cases the vector-based artwork has to be rasterized first, or at least simplified, to make the trip. The way you move artwork between the two programs will depend on what sort of artwork you're moving and which of its properties are most important to preserve. Because each program can produce such a wide range of type and vector art, it's hard to come up with a set of hard-and-fast rules for making the transfer. With as many exceptions as rules, exact results can be hard to predict. But here's a generalized list of options for moving artwork (see page 430 for type options):

In Illustrator CS/CS2, the AICB option must be checked in the Files & Clipboard section of the Preferences dialog box in order to paste shapes or paths into Photoshop.

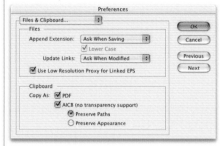

Then when you paste from the clipboard into Photoshop, the Paste dialog box will let you choose to rasterize the clipboard contents (turn it into pixels), or bring it in as a path, or import it as a Shape layer. In CS2 you can also paste as a Smart Object, with the option for further editing in Illustrator later and automatic updating of the Photoshop file.

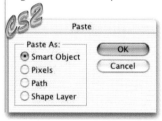

Of course, Illustrator isn't the only Post-Script drawing program that produces files Photoshop can handle. Files from Macromedia FreeHand (version 8 and later) can be rasterized as pixel-based images in Photoshop format.

CorelDraw files can be rasterized and exported as Photoshop files or saved in Adobe Illustrator format and processed through Illustrator to Photoshop. Translation of a complex file from CorelDraw to Illustrator may not be completely accurate, though.

Drag-and-drop (for paths and shapes). By default, Illustrator artwork will be rasterized when it's dragged from Illustrator and dropped into Photoshop, but you can keep editable paths if you hold down the Ctrl/⌘ key as you drag. In the other direction, Photoshop paths and shapes retain their vector character and editability when you drag-and-drop them into Illustrator.

Copy and paste (for pixels, paths, and shapes). With Preferences set correctly (as described in "Pasting from Illustrator" at the left), when you copy an Illustrator object to the clipboard and paste it into a Photoshop file, the Paste dialog will offer you the choice to paste as Pixels, a Path, or a Shape Layer. In CS2 you also have the opportunity to paste as a Smart Object, with a link back to Illustrator for editing, and automatic updating of the Photoshop file.

Going from Photoshop to Illustrator, simply select and copy the element you want in Photoshop, then paste it into your Illustrator document. Its pixel or vector character will be retained.

Files (for shapes and multiple layers). To move an **Illustrator file to Photoshop**, choose Photoshop (PSD) in Illustrator's File > Export dialog box. In saving in PSD format, Illustrator tries to retain as much editability as possible (live type and layer structure, which keeps objects separate and easy to select in Photoshop) without sacrificing appearance.

To move **Photoshop files to Illustrator**, for paths, choose File > Export > Paths to Illustrator. For Shape layers, save the file in Photoshop (PSD) format, and then open it in Illustrator (File > Open). In Illustrator's Photoshop Import Options dialog choose "Convert Photoshop layers to objects and make text editable where possible" and click "OK."

When you Open or Place (embed) a PSD file in Illustrator, choose the "Convert Photoshop layers to objects. . ." option to preserve as much of the layer structure as can be done without compromising the appearance of the document. The rules governing which layers are merged (and what parts of the artwork are rasterized) are complex, but in general, layers with features that Illustrator doesn't support will be merged.

Importing complex graphics. One often used workflow is to construct a complex graphic in Illustrator and then bring it into Photoshop to apply Layer Styles to individual components.

The original Illustrator art **A** was imported as a Shape layer, which was duplicated three times **B**. Then different subpaths were deleted from each layer **C** and Layer Styles were applied **D** (see page 460).

The original Illustrator artwork was pasted into Photoshop as a Shape layer, and a layer style was applied **A**, **B**. Then some of the component paths were selected, cut, and pasted into new layers, so the color of the neon could be changed **C**, **D** (see page 546).

Since each layer can have just one Style, the goal is to separate all the elements that need different Styles onto their own layers in Photoshop, keeping the elements in register as in the original graphic. One approach is described in "Coloring Clip Art" on page 474. A layered Illustrator file is saved in PSD format, with the elements sorted onto layers according to how they will need to be treated in Photoshop.

A second approach is to select and copy the desired artwork to the clipboard in Illustrator, and then paste it into a Photoshop file as a single Shape layer; next duplicate this Shape layer as many times as you need layers, and then delete the unwanted elements from each layer. This method results in vector-based artwork and is described in "Designing for Scalability & Animation" on page 460.

And here's a third option. Once you've copied and pasted a Shape layer, in your pasted layer, select the path that you want to put on a layer of its own and cut it to the clipboard. Then add a Solid Color Fill layer, add a vector mask, and paste. The path will appear in the new layer in exactly the same position where it was when you selected and copied it. This method is demonstrated in "Crafting a Neon Glow" on page 546.

In Creative Suite 2 there's another option. Create the artwork in Illustrator, copy it to the clipboard, and paste it into Photoshop as a **Smart Object**.▼ You can then treat it like any regular layer in Photoshop, applying a Style and transforming it repeatedly without deterioration. If you want to edit the artwork, double-clicking the Smart Object's thumbnail in the Layers palette reopens the file in Illustrator, where you can make changes. Saving the edited file in Illustrator automatically updates the Photoshop file.

FIND OUT MORE

▼ Working with Smart Objects **page 39**

PHOTOSHOP & PAGE LAYOUT PROGRAMS

When you need to create a multipage document, move to Adobe InDesign or QuarkXPress. These programs have such features as paragraph styles, more sophisticated "find and replace" functions, automatic page and figure numbering, and automated table of contents and indexing, which will make your multipage documents easy to create and update. A page layout program also provides an easy way to assemble Photoshop files of different resolutions.

To use a path to silhouette a Photoshop image for placement in a page layout document, you can create the path and then designate it as the *clipping path* that will hide the parts of the image you don't want to show:

- Make a path based on the transparency of a type or Shape layer (by targeting the layer in the Layers palette and then clicking the "Make work path from selection" button ⟠ at the bottom of the Paths palette).

- Draw a *Work Path* that surrounds the area you want to retain and save the path (double-click the *Work Path* name in the Paths palette). (Of course, if you have an appropriate path that you've saved already, you can just click its name in the Paths palette, rather than drawing a new path.)

DESIGNING ILLUSTRATOR ARTWORK FOR SMART OBJECTS

Every Smart Object has **contents** that can be edited and a **"package"** (or bounding box) that's established when the Smart Object is created, and can't be changed later. When you create artwork in Illustrator **A** and paste it into Photoshop as a Smart Object **B**, the package is the smallest rectangle that can include the art. If you later enlarge the artwork outside the original bounding box, Illustrator will seem to be enlarging the package **C**, but when you save the edited file, Photoshop will scale as necessary (often disproportionately) to fit the edited contents within the original Smart Object bounding box **D**. This scaling is rarely desirable. To avoid it, there's something you can do when you first create the Illustrator artwork, to ensure that Photoshop will create a bigger package that can accommodate more changes without distorting the art.

In Illustrator, after you've created the art, add an invisible (no-stroke, no-fill) bounding box shape that's bigger than the artwork itself **E**. Align the center of this object with the center of the artwork itself, so that if the Smart Object is rotated or scaled in Photoshop, it will be transformed correctly around the center of the graphics.

If you later edit the Smart Object contents in Illustrator, you can add elements anywhere inside the bounding box without having the artwork distorted in Photoshop when you save your Illustrator edits **F**. (When you edit the artwork in Illustrator, you may want to realign the center of the edited artwork with the center of the unchanged bounding box. Do this if you want Photoshop to use the new center of the graphics when the Smart Object "remembers" previous transformations in the Photoshop file.)

A The original graphics in Illustrator (part of Don Jolley's graphics for "Rusted & Pitted" on page 517)

B

Pasted into Photoshop as a Smart Object, with a Layer Style added for color and texture

C

Edited in Illustrator

D

Updating the Photoshop file causes distortion.

E

Adding an invisible rectangle when the graphics are first created, to establish a larger "package" for the Smart Object

F

The graphics can be edited within the "oversize" bounding box, and updating the Photoshop file doesn't cause distortion.

If you import a layered Photoshop (PSD) file into InDesign with InDesign's File > Place command, the placed version of the file, layer(s), or layer comp is flattened. (The original Photoshop file is not flattened — just the placed version.) If you hold down the Shift key during the import process, you can choose whether to apply the clipping path (if one was saved with the file).

If a Photoshop file imported into InDesign has at least one path in it, choosing InDesign's Object > Clipping Path command opens a dialog box that lets you choose a path to use as a clipping path, even if you haven't designated a clipping path in Photoshop. The same image can be placed more than once with different clipping paths.

Then in the Paths palette, click the ⊙ in the upper right corner of the palette and choose Clipping Path from the menu. In the Clipping Path dialog box, leave the Flatness blank, to be set by the output device, or use the setting of 8 to 10 that Adobe recommends for high-resolution printing, or 1 to 3 for low-resolution (under 600 dots per inch). Choose from the menu of named and saved paths in the file. Then Click "OK" to close the box. Save the file (File > Save As) in Photoshop format for maximum flexibility.

If your Photoshop artwork is destined for an InDesign document, the PSD file you've saved will be perfect. In InDesign choose File > Place. In the Image Import Options dialog box, turn on the "Apply Photoshop Clipping Path" option if you want to use the clipping path you've made, and click "OK." The placed artwork will be flattened and clipped. But you can change the clip by choosing Object > Clipping Path and choosing a different option in the "Type:" menu of InDesign's Clipping Path dialog (a different Photoshop path or an alpha channel,▼ for example).

FIND OUT MORE

▼ Alpha channels
page 67

If your Photoshop artwork is destined for a QuarkXPress document, after you designate a clipping path, *save in Photoshop format to preserve editability of the clipping path* in case you want to make changes later. Then *save the file again under a different file name* in Photoshop DCS 2.0 format (File > Save As) with the "Include Vector Data" option turned on in the DCS 2.0 Format dialog box.

THE LINKS PALETTE

InDesign CS/CS2 and Illustrator CS/CS2 have a Links palette that lists each image linked to the document and helps you manage those images:

• You can open a Photoshop image in Photoshop for editing, and the Illustrator or InDesign file will be updated automatically when you save the edited file in Photoshop.

• A warning appears when an image is missing or has been modified since the last time it was linked.

• You can sort the list of images by name or other characteristics.

The Links palette from InDesign CS is shown at the right.

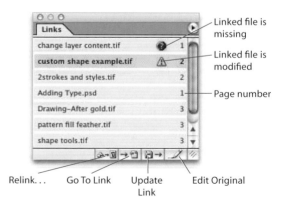

Type Layers

Lance Jackson designed the artwork below for a holiday card for the *San Francisco Chronicle* newspaper, using the Electra font (www.linotype.com). Here, with his and the *Chronicle's* permission, we use it as a model to explore the kinds of typesetting that can be done within a single type layer in Photoshop, and other type tasks that require separation of the characters onto more than one layer.

Managing type in Photoshop is a challenge that's well worth the effort. Success depends partly on understanding the typesetting controls, most of which are available through the Options bar. But there are also some important tricks to learn about managing type *layers.* This type exercise covers:

- How to set type
- How to make global changes that apply to an entire type layer
- How to make character-by-character changes
- How to start a new type layer (rather than typing into an existing one)
- How to make a mask for type
- How to get free of that "trapped in a type layer" feeling (see "Escaping from a Type Layer" at the right)

We've used the Georgia font for our example (at the bottom) because it's "native" to both Mac and Windows Systems.

LANCE JACKSON /
SAN FRANCISCO CHRONICLE

AFTER LANCE JACKSON,
WITH PERMISSION

1 Setting Type

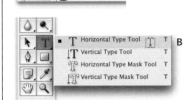

A

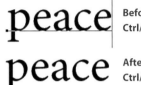

B

peace
**Before pressing
Ctrl/⌘-Enter**

peace
**After pressing
Ctrl/⌘-Enter**

To follow our example, start a Photoshop document (File > New) 6 inches wide by 3 inches high, at a resolution of 225 pixels/inch, in RGB mode with a white background. Before beginning to set type, choose the Move tool ▸⊕ and in the Options bar, *turn off the Auto Select Layer option* **A**. This will make it easier to manage the type layers.

Choose the Horizontal Type tool (**T**) **B**. (We'll call it simply the Type tool.) Without worrying about the settings in the Options bar, click in the working window and type the word "peace," using whatever font and size your Options bar is set at; we typed ours in a Minion font at 24 pt size.

Now *press Ctrl/⌘-Enter*. The Type tool will still be chosen, but the blinking *insertion point cursor* and the baseline indicator will have disappeared from the line of type, as shown above. When there is no insertion point in the type, the choices you make in the Options bar (as you will in a moment) will affect *all the type on the layer.*

THE FINISHED TYPE CAN BE FOUND
in 🔵 > Wow Project Files > Chapter 7 > Exercising Type Layers

"ESCAPING" FROM A TYPE LAYER

When you've finished making changes to type and you want to have access again to all of Photoshop's tools and menus and the other layers in your file:

- To accept the changes, press Ctrl/⌘-Enter key.
- To move on without making the changes, press the Escape key or type Ctrl/⌘-period.

2 Changing the Layer's Type Specs

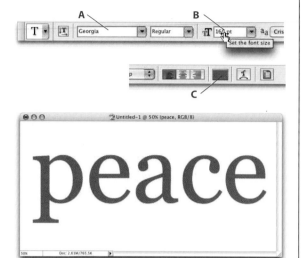

Click the ⏷ button next to the font name near the left end of the Options bar, and choose Georgia **A**. (If you don't have Georgia, you might try Arial.)

One way to make the type bigger than the sizes offered by the Options bar's pop-up size menu is to hold down the Ctrl/⌘ key, put the cursor over the number in the "Set the font size" box, and "scrub," dragging to the right to increase the size (we used 160 pt) **B**. Don't worry if the type extends beyond the edge of the working window. Just hold down the Ctrl/⌘ key to toggle to the Move tool ▸⊕, drag on the type to move it into position, and release the Ctrl/⌘ key to toggle back to the Type tool.

Next, change the color: Click the color swatch in the Options bar **C** to open the Color Picker, click on a bright red, and click "OK" to close the picker.

CHANGING SEVERAL TYPE LAYERS AT ONCE

To change the color, font, or other characteristics of more than one type layer at a time, first target one of the layers by clicking its thumbnail in the Layers palette. In Photoshop CS click in the column next to the 👁 for each of the other layers to link them 🔗; in CS2 Shift-click or Ctrl/⌘-click to target the other layers. With the Type tool chosen but no insertion point (if the insertion point is visible, pressing Ctrl/⌘-Enter will turn it off), in CS hold down the Shift key and make the changes you want in the Options bar (in CS2 the Shift key isn't needed).

3 Trying Other Fonts

peace — **Minion Pro**

peace — **News Gothic Std**

peace — **Nueva Std**

peace — **Georgia**

If you want to try out other fonts for your type at this point, it's easy. With the type layer targeted (highlighted in the Layers palette) and the Type tool chosen, but with no insertion point active, you can change the font for all the type on the layer by choosing a different font from the pop-up list in the Options bar. To try out all the fonts in this menu, one after another, use the method in "Automated Type Showings" below.

If you choose a font other than Georgia, the kerning values later in this exercise may be different than the ones you will need to use.

AUTOMATED TYPE SHOWINGS

It's easy to try out a whole series of different fonts for your type. Make sure your type layer is targeted in the Layers palette. Choose the Type tool but make sure the insertion point is *not* present (if you see it, press Ctrl/⌘-Enter key to turn it off). In the Options bar, click in the "Set the font family" entry field. Now press the up or down arrow on the keyboard (⬆ or ⬇) to step through the available fonts.

Holding down the Shift key as you press the ⬆ key will change the font to the one at the top of the pop-up list; Shift ⬇ will change to the last font in the list.

4 Adding a Stroke

To add a stroke to all the type in a Photoshop layer, you can use a Layer Style. With the type layer targeted in the Layers palette, click the "Add a layer style" button 🖋 at the bottom of the palette and choose Stroke from the pop-up menu. When the Layer Style dialog box opens, click the color swatch to choose a stroke color (we chose a bright green). Then experiment to arrive at a Size and Position; we chose a narrow stroke (3 px) and chose Inside (so the stroke wouldn't fatten the type). When your stroke is in place, click "OK" to close the Layer Style dialog box.

5 Changing an Individual Letter

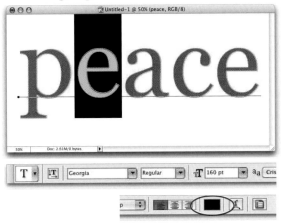

So far, we've made all of our changes to the entire type layer. Now we'll change the color, as well as the position, of a single letter. When some of the type is selected, any changes made in the Options bar apply to the selected type only. With the Type tool active, click between the "p" and the "e" and drag right to select the "e." Using the color swatch in the Options bar, change the color to black. Don't press Ctrl/⌘-Enter yet. Notice that the Stroke is still present.

HIDING THE HIGHLIGHT

When you select characters on a type layer, a highlight box appears to show you what's selected. But the inverted colors in the selection highlight can make it hard to evaluate your type changes. To hide the highlight, press Ctrl/⌘-H. Pressing Ctrl/⌘-H again restores the highlight.

It can be hard to interpret the type characteristics of selected type (left). To keep the type selected but hide the selection highlight (right), press Ctrl/⌘-H.

6 Rotating a Character

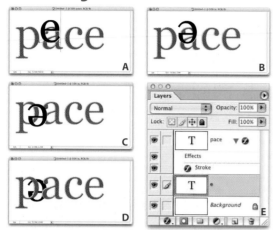

In Photoshop, you can *transform* an entire layer of type (resize, rotate, or skew it), but you can't select and transform only some of the characters. So to rotate the "e," we'll put this letter on a type layer of its own.

With the "e" selected (as we left it in "5 Changing an Individual Letter"), cut it from the current layer (Ctrl/⌘-X); then press Ctrl/⌘-Enter to complete the change. Now start a new type layer for the "e": ***Hold down the Shift key*** and click where the "e" used to be. Since you pressed Ctrl/⌘-Enter key to turn off the insertion point, and since you held down the Shift key before clicking with the cursor, a *new type layer* will be added when you paste the "e" (Ctrl/⌘-V); don't worry if the "e" isn't in the right spot **A**. (Notice that the stroke didn't come with the cut-and-pasted letter. A Layer Style disappears in transit when an element is cut and pasted to a brand-new layer. This is fine for the "e" in Jackson's design. We'll see how you can keep a Style if you want to in "8 Overlapping & Restoring a Style" on page 451.)

To rotate the "e" and move it into place, first press Ctrl/⌘-Enter to let Photoshop know you're finished with typesetting. To turn the letter around, choose Edit > Transform > Rotate 180° **B**. Hold down the Ctrl/⌘ key to toggle to the Move tool ▸₊, and drag the letter where you want it **C**. (For his "peace" design Jackson used a font whose "e" has a higher bar than the Georgia font used here. So we moved the "e" down a bit to allow for the interweaving to come.)

To continue to build Jackson's design, we'll need to move the "e" behind the other characters: Drag its thumbnail down below the "pace" layer in the Layers palette **D**, **E**.

7 Kerning

Now that the "e" has been moved to another layer and rotated, we can adjust the spacing of the "p" and "a" so we can intertwine them with the "e." In the Layers palette target the "pace" layer by clicking on its thumbnail. With the Type tool chosen, click in between the "p" and the "a" **A**.

Near the right end of the Options bar, click the 📄 button to open the Character palette. Now tighten the space between the two letters as much as possible without overlapping them. You can do this by entering a negative number in the **kerning** field and pressing Enter **B**. We zoomed in to the 100% view; this can be done by pressing Ctrl-Alt-0 (Windows) or ⌘-Option-0 (Mac; that's a zero). Then we experimented with bigger negative numbers until the outlines of the two characters seemed to be touching at –93. (To change the kerning, you can use the "scrubbing" method described for the font size in "2 Changing the Layer's Type Specs" on page 448. But for precise control, drag-select the number in the kerning entry field and type in a new number; then press Enter to complete the kerning operation.) Notice that if you kern too tightly, the two characters merge and the stroke disappears where they overlap. That's because the Stroke effect in the Layer Style follows the outline of the *layer contents,* and when you merge the two characters, the outline changes and the Stroke reflects this.

When you've pressed Enter to complete the kerning, press Ctrl/⌘-Enter to let Photoshop know you've finished editing **C**.

8 Overlapping & Restoring a Style

To pull the "a" and "e" together and put the "c" on top, drag the insertion point across the "c" to select it and cut it (Ctrl/⌘-X); then click between the "a" and "e" and kern the "ae" pair **A** as in "7 Kerning" on the facing page; we used a kerning value of −129. Finally, **press Ctrl/⌘-Enter and then Shift-click** with the Type tool to start a new type layer. Paste the "c" (Ctrl/⌘-V) and then press Enter again. Toggle to the Move tool ▶⊕ by holding down the Ctrl/⌘ key, and drag the "c" into position **B**.

Like the "e" in "6 Rotating a Character" on the facing page, the "c" has lost its stroke in transit. But we can restore it. In the Layers palette, copy the layer Style from the "pae" layer by right/Ctrl-clicking on the *f* *for the layer* and choosing Copy Layer Style from the context-sensitive menu that pops up **C**. Then right/Ctrl-click in about the same position on the "c" layer's entry in the Layers palette and choose Paste Layer Style to add the Style to the "c" layer **D**, **E**.

9 Interweaving the Type

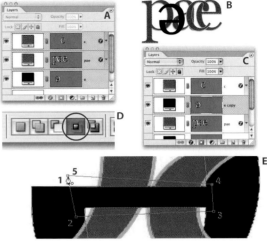

Now that we've made final adjustments to the spacing, we'll convert the type to Shape layers. By converting, we can be sure to avoid any font complications when the file is output on a system other the one that originated it. To make the conversion, start by targeting the type layers: In CS2, click the top type layer and Shift-click the bottom type layer to target all of them. Then choose Layer > Type > Convert to Shape **A**. In CS, target and convert each layer separately.

To bring the bar of the black "e" in front of the "p" and "a," we'll put a duplicate of the black "e" above the red "pae" layer and hide all but the bar. Click the black thumbnail for the "e" layer and type Ctrl/⌘-J to duplicate the layer. Drag the thumbnail for the new layer up the Layers palette until it's between the "c" and "pae" layers. Now make sure the vector mask for this layer is active (click the mask thumbnail in the Layers palette once or twice — until the double border appears around it) **B**, **C**.

To hide all of the "e" except the bar, choose the Pen tool ✎, and in the Options bar **D** click the "Intersect shape areas" button ▣ so that when you draw a shape with the Pen, only the intersection of the "e" and the new shape will show. Zoom in (Ctrl/⌘-+) and click from point to point with the Pen, to make a path that surrounds the bar **E**; it's OK to include some of the body of the "e" within the path, as long as you don't include any that should be hidden by the overlapping "p" and "a." When you click on your starting point to complete the path (a tiny circle ✎ will indicate that clicking will close the path), most of the "e" will disappear, leaving the bar to complete the interweaving effect. Our final "peace" model is shown at the bottom of page 447.

Don Jolley Demos an Antique Technique

YOU SEE IT ALL THE TIME — type wrapped around a circle, some of it above and some below, both settings reading left to right. How do they do that? We first encountered this quick, reliable method back in 1994, when Jim McConlogue of Warner Design Associates used it to design a commemorative medallion in Adobe Illustrator. Now that Photoshop can put type on a path, we asked Don Jolley to revive this "ancient" technique for us.

The **Circle Type.psd** file is provided on the Wow DVD-ROM (in the Wow Goodies folder). If you don't have the Schneidler Initials font, you'll need to substitute a font of your own choosing in order to edit the text.

1 Use the Ellipse tool ⬭, with the Paths option chosen in the Options bar, to draw a circle. Don put the cursor approximately at the center of the butterfly and started to drag, then depressed the Shift and Alt/Option keys to draw a perfect circle centered at the starting point. (If you need to move the circle a little as you draw, to get it centered exactly right, press the spacebar and drag, then release the spacebar and continue to Shift-Alt/Option-drag.)

Don drew a circular path around the butterfly.

2 Now choose the Type tool (T). In the Options bar, choose the "Center text" option and choose the font, size, and color you want.

Setting up the type specifications, including "Center text"

3 Click on the top of the circle and type the text you want there.

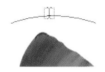

Positioning the cursor on the top of the circle

As the text is typed, it spreads out, centered at the top of the circle.

ORIGINAL PHOTO: PHOTOSPIN.COM

The finished type layer for the top of the circle

4 You'll need a second circle path for the bottom text. Here's how to get one that's exactly the right size and centered in the same place as the first: Duplicate the type layer (Ctrl/⌘-J). Then choose Edit > Transform Path > Flip Vertical. Now you have a copy of your top type at the bottom of the circle, right-side up and facing the right direction, but *inside* the circle rather than outside.

Copying the type layer and flipping the copy puts type inside the circle at the bottom.

5 Before moving the type outside, replace it with the text you want on the bottom. Select all by putting the cursor in the type and pressing Ctrl/⌘-A. Then go ahead and type the new text.

Selecting the text for replacement

After typing the new text

6 To put the type outside the circle where it belongs, all you have to do is lower the baseline. With all the type selected, you can do that by entering a negative number in the baseline shift field of the Character palette (Window > Character). Experiment with the setting until you get it right. You may want to track and kern the type also. ▼

Besides changing the baseline, Don added bullet characters and spaces. Then he drag-selected the type and changed its color.

7 Rotating the type around to the left is a lot easier in Photoshop CS2 than in CS.

In CS2 the two circles of type can be rotated together: In the Layers palette, click the thumbnail for one type layer and Ctrl/⌘-click to

Targeting both type layers and rotating the type in Photoshop CS2

also target the other layer. Then choose the Move tool ▸⊕, type Ctrl/⌘-T, and drag to turn the type; pressing the Enter key completes the rotation.

In CS, you can rotate one type layer and then the other, but without a live preview during the rotation. Click one layer's thumbnail to target the layer and choose the Move tool ▸⊕; type Ctrl/⌘-T, drag to rotate, and press the Enter key. Target the second layer, type Ctrl/⌘-Shift-T (for Transform Again), and press Enter.

FIND OUT MORE

▼ Kerning & tracking
page 454

DONAL JOLLEY

Neon Type

"Crafting a Neon Glow" on page 546 tells step-by-step how to construct a neon sign using a Shape layer, make it glow with a Layer Style, and finally add details like pinches in the tubing and supports to hold it to the wall. And page 397 tells how Bert Monroy, master of photorealism, hand-crafts his neon, complete with the "grunge" of the city environment. Here we see some simpler examples of quick neon styling for type.

The **Quick Neon Type** files (see below) include all the examples shown here (with the type rasterized) so you can easily explore the settings for the Layer Styles (in the Layers palette simply double-click on the ⊘ for a layer to open the Layer Style dialog box). The Quick Neon Type files can also serve as a source of neon for copying a Style, which you can then paste into another file.

YOU'LL FIND THE FILES
in ⓦ > Wow Project Files > Chapter 7 > Quick Neon Type

VIEWING CHARACTERS

How do you know what the characters in a particular font look like? Here are some ways to find out:

• In Photoshop CS2, the font menu in the Type tool's Options bar includes a **"Sample" column** that gives you a peek at these six characters in every font.

• Both Windows and Mac provide a way to look at font content. **Windows's Character Map** utility (found in the **Start, Accessories,** or **System Tools** menu in different versions) lets you see all the characters of a font, and copy and paste them into a Photoshop type layer. In **Mac OS X** the **Character Palette** shows all the characters in a particular font, or the same character in all the fonts in your System. In **Mac OS 10.3** and **10.4,** choosing **Edit > Special Characters** opens the palette. In **Mac OS 10.2,** add it to the **"flag"** menu near the right end of the Finder menu bar by choosing **System Preferences > International > Input Menu** and checking the box next to Character Palette.

"Made-for-Neon" Fonts

CERTAIN DISPLAY FONTS, such as **Eklektic** (used for "space bar" above) and MiniPics **Confetti** (an icon font, used for the swirl), are ideal for simulating neon tubing. Their characters are formed with a single monoweight stroke (neon tubes have a consistent diameter) and with rounded ends. Lighting up such a font is simply a matter of typing the text (choose the Type tool **T**, click in the working window, and type) and then applying a Layer Style like any of those used in "Crafting a Neon Glow," scaling the Style if necessary (Layer > Layer Style > Scale Effects).

In this case we drew a path with the Pen tool ⬯ and set type on the path by clicking on it with the Type tool and typing the word "space." Then we duplicated the type-on-a-path layer (Ctrl/⌘-J). On the new layer we held down the Ctrl/⌘ key and dragged the type down so the two words were stacked. We selected the type by dragging the cursor over it and then typed "bar." On both layers we tracked and kerned the type, and adjusted its position.▼

We added a new empty layer (Ctrl/⌘-Shift-N, or add the Alt/Option key to bypass the New Layer dialog box) and turned it into a third type layer by typing on it, adding a symbol from the MiniPics Confetti font. Then, to fit the swirl with the two lines of Eklektic, we resized and rotated the swirl (by pressing Ctrl/⌘-T, Shift-dragging on a corner handle to resize, and then dragging around outside a corner handle to rotate).

FIND OUT MORE

▼ Adjusting type along a path **page 425**

 Made for Neon.psd

KERNING & TRACKING

To **kern**, put the Type tool **T** cursor between two characters, hold down Alt/Option, and use the → or ← key to widen or narrow the space. To **track**, drag the Type tool **T** cursor over the type you want to affect, hold down Alt/Option and use the → or ← key.

Almost "Made-for-Neon"

MANY OTHER MONOWEIGHT TYPEFACES, though not quite perfect, can still successfully suggest neon. In the examples above:

- The **Pump Tri D** font (used for "zebra room"), **Harpoon** (for "city deli"), and **Chunky Monkey** are practical candidates even though they have square rather than round ends on their strokes.

- For "Motel 5" we used the **Balloon** font, pairing sizes (36-point Bold and 80-point Light) that gave a visually consistent diameter to the neon tubing. In this font family the strokes have round ends. The characters lack the breaks between strokes that you would see in real neon, but for suggesting neon, the font works.

- The **Circle D** font used for "joe's" is monoweight with round ends. But it was too thin by itself to make neon tubes. So after setting the type and pressing the Enter key, we thickened the strokes: We clicked the toggle for the Character and Paragraph palettes on the Type tool's Options bar to open the Character palette, then clicked the ⊙ at the top right corner of the palette and chose Faux Bold from the fly-out menu; the tubes gained the weight we wanted, and the type was still live.

- The rainclouds icon is from **Inkfont Dingbats**. To get the purple color we added a Hue/Saturation Adjustment layer above this type layer (by clicking the "Create new fill or adjustment layer" button ⬮ at the bottom of the Layers palette and moving the Hue slider). This recoloring method changes both the Inner Glow and the Outer Glow. It's successful in this case because the rainclouds layer is below all the other type layers and because the *Background* is black (it has no hue), so none of these other layers are affected by the Hue/Saturation layer.

 **Almost Made for Neon.psd**

"Outlining" with Neon

YOU CAN BEND NEON TUBING to fit type outlines by using a Layer Style that includes a gradient Stroke effect. You can type your text in any color, because the Layer Style will hide the fill. Click the "Add a layer style" button ⬮ at the bottom of the Layers palette and choose **Blending Options** at the top of the pop-up list. When the Layer Style dialog box opens, in the Advanced Blending section set the **Fill Opacity** to **0**, to make the type transparent. Also make sure the **Blend Interior Effects As Group** option is *not checked*. This will ensure that for the Stroke (which we'll add next), the part that falls inside the body of the type will show, even though the Fill Opacity is 0.

From the list on the left side of the Layer Style box, click on the word "Stroke." In the Stroke panel, for the **Position** choose **Center** so the Stroke will straddle the edge and won't make the characters too fat or too thin. For the **Fill Type** choose **Gradient** and for the **Style** choose **Shape Burst**. You'll need a gradient that goes from a light color or white in the center to the same bright color at each end. To get the tubes to glow just right, experiment with the Stroke's **Size** slider. For the glow around the tubing, we added Inner Glow and Outer Glow effects, both in Screen mode.

- For "crow bar" we used the **Fluf** font.

- We typed "blue" and "hippo" in the **Beeswax** font and used the **Animal** font for the outline of the hippo. The dots are type-on-a-path (the period character) with the Justify All option turned on in the Paragraph palette to space them evenly from one end of the path to the other, and with a Style like those in "Almost 'Made for Neon.'"

- The first character of "ink" is from the **Hygiene** font, and the "nk" is set in **BubbleSoft**.

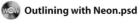 **Outlining with Neon.psd**

EXERCISING
Drawing Tools

With Photoshop's drawing tools — the Shapes, Pen, and path-editing tools — you can create vector-based elements that you can then stretch or otherwise reshape with no deterioration of the edge quality.

The aim of this exercise is to create a sun figure like the one below, all in one Shape layer so you can save it as a Custom Shape. You'll learn:

- How to work with a Grid, Guides, and the Transform command.

- How to set up the Options bar to make a new Shape layer or modify an existing one.

- How to draw with the Shape tools and the Pen.

- How to modify shapes.

- How to copy shapes, within one layer or from layer to layer.

- How to take advantage of ImageReady's extra Shape tools.

- How to define a Custom Shape so you can use it again later.

Read the tips as you go along!

YOU'LL FIND THE FILE
in 🟡 > Wow Project Files > Chapter 7 > Exercising Drawing Tools

1 Setting Up to Draw

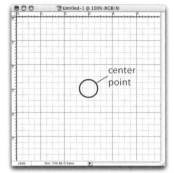

Start a new file (File > New; ours was 6 by 6 inches; 72 pixels/inch gave us a nice-sized on-screen view at 100%). To set up a Grid, open the Preferences dialog box (type Ctrl/⌘-K) and choose Guides, Grid & Slices from the top menu. Set up a Grid (we used a Gridline every 1 inch and 4 Subdivisions) and click "OK." Make sure View > Show > Grid is turned on.

Now in your working window, set a center point: Press Ctrl/⌘-R to display the rulers. Set a vertical Guide by dragging from the left-hand ruler to a point near the center, and set an intersecting horizontal Guide by dragging down from the top ruler.

In the View menu, make sure Snap has a check mark (if it doesn't, click Snap to turn it on). Choose View > Snap To and turn on Grid and Guides (click to show the check mark). This will make the Grid and Guide lines "magnetic," so they'll attract the cursor when it gets close, making it easier to draw with geometric precision.

2 Drawing a Shape

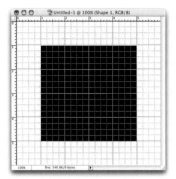

Choose the Rectangle tool ▢. Make sure the Options bar is set to create a Shape layer **A**. Click the Geometry Options button **B** and make sure "Unconstrained" is the only option checked **C**. This will allow you to use modifier keys to change how the shapes are drawn while you're drawing them (see below). If the color swatch isn't black, click it and choose black from the Color Picker.

Put the cursor on the center point, and drag outward, pressing and holding down the Shift and Alt/Option keys once you get started. The Shift key will constrain the shape to a square; the Alt/Option key will cause the shape to be drawn outward, using your starting point as the center.

MODIFIER KEYS FOR DRAWING

Start to draw with a Shape tool and *then* press:

- **Shift** to constrain to a 1:1 ratio of width to height.

- **Alt/Option** to draw from the center.

- **Spacebar** to move the path; then release the spacebar to continue drawing.

3 Adding to a Shape

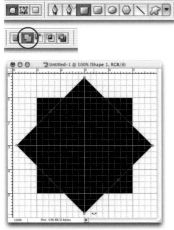

To add a second, rotated, square to complete the sun's corona, click the "Add to shape area" button 🔲 in the Options bar. To copy the square and rotate the copy 45°, all at once, press Ctrl-Alt-T (Windows) or ⌘-Option-T (Mac) and drag around outside the Transform frame to rotate 45°, pressing the Shift key once you get started. (Adding the Alt/Option key creates the copy to transform, and the Shift key constrains the rotation to certain angles, including 45°.) Double-click inside the Transform frame (or press the Enter key) to complete the transformation.

4 Subtracting a Shape

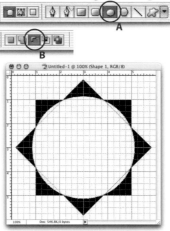

Now in the View > Snap To menu, turn off the Grid, so it won't be magnetic and you'll have more freedom to choose where the circle cuts the squares; but leave Guides turned on so that your center point will still "snap." To choose the Ellipse tool ⬭ quickly, click its button in the Options bar **A**; also click the "Subtract from shape area" button 🔲 **B**. Draw a circle outward from your center point, again pressing Shift and Alt/Option once you get started. Make the circle extend all the way out to the "joints" of the corona.

5 Duplicating a Path

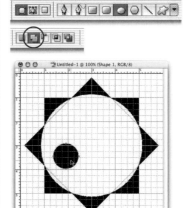

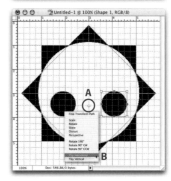

To add the cheeks, click the "Add to shape area" button 🔲 in the Options bar, hold down the Shift key, and drag the Ellipse tool ⬭ to make one of the circular cheeks. Then hold down the Ctrl/⌘ key to toggle to the Path Selection tool ▶ and drag the cheek into position where you want it.

Make the second cheek by duplicating the first: Press Ctrl-Alt-T (Windows) or ⌘-Option-T (Mac). In the Transform frame, drag the center point onto the vertical Guide **A**. Then right/Ctrl-click in the window to open a context-sensitive menu, and choose Flip Horizontal **B**. Double-click inside the Transform frame to complete the move.

NOTHING BUT NEW!

You may find yourself working on a Shape layer and wanting to add to or take away from it, but "Create new shape layer" ⬛ is the only one of the five drawing mode buttons available. This may be because you accidentally "detargeted" your Shape layer's mask. To remedy the situation, in the Layers palette, click the vector mask thumbnail once or twice, until you see the frame around it.

A double border shows that the Shape layer's built-in vector mask is active. In CS2 the outer border is a dashed line.

6 Pen Drawing 1

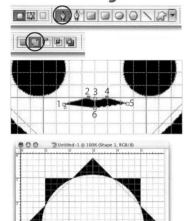

To add the upper lip, made from a series of straight segments, choose the Pen tool ✒ and make sure the "Shape layer" and "Add to shape layer" options are chosen in the Options bar. Then click from point to point, without dragging (you can follow the numbers above), finishing by clicking the starting point again.

If you want to reshape the lip, choose the Direct Selection tool ▶ (it shares a space in the Tools palette with the Path Selection tool ▶). Shift-click the points you want to move, and drag them. We dragged points 2 and 4 up.

RESHAPING A PATH

To reshape a path, select the Direct Selection tool ▶. Then:

• Drag a path segment to reshape it.

• Click or drag-select a point (it will look solid while the other points look empty) and then drag the point to move it.

7 Pen Drawing 2

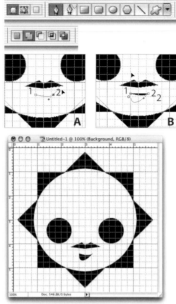

To make the shadow that defines the lower lip, you might want to read these directions all the way through, and then start, but here's the "executive summary": Click at 1, click-drag at 2, Alt/Option-click point 2, click-drag at point 1.

To start, click with the Pen ✒ to make the first point (1), then click and drag up and to the right a little to make the next point (2), using the drag motion to shape the curve segment between points 1 and 2 **A**. Since this last segment was a curve, Photoshop thinks you're going to go on drawing curves, so it makes the new point (2) a curve point. But, in fact, to define the lower lip, you want point 2 to be a sharp cusp, or "hinge." To tell Photoshop to change point 2 to a cusp, hold down the Alt/Option key (a tiny "convert point" icon ▶ will be added to the Pen cursor) and "re-click" point 2. Then click at point 1, and drag out a handle (a little up and to the left) to shape this curve segment and complete and close the path **B**.

8 Pen Drawing 3

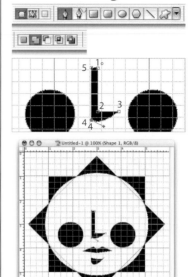

To make the nose, follow the numbers as you draw it as described below, centered around the vertical Guide. (To work close to the Guide without snapping to it, you may want to zoom in — press Ctrl/⌘-+.)

Start by clicking with the Pen ✒ to make the point at the top of the right side (1). Shift-click below the first point to make the tip of the nose (2). Shift-click to the right to make the outside corner of the nose (3). Then click and drag (4) to make the bottom curve. Since this last segment was a curve, you need to tell Photoshop that you want point 4 to be a cusp instead of a curve point. So hold down the Alt/Option key and re-click point 4. Now when you click at the top (5), you'll get a straight segment. Click point 1 again to close the path.

CLOSE ENOUGH TO CLOSE

When you draw with the Pen, the cursor signals you with a little "o" when it's close enough to the first point to close the path.

9 Borrowing a Shape

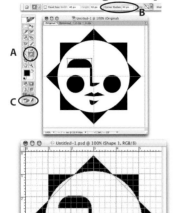

You could use Photoshop's Pen and Grid to create a symmetrical eyelid shape, but another option is to borrow a ready-made version from ImageReady. Click the "Edit in ImageReady" button at the very bottom of Photoshop's Tools palette. Then in ImageReady choose the Tab Rectangle tool ▢ **A**, and in the Options bar set the Corner Radius (we used 40 px) **B**. Drag to make the eye.

ImageReady's Options bar doesn't offer the adding and other options that Photoshop's does; when you draw a Tab Rectangle, a new layer is created. To move the new eyelid to the layer with the other shapes, click the "Edit in Photoshop" button **C**. In Photoshop choose the Path Selection tool ▸ and click on the eyelid. Copy it (Ctrl/⌘-C), then in the Layers palette, target your main Shape layer *by clicking its vector mask thumbnail once or twice*. Paste (Ctrl/⌘-V) and click the "Add to shape layer" button ▢ in the Options bar. (To delete the imported layer, in the Layers palette drag its thumbnail to the 🗑 button at the bottom of the palette.)

10 Combining Two Paths

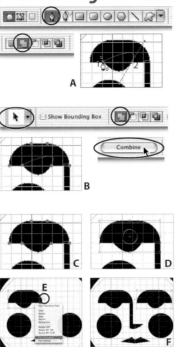

Use the Pen ◊ to add an eyeball, overlapping the eyelid: Make sure the "Add to shape layer" option ▢ is chosen. Click to make a point (1), click and drag (2) to make a curve, and click again on point 1 to close the shape **A**.

To combine eyelid and eyeball into a single shape, choose the Path Selection tool ▸, Shift-click the two paths, and click the "Combine" button in the Options bar **B**, **C**.

To make the other eye, zoom in (Ctrl/⌘-+) for finer control, and press Ctrl-Alt-T (Windows) or ⌘-Option-T (Mac) to make a copy and bring up the Transform frame **D**, as you did for the cheeks. As before, reposition the Transform center point over the vertical Guide **E**. Then right/Ctrl-click in the window to open the context-sensitive menu, and choose Flip Horizontal to finish the eyes **F**. Double-click inside the Transform frame to commit the transformation.

11 Defining & Saving

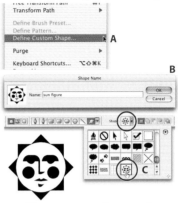

To add your new sun figure to the Shapes that can be drawn with the Custom Shape tool, make sure its vector mask thumbnail is still targeted, and choose Edit > Define Custom Shape **A**. Name the shape and click "OK" **B**. Now if you choose the Custom Shape tool 🐾, you can find your new shape at the bottom of the flyout Custom Shape picker **C**. When you draw, Shift-drag to keep the figure in proportion. (For safekeeping, it's a good idea to use the Preset Manager ▼ to save a set that includes any new shape you create.)

FIND OUT MORE

▼ Using the Preset Manager **page 47**

STYLING AS YOU DRAW

With the path-drawing tools (Shapes and Pens) you can add a Layer Style *as you draw*: In the Options bar, make sure the ⓘ isn't depressed (dark). Open the Style picker, and choose a Style. Now every filled path you draw will automatically include that Style.

Designing for Scalability & Animation

YOU'LL FIND THE FILES

in 🌀 > Wow Project Files > Chapter 7 > Scalability and Animation:
- Scalable Design-Before.psd (to start)
- Scalable Design-After.psd (to copy Layer Styles and to compare)
- Scalable Design 100-After.psd (to compare)

OPEN THESE PALETTES

from the Window menu:
- Tools • Layers

OVERVIEW

Import graphics created in Adobe Illustrator • "Deconstruct" the graphics to put individual elements on separate layers • Copy and paste Layer Styles for the graphics layers • Create a separate layer for each position needed to rotate the graphics in an animation • Distort the rotation graphics • Collect the rotation graphics in a layer set/group and apply a vector mask • Duplicate the file • Resize the copies, scaling the Layer Styles along with the graphics

FIND OUT MORE

▼ Using Smart Objects
page 39

A TYPICAL LOGO PROJECT MIGHT START OUT as color graphics designed for a business card and stationery — about an inch to an inch-and-a-half across at 300 dpi. But then you might need a version for a CD-ROM splash screen, which means it can be the same pixel size (about 350 pixels) but at 72 dpi. And now the client wants it animated. You might as well use the animated version on the web site, too, but it will have to be smaller — say about 100 pixels. Next you'll need a brochure cover, a poster, and — who knows? — maybe a billboard!

Because of the scaling required for the CAFFEIN³ logo's different uses, and because we would need to distort and rotate portions of it for the animation, the smart approach was to create the design using Shape layers and Layer Styles, both of which can be changed repeatedly without the deterioration that's typical when you manipulate pixel-based images.

The new Smart Object technology in Photoshop CS2 provides some of the benefits of vector graphics even for pixel-based elements. Turning an element into a Smart Object can protect it from the *cumulative* effects of *repeated* transformations such as rotation or distorting. ▼ But the fact remains that the pixel-based element will still be subject to one round of softening or pixelating if you scale or otherwise transform it, even if you've turned it into a Smart Object first. So for this project, vector graphics with Layer Styles is a good choice even in CS2. (You can find an example of Smart Objects used to avoid deterioration with repeated transformation in Sharon Steuer's "claymation" approach to animation in the Chapter 10 "Gallery.")

The original graphics, selected for copying in Illustrator

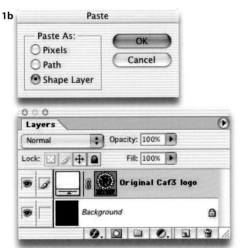

1b

Pasting the copied graphics into the Photoshop file from Illustrator created a Shape layer. This is the **Scalable Design-Before.psd** file.

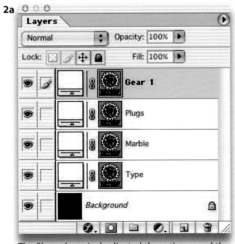

The Shape layer is duplicated three times, and the layers are renamed.

1 Importing the graphics. We wanted to take our flat logo **1a** and turn it into something dimensional and dynamic. Even in its flat state, the graphics implied energy and motion. But by combining the central parts of the design into a glowing sphere and tilting the gear wheel forward to rotate around it as shown on the facing page, we could give all that energy more purpose and direction. Getting the gear wheel to rotate in perspective takes some advance thinking and planning — you have to create the rotation frames *before* you tilt the gear into position. That's because in Photoshop it's easy to rotate a graphic in the plane of your canvas, but it's much harder to do the rotation in any plane that extends into and out of the image.

Create or import the graphic you want to "dimensionalize." Working in Adobe Illustrator we designed the logo components. After making sure that the AICB option was turned on in the Files & Clipboard section of Illustrator's Preferences dialog,▼ we selected all (Ctrl/⌘-A) and copied to the clipboard (Ctrl/⌘-C). In Photoshop we set the Foreground color to white (you can do this by typing D for "Default colors" and then X for "eXchange colors"). Then we started a new file with a black-filled *Background* (File > New, with RGB Color chosen as the Mode in the New dialog box, and Background Color chosen as the Background Contents; 375 pixels wide by 426 high at 300 pixels/inch). We pasted the copied graphics as a Shape layer (Edit > Paste > Paste As: Shape Layer). Because white was the current Foreground color, the Shape layer was white, and therefore so were the graphics. After the graphics are pasted in, you can scale them if necessary (press Ctrl/⌘-T for Edit > Free Transform Path, Shift-drag a corner handle to scale, and double-click in the Transform box to complete the transformation) **1b**.

FIND OUT MORE

▼ Copying & pasting from Illustrator
page 443

2 Deconstructing the graphics into components. To separate the individual elements of the current single Shape layer into multiple Shape layers, you can first duplicate it to make as many layers as you will have parts. Then delete all the unwanted elements from each layer, leaving behind the appropriate component. For instance, we wanted to be able to handle the gear wheel, the atom surrounded by the electric plugs, the circle-soon-to-be-sphere, and the logotype with its horizontal bars — all separately, so we needed a total of four Shape layers. You can make the duplicate layers simply by pressing Ctrl/⌘-J (for Layer > New > Layer via Copy). If you want to rename a layer, double-click its name in the Layers palette and type **2a**.

2b

On one of the Shape layers, which we renamed "Type," drag-selecting with the Direct Selection tool ▸ at least partially selected most of the elements we wanted to remove (top). Then, pressing Backspace/Delete twice removed all the elements that had been completely or partly selected, leaving only the logotype (bottom).

2c

For the "Plugs" layer, deleting the gear path from the compound shape made the circle white, since it was now the outermost path in the compound (left). Then deleting the circle itself made the plugs-and-atom unit white, and deleting the logotype completed the layer (right).

To delete parts from a layer, in the Layers palette, click the vector mask thumbnail (next to the layer name) for that layer once or twice — just until you see a double border around the vector mask thumbnail. Then, so you're not confused by seeing other intact layers as you delete, click the ◉ icon for each of the other Shape layers to turn off their visibility.

Now choose the Direct Selection tool ▸ and use it to select the element(s) you want to remove: Click on the edge of an element you want to delete, or drag across more than one element at once, enclosing part of each element you want to remove. Once the elements are selected for removal, you can delete them by pressing the Backspace/Delete key twice; the first Backspace/Delete removes the specific segment(s) of the path(s) you drag-selected, and the second removes the rest of the path(s) **2b**. As we deleted parts, the positive/negative relationship of the parts of the compound shape changed. For instance, for the "Plugs" layer, when we deleted the outer positive (white) gear shape, the interior circle became the positive shape and filled with white; the elements inside (atom and plugs) became negative (transparent), allowing the black background to show through **2c**. Then, as we selected part of the white circle and pressed Backspace/Delete twice, the atom and plugs became white again; selecting and deleting the logotype completed the layer isolating the plugs and atom.

3 Styling the parts. With the separate graphics layers prepared **3a**, you can now add color, dimension, and lighting by applying a Layer Style to each of your graphics layers. To "borrow" the Styles we used, open the **Scalable Design-After.psd** file and in the Layers palette, right-click/Ctrl-click on the ◉ icon for the corresponding layer to open a context-sensitive menu, and select Copy Layer Style. Switch back to your developing file, and for the layer you want to apply the Style to, in the Layers palette, right-click/Ctrl-click in the empty space to the right of the layer name and choose Paste Layer Style **3b**.

When we developed these particular Layer Styles, we knew that we wanted to be able to scale our Styles along with the graphics, possibly quite large or small, so we were careful not to use any pixel-based effects. For instance, we didn't use the Pattern Overlay and Texture effects, because they include pixel-based patterns and consequently are subject to the same "softening" or deterioration that any pixel-based elements would suffer.

4 Creating the "frames" for the animation. Now the planning that was done in step 1 comes into play. In the CAFFEIN[3]

3a

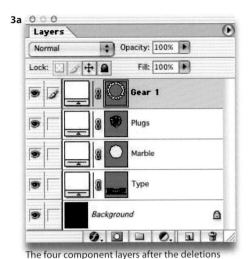

The four component layers after the deletions

3b

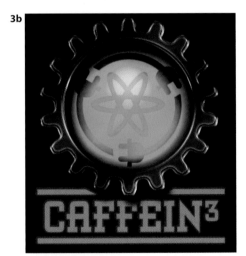

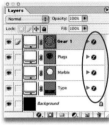

Layer Styles are applied to the shape layers by copying each one from the **Scalable Design-After.psd** file and pasting it into the corresponding layer in the developing file.

logo the layers required for animating the gear wheel need to be made at this point, while the wheel is still parallel to the plane of the canvas. We need only enough frames to produce a smooth clockwise rotation of the gear from one position to the next — that is, to rotate the gear wheel until the tooth in the top position has moved to coincide with the next tooth position. When we animate the rotation, we can simply replay these frames continuously for a smooth, continuous revolution. The total angle we need to rotate is 20° (360° in a circle ÷ 18 teeth = 20° per tooth position). To keep the animation file small, we want the smallest number of frames that will (a) produce a smooth rotation and (b) divide into 20 evenly. Four frames should do the trick (20° ÷ 4 frames = 5° per frame).

The "Gear 1" layer itself will serve as the first frame. To get the second frame, we duplicate the layer (Ctrt/⌘-J) and rename the new layer "Gear 2." To rotate this new layer we choose Edit > Free Transform Path (or press Ctrl/⌘-T), type "5" for the Rotate value in the Options bar **4a**, and click the ✔ button at the right end of the Options bar.

We make the "Gear 3" layer by duplicating "Gear 2" (Ctrl/⌘-J). To rotate this new layer 5° more, we use Transform Again (you can choose it from the Edit > Transform Path menu, or press Ctrl/⌘-Shift-T) **4b**. We create the fourth "Gear" layer by duplicating "Gear 3" and rotating the copy another 5°.

4a

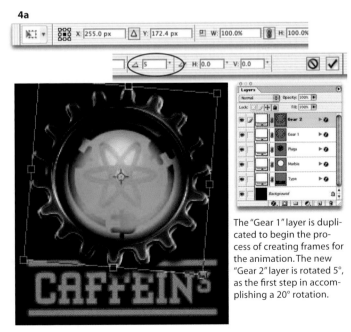

The "Gear 1" layer is duplicated to begin the process of creating frames for the animation. The new "Gear 2" layer is rotated 5°, as the first step in accomplishing a 20° rotation.

Rotating the "Gear 3" layer using Transform Again

5 Putting the rotation in perspective. Once all the rotation layers are complete, you can identically scale and skew all the rotating elements (the gear wheels in this instance):

- In Photoshop CS, start by linking the layers, as follows. In the Layers palette, click the thumbnail of one of the "Gear" layers and then click in the link column (to the right of the ☻ column) of the other "Gear" layers.

- In CS2, simply target the top "Gear" layer by clicking its thumbnail in the Layers palette, and then Shift-click the bottom "Gear" layer to select all the others as well.

Now type Ctrl/⌘-T (for Edit > Free Transform Path). To enlarge the gear wheel to put a little more space between the gear wheel and the sphere, in the Options bar click the link button between the W(idth) and H(eight) boxes, for proportional scaling and enter a value for either parameter (we used 110%) **5a**. Next click the Options bar's button again to *unlink* the two dimensions, and enter a reduced "H" value (we used 40%) **5b**. Finally, enter a Rotate angle value (we used −30°) **5c**, and finalize the transformation by clicking the ✔ at the right end of the Options bar.

5a

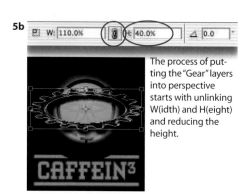

Using Free Transform and the Options bar to enlarge the "Gear" layers. With W(idth) and H(eight) linked in the Options bar, the gear wheels stay in proportion as they are resized. (We've turned off visibility for all but one "Gear" layer here.)

6 Cleaning up. At this point you may need to rearrange or adapt some of the elements of your design to fit with the new orientation of the rotating element. For instance, we chose the Move tool ▸⊕, targeted our "Type" layer, and dragged the logotype upward, closer to the bottom of the sphere. We also used the Rectangular Marquee ⬚ to select the entire logo, including logotype, and just a little space around it, then chose Edit > Crop to get rid of the extra margins **6**.

5b

The process of putting the "Gear" layers into perspective starts with unlinking W(idth) and H(eight) and reducing the height.

7 Masking the rotating element. The next challenge is to make the rotating element (our gear wheel) seem to surround the central "marble." To make a single mask that will accomplish this for all four layers that comprise the rotating gear wheel, we collected the "Gear" layers in a set/group (represented

5c

6

The "Gear" layers are tilted by setting the Rotate angle.

The rearranged and cropped logo

7a

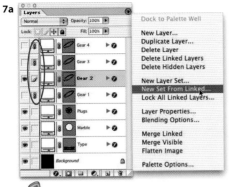

Making a layer set/group from the linked "Gear" layers

7b

Selecting the vector mask of the "Marble" layer, to be copied and pasted as the vector mask for the set/group

7c

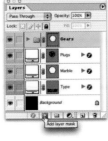

The vector mask allows the gear wheel to show only inside the bounds of the marble.

in the Layers palette by a folder icon ⬛) and applied the mask to the "folder." To make the layer set/group **7a**:

- In CS, with the Gear layers still linked (from step 5), click the Layers palette's menu button ⊙ and choose New Set From Linked.

- In CS2, with all the Gear layers still targeted in the Layers palette (from step 5), click the palette's menu button ⊙ and choose New Group From Layers.

At this point we color-coded the other elements in the composition by right-clicking/Ctrl-clicking on each layer's name and choosing Layer Properties from the context-sensitive menu to open the Layer Properties dialog box, where we could choose a color.

Next we can use the path from the "Marble" layer as the basis for creating the mask for the new set/group, as follows: Target the vector mask for the "Marble" layer (click its thumbnail once or twice, just until it has the double border around it). With its path showing in the working window we can use the Path Selection tool ▶ to select the path **7b** and then copy the path to the clipboard (Ctrl/⌘-C). With the path waiting in the clipboard, we first click on the folder thumbnail for the layer set/group at the top of the stack of layers in the Layers palette and then Ctrl/⌘-click the ⬛ button at the bottom of the palette to add an empty vector mask to the folder (without the Ctrl/⌘ key a pixel-based layer mask would be added instead of a path-based vector mask; a vector mask will work better here because, like the graphics it masks, it will be scaled without deterioration and will continue to fit the graphics exactly).

As the next step in making the mask, paste the copied path (Ctrl/⌘-V). At this point the mask "clips off" the edges of the gear wheel, so it shows only *inside* the circular outline of the marble **7c**. With the new vector mask still active, we invert the mask so that what is currently revealed becomes hidden and vice versa, by clicking the "Subtract from shape area" button ▯ in the Options bar **7d**.

Now we need to modify the vector mask so it hides only the part of the gear wheel "behind" the marble and reveals the front part. We can remove half of the circle from the vector mask by deleting one of the four control points from its path. To remove a "tilted" half, we first rotate the circular path to the same −30° tilt as the gear wheel so the bottom point will be in the right place in relation to the tilt of the wheel (with the vector mask active, press Ctrl/⌘-T and enter −30° for the Rotate angle

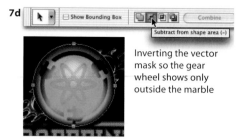

7d

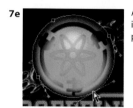

Inverting the vector mask so the gear wheel shows only outside the marble

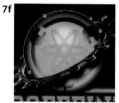

7e

After the vector mask is rotated, its "bottom" point is selected.

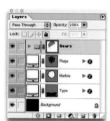

7f

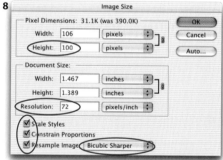

When the bottom point is deleted, the lower part of the gear wheel is revealed in front of the marble.

8

Scaling the graphic, including the Layer Styles: Turn on all three check boxes at the bottom of the Image Size box. Then set the Resolution. Then set the Height. Try Bicubic Sharper to keep the reduced image crisp.

FIND OUT MORE

▼ Settings for Layer Style effects
page 498

in the Options bar; then click the ✔). Next we choose the Direct Selection tool ⟨ again and select the bottom point (and deselect all the other points on the path) by dragging a marquee around it **7e**; then press Backspace/Delete to remove the selected point **7f**. The result is shown at the top of page 460.

8 Resizing the file. To make the 100-pixel-high file we want for the web site, we need to resize the file without messing up the Layer Styles and having to scale the Style for each layer to get our effects back. This used to be tricky, but now with Photoshop CS/CS2, it's easy. We can first duplicate the layered file (choose Image > Duplicate and click "OK"), and then choose Image > Image Size. At the bottom of the Image Size dialog box, make sure that Scale Styles, Constrain Proportions, and Resample Image are all checked. Then do the following, in order: In the Document Size section in the middle of the dialog box, change Resolution from 300 to 72 pixels/inch. In the Pixel Dimensions section at the top of the dialog box, enter 100 for the Height value. Back at the bottom of the box, choose Bicubic Sharper for the Resample Image option because we want to keep as much detail as possible when the file size is reduced **8**; then click "OK." (If using Bicubic Sharper produces an oversharpened image, press Ctrl/⌘-Z to undo, and then redo the Image Size command, using Bicubic instead.)

We now have our 100-pixel-high file for animating. Starting with the original file again, we can go through a similar process to make the 600-pixel-high file for print, but enter 600 for the Height under Pixel Dimensions, leave the Resolution at 300 pixels/inch, and choose Bicubic Smoother for the Resample option to prevent introducing artifacts as the image is scaled larger.

Developing the animations. Animating the two versions of the graphics (300 and 100 pixels) is described in "Animating with Actions" on page 701. 🖋

RESIZING A "STYLED" FILE

A Layer Style's Size, Distance, and other pixel-based settings have to be in *whole pixels*. So when a file that includes Styles is resized (by choosing Image > Image Size and turning on Scale Styles), there can be some "rounding error." For instance, if the Distance setting for a Drop Shadow is 15 pixels for a 400-pixel-high file and you reduce the file to 100 pixels high (25% of its original height), the new Distance value would be 4 pixels because it can't be 3.75 (15 x 0.25 = 3.75). The shadow would look a little more offset than in the original, and you might want to do some fine-tuning to balance the settings. ▼

Organic Graphics

YOU'LL FIND THE FILES

in 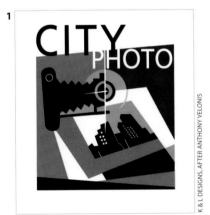(wow) > Wow Project Files > Chapter 7 >
Organic Graphics:
- Organic Graphics-Before.psd (to start)
- Wow-Organics.pat (a Patterns preset file)
- Organic Graphics-After.psd (to compare)

OPEN THESE PALETTES

from the Window menu:
- Tools • Layers

OVERVIEW

Starting with graphics (black and flat colors on white), make a duplicate layer in Multiply mode and shade the edges with the Photocopy filter • Separate the black and colors to two layers • Add a patterned background and a texture layer in Overlay mode

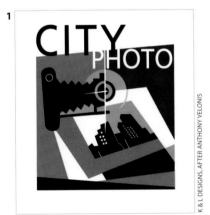

The original Adobe Illustrator artwork is duplicated to a new layer.

K & L DESIGNS, AFTER ANTHONY VELONIS

The Photocopy filter is run on the duplicate artwork layer. (Here we've hidden the filter thumbnails by clicking the arrow button to the left of the "OK" button, to make the preview window bigger.) Detail is set at 12, and Darkness at 10.

THERE ARE TIMES WHEN YOU WANT to take a crisp vector-based graphic out of its slick-lined, flat-colored environment and bring it into a space with a little more texture and personality. Whether you start with clip art or with your own artwork, once you develop a treatment that you like, you can use it to stylize an entire series of graphics. The step-by-step process presented here allows you to treat line work, color, and background separately. (For a quicker though less sophisticated approach to customizing clip art, see "Fast Filter Embellishing" on page 471.)

1 Importing the PostScript artwork. Open or place your PostScript artwork in Photoshop.▼ We opened an Illustrator file, rasterizing it at 1000 pixels wide and high **1**. Our artwork was on a white background, which can be important, since some filters work differently on transparency. (An approach for enhancing PostScript art using a layered file with transparency is presented in "Coloring Clip Art" on page 474.)

It's a good idea to keep an untouched version of the artwork available throughout the process of developing the Photoshop file. You can use it as the master graphic for duplicating and manipulating later, and it can also be the

FIND OUT MORE

▼ Working with Post-Script artwork
page 442

2b

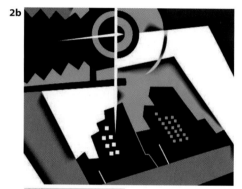

The filtered layer is put in Multiply mode, which makes the white parts transparent. Opacity is set at 75%.

3a

Using the Magic Wand to select the black on a second copy of the original artwork.

quickest way to recover from a mistake. So start by duplicating the artwork (one way is to press Ctrl/⌘-J, for Layer > New > Layer Via Copy). We renamed the layers at this point, "Original" and "Photocopy," which is what the new layer would soon contain. To rename a layer, in the Layers palette, double-click on the layer's name and type the new name.

2 Shading the edges. In the Layers palette, make sure the "Photocopy" layer is targeted by clicking its thumbnail. Also make sure black and white are the default Foreground and Background colors by typing D. Then instantly turn the "Photocopy" layer into a shaded black-and-white version of the art by running the Photocopy filter (Filter > Sketch > Photocopy; we used Detail 12, Darkness 10) **2a**. To let the color show through from below, put this "Photocopy" layer in Multiply mode. To soften the Photocopy effect, we reduced the Opacity of the layer to 75% **2b**.

3 Separating the black from the colors. The next step is to isolate the black artwork on one layer and the colors on another so you can easily treat them separately. In the Layers palette, click on the thumbnail for the "Original" layer and duplicate this layer again (Ctrl/⌘-J). We renamed this new layer "Colors," which is what it would soon contain. In this new "Colors" layer, select the black, using the Magic Wand with the

WHAT IS THE PHOTOCOPY FILTER DOING?

Here's what the Photocopy filter (Filter > Sketch > Photocopy) does to graphics:

• Photocopy has no effect on **white** areas; it leaves them white.

• For **black** elements, the filter turns the middle of the shape white and creates black shading extending inward from the edges. However, if the original black shape is narrow — as in type, for instance — the shading from the edges may extend all the way to the middle, so little or no white shows.

• **Colors** and **grays** respond according to how light or dark they are compared to their surroundings. Where they are next to a lighter color or white, the filter treats them more like black, creating shading that extends inward from the edges. But where they are next to a darker color or black, the filter treats them more like white, producing little or no shading. A color shape will show stronger shading if it doesn't have a black outline.

• The **Detail** setting for the Photocopy filter controls how far the shading extends inward from the edges. The **Darkness** setting determines how dense the shading is. (If you've worked with the Shadow and Glow effects in Layer Styles, it may help to think of Darkness as similar to Size, and Detail as similar to Choke or Spread.)

3b

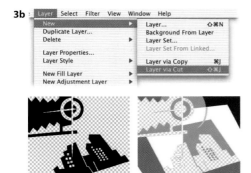

Cutting the selected black artwork to a new layer also leaves the color on a layer of its own. Here each new layer is viewed alone.

4a

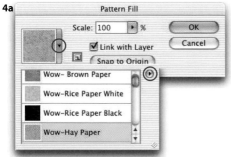

Adding a Pattern Fill layer with the Wow-Hay Paper pattern.

4b

A Pattern Fill layer was added to provide an organic background. The Black layer's Opacity was reduced to 50%, and the Colors layer was put in Multiply mode. (This produces a nice-looking result, even without proceeding further.)

Options bar settings shown in **3a**: **Tolerance** set to 0, so that only 100% black will be selected when you click on a black pixel; **Anti-aliased** turned on, for a smooth edge; and **Contiguous turned off**, so that all black will be selected, whether or not it's connected to the pixel you click on. With these settings the Magic Wand selection won't be perfect. It will be slightly smaller than the original line work overall, leaving behind thin dark edges around the color areas. But this won't be a problem because the "Photocopy" layer above will actually define the black edges. After clicking on black to make the selection, separate the black onto its own layer by choosing Layer > New > Layer Via Cut (or use the shortcut, Ctrl/⌘-Shift-J) **3b**. We named this new layer "Black."

4 Adding a background. Putting a new background in place now will help you see the "organic" treatment as it develops. One way to add a background is to use a Pattern Fill layer. In the Layers palette, target the "Original" layer by clicking its thumbnail. Then click the "Create new fill or adjustment layer" button ⬤ at the bottom of the palette and choose Pattern from the pop-up list. In the Pattern Fill dialog box **4a**, click the little black triangle to the right of the pattern swatch to open the palette of available patterns. We chose **Wow-Hay Paper** from the **Wow Organic Patterns** set. If you haven't yet loaded the Wow presets from the DVD-ROM that comes with this book,▼ click the ⓡ button to the right of the pattern menu, choose Load Patterns, and navigate to the **Wow Organics** (see "You'll Find the Files" on page 467). In the Caution box, click the "Append" button to add the Wow Organic Patterns set to the currently available swatches.

> **FINDING PATTERNS BY NAME**
>
> Looking for a particular pattern? Wherever the Patterns palette occurs in Photoshop, you can see all the pattern names as well as the swatches by choosing Large List from the palette's pop-up menu. But even without using one of the List modes, if you have Show Tool Tips turned on in Preferences > General (Ctrl/⌘-K is the shortcut), you can see the name of a particular pattern by pausing your cursor over the swatch.

Target the "Colors" layer and put it in Multiply mode (at the upper left corner of the Layers palette) to let the Pattern Fill show through. At this point you can experiment by adjusting Opacity; we left the Opacity of the "Colors" layer at 100%, but reduced the Opacity of the "Black" layer to 50% to get a look that we liked **4b**.

> **FIND OUT MORE**
>
> ▼ Loading the Wow presets
> **page 5**

5 "Airbrushing." For a soft, subtle airbrushing effect, target the "Colors" layer and choose Filter > Blur > Gaussian Blur; we set the Radius to 10 pixels to get the degree of blurring we wanted **5**.

6 Adding texture. To add an overall texture to the graphics, try the Stucco pattern from the Patterns 2 presets file that comes with Photoshop: In the Layers palette click on the "Photocopy" layer to target it. Then click the "Create new fill or adjustment layer" button ⊘ and choose Pattern. In the Pattern Fill dialog box, click the little triangle to the right of the swatch to open the Pattern Preset picker; then click on that palette's ⊙ button and choose Patterns 2 from that list. In the Caution box that pops up, click "Append." The Patterns 2 set will be added at the bottom of the list of swatches, and you can choose Stucco.

Now change the blend mode of your new gray-stucco-filled layer to Overlay or one of the other modes immediately below it in the list. We chose Vivid Light because it brightened the background color and intensified the texture **6**. The result is shown at the top of page 467.

Experimenting with other textures. With your texture and background in Pattern Fill layers, it's easy to try out other textures — almost like having "live" filter layers. Double-click the thumbnail for the Pattern Fill layer and choose other patterns from the various Wow presets. You can also experiment by turning on and off visibility or changing Opacity for various layers. *Wow*

5

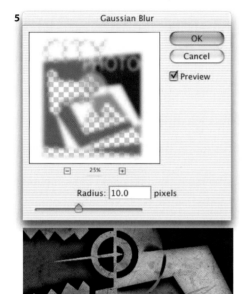

Blurring the "Colors" layer for a softer "airbrushed" look produces another nice-looking result.

6

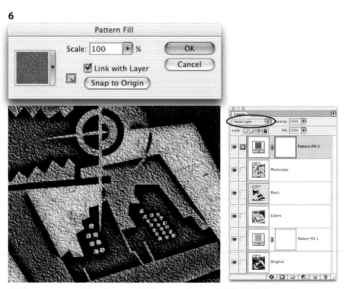

Adding texture with a Pattern Fill layer at the top in Vivid Light mode

Filter Treatments

Some of the options in Photoshop's Filter menu and Filter Gallery are especially good for turning flat PostScript line art or rasterized Shape layers into something that looks more organic, textured, or dimensional. The treatments shown on these three pages are designed to offer quick solutions, applied to one graphic or to a series.

To create any of the effects shown here, go to Photoshop's Filter menu and make the choices shown in the caption. An "**FG**" in the caption means the effect can also be carried out by choosing Filter > Filter Gallery.

In the Tools palette the Foreground and Background colors were set to the default black and white before the filters were run. You can set the default colors by typing D.

We started with this logo, which was cre-ated in Illustrator and rasterized in Photoshop at 1000 pixels square (in-cluding the white border) as described in "Organic Graphics" on page 467.

YOU'LL FIND THE FILE

in wow > Wow Project Files > Chapter 7 > Organic Graphics:

• Organic Graphics-Before (to start)

Roughening the Lines

The following filter treatments act on the quality of the lines and edges.

Brush Strokes > Spatter (Spray Radius 5, Smoothness 10)   FG

Distort > Glass (Distortion 3, Smooth-ness 5, Texture: Frosted, Scaling 100)   FG

Artistic > Poster Edges (Edge Thickness 2, Edge Intensity 6, Posterization 2)   FG

Artistic > Rough Pastels (Stroke Length 6, Stroke Detail 4, Texture: Canvas, Scaling 100, Relief 20, Light: Top Left)   FG

Pattern & Texture

The filters shown here add pattern to the artwork.

Artistic > Sponge (Brush Size 0, Definition 25, Smoothness 1)   FG

Distort > Diffuse Glow (Graininess 10, Glow Amount 5, Clear Amount 10)   FG

Pixelate > Color Halftone (Max. Radius 6, Default Angles)

Texture > Grain (Intensity 30, Contrast 50, Grain Type: Contrasty)   FG

Monochrome Effects

Most of the filters in the Sketch menu render artwork in the current Foreground and Background colors.

Sketch > Chalk & Charcoal (Charcoal Area 6, Chalk Area 6, Stroke Pressure 1)   FG

Sketch > Halftone Pattern (Size 1, Contrast 10, Pattern Type: Line)   FG

Sketch > Reticulation (Density 12, Foreground Level 15, Background Level 5)   FG

Sketch > Conté Crayon (Foreground Level 11, Background Level 7, Texture: Canvas, Scaling 100, Relief 4, Light: Top Right)   FG

Dimensional Effects

Some filters simulate light and shadow to add thickness to graphics.

Render > Lighting Effects (Style: Default, Texture Channel: Green, Height 100)

Artistic > Plastic Wrap (Highlight Strength 20, Detail 7, Smoothness 7)   FG

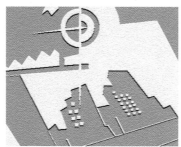

Sketch > Note Paper (Image Balance 20, Graininess 5, Relief 10)

Sketch > Plaster (Image Balance 29, Smoothness 1, Light: Top Right)   FG

Lighting

Photoshop's built-in lighting studio (Filter > Render > Lighting Effects) and other filters can light up your graphics.

Render > Lighting Effects (Style: Triple Spotlight, Intensity 100)

Sharpen > Unsharp Mask (Amount 400, Radius 75, Threshold 0)

Render > Lens Flare (Brightness 100, Flare Center moved, Lens Type: 50-300mm Zoom)

Artistic > Neon Glow (Glow Size 5, Glow Brightness 20, Glow Color yellow-green)   FG

Artistic > Neon Glow (Glow Size –5, Glow Brightness 20, Glow Color yellow-green)   FG

Distorting the Artwork

To distort an entire graphic without having the distortion "flatten out" at the edges, you need empty space around the artwork, as in our example, shown on page 471.

Distort > Twirl (Angle –30)

Distort > Pinch (Amount 50)

Distort > Spherize (Amount 100, Mode: Normal)

Filtered Over Original

You can get eye-catching effects by layering a filtered version over the original and changing the filtered layer's blend mode or Opacity.

Render > Fibers (Variance 16, Strength 64) in Overlay mode at 50% Opacity, over the original image

Blur > Average in Hue mode at 100% Opacity, over the original image

Stylize > Find Edges in Multiply mode at 100% Opacity, over the original image

Layering Filters

For other interesting combinations, layer a filtered version, at reduced Opacity or in a different blend mode, over another filtered version.

Other > High Pass (Radius 30) in Linear Light mode at 100% Opacity, over Sketch > Photocopy (Detail 7, Darkness 8)

Sketch > Halftone Pattern (Size 1, Contrast 10, Pattern Type: Line) in Color Burn mode at 100% Opacity, over Other > High Pass (Radius 30)

Artistic > Neon Glow (Glow Size 5, Glow Brightness 20, Glow Color yellow-green) in Normal mode at 60% Opacity, over Artistic > Plastic Wrap (Highlight Strength 20, Detail 7, Smoothness 7)   FG

DONAL JOLLEY

Coloring Clip Art

YOU'LL FIND THE FILES
in <wow> > Wow Project Files > Chapter 7 >
Coloring Clip Art:
   • Coloring Clip-Before.psd (to start)
   • Checkered.pat (a Pattern presets file)
   • Coloring Clip-After.psd (to compare)

OPEN THESE PALETTES
from the Window menu:
   • Tools • Layers • Channels

OVERVIEW
Divide the artwork into the layers you'll
need for treating elements separately
• Create layers with linework only and
white-filled base layers • Add color on
new layers in Multiply mode • Add a
Pattern Fill layer • Apply Layer Styles to
add dimension

START WITH YOUR OWN ARTWORK created in a PostScript drawing program, or take advantage of the zillions of clip art files
out there just waiting for the kinds of coloring and special effects that Photoshop can do so well. We started with a logo
designed by Don Jolley in Adobe Illustrator. The exact step-
by-step coloring process will depend on the complexity of your
original artwork and how it was created. But several concepts
covered here can be useful regardless of the file you start with:

• Isolating the black "linework" in a way that doesn't produce
a gray "halo" at the edges of the lines

• Isolating shapes that can be filled with color on a separate
layer in Multiply mode so there are no gaps between the
color and the black linework

• Using Photoshop's toning tools and Airbrush to enhance
the color

• Locking transparency to make it easy to paint the black
linework itself

1a

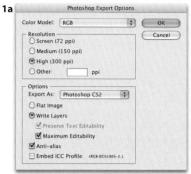

Exporting the file in Photoshop PSD format from Adobe Illustrator

1b

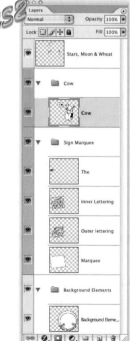

The layered file opened in Photoshop, with layer sets/groups added to help organize the layers for the three main parts of the art — the cow, the sign, and the background.

- Coloring with a Pattern Fill layer
- Adding dimension with Layer Styles

Use artwork of your own choosing, or open **Coloring Clip-Before.psd** and follow along.

1 Preparing the art. The first step is to create and organize the artwork in Illustrator and save it in Photoshop PSD format. Jolley had set up the Illustrator file as an RGB document (File > Document Color Mode). In Illustrator we sorted the objects that made up the file into layers, using as few layers as we could that would still isolate the areas that would need independent color fills, painting, or different Layer Styles. We ended up with six layers — from bottom to top, a layer for the background elements, four layers for the marquee and lettering, a layer for the cow, and a layer for the stars, moon, and wheat straw. We decided to keep the cow, the marquee and its lettering, and the background elements separate — essentially as different pieces of clip art. That way we could layer them and adjust their spatial relationships, and we could also use the cow and marquee alone as spot illustrations.

We exported the file in Photoshop CS PSD format **1a**, choosing RGB for the Color Mode, setting the Resolution at High, and clicking the check boxes to turn on Anti-alias (for smooth edges) and Write Layers (to translate the Illustrator layers directly into Photoshop layers). The resulting file, opened in Photoshop, kept the same layer names. We made a layer set/group for each of our three sections — Cow, Sign, and Background **1b**. ▼

FIND OUT MORE

▼ Layer sets/groups
page 583

2 Making black-on-transparent artwork. The original Post-Script artwork for "Bellowing Bluegrass Stampede" had been composed of stacked black-filled and white-filled shapes. But in our Photoshop file we wanted to isolate most of the black artwork on its own transparent layers so we could use its shapes to apply Layer Styles to add a little dimension.

To isolate the black linework, load the luminosity of the artwork layer as a selection (start with the "Cow" layer in this case), as follows: First click the 👁 icons in the Layers palette to turn off visibility for all layers except the one you want to make lines from **2a**. Then in the Channels palette, Ctrl/⌘-click on the RGB composite channel's name to load its luminosity as a selection **2b**. That will select all the white areas in the layer and leave the black unselected. Invert the selection (Ctrl/⌘-Shift-I) to select

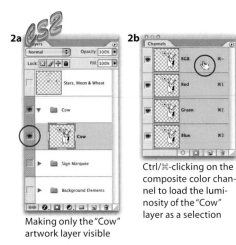

2a

2b

Ctrl/⌘-clicking on the composite color channel to load the luminosity of the "Cow" layer as a selection

Making only the "Cow" artwork layer visible

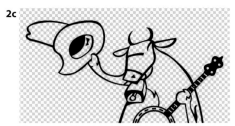

2c

The inverted luminosity selection filled with black on a new transparent layer to make artwork that can be acted on by a Layer Style later. Part of the new "Cow Lines" layer is viewed alone here.

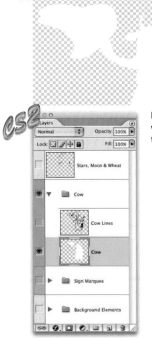

3a

Part of the finished white base layer for the cow, viewed alone

the black. Now add a new layer above the artwork layer by targeting the artwork layer (in our example, click the "Cow" layer's thumbnail in the Layers palette) and then Alt/Option-clicking the "Create a new layer" button 🔲 at the bottom of the Layers palette so you can name the layer as you create it; we named ours "Cow Lines." In this new layer, with black as the Foreground color (type X to restore the default colors), press Alt-Backspace (Windows) or Option-Delete (Mac) to fill the selection with black **2c** and then deselect (Ctrl/⌘-D). (By selecting and filling rather than simply cutting or copying the selected linework to a new layer, you avoid bringing along shades of gray in the antialiasing at the edges of the lines.)

3 Making a white base layer for the art. Now the black linework is isolated on its own new "Cow Lines" layer, and the black-and-white art is on the original "Cow" layer below. The process of adding color to the artwork (in step 4) depends on using Multiply mode so that solid color will extend all the way to the black "lines," and there won't be a "fringe" of antialiasing between the color and the black. But for Multiply mode to work, there has to be something opaque underneath for the color to affect. We need a white-filled shape under the linework.

To turn the original black-and-white artwork into a white base for the color, target the layer by clicking its thumbnail in the Layers palette; we targeted the "Cow" layer. With white as the Background color in the Tools palette and no selection active, press Ctrl-Shift-Backspace (Windows) or ⌘-Shift-Delete (Mac) to fill all the nontransparent areas on this layer with white **3a**. (Including the Shift key in the keyboard shortcut temporarily turns on the "Lock transparent pixels" function, which can also be set at the top the Layers palette. This way the transparent areas stay transparent and all partially transparent pixels, in the antialiasing in this case, are recolored but with their partial transparency maintained.)

To ensure that a white fringe doesn't peek out from behind the black linework in the layer above, we can trim off the edges of the white: Ctrl/⌘-click its thumbnail to load it as a selection. Then choose Select > Modify > Contract (1 pixel) to shrink the selection **3b**. Invert the selection (Ctrl/⌘-Shift-I) and press the Backspace/Delete key to trim; then deselect (Ctrl/⌘-D).

Repeat the process of isolating the linework and making and trimming a white backing; we created additional black linework and white base layers for the "Background Elements" layer, the "Marquee" layer, and the word "The" **3c**.

3b

We contracted the selection of the white base layer by 1 pixel all around (above). Then we inverted the selection and deleted the 1-pixel edge.

3c

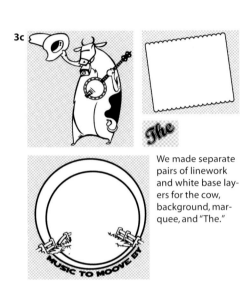

We made separate pairs of linework and white base layers for the cow, background, marquee, and "The."

4a

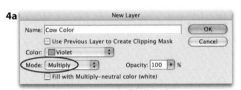

Starting a new layer to hold the color

4b

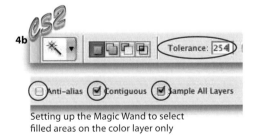

Setting up the Magic Wand to select filled areas on the color layer only

4 Coloring the artwork. For each pair (linework layer and base layer), you'll need a layer above for the color. Target a linework layer (click its thumbnail in the Layers palette); we started with the "Cow" layer. Then add a new layer above it (Alt/Option-click the "Create a new layer" button ▣; in the New Layer dialog box, choose Multiply for the new layer's blend mode) **4a**.

The next step is to select and color each enclosed shape in the artwork. First choose the Magic Wand ✺ and set it up as follows **4b**: In the Options bar turn on **Contiguous** and **Use/Sample All Layers**, turn off **Anti-alias**, and set the **Tolerance at 254**.

- The **Contiguous** setting will limit the selection to the single black-line-enclosed area you click with the Wand.

- The **Use/Sample All Layers** setting will let you work on your new transparent layer while allowing the Wand to "see" the artwork in all layers to make the selection.

- **Turning off Anti-alias** will make a selection that will fill entirely with color, rather than adding partial transparency at the edges. This will prevent the edge from getting messy if you select and reselect, fill and refill a selection as you experiment with color.

- Setting the **Tolerance at 254** (1 less than the maximum 255 tones) means that if you click on a white area, all pixels except solid black ones will be included in the selection — in other words, the selection will encroach into the black linework to include its antialiasing pixels. This makes the color-filled area overlap the black linework slightly, "trapping" the color-and-line interface so there's no gap between them.

In the Layers palette, turn on visibility (the 👁 icons) for the linework layer and the base layer; we started with the cow, so we had visibility turned on for the "Cow Color," "Cow Lines," and "Cow" layers, and turned off for the other layers. Click each black-line-enclosed area with the Magic Wand ✺, Shift-clicking if you want to add another area to be filled with the same color. Then choose a Foreground color (double-click the Foreground swatch in the Tools palette to open the Color Picker, and choose a color); then press Alt-Backspace or Option-Delete to fill the selection **4c**. (The reason we used the Magic Wand and then filled, rather than using the Paint Bucket at the same settings mentioned, is that we could "multiselect" areas to fill, as described above, and we could be sure of what areas would be filled *before* filling.) You can temporarily switch the color

4c

The "Cow Color" layer with all the basic fills in place, viewed alone (top left) and with the "Cow Lines" and "Cow" white base layer (top right)

5a

Setting up the Gradient tool's ▣ options to color the sky in the "Background Elements Color" layer

5b

Color fills and gradient in place for the Background Elements

6a

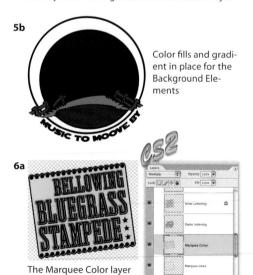

The Marquee Color layer with the "Marquee," "Marquee Lines," and the two "Lettering" layers visible

layer from Multiply to Normal mode (in the list at the upper left of the Layers palette) to see how the edges of the colors overlap the black lines.

5 Coloring with a gradient. When the "Cow Color" layer had all its color fills, we turned off visibility for the "Cow" layer set/ group and turned on visibility for the "Background Elements" layer. We added a new transparent layer in Multiply mode to hold the colors for this group. We used the same technique for coloring the fence and grass in the "Background Elements" layer as we had for the cow. To fill the sky with a blue gradient, we Shift-selected the areas that made up the sky and chose two shades of dark blue as Foreground and Background colors (to set the Foreground or Background color, double-click its swatch in the Tools palette and choose a color). We used the Gradient tool ▣ with the Foreground to Background Linear gradient **5a**, dragging from top to bottom of the selected areas.▼ We left the circular border uncolored **5b**; we would apply a pattern to this area later (at step 8).

FIND OUT MORE

▼ Working with gradients **page 160**

6 Adding a slanted stripe of color. For the sign marquee, we used the same selecting-and-filling technique from step 4 to color the sign yellow. In addition to our linework, base, and color layers for the Marquee, we turned on visibility for the lettering layers so we could see exactly where to build a green band behind the word "BLUEGRASS" **6a**. We needed to make a tilted rectangular selection in order to fill the band. Here's one way to select a tilted rectangle: To figure out the tilt angle, choose the Measure tool ⬩ and drag it along one edge of the sign — for instance, position the cursor near the bottom of the right edge of the sign and drag up the edge **6b**. This draws a nonprinting line, and the "A" (angle) value in the Options bar and the Info palette reports its angle; make a note of this number, because you'll need it in a minute. Choose the Rectangular Marquee ⬚ and drag to select a rectangle of any dimensions. Choose Select > Transform Selection and in the Options bar, type into the "Set rotation" field a value equal to but opposite the value you noted for the Measure tool **6c**; in other words, if the value was 97.4, you would type –97.4; or if the value was –50, you would type 50. Then use the handles of the Transform frame to stretch or shrink the selection

RECALLING MEASUREMENTS

It's easy to recall the length, width, origin, and angle values for the most recent line you've drawn with the Measure tool ⬩. Simply choose the tool again and check the Options bar or Info palette.

6b

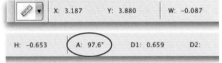

Using the Measure tool ![measure tool] to find the tilt angle for the sign marquee

6c

Entering the negative of the angle measurement after choosing Select > Transform Selection

6d

The tilted rectangular selection

6e

After choosing a green for the Foreground color and pressing Alt-Backspace (Windows) or Option-Delete (Mac) to fill the selected stripe with color

7a

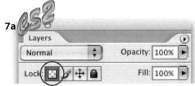

Locking transparency for the color layer

to fit the area you want to color **6d**. Complete the transformation (press Enter/Return, or double-click inside the Transform frame) and then fill the selection with color **6e**.

7 Refining the color. To "tune" the color on each color layer, you can use the Dodge tool ![dodge] for highlighting and the Burn tool ![burn] for shading, or add highlights or shadows with the Brush tool ![brush] with Airbrush mode ![airbrush] turned on in the Options bar. First, lock the transparent pixels for the color layer (by clicking the ☐ button near the top of the Layers palette) **7a** to prevent "coloring outside the lines." If you need a selection to fill, use the Magic Wand ![wand] again to select the individual color patches, **but this time turn *off* Use/Sample All Layers** in the Options bar **7b**, so the Wand will only "look at" the active layer — the color layer in this case — as it makes selections. Leave **Contiguous turned on** and leave the **Tolerance at 254** so that each click of the Wand selects *all* the color that's inside the clicked area and surrounded by the transparent gaps — even if you've filled it with a gradient or modified the color with other shades and tones. Select and tone, paint, or refill as you like. We used the Burn tool ![burn] with a soft brush tip to darken various areas of the cow and the hat **7c**. We also used the selection of the cow to contain the gray paint as we used the Brush ![brush] to paint the hooves and the brown paint for the tail.

We used the Brush ![brush] with the Airbrush feature ![airbrush] turned on in the Options bar to highlight the fence rails and posts **7d**.

7b

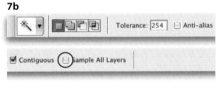

Setting up the Magic Wand ![wand] for selecting patches of color to fine-tune

7c

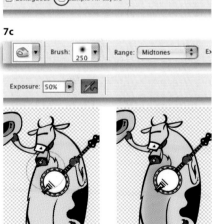

We used the Brush ![brush] to paint the hooves and tail, and the Burn tool ![burn] to tone the cow's body and hat. For the body we started with a large soft brush tip (left), made a vertical stroke downward to "burn" the color, and then reduced the size of the brush tip and the Exposure, and painted to tone the edges of the area.

7d The "Background Elements Color" layer is fine-tuned by using the Brush tool 🖌 with the Airbrush option 🖌 turned on to spray the fence rails and posts with a lighter brown for highlighting.

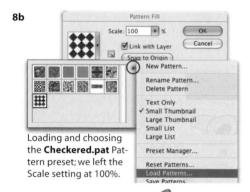

8a Selecting the parts of the ring (left) and adding a Pattern Fill layer

8b Loading and choosing the **Checkered.pat** Pattern preset; we left the Scale setting at 100%.

8c The Pattern Fill layer in place

8d After turning on visibility for the "Cow" layer set/group, we adjusted the position of the Pattern slightly within the ring.

8 Using a Pattern Fill layer. For the ring that frames the sky and ground, we wanted to use a checkered pattern. Instead of simply selecting and filling the ring, we used a Pattern Fill layer for more control of the positioning and scale of the pattern. Here's how to do it: Target the "Background Elements" layer and use the Magic Wand ✨ with settings as in step 4 (Use/ Sample All Layers turned on), Shift-clicking to select all parts of the ring. Once the selection is complete, click on the "Create new fill or adjustment layer" button ⬤ at the bottom of the Layers palette and choose Pattern **8a**. In the Pattern Fill dialog, click the tiny triangle next to the pattern swatch to open the Pattern picker **8b**. Then click the ⊙ button and choose Load Patterns from the menu. Load **Checkered.pat** (supplied with the other files for this section) and watch the working window as you move the pattern (by dragging in the working window) or adjust its size with the Scale slider **8c**; scale by a factor of 2 (50% or 25%, for example) to prevent "softening" of the pattern. (If you decide later that you want to change the scale or position of the pattern, you can simply double-click the Pattern layer's thumbnail in the Layers palette to reopen the Pattern Fill dialog) **8d**.

9 Coloring some of the black artwork. We wanted to color the stars, moon, and wheat, the "Bellowing Bluegrass Stampede" (the "Inner Lettering" layer), the marquee lights and stars, and the word "The," all of them parts of the black artwork.

- For the stars, moon, and wheat, we targeted the layer and locked its transparency (click the ⬚ button). We painted with the Brush tool 🖌 with a hard round brush tip and 100% Opacity **9a**, sampling colors by Alt/Option-clicking the colors already used for coloring the art. We shaded the moon with the Burn tool ✋ as described in step 7; you can see the result on page 474.

- On the "Inner Lettering" layer, we chose the color and with transparency locked (click ⬚) pressed Alt-Backspace (Windows) or Option-Delete (Mac) to fill the lettering, the round marquee lights, and the three stars with color all at once **9b**. Then we changed the color of the lights and stars to white by using the Brush tool 🖌, white paint, and a hard round brush tip **9c**: With a brush tip larger than the circles, we clicked to the left of the top row of lights, then Shift-clicked past the right end; the process was repeated for the bottom row of lights and (top to bottom) for the three stars.

9a

Painting the stars

9b

We locked transparency for the "Inner Lettering" layer and filled it with color.

9c

With transparency still locked, we painted over the dots and stars with white.

9d

Setting up options for the Paint Bucket

9e

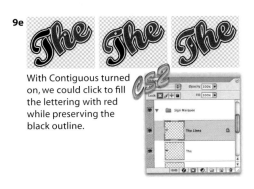

With Contiguous turned on, we could click to fill the lettering with red while preserving the black outline.

- To color the word "The" red, but preserve its black outline, we locked transparency for the "The Lines" layer and chose the Paint Bucket tool. In the Options bar we set Tolerance to 254 and turned on Contiguous **9d**; it took three clicks on different parts of the lettering to turn all the black pixels red instead, including those that were partly transparent for antialiasing **9e**. The black outline, though, didn't change, since it wasn't touching (contiguous with) the central parts of the lettering that had been clicked.

10 Adding Layer Styles. When you think the coloring is complete — because of the way you've constructed the color layer, you can always go back and recolor later — you can add dimensionality with Layer Styles; we added only a subtle bevel to emboss the "Cow Lines" layer by targeting the layer, clicking the "Add a layer style" button at the bottom of the Layers palette, and choosing Bevel and Emboss **10**. We copied and pasted the Style to the "Background Elements Lines" and "Marquee Lines" layers and also to the colored linework in the "Stars, Moon, and Wheat" and "Inner Lettering" layers. To copy and paste a Style, in the Layers palette, right/Ctrl-click on the icon for the "styled" layer and choose Copy Layer Style from the context-sensitive menu. Then right/Ctrl-click in about the same area of the entry for another layer you want to style, and choose Paste Layer Style. (In Photoshop CS2 you can paste a copied Style to several layers at once by Shift-clicking or Ctrl-clicking the layers' thumbnails to multitarget them, and then pasting to one of the targeted layers.)

To complete the illustration on page 474 with a subtle layered look, we added a Style with only a Drop Shadow to the white base layers for the cow, marquee, and background.

10

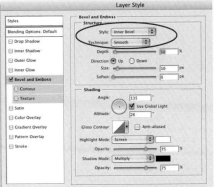

When the Bevel and Emboss panel of the Layer Style dialog opened, we used the default Smooth Inner Bevel, adjusting the Depth and Size to give the linework just a slight "bump."

PERSUASION: RECEPTION AND RESPONSIBILITY

Charles U. Larson 10th Edition

JOHN ODAM

In developing the cover illustration for ***Persuasion: Reception and Responsibility, Tenth Edition***, by Charles U. Larson (Wadsworth), designer **John Odam** used type to mask photos. He started by setting the Futura Extra Bold type, one letter per layer, in black (see "Starting a New Type Layer" below). Many of the changes Odam planned to make to the type — scaling the characters and changing their baselines, for instance — could have been done with a single type layer. But to tilt (rotate) the letters individually, overlap them in any order, and add a separate drop shadow to each letter, even when letters overlapped, he had to put his characters on different layers.

Odam didn't need the type to remain editable — the title of the book wasn't going to change at this point, and by eliminating the live type he could avoid any font problems during output. Faced with converting a type layer, you can choose either to make it a Shape layer (by clicking its thumbnail in the Layers palette to target the layer and then choosing Layer > Type > Convert to Shape from the main menu) or to rasterize it into pixels (by targeting it and choosing Layer > Rasterize > Type). The Shape layer will preserve the sharp letter outline, even if the file is resized.

After converting the type and targeting one of his letter layers by clicking its thumbnail in the Layers palette, Odam transformed the individual black letter (by pressing Ctrl/⌘-T for Edit > Free Transform Path and dragging — outside a corner to rotate, or on a corner handle with the Shift key held down to scale proportionally, or inside the Transform box to reposition).

When the layout was complete **A**, he began to add photos; some he shot himself with a digital camera and some were purchased as stock photography. He opened the photo files and then clicked in the working window of the layout file to activate it. If you target a letter layer, and then drag the photo you want to mask with that layer into the file, the photo becomes a layer just above its letter. Then by Alt/Option-clicking on the line between the photo and letter layers in the Layers palette, you form a clipping group that masks the photo inside the letter **B**. Using the Move tool ▶⊕, you can drag in the working window to move the photo until the part of the image you want shows in the letter.

When all the photos had been clipped inside letters, Odam targeted one of the letter layers and added Photoshop's default drop shadow by clicking the "Add a layer style" button ⓕ at the bottom of the layers palette, choosing Drop Shadow from the pop-up list, and clicking "OK" to close the Layer Style dialog box. Then he duplicated the drop shadow to the other letter layers **C** (see "Drag-and-Drop Effects" at the right).

A finished file composed of clipping groups and Layer Styles offers a great deal of flexibility, because you still have separate access to each of the photos, letter shapes, and effects.

When Odam had finished his illustration, he made a single-layer copy of it (Image > Duplicate, choosing Duplicate Merged Layers Only), saved it in TIFF format, and placed it in a page layout file, where he added type for the title and author.

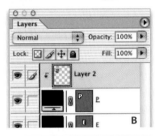

A

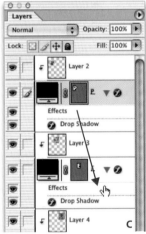

B

C

STARTING A NEW TYPE LAYER

One easy way to let Photoshop know that you want to start a new type layer rather than adding characters to an existing one is to add a new empty layer (click the "Create a new layer" button ◻ at the bottom of the Layers palette, or Ctrl/⌘-click it to add the new layer *below* the original); then with the Type tool **T** chosen, click in your working window and start typing. The empty layer you just added will automatically become a type layer.

DRAG-AND-DROP EFFECTS

One quick way to copy the effects in a Layer Style to another layer is simply to drag the "Effects" entry in the Layers palette to the other layer's entry (in CS2, Alt/Option-drag). **Note:** Only the *effects* — such as Drop Shadow, Inner Glow, Outer Glow, or Pattern Overlay — are added when you drag and drop the "Effects" entry. Any *blending options* — such as blend mode or Fill opacity — that may also be built into a Layer Style are *not* copied when you drag and drop.

For both **Luna Surf** (this page) and **Taste of Style** (opposite) **Mike Kungl** began with a pencil sketch, scanned it, and used it as a template in Adobe Illustrator, where he drew shapes and filled them with flat colors to make a design comp, as shown in the small illustration on the facing page. When he finished in Illustrator, Kungl turned on the AICB Preserve Paths option in Illustrator's Preferences (File Han-

dling & Clipboard) dialog so he could copy the artwork to the clipboard and paste it as paths into a Photoshop file he had set up with the same height and width dimensions as the Illustrator file.

Working in Photoshop, Kungl turned each subpath into an alpha channel — for each subpath in turn, he clicked it with the Path Selection tool ▶, then clicked the "Load path as a selection" button ◉ at the bottom of the Paths

palette, and finally saved the selection as an alpha channel by clicking the "Save selection as channel" button ◻ at the bottom of the Channels palette. When he had converted all the paths to alpha channels, he had a file with a single empty layer and many channels, which he saved in Photoshop (PSD) format and opened in Corel Painter. He also imported his original Illustrator comp into Painter to use as a visual guide as he turned

the channels into selections and used them as friskets to limit the gradient fills he combined with paper textures and brushwork applied with Painter's natural media brushes.

When he had finished in Painter, Kungl saved the file in PSD format again and reopened it in Photoshop, where the layer hierarchy created in Painter was preserved. In this layered file, he touched up the artwork — for instance, he used the Eraser ⬛ to

create "holes" in the surf foam. He made color adjustments with Levels, Hue/Saturation, and Selective Color,▼ and changed layer Opacity to blend elements. Finally, he converted the file to CMYK for output.

Luna Surf was produced as a limited edition fine art Giclée print in several sizes, from 18 to 43 inches high, on 330# German Fine Art Soft archival paper with archival inks.

Taste of Style is one of seven illustrations commissioned by Resorts Casinos in Atlantic City, New Jersey, that were applied to everything from matchbook covers and towels to light pole banners and billboards.

FIND OUT MORE

▼ Adjusting tone & color **page 165**

WINTER SPRING SUMMER FALL

THE SEASONS OF A SOUL RHYME WITH HOT WARM COOL AND COLD.

To create the abstract background for his type in *Seasons of the Soul,* **Steven Gordon** opened a photograph **A** and turned it into a pattern (Edit > Define Pattern). He closed the photo file and created a new document at 72 pixels/inch. Gordon chose the Pattern Stamp tool, clicked the Tool Preset picker at the left end of the Options bar, and chose the **Wow-PS Dry Brush-Large** preset from the **Wow Pattern Stamp Brushes** set of presets.▼ In the Options bar he lowered the brush's Opacity to 50%, but he kept the pattern Aligned and kept Impressionist turned on. On the canvas Gordon painted short, overlapping strokes **B**.

Because the source image was larger than the document on which he was painting, only the upper left corner of the source contributed to his Pattern Stamp strokes.

When he finished painting, Gordon added a Hue/Saturation layer (clicking at the bottom of the Layers palette) and increased the Saturation to make the colors more vibrant. He increased the document's resolution to 288 pixels/inch (Image > Image Size, with Resample Image checked) and used Unsharp Mask to sharpen the definition of the brush marks.▼

To create the four-seasons type, Gordon selected the Horizontal Type tool T. In the Options bar's font list he chose Cancione, an all-capitals font designed by Brenda Walton (www.itcfonts.com). To make a solid block of type that would hold together well as he warped it, he clicked the Options bar's "Toggle Character and Paragraph palettes" button 🔲 and set the font size and leading the same, which would leave little space between the lines of type. He clicked in the working window, automatically creating a new type layer, and keyed in the text, beginning with "WINTER" and pressing the Enter/Return key at the end of each

word. When the type was set, he clicked the "Create warped text" button 🔲 in the Options bar, and chose the Twist style in the Warp Text dialog box **C**. He adjusted the Bend and Distortion controls until he had the geometry he wanted **D**. In the Layers palette, Gordon changed the blend mode for the layer to Overlay so the background colors of the painting affected the color of the type. Finally, he set off the type by clicking the 🔲 button at the bottom of the Layers palette and adding a Drop Shadow, changing its color to white, its Mode to Normal, and its Opacity to 30%. To fade the type on the right side, he added a layer mask 🔲 and applied a gradient to it.▼

For the verse, Gordon used paragraph type: He dragged with the Type tool T to create a rectangle for the type, then moved the cursor outside a corner of the type box and

dragged counterclockwise to rotate the box to the angle he wanted for the verse. In the Options bar he chose the OpenType LithosPro font and the right-aligned option. In the Character palette he chose type size and Auto leading, and typed the verse, pressing Enter/Return whenever he wanted to start a new line **E**. Clicking the ✔ button on the Options bar completed the text **F**.

> You'll find a low-resolution version of Steven Gordon's **Seasons.psd** file in Wow Goodies so you can inspect its construction and experiment with type.

FIND OUT MORE

▼ Loading the Wow presets **page 5**
▼ Using Unsharp Mask **page 326**
▼ Masking with Gradients **page 75**

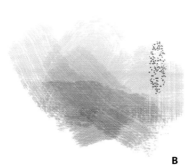

A

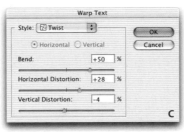

Warp Text

Style: Twist

Horizontal Vertical

Bend: +50 %

Horizontal Distortion: +28 %

Vertical Distortion: -4 %

C

THE
SEASONS
OF A SOUL
RHYME
WITH
HOT
WARM
COOL
AND
COLD.

E

B

D

Layers

Normal   Opacity: 100%

Lock: Fill: 100%

T THE SEASONS OF A SOUL RHYME I

T winter spring summer fall

Effects

Drop Shadow

Hue/Saturation

Background   F

Special Effects for Type & Graphics

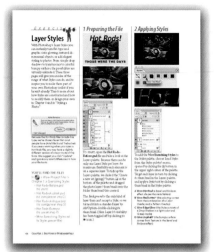

If you haven't worked extensively with Styles and you haven't yet absorbed "Exercising Layer Styles" (pages 44–47), you might want to look at that section now, as a quick introduction to the subject. It includes some important tips for applying, copying, and saving Styles.

"Honoring a Style's 'Design Resolution'" on page 47 tells how to keep a Wow Style looking the way it was designed to look, even if you apply it to a file whose resolution is very different from the file in which the Style was designed. Knowing this little secret can make the difference between the result on the left (the Wow-Clear Orange Style applied to a file at 72 pixels/inch) and the one on the right (with the same Style applied to a file at its design resolution of 225 pixels/inch).

Turning a flat graphic or type into a translucent dimensional object is just one of the things you can accomplish with a Layer Style. The Layer Style used for the type above is described in "Anatomy of Clear Color" on page 513.

MOST OF THE SPECIAL EFFECTS in this chapter are designed to simulate what happens when light and materials interact — from a simple drop shadow to the complex reflections and refraction of chrome, brushed metal, or glass. In Photoshop, creating "live" special effects for graphics and type is almost exclusively the province of Layer Styles, with occasional help from Adjustment layers, masks, and filters.

One important change to Layer Styles in Photoshop CS/CS2 is that you can now choose whether to **resize Layer Styles along with the file** when you scale an image up or down. If you want all the shadows, textures, bevels, and other Style components to shrink or expand along with the size of your image, turning on **Scale Styles** in the Image > Image Size dialog box will make these changes happen automatically as you resize.▼

FIND OUT MORE
▼ Resizing an image
page 73

WORKING WITH LAYER STYLES

With Layer Styles you can create entire dimensional lighting and color treatments to apply wherever you want them. Because Styles are such a powerful component of Photoshop's bag of tricks, they were introduced in Chapter 1 in "Exercising Layer Styles" (page 44). But here's a brief recap of some of the important features of Styles.

A **Style**, with all its component effects, **can be copied** to other layers or other documents — it can even be named and saved as a **preset** for future use. When you apply these portable Styles to other layers, they can be **scaled to fit** the new elements you apply them to, with a single easy **scaling** operation that adjusts all the component effects at once.

A Layer Style can be added to any layer that isn't locked, and you can edit and re-edit your special effects without degrading the interior or edge of the element you've "styled." That edge is defined by the **outline of the layer's content** — in other words, the "footprint" of the layer's pixels, type, or Shape — the demarcation between what's transparent and what's opaque on a layer. The outline may be modified by a layer mask or vector mask.▼ As the default, both of these masks help define the edge for the Layer Style.

FIND OUT MORE
▼ Using masks
page 68

A Layer Style can consist of as many as 12 different component **effects**, along with the **Blending Option**s that govern how the

The same Style used for the type was applied to the splash graphic. Then several of the Style's component effects were adjusted to make the splash look thinner than the "H2O," as described in "A Logo in Clear Color" on page 509.

effects interact with the layer's content and how the layer itself interacts with other layers in the file. Most of the effects (and the Blending Options) have several parameters you can change, and there are *millions* of possible combinations of settings.

Photoshop comes with collections of **preset Styles** that can be loaded for use by opening the Styles palette (Window > Show Styles) and choosing from the menu that pops out from the upper right corner of the palette ⊙. The bottom part of the menu lists all the preset files that are currently in the Styles folder (created inside the Presets folder in your Photoshop application folder when you install the program).

To **develop your own custom Styles**, you can start by applying an existing Style and then edit it in the Layer Style dialog box. Or build a Style from scratch by targeting any unlocked and "unstyled" layer in the Layers palette and opening the Layer

Continued on page 493

GETTING INSIDE THE BOX

There are several ways to open the Layer Style dialog box. Once you're "inside the box," you can use the list on the left side to move from effect to effect or to set up the Blending Options (as shown on page 493).

Note: The menu and palette shown here are from CS2; CS works the same way.

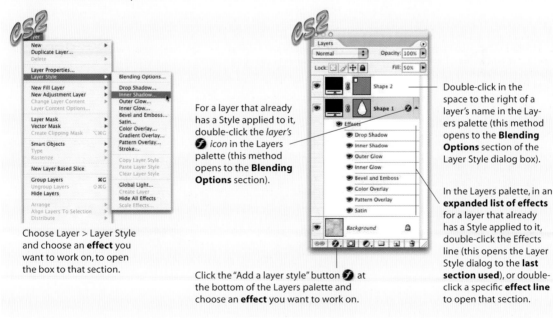

Choose Layer > Layer Style and choose an **effect** you want to work on, to open the box to that section.

For a layer that already has a Style applied to it, double-click the *layer's* 𝒇 icon in the Layers palette (this method opens to the **Blending Options** section).

Click the "Add a layer style" button 𝒇 at the bottom of the Layers palette and choose an **effect** you want to work on.

Double-click in the space to the right of a layer's name in the Layers palette (this method opens to the **Blending Options** section of the Layer Style dialog box).

In the Layers palette, in an **expanded list of effects** for a layer that already has a Style applied to it, double-click the Effects line (this opens the Layer Style dialog to the **last section used**), or double-click a specific **effect line** to open that section.

APPLYING A PRESET STYLE

"Exercising Layer Styles" on page 44 provides a quick but thorough introduction to working with Styles. But here's a summary of how to apply a Style from the Styles palette. With both the Layers palette and the Styles palette open (they're available through the Window menu):

Note: The palettes shown here are from CS2; CS works the same way.

1 Target any unlocked layer (click the layer's thumbnail in the Layers palette).

A Style can't be applied to a *Background* or to any other locked layer.

2 Click the Style of your choice in the Styles palette, which holds Styles that you've loaded and any new ones that you've saved. (Page 5 tells how to load the Wow Styles.)

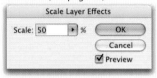

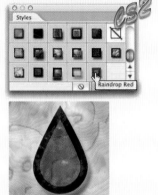

3 In the Layers palette, right-click/Ctrl-click on the *f* for the "styled" layer and choose Scale Effects from the context-sensitive menu. Experiment with the Scale slider to get the best "fit." Styles that include patterns should be scaled with care (see page 45).

COPYING A STYLE FROM ANOTHER LAYER

You can copy a Style from a layer to which it has already been applied, whether that layer is in the same file or another open file:

Note: The palettes shown here are from CS2; CS works the same way.

1 In the Layers palette right/Ctrl-click on the *f* for the "styled" layer and choose Copy Layer Style from the context-sensitive menu.

2 Right/Ctrl-click to the right of the unstyled layer's name in the Layers palette and choose Paste Layer Style.

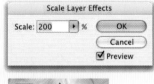

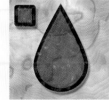

3 Check the scale of the Style, as described in step 3 above.

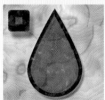

THE LIST IN THE LAYER STYLE DIALOG

All the effects that you can incorporate in a Layer Style are listed at the left side of the Layer Style dialog box.

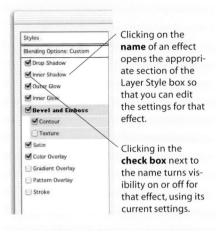

Clicking on the **name** of an effect opens the appropriate section of the Layer Style box so that you can edit the settings for that effect.

Clicking in the **check box** next to the name turns visibility on or off for that effect, using its current settings.

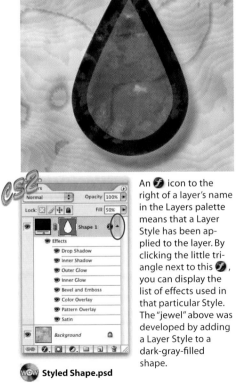

An 🅕 icon to the right of a layer's name in the Layers palette means that a Layer Style has been applied to the layer. By clicking the little triangle next to this 🅕, you can display the list of effects used in that particular Style. The "jewel" above was developed by adding a Layer Style to a dark-gray-filled shape.

Styled Shape.psd

Style dialog box. To open the Layer Style box, simply click the "Add a layer style" button 🅕 at the bottom of the Layers palette (or use one of the other methods in "Getting Inside the Box" on page 491), and choose an effect from the pop-up menu. In the Layer Style dialog box adjust the settings for the effect you chose, and then choose another effect, if you want, from the list on the left side of the dialog box. You can go on this way, choosing effects and setting parameters for as many effects as you want in your Style.

UNDERSTANDING STYLES

The next few pages show how the component effects of Photoshop's Layer Styles work. Then the "Anatomy" sections of the chapter provide examples of exactly how the effects in a Style work together to create different materials, dimensionality, and lighting. The layered-and-styled "Anatomy" files on the Wow DVD-ROM offer a compact, interactive, and interesting way for you to pick up the details. All of a Style's different effects and Blending Options interact with one another, and a slight difference in the combination can make the Style turn out very different than you expect. If one or two little settings are left unmodified, or if your Blending Options are set up differently, instead of translucent blue glass, you could end up with slick black plastic!

The step-by-step special-effects techniques in the chapter show how to develop these highly tactile dimensional treatments even further with additional image layers and Adjustment layers. When you start one of these step-by-step techniques, you may want to **open not only the "before" version of the artwork from the Wow DVD-ROM, but also the "after" file**, so you can refer to it as you work. Also, if your goal is simply to *use* a particular Style from the "after" file rather than learning exactly how it's put together, you can apply the Style by copying and pasting from the file, as described on page 492.

Exploring the Layer Style Dialog Box

One way to learn about how the settings work in a Shadow or Glow or any other effect is to make a type or Shape layer, then open the Layer Style dialog box and for each effect that you want to explore, click its name in the list on the left side of the dialog box to open its section of the box. Then try setting Opacity to 100%, setting Blend Mode to Normal, and setting all other parameters at their minimum settings. Experiment by changing the settings one at a time and in combination, seeing what each one does and how it interacts with the others.

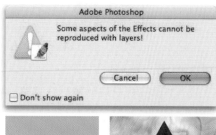

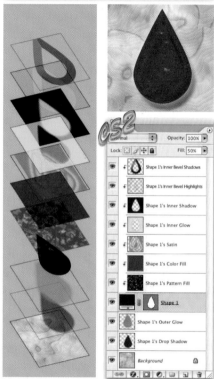

The Create Layers command renders the effects in a Layer Style as separate layers. As shown here for the **Styled Shape.psd** file shown on page 493, sometimes with a Layer Style the whole is greater than the sum of the parts, and the combination of effects you can create with a Style can't be successfully rasterized into separate layers.

LOST IN TRANSLATION

When you choose the **Create Layers** command, a Caution box will warn you that some effects may be lost in translation. For safekeeping, save your Style before you Create Layers: Click the "Create new style" button ▣ at the bottom of the Styles palette, name the Style if you like, and click "OK." It will be added to the Styles palette.

Taking a Style Apart

Another interesting experiment is to set up several effects to create a Style and then rasterize the effects (right/Ctrl-click the layer's *ƒ* icon and choose Create Layers from the context-sensitive menu). Each effect will be separated into a layer of its own — some effects may even need two layers. Notice where the new layers fall in the Layers palette — some will be above and some below the layer you applied the Style to. The order of the layers can be enlightening. The "effects" layers that are above the original "styled" layer will be included in a clipping group ▼ with your original layer serving as the base (as shown in the Layers palette at the left), so the effects show only *inside* the outline created by the original layer. If you now Alt/Option-click in the Layers palette on the border between the original layer and the one just above it in the Layers palette, the layers will be released from the clipping group, and you'll be able to see what the clipping group was accomplishing. Now experiment by clicking the ◉ icons for individual layers.

FIND OUT MORE

▼ Clipping groups **page 70**

LAYER STYLE COMPONENTS

Many of the individual components of a Layer Style are named for the specific effects they were designed to create — Drop Shadow, Inner Shadow, Inner Glow, Outer Glow, and so on. Examples of these effects are shown in "Layer Style Options" on page 495. But a *brightly colored* Drop Shadow can also be put to work as part of a glow (as in "Crafting a Neon Glow" on page 546), and a *dark* Inner Glow can help build realistic shadows (as in "Anatomy of Clear Color" on page 513). If you can get beyond the names and understand how each effect can interact with the others, you'll greatly expand the creative potential that Styles offer.

Another important aspect of Styles is lighting — what direction the light comes from, whether it's directly overhead or more oblique, and how strong it is. Let's start with the simplest of the effects — the Color, Gradient, and Pattern Overlays, then explore lighting and the effects in which lighting plays a role.

OVERLAYS

The three **Overlay** effects provide an easy, flexible way to add a solid color, pattern, or gradient, with complete freedom to change it at any time, regulating the content, opacity, and blend mode. The Overlays interact as if they were stacked in the same

Continued on page 496

LAYER STYLE OPTIONS

A Layer Style can be made up of any of the effects shown here: There are three **Overlays** for coloring the surface, two **Shadows** and two **Glows**, a **Satin** effect, and a **Stroke**. The **Bevel And Emboss** effect has five different kinds of bevel structures, as well as a **Contour** to shape the bevel. The structure and lighting in the Bevel and Emboss effect also control the "bump mapping" added by the **Texture** effect.

 Style Samples.psd

Inner Shadow

Bevel And Emboss: Inner Bevel

Outer Glow

Bevel And Emboss: Outer Bevel

Color Overlay

Inner Glow: Edge

Bevel And Emboss: Emboss

Gradient Overlay (Solid, 90°, Reflected)

Inner Glow: Center

Bevel And Emboss: Pillow Emboss

Gradient Overlay (Noise, 27°, Linear)

Satin

Bevel And Emboss: Stroke Emboss

Pattern Overlay

Stroke: Color

Bevel And Emboss with Contour

Drop Shadow

Stroke: Shape Burst Gradient

Bevel And Emboss with Texture

LAYER STYLE COMPONENTS   **495**

A shadow created with the Drop Shadow component of a Layer Style can be separated from its graphic element and rendered as a layer of its own (one way is to choose Layer > Layer Style > Create Layer). Then it can be distorted with the Free Transform command (Ctrl/⌘-T) to produce a cast shadow. Another Layer Style, including a Drop Shadow, can then be added to the graphic element to create dimensionality and surface characteristics that remain "live" and editable.

A Layer Style was used to add a **Drop Shadow** to the Shape layer. Then the Style was separated to create an independent shadow layer that could be manipulated to make a cast shadow. A new Style, including a Drop Shadow with its Distance set to 0 to make a "dark halo," was added to the Shape layer to build dimensionality, lighting, and surface characteristics.

By changing the **Color Overlay**, you can adapt a single button Style for different navigation functions. See Chapter 10 for more about Styles for buttons.

 **Color Overlay.psd**

order they occur in the Layer Style dialog's list: Color Overlay (a solid color fill) is on top, then Gradient, then Pattern. Here are a few of the things you can do with **Color Overlay**:

- Darken a recessed element, as if it were in a shadow created by carving it into the surface. The two **Wow-Carved** Styles (shown in Appendix B) are examples.
- Create a series of matching buttons by copying a layer with a button graphic that has been treated with a Style composed of several effects and then changing only the Color Overlay of each one, as shown at the bottom of this page.
- Store color information that you have to apply often — the corporate color for a logo, for instance — so you can apply this Color Overlay wherever you need it.

For the **Gradient Overlay** if the **"Align with Layer"** box is **checked, the gradient starts at the edge of the layer content**. With the box checked it's as though the entire gradient is "poured into" the outline created by the layer content. With the box **unchecked, the gradient will be aligned with the edge of the *document*,** and it may be that only part of the gradient will fall within the outline. (The edge of the document may be outside the canvas if any layers are oversized or have been moved partly "offstage.") **Angle** sets the direction of the color changes, and **Style** offers the five gradient types (these are demonstrated on page 160). The **Scale** slider can be used to compress or expand the gradient, extending the end colors to fill the edges when the Scale is less than 100%. Anytime the Layer Style dialog is open to the Gradient Overlay section, you can adjust the gradient's position by dragging in the image window.

For the **Pattern Overlay** if the **"Link with Layer"** box is **checked** when you apply the effect, the pattern starts at the upper left corner of an imaginary bounding box around the **layer content**. With the box **unchecked**, the pattern starts at the upper left corner of the **document** instead. *After* you apply the pattern, however, checking or unchecking the "Link with Layer" box doesn't by itself shift the pattern's position. You have to uncheck the box, and then click the "Snap to Origin" button. You can also change the pattern's position by dragging in the image window. Checking the "Link with Layer" box also binds the pattern to the layer. If you move the layer content around (after closing the Layer Style box), the pattern will move along with it. The **Scale** slider lets you shrink or enlarge the pattern without resizing the layer content.

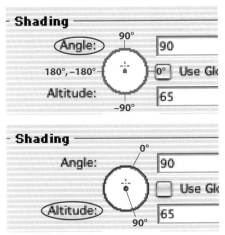

In the lighting diagram found in many of the effects in the Layer Style dialog box, the compass direction around the circle determines the direction of the light source. The distance from the center of the circle determines the height of the light source, with the center (90°) being highest and around the edge of the circle being at "ground level" (0°).

SEEING THE NAMES OF PRESETS

If you turn on Tool Tips (type Ctrl/⌘-K for Preferences > General and check Show Tool Tips) you can see the name of each Pattern, Contour, Style, or other preset when you pause the cursor over its thumbnail in a palette.

Note: Since patterns are pixel-based rather than instruction-based like most other effects, a Pattern Overlay can "soften" with scaling. This is also true of the Texture effect and for a patterned Stroke. ▼

FIND OUT MORE

▼ Scaling Styles that include patterns
page 45

LIGHTING IN LAYER STYLES

To understand lighting in a Layer Style, imagine that the little circle you see in the lighting setup for many of the layer effects (as shown at the left) represents a half-sphere dome sitting over your image. The **Angle** setting determines where around the circle the light is positioned. The **Altitude** determines how far up the dome the light is hung — from 0° (at "floor level") to 90° (at the top of the dome).

Global Light

Every Photoshop file that can accept Layer Styles — even a brand-new empty file you just created — has built-in **Global Light** settings for Altitude and Angle. The **Use Global Light** option, found in the Drop Shadow, Bevel and Emboss, and other sections of the Layer Style dialog box, was designed to make it easy to coordinate lighting for all of the effects in a Style and for all Layer Styles in a file, so the light will seem to come consistently from a single direction.

When you apply a Layer Style to a file, if Use Global Light is already turned on for any of that Style's effects, these effects *automatically take on the Global Light settings that already exist* in the file. These could be Adobe's default settings (Angle, 120° and Altitude, 30°), or they could be custom settings. You can see what the Global Light settings are, or customize them, by choosing Layer > Layer Style > Global Light.

If Use Global Light is turned on for any effect in any Layer Style in your file and then you change the Angle or Altitude for this effect, *your new Angle and Altitude settings become the new Global Light values, affecting all other effects in the file that have Use Global Light turned on.* Since "on" is the default state for Use Global Light in the Layer Style dialog box, *it's easy to accidentally reset the lighting for your entire file as you experiment with settings for one effect on one layer.* (See "Lighting: Global or Not" on page 498 for tips on working with lighting.)

Other Lighting Controls

Besides Altitude and Angle settings and whether Global Light is turned on, there are other settings that change the lighting

Turning on **Global Light** works well for coordinating the lighting Angle for all Styles in a file, but it can ruin the **material characteristics** that can be simulated with the **Altitude** setting. For instance, a shiny surface that depends on a high Altitude setting in the Satin effect can become dull if the Global Light setting forces it to use the same Altitude setting as in the Bevel and Emboss effect.

Let's say you design a Layer Style that takes advantage of Global Light. You run the risk, using it in another situation, that the Global Light already built into that file could produce different material characteristics than you want, since only one Global Light is allowed per file, and the file's existing Global Light setting will "take over" the Layer Style. To protect your Altitude settings, your best bet is to **turn off the Global Light option** before you experiment with the settings for any single effect.

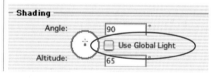

A yellow Stroke was added to the green type. To create the hard-edged black shading, the Inner Shadow and Drop Shadow were used with Choke and Spread (respectively) set to 100%. For details, see page 539 in "Anatomy of Bevels."

for the effects in a Layer Style. These are the color, Blend Mode, and Opacity settings for Shadow and Highlight controls for individual effects, as well as Gloss Contour. These parameters are described in the effects sections that follow.

SHADOWS & GLOWS

Like most of the effects in a Layer Style, both Shadow and Glow effects work by duplicating the outline of a layer's contents — whether pixels, vector outline, or a combination created by masking. The duplicate is then either filled with color (for a Drop Shadow, an Outer Glow, or an Inner Glow from the Center) or used as a hole in an overlay that's filled with color (for an Inner Shadow or an Inner Glow from the Edge); the copy is usually resized and blurred somewhat. Once you visualize the blurred copy as the starting point (the expanded Style shown on page 496 can help with this), you can begin to look at the differences between Shadow and Glow effects. The two main differences between Shadow effects and Glow effects are:

- A **Shadow can be** *offset*, but a Glow radiates evenly in all directions.
- A **Glow can use a** *gradient* or a solid color; a Shadow can only use a solid color.

Distance & Angle

The **Distance** setting in a **Shadow** effect determines how far the shadow will be offset in one direction. You can change the Distance setting by using the slider, typing a value into the box, using the arrow keys on the keyboard (↑ and ↓), or simply dragging in the working window while the dialog box is open.

You can individually set the **Angle** that determines where the light source is located for each Shadow effect and for other effects in your Style, such as Bevel and Emboss. Or you can turn on **Global Light**, which will **apply the same lighting Angle to all of the effects**. See the tip at the left for pointers.

Glows cannot be offset. If you choose one of the Glow effects in the list on the left side of the Layer Style dialog box, you'll see that there's no Distance setting and no Angle, and they aren't subject to Global Light.

Blend Mode, Color & Gradient

We think of shadows as dark and we think of glows as light, but both Shadow and Glow effects can be either dark or light, depending on the color and Blend Mode setting you choose.

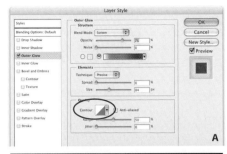

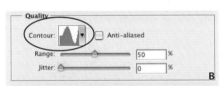

A straight-line Contour **A** is the default for a Shadow or Glow effect. But the Contour setting can be used to "remap" the tones, as shown for this Outer Glow **B**.

 **Glow Contour.psd**

By default, Shadows are set to dark colors and are in Multiply mode, and Glows are light colors in Screen mode. But you can reverse that if you want to, or use other modes. ▼ A light-colored Shadow in Screen mode with a Distance setting of 0 creates a glow. A dark-colored Outer Glow in Multiply mode becomes an evenly radiating shadow or "dark halo."

FIND OUT MORE

▼ Blend modes
page 173

What **Glows** lack in offset ability, they more than make up for in their capacity for using **gradients**. Instead of simply offering a color swatch (as in the Shadow sections), the Glow sections also offer a gradient choice, which, with the right combination of colors and transparency in the gradient, can be used for some great multicolor radiant effects. There are three additional controls for **Gradient glows**. **Noise** introduces a random pattern of light-dark variation that can prevent the obvious banding that sometimes happens when gradients are reproduced in print. **Jitter** mixes up pixels of the colors in the gradient so the color transitions are less well-defined. If you push the Jitter slider all the way to the right, you'll reduce the gradient to a mixture of color sprinkles. The **Range** setting determines what part of the gradient is used for the Glow.

The Difference Between Inner & Outer

Logically enough, the outer effects (Outer Glow and Drop Shadow) extend *outward* from the edge of the layer content you apply them to. You can think of them as filled and blurred duplicates of the outline, placed *behind* the layer — that is, below it in the layer stack.

Inner effects (Inner Shadow and Inner Glow) happen *inside* the edge. The **Inner Shadow** and the **Inner Glow** with **Edge** as the Source radiate inward from the edge, getting thinner toward the center. The **Inner Glow** with **Center** as the Source radiates color from the center outward; the color gets thinner as it extends toward the edge.

Size, Spread & Choke

In shadows and glows the **Size** determines the **amount of blur** that's applied to the color-filled copy that makes the shadow or glow. The greater the Size setting, the more the shadow or glow is blurred into the surroundings, so at higher Size settings, the shadow or glow is more diffuse — it's thinner and it spreads out farther.

Spread and Choke interact with the Size setting. Increasing the **Spread** of an outer shadow or glow, or the **Choke** of an inner

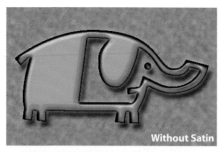

Without Satin

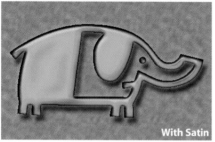

With Satin

Without Satin

With Satin

The interior lighting added by the Satin effect can be subtle (top) or dramatic. Shown here are two examples of "styled" graphics before and after the Satin effect was added to the Layer Style.

 Satin.psd

one, makes the effect denser, or more concentrated, by controlling where and how abruptly the transition is made from dense to transparent within the range established by the Size.

Contour

A **Contour** setting is like a Curves setting. It **"remaps" the intermediate tones** that are created by the blur used to make a Shadow or Glow. If the default **Linear** (45° straight-line) Contour is chosen, the tones or colors stay the same as when they were generated by the blur, proceeding from opaque to transparent as they extend away from the outline — either inward or outward (except for the Inner Glow with Center as the Source, which is more opaque in the center and gets "thinner" as it goes from the center to the outline).

If you choose a Contour other than the default, the intermediate tones are changed according to the Curve. By applying a Contour with several extreme peaks and valleys, you can get some fairly wild "striping" in a Glow or Shadow (see page 499).

SATIN

The **Satin** effect is created by the intersection of two blurred, offset, reflected copies of the outline of the layer content. It can be useful for simulating **internal reflections** or a **satiny finish**. **Size** controls the amount of blur as in other effects. **Distance** controls how much the two blurred and offset copies overlap, and **Angle** determines the direction of offset. As in other effects, the **Contour** remaps the tones created by the blurring according to the Curve you choose.

To get an idea of what's happening when you change the settings for the Satin effect, try this:

1 Choose the Ellipse tool ⬭, choose the "Shape layers" option in the Options bar, and drag the cursor to create a layer with a filled circle or oval.

2 Double-click to the right of the layer's name in the Layers palette to open the Layer Style dialog box to the Blending Options section. In the Advanced Blending area, make sure the Blend Interior Effects As Group box is *not* checked, and set the Fill Opacity to 0. (The filled circle will disappear.)

3 Open the Satin section of the Layer Style dialog box by clicking the Satin entry in the list at the left side of the box. Experiment with the Size (blur), Distance (amount of overlap), and Angle. Pop open the Contour palette by clicking

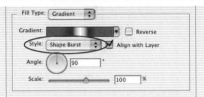

This button was created by reducing the Fill Opacity of the white graphic shown on the left to 0, and adding a Stroke made with a Shape Burst Gradient. The difference between the two button states on the right is the color of the gradients and the Inner and Outer Glows. The technique is described in "Outlining with Neon" on page 455.

Neon Stroke.psd

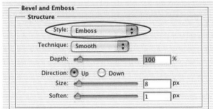

The Emboss style of the Bevel and Emboss effect builds the bevel partly inward and partly outward, letting the color from the layer below show through as well as the color of the current layer. Here the Emboss was applied to the layer with the type, but the beveling also affects the layer below.

License Bevel.psd

the little triangle to the right of the Contour swatch, and try different Contours. For some fun, watch what happens when you choose a really complex Contour, such as Ring-Double (one of the presets that come with Photoshop) and vary the Distance.

STROKE

For the **Stroke** effect, the **Size** sets the width of the stroke that outlines the layer content. The **Position** determines whether the stroke is built from the edge outward or inward, or is centered on the edge. The Stroke's width is filled according to the **Fill Type** you choose: solid color, pattern, or any of the usual five gradient styles (Linear, Radial, Angle, Reflected, or Diamond). There's also one more gradient form that occurs nowhere else in Photoshop — the **Shape Burst** gradient. With a Shape Burst gradient the colors follow along the outline, which can create a quick neon effect (see page 455), an inline/outline effect for type (see page 190), or a multicolor glow if the gradient includes transparency at the outer edge. Patterns and gradients can be scaled within the Stroke width. A solid-color Stroke effect can be useful for filling in an Outer Bevel when you don't want the layer below to show through it, as illustrated on page 538.

BEVEL AND EMBOSS

The **Bevel and Emboss** dialog box is complex, but if you remember the filled, blurred duplicate idea, it can be easier to grasp how it works. To create the highlight and shadow effects that simulate the bevel shading, Photoshop offsets and trims blurred light and dark duplicates. Because of the blur, the highlights and shadows are partly transparent, even when you set the Opacity at 100%, so they blend with the color underneath, creating the illusion of the bevel.

Like the Shadows and Glows, the Bevel and Emboss effect has tremendous potential beyond what its name implies. Some of its possibilities are explored in "Anatomy of Bevels" on page 537. Experiment in the Structure panel of the Bevel And Emboss section. Then move on to the Shading section, which controls the lighting.

Structure

When you start to experiment with Bevel and Emboss, an obvious place to begin is with the **Direction**: The default **Up** raises the object from the surface; **Down** sinks it into the surface.

Altitude.psd

A high Altitude setting (70°, used in the Bevel and Emboss effects on both the frame and lens layers for the glasses at the right) can add thickness and can simulate a strong reflection from the surface. The Bevel and Emboss effects for the glasses at the left use Photoshop's default Altitude setting, 30°.

The Gloss Contour in the Bevel and Emboss section of the Layer Style dialog box was important in creating the dark and light "reflections" that make the surface of the Chrome look shiny and curved, as described in "Anatomy of 'Shiny'" on page 531.

The type was colored with a red Color Overlay and then "lit" with a Bevel and Emboss effect. In the Bevel and Emboss section of the Layer Style dialog box, yellow in Screen mode was used for the bevel highlights and purple in Color Mode for the shadows, to simulate two colored light sources shining on the red type. See page 539 for details.

Then choose the **Style:** The **Inner Bevel** builds the beveled edge *inward* from the outline of the layer content, so the element itself appears to get thinner, and the highlight and shadow the bevel generates will blend with the color of the layer content. The **Outer Bevel** builds the beveled edge *outward* from the outline and blends with whatever is "beyond" the layer content. The material that's beyond the outline can be supplied by the layers below, or it can be a band of color created by the Stroke effect. In the **Emboss** Style, the bevel "straddles" the outline, building the bevel half outward and half inward to create the kind of bevel seen in license plates and street signs. **Pillow Emboss** is a kind of double bevel, with a bevel extending away from the outline in both directions, like a quilted effect. If you've added a Stroke effect, the **Stroke Emboss** builds the bevel using only the width of the Stroke.

Size, which again is the degree of blurring used to create the effect, determines how far inward or outward the bevel goes — that is, how much of the shape or the background is consumed by the bevel. **Soften** controls what happens to the edge that's away from the outline — whether this edge is abrupt and angular or rounded. A higher Soften value makes it rounder.

Depth determines how steep the sides of the bevel are. A greater Depth setting increases contrast between the tones used for the highlights and shadows and makes the beveled element appear to stick up from the surface farther or sink into it more.

Shading

The **Angle** setting operates the same way as for the Shadows. It determines the direction of the light. By increasing the **Altitude**, you can move the "bevel highlight" farther onto the front (top) surface of the element to which the Style is applied. The result is that surfaces seem more polished with the harder highlights created by higher Altitude settings.

Gloss Contour remaps the tones in the bevel highlight and shadow to make the surfaces seem more or less glossy and reflective. The Gloss Contour can be useful for imitating highly polished surfaces with multiple highlights.

The **Color**, **Mode**, and **Opacity** settings let you control the characteristics of highlighted edges and shadowed edges independently. So if you like, you can use them to simulate two different-colored light sources as shown in the colorful type at the left, rather than simulating a single highlight and a shadow.

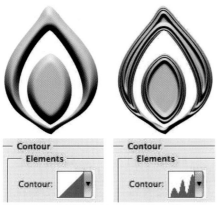

The Contour of the Bevel and Emboss effect can be used to shape the bevel "shoulder." Here the default Linear Contour is shown on the left and a custom Contour on the right.

Bevel Contour.psd

Contour

Indented just below Bevel and Emboss in the list on the left side of the Layer Style dialog box you'll find **Contour.** This Contour has to do with the Structure of the bevel. It defines the shape of the bevel's "shoulder." To explore its effect, you can start with a gray Shape, such as the one in **Bevel Contour.psd,** shown at the left. Then add the default Bevel and Emboss, and increase the Size to make the bevel wider. Click Contour in the list at the left side of the box and make choices from the Contour palette that pops out when you click the little triangle to the right of the Contour swatch. You'll be able to see that the Contour changes the cross-section of the bevel. Experiment with the **Range** slider, which controls how much of the bevel is "sculpted" by the Contour — in other words, how much of the bevel is consumed by the "shoulder." Low Range settings make the "shoulder" smaller and move it away from the outline created by the layer content.

SETTINGS FOR BEVEL AND EMBOSS

The **Style** setting of **Bevel and Emboss** determines where the bevel will be built — inside, outside, or overlapping the outline of the layer content.

The **Technique** controls the smoothness of the bevel walls. The Smooth setting produces the smoothest walls, and the Chisel Soft produces the most gouged.

Depth controls the contrast between the highlighted and shaded walls of the bevel. The greater the Depth setting, the greater the contrast, and therefore the steeper the walls will look.

The **Direction** setting determines whether the beveled element seems to rise from the surrounding surface (Up) or sinks into it (Down).

Size controls how wide the bevel is.

Soften controls the rounding/sharpness of the edge of the bevel that's away from the layer content's outline.

Angle controls the direction of the lighting that causes highlights and shadows. **Altitude** controls how high above the surface the light source is. The **Use Global Light** option unifies the lighting in all effects that use Angle or Altitude in all Layer Styles throughout the file.

Gloss Contour controls the shininess of the surface, from matte to highly polished, by remapping the tones in the bevel highlights and shadows.

Mode, Color, and **Opacity** settings can be controlled independently for the bevel highlights and shadows.

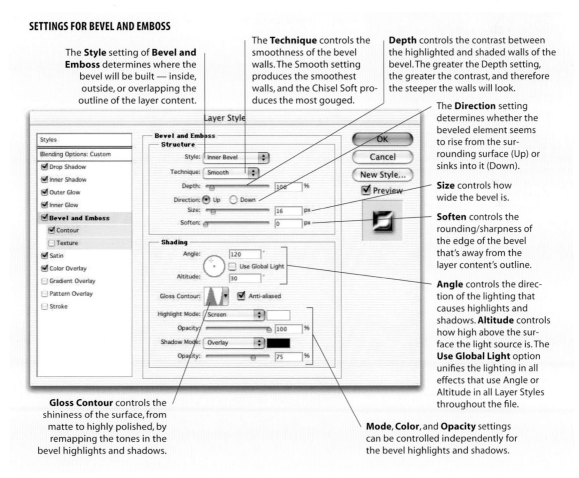

Inner Bevel

Outer Bevel

Emboss

Pillow Emboss

Stroke

When you add **Texture** to a Bevel and Emboss effect, the Style setting within the Bevel and Emboss panel in the Layer Style dialog determines where the texture shows up, as shown above. Only the bottom example has an added Stroke effect, so that the Stroke style of Bevel and Emboss will work and the Texture will appear on the Stroke.

Texture

Below Contour in the effects list is **Texture**. The Texture effect embosses the pattern you choose from the **Pattern swatch** in the Texture section of the Layer Style dialog box. This swatch is like the one in the Pattern Overlay section of the dialog box except that here the pattern appears in grayscale. That's because Photoshop uses only the lights and darks of the pattern — to simulate bumps and pits in the surface. By using the same pattern for the Pattern Overlay and the Texture, you can match the surface texture to the surface patterning.

For an **Inner Bevel** the embossed pattern goes inside the outline of the layer content (and so does the Pattern Overlay). For the **Outer Bevel** the embossed pattern goes outside, so it appears on whatever is in the image below the layer with the Style. For **Emboss** and **Pillow Emboss** the embossed pattern extends both inside and outside, and for **Stroke** it appears only within the stroke width. The "embossing" of the pattern is affected by the Depth and Soften settings for Bevel and Emboss and by all the settings in its Shading section.

BLENDING OPTIONS

The **Blending Options** section of the Layer Style dialog box (shown on page 505) governs how the layer interacts with other layers. In the **General Blending** section at the top of the box you can change the Blend Mode and the Opacity. These changes are reflected in the **Blend Mode** and **Opacity** settings at the top of the Layers palette and can also be controlled there.▼

Advanced Blending

Also reflected in the Layers palette is the **Fill Opacity** setting, the first of the **Advanced Blending** settings. It allows you to reduce the Opacity of the layer's "fill" without reducing the opacity of the entire layer. That means, for instance, that you can make the layer content partly transparent but leave the shadows or glows around it at full strength.

The other settings in the **Advanced Blending** section are a bit more complex. The two check boxes under the Fill Opacity slider control whether certain inner effects are considered part of the Fill for purposes of adjusting Fill Opacity. With the **"Blend Interior Effects as Group"** box checked, the Inner Glow, any interior bevel highlights and shadows, the three Overlays, and the Satin effect — all of which fall within the layer content's outline — are considered part

FIND OUT MORE

▼ Using blend modes
page 173

of the fill when the Fill Opacity is reduced. (The Inner Shadow isn't considered an Interior Effect for purposes of blending, perhaps because it's from an *outside* light source.)

The **"Blend Clipped Layers as Group"** check box controls whether any layers that are part of a clipping group with the "styled" layer as the base are treated as if they became part of the layer *before* or *after* the Layer Style was added. With this option *turned on*, it's as if any clipped layers became part of the fill *before* the Layer Style's effects are applied. So a Color Overlay, Gradient Overlay, or Pattern Overlay will hide or change the clipped image (see page 506). Blend modes of the various layers also play a role, of course, and it gets complicated quickly.

If you want a layer to cut a hole in the layers below, you can reduce the Fill Opacity to 0% and choose the appropriate option for **Knockout**:

- If you choose **Deep**, the knockout can go all the way down to (but not through) the *Background* at the bottom of the layer stack, or to transparency if there is no *Background*.

BLENDING OPTIONS

In the **General Blending** section of Blending Options you'll find **Blend Mode** and **Opacity** settings. These are the same controls that are found at the top of the Layers palette. Changing a setting here also changes it in the Layers palette and vice versa.

The Layers palette shows no evidence of the customized settings in the **Advanced Blending** section.

The tricky thing about **Fill Opacity** is specifying what constitutes the Fill. With both of the "Blend...as" options unchecked, the original layer content constitutes the entire fill. With the **Blend Interior Effects as Group** option turned on, any Overlay effects, the Inner Glow, and the Satin effect are considered part of the Fill. With the **Blend Clipped Layers as Group** option turned on, any clipped layers are also treated as part of the Fill.

Blending Options can be controlled in the Layer Style dialog box.

Applying any of the **effects** in this list causes an 🅕 icon to appear to the right of the layer's name in the Layers palette.

The **"Blend If"** sliders define the ranges of tone or color where a pixel from the active layer has priority over the pixel from the image underneath, and vice versa. The black and white sliders can be split by holding down the **Alt/Option** key. This makes a softer transition so the pixels blend rather than completely replace each other.

The **Shallow** and **Deep Knockout** options can make a "hole" in underlying layers. So if you reduce the Fill Opacity, you'll be able to see through them to what lies below.

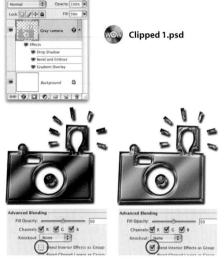

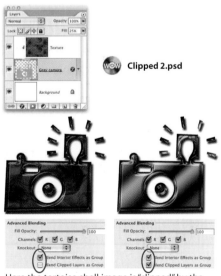

When **Blend Interior Effects as Group** is turned **off** (left), only the original color's opacity is reduced when Fill Opacity is reduced to 50%; we don't see any reduction because the Gradient Overlay in the Style covers it. When **Blend Interior Effects as Group** is turned **on** (right), the Gradient Overlay is treated as if it became part of the surface of the shape *before* the Fill Opacity was reduced.

Here the tortoise shell image is "clipped" by the graphic. With **Blend Clipped Layers as Group** turned **off** (left), it's as if the tortoise shell surface goes on top of the Gradient Overlay and hides it. If **Blend Clipped Layers as Group** is turned **on** (right), it's as if the tortoise shell surface became part of the original graphic first and then the Gradient Overlay was added.

- If the **Shallow** option is chosen, the knockout goes only as far as the first logical stopping point — through the bottom of the clipping group or layer set/group, for instance. If there is no clipping group or layer set/group, then the knockout goes all the way to the *Background* or transparency, just as Deep does.

- If the Knockout setting is the default **None**, then no hole is made in the layers below.

The results of the Knockout settings are modified by the settings in the two **"Blend. . . as"** check boxes and by whether the layer set is in Pass Through mode, not to mention the blend modes of the individual layers or whether there are nested layer sets/groups. Again, it gets complicated quickly!

The "Blend If" Settings

At the bottom of the Blending Options dialog are the **"Blend If"** sliders, which provide a way to blend a layer with the image formed by the layers below. ▼ With these sliders you can control which tones and colors in the active layer contribute to the composite, and which will act as if they are transparent, allowing the image underneath to show

FIND OUT MORE

▼ Using the "Blend If" sliders **page 70**

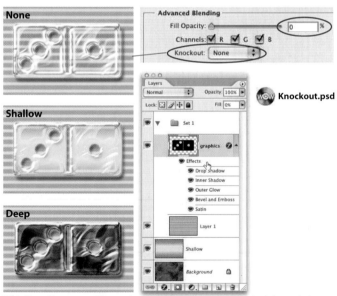

With **Knockout** set to **None**, the striped surface shows behind the styled "glass" graphic. With Knockout set to **Shallow**, the graphic knocks out through the striped surface since it's included in the layer set/group with the graphic, but it doesn't knock out the gradient beneath the set. With Knockout set to **Deep**, the graphic knocks out all the way to the *Background*.

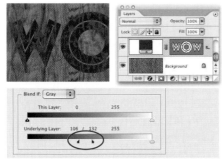

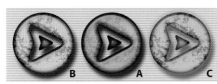

If your background has a mix of light and dark tones, it's easy to "distress" type or graphics by eliminating the active layer's contribution in either the light or the dark areas. Here the "Blend If" sliders are set so the black graphics don't cover the dark areas of the woodgrain. Splitting the sliders (by holding down the Alt/Option key as you drag) makes a smooth transition.

 Style Samples.psd

Sometimes you can change the colors in a Layer Style without editing the individual effects. The middle button **A** shows the original color of all three buttons. To change the color of the left button, a Hue/Saturation Adjustment layer was made part of a clipping group with the button layer as the "clipper" **B**. Notice that the color of the "shadow" hasn't changed, since it's outside the button graphic. To change the color of the right button **C**, we used a Hue/Saturation Adjustment layer with the same settings, but it was included in a layer set/group whose mode was changed from the default Pass Through to Normal. Notice that in this case, since the Adjustment layer is not clipped by the button graphic, it also changes the color of the shadow.

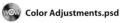 **Color Adjustments.psd**

through. These controls provide a great way to "distress" or weather type or graphics applied to a surface.

ENHANCING LAYER STYLES

Once you have a Layer Style in place, it may be easier to make a color or lighting change by adding an Adjustment layer or using the Lighting Effects filter than to "remix" all the effects in the Style. For highly polished surfaces created with Layer Styles you can also add "environmental" reflections by using Distort filters to bend a reflected image to fit the styled element. Filters can also be useful for roughening the edges of a surface to which a Style with texture has been applied, for a more realistic look.

Adjustment Layers

In some cases Levels, Curves, Color Balance, and Hue/Saturation can be varied through Adjustment layers to change the color or brightness of a layer to which a Style has been applied, without the need to go back into the Layer Style box and make changes (examples are shown at the left). You can set the Adjustment layer to affect just the interior of the styled element, or the interior and exterior effects, or the interior, exterior, and all visible layers below. Just be sure that the two "Blend. . . as" check boxes in the Blending Options panel of the Layer Style box are set up so the Adjustment layer will act on the interior effects and clipped layers if that's what you want:

- **If the Adjustment layer is made part of a clipping group** with the styled layer serving as its base, the Adjustment Layer will **act only on the interior of the element**. If "Blend Interior Effects as Group" is turned on, it will affect any Overlay, Inner Glow, or Satin effects along with the original fill.

- **If the Adjustment layer is not "clipped,"** it will affect not only the **interior** of the element but also any **exterior effects**, such as Drop Shadow or Outer Glow, as well as any **other layers** that are visible below it.

- You can set up your file so **the Adjustment layer affects a number of consecutive layers, even if they are not at the bottom of the layer stack and are not clipped.** To do this, make a layer set/group, with the Adjustment layer as the top layer in the set and make the blend mode of the layer set/group Normal. (In Photoshop CS, a layer set can be made by activating one of the layers and linking all the others you want in the set by clicking in the links column next to the 👁 in the Layers palette; then choose New Set From Linked from the pop-out menu ⊙ in the upper right corner

A landscape photo was treated with the Glass filter and layered above the styled graphic in this chrome treatment. The techniques are described in "Custom Chrome," which starts on page 525.

The initial "carving" of the rock was done by applying a Layer Style to graphics on a transparent layer, using Bevel and Emboss, Shadow, and Overlay effects. The "styled" layer was modified with the Displace filter to make the beveled edge follow the features of the rock surface. The Lighting Effects filter was used to add a spotlight to enhance the lighting. (These Style, Displace, and Lighting Effects techniques are presented step-by-step in "Carving" on page 540.)

In this corroded metal effect, after the same **Wow-Rust** Layer Style was applied to both the chicken graphics and the background shape, two Adjustment layers were used to brighten and "neutralize" the color of the chicken. Then the Spatter filter was applied to a matching layer mask to "roughen" the edge so it matches the surface corrosion that had been applied by the Style. An "environment" image was added to further "weather" the metal. The technique is described step-by-step in "Rusted & Pitted" starting on page 517.

of the Layers palette. In CS2 simply Shift-click or Ctrl/⌘-click all the layers you want in the group, and then choose New Group from Layers from the palette's menu ⊙.)

Lighting Effects

With the Lighting Effects filter you can create pools of light exactly where you want them by adding Spotlights. A way to apply Lighting Effects with flexibility is to add a 50%-gray-filled layer in Overlay mode and run the filter on that. Because 50% gray is neutral (invisible) in Overlay mode, only the lightened or darkened areas of the layer show up to light the composite. You'll find an example of this use of Lighting Effects on page 542. Once you run the filter on the gray-filled layer (Filter > Render > Lighting Effects), you can fine-tune the lighting: Add a layer mask, change the Opacity of the spotlight layer, or even reposition the spotlight with the Move tool ⊹.

Other Filters

The **Glass** filter (Filter > Distort > Glass) can be extremely useful in distorting environmental images to look like reflections in polished metal or glass surfaces, as shown at the left. You can find examples on pages 530 and 534 in this chapter. The **Displace** filter, also in the Distort "family," can augment carved and chiseled effects by distorting the layer content to make it conform to the textured surface you want to "carve" into, as shown at the left.

Other filters, such as **Spatter**, can be used to modify the edge of a graphic so its texture matches the roughness introduced by the Texture effect in a Layer Style, as in "Rusted & Pitted," starting on page 517. And the **Texturizer**, **Add Noise**, **Clouds**, **Fibers**, **Tile Maker**, and other filters can be very useful for producing backgrounds, textures, and patterns, as shown in "Quick Backgrounds & Textures" on page 555 and "Quick Seamless Patterns" on page 562.

STEVEN GORDON

2006 CLEAN WATER FESTIVAL

A Logo in Clear Color

YOU'LL FIND THE FILES
in (wow) > Wow Project Files > Chapter 8 >
Logo in Clear Color:
  • Clear Logo-Before.psd (to start)
  • Clear Logo-After files (to compare, or
    as a source for the Layer Style)

OPEN THESE PALETTES
from the Window menu:
  • Tools • Layers • Styles

OVERVIEW
Type the first character • Apply a Layer
Style • Duplicate & edit the "styled" type
• Import graphics • Copy & paste the Style
• Color the styled graphics using an
Adjustment layer & a layer set/group

1

The letter "H" was set in
the BeesWax font at 180
points. It's shown here
at about half-size.

ONE OF THE FEATURES that make Photoshop's Layer Styles so useful is that once you've developed a Style you like, it's so easy to apply it to other elements. We manufactured the logo above by developing a Layer Style that we could then simply and quickly scale to fit another element in the logo ("Anatomy of Clear Color" on page 513 shows how the components of this Style work together.) We used an Adjustment layer in a layer set/group as a quick, easy way to change the color and thickness of one of the "styled" elements.

1 Typing the first character. Open a new 225-dpi file with a white *Background.* Choose the type tool (T). In the Options bar, choose the font, size, and style of type you want. In **Clear Logo-Before**, we used BeesWax, a shareware TrueType font for Windows by Ken Woodward, available from **fontfiles.com** and other web sites; we used the TTFConverter utility (a web search should turn up sources) to convert it for the Mac. If you don't have BeesWax, you may want to substitute an ExtraBold or Black typeface. Click with the Type tool T in the working window where you want your first character to be, and type it **1**. If you look at the Layers palette, you'll see that a new type layer (represented by a "T" icon) has been added to your file, and that its name consists of the letter you typed.

If you want to change the specifications for your type, highlight the letter by dragging over it with the Type tool, and then make the changes in the Options bar.▼

FIND OUT MORE

▼ Operating the
Type tool **page 418**

2

3a

3b

The **Wow-Clear Blue** Layer Style (found on the DVD-ROM that comes with this book) was applied to the "H." "Anatomy of Clear Color" on page 513 tells how the effects in this Style create the clear blue.

The second "H" was repositioned with the Move tool ▸⊕, drag-selected with the Type tool **T**, (above left), and changed to a "2."

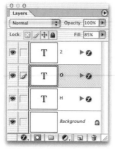

Another copy of the "H" layer was turned into the "O." (Clicking the little triangle next to the 🅕 for a layer hides the list of effects, for a more compact Layers palette.)

2 Adding a Style. Now you can turn your flat black type into a translucent blue by assigning a preset Style. If you've already installed the **Wow Presets**, ▼ pop-out the Styles palette's menu ⊙ and choose the **Wow-Plastic Styles** listed at the bottom. Then click on **Wow-Clear Blue** from the newly loaded set in the Styles palette **2**. If you haven't installed the Wow presets and therefore don't see **Wow-Plastic Styles** in the Styles palette's menu, you can copy the Style instead from the **Clear Logo-After.psd** file (copying and pasting a Style is described in step 4).

FIND OUT MORE

▼ Installing the Wow presets **page 5**

Whichever way you choose to apply the Style, if the type you've used is very different in size or structure from the BeesWax used in our example, you may need to scale the Style: Right-click (Windows) or Ctrl-click (Mac) on the little 🅕 icon *to the right of the layer's name* to bring up a context-sensitive menu, and choose Scale Effects. Now, with the Preview box checked, you can change the Scale number and watch your image change as you experiment with different percentages.

3 Adding more characters. To add a second letter to the logo, you can copy the first and then edit the copy: We duplicated our type layer (Ctrl/⌘-J) and used the Move tool ▸⊕ to drag the upper "H" into position approximately where we wanted our "2" to be. We used the Type tool (**T**) to select and edit the type we had moved, changing the character from "H" to "2" and pressing the Enter key to commit the type **3a**. If you need to fine-tune the position of the new character, activate the Move tool again (holding down the Ctrl/⌘ key will do it); pressing the arrow keys will move the character in small steps.

To complete the "H2O," target the "H" layer again in the Layers palette, duplicate it (Ctrl/⌘-J), and drag the new copy to the right with the Move tool ▸⊕, as you did for the "2." Then select this new "H" and type the letter "O" **3b**.

4 Adding and styling another component. Now add the next element to your logo. We had produced our water splash in Adobe Illustrator, so we copied it there, targeted the *Background* of our developing logo file in Photoshop, and then pasted (Edit > Paste As: Pixels). This put the splash on a layer above the *Background* and below the type **4a**. In Photoshop CS2 another option would be to paste the artwork as a Smart Object, ▼ which would allow you to return to Illustrator to edit the shape if you wanted to.

FIND OUT MORE

▼ Working with Smart Objects **page 39**

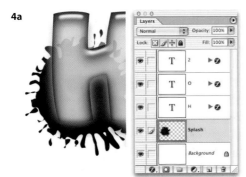

4a

The splash graphic, created in Illustrator, is pasted into the Photoshop file.

4b

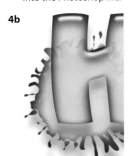

The **Wow-Clear Blue** Style is copied from one of the type layers and pasted to the "Splash" layer, where it obviously will need some scaling.

4c

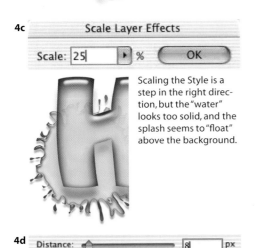

Scale Layer Effects

Scale: 25 % OK

Scaling the Style is a step in the right direction, but the "water" looks too solid, and the splash seems to "float" above the background.

4d

Distance: 8 px

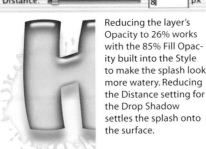

Reducing the layer's Opacity to 26% works with the 85% Fill Opacity built into the Style to make the splash look more watery. Reducing the Distance setting for the Drop Shadow settles the splash onto the surface.

To start with the same "material" and lighting specifications for your new element, copy the Style you used for the type: Right/Ctrl-click directly on the 𝑓 icon *for one of the type layers* and choose Copy Layer Style from the context-sensitive menu that pops out; then in the Layers palette for the file where you want to add the Style, right/Ctrl-click in about the same place on the entry for the layer that you want to "style," and choose Paste Layer Style **4b**.

Now examine the newly styled artwork to consider what changes you'd like to make. We wanted to make the splash look thinner than the "H2O" and to make it appear to be behind the type and a slightly different color. Also, it was obvious the Style needed adjusting in order to work with the narrow "rays" of the splash.

Reducing the Scale (as described in step 2) pushes the dark shading away from the center, which brings some dimension to the splash's projections; we settled on a Scale setting of 25%. **4c**.

Reducing the Opacity lightens the color overall, both the interior of the splash and the drop shadow and glow; we reduced the Opacity to 26%, using the slider in the Layers palette. Even with the Scale and Opacity reduced, the Drop Shadow effect makes the splash seem to "float" above the background. To put the splash flat on the surface, in the Layers palette double-click the Drop Shadow entry in the Effects list under the "Splash" layer's name; this opens the Layer Style dialog box to the Drop Shadow control panel. There you can **reduce the Distance setting** until the image looks the way you want it to; we set the Drop Shadow's Distance to 8 px **4d**.

5 Adjusting color. To change the color of the splash without having to recolor each of the effects that make up the Style, you can use a Hue/Saturation Adjustment layer. To shift the color of the splash toward green, we added the Hue/Saturation layer immediately above the splash by clicking the "Create new fill or adjustment layer" button 𝑂 at the bottom of the Layers palette, clicking Hue/Saturation in the list of choices, and changing the color by moving the Hue slider **5a**.

With our splash layer on the bottom of the layer stack, that would have completed the coloring. However, the type, though translucent, was dense enough to obscure the splash more than we liked. To see more detail in the splash, we dragged the "Splash" layer and the Adjustment layer up to the top of the Layers palette. The Opacity of the Splash layer had been reduced

5a

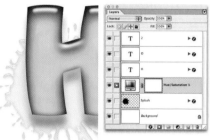

A Hue/Saturation Adjustment layer is added to change the color of the splash. The white Background isn't affected since it has no color to change.

5b

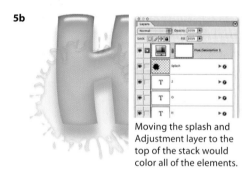

Moving the splash and Adjustment layer to the top of the stack would color all of the elements.

5c

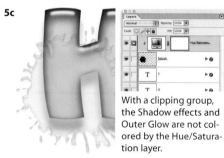

With a clipping group, the Shadow effects and Outer Glow are not colored by the Hue/Saturation layer.

5d

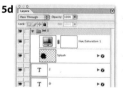

A layer set/group in Pass Through mode passes the effect of the Adjustment layer through to the layers below, to produce the same result shown in **5b** above.

enough so we could see more detail in the edges, as we wanted. But because the Hue/Saturation layer was now above the type layers, it was also coloring the type **5b**.

To restrict the color change to the "Splash" layer, we did some experimenting, trying to think like Photoshop:

- If we made a **clipping group** (by Alt/Option-clicking on the border between the "Splash" layer and the Hue/Saturation layer in the Layers palette), the color change would be clipped inside the outline of the splash and wouldn't affect the type layers. But this clipping would color only the *inside* of the splash, leaving the Inner Shadow, Drop Shadow, and Outer Glow unchanged **5c**, so this wasn't what we wanted.

- We tried putting the "Splash" layer and the Adjustment layer in a layer set/group (in CS this can be done by clicking the thumbnail of one layer and clicking in the Links column next to the 👁 for the other layer to link the two, then choosing "New Set from Linked" from the palette's ⊙ menu; in CS2, click one thumbnail, Ctrl/⌘-click the other, and then choose "New Group from Layers" from the palette's ⊙ menu). But the default Pass Through mode for the set passed the color change through to the type layers below, so this wasn't what we wanted **5d**.

- When we changed the blend mode of the **layer set/group to Normal**, we got exactly the result we were looking for. The Adjustment layer modified the color of the "Splash" layer, and the layer set/group contributed to the composite image as if the set/group were a single merged layer **5e**.

6 Adding more type. To finish the logo we clicked with the Type tool (**T**) to add a new type layer. In the Options bar we chose Myriad Pro, 32 pt, and clicked the color swatch; we clicked on the letter "H" to sample a blue. Pressing the Caps Lock key, we typed "2006 CLEAN WATER FESTIVAL" **6**, then held down the Ctrl/⌘ key, and dragged to position the type. *Wow*

5e

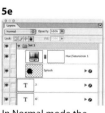

In Normal mode the layer set/group produces the result shown at the top of page 509.

6

2006 CLEAN WATER

The final type layer was added in a color sampled from the larger, dimensional type.

Clear Color

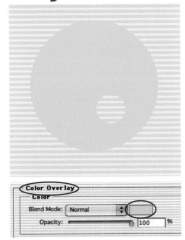

In the **Wow-Clear Blue** Layer Style used in "A Logo in Clear Color" on page 509, the component effects work together to turn type or graphics into dimensional, translucent objects. To explore the individual effects that make up this Style, open the **Plastic O.psd** file, then open the Layers palette and double-click the ⓕ **symbol to the right of the "O" layer's name** to open the Layer Style dialog box. **In the list on the left side of the Layer Style box**, click on the name of each individual effect as you read its description here, to open the "control panel" for that particular effect.

YOU'LL FIND THE FILE
in ⊚ > Wow Project Files >
Chapter 8 > Anatomy of
Clear Color

Layer Content

WE STARTED by typing the letter "O" in the BeesWax font above a striped *Background*. The Layer Style could have been applied directly to the live type. But in the **Plastic O.psd** file the type has been converted to a Shape layer, so you can explore the Layer Style without encountering a Caution box if you don't have the font installed on your system.

Taking Over the Color

WHEN YOU PUT TOGETHER a Layer Style, it's good to start with the effect that will bring about the biggest change. Then you can watch the Style develop as you build it up by adding the subtler effects.

In this case we started by applying color using the **Color Overlay** effect. We clicked "Color Overlay" in the list on the left side of the Layer Style dialog box, then clicked the color swatch to open the Color Picker and chose a light blue. By applying the effect in Normal mode at 100% Opacity, we could ensure that the Style would always produce the light blue color, completely replacing the original color of the type or graphics.

Blending

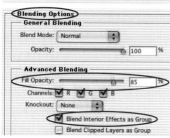

SINCE WE WOULD BE BUILDING a Style that included several interior effects — the Color Overlay, Inner Glow, and Satin — we made sure that **"Blend Interior Effects as Group"** was turned on in the **Blending Options** section of the Layer Style box. With this choice, the Blending Options settings such as Fill Opacity would act on the interior of the "O" as a blended unit, applying to all the interior effects combined. For instance, reducing the Fill Opacity to 85% to make the "O" partially transparent also makes the Color Overlay, Inner Glow, and Satin partially transparent. (Without the "Blend Interior Effects as Group" setting, the Color Overlay, for instance, would stay at its 100% Opacity setting, making the "O" a solid blue even if Fill Opacity for the layer was reduced all the way to 0%!)

Color Drop Shadow

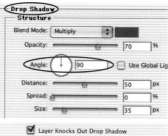

THE **DROP SHADOW** was a good next step, to start creating dimensionality by making a blurred offset copy "behind" the "O." We could use the Drop Shadow to contribute to the illusion of transparency by making it look as if light is passing through the blue "O" and coloring the shadow. We clicked the color swatch to open the Color Picker and chose a darker, less saturated blue. To light the "O" from the top, we set the Drop Shadow's **Angle** at 90°. It would have been convenient to turn on Use Global Light so this Angle would automatically carry over to all other effects that use a lighting Angle setting. But Use Global Light is risky when the Altitude setting is important in creating a shiny surface (see "Lighting: Global or Not?" on page 498). At the bottom of the Drop Shadow panel, we made sure the default **Layer Knocks Out Drop Shadow** was turned on, so the shadow wouldn't darken the partly transparent "O."

Shading the Edge 1

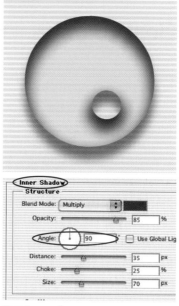

THE **INNER SHADOW** EFFECT, a blurred offset copy that's created *inside* the edge, was used here to help round the edges of the "O." We made a soft transition for a gentle rounding (the **Size** setting controls how soft, or diffuse, a blurred effect will be). So it would darken the color already established by the Color Overlay, we left the Inner Shadow in its default Multiply mode, though we chose a slightly brighter blue for the color. We set the **Angle** at 90°, the same as for the Drop Shadow. (The Inner Shadow is often used for a cutout or carved-in, effect. But because a drop shadow was already in place making the "O" look like it was floating above the background, the Inner Shadow didn't create that illusion.) *Note:* Consistent with its nature as a shadow, **the Inner Shadow doesn't blend with other interior effects** (Overlays, Inner Glow, and Satin) when you turn on the "Blend Interior Effects as Group" option.

Shading the Edge 2

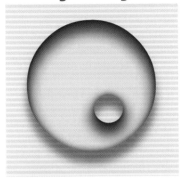

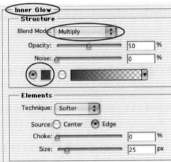

WE USED THE **INNER GLOW** to enhance the rounding of the edge that had been started with the Inner Shadow. We changed the Blend Mode from the default Screen to **Multiply** and used approximately the same blue as for the Inner Shadow. In Multiply mode the dark Inner Glow darkens the shading already established inside the "O" by the Inner Shadow. But unlike the Inner Shadow, the Inner Glow is not an offset effect, so its dark "halo" applies evenly around the edges, darkening the edge areas that were not shaded by the Inner Shadow — for example, the lower edges of the "O."

Adding a Highlight

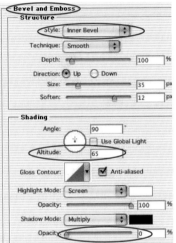

HERE WE USED the **Bevel and Emboss** effect, not so much for bevelling but to add reflective highlights on the surface of the "O." We used **Inner Bevel** for the Style and the default white in Screen mode for the Highlight. But because we had used the Inner Shadow and Inner Glow to control the shading, we didn't need the bevel's Shadow, so we could effectively turn it off by setting its Opacity at 0 (using the bottom slider in the box). Changing the **Altitude** setting to 65° was very important, because it pulled the highlight off the top edge of the plastic "O" and onto the front surface. Again we set the **Angle** at 90° to keep the lighting consistent with the Drop Shadow and Inner Shadow.

Refining the Shine

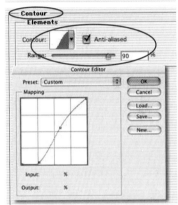

IN THE LIST OF EFFECTS at the left side of the Layer Style dialog box and just below Bevel and Emboss, we clicked on **Contour**. In the Contour section we clicked the Contour thumbnail and customized the curve in the Contour Editor box as shown above. We also changed the Range to 90%. These changes sharpened and narrowed the highlight and pulled it farther up and off the edge of the "O," so it looked even more like a reflection on a hard surface.

Mottling

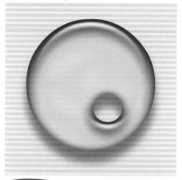

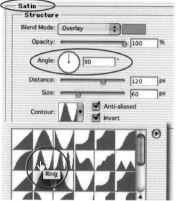

TO ADD THE LOOK of subtle streaks and spots to the color, we applied the **Satin** effect in light blue in Overlay mode, creating an offset, manipulated copy of the "O." The **Distance** setting scaled the copy, reducing it vertically because of the 90° **Angle** setting. This setting determines the angle of distortion of the Satin duplicate. A 90° setting squashes the duplicate vertically, making it shorter and fatter. As in the other sections of the Layer Style box, the **Size** setting controls the amount of blur, making the effect subtler by blurring the copy. We clicked the little triangle to the right of the Contour thumbnail and chose a Contour ("Ring" from Adobe's default set) that provides light-dark-light variation in the blurred, squashed duplicate, making it look as if light is bouncing around inside the plastic.

Creating Refraction

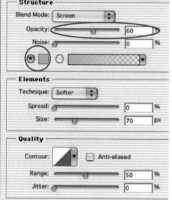

FINALLY, the **Outer Glow** effect in light blue was applied in its default Screen mode. We used **Softer** for the Technique for a more diffuse and irregular look than the alternative Precise setting would have produced. Because the glow is in Screen mode, it affects only the parts of the shadow that are darker than itself, and it affects the light background only slightly. As a result, it lightens and colors the Drop Shadow close to the edge of the "O." This makes it look as if light is being focused through the plastic, brightening the shadow beneath. The degree of brightening was controlled by adjusting the glow's **Opacity**.

To reduce the opacity of an element without reducing the opacity of the Drop Shadow, Inner Shadow, or Outer Glow, reduce Fill Opacity rather than Layer Opacity. Both of the Opacity controls can be found at the top of the Layers palette and in the Blending Options section of the Layer Style dialog. Changing the setting in one of these places also changes it in the other.

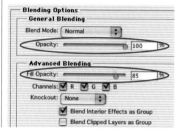

When you apply a Layer Style, it's a good idea to check the scale, to see if you're getting the best "fit" for the element you're applying it to. One way to open the Scale Layer Effects dialog is to choose Layer > Layer Style > Scale Effects. Once the box is open, pop out the Scale slider and try out various settings.

The **Wow-Clear Blue** Style looks very different (top left) until it's scaled down to fit the buttons (top right).

DONAL JOLLEY

Rusted & Pitted

OPEN THESE PALETTES

from the Window menu:

- Tools • Layers • Styles

OVERVIEW

Create or import vector graphics • Apply a Layer Style to add dimension, texture, and lighting • Roughen the edges with a filtered layer mask • Use Adjustment layers in a clipping group to change the color and texture of the "styled" element • Add an environment photo for atmosphere

USING LAYER MASKS WITH VECTOR-BASED ARTWORK, along with the Pattern and Texture effects in Layer Styles, allows for a tremendous amount of flexibility in creating realistic surface and edge effects. You can use this "weathered metal" technique with graphics, as we have, or with live type (although you might want to read about the advantages of converting type to shapes on page 428).

1 Setting up the file. Open the **Rusted-Before.psd** file, or start your own RGB Photoshop file with a white *Background* (File > New) and add type, draw vector graphics, or import a design element. Our logo artwork was created in Adobe Illustrator, where the type was converted to paths. The artwork was then selected **1a**, copied to the clipboard, and pasted into Photoshop as a Shape layer **1b**. It came in as large as it would fit, and we scaled it down (Ctrl/⌘-T and Alt/Option-Shift-drag a corner handle to scale proportionally while keeping the graphic centered) **1c**. In Photoshop CS2 you also have the option of pasting as a Smart Object so you can update the artwork in Illustrator and have the update automatically carry over into the Photoshop file.▼ The weathering process described here works the same for a Smart Object as for a Shape layer.

In Photoshop, we added a skewed plaque behind the logo: First we targeted the *Background* by clicking on it, so the Shape layer

FIND OUT MORE

▼ Importing Smart Objects from Adobe Illustrator **page 443**

1a

The artwork was drawn in Adobe Illustrator, selected, and copied to the clipboard.

1b

Pasting the artwork into Photoshop as a Shape layer

1c

Reducing the size of the artwork in the Photoshop file

1d

Setting Options for the Rounded Rectangle tool

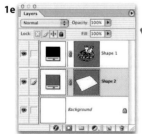

1e

The imported artwork and the added plaque shape

we were about to add would be between the *Background* and the imported graphic. We chose a Shape tool (by typing U), and in the Shape Tools Options bar made sure the Shape Layers option, the Rounded Rectangle option, and the Create New Shape Layer option were all chosen; we set the corner Radius to 30 px and clicked the color swatch and chose a medium gray **1d**. Dragging in the working window created a rectangle. Then we typed Ctrl/⌘-T (for Edit > Free Transform) and dragged around outside the Transform box to rotate the shape. We reshaped the rectangle by holding down the Ctrl/⌘ key and dragging the individual corner handles of the box in turn to distort the plaque. We dragged inside the Transform box to move the shape into position and then double-clicked inside the box to complete the transformation **1e**.

2 "Rusting" the logo and plaque. To add color, surface texture, and a beveled edge to both layers, you can use the **Wow-Rust** Style. ("Anatomy of 'Bumpy'" on page 522 shows how the individual effects in **Wow-Rust** work together to produce the Style.)

- In Photoshop CS, to target your graphics layer (the logo in the **Rusted-Before** file), click on its thumbnail in the Layers palette.

- In CS2 you can "style" both layers at once: Click the thumbnail for the logo layer and then Shift-click the thumbnail for the plaque layer.

To apply the Style, in the Styles palette click the ⊙ button near the top right corner and choose **Wow-Metal** Styles. If you haven't yet loaded the Wow presets ▼, the **Wow-Metal** Styles won't appear in the menu. To load just the two Styles associated with this project, choose Load Styles and navigate to **Wow-Rust Project.asl** (in Wow Project Files > Chapter 8 > Rusted). Once you've loaded one of these sets of Styles, just click on the **Wow-Rust** thumbnail **2a** to apply the Style.

In Photoshop CS2, if you Shift-selected both graphics layers, both are now "styled." In CS, you'll need to target the second layer and apply the Style to it separately **2b**. (If you're using your own artwork, you may need to scale the Style to fit after you apply it: In the Layers palette right/Ctrl-click on the 🎨 for the layer where you applied the Style, choose Scale Effects from the context-sensitive menu, and adjust the Scale value until the Style looks right.)

<table>
<tr><td>**FIND OUT MORE**</td></tr>
<tr><td>▼ Loading the Wow presets **page 5**</td></tr>
</table>

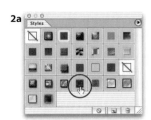

2a Choosing **Wow-Rust** from the Wow-Metal presets in the Styles palette

2b

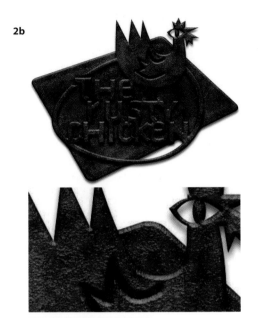

The Wow-Rust Style is applied to both graphics layers. You can make the Layers palette more compact, as shown here for the top layer, by clicking the little arrow next to the 𝑓 for the layer to hide the list of effects.

HIDING A SHAPE'S PATHS

If seeing the outlines of your Shape layer on-screen interferes with your view of the edges of your Styled graphic, you can toggle the paths off by typing **Ctrl/⌘-Shift-H** (for View > Show > Target Path) once or twice. Repeat to toggle the path view on again.

3 Eroding the edges of the logo. The next step is to roughen the edges of the logo. An effective way to do that, without actually doing any damage to the artwork, is to add a pixel-based layer mask to the Shape layer and erode the edge of this layer mask. The Layer Style that we added at step 2 will then apply the bevel, drop shadow, and other effects to the shape defined by a combination of the layer mask and the layer's built-in vector mask.

To add a layer mask, make sure the logo layer is targeted (click its thumbnail in the Layers palette). Then load the outline of the artwork as a selection: In the Layers palette, Ctrl/⌘-click the vector mask thumbnail or the Smart Object thumbnail **3a**. Then click the "Add a layer mask" button at the bottom of the palette.

To roughen the edges of the new layer mask, apply the Spatter filter (Filter > Brush Strokes > Spatter). In the Spatter dialog box, first set the lower slider (Smoothness) at the maximum (15) so you can get a rough but not crumbly edge, and then adjust the Spray Radius until you get the edge effect you want (we used 8; with higher settings the thin lines and sharp points on the chicken began to break up) **3b**. As you look at the preview in the Spatter dialog, you won't be seeing exactly what will happen to the edge outline of your graphic or type. That's because *two* masking elements will work in concert to define the edge — the roughened layer mask and the hard-edged vector outline. Where the filter "eats *into*" the edge of the layer mask, its effects will show in the final artwork. But anywhere the filter spreads the edge of the mask *outward*, the layer mask edge *won't* have an effect, because the hard edge of the vector outline will mask out these protrusions **3c**. This works well for our degrading effect; when a metal edge erodes, it's eaten away, not splattered outward. Click "OK" to close the Filter Gallery. If you need to rerun the filter with a different setting, type Ctrl/⌘-Z to undo and then Ctrl-Alt-F (Windows) or ⌘-Option-F (Mac) to reopen the Filter Gallery so you can change the settings.

Repeat the masking and filtering on the plaque layer.

3a

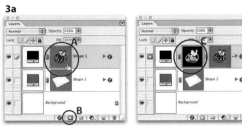

Ctrl/⌘-clicking the vector mask thumbnail for the Shape layer **A** and then clicking the "Add layer mask" button **B** created a matching layer mask **C**.

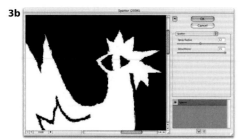

3b

Running the Spatter filter on the layer mask for the logo graphics layer; choosing Filter > Brush Strokes > Spatter automatically opens the Filter Gallery.

3c

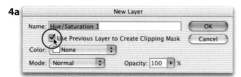

The roughened edge of the layer mask was "clipped" by the vector mask (top). This "ate away" at the edge of the styled graphic.

4a

Adding a Hue/Saturation Adjustment layer clipped to the logo below it in the layer stack

4b

Reducing Saturation to the minimum removes the color from the logo.

4 Changing the surface characteristics. With both graphics elements styled, it's easy to experiment with the texture and color of either layer. To turn the rusted logo into pitted (but not rusted) metal, you can remove the color in the logo layer and increase its contrast to emphasize the texture, as follows: To remove the color, target the logo layer in the Layers palette; then create a Hue/Saturation Adjustment layer above it by Alt/Option-clicking the "Create new fill or adjustment layer" button ⬤ at the bottom of the Layers palette and choosing Hue/Saturation from the menu. Using the Alt/Option key opens the New Layer dialog box **4a**, where you can choose "Use Previous Layer to Create Clipping Mask" so the Hue/Saturation adjustment will affect only the logo layer, not the layers below it in the stack. Click "OK" to close the New Layer box. When the Hue/Saturation dialog opens, reduce the Saturation to −100 (the minimum setting) and click "OK" **4b**, **4c**.

To increase the contrast, Alt/Option-click the ⬤ button again to add another Adjustment layer, this time choosing Levels, and again choosing "Use Previous Layer to Create Clipping Mask" so the Levels layer will be added to the clipping group and won't affect the plaque shape. In the Levels dialog box, move the Input Levels white point slider to the left to increase the contrast until you have some true white highlights **4d**.

5 Adding "atmosphere." You can give your styled elements an even more realistic look by adding "atmosphere." Drag-and-drop or copy-and-paste a blurred environment photo above the graphics; the **Rust-After.psd** file includes such a layer. Change this layer's blend mode (we used Hard Light), and reduce its Opacity to taste (we used 30%). A hint of "environment" can add to a weathered look. (If needed, it can also help disguise the repeat in a texture pattern.)

Creating the mask for the environment layer was a tricky but logical process. First we Ctrl/⌘-clicked the *logo layer's vector*

4c

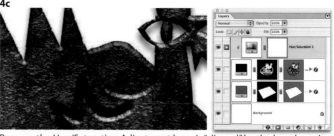

Because the Hue/Saturation Adjustment layer is "clipped" by the logo layer, it doesn't affect the color of the plaque. The indent and downward arrow in the Layers palette indicate that the layer is clipped.

4d

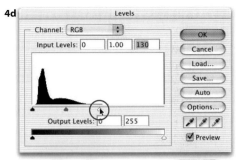

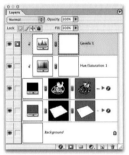

Moving the white point slider in a Levels Adjustment layer brightens the highlights in the metal. If you like, you can also move the black point slider to the right a little to bring back some internal contrast.

5

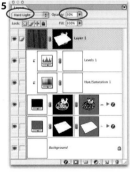

A carefully masked blurred photo is added in Hard Light mode at 30% Opacity to add more weathering. A "composite" layer mask hides the image except on the logo and plaque. The finished image is shown at the top of page 517.

mask thumbnail (if you're using a Smart Object, Ctrl/⌘-click its thumbnail); this loaded the mask's outline as a selection. The next step in developing the mask was to Ctrl-Alt-Shift-click (Windows) or ⌘-Option-Shift-click the *logo's layer mask* thumbnail (this changed the selection to the intersection of the layer mask and vector mask, eliminating any parts that extended outside the overlap of the two). Finally we Ctrl/⌘-Shift-clicked the *plaque's vector mask* thumbnail (this added the plaque outline to the selection). With this combined selection active, we clicked the thumbnail for the photo layer and clicked the ▢ button at the bottom of the Layers palette to add a layer mask **5**.

Experimenting. Here are two more options to try on your styled graphics:

- To take away the rust color entirely, release the Adjustment layers from the clipping group so the Saturation and Levels adjustments will affect both the logo and the plaque. You can release a layer from its clipping group by Alt/Option-clicking on the boundary between it and the layer below; any layers above it in the clipping group will also be released from the clipping group.

- For the look of hot, glowing metal, turn off visibility for the photo layer and Adjustment layers by clicking their ◉ icons in the Layers palette. Then target each of the graphics layers in turn (or in CS2, you can Shift-click to target both layers at once) and click **Wow-Hot Metal** in the Styles palette. *Wow!*

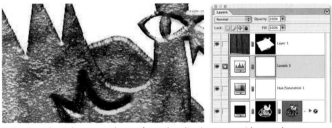

Releasing the Adjustment layers from the clipping group (they no longer appear indented) allows the Adjustment layers to work on both graphics layers.

The **Wow-Hot Metal** Layer Style heats up the metal.

A N A T O M Y   O F
"Bumpy"

In the **Wow-Rust** Layer Style shown here and used in "Rusted & Pitted" on page 517, the component effects create a weathered metal surface texture. To explore how the effects combine to make this Style, open the **Bumpy.psd** file, then open the Layers palette and double-click the 🌀 **symbol to the right of the "Graphic" layer's name** to open the Layer Style dialog box. **In the list on the left side of the Layer Style box**, click on the name of each individual effect as you read its description here, to open the "control panel" for that effect.

YOU'LL FIND THE FILE
in 🔵 > Wow Project Files > Chapter 8 > Anatomy of Bumpy

Layer Content

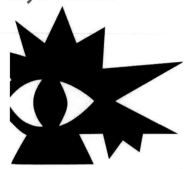

WE STARTED WITH ARTWORK copied to the clipboard in Illustrator and then pasted into a Photoshop file (Edit > Paste > **Paste As Shape**). In Photoshop CS2 you also have the additional choice of pasting from Illustrator as a Smart Object. This gives you the option of returning to Illustrator to make changes to the original artwork later and then automatically updating the Photoshop file to reflect the changes. (For tips on getting the results you expect when you edit a Vector Smart Object in Illustrator, see page 445.)

SMART OBJECT OR NO?

One thing to consider in CS2 when choosing whether to Paste As Shape Layer or Paste As Smart Object is that if you Paste As Smart Object, someone opening the file in a previous version of the program will be able to import it only as a pixel-based layer, not as a vector-based Shape Layer.

The warning that appears in Photoshop CS when you open a file containing a Vector Smart Object from CS2 isn't as dire as it may seem. Clicking "OK" doesn't discard the pasted element itself; it simply rasterizes it, eliminating its Vector Smart Object qualities.

Color & Pattern

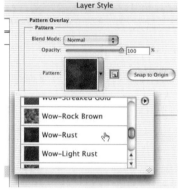

THE **PATTERN OVERLAY** EFFECT provides the surface color and pattern in the **Wow-Rust** Style. With the Pattern Overlay in place, it would be easier to see how the other effects were developing later. We turned on the Pattern Overlay by clicking its checkbox in the list on the left side of the Layer Style dialog box; to see the settings, click its name.

We clicked the **Pattern** swatch and chose the **Wow-Rust** pattern from the palette (**Wow-Rust** is part of the **Wow-Misc Surface Patterns** set from the DVD-ROM that comes with this book.)▼

We left "Link with Layer" checked (the default setting).▼

FIND OUT MORE

▼ Installing Wow presets **page 5**
▼ Link with Layer **page 496**

Blending Options

Layer Style

WHAT WE DID NEXT had no immediate effect on the artwork, but it would make a big difference in the Style's versatility. Clicking **"Blending Options"** in the list on the left side of the Layer Style dialog box opened that panel. We used these settings in the **Advanced Blending** section:

- We turned **"Blend Interior Effects as Group" on** so the Pattern Overlay we were using in the Style would completely replace the styled layer's "native" coloring.

- We turned **"Blend Clipped Layers as Group" off**. That way we could use an Adjustment layer in a clipping group to modify the color of the Layer Style, as described in step 4 of "Rusted & Pitted" on page 520. (If "Blend Clipped Layers as Group" were turned on, any Adjustment layers we might include in a clipping group would affect the native coloring of the layer *before* the Layer Style could come into play — so the effect of the Adjustment layers wouldn't show, because they would be "covered" by the Pattern Overlay.)

Drop Shadow

Layer Style

TO ADD TO THE ILLUSION of a solid object, we clicked **"Drop Shadow"** in the list and adjusted its settings so it looked like a shadow cast onto the surface by a metal cutout:

- We moved the cursor into the working window, grabbed the shadow with it, and dragged straight down. We ended up with a 90° **Angle** (this made it look as if the light was positioned at 12 o'clock) and a **Distance** of 10 px. We turned Use Global Light off, for reasons having to do with the bevel.▼

- We reduced the **Opacity** to 60%, and increased the **Size** setting from the default (to 10 px), both of which softened the shadow a little — the larger the Size setting, the more diffuse the shadow.

The combination of Distance, Angle, Size, and Opacity helps characterize the ambient light.

Bevel Structure

Layer Style

TO ADD DIMENSION, we clicked on **"Bevel And Emboss"** and in the **Structure** section of the panel set up an **Inner Bevel** in the **Up** direction. This starts the bevel at the edge of the graphic and raises it inward from there.▼ We chose **Chisel Hard** for Technique to create subtle chisel marks in the edge. (The Smooth Technique doesn't produce chisel marks, and Chisel Soft makes the marks very pronounced, as if the edge were being chiseled in relatively soft material.) We raised the **Depth** to 300% for a larger bevel.

At this point the Shading section of the Bevel and Emboss section was still set to its defaults. But we would change that next.

FIND OUT MORE

▼ Turning off Use Global Light **page 498**
▼ Bevel structure **page 501**

Bevel Shading

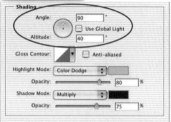

STILL WORKING in the **Bevel and Emboss** panel of the Layer Style dialog box, we turned to the **Shading** section. For the **Highlight** we chose a yellow by clicking the color swatch and choosing from the Color Picker when it opened. Putting the yellow Highlight in Color Dodge mode and raising the Opacity to 80% created warm lighting.

To keep the lighting consistent, we used the same 90° **Angle** as we had used for the Drop Shadow. Increasing the **Altitude** to 40° moved the light farther up onto the surface of the graphic, as if the light were higher overhead. We turned **Use Global Light** off. If Use Global Light had been on, whenever the Style was applied to a different file, the existing Altitude setting for the file — often Adobe's default 30° — would have changed the character of the bevel.

For the bevel's **Shadow** we clicked the color swatch and then clicked on the patterned surface of the graphic to sample a dark brown for the shaded faces of the bevel.

Surface Texture

BESIDES THE EDGE, the **Bevel and Emboss** effect also controls the "embossing" of surface texture. We clicked on **"Texture,"** one of the subcategories under "Bevel and Emboss" in the list in the Layers palette.

We used the **Wow-Rust** pattern from the Texture panel's Pattern palette. The swatch showed the pattern in grayscale because only the brightness (or luminance) information — not the color — is used to create the surface texture.

We were embossing the same pattern used in the Pattern Overlay, so we left the **Scale** at 100% to match the default 100% used there. And we left **"Link with Layer"** checked, as we had for the Pattern Overlay, so the embossing would align with the Pattern Overlay. (If you wanted to break up the pattern with a different texture, you could uncheck the "Link with Layer" box and drag in the working window until the texture interrupted the pattern as you wanted it to.)

The **Depth** slider controls how deeply the texture is embossed; our 50% setting produced a fairly shallow emboss.

Edge Definition

AN **INNER GLOW** of a sampled gray color in Multiply mode added shading inside the edge to increase contrast and improve edge definition.

Shading & Weathering

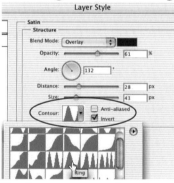

THE **SATIN** EFFECT completes the Style (see the bottom of page 522). Using a complementary color, Overlay mode, and an Angle we arrived at by experimenting, Satin creates tonal variation that's based on the **Contour.** Like a Curves setting, the Contour "remaps" the tones in a blurred copy of the layer content. Satin can change the surface lighting in a way that adds weathering here and helps hide repetition in the Pattern Overlay and Texture.

Custom Chrome

YOU'LL FIND THE FILES

in (wow) > Wow Project Files > Chapter 8 > Custom Chrome:

- Chrome-Before.psd (to start)
- Wow Chrome Project.asl (a Style presets file)
- Cloud Reflection.psd (for creating the reflection)
- Chrome-After.psd (to compare)

OPEN THESE PALETTES

from the Window menu:

- Tools • Layers • Channels • Styles

OVERVIEW

Prepare an RGB file with a background image and a graphics layer • Apply the Wow-Chrome 03 Layer Style to add shine and dimension to the graphics • Build a displacement map from the graphics • Use the displacement map with the Glass filter to apply a reflected image onto the surface of the graphics • Touch up the chrome surface • Create a dimensional surface for the graphics to sit on • Apply and modify a Style for this surface

THE CHALLENGE IN IMITATING the uniquely shiny surfaces of chrome is to get the reflections right — to re-create the complex distortion of the environment that's mirrored in the rounded, curving surfaces of the polished object. One way to create convincing chrome in Photoshop is with a Layer Style that turns a flat graphic or type into a highly reflective, dimensional object. This transformation is the subject of step 2 below. The "Anatomy of 'Shiny'" section on page 531 dissects this particular Style and tells how it works. And "Chrome" in Appendix B shows 19 more chrome variations that you can apply instantly — some flat, some round, some with sharp bevels, even some with simulated environment reflections.

Here we take a chrome simulation beyond the effects of the Layer Style by using the Glass filter to warp an image of the outside world so it seems to be mirrored in the shiny surface. Then we use another Layer Style, modified for our blue color scheme, to add a gemstone base for the chrome lettering.

1 Preparing the file. Open the color file that you want to use for the background behind your chrome object, or open the **Chrome-Before.psd** file provided. If your file isn't in RGB Color mode, convert it now (Image > Mode > RGB Color), since the Glass filter won't work in CMYK. Import the graphics or type that you want to turn into chrome, or create them in Photoshop on a transparent layer. We started with a 1000-pixel-wide scan of marble that had been colored blue▼ and added the "Orbit" logo, which had been created in Adobe

FIND OUT MORE

▼ Colorizing an image **page 200**

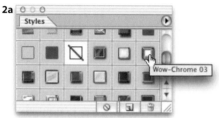

The Cooper Bold Italic type and the ellipse were created in Illustrator, copied to the clipboard, and pasted-as-pixels into the marble file.

Choosing the **Wow-Chrome 03** Style

When the **Wow-Chrome 03** Style is applied, its component effects are listed under the "Orbit logo" layer in the Layers palette.

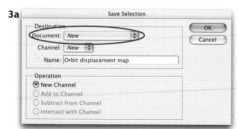

Ctrl/⌘-clicking the "Orbit logo" layer's thumbnail in the Layers palette and choosing Select > Save Selection to start the displacement map file

Illustrator, copied to the clipboard, and pasted into the Photoshop file (Edit > Paste > Paste As: Pixels)▼ **1**.

2 Adding the chrome. Click on the thumbnail for your graphics layer to target it. To create the dimensionality and shine of the chrome, we built a Layer Style for the graphic. The building process is described in "Anatomy of 'Shiny'" on page 531, in case you'd like to build it from scratch or simply examine how the effects work together to make the Style. To use the Style without having to build it, in the Styles palette click the ⊙ button near the top right corner of the palette and choose **Wow-Chrome Styles**. If you haven't yet loaded the Wow presets,▼ the **Wow-Chrome Styles** won't appear in the menu. To load just the Styles associated with this project, you can choose Load Styles and navigate to **Wow-Chrome Project.asl** (in Wow Project Files > Chapter 8 > Custom Chrome). Once you've loaded one of these sets of Styles, click on **Wow-Chrome 03** in the palette **2a**, **2b**. (If you're using a file other than **Chrome-Before.psd,** you may need to scale the Style after you apply it;▼ in the Layers palette, right/Ctrl-click on the ⊘ for the layer where you applied the Style, choose Scale Effects from the pop-up menu, and adjust the slider until the Style looks good.)

VIEWING STYLE NAMES

If you don't see names in the Styles palette — only swatches — you can display the names also by clicking the ⊙ button in the upper right corner of the palette and choosing Large List.

3 Building a displacement map. The strategy in reflecting an "environment" in the chrome is to warp a version of the environment photo onto the surface of the chrome object. The first step is to make a *displacement map* (a separate file) from the graphic, to be used in the distortion. Besides creating the subtle highlights and shadows that simulate the reflections and refractions of glass, Photoshop's Glass filter works like its cousin the Displace filter, used in "Carving" on page 540. The Glass filter moves the pixels of the layer it's applied to. The distance each pixel is moved depends on the luminance (or brightness) of the corresponding pixel in the displacement map. Any image in Photoshop format (**.psd**) except one in Bitmap mode can serve as a displacement map. When you use a grayscale file, white pixels move their corresponding pixels in the filtered image the maximum distance in one direction, black pixels produce the maximum displacement in the

FIND OUT MORE

▼ Pasting from Illustrator **page 443**

▼ Loading the Wow presets **page 5**

▼ Scaling Layer Styles **page 45**

3b

The Save Selection command opens a new file with the graphics in black-and-white.

3c

Blurring the displacement map image

3d

The displacement map, shown here, must be saved as a Photoshop file (remember where you put it!) before it can be used with the Glass filter.

4a

ORIGINAL PHOTO: JHDAVIS

The imported clouds image is positioned and stretched.

opposite direction, and 50% brightness produces no displacement at all.

To begin making the displacement map, make an active selection from the outline of the original graphic by Ctrl/⌘-clicking the thumbnail for the "Orbit logo" layer in the Layers palette. Save the selection as a new file by choosing Select > Save Selection and choosing *New* in the Document menu of the Save Selection dialog box, naming the file (we called ours "Orbit displacement map"), and clicking "OK" **3a**, **3b**.

To produce smooth, rounded edges, the displacement map has to have a soft transition from black through grays to white. To produce the gray tones, blur the new file (Filter > Blur > Gaussian Blur); a good rule of thumb is to use a Radius that's half the Size setting for the Inner Bevel of the chrome Layer Style. Since the Size setting for **Wow-Chrome 03** is 16 pixels, we used an 8-pixel Radius **3c**. (You can check the bevel size setting by double-clicking "Bevel and Emboss" in the list of effects in the Layers palette to open the Layer Style dialog box.) Now save the displacement map file, since it can't be used with the Glass filter until it's saved (File > Save As) **3d**.

4 Adding the reflection. In this next step, when you add the image you want to use as the reflected environment, it's important that it end up exactly the same pixel size as the canvas of the developing chrome file, in order for the Glass filter to work correctly.

Open the image you want to use (we used the **Cloud Reflection.psd** file from the Wow DVD-ROM) and drag with the Rectangular Marquee ⌷ to select the part you want to use, or select

---

ALIGNMENT IS IMPORTANT

When you apply a filter that uses a displacement map, such as Displace or Glass, Photoshop aligns the displacement map with the **upper-left corner of the layer** you apply it to. It can cause problems if your layer is oversize and extends above or to the left of the canvas, or if it falls short of the corner. In that case the displacement map will line up differently than you expect when you run the filter. For instance, if you've made the displacement map from a graphic in the file and you run it on a layer that's bigger or smaller, the distortion the filter produces won't align with your graphic. In order to avoid the problem, you can trim away excess on a layer before running the filter by selecting all (Ctrl/⌘-A) and choosing Image > Crop. For a layer whose pixels don't fill the canvas, you'll need to fill in the empty space or select all (Ctrl/⌘-A) before running the filter.

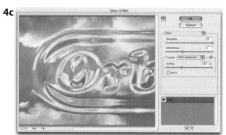

4b Blurring the clouds image slightly

Running the Glass filter on the blurred clouds layer

4c

4d The clouds layer at full opacity after running the Glass filter

4e

A clipping group allows the clouds to show only on the chromed graphic. Opacity of the clouds layer is reduced until the reflection is the right strength.

5a

Before (left) and after using the Blur tool 🜄 to smooth a pixelated color break

all (Ctrl/⌘-A), and then copy (Ctrl/⌘-C). Activate the graphic layer in the chrome file by clicking on its thumbnail in the Layers palette, and paste (Ctrl/⌘-V). In the Layers palette, reduce the Opacity of the new layer so you can see the "styled" graphic below. To give yourself some extra room to work by reducing the view of your image without reducing the window size, drag the lower right corner of the window frame down and to the right, so the gray apron appears around the image. Use Free Transform (Ctrl/⌘-T) to enlarge the image until it more than fills the canvas (Alt/Option-Shift-dragging on a corner handle of the bounding box enlarges proportionally from the center in all directions at once) and position it (by dragging inside the Transform box) **4a**; double-click inside the Transform box to complete the transformation. To trim off the parts of the image that bleed off the canvas, select all (Ctrl/⌘-A) and choose Image > Crop.

When the image is in place, blur it if you like (Filter > Blur > Gaussian Blur). Sharp detail can distract from the shape of the graphic or produce a pixelated result when the Glass filter is run. For the soft image of clouds that we used, we set the Gaussian Blur Radius to 4 pixels, which made the edges of the clouds even softer and hid the film grain **4b**.

Now run the Glass filter (Filter > Distort > Glass) **4c**. For the Texture, choose Load Texture from the pop-up menu, locate the displacement map you made at step 3, and click "Open." We used the maximum setting (20) for Distortion and 6 for Smoothness. Lower Smoothness settings produce sharper edges, but may also produce pixelated breaks in the image; higher settings make smoother distortions, but the edges are softer. We left Scaling at 100% and Invert turned off. When you have a result you like, even if there are a few small areas of pixelation, click "OK" to apply the filter **4d**. We can touch up those few spots in step 5.

To limit the distorted environment image to the graphic itself, make a clipping group: In the Layers palette, Alt/Option-click on the border between the image layer and the graphic layer. Because of the way the Blending Options have been set in the **Wow-Chrome 03** Layer Style,▼ the clipped image will interact with the edge effects applied by the Style of the graphic layer below **4e**. Experiment with reducing the Opacity of the image layer to arrive at the right blend of the image and the light/dark "striping" created by the Satin effect; we settled on 60% Opacity.

FIND OUT MORE

▼ "Anatomy of 'Shiny'" **page 531**

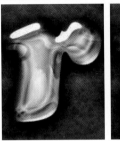

5b

Before (left) and after using the "Blend If" settings to bring back some of the sharp specular highlights that had been reduced by overlaying the clouds image

6a

Setting up the Magic Wand ✺ to select the empty space inside the oval on the "Orbit logo" layer

6b

You can add the letters to the oval selection by Shift-clicking to surround them with the Polygonal Lasso ☙.

6c

A new layer is added, and the oval selection is filled with blue.

5 Touching up. To smooth pixelated spots in the reflected image — for example, in the dot of the "i" in our example, choose the Blur tool ◌; in the Options bar, click the "Brush:" swatch and choose a small, soft brush tip, and reduce the Strength (we used a 13-pixel brush tip and 80% Strength). Make short strokes in the pixelated area to eliminate the rough edges **5a**.

If you want to keep the cloud image from dulling the brightest specular highlights in the chrome, you can double-click the cloud layer's thumbnail in the Layers palette to open the Blending Options dialog box. Then Alt/Option-drag the left part of the white point slider of the "Underlying Layer" to the left slightly **5b**. With a setting of 251/255, the whitest highlights are partially protected from the clouds image.

6 Adding an internal surface. At this point we'll add a stone surface inside the chrome oval and behind the "Orbit" lettering, as follows: First sample a blue color: Click the Foreground color swatch in the Tools palette to open the Color Picker, then click on a blue in the marble background, and finally click "OK" to close the Color Picker.

Next select the oval: We chose the Magic Wand ✺ and targeted the "Orbit logo" layer. With Use/Sample All Layers turned **off** in the Options bar **6a**, we clicked once in the area inside the oval but outside the letters. To add the letters to the selection, we used the Polygonal Lasso ☙ *with the Shift key held down,* clicking several times to build a selection border that added the letters to the existing selection **6b**. (We could have used a different selection tool, but the ☙ was quick and easy to control.) When the selection is complete, add a new layer *below* the "Orbit logo" layer by Ctrl/⌘-clicking the "Create a new layer" button ◙ at the bottom of the Layers palette, and fill the selection with your blue color by pressing Alt/Option-Delete, the shortcut for filling with the Foreground color, and then deselect all (Ctrl/⌘-D) **6c**.

7 Modifying a Style. Next we'll create a patterned, polished surface for the stone by applying the **Wow-Red Amber** Style and changing its settings to keep the intricate patterning but eliminate the red-orange color. Click the **Wow-Red Amber** swatch in the Styles palette; it's found in the **Wow-Gems** Styles and also in the **Wow-Chrome Project** Styles (from step 2) **7a**. (If you notice that the shadow outside the chrome oval gets a bit denser, it's because Wow-Red Amber's Drop Shadow has Distance, Size, and Spread settings large enough so the shadow shows around the edges of the graphic.)

7a

The **Wow-Red Amber** Style is applied to the blue oval.

7b

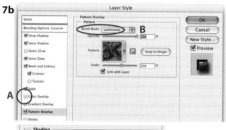

A

B

C

Turning off the Color Overlay effect **A**, changing the Pattern Overlay to Luminosity mode **B**, and lowering the Altitude slightly for Bevel and Emboss **C** produces the gemstone effect shown at the top of page 525.

Now to change the settings: In the Layers palette, double-click the "Color Overlay" listing for the Style you just added to the blue oval; this opens the Layer Style dialog box to the Color Overlay section. We can see that the red color comes, at least in part, from this Color Overlay. Since our oval is already the blue we want it to be, we don't need the Color Overlay. Click on the check mark next to Color Overlay in the list on the left side of the dialog box to turn off this effect.

Turning off Color Overlay doesn't remove the red entirely. Since the Pattern Overlay is now the only overlay effect that's turned on, we can deduce that the color is probably coming from there. In the list on the left side of the dialog box, click "Pattern Overlay" (the name, not the check mark). We can see by looking at the swatch that the red-orange color is built into the pattern; to change it would be a project that we don't need to tackle. Instead, since we have the blue color we want in the layer itself, we can simply change the Blend Mode to Luminosity, so the pattern will contribute its light-and-dark detail but not its color **7b**.

One more change: To flatten the top of the gemstone so the chrome letters rest on it comfortably, we can move the highlight a little farther toward the edge. Click "Bevel and Emboss" in the list of effects, and reduce the Altitude setting slightly; we used a setting of 58°.

Variations. The "environment" image you choose can make a big difference in the way your chrome looks. The examples below were made from the "negative" version of the Orbit logo graphics with the **Wow-Chrome 03** Style applied. A displacement map made from the new graphics was used with the Glass filter to distort the environment photo in step 4. The only difference from one example to another is that a different environment image was used. *Wow*

The displacement map for the modified logo

The same clouds image used in step 4, but with the layer at 100% Opacity

A landscape photo (from Corbis Royalty Free), also used in "Painting 'Wet on Wet'" on page 376

A photo of the Arc de Triomphe (by E. A. M. Visser)

The **Chrome Reflections.psd** file on the Wow DVD-ROM (Wow Project Files > Chapter 8 > Chrome Reflections) includes these three custom chrome treatments.

A N A T O M Y   O F
"Shiny"

The next three pages examine the **Wow-Chrome 03** Layer Style, looking at how the component effects interact in this and other shiny Styles. The goal is to show you how to create or modify a Layer Style that adds both dimension and shine. To follow along, you can open **Chrome Anatomy-Before.psd** and build the Style step-by-step, or open **Chrome Anatomy-After.psd** and examine the effects as they're described.

"Custom Chrome" on page 525 tells how to add an environmental reflection to this chrome using a photo. And "Chrome" in Appendix B shows all 20 of the chrome Styles on the Wow DVD-ROM.

Before

After

YOU'LL FIND THE FILES

in 🅦 > Wow Project Files > Chapter 8 > Shiny:

- Chrome Anatomy-Before.psd (to build the Layer Style from scratch)
- Wow-Chrome.shc (a Contours file)
- Chrome Anatomy-After.psd (to inspect the finished Style)

Taking Over the Color

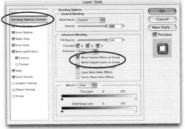

WITH THE LAYERS PALETTE OPEN (Window > Layers), we double-clicked on the thumbnail for the "Orbit logo" layer to open the Layer Style dialog box to begin building a Style for this layer. In the Advanced Blending section, we turned **"Blend Interior Effects as Group" on** and turned **"Blend Clipped Layers as Group" off**. These settings give us the option of adding an image to be reflected in the chrome, as described in step 4 of "Custom Chrome" on page 527. Without these settings, the reflection wouldn't show up.

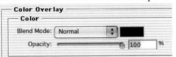

Although the "Orbit logo" graphic is already black, we used a **Color Overlay** effect to set the color for our Layer Style, to build a Style that could be applied to type or graphics of *any* color without surprises. From the list of effects on the left side of the Layer Style dialog, we chose **Color Overlay**. In the Color Overlay panel we left the Blend Mode set at Normal and Opacity at 100%. But we clicked the color swatch to open the Color Picker and clicked on black as the basis for the Style.

Adding a Drop Shadow

TO START THE ILLUSION of physical objects in a space, we chose **Drop Shadow** from the list in the dialog box. We entered a setting of 10 pixels for the **Distance** (how far the shadow is offset) and 20 pixels for the **Size** (how far the shadow extends out from the edge), leaving the **Spread** at 0. The Spread setting controls whether the shadow is soft and diffuse (a low setting) or dense and sharp-edged (a high setting).

We left the **Angle** at the default 120° but turned **Use Global Light off** so our lighting angle would be independent of any other Layer Style in the file. It works like this:

When you turn on Use Global Light for an effect in a Layer Style, the Angle setting you then choose will reset the lighting for any other Layer Styles already in the file that have Use Global Light turned on. Likewise, if you later add to the file another Style that has Use Global Light turned on, the lighting angle will be reset again, to match the newly introduced Angle.

Adding Thickness

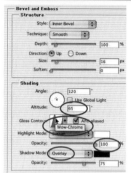

TO CREATE A ROUNDED EDGE for the chrome, we clicked on **Bevel and Emboss** in the list of effects. In the Structure section we chose Smooth for the **Technique**. For the bevel **Style** we chose Inner Bevel, to build the bevel inward from the edge of the graphic, and we increased the **Size** to 16 pixels. In the Shading section we again turned **Use Global Light off**. We chose a high **Altitude** setting of 65° to position the highlight up on the "shoulder" of the bevel, and selected our own custom contour (Wow-Chrome) for the Gloss Contour. This contour makes the highlight bright and sharp. (If you're building the Style, click the tiny triangle to the right of the Contour swatch to open a palette of Contours. Click this palette's ⊙ button, load **Wow-Chrome.shc**, and click Wow-Chrome in the palette.)

We changed the **Highlight Opacity** to 100% and the **Shadow Mode** to Overlay. The Mode makes no difference now, but when we add the Satin effect, using Overlay for the Shadow will increase the contrast of the light/dark banding that Satin creates.

Shaping the "Shoulder"

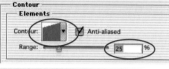

WE NEXT CLICKED on the **Contour** option, under **Bevel and Emboss** in the list on the left, to open its panel. This Contour interacts with other bevel characteristics to control the shape and lighting of the edges. In this case, we customized the contour by clicking on the contour thumbnail to open the Contour Editor and dragging up on the left end of the curve. The **Contour Editor** has a live preview, so we could see the effect of the new curve as we created it.

Back in the Contour panel, we reduced the **Range** percentage in order to increase the complexity of the highlight and to let some of the highlights "pop up" on the shaded side of the object.

GRID SCALE

To switch between a coarse and a fine grid in the Contour Editor anywhere you encounter it in the Layer Style dialog, Alt/Option-click in the Mapping box. (This also works in Photoshop's Curves dialog box.)

Creating Reflections

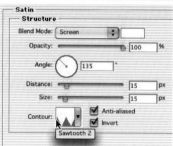

NOW WE WERE READY to use the **Satin** effect to do the magic of the reflections. We chose white for the **color** and Screen for the **Blend Mode**, in order to lighten the object overall. We used 100% **Opacity** for the fullest lightening effect we could get. For the **Contour**, we chose Sawtooth 2 in order to get the light/dark striping that's characteristic of multiple light sources reflected in a polished, curved surface. We experimented with the **Angle** of the effect, changing it from the default of 19° to 135° to position the brightest highlights where we wanted them. We wanted to use Satin's full potential for interacting with the shape of the graphic it's applied to, so we also experimented with **Distance**. We kept the setting low enough (15 pixels) to get well-defined repeats of the graphic's shapes inside the letters and the oval ring, and sharp specular highlights on the letters. We increased the **Size** enough to nicely blur the repeats (also 15 pixels), without blowing them out entirely.

Deepening Reflections

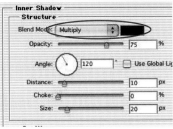

WE EXPERIMENTED with the Inner Shadow and Inner Glow to increase the complexity of the highlights and shadows in the chrome, and to enhance the edge definition.

For the **Inner Shadow** we left the **Angle** at 120° and again turned **Use Global Light off**. The Distance and Size settings were adjusted until the interaction of these two characteristics with the Satin had restored some of the gray in the metal, and had further defined but also softened the bands the Satin effect had created. We settled on 10 pixels for **Distance** and 20 pixels for **Size**.

Enhancing Roundness

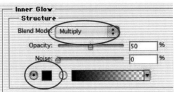

UNLIKE THE INNER SHADOW, which is applied at an angle so that some aspects are darkened and others are not, the Inner Glow is applied evenly, extending inward from the edges of the graphic. Though the defaults for the Inner Glow are set to produce a light glow, we chose black for the **color** and set the **Blend Mode** to Multiply. We chose a moderate **Opacity** setting of 50% — just enough to throw the edges into shadow, enhancing the illusion of roundness in the object as the edges fall away from the light.

Additional Shading

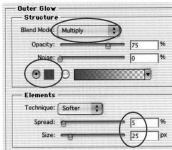

FINALLY, TO MAKE THE CHROME look more like it's sitting on the surface of the stone rather than floating above it, we added an **Outer Glow**, using a medium gray in Multiply mode. (By using gray rather than black, we gave ourselves finer control of the shadow density through the Opacity slider.) With Size reset to 35 and Spread to 5, the Outer Glow created a diffuse darkness around the graphics, defining the shiny forms even more and creating the interacting shadows between pairs of solid letters and between the letters and the rim. At this point, our chrome Style was complete, so we clicked "OK" to close the Layer Style dialog box.

BUILT-IN "REFLECTIONS" FOR SHINY STYLES

In a Layer Style, the three Overlay effects interact with one another as if they were "stacked" in the order they appear in the list in the Layer Style dialog box, with Color on top, then Gradient, then Pattern. So when a Pattern or Gradient Overlay is added to create reflections in a shiny style, the Opacity or Blend Mode of the Color Overlay is typically adjusted to allow the gradient to show.

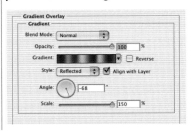

In the **Wow-Chrome 05** Style a reflected environment is simulated with a Gradient Overlay. The white Color Overlay's Opacity is reduced to let the steel-blue gradient "beneath" contribute to the look.

Don't miss the other Style-based chrome treatments shown in "Chrome" in "Appendix B: Wow Layer Styles." You can apply any of them to your own type or graphics with one click in the Styles palette, or by copying and pasting from the **Wow-Chrome Samples.psd** file as explained on page 492.

Custom Glass

YOU'LL FIND THE FILES

in **wow** > Wow Project Files > Chapter 8 > Custom Glass:
- Custom Glass-Before.psd (to start)
- Displace.psd (a displacement map for the Glass filter)
- Earth.psd (for the reflection)
- Custom Glass-After.psd (to compare)

OPEN THESE PALETTES

from the Window menu:
- Tools • Layers

OVERVIEW

Apply the **Wow-Chrome 03** Style to graphics • Add, clip, and distort a copy of the background image • Adjust the Layer Style • Add glare and a reflected image

1

The graphics, treated with the **Wow-Chrome 03** Layer Style, over a background image

THE GLASS PLAQUE SHOWN HERE is produced using a variation of the "Custom Chrome" technique on page 525. The main difference in construction between chrome and this glass is the addition of a distorted copy of the background image, clipped by the logo, which makes it seem as if we're seeing the background through a transparent object. Also, the Opacity of the "environment" photo reflected in the surface is lower than with chrome, since glass is not as reflective. A few strategic changes to the Layer Style complete the character of the glass.

1 Setting up the file. Open the file you want to use as the background behind your glass object. On another layer create or import graphics. Our **Glass-Before.psd** file is a 1000-pixel-wide background with a logo on another layer. To build your new glass Style, you can start by applying the **Wow-Chrome 03** Style on your graphics layer as described on page 526. Or open the **Custom Glass-After.psd** file and copy the Style from there. ▼ You may need to scale the Style to fit your graphics; right/Ctrl-click the 𝑓 for the styled layer, choose Scale Effects, and adjust the slider until the chrome surface looks right **1**; you don't need to be concerned about the exterior shadows, since they'll be changed in step 3.

FIND OUT MORE

▼ Copying a Layer Style **page 492**

2 Making the object transparent. In the Layers palette, duplicate the background image — click its thumbnail to target it, and then type Ctrl/⌘-J. Drag the new layer's thumbnail up in the palette so it's above the graphics, and Alt/Option-click the border between this copy and the graphics layer below it, to "clip" the "Background copy" inside the graphics shape **2a**.

To distort the background as seen through the glass, you'll need a displacement map made from the graphics, as described in

2a

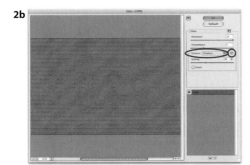

A copy of the background image is clipped by the graphics.

2b

Running the Glass filter on the background copy distorts the image as if it were being viewed through the rounded glass logo.

step 3 of "Custom Chrome"; our displacement map is the file **Displace.psd**. Use the displacement map with the Glass filter (Filter > Distort > Glass) to "glassify" the "Background copy" layer, clicking the ⊙ button in the Glass dialog, choosing Load Texture, and loading the displacement map file; we used Distortion and Smoothness settings of 20 and 5 respectively **2b**.

3 Adjusting the Style. To make the graphics more glasslike, make these changes to the Style on the graphics layer:

- In the Layers palette, if you don't see the list of effects for the styled layer, click the tiny arrow next to the layer's 𝑓 icon. Double-click the **Inner Shadow** entry to open the Layer Style dialog to that panel. Change the Inner Shadow's Blend Mode to **Overlay**. This will brighten the edges of the glass graphic **3a**, because Overlay darkens less than Multiply does. We liked the results for Overlay, but you might also try Soft Light or another of the contrast-enhancing modes grouped with Overlay in the Blend Mode list.▼

FIND OUT MORE

▼ Using blend modes **page 176**

- Click on the name **Outer Glow** (not the check box) in the list of effects at the left of the Layer Style dialog. To change the Outer Glow from a "dark halo" to a glow that simulates light being refracted through the glass to light up the surface beneath, click the color swatch and change the color to white; change the Blend Mode to **Overlay**, which lightens, but not as intensely as Screen would; and experiment with reducing the Size setting; we reduced the Size to 20 pixels **3b**. Even with the Outer Glow lightened, the glass graphics will still cast a slight shadow, thanks to the Drop Shadow. This helps with the illusion of a clear but solid material.

3a

After modifying the Inner Shadow

Changing the Outer Glow

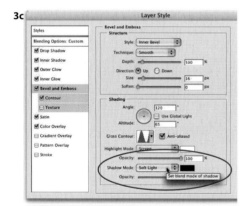

Changing the Bevel and Emboss Shadow

- Depending on your background image, your glass may look too much darker or more saturated than the background. If so, click on **Bevel and Emboss** in the list at the left and reduce the Opacity of the **Shadow** in the Shading section of the Bevel and Emboss panel, or change the Mode from Overlay to **Soft Light**; we changed the Shadow Mode to Soft Light and left the Opacity at 75% **3c**.

4 Creating glare. You can "reflect" diffuse light from the surface of the glass graphics by lowering the Opacity setting for the glassified background copy; we settled on 85% Opacity for the "Background copy" layer **4**.

5 Reflecting an environment. To reflect an image on the glass, target the "Background copy" layer by clicking its thumbnail; then open a photo file and drag and drop the image; we used the **Earth.psd** image. Then add this new layer to the clipping group by Alt/Option-clicking its lower border in the Layers palette. We renamed our imported image layer by double-clicking its name in the Layers palette and typing "Reflection."

Before you "glassify" this layer, *be sure to crop off any excess* from the layer so the displacement map will line up with it correctly (type Ctrl/⌘-A to select all, and choose Image > Crop). To run the Glass filter again with the same settings and the same displacement map, you can simply type Ctrl/⌘-F **5**. Then reduce the Opacity of this glassified "Reflection" layer until the reflection is the strength you want; we used 10% for the result shown at the top of page 534. *Wow!*

4

Reducing the glassified "Background copy" layer's Opacity creates a slight surface glare.

5

A photo for reflection is added and modified with the Glass filter.

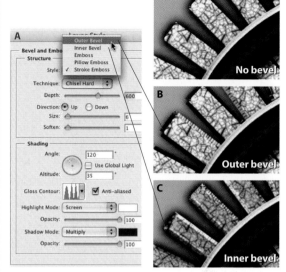

497936

ANATOMY OF

Bevels

Photoshop's Bevel and Emboss is one of the most valuable
effects in a Layer Style for turning type and graphics into
tangible objects. It plays a role in most of the special effects in this chapter, contributing everything from a
smooth and rounded look to a rough and angular appearance. The fundamentals of the settings for the Bevel and
Emboss effect are covered starting on page 501, along with
their relationship to Contour (which shapes the "shoulder" of a bevel; page 503) and Texture (which adds an embossed surface, the location of the texture being determined by the type of bevel; page 504). This "Anatomy of
Bevels" section explores the potential of some of the nu-
ances of Bevel and Emboss that aren't covered elsewhere
in the chapter.

The essential tools for beveling are found in the Bevel and
Emboss panel of the Layer Style dialog box, and in the related Contour and Texture panels. But the Stroke effect is
also very useful for building bevels.

In the Layer Styles applied to the four graphics layers that make
up **Star.psd**, the Bevel and Emboss effects are key to creating
the illusion of solid, dimensional objects. Use this file to explore
the importance of bevel position and Stroke in establishing a
beveled look.

 Star.psd

YOU'LL FIND THE FILES

in (wow) > Wow Project Files > Chapter 8 > Anatomy of
Bevels

Bevel Position

IN THE BEVEL AND EMBOSS PANEL of the Layer Style dia-
log box **A**, you can set the **Style**, or position, of the bevel in
the **Structure** section. The choice you make determines
where the bevel will be built relative to the edge of the layer
content. The Inner Bevel and Outer Bevel extend inward
and outward, of course; Emboss straddles the outline, and
so does Pillow Emboss; the position of a Stroke Emboss
depends entirely on the position of the Stroke (see "Bevels
& Strokes" on the next page).

Below are some things to consider when choosing a bevel's
position. To follow along, turn off visibility for the Stroke
effect for the "Spokes" layer (click the Stroke's 👁 in the
Layers palette). *Note:* For a simpler view of the beveling,
you may also want to turn off visibility for the Shadow and
Glow effects (we did not).

• An **Outer Bevel extends** outward **B**, so you may need to
add extra space between characters if you use it on type.
Also, the **Outer Bevel** is **semi-transparent** and allows
whatever is below it in the Layer stack to show through
the bevel (as the yellow does here), unless you use the
Outer Bevel with a Stroke effect, as described on page 538.

• The **Inner Bevel** takes characteristics (such as color or pattern) from the element itself, so it **creates a solid edge** that
doesn't let a background show through **C**. An **Inner Bevel**
"consumes" part of the shape it's applied to, which can
be a problem if you use it on a delicate shape or on type.

• An **Outer Bevel is rounded** around any sharp points,
while an **Inner Bevel has sharp corners**. An **Emboss**
bevel creates **intermediate rounding.**

Bevels & Strokes

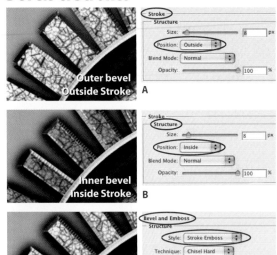

Outer bevel / Outside Stroke A

Inner bevel / Inside Stroke B

Stroke Emboss / Inside Stroke C

THE COMBINATION of a Bevel and Emboss effect and a Stroke effect can help you tailor the edge profile and lighting for the bevels you apply:

• An **Outer Bevel**, which is otherwise semi-transparent, can be filled in by adding a **Stroke** with **Outside** chosen as the position. Notice that with a Stroke in place **A**, the yellow background no longer shows through as it does for the Outer Bevel on page 537. For a good fit between bevel and Stroke, try **matching the Size** setting of the Stroke to the Size setting for the Bevel and Emboss and then adjust as needed. (Another option for a solid outer bevel is to use the **Stroke Emboss with an Outside Stroke**.)

• For an **Inner Bevel**, adding an **Inside Stroke** creates a cleanly "cut" edge by keeping any Overlay effects (Color, Gradient, or Pattern) from "spilling over" onto the bevel **B** (to see the effect, compare **B** to the Inner Bevel on page 537, in which the Overlay effects extend from the top surface onto the bevel). A **Center Stroke** can be used in the same way for an **Emboss** or **Pillow Emboss** bevel. (Note that a Stroke *doesn't* hide a Texture effect applied in conjunction with Bevel and Emboss.)

• The Shading settings for an Inner Bevel affect not only the bevel itself but also the "top surface" of the element you apply the bevel to; for instance, in **B** the Bevel and Emboss Shadow darkens the surface. But if you use the Inside Stroke with a **Stroke Emboss** instead of an Inner Bevel, you get the same bevel effect without the shading on the top surface **C**.

Bevels & Lighting

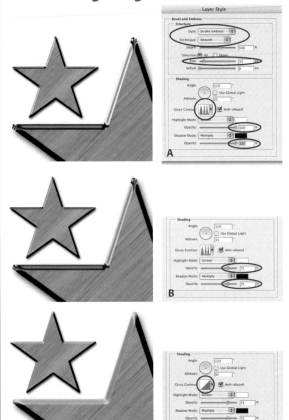

THE LIGHTING FOR BEVELS is set up in the Shading section of the Bevel and Emboss panel, using the Gloss Contour and the Mode, Opacity, and colors of the highlights and shadows. With the Stroke Emboss and Stroke (as described at the left), the characteristics of the bevel and the top surface are independent of each other. You may want to turn off visibility for the Satin effect (as we did here) as you "deconstruct" the Bevel and Emboss for the "Small Star" layer, which has a **Stroke Emboss** (15 pixels) backed up with a **Center Stroke** (10 pixels).

The **highly reflective edge** with alternating high-contrast lights and darks results in part from choosing a **complex Gloss Contour** with multiple ridges, such as Adobe's Ring-Triple **A**. Also, with **Highlight Mode** and **Shadow Mode** set to their default Screen and Multiply, using higher **Opacity** settings makes the beveled edges **more reflective** — shinier. See the difference by reducing both Opacity settings to 75% **B**, and then also compare the effect of using the default Gloss Contour **C**.

Bevels & Color

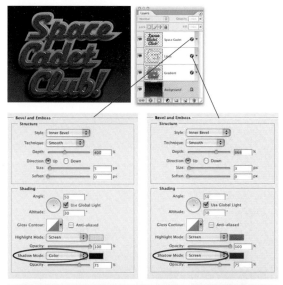

YOU CAN USE THE BEVEL AND EMBOSS effect not only to add thickness and lighting direction to type or graphics but also to set the color of the lighting. Two examples are shown here; the type and border were created on separate layers so that each could have its own Layer Style:

- With an **Inner Bevel** chosen for the "Space Cadet" layer, we used yellow for the Highlight and a bright purple for the Shadow. We put the Shadow in Color mode to override the color on the shaded edges of the bevel, to make it look as if another light source was shining from below.

- For the black outlines that make up the "Lines" layer, the **Inner Bevel** was used with a magenta Highlight in Screen mode and a violet Shadow, also in Screen mode, again to simulate additional light sources.

(Using a higher Size setting for the Bevel and Emboss effect on the "Space Cadet" logotype — 5 instead of the 3 used for the "Lines" layer — makes the logotype look thicker, as if it stands up farther off the background.)

 Space.psd

A Bevel That Isn't a Bevel

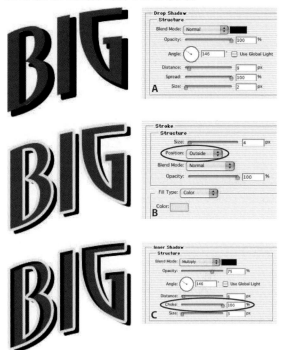

WHEN IS A BEVEL not a bevel? When you create it with other effects in a Layer Style. With the "multiple-stroke" approach described here, you can create an old-fashioned dimensional look, with built-up "square" bevels. We started with graphics to which a Color Overlay effect had been added, as well as a **Drop Shadow** with the **Spread at 100%** to ensure a hard edge **A**; the Drop Shadow's Distance setting determines the offset. Then we built the "bevel":

- A light-colored **Stroke** effect is added **B**; it will create the flat top surface of the straight bevel. In the Structure section of the Stroke settings, the **Outside** choice for the Position **thickens the letters.**

- The **Inner Shadow** adds a cast shadow, to turn the Stroke into a built-up edge **C**. In the Structure section of the Inner Shadow settings, we set the **Choke at 100%** for a hard-edged shadow. We also made sure to use the same Angle as for the Drop Shadow, to keep lighting consistent. (If you toggle the 👁 for the Drop Shadow effect on and off, you'll see that it's important in establishing the letters as solid objects. Also notice that even though the "cast shadow" illusion isn't perfect at the corners, the dimensional impression works!)

 Big.psd

Carving

YOU'LL FIND THE FILES

in  > Wow Project Files > Chapter 8 > Carving:

- Carving-Before.psd files (to start)
- Wow-Carving.asl (a Style presets file)
- Carving-After.psd files (to compare)

OPEN THESE PALETTES

from the Window menu:
- Tools • Layers • Styles

OVERVIEW

Add a Layer Style to a graphic to "carve" it into a plain background • Use the Lighting Effects filter to enhance the dimensionality of the carving • Switch to a smooth, patterned background image; offset a copy of this surface image, masked with the graphic, to add to the Illusion of depth • Switch to a textured background image; make a displacement map from this image, and use the Displace filter to roughen the carving

SOMETIMES ALL YOU NEED in order to create the illusion of the third dimension is an edge, defined by subtle highlights and shadows that can make a shape look carved or cut-out. In Photoshop an excellent way to accomplish this is to use a Layer Style consisting of a **Bevel and Emboss** effect to create the cut edges, an **Inner Shadow** to add depth to the carving, and a **Color Overlay** to control the overall shading of the recessed areas. That may be all you need if the carved surface is smooth and plain, although adding lighting with the **Lighting Effects** filter can reinforce the effect.

If the smooth surface has distinct color markings such as wood grain, you can add to the illusion by **offsetting** the interior of the carving. This creates an obvious "jump" in the markings that adds to the appearance that the carved area is recessed.

For a third type of background image, with a rough surface like the rock above, treating the graphics with the **Displace** filter can make the difference between a convincing illusion and a "near miss." Used with a displacement map made from the surface image, this filter can "disrupt" or bend the edges of the carved graphic to conform to the surface texture.

1

The **Carving Smooth-Before.psd** file consists of graphics on a transparent layer over a smooth surface that was created by applying a Layer Style to a color-filled layer.

2a

Loading a Layer Style presets file into the Styles palette

2b

In the **Wow-Carved Sharp** Style, a black Color Overlay replaces the native color of the element it's applied to (in this case the graphics were black already anyway, so it made no difference); the reduced Fill opacity (25%, also built into the Style) makes the black graphics partly transparent, so the effect is to shade the recessed areas of the carving.

2c

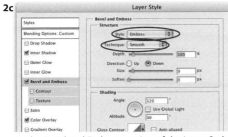

In the Bevel and Emboss section of the Layer Style dialog box, we changed the Style to Emboss and the Technique to Smooth.

1 Preparing to carve a smooth surface. Open or create an image of a smooth surface, without distinct markings or texture. Add the graphics you want to carve, as a transparent layer in this file; you might copy-and-paste or drag-and-drop the artwork from another file, or create it with one of Photoshop's drawing tools. Or open the **Carving Smooth-Before.psd** file **1**. The red surface is created with a Layer Style (**Wow-Red**, one of the **Wow Plastics** Styles shown in Appendix B); the graphics are old-fashioned clip art, scanned, modified, and isolated from the white background. ▼

2 Adding a Layer Style to the graphics. To carve the graphics into the surface, we began by targeting the graphics layer (by clicking its thumbnail in the Layers palette) and applying the **Wow-Carved Sharp** Layer Style from the **Wow Halos & Embossing** Styles on the DVD-ROM that comes with this book; "Anatomy of Bevels" on page 537 tells how the effects in this and other Styles work together to create dimensional edges. To apply the Style, you can either click on it in the Styles palette (if you've installed the Wow presets as explained on page 5), or you can choose Load Styles from the palette's menu ⊙ **2a** and load the **Wow-Carving.asl** file from the folder with the other files for this project; once it's loaded into the Styles palette, click on the **Wow-Carved Sharp** Style to apply it **2b**.

Depending on the size and type of graphics you're using, you may want to scale the Style overall (we did not), ▼ or you may want to modify some of its effects. We didn't change the Inner Shadow (which creates the shadow cast by the carved edge) or the Color Overlay (which darkens the recessed areas overall). But the Bevel and Emboss effect seemed too heavy for our graphics on this surface, so in the Layers palette we double-clicked the Bevel and Emboss listing for the graphics layer and made some changes **2c**: We changed the Outer Bevel, which builds the carved edge outward from the black graphics, to **Emboss**, which creates half the width of the edge by building outward,

2d

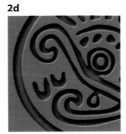

and half by building inward. We also changed the Chisel Hard setting to Smooth for a "machined" look **2d**. (If you want to experiment with the Inner Shadow or the Color Overlay, click

The carved graphics after the change in the Style

FIND OUT MORE

▼ Isolating graphics on a transparent layer **page 474**

▼ Scaling Styles **page 492**

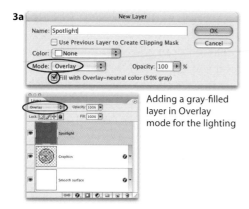

3a

Adding a gray-filled layer in Overlay mode for the lighting

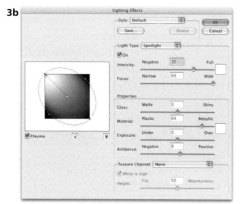

Setting up a spotlight

3b

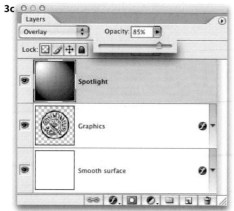

3c

The lighting in place; the result is shown on page 540

its name in the list on the left side of the Layer Style dialog box; the check marks indicate which effects are turned on and contributing to the Style, but you'll need to click the *name* of the effect to get to the right section of the dialog box to make changes.)

3 Making a "lighting" layer. To liven up the carved image, we applied a Spotlight with the **Lighting Effects** filter, but we kept it on a separate "lighting" layer for greater control of the effect: With the graphics layer targeted, add a new layer in Overlay mode by Alt/Option-clicking the "Create a new layer" button at the bottom of the Layers palette; using the Alt/Option key opens the New Layer dialog box, where you can choose **Overlay** for the Mode and click the check box for **"Fill with Overlay-neutral color (50% gray)" 3a**. Since the gray is neutral (invisible) in this mode, your image won't change when you click "OK" to close the box, but you'll see the gray-filled layer in the Layers palette.

To create the Spotlight, choose Filter > Render > Lighting Effects and set up your lighting **3b**. We started with the Default lighting, reoriented the light so it was most intense in the upper left corner, and made it closer to circular by dragging inward on the bottom handle.▼ The Lighting Effects preview will show only the gray layer, and you won't be able to preview the effect on your image in the working window, but having the light on a separate layer will give you a great deal of control to modify it once you click "OK" to close the Lighting Effects dialog.

FIND OUT MORE

▼ Using Lighting Effects **page 259**

In the Layers palette you can experiment by choosing other blend modes for the spotlight layer (from the menu at the upper left of the Layers palette) or by reducing the Opacity setting (at the upper right) to decrease the spotlight effect, or by doubling the layer (Ctrl/⌘-J) to increase the lighting contrast. You might try a different blend mode, such as Soft Light, Hard Light, Linear Light, Screen, or Multiply; we stayed with Overlay but reduced the Opacity to 85% **3c**.

4 Carving a patterned surface. To carve a patterned surface, either open your own image file and add graphics (as in step 1), then apply the **Wow-Carved Sharp** Style (step 2), and add lighting (step 3). Or open the **Carving Patterned-Before.psd** file; the **Wow-Carved Sharp** Style has been applied (we found that this Style worked well for the wood carving without changes), and a "Spotlight" layer has been added **4a**.

4a

The **Carving Pattern-Before.psd** file, with the **Wow-Carved Sharp** Style applied to the graphics

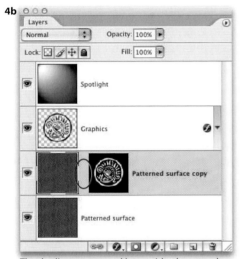

4b

The duplicate patterned layer with a layer mask applied and unlinked

4c

Before

After

Offsetting the masked duplicate layer slightly to create a "jump" in the pattern

To shift the recessed area to enhance the illusion of depth, **create a masked duplicate** of the surface image: Target the surface image in the Layers palette and press Ctrl/⌘-J to duplicate it; then load the graphics layer as a selection by Ctrl/⌘-clicking the graphics layer's thumbnail in the palette, and click the "Add a layer mask" button ◻ at the bottom of the Layers palette. The next important step is to **unlink the mask** in this duplicate layer (by clicking the 🔗 icon between the layer's image thumbnail and its mask thumbnail) **4b**. This will allow you to move the wood image while the mask stays right in place: Target the image rather than the mask. Choose the Move tool ▶⊕ and nudge the image by tapping the arrow keys on the keyboard until the image is shifted as much as you like **4c**.

5 Carving a textured surface. If the surface you're carving has some roughness to it, there's something else you can do to add to the illusion. To follow our example, open the **Carving Rough-Before.psd** file **5a**, or if you're using your own image and graphics, follow steps 1 through 4, but in step 2 instead of using the Wow-Carved Sharp Style, you may want to try **Wow-Carved Smooth**, to make the carving look "rounder" as if worn with age **5b**.

LAYERING TWO MATERIALS

When you "carve" a patterned surface, the mask you create (in step 4 of "Carving") can be used not only for shifting the recessed surface, but also for *replacing* it with a different material, as follows: Target the layer with the mask by clicking its thumbnail in the Layers palette. Open the image file you want to use for the second surface, and with the Move tool ▶⊕ drag-and-drop it into the carving file; it will come in as a layer above the masked layer. Now "copy the mask" to your new layer by clicking the mask thumbnail for the masked layer and then clicking the ◻ button at the bottom of the palette; in Photoshop CS2, you can simply Alt/Option-drag the mask thumbnail to the imported layer.

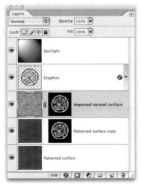

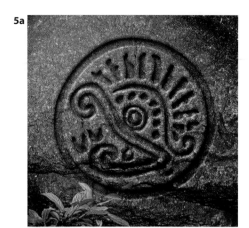

5a

The **Carving Rough-Before.psd** file, with the **Wow-Carved Smooth** Layer Style applied to the graphics layer. Some of the leaves in the foreground are "caught" in the carving, but that will be fixed in step 6.

5b

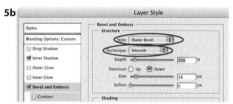

In the Bevel and Emboss section of the Layer Style dialog box, a higher Size setting (16 for Wow-Carved Smooth, instead of the 9 used for Wow-Carved Sharp) and the Smooth setting for Technique make a softer, rounder edge on the bevel.

6a

The carving file, with only the stone image layer visible, is duplicated to start making the displacement map.

6b

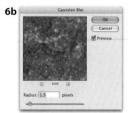

After converting the displacement map file to grayscale, we blurred it slightly to smooth out details in the texture.

6 "Roughening" the carving. For the rough surface, the next step is to create a displacement map to use with the Displace filter to make the carving look like it's affected by the depressions (dark areas) and rises (lighter areas) in the surface topography. (The Displace filter works on an image by "pushing" pixels up or down and right or left. For each pixel the direction is decided by whether the corresponding pixel in the displacement map is dark or light, and the relative amount of displacement is affected by the degree of darkness or lightness.▼

FIND OUT MORE

▼ How the Displace filter works **page 578**

At this point, in case there might be any layers that extend beyond the canvas, it's a good idea to select all (Ctrl/⌘-A) and choose Image > **Crop**, so the displacement map you're about to make is sure to match up with the surface image when you apply the Displace filter. Then in the Layers palette, temporarily turn off visibility for all but the surface image layer (Alt/Option-click its ● icon), choose Image > Duplicate, and turn on the Duplicate Merged Layers Only option **6a**.

To make it easier to see how the contrast in the new image will work as a displacement map, convert the file to Grayscale (Image > Mode > Grayscale). Then you may want to get rid of unwanted detail by blurring **6b**, **6c**, and increase the contrast to exaggerate the light/dark differences in major features of the surface **6d**. **Save the file in Photoshop (PSD) format**, since the Displace filter requires a saved Photoshop file.

To "roughen" the carving, target the graphics layer in the Layers palette and turn on its visibility (click in the Visibility column in the Layers palette to bring back its ● icon). Choose Filter > Distort > Displace. In the Displace dialog box, put in values for the Horizontal and Vertical Scale (we used 6 for both) **6e**, and click "OK" to close the box; navigate to the displacement map you just made, and click "Open." Since the Displace filter has no preview you may need to look at the result, undo (Ctrl/⌘-Z), and reapply the filter with new settings; Ctrl-Alt F (Windows) or ⌘-Option-F (Mac) reopens the dialog for the last filter used, with the settings as they were so you can increase or decrease them to get a more pronounced or less pronounced effect.

7 Bringing foreground elements in front of the carving. Whether your carved surface is smooth, patterned, or textured, if there is a subject in your surface image that needs to appear

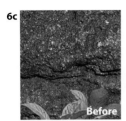

6c

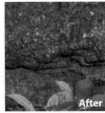

The effect of blurring the displacement map

6d

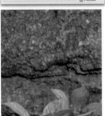

Using a Levels Adjustment layer and the "Blend If" sliders to increase contrast in the darkest tones, to emphasize the dark crevices without exaggerating the "grain" of the rock. (Right/Ctrl-click the Adjustment layer's thumbnail to open to Blending Options.)

6e

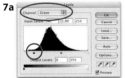

Applying the Displace filter distorts the carved graphics to match the surface.

7a

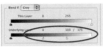

A Levels adjustment targeted to the Green channel increases color contrast between the leaves and the rock, which makes it easier for the Magnetic Lasso to follow the edge.

7b

Once the selection is made, visibility for the Adjustment layer is turned off (or the layer can be deleted, as here). The selection is used to copy the foreground elements to a separate layer above the graphics.

in front of the carving, you can make that happen by selecting the subject and duplicating it to a new layer.

Use a selection method appropriate to your subject. ▼ To keep our work to a minimum, we would select only those few leaves that actually overlapped the carving. Because of the variation in tone and saturation of the leaves and the speckled nature of the stone, it would be hard to select by color with the Magic Wand or the Color Range command. So we decided to use the Magnetic Lasso 🖉, operating the tool magnetically wherever the edge was distinct enough by "floating" it along without depressing the mouse button, ▼ and then clicking or Alt/Option-dragging where the tool needed help following the edge. But before we started, we increased the color contrast between the leaves and rocks to make it easier for the Magnetic Lasso to "see" the edge: We clicked the "Create new fill or adjustment layer" button ◓ at the bottom of the Layers palette) and chose Levels. Sometimes simply increasing contrast by moving the Input Levels black and white sliders inward is all that's needed. In this case, however, we decided to use the fact that we had green leaves on a neutral background. We chose Green from the Channel menu at the top of the Levels dialog and moved the black slider inward, turning the rock a dark magenta **7a**, which made it easier to select the leaves. When the selection was finished, we deleted the Levels layer, targeted the image layer again, and copied the leaves to a new layer (Ctrl/⌘-J). Then it was just a matter of dragging the leaves up the stack in the Layers palette until they were in front of the carving, and turning on visibility for the spotlight layer again **7b**.

Finishing touches. To tone down the bevel highlight at the bottom of the carving where the rock is undercut, we added an empty layer (Ctrl/⌘-Shift-N), put it in Multiply mode, and painted with black, using the Brush ✐ with a soft tip and low Opacity. If your image has a color cast in the shadows, you can modify the Layer Style to match. For any shadow effect, in the Layer Style dialog box, click the color swatch and click in a shadowed area of the image to sample color. To further exaggerate displacement of some elements, make a flattened copy of the file (Image > Duplicate, Duplicate Merged Layers Only), and try Liquify. ▼ Finally, to further unify the carved graphics and the surface, sharpen the flattened image slightly. ▼

FIND OUT MORE

▼ Choosing a selection method **page 55**

▼ Operating the Magnetic Lasso 🖉 **page 61**

▼ Using Liquify **page 615**

▼ Sharpening **page 326**

Crafting a Neon Glow

YOU'LL FIND THE FILES

in > Wow Project Files > Chapter 8 > Neon Glow:

- Neon Glow-Before.psd (to start)
- Wow-Neon Glow.grd (a gradient preset file)
- Neon Glow-After.psd (to compare)

OPEN THESE PALETTES

from the Window menu:

- Tools • Layers • Styles • Paths

OVERVIEW

Set up a file with a dark background • Import or draw artwork for the neon tubes • Create a neon Layer Style • Fine-tune the artwork and add supports for the tubes • Separate some neon elements to new layers and change their coloring

1a The paths were drawn in Illustrator, where they were stroked and given round end caps and joins.

1b Uniting the paths after outlining the strokes

THERE ARE MANY WAYS TO CREATE NEON effects for type and graphics, including the fast methods shown in "Quick Neon Type" on page 454. But if the neon is vector- and Style-based, its shapes can be edited, it can be scaled up or down without deterioration, and you can change the Style to change the color, or create an "off" state to animate the sign. The neon shown above comes from paths imported from Adobe Illustrator, turned into vector masks, and treated with Layer Styles. The basic Style consists of an Inner Glow based on a gradient to simulate the neon gas glowing inside the glass tubes, as well as a solid-color Outer Glow combined with a Drop Shadow in Color Dodge mode to light up a dark textured surface. Here the goal is to communicate the *concept* of neon lighting, but with additional hand-detailing the neon could be made more photorealistic. (Bert Monroy, master of photorealism, adds the "grunge" and other detail needed to make neon tubes look real, as described on page 397.)

1 Preparing the "tubes." This step builds the tubes for the neon. Start with a file with a dark *Background*; ours was a scanned texture with lighting added with the Lighting Effects filter. ▼ Then import shapes to serve as the basis for your neon tubing, or draw them in Photoshop with the Pen ⬥ or use the Type tool **T** to set monoweight type. (Instead of building your own tubes according to the description that follows, you can open the **Neon Glow-Before.psd** file, then simply read the rest of this step to see how it was created, and then go on to step 2.)

FIND OUT MORE

▼ Working with Lighting Effects
page 259

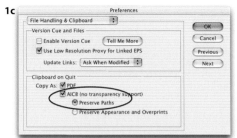

1c

Setting Preferences in Illustrator so that copied graphics can be pasted into Photoshop as paths

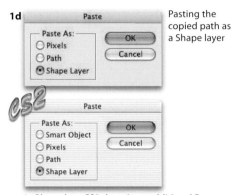

1d

Pasting the copied path as a Shape layer

In Photoshop CS2 there is an additional Paste As option (Smart Object) for artwork copied from Illustrator, but for this project, in which the artwork is imported and then separated into parts, the Shape Layer option is still a good choice.

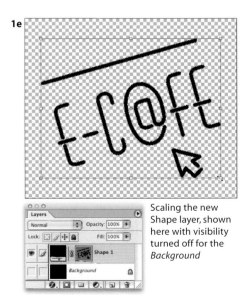

1e

Scaling the new Shape layer, shown here with visibility turned off for the *Background*

We drew the custom lettering and symbols in Adobe Illustrator, using a series of stroked, single paths, with round corners and round end caps, set in Illustrator's Stroke palette **1a**.

To create the tubes in a way that would let us reshape them in Photoshop if we wanted to, we converted the stroked paths into outlined shapes (Object > Path > Outline Stroke). Next, to make the shapes into a unified graphic without overlapping paths, still in Illustrator we selected all the paths (Ctrl/⌘-A) and clicked on the "Add to shape area" button in the Pathfinder palette **1b**.

Before moving the paths to Photoshop, we made sure that Illustrator's Preferences were set for copying paths for use in Photoshop by choosing Illustrator > Preferences > File Handling & Clipboard and turning on the "AICB" and "Preserve Paths" options **1c**. Then we copied the selected graphic (Ctrl/⌘-C). We opened a Photoshop file and pasted (Ctrl/⌘-V, choosing Paste As: Shape Layer in the Paste dialog box) **1d**. If you need to scale the Shape layer after pasting, use Free Transform (Ctrl/⌘-T) and Shift-drag a corner handle **1e** (if the Transform box extends outside the working window so you can't see the corner handles, press Ctrl/⌘-0 — that's zero — to enlarge the window enough to show all the handles of the box). Double-click inside the box or press the Enter key to finish the transformation.

2 Creating the neon Layer Style. With your graphic in place and its layer active, click the "Add a layer style" button 🇫 at the bottom of the Layers palette and choose **Inner Glow** from the pop-up menu to open the Layer Style dialog box to the **Inner Glow** panel. In the Structure section of the panel, set the **Blend Mode** to **Normal** and the **Opacity** to 100%, so the neon gradient you are about to add will completely override the existing color of your graphic. Click to choose the gradient option rather than the solid color. Now you can choose or create a gradient that goes from white-hot to your darkest color (in our gradient this was hot pink), through one or more intermediate colors (in this case a softer pink). Click the tiny triangle to the right of the gradient swatch to open the Gradient palette, where you can choose a gradient or load other gradients into the palette by clicking the ⊙ button and choosing from the list of presets or choosing Load Gradients. (The Wow Gradients include several that are good for neon,▼ or you can load the **Wow-Neon Glow.grd** file from the Neon Glow folder that has the files for this technique. Or double-click

FIND OUT MORE

▼ Loading the Wow presets **page 5**

2a

Lighting and rounding the tubes with an Inner Glow

2b

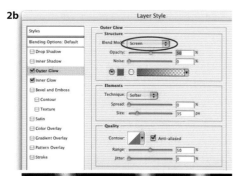

Casting light on the wall with an Outer Glow

2c

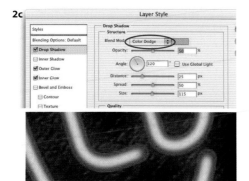

Brightening the detail in the background with a Drop Shadow effect

the gradient swatch itself to open the Gradient Editor, and create your own gradient.▼

FIND OUT MORE

▼Creating gradients **page 161**

In the Elements section of the Inner Glow panel **2a**, for the **Technique** choose **Softer**, because this choice will apply the gradient to look less like parallel stroking and more like variable glowing. For the **Source** choose **Center** (so the gradient goes from white in the center to color at the edges); if you've accidentally built your gradient in reverse, you can choose Edge instead of Center. In the Quality section, set the **Range** to **100%** so the entire gradient will be used to color the tube. Then, back in the Elements section, set the **Choke** at **0** temporarily and **adjust the Size** until the white-to-color transition of your neon looks right; then **adjust the Choke** to control how wide the outermost color will be, before the gradient transition begins. You can "jockey" the Size and Choke until you get the result you want. We found that for our thin neon tubes and our gradient, using a Choke setting of 30% worked well to "round" the tubes.

When the Inner Glow is as you like it, click on the words **"Outer Glow"** in the list at the left side of the Layer Style dialog box. Because the **Blend Mode** is set to **Screen,** the glow will light up the dark background behind the neon **2b**. We used a solid pink color, with a **Size** set at **35 px** and the **Spread** set to **0** to make the glow as diffuse as possible and minimize any abrupt halo effect. We set the **Opacity** at **50%**; you can increase this if you're working on a very dark background or if you want a more dramatic glow. We experimented with the **Range** and settled on the **50%** default setting.

To make the glow outside the tube more realistic, we chose **Drop Shadow** from the list at the left edge of the box, setting the shadow's color to pink and its **Blend Mode** to **Color Dodge**, which lightens the color in layers underneath and increases contrast by lightening the light colors even more than the dark colors **2c**. The Drop Shadow worked with the Outer Glow and the lighting built into the *Background* to create the effect of the neon tubing lighting up the surface and showing off the surface detail. For a "straight-on" view, the Distance (the offset) would be set at 0, but we set the **Angle** and **Distance** to 25 px to shift this additional glow to the right and down, to suggest the illusion of looking up at the sign.

3 Fine-tuning the tubes. With the tubes lit, you can now make adjustments to their shapes to add realism. In the Layers palette, activate the Shape layer by clicking its rightmost (vector

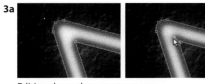

3a

Editing the path to create creases

3b

The completed neon tubing

4

A "Connectors" layer was added. The "styled" connectors are shown here without (top left) and with the neon layer.

mask) thumbnail; the path will also show in the working window. (If you started with live type in Photoshop, you can convert it to a Shape layer in order to alter the characters; choose Layer > Type > Convert to Shape.) Choose the Pen tool ⬥. Hold down the Ctrl/⌘ key to toggle the Pen to the Direct Selection tool ⬥, click on the path to show its control points, and release the Ctrl/⌘ key. To make the Layer Style follow the creases characteristic of bent tubing, we added points by clicking with the Pen ⬥ on each side of each point that controlled a sharp inner corner of our neon arrow cursor. Then by holding down the Ctrl/⌘ key again, we could move the original point, and the new points if necessary, to make the crease **3a** and complete the neon tubes **3b**.

4 Connecting the tubing to the wall. To simulate the connections to the wall, you can simply create round dots at the attachment points and add a Layer Style **4**. We made ours by activating the *Background* and adding a layer above it by Alt/Option-clicking the "Create a new layer" button ⬜ at the bottom of the Layers palette, naming the layer and clicking "OK" in the New Layer dialog box. We then clicked at various spots with the Brush tool ⬥ using the 19-pixel hard round brush tip and black paint (if you use a stylus instead of a mouse, turn off Shape Dynamics in the Brushes palette). We added a Style with a Color Overlay to color the dots (we used a purplish brown that would take on some of the color of the neon) and applied a simple bevel and shadow for dimensionality. You can see the settings for the Style in the **Neon Glow-After.psd** file.

5 Adding colors. To enliven your sign, you can highlight individual elements giving each one a unique color. One way to do this — **making a layer set/group** and using a Hue/Saturation Adjustment layer within it to change the color and then changing the mode of the set/group from Pass Through to Normal — is described on page 507. This technique is great, because it requires only a single color adjustment to fix all the color-based effects. But it **won't work in this case** because the Color Burn mode used for the Drop Shadow is essentially lost in the process of putting the layer set/group into Normal mode; it makes the glow on the wall look more like spray paint.

Here we'll take a different approach. First we'll copy subpaths from the Shape layer and make new layers from them. Then we'll copy and paste the original neon Layer Style and adjust the color of the individual effects in the Style to change the color of the neon.

5a

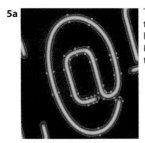

The subpath for the @ sign is selected with the Path Selection tool ▶.

5b

The @ sign is cut to the clipboard, a new path is started, and the cut subpath is pasted into it.

5c

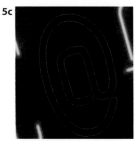

With the new path active, adding a Solid Color Fill layer automatically creates a vector mask.

5d

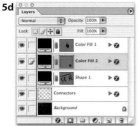

After cutting the arrow cursor to a separate layer also, we copied and pasted the Layer Style and then modified the pasted Styles.

5e

To paste a Style to more than one layer at a time in Photoshop CS2, click the thumbnail of one, Ctrl/⌘-click or Shift-click to target the others as well, and then choose Paste Layer Style.

In the Layers palette, click on the vector mask thumbnail for the Shape layer with the graphic, and then use the Path Selection tool ▶ to click on the individual subpath you want to move to another layer (Shift-click to choose more than one subpath at a time) **5a**. Use the Edit > Cut command (Ctrl/⌘-X) to remove the path from the document and store it on the clipboard. In the Paths palette, click the "Create new path" button ▣, then Edit > Paste (Ctrl/⌘-V) the artwork you just cut to make a new path **5b**.

With the pasted path still active (highlighted in the Paths palette), add a Solid Color Fill layer by clicking the "Create new fill or adjustment layer" button ⏺ at the bottom of the Layers palette, choosing Solid Color from the pop-up list, and clicking "OK." When the Color Picker opens, you can just click "OK" to close it, since the color doesn't matter — our neon Layer Style's Inner Glow in Normal mode will hide any native color. The new layer that's added to the file has a vector mask made from the subpath you cut and pasted **5c**. Repeat the process of cutting and pasting a subpath and then adding a new Fill layer to make as many separate layers as you want separate neon colors. We added another new layer for the arrow cursor.

Rather than build new Layer Styles for the different colors of neon from scratch, it makes sense to copy, paste, and modify the one we already have. Start by right/Ctrl-clicking the ⏺ icon to the right of the name of the original Shape layer and choosing Copy Layer Style from the context-sensitive menu. Then for each of your other neon layers, in Photoshop CS right/Ctrl-click to the right of the layer's name and choose Paste Layer Style **5d**. In CS 2 you can paste a Style to several layers at once **5e**. To change the neon color for a layer, double-click the ⏺ that appears to the right of the layer's name to open the Layer Style dialog, where you can open the panel for each of the Style's effects in turn and change colors. The result is shown at the top of page 546, and you'll find our changes in **Neon Glow-After.psd**, where you can double-click the ⏺ icon for the yellow and green neon layers and explore the effects. *Wow!*

FX: Wow Actions

The **Wow-Graphix Enhance Actions** are "miniprograms" designed to give type or graphics a "special effects" treatment that's more complex than you can achieve with a Layer Style. You interact with each Wow-Graphix Enhance Action as it runs, if only to make sure that your file is configured the way the Action expects — as a two-layer file with the graphics or type on the top, active layer and an image layer on the bottom, though the "image" can be a pattern or gradient instead of a picture.

 FX.psd

If you haven't yet installed the **Wow Actions,** do that now (see page 5). Then open the Actions palette (Window > Actions) and open the palette's menu ⊙ and choose the **Wow-Graphix Enhance Actions** set.

To run an Action, click its name in the Actions palette and click the "Play selection" button ▶ at the bottom of the palette. (If your Actions palette is set to Button mode, simply click the Action's button to start running it.)

Whenever a "Stop" message appears during an Action, read and follow its instructions — the Action needs your undivided attention at this point to ensure the expected results.

Each Action produces a layered file, so you can customize the results.

YOU'LL FIND THE FILES
in > Wow Project Files > Chapter 8 > Quick FX

Wow-Silvery

IN THE **WOW-SILVERY** ACTION, as in the -Golden, -Streaked Metal, -Streaked Steel, and -Oily Steel Actions, the Lighting Effects filter adds dimension, using a blurred copy of the graphics, and creates an initial play of light. After you try out the settings built into the Action by running it on the **FX.psd** file or a file of your own, you might want to choose File > Revert and run it again, this time making some changes when the Lighting Effects dialog opens — such as rearranging the lights (by dragging their center points) to change which parts of the graphics are highlighted.

In the finished layered file, you can alter the effect by changing the blend mode or Opacity of the "Graphic Wrapped" layer. Or change the Color Balance settings as described for Wow-Golden at the right.

Wow-Golden

IN THE **WOW-GOLDEN** ACTION the metal qualities are added to the graphics with a Lighting Effects treatment and a Layer Style. Then a Color Balance Adjustment layer is applied to enhance the color. The gold color can be altered after running the Action: In the Layers palette double-click the thumbnail for the Color Balance layer and use the three check boxes and sliders to change the color for Highlights, Midtones, and Shadows.▼

FIND OUT MORE

▼ Using Color Balance **page 166**

Note: The **Wow Graphix Enhance** Actions are designed to create their special effects and still leave any type or vector graphics "live" and intact. Some of them duplicate the graphics layer before rasterizing it. Others duplicate the entire file and run the Action on a copy. For safekeeping, though, it's always a good idea to run an Action on a duplicate of a file rather than on the original.

Wow-Streaked Metal

THE **WOW-STREAKED METAL** Action adds a "burnished" metal surface with rounded edges. To do this it adds a layer in Overlay mode, filled with Overlay-neutral 50% gray. The Noise filter adds the raw material that the Motion Blur filter then turns into streaks.

Note: Some of the Wow-Graphix Enhance Actions make use of Photoshop filters whose parameters are set as numbers of pixels. If your graphics are much larger or smaller than ours (our file is 1000 pixels wide), you may get different results. "Examining an Action" on page 554 has pointers for changing the filter settings to work with your file.

Wow-Streaked Steel

THE **WOW-STREAKED STEEL** Action adds a sharply detailed "brushed" surface that doesn't extend into the beveled edges. The bevel's size and its protection from the texture are controlled by three steps, which you can locate if you click the tiny arrow in front of the Action's name in the Actions palette and scan the list. The first "Gaussian Blur" step creates dimension (the second one simply smooths the edges). Later in the Action the two "Contract" steps are important in making a clean edge. To change the width of the beveled edge, enter different values in the dialog boxes for these commands, as follows: Click in the "Toggle dialog on/off" box to the left of each of the commands. Then play the Action, and when these dialog boxes open, enter your own values. For **Gaussian Blur** enter a larger value for a wider bevel, or a smaller value for a narrower one. For a smooth trim that doesn't let the brushed texture spill onto the bevel, we set the **first Contract value** at 1 pixel less than the Gaussian Blur setting and **the second Contract** value at 1 pixel more.

CHANGING THE BACKGROUND

After you run a Wow Action, you may want to change the background for your creation or move the creation itself into a different file. Here are some ways to make those kinds of changes:

• Change the background image by targeting the bottom layer of your file and then dragging and dropping a different background into the file.

• If you "package" the layered results of your Action by enclosing them in a layer set/group, you can duplicate the set/group into another file.

To make a layer set in Photoshop CS, target one of the layers by clicking its thumbnail in the Layers palette; then click in the Links column (next to the 👁) for each of the other layers you want to move (perhaps all the layers or all but the background image); finally, from the palette menu ⊙, choose New Set From Linked.

In CS2's Layers palette, Ctrl/⌘-click the names of the layers you want to include; from the palette menu ⊙ choose New Group From Layers.

Now you can simply drag and drop the entire folder to move the "package" to another file.

• Instead of moving the layered result, you can merge it to one layer before dragging and dropping. With the layer set/group targeted in the Layers palette, duplicate it (to preserve the layers in your original file) by choosing Duplicate Layer Set/Group from the palette's menu ⊙. Then type Ctrl/⌘-E to merge the set/group into a single layer.

Wow-Oily Steel

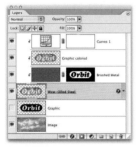

THE **WOW-OILY STEEL** ACTION is similar to Wow-Streaked Steel, with a couple of interesting differences. The "oil slick" colors result from the combination of the more saturated color in the "Graphic colored" layer and differences in the Curves Adjustment layer — the curve itself is a different shape, and the layer is applied in Normal mode rather than Luminosity mode, which is used in the Wow-Streaked Steel result.

In the **Wow-Oily Steel** result, the brushed texture is cleared from the bevel edges, but the color is not. You can remove the color from the bevel with a layer mask: In the Layers palette, Ctrl/⌘-click the mask thumbnail for the "Brushed Metal" layer to load it as a selection. Then invert the selection (Ctrl/⌘-Shift-I), target the Curves layer by clicking its thumbnail, and fill the selection with black (Edit > Fill > Use Black).

Wow-Chromed

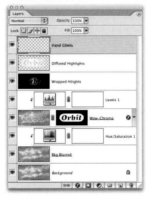

THE **WOW-CHROMED** ACTION uses the "image" layer to create a reflection on the surface of the chrome. It produces a result similar to the examples in "Variations" on page 530. As you run the Action, when the Glass filter's dialog box opens, you're asked to load the **Displace.psd** file (which the Action will have made for you) as the Texture.

In the finished file, the "Bkg Blurred" layer and the "Hue/Saturation 1" Adjustment layer that colors it are used simply to make a dark contrasting background for the chrome. The color was chosen to match highlight and shadow colors used in the Layer Style. You can replace the blurred and colored background as described in "Changing the Background" on page 552.

Wow-Crystal

THE **WOW-CRYSTAL** ACTION simulates both reflected light at the surface and refracted light inside the crystal object. Run the Action, and then try changing the material characteristics of the object by changing the blend mode of the "Reflection" layer to one of the other "contrast" modes (the ones grouped with Overlay in the Layers palette's blend modes list) or to Screen or Multiply.▼

FIND OUT MORE

▼ Blend modes
page 174

Also try reducing the Fill opacity for the "Wow-Crystal" layer; this makes the object more translucent without reducing the glow at the edges that simulates light passing through the crystal.

Wow-Distressed

THE **WOW-DISTRESSED** ACTION can be used to "roughen" type or graphics before applying a Layer Style, such as **Wow-Heavy Rust** from the **Wow-Metals Styles**.

SLOWING THE PACE

By default Photoshop runs Actions faster than it can show you what's happening. But if you want to see each step as it happens, open the Actions palette's menu ⊙, choose **Playback Options**, and set the Performance to **Step by Step** or **Pause For** 1 or 2 seconds.

Wow-Fire

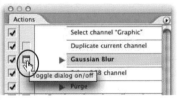 **FX2 files**

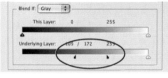

THE **WOW-FIRE** ACTION adds stylized flames around the edges of the type or graphics. Here we've also run it on a black "i" shape. To bring some flame in front of the "i," after running the Action we double-clicked the thumbnail for "Layer 1" in the Layers palette and worked with the "Underlying Layer" black slider, holding down the Alt/Option key to split the slider.▼ We also increased the Size and Spread of the Inner Glow.

Wow-Fire is an interesting Action to observe step-by-step for its use of filters (see "Slowing the Pace" at the left).

EXAMINING AN ACTION

To play an Action one step at a time so you can explore what each step does before going on to the next one, first expand the list to show all the steps by clicking the tiny arrow in front of the Action's name in the Actions palette. Then target the first step by clicking on it; hold down the Ctrl/⌘ key and click the "Play selection" button ▶ at the bottom of the palette. The single step will be carried out, the next step will be targeted, and the Action will stop and wait. Continue to Ctrl/⌘-click the ▶ button to carry out each step. You can see the settings for any step that has a tiny triangle in front of its name by clicking the triangle to expand the list of settings.

If you'd like to change the settings inside the dialog box for a step you just played, type Ctrl/⌘-Z to undo the step, then click in the "Toggle dialog on/off" box for that step, if needed, to add a dialog box icon for that step.

At the bottom of the palette, Ctrl/⌘-click the ▶ button again, and the dialog box will open. Any changes you make inside the dialog will be carried out in this run of the Action, but the Action itself won't incorporate the changes for future use. To do that, you need to edit the Action by recording the changes.▼

FIND OUT MORE

▼ Working with "Blend If" **page 70**
▼ Editing Actions **page 115**

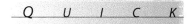

Backgrounds & Textures

Photoshop gives you a magician's kit of filters, patterns, and Layer Styles — all great places to start when you're looking for some "raw material" to support a concept or extend an image. With these tools you can invent patterns and textures out of thin air, either for making backgrounds or for turning plain flat type or graphics into believable solid objects. On the next seven pages are some examples to get you started.

Before you begin, be sure to load the **Wow Presets** (at least the Patterns and Gradients) as described on page 5.

In addition to the methods shown here, using a pattern in a Layer Style — as both the Pattern Overlay effect and the Texture for the Bevel and Emboss effect — can generate some great surface textures. "Anatomy of 'Bumpy'" on page 522 shows exactly how this works.

FIND OUT MORE

▼ Using Gradient Map **page 208**
▼ The Gradient Editor **page 161**
▼ Using Lighting Effects **page 259**

Marble

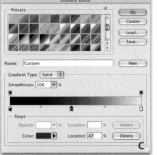

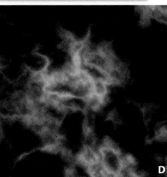

THE MORE YOU RUN the **Difference Clouds** filter, the less "cloudlike" the result becomes, and it can be the source of some great marble and stone backgrounds: In the white-filled *Background* of an RGB file, with black and white as the Foreground and Background colors, choose Filter > Render > Difference Clouds **A**. Then press **Ctrl/⌘-F** repeatedly to rerun the filter and build the veins for the degree of marbling you want **B**.

One way to color the marble is to click the "Create new fill or adjustment layer" button ⬤ at the bottom of the Layers palette and choose Gradient Map. Click the gradient bar to open the Gradient Editor, and design a gradient to color your marble **C**. ▼

Rougher Rock

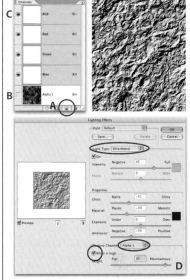

YOU CAN GENERATE a variety of stone surfaces by starting with the **Clouds** filter or the **Difference Clouds** filter as used in "Marble" at the left, and then applying the **Lighting Effects** filter to "emboss" and color the surface. Start a new RGB file (Ctrl/⌘-N) with a white *Background*. In the Channels palette, add a new channel (Alpha 1) by clicking the "Create new channel" button ⬛ **A**. With this new channel active, choose Filter > Render > Difference Clouds. Repeat the filter (Ctrl/⌘-F) until you get a light/dark pattern that you like **B**, keeping in mind that the dark areas will make depressions and crevices and the light areas will make "hills."

Then activate the composite RGB channel again (Ctrl/⌘-~) **C**, and choose Filter > Render > Lighting Effects **D**. Set up the Lighting Effects dialog box with a Directional light, and choose colors in the Light Type and Properties sections. ▼ In the Texture Channel menu, choose "Alpha 1" and turn on White Is High. To develop the surface, work with the position and Intensity of the light source as well as the Properties settings.

CLOUDY SKIES

Filter > Render > Clouds creates clouds and sky. By itself, the result isn't necessarily convincing. But to add clouds to a background sky, try running the Clouds filter on a layer above the image, using a blue that you sample from the sky as the Foreground color and white as the Background color. If you first make a mask to reveal the sky area only (for instance, by clicking on the blue sky with the Magic Wand ✦ and then clicking the "Add a layer mask" button ◻ at the bottom of the Layers palette), you can watch the sky develop as you type Ctrl/⌘-F to rerun the filter to generate a new array of clouds. You can also change the blend mode and Opacity of the clouds layer to suit. Or paint the mask with black to diminish the clouds: Choose the Brush tool ✎, black paint, and a large, soft brush tip, set at low Opacity.▼

PETER CARLISLE

Noise to Metal

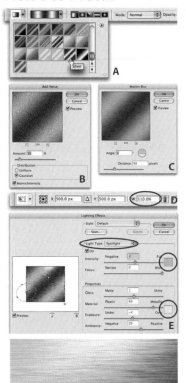

THE ADD NOISE FILTER can be a starting point for streaks to simulate brushed metal. Start from scratch with a white *Background*, or use the Gradient tool ◻ and a metallic gradient to establish a base sheen; we used Adobe's **Silver** gradient from the **Metals** Gradient presets **A**, dragging diagonally across a layer.▼

To start the texture use Filter > Noise > Add Noise **B**. Then convert the noise to streaks with Filter > Blur > Motion Blur **C**; we made horizontal streaks (Angle 0°, Distance 50 pixels). Because Motion Blur leaves odd edges, we next used the Edit > Transform command (Ctrl/⌘-T) and set the Width in the Options bar to 110% **D**, then clicked the ✔ to commit the transform. For color and shine, we used Filter > Render > Lighting Effects, with colored Spotlights **E**.▼

MIXED METALS

For some interesting metallic luster effects, try using the Gradient tool ◻ to apply Adobe's Metal gradients on two different layers and at two slightly different angles, with or without Transparency (you can turn Transparency on or off in the Options bar when the Gradient tool is active). In the Layers palette, set the blend mode for the upper layer to Overlay, Soft Light, or another blend mode, as shown below.

FIND OUT MORE

▼ Using the Brush ✎
page 361
▼ Using Gradients
page 160
▼ Using Lighting
Effects **page 259**

Noise to Paper

A
B

C

D

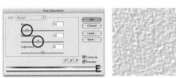

E

TO MAKE ROUGH PAPER or wall surfaces, create a new file (File > New) with a white *Background.* Generate some noise (Filter > Noise > **Add Noise**) at a low setting **A**. Then blur the result slightly — we used Filter > Blur > **Gaussian Blur B**. Next, emboss the noise pattern (Filter > Stylize > **Emboss**) **C**.

With the texture defined, it's easy to adjust tone and color by using Adjustment layers or choices from the Image > Adjustments menu, but using Adjustment layers offers more flexibility. We used a **Levels** Adjustment layer to whiten the paper **D** and then added a **Hue/Saturation** Adjustment layer with the **Colorize** option turned on to tint our surface **E**.

Texturizing

A

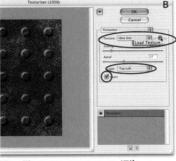

B

THE **TEXTURIZER** FILTER (Filter > Texture > Texturizer) can be used to create surface relief. This filter lacks the full "lighting studio" sophistication of the Lighting Effects filter — its single light source is directional. But it can load any Photoshop (**.psd**) file as a repeating embossing texture. You can Scale your pattern down to 50% or up to 200%, so you can control how many times it repeats. To get a smaller pattern with more repetitions, start with a texture file that's smaller in relation to your background image. To get a rounder edge, apply a slight Gaussian Blur to the texture file before you run the Texturizer filter.

Here we started with a small file with a single dot on a transparent layer **A**; it was made with the Brush tool and black paint, with a 45-pixel brush tip with Hardness set at 50% in the pop-out Brush Preset picker in the Options bar, and the file was then saved in .psd format (File > Save). To texturize our rust image **B**, we clicked the dialog's ⊙ button, chose Load Texture, and loaded the One Dot.psd file as the Texture. We chose Top Left for the Light setting and turned on the **Invert** option, since the filter raises white elements by default, and ours was black.

TEXTURES TO GO

The Textures files that Adobe supplies (installed in the Presets folder in your Photoshop application folder) make good "bump maps" for creating surface relief for the Texturizer filter to act on.

Some of the files in the Textures folder are already in the **.psd** format required by Texturizer. Others are in **.jpg** format, but to be able to use them with Texturizer (as well as Displace▼ and other filters that use .psd files for creating and enhancing textures), all you have to do is open them in Photoshop and resave them in .psd (Photoshop) format.

To use Textures with Texturizer (as described in "Texturizing" at the left), choose Filter > Render > Texturizer, click on the ⊙ button to the right of the dialog box's Texture menu, and choose Load Texture. Navigate to the Textures folder (or whatever folder you have that contains suitable files in .psd format), choose a texture, and click the "Load" button.

FIND OUT MORE

▼ Using the Displace filter **page 544**

Embossing a Pattern

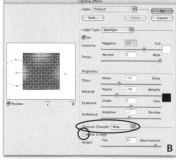

A **PATTERN PRESET** can be a great resource for creating a surface texture. You can generate the dimensionality you need by running the **Lighting Effects** filter using one of the color channels (Red, Green, or Blue) as the Texture Channel. The Lighting Effects filter lets you blend the effects of several kinds and colors of lights with the environmental ambience. We made our textured bricks by filling a layer with the **Wow-Brick** preset Pattern fill (from the **Wow Misc Surface** patterns); to do this choose Edit > **Fill** > Use Pattern and choose Wow-Brick **A**. Then we chose Filter > Render > Lighting Effects, and set the Light Style and Properties parameters **B**.▼ We established a blue Directional light from the upper left and added three white Spotlights. We chose the **Blue channel** as the Texture Channel because it showed good contrast. We made sure White Is High was set appropriately — off in this case, since we wanted the light-colored mortar to recede **C** — and clicked "OK."

Resurfacing

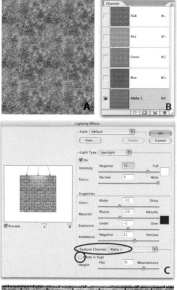

TO KEEP the basic brick structure but change the material, we opened a new file and filled it with **Wow-Sandstone** from the **Wow-Misc Surface** patterns **A**. To get the Wow-Bricks into a channel we could use with Lighting Effects, we added an **alpha channel** (by clicking the "Create new channel" button ▣ at the bottom of the Channels palette) and filled it with **Wow-Brick** (Edit > **Fill** > Use Pattern) **B**. Now we targeted the sandstone image again (by clicking the thumbnail for the RGB composite at the top of the Channels palette) and chose Filter > Render > **Lighting Effects C**.▼ For a golden color with fairly uniform lighting, we used a warm-colored Directional light and one soft Spotlight. As the Texture Channel we chose "Alpha 1," our brick pattern, turning off White Is High **D**.

FIND OUT MORE

▼ Using Lighting Effects **page 259**

Whitening the Mortar

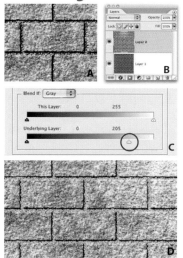

IN THE "SANDSTONE BRICK" created in "Resurfacing" (at the left), the mortar is the same color as the stone **A**. To bring back the white mortar, we would add a layer below the sandstone, filled with the brick pattern, and allow the white mortar of this layer to show through the sandstone brick layer above. The sandstone was a *Background,* so we had to first turn it into a regular layer (by double-clicking its thumbnail in the Layers palette and clicking "OK" in the New Layer dialog). Then we could add the new layer (Ctrl/⌘-clicking the Layers palette's "Create new layer" button ▣ adds a layer *below* the current layer). We filled this layer with the brick pattern **B**; at this point it was entirely hidden by the sandstone bricks in the layer above.

We double-clicked the thumbnail for the sandstone layer to target the layer and open the Layer Style dialog. In the **"Blend If"** section we moved the "Underlying Layer" white point slider inward to 205 **C**, which kept the sandstone layer from covering up anything in the brick layer that was very light, allowing the lightest mortar to show through **D**.

Fibers to "Nubby"

THE **FIBERS** FILTER can be a good start for carpet and nubby fabrics. When you choose Filter > Render > Fibers, the Fibers dialog offers two sliders — Variance and Strength. When Variance and Strength are set low, the fibers generated are long and very fine — so fine that you can't really see the separate fibers. As you increase Variance, the fibers can get shorter; and as you increase Strength, the contrast between fibers increases and you can see the individual fibers better as they get "thicker."

To create a nubby fabric, with short, dense fibers, we first started a new file and set black and white as the Foreground and Background colors (type D). We opened the Fibers dialog and set Variance as high as possible (64) and Strength as low as possible (1) **A**, and clicked "OK" to close the dialog box. To color the "carpet," we added a Color Fill Layer (by clicking the "Create new fill or adjustment layer" button ⊘ at the bottom of the Layers palette) and changed its blend mode to Color **B**.

Fibers to Wood

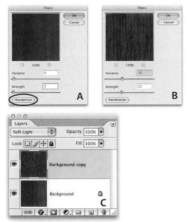

THE **FIBERS** FILTER can create a subtle or dramatic woodgrain surface. We clicked the Foreground swatch in the Tools palette and chose a dark reddish brown, and then clicked the Background swatch and chose a pale reddish brown. We opened a new file and chose Filter > Render > Fibers and used very low settings (Variance 4 and Strength 3) for long, fine streaks, clicking the "Randomize" button until we had a smooth mix of colors **A**. We then duplicated the layer (Ctrl/⌘-J) and ran the Fibers filter at settings of 23 and 22 this time, for a rougher effect **B**. (The new fibers completely replaced the old in this layer.) Then we blended the two versions by putting the upper layer in Soft Light mode **C**; blending in this way can produce a more complex and realistic grain than using a single layer.

Customizing the Wood

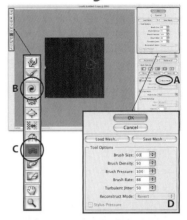

TO ADD MORE CHARACTER to the grain, we first made a merged copy of the two Fibers-treated layers so we would have a single layer to use with the Liquify filter; to make a merged layer, hold down Ctrl-Alt-Shift (Windows) or ⌘-Option-Shift (Mac) and type N, then E (in CS2, you can skip the N).

We chose Filter > Liquify, and turned off visibility for the Mesh **A** so we could see the grain better. We used the Twirl **B** and Turbulence **C** tools to simulate wood grain, adjusting the Brush Size frequently for variation **D**. We didn't worry about working close to the edges and creating a little transparency on the layer, since the layers below would fill any "holes" this might create.▼

FIND OUT MORE

▼ The Liquify filter
page 616

Fibers to Weave

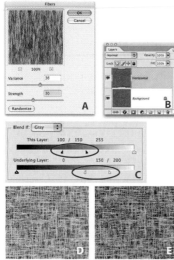

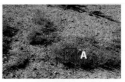

THE **FIBERS** FILTER can also generate rough meshes and weaves. To control the contrast, we started with a light gray and dark gray (set by clicking the Foreground and Background squares and choosing from the Color Picker). To produce a set of vertical threads, we chose Filter > Render > Fibers and set the Variance fairly high (38) for fairly short fibers, thinking it would be easier to achieve a woven appearance that way. We set Strength at 30; with the high Variance setting this Strength would produce fibers that were thin to medium-thick **A**. We duplicated the layer (Ctrl/⌘-J) and rotated the duplicate (Edit > Transform > Rotate 90° CW, pressing the Enter key) **B**. To get these horizontal threads to interact with the vertical ones, we double-clicked the top layer's thumbnail (for Layer > Layer Style > Blending Options) and worked with the "Blend If" sliders, holding down the Alt/Option key to split the sliders for smooth transitions **C**, **D**. We then added a Color Balance Adjustment layer (by clicking the ⬤ button and choosing) and used the sliders in the Color Balance dialog to tint highlights, midtones, and shadows **E**.

Weave to Pattern

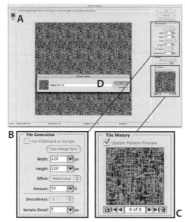

ONE OF THE THINGS Photoshop's **Pattern Maker** filter can do is to generate wallpaper- or fabric-style patterns (with obvious repeats) based on a selection from an image. We used it with a weave from "Fibers to Weave" (at the left) to generate a series of more complex woven patterns **A**. First we made a duplicate of the file we wanted to make the pattern from (Image > Duplicate, choosing Duplicate Merged Layers Only). In the new file we chose Filter > Pattern Maker. In the Pattern Maker dialog, we Shift-dragged to select a square area to repeat. In Pattern Maker, the selection size, Tile Size, Sample Detail, and Offset, as well as the random factor behind the "Generate" button, all determine the pattern. In the File Generation section **B** we set Tile Size to 128 pixels square and Sample Detail as low as possible (at 3; higher settings preserve large features within the selection but take longer to render). We set a 50% Vertical Offset, and clicked the "Generate" button; the preview window filled with pattern. Clicking the "Save Pattern Preset" button at the bottom of the dialog box **C** lets you name and save a pattern you like **D** before you hit the "Generate Again" button to try a new one. You can use the arrow buttons to review recent patterns; saving any you decide to keep.

Textures from Photos

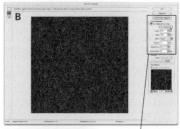

BESIDES MAKING PATTERNS with an obvious repeat (as in "Weave to Pattern" at the left), the **Pattern Maker** filter is great for filling an entire layer with a *non*repeating background texture made from a selected area of an image. You can either replace the content of your source layer with the background fill, or you can copy your source material from one file or layer, and create the fill in another. Here we started with a clump of grass selected in one photo **A** by Shift-dragging the Rectangular Marquee [ ], with Feather set at 0 in the Options bar; we copied the selection to the clipboard (Ctrl/⌘-C).

We opened a new file and chose Filter > Pattern Maker **B**. We clicked to turn on the **"Use Clipboard as Sample"** option, and also clicked on the **"Use Image Size"** button (to generate a fill that wouldn't repeat within the size of the image) **C**. When we clicked the "Generate" button, the preview filled with grass. We could look at more options by clicking "Generate Again" and save those we wanted, as described at the left.

Color Blends

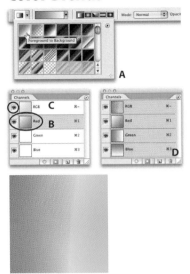

FOR A BACKGROUND of free-flowing color, create an RGB file with a white *Background* (File > New). In the Tools palette choose the Gradient tool ▭.▼ For pastel colors, choose gray and white for the Foreground and Background colors (type D and then click the black Foreground swatch and choose a gray; for brighter colors, use the default black and white.) In the Options bar for the Gradient tool, choose the Foreground to Background swatch **A**.

In the Channels palette (Window > Channels) click on one of the color channels — we started with Red **B** — and also click in the Visibility column of the RGB channel (to the left of the top thumbnail) **C** so you can see the color as it develops. Now drag diagonally across the working window to make a gradient in the Red channel (you can see this gradient in the Red thumbnail in the Channels palette, but the effect in the working window is a color ramp). After drawing the Red diagonal, we targeted the Green channel and filled it with a horizontal left-to-right gradient, then the Blue channel with a top-to-bottom gradient **D**.

Filtered Color

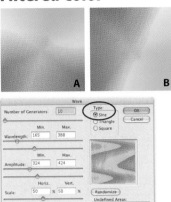

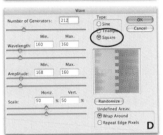

ONCE YOU HAVE a color blend (left), you can modify the color with an Adjustment layer. Adding a Hue/Saturation layer and moving the Hue slider creates rotating wedges of color **A**, **B**. Or duplicate the color-filled layer and run a filter. We used Filter > Distort > Wave in Sine mode **C** and Square mode **D**, and experimented with Filter > Distort > Glass followed by Filter > Distort > Twirl **E**. Applying this color as a layer in Overlay mode, or one of the other modes in the Overlay group, can provide an interesting way to tint a background image.

FIND OUT MORE

▼ Gradients **page 160**
▼ Noise Gradients **page 189**
▼ Patterns **page 562**

Noise Gradient Plaids

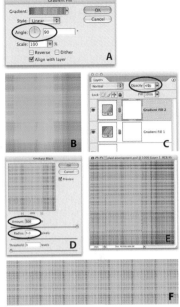

TO MAKE A **PLAID**, we opened a new file and added a Gradient Fill layer (by clicking the "Create new fill or adjustment layer" button ◑ at the bottom of the Layers palette and choosing Gradient). We chose a Noise gradient **A**, left the **Angle at the default 90°**, and clicked "OK" to close the dialog box.▼ We duplicated the layer (**Ctrl/⌘-J**) and in the Layers palette double-clicked the thumbnail for the new layer, to reopen the Gradient Fill dialog; there we set the **Angle at 0°** and clicked "OK." In the Layers palette we then reduced the Opacity of this second layer until we liked the blend **B**, **C**.

We made a merged copy (one way is to click the ▣ button at the bottom of the Layers palette and type Ctrl-Alt-E in Windows or ⌘-Option-E on the Mac); we sharpened the merged copy heavily **D**. Then we Shift-dragged with the Rectangular Marquee ⬚ to select a square area as the repeat for the design **E**, and chose Edit > Define Pattern to make a seamless pattern we could apply elsewhere **F**.▼

Seamless Patterns

With the myriad ways to use patterns in Photoshop, it's good to know how to generate your own. If you want to turn an image (such as one of those from "Quick Backgrounds & Textures" on page 555) into a seamlessly tiling pattern, you need to first assess the seams that would be generated if you simply defined the entire image as the pattern tile. Then, if necessary, choose a method for hiding the seams.

Some kinds of pattern images will be seamless automatically. For instance, the plaid created on page 561 consists of lines that extend straight from left to right and from top to bottom, so the edges automatically line up perfectly when the pattern tile is repeated. Other examples are the "Joy" pattern and its "relatives" (assembled from graphic elements, on page 39 and page 572) and the design created in "Creating an Obvious Repeat" on page 565. Most pattern material, however, even with fine-grained textures like the rock pattern from page 555 and the paper pattern from page 557, requires some editing to hide the seams between tiles.

Once you've assessed the seams as described at the right, use one of the three methods on the next two pages (blending, healing, or patching) to remove the seams. Then recheck for seams and do further hiding if necessary. Finally, define the altered image as a pattern tile, as in "Defining & Applying Patterns" on page 565.

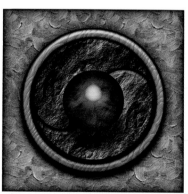

To make the illustration above, patterns were applied to graphics layers as the Pattern Overlay and Texture components of Layer Styles. Open the file to explore the patterns or to capture them for your own use, as described on page 565.

wow Seamless Patterns.psd

YOU'LL FIND THE FILES
in **wow** > Wow Project Files > Chapter 8 > Quick Seamless Patterns

Assessing the Seam

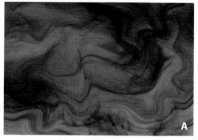

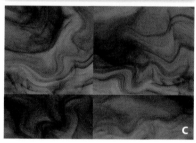

TO MAKE A PATTERN TILE, you'll need a **single-layer file** that includes only the area you want to use for the tile; here we've used a 300-pixel-high file. If your file is multilayer or if you want to use less than the entire image as your pattern tile, duplicate the file (Image > Duplicate, turning on Duplicate Merged Layers Only if it's available); in the duplicate file, if you want to use only part of the image, choose the Rectangular Marquee ⌞⌝, drag to select the area for your tile, and choose Image > Crop.

Next use the **Offset filter** to find out how bad the seam would be if you did nothing to hide it **B**: Choose Filter > Other > Offset and enter pixel dimensions for Horizontal and Vertical that are roughly a third to half the width and height of your file; set the Undefined Areas to Wrap Around and click "OK" to run the filter. Any unmatched "seams" will now be shifted to the interior and will be plainly visible near the middle of your image **C**. If you don't see any seams, you can go directly to "Defining & Applying Patterns" (page 565). Otherwise, choose one of the three seam-removal methods on the next two pages, depending on the nature of your developing pattern tile.

Blending the Edges

IF YOUR IMAGE IS FLUID and amorphous like the one on the facing page, the "Marble" from page 555, or the wood from page 559, you may be able to hide the seams by blending the edges with the Tile Maker filter. If you did the test with the Offset filter (on the facing page), undo the offset (press Ctrl/⌘-Z or Edit > Step Backward). If your image is a *Background*, convert it to a regular layer **A** (double-click its name in the Layers palette and click "OK" in the New Layer dialog box).

To run the Tile Maker, choose Filter > Other > **Tile Maker** (if you don't see Tile Maker in the Filter > Other submenu, see the "Loading Tile Maker" tip at the right). In the Tile Maker dialog box, make sure **Blend Edges** is chosen **B**. This option will blend material from the right edge of the image into the left edge and vice versa, and will do the same for the top and bottom edges, resulting in a tile whose edges show no seams when repeated. The **Width** determines how far into the image the blending will extend **C**; the default 10% is often enough to make a good blend without consuming too much of the image. (The "Resize Tile To Fill Image" option can be turned off. Turning it off will make a tile that's a little smaller than the original, because of the overlap the filter uses to blend the edges. But with it turned on, the image is enlarged slightly to make up for the overlap, and this often causes overall blurring.) Click "OK" to complete the filtering **D**.

Eliminate any empty space at the edges by choosing Image > **Trim** and trimming the **Transparent Pixels** from all four sides **E, F**. Check for seams by running the Offset filter again if you like, and proceed to "Defining & Applying Patterns." Here we've used it to fill a 500-pixel square **G**.

LOADING TILE MAKER

The Tile Maker filter that comes with ImageReady is designed for making seamlessly tiling patterns for web page backgrounds. But you can also use it in Photoshop. Locate the Tile maker plug-in (in the Adobe Photoshop CS or CS2 > Plug-ins > Adobe ImageReady Only > Filters folder) and drag the icon into the Filters folder (Adobe Photoshop CS or CS2 > Plug-ins > Filters), which holds plug-ins that are shared by Photoshop and ImageReady; then restart Photoshop. Now you'll find Tile Maker in the Filter > Other submenu.

TILE MAKER'S OTHER MODE

The Tile Maker filter offers two ways to create tiles: Blend Edges (described in "Blending the Edges" at the left) and Kaleidoscope Tile. The Kaleidoscope Tile option makes a tile from multiple reflections of a selected area of an image, or from the entire image if there's no active selection. Working with a duplicate of your image file, select an area with the Rectangular Marquee [ ]. Choose Filter > Other > Tile Maker, and in the Tile Maker dialog box, choose Kaleidoscope Tile and click "OK."

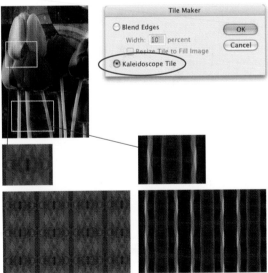

Two pattern tiles were made from rectangular selections in the image above, using Tile Maker's Kaleidoscope Tile option. Each was then defined as a pattern (Edit > Define Pattern) and used with the Edit > Fill command.

"Healing" the Seam

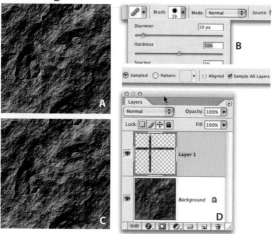

IF THE TEXTURE in your image is quite random and "fine-grained," after running the Offset filter **A** (page 562) you can probably hide the seam by "healing" it. To make it easier to fix any mistakes you might make in the seam-hiding process, add an empty "repairs" layer (Ctrl/⌘-Shift-N). Choose the Healing Brush 🖌 and in the Options bar **B**, set the Mode to Normal, and turn on Use/Sample All Layers. Open the Brush picker (click the tiny triangle to the right of the brush footprint); for our seam we used a 19-pixel brush with Hardness set at 50%.

To sample and paint, hold down the Alt/Option key and click somewhere away from the vertical seam and near (but not right at) the top edge of the image to "load" the tool with "source" image material; then release the Alt/Option key and click on the seam at about the same height as you sampled. Shift-click near (but not right at) the bottom of the vertical seam to "paint" a straight stroke that covers the seam. Repeat the process for the horizontal seam **C**. Inspect the repairs for obvious edges or repeating elements. If you see any, you can use the Eraser 🖉 or Lasso ⚲ to remove a mistake, or simply use the Healing Brush 🖌 to Alt/Option-click away from the seam to sample, and then click on the seam to "dab" over the problem area.

Flatten the file (Layer > Flatten Image), run the Offset filter again with the same settings as in "Assessing the Seam" on page 562, and again check for seams in the middle (there shouldn't be any if you were able to stay away from the edges). If any subtle corrections are needed, use the Healing Brush 🖌 on another repairs layer to make them, and again flatten the image. When the image is "seamless," proceed to "Defining & Applying Patterns."

FIND OUT MORE

▼ Smart Objects
page 39

Copying Bits & Pieces

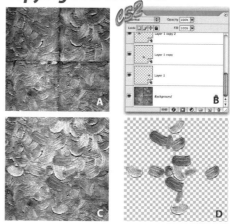

IF YOUR IMAGE **A** is a texture that isn't especially fine-grained and doesn't lend itself to blended edges, the best way to cover the seam may be to select, copy, and overlay parts of the image. This method often works well for photos of discrete items, from pebbles to cherries, clouds, or brush strokes. Start by selecting a feature; we used the Lasso ⚲ to select one of the paint dabs in our scan of a hand-painted canvas. Then copy the selected element to a new "patch" layer (Ctrl/⌘-J); if you're working in Photoshop CS2, you can turn this layer into a Smart Object to protect it from blurring in case you want to copy and transform it again. ▼ Use the Free Transform command (Ctrl/⌘-T) and drag the element over the seam (try to keep your "patch" from touching an edge of the image). You can also rotate, scale, or flip the patch by right/Ctrl-clicking inside the Transform box and choosing from the menu of transform options, then dragging on a handle; be careful not to change the apparent direction of the light for the copied element in a way that would clash with the lighting in the original image; press the Enter key to complete the transformation. You can now duplicate this element (Ctrl/⌘-J) and move and transform the new copy to cover another part of the seam. If you use the same selected element too many times, the repair will be obvious, and unless you've made it into a Smart Object, the element can become blurred from repeated transforming. So instead you can target the original image layer again by clicking its thumbnail in the Layer palette, then make another selection, copy it to a new layer, and so on. When your seam is hidden **B**, **C**, **D**, flatten the file (Layer > Flatten Image) and run the Offset filter again with the same settings as in "Assessing the Seam" on page 562 to check for new seams. If necessary create more "patches," and flatten the file again. Then proceed to "Defining & Applying Patterns."

Defining & Applying Patterns

ONCE YOU'VE PREPARED AN IMAGE for use as a pattern tile, choose Edit > **Define Pattern A**, name it in the Pattern Name dialog box **B**, and click "OK." Your new pattern will appear as the last pattern swatch anywhere the Patterns palette appears in Photoshop.

You can now apply the pattern as a **Pattern Fill layer C**, an effect in a **Layer Style D**, the "paint" for the Pattern Stamp tool, or a fill for a regular layer or a selection (with the **Edit > Fill** command). See Appendix C for more.

"CAPTURING" A PATTERN

Any pattern that's used in a Pattern Fill layer or a Layer Style can easily be "captured" and added to the Patterns palette for use elsewhere. To capture a pattern, the first thing you have to do is to find it: In the Layers palette, double-click the thumbnail for the Pattern Fill layer, or double-click on the Pattern Overlay, Texture, or Stroke (wherever the pattern is used) in the list of effects in a Layer Style. When you see the swatch of pattern you want to capture, click the little "Create a new preset from this pattern" button that's right next to the swatch. The pattern is added to the Patterns palette, available anywhere in Photoshop that patterns are used.

SAVING A PATTERN

To save the pattern permanently, along with other patterns currently in the Patterns palette, choose **Preset Manager** from Photoshop's Edit menu or from the Patterns palette's ⊙ menu. In the Preset Manager dialog box, choose Patterns for the Preset Type. Shift-click or Ctrl/⌘-click to select all the patterns you want to save together in a new Patterns preset file, and click the "Save Set" button.

CREATING AN OBVIOUS REPEAT

To make a pattern with an obvious repeat:

1 Create your pattern element on a transparent layer. Then select it with the Rectangular Marquee, with half as much space around it as you want between the repeating elements of your pattern; choose Image > Crop to trim away excess space.

2 Choose Edit > Define Pattern; in the Pattern Name dialog box, name the pattern and click "OK." You can stop there, or build a more complex pattern as described in steps 3 through 5.

3 To set up the pattern so elements in alternate columns are offset, do this: Start a new file that's twice as wide and twice as high as your pattern element with its surrounding space from step 1 (choose File > New, with Transparent chosen in the Background Contents section of the New dialog box). Fill with the pattern you defined in step 2 (Edit > Fill).

4 In your pattern-filled layer use the Rectangular Marquee to select one column of your pattern, and choose Filter > Other > Offset (with Undefined Areas set to Wrap Around). Set the Horizontal Offset at 0 and use the up or down arrow key (↑ or ↓, with the Shift key held down for bigger steps) to offset the pattern elements as much as you like.

5 Deselect (Ctrl/⌘-D) and choose Edit > Define Pattern. Now you can apply your pattern over any background; to change its color, you can also use a Color Overlay effect in a Layer Style or an Adjustment layer, as shown here.

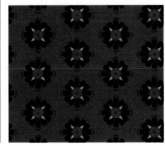

Altered Repeat.psd

from far away she looked like jesus

wild mane of hair
crown of thorns
from far away she looked like jesus
crucified, suffering
now close I can see
she is an angel
her disguise translucent as tissue paper
laid in wet strips over her breaking heart
the pain of her possession
how much she wants to have it

comfort comes only
in the shape of a lover
the size of the earth
who sees the beauty of sadness
who sees love inside fear
who pushes through her like the ocean
and changes the tide forever

this cocoon falls away
I can see what I've been seeing
hear what I've been hearing
touch what I've been touching
lavish heart
perfect beauty
turning everyone inside out
her music still resonating
within me

Fig 97

now close I can see
she is an angel

For the CD cover *From Far Away She Looked Like Jesus*, **Alicia Buelow** used a scanned photo of a stucco wall to lend an organic feel to the background. Next, she used the Move tool ⬉ to drag and drop photos of a tree and roots into her working file, blending their layers into the background by choosing the Color Burn blend mode at 50% Opacity for the trees, and Luminosity at 90% for the roots.▼

To make the central ghostly figure, Buelow used three images — photos of a child's head and a youth's body, and a scan of her own hand. She inverted the color of the head and body images (Ctrl/⌘-I). Then for each of the three subjects in turn, she made a feathered selection and used the Move tool ⬉ to drag each selected part into the working file. She set the blend mode for the head and body to Screen and the hand's blend mode to Luminosity. She further blended the three together by adjusting the layers' Opacity settings and using layer masks (added by clicking the "Add layer mask" button ⬚ at the bottom of the Layers palette, and then painted with the Brush tool ✎ with a soft tip, black paint, and a low Opacity setting chosen in the Options bar) .

Using an image of a wing from Getty Images, Buelow dragged it into the working file, copied this wing layer, and flipped the copy to compose the matching pair. She then duplicated

each wing layer and blurred the bottom copy of each (Filter > Blur > Motion Blur).

Drawing a white cube in Adobe Illustrator, Buelow copied it to the clipboard and pasted it into Photoshop as pixels.▼ She set the cube layer's blend mode to Overlay, then clicked the "Add a layer style" button 🅕 at the bottom of the Layers palette and chose the Outer Glow effect, using the default light yellow color but setting the effect's blend mode to Overlay and its Opacity to 80%.

To complete the illustration, Buelow selected the Type tool and typed numbers and words on several layers, blurring some layers slightly (Filter > Blur > Gaussian Blur). For the drop shadow behind the block of text on the left, she duplicated the type layer, and chose a dark gray for the lower layer by clicking the color swatch in the Type tool's Options bar. After using the Move tool ⬉ to drag the shadow layer down and to the right, she applied a strong blur with the Gaussian Blur filter and set the layer's blend mode to Color Burn. Because the shadow was a layer of its own

COPY & TRANSFORM

To copy a layer and transform the copy at the same time, hold down the Alt/Option key as you transform — for instance, by choosing Edit > Transform > Flip Horizontal.

rather than a Drop Shadow effect on the original type layer, she could add a layer mask and paint it with black to obscure parts of the shadow, giving it an eroded appearance.

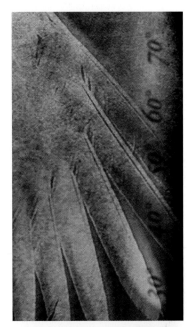

FIND OUT MORE

▼ Using blend modes **page 173**

▼ Copying & pasting from Adobe Illustrator **page 443**

For illustrator **Rob Magiera,** the acorn-to-oak metaphor was the perfect expression of the sprouting of hundreds of acronyms that have accompanied the growth of the Internet. Magiera began **Seeds of Internet Growth** in the 3D program Alias Maya, painting key parts of the image with Maya's Paint Effects tools. Working in Maya, Magiera benefited from the software's option to generate an alpha channel when rendering. This made it easy to isolate the trees in Photoshop. He could load the alpha channel as a selection (Select > Load Selection), then invert the selection (Ctrl/⌘-Shift-I), and press the Delete key to remove the black background. To remove all remaining traces of black from the edges of the trees, Magiera used Photoshop's

Layer > Matting > Remove Black Matte, which replaces any black at the edges with transparency. (He had chosen black for the background in Maya with this command in mind.)

To get the image of the ground, Magiera threw a scoop of dirt on his flatbed scanner and scanned it, having first stretched a piece of clear plastic wrap over the glass to avoid scratches and make cleanup easier. For the sprouted acorn, he opened a stock image in Photoshop, painted roots on it, and added a shadow by clicking the "Add a layer style" button at the bottom of the Layers palette and choosing Drop Shadow.

Magiera next opened the rendered main tree file and copied and pasted the other trees, the acorn artwork, and the dirt scan. To help keep track

of his various elements, he created a layer set/group for the far trees and one for the near tree. (To collect layers into a set/group, target one of the layers by clicking its thumbnail in the Layers palette; then link the other layers: In CS click in the column to the right of the 👁 icon for each one and then click the ⊙ button in the upper right corner of the palette and choose New Set from Linked; in CS2 Ctrl/⌘-click or Shift-click the layer thumbnails and then Shift-click the "Create a new group" button 🗀 at the bottom of the palette.)

To make the acronym text, Magiera selected the Horizontal Type tool T and dragged a rectangle larger than the main tree to create paragraph type. (Photoshop automatically creates a type layer when you click or drag with the Type tool with a layer targeted that already contains non-type artwork.) He set the font, size, and color in the Options bar and began typing. He added a Layer Style to make the type glow, clicking the button at the bottom of the Layers palette and choosing Outer Glow from the pop-up list. To light up the type and its glow, he put the layer in Screen mode, using the blend mode pop-up menu in the upper left corner of the Layers palette.

Magiera duplicated the type layer (Ctrl/⌘-J) and dragged the copy's thumbnail in the Layers palette to a position above the layer with the far trees. He reduced the size of the duplicate type (by pressing Ctrl/⌘-T for Edit > Free Transform, and then Shift-dragging inward on a corner handle of the Transform frame). He rasterized the type layers so the font wouldn't be needed for output.

With all of the elements assembled in Photoshop, Magiera began modifying them, using layer masks and clipping groups and adding Adjustment layers, to preserve as much editability as possible. He masked the acorn root and a painted shadow at the base of the tree inside the dirt layer by creating a clipping group with the dirt as its base, so the parts of the shadow and root that extended above the dirt surface were hidden. Also in this clipping group was a Hue/Saturation layer that brightened the dirt around the acorn. (To create a clipping group, target the layer you want to use as the mask and then Alt/Option-click the border between this clipping layer and the next one above it. If you like, you can continue up the layer stack, masking consecutive layers inside the "footprint" of the clipping layer.)

He added a layer mask to each of the type layers so the type would show up only on the trees' leaves. Layer masks worked better than clipping groups in these cases, because he could modify the masks — blurring the edges slightly and painting with black to hide the type in some places, allowing the branches and trunk to show. He made each mask by Ctrl/⌘-clicking the thumbnail for the tree, then targeting the type layer and clicking the "Add layer mask" button at the bottom of the Layers palette. Once the mask was made, he used Filter > Blur > Gaussian Blur on it to soften the edges of the leaves. By clicking the link icon between the layer thumbnail and mask thumbnail, he could decouple the type and the mask, so he could move the type around until he got the placement he wanted.

Magiera used several layers to create the atmosphere in his image, starting with a gray-filled layer at the bottom of the stack. He put a white-filled layer at reduced opacity between the far trees and the near tree to create atmospheric fog that adds depth. Then he used a Hue/Saturation Adjustment layer to colorize the fog and a gradient-filled layer in Overlay mode to darken it at the top and change the green, using layer masks to protect the near tree from the color.

To add more atmosphere immediately around the near tree, Magiera created a softened, dark green copy of the tree by adding a Drop Shadow to the layer (as described earlier for the acorn). Then he separated the shadow to its own layer (Layer > Layer Style > Create Layer), where he adjusted Opacity.

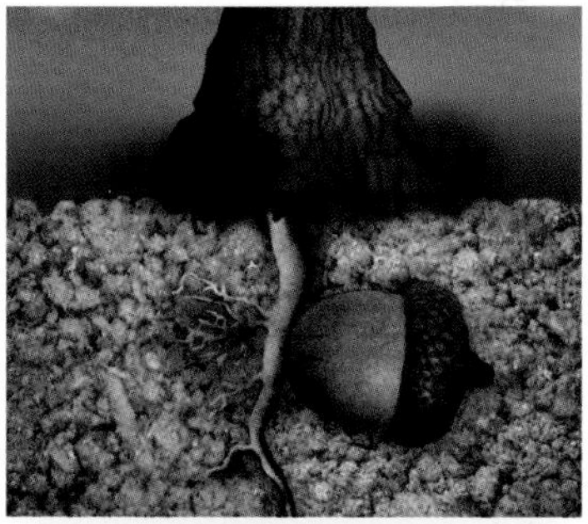

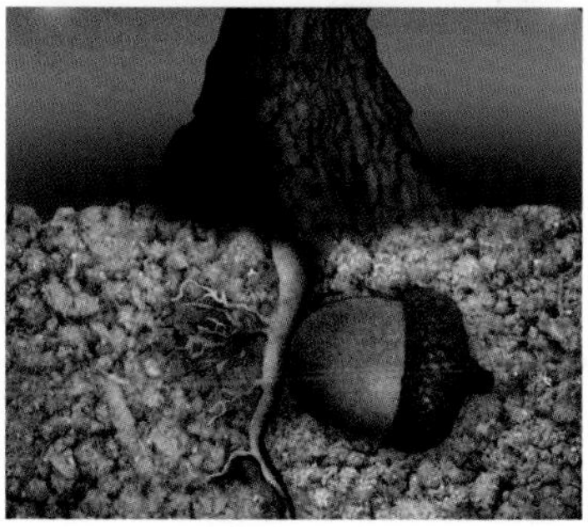

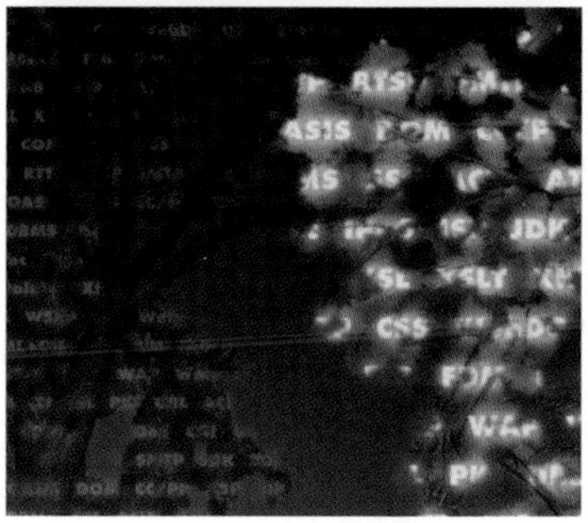

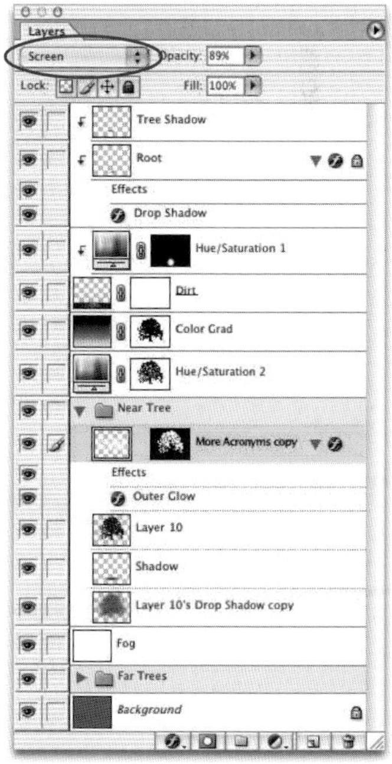

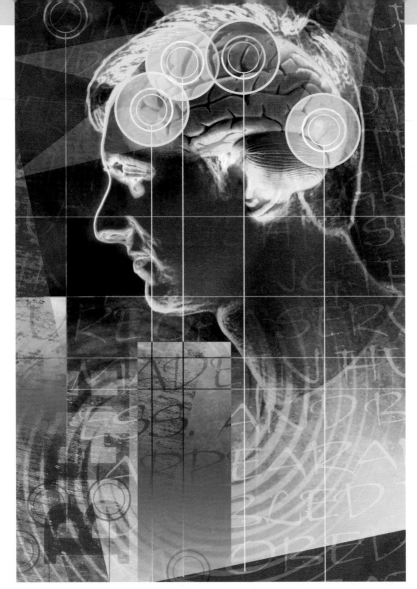

The depth and color of **Don Jolley's** striking editorial illustration *Behavior* were achieved with layered photos and Adobe Illustrator artwork, masks, blend modes, and Adjustment layers. The single Layer Style in the file is there not to create a dimensional effect but as a design solution for a challenge that arose as the image developed.

To create his composition, Jolley layered a filtered copy of his photo of a friend over the original **A**, and added several copies of a photo of a brain model **B**. He dragged in images from his own texture library (described on page 147) and added transparent layers, which he painted with the Brush tool ✐,▼ and masked Adjustment layers▼ for tweaking color **C**. From Illustrator he brought in a page of text and the vertical title type, as well as a dynamic spiral element made by drawing a 20-arm star and applying Illustrator's Filter > Distort > Twist to the figure; in Photoshop he added layer masks to mostly hide the text and spiral where they overlapped the man's face **D**.▼

Jolley also pasted in a grid of lines and circles that he had drawn in Illustrator to highlight four areas of the brain **E**; he had used a flattened version of his developing composition as a template in Illustrator in order to put the circles and lines where he wanted them. With the grid in place, he added a series of geometric selections filled with color as well as copies of parts of the grid.

To highlight each of the four regions of the brain with color, Jolley needed to select a circular area larger than the circles imported from Illustrator, but centered at the same spot. In order to

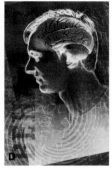
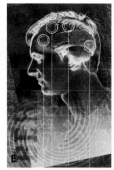

A   **B**   **C**   **D**   **E**

do that, he found the center of each existing pair of concentric circles so that he could then draw a selection outward from that center. Here's a way to do it that takes advantage of the Transform frame's center point, which "attracts" Guides: He turned on the Rulers (Ctrl/⌘-R) and dragged a Guide from the vertical ruler to line up with the "stalk" of the pair of circles **F**. Next he used the Rectangular Marquee 🔲 and his new Guide to draw a selection from the top of the outer circle to its bottom (the width of the rectangle didn't matter, just the height). Pressing Ctrl/⌘-T brought up the Transform frame **G**. With the Snap feature turned on in the View menu, he dragged a Guide down from the top ruler until it snapped to the center of the frame **H**. At this point he could escape from the Transform (Ctrl/⌘-period) and the selection (Ctrl/⌘-D), leaving only the new Guides, which intersected at the center of the circles.

With the center of the circles marked by the intersection of the Guides, Jolley chose the Elliptical Marquee tool ⬭ and Alt/Option-Shift-dragged outward from the intersection to make a circle the size he wanted **I**. Then he clicked the "Create new fill or adjustment layer" button ◑ at the bottom of the Layers palette and chose Hue/Saturation. He turned on the Colorize option in the dialog box and adjusted the Hue slider, also increasing the Lightness. The circular selection he had made became a mask that targeted the Hue/Saturation change.

For the additional highlights, Jolley added more masked Hue/Saturation layers. Drawing intersecting Guides to find the center of each pair of circles as he had for the first pair, he then recalled the circular selection (in the Layers palette, Ctrl/⌘-click on the thumbnail for the Hue/Saturation layer's mask) and moved it into position on another pair of circles **J**. One way to do that is to choose Select > Transform Selection and drag inside the selection boundary to move it until the center of the Transform frame snaps to the intersecting Guides, and then press the Escape key to release the transform. In Photoshop CS2 the Transform frame isn't needed; the center of the selection snaps to the intersection automatically as the selection is moved into place.

With the Hue/Saturation layers in place, Jolley decided he needed a stroke around each of these larger circles. This is where the Layer Style came in. He targeted one of the Hue/Saturation layers and clicked the "Add layer style" button ƒ at the bottom of the Layers palette, choosing Stroke from the list of effects; the Stroke automatically followed the edge of the layer mask. He could experiment with Size (he chose 10 pixels for this 1700-pixel wide image), Position (he chose Outside), and Color until he had exactly the look he wanted **K**, **L**, **M**. He could then copy the Style and paste it to the other Hue/Saturation layers. ▼

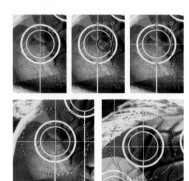
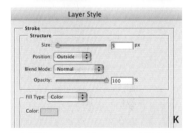

Layer Style

K

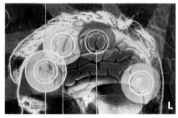

L

M

FIND OUT MORE

▼ Using the Brush 🖌 **page 362**

▼ Adjustment layers **page 164**

▼ Masks **page 68**

▼ Copying & pasting Styles **page 492**

When **Cristen Gillespie** developed *Lady with a Harp*, the second piece in the *Joy of Music* series, it was important to maintain a visual relationship between the illustrations, but she didn't want to use identical patterns. Because she had used Smart Objects when creating the patterns for the first illustration (above left) and had saved the .psd pattern development file with layers and Smart Objects intact, all she had to do to make new but related patterns was to change a few elements in this file. (For the "how to" of making the original patterns, see "Exercising Smart Objects" on page 39.)

Gillespie decided to make the new patterns on transparency, so they could be applied over any back-

ground. She opened her pattern development file (**Exercising SO-After.psd** from page 39) and turned off visibility for the *Background* and the Solid Color Fill layer by clicking their 👁 icons in the Layers palette. To make the new pattern for the harp, she wanted independent control of the "JOY" type and the dancing figures. She decided she would actually make two separate patterns, one with "JOY" and another with the dancers, that would look like a single pattern when used together. To start with "JOY" she also turned off visibility for the "Leaping Lady" Smart Object, leaving only "JOY" visible **A**.

She made changes to the Layer Style for the "JOY" Smart Object, adding a Color Overlay and a Satin effect.▼ To capture the pattern, she Ctrl/⌘-clicked

on the Solid Fill layer's mask to load it as a selection (this mask had been designed as the square tile for defining the pattern, as described on page 40) **B**. With the selection active, she chose Edit > Define Pattern, and saved and named the pattern.

Gillespie next changed the dancing figures part of the pattern **C**: She restored visibility to the "Leaping Lady" Smart Object and turned off visibility for "JOY." She double-clicked the thumbnail for the "Leaping Lady" Smart Object to open its .psb file and then also double-clicked one of the Smart Object instances nested within that file. When that second .psb file opened, she added a new layer with a different character rasterized from the Pedestria PictOne font and turned off the 👁 icon for the layers below. Using

Ctrl/⌘-T for Free Transform, she resized the new character to fit within the document so its edges wouldn't be cropped off; she added a Layer Style with a Gradient Overlay effect to color the new character.

Then she worked backwards to update the nested Smart Objects: When she saved the Smart Object file (Ctrl/⌘-S) all instances of the dancing couple character in the "super" Smart Object file were automatically updated. Happy with how the characters looked as a group, she also saved this "super" Smart Object file (Ctrl/⌘-S) to update it. She defined a pattern with the dancing figures on transparency

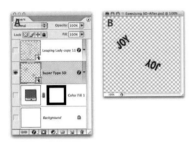

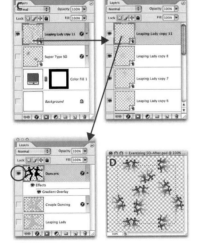

by using the same method she had used for the "JOY" pattern **D**.

To define a pattern with the leaping lady on a transparent background, Gillespie opened nested Smart Objects until she got to the one where she could turn on visibility for that figure only **E**, then saved the file for automatic updating. To substitute the leaping lady for all of the pattern elements, she had to do this series of operations twice — once to substitute the leaping lady in the "Leaping Lady" super Smart Object and once to substitute it in the "JOY" super Smart Object. Back in the main pattern development file with visibility turned on for both of these Smart Objects and turned off for all other layers, she could capture a "leaping ladies" pattern on transparency **F**.

Now Gillespie could apply the new patterns to her *Lady with a Harp* illustration. Targeting the *Background* of the image, she used the Magic Wand ✦ with Contiguous unchecked to select all of the blue background.▼ She Alt/Option- clicked on the "Create new fill or adjustment layer" button ⊘ at the bottom of the Layers palette, and chose Pattern Fill. In the Pattern Fill dialog box **G** she chose the new "leaping lady" pattern she had just made, scaled it to 50%, and clicked "OK." The wallpaper seemed too bright, so she reduced the Opacity of the Pattern Fill layer to 80%.

Targeting the *Background* again, Gillespie clicked and Shift-clicked with the Magic Wand ✦ to make a selection that included all three parts of the golden harp. Then she made another Pattern Fill layer, choosing the "dancing figures" pattern. She duplicated this layer (Ctrl/⌘-J) and double-clicked the new duplicate layer's thumbnail in the Layers palette to reopen the Pattern Fill dialog box. There she chose the "JOY" pattern. Because Photoshop defaults to starting each pattern at the upper left corner of the document, the "JOY" and "dancing figures" pattern layers

aligned with each other perfectly, to give the impression of a single pattern. The benefit of having them separate, though, was that Gillespie could change the blend mode of the "JOY" layer independently of the dancing figures, putting it in Hard Light mode for a more interesting blend.

Finally, to balance the patterns and subdue the grayish streak in the Lady's hair, Gillespie added another Pattern Fill layer to fill the streak with the "leaping lady" pattern scaled to 25%. She used Luminosity as the blend mode (so the pattern's color had no effect), and reduced the layer's Opacity to mute the pattern even more **H**.

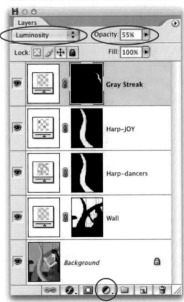

FIND OUT MORE

▼ Layer Style components **page 494**

▼ Using the Magic Wand ✦ **page 57**

YOU'LL FIND THE FILE

in **wow** >Wow Goodies > Lady with Harp.psd

Putting It All Together

9

"Adding Type to an Image" on page 596 demonstrates Photoshop's versatile masking and blending techniques for combining images, type, and graphics.

When **Auto Select Layer** is turned on in the Move tool's ▶⊕ Options bar in Photoshop CS or CS2, clicking in the working window automatically targets the uppermost layer with content under the cursor, as long as that layer's Opacity is 50% or more. In CS2 you can target the uppermost layer and any other layers in its group if you turn on the **Auto Select Group** choice before you click. Check page 583 for more about layer sets/groups.

WHAT AUTO SELECT LAYER "SEES"

A layer may be invisible because of its blend mode, but the Move tool's ▶⊕ Auto Select Layer option can still see it, as long as its visibility 👁 is turned on in the Layers palette. Auto Select Layer doesn't "see" a layer if its Opacity is less than 50%. But if you can **regulate transparency with Fill opacity** instead of Opacity, the Auto Select Layer option *will* see the layer.

WITH PHOTOSHOP'S EXTRAORDINARY ability to combine elements, you can create any kind of combination — from a seamless "faked" photo to an obvious montage or a page layout. In this chapter the skills and techniques covered in earlier chapters are brought together to combine photos with each other and with nonphotographic elements.

COMPOSITION METHODS

Of prime importance in the Photoshop compositing process are the **selections, masks, clipping groups**, and **blending options** covered in Chapter 2, as well as the **blend modes** and **Adjustment layers** detailed in Chapter 4. Many of these and other combining functions can be set up and organized through the Layers palette, as shown in the illustration on page 577.

The following Photoshop tools and commands are among the most useful for making composites:

- With the **Move tool** ▶⊕ you can slide layers around until you're happy with the composition. Photoshop even preserves the parts of layers that you move outside the margins of the canvas. So if you change your mind, the entire element will still exist and you can move it back into the image frame.

- In conjunction with the Move tool, the **Smart Guides** in Photoshop CS2 and in ImageReady CS/CS2 will help align elements as you compose. The Align and Distribute commands in the Layers menu can arrange several elements at once. In Photoshop CS the commands work on linked layers, but in CS2, where you can target more than one layer at a time, the layers need not be linked (see page 582 for linking and "multitargeting").

- The **Patch Tool** 🖾 and Clone Stamp ♣ can copy image material from one part of the composite and repeat it in another area.

In Photoshop CS2's **Vanishing Point** interface, you can start by clicking with the Create Plane tool ▦ to set the four corners of a perspective plane. With the grid in place and adjusted, pasted elements such as the sign graphics above can be dragged onto the grid to automatically fit the perspective. With Vanishing Point you can also paint and clone in perspective. "Exercising Vanishing Point" on page 588 shows how to get the most from Vanishing Point's set of tools.

The kinds of components typically used in a composite like the one above are identified and explained in the Layers palette on the facing page. The layout was assembled with masks, clipping groups, and layer sets/groups. Techniques for a similar construction are presented step-by-step in "Building a Layout with Masks & Clipping Groups" on page 635. The final template was produced in a form that allows new images and type to be substituted automatically into a layout for a series of website splash screens, postcard ads, or brochure covers.

- The **Filter > Extract** command excels at making clean selections of elements with difficult organic edges, such as hair, so they can be seamlessly combined with a new background. You'll find an example of its use in "Swapping a Background" on page 628.

- The **Edit > Transform** and **Free Transform** commands are often essential in resizing or distorting elements to fit into the overall picture. ▼ And in Photoshop CS2 turning a component into a **Smart Object** allows you the freedom to experiment as you build a composition. You can transform several times if needed, with no more reduction in image quality than a single transformation would cause. ▼

- Photoshop CS2's **Vanishing Point** filter allows you to automatically paste an element into the perspective of the image you add it to. "Exercising Vanishing Point" on page 588 takes you through this process step-by-step.

- To make one image conform to a surface depicted in another image, the **Liquify** filter, the **Displace** filter, and in Photoshop CS2 the **Edit > Transform > Warp** command are important resources (page 578). Another tool for molding elements to fit is Warp Text (page 480).

- The **Photomerge** command helps with piecing together a panorama from a series of images shot for that purpose. Its operation is described on page 580, and its use is demonstrated in "'Photomerging' a Panorama" on page 604.

- The **Image > Variables** command in Photoshop CS2 (and ImageReady CS/CS2) allows you to make a template that will automatically substitute alternate sets of images and text into the same layout. "Building a Layout with Masks & Clipping Groups" on page 635 shows how.

CHOOSING & PREPARING COMPONENTS

One requirement for creating a successful "seamless" photo montage, when that's your goal, is choosing component images that match one another in several key respects. For example, the light should be coming from the same direction, the color and amount of detail in the shadows and highlights should be about the same, and the "graininess" of the images should match. Some of these factors are more important than others:

- **Highlight and shadow detail can be manipulated** by using the Image > Adjustments > **Shadow/Highlight** command, or with

Continued on page 578

FIND OUT MORE

▼ Transforming **page 71**

▼ Smart Objects **page 39**

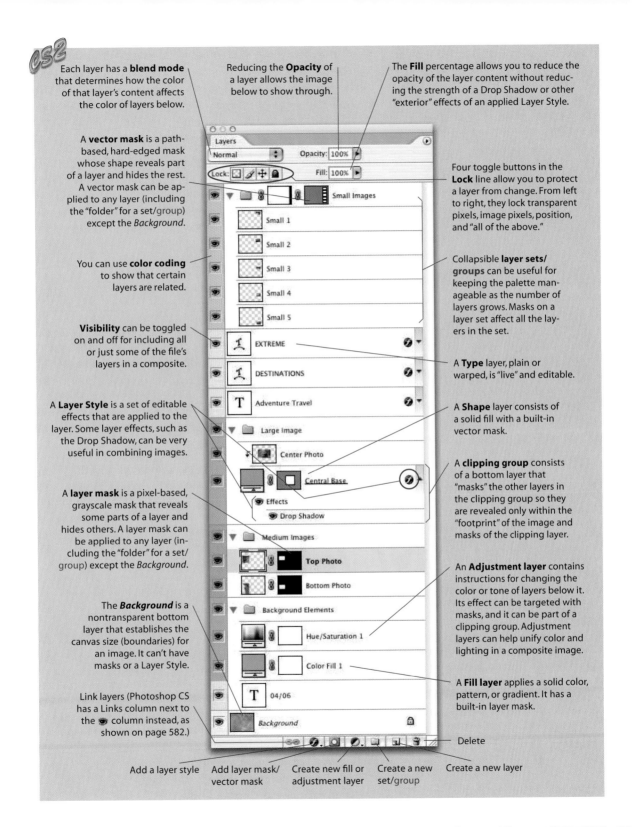

Each layer has a **blend mode** that determines how the color of that layer's content affects the color of layers below.

Reducing the **Opacity** of a layer allows the image below to show through.

The **Fill** percentage allows you to reduce the opacity of the layer content without reducing the strength of a Drop Shadow or other "exterior" effects of an applied Layer Style.

A **vector mask** is a path-based, hard-edged mask whose shape reveals part of a layer and hides the rest. A vector mask can be applied to any layer (including the "folder" for a set/group) except the *Background*.

Four toggle buttons in the **Lock** line allow you to protect a layer from change. From left to right, they lock transparent pixels, image pixels, position, and "all of the above."

You can use **color coding** to show that certain layers are related.

Collapsible **layer sets/ groups** can be useful for keeping the palette manageable as the number of layers grows. Masks on a layer set affect all the layers in the set.

Visibility can be toggled on and off for including all or just some of the file's layers in a composite.

A **Type** layer, plain or warped, is "live" and editable.

A **Layer Style** is a set of editable effects that are applied to the layer. Some layer effects, such as the Drop Shadow, can be very useful in combining images.

A **Shape** layer consists of a solid fill with a built-in vector mask.

A **layer mask** is a pixel-based, grayscale mask that reveals some parts of a layer and hides others. A layer mask can be applied to any layer (including the "folder" for a set/ group) except the *Background*.

A **clipping group** consists of a bottom layer that "masks" the other layers in the clipping group so they are revealed only within the "footprint" of the image and masks of the clipping layer.

An **Adjustment layer** contains instructions for changing the color or tone of layers below it. Its effect can be targeted with masks, and it can be part of a clipping group. Adjustment layers can help unify color and lighting in a composite image.

The *Background* is a nontransparent bottom layer that establishes the canvas size (boundaries) for an image. It can't have masks or a Layer Style.

A **Fill layer** applies a solid color, pattern, or gradient. It has a built-in layer mask.

Link layers (Photoshop CS has a Links column next to the 👁 column instead, as shown on page 582.)

Delete

Add a layer style
Add layer mask/ vector mask
Create new fill or adjustment layer
Create a new set/group
Create a new layer

A spotlight created with the Lighting Effects filter helps to unify this composite, adding to the lighting provided by Layer Styles on the "Mat" and "Frame" layers. For more about the construction of the image, see page 666.

Framed Photo.psd

Curves or **Levels**, both of which are especially effective as Adjustment layers. ▼

- A **color cast** — in a shadow, for instance— can be identified with the RGB or CMYK readings in the Info palette (you can choose Window > Show Info to open it, or use the F8 default keyboard shortcut).▼ Then the color cast **can be adjusted** — with Curves, Levels, Color Balance, or Match Color.▼ "Swapping a Background" on page 628 uses the Match Color command for this purpose.

- **Changing the direction of the light can be much more difficult** than managing shadow detail or a color cast. If the elements you want to blend are fairly flat (like pictures on a wall), you may get good results with the Lighting Effects filter or a Layer Style's Bevel And Emboss or Shadow effect, or a combination of these. If the final effect you're looking for will tolerate it, you may be able to "overpower" the varied "native" lighting of the elements of a composite image by applying the same lighting effect to all the parts. You can also dodge and burn to create highlights and shadows.▼ But if quick Lighting Effects or dodging-and-burning fixes won't work, you'll generally get better results if you continue your search for photo elements whose lighting matches, rather than trying to make further adjustments to correct the lighting direction.

- **Film grain or digital noise can be simulated** to match the grain of other image components by using the Lens Blur filter (as described in step 3 of "Focusing Attention on the Subject" on page 288) or one of the Wow Noise patterns (as in step 4 of that same section).

FITTING AN ELEMENT TO A SURFACE

When you want an image to take on the contours or surface texture of another image below it in the layer stack, Photoshop offers two main methods (three in Photoshop CS2) for distorting the top image to fit. These are the Displace and Liquify filters and in CS2 the Warp command.

Displace

The **Displace command** (Filter > Distort > Displace) requires a third image, called (appropriately enough) a *displacement map* to distort the upper image to fit. It uses differences in brightness to determine the amount of shifting that should take place in various parts of the image. Dark

FIND OUT MORE

▼ Using Levels & Curves **page 249**

▼ Using the Info palette **page 162**

▼ Dodging & burning **page 254**

DONAL JOLLEY

When Don Jolley applied the sign graphics to the wall and aged the sign in place, the Displace filter played a role in "painting" the graphics onto the bricks. The techniques he used are presented step-by-step in "Applying an Image to a Textured Surface" on page 611.

The Liquify command is great for "massaging" an image or graphic to fit organic contours such as the facial features in this photo. The process is presented in "Applying an Image with Liquify" on page 615.

pixels in the displacement map will push the image pixels down and to the right; light pixels will push them up and to the left. In many cases a displacement map made from the surface image itself will successfully distort the applied image so it appears to dip where it goes over crevices and indentations, which are dark because they are in shadow; likewise the image will appear to rise where it goes over raised, highlighted areas. This won't work right, of course, if there are pronounced lights and darks on the surface that have nothing to do with depth changes — patterns or cast shadows, for instance. In a case like that you can paint your own grayscale displacement map, brushing in the dark dips and highlighted "hills."

Rasterized type, familiar shapes, or bold patterns with strong vertical or horizontal motifs are great choices for images to apply with the Displace filter, because they easily show distortion. In contrast, busy images or patterns may show almost nothing of the displacement applied. "Applying an Image to a Textured Surface" on page 611 shows an example of combining images with the Displace filter.

Liquify

Unlike Displace, which has no preview, **Liquify** employs a warping process that's completely visible while you work. Using Liquify, you mold the upper image to the contours of the lower by "fingerpainting," warping the image to the picture below to whatever degree you like. You can set up the filter to show both the warped image and the rest of the composite, so you can watch the combination. Though the on-screen preview shows the changes to the image, no changes will actually be made to the "Liquified" layer itself until you click "OK" to close the Liquify dialog box. This means that the pixels won't suffer from being worked and reworked as you use the filter.

As you work you are actually distorting the Liquify *mesh,* which then distorts the image itself. Since Liquify is applied to a single layer at a time, saving the mesh before you close the Liquify dialog and then reloading it for use on another layer provides a way to bend several components to match the same surface.

Warp

Photoshop CS2's **Edit** > **Transform** > **Warp** command is ideal for applying graphics or images to shapes that are curved and geometric or nearly so. Unlike the Displace and Liquify filters, which can be used on pixel-based layers only (the filters will offer to rasterize any other kind of layer you try to apply them to), the Warp command can be used on pixel-based or Shape

Tips on taking photos to make a seamless panorama, as well as step-by-step instructions for using the Photomerge interface, can be found in "'Photomerging' a Panorama" on page 604. Even when the Photomerge command can't successfully merge a series of images, its interface is helpful for arranging the images in position on separate layers so you can merge them with masking (as in this case).

layers and on Smart Objects. Used on a Smart Object, the Warp command offers a kind of "surface template" that allows you to quickly substitute different images or graphics as surface art, as in "'Warping' Graphics to a Surface" on page 620.

Combining Techniques

For the most realistic blend of an image over complex topography, when it matters that the warping appears real and the image and topography are one, it often makes sense to start with the Displace filter, or even Warp or Warp Text, and then use Liquify to "touch up" the image to help some of the contours show up more clearly.

USING PHOTOMERGE

Choosing the **Photomerge** command (via Photoshop's File > Automate menu or through File Browser or the Bridge program) opens a first Photomerge dialog box, where you can choose the images you want to blend together into the panorama. Here you can also indicate how much help you want from Photomerge in assembling these components. When you click "OK," a second Photomerge dialog box opens, where you and Photoshop actually assemble the panorama. This dialog

Continued on page 582

THE PHOTOMERGE INTERFACE

You can choose the Photomerge command from File > Automate in Photoshop or from the Automate menu in File Browser (in CS) or Tools > Photoshop > Photomerge in Bridge (in CS2). This opens the first Photomerge dialog box (shown below).

Any file listed in the first Photomerge dialog box will be used for the panorama, so delete any extra files in the list by clicking their names (Shift-click or Ctrl/⌘-click to multi-select) and clicking the "Remove" button. You can choose whether to have Photomerge automatically assemble the component images. Clicking "OK" opens the second Photomerge dialog, shown at the right.

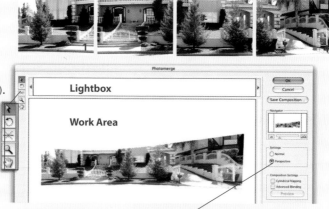

In the second Photomerge dialog, you can move files from the **Lightbox** at the top to the **Work Area** below (or vice versa) with the **Select Image** tool ↖. Use the **Rotate Image** tool ↻ to tilt a component for better fit.

Choosing **Perspective** makes a panorama that accounts for the camera's location. By default a center image is chosen as the one directly in front of the camera and the perspective of the others is adjusted accordingly. In case you shot more images to one side of the center than the other, Perspective allows you to click one image with the **Set Vanishing Point** tool ✻ to rebuild the panorama using that image as the one directly in front of the camera.

ADJUSTING A PANORAMA

The **Advanced Blending** option (available whether you choose Normal or Perspective in the second Photomerge dialog) may improve the "joins" between component images. For Perspective only, choosing **Cylindrical Mapping** "curves" the panorama to correct the "bowtie" expansion of the end images seen on the facing page. After choosing Advanced Blending or Cylindrical Mapping, click the **"Preview"** button to see the changes.

For comparison of Photomerge options, each of the panoramas below was assembled using the Normal option or the Perspective option, along with the Composition Settings indicated below. Then each panorama was cropped to the largest rectangle possible without including empty space at the edges. The four component images are provided on the Wow DVD-ROM so you can experiment.

Panorama

Normal

Perspective (cropped from the arrangement shown on the facing page)

Perspective & Cylindrical Mapping

Perspective with Vanishing Point changed from Image 2 (the default) to Image 3

Perspective & Cylindrical Mapping with Vanishing Point changed as above

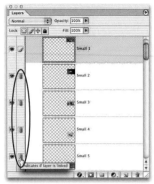

In Photoshop CS, link layers by clicking one layer's thumbnail in the Layers palette and then clicking in the Links column (next to the 👁) of the other layers. To add layers that are sequential in the palette, you can simply drag up or down the Links column. To unlink a layer, click its 🔗 icon.

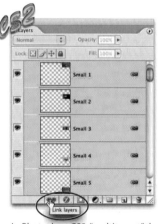

In Photoshop CS2, "multitarget" the layers you want to link (by clicking the thumbnail of one in the Layers palette and Shift-clicking or Ctrl/⌘-clicking the others). Then click the "Link layers" button 🔗 at the bottom of the palette. To unlink, select any thumbnails whose layers you want to remove from the "linkage" and click the 🔗 at the bottom of the palette.

GROUPING SHORTCUTS

To quickly group multitargeted layers into a "folder" 📁 in Photoshop CS2, type Ctrl/⌘-G. To disband a group and delete the folder but keep the layers, type Ctrl/⌘-Shift-G.

box offers several ways to "correct" the perspective of the assemblage and to better blend details where the components join.

OPERATING ON SEVERAL LAYERS AT ONCE

Some of Photoshop's operations can be carried out on more than one layer at a time. To work on two or more layers together, you can link them together in the Layers palette, group them into a layer set/group, or in CS2 simply target several layers at once by Shift-clicking or Ctrl-clicking their Layers palette thumbnails.

Linking & "Multitargeting"

In both CS and CS2, layers can be linked using the linking mechanism in the Layers palette; it works a little differently in the two versions, as described at the left.

• Moving or otherwise transforming one linked or "multitargeted" layer also transforms the others. ***Note:*** In Photoshop CS, transforming linked layers may not work if all the linked layers are Shape layers; but you can do the job by adding an empty regular (transparent) layer, linking it to the Shape layers, and transforming it to transform all of them together.

• Dragging one linked layer from the *working window* and dropping it into another file drags the other linked layers along. However, dragging-and-dropping a layer's thumbnail from the *Layers palette* doesn't bring linked layers with it. This difference gives you an option if you do or don't want to bring linked layers along.

• You can lock or unlock all the linked or multitargeted layers at once by choosing Lock All Linked Layers/Lock Layers from the Layers menu or the Layers palette's ▶ menu.

• You can also paste the same Layer Style to linked layers in Photoshop CS by copying the Style from a "donor" layer, then pasting to one of the linked layers. In CS2, copy and paste to multitargeted layers; for linked layers, multitarget before pasting by clicking the thumbnail for one of them and choosing Select Linked Layers from the Layers palette's ▶ menu.▼

FIND OUT MORE

▼ Copying & pasting Layer Styles
page 492

Although layer sets/groups offer certain advantages over linked layers, as described next, linking has an advantage of its own — you can link layers even if they aren't stacked consecutively in the Layers palette, while a set/group's layers have to be consecutive.

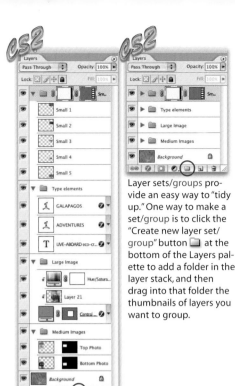

Layer sets/groups provide an easy way to "tidy up." One way to make a set/group is to click the "Create new layer set/group" button ▢ at the bottom of the Layers palette to add a folder in the layer stack, and then drag into that folder the thumbnails of layers you want to group.

A quick way to make a layer set from existing layers in Photoshop CS is to link them (as described on the facing page) and then choose New Set From Linked from the Layers palette's ⊙ menu.

To group layers in CS2, Shift-select them in the Layers palette and then either choose New Group from Layers from the palette's ⊙ menu, or Shift-click on the "Create a new group" button ▢ at the bottom of the palette.

Layer Sets/Groups

The **layer set/group** is a great way to organize layers — you can hide several layers inside a single "folder" in the Layers palette, making the palette more compact and organizing associated layers together. By clicking the little triangle to the left of the folder icon in the Layers palette, you can hide or show the thumbnails of all the layers inside the set/group. In a file with many layers, closing a folder can make it easier to locate and work with other layers in the file.

You can start a layer set/group "from scratch" as described at the left, or quickly make one from linked or multitargeted layers. In CS, click on one of the linked layers in the Layers palette and choose Layer > New > Layer Set From Linked, or choose it from the Layers palette's menu. In CS2, you make the group from multitargeted layers: Layer > New > Group from Layers. If you're starting with linked layers that aren't multiselected, you can quickly select them all (Layer > Select Linked Layers) and then group them. Once a set/group is established, you can add more layers by dragging the layer thumbnails to the folder's thumbnail, or directly to the position where you want the layer in the stack. And you can add a brand-new layer to a set by targeting the folder in the Layers palette and then clicking the "Create a new layer" button ▢ at the bottom of the palette.

A folder can't have image content of its own. But a layer set/group is definitely more than just a "housekeeping" feature. It lets you control certain layer attributes for the entire set/group at once, and it can also have its own layer mask and vector mask. When a mask is applied to a set, any individual masks on the layers also remain in effect; you can see an example of this "double masking" on page 584.

The Opacity and blend mode for the folder don't *replace* the settings for the individual layers; they *interact* with them:

- **The folder's Opacity is a multiplier** for the Opacity of each layer in the set. At 100%, the folder's Opacity setting makes no change to the look of the composite. Below 100% the folder's Opacity reduces the opacity of the layers proportionally. So, for instance if you have a set with some layers at 50% Opacity and some at 80%, if you reduce the folder's Opacity to 50%, the cumulative effect is that some layers are now only 25% opaque (50% of 50% is 25%) and some are 40% opaque (50% of 80% is 40%).

To reposition all the layers in a layer set/group at the same time, target the folder in the Layers palette, choose the Move tool ▸⊕, and then do one of the following:

• If all the layers in the layer set are linked, simply drag in the image window to move the set.

• If some of the layers in the set are *not* linked, you can make choices in the Options bar that allow you to move them all. In Photoshop CS *turn off the Auto Select Layer option* and drag in the working window to move the set.

In CS2, turn on the Auto Select Groups option (it's only available if Auto Select Layer is on) and drag in the working window to move the group.

• **The folder's default blend mode is Pass Through,** which simply means that each layer in the set/group keeps its own blend mode, the same as if it weren't in a set. If you choose any other blend mode for the folder, the result is as if you had merged all the layers in the set/group (with their existing blend modes) into a single layer and then applied the folder's blend mode to the merged image.

With the ability to nest sets/groups within others, you can do some complex masking and blending. However, not everything you can do to a layer can be done to a layer set/group. For instance, you can't apply a Layer Style to a folder, even if the folder has a layer mask or vector mask of its own. And a folder can't be part of a clipping group. Also, a folder's masks aren't subject to the Layer Styles of any layers in the set/group.

You can remove a layer from a set/group by dragging its thumbnail to a position above or below the set/group in the Layers palette. You can remove an entire set from the file by dragging its 🗀 icon to the 🗑 button at the bottom of the Layers palette. To delete the folder, releasing the layers from the set/group but not deleting the layers themselves, hold down the Ctrl/⌘ key as you drag the 🗀 to the 🗑 button. ***Note:*** When you disband a

A layer set/group can do more than organize or mask several layers. Used with a single layer, it can provide a way to combine the effects of two different layer masks on that one layer, as in this composite. To mask the layer itself, target the image by clicking its thumbnail in the Layers palette. Then in the working window select the area of the image that you want to remain visible, and click the "Add a layer mask" button ▢ at the bottom of the Layers palette. With the layer still targeted in the Layers palette, add a new set/group (in both versions CS and CS2, you can do this by clicking the "Create a new set/group" button 🗀 at the bottom of the palette). Then drag your masked layer's thumbnail to the folder thumbnail. Now you can add a mask to the set/group: Select the area you want to remain visible, target the folder icon in the Layers palette and click the ▢ button again; the second mask is applied.

In this montage, the mask on the "Ryan" layer hides the background of that photo so the scenic *Background* image can show through. The additional layer mask on the "Ryan Xtra Mask" set/group hides part of the raft and the water in the foreground of the "Ryan" layer to "sandwich" the layer in between the foreground and background of the *Background* layer, maintaining some leeway for moving or rotating him a little to the right or left. See pages 614 and 670 for examples of masked sets/groups.

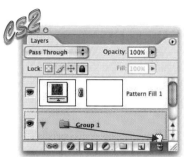

Dragging a set/group's thumbnail to the "Delete" button 🗑 is often the quickest way to remove it from the file; Photoshop doesn't stop you to ask if you really mean it. Ctrl/⌘-drag to merely disband the set/group, removing the folder but leaving the layers in place.

Targeting a layer set/group and then clicking the "Delete" button 🗑 at the bottom of the Layers palette opens a Caution box where you can choose to remove the "Set/Group and Contents" or disband the "Set/Group Only," keeping the layers.

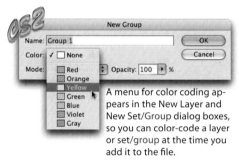

A menu for color coding appears in the New Layer and New Set/Group dialog boxes, so you can color-code a layer or set/group at the time you add it to the file.

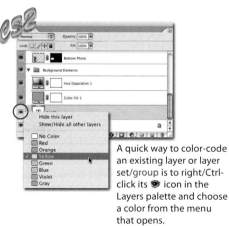

A quick way to color-code an existing layer or layer set/group is to right/Ctrl-click its 👁 icon in the Layers palette and choose a color from the menu that opens.

set/group, any layer mask or vector mask it had is discarded without being applied.

Color Coding

You can color-code layers in the Layers palette, assigning the same color to layers that are somehow related. Color coding has no effect on the layers or folders you apply it to — it's simply a visual organizing tool for the palette.

QUICK COLLAPSE OR EXPAND

Quickly open or close any or all layer sets/groups by right/Ctrl-clicking the tiny arrow to the left of a folder 📁 in the Layers palette and choosing from the menu.

Here are some ideas for using color coding:

- You might color all the members of a **layer set/group** with the same color, so you can quickly see where sets begin and end when they are expanded in the palette.

- Or use a color to identify all the layers that were duplicated from a single **original layer**. (When a layer is duplicated, the new copy keeps the same color code.)

- Or use the same color to identify **related elements** in several different files; for instance, you might routinely make all "live" type layers yellow so you can quickly locate them when you want to simplify your file by converting them to Shape layers or rasterizing them.

You can color-code a layer or layer set/group at the time you create it or afterwards:

- When you create a layer or layer set/group, hold down the Alt/Option key as you click the 🔲 or 📁 button at the bottom of the Layers palette; this will open a dialog box where you can choose a Color.

- To color-code an existing layer (or layer set/group), choose Layer > Layer Properties (or Layer > Set/Group Properties), or use the context-sensitive menu as shown at the left.

- When you color-code a set/group, you automatically color all the layers within the set. But when you move a layer into a set/group, the layer keeps its own color if it has one, or takes on the set's/group's color if it hasn't yet been color-coded.

LAYER COMPS

For a many-layered, complex file with masks and Layer Styles, **layer comps** can be invaluable for keeping track of alternatives for the final composition. A layer comp is a "snapshot" of the

The Layer Comps palette provides a way to save alternate versions of multilayer compositions such as Sharon Steuer's *Oil Spirit*, shown here. Starting with a photo of her original sculpture (top left), Steuer duplicated the image several times, and applied filters and other effects, using blend modes and masking to combine the results. As she developed alternative composites, Steuer "collected" them as layer comps. For each promising composite, she generated and named a new layer comp. This made it possible to go back later and, with one click, turn on visibility for all the layers and masks that make up a particular version of the image.

current state of the Layers palette, made by choosing New Layer Comp from the Layer Comps palette's ⓘ menu, or by clicking the "Create New Layer Comp" button ⬛ at the bottom of the palette. Your new layer comp captures the position, visibility and masking, opacity, and blend mode of each layer. Also, it captures anything that can be set in the Layer Styles dialog box — blend mode, "Blend If" settings, and other blending options, as well as the effects in Layer Styles. Once you capture a layer comp, if you make changes to any of these properties, your existing comp will be protected from change. You can try out options by changing visibility, position, or effects, then making another comp, and so on. To bring back the state of the file represented by any comp, you simply click in the column to the left of that comp's name in the Layer Comps palette.

A layer comp *doesn't* freeze image *content*. So, for instance, if you add or take away pixels, edit Shape layers, move a layer up or down the stack in the Layers palette, or change the text in a type layer, these changes *will* also be made to any existing comp that includes the layers you changed. Of course, there's a way to change content without changing your comps. You simply make your changes in a new layer — for instance, duplicate a type layer in the Layers palette, turn off visibility for the original type layer, and change the copy — and then use the Layer Comps palette to make another comp.

Assigning meaningful names to layer comps can be helpful later, when you want to quickly find a particular comp. A comp can be modified (updated) by clicking on its name in the Layer Comps palette, then adjusting visibility, layer position, or effects, and clicking the "Update Layer Comp" button ⟳ at the bottom of the palette.

The use of layer comps is shown at the left and is covered step-by-step in "Focusing Attention on the Subject" on page 285 and "Animating with Layer Comps" in Chapter 10. Layer comps exist in both Photoshop and ImageReady; for RGB files, they travel with the file from one program to the other.

REORDERING LAYERS

To change the stacking order of layers in your file, you can drag their thumbnails up or down the Layers palette. Or use keyboard shortcuts: **Ctrl/⌘-]** moves the targeted layer **up** one position in the stack, and **Ctrl/⌘-[** moves it **down**. Move a layer to the **top or bottom** of the entire stack by typing **Ctrl/⌘-Shift-]** or **Ctrl/⌘-Shift-[**.

Several options for merging visible layers are available in the Layers palette's menu and in the main Layer menu. Others are available elsewhere, as noted below. The same keyboard shortcut (Ctrl/⌘-E) works for many of them.

- In Photoshop CS, **Merge Linked (Ctrl/⌘-E)** combines the active layer and any visible layers linked to it, **discarding any hidden linked layers**. In CS2, first select the linked layers (choose Select Linked Layers from the palette's ⊙ menu) and then **Merge Layers (Ctrl/⌘-E)**.

- When the "folder" of a layer set/group is targeted in the Layers palette, **Merge Layer Set/Merge Group (Ctrl/⌘-E)** combines all the visible layers of the set/group, **discarding its hidden layers**.

- **Merge Down (Ctrl/⌘-E)** combines the active layer with the very next layer below it in the stack; the bottom layer of the "merge" has to be a pixel-based layer.

- **Merge Visible (Ctrl/⌘-Shift-E)** combines all visible layers and also **keeps all the hidden layers**.

- **Edit > Copy Merged (Ctrl/⌘-Shift-C)** makes a copy that includes the selected area of all visible layers, as if they were a single layer. Then Edit > Paste (Ctrl/⌘-V) can be used to turn the copy into a new layer.

- The **Image > Duplicate** command offers the **Merged Layers Only** option, which makes a merged copy of the file, ignoring invisible layers.

- Unchecking the Layers box in the **Save As** dialog box saves a merged copy of the file.

MERGING & FLATTENING

Merging combines two or more visible layers into a single layer. You might want to merge a series of layers when you've finished working on them and you no longer need to keep them separate and "live." Since merging reduces the number of layers, it also reduces the amount of RAM needed for the file. When you merge layers, any Layer Styles and masks are applied and then discarded, and type is rasterized. The new combined layer takes its blend mode and opacity from the bottom layer of the merging series; it becomes a *Background* only if the bottom layer of the merging series is a *Background*.

Certain file formats require a *flattened* file. Even a single-layered file with the capacity for transparency won't do. Flattening (Layer > Flatten Image) combines all visible layers into a *Background*. A Caution box warns that hidden layers will be discarded, so you can reconsider. Any transparency in the combined image is filled with the current Background color. Alpha channels are retained. *New!*

Even when you want to keep all your layers live and separate for maximum flexibility, there are times when a merged (single-layer, combined) copy of a developing image can be helpful. For instance, you may want to apply a filter or some other modification to an image that's composed of multiple layers; combine them into one and then modify the one. To make a merged copy as a separate layer, turn on visibility for all the layers you want to include in the composite copy, hold down the Ctrl/⌘, Alt/Option, and Shift keys, and type N, then E.

We made a merged copy of the three masked layers in order to apply the Image > Adjustments > Shadow/Highlight command to the entire blended image.

Vanishing Point

Photoshop CS2's new Vanishing Point "megafilter" allows you to paste, paint, and clone in perspective. Once you create a perspective grid to work on, it stays with the file, so you can work back and forth between Vanishing Point and Photoshop, returning to the grid when you need it.

This project demonstrates the basics of Vanishing Point — setting up grids, pasting a new sign in place, repainting an existing strip of wood trim and extending it to another wall, removing the alarm bell, and performing a variety of clean-up operations to produce the composite below.

Vanishing Point can paste, paint, and clone on empty layers, so you can protect the rest of the file from changes and keep your edits available for further changes in Photoshop. And Vanishing Point allows for multiple undo's (type Ctrl/⌘-Z to step backwards through your edits).

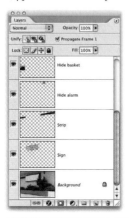

As you work, it's a good idea to make changes on separate layers and name your layers according to their content (double-click a layer name in the Layers palette and type the new name).

YOU'LL FIND THE FILES
in ⓦⓞⓦ > Wow Project Files > Chapter 9 > Exercising Vanishing Point

 VP-After.psd

1 Assemble the Components

A

ⓦⓞⓦ **VP-Before.psd**
Sunrise Bakery.psd

B

GRAPHICS: DONAL JOLLEY

C

Open the **VP-Before.psd** and **Sunrise Bakery.psd** files. You'll see that we've done some advance preparation to the **VP-Before.psd** file **A**. We removed the existing logo to create a blank signboard. We also isolated the green leaves in front of the sign by making a Rectangular Marquee selection of the area where the plants appear in front of the sign, and then running the Select > Color Range command on the selected area; we copied the selected leaves from the *Background* to a new layer (Ctrl/⌘-J) **B**. Now all of our Vanishing Point changes can be made on other layers that we'll add between the two. In the Layers palette we can turn visibility for the "Plants" layer off and on as needed by clicking its 👁 icon.

The new sign graphics were designed in Adobe Illustrator to fit the estimated measurements of the actual sign space so we wouldn't have to stretch the artwork out of proportion to fit it onto the signboard. The file was saved in EPS format and opened in Photoshop at the same resolution as the photo (225 ppi) and close to the size of the sign in the image (almost 3 inches by a little over 1 inch) **C**, so that when we copied and pasted it into the image in Vanishing Point, it would come in at a size that would be easy to manage.

2 Establish the Perspective Plane

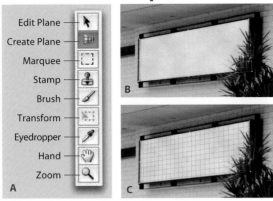

In **VP-Before.psd** open the Vanishing Point interface (Filter > Vanishing Point). Everything that happens in Vanishing Point begins with a grid you draw, called the ***perspective plane***. The image-altering tools **A** automatically change the proportions of any editing you do to match this perspective. To establish a grid for an image, you start by placing an anchor on each of four corners of something that you believe is rectangular and represents the image perspective, such as a door or window, or the signboard in our image, and then adjust the corner positions as needed. Before you begin to place the points, read "Grid Gymnastics" at the right for some insight into the process.

Success depends on drawing and adjusting the grid. As you use the **Create Plane tool** to place the corner anchor points, holding down the **X key temporarily zooms** in so you can see more precisely (the X shortcut also works when the other Vanishing Point tools are active). As soon as you place the fourth point and release the cursor, you'll see a red, yellow **B**, or blue grid **C**. Although you can use the tools on red or yellow, the color warns you that Vanishing Point might not accurately scale and proportion elements on it; a **blue grid** is what you're aiming for. Setting the fourth anchor automatically chooses the **Edit Plane tool**, and you can move the anchors to adjust the grid. In **VP-Before.psd**, we could see that the sign wasn't badly distorted by perspective, so we chose and then edited the position for the fourth point to generate a grid whose cells weren't very distorted from square (the blue grid shown here). To make it easier to see how elements in your image relate to the Vanishing Point perspective plane, you can change the **Grid size** (at the top of the Vanishing Point interface) and use the Edit Plane tool to **align the grid** by dragging on a grid line.

With the grid established, click "OK" to return to the main Photoshop interface.

GRID GYMNASTICS

If we were to create a Vanishing Point perspective plane on a surface that was facing us directly, it would consist of square cells **A**.

The more skewed the surface is, the more pronounced the perspective distortion is, and the more distorted the squares become. For instance, with a wall that instead of facing us is sharply angled, the cells are distorted into tall skewed rectangles as the grid is foreshortened **B**.

As shown below, when you create a perspective plane in Vanishing Point, a very small difference in the placement of a single point can make a big difference in the grid and in the results you get when you use it.

Placing the four anchors precisely on the corners of your rectangular element is less important than making sure they generate a grid that makes sense for the image, even if this involves some creative tweaking of the anchor positions. Some reasons that you and Vanishing Point might generate a grid that needs tweaking in order to work right are:

- Despite your best efforts, you may have positioned one of your points a little off the exact corner of your rectangular element.
- The "rectangle" you're using might actually have been not-quite-rectangular in real life.
- The camera lens may have caused distortion.
- Any combination of the above factors could be at work.

3 Paste in Perspective

To bring in the new sign, in the **Sunrise Bakery.psd** file, select the entire sign graphic (Ctrl/⌘-A) and copy it to the clipboard (Ctrl/⌘-C). In the **VP-Before.psd** file, target the *Background* by clicking its thumbnail in the Layers palette, and then add a new layer above it (Ctrl/⌘-Shift-N). This layer will hold the sign when you paste it into the file in Vanishing Point.

With the new layer active, reopen Vanishing Point (Ctrl-Alt-V is the shortcut in Windows; ⌘-Option-V on the Mac) and paste the copied sign graphics (Ctrl/⌘-V). The pasted element will appear in the upper left corner **A** and the Marquee tool will be active. Drag inside the pasted element to move it into the plane — its perspective will change to match **B**. *Note:* If your grid is different from ours, you'll get a different result than you see here. You can tweak the pasted sign (see "Cheating a Little" at the right) and expect that your results from here on might be slightly different from ours. Or you can open the ⊕ **VP-with grid.psd** file, open Vanishing Point, paste the sign graphics, and follow along from there.

Now choose the Transform tool to adjust the pasted and moved logo graphics. As with Photoshop's Transform function, Shift-dragging inward on a corner handle of the Transform box will shrink the logo proportionally. Putting the cursor inside the Transform box and dragging will reposition the logo. We reduced the graphics just enough so they weren't taller than the sign space, and we moved them until we had a balance of white space on the two sides of the graphics **C**. With the sign completed, go on to step 4 without leaving Vanishing Point.

4 Expand the Perspective Plane

Once you've created the perspective plane in Vanishing Point (as you did in step 2), you can use the Edit Plane tool at any time to adjust or expand it. Editing the plane doesn't change the perspective of any changes you've already made, only those that you make afterwards.

In our image the perspective for the sign is probably just slightly different from the perspective of the wall it's on and from that of the wall on the left side, which is set farther back. But the perspectives are close enough so that we can probably use the same grid for all three surfaces rather than make separate but overlapping grids, which can be a little harder to manage than a single one.

To expand the plane to cover the wall surfaces, drag each midpoint handle outward. To zoom out so you can see the entire image, Type Ctrl/⌘-0 (that's zero; the Photoshop shortcuts for zooming in stages are also available in Vanishing Point — Ctrl/⌘-hyphen to zoom out and Ctrl/⌘-+ to zoom in).

With your grid established and expanded as shown above, click "OK" to leave Vanishing Point. In Photoshop proper, set up a new empty layer for painting the strip of wood trim (Ctrl/⌘-N). Then go back into Vanishing Point (Ctrl-Alt-V or ⌘-Option-V).

5 Brush To Paint

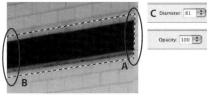

If you need to keep the paint from spilling over an edge like the one at the right side of our blue strip of wood trim, it's easiest to first make a selection with the **Marquee** tool to limit the paint; we used the default Feather setting (1 pixel). The Marquee can leave pixels at the edge of the image partly unselected if you don't select a bit beyond the document bounds. If you're already zoomed in and can't select beyond the document bounds (the left edge in this case), marquee more on the opposite side than you want, then place the cursor inside the selection, and drag until the edge of the selection boundary lines up with the edge you want to preserve **A**. The other end of the marquee will "disappear" into the document edge **B**, indicating that the selection now extends beyond the edge.

Setting the color for the Brush tool to use for painting works a little differently in Vanishing Point than in Photoshop proper. If you want to sample a color to use with Vanishing Point's Brush, you do it *before* choosing the Brush tool. Choose the **Eyedropper** and click on the red in the word "Bakery." Then choose the **Brush**. To completely cover the blue, use **Heal:Off** and leave Hardness set at 100% **C**. Put the cursor at the point where you want to begin to paint, and set the Diameter — use the left and right bracket keys ([and]) and watch the footprint "preview" to get close to the size you need. (For finer adjustment, scrub over the word "Diameter" or drag-select the number and change it.) We started at the left end of the wood trim with the Diameter set at 81 (your diameter may be different, depending on your grid). The brush will automatically adjust its size to match the perspective plane as you paint. Click where you want to start painting **D**, and Shift-click at the other end (the Shift key constrains the Brush to straight lines) **E**, **F**. Type Ctrl/⌘-H to turn off "Show Edges," hiding the selection marquee so you can see the right edge. If you need to try again, type Ctrl/⌘-Z to step backwards.

"HEAL" MODES MAKE THE TOOLS

Vanishing Point's **Marquee**, **Stamp**, and **Brush** tools, when you operate them in **Heal:Off** mode, will copy, clone, or paint much the same as the tools with the same names in Photoshop proper. But they can also operate in two other modes — **Heal:On** and **Heal: Luminance**. With these options, Vanishing Point's Marquee operates as a combination Marquee and Patch tool, the Stamp as Stamp plus Healing Brush, and the Brush as Brush plus Spot Healing Brush.

The **Brush** tool paints. In **Heal:Off** mode it paints with the chosen color, covering up whatever is below it. In **Heal:Luminance** mode, the brush paints with the chosen color, but it uses the luminance of the area it covers (the brush footprint "preview" is also shown here). In **Heal:On** mode, the brush ignores the chosen color and instead samples color and luminance from the area you're painting.

In **Heal:Off** mode the **Marquee** (shown below) and **Stamp** cover the image by cloning the source you designate. The Opacity and the amount of Feather (Marquee) or Hardness (Stamp) control how completely the image is covered. While the Stamp tool requires you to set a source first, the Marquee tool has two **Move Modes** — Destination and Source. We find it easiest to leave the Move Mode set to Destination and use helper keys to change the mode of operation — Ctrl/⌘-drag to copy material from outside *into* the selection, or Alt/Option-drag to copy the selected area to another place in the image. With **Heal:Off** the Marquee and Stamp copy the selected material (here a part of the brick wall) to hide the area you copy into. With **Heal:Luminance** checked, these tools preserve the luminance of the area you copy into. With **Heal:On**, they use the source area for the details, but blend it with the color *and* the luminance of the area you copy into.

6 Marquee to Copy

The next step is to copy the red strip to the righthand side
of the wall and also add a bit to the left side by the sign. If
you turned off "Show Edges" in step 5, turn it back on now
(Ctrl/⌘-H). Starting with the copy for the far right, and
using the default settings for the **Marquee** tool ⬚ (Feather
1, Opacity 100, Heal:Off), select most of the strip on the
left, including the shadowed bottom edge. Then hold
down the Alt/Option key (to make a copy) and begin
dragging to the right (to move the copy). As you drag, also
depress the Shift key (to keep the copy aligned with the
original strip). The strip will grow proportionally larger as
you move the copy along the wall **A**. You'll cover part of
the alarm, but that's fine because we'll be removing it anyway. Align the left edge of the copied strip with the sign
(use Ctrl/⌘-H to check), and release the mouse and keys
to "commit" the copy — but don't deselect it yet.

To extend the strip, rather than copy again (which might
leave a mark where the two copies join), you can simply
stretch your copy, since there isn't any texture or detail to
worry about. With the copy still selected, choose the
Transform tool ▦, grab the midpoint anchor on the right
side, and drag just beyond the right edge **B** (zoom out
with Ctrl/⌘-hyphen if necessary to get beyond the edge).

To copy the original red strip into the area just to the left
of the sign, operate the Marquee tool ⬚ like Photoshop's
Patch tool: Drag with the Marquee around the small area
you want to replace, offsetting this selection just a little upward to hint that the two sections of the wall are separate,
and including enough room in the selection marquee for
the shaded bottom edge of the strip. Then Ctrl/⌘-drag
into the original strip to clone into the selection **C**. If
necessary, type Ctrl/⌘-H and use the Transform tool ▦
to adjust **D**. With the red strips completed, click "OK" **E**.

7 Stamp to Remove an Object

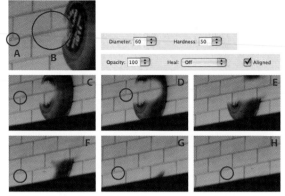

Back in Photoshop, add another new empty layer and reopen Vanishing Point. To remove the alarm bell, we'll cover
it with bricks. The Marquee tool would seem to be a natural for copying bricks from another area. However, the only
area large enough to fill a selection that will cover the alarm
is brighter than the bricks near the alarm, and because the
alarm is very dark, neither Heal:Luminance nor Heal:On
will work.

Instead, to match the bricks around the bell, choose the
Stamp tool ⬚, hold down the Alt/Option key, and line up
the crosshairs with an intersection of a vertical and a horizontal mortar line in the bricks just to the left of the alarm
A; this way you'll avoid the lighter bricks to the right and
the shadow near the edge of the sign.

Because you can't get a footprint "preview" of the Stamp's
"loaded" brush tip **B** until you Alt/Option-click on your
source point, it's easier to size the brush after setting the
source. Set the Size to cover an area large enough to make it
easy to line it up with the existing bricks, but small enough
so that you don't pick up any of the alarm bell; we used a
Diameter of 60. We also chose a soft brush (Hardness
50%), which would make it easy to see how the cloned
bricks were blending with the original, and would prevent
any telltale hard edges; and we chose Aligned to automatically resample as we moved the cursor along.

Once the Stamp is loaded, move the cursor to the right to
the next "mortar intersection" and click. A few more clicks
to the right **C**, **D**, **E** will cover the middle of the alarm. Because you started sampling at the left, working left-to-right
should ensure a "clean" dab source each time you click.
Then you can repeat the left-to-right process for the top
and for the bottom **F**, **G**, **H**. If you get some smudges nevertheless, you can even out the tone by setting a new source
to the right and cloning back over the "smudgier" areas.
Then click "OK" and return to Photoshop.

8 Marquee & Stamp To Cover Up

To remove the market basket, add another layer and open Vanishing Point (Ctrl-Alt-V or ⌘-Option-V). Since we have several straight edges to work with (the document edge on the left, the edge of the sign's wall on the right, and the top of the planter wall at the bottom), we decided the Marquee tool might be a quick way to start the cover-up. We could then use the Stamp for details if necessary.

With the **Marquee** ⸢⸥, select the area you want to replace, extending the selection outside the document to make sure all edge pixels are included **A**. To copy from another area into your selection, hold down the Ctrl/⌘ key while dragging the cursor to the bushes you want to use to replace the basket; adding the Shift key as you drag will constrain the move to follow the perspective grid, which will make it easier to keep the planter edge lined up. When you like the way the basket is covered in the "preview," release the mouse to set the "clone" **B**. If you want to undo and try again, you need to also step backwards (Ctrl/⌘-Z) an extra time, until Move Mode is no longer grayed out. When you've finished, type Ctrl/⌘-D to deselect.

The **Stamp** tool 🖳 works well to clone small areas over the hard edges or over repeating elements that are a dead giveaway that we've been cloning. Select the Stamp 🖳, Alt/Option-click to "load" it, and click to add new bits and pieces of shrubbery and bricks, "reloading" as needed; use a small, hard-edged brush tip to clone the bush where it meets the bricks, and a larger, softer brush to tidy up any areas within the bush or bricks that look cloned and unnatural **C**. If needed, use Ctrl/⌘-Z and try new options until you're comfortable that your cover-up of the basket no longer looks fake. When you've finished, click "OK."

9 Cleanup

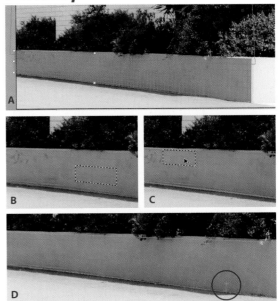

Again add an empty layer and reopen the filter dialog. The planter wall is marred, but the **Marquee** tool ⸢⸥ will make quick work of cleaning up large spaces, as you can select and drag clean areas over marred ones. Any textures will automatically be scaled to fit the perspective.

If you use the Edit Plane tool ▸ to drag the bottom middle handle of the grid down, you can see that the original grid doesn't fit the perspective of the planter wall. For the kind of clean-up that we want to do here (a blank wall with some texture), the existing grid would probably work anyway. But since, in general, this situation might call for a new plane, let's create one for the planter wall; use the **Create Plane** tool ▦ to set the anchors and the **Edit Plane** tool ▸ to adjust the grid **A** (as in step 2).

To remove the marks from the wall without losing the luminosity and color of the original, we used the **Marquee** ⸢⸥ with **Heal:On**, selecting a clean area **B** and then Alt/Option-dragging repeatedly to cover up the worst of the marks in other areas **C**. After deselecting (Ctrl/⌘-D) we used the **Stamp** tool 🖳 with a soft tip, small size, and 60% Opacity with **Heal:On** to work at the bottom of the wall without allowing the nearby shadow on the sidewalk to darken our repairs **D**. When the touch-up is finished, click "OK."

"REDO"

In Vanishing Point, if you undo a change and then decide you want it back, press **Ctrl-Shift-Z** (Windows) or **⌘-Shift-Z** (Mac) to undo the undo.

10 Turn a Corner in Perspective

In order to "paint" our sign on the planter's side wall, copy **Sunrise Bakery.psd** to the clipboard again (or perhaps it's still there), add a new layer to your developing **VP-Before.psd** file, and reopen Vanishing Point. We can try adding to the planter grid so it "turns the corner" to match the perspective of the side wall; if that fails, we can start another grid.

Hold down the Ctrl/⌘ key and with the Edit Plane tool, drag the right-hand middle anchor to the right. This "tears off" a new plane at right angles. If this grid doesn't fit the planter's side wall (ours didn't quite), you have a choice:

- Move the corner anchors of this tear-off grid to align them with the side wall. If you do this, the original planter grid, which is connected to the tear-off grid, will change also, but any painting, pasting, or cloning you've already done won't change (see "Working with More than One Plane" at the right).

- Or choose the Create Plane tool 🖽 and use it to set four corners for a new plane on the planter side wall.

Our tear-off grid almost fit, so we adjusted its anchors **A**. Since the side wall seems to be facing us almost straight on, the grid cells are close to square.

When the grid is aligned with the side wall, type Ctrl/⌘-V to paste the sign into Vanishing Point. Then drag the sign over the planter. You'll see the sign adjust for each perspective plane the cursor passes through. When the sign is roughly where you want it **B**, use the Transform tool 🔣 to move it into position and, with the Shift key held down (to scale proportionally), drag a corner to resize the sign to fit **C**. Click "OK" to return to Photoshop.

11 Finishing Touches in Photoshop

Because you've kept your Vanishing Point edits on separate layers, you can now refine them further in Photoshop proper. Open the **VP-After.psd** file to examine our final result (shown on page 588). To finish this image, we used a Levels Adjustment layer in a clipping group to darken the red strips.▼ We used another Levels layer in a clipping group to lighten the sign on the planter wall to match the glare on the wall; we also added a Layer Style to simulate the wall's texture on this painted sign.▼ The larger sign seemed too sharp and bright for the image, so we also added a masked Solid Color Fill layer in a light gray sampled from the brick wall, with Opacity reduced to 15%.▼

> **FIND OUT MORE**
> ▼ Using Adjustment layers **page 165**
> ▼ Using Layer Styles **page 44**
> ▼ Using Fill layers **page 159**
> ▼ Masking **page 75**

WORKING WITH MORE THAN ONE PLANE

After you use the Create Plane and Edit Plane tools to make the first perspective plane In Vanishing Point, you can either build other related planes or start completely new ones. Tools will automatically work in the perspective of the plane the cursor is in.

To start a new plane, click with the Create Plane tool 🖽 to make four new corner anchors, and adjust them with the Edit Plane tool ▸ to make the plane.

To create a secondary plane that turns a corner at right angles to the currently active plane, use the Edit Plane tool ▸ to Ctrl/⌘-drag on a midpoint handle. If the new secondary plane *almost* fits the elements you want to match, you might want to adjust the corner anchors until it fits. Keep in mind, that the adjustments will "ripple" back through any other connected planes. So if it's important to preserve your original plane, you may want to undo and start a new independent plane instead.

To delete a plane, click with the Edit Plane tool to highlight it and then hit the Backspace/Delete key.

If you've created overlapping perspective planes, you can **activate the plane you want** by repeatedly Ctrl/⌘-clicking inside it, activating planes in the "stack" until you get to the one you want.

If you use the Marquee with Ctrl/⌘ or Alt-Option to clone from one plane to another, the clone will sometimes flip (horizontally) or flop (vertically) as it makes the transition. To straighten this out, choose the Transform tool 🔣 and click the appropriate correction (Flip or Flop) at the top of the dialog box.

Katrin Eismann Gives New Meaning to the Word "Composite"

WHEN SOMEONE SAYS "COMPOSITE," Photoshop users are likely to think of photos of different subjects — either combined seamlessly into a single "fake," or assembled as a collage with their separate origins obvious. But when you say "composite" to photographer Katrin Eismann, she tends to think a little more broadly. The photo at the bottom of the page is optically impossible. To get sharp focus for both the extreme close-up of the fish and the far-away sky required a composite — but maybe not the composite that would first come to mind.

Katrin set up her "Horse Mackerel Beauty" photo on the balcony of her home using a tripod to steady the Nikon D100 camera just a few inches above a market fish she had set on a mirror. Aiming the camera at this still life, she focused at infinity to get a clear picture of the mirrored sky **A**, knowing that for the image reflected in the mirror, she would need to set the focus based on how far away the sky was from the mirror rather than the short distance between the mirror and the camera.

After taking the sky photo, Katrin focused her macro lens on the skin of the fish. Since the lens has a very shallow depth of field when used close up, she took three photos, each focusing at a slightly different distance, to capture the detail of the skin on the back **B**, fin **C**, and belly **D**.

Katrin layered the four images in a single file with the sky layer at the bottom. Then she added layer masks to all but the sky layer and painted the masks with black to hide the out-of-focus areas of each layer. The result was a composite with everything in focus. To complete the image, Katrin brought out color and detail by adding Adjustment layers and manipulating blend modes.

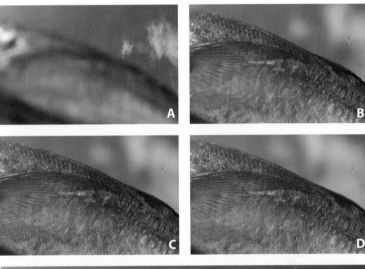

Horse Mackerel Beauty is one of Katrin's *Silent Beauty* series of images. You can see others from the series in the "Gallery" section at the end of this chapter, where you can also learn more about the techniques she uses to optimize color, tone, and image detail.

We promise beaches like this one.

Believe it or not, beaches like this still exist. Where the waves are gentle, the sand is soft, and marine life is everywhere in abundance.

For a vacation in unsurpassed natural beauty with wonders that never cease, come to La Playa Island Resorts. You'll find us on the Web at www.laplaya.com.

1.800.555.2323

LA PLAYA ISLAND RESORTS

Adding Type to an Image

YOU'LL FIND THE FILES

in (wow) > Wow Project Files > Chapter 9 > Adding Type:

- Adding Type-Before.psd (to start)
- Wow Sun Logo.csh (a Custom Shape presets file)
- Adding Type-After.psd (to compare)

OPEN THESE PALETTES

from the Window menu:

- Tools • Layers • Character • Paragraph

OVERVIEW: Expand the image background • Add image-filled headline type • Lighten part of the background and set paragraph text over it • Import a logo and add a Layer Style • Set type around a circle • Set type and "carve" it into the sand.

BEFORE PHOTOSHOP CS/CS2, DESIGNING AN AD often started with editing the photo in Photoshop, but then required moving into another program to set the type. Now, however, with type on a path and within a path, combined with Photoshop's expert typesetting engine, it's easy to design an ad, from logo to body text, without ever leaving Photoshop.

1 Choosing a photo. We began our ad by choosing a photo that suited our theme and that we could adapt to accommodate the text, headline, and logo we wanted to use **1**. As often happens, the layout of the photo didn't quite fit with the way we wanted to use it. We had more photo on the left than we needed, less on the right, and a bit too little at the top of the image to fit the headline well. But because the background of the image was fluid and organic, we could "reproportion" the photo to the dimensions we wanted.

2 "Reproportioning" the image. We opened our photo file and also started a new RGB file at the size we wanted for our small ad (File > New, at 7.2 inches wide by 5.5 inches high and

The original photo

This is **Adding Type-Before.psd**. A file has been created for the small ad, and the photo has been dragged into position and merged with the *Background*.

Individual groups of shells are copied to new layers so they can be preserved, undistorted, when the background is stretched.

The top of the image (but not the white space above it) is selected and stretched to the top of the canvas.

CANDIDATES FOR STRETCHING

You don't necessarily have to reject an image just because its proportions don't match the space you plan to fill in a layout. For many images with fluid, organic backgrounds or portraits shot against a drape or an abstract backdrop, it's possible to stretch the background areas beside, above, or below the subject. Obviously this won't work for backgrounds that show a lot of detail or that include large features with definite proportions (such as a car), since these will show the distortion. And in a photo with a pronounced grain, stretching can turn the grain into streaks.

225 pixels/inch). We used the Move tool ⤧ to drag the photo into our new file and offset it to the left. (If it had been necessary to resize the image to fit the ad file, we would have done it at this point▼, but it wasn't needed.) To tidy up the file, we merged the new image layer with the *Background* (Layer > Merge Down, or Ctrl/⌘-E) **2a**. As well as reducing the file to a single *Background* layer, this trimmed away the extra image beyond the canvas.

FIND OUT MORE

▼ Resizing **page 73**

Before you stretch a background, you may want to preserve some features in their original proportions so you can use them to replace obviously stretched elements later. To preserve a few of the shells in this image, you can use the Lasso tool ⟲ to select a group of shells (we set the feather at 2 pixels in the Options bar), and copy it from the *Background* to a new layer (Ctrl/⌘-J). Then target the *Background* again by clicking its thumbnail in the Layers palette, and select and copy another group of shells. We continued until we had "preserved" the three pairs of shells that were biggest and farthest forward **2b**.

Now for the stretching. Target the *Background* again and also Alt/Option-click on the *Background*'s visibility icon ⬉ to view the *Background* alone. Drag with the Rectangular Marquee ⬚ to select the top of the photo, above the child's head. Then stretch the selected area to the top of the canvas by pressing Ctrl/⌘-T (for Edit > Free Transform) and dragging up on the top center handle of the Transform frame to fill the top of the canvas with image **2c**; press the Enter/Return key to complete the transformation. Next select as much of the right side of the image as you can without selecting the child (the wider the selection, the less you'll have to stretch it), and transform that area, stretching until it reaches the right side of the canvas **2d**.

3 Repairing the details. Now, to remove shells that are obviously stretched, use the Clone Stamp tool ⬆ on the *Background*,

2d

The *Background* after the top and right side have been stretched

3a

Using the Clone Stamp to remove an obviously stretched detail

3b

Turning on Auto Select Layer for the Move tool ▶⊕ makes it easy to drag the "preserved" shell layers into place.

4a

Setting up the Options bar for typing the headline

Alt/Option-clicking to sample an area of empty beach to "paint with" and then releasing the Alt/Option key and painting over the stretched shells **3a**. In the Layers palette, Alt/Option-click on the ◉ for the *Background* to make all layers visible again. Use the Move tool ▶⊕ with Auto Select Layer turned on in the Options bar to drag the copied shells into their new positions on the transformed beach **3b**. Now check for obvious signs of manipulation. (If there are any, you can add an empty layer by typing Ctrl/⌘-Shift-N, and then use the Healing Brush ⬚, the Spot Healing Brush ⬚ in CS2, or the Clone Stamp ⬚, with Use All Layers/Sample All Layers turned on in the Options bar.)▼ Finally merge all the layers into the *Background* (Ctrl/⌘-Shift-E).

4 Typing and "styling" the headline. For the headline, select the Type tool **T**. In the Options bar choose a bold font (we used Trebuchet MS Bold at 28 pt for our small ad), set the Alignment option to Center text, and click the color swatch to choose a color that's easy to see against the image (we used white) **4a**. For **centered point type**, click once where you want the line to be centered (in our case, halfway across the image) and type. When you finish typing, hit Ctrl/⌘-Enter **4b**. With the Type tool still selected, you can adjust the position of the type if necessary by holding down the Ctrl/⌘ key (to turn the Type tool into the Move tool temporarily) and dragging; if you turned on Auto Select Layer (in step 3), either be careful to drag exactly on the type, or turn off the Auto Select option.

To help the type stand out, you can add a Layer Style, building it *before* fine-tuning the spacing of the headline, since it may change the way the spacing looks. Click the "Add a layer style" button ⬚ at the bottom of the Layers palette and choose Drop Shadow. Turn off "Use Global Light"▼ and set the Angle (we used 45° to cast the shadow to the left and down) and the Distance (we offset the shadow 13 px). Adjust the Size (to determine how far the shadow extends; we used 12 px) and Spread (to determine how dense the shadow will be; we used 23%). We left the Blend Mode and Opacity at their default settings of Multiply and 75%. Click "OK" to close the Layer Style dialog box.

Now that you can see how the Layer Style affects the spacing of the type **4c**, you can interactively fine-tune the headline if you think it needs it. Click to make an insertion point between two letters whose spacing needs adjusting (kerning), or drag-select

FIND OUT MORE

▼ Using the Healing Brush ⬚ **page 318**

▼ Using the Spot Healing Brush ⬚ **page 319**

▼ The "Use Global Light" option **page 497**

4b Headline type set

4c Drop shadow added

5a

Drawing a rectangular selection big enough to include the type

5b

Making a clipping group to mask the image inside the type. Since the masked image and the background are identical, only the Drop Shadow effect defines the characters at this point.

5c

Adding a Levels Adjustment layer to the clipping group to lighten the image inside the type

several characters if you want to change their spacing overall (tracking). Hold down the Alt/Option key and hit the → or ← key for more or less space, respectively. Or use the Character palette (click the ▤ button in the Type tool's Options bar) to type in an amount, or to "scrub" to make the change. When you're satisfied with the spacing, type Ctrl/⌘-Enter to commit the type.

5 Filling the headline. The next step is to fill the headline with the background image. With the Marquee tool ⬚, drag a rectangle around the type **5a**. Then in the Layers palette, turn off visibility for the type layer by clicking its ◉ and target the *Background.* Copy the selected area (Ctrl/⌘-C), and then target the type layer and paste (Ctrl/⌘-V); because the type layer is targeted, the copied selection will be pasted as a layer just above it. Now restore the type, which has been hidden by the pasted layer: In the Layers palette, Alt/Option-click on the border between the type layer and the pasted layer to make a clipping group, which allows the pasted layer to show only inside the type **5b**.

The area you selected and clipped inside the headline type is identical to the background, but lightening it will make the type stand out more. Alt/Option-click on the "Create new fill or adjustment layer" button ◑, choose Levels, and check the box for "Use Previous Layer to Create Clipping Mask" so that only the image that's clipped inside the type will be affected by the Levels adjustment. Click "OK" to close the New Layer dialog box, and in the Levels dialog box lighten the type; we moved the Input Levels white point slider to the left to brighten the type by both lightening it and boosting contrast, and moved the Output Levels black point slider to the right to lighten the type more without further increasing contrast **5c**. Click "OK" to close the Levels dialog box **5d**.

5d

In the clipping group the type layer is the base that masks both the image rectangle and the Levels adjustment.

6a

Setting up the gradient for the Gradient Fill layer

6b

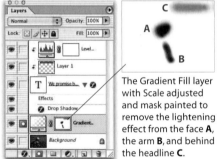

The Gradient Fill layer with Scale adjusted and mask painted to remove the lightening effect from the face **A**, the arm **B**, and behind the headline **C**.

7a

A text box for paragraph type is defined by dragging with the Type tool T. If necessary, the box can be adjusted to fit the text better later.

6 Preparing an area for text. A Gradient Fill layer is a flexible way to lighten part of the photo so it's easier to read dark text over it, and to provide the kind of effect we want here. ▼ Select white as the Foreground color (you can do this by typing D and then X). Again target the *Background* and click on the "Create new fill or adjustment layer" button ◑ at the bottom of the Layers palette and choose Gradient from the pop-up list. In the Gradient Fill dialog box, make sure that the gradient shows white to transparent (if it doesn't, click on the gradient and in the Gradient Preset picker, click on the Foreground to Transparent swatch). Then set up the gradient this way **6a**:

- For a simple left-to-right transition from clear to white, select Linear as the Style and set the Angle at 180°.

- With the Gradient Fill dialog box still open, you can move the gradient and adjust its density to make the background right for the type, as follows: Move the cursor into the image window, where it automatically becomes a temporary Move tool, and drag the gradient to the right in the image window until the lightening effect begins just over the child's cheek (you can remove the gradient from the child's face and arm later).

- Adjust the Scale in the Gradient Fill dialog (we used 75%) to make the gradient go from clear to white over a shorter distance, creating a light enough background for the type.

When you're satisfied with the gradient's position and scale, click "OK." You can leave the blend mode for the Gradient Fill layer at Normal since the gradient is white, but if you were using a color instead, you might try Screen or Lighten.

You can take advantage of the automatic mask created with the Gradient Fill layer to fix areas that are lightened too much. In our image, for instance, the edge of the child's face and her arm seemed too light. We chose the Brush tool ✐, clicked on the brush footprint in the Options bar, and picked a soft brush tip from the Brush Preset picker; also in the Options bar we lowered the Opacity to 50% (for more control in building density), and changed the Foreground color to black (typing D or X will do it). We painted on the mask just over the face and arm to remove the screen effect. We also brushed the area behind the right end of the headline type, for more contrast between the lightened type and the background **6b**.

7 Typing the text. For **paragraph type** aligned with the right edge of the headline, turn on the rulers (Ctrl/⌘-R) and drag

FIND OUT MORE

▼ Gradient Fill layers
page 188

7b

Specifying type in the Options bar

7c

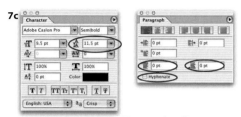

Using the Character and Paragraph palettes to add to the type specs

7d

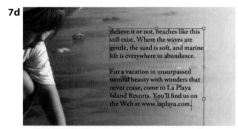

The body text is typed into the text box. Although it's possible to set interparagraph spacing in the Paragraph palette, we simply pressed the Enter/Return key to add space between paragraphs.

SPELL-CHECKING

When you've entered all of your text, to ensure that you didn't make typing mistakes, choose Edit > Check Spelling, and Photoshop will bring up the Check Spelling dialog box, listing words it doesn't know one at a time. Here you can replace words with ones from Photoshop's dictionary. Or ignore the suggestions, or add words to the dictionary (such as "www" or a brand name) so the spell checker won't ask about them every time they appear. You can also choose to check *all* the live type in the document.

a guide from the ruler on the left, lining it up with the last letter of the headline. With the guide in place, select the Type tool T. Start at the guide and at the level of the child's eyes, and drag left and down to make a box to hold the text **7a**; if you need to move the box, hold down the Ctrl/⌘ key and drag.

In the Type tool's Options bar, select a typeface for the body that's bold enough to show up against the background (we chose Adobe Caslon Pro Semibold); we chose 9.5 pt for the Size and clicked the "Left align text" button **7b**. Set leading in the Character palette (we chose 11.5 pt) **7c**. In the Paragraph palette, we made sure that Hyphenate was unchecked and that both "Add space before paragraph" and "Add space after paragraph" were set to 0 because we preferred to separate the paragraphs of our text with a full line space. Type the body text **7d**. If you want to check spelling, now is a good time, before you fine-tune the spacing (see the "Spell-Checking" tip at the left). If the text doesn't fit the text box, adjust the spacing as described in the "Type-Fitting" tip on the next page.

8 Adding a stored logo. The next step is to add the logo, which has been stored as a Custom Shape preset and will be added as a Shape layer. Choose the Custom Shape tool ☁. Click the "Shape" icon in the middle of the Options bar to open the Custom Shape Preset picker **8a**, where you can then click the ▸ button in the upper right corner to open the palette menu. Choose Load Shapes and load the **Wow Sun Logo.csh** file from the **Adding Type** folder of files for this project. Now you can find the Wow Sun Logo listed at the bottom of the open palette; click on it. Click the ▾ a little to the left on the Options bar to open the Custom Shapes Options menu **8b**, and make sure Defined Proportions is checked so the logo's proportions will be maintained; click the "Shape layers" button ▢ at the left end of the Options bar. Click the color swatch in the Options bar and choose a color; we sampled a dark warm brown from a shadow on the child's leg. To position the logo, we added a horizontal guide in line with the bottom of the child's lower sandal. Now drag the Custom Shape tool to draw the logo at the size you want. With the Ctrl/⌘ key held down to temporarily access the Move tool ▸⊕, you can position the logo **8c**.

We added a drop shadow to the logo to pop it off the page a bit. To construct this Style, click the "Add a layer style" button ⊘ at the bottom of the Layers palette and choose Drop Shadow. Turn off Use Global Light and set the parameters for the shadow; we used Angle 45°, Distance 3 px, Spread 1%, and Size 7 px **8d**.

Here's a series of adjustments you can make to get paragraph text to fit better in the space available for it:

1 Photoshop uses the InDesign type engine for letterspacing and word spacing. With the **Adobe Every-line Composer** selected from the flyout menu in the Paragraph palette, Photoshop can adjust spacing anywhere in a paragraph to solve a spacing problem in any one line. When your design allows you the flexibility to **make the text box a bit larger or smaller,** you can often get professional-looking typesetting simply by adjusting the size of the box and letting the Adobe Every-line Composer reflow the type.

2 If you still don't like the way the type is set and can't adjust the text box any more, you can **change the font size or leading** in the Character palette to help the type fit the box; the size and leading boxes accept numbers to two decimal places.

3 Turn on **Hyphenate** if your project allows you to use it.

4 As a last resort, manually adjust the **tracking** and **kerning** of the paragraph in the Character palette.

8a

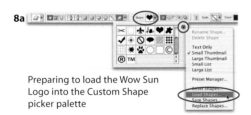

Preparing to load the Wow Sun Logo into the Custom Shape picker palette

8b

Choosing the Defined Proportions option

9 Adding type on a circle. To set the type around the logo, first make a circular path: Choose the Ellipse tool ⬭ and click on the "Paths" button 🔲 near the left end of the Options bar. Starting at the center of the logo shape, begin to drag outward. Then hold down the Shift and Alt/Option keys to draw a perfect circle centered at your starting point; if you notice that the circle is forming off-center, add the spacebar to the keys you're holding down, drag to reposition the circle, and then release the spacebar so you can continue drawing the circle.

Choose the Type tool **T** and set your type specs. In the Options bar we chose Trebuchet MS Bold at 11 pt and clicked the "Center text" button. We clicked the color swatch and clicked on the logo to sample color. We also clicked the Character palette's "Small Caps" button and chose a value of +25 from its menu for tracking. Move the Type tool cursor to the center of the top of the path; when it turns into the **type-on-a-path** icon, click and type the company name. Type Ctrl/⌘-Enter to commit the type **9**. Adjust type size in the Options bar if necessary for fit.

To "style" the type to match the logo, in the Layers palette right-click (Windows) or Ctrl-click (Mac) on the 🞊 for the logo layer and choose Copy Layer Style. Then right/Ctrl-click in the same area of the palette's entry for the type layer and choose Paste Layer Style.

You may need to do some more tracking or kerning at this point to make the type fit around the circle better, using the same method as with the headline. If you need to reposition the type around the circle after kerning, choose the Path Selection tool ▸, hover the cursor over the top center of the type circle until it turns into the I-beam with the double arrow, and then drag. (If you need to reposition the entire circle of type relative to the logo, you can do it by dragging with the Move tool ▸⊕.)

The phone number was set as **point type** in Trebuchet MS Bold, 10 pt. We clicked the color swatch in the Options bar and clicked on the logo to sample color. We used the guide as our baseline.

10 "Carving" type into the sand. Next we added a photo credit, distorted to suggest that it was drawn in the sand: Choose the Pen tool ⬭ and click the "Paths" button in the Options bar; then click and drag to draw a path that curves below the child's right foot **10a**. ▼ Choose the Type tool **T** again. Set the type specs in the Options bar: We chose Trebuchet MS, Bold, 9 pt, and "Left aligned"; we clicked the color swatch and sampled a dark wet-sand color from the image. Click on the path, type the photographer's name, and press Ctrl/⌘-Enter **10b**.

FIND OUT MORE

▼ Using the Pen tool ⬭ **page 435**

8c

The scaled logo in place, aligned with the bottom of the child's foot.

8d

A Layer Style consisting only of a Drop Shadow effect is added to the logo.

9

Using capital letters will make the circling "band" of type more uniform. Choosing small caps kept the letter height in proportion to the sun without reducing point size and decreasing legibility. Positive tracking (here +25) often improves the look of type set on a circle.

To distort the type, we would use the Distort command, which we found easier to control than Warp Text (or Edit > Transform > Warp in CS2). Distort is one of the Transform commands that can't be used on live type, so first convert the type to pixels (Layer > Rasterize > Type). Then choose Edit > Transform > Distort and drag the individual handles of the Transform frame to spread the type out on the sand; double-click inside the Transform frame to complete the distortion **10c** (if your distortion goes awry and you want to start over, you can type Ctrl/⌘-period or hit the Escape key instead of double-clicking, and then use Edit > Transform > Distort again).

Next we used the Ripple filter to distort the letters slightly and a Layer Style to add shading to create depth. Choose Filter > Distort > Ripple, set the parameters (we used Small for the Size and 70% for the Amount) **10d**, and click "OK." Then click the "Add a layer style" button 𝑓 at the bottom of the Layers palette and choose Bevel and Emboss; choose Inner Bevel and Smooth, and turn off Use Global Light; choose **Down** for the **Direction** and set the parameters so the shadows inside the type match the shadows caused by small lumps of sand in the image (we used 35° for the Angle, 16° for the Altitude, a Depth of 50%, and Size and Soften settings of 0); click "OK." In the Layers palette we reduced the Fill opacity for this "carved" layer to 80% **10e**, which lightened the letters without affecting the bevel shadows and highlights of the Style as much as if we had reduced the overall layer Opacity.

10a

A path is drawn for the type.

10b

The type is set on the path.

10c

The rasterized type is flattened onto the sand with the Distort command.

10e

The "drawn in the sand" look, after applying the Ripple filter, adding a Style, and reducing the Fill opacity

10d

Adding a slight ripple to the lettering

"Photomerging" a Panorama

OVERVIEW
If necessary, match the color of the images in the series • Try Photomerge for an automated panorama or as a working window for aligning layers • Blend aligned layers with layer masks • Check the blend with Shadow/Highlight • Adjust overall color & tone

WHEN IT COMES TO PIECING TOGETHER a series of images to make a panorama, Photoshop's Photomerge command can often do much of the work for you.▼ And for panoramas like this one that defy automation, Photomerge still provides a great interface where *you* can do the "merging" work that it can't.

FIND OUT MORE
▼ Using Photomerge
page 580

The Match Color command is also a boon for piecing panoramas, since it can shortcut the process of matching colors between the series images. Automated cameras, both digital and film, change their exposure settings as the light changes, and often this is what the photographer wants. But when you shoot a panoramic series, the different automatic exposure settings that happen as you point the camera more directly into the light can cause color mismatches between images in the series.

1a

The three original images in the panorama series

ORIGINAL PHOTOS: JHDAVIS

SHOOTING FOR A PANORAMA

When you shoot photos for a panorama, here are some things you can do to make the eventual merging process easier:

• Check to see if your camera has a special setting for shooting images for a panorama.

• If not, set the exposure manually if you can, setting it once and leaving it at that setting for the entire series.

• Keep the camera in one spot if you can, turning it rather than moving it around. And keep it level, both side-to-side and front-to-back. A tripod can be a great help.

• Shoot for an overlap of about 25%. More requires too many photos, but less might not leave enough overlap for merging.

• For the typical horizontal panorama, shoot "taller" than you think you will need, allowing plenty of top and bottom edge space, so you won't wind up cropping off something important at the top or bottom of your panorama when photos are moved up or down or distorted in order to align them.

1b

Choosing the Match Color command. Match Color is an adjustment that can be applied via the Adjustments menu but not as an Adjustment layer.

1c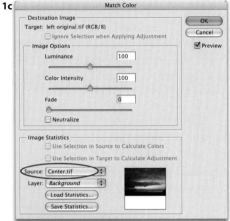

The color of **Left.psd** is matched to that of **Center.psd**.

2

Choosing to merge the open files

3a

Photomerge aligns the Center and Right images **A** but can't align the Left **B**.

This kind of color shift can be the main problem you need to address when you piece the panorama together, as it was in this series of three photos.

1 Preparing the images. Check the color of your images to see if color matching is needed. If your photos were taken specifically for a panorama (see "Shooting for a Panorama" on the facing page), you may not need to correct color, and you may want to use File Browser/Bridge to multi-target the images (by Ctrl/⌘-clicking or Shift-clicking) and then open them in Photomerge directly from there (in File Browser, use Automate > Photomerge; in Bridge, use Tools > Photoshop > Photomerge). If no color matching is needed, you can go to step 3.

For our sunset images, it's clear that **Left.psd** will need to be color-corrected to match the other two photos **1a**. So if you're following along with our files (or are using other images that need to be color-matched), open the files in Photoshop.

With **Left.psd** active choose Image > Adjustments > Match Color **1b**. In the Match Color dialog box, for the **Source** (in the lower left corner of the dialog box) choose the image whose color you would like to match **1c**; we chose **Center.psd** and checked the result in the working window. If the recoloring effect is too strong (ours wasn't), modify it with the Fade slider. Then click "OK" to close the dialog box. Save the altered file (use File > Save if you have the original safely stored somewhere else for safekeeping; or use File > Save As and a new file name).

2 Starting Photomerge from Photoshop. With your files open in Photoshop, choose File > Automate > Photomerge, and in the first Photomerge dialog box **2**, for the "Use" function, choose "Open Files." If you have extra files open, Ctrl/⌘-click to highlight the names of the extras and click the "Remove" button to take them out of the list. Then click "OK."

3 Working in Photomerge. Once you activate Photomerge (from Photoshop, File Browser in CS, or Bridge in CS2), it goes to work, doing its best to overlap and align the component images. If it isn't completely successful (as we found to be the case with this series), a warning box will let you know; click "OK" to continue **3a**. In the Photomerge dialog, photos that Photomerge can align will appear in the large lower panel. Any that couldn't be aligned will appear in the "lightbox" band at the top of the window, and the Select Image tool ▸ will be active. A Navigator slider in the upper right corner of the Photomerge dialog lets you enlarge the view **3b**.

3c

3b

"Snap to Image" provides an automatic assist to manual alignment.

Enlarging the view in the Photomerge dialog box

3d

Rotating the Left image slightly

3e

The images are aligned but not well-blended in Photomerge. Choosing "Keep as Layers" will allow you to use layer masks to blend the images in Photoshop.

4a

The Center image is positioned as the bottom layer. The Left and Right layers will be masked.

4b

Choosing the "Black, White" gradient, to be applied in the Linear style with the Reverse option turned off

Drag each image in the upper band into the lower panel, where it will look partly transparent so you can see to align it manually by overlapping. With the "Snap to Image" option turned on (in the lower right corner) **3c**, Photomerge will take over and align the images if you get close; turn this option off if you want finer control.

If you need to rotate an image slightly to make it line up, use the Rotate Image tool ⟳ (the keyboard shortcut is **R**) and drag the cursor to turn the photo **3d**; we rotated the left image slightly counterclockwise to straighten the horizon and then turned off "Snap to Image" and moved this photo up slightly to align it with the center image.

When you and Photomerge have overlapped and aligned all the images, you have several options for completing the panorama. Since it's obvious from our Photomerge preview that the sunset panorama will need more work to get smooth transitions **3e**, click the check box at the lower right to "Keep as Layers" so you'll be able to use layer masks to blend the images; then click "OK." Photomerge will automatically produce a file that's wide enough to hold the panorama, with each component image as a separate layer.

CAN'T ALIGN?

If the alignment of details can't be resolved by simply overlapping the images in a panoramic series, here are some things you can try. **First, within the Photomerge interface:**

If you **aren't getting a good alignment** in Photomerge's default mode, try both Perspective alone and Perspective with Cylindrical Mapping. To see the results of Cylindrical Mapping, you must click the "Preview" button.

On the other hand, if you're getting a **pretty good alignment**, but it isn't perfect, you can try Advanced Blending, which will take greater care to align objects through the center of the image, but at the expense of the edges; click "Preview" to see the result. Advanced Blending doesn't allow you to keep the individual images on layers, though, so it can be harder to resolve any remaining problems. (To "undo" Advanced Blending click "Exit Preview.")

Outside the Photomerge dialog box, if you can't adjust alignment of an element that continues from one part of the panorama to another, you can try this: In the Layers palette, reduce the Opacity of the upper of the two layers, so you can see the element on both layers at once. Then select the element on one of the two layers and use the Edit > Transform > Distort command (or press Ctrl/⌘-T, and then hold down the Ctrl/⌘ key); drag any of the corner points to distort the element and bring it into alignment with its twin in the other part.

4c

Dragging the Gradient tool ▨ to create a blending mask; the effect is shown below.

4d

Checking the effectiveness of the top layer's mask. The result looks good.

4e

Making the blending mask for the "Right.psd" layer

4 Blending with layer masks. You may want to change the "stacking order" of the layers to an order that seems logical for the kinds of repairs that are needed. Just drag the individual layer thumbnails up or down the Layers palette. For this panorama we put the "Center" layer on the bottom **4a**. We would mask the "Left" and "Right" layers to reveal the "Center" layer.

Now you'll create layer masks to control how each layer's image blends with the next one in the series in the area where they overlap. A black-to-white gradient will form the basis of each mask, with details hand-painted if necessary. Target the top layer in your stack by clicking its thumbnail in the Layers palette; for our file, this was the "Left" layer. Change its Opacity to 90% (with the slider at the top of the palette) so you can see the overlap. Click the "Add layer mask" button ▣ at the bottom of the palette.

To make the blending mask, choose the Gradient tool ▨. In the Options bar click the "Linear" button, and open the Gradient palette by clicking the tiny arrow to the right of the sample Gradient **4b**; choose the "Black, White" gradient (it's the third one in the default palette).

Drag the Gradient tool's cursor across the overlap, starting just inside where you want this layer's image to disappear completely and ending just inside where you want this layer to completely hide the underlying image **4c**. Restore the layer's Opacity to 100% to check the blend **4d**. If the first try hasn't produced a smooth transition in the lighting and color of the two layers, you can reduce the layer's Opacity to 90% again and make another try at drawing the gradient. If the blending has caused ghosting of details that don't overlap perfectly, you can hand-paint the gradient mask with black to give priority to the lower layer, or with white to give priority to the upper layer. ▼

FIND OUT MORE

▼ Painting a layer mask **page 75**

4f

The blended panorama, with two gradient-based layer masks

5a

Checking details by lightening a merged copy of the image with the Shadow/Highlight command. Depending on your image, you might use a different Adjustment command (such as Levels) to check for problems.

5b

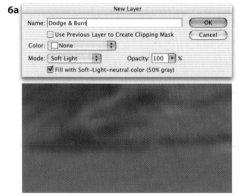

After undoing Shadow/Highlight

6a

A "Dodge & Burn" layer in Soft Light mode is added and painted (shown here viewed @ alone).

Repeat the masking operation for all other layers except the bottom one. We added a gradient mask to the "Right" layer **4e**, but no other changes were needed **4f**. (If you need to make additional individual color adjustments to the layers, you can do so by adding Adjustment layers, limiting their effects to a single layer by making a clipping group.)▼

FIND OUT MORE

▼ Using a clipping group **page 70**

5 Checking the blend. For this sunset panorama, much of the foreground of the image is dark by design. But just to make sure we weren't missing any jolting discontinuities or "double exposures" that might show up in print, we did the following check. We created a merged copy of the image (in Photoshop CS, hold down Ctrl-Alt-Shift (Windows) or ⌘-Option-Shift (Mac) and type N, then E; in CS2 you can do the same, or skip the N). Then we ran the Shadow/Highlight command on this new composite layer (Image > Adjustments > Shadow/Highlight), moving the Shadows Amount slider all the way to 100% to get a better look at details **5a**. Had we found problems (we didn't), we would have addressed them by painting on one or more of our gradient-based layer masks, as described at the end of step 4. After checking with Shadow/Highlight, we used Undo (Ctrl/⌘-Z) to remove the adjustment **5b**.

6 Adjusting overall color and tone. For this image, the clouds were "the star of the show." To make them even more dramatic, we used a dodge-and-burn layer and a Hue/Saturation layer.

We added the dodge-and-burn layer by Alt/Option-clicking the "Create a new layer" button ▣, choosing Soft Light for the Mode in the New Layer dialog box, and checking the box for "Fill with Soft Light-neutral color (50% gray)" **6a**. Then we painted this new layer with the Brush tool ✎; in the Options bar we chose a soft brush tip, set Opacity low, and turned on the Airbrush option. We painted the layer with black to darken the color of the cloud faces, and with white to lighten their undersides. Because the layer was in Soft Light mode, the colors, especially the midtones, were intensified **6b**.

Finally we added a Hue/Saturation layer by clicking the "Create new fill or adjustment layer" button ◔ at the bottom of the Layers palette and choosing from the pop-out list. We increased the Saturation to make the cloud color more brilliant and moved the Hue slider slightly to the right to warm the colors **6c**. We turned on the Gamut Warning (in the View menu) so we could

6b

The "Dodge & Burn" layer adds drama to the sky.

6c

A Hue/Saturation Adjustment layer makes the sky colors more vivid.

be warned if Photoshop determined that the colors were getting too saturated for printing. When that happened, we could choose the problem color range from the Hue/Saturation dialog's Edit menu and reduce Saturation until the warning color (gray) disappeared. Because we've found that some technically "out of gamut" colors print fine, we allowed some colors to stay "hot," not bringing them completely back into gamut.

UNPRINTABLE COLORS?

If you plan to increase color saturation, either with the Hue/Saturation dialog box or with the Sponge tool in Saturate mode, it's a good idea to turn on the **Gamut Warning** so you can see where you may have intensified the color beyond what it's possible to print with the current CMYK Color Settings.

To toggle the Gamut Warning on or off, first make sure the Working CMYK color space is chosen (View > Proof Setup). Then choose View > Gamut Warning (or press Ctrl/⌘-Shift-Y). "Unprintable" colors are displayed as flat gray patches by default, though you can change the warning color by choosing Preferences (Ctrl/⌘-K) and then choosing Transparency & Gamut (Ctrl/⌘-4) and picking a new color.

Both choosing View > Gamut Warning and using the Ctrl/⌘-Shift-Y shortcut will work even if a dialog box is already open. So if you forget to set up the Gamut Warning before you open the Hue/Saturation dialog, you can still get to it.

Note: The Gamut Warning tends to be conservative, telling you that some colors are outside the printable gamut when in fact they may print quite nicely.

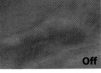 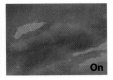

Off **On**

---

7 Fixing the edges. To tidy up the edges, we dragged the Rectangular Marquee ⌷ to surround the biggest area we could and still exclude the uneven edges **7**, and then chose Image > Crop. (Another option is to use the Clone Stamp ▲ to copy material to fill in the empty spaces at the edges.) *wow*

Cropping with the Rectangular Marquee ⌷

7

Reflections

REFLECTIONS can lend serenity or elegance to a scene. Simulated in Photoshop, reflections can also make a composed image more photorealistic and three-dimensional by integrating the subject into its environment. Here are three approaches to "capturing" reflections.

Real: One way to capture a gorgeous and convincing reflection is to hike 20 miles in and 10,000 feet up, sit down, point your camera, and take the shot.

This method registers a high serenity factor.

Photoshop: Another approach is to duplicate and flip an image of your subject, fading the flipped copy with a layer mask, as described in "Tweening a Type Warp" on page 699.

Unlinking the layer mask from its type allowed the "reflection" to be moved into position just below the "real" type, without disturbing the "atmosphere" provided by the mask.

"Real": A third way is to carry your lake, ocean, or mist in your pocket in the form of a mirror. Rod Deutschmann teaches this third approach. Used with or without a polarizing filter, a mirror — flat, with no bevels at the edges — is held perpendicular to the lens. With a digital camera it's easy to preview the image as you tilt the camera and the mirror to get the composition you want.

The first step is to find the image in the broader scene.

Deutschmann chose the tops of the palms.

With a friend supplying the third hand to hold the polarizer, Deutschmann worked out the right combination for the camera, polarizer, and mirror positions, previewing the shot on his LCD screen.

The image with reflections. To create the slight "motion blur" in the "water," Deutschmann had used a citrus-based cleaner to partially remove the silver from some areas of the back of the mirror.

A structure takes on a new geometry.

Mirror work enhances the St. Louis skyline.

Applying an Image to a Textured Surface

OVERVIEW

"Apply" graphics on one layer to a surface image in another layer, using the luminance of the surface layer to distort the graphics to conform to the surface • Adjust blend mode and opacity • Add masks as needed

BENDING, SUBTLY DISTORTING, AND "AGING" an image or graphics so they appear to be part of a textured surface in another image can create a unified visual illusion that can be very powerful in presenting a concept. A fast, flexible and convincing way to do this in Photoshop involves applying the image or graphics with the right blend mode, transparency, and masking, and using the Displace filter with a *displacement map* that's made from the surface image itself. (The Liquify filter, so successful for "massaging" one image to fit the organic contours of another, as on page 615, couldn't begin to do the precise, practical work needed to paint the graphics onto the deteriorating bricks and mortar of this image.)

1 Preparing the components. Choose the image or graphics you want to apply — in this case the sign started as a clip art file, which Don Jolley opened and modified in Adobe Illustrator **1a**. Also open the file with the surface you want to apply it to — here Jolley's photo of a shaded, deteriorating brick wall behind brightly lit posts **1b**.

1a

The sign graphics in Adobe Illustrator

1b

The photo

DONAL JOLLEY

2a

The sign pasted in position

2b

Using the Overlay blend mode and 50% layer Opacity to apply the sign

2 Combining the elements. Add the graphics to the surface image file as a new layer. Jolley copied the graphics in Illustrator and pasted them into the file (Edit > Paste > Paste As Pixels), positioning and sizing the pasted element to fit the space available **2a**; this is the **Apply Image-Before.psd** file.

In the pop-out blend mode list at the top left of the Layers palette, choose Overlay, and try reducing the Opacity (at the top right of the palette) until the graphics and the background image blend as you want; we liked 50% Opacity **2b**. (For the moment, ignore the parts of the image that should be in front of the applied element — here the two posts; we'll deal with them in step 5.) You may want to experiment with other blend modes, such as Multiply, Soft Light, Hard Light, or Color for different visual effects. We tried Soft Light, which lightened and faded the sign **2c**, and Multiply, which darkened and faded it **2d**, but we liked Overlay at 50% the best, so we restored these settings.

3 Making the displacement map. The next step is to prepare a grayscale displacement map from the surface image layer. You'll use it with the Displace filter in step 4 to distort the graphics so they look as if they're affected by the surface topography (in this case the deteriorating bricks). **Note:** If your graphics extend beyond any of the edges of your image, you'll need to trim away any excess at this point in order for the displacement to work right in the next step. To do this, select all (Ctrl/⌘-A) and then choose Image > Crop. And once you've made the displacement map, the file shouldn't be cropped again or resized — at least until after you've run the Displace filter.

To make a grayscale displacement map from the photo layer, in the Layers palette, Alt/Option-click its 👁 icon to make it the only visible layer. Then choose Image > Duplicate, check the "Duplicate Merged Layers Only" option in the Duplicate dialog box, and click "OK." In the new image, choose Image > Mode > Grayscale. To make the grayscale image work better as a displacement map, you may want to get rid of the finest detail by blurring (although we didn't for this image, since the mortar lines themselves were quite small and our displacement would be subtle), and perhaps increase the contrast to exaggerate the light/dark differences (we used Image > Adjust > Levels), moving the black and white Input Levels sliders inward and the gamma slider to the right **3**. (Although we didn't for this project, you may also want to paint over with gray any especially dark or light marks that aren't part of the surface texture. You can sample a medium gray for the paint by

2c

The sign layer in Soft Light mode at 65% Opacity

2d

The sign layer in Multiply mode at 100% Opacity

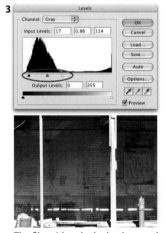

3

The file, with only the background photo visible, is duplicated and converted to Grayscale. Then a Levels adjustment increases contrast between the mortar lines and the bricks.

4a

Running the Displace filter. For a higher-resolution file or more displacement, you would use higher Scale settings.

Alt/Option-clicking in your image with the Brush tool ✎ before you paint.) When your grayscale image is adjusted, **save in Photoshop (PSD) format** (File > Save As, or Ctrl/⌘-S) since the Displace filter uses only saved Photoshop-format files.

4 Applying the displacement map. Back in your composite image, in the Layers palette click on the graphics layer's thumbnail to target this layer, and turn its visibility back on by clicking in its ☻ column. Then choose Filter > Distort > Displace (if your graphics are a Shape or type layer or a Smart Object, you'll be warned at this point that they will be rasterized). In the Displace dialog box **4a**, choose values for the Horizontal and Vertical Scale of the displacement; the higher the numbers, the farther the pixels of your graphics will be nudged by the corresponding dark and light pixels in the displacement map file. Since we needed only subtle nudges to "push" the paint into the troughs of the mortar, we used small values — Horizontal 2 and Vertical 1. (In the Displace dialog, the Displacement Map and Undefined Areas settings are irrelevant because the two files are exactly the same dimensions and the displacement is very small.) Click "OK," locate the displacement map file you just made, and click the "Open" button. The filter will displace the graphics **4b**.

5 Masking the graphics. To put the graphics "behind" any elements in the image that are supposed to appear in front, you can use a layer mask. To make the mask, target the surface photo layer and select the forward elements.▼ To select the two wooden supports, Jolley chose the Magic Wand ✸; in the Options bar he set Tolerance to 32 (for smooth edges), turned off the Contiguous option (to be able to select throughout the image), and also turned off Use All Layers/Sample All Layers (so the Magic Wand would be "looking at" the photo only, not the sign graphics) **5a**.

FIND OUT MORE

▼ Choosing a selection method
page 55

To start the selection he clicked on a bright white area of the larger support, saw what had been selected, and Shift-clicked on an almost-white area to expand the selection. Rather than try to add the shaded area of the post with the Magic Wand, which also would have selected much of the brick wall, he switched to Quick Mask mode at this point (by clicking the "Edit in Quick Mask mode" button ◙ near the bottom of the Tools palette) and used the Brush ✎ with a hard round tip (9 pixels) and white paint (type D, then X) to erase the mask in the shaded area of the larger post. For the thinner post Jolley

4b

Before (left) and after running the Displace filter

5a

Setting up the Magic Wand ✺

5b

The Quick Mask is erased over the posts and a few small features on the wall.

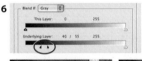

6

Before   After

The black point slider is moved inward for the Underlying Layer so the darkest marks on the wall show through the sign more, adding to the worn and stained look. Holding down Alt/Option splits the slider to make a smooth transition in these areas.

7a

Making a set/group with a mask to fade the lower right corner of the sign

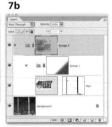

7b

The masked folder is nested inside another set/group, which is masked to "erode" the sign so more of the wall shows through.

held down the Shift key as needed as he used the Brush to erase in vertical lines **5b**; he also erased over a few small features on the wall. He could have used black to mask the white dashed line on the wall, but since it was too low to interfere with the sign, he left it. With the mask complete, he clicked the "Edit in Standard Mode" 🔲 button to go back to an active selection. In the Layers palette he targeted the graphics layer and Alt/Option-clicked the "Add layer mask" button 🔲 at the bottom of the palette; adding the Alt/Option key created a mask that hid the sign in the selected areas and revealed the rest of it — the posts popped in front of the sign.

6 Experimenting with Blending Options. To try "wearing away" parts of the applied graphics, in the Layers palette, right/Ctrl-click the thumbnail for the graphics layer to open a menu where you can choose Blending Options to open the Layer Style dialog box; then adjust the "Blend If" sliders **6**. ▼

7 Adding a "lighting" mask and a "grunge" mask. Putting your graphics layer in a set/group, ▼ as Jolley often does, will give you a way to add a second layer mask: Click the "Create a new set/group" button 🗀 at the bottom of the Layers palette and drag the thumbnail of the graphics layer into the new "folder layer" this creates. Then target the new folder and add a mask by clicking the 🔲 button at the bottom of the palette; filling the mask with a gray-to-white gradient will fade the bottom right corner of the sign **7a**. ▼

Nesting this set/group inside another one and adding a layer mask to the new outer folder gives you still another separate masking opportunity, which can be used to apply some "grunge" to the sign. With the first set/group targeted, click the 🗀 button again, and drag the existing folder's thumbnail into the new folder. Stored in an alpha channel in the **Apply Image-Before.psd** file is one of the many photos in Don Jolley's texture collection. You can turn it into a mask for the new set/group as follows: In the Channels palette, Ctrl/⌘-click on the "Alpha 1" thumbnail to load the luminosity of the channel as a selection. In the Layers palette, target the new folder and click the 🔲 button. To control how much this mask "erodes" the sign, use Image > Adjustments > Levels to adjust Input Levels or Output Levels. With the "grunge" mask in place **7b**, you may also want to brighten the sign layer itself; we increased Opacity to 80% to get the result on page 611. 𝓦𝓸𝓦!

FIND OUT MORE

▼ Using the "Blend If" sliders **page 70**

▼ Layer sets/groups **page 583**

▼ Masking with gradients **page 75**

Applying an Image with Liquify

YOU'LL FIND THE FILES

in 🌀 > Wow Project Files > Chapter 9 > Applying with Liquify:
- Liquify Wrap-Before.psd (to start)
- Liquify Wrap-After.psd (to compare)

OPEN THESE PALETTES

from the Window menu:
- Tools • Layers • Channels

OVERVIEW

Select and align the images as layers in a single file • Create a layer mask to limit the image you're applying to the area where you want it to show • Use the Liquify filter to "mold" the applied image • Adjust color and contrast • Convert to a black-and-white with Channel Mixer

JH DAVIS / MODEL: JENNIFER LUTTRELL / AGENCY: ANDERSONPHOTOGRAPHICS.COM

1a

JHDAVIS

JULIANNE KOST

The original photos of the model (712 pixels wide) and the zebra

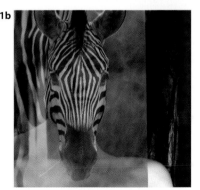

1b

The "Zebra" layer's Opacity is reduced and the layer is flipped, stretched, and moved to more closely fit the model's face.

WHEN YOU MERGE ELEMENTS in Photoshop, often it's the subtle adjustments — like molding one image to fit the surfaces of another using the Liquify filter — that make the result convincing. Liquify is a powerful, practical hands-on tool for projects like the "Wild" image shown here.

1 Select and align the images. In choosing the photos you want to combine, make it a point to find images that share compatible lighting, perspective, and sharpness. The view angle in both of our photos was almost straight on **1a**, and the lighting for the zebra was flat enough that it could work effectively with almost any other image.

To re-create the image above, open the **Liquify Wrap-Before.psd** file. The zebra photo has already been dragged from its own file and dropped onto the shot of our jungle-inhabiting model. To get an even better match of the viewing angles of the two photos, we flipped the "Zebra" layer (Edit > Transform > Flip Horizontal). We reduced its Opacity so we could see through it to line it up with the "Jennifer" photo layer below. Then we moved it into place and stretched it to fit: With the Edit > Free Transform command (Ctrl/⌘-T) we moved the cursor inside the Free Transform frame and dragged to move the zebra into position. We dragged a corner handle to resize, holding down the Shift key to constrain proportions while scaling. We worked

1c

The "Zebra" layer is set to 60% Opacity, and Overlay is chosen as the blend mode that best combines the two images.

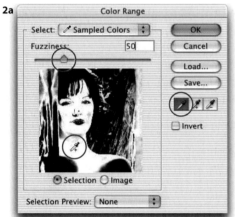

2a

Using Color Range to create a selection based on the skin tones of the model

2b

A layer mask is created from the Color Range selection and refined with the Brush tool 🖌, to limit where the stripes will appear.

with Free Transform until we had the best alignment possible, and then pressed the Enter key to lock in the transformation and close the frame **1b**.

To get the striped tattooing effect, experiment with the Opacity and blend mode of the "Zebra" layer. Powerful modes to try when combining images include Overlay, Soft Light, Hard Light, Vivid Light, Linear Light, and Pin Light — all of which use the light and dark areas of the active layer (but not its middle-tone grays) to affect the layers below.▼ We chose 60% Opacity and the Overlay blend mode **1c**.

2 Selecting and masking. Our next challenge is to limit the zebra stripes to the model's face. To isolate the skin tones, turn off visibility for the "Zebra" layer by clicking its 👁 icon, and choose Select > Color Range. Once the dialog box is open, choose "Sampled Colors" from its Select menu. Then click on the face with the dialog's Eyedropper tool 🖊 and then Shift-drag over all the colors you want to select, avoiding the eyes, mouth, and hair **2a**. (If you accidentally select colors you don't want, hold down the Alt/Option key and click on the color you want to deselect.) Set the Fuzziness fairly high (we used 50), to keep a smooth transition between what will be included in the selection and what will be omitted. When you finish, click "OK."

With the skin tones selected, click the "Zebra" layer's thumbnail to activate it, and then click the "Add layer mask" button 🔲 at the bottom of the Layers palette. This creates a mask identical to the preview we saw in Color Range. The white parts of the mask allow the zebra stripes to show through and combine with the "Jennifer" image, and the black areas hide the rest of the "Zebra" layer.

To fine-tune this mask, choose the Brush 🖌 tool and choose a soft-edged brush tip in the Options bar.▼ Make sure the mask, not the image itself, is active (in the Layers palette, click the mask thumbnail for the layer). With black as the Foreground color (you can set it by typing D or X), paint on the "Zebra" layer's mask to hide more of the animal (on the model's neck for instance) **2b**. While you work, you can Alt/Option-click on the mask thumbnail in the Layers palette to toggle between the image view and the mask view **2c**.

3 Setting up the Liquify window. Now for the fun part! In the Layers palette, click the thumbnail for the "Zebra" image to

FIND OUT MORE

▼ Using blend modes **page 176**

▼ Choosing and sizing brush tips **page 363**

2c

A view of the fine-tuned layer mask alone (left) and at work on the image

3

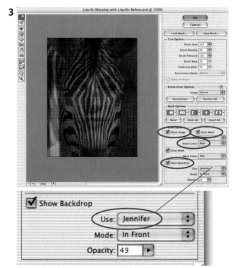

The Liquify window is set up to show the "Jennifer" layer as the Backdrop and Blue as the Mesh Color (for better contrast).

4a

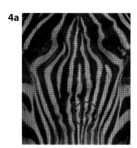

The Forward Warp tool is used, first with a large Brush Size to move the stripes inward from the eyes and outward on the cheeks. Then a smaller brush (shown here) fits the stripes around the nose and mouth.

4b

To "undo" distortion in some areas, use the Reconstruct tool with Revert chosen in the Reconstruct Options area of the Liquify window.

---

target the image rather than the mask. Choose the Rectangular Marquee tool and drag to select the face area. Then choose Filter > Liquify. In the Liquify window, set the View Options so you can see the Image and the distorting Mesh, with the "Jennifer" layer chosen as the Backdrop **3**. That way you can see both the "Zebra" layer you're filtering and the model's face, so you can distort the stripes to conform to the face. Experiment with the Backdrop's Mode and Opacity settings for the best view.

SELECTING THE AREA TO LIQUIFY

If you want to Liquify only part of an image, it's better to make a selection of the limited area you want to work on before you choose Filter > Liquify. That way Liquify won't have to manage the entire image, and it can work faster.

SETTING UP THE BACKDROP

The **Backdrop** in Liquify is the wonderful feature that lets you see other layers in addition to the one you're Liquifying. The Backdrop setting offers two basic choices — a single layer of your choice, or **All Layers**, in which case you see all visible layers *including the original condition of the layer you're Liquifying*. For a multilayer file, you may want to use the All Layers choice in order to see the entire image. But this can be confusing because All Layers includes the "before" version of the layer you're Liquifying, and it can be hard to see which is the original and which is the Liquified version, especially if you're making subtle changes.

If you don't want to "see double" when it comes to the Liquified layer, try making a merged copy of the "backdrop" you want *before* you run the Liquify filter: Turn on visibility for the layers you want to include in the backdrop (but not the layer to be Liquified). Then make a merged copy by holding down Ctrl-Alt-Shift (Windows) or ⌘-Option-Shift (Mac) and typing N, then E. (In CS2 you can shortcut the process, leaving out the N.) Then choose Filter > Liquify and choose the merged-copy layer as your Backdrop.

4 Liquifying the details. Start with Liquify's Forward Warp tool with a large Brush Size (we used 100 for this image) and Medium Brush Pressure (50), and move the zebra stripes around in relation to the major contours of the face below. To increase the believability of the stripes, move the ones over the eyes inward toward the nose, and the ones over the cheeks slightly outward toward the ears. Then reduce the brush size (we used 25) and adjust areas of detail around the eyebrows, nostrils, and lips, adjusting the Backdrop settings to give you the best view as you work **4a**.

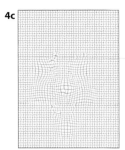

4c

Checking the distortion by toggling on and off visibility for the Backdrop, Image, and Mesh

4d

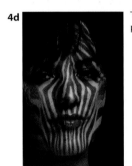

The Liquified stripes in position

5a

A merged-copy layer is added.

5b

The merged-copy layer is blurred, and Soft Light is chosen as the blend mode.

Finish by changing to the Bloat Tool ⬦ and just clicking on areas like the tip of the nose and chin to make the stripes appear to come forward **4a**. If you want to make corrections, use the Freeze Mask tool 🖌 to freeze the areas you want to keep, and then use the Reconstruct tool 🖌 with the Mode set to Revert **4b** to stroke over the unwanted distortion. Check your work **4c**, click "OK," and deselect (Ctrl/⌘-D) **4d**.

"MASK" = "FREEZE"

The "Mask" functions in the Liquify window let you specify which parts of your image are "frozen" (protected from the effects of Liquify's warping tools) and which parts are "thawed" (exposed to the changes). *By default a layer mask has no effect within the Liquify filtering process.* But you *can* use it for freezing by choosing Layer Mask from any of the pop-up menus in the

Mask Options section of the Liquify dialog box. Black parts of the mask protect and white parts expose. You can alter the mask with the Freeze Mask 🖌 and Thaw Mask 🖌 tools.

---

5 Unifying the parts. With the Liquified stripes in place, we decided that our combined image could benefit from slightly softening the focus and at the same time enhancing the color and contrast. First, we needed to make a copy of the composite so we could work on the "tattooed" face as a unified image. To make a composite copy, hold down Ctrl-Alt-Shift (Windows) or ⌘-Option-Shift (Mac) and type N, then E. (In CS2 you can shortcut the process, leaving out the N.) This turns the new layer into a merged copy of what's currently visible *but also leaves the other layers intact* **5a**. (Without the Alt/Option key, the other layers would have been swallowed up into the new layer.)

To soften this layer, we'll blur it and then do some fancy compositing with the layers below. Choose Filter > Blur > Gaussian Blur and set the Radius (we used a setting of 5, because we guessed from experience that this setting would work well for the degree of softening we wanted in this size image); then click "OK." Next change the layer's blend mode. We chose Soft Light, which lets the layers below provide the sharp image while the new layer adds the glow and color intensity **5b**.

The blurred layer provides the right atmosphere, but it also hides some of the shadow detail in the image. A quick fix for this problem is to use the "Blend If" feature within the Layer Style dialog box to keep the darkest areas of the blurred layer

5c

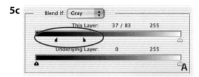

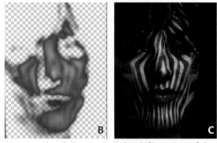

By using the sliders in the "Blend If" section of the Layer Styles dialog **A**, you can limit the contribution of the dark areas of the Soft Light layer (viewed alone in **B**) so your image maintains its shadow detail (shown with all layers visible in **C**).

6a

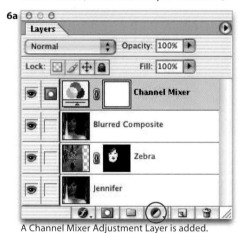

A Channel Mixer Adjustment Layer is added.

6b

The Monochrome box is checked, and experimenting with the sliders produces the result shown at the top of page 615.

from contributing to the combined image. In the Layers palette, double-click on the "Blurred Composite" layer's thumbnail to bring up the Blending Options panel of the Layer Style dialog. Next, in the "This Layer" section of the "Blend If" options at the bottom of the dialog **5c**, drag the black triangle. As you move the triangle slider to the right, you'll begin to see the effect of the dark areas of the "Blurred Composite" layer begin to disappear. To soften the transition between what's being hidden and what's continuing to contribute to the image, you can split the sliders by Alt/Option-dragging one half of the triangle away from the other. When the shadow detail of the layer below is visible again, click "OK."

6 "Translating" to black-and-white. Next we'll use a Channel Mixer Adjustment layer to translate the full-color image to black-and-white. Inspect the Channels palette; notice that the Red channel is brightest and the Blue channel is darkest. To add a Channel Mixer layer, click the "Create new fill or adjustment layer" button ⊘ at the bottom of the Layers palette and select Channel Mixer **6a**. In the dialog box, click the "Monochrome" check box. Now you can use the sliders to mix the color channels to create a black-and-white version you like. We found that reducing the Red channel from its default +100% to +50%, leaving Green at 0%, and boosting the Blue channel to +60% reduced the brightness of the white stripes and increased the density of the dark ones **6b**. The result is shown at the top of page 615.

Variations. Changes in the Channel Mixer settings can make a big difference in how a color image is "translated" to black-and-white. Shown below are two other possibilities. 𝒲𝑜𝓌!

Red: +100%; Green: 0%; Blue: 0% The lips and the dark stripes are lightened because there are no Green and Blue to tone down the Red, which is strong in the lip color and skin tones.

Red: −30%; Green: +200%; Blue: +100% Reducing the Red below 0 darkens the lips. Increasing the combined Green and Blue percentage to nearly 300% boosts the white in the stripes, the eyes, and the highlight on the lips.

ORIGINAL PHOTO: PHOTOSPIN.COM

ORIGINAL GRAPHICS: DONAL JOLLEY

CS2 "Warping" Graphics to a Surface

YOU'LL FIND THE FILES
in [wow] Wow Project Files > Chapter 9 >
Warping Graphics
  • Warp Mug-Before.psd (to start)
  • Warp Graphics files (to apply)
  • Warp After files (to compare)
  • 3D Transform Files (for a warping
    technique to use in Photoshop CS)

OPEN THESE PALETTES
from the Window menu:
  • Tools • Layers

OVERVIEW
Draw a grid • Turn it into a Smart Object
• Scale, position, warp, and blend it • Open
the Smart Object file, add graphics, and
save to update the main file • Duplicate
the main file and fine-tune the copy

PHOTOSHOP CS2'S WARP COMMAND can be the perfect tool
for applying artwork to the smoothly curving surfaces of a
bottle, a car, or a coffee mug, for instance. For top quality and
efficiency, combine the warping with Smart Object technology, and use blend modes and masks to reinforce the illusion.
Here we use Warp and Smart Objects to mock up three mugs.
We use one file to set up the warping but then "spin off" each
individual mug design as a separate file to apply the finishing
touches particular to that design. (Photoshop CS doesn't have
the Warp command or Smart Objects, but its 3D Transform
filter can be useful for this kind of application, as long as the
object you want to apply the graphics to is generally cylindrical; see the 3D Transform files on the Wow DVD-ROM.)

1 Creating a Smart-Object grid. Open the file with the object you want to apply graphics to, or use the **Warp Graphics-
Before.psd** file **1a**. This mug is basically a cylinder, slightly
pinched in at the "waist."

To get a good sense of the size of the graphics area (the graphics will be applied to the side facing us) and the geometry of

1a

The **Warp Mug-Before.psd** file

CORBIS ROYALTY FREE

1b

Choosing the Grid from the Tiles set in the Custom Shape picker

1c

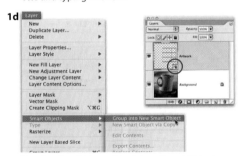

Draw the Grid by Shift-dragging. To help make the Layers palette easier to interpret, we renamed the layer by double-clicking its name in the palette and typing "Artwork."

1d

Turning the Grid graphics into a Smart Object puts an identifying mark on its thumbnail in the Layers palette.

2a

Rotating, scaling, and positioning the Grid with the Edit > Free Transform command

the warping, start by fitting a grid element to the object: Choose the Custom Shape tool. At the left end of the Options bar, click the "Shape layers" button. Click the tiny arrow to the right of the in the Options bar to pop out the Custom Shape picker, and choose the Grid shape that comes with Photoshop **1b** (it's in the Tiles set available from the picker's menu). To make a square Grid, begin dragging, then press the Shift key as you drag to make a square figure almost as tall as the mug **1c**.▼

Before you fit the Grid to the surface, turning it into a **Smart Object**▼ will protect the graphics from deteriorating as you experiment with transforming them, and will also let you substitute different graphics without having to repeat the warping steps: With the Grid layer targeted, choose **Layer > Smart Objects > Group Into New Smart Object 1d**.

2 Warping the Smart Object. To fit the Grid to your object (in this case the mug), choose Edit > Free Transform (Ctrl/⌘-T). Start with the big, general adjustments and move to the finer ones. For instance, for the mug, we'll first orient and scale the Grid, and then warp it to the cylindrical shape, then "pinch the waist," and finally fine-tune the warp.

To get the left side of the Grid into position **2a**, start by dragging inside the Transform frame to move the Grid. Drag outside a corner of the Transform frame (the cursor turns into a curved, double-headed arrow) to rotate the Grid to match the tilt of the object. If necessary, Shift-drag on a corner handle to adjust the size. To bend the Grid, switch from the Transform frame to the Warp mesh (right/Ctrl-click inside the Transform frame to open a menu where you can choose Warp **2b**, or click the "Switch between free transform and warp modes" button in the Options bar).

The Warp mesh is anchored by control points at all four corners of the mesh. The two handles attached to each control point are designed to work as levers to bend the curve between these points and reshape the mesh. Feel free to make adjustments as you go, or come back and adjust later. The Smart Object will "collect" all the transformation info and apply it without degrading the image any more than if you had done it in a single Transform/Warp session. Here's the process we used to warp the mesh and Grid to the mug:

- Drag the two right-side control points into position where you want them on the mug **2c**.

FIND OUT MORE

▼ Using drawing tools **page 456**

▼ Smart Objects **page 20**

2b

Switching from Transform to Warp, using the Transform frame's context-sensitive menu

2c

Moving the control points for the two right-side corners

2d

Using the horizontal handles for the corner points to curve the top and bottom edges of the mug

2e

"Pinching" the left and right sides by dragging the vertical handles for the corner points

- To make the top and bottom of the Grid follow the top and bottom curves of the mug **2d**, drag down on each of the two handles on the top line of the mesh (also drag a little outward toward the side edges if needed). Then also drag down (and slightly outward) on each of the handles on the bottom line of the mesh.

- To "pinch the waist," drag inward just a little on the two handles on the left edge of the mesh. Then also drag inward on the two handles on the right edge **2e**.

- The middle "column" of the mesh is closest to us and the two side columns are receding as the surface of the mug curves away. Drag each of the top horizontal handles a little outward, so the center column becomes a little wider than the side columns. Repeat with the bottom handles.

- Since the middle "row" of the mesh is "pinched" away from us, make it slightly shorter than the top and bottom rows — on each side, drag the top handle down a little and the bottom handle up.

- At this point we dragged on the internal spaces and lines of the mesh to finalize the shaping **2f**. We wanted to keep the center column of squares aligned directly above one another (allowing for the tilt of the mug, of course).

When the mesh and Grid look about right to you, look at the Grid figure without control points and handles for a clearer view **2g**: Make the mesh invisible by choosing View > Extras or typing Ctrl/⌘-H (it's a toggle, and you may have to use it twice). When we did this, we decided the upper left corner needed to be moved a little to the left, which we could do by dragging the corner, even though the mesh was invisible.

When the Grid looks right, press the Enter key (or click the "Commit transform" button ✔ in the Options bar). The mesh will become an invisible template that will scale, orient, and warp any other graphics that you substitute in the Smart Object (coming up in step 5). But the Warp mesh will also remain live, so you can reactivate it later to adjust it if needed.

3 Blending the applied graphics into the surface. Now you can experiment with the blend mode and Opacity for the "Artwork" layer, to allow the character of the object's surface (noise, grain, texture, or lighting) to show through, making the artwork look like it's part of the surface finish rather than "pasted on" **3**. We used Overlay mode and reduced the Opacity to 90%.

2f After adjusting by dragging inside individual cells of the Warp mesh

2g The view of the mesh is turned off and a final adjustment is made to the upper left corner.

3 Changing the "Artwork" layer's blend mode to Overlay and reducing Opacity to 90% brings the glare onto the graphics, blending the Grid into the surface of the mug.

4a The Smart Object is duplicated, and the copy is flipped vertically; we renamed the new layer "Reflection."

4b The duplicate Grid is dragged downward

4 Adding a reflection. To extend the illusion that the artwork is printed on the mug, we can also add it to the mug's reflection. If we make the artwork's reflection from a duplicate of the Smart Object, then the reflection will change automatically when we change the main graphics for the mug. To add the reflection, duplicate the Smart Object layer (Ctrl/⌘-J); rename the new layer if you like; we called it "Reflection." Flip the layer vertically (Edit > Transform > Flip Vertical) **4a**. Then reorient the reflected copy by dragging it down and rotating it **4b**. Adjust the mesh to reshape at least the visible part of the Grid reflection **4c**.

To hide the reflected Grid where the spoon handle blocks our view of it, add a layer mask: Click the "Add a layer mask" button ◻ at the bottom of the Layers palette. To mask the handle, we painted the mask with the Brush tool ✎ and black paint (press X if necessary to make black the Foreground color) using a round brush tip with Hardness set to 50% and Opacity at 100%. ▼ For less contrast in the reflection, we put the "Reflection" layer in Soft Light mode and reduced Opacity to 40% **4d**.

FIND OUT MORE

▼ Painting layer masks **page 75**

5 Substituting graphics in the Smart Object. We can now experiment with substituting graphics for the Grid. In the Layers palette, double-click on the thumbnail for either copy of the Smart Object ("Artwork" or "Reflection") to open the Smart Object "subfile" (**Artwork.psb**). Then add graphics; we opened the first of the three files of artwork for the mug — **Cow Graphics.psd** (derived from Coloring Clip Art-After.psd on

4c The warping is changed to match the mug's reflection. Pressing Ctrl-Alt-hyphen (Windows) or ⌘-Option-hyphen (Mac) shrinks the window so you can reach parts of the mesh that extend below the bottom of the image.

4d A layer mask is added to the "Reflection" layer to bring the spoon handle in front of the reflection. The blend mode for the layer is changed to Soft Light, and the Opacity is reduced to 40%.

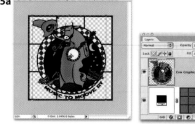

5a

The Cow Graphics are imported into the Artwork.psb file and scaled. Viewing the Grid at the same time helps to position the graphics.

5b

The .psb file, with the graphics scaled and Grid visibility turned off, is ready to Save.

5c

After saving the .psb file, clicking in the working window of the main file automatically replaces the Grid with the Cow Graphics in both copies of the Smart Object layer.

6

Duplicating the developing mug file before fine-tuning the Cow Graphics design

7a

Using the white point slider for "This Layer" to "drop out" the white from the "Artwork" layer in the Warp Cow file. The same change is applied to the "Reflection" layer.

page 474). Using the Move tool ▸⊕, drag the artwork into the .psb file **5a**. As long as you scale the artwork (Ctrl/⌘-T and Shift-drag a corner) to fit entirely within the "canvas" that the Grid element has established, the graphics won't be cropped when applied to the mug.

With the new art in place in the .psb file, turn off visibility for the Grid layer by clicking its 👁 icon in the Layers palette **5b**, and save the file (Ctrl/⌘-S). Then simply click in the working window of the main file. The new artwork will replace the Grid — automatically warped to fit both the mug and the reflection **5c**.

6 "Spinning off" a separate file. The fine-tuning needed for the "Cow Graphics" is likely to be different than what's needed for the "Horses" photo or the "Indifferent" graphics. So it makes sense to save a copy of the "Cow Graphics" version of the file separately to do the final tweaking that may not apply to the other designs. (If you continued in the same file for all three versions of the mug, your most current fine-tuning would affect all three designs.) A quick, safe way to "spin off" a version of the file — keeping the Smart Object layers live — is to copy the file (Image > Duplicate, *without choosing Duplicate Merged Layers Only*) **6**; we named the file "Warp Cow."

7 Fine-tuning the applied graphics. In the Warp Cow file, we can see that the white in the artwork is too bright for the shading on the mug. To make it appear that the white in the artwork has simply been left unprinted so the white surface of the mug shows through, try this: With the "Artwork" Smart Object targeted in the Layers palette, choose Blending Options from the palette's ⊙ menu. At the bottom of the dialog box in the "Blend If" section **7a**, move the white-point slider for "This Layer" a little to the left, until the white in the checkered pattern and in the banjo disappears except at the edges of the white areas; we stopped at a setting of 235, which told Photoshop that any pixels in this layer lighter than 235 (bright white is 255) should be blocked from contributing to the image. Then hold down the Alt/Option key and drag farther left on the left half of the white point slider to remove the white fringes; we used a setting of 130. Splitting the slider allows a partial contribution from pixels that are light but not bright white, such as the anti-aliasing at the edges of the whites; this partial transparency makes a smooth (rather than abrupt) transition. To remove white from the "Reflection" layer, repeat the "Blend If" adjustment on that layer **7b**. These adjustments have made the light colors in the graphics paler than we'd like, but we can address that next.

7b

The lightest tones in the "Artwork" and "Reflection" layers are dropped out with "Blend If," to allow the "white" of the mug to show through.

8a

To change the colorful background but not the neutral mug, a Hue/Saturation Adjustment layer is applied in Hue mode.

8b

Moving the Hue slider to recolor the abstract background

8c

8d

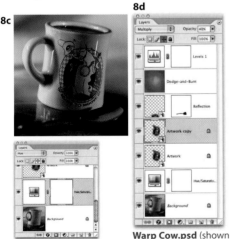

The recolored background

Warp Cow.psd (shown on page 620) is completed with a duplicate "Artwork" layer in Multiply mode, a dodge-and-burn layer, and a Levels Adjustment.

8 Finishing the first mug file. To complete the mock-up, we can change the background color to pick up color in the graphics. We can also restore color density that suffered when we dropped out the white, and we can light up the graphics a bit where they're in the shadows. To change the background color, we used a Hue/Saturation Adjustment layer in Hue mode because it would change the colorful background without affecting the grays of the mug (neutral colors aren't affected by adjustments in Hue mode).▼ In the Layers palette, Alt/Option-click the "Create new fill or adjustment layer" button ◐ and choose Hue/Saturation. When the New Layer dialog box opens, choose Hue for the Mode **8a** and click "OK." In the Hue/Saturation dialog box **8b**, move the Hue slider to the right (we stopped at +158) to change the background from green to blue; click "OK" **8c**.

To brighten the graphics on the mug, we first targeted the "Artwork" layer and duplicated it. We put the duplicate layer in Multiply mode and reduced its Opacity to 40%.

We added a gray-filled "dodge-and-burn" layer in Overlay mode by Alt/Option-clicking the "Create a new layer" button 📄 at the bottom of the Layers palette, choosing Overlay mode in the New Layer dialog, checking the "Fill with Overlay-Neutral Color (50% gray)" box, and clicking "OK." Where we wanted more light, we painted the new layer loosely with a large soft brush and white paint, with a low Opacity set in the Options bar; for deeper shading around the edges we used black paint.▼ To improve contrast and complete the mock-up shown on page 620, we clicked the ◐ button at the bottom of the Layers palette, chose Levels, and clicked "Auto" in the Levels dialog **8d**.▼

When you've applied the final touches, save the file (File > Save As) in Photoshop format; its own Smart Object "subfile" (.psb) will be saved with the file. If you want to make changes to the warping, blending, or tone and color, or even the Smart Object graphics in the future, you can do so without affecting your original working file (the developing **Warp Mug-Before.psd** in this case). If you want to make changes to the graphics, clicking on one of the Smart Object layers in the **Warp Cow.psd** file will open the Smart Object file with the Grid and Cow Graphics layers.

9 Using a photo for the second mug. To apply a photo, go back to your main working file as you left it after step 5 (in

FIND OUT MORE

▼ Using blend modes **page 177**

▼ Making a dodge & burn layer **page 329**

▼ Using Auto Levels **page 268**

9a

The photo from **Horses.psd** is dragged into the .psb file and scaled. In scaling and positioning the photo, we allowed some of the image to extend beyond the top and bottom edges of the Grid; this would crop the photo when it was automatically applied to the mug.

9b

Saving the .psb file automatically applies the photo to the mug in the developing **Warp-Before.psd** file.

9c

Stretching the photo sideways in the Warp Horses file to fill more of the available space. The stretching becomes part of the "single" transformation stored in the Smart Object layer.

9d

Tinting the mug and background with the Colorize function in a Hue/Saturation Adjustment layer

this example, it's the developing **Warp Mug-Before.psd** file). In the Layers palette, double-click the thumbnail for the "Artwork" or "Reflection" layer; either will open the Artwork.psb file. Open the file that holds the photo you want to apply; we used **Horses.psd**. Drag the photo into the .psb file and scale it (Ctrl/⌘-T) **9a**. Turn off visibility for all layers except the photo, and save the .psb file (Ctrl/⌘-S); then click in the working window of the developing **Warp Mug-Before.psd** file to see the photo on the mug and in the reflection **9b**.

Duplicate the **Warp Mug-Before** file (as in step 6; Image > Duplicate); we named our duplicate file "Warp Horses." To fine-tune this mug design:

• With the photo in place on the mug, we wanted to widen it to fill more of the surface. We could stretch the photo by typing Ctrl/⌘-T (for Edit > Free Transform) and dragging the right-side middle handle outward **9c**. (This is an example of fine-tuning that's better done in a "spun-off" file; it will change the Horses image, which can be stretched slightly without looking distorted, but it won't change the fit of the Cow Graphics.) We stretched the "Reflection" layer also.

• We simulated applying the photo to a tan mug by tinting the background image with a Hue/Saturation layer in Normal mode with Colorize turned on **9d**.

• We liked the result we got for blending the photo into the mug surface when we changed the blend mode for the Horses layer to Soft Light and restored the Opacity to 100%, then duplicated this layer (Ctrl/⌘-J) and put the copy in Multiply mode at 40% Opacity **9e**. We left the white parts opaque as if white ink had been "printed" onto the mug.

• We added a Levels Adjustment layer as in step 8, but not a dodge-and-burn layer; the result is shown on page 620.

10 Making the "Indifferent" mug. We went back to the developing **Warp Mug-Before.psd** file and double-clicked the "Artwork" layer to open the .psb file. We brought in the converted type from the **Indifferent.psd** file **10a** by dragging the entire group ▭ from the Layers palette into the working window of the .psb file. Scaling it to fit the Grid, we purposely let the "t" in "Different" extend a little beyond the right edge so it would appear to curve out of sight around the mug **10b**. Once again, saving the .psb file and clicking in the working window of the main file updated the composite image.

We spun off the third version of the file (File > Save As), naming it "Warp-Indifferent." Targeting the "Artwork" layer, we used

9e

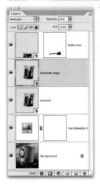

Two layers — in Soft Light and Multiply modes — are used to blend the photo with the mug.

the Move tool ⯭ to reposition the graphics, and adjusted the layer's Opacity (85%). To reinforce the subject matter in this illustration, we added a Hue/Saturation Adjustment layer above the photo layer and reduced Saturation to dull the background. We left the face of the mug in shadows, but added a Levels Adjustment layer at the top of the stack and clicked "Auto" to improve contrast; the result is shown at the top of page 620. *Wow!*

10b

Positioning the graphics in the **Artwork.psb** file so the type would appear to curve out of sight

10a

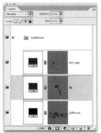

To build **Indifferent.psd** we set, tracked, and kerned two layers of type ("IN" in red and "Different" in black), and converted them to Shape layers (Layer > Type > Convert to Shape). ▼ The "not" symbol (from Photoshop's Symbols set of presets) was added with the Custom Shape tool ⬠; the blend mode for this Shape layer was changed to Color Burn so the slash would disappear where it crossed the black dot, seeming to cross behind it. All three parts of the design were targeted by clicking and Shift-clicking their thumbnails in the Layers palette and were collected in a group by choosing New Group from Layers from the palette's ▶ menu.

FIND OUT MORE

▼ Working with type
page 418

APPLYING LABELS TO GLASS

To mock up a label on a glass container, you can add details that make the transparency of the glass more photorealistic:

• Using two layers, construct a label with a solid-filled label shape in one layer and another layer above it with the type. Reduce the Opacity of the label shape layer until you get the translucent effect you want, with the image below showing through. Then with the type layer targeted in the Layers palette, merge it with the layer below (Ctrl/⌘-E). This combines the two parts of the label, preserving both the partial transparency of the label shape and the full opacity of the type.

• If there's something inside the container, a drop shadow on the contents adds to the illusion: Click the "Add a layer style" button ⓕ at the bottom of the Layers palette and choose Drop Shadow from the pop-out list. In the Drop Shadow section of the Layer Style dialog box, click the color swatch and sample a shadow color from the image. Choose the Opacity, Spread (density), and Size (softness) to match the light in your photo; experiment with Distance and Angle by dragging in the image to move the shadow, creating the appropriate physical space between the label and the material it falls on.

The label was made with type in one layer and a label shape in a 70%-opaque layer below (left). The two were merged, the merged layer was warped, and a Drop Shadow was added.

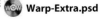
Warp-Extra.psd

Swapping a Background

YOU'LL FIND THE FILES
in 🔵 > Wow Project Files > Chapter 9 >
Swap Background:
  • Swap-Before 1 & 2.psd (to start)
  • Swap-After.psd (to compare)

OPEN THESE PALETTES
from the Window menu:
  • Tools • Layers

OVERVIEW
Extract the subject from its background
• Improve the edge of the extracted
subject with a layer mask • Import the
new background • Use the Match Color
command and other adjustments to
modify the lighting on the subject to
make the two layers match

1

ORIGINAL PHOTOS: CORBIS ROYALTY FREE

The original subject and background photos

WHEN YOU WANT TO COMBINE a subject from one photo with
a background from another, one of the main tasks is making a
clean selection of the subject from its original background. If
you're working with a portrait, that usually means solving "the
hair problem": How do you make a selection that separates the
hair from the background with a result that looks natural instead of too smooth or too spiky? There's no simple one-size-
fits-all solution to this problem. The approach that works best
depends on whether the hair color contrasts strongly with the
background, and whether the wisps of hair are in sharp focus
or soft, among other things. In Photoshop, the Extract filter
often provides the best solution.

Even when the hair problem is solved and the selection is made,
there are other important factors that will help to make the
subject at home in its new environment so the composite will
be convincing:

• The ambient lighting has to look the same for both the subject and the background.

• The directional lighting also has to be consistent.

• The depth of focus has to look realistic. If the subject is entirely sharp and in focus, the background can be either in
  focus or blurred. But if the subject shows a short depth of
  field, with some parts in sharp focus and others soft, the
  background will need to be soft.

2a

Before the Extract command was used, we made a copy of the image for safekeeping.

• The film grain or "noise" in the component images has to match. (Simulating or adjusting film grain is covered in step 4 of "Focusing Attention on the Subject" on page 288.)

1 Analyzing the photos. Select the two photos you want to combine, and crop if necessary. In choosing the subject and background, look for images whose lighting doesn't "fight" uncontrollably. The sunset sky we chose for our ad image had ambient lighting that was opposite in color from the lighting in our portrait — a warm golden brown instead of a cool green **1**. But we knew we would be able to fix this difference by adjusting the color of the portrait (in step 5). The direction of the lighting in the background photo was straight into the camera, while the basic directional lighting in the portrait came from behind the woman and from her left (our right; notice the highlights on the shoulders and forehead). We were confident we could adjust the lighting to make the two images into a convincing composite.

2 Starting the extraction. The Extract command (Filter > Extract) is often Photoshop's best tool for solving the hair problem and other selection challenges. But using this command is a "destructive" process — it permanently removes pixels. So before you Extract, duplicate your image layer for safekeeping (type Ctrl/⌘-J). Then click the icon of the bottom image layer to turn off its visibility **2a** so you'll be able to see the result of your extraction.

Next open the Extract dialog box from the Filter menu. From the dialog's Highlight menu choose a color that contrasts with the subject and background so you'll be able to see the highlight clearly as you trace the edge. We changed the default Green to Red, since the background of the photo was green.

With the Edge Highlighter tool chosen, set the Brush Size: A large brush works well for soft or fuzzy edges. We chose a relatively large Brush Size (40) to select the hair. Although on first inspection the contrast between the green background and the black hair looks strong, the depth of field for this photo is short, so

2b

Using the Edge Highlighter ✍ with a large brush size and Red as the Highlight color for areas that have transparency or have the background color showing through

2c

Tool Options	
Brush Size:	40 ▶
Highlight:	Red
Fill:	Blue
☑ Smart Highlighting	

Turning on Smart Highlighting to trace the edge "magnetically"

REPAIRS ON-THE-FLY

If you make a mistake with the Edge Highlighter ✍, you can repair it:

- You can quickly add by dragging the tool back over an area you missed.
- Or to remove some of the edge material you've applied, hold down the Alt/Option key to temporarily turn the Edge Highlighter into an eraser.

2d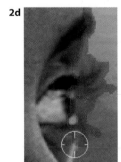

2e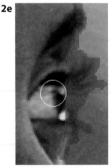

When the Edge Highlighter ✍ is in Smart Highlighting mode, the cursor changes.

Holding down the Alt/Option key turns the Edge Highlighter ✍ into a highlight eraser.

some of the hair is out-of-focus and soft; also, the green background has created green highlights in the hair. A large brush would allow us to drag along the edge quickly, catching all the fine curls of hair in one sweep. Drag the Edge Highlighter to draw a highlight that overlaps both the subject and the background where they meet **2b**. This highlight defines the band where the Extract function will look for the edge when it selects the subject. In the extraction process that follows, anything within the highlight band may be made partly transparent. In our image the broad strokes would help with selecting the fine detail, and would allow the hair to be selected as partially transparent, without the color cast from the background. When the extracted image was put against the new background, this semi-transparency of the hair would allow the new background to add its own color cast.

A smaller brush is better for a hard edge, or if there are two edges close together. In our image, we could have used a small brush to make a sharp selection of the neck on the left side of the photo. But instead of resetting the Brush Size, we clicked the Smart Highlighting check box **2c**. With Smart Highlighting turned on, the cursor changes and the Edge Highlighter becomes "magnetic," automatically clinging to the edge as you drag the tool and *automatically narrowing the brush whenever possible.*

In our portrait there were really two high-contrast edges on the woman's profile—the green-against-white edge between the background and the highlight, and the white-against-brown edge between highlight and normal skin tone. We zoomed in as described in the "Navigating the Preview" tip on page 629 for a close-up, in order to follow the edge **2d**. We had to switch back to "manual" operation of the Edge Highlighter (by holding down the Ctrl/⌘ key), and we reduced brush size to 10 (using the bracket keys)

THE DUMB/SMART TOGGLE

Unfortunately, "Smart Highlighting" is really only smart about sharp, high-contrast edges. So as you drag from an area with a high-contrast edge to an area of low contrast, you'll need to turn off Smart Highlighting and operate the Edge Highlighter ✍ "by hand." Holding down the **Ctrl/⌘** key automatically switches out of Smart Highlighting if you have it turned on, or switches into it if you have it turned off. Release the key to toggle back again.

CHANGING BRUSH SIZE

The control keys for resizing the brush tip for the tools in the Extract dialog box are the bracket keys, the same as for Photoshop's painting tools: Press [to shrink the brush, or] to enlarge it.

3a

Filling the completed highlight with the Fill tool ✋ makes the "Preview" button available in the top right corner of the dialog box. A high Smooth setting will blur the edges more than a low one, which is what we want for extracting the hair.

3b

Choosing a contrasting color for the Preview background

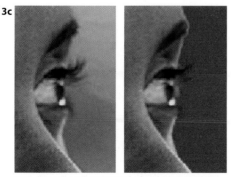

3c

Switching the "Show" setting from Original (left) to Extracted to check the edge

to follow the highlight on the shoulders in order to "tell" the Edge Highlighter that we wanted to keep, not cut away, the hot white edges. Left to its own devices, Smart Highlighting would have followed the higher-contrast edge between the white highlight and the darker skin. To clean up the edge, we held down the Alt/Option key to erase extra highlighting **2e**.

The highlighting is complete when the subject is entirely enclosed within the highlight, except that you don't have to drag along the outside edges of the image. For instance, in this photo the highlight extended from the bottom edge of the photo on the left, up and around the profile to the right edge of the photo; we didn't need to trace the bottom edge.

3 Completing the extraction. Before you can preview the selection you've made with the Edge Highlighter, you need to add a fill. Select the Extract box's Fill tool ✋ and click inside your highlight to fill the enclosed area and make the "Preview" button available **3a**. In the Extraction section of the dialog box, you can set the Smooth value to 100 to make an extraction with as little "debris" at the edge as possible; you'll be able to smooth it more later with the Edge Touchup tool if needed, as described below. Click the "Preview" button to make the background disappear.

In the Preview section at the bottom of the dialog box, you can change the Display setting to a color that contrasts with the original background of the photo. This will give you the best indication of how good your extraction is. If you don't find a workable color in the Display menu, choose Other and pick a color; we picked a red to contrast with the original green background of the photo **3b**. By switching back and forth between Show Extracted and Show Original in the Preview section, you can compare the extracted edge with the original **3c**.

To make repairs, in the Extracted view use the Cleanup tool ✍ ("C" is the keyboard shortcut) on the edge to erase excess material **3d**. What's really exciting is that *you can also use the Cleanup tool with the Alt/Option key held down, to bring back material that was lost in the extraction.* Besides using the bracket keys to change brush size, you can change the pressure (or opacity) of the tool as you work by pressing the number keys ("1" through "9" for 10% to 90%, and "0" for 100%). Use a low opacity setting for a softened edge. In general, using a fairly low opacity and "scrubbing" with the tool gives good results. The Edge Touchup tool ✍ can be used to smooth the edge. It automatically removes or consolidates edge pixel debris.

3d

The Cleanup tool ✐ (shown here) and the Edge Touchup tool ✐ (below it in the Extract tool palette) become available after you click the "Preview" button, so you can refine the edge before finalizing the extraction.

3e

The subject layer after extraction

4a

Bringing in the new background image

As you touch up the edge and get ready to leave the Extract dialog box, keep in mind that it's better to have too much image material than not enough, because you can further trim the edge after extraction (as described in step 4), but it can be harder to add back, even with the spare original you kept at step 2. When you've examined and fine-tuned the entire edge as well as you can, click "OK" to finalize the extraction and close the Extract dialog box **3e**.

4 Combining the subject with the new background. Use the Move tool ▶⊕ to click in the image you want to use for your new background; then drag it into the working window of the portrait file. In the Layers palette drag the imported layer's name to a position under the extracted layer **4a**; to rename the layer (we called it "Sunset"), double-click on its name and type a new one. Use the Move tool to reposition the image if you like. Or scale it by pressing Ctrl/⌘-T (for Edit > Free Transform) and Shift-dragging a corner handle. You can also blur the image (Filter > Blur > Gaussian Blur or Lens Blur)▼ to soften the focus if needed, as we did here.

FIND OUT MORE

▼ Using Lens Blur
page 291

Now that the new background is in place, you may want to further refine the edge of your extracted subject. A flexible, non-destructive way to do that is to make a layer mask that exactly fits the subject and then modify the edge of the mask. First make a selection by loading the transparency mask that's inherent in the subject layer (Ctrl/⌘-click on the layer's thumbnail in the Layers palette) **4b**. Then add a layer mask based on the selection (click the "Add layer mask" button ◻ at the bottom of the palette) **4c**. Because of the semi-transparency at the edge of the transparency mask, the layer mask that you've made

4b

The transparency mask loaded as a selection

A layer mask, made from the transparency mask selection, added to the subject layer

The silhouetted subject before (left) and after adding the layer mask

Blurring the mask (Radius 2 pixels) to soften the edge

The duplicate subject layer, ready for applying the Match Color command

from it will automatically trim the edge slightly. This change by itself may smooth the edge or get rid of unwanted background color **4d**.

If you need to refine the edge further, you can now use Filter > Blur > Gaussian Blur to soften the entire edge **4e**, or just a selected part of it. Or paint black on the layer mask to hide more of the extracted image (try the Brush tool 🖌 with the Airbrush feature turned on in the Options bar, and with a low Pressure setting).▼ If you don't like what your painting or blurring did, choose Edit > Step Backward (Ctrl/⌘-Shift-Z) to erase the changes step-by-step to restore parts of the original extraction edge, or paint on the mask with white.

FIND OUT MORE

▼ Painting a mask
page 75

5 Adjusting the lighting. Now you can make changes to the color and intensity of the lighting to make the subject look more at home in the background. The Match Color command can work well for this kind of change, but since it doesn't exist as an Adjustment layer, using it will change the image itself. To protect the work you've done so far, duplicate the extracted layer by typing Ctrl/⌘-J, and then turn off visibility for the lower of the two layers (click its 👁 in the Layers palette) **5a**.

Click the image thumbnail for the duplicate extracted layer and choose Image > Adjustments > **Match Color**. In the Match Color dialog box, start at the bottom of the box in the Image Statistics section. For the **Source**, choose the name of the current file from the pop-out menu. Then in the **Layer** menu, choose the "Sunset" layer. The color in the working window will change dramatically **5b**. Use the Match Color dialog's **Fade** slider to reduce the coloring to a level that looks right (we used

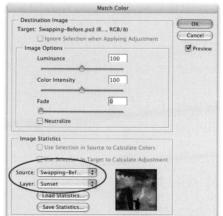

After choosing the "Sunset" layer as the Source in the Match Color dialog box

5c

Fading the intensity of the matched color

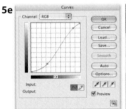

5d

Using Edit > Fade to put the color-matched layer in Color mode

5e

Shading the subject with a Curves Adjustment layer in Luminosity mode

6a Using a Levels Adjustment to lighten the sky on the right

6b A masked Levels layer locates the sunset on the right **A**, and a painted mask on the Curves layer **B** increases the directional lighting on the face.

a Fade setting of 75) **5c** and click "OK." To experiment with blend mode, choose Edit > Fade Match Color (available only immediately after using the Match Color command) and try the Color and Hue modes; we decided on Color — it removed some of the overall lightening of the image but kept the overall warmth that an intense sunset like this one would produce **5d**.

(The bright color of the sunset would affect the full range of tones — highlights, midtones, and shadows — of almost any subject in its environment. But for a subtler background image, you might want to restrict the color matching to the shadows or highlights, or tint both shadows *and* highlights but protect the midtones from change. For managing that kind of change, see examples of using the "Blend If" sliders on pages 75, 327, 337, and 619.)

Next, since the subject would naturally be in shadow against the bright sky, we darkened it with a Curves Adjustment layer, masked so it would affect only the subject and not the sunset: In the Layers palette, Ctrl/⌘-click the layer mask thumbnail for the subject layer to load it as a selection; then click the "Create new fill or adjustment layer" button ⬤ at the bottom of the Layers palette and choose Curves from the list **5e**. In the Curves dialog, move the midpoint of the curve down to darken the image; we found that making an "S" curve (by also moving this point left and adding another point for the highlights) kept detail in the highlights that would improve the printing of the image.▼ The Curves adjustment increased color intensity as it darkened the portrait; to prevent that, we changed the blend mode for the Curves layer to Luminosity.

FIND OUT MORE

▼ Using an "S" curve
page 332

▼ Gradient masks
page 79

▼ Painting a mask
page 75

6 Adjusting the directional light. To match the directional lighting in our two image components, we would modify both of them. Since in the original portrait there seemed to be light coming from the right, we created the impression of a setting sun beyond the right side of the "Sunset" image: We targeted the Sunset layer and clicked the ⬤ button to add a Levels Adjustment layer above it; we moved the Input Levels gamma slider to the 1.35 to lighten the image **6a**. Then we used the Gradient tool ▣ with the Black, White Gradient and the Radial style and the Reverse option chosen in the Options bar, and dragged inward from the right edge to create a mask for our "lighting."▼ We also painted soft black strokes on the mask for the Curves layer to "catch the light" of the sunset on the forehead and neck **6b**.▼ The finished image appears on page 628. *Wow*

Building a Layout with Masks & Clipping Groups

YOU'LL FIND THE FILES
in 🔵 Wow Project Files > Chapter 9 > Building a Layout
- Layout-Before files (to start)
- Layout-After.psd (to compare)

OPEN THESE PALETTES
from the Window menu:
- Tools • Layers

OVERVIEW
Create a layout with Shape layers, layer masks, type layers, and Layer Styles
• Populate the layout with photos, each one on a layer above its placeholder • Clip each photo to its placeholder • Use the same layout with new photos and edited type, adjusting Styles as needed

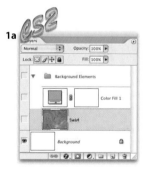

1a The **Layout-Before.psd** file has the default white *Background* and two layers that form the backdrop for the layout. But as we begin to design the layout, only the *Background* is visible.

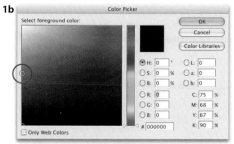

1b Choosing a medium gray for drawing the place-holders

FOR A WEBSITE SPLASH SCREEN, a postcard ad, or other small design projects, Photoshop is a practical layout tool. You can design your layout — including image placeholders, masking effects, and added Layer Styles — and also set your display type. Then just add your photos, each on its own layer, and "clip" each one with its placeholder layer. With this approach, it's easy to use your layout file again with other text and images. (If you want to create several additional compositions from the layout, consider turning your layout file into an automated template; "Many Versions from One Template" on page 643 tells how.)

1 Setting up the file. Start your layout by opening a new file (File > New) with a white *Background*; or use the **Layout-Before.psd** file. It's an RGB file 1000 pixels wide and 750 pixels high at 225 pixels per inch, and it also includes a swirling background image and a Solid Color layer in Screen mode to color it, but visibility for these elements has been turned off **1a**.

Choose a medium gray to use for your placeholders (one way is to double-click the Foreground square in the Tools palette, and then click about halfway down the left edge of the large color square in the Color Picker) **1b**. For each placeholder the gray will later be entirely hidden by a photo, but in the meantime the placeholders will let us design the layout and see the effects of masking and of any Layer Styles.

For our adventure travel postcard series (the first card design is shown above), we wanted a main photo in the center, a column of five evenly spaced photos on the right, and two vignetted photos on the left. "Zooming" type would tie the photos together and draw the viewer into the layout.

2a

The Rectangle tool's Options bar, set up for creating a Shape layer

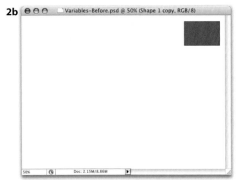

2b

The placeholder for the first small photo, drawn with the Rectangle tool ▢. Our placeholder was a little more horizontal than a typical 35 mm or digital photo, so we could expect that it would "trim" the top and bottom edges of such a photo even without any enlarging we might do for the sake of our design.

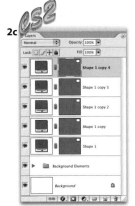

2c

After duplicating the small rectangle four times

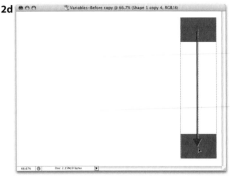

2d

Moving one placeholder to the bottom position

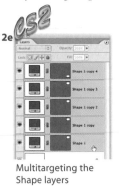

2e

Multitargeting the Shape layers

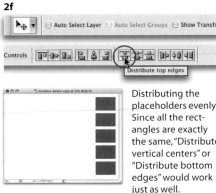

2f

Distributing the placeholders evenly. Since all the rectangles are exactly the same, "Distribute vertical centers" or "Distribute bottom edges" would work just as well.

We'll build placeholders for the five small photos first, spacing them evenly in a column. The large central placeholder can then be drawn to match the combined height of the three middle photos in the column, and we can also align the two soft-edged placeholders on the left with the central photo.

2 Making placeholders for the five small photos. Choose the Rectangle tool ▢ and click the "Shape layers" button ▢ in the Options bar so the shape you draw will make a new layer **2a**. Drag to create one of the small rectangular placeholders. Use the Move tool ▶⊕ to drag the rectangle into position where you want the topmost of the five photos to be, near the top right corner of the working window **2b**.

Make the other four placeholders by duplicating this layer (Ctrl/⌘-J four times) **2c**. To space the rectangles evenly in the column, use the Move tool ▶⊕ again. Shift-drag a rectangle down to where you want the bottom photo to be **2d**. Then in the Layers palette:

- In CS, click in the Links column (next to the 👁) of the other four rectangle layers.

- In CS2, where you can target more than one layer at a time, simply Shift-click the thumbnail for the top rectangle to also target it and the three layers in between **2e**.

With the Move tool ▶⊕ chosen and the five layers linked or "multitargeted," the Options bar will show the Align and Distribute buttons **2f**. Click the "Distribute top edges" button ≣ to equalize the spacing between the rectangles.

3 Fading one edge of the small photos. To fade the right edge of all five placeholders (and the images that will replace them), first collect the still linked or multitargeted layers in a layer set/group:

3a

Making a new group from the Shape layers; in Photoshop CS, the command is New Layer Set from Linked.

3b

A layer mask is added to the layer set/group

3c

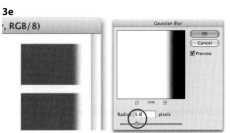

Setting up the Gradient tool ▣ to draw on the layer mask

3d

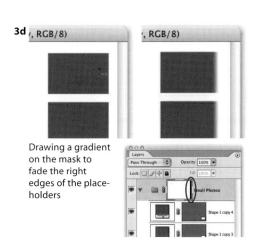

, RGB/8)   , RGB/8)

Drawing a gradient on the mask to fade the right edges of the place-holders

- In CS, choose "New Set From Linked" from the Layers palette's ▶ menu.
- In CS2, choose "New Group from Layers" from the Layers palette's ▶ menu **3a**.

Then add a mask that applies to the entire set/group by clicking the "Add layer mask" button ▣ at the bottom of the palette to add a mask to the new "folder" **3b**. To create the fade, choose the Gradient tool ▣; in the Options bar choose the Black, White gradient (the third one in the Gradient picker by default) and the Linear form **3c**. From a little inside the right edge of the rectangles, Shift-drag to the left, to where you want the image to be solid **3d**. ▼ We extended the fade slightly by running the Gaussian Blur filter on the mask **3e** with a Radius setting of 5 (see "Modifying Soft-Edged Masks" on page 638).

FIND OUT MORE

▼ Making Gradient masks **page 75**

4 Making a placeholder for the central photo. Setting up Guides will make it easier to align the central photo with the side photos. (Photoshop CS2's automated Smart Guides are designed to help with alignment, but in this situation we found them a bit less reliable than the "old-fashioned" Guides that have been around for several versions.) To set up Guides, type Ctrl/⌘-R to display the rulers, and drag a Guide down from the top ruler to align with the top of the second small rectangle. Drag another guide down to align with the bottom of the fourth rectangle **4a**.

Choose the Rounded Rectangle ▢ (another of the Shape tools) **4b** and drag to make a round-cornered rectangle **4c**. Then choose the Rectangle tool ▢ (sharp-cornered), click the "Subtract from shape area (-)" button ▣ in the Options bar, and

3e

, RGB/8)

Using Gaussian Blur to soften the fading edge. Your Radius setting may differ, depending on how you drew the gradient and how soft you want the edge to be.

To adjust the edge of a soft-edged mask,

you can use either of these methods to experiment with changes as you watch the effect of the changes on your masked element in the working window:

• Make the transition more gradual by choosing Filter > Blur > Gaussian Blur and watching the fade change in the working window as you experiment with the Radius setting;

A Gaussian Blur spreads out the transition at the edge of the mask.

• Make the transition more abrupt or shift it right or left by choosing Image > Adjustments > Levels and working with any of the Input Levels sliders.▼

Using Image > Adjustments > Levels on the original gradient mask and moving the black point and gamma sliders to the right shifts the edge to the left and "hardens" it somewhat.

drag a rectangle that trims the right edge of the round-cornered shape so it has sharp corners on the right **4d**.

Now use the Drop Shadow effect to add a bar at the trimmed right edge: Click the "Add a layer style" button 🔷 at the bottom of the Layers palette and choose Drop Shadow. In the Drop Shadow panel of the Layer Style dialog box **4e**, change the Blend Mode to Normal, increase the Opacity to 100%, and either leave black as the color (as we did), or click the color swatch and choose a different color for your bar. Set the Angle at 180° (which will cast the "shadow" directly to the right), set the Size to 0 (which will keep the shadow from being any bigger than the shape it's applied to), and set the Spread to 100% (which will make a sharp, rather than soft, edge on the shadow); set the Distance to make the band as wide as you like; our Distance setting was 20 pixels. Click "OK" to close the Layer Style dialog box.

5 Adding placeholders for the two vignetted photos. To make placeholders for the two vignetted photos on the left, first turn on the Snap To function (in the View menu make sure there's a check mark beside the Snap command). Then set up a Guide to mark half the height of the large rectangle: Drag a Guide down from the top ruler until it snaps into place halfway

4b

Setting up the Rounded Rectangle tool ▢ to draw the placeholder for the center photo; we used a corner Radius of 20 pixels.

4a

Setting up Guides to establish the height of the central placeholder

4c

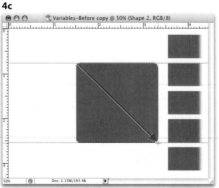

Drawing with the Rounded Rectangle tool ▢ to start the center placeholder

FIND OUT MORE

▼ Using Levels
page 250

4d

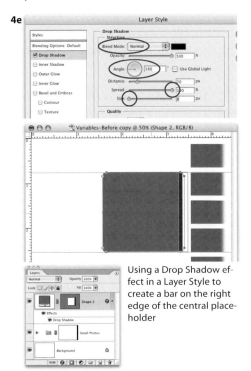

Subtracting with the Rectangle tool ▣ to make sharp corners on the right side of the central placeholder

4e

Using a Drop Shadow effect in a Layer Style to create a bar on the right edge of the central placeholder

down the shape. Now use the Rectangular Marquee ⬚ to make a selection whose bottom aligns with the bottom of the large rectangle and whose top is below the new center Guide **5a**.

When you've made the rectangular selection, click the "Create new fill or adjustment layer" button ◑ at the bottom of the Layers palette and choose Solid Color from the list of layer types; when the Color Picker opens, click on one of your gray placeholders in the working window to sample the medium gray, and click "OK." If you want to soften the edges of the rectangular mask on the Solid Color layer, choose Filter > Blur > Gaussian Blur and set an Amount that softens the edge as much as you like; we used Radius 10. Click "OK" to close the dialog box.

Duplicate the layer (Ctrl/⌘-J) and use the Move tool ⊹ to Shift-drag upward until this second vignetted placeholder clicks into alignment with the Guide at the top of the large central rectangle (the middle of the feather on the top edge will align with the sharp edge of the large rectangle) **5b**.

6 Adding display type. The next step is to add, warp, and stretch the type, leaving it "live" so we can make changes if needed, once the photos are in place.▼ Choose the Type tool **T**; in the Options bar choose a font and size. We used Trebuchet (a font that's standard on both Windows and Mac) in the Bold style, and set the font size at 48 pt. To follow our example, press the Caps Lock key, type the word "EXTREME" **6a**, and press the Enter key to commit (finalize) the type. (If you've started your own layout file rather than using ours, you may want to start with a different font size, especially if the resolution of your file is very different from the 225 ppi we used in our file.)

> **FIND OUT MORE**
> ▼ Working with type
> **page 418**

5a

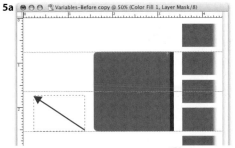

Dragging the Rectangular Marquee ⬚ to select the area for the first of the vignetted placeholders

5b

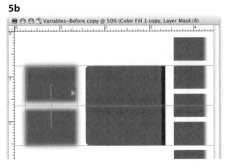

Moving the second vignetted placeholder into position

6a

Setting the first line of display type

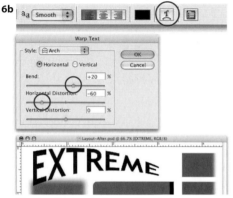

6b

Warping the type to form a distorted arch

6c

Moving, tilting, and stretching the type with the Edit > Free Transform command

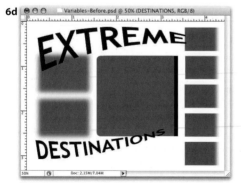

6d

"DESTINATIONS" is added in 27 pt type, warped into an opposite arch, and stretched to fit the layout.

To add depth and motion to the design, with the "EXTREME" layer still targeted, choose the Type tool **T** and then click the "Create warped text" button **⊥** in the Options bar **6b**. In the Warp Text dialog box, choose Arch from the Style menu; leave the default Horizontal option but change the Bend setting from the default +50% to +20% to make the arching less extreme. Set the Horizontal Distortion at −60% to make the type appear to travel into the layout, leave the Vertical Distortion at 0, and click "OK" to close the Warp Text box; then press the Enter key again to commit the warped type.

To complete this type, press Ctrl/⌘-T (for Edit > Free Transform). Now you can experiment with dragging inside the frame to move the type; or move the cursor outside the Transform frame and drag the curved double-headed arrow to rotate the type counterclockwise; drag a side or corner handle to stretch the type **6c**. Press the Enter key to commit the transformation.

Make a new type layer for "DESTINATIONS" by Shift-clicking with the Type tool **T** (adding the Shift key ensures that the click will start a *new* type layer, rather than positioning the cursor in an existing type layer for editing). We typed the word "DESTINATIONS" in the same Trebuchet Bold font but at 27 pt. We warped the type, again using the Arch style, but with a negative Bend setting (−15%) this time, and again rotated and stretched it **6d**. Because the type is live, you'll be able to come back to it and easily adjust its position, size, and warping, if needed, to suit the photos once they're in place.

7 Adding the subhead and date. To add the subhead "ADVENTURE TRAVEL" and a small date code **7**, for each one start a new type layer by Shift-clicking with the Type tool **T**. We used Arial Bold Italic 12 pt for the subhead "ADVENTURE TRAVEL," putting "ADVENTURE" and "TRAVEL" on two separate layers. (We could have set the two words on separate lines in a single layer, but two layers (one line per layer) will make it easier to

---

USING THE HIGHLIGHT

Photoshop's text warping works on an entire layer of type. You don't have to select (highlight) the type in order for warp to work. But sometimes it can be easier to get an overall understanding of what the warping settings are doing if you select the type and watch how the "sheet" of highlighting changes as you operate the Warp Text controls.

7

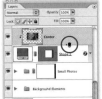

The layout file with all type in place and with visibility turned on for the "Background Elements"

8a

In the layout file we targeted the placeholder for the center photo. We dragged the photo into the file, renamed the new layer, and clipped it to its placeholder. We repositioned the image and scaled it proportionally.

8b

The layout with all the photos in place

use the Variables command in "Many Versions from One Template," page 643.)

We used Arial Regular 6.5 pt for the date. With the type in place, we turned on visibility for the "Background Elements" folder by clicking its 👁 in the Layers palette.

8 Bringing in the photos. Now that the design is complete, open the photos to "populate" the layout: One way is to choose File > Open, navigate to the **Layout-Before** folder (page 635 tells its location); select all the files in the folder except **Layout-Before.psd**, and click the "Open" button. Now you can drag each of the images into your layout file, as described next. *Note:* If you're using Photoshop CS2, in the Options bar turn off Auto Select Group; in fact, you may find it helpful to turn off Auto Select Layer also, in both CS and CS2.

In the Layers palette for the layout file, target the placeholder layer you want to "fill" with a photo by clicking its thumbnail; we started with the placeholder for the large central photo. Then choose the Move tool ►♦. Click in the working window of your photo file, and drag the image into the working window of the layout file and onto its placeholder; we started by dragging the **windsurfer.tif** image. In the Layers Palette the photo will appear above the placeholder layer. Double-click the layer's name and type a new name, such as "Center," that will help you keep track of what's on each layer. To "clip" the photo to the size and shape of the placeholder, Alt/Option-click the border between the two in the Layers palette **8a** to form a *clipping group*.

If you need to adjust how the photo fits the space allotted by the placeholder, use Ctrl/⌘-T and Shift-drag a corner handle to proportionally scale the imported photo to better match the size of the placeholder. Or drag with the Move tool ►♦ to adjust the "crop." Make sure no gray from the placeholder is showing around the edges.

For each of the other photo files, repeat the importing process: Target the appropriate placeholder layer in the layout file, drag the photo in, Alt/Option-click to make the clipping group, and adjust the position and size of the image to get the "crop" you want for the photo **8b**.

9 Styling the type. Now add a Layer Style to color and style the display type. In the Layers palette we targeted the "EXTREME" layer, clicked the "Add a layer style" button 𝒇 at the bottom of the palette, and chose Color Overlay. We clicked the color swatch and then clicked to sample a bright yellow in the rock-climbing

9a

Adding a Color Overlay to the "EXTREME" type layer

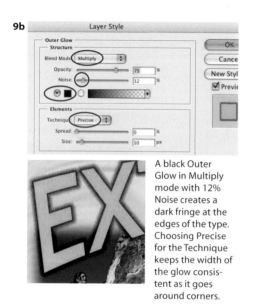

9b

A black Outer Glow in Multiply mode with 12% Noise creates a dark fringe at the edges of the type. Choosing Precise for the Technique keeps the width of the glow consistent as it goes around corners.

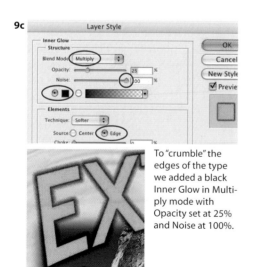

9c

To "crumble" the edges of the type we added a black Inner Glow in Multiply mode with Opacity set at 25% and Noise at 100%.

photo to sample color **9a**. To make the type stand out from the background, we added an Outer Glow in black with a Noise component **9b**. To "erode" the edge, we added an Inner Glow, also in black with more Noise **9c**.

After clicking "OK" to close the Layer Style dialog box, we copied the Style (in the Layers palette, right/Ctrl-click the ⬤ for the "EXTREME" layer and choose Copy Layer Style from the context-sensitive menu) and pasted it to the "DESTINATIONS" layer (right/Ctrl-click the position where the layer's ⬤ would be if it had one, and choose Paste Layer Style).

We added a Layer Style consisting of a white Outer Glow in the default Screen mode to the "adventure" and "travel" layers to help the type stand out. The result can be seen on page 635.

Housekeeping. At this point there are some things you can do to organize the Layers palette and to make it easier to identify layers when you substitute other images. Rename the photo layers according to their positions in the layout (the Type layers and "Center" already have meaningful names), and collect them in layer sets/groups (the process is described in step 3). We named the small photo layers "Small 1" through "Small 5," from the top position in the column down, and we named the two vignetted photos "Left top" and "Left bottom." Color-code the layers and groups if you like by targeting a layer or a set/group and choosing the Layer Properties or Layer Set/Group Properties command from the Layers palette's ⊙ menu. The **Layout-After.psd** file includes the names and color codes we chose.

Using the layout again. It's fairly easy to substitute new images in the layout. For each new photo, proceed as follows: Open the file and select all (Ctrl/⌘-A). In the layout file, target one of the placeholder layers in the Layers palette, and turn off visibility for the photo layer that's currently clipped to it. From the photo file, use the Move tool ▶₊ to drag and drop the new photo into the layout. (It's necessary to make the selection in the photo file to keep the clipping group in the layout from releasing when you drag the photo in. And it's necessary to turn off visibility for the old photo so you can see your new one after you drag-and-drop it.) You can either keep the old photo or remove it (drag it to the "Delete" button 🗑 at the bottom of the palette).

The type in the layout is live, so you can edit it, or reshape it with the Transform and Warp Text commands. Or change any Layer Style in the layout to match the photos, as described in step 9 on page 641. 🎨

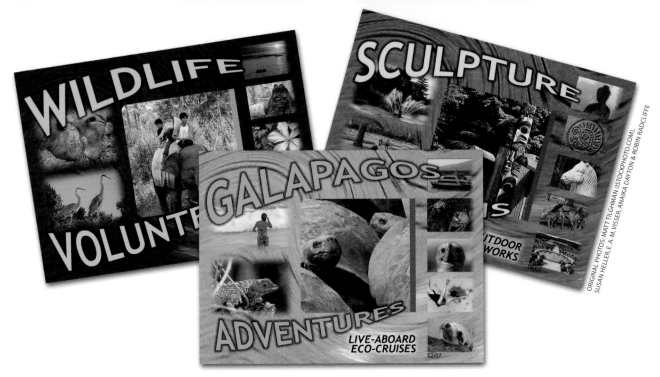

ORIGINAL PHOTOS: MATT TILGHMAN (ISTOCKPHOTO.COM),
SUSAN HELLER, E. A. M. VISSER, ANAIKA DAYTON & ROBIN RADCLIFFE

Many Versions from One Template

YOU'LL FIND THE FILES

in **wow** > Wow Project Files > Chapter 9 > Variables
- Variables-Before.psd (for steps 1 & 2)
- Postcards in Progress files (for steps 3, 4 & 5)
- Variables-After files (to compare)

OPEN THESE PALETTES

from the Window menu:
- Tools • Layers

OVERVIEW

Starting with a layout file that includes type and image layers, define variables for layers that will change in new versions of the layout • Create a data set by browsing for images and replacing type • Import other premade data sets • Apply the data sets to create the new versions of the layout • Adjust the layouts in Photoshop

FOR PROJECTS THAT REQUIRE MANY VERSIONS of the same layout — for instance, the name, a photo, and a short bio of each member of an organization for a website — the Image > Variables command can generate the different versions automatically. (Photoshop CS2 has Variables; in CS you must jump to ImageReady to access this command.) Here we use Variables to create three more of our series of postcard layouts from "Building a Layout with Masks & Clipping Groups" on page 635. After replacing the images and text, we adjust each new version in Photoshop.

1 Understanding Variables. Replacing images or text using Photoshop's **Variables** command is a three-step process:

- First, **define the variables 1a** so Photoshop knows which elements in the layout file can be replaced and how to treat the replacements in the new version of the file (to make them visible or not, scale them, or crop them). Once you've defined the variables, saving the file also saves the variables.

- Second, for each new version of the layout you want to make, **create a data set** that tells Photoshop what images or text to substitute for the variables **1b**. You can create a data set "on the fly" from the Variables dialog box by **browsing** for the new images and typing the substitute text. Or, outside Photoshop, prepare one or more data sets as a text file and **import** the file to bring in the new images and text.

1a

The process of assigning variables begins with the **Image > Variables > Define** command.

1b

Once the variables are defined, you can start to assemble data sets that will automatically substitute new images and text for the variables, to make new versions of the layout.

2a

The **Variables-Before.psd** file is a layout with photos in clipping groups and with live type layers. Layer Styles are used for the bar at the right edge of the central photo and for the type in the heading and subheading.

• Third, **apply the data set.** Once you've created or imported a data set and previewed the changes in the Variables dialog, you can export the alternate version of the layout.

Let's explore the process step-by-step.

2 Defining the variables and saving the file. Open a simple layout file of your own, or use **Variables-Before.psd 2a**. If you're working **in Photoshop CS, you'll need to jump to ImageReady at this point;** in CS2 the Variables command has also been added to the Image menu.

To make a template of the file, choose Image > Variables > Define. In the **Variables** dialog box you'll specify which layers are variables — that is, which can be automatically hidden or shown, or can have alternate text or images substituted. In defining the variables, you identify which layers you'll want to change, and name these variables. First choose from the Layer menu at the top of the box the name of a layer that holds something you'll be replacing **2b**. For instance, in the **Variables-Before.psd** file choose the "Center" layer, which is the central photo in the layout. In the **Variable Type** section of the dialog box, for an image layer such as "Center," you can choose to control whether the layer shows up at all (**Visibility**) and whether its contents will be replaced by another image (**Pixel Replacement**):

• For our postcard series, we want the photo on the "Center" layer to be replaced for each card, so turn on the **Pixel Replacement** option. For the **Method**, choose **Fill**, and leave the Alignment centered. (We'll use Pixel Replacement and Fill for all of the photos in the layout.) Once you've chosen a Method, if you pause the cursor over that choice, a diagram at the bottom of the dialog box will show how that Method works **2c**. For instance, **Fill** will proportionally scale the substituted photo so it at least fills the space occupied by the photo currently on the layer. This option does some initial resizing but also leaves a great deal of flexibility for cropping or scaling the photo to adjust it to the layout, which makes it a good choice for our postcard project.

• Also for flexibility, leave **"Clip to Bounding Box" turned off** so the entire photo will be available in the file, without being permanently cropped on the way in. Our layout file is set up so the gray placeholder layers will mask the photos to the right shapes, and with "Clip to Bounding Box" turned off, you'll be able to frame the part of the image you want by moving the photo around.

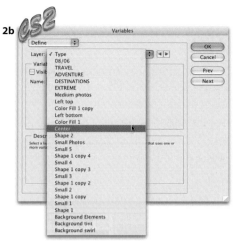

2b

In the **Variables** dialog box, the Layer menu for **Variables-Before.psd** shows all the entries in the Layers palette: type layers, image layers, placeholders ("Shape" layers), folders for layer sets/ groups, and the Color Fill layer ("Background tint") that recolors the "Background swirl" image. We will define variables only for the photos and type layers.

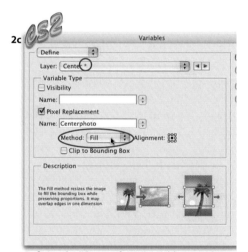

2c

Defining the **"Centerphoto"** variable (to replace the large central photo in the layout). The **asterisk after a name** in the Layer menu shows that this layer has been defined as a variable. With the **Fill** option chosen and **"Clip to Bounding Box" turned off,** the replacement image will be proportionally scaled to fill the bounding box of the original layer contents. Usually this means that the image will extend beyond the bounding box; when the **center Alignment** is chosen, the extra appears evenly divided, either top or bottom (as shown in the diagram) or left or right. **Visibility** will be left unchanged.

- For our postcard series, we won't be using the Visibility option (it allows you to have a layer appear in some versions of your file but not in others). Leave the **Visibility box unchecked**; Photoshop/ImageReady will interpret this to mean that visibility for the layer should stay as it was in the original template.

- Before moving on to the next variable, enter a **name** for this one; we used "Centerphoto." **Variable names can't include spaces or unusual characters.**

Now define a variable for the "EXTREME" layer **2d**: Choose it from the Layer menu. In the **Variable Type** section of the dialog box, once again leave the **Visibility box unchecked** since visibility won't vary. Check the **Text Replacement** box, since we'll want to change the display type for each postcard in the series. Name the variable; we called it "Head1" since it's the first line of the heading.

Repeat the process of defining and naming for all the other type and photo layers in the file, but not the folders, placeholders (Shape layers), "Background Elements" layers, or *Background* (no substitutions will be made in these layers or layer sets/groups). We used the same Pixel Replacement settings (**Fill, with clipping off**) for all the photo layers; we named them the same as the layer names, but without the spaces between words. For the type layers, we named the "DESTINATIONS" layer "Head2," the "ADVENTURE" and "TRAVEL" layers "Subhead1" and "Subhead2," and the "08/06" layer "Date."

When you've defined all the variables you want in the file, save it (File > Save As); we called our file **Variables-Defined**.psd.

3 Creating and applying a data set. A **data set** tells Photoshop/ImageReady what images and text you want to substitute for the variables in the file. You can create a data set by *browsing* (to find each image where it's stored) and by typing any replacement text. Or instead, *import* a text file that lists the new text and the alternate images to be substituted in the file.

2d

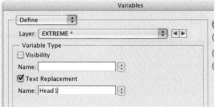

Setting up the variable for the "EXTREME" type layer, called "Head1." Again, the Visibility option is left unchecked.

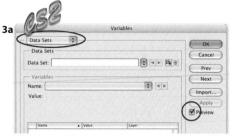

3a

Opening the Variables dialog to the Data Sets panel

3b

We started a new data set based on the variables that had been defined and named it "Galapagos Adventures."

3c

Setting a new Value for the "Head1" variable in the "Galapagos Adventures" data set. With the Preview option checked, you can see the change in the working window for the file.

- You might use **browsing** if you have a collection of many images you want to review and choose from.

- You might **import** instead if you (or someone else) can choose the photos in advance and prepare a text file listing their file names, along with any substitute text. Importing allows you to make all the substitutions at once simply by choosing the text file.

Creating a data set by browsing and typing. Start by opening a file for which variables have been defined. If you're following along with our example, copy the **Postcards in Progress folder** from the Wow DVD-ROM (see "YOU'LL FIND THE FILES" on page 643) onto your hard drive and open the **Variables-Defined.psd** file. Using our Variables-Defined.psd will ensure that the variable names will exactly match the values we've used in the sample data sets. Choose Image > Variables > Data Sets **3a**. In the Variables dialog box, turn on the **Preview** option so you'll be able to see the new layout developing.

In the **Data Sets** section at the top of the dialog box, click the **"Create a new data set"** button 🔳 **3b** (in ImageReady the first data set is created automatically). Change the default "Data Set 1" name if you like; we used "Galapagos Adventures."

In the **Name** column of the dialog box is a list of all the variables defined for the layers in the file (from step 2). For each text variable, the **Value** column shows the text that's currently on that layer. To change the value of a text layer for the new data set you're building, click the text layer's name in the Layer list at the bottom of the dialog box; then select the text that appears in the **Value** box and type the replacement text in its place **3c** (don't press the Enter/Return key; Photoshop will respond as if you had clicked "OK" to close the Variables dialog box). We changed "Head1" and "Head2" to "GALAPAGOS" and "ADVENTURES"; "Subhead1" and "Subhead2" became "LIVE-ABOARD" and "ECO-CRUISES"; we changed "Date" to "02/07." (If you have trouble selecting the text, press Backspace/Delete to erase, and then type the new text.)

For each of the **Pixel Replacement variables**, click on it in the Layer list at the bottom of the dialog box. Then click the **"Select File"** button in Photoshop CS2 **3d** (if you're working in ImageReady the button is "Choose" or "Browse") and browse to find the file you want. Find the **Galapagos folder** of images in the **Postcards in Progress folder**; for the "Centerphoto" variable, choose the **tortoises.jpg** file, and choose other photos for

3d

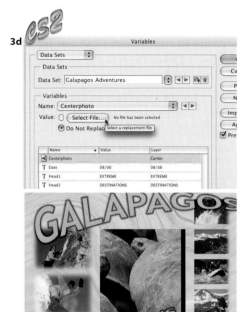

Browsing to choose a replacement (set a Value) for the "Centerphoto" variable. The change is previewed in the file's working window.

3e

After browsing and typing to change the photo and text variables

3f

Importing data sets begins with clicking the **Import button** in the **Variables** dialog box.

3g

In Photoshop CS2's **Import Data Set** dialog box (in ImageReady it's **Import Variable Data Sets**), **turn off the Replace Existing Data Sets option** to keep any existing data sets (in this case "Galapagos Adventures") when the new data sets are imported.

---

the other image variables. When you select a file, its **name** (**along with the path** that tells where it's located on your system) appears in the **Value** column.

When you've changed the values for all variables, the preview will show you the file with all text and image substitutions **3e**. Don't click "Apply" or "OK" yet.

Importing data sets: If a data set text file with one or more data sets has been prepared in advance, you can change the images and text simply by importing this text file. We've made the **Postcard.txt** file for this purpose.

In the **Variables** dialog box, click the "Import" button to open the Import Data Set dialog box **3f**, **3g**. Click the "Select File" button and navigate to the **Postcard.txt** file in the **Postcards in Progress** folder. After you load the Postcard.txt file, click "OK" in the Import Data Set dialog. *Note:* In the process of using a data set file with the Variables command, you won't ever see the content of the .txt file, but "Building Data Sets" (on page 648) tells what constitutes a data set and how to create one.

When you find yourself back in the Variables dialog, notice that the imported image file names appear in the Value column without a path telling where they're found. We didn't have to include the path information in our data set lines because we stored the images in the same folder as the text file for the data set. When the images are not in the same folder, the path must be included as part of each file's listing — for instance, My Hard Drive/Projects/Postcards in Progress/red lizard.jpg — so Photoshop will know where to find the file.

BUILDING DATA SETS

To prepare a data set to use with Photoshop CS2's or ImageReady's Variables command, you can use any word-processing or text-editing software that can save a plain text (.txt) file. Use commas or tabs to separate the entries. End each "line" (defined at the right) by pressing the Enter/Return key.

Shown at the right is the text file, created in Microsoft Word, that's used to import two data sets for the example in step 3 of "Many Versions from One Template" (page 647).

In these data sets, each image name appears without a path that tells where it's stored. But the path information must be included unless, as is the case here, the image files and .txt file are together in the same folder.

Line 1 of the text file is always a list of the variable Names that have been assigned in the Variables dialog box.

Each of the other lines in the file is a **data set** that lists the **substitute Values** (the file names/paths and the text). These values appear in the same order as the variables in Line 1, so Photoshop/ImageReady will know how to match them up for substitution. Here Line 2 (highlighted to help you distinguish it) and Line 3 list the substitute Values to be used for two different versions of the layout. Line 2 has the values for a "Sculpture Gardens" version, and Line 3 has the values for a "Wildlife Volunteers" version.

```
Centerphoto,Date,Head1,Head2,Leftbottom,Lefttop,Small1,
Small2,Small3,Small4,Small5,Subhead1,Subhead2
totems.jpg,06/07,SCULPTURE,GARDENS,chained
trees.jpg,fountain.jpg,buddha.jpg,carving.jpg,horse.jpg
,three seated.jpg,formal garden.jpg,OUTDOOR,ARTWORKS
elephant riders.jpg,04/
07,WILDLIFE,VOLUNTEERS,herons.jpg,rhinos.jpg,sunset.jpg
,frog.jpg,flower.jpg,small
mammal.jpg,duck.jpg,HABITAT,RECOVERY
```

Exporting the three new postcard layouts

Shown here is the "Wildlife Volunteers" version of the layout as produced by the Export Data Sets as Files command. In the files produced by exporting the data sets, the photos needed to be reframed, and type and color needed adjusting.

Click "OK" to close the Variables dialog box. The original "Extreme Destinations" images and text will be restored to the layout, but when you save the file (Ctrl/⌘-S) the data sets you made or imported will be saved along with it.

4 Applying the data sets. To automate production of the new versions of the layout, use your file from step 3 or open our **Variables-Data Sets.psd**, which includes the three data sets added in step 3. Choose **File > Export > Data Sets as Files**. In the **Export Data Sets as Files** dialog box, click the "Select Folder" button in Photoshop CS2 (in ImageReady it's "Choose") and choose a location for your new postcard files, creating a new folder if you like. Then from the **Data Set** menu, choose **All Data Sets 4**. Make any changes you want in the file-naming section of the dialog box (we left the default settings) and click "OK." Three new Postcard files will be produced but not opened.

5 Fine-tuning the new postcards. After the automated substitutions, the three new versions of the postcard file will need individual fine-tuning **5a**. Open the files in Photoshop and make any of the following changes:

- For each of the photo layers, target the layer by clicking its thumbnail in the Layers palette. Choose the Move tool ▸⊕; turn Auto Select Layer on and off in the Options bar as

5b

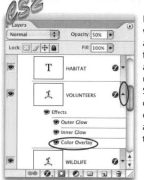

Photos and type were proportionally scaled and flipped as needed, and the colors used in Layer Styles were changed to recolor the type and the bar on the center photo.

5c

Unifying the "Wildlife Volunteers" version of the postcard (see page 643). A Hue/Saturation Adjustment layer is used at reduced Opacity (50%) to unify the composition by tinting all the layers below it.

needed, but in Photoshop CS2 be sure to **turn off the Auto Select Group option**. Use Free Transform (Ctrl/⌘-T) to scale the photo proportionally by Shift-dragging a corner handle, or to move it around within the framing provided by its clipping group. In some cases we flipped images horizontally (Edit > Transform > Flip Horizontal) for better composition.

- Scale the display type or change the warping if needed. Step 6 of "Building a Layout with Masks & Clipping Groups" on page 639 tells about transforming and warping the type.

- Make color adjustments. For instance in the Layers palette for each new postcard file we double-clicked the "Background tint" layer's thumbnail and chose a new color; we also experimented with this layer's blend mode and Opacity.

In the Layers palette we expanded the list of effects for a layer by clicking the small downward arrow beside the 🎨 for the layer in the Layers palette **5b**. We then double-clicked on the name of an effect to open the Layer Style dialog box. To change the color of the Color Overlay for the type, double-click the Color Overlay effect for the first line of the heading, click the color swatch, and click on one of the photos to sample a color. For the second line of the heading, sample from the newly colored first line, so the color will match exactly. We also changed the color of the Drop Shadow effect that produces the bar on the right edge of the center photo.

One approach to turning a diverse collection of images into a unified set is to slightly tint the entire assemblage with a single color. We added a Hue/Saturation Adjustment layer above all other layers in the "Wildlife Volunteers" version of the postcard and reduced this layer's Opacity to taste **5c**. We used a similar subtle tint for the "Sculpture Gardens" layout.

The final postcard layouts are included in the **Variables-After folder** and are shown at the top of page 643. *Wow!*

Mark Wainer's *Oregon Beach* is a composite of three photos. He opened the two beach photos (shown at the right) with Photoshop's Camera Raw plug-in, where it was easy to experiment with changes in the Temperature, Tint, and other controls in the Adjust panel to boost the color.▼

He increased each digital file's size to 29 MB.▼ Then, starting with the main photo **A**, Wainer added extra canvas at the bottom (Image > Canvas Size) and then stretched the photo vertically and flipped it horizontally. One way to do this is to use the Rectangular Marquee ⬚ to select the image, press Ctrl/⌘-T for Free Transform, and drag the bottom center handle down to stretch the image;

FIND OUT MORE

▼ Using Camera Raw **page 102**
▼ Enlarging a file **page 73**

then before pressing Enter to complete the transform, right/Ctrl-click to open a context-sensitive menu where you can choose Flip Horizontal.

Wainer built up the large rock formation in the background with the Clone Stamp ⬚. Then he used a feathered Lasso ⬚ to copy the rock with the starfish from the second image **B** and pasted it into the first. He flipped this new layer as well so the lighting would match (Edit > Transform > Flip Horizontal), and used the Move tool ⬚ to position it. He used the methods described on page 407 to adjust tone and color and to change the composite into a painted image.

Then he added the sky from the third photo (not shown here). One way to do this is to select and copy the replacement sky image (Ctrl/⌘-A, Ctrl/⌘-C), then select the sky to be replaced (for a continuous monotone

expanse like this, the Magic Wand ⬚ works well), and choose Edit > Paste Into. Paste Into creates a stationary mask in the new pasted layer, and you can use the Move tool ⬚ to drag the pasted image until the mask reveals the area you want.

A

B

The photos that **Katrin Eismann** used to develop her *Silent Beauty* series were set up outside, with fish placed on a mirror, and were shot with a Nikon D100 camera fitted with a macro lens and set on a tripod. For *Long Mackerel* (above) she photographed her setup four times, first focusing on the sky in the mirror, and then focusing at different depths, so that every part of the fish was in focus in at least one of the photos.

Once the files were open in Photoshop, Eismann used layer masks to composite the four versions, painting the masks with black and white to hide the blurred parts and reveal the sharp areas of each image.▼

Eismann brightened each eye with its own Curves Adjustment layer,▼ one in Color Dodge mode and one in Lighten,▼ painting the layers' built-in masks to limit the changes to the eyes. To enhance the colors in the fish's skin, she simply painted streaks of gold and blue with the Brush tool at low-opacity on a transparent layer and put the Layer in Overlay mode, one of the blend modes that boosts color contrast. Another Curves Adjustment layer was added and set to lighten the Blue channel, with a mask that restricted the brightening to the sky. And one more Curves layer (with an "S" curve to increase midtone contrast) was added and masked to brighten the clouds.

FIND OUT MORE

▼ Painting layer masks **page 75**

▼ Using Curves **page 250**

▼ Using blend modes **page 176**

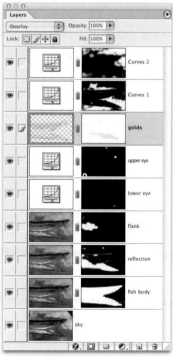

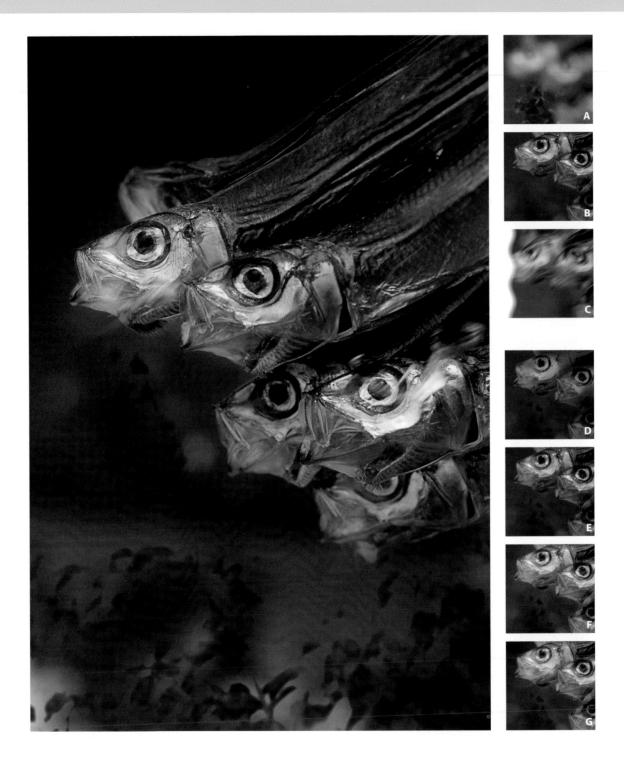

For **Blue Guys**, **Katrin Eismann** set up six fish on a mirror near a ficus plant. Using a Nikon D100 with a macro lens, as she had for the other photos in her **Silent Beauty** series, she chose to shoot one photo with the ficus tree's reflection in the mirror slightly out of focus. Then she shot another with the macro lens focused on the fish.

She had set the camera to use Nikon's raw file format (.nef), which stores the raw data the camera captures separate from the processing instructions the camera uses to refine the image. When she opened the raw photos in Photoshop, the Camera Raw plug-in's interface automatically appeared on-screen (the raw image of the fish is shown below, before adjustments were made).▼

Camera Raw allowed Eismann to work with the raw data, adjusting the color of the photos by changing the White Balance setting. The photo was taken outdoors in daylight, but by choosing Fluorescent, she could shift the color of the fish to blue and then make a small adjustment with the Temperature slider. Direct control of Temperature is one of the advantages of shooting in raw format and using Camera Raw, since there's no directly comparable adjustment you can make in Photoshop without the Camera Raw plug-in. Eismann also adjusted Exposure to brighten the colors. The same kinds of adjustments were used to boost color in *Horse Mackerel,* shown on page 595.

Clicking Camera Raw's Advanced button gave Eismann access to the Calibrate panel, where she could adjust the hues in her image and boost the saturation (this can also be done in Photoshop's Hue/Saturation dialog box, but Camera Raw presents the sliders for Red, Green, and Blue all at once, while in the Hue/Saturation dialog box you do the work color-by-color). Another advantage of doing this sort of work in Camera Raw is the opportunity to work interactively with several different color adjustments.

Blue Guys is essentially a composite of three images, as shown in the progressive details on the facing page. The three "originals" are the background shot **A**, several copies of the sharp photo of the fish **B**, and a version of the sharp photo treated with the Distort > Wave filter **C**. In addition to the masking used in other images in the series (shown on pages 595 and 651), Eismann used blend modes to combine the background layer with the fish layer.▼ An unmasked layer in Darken mode gave a painted look to the ficus **D**. A layer in Lighten mode (masked to protect the background) filled in most of the rest of the fish image **E**, and a layer in Screen mode added a bright glow **F**. To add "neon" streaks, Eismann masked the Wave-filtered image on a layer just above the Darken layer. With the blend mode for this streaky layer set at Pin Light, its bright streaks replaced some of the darker pixels in the composite **G**.

FIND OUT MORE

▼ Using Camera Raw
page 102

▼ Using blend modes
page 173

To finish the composition, Eismann "burned" the upper left corner, using the method described on page 349. (The Layers palette below shows the file at this stage.)

To boost detail in the image, she used PixelGenius's PhotoKit Sharpener, a plug-in that offers sharpening routines through Photoshop's File > Automate menu. Individual sharpening processes, which operate without permanently changing any pixels in the file, are designed for a wide range of input sources, creative treatments, and output devices, such as inkjet printers and halftone printing at various image resolutions and print line screens (www.pixelgenius.com).

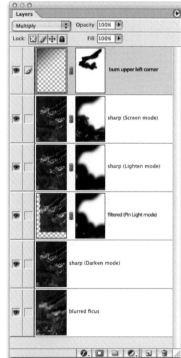

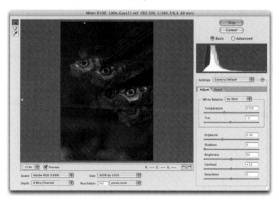

Before Sharpening   After Sharpening

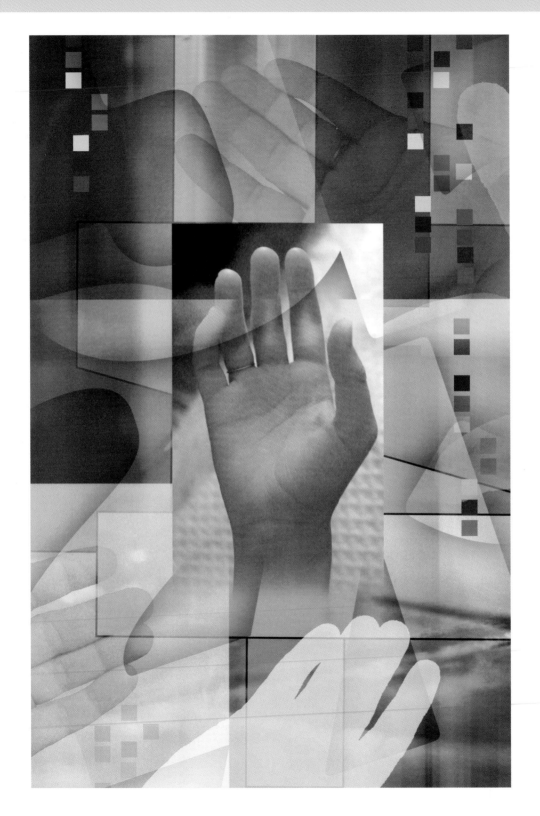

Don Jolley applies masks, blend modes, and Adjustment layers to weave his photo and graphic elements into layered compositions with a dynamic "push-pull" tension that holds the viewer's attention. To make the "background" for **Hannah's Hand**, Jolley started with an abstract photo, tinted it green, and selected and lightened a rectangle in one corner.▼ On top of this he layered two versions of the same silhouetted hand,▼ rotated to different angles, tinted to match the photo, and with layer Opacity reduced to about half to let the abstract image filter through **A**. Next he added an out-of-focus photo of candles in Color mode **B**. And finally, graphics created in Adobe Illustrator, copied to the clipboard, and pasted into Photoshop as pixels▼ provided geometric structure to anchor the central figure — the hand **C**.

The hand image itself is a composite of three copies of the same photo, all in Normal mode. Working with a photo he had dragged into the composite file with the Move tool ▶⊕, Jolley

used the Rectangular Marquee ⌞⌟ to select the area he wanted to show in the image, and then clicked the "Add a layer mask" button ⬤ at the bottom of the Layers palette to make a black-filled mask with a white rectangle that revealed the selected area. With the new mask targeted in the Layers palette, he used the Gradient tool ▨ with a Foreground (black)-to-Transparency gradient to fade the lower edge of the photo to blend it with the background **D**.▼ Jolley then duplicated the masked layer (Ctrl/⌘-J). Where the masked image was fully opaque or fully transparent, the duplicate layer made no difference. But in the partly transparent area, the density of the image was built up **E**.

REGULATING TRANSPARENCY

One way to modify a transition from opaque to transparent is to layer two copies of the partly transparent image; in the Layers palette move the Fill or Opacity slider for the upper layer as you watch the effect in real time, stopping when you see the transition you want.

Jolley duplicated the hand layer again (Ctrl/⌘-J) and added a Hue/Saturation layer as part of a clipping group, so it would apply only to the top hand layer.▼ In the Hue/Saturation dialog box he moved the Hue slider to turn the hand blue. By using the Gradient tool ▨ to alter the layer mask, Jolley hid more of this blue hand, to blend it with the hand on the lower layers **F**.

Large numerals "2" and "4" were set and colored in Illustrator, then copied to the clipboard, and pasted into the Photoshop file as pixels. Clicking the "Add a layer style" button ⬤ at the bottom of the Layers palette, Jolley added a Drop Shadow effect to the new layer. By reducing the Fill opacity (via the Layers palette) for the numbers layer, he allowed the image below to show through. He used the same process to add another layer with numerals "5" and "3." Because he reduced the *Fill* rather than the overall *Opacity* of these layers, the intensity of the drop shadow was not affected, and the shadows still clearly defined the number shapes.

Layers with small square color swatches and additional hands (at the bottom and on the right edge) completed the montage. Finally, Jolley created a transition from bright colors at the top of the composition to a warm monochrome at the bottom. To do this he added a Hue/Saturation Adjustment layer at the top of the layer stack with Colorize turned on, and then used the Gradient tool ▨ on the layer's built-in mask so this tint effect was hidden at the top of the composition and revealed at the bottom.

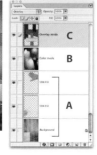

A

B

C

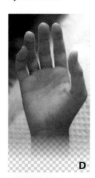

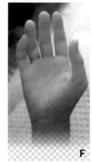
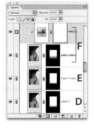

D

E

F

FIND OUT MORE

▼ Quick tinting methods **page 200**

▼ Jolley's silhouetting technique **page 50**

▼ Copying & pasting from Illustrator **page 443**

▼ Masking with gradients **page 75**

▼ Using clipping groups **page 79**

E xperimenting with Photoshop's Photomerge command, **John McIntosh** proved that this command has potential beyond piecing images together in a panorama. For each of the symmetrical images on this page, McIntosh started with a copy of a photo without strong directional shadows. Then he used the Rectangular Selection tool ⌞⌟ to select a little more of the photo than he wanted for one half (either left or right) of the final image, and cropped (Image > Crop). He duplicated the cropped photo (Image > Duplicate), selected all (Ctrl/⌘-A), and flipped the duplicate image (Edit > Transform > Flip Horizontal). He saved both files, since Photomerge works only on saved files, and chose File > Automate > Photomerge. In the Photomerge dialog box he chose "Use: Open Files," turned on "Attempt to Automatically Arrange Source Images,"

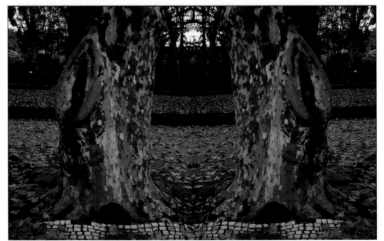

and clicked "OK." Photomerge used the overlap that McIntosh had included to align the mirror images perfectly.

In **Tomar Twin Castle Stairs** (top) the symmetry is believable at first glance because the architecture is manmade. The merged details are just as believable in **Tomar Park Trees** but the perfect symmetry of the pair of trees tips us off that Nature didn't produce this scene by herself.

John McIntosh's *Rosenquist Opening at the Guggenheim* is a montage of seven overlapping photos he shot from up high in the museum and assembled by hand with Photomerge. Before beginning to photograph, McIntosh set his camera's exposure manually so the lighting would stay as consistent as possible from photo to photo. (With automatic exposure, the camera adapts as you point it closer to or farther from the light source. This can change the color from one image to the next. For an example of how to correct for this after the fact, see "'Photomerging' a Panorama" on page 604.)

McIntosh opened all of the museum photos and used Image > Adjustments > Shadow/Highlight to make minor adjustments to balance the exposure from image to image.▼ Using Photomerge as a compositing tool, he chose File > Automate > Photomerge and turned *off* the "Attempt to Automatically Arrange Source Images" option, so that when he clicked "OK" the Photomerge window opened with all the images side-by-side in the lightbox strip at the top. From there he could drag the photos into position in the main Photomerge window with the Select Image tool ꕙ, adjusting the overlap and using the Rotate Image tool ⟳ as needed. He returned to the thumbnail strip any photos he decided not to include in the montage.

By turning on Advanced Blending and clicking the "Preview" button, McIntosh could check on how the montage was developing, then click "Exit Preview," adjust the composite, preview again, and so on until he had the composition he wanted. Though truncated in spots when Photomerge couldn't match them, the smooth, sharp curves of the walls and the adjusted tone and color unified the parts into a single image.

After completing the merge, he added a black outline: He Ctrl/⌘-clicked the thumbnail in the Layers palette and chose Edit > Stroke, set the stroke's position and width and clicked "OK."

FIND OUT MORE

▼ Using Shadow/Highlight **page 169**

Designer **Wayne Rankin** brought images and Photoshop effects together to make a series of posters for **The Ultimate Journey**, a new live entertainment concept based on a theme of time travel. To start, he opened a long-exposure photo of a landscape and star trails, chosen to hint at a time tunnel. To create the aurora at the top of the image, he added new layers and used the Brush tool with the Airbrush option turned on in the Options bar to make brush footprints in bright colors. Then he used Filter > Blur > Motion Blur with the Angle set at 90°, adjusting the Distance as he watched the filter's preview window, to stretch the dabs of color into vertical curtains of light.

He selected the moon from another image, holding down the Alt/Option and Shift keys as he dragged with the Elliptical Marquee (Alt/Option to draw the selection from the center; Shift to constrain it to a circle). Then he used the Move tool to drag the selected moon into the background photo at the center of the concentric star trails. Rankin set the moon layer's blend mode to Linear Dodge, which lightened the light colors in the image underneath, allowing the star trails and aurora to appear in front of the moon.▼ He also added a layer mask and painted it with the Gradient tool , to hide the lower part of

the moon, fading it into the black sky in the image beneath.▼

For the bright streaks at the bottom of the illustration, Rankin dragged in a photo of medical capsules on a black background, applied the Motion Blur filter to it, and colored it, choosing Image > Adjustments > Hue/Saturation; he turned on the Colorize option, choosing a color with the Hue slider and moving the Saturation slider to the right to make the color more intense. He selected the band of streaks with a feathered Lasso , inverted the selection, and pressed the Delete key to remove most of the black background. Then he copied the streak layer (Ctrl/⌘-J) several times. He repositioned the new layers with the Move tool and reduced their opacity different amounts. He used the Hue/Saturation command again on some of the layers to change their colors. On one layer he bent the glowing lights slightly with the Spherize filter (Filter > Distort > Spherize).

For the title, Rankin selected the Type tool T, clicked on the image (to create a new type layer), and chose the Trajan font from the pop-up list in the Options bar. After typing "The Ultimate Journey," Rankin wanted to put it into perspective. Although you can use Edit > Transform on a live type layer, not all of the transforming options are available: Scale, Rotate, and Skew will work, but not Distort or Perspective. So Rankin right/Ctrl-clicked

on the type layer's name in the Layers palette to open a context-sensitive menu, and selected Rasterize Layer. Then he chose Edit > Transform > Perspective and dragged one of the upper corner handles of the Transform box toward the center to achieve the perspective.

To create the "ghosted" type behind the title, Rankin duplicated the layer and applied the Motion Blur filter, again setting the Angle at 90° and experimenting with Distance.

For the subtitle "Where Time Has No Limit!" Rankin selected the Type tool T and clicked the "Center text" button in the Options bar, clicked on the image, and typed the first line; then he held down the Shift key and pressed the Enter/Return key, and typed the second line. He added a layer mask and used the Gradient tool to drag vertically so the type was progressively masked from top to bottom.

For other posters in the series, Rankin used Hue/Saturation adjustments to change the colors of the aurora and streaks. And he changed the subtitle by dragging with the Type tool T to select the text, and retyping.

FIND OUT MORE

▼ Blend modes **page 176**
▼ Masking with gradients **page 75**

For ***Whispers in the Forest,*** which **Darryl Baird** composed as a tribute to old photographs for his series *Transcending Loss,* the artist developed the image in black-and-white, then used Duotone color to approximate the look of an old albumen or kallitype (sepia) print, and finally converted this "enriched" image back to RGB color, since he wasn't planning to print the file with two custom inks and therefore didn't need the two-plate Duotone file structure. Here's the process he used.

Starting with his 35mm black-and-white photograph of a mausoleum in the woods of San Juan Island, Washington, Baird had the photo processed as Kodak Photo CD and opened it in RGB mode in Photoshop. He also scanned as two separate files

a tintype photo and a picture frame placed directly on his flatbed scanner. Then he used the Move tool to drag and drop the tintype scan into the frame file. He began the process of integrating these two images by removing the color but still keeping the file in RGB mode (one way to do this is to use a Channel Mixer with the Monochrome option turned on).▼ He applied the Edit > Free Transform command (Ctrl/⌘-T) to the tintype layer to resize and position it so it would fit the frame, Shift-dragging a corner of the Transform frame to keep proportionality. After pressing the Enter key to finish the transformation, he trimmed each of the two layers by using the Rectangular Marquee to select the area he wanted to keep, then inverting the selection (Ctrl/⌘-Shift-I) and pressing the Delete key to trim away the edges he didn't want. He merged the two layers, targeting the tintype layer by clicking its thumbnail in the Layers palette and then pressing Ctrl/⌘-E (for Layer > Merge Down) to combine it with the frame layer below it.

He dragged and dropped the framed tintype image into the main photo file and used Free Transform to scale and

position it in the space created by the broken column.

To heighten the quiet drama of the scene and to unify the frame and tintype, he applied the Lighting Effects filter.▼ He targeted the framed tintype layer, then chose Filter > Render > Lighting Effects and set up a custom Spotlight to fall across the picture-and-frame composition.

Once he was finished with the Lighting Effects filter, which works only in RGB mode, he could convert the file to Duotone mode (Image > Mode > Grayscale and then Image > Mode > Duotone, since the only way to Duotone mode is through Grayscale). In the Duotone Options dialog box, he chose Duotone for the Type. He loaded a Duotone preset that Adobe supplies with Photoshop, one that uses Black and Pantone 478, a warm brown. In the Duotone Options box he clicked on the Duotone Curve thumbnail for the Pantone color and experimented with the Brown curve to arrive at a solution like the one shown below, with brown in the midtones. When he was satisfied, he clicked "OK" to close the box and then converted the file back to RGB (Image > Mode > RGB Color).

FIND OUT MORE

▼ Converting from color to gray
page 213

▼ Using the Lighting Effects filter
page 259

For the 40th Anniversary Commemorative Issue of *Footprints,* the newsletter of Adventure 16 Outdoor & Travel Outfitters, **Betsy Schulz** designed the cover and inside spreads as layered Photoshop files. For each spread she set up a full-size RGB file in Photoshop (22 x 12 inches) at the resolution she wanted for printing (300 pixels/inch). Using Photoshop's File > Import command, she scanned various photo and drawing files and dragged-and-dropped them into the layout file. She tinted some of these layers▼ and used Edit > Free Transform (Ctrl/⌘-T) to reduce them to the appropriate sizes, rotate them, and move them into position.

For the *Footprints* nameplate on the cover, she dragged and dropped an image of rusted metal from MindCandy's *Textures* collection (www.mindcandy.com). She used the Pen tool ◊ to draw a path for the shape she wanted for the plate, first making sure to select the "Paths" 🔲 and "Add to path area" 🔲 settings in the Options bar.▼ Then she made a selection from the path (by clicking the "Load path as a selection" button ⊙ at the bottom of the Paths palette)

and clicked the "Add a layer mask" button 🔲 at the bottom of the Layers palette to create a layer mask (with an active selection, clicking 🔲 adds a mask that hides all but the selected area). With the layer mask active, she "knocked out" the type: First she used the Horizontal Type Mask tool ▼ to set the type, pressing Ctrl/⌘-Enter to complete the setting.▼ Then she pressed Delete to fill the type with black (when a mask is active, black is the Background color by default, and pressing Delete fills the selection with black).

She created a shadow for each photo by clicking the 🅯 at the bottom of the Layers palette and adding a Drop Shadow effect, then rendering the shadow onto a separate layer so that she could modify it. (To render the effects in a Layer Style, you can right-click/Ctrl-click on the 🅯 for the layer in the Layers palette and choose Create Layer.) With each shadow on a separate layer, she could distort it (Edit > Transform > Distort), to make it look as

though the snapshot was curled slightly.

For the pieces of paper that would hold the text (to be set in QuarkXPress), Schulz scanned a textured sheet and added a Drop Shadow effect. For each piece of paper she needed, she duplicated this paper layer, sometimes tinting the duplicate. Then she used the Pen tool to draw a path that defined the shape of the piece of paper she needed. As she had done for the *Footprints* nameplate, she made a selection from the path and added a layer mask that revealed the image only in the selected area. The Drop Shadow automatically conformed to the shape defined by the mask.

Schulz saved each completed file in Photoshop EPS format and imported it into her QuarkXPress file, where she added logos and other graphics to the pages and set the type in fonts from the VTypewriter family by Vintage Type (www.vintagetype.com).

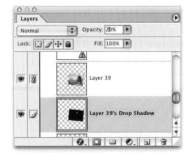

FIND OUT MORE

▼ Tinting images **page 200**
▼ Using the Pen tools **page 435**
▼ Using the Type tools **page 418**

ODE TO A ROCKCOD

BANJO MAKES A RIGHT NICE BAIT

...and other Fine Fish Stories

ALFIE MEEK

n his ***Ode to a Rockcod*** book cover, **Don Jolley** really "puts it all together." The background is a blend of two photos from the artist's "grunge" library (see page 147), layered in Overlay mode over a color-filled layer **A**. Jolley added copies of a silhouetted banjo photo in Multiply mode in the middle and at the corners **B**. Then he added another layer with just the center banjo in Overlay mode, from which he removed the

color (one way is to use Image > Adjustments > Desaturate). Finally he added the center banjo again on yet a third layer, also in Overlay mode but this time with its color intact **C**. By using separate copies, with and without color and in different blend modes, he was able to work in the Layers palette to adjust Fill opacity for each layer to get exactly the blend of contrast and color that he wanted **D**.

He marked the center of his background composition with Guides (see "No Measuring, No Arithmetic" on the facing page) and used the Guides with the Rectangular Marquee [ ] to develop a mask for a Hue/ Saturation layer that he added in order to color opposite quadrants of his background composition (the masking method is shown on page 211.)

The type layers for title, subtitle, and author were given color and dimension primarily with Layer Styles. For the "hand-written" story text, he first used the Pen tool ✎ to draw a series of curved component paths **E** and converted this *Work Path* to a permanent path by dragging the *Work Path* thumbnail to the "Create new path" button ⬛ at the bottom of the Paths palette. By targeting this Path in the Paths palette, and then clicking on a component path with the Type tool **T**, he could type a layer of text for each line, using each component path as a baseline.

To combine his own portrait with the fish, Jolley layered two images **F**, then used layer masks to isolate the single fish and to mask the face to blend with it **G**.

To refine the face-fish blend Jolley used one desaturated fish layer in Overlay mode and one full-color layer in Normal mode, to achieve the combination of color and contrast he wanted. He started with a black-filled layer mask on each of these layers and painted it with white to bring in

fish characteristics where he wanted them **H, I, J**. Jolley also added other transparent layers in Multiply mode on which he painted a drop shadow for the fish and a shadow for the ear.

To balance the horizontal elements in the composition, he added a layer with vertical black stripes in Overlay mode just above the background composition. He also added a layer in Normal mode with strips of black at the side edges to frame the finished book cover.

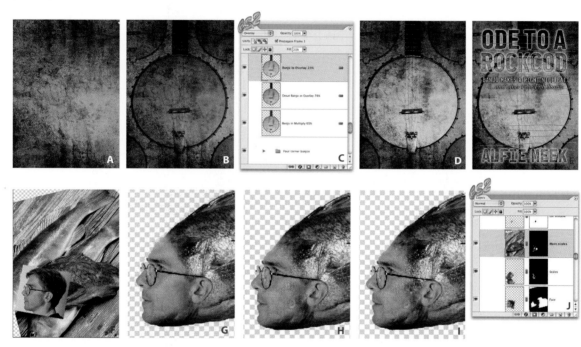

NO MEASURING, NO ARITHMETIC

Have you ever wanted to find and mark the center of a layer or a selected area so you could use this point as a starting point to select or draw from the center? Here's a quick way that works on any pixel-based layer (a *Background* has to be converted to a regular layer first; double-click its name in the Layers palette). First target the layer by clicking its image thumbnail in the Layers palette (make a selection if you like). Turn on the Rulers (Ctrl/⌘-R), and bring up the Transform frame (Ctrl/⌘-T, or in Photoshop CS2 with the Move tool ▶⊕ chosen, just turn on Show Transform Controls in the Options bar).

The Transform frame has a small circle with vertical and horizontal tick marks that indicates the center of the bounding box for the layer. Turn on the Snap feature in the View menu. Now when you drag a Guide from each Ruler, it will "snap" to the center of the Transform frame.

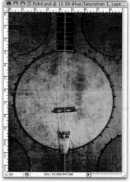

The center point of the Transform frame (above) can be used to "attract" Guides dragged in from the Rulers to mark the center of a layer or a selected area.

To create *Rainy Day*, **Marie Brown** started by layering Beverly Goward's photo of the girl in the rain with another photo (the frame) and two elements constructed with Layer Styles (the mat and the wall). To unify the composition, she made a merged copy of the image and treated it with the Lighting Effects filter. (The finished file is included on the Wow DVD-ROM, so you can examine it as you read about its construction if you like.)

Starting at the bottom of a new file, Brown targeted the white *Background* and turned it to a regular layer (Layer > New > Layer from Background) **A** so she could add a Layer Style to define

You can experiment find the **Rainy Day.psd** file in Wow Goodies on the Wow DVD-ROM.

the wallpaper. To add the Style, she clicked the "Add layer style" button 🔘 at the bottom of the Layers palette and chose Pattern Overlay from the pop-out list, choosing a pattern and scaling it to 20% of its normal size **B**. From the list on the left side of the Layer Style dialog box, she then chose Color Overlay and chose a tan color; she changed the Blend Mode for the Color Overlay to Color so it would tint the pattern rather than covering it up **C**. ▼

She opened Goward's photo file and used the Move tool ▶♦ to drag it into the developing composite file **D**. The next step was to open and drag in the frame, which had been isolated on a transparent layer. Having the frame in place **E** would allow her to establish the lighting for the composite and would give her the visual cues she needed for constructing the mat.

With the frame layer active, Brown opened the Layer Style dialog by clicking the 🔘 at the bottom of the palette and choosing Drop Shadow. The lighting on the frame was quite direct and the gilt reflected the light, so the lighting of this element was adaptable, and she could choose from a wide range of lighting Angle settings for the Drop Shadow. She left the default 120° Angle, with "Use Global Light" turned on so she could easily change the angle for both the frame and the mat layer that she would add next, by changing it for either one. Before leaving the Layer Style dialog, she added dimension with even, narrow shading around the entire frame, choosing Outer Glow from the menu on the left side of the dialog box. To make a dark shadow instead of a bright glow, she clicked the color swatch, clicked a

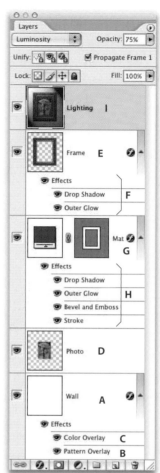

shadow in the image to sample a dark color, and changed the blend mode for the Outer Glow to Multiply **F**.▼

To draw the mat, Brown targeted the "Photo" layer (by clicking its thumbnail in the Layers palette) so the Shape layer she was about to add would be above it, between the photo and the frame. She used the Rectangle tool ☐ to draw a Shape layer.▼ She drew a large enough rectangle so it filled the opening in the frame and extended a bit beyond so she could be sure there were no gaps. Then she reduced the Opacity of the Shape layer so she could see the photo through it, and used the Rectangle tool ☐ again in "Subtract from shape area" mode ☐ to make the opening in the mat just big enough for the photo; she then restored the Opacity of the mat layer to 100% **G**.

The cut edge of the mat was made by adding a Layer Style consisting of a narrow Drop Shadow, a Stroke effect and a Bevel and Emboss, set to Stroke Emboss and with "Use Global Light" turned on so the lighting direction matched the drop shadow on the "Frame" layer **H**.▼ An Outer Glow was used in the same way as for the frame.

Brown wanted to use the Lighting Effects filter to help unify the image. To make a single layer to use with the filter, she made a merged copy of the composite (this can be done by holding down Ctrl-Alt-Shift in Windows or ⌘-Option-Shift on the Mac and typing first N for the new layer and then E to turn it into a merged copy of all that's visible). She then chose Filter > Render > Lighting Effects. Finding it hard to see exactly what the effect

would be (the preview in the Lighting Effects dialog box is small), Brown added a Spotlight that lit the image from the upper left (consistent with the lighting established by the Layer Styles); she made it stronger than she knew she wanted **I**. After clicking "OK" to leave the dialog box, she reduced the new layer's Opacity until she had the effect she wanted (shown on the facing page).

FIND OUT MORE

▼ Overlay effects in a Layer Style
page 494

▼ Shadow & glow effects in a Layer Style
page 498

▼ Using the Shape tools **page 433**

▼ Bevels **pages 501 & 537**

ORIGINAL PHOTOS: BEVERLY GOWARD

For each of a series of **wedding *keepsake prints*** for the members of the bridal party, photographer **Beverly Goward** wanted to assemble a portrait of the bride with four candid shots. Working with Goward's photos, **Marie Brown** approached the project with Photoshop's Picture Package, starting with the page for the flower girl.

Brown began by opening Bridge (this can be done from Photoshop by clicking the "Go to Bridge" button

> The **Bridal Party layout** is included in the Wow Goodies folder, along with **Creating a Mat.psd**, a smaller file that shows the construction of the beveled mat.

near the right end of the Options bar).▼ In Bridge, she navigated to a folder that contained the main portrait of the bride, cropped to a 5 x 7 horizontal format.▼ She clicked on the portrait to select it and chose Tools > Photoshop > Picture Package to open the Picture Package interface. (In Photoshop CS's File Browser or in Photoshop's own File menu, the choice would be Automate > Picture Package).

In the Picture Package window, Brown set the Page Size at "8.0 x 10.0 in" **A** and the resolution at 300 pixels/in **B**. She chose the "(1)5x7 (4)2.5x3.5" option from the Layout menu **C** — it was closest to the layout she wanted. Each of the five zones in the Layout displayed the portrait **D**.

Photoshop's Picture Package routine is designed to maximize space on the output page and to make it easy to cut the photos apart. But Brown and Goward wanted a different result — a balanced arrangement with space between the images so a "mat" could be added to the print. Before substituting the four photos of the flower girl, Brown modified the layout. She clicked the "Edit Layout" button **E** to open the Picture Package Edit Layout dialog.

In the upper left corner of the Edit Layout dialog, Brown named her layout "Bridal Party" **F** and set the Units to "inches" **G**. To make it easier to resize and align the zones, she turned on the Snap To function **H** to

display the "magnetic" grid; she set the grid Size to 0.25 in, the smallest division **I**.

She dragged the side handles of the large zone to reduce it so there was space around it. Then she put the cursor inside the image and dragged to center the zone near the top of the page. Next she used the side handles to reduce the smaller zones, and then dragged inside each one to align its outside edge with a side edge of the large photo **J**. With the side edges aligned, she could drag the zones up or down, using the white space at the tops and bottoms of the zones (rather than the zone boundaries themselves) as the predictors of how much space there would be between photos.

"I noticed some interesting behavior in Picture Package," says Brown. "First, if I wanted to both edit the layout *and* replace some of the photos, it was important to **do the editing before** I substituted the photos, because if I did things in the reverse order, the substitutions would be lost as soon as I clicked the 'Edit Layout' button.

"Second, resizing a zone in Picture Package works differently than scaling with Photoshop's Transform command. In Picture Package, no matter which handle you drag, the photo is always resized proportionally. But if you use a mid-side handle, then the width seems to become the

critical dimension, and empty space is added at the top and bottom of the photo to fill the zone. I use mid-side handles when I want the side edges of photos to align. Using a center top or center bottom handle makes height the critical dimension, and space is added at the sides; if I want to align top or bottom edges of photos, I resize the zones using the center top or bottom handle."

When Brown clicked the "Save" button **K** and the "Enter the new layout file name" dialog box opened, she named the layout and clicked "Save." The main Picture Package dialog opened again, showing the new layout; its name was also available in the Layout menu so she could use it for other prints in the series.

To substitute for the small photos, Brown went back to Bridge to the folder that held photos of the flower girl. These had been cropped to a 5 x 7 horizontal format, which is the same aspect ratio as 2.5 x 3.5. In Bridge she clicked on one of the images and dragged it into the Picture Package dialog and onto the zone where she wanted it, repeating the process until she had all the photos in place **L**. (In Photoshop CS, you can't drag and drop from File Browser, but you can do so from a folder open on the Desktop. Also, in either CS or CS2, simply clicking one of the zones opens the "Select an image" dialog, and you can navigate to the photo you want.)

With the Flatten All Images option chosen in the Document panel of the dialog box, Brown clicked "OK" and watched as Photoshop built a file named "Picture Package 1," with all the photos in place on a single layer.

To this file she added a mat. Targeting the file's *Background* in the Layers palette, she clicked the "Create new fill or adjustment layer" button ⬤ at the bottom of the palette and chose Solid Color, then sampled a color from one of the assembled photos.

To "cut" the mat, she targeted the photo layer again by clicking its thumbnail in the Layers palette, then clicked the "Add a layer style" button 🌀 at the bottom of the palette and chose the Bevel and Emboss effect. Setting up an Outer Bevel, she built a semitransparent rise from the edge of each photo *outward,* so the mat, rather than the photo, seemed to be beveled.▼

FIND OUT MORE

▼ Using Bridge **page 128**

▼ Cropping **page 498**

▼ Building bevels **pages 501 & 537**

To make the **Waikiki Kids** composite image, **Jack Davis** started with separate photos of the two kids. For the main shot he chose the one of Rachel with Diamond Head in the background **A**. The masking challenge was to tuck Ryan **B** in between Rachel and the background. To allow some flexibility in positioning, Davis did the masking in two stages.

First he used the Pen tool ✎ to make a *Work Path* outlining Ryan and the air mattress, not worrying about the foreground because that would be hidden with a second mask. He converted the path to a selection by clicking the "Load path as a selection" button ● at the bottom of the Paths palette. Then, with Ryan's layer targeted in the Layers palette, he clicked the "Add layer mask" button ▣ at the bottom of the palette to

turn the selection into a mask that showed Ryan and hid the background behind him **C**.

Second, he made a similar selection of Rachel, her air mattress, and the water in the foreground. But rather than using this selection to modify the mask on Ryan's layer (which would have "locked" him into position relative to Rachel), Davis added a layer set (a *group* in CS2) by clicking the ▢ button at the bottom of the Layers palette. In the Layers palette he dragged the thumbnail for Ryan's layer into the new folder. Then he clicked the folder's thumbnail and, with the selection still active, added a mask by once again clicking the ▣ button **D**. Having a separate mask on the folder meant that Davis could scale and reposition Ryan's layer without affecting the edge that was hiding the overlap with Rachel.

Working with photos taken more than 30 years ago, Marv Lyons produced ***Woman Waiting in Papeete*** (above) and ***Three Girls*** (right) by scanning and layering them. In each case Lyons combined the original photo with an image of palm trees overhead, which he had photographed through a chandelier prism. Lyons often takes "ambience" photos like the one of the palm trees and uses them to add atmosphere to photos taken in the same location. He developed his original compositing technique in the darkroom, and later "translated" it to Photoshop, layering scanned images with varied blend modes and opacities.

In ***Woman Waiting*** the "Palm Trees" layer is in Overlay mode at 100% Opacity. Lyons manufactured a "warming filter" by choosing a gold as the Foreground color, adding an empty layer, and filling it with color (Alt-Backspace in Windows; Option-Delete on the Mac). He put the layer in Multiply mode and reduced its Opacity to 17%.

For ***Three Girls***, Lyons used the "Palm Trees" layer twice, once in Overlay mode at 100% and again above that in Multiply mode at 41%.

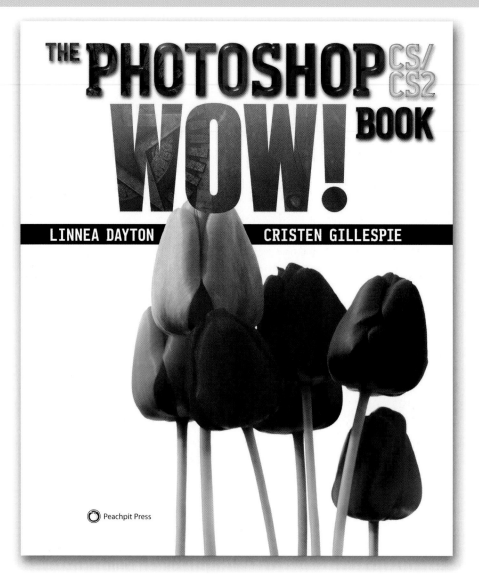

In designing the title page of *The Photoshop WOW! Book,* **Don Jolley** used two versions of each file — one for the title type and another for the rest of the design. The two were saved in EPS format and assembled in Adobe InDesign. To make the EPS for the type, Jolley created the type in Adobe Illustrator, converted it to outlines to avoid font problems at output, and copied the result to the clipboard. He pasted it into Photoshop as paths, so that it appeared in the Paths palette as the *Work Path.* Then he preserved this

path by dragging the *Work Path* thumbnail to the "Create new path" button ▣ at the bottom of the Paths palette to make Path 1. With this path targeted in the Paths palette, he chose Clipping Path from the palette's ⊙ menu. When he saved the file as an EPS with clipping path, Path 1 would hide the rest of the image, cutting the sharpest outline the output device was capable of, to make crisp edges on the lettering.

For the second file, the background, Jolley turned off visibility for all the

lettering, but left the soft elements such as the combined drop shadow and refracted light behind the blue type and the yellow "CS/CS2."

The two files were aligned in InDesign to make the complete title page, and the author names and Peachpit logo were added there.

To ensure that the antialiased edges of the lettering wouldn't pick up the background color when they were "clipped," Jolley made the lettering just a little bigger all around than the path that would be trimming it, so

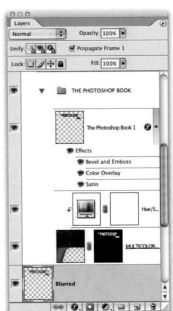

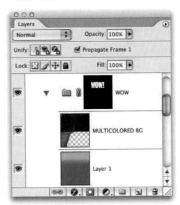

that any semitransparent antialiasing that was created by the clipping path was filled in with the same color as the lettering. To make the lettering slightly bigger than the clipping path (as shown above), Jolley loaded the path as a selection by Ctrl/⌘-clicking on its thumbnail in the Paths palette, and then enlarged the selection by choosing Select > Modify > Expand and entering 5 pixels for the amount of expansion. He then used this larger selection to create a layer mask for the layer set/group that held the

image and Adjustment layers that filled and colored the lettering.

The "Wow!" lettering on the title page is a two-layer composite of the background image from the cover in Overlay mode and a gold gradient, masked by the layer mask on the layer set/group.

The construction of the lettering for "THE PHOTOSHOP BOOK" is more complex. The same background image is masked inside the lettering, but with a Hue/Saturation layer tinting it blue.

On top of that is a copy of the lettering in black, but with Fill Opacity reduced to 16%; this layer is treated with a Layer Style to create the beveling and highlights, so the lettering looks like a clear solid over the blue image.

To complete the illusion of translucency, Jolley applied the Gaussian Blur filter to a copy of the image-filled lettering to create the mottled light of a combined drop shadow and refracted light.

The Web & Animation

10

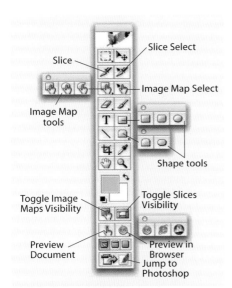

Slice Select

Slice

Image Map Select

Image Map
tools

Shape tools

Toggle Image
Maps Visibility

Toggle Slices
Visibility

Preview
Document

Preview in
Browser
Jump to
Photoshop

Unique to ImageReady's Tools palette are tools for creating and previewing image maps and for previewing rollovers. ImageReady's movable "tear-off" palettes allow you to see all the tools that share a spot. Two Shape tools found in ImageReady but not in Photoshop are the Tab Rectangle ▢ and Pill Rectangle ◯.

Photoshop's Tools palette includes the same Slice ✒ and Slice Select ✒ tools as in Image-Ready, and a "Jump to ImageReady" button at the bottom (not shown). The "Preview in default browser" and "Slice visibility" ▣ buttons that appear in ImageReady's Tools palette are found in Photoshop's Save for Web dialog box instead.

WITH PHOTOSHOP AND IMAGEREADY you can take a web project all the way from the first "sketch" to finished HTML and JavaScript. In version CS both programs showed some big improvements for making artwork "web-ready" and making website design and maintenance more efficient. As the artist, you can spend most of your time creating the art, and then quickly convert your work into a series of web graphics or pages. Photoshop CS2 has gained Smart Guides, Variables, and animation, which in previous versions were in ImageReady only. If you're working in CS, you'll be able to do all the web work that you can do in CS2, but you'll be jumping back and forth between the two programs more often than in CS2.

THE BASIC WORKFLOW

A basic web workflow includes planning, designing and building, and then optimizing (making the files as small as you can without losing the image quality you want), previewing, and saving. With an efficient workflow you can move comfortably from Photoshop to ImageReady to an HTML editing and site-creation tool. In fact, if you use Adobe GoLive, you can quickly incorporate your pages from Photoshop and ImageReady into a website with very little postprocessing.

Given the variety of projects you can create with Photoshop and ImageReady, there's no one "best" way to work. But as a general rule it makes sense to start your artwork in Photoshop. In CS you'll need to jump to ImageReady to animate your work (in CS2 Photoshop has the same Animation palette as Image-Ready). In either version ImageReady can add sophisticated buttons, or can output several web-ready versions from a single file. If you need to do something that ImageReady can't do well, such as making targeted tone and color adjustments, you can jump back to Photoshop for these, and then jump to Image-Ready again just as easily. Whenever you jump, the elements

Continued on page 677

SOME TYPICAL WEB WORKFLOWS FOR PHOTOSHOP & IMAGEREADY

Start creating your artwork in Photoshop as you would for any other project. Where you go from there depends on the type of web graphics you're creating.

Most single graphics, whether flat-color or continuous-tone, can be started and finished in Photoshop, without the help of ImageReady. Photoshop's Save for Web dialog (see page 679) allows you to save a file as JPEG, GIF, or HTML with color compression and with any associated slices.

In version CS, animations must be created in ImageReady, but in CS2 you can also do animation in Photoshop. You can animate by "tweening" to create several intermediates between two frames (above; for more see page 699), by manually editing each separate frame (page 710), or by creating frames automatically from layers or layer comps (page 705).

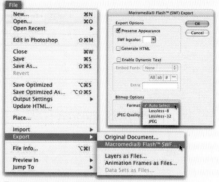

To export in Macromedia Flash SWF format, use ImageReady's File > Export > Macromedia® Flash™ SWF command (see page 684 for more about exporting Flash animations).

Use ImageReady to produce and apply combined rollover Styles for button interactivity. Rollover Styles can be dimensional like the 15 Wow Button Styles applied to "pill rectangle" shapes here (see page 767 for these and 35 more rollover Styles included on the Wow DVD-ROM), or "paper thin" like the tabs above. "Quick Rollover Styles" on page 716 tells how to make interactive buttons.

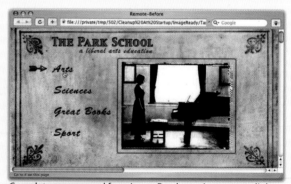

Complete pages saved from ImageReady can incorporate links, rollovers, and slices. Create the elements of the web page in Photoshop, and then move to ImageReady to add these interactive options, as in "Creating Remote Rollovers" on page 721.

In ImageReady, as in Photoshop, preset Layer Styles can be applied by choosing from the Styles palette. A black upper left corner on a thumbnail in ImageReady's Styles palette indicates a combined rollover Style, with the interactivity and slicing built-in. For more about rollover Styles, see page 716.

TRAVELING LAYER STYLES

Photoshop and ImageReady keep track of Layer Styles independently of each other. Loading a set of Styles into Photoshop — or saving Styles that you create — won't automatically make them available in ImageReady, and vice versa.

When you jump from one program to the other, any Styles you've applied will travel along with the file and you'll be able to edit, copy, and paste them, but you won't find your imported Styles listed in the Styles palette.

To add a Style to the Styles palette, after you jump, in the Layers palette click on the layer that has the Style you want, and then in the Styles palette click on the "Create new style" button ▣. For consistency, give the Style the same name it has in the other program.

Note: If you jump a combined rollover Style from ImageReady to Photoshop, only the Normal state of the Style will make the trip.

you've added to the file in the other program are maintained, so all you lose is the time it takes to switch.

Planning, Designing & Building

Here are some general tips for designing and building web graphics:

- While you're thinking about how to make a website appealing and easy to navigate, **think small**. Faster downloading is becoming more widely available, but it still pays to think about how to make your artwork look good while keeping file size small. At the planning stage consider what file formats are available to you (JPEG, GIF, or Flash in particular), since not all formats do well with all kinds of artwork.

- **Build in flexibility**. Keep as much of your work as you can in an easily editable form, working with the layers, layer sets/groups, layer comps, Layer Styles, and Adjustment layers that contribute to flexibility in all Photoshop artwork and that you've encountered throughout this book. With Layer Styles, for instance, you can quickly create a "look" (a set of effects such as a drop shadow, a dimensional edge, or a glow) for the elements on any layer, and then apply it to other layers for a consistent look and feel. Also take advantage of well-crafted slices and slice sets (described on page 688). You can find examples in "Creating Remote Rollovers" on page 721.

- **Use Guides, Smart Guides, and other align-and-distribute options** to quickly line up your type and graphics and to structure your pages.

- **Take advantage of Type options.** In both Photoshop and ImageReady, the **Type tool's** Options bar and the **Character palette** have features designed especially for producing good-looking, readable type on-screen, particularly at small sizes. The **Sharp** and **Strong** antialiasing options in the Options bar can make type look sharper or heavier, respectively. For smaller point sizes, **Crisp** gives the type a lighter-weight appearance (**Smooth** can make small type look blurred or badly spaced.) Turning off the **Fractional Widths** option (in the

TYPE FOR THE SCREEN

For crisp, readable small type, you can use a bitmapped font, designed to look good at small sizes without the need for anti-aliasing. A search on the web will turn up many possibilities.

The Sevenet font by Peter Bruhn is ideal for tiny labels that are revealed on rollover. You can download it free from the "Pro Bono fonts" section of **www.fountain.nu**.

The Type tool's Options bar and the Character palette offer several antialiasing methods designed especially for type that will be viewed on-screen.

Distribute layer horizontal space

ImageReady's Options bar for the Move tool offers two useful distribution options that Photoshop doesn't have. After you've targeted the layers whose contents you want to distribute, in the "Space between distributed objects" field choose or enter the number of pixels you want between the elements. Then click the button for either "Distribute layer horizontal space" (as shown here) or "Distribute layer vertical space." Image-Ready will leave the leftmost or top element where it is and arrange the others in a row or column with the gaps you've specified (page 716 has an example).

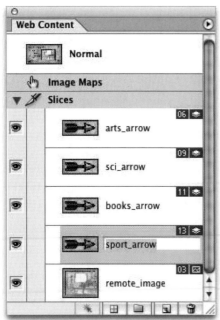

The Web Content palette in ImageReady organizes all of a file's slices, rollovers, and image maps in one location.

ATTRACTING A CLICK

Using The **Underline** option for type (available from the Character palette's pop-out menu) and turning off anti-aliasing can make a word that's really part of a graphic look "live" and interactive, to attract the site visitor to click on it and trigger the link for the graphic's slice or hot spot.

Character palette's ⊙ menu) can prevent small type from running together on-screen.

- **Know which program has which tools.** Photoshop and ImageReady have many tools and operations in common. But there are some differences in the two programs. **Photoshop has better selecting, image-editing, and painting** tools and commands than ImageReady does. Photoshop allows you to sample color from your file when the Color Picker is open. And Photoshop also has **more vector-based drawing and editing tools** than ImageReady. For instance, only Photoshop can create and edit custom shapes with drawing tools like those in Adobe Illustrator. ImageReady's vector drawing tools are limited to five basic shapes — the Rectangle, Rounded Rectangle, and Ellipse, and **two popular button shapes (new in ImageReady CS), the Tab Rectangle and Pill Rectangle,** which Photoshop doesn't have. ImageReady can resize or rotate a shape created in Photoshop, but it can't create or edit custom shapes.

  Adjustment layers, those image-editing gems that let you make easily editable changes to your artwork without permanently changing the pixels, can be added or changed in Photoshop. Adjustment layers *do* travel to ImageReady, but it will mean jumping back to Photoshop if you want to edit them in any way other than to turn off their visibility or delete them.

  Only ImageReady has **Image Map tools,** which allow you to create nonrectangular "hot spots" (links) in a file (see page 687 for more about image maps).

  ImageReady is the only program that allows you to create **combined rollover Styles,** which are Layer Styles that change in response to cursor movement or clicking. "Quick Button Rollovers" on page 716 tells how to design, save, and apply combined rollover Styles.

If you choose Edit > Preferences > Optimization in ImageReady, you can choose to have the program automatically make its best compromise between file size and image quality when optimizing, including whether to use GIF or JPEG. You can override this automatic choice at any time by making entries in the Optimize palette.

PROGRESSIVE DISPLAY

For very large JPEG images, you can avoid subjecting the viewer to a long wait before anything happens on-screen by choosing the Progressive option in the Optimize palette. The image will appear quickly (though pixelated) and then build sharp detail.

Optimizing, Previewing & Saving

Both Photoshop and ImageReady have tools for **optimizing** — choosing the best file format and compression scheme. **Photoshop has the Save for Web dialog box**, and **ImageReady has the Optimize palette and Color Table palette**. These tools let you experiment with target file sizes, file formats, number of colors, or degree of compression, and preview the different options before you make a choice.

Both programs have **weighted optimization** using alpha channels, type layers, or Shape layers to control which parts of a file are considered most important in creating a color palette, and to protect some parts when color compression is applied. Weighted optimization helps minimize unwanted artifacts in areas where they would be most obvious or jarring. "Animating with Layer Comps" on page 705 demonstrates the use of an alpha channel for weighted optimization using Lossy GIF compression.

Continued on page 681

OPTIMIZING VIEWS

Photoshop's **Save for Web** interface is designed to help you balance image quality and file size. It includes the same views available in ImageReady's working window — the Original alone, the current Optimized version alone, 2-Up (the Original and the current Optimized, side-by-side for comparison), and 4-Up (the Original and three optimized versions). You can zoom in and out in all windows at once for comparison — use the standard Ctrl/⌘-+ and Ctrl/⌘-hyphen keyboard shortcuts.

In the 4-Up view (shown here) you see your original image, the format and compression currently shown in the Optimize panel/palette, and two other compression options. The display for each preview includes a listing of file sizes and conservative download times. The tools in Photoshop's Save For Web toolbox — for moving or magnifying the view and sampling color — are also found in ImageReady, but in the standard Tools palette.

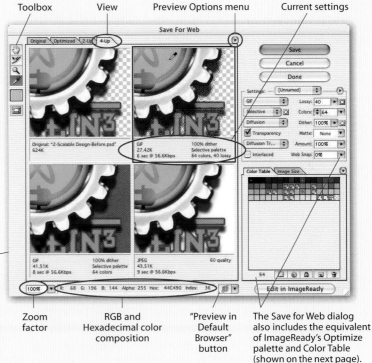

Toolbox   View   Preview Options menu   Current settings

Zoom factor

RGB and Hexadecimal color composition

"Preview in Default Browser" button

The Save for Web dialog also includes the equivalent of ImageReady's Optimize palette and Color Table (shown on the next page).

THE OPTIMIZE PANEL/PALETTE

In Photoshop's Optimize panel or ImageReady's Optimize palette you can choose a preset compression scheme or design your own, including the file format, the type of color reduction, the number of colors to be used, and the kind and extent of dithering that will be produced. The Web Snap setting determines how close the original color has to be to a web-safe color before it will automatically snap to the web-safe palette. With the Transparency box checked, fully transparent pixels remain transparent; with Transparency unchecked, the Matte color is substituted for transparency.

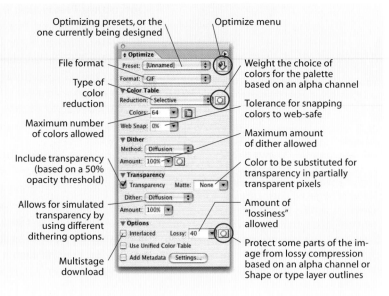

Optimizing presets, or the one currently being designed

Optimize menu

File format

Type of color reduction

Maximum number of colors allowed

Include transparency (based on a 50% opacity threshold)

Allows for simulated transparency by using different dithering options.

Multistage download

Weight the choice of colors for the palette based on an alpha channel

Tolerance for snapping colors to web-safe

Maximum amount of dither allowed

Color to be substituted for transparency in partially transparent pixels

Amount of "lossiness" allowed

Protect some parts of the image from lossy compression based on an alpha channel or Shape or type layer outlines

THE COLOR TABLE

In the **Color Table** you can select and sort colors. To keep colors from being eliminated as you reduce the number of colors in the file, you can lock them.

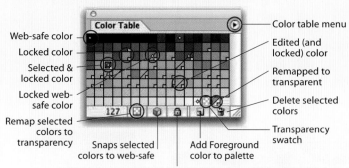

Web-safe color

Locked color

Selected & locked color

Locked web-safe color

Remap selected colors to transparency

Snaps selected colors to web-safe

Add Foreground color to palette

Color table menu

Edited (and locked) color

Remapped to transparent

Delete selected colors

Transparency swatch

Locks/unlocks selected colors; locked colors can't be changed and can't be dropped until all unlocked colors have been eliminated.

A thick outline means that a color swatch is currently **selected**, so you can lock or unlock it or shift it to or from "web-safety."

A small square in the lower right corner shows that a color is **locked** and won't be eliminated during reduction until all unlocked colors are gone.

A small white diamond indicates a **web-safe** color.

If the Transparency box is checked in the **Optimize** palette, the transparency swatch appears in the Color Table.

MASKING COMPRESSION

In ImageReady's Optimize palette and Photoshop's Optimize panel in the Save for Web dialog, "mask" buttons allow you to use outlines of type and Shape layers (both vector-based), as well as any alpha channel you choose, to protect some areas of your artwork from compression artifacts. This means you can take advantage of compression to reduce file size, but still keep areas of solid color intact and can keep hard-edged graphics crisp-looking.

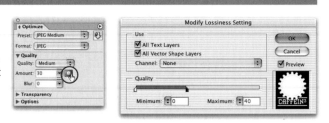

You can often get better-looking results if you set up your file in Photoshop at twice or four times the pixel dimensions you need and then scale your finished graphics down, rather than starting small in the first place. A side benefit of designing large is that you can quickly repurpose your projects for print.

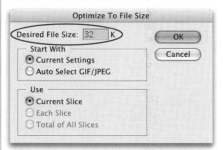

When you're ready to reduce the artwork to its final size, you can do it by choosing Image > Image Size. Or use the **Optimize To File Size** dialog box, which you can choose from the (▶) menu of the Optimize panel/palette. Here you can enter a **Desired File Size** as a target. If you choose the **Current Settings** option, Photoshop will use the file format, type of palette, and Dither currently in the Settings section of the Optimize panel/palette as a starting point for reducing the file size to hit the target. On the other hand, if you choose the **Auto Select** option, Photoshop will analyze the colors in the image and choose a GIF or JPEG profile based on the analysis.

The Image Size panel in Photoshop's Save for Web dialog box lets you size to particular pixel dimensions or a percentage of the file's original dimensions. Choose Bicubic Sharper as the Quality setting to sharpen the image as you scale it down.

Accurate previewing is done with the "Preview in Default Browser" button (identified with an icon for your default browser). This button is found near the bottom right corner of Photoshop's Save For Web dialog box and in the bottom right corner of ImageReady's Tools palette. It's great for seeing how your artwork will behave on a web page. This kind of preview is especially important for checking the motion in animations and the operation of rollovers, for instance. In addition, ImageReady has a **Preview Document** button 🐾, which lets you preview rollovers in operation, without leaving Image-Ready.

Saving in Photoshop is done by clicking the "Save" button in the Save for Web dialog once you have the optimization set up the way you want it; this opens the Save Optimized As dialog box. In ImageReady, choose File > Save Optimized As to get to the Save Optimized As dialog. In the Save Optimized As dialog, you can choose the format(s) you want to save.

As with creating artwork, although Photoshop and ImageReady share many of the same optimizing, previewing, and saving functions, there are some important differences between the two programs:

- In ImageReady you can choose File > Export > Macromedia **Flash SWF**, or File > Export > **Layers as Files**.
- Photoshop's File > Automate > **Web Photo Gallery** comes with templates that can be used "as is" or customized to create your own "portfolio" Web site. "Making a Web Photo Gallery" on page 692 includes some suggestions for modifying the frame-based and table-based galleries produced with Web Photo Gallery.

For simple web pages, you can add the whole Photoshop file to an opened HTML page in Adobe GoLive. GoLive will create HTML, JavaScript, and web-ready files from the Photoshop file. Any layers or slices that are not visible will be ignored. If you make a change to the page in Photoshop or ImageReady later and save the file, GoLive can automatically update the HTML for you.

CHOOSING A FILE FORMAT FOR STATIC WEB GRAPHICS

Choosing a format for web graphics is a matter of analyzing the content of the file and knowing a bit about how the different file types handle compression. **JPEG** (.jpg) excels at compressing photos and other continuous-tone images because it supports a **full range of colors**. For **flat-color art**, **GIF** (.gif) is great and it offers **transparency** options that make it worth considering even for silhouetted photos.

For **color graphics** such as logos or drawings, GIF allows you to reduce the file size by reducing the number of colors, as described in "Quick GIF Optimizing" on page 693. The GIF format allows for transparency, so your artwork doesn't have to be rectangular.

For a **rectangular photo** or other continuous-tone image that doesn't have any areas that need to be transparent, plan to use JPEG. Try several Quality settings, comparing image quality and loading time. Often Low quality works for photos, while Medium may be needed for color gradients. If your goal is to save continuous-tone images that will then be used in the Macromedia Flash program, JPEG is an option, but you may also want to consider PNG (.png). The PNG-24 file format supports both high-quality color and transparency (through alpha channels, which can be full grayscale masks).

If your photo or continuous-tone image has a shape other than rectangular — especially if it has a soft, feathered edge or internal transparency, JPEG is still an option if your web-page background consists of a seamless, randomized texture that doesn't require precise alignment. The same randomized pattern that was used to make the seamlessly tiled web-page background was incorporated into each of the graphics on this web page. The graphics were saved as JPEG files with the same compression settings used for the background tile.

If your continuous-tone non-rectangular image is small and silhouetted, you may want to use the GIF format. This is true especially if you can't match the web-page background as described above. With GIF you may have to compromise color richness to get transparency, but that may be acceptable if your image is small.

The Flash (.swf) format is now an option if you want to use a solid-color logo or type directly on top of a photograph. Neither GIF nor JPEG can do a great job with this combination, but if you move the layered file to ImageReady you can instead export the layer with the solid-color element and the layer with the continuous-tone image to Flash separately and combine them there.

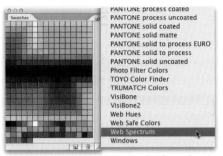

In either Photoshop or ImageReady (shown here) you can choose a set of Swatches from the list at the bottom of the Swatches palette's pop-up menu.

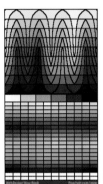

The **Web Wow Color Pal.gif** file in the Wow Goodies folder on the Wow DVD-ROM provides two "spectrum" layouts of web-safe colors. It also isolates the four pure grays that exist in the web-safe palette and provides extra "wells" where you can put colors that are important for a particular job.

Web Wow Color Pal.gif

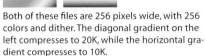

Both of these files are 256 pixels wide, with 256 colors and dither. The diagonal gradient on the left compresses to 20K, while the horizontal gradient compresses to 10K.

When you optimize for the JPEG format, you can choose from three Preset settings or five Quality settings. You can choose an alpha channel to protect some areas of the image from compression (see page 705). Blurring the image slightly before compressing can result in a smaller file. With the Blur setting in the Optimize palette, experiment to see how different degrees of blurring reduce file size (and affect image quality). Adobe suggests a Blur setting of 0.1 to 0.5.

STATIC IMAGES OR GRAPHICS

Many of the same basic rules of design and composition apply whether you're designing for the screen or for print. But creating artwork for the web and related on-screen applications always involves file-size considerations. Even at the planning stage, there are some important things you can do to minimize file size for downloading.

- Plan to have each photo or graphic element appear as **small** as you can make it and still achieve the impression you want.

- For graphics, use as **few colors** as you can without compromising your design.

- Choosing colors from the 216-color **web-safe palette** used to be important because so many people had computers that could only display 256 colors, and only 216 of those were common to all computers. "Web-safety" isn't as important as it used to be because it's unusual today to find a monitor or web browser that can't handle at least thousands of colors, if not millions. But if you need to work with a web-safe palette (for wireless computing applications, for instance), you can choose from a browser-safe Swatches palette such as the Web Safe Colors (in order by the hexadecimal code numbers that identify the colors) or Web Spectrum, both provided on the Adobe Photoshop application CD-ROM. Or open the **Web Wow Color Pal.gif** file provided on the Wow DVD-ROM that comes with this book and use it to sample colors. When you don't have to match a particular color in the graphics you're designing for the web, consider choosing from the web-safe palette just to keep color compression as simple as possible.

- Avoid diagonal gradients if you'll be saving files in the GIF format. Because of the methods used to compress GIF, diagonal gradients take more file space.

Optimizing, Previewing & Saving Static Graphics

For static web graphics, **JPEG, GIF,** and now **Flash** (**SWF**) are the most useful file formats. PNG, which offers the best options for transparency, is also appropriate in certain cases, and WBMP is useful for simple 1-bit ("black-and-white") displays. "Quick GIF Optimizing" on page 693 tells step-by-step how to reduce file size for a graphic element in GIF format. Optimization for JPEG is very similar to that explained in the "Preparing an Image for Emailing" tip on page 121.

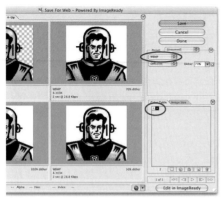

If you are designing artwork that will be converted to the 1-bit (black-and-white-only) WBMP format for use with single-color displays, use high-contrast, low-detail art. Keep in mind that fine lines can disappear and that gradients that depend on color to be effective may not translate well.

Photoshop CS2 has the same Animation palette that ImageReady CS/CS2 does. As in ImageReady, you can set up your animation so that any new layer that you add will appear only in the frame that's active when you add it, or so it will be added to every frame. To make a layer appear in all frames, select the "New Layers Visible in All Frames" option from the Animation palette's menu.

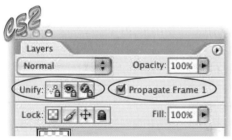

Photoshop CS2's Layers palette has the same series of "Unify" buttons as in ImageReady for adding the content, position, or Layer Style of the current layer to all frames in an animation. You can also choose to carry any changes made in the first frame to all frames in the animation. In Photoshop, by default, the "Unify" buttons and "Propagate" option appear only when the Animation palette is open.

ANIMATIONS

An animation consists of a series of still images called *frames*. Usually each frame is almost the same scene as the frame before, with just a small change applied. Playing all the frames in sequence, if you have enough of them and you swap them fast enough, creates the illusion of motion. Many of the planning and design strategies that apply to single graphics also apply to animations. But because graphics in motion are more complex, there are also other things to consider.

Planning an Animation

Your animation file will consist of several graphics rather than just one, so it's especially important to keep graphics small and color relatively simple. The way you create your graphics will depend on whether you plan to save your file as an animated GIF or take advantage of ImageReady's ability to export to Flash (SWF) format. So it's best to choose a format before you begin.

If your project is made of primarily **vector-based shapes or type** (without Layer Styles), then Flash will be a good choice, because it will keep the file size small, especially if your animation has more than a few frames. When Flash animates a vector-based shape, it uses math instructions to do so. GIF, on the other hand, has to deal with pixels, which are "bulkier" than math. For a long or complex animation, this can mean a dramatic file-size difference in favor of Flash. Photographs may be better animated as Flash, because Flash supports JPEG compression. In general, the more complex your animation becomes, the more Flash becomes an attractive choice.

However, Flash has some requirements that are worth considering. First, for a browser to play a Flash file, it has to have the Flash Player plug-in. Many people have the free Flash Player, but some don't, and some of your intended audience may not be willing to download a plug-in just to view a Flash-animated banner ad, for instance. If your animated element is **simple, with just a few frames,** animated **GIF** is probably a better way to go, since virtually every browser will be able play it without a plug-in. By doing things like isolating the moving elements to a specific area of the animation, using solid colors, and avoiding gradients, you can create a very small animation with GIF.

If you're planning a **Flash** animation, keep the strengths of the Flash format in mind. Flash files are smallest when the content is primarily vector-based (type and shapes). The more pixels (non-vector-based art) you use in a project, the larger the Flash file will be, increasing the download time and also the time it takes for the Flash player to deliver the frames of the anima-

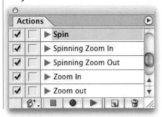
tion to the screen. When exporting to Flash, ImageReady will keep any shape or type as vector art — unless you've added a Layer Style. This doesn't mean you can't use Styles in art destined for a Flash animation; it just means you should do so with the understanding that it will increase the file size and slow the rendering speed.

Plan to export to Flash (File > Export > Macromedia Flash SWF) if your animation will consist of a vector-based logo or type directly on top of a photograph. When you export this project to a Flash file, you'll set the compression for both the vector-based elements and the pixel-based images and create a file that you can use directly or take into Flash and edit further. ImageReady applies the same type of compression to all the pixel-based images in a given Flash export, so, if you choose JPEG then all the JPEG images will be compressed at the same quality. If your artwork includes pixel-based elements that should use different compression settings, consider saving them separately as JPEGs or PNGs rather then export them in Flash format; then open them in Flash and assemble them there.

Designing & Building an Animation

Photoshop is a great environment for creating the art for an animation. In CS the animating itself is done in ImageReady's Animation palette. But in CS2 the Animation palette has been added to Photoshop as well. Here are three ways to create the frames of an animation:

• **Animating by hand.** Create a single frame. Then copy the frame and make changes to the artwork so this new frame now looks slightly different. Then copy this frame to make the next one, make more changes, copy again, change again, and so on. ImageReady CS/CS2 and Photoshop CS2 have a "Create New Layer for Each New Frame" option on the Animation palette. When you choose this option, ImageReady will automatically add a new empty layer, ready for you to add artwork, every time you add an animation frame.

• **Making frames from layers or layer comps.** Another option is to create the artwork for all of your frames ahead of time, as separate layers or layer comps in your Photoshop file. Then use the Make Frames From Layers command from the Animation palette's ▶ menu, or use the Layer Comps palette, to create the animation.

• **Tweening.** Instead of hand-crafting each frame on the fly or creating a separate layer for every frame, you can make starting and ending frames for an animation sequence and

Thinking smart and using keyboard shortcuts, Geno Andrews produced his "SPIN" animation almost as quickly as if he could have tweeened it (transforming isn't tweenable). He typed "SPIN" above his image layer and chose **(Layer > Type > Rasterize)**. Then he duplicated this "SPIN" layer and rotated it 45° all in one step using the shortcut for **copy-and-transform: Ctrl-Alt-T (Windows); ⌘-Option-T (Mac)**. He used **Filter > Blur > Radial Blur (Spin)** to blur the word, and then copied and rotated the blurred result six more times using the shortcut for **copy-and-transform-again: Ctrl-Alt-Shift-T (Windows); ⌘-Option-Shift-T (Mac)**. In the Layers palette he Shift-selected all the "SPIN" layers and distorted them (Edit > Transform > Perspective and Scale) to fit the spin into the face (this had to be done *after* the rotation in order for the whole rotation to be tilted correctly). **Make Frames from Layers** from the Animations palette's ⏵ menu made the frames. Finally, he clicked on the thumbnail for his image layer, made sure it was visible 👁, and clicked on the "Unify layer visibility" button (see "Retroactive Additions" at the right). He deleted the extra first frame (the one made from the image layer alone) and adjusted the timing so the spinning would stop briefly after each full rotation.

 Spin.psd

let the Animation palette automatically generate a number of frames in between. This automated process is called *tweening* (short for "in-betweening"). You can tween all layers or just certain ones you select. Three kinds of properties of each layer can be tweened: **Position**, **Opacity**, and **Effects** (Layer Styles and warped text). The "Unify" buttons on the Layers palette let you select a layer and lock it so its position, visibility, or Layer Style will stay the same, not subject to tweening, as frames are tweened. (The "Create Layer for Each New Frame" option doesn't add new layers when you tween.)

Once you've created your frames, in the Animations palette set the timing and looping options, and then use the palette's Play button ▶ to preview the animation so you can adjust the timing; this process is presented step-by-step in "Animating Frame-by-Frame" on page 710.

Optimizing, Previewing & Saving Animations

When you choose Optimize Animation from the Animation palette's pop-up menu, the dialog box offers you two default choices that can dramatically reduce the number of pixels in a frame, which cuts the file size, without affecting image quality at all:

- **Bounding Box** effectively crops the frame to include only the area that has changed since the previous frame.

- **Redundant Pixel Removal** reduces the size even more by making transparent all pixels that are the same as they were in the preceding frame. For this to work, the frame disposal method has to be set to Automatic, which is the default.

In older browsers (before versions 3.x), such an Optimized GIF might render incorrectly, but today, it's fine to leave these options on.

To rotate points around the edge of an oval (above) rather than a circle, or to rotate an element in perspective (as in the "Spin" type on the facing page), you have to do the **rotation first and then the transformation**. To make the points of this burst "travel" around the edge, we first made and rotated several copies of a spiky circle on separate layers, then linked all the layers and scaled them vertically to turn the circles into ovals. The transforming process is the same one used in "Designing for Scalability & Animation" on page 460.

Oval Anim files

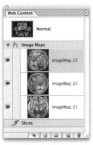

For this image, circular "hot spots" fit the content better than rectangular slices would. We drew the hot spot for the large central tiger by Alt/Option-dragging ImageReady's Circle Image Map tool outward from the nose. We drew the hot spot for the lion on the left the same way but then dragged it a little to the left to align it better. For the cheetah on the right, in the Web Content palette we dragged the thumbnail for the lion's hot spot to the button at the bottom of the palette to make a duplicate, dragged it into position, and dragged a corner handle outward to enlarge it slightly.

SPINNING OFF "STILLS"

The opposite of animating is to produce "snapshots" from your animations — exporting each frame as a single file. In Image-Ready you can do this by choosing **File > Export > Animation Frames As Files** to create a series of files. This is a handy way to produce "stills" for web pages or to create files for use in other animation programs. The export dialog box allows you choose a file format appropriate for your needs.

Once you've clicked "OK" in the Optimize Animation dialog box, turn to the Optimize panel/palette and choose GIF for the Format. To prevent "flashing" (color shift from frame to frame), for Color Table Reduction choose Adaptive, Perceptual, or Selective. Preview the animation in a browser (described in "Animating with Layer Comps") and save the animation (File > Save Optimized).

INTERACTIVITY FOR WEB PAGES

Like animation, interactivity has some specialized terminology associated with it:

- A **link** is a set of HTML instructions associated with a region on a web page. When that region is clicked, the on-screen display jumps to another location — on the same web page, a different page at the same site, or even an entirely different site. Buttons, for example, are regions with links. A region can be either a *slice* or an *image map* (these terms are defined next).

- A **slice** is a "snapshot" of a rectangular piece of an image. Each slice can become a clickable link to a specific web address, or *URL*. Each slice can also have rollover states so it responds when the cursor moves over it, clicks on it, or moves away. When you create slices and save the file, a *table* is automatically set up in an HTML file. The table holds the directions that tell a browser how to reassemble the slices on-screen and also includes the URLs for the links.

- An **image map** is a single image that can contain several "hot spots" (clickable regions that link to other locations). An advantage of image maps over slices is that the hot spots of an image map don't have to be rectangular.

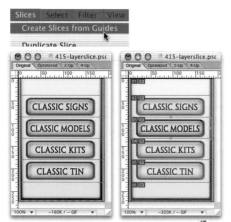

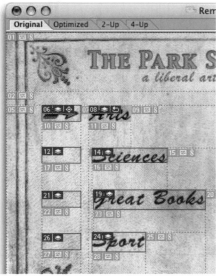

User slices can be drawn with the Slice tool ✂, constructed from guides pulled in from the rulers as shown here, or in ImageReady, created from an active selection. Each user slice is identified by a blue tag in the upper left corner containing the slice number. The currently active slice is outlined in yellow.

Photoshop or ImageReady automatically fills empty space with auto slices, which are identified by gray slice numbers and dotted gray outlines. Every time you create a new slice, ImageReady redraws the auto slices to fill in the gaps. In "Creating Remote Rollovers" on page 721 layer-based slices were made for the four arrow layers and four subject layers, and ImageReady filled in the auto slices around them, as shown here.

- A **rollover** is JavaScript code embedded in the HTML file. The JavaScript can swap one image for another in a slice. This makes it possible (in ImageReady only) to create a button that changes when a site visitor rolls the cursor over it, clicks it, or moves on. ("Quick Button Rollovers" on page 716 tells how to construct a combined rollover Style. See "Wow Button Styles" on page 767 and the associated layered Photoshop file on the Wow DVD-ROM for inspiration and for practical Layer Styles for creating buttons.)

- ImageReady alone also has the **remote rollover**: When the cursor rolls over a slice, the image in a *different* slice is swapped for another. The process is presented step-by-step in "Creating Remote Rollovers" on page 721.

Planning Pages for Interactivity

Most web pages are collections of single graphic elements "knitted" together. Web pages often have photos and logos sitting beside each other. It's efficient to design an entire page as a single file, with all the elements at hand so you can edit them or realign them, and see how these changes affect the page overall. But often if you had to choose one format for the whole page, some parts might not look good in the format you chose. By breaking the page down, you can set the photos to use JPEG compression while creating GIF files from the logos.

Designing & Building Interactive Pages

To help visitors get the information (or just plain fun) they seek from a website, easy-to-interpret buttons and other navigational controls are essential. Equally important in building pages is making them easy to maintain, so the site's content can be changed without completely rebuilding pages.

Slicing. There are three types of slices you can make in Image-Ready; two of these — user slices and auto slices — can also be made in Photoshop:

- **User slices** are the ones that you (the user) draw with the Slice tool ✂ or define with guides (as shown at the left). In ImageReady you can also make user slices by selecting an area and choosing Select > Create Slice from Selection.

- **Layer-based slices** (recall that they're only available in ImageReady) are made when you click on a layer's thumbnail in the Layers palette and choose Layer > New Layer Based Slice. The rectangular slice is automatically based on the smallest possible bounding box that includes all the nontransparent pixels in the layer. Layer-based slicing can

be used whenever you're slicing an item that's isolated on its own layer. It's quicker and more accurate than drawing slices with the Slice tool, and it makes slices that will automatically change with the artwork, so you won't need to reslice if you redesign. Layer-based slices can't be manually adjusted — they're locked to the layer content. But if you want **to move or reshape a layer-based slice,** first click it with the Slice Select tool ✄ and then choose Slices > **Promote to User Slice**; it will now be a user slice, without its layer-based properties.

- **Auto slices** are the ones that Photoshop or ImageReady makes to fill in the rest of the canvas around the user slices and layer-based slices you've made.

In Photoshop the URL for a link can be assigned to a slice by clicking the "Slice Options" button in the Slice Selection tool's ✄ Options bar. In ImageReady, the URL can be added in the top panel of the Slice palette.

ImageReady's **Table palette** and **Web Content palette** have a robust set of table tools:

- In ImageReady's Table palette you can set the table width and height as **percentage values** — not just pixels. Percentages allow the table to stretch or shrink as needed to fit the browser window. You can also predetermine the **attributes** of the cells (slices) in the table by setting values for the border, pad (space between the border and the cell content), and spacing (space between cells); these are useful only for cells that hold text but no image.

- Tables can be complex. You can group slices together, creating a **nested table**, by Shift-selecting (or Ctrl/⌘-selecting) slices in the Web Content palette and clicking the "Group Slices into Table" button at the bottom of the Web Content palette.

Grouping related slices together into a nested table isolates elements in the HTML code. This makes the code more modular, so someone who wants to edit it can more easily find the right section. Also, tables are often used just to hold objects in a certain place on the page. By nesting tables, you can create a small table to hold the parts of a graphic element together, and then place that into a larger table that positions the whole graphic on the page. This makes it easier to move or resize the graphic. And here's one more advantage of using nested tables: With layers, you can turn various content on or off. If you create slices based on content

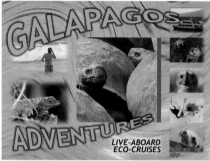

In "Many Versions from One Template," starting on page 643, the Image > Variables command was used to define variables and to make three new versions of the postcard that was designed in "Building a Layout with Masks & Clipping Groups" on page 635. The original design is shown here at the top. The Galapagos version was made by choosing new values for the variables (images were chosen from folders and text was typed into the Variables dialog box). The other version was created by importing a text file containing the variable names and a new value (text or an image file name) for each variable. Importing the data set automatically "repopulated" the layout to make the new version.

and save the slices as a *slice set* (as described next), you can then isolate sets into a nested table so that when you change the content, you can change the slicing without affecting other elements on the page.

- **Slice sets** are similar in function to layer comps. You can use them to change the slicing of a single document to match the content, so you don't need to create multiple files to represent different pages in a web site. For example, if you have a page design that can hold information about a variety of different products, you might create a layer comp to hide or reveal each product photo. Because each product is a different shape and color, each photo might require a different set of slices for the best optimization. When you activate a particular layer comp to export a page (in the Save Optimized As dialog box), in the Slices pop-up menu you can choose the slice set that works for that content.

Variables. In ImageReady and in Photoshop CS2 you can add *variables* to your document. With variables you can create a page "template" file and automatically generate several different pages from it by swapping in new images or text, defined in a ***data set***. There are three things about a layer that can be designated as variables: **Visibilit**y (the layer can be visible or hidden), **Pixel Replacement** (the layer content will be replaced by the file specified in the data set), and **Text Replacement** (the text in the layer will be replaced by the text specified in the data set). There are some logical limitations on variables: Variables can't be assigned to the *Background*, Text Replacement can only be assigned to a type layer, and Pixel Replacement *can't* be assigned to a type layer.

To create variables for a layer, open the Variables dialog box (choose Image > Variables > Define). Next choose the layer you want to define or import variables for, and choose the variable type. Within the Variables dialog box you can specify the images and text to use for the page by choosing **Define** from the menu at the top of the box, or import a tab- or comma-delimited text file by choosing **Data Sets** from this menu. "Building a Template with Masks & Variables" in Chapter 9 includes a step-by-step example.

Rollovers. Rollover effects can be created in the **Web Content palette**. After you create a rollover for a slice, you can capture it as a rollover Style preset and apply it to other slices in your project. Since ImageReady's combined button rollover Style presets can incorporate only changes made entirely with Layer

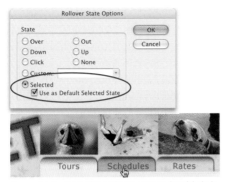

To suggest where the website visitor should click first, you can make the Selected state of a button (rather than its Normal state) the default. To do this, in the Web Content palette double-click on the Selected state for a button to open the Rollover State Options dialog box and click to turn on **"Use as Default Selected State."** Here the "Tours" button's Selected state suggests that the website visitor start by looking at the list of tours offered before checking schedules or prices.

To set up a remote rollover, you start by targeting a button state in the Web Content palette. Then in the Layers palette set up visibility for the way you want the remote slice to appear. Finally drag a target line from the state in the Web Content palette to the remote slice in the working window. Step 6 of "Creating Remote Rollovers" on page 726 tells exactly how to do it.

For more about designing and building for the web, check **How-to-Wow: Photoshop for the Web.**

Styles, design your rollover states with color, pattern, and gradient fill applied as Overlay effects in Layer Styles. "Quick Button Rollovers" on page 716 presents a step-by-step method for constructing a rollover Style. Another way to design rollover Styles is to assign an existing layer-based rollover Style, such as one of the Wow Button Rollovers from the Wow DVD-ROM (see page 767) to your button layer, and then modify the rollover states and save the new rollover Style.

Remote rollovers. The changes you apply to a slice in a rollover state aren't limited to that slice. You can make a web page much more engaging by adding a *remote rollover* effect: The site visitor's cursor rolls over one area and — as if by magic — some other area on the page changes! Drag the Web Content palette's target slice icon (which appears whenever you create a rollover) into the working window to specify the remote slice that will change; see page 721 for more about remote rollovers.

Optimizing, Previewing & Saving Interactive Files

Before you save your work (and probably many times during the creation process), you'll want to preview it. The **Preview in Browser** option in ImageReady's Tools palette and Photoshop's Save for Web dialog box is the most accurate preview, because it creates the HTML, JavaScript, and image files and hands them to a browser on your computer, to present them as a website visitor would see them.

If you have a file with layer comps that represent different pages of a site, it's a good idea to preview each of these in succession, rather than assuming that because one looks good they all will. The same is true for data sets. Load each data set in succession and preview it to make sure it looks and acts the way you intend.

When you save your work (with ImageReady's File > Save Optimized command) you can choose to have the program produce HTML code for you, with all the information required for the links, slices, and image maps to work. If your file includes rollovers, JavaScript will be embedded in the HTML. ImageReady can also automatically save several HTML pages based on slice sets that you have created (choose a slice set from the Slices pop-up menu in the Save Optimized dialog box).

MAKING A WEB PHOTO GALLERY

Photoshop's **Web Photo Gallery** command automatically makes a "portfolio" website from all the image files in a folder or from files selected in File Browser/Bridge. The portfolio has

HTML supports the use of frames in a browser, to create a modular site that lets you reuse elements and thereby reduce download times. With frames you can display different HTML files in various regions of the same browser window. If, for example, your web site has a set of navigation buttons that will stay on-screen regardless of what page is showing, you can create a separate HTML file for the buttons, and put them into their own frame on the page. Within a frame, your HTML page may be sliced to help keep the contents of the frame small. In a Photoshop-ImageReady workflow, you'll be able to create HTML for each frame, but you can't produce the file that actually sets up the frames.

The only way Photoshop or ImageReady works with frames directly is through File > Automate > Web Photo Gallery. The Web Photo Gallery's frames have already been created for you. You can customize their content, or even change the layout.

Jack Davis customized a Web Photo Gallery of some of his paintings by making the thumbnails square. See page 729 for his method.

The Security feature in Web Photo Gallery allows you to label or watermark the images in your site.

interactive thumbnail buttons, each of which brings up a larger, potentially captioned version of its image when clicked. The Web Photo Gallery command is available through Photoshop's File > Automate menu, File Browser's Automate menu (in Photoshop CS), and Bridge's Tools > Photoshop menu (in CS2). The Web Photo Gallery templates provide all the resizing, compression, linking, and HTML coding for the placement and interactivity needed for the site. Eleven templates come with Photoshop CS; CS2 has 20, including two Flash templates.

If you're comfortable working with an HTML editor, you can customize a copy of any of the Web Photo Gallery templates to make your own template. But you can also do some customization *without* coding. For instance, for each artwork file, you can use the Description section of the File Info dialog box (File > File Info) to create the caption you want for the image itself or for its thumbnail. You can also watermark the images in your site with the Security option. *Wow!*

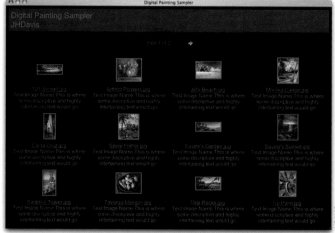

You can caption the thumbnails in a Web Photo Gallery by entering text in the Description section of the File Info dialog box for the artwork image files before you run the Automate > Web Photo Gallery command. Shown here is a gallery made from the **Simple** template.

GIF Optimizing

The challenge in optimizing a GIF is to reduce the number of colors in the file (and thus reduce the file size for fast downloading), but still keep the artwork looking good. Here we started with a space man on transparency. We chose the GIF format because we could retain transparency to silhouette the space man. (JPEG doesn't allow transparency; PNG was an option, but not all browsers can handle it.) If your file has transparency, find out the color of your web page background before you start optimizing your graphics. One way is to click on the background image or tile, then double-click the Foreground swatch, and read the hexadecimal code in the Color Picker; ours was 000099. (If the background is not a solid color, sample an "average" color with the Eyedropper tool's 🖊 Sample Size set to "5 by 5 Average" in the Options bar.)

Open a graphics file of your own, or open our **Space Man.psd** file in either Photoshop or ImageReady. Do one of the following:

• In Photoshop (shown here) choose File > **Save for Web**.

• In ImageReady open the **Optimize** palette (Window > Optimize) and the **Color Table** (Window > Color Table). If you don't see colors in the Color Table, click the little yellow Caution triangle near the bottom of the table.

In the working area, click the 2-Up or 4-Up tab (with 4-up, you can compare three different optimized versions and the original); here we've used the 2-Up tab.

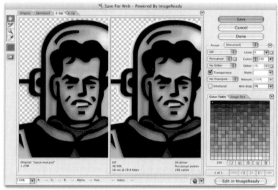

The **Space Man.psd** file open in Photoshop's Save for Web dialog box. With Colors set at 256, choosing Sort by Luminance in the Color Table's ▶ menu arranged the colors as shown.

YOU'LL FIND THE FILES

in 🅦🅞🅦 > Project Files > Chapter 10 > Quick GIF Optimizing

1 Reduce the Dimensions

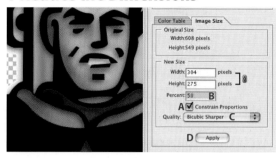

If you've made your artwork bigger than you need it,▼ start by reducing its size. In Photoshop, there's no need to leave the Save for Web dialog to use the Image > Image Size command — you can simply click the tab of the Image Size panel nested behind the Color Table. In Image-Ready, choose Image > Image Size. Make sure **Constrain Proportions** is on **A**. You can specify a particular width or height, or a percentage of the original size **B**; we entered 50%. For Quality, try the **Bicubic Sharper** option, which will keep the image crisp as it's sized down **C**. In Photoshop, click the "Apply" button **D**; in Image-Ready, click "OK."

FIND OUT MORE

▼ Benefits of working large **page 681**

2 Choose a Reduction Algorithm

For the **Colors** setting, start with 256 (the maximum number) **A**. Choose one of the adaptive palettes (Adaptive, Perceptual, or Selective), based on the nature of the art:

• An **Adaptive** palette is optimized to reproduce the colors that occur most often in the image.

• A **Perceptual** palette is like an Adaptive palette, but it also takes into consideration the parts of the spectrum where the human eye is most sensitive.

• A **Selective** palette — often a good choice — is like the Perceptual but also favors web-safe colors and colors that occur in large areas of flat color.

For this art we chose Selective **B**.

3 Lock Important Colors

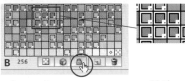

To select the colors that are important to preserve, Shift-click them or Shift-drag over them in the image with the **Eyedropper tool** ✐ (in Photoshop it's in the small palette of tools in the upper left corner of the Save for Web dialog **A**; in ImageReady, it's in the main Tools palette). In the **Color Table** the swatches of the colors you choose will be outlined (selected).

Click the **Lock** button at the bottom of the Color Table **B**, so the colors you selected will be the last to be deleted from the palette as you reduce the number of colors.

USING TRANSPARENCY AS A MARKER

Even if your file has no transparent pixels, it can be helpful to temporarily turn on the Transparency option in the Color Table. You can use it to make sure you don't delete any locked colors as you reduce the number of colors in the file. The transparency swatch ⊠ has a priority that's in between locked and unlocked colors. As you reduce the number of colors, transparency will be retained until all unlocked colors have been eliminated:

- If you reduce the number of colors and find that all the remaining colors are locked but the transparency swatch is still there, you know that you haven't lost any locked colors.

- If you reduce the number of colors and find that the transparency swatch is gone (right), restore colors one by one until transparency comes back, indicating that all locked colors are also present.

4 Reduce the Number of Colors

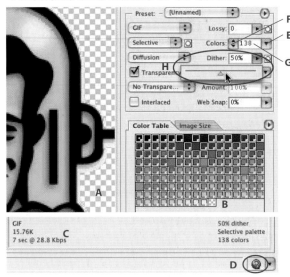

To remove nonessential colors (and thus decrease file size) **watch the changes** in the optimized version **A** as you **reduce the Colors** number in the Optimize panel/palette (as described below). Also keep an eye on the **Color Table** to see when you start losing colors you've locked (see "Transparency as a Marker" at the left) **B**. And watch the **file size and download time C**. As you work, experiment with Dither settings also (see below). Keep going just until the image quality doesn't look good to you anymore. Then increase the number of colors until it looks good again. Click the "Preview in browser" button **D** (in ImageReady it's in the Tools palette) to preview, and then click again to leave the browser; adjust your Optimize settings, preview again, and so on until you like the result.

- **To reduce the number of colors** in large steps, use the pop-up Colors menu **E** (each choice is half the one below it).

- **To increase or decrease by one color at a time,** use the arrows left of the Colors field in Photoshop CS2 **F**, or click in the Colors field itself **G** and tap the up or down arrow key on your keyboard. Add the Shift key to either method to increase or decrease by 10 colors at a time.

Dither intersperses dots of two different colors to create the illusion of a third color. It can smooth the transitions between colors to prevent "banding." But because it can interfere with compression, it sometimes *increases* the size of a GIF file even though it allows you to reduce the number of colors. Balancing Dither with color reduction is a matter of experimenting **H**. To protect some areas from dithering, see "'Weighting' Certain Areas" on page 695.

5 Deal with Transparency

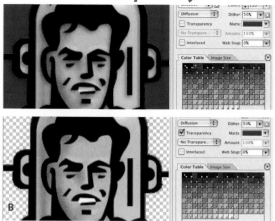

In a GIF file, transparency is different than in Photoshop in general — we can think of it as just one of the colors in the Color Table. Each pixel in a GIF file has to be either fully transparent or a solid color. But there are ways to "fake" partial transparency — to keep the antialiased edges of your artwork smooth, or to allow soft edges to fade into the web page background. Click the **Matte** swatch to open the Color Picker and set the color to your web page background color (we typed in 000099).

If you turn **Transparency off**, all the full transparency in your artwork will be replaced with the Matte color, which will also be blended into existing color to give each partly transparent pixel a solid color **A**.

On the other hand, if you turn **Transparency on**, the Matte color will still be blended into the partly transparent pixels (such as those in the antialiasing here), but any fully transparent pixels will stay transparent **B**.

Transparency Dither helps simulate partial transparency in soft-edged graphics such as drop shadows that need to appear over different colored backgrounds; **Diffusion** Transparency Dither is often the

most effective. A low Amount setting makes more of the partly transparent pixels fully transparent, while a high setting makes more of them fully opaque.

6 Check Lossy Compression & Save

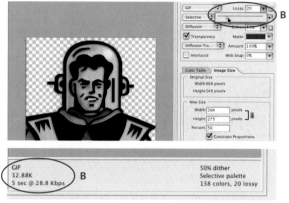

Lossy compression allows some image deterioration as file size is reduced. But a setting between 10% and 40% often doesn't degrade the image too much **A**. If you like, you can mask certain areas to protect them from compression (see below). When you're happy with color and file size **B**, click the "Save" button in Photoshop, or in Image-Ready, choose File > Save Optimized As. **Space Man.gif** is our finished file.

The three mask symbols ⊙ in the Optimize panel/palette are there to give more weight to certain areas of the image as you reduce file size. Clicking any of the three opens a dialog where you can choose to mask with an alpha channel, live type, or vector graphics. White areas of the mask are the selected areas, black areas are unselected, and gray areas are partly selected.

- The ⊙ next to the **color-reduction algorithm** gives priority to retaining colors in the selected area as you reduce the number of colors in the file.

- The ⊙ next to the **Dither** setting protects the selected area from dithering. Clicking this button opens the Modify Dither Setting dialog, where you can set the Minimum amount of Dither. Unselected areas receive the Maximum (the amount that appears as the Dither setting).

- The ⊙ next to **Lossy** protects the selected area from compression. Maximum and Minimum work the same way as for the Dither protection described above.

Tweening

Tweening is the process of creating the intermediate frames between the starting and ending frames of an animation sequence. For many GIF animations you can save a great deal of time by letting ImageReady CS/CS2 or Photoshop CS2 do the tweening automatically. To fine-tune the animation, you may want to go back and make changes to individual frames.

The automated tweening process goes like this: In the Animation palette first select the frame that you want for the beginning or end of your tweened sequence. Then click the "Tween" button at the bottom of the palette and choose whether to tween this frame with the Previous Frame, the Next Frame, or back to the First Frame. Choose which properties you want to tween — Position, Opacity, or Effects — and whether to tween all layers or just some of them. Click "OK" to create the tweened sequence.

YOU'LL FIND THE FILES

in  > Wow Project Files > Chapter 10 > Quick Tweening

Tweening Position

Tug-O-War Banner.psd and .gif

Our file's *Background is* filled with solid color. The silhouetted tugging hands were dragged-and-dropped from a larger file; when centered they extended beyond the left and right edges of the canvas.

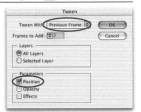

In the Animation palette we duplicated the first frame **A** to make the second. Then we shifted the hands layer 4 pixels to the right **B** by choosing the Move tool and tapping the → key four times.

A Position Tween of just two steps was carried out by selecting the second frame and choosing to tween with Previous Frame. This made a total of four frames.

To set up the tug back to the left, the fourth frame was duplicated to make the fifth, and the Move tool and arrow keys were used to shift the hands layer 8 pixels to the left **C**, to a position 4 pixels to the left of the original starting point.

Another tween with Previous Frame using Position created two in-between frames for the quick tug to the left.

Loop

To complete the basic animation, a two-frame tween with the First Frame was created to bring the hands back to their starting position, and the animation was set to loop Forever. Clicking on individual frames and using the Move tool and arrow keys to nudge each frame up or down added to the struggle in the tug of war.

Tweening a Style

 **Bolt Bulb anim.psd and .gif files**

The goal for this animation was to move the position of an apparent light source. We did it by changing just one attribute — the Global Light Angle — of a Layer Style that consisted of a Drop Shadow and a Bevel and Emboss effect. We turned on Use Global Light for both the Drop Shadow and Bevel and Emboss, and set the Angle at 90° to start, so the light appeared to be positioned at 12 o'clock **A**.

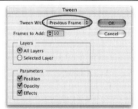

In the Animation palette, we duplicated the first frame to make frame 2. Next we double-clicked on the Drop Shadow's label in the Layers palette to open the Drop Shadow section of the Layer Style dialog box. Then all we had to do to move our "light source" to a position exactly opposite was to change the Angle setting to –90° (6 o'clock). Since we had turned on Use Global Light, changing the Angle for the Drop Shadow also changed it for the Bevel and Emboss. The shadow and the edge highlights and shading all moved together in response to the change in Angle **B**.

With the second frame selected, we clicked the Tween button and created a 10-frame tween with the Previous Frame.

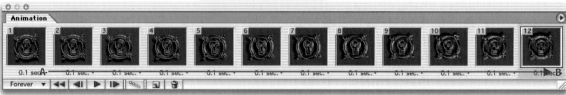

We clicked the Tween button again, this time setting up a tween to the First Frame, again in 10 frames, to complete the rotation of the light.

Tweening Position & Style

 **Tween Style Ball.psd and .gif files**

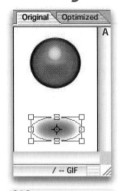

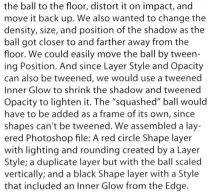

A

B

C

To animate a bouncing ball, we wanted to drop the ball to the floor, distort it on impact, and move it back up. We also wanted to change the density, size, and position of the shadow as the ball got closer to and farther away from the floor. We could easily move the ball by tweening Position. And since Layer Style and Opacity can also be tweened, we would use a tweened Inner Glow to shrink the shadow and tweened Opacity to lighten it. The "squashed" ball would have to be added as a frame of its own, since shapes can't be tweened. We assembled a layered Photoshop file: A red circle Shape layer with lighting and rounding created by a Layer Style; a duplicate layer but with the ball scaled vertically; and a black Shape layer with a Style that included an Inner Glow from the Edge.

By adjusting Opacity, Style, and layer visibility, we could produce these three frames:

A The round ball high in the frame with a low-Opacity shadow layer and a large (20-pixel) Size for the shadow's Inner Glow

B The round ball on the floor with the shadow moved down, shadow Opacity increased, and a reduced (10-pixel) Size for the Glow

C The "squashed " ball on the floor with the same shadow and Glow as for **B**

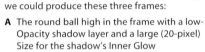

The first frame was set up with the red circle and shadow layers visible, the Opacity of the shadow layer reduced, and the squashed circle layer hidden. This frame was duplicated to make the second frame, and the ball was moved down (with the Move tool and arrow keys). The Opacity of the shadow layer was increased, and the Size of its Inner Glow was reduced. Then we clicked the Tween button and made a five-frame tween with the Previous Frame.

The last frame was duplicated, and the visibility of the layers was adjusted: Visibility for the top (red circle) layer was turned off and visibility for the squashed circle layer was turned on.

The "ball down" frame **B** was then Alt/Option-dragged to the right of the "squashed ball" frame **C** to copy it to the next frame.

We clicked the Tween button again and set up a tween with First Frame to make five more frames to finish the sequence.

To roughly imitate the acceleration and deceleration of a real bounce, a delay of 0.2 second was set for the first frame. The second, last, and "squash" frames were set to 0.1.

Loop

Tweening a Type Warp

 Type Warp tween.psd and .gif

Text Warp is among the effects that can be tweened in the Animation palette. Starting with a gradient-filled *Background*, we used the Type tool T to set the word "HULA." We added dimension and lighting with a Layer Style. Then we duplicated the layer and flipped the copy, all in one operation, by using the keyboard shortcut for duplicate-and-transform (Ctrl-Alt-T in Windows or ⌘-Option-T on the Mac) and then dragging the top center handle of the Transform frame down to the bottom of the canvas. A gradient-filled mask on the duplicate layer faded the "reflection" **A**.

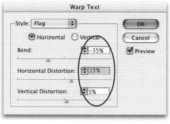

In the Animation palette, frame 1 was duplicated to start frame 2. Then the original type layer was distorted by clicking the "Create warped text" button in the Type tool's Options bar, choosing the Flag Style and setting the Bend and Vertical and Horizontal Distortion parameters, and clicking "OK" to apply the warp to make the "H down" position. The same Flag warp was applied to the duplicate layer, but with opposite Bend and Distortion settings — negative values were substituted for positive and vice versa **B**.

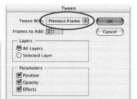

With the second frame selected and both type layers visible, we clicked the Tween button and set up a five-frame tween with the Previous Frame (the straight type) to tween the position of the letters in both type layers.

The last frame was duplicated to make another. The text warp was changed again to set up the "H up" position **C**. Again the warp for the reflection layer was set with opposite numbers. Then this frame was tweened with the Previous Frame to add 11 frames, and then with the First Frame to add five more frames to complete the animation sequence. The complete, looping animation consisted of 24 frames.

Geno Andrews Animates a "Shape Shift"

THE TWEEN FUNCTION in the Animation palette of ImageReady CS/CS2 and Photoshop CS2 can tween position, Layer Styles, text warp, and opacity, but it can't tween from one shape to another. To "morph" the word "Act" to the word "Now" for a GIF animation, Geno Andrews called on some of Adobe Illustrator's talents and then moved to Photoshop/ImageReady to complete the animaton, as described below.

> **WOW** To enjoy Geno's **Act-Now.gif** animation, open it in a browser or in ImageReady. You can also examine the **Act Now.psd** file used to build it. Look in the Wow Goodies folder on the Wow DVD-ROM.

After typing "Act" and "Now" in Illustrator, Geno converted the type to outlines, then used Illustrator's Blend tool to make six intermediate steps in the change from one word to the other. He chose Object > Expand to separate the blend elements. Then he put the eight stages — two originals and six blend steps — onto separate layers. He exported the file as a layered Photoshop document▼ and opened it in Photoshop. He applied the same Layer Style to each layer▼ and added a background. (In version CS, he would have jumped to ImageReady at this point, since Photoshop didn't have an Animation palette until CS2.)

From the Animation palette's ⊙ menu, Geno chose **Make Frames from Layers** to automatically generate the animation to morph the word "Now" to "Act."

To add the background to every frame, he clicked the *Background* thumbnail in the Layers palette and clicked the **"Unify layer visibility"** button at the top of the palette. **Then he clicked it off again**. He deleted Frame 1 (the background by itself) by clicking its Frame thumbnail in the Animation palette and clicking the "Deletes selected frames" button 🗑 at the bottom of the palette. The old Frame 2 became the new Frame 1, Frame 3 became Frame 2, and so on.

> **FIND OUT MORE**
>
> ▼ Moving files from Illustrator to Photoshop **page 442**
> ▼ Working with Layer Styles **page 44**

To get from "Act" back to "Now," Geno clicked on the new Frame 2 thumbnail and then Shift-clicked on Frame 7's to select all frames from 2 through 7. He copied them by choosing **Copy Frames** from the Animation palette's ⊙ menu. Then he added the copied frames to the existing animation by clicking on Frame 8's thumbnail, choosing **Paste Frames** from the ⊙ menu, and choosing **Paste After Selection** in the **Paste Frames** dialog box.

With the newly pasted frames still selected in the Animation palette, he chose **Reverse Frames** from the ⊙ menu.

Finally, he changed the timing for Frame 1 and Frame 8 to 1 sec, to pause the animation briefly at the word "Now" and the word "Act."

After choosing Make Frames from layers and before deleting the empty first frame

Geno selected all but the starting and ending frames and copied them.

For smooth morphing back and forth, he pasted the copied frames and reversed their order.

Animating with Actions

YOU'LL FIND THE FILES
in  > Wow Project Files > Chapter 10 >
Animating with Actions:
- Animated Design-Before files (to start)
- Animated Design-After files (to compare)
- Caffein-355.gif & Caffein-100.gif (to compare)

OPEN THESE PALETTES
from the Window menu:
- Tools • Layers • Actions • Animation

OVERVIEW
Optimize the first version of a file that has been duplicated and scaled to two or more sizes • Save the optimization settings • Record an Action as you apply the optimization and set up the frames, timing, and looping for the animation • Export the file • Open the second file, run the Action, and export the file

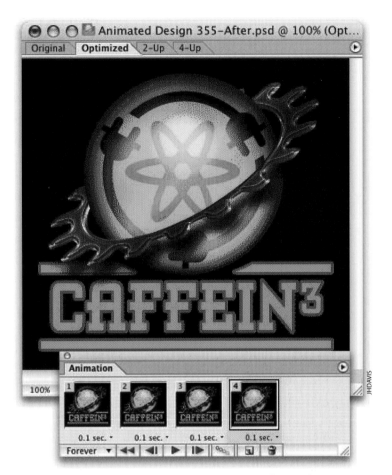

1a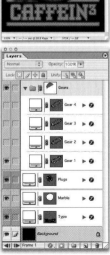

The **Animated Design355-Before .psd** file, opened in ImageReady and set up with the Gear 1 layer visible and all other Gear layers hidden

IF YOU WANT TO PRODUCE THE SAME GIF ANIMATION in more than one size, you can save some time — while maintaining high quality — if you produce the different-size files first, next record an Action as you animate one of the files, and then open another version of the file and play the Action back to animate that one as well. Here we've animated two sizes of the file produced in "Designing for Scalability & Animation" on page 460. Since Photoshop CS2 has an Animation palette, and since this project doesn't use Conditional Actions (found only in ImageReady), if you're working in CS2 you can use either Photoshop or ImageReady; here we've used ImageReady.

1 Optimizing the larger file. When you've finished building your layered file in Photoshop and have saved it in the two or more sizes you want to animate, open the largest version in ImageReady. We had 355-pixel-high and 100-pixel-high versions of our file, so we opened the larger file (**Animated Design 355-Before.psd**) **1a**.

1b

Choosing **GIF 32 Dithered** loads one of Adobe's optimizing presets as a starting point for optimizing the file.

1c

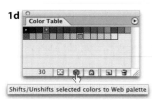

To reduce file size we increased the Amount of Dither, reduced the number of colors and turned off Add Metadata.

1d

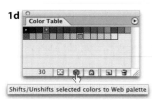

Snapping the orange color used for the logotype to a web-safe color

Open the Optimize interface (in ImageReady, choose Window > Optimize; in Photoshop CS2, File > Save for Web). Now click the **Optimized** tab in the working window so you can preview the optimized image as you reduce file size. You can either start the reduction from scratch (use the optimizing method described in "Quick GIF Optimizing," page 693) or begin with a choice from the **Presets** menu **1b**; we chose **GIF 32 Dithered** from the menu

GIF 32 Dithered uses a **Selective** palette, which gives priority to the colors the human eye is most sensitive to *and* to any large areas of flat color, such as the orange logotype in our file. This preset also uses **Diffusion Dither at 88%**; dithering reduces the number of colors needed by simulating some colors with a mixture of dots of others (blue and red to make purple, for instance). In this image, preserving smooth color transitions *without* dithering would take many more colors than *with* dithering, so overall, dithering reduces file size.▼

FIND OUT MORE

▼ How Dithering affects file size **page 694**

Now experiment with changing the settings **1c**:

- Try **increasing Dither to 100%**; although it increases file size a little, we found it reduced color banding and made the image look significantly better.

- To see if you can **reduce the number of colors**, click in the Colors field and watch the image as you tap the ⬇ key; the shadow of the gear wheel on the orange bar looked significantly worse when we went from 30 to 29 colors, so we tapped the ⬆ key to return to 30.

- In the Options section, turn **Add Metadata off** (if you don't need copyright and other info in the file) to reduce file size further.

- Set **Lossy at 0**, effectively turning off this option. Lossy compression generates "noise" in the process of compressing the image. This isn't necessarily a problem in the parts of the animation that are moving anyway and therefore changing. But the noise can also cause subtle variation in the static parts of the image, which can be distracting.

In the **Color Table** palette (in ImageReady; choose Window > Color Table; in Photoshop it's part of the Save For Web interface) click on the swatch for the orange of the type, and click the ⬢ button at the bottom of the palette that "Shifts/Unshifts selected colors to web palette" **1c**. This will ensure that this orange won't dither. Then choose **Save Color Table** from the

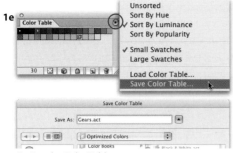

1e

Saving the Color Table

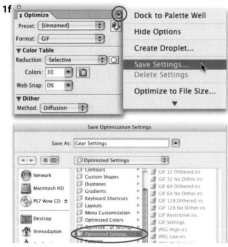

1f

Saving the optimization settings as a preset in the Optimized Settings folder so the preset will be listed in the Optimize palette's Preset menu.

2a

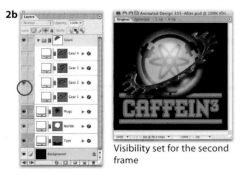

2b

Visibility set for the second frame

palette's pop-out menu ⊙ **1d**. So that you can apply the same optimization settings to the smaller file later, including your customized Color Table, save the settings by choosing **Save Settings** from the Optimize palette's ⊙ menu **1e**; give the setting a new name.

2 Animating the file and recording the Action. In the Layers palette, **set up visibility** in your layered file to show the image you want to use for the first frame of your animation: Click the ◉ column for each layer to turn its visibility on or off. We made all the component elements of the logo visible, including the folder at the top that included the layer mask, but **only one of the Gear layers**.

We made the ***Background***, which would appear in all frames, the active layer by clicking its name in the palette (refer to **1a**). Turning on and off different Gear layers for the different frames of the animation (as described next) will achieve the rotation we had planned. Making the *Background* the active layer will prevent the situation in which the active layer is invisible, which can cause problems in recording an Action.

When the file is set up for the first frame, in the Actions palette click the "Create new action" button ⊡ at the bottom of the palette. In the New Action dialog box, name the Action **2a**, assign it an F-key shortcut if you like, and click "Record."

As Photoshop/ImageReady automatically records what you do, in the **Settings** menu at the top of the Optimize interface, choose a different option, and then **"rechoose" the new custom Settings preset** you saved in step 1. Applying it while the Action is being recorded will ensure that its settings will become part of the Action. Also, for the same reason, **reload the custom Color Table** you saved in step 1 by choosing Load Color Table from the Color Table's ⊙ menu.

Then **duplicate the first frame** in the Animation palette to start the second frame: Click the "Duplicates current frame" button ⊡ at the bottom of the Animation palette. Adjust the visibility of your layers to show the image you want for the second frame **2b**. We turned off visibility for the Gear 1 layer and turned on visibility for Gear 2. ***Caution:*** As you record the Action, wait for the screen to be refreshed to show changes in visibility before clicking on the ⊡ button to make a new frame. On slower computers, this can take some time!

Continue to add new frames by duplicating the current frame and changing visibility until you have all the frames you need.

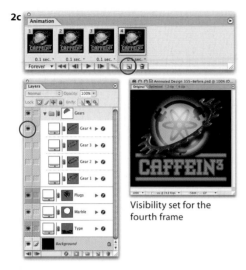

2c

Visibility set for the fourth frame

2d

All four frames were selected and a delay of 0.1 second was assigned.

2e

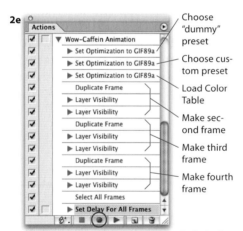

Choose "dummy" preset

Choose custom preset

Load Color Table

Make second frame

Make third frame

Make fourth frame

The Action that was recorded as the Optimization settings were chosen, the frames were made, and the timing was set

3

Exporting the second animated GIF

We made a frame with the Gear 3 layer visible **2c** and another with Gear 4. These four frames will be all you'll need, since the graphics were designed in such a way that the animation will loop to continue the rotation of the gear (as described in step 4 of "Designing for Scalability & Animation" on page 462).

With the Action still being recorded, set the timing for the animation: Select all the frames of the animation by choosing Select All Frames from the Animation palette's ⊙ menu, click the time value at the bottom of one frame, and choose from the pop-out list **2d**. We chose **0.1 second** — the shortest interval available — to prevent the animation from playing back at the fastest speed that any particular computer system can achieve. Set the looping option (in the lower left corner of the Animation palette). Since we wanted the animation to loop continuously, we left the setting at the default, **Forever**.

When you've completed the animation, stop the recording of the Action by clicking the "Stop playing/recording" button ■ at the bottom of the Actions palette **2e**. You can check the animation by clicking the Play button ▶ at the bottom of the Animation palette. (If you like, you can remove the first "Set Optimization to GIF89a" step from your Action by dragging it to the 🗑 button at the bottom of the Actions palette; this was the step that chose a dummy optimization Preset so that you could "rechoose" your custom settings. But leaving the now unnecessary step in place won't affect the final result.)▼

FIND OUT MORE

▼ Editing Actions **page 115**

Preview the animation in a browser by clicking the "Preview in" button (it shows a browser icon) near the bottom of the Tools palette (in Photoshop, it's near the bottom right corner of the Save for Web dialog). To stop, close the browser window. Export the animation file (File > **Save Optimized As**; in Photoshop click the "Save" button); in the Save Optimized As dialog, choose **Images Only** for the Format.

3 Optimizing and animating a smaller version. Open the second version of the file, set the visibility for the first frame, and activate a layer that will appear in all frames (such as the *Background* in our file). In the Actions palette, click the name of your Action, and click the "Play selection" button ▶ at the bottom of the palette. Photoshop/ImageReady will load the optimization settings, create the frames for the smaller animation, and set their timing. If the larger file you animated was much bigger than the second, smaller version, you may be able to economize on file size by using fewer Colors in the Optimize palette. After adjusting, preview in a browser and export **3**. *Wow*

Animating with Layer Comps

YOU'LL FIND THE FILES

in ⊙ > Wow Project Files > Chapter 10 > Animated Neon:

- Animated Neon-Before.psd (to start)
- Animated Neon-After.psd & Animated Neon.gif (to compare)

OPEN THESE PALETTES

from the Window menu:

- Tools • Layers • Layer Comps
- Animation

OVERVIEW

Make and alpha channel to protect the background during optimization • Adjust layer opacity and Styles to make layer comps • Create frames from layer comps • Optimize using Lossy compression with the alpha channel • Preview in browser against web-page background color

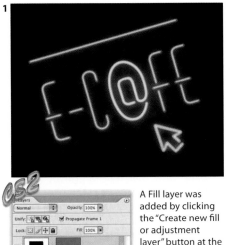

A Fill layer was added by clicking the "Create new fill or adjustment layer" button at the bottom of the Layers palette. When the Color Picker opened, we typed the hexadeximal number for the web page background color (330000) into the # field.

IF YOUR ANIMATION PROJECT involves artwork that's organized in layers, and if changing layer opacities, blend modes, or Layer Styles play a role in the changes from frame to frame, layer comps can be useful for collecting the various states of the artwork. Layer comps can be especially helpful for animations in which frames repeat at various spots within the animation. It will be easier to understand the goal of this technique if you play the Animated Neon.gif before you begin. Open the file in ImageReady; click the "Preview document" button 🖑 in Image-Ready's Tools palette to put the neon into action, or click the "Preview in browser" button to view it in a browser.

1 Preparing the graphics. Neon Animation-Before.psd is derived from "Crafting a Neon Glow" on page 546. It's smaller than the original, and the Layer Styles have been adjusted to go with the solid dark brown (hexadecimal 33000) used for the background of the web page **1**.

2 Making an alpha channel for weighted optimization. In the "on" state, the neon sign lights up the background for quite a distance from the tubing itself. This results in many different shades and tones of color. The Lossy compression that's available in the Optimize panel/palette for reducing file size can handle varied color quite well, but it often introduces "streaking" in flat color. To protect the solid background color from streaking, we made an alpha channel to use as a mask that would restrict Lossy compression to the areas where a lot of color variability already existed, such as the neon tubing and the glow around it.

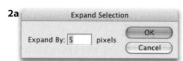

2a

After selecting the neon, choosing Select > Modify > Expand opens a dialog box where you can set the amount of expansion.

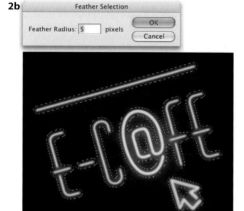

2b

Feathering the expanded selection

2c

The selection is inverted to select the background and saved as an alpha channel, to be used as a mask to protect the background from Lossy compression.

To start the alpha channel mask, load the graphics as a selection by Ctrl/⌘-clicking on the Layers palette thumbnail for one of the graphics layers, then Shift-Ctrl/⌘-clicking on each of the other two graphics layers' thumbnails. To make some space around the graphics (for the glow), expand the selection (choose Select > Modify > Expand; we used 5 pixels) **2a**. To soften the transition between the areas that will and won't be protected by the weighted optimization mask, feather the selection (Select > Feather; we used a Feather Radius of 5 pixels) **2b**. Finally, invert the selection so the background is now selected (Ctrl/⌘-Shift-I), and turn the selection into an alpha channel (Select > Save Selection) **2c**.

3 Making the layer comps. To suggest flashing neon, we'll set up layer comps for an "all on" state, an "all off" state, and two others — one with only the @ sign on, and one with the @ sign and the cursor on.

- To set up the layer comp for **"all on,"** make sure all layers of the file are visible and click the "Create New Layer Comp" button ▣ at the bottom of the Layer Comps palette. In the New Layer Comp dialog box, make sure Visibility and Appearance are turned on **3a**. **Visibility** controls whether the layer shows up, and **Appearance** controls everything that can be controlled inside the Layer Style dialog, including layer Opacity. Name the layer comp "all on" (descriptive names will help you find the right comps later) and click "OK" to close the dialog box.

- To set up the **"all off"** layer comp, in the Layers palette, reduce the Opacity of each of the neon graphics layers; we used 50%. Also in the Layers palette click the 𝑓 icons to expand the Style listing for each Drop Shadow and Outer Glow and turn these effects off **3b**. Reducing our view of the image on-screen (Ctrl/⌘-hyphen) convinced us that this "off" state would be effective when the file was reduced for the web. Click the Layer Comps palette's ▣ button, name the comp, and click "OK" to save it.

3a

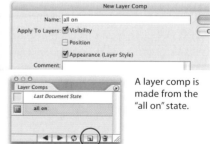

A layer comp is made from the "all on" state.

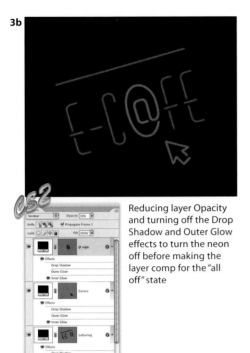

3b

Reducing layer Opacity and turning off the Drop Shadow and Outer Glow effects to turn the neon off before making the layer comp for the "all off" state

3c

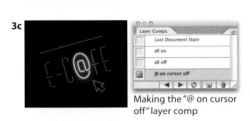

Making the "@ on cursor off" layer comp

3d

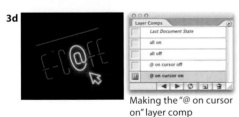

Making the "@ on cursor on" layer comp

4a

The Image > Trim command

- Make an "@ on cursor off" state by restoring 100% Opacity for the @ sign layer only and turning its Drop Shadow and Outer Glow on again. Click ◻, name the comp, and save it **3c**.

- The last state we need is "@ on cursor on." With the @ layer at full Opacity and all others reduced from the "@ on cursor off" state, restore full Opacity to the cursor layer and turn on its Drop Shadow and Outer Glow. Click ◻ and name and save the comp **3d**.

4 Reducing dimensions. To reduce file size but still keep a seamless transition from the graphics to the web-page background, trim away excess background, but without abruptly cutting off the soft edges of the glows: Return the neon to its fully lit state by clicking the box to the left of the "all on" comp in the Layer Comps palette, since this is the state with the broadest glow. Choose Image > Trim; choose Bottom Right Pixel Color (or Top Left would work also) and turn on all the Trim Away options **4a**.

To scale the file down (our target height was 200 pixels), choose Image > Image Size **4b**. Make sure all three options in the lower left corner (Scale Styles, Constrain Proportions, and Resample Image) are turned on. Then type "200" in the Height field at the top of the Image Size dialog box.

5 Making the animation frames. If you're working in CS2, stay in Photoshop. If you're working in version CS, click the "Edit in ImageReady" button at the bottom of Photoshop's Tools palette to jump to ImageReady, since Photoshop CS doesn't have the animation palette; the layer comps you made in step 3 will go along with the file.

In either program, use the layer comps to produce the animation frames:

- **First frame.** In the Animation palette the first (and only) frame will be targeted. In the Layer Comps palette, for Frame 1 click in the box to the left of the "all on" listing to choose this comp and thus turn on all the neon **5a**.

- **Second frame:** Click the "Duplicates selected frames" button ◻ at the bottom of the Animation palette to add a second frame just like the first. To change the content of this frame, click in the box next to the "all off" layer comp.

- **Third frame:** In the Animation palette, click the ◻ button to add another frame. In the Layer Comps palette, choose the "@ on cursor on" comp **5b**.

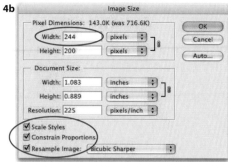
Reducing pixel dimensions to reduce file size

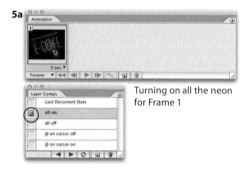
Turning on all the neon for Frame 1

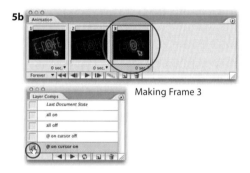
Making Frame 3

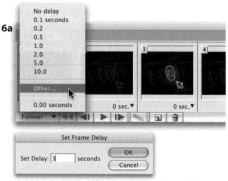
Setting the timing for Frame 1 to 3 seconds

- **Fourth frame:** Add another frame and use the "@ on cursor off" comp.

- **Fifth frame:** Add the final frame using "@ on cursor on" again.

6 Setting the timing. Next set the timing for your animation by clicking on the time setting beneath each of the frames in the Animation palette to open the pop-up menu, where you can choose a display time for that frame. We wanted to set our timing so the cursor flickered on and off but so the other pauses for the flashing of the entire sign and the "@" were long enough to make the animation interesting rather than annoying. We set the first frame for 3 seconds by choosing Other and typing 3 into the Set Frame Delay box **6a**. We set the second frame for 2 seconds, the third for 0.5, the fourth for 0.1 (the flicker), and the fifth for 0.5 (the @ stayed lit in frames 3 through 5, more than 1 second, so the cursor was the only thing that flickered).

Choose a looping option for the animation, from the lower left corner of the Animation palette; we chose **Other** and entered 5 in the **Set Loop Count** box **6b**. You can preview the animation by clicking the Play button ▶ at the bottom of the palette. Make any adjustments you need by resetting the times for individual frames, and Play ▶ to test again.

7 Optimizing. To reduce the file size for quick downloading, first choose Optimize Animation from the Animation palette's ⊙ menu, and make sure that both options are turned on. If you're working in Photoshop CS2, open the Save for Web dialog (File > Save for Web). In either Photoshop or ImageReady, target the frame with the most color variation (Frame 1 in this case) and click the Optimized tab at the top of the window so you can preview the changes you'll make next, as you make them.

In the Optimize panel/palette **7a**, choose a reduction method; we chose Selective, appropriate for a file with a variety of colors and tones. Choose 100% Diffusion Dither to help break up the banding that will otherwise happen in the glows when you drastically reduce the number of colors. Then select and lock the important colors using the Eyedropper ✐ Shift-click method in "Quick GIF Optimizing" on page 694; be sure to include the background color. For this animation, we repeated the selecting and locking process for the "all off" state in Frame 2. Between the two states, we felt confident we had the important colors. We then reduced the number of colors **7a** to 64.

Check to see if the Lossy setting can help reduce the file size even more. Click on the mask button ▣ next to the Lossy field

6b

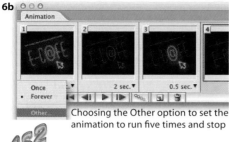

Choosing the Other option to set the animation to run five times and stop

7a

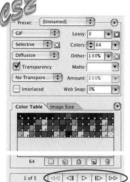

Optimizing with Selective color reduction, locked colors from Frames 1 and 2, with 64 colors total. In Photoshop CS2, you can use the controls under the Color Table to play the animation to preview it, or to switch from frame to frame for optimizing.

7b

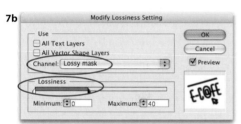

Minimum is set to 0 to protect the areas represented by the white in the mask. We chose 40 as the Maximum.

8

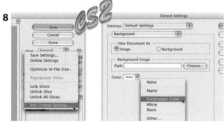

Setting the background color for previewing in a browser

9

Previewing in the browser against the web-page background

in the Optimize panel/palette, and in the Modify Lossiness Setting dialog box, choose the alpha channel you made in step 2. Experiment with the settings **7b**, with the left slider at 0 and the right slider at a setting low enough to keep the image from looking too "noisy" **7b**. Our alpha channel concentrated the Lossy compression in the areas around the neon (the black areas of the alpha channel) and protected the background (the white part of the mask) from streaky compression artifacts. When you have the setting you like, click "OK" to close the dialog box.

8 Previewing in a browser. With the compression set, preview in a browser, against the background color of your web page, to make sure the entire animation looks good **8**:

- In Photoshop CS2 use the Save for Web Eyedropper 🖋 to click on a corner of your image to sample the background color again, and choose Edit Output Settings from the Optimize panel's ⊙ menu. When the Output Settings dialog opens, choose Background from the second menu from the top and then choose Eyedropper Color from the menu that pops out from the color swatch.

- In ImageReady click with the Eyedropper 🖋 to sample the background color, then choose File > Output Settings > Background, and choose Foreground (meaning Foreground Swatch) from the BG Color swatch menu.

Click "OK" to close the box and click the "Preview in Browser" button in the bottom right corner of the Save for Web dialog or the ImageReady Tools palette. If the browser test shows problems, go back and adjust the settings for the Lossy compression or the number of colors.

9 Exporting the animation. If the browser test looks good, you're ready to save the animated GIF file:

- In Photoshop, click the Save for Web dialog's "Save" button.

- In ImageReady, choose File > Save Optimized As.

In the Save Optimized As dialog, enter a file name and choose Images Only for the Format (since you're saving a file with no links). Then click the "Save" button. 🖋

ADAPTIVE MAY BE IDEAL

In the Optimize panel/palette, try the Adaptive reduction method for graphics with a limited range of hues but many shades and tones. It gives priority to the colors most common in the image.

Animating Frame-by-Frame

YOU'LL FIND THE FILES in  wow > Wow Project Files > Chapter 10 > Frame-by-Frame:
- Catanimation-Before.psd (to start)
- Catanimation-After.psd & Catanimation.gif (to compare)

OPEN THESE PALETTES from the Window menu:
- Tools • Layers
- Animation

OVERVIEW
Compose the frames of an animation by moving, transforming, and editing components • Adjust timing • Create a layer for each frame • Duplicate each layer, filter the copy, and combine with the original • Optimize and save the animation

WHILE THERE ARE CERTAINLY more sophisticated ways of animating for the web (vector-based Flash animation, for example), a simple "hand-crafted" animation exported in GIF format can be viewed by any browser that supports graphics. Here we started with drawn elements that we assembled, modified, and animated to produce a six-frame cat-and-mouse "cartoon." We then added a little dimension and subtle motion with the Photocopy filter. In order to have some flexibility in the final size of our animation, we started working at about 200% of what we thought would be our final frame dimensions.

There are many ways to control the timing of the motion in an animation. To see the animation in **Catanimation.gif**, open it in ImageReady and then click the "Preview in browser" button at the bottom of the Tools palette and notice the timing:

- The speed of the white mouse varies as it runs across the stage. The variation comes mostly from **moving** the little animal farther in some frames than others. Similar speed effects are achieved by turning the cat's head, paw, or tail through a greater or smaller arc from one frame to the next. These changes were made as the frames were composed and captured one by one.

- A long pause occurs before the mouse appears, and there's a short pause when the cat bats at the mouse. These were accomplished after all the frames were made, by increasing the **timing** setting for these two frames.

- The "small motion" of the muscles comes from applying the **Photocopy filter** to the finished art for each frame, varying the setting slightly for one of the frames.

1 Preparing the graphics. You can use Photoshop CS2 as we did (it has the Animation palette) or use ImageReady, which works the same way with a few exceptions, noted in the steps that follow. Open a file with the essential graphics for your own animation, or use the **Catanimation-Before.psd** file **1a**.

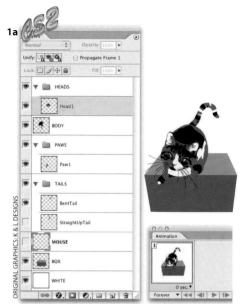

1a

In the **Catanimation-Before.psd** file, layer visibility is set up to show the image that will appear in Frame 1. If you're working with a file of your own, use the 👁 column in the Layers palette to turn each layer's visibility on or off, depending on whether or not you want that layer to show in the first frame.

1b

In the Layers palette the Propagate Frame 1 option is turned off so the first frame can be edited later without having the changes "ripple" through the other frames that will be added.

1c

Clicking the "Duplicates selected frames" button ⬒ copies Frame 1 as a start for Frame 2. Any changes you make to your image now will be reflected in Frame 2.

FIND OUT MORE

▼ Using the Brush tool 🖌 **page 362**

Our file includes the cat's head, its body, a paw, two versions of the tail (bent and straight up), a mouse, the box the cat sits on, and a white background, each on its own layer, and with layer sets/groups set up to keep like parts together as we develop the animation. The body and box will remain visible for all frames and won't change position. You can duplicate and change the other elements as needed, and turn visibility on and off to set up the frames to create motion.

Before you begin to make frames, turn off "Propagate Frame 1" near the top of the Layers palette in CS2 **1b**; in ImageReady turn off "Propagate Frame 1 Changes" in the Layers palette's ⊙ menu. That way, if you find yourself returning to Frame 1 to edit it, you won't accidentally change the other frames as well. (Make sure you turn it off whenever Frame 1 is active, unless, of course, if you want to add something to all frames of your animation; then you can turn the "Propagate" option back on temporarily.) Also turn off "New Layers Visible in All Frames" in the Animation palette's ⊙ menu.

To preserve your "scene" as the first frame, create a second frame that will then become the active one: **Click the "Duplicates selected frame" button ⬒ at the bottom of the Animation palette 1c.** Now your first frame won't change as you rearrange and modify your artwork and change layer visibility to set up the second frame.

2 Animating by transforming: Frame 2. Now transform the components of your artwork as needed to create the frames of the animation. The changes in **Frame 2** of Catanimation are the appearance of the mouse and the movement of the head, as the mouse catches the cat's attention. In the Layers palette, turn on visibility for the "MOUSE" layer by clicking in its 👁 column. Click on the thumbnail for the "Head1" layer and duplicate it (Ctrl/⌘-J) **2a**. Rotate the head counterclockwise to look at the mouse at the right, by pressing Ctrl/⌘-T (for Edit > Free Transform) and dragging the curved double-headed arrow cursor counterclockwise outside the Transform frame **2b**; then double-click inside the frame to close it. We used the Brush 🖌 to paint changes in the eyes **2c**, holding down Alt/Option to sample colors as needed. ▼ With the second frame complete, **click the ⬒ button in the Animation palette to move on to the third frame 2d**.

3 Animating by transforming: Frame 3. In Frame 3, use the Move tool ⊹ to drag the "MOUSE" layer a little farther to the left **3a**. **Click ⬒ at the bottom of the Animation palette** to start the fourth frame **3b**.

"Head2" is rotated toward the mouse.

The eyes are repainted to look at the mouse, using color sampled from the artwork.

After completing Frame 2, duplicate it to start Frame 3.

For Frame 2, visibility is turned on for the "MOUSE" layer. The "Head1" layer is duplicated, and the copy is renamed (by double-clicking the layer name and typing "Head2"). Visibility for the original "Head1" layer is turned off.

4 Animating by transforming: Frame 4. For this frame, use the Move tool ⇖ to drag the mouse directly in front of the cat. Target the original "Head1" by clicking its thumbnail in the Layers palette, duplicate it (Ctrl/⌘-J) to make the "Head3" layer, turn on visibility ⬤ for this copy, and turn off visibility for "Head2." Rotate your new "Head3" and paint the eyes to look down at the mouse. Turn off visibility for the "BentTail" layer and turn on visibility for "StraightUpTail" **4a**.

To extend the paw, duplicate the "Paw1" layer to create "Paw2," turn off visibility for "Paw1," and type Ctrl/⌘-T to open the Transform frame. Drag the center of rotation (the little "target" in the middle of the Transform frame) to the shoulder area, where the limb would be articulated **4b**. Now when you drag counterclockwise outside the frame to rotate until the paw

A **painted guideline**, a **Grid**, and reduced layer Opacity ("**onion-skin-ning**") help produce smooth, even motion. Once the elements are in position, visibility for the guide and Grid can be turned off and layer Opacity adjusted for each frame.

USING GUIDES FOR MOTION

A temporary **guide** can help to keep the motion smooth, when that's your goal, as an object moves across the stage of your animation. To make a temporary guide, activate the top layer of the file, click on the "Create a new layer" button ⬛ at the bottom of the Layers palette and use the Pen tool ✎ in Paths mode to draw an arc. ▼ To make the arc easier to see, stroke the path with paint by choosing the Brush tool ✐ and clicking the "Stroke path with brush" button ○ at the bottom of the Paths palette. Turn off visibility for the paint stroke layer when you've finished using it so it won't appear in your animation.

To regulate the speed of motion, a **Grid** that divides the stage into equal sections can help with estimating the distance an element should move in each frame. Choose View > Show > Grid to display the Grid. Then choose Photoshop > Preferences > Guides, Grid & Slices and in the Grid section of the Preferences dialog, set "Subdivisions" to 1 and adjust the "Gridline every" setting, checking the working window until you have as many grid units as the number of frames you want for the motion.

To align the current layer with an element you've used in a previous frame, try the Photoshop/ImageReady version of the classic **"onion-skinning"** technique. Turn on visibility for the current layer and any layers you want to compare with it. Then reduce the Opacity (try 50%) for one or more layers, and align as needed. After aligning, return the current layer to 100% Opacity and turn off visibility for the layers that won't appear in the frame.

JHDAVIS GRAPHICS: HAVANA STREET, IN THE MOOD

FIND OUT MORE

▼ Using the Pen tool
✎ **page 435**

3a

In Frame 3, the "MOUSE" layer is moved slightly.

3b

Duplicating Frame 3 to start Frame 4

4a

In Frame 4, the mouse moves a longer distance, the head rotates, the eyelids are lowered, and the "StraightUpTail" layer is visible.

4b

In the "Paw2" layer, move the center of rotation to the shoulder (top left). Then rotate the layer (top right), and stretch the paw down to reach the mouse.

4c

A new frame is added to start Frame 5.

is pointing down, the shoulder will be the pivot point for the swiping motion. After rotating the paw, drag the center bottom handle to stretch it down to touch the mouse. This completes Frame 4, so **click ◰ at the bottom of the Animation palette** to start the fifth frame **4c**.

5 Animating by transforming: Frame 5. Move the mouse a little farther along. Turn off visibility for "Head3" and turn on visibility for "Head1," the head's original position.

Make another copy of "Paw1"; turn on visibility for this new "Paw3" and reduce the Opacity for the "Paw1" and "Paw2" layers. With the "Paw3" layer targeted, open the Transform frame (Ctrl/⌘-T), move the center of rotation to the shoulder again, and rotate the limb to a position between the angle of "Paw1" and the stretched "Paw2"; drag inside the Transform frame to move the limb down slightly **5a**. Restore Opacity for "Paw1" and "Paw" and turn off their visibility.

To swish the tail, turn on visibility for "BentTail" and duplicate it. With the new layer targeted, type Ctrl/⌘-T, move the center of rotation to the base of the tail where it attaches to the body, and rotate the tail to a position between its original and the "StraightUpTail" **5b**. Then use Edit > Transform > Flip Horizontal **5c** and drag to adjust the tail's position if necessary. Restore Opacity for "BentTail" and "StraightUPTail," turn off their visibility, and in the Animation palette, create a new frame ◰ **5d**.

6 Animating by transforming: Frame 6. In this frame the mouse moves farther left, to the edge of the frame. Duplicate the "BentTail copy" layer from step 5, move the center or rotation, and rotate it farther to the left **6**. Adjust visibility.

5a

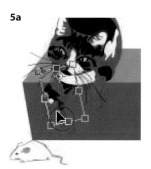

It's easier to position "Paw3" between them, using a form of "onion-skinning" (see the tip on the facing page).

5b

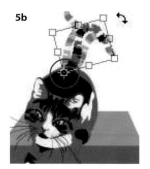

The "BentTail" layer is duplicated to make "BentTail copy," and the copy is rotated.

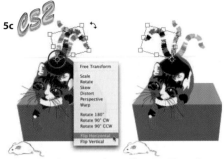

5c

Flipping the "BentTail copy" layer. In Photoshop CS2, while the Transform frame is open you can right/Ctrl-click and choose Flip Horizontal from a context-sensitive menu.

5d

Duplicating frame 5 to start Frame 6

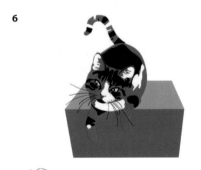

6

Frame 6 completes the motion as the mouse escapes.

7

Changing the timing for Frame 1

8a

Making a single layer from each frame

7 Testing the animation and setting the timing. At this point, click the "Play" button ▶ at the bottom of the Animation palette to display the action frame-by-frame. Click the ■ button to stop it, and change the timing for some of the frames as needed: Click the tiny arrow in the bottom right corner of the frame and choose from the menu; we used 2 sec for Frame 1 (a long pause), 0.5 sec for Frame 2, 0.1 sec for Frame 3, 0.3 sec for Frame 4 (a slight hesitation for the strike), and then back to 0.1 for Frames 5 and 6 (for the quick escape).

Now check the timing: In Photoshop, open the Save For Web dialog (choose File > Save For Web and use the "Play" button ▷ underneath the Color Table. Also look at the animation in a browser by clicking the "Preview in Browser" button in the lower right corner of the dialog box. To leave the Save for Web dialog and get back to Photoshop, click the Cancel button; in Image-Ready, find both the "Preview Document" button 👆 and the "Preview in Browser" button near the bottom of the Tools palette.

At this point you can adjust the timing in the Animation palette if needed, preview again, and so on until you're happy with the motion. If you want to change the artwork in a frame, click the frame in the Animation palette, arrange position and visibility to your liking in the working window and Layers palette, and preview again.

8 Adding a little dimension. The Photocopy filter can add shading and edge definition. Because you can't run a filter on a frame — you need a layer — make a layer from each of your frames by choosing Flatten Frames Into Layers from the Animation palette's ⊙ menu **8a**. At the top of the layer stack, a new layer will be added for each frame in the animation **8b**.

Modify each of these new layers in turn with the Photocopy filter as described next. But first choose the Move tool ▸⊕ so you can control the blend mode with a keyboard shortcut (with the Move tool or any selection tool chosen, Shift-+ steps through the blend modes for the active layer). Also, reset the Foreground and Background colors (type D for "Default"). If you had many frames in the animation, recording an Action would speed the process of filtering (as in "Creating an Action to Animate a Video Clip" on page 134), but because we had just a few frames, we simply used keyboard shortcuts instead.

To begin the filtering process, click on the first frame in the Animation palette. In the Layers palette, visibility for the corresponding layer (called Frame 1 in Photoshop) will be turned

8b

After choosing Flatten Frames Into Layers but before targeting the layer corresponding to Frame 1

8c

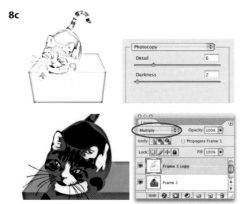

Running the Photocopy filter on a copy of the "Frame 1" layer (top). In Multiply mode, the filtered layer adds shading.

9a

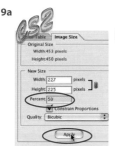

Reducing Image Size to 50% in Photoshop's Save for Web dialog. Clicking the "Apply" button reduces the size for the GIF that will be saved but doesn't permanently change the size of the **.psd** file.

9b

We used the Selective reduction method, 64 colors, Diffusion Dither at 50%, and a Lossy setting of 0, reducing download time to 9 sec.

on automatically, but you'll still need to *target* the layer in the Layers palette to make it the active one — click its thumbnail. Duplicate the layer (Ctrl/⌘-J) Then choose Filter > Sketch > Photocopy and set the Detail (we used 6) and Darkness (we used 2); click "OK" to leave the filter dialog; if you don't like the result, undo (Ctrl/⌘-Z), reopen Photocopy (Ctrl-Alt-F in Windows or ⌘-Option-F on the Mac), change the settings, and click "OK." After filtering, put the copy in Multiply mode (to get from Normal to Multiply hold down Shift and type +++) **8c**. Then press Ctrl/⌘-E to merge the Photocopy layer with the original; the corresponding animation frame is updated automatically.

Advance to the next frame (you can do that by clicking the "Select next frame" button ▐▶ at the bottom of the Animation palette) and repeat the keyboard shortcuts: Alt/Option-⑦ targets the layer, Ctrl/⌘-J duplicates it, Ctrl/⌘-F repeats the filter, and Shift-+++ puts the filtered layer in Multiply mode. We repeated the process for Frame 3 but departed from this routine for Frame 4, using Ctrl-Alt-F (Windows)/⌘-Option-F (Mac) to open the Photocopy dialog so we could change the settings to Detail 10, Darkness 2 to emphasize the strike at the mouse. When filtering the next frame's layer copy we used Ctrl-Alt-F/⌘-Option-F again, to restore the Detail 6, Darkness 2 settings; then we used Ctrl/⌘-F to keep these settings for the last frame.

9 Optimizing and saving. Choose Optimize Animation from the animation palette's ⊙ menu, and make sure both Bounding Box and Redundant Pixel Removal are checked. Beyond that, optimizing this GIF animation is much like optimizing any GIF, described step-by-step in "Quick GIF Optimizing" on page 693. Start by reducing the dimensions of the file (recall that the artwork had been designed twice as big as we wanted it) in the Image Size panel (nested behind the Color Table in the Save for Web dialog) **9a** or with ImageReady's Image > Image Size command.

For color reduction, use the frame with the most color complexity — the most colors and the most broken-up distribution of the color patches; in Catanimation, the colors don't vary much, but we used Frame 4 because it included the mouse and had more shading at the edges **9b**.

When you've optimized the file, previewed it in a browser, and decided it's ready, click the "Save" button in Photoshop's Save for Web dialog, or choose File > Save Optimized As in Image-Ready. In either program, choose Images Only to save the file as an animated GIF. *Wow*

Button Rollovers

FOR THE NAVIGATION BAR for a travel website, we wanted a low-tech look like the tabbed pages in a notebook. Layer-based rollover Styles would make the styling portable from one button to the others and to other buttons later on. Our button rollovers would have three states: Normal (unselected), Over (as the cursor moves over the button), and Selected (when the button is clicked and until another button is clicked). Selected is like Down, which responds to a click, except that the Down state ends immediately after the click, while Selected persists.

To visually simplify this exercise, we've rasterized a mock-up of all the elements except the buttons (the tabs) and flattened them into a *Background* with a yellow page. We added a layer holding the (rasterized) text that will appear on the buttons in an orange-red color. Both the yellow and the orange-red had been chosen from the web-safe palette.

We used ImageReady's Tab Rectangle tool 🔲 to draw one button and then copied that layer (Ctrl/⌘-J) twice to make the other two buttons. We double-clicked on each button layer's name and renamed it to match the text that would appear over it. Since ImageReady uses the layer names when it writes the code for the rollover buttons, we avoided using spaces or unusual characters that might be problematic in HTML.

ORIGINAL PHOTOS:
MATT TILGHMAN (ISTOCKPHOTO.COM)
SUSAN HELLER (SEAL)

The **Rollovers-Before.psd** file has three identical tab-shaped buttons, each on its own layer, stacked directly on top of one another. We drew one button as a gray Shape layer, rasterized it, and duplicated it (Ctrl/⌘-J) twice. The Layer Styles we would use to make the Normal, Over, and Selected states of the buttons would replace the gray.▼

YOU'LL FIND THE FILES
In 🌀 > Wow Project Files > Chapter 10 > Quick Rollovers

1 Spacing the Buttons

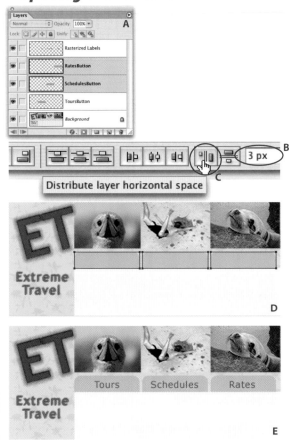

To follow along with our example, open the **Rollovers-Before.psd** file in ImageReady. Shift-click or Ctrl-click on the thumbnails in the Layers palette to target all the button layers **A**. Choose the Move tool ▶⊕, and in the Options bar, type 3 px (for the space between the buttons) in the box just to the right of the Align and Distribute buttons **B**. Next click on the "Distribute layer horizontal space" button **C**. The leftmost gray tab will stay where it is, and the other two will be automatically spaced with 3-pixel gaps between tabs **D**. (At this point, turn on visibility for the rasterized text layer, since text would be added at this point **E**.)

FIND OUT MORE

▼ Working with Shape
tools **page 433**

---

2 Starting a Rollover Style

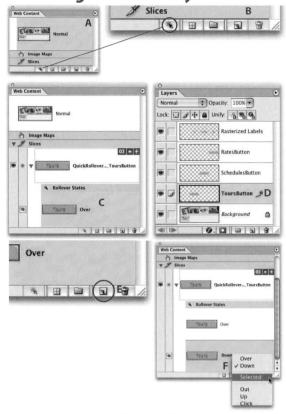

3 Matching Colors in ImageReady

To get ready to start building the rollover Style, target the "Tours" button in the Layers palette, then open the Web Content palette (Window > Web Content) and take a look. It shows an entry for the targeted layer in its Normal state, before any rollover capacity is built-in **A**. Click the "Create layer-based rollover" button ✳ at the bottom of the Web Content palette **B**. ImageReady will automatically add one rollover state — Over — to the Web Content palette **C** and will also add a Slice icon ✐ to the layer in the Layers palette; this shows that the content of this layer defines a layer-based slice **D**.

Add another rollover state by clicking the "Create rollover state" button ▣ at the bottom of the Web Content palette **E**. The next state in ImageReady's list of states (Down in this case) is automatically added to the button, but we want the Selected state instead. An easy way to swap a different state for one already in the palette is to right/Ctrl-click on the state's name in the Web Content palette, and then choose the state you want—in this case, Selected **F**.

Unlike Photoshop, ImageReady can't sample colors from open documents with the Eyedropper tool once the Color Picker is open. So it's a good idea to identify any colors from the background that you may want to match in your rollover Styles *before* you start creating the Styles, writing down the hexadecimal codes for these colors; you can even store one of the colors in the clipboard.

Using the Eyedropper ✐ with Point Sample chosen in the Options bar **A** so you get the exact color of the pixel you click on, sample the orange-red of the rasterized type on the tabs **B**, making this the Foreground color **C**. Then choose Edit > Copy Foreground Color as HTML to store the color in the clipboard **D**. (To be on the safe side, in case you need to use the clipboard for something else, also double-click the Foreground square in the Tools palette and when the Color Picker opens, find the hexadecimal code **E** and write it down.)

Use the Eyedropper ✐ again to click on the "paper yellow" **F** but this time don't copy the number to the clipboard. Instead, click the Foreground swatch in the Tools palette, find the hexadecimal code **G,** and write it down. Sample a blue from the background and write down its code also.

4 "Styling" the Normal State

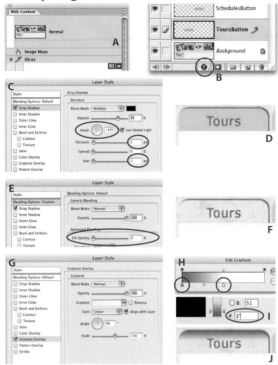

5 "Styling" the Over & Selected States

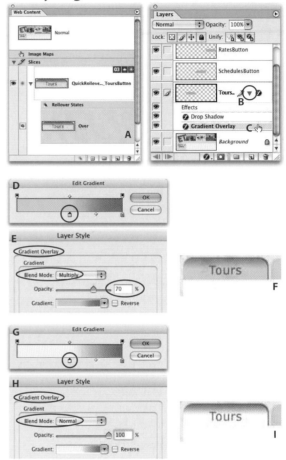

Now create a Style for the Normal state: In the Web Content palette, target the Normal state **A**. To outline the "notebook tab," click the "Add a layer style" button ⨍ at the bottom of the Layers palette **B**, and choose **Drop Shadow**. In the Drop Shadow panel **C** of the Layer Style dialog **C**, set the Angle to approximately match the shadow cast by the type in the background; we used −135°, setting the Distance at 2 px, Spread at 0%, and Size at 2 px **D**.

Choose **Blending Options** from the list at the left of the dialog box **E**; reduce **Fill Opacity** to 0 to remove the gray so the tab takes its color from the background **F**.

To further define the tab, choose **Gradient Overlay** from the list at the left. Leave the Angle set at 90° for a vertical gradient **G**, with Blend Mode set to Darken. Click the Gradient bar to open the Edit Gradient dialog and make the following changes **H**: Double-click the left color stop below the bar and choose white; to restrict the gradient to the top of the tab, drag the white stop halfway across the bar. Double-click the right stop, then double-click the hexadecimal number in the Color Picker, paste in the number you noted in step 3 for the orange-red (Ctrl/⌘-V; the pasted number may look incomplete **I**, but it will work fine). Click "OK" to close the dialog **J**.

The Style assigned to the Normal state is automatically assigned to the other states in the rollover also. Now change the Over state so the tab will signal the user that it's a button when the cursor rolls over it: Target the Over state in the Web Content palette **A**; if the list of effects in the Style isn't already showing in the Layers palette, twirl down the arrow for the layer **B**; double-click on Gradient Overlay entry **C** to open the Layer Style dialog to that effect. Click on the Gradient bar to reopen the Edit Gradient dialog **D**, and double-click on the white color stop to open the Color Picker. From there enter the hexadecimal code you noted at step 3 for the blue and click "OK." Darken mode will cover up the subtle background pattern, so switch to Multiply and then reduce the Opacity to 70% **E, F**.

Target the Selected state in the Web Content palette and change it by replacing the white in the Gradient Overlay with the background yellow (identified in step 3) **G**; change the Blend Mode to Normal **H, I**.

6 Previewing & Saving the Style

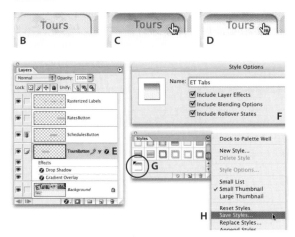

With your rollover Style completed, it's a good idea to use the Tools palette's Preview Document button 🖑 to check that you're happy with the rollover Style you've created **A**. With the cursor away from the button, the preview should show the button in the Normal state **B**. Move the cursor over the tab to view the Over state **C**, then click on the tab to see the Selected state **D**; when you move the cursor off the button, the Selected state should persist. If you're satisfied with the effects, click the 🖑 again to leave the preview.

Next save the rollover Style: First make sure the "styled" layer is targeted in the Layers palette **E**. Open the Styles palette (Window > Styles) and click the "Create new style" button 🔲 at the bottom of the palette. When the Style Options dialog box opens, make sure all three boxes are checked **F**, so that the effects, blending options, and rollover states will all be included in the Style. Name the new Style, and click "OK" to close the Style Options dialog box. The new Style will appear in the Styles palette, marked in the upper left corner to show that it's a rollover **G**. To ensure that the combined rollover Style will be permanently saved as part of a set of Styles, choose Save Styles from the Styles palette's ⓘ menu **H**.

7 "Styling" the Other Buttons

To add the new rollover Style to the other buttons, in the Layers palette simply target the layer for each button and then click on your saved rollover Style in the Styles palette. ImageReady will automatically create the layer-based slice for each button, add the same states, and apply the appropriate effects and blending options to each one.

8 Designating a Default Selected Button

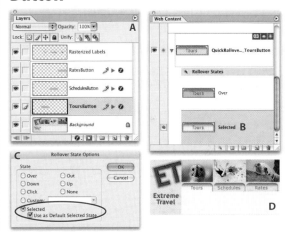

By default, all buttons will display the Normal state when the document is loaded into a web browser and is awaiting user interaction. But it's possible to display a button's Selected state instead of Normal. To encourage the user to start with the "Tours" button, target its layer in the Layers palette **A** and double-click its Selected state in the Web Content palette **B**; in the Rollover State Options dialog box **C**, choose Use as Default Selected State.

Preview again, with Preview Document 🖑 and with the Preview in Browser button next to it in the Tools palette, to make sure the set of buttons operates as you expect. The "Tours" button should be yellow to begin with **D**, and should remain yellow until you click one of the other buttons.

9 Optimizing the Buttons

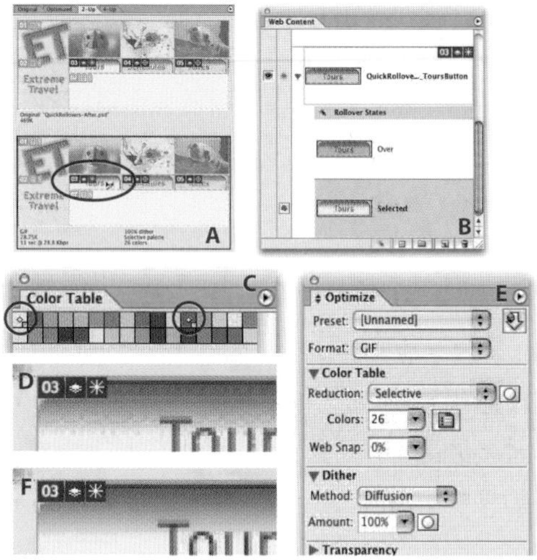

The final step is to optimize your buttons for the smallest file size that still looks good. If the Optimize palette isn't already open, choose Window > Optimize; click the tab for the 2-Up view so you can compare the Original as you develop the Optimized version. Choose the Slice Select tool and click on one of your buttons in the Optimized window **A**. In the Web Content palette, click on the state in which color is most critical, in this case the yellow "Selected" state **B** — we want to preserve the match with the background yellow and also preserve smooth transitions in the gradient.

In the **Color Table**, lock any colors that must be preserved ▼; we locked the background yellow and the orange-red **C**. In the Optimize palette, choose the **Gif 32 Dithered** Preset as a starting point, and increase Diffusion Dither to 100% to help prevent banding in the gradient. Since 32 colors produces a smooth gradient, try choosing 16 from the pop-out Colors list; artifacts are now plain to see **D**. Click in the Colors box and tap the ↑ key until the artifacts disappear (26 colors did the trick) **E**, **F**. In the Web Content palette, target each of the other states in turn to make sure the optimization works for them also.

Next choose **Save Settings** from the Optimize palette's menu and give your settings a distinctive name. If you save them in the default location, you can now select the next button with the Slice Select tool and apply your settings from the Optimize palette's Preset menu. Finally, preview your rollovers again in your browser, save the file in .psd format (File > Save As; compare **Rollovers-After.psd**), and then choose File > Save Optimized As, and choose HTML and Images to save everything needed for the buttons to operate (compare **Rollovers-Operational**).

MODIFYING A PRE-EXISTING STYLE

It's easy to create your layer-based rollover buttons from scratch when you want a fairly simple look, as in "Quick Rollover Styles." If you want a more complex look, however, such as a metallic, plastic, or glass button, or if you simply want a variant of any rollover Style you've already saved, you can speed up the process by beginning with an existing rollover Style. To modify a preset rollover Style, you'll need to open the Styles, Layers, and Web Content palettes.

1 Target a button layer by clicking its thumbnail in the Layers palette. In the Styles palette, click on the rollover Style you want to start with (here we used Wow Button 05; see page 767).

2 Change or add any states that you want in the Web Content palette; for instance, here Down is changed to Selected (one way is to double-click the "Down" entry to open the Rollover State Options dialog box, and choose Selected).

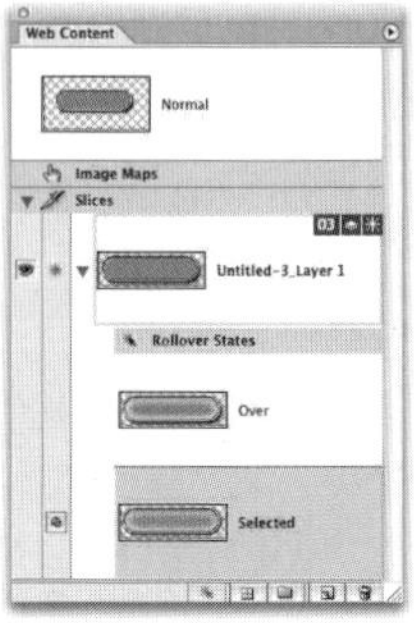

3 For each of the states in turn, target the state in the Web Content palette; in the Layers palette, double-click the for the layer to open the Layer Style dialog; make any changes you want in the effects for that state, ▼ and click "OK" to close the Layer Style dialog. Here the Color Overlay was changed for the Normal state, and both Color Overlay and Inner Glow were changed for the Over state.

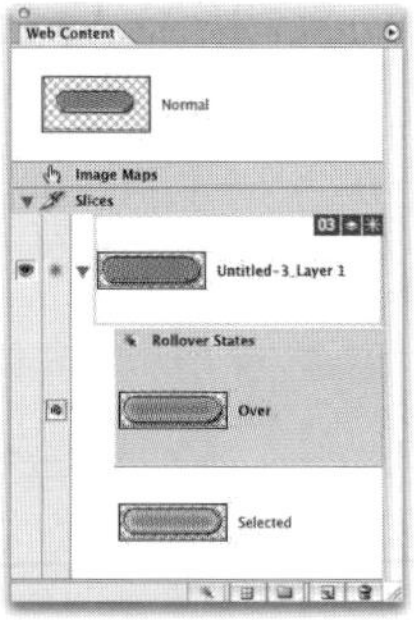

4 Now click the "Create new style" button at the bottom of the Styles palette, name your modified rollover Style, and click "OK" to save it.

FIND OUT MORE

▼ Locking colors **page 694**
▼ Effects used in Layer Styles **page 494**

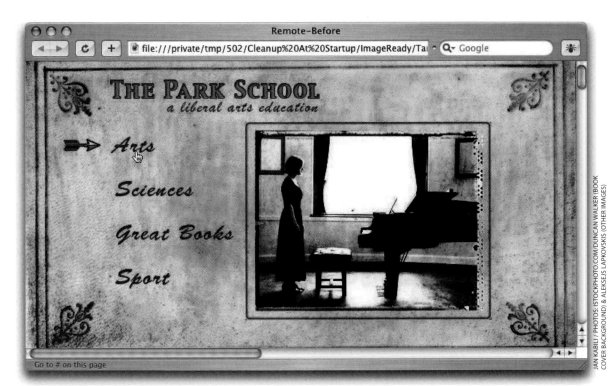

Creating Remote Rollovers

YOU'LL FIND THE FILES
In (wow) > Wow Project Files > Chapter 10 > Creating Remote Rollovers:
- Remote-Before.psd (to start)
- Remote-After.psd (to compare)
- Remote Output folder (to compare)

OPEN THESE IMAGEREADY PALETTES
from the Window menu:
- Tools • Layers • Web Content
- Optimize

OVERVIEW
In ImageReady, open a web page layout file • Slice each button & remote area separately • Program each button to trigger two remote events when a viewer mouses over the button • Optimize the slices • Save the optimized slices along with an HTML file that contains JavaScript to make the rollovers work

YOU CAN PROGRAM A BUTTON IN IMAGEREADY to trigger an event elsewhere on a web page when the cursor rolls over the button. Such a *remote rollover* is a great way to liven up the page and offer extra information about your navigation scheme in the form of graphics, images, or text. Photoshop expert Jan Kabili used remote rollovers in this web page layout to point to each text button as it becomes active, letting site visitors know that the cursor is on the button (an arrow appears next to the button as shown for the "Arts" button above). Another remote event is also triggered by the same rollover — the framed photo changes to show visitors where they will go from here if they click the button.

1 Designing the layout in Photoshop. Photoshop can't program rollovers; that needs to be done in ImageReady. But because Photoshop offers more options for designing the layout, Kabili started this page in Photoshop's File > New dialog box **1a**, where she set the page width to 760 pixels and the height to 410 pixels to leave room on an 800 x 600-pixel monitor for the scroll bars and tool bars of a typical web browser. She set the Mode to RGB Color and the Bit Depth to 8 bit. She clicked "Advanced" and chose Color Profile: sRGB IEC61966-2.1 to set the color of the file in Photoshop to resemble color in a typical web browser on a Windows computer.

1a

Starting the page layout in Photoshop's New dialog box

1b

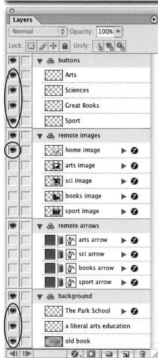

The **Remote Before.psd** file includes all the artwork needed for setting up the remote rollovers. Visibility of the individual artwork layers is set so the file looks as it will appear when it first loads in a site visitor's web browser. The background image, title, and subtitle are showing; all four buttons are visible; the "home Image" is showing; and no arrows appear.

Before you design a web page in Photoshop, you can gather some information about your target audience that will help you size the layout. Do your best to determine what platform, web browser, and monitor display size your audience is likely to use. Take a screen shot of the browser (check your operating system's Help files for a keyboard shortcut for taking a screen shot) and crop away the scroll bars, tool bars, and anything outside them, leaving just the browser window; one way is to use the Rectangular Marquee to select the area, and then choose Image > Crop. Now choose File > New and choose the name of your open cropped file at the very bottom of the Preset menu. This will automatically set your new file to the same size.

Open the **Remote-Before.psd** file in ImageReady and take a look at how it was constructed. In building the layout, Kabili placed each text button, remote image, and remote arrow on a separate layer so these items could be programmed independently. In ImageReady she collected the layers into groups (by Shift-selecting them and typing Ctrl/⌘-G) to make it easier to find them in the Layers palette **1b**.

Click the ▶ next to each layer group to see its contents.

- The four type layers in the "buttons" layer group were set in 30 pt Brush Script Medium. ▼ "The Park School" headline in the "background" layer group was set in 30 pt Capitals, and a Layer Style with two effects — an inner shadow and a stroke — was applied to that layer. ▼ The tag line "a liberal arts education" was set in 24 pt Brush Script MT. All of the type layers were rasterized (Layer > Rasterize > Type), so they'll look correct on your computer even if you don't have the fonts Kabili used.

- The "old book" layer in the "background" layer group is a photo of a book cover.

- The "remote images" layer group contains five layers of photographs, all in the same location. A rectangular selection of the "old book" layer, slightly bigger than the photographs, was copied onto a separate layer (Ctrl/⌘-J) five times, and in the Layers palette each copy was dragged into place beneath a photo layer. The photo layers were set to the Hard Light blend mode (except the "home image" layer, which was set to Screen for a lighter look). ▼ Each photo layer was merged with the layer below it (Ctrl/⌘-E for Layer > Merge Down). A Layer Style

FIND OUT MORE

▼ Using type
page 418

▼ Adding Layer
Styles **page 44**

▼ Blend modes
page 173

2a

2b

Choosing the
Slice tool

With all the layers in the "remote
images" layer group made visible,
you can see where to draw a slice
big enough to include the largest
of them.

2c

Drawing a slice with the Slice tool around the remote images. The slice you draw is called a **User
slice**. It's identified by a **blue slice number and
symbol** in its top left corner and by its **solid border**. ImageReady created some additional slices
to fill in the space around this User slice. These are
called **Auto slices** and are identified by **gray slice
numbers and symbols, dotted borders,** and a
faded appearance. Every time you create a new
slice, ImageReady redraws the Auto slices to fill in
the space that isn't occupied by User slices.

2d

The Web Content palette displays each slice as
it's created. You can manage all your slices and
rollover states in this palette.

with an Inner Shadow effect was applied to each of the resulting composite layers to frame its photo.

• The "remote arrows" layer group contains four Shape
layers,▼ each with the same arrow, made with the Custom
Shape tool 🐾 and the Arrow 1 shape.

Starting with this **Remote-Before.psd** file or a layout of your
own, follow along to create slices, then program remote rollovers inside the slices, optimize the slices, and generate individual files for each rollover state along with an HTML file
containing the JavaScript that makes the rollovers work.

2 Slicing the remote image area. Each of the areas involved
in the rollovers — the remote image area, the remote arrows,
and the text buttons themselves — must be sliced in preparation for generating rollover graphics. Slicing▼ can be done in
either Photoshop or ImageReady, but we'll slice this file in
ImageReady because we'll be working there anyway to program
the rollovers. (If you're working on a file of your own in
Photoshop, click the "Edit in ImageReady" button at the bottom of Photoshop's Tools palette to move to ImageReady.)

We'll set up our rollovers so that when a web-page visitor
mouses over one of the four text buttons, two things will happen in two locations *away* from the button (which is why we
call these *remote* rollovers). An arrow will appear to the left of
the text button, and the image will appear at the right that represents the destination to be reached by clicking the button.
We'll start by creating a slice around the remote area in which
the images will appear.

Select the Slice tool 🔪 in ImageReady's Tools palette **2a**. We're
using the Slice tool in this step, rather than layer-based slicing
(which we'll use shortly), because the remote images are not
all the same size. We want to encompass all of them in a single
slice so we don't end up with the unnecessary complication of
overlapping slices. It's more efficient to make all the remote
image layers visible and slice manually around the largest than
to try to estimate which is biggest for purposes of layer-based
slicing. In the Layers palette, make all five images in the group
visible **2b** by clicking to turn on the 👁 icon to the left of each
thumbnail. It doesn't matter which layer
is targeted, because the Slice tool will cut
through all layers in the file. In the working window, drag with the Slice tool to
draw a rectangular slice big enough to encompass the largest of the remote images,

FIND OUT MORE

▼ Using Shape layers
page 431

▼ What a slice is
page 687

3a

So that you can create layer-based slices around all the arrows at once, Shift-click to select all the "remote arrows" layers. Here visibility for all the layers has been turned on as well.

3b

Layer-based slicing automatically creates a slice around the content of each selected layer in the "remote arrows" layer group.

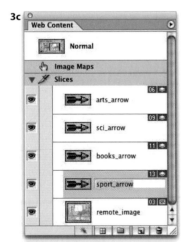

3c

The layer-based slices around the arrows automatically appear in the Web Content palette, where you can give them more manageable names.

being sure to include a little of the background image outside the frame also **2c**. To adjust the fit of the slice, drag on any of the slice borders. After creating the slice, Kabili clicked the 👁 icons of all the layers in this group except the "home image," so that "home image" was the only one left visible.

The slice you drew appears in the Web Content palette with a default name. To follow Kabili's well-thought-out naming scheme, double-click the slice's name in the Web Content palette and type **remote_image** to rename it **2d**. The Web Content palette will eventually list every slice and every rollover state in this file. Slice names become part of the file names ImageReady generates. To ensure that file names will be readable by all browsers, in naming slices use an underscore (Shift-hyphen) rather than a space, avoid unusual characters, and keep slice names short, because ImageReady truncates file names by default.

3 Slicing the remote arrows. When a site visitor mouses over any of the text buttons, in addition to the image on the right changing, an arrow will appear to the left of the button. As the viewer moves the cursor down the column of buttons, it may look like one arrow is moving down the list, but there are actually four identical arrows in this layout, each located next to one of the buttons. Rolling over a button will actually cause an arrow to take the place of a plain background graphic that contains no arrow. Each of the areas containing a remote arrow must be sliced (so we can turn it into a remote rollover at step 6). This time we'll use automatic layer-based slicing, rather than the Slice tool, as a quick way to create several slices at once.

Layer-based slicing can be used whenever you're slicing one or more items that are isolated on their own layers. Layer-based slicing is usually preferable to the Slice tool, especially if the items don't overlap, because it's quick and accurate, it can create many slices with one click, and it makes slices that will move with the artwork, so if you change the design after you slice, the slices will automatically adjust.

Select all the layers in the "remote arrows" layer group by clicking on the top layer ("arts arrow") and then Shift-clicking on the bottom layer ("sport arrow") **3a**. (To see the arrows in the working window, click in the visibility fields so the 👁 icons appear for all four layers, making them all visible.) Choose Layer > New Layer Based Slices from the menu bar. A blue slice boundary appears around each of the four arrows in the page layout, and the gray Auto slices are redrawn **3b**. The four new slices are listed in the Web Content palette. Type more new names

CUSTOMIZING LAYER-BASED SLICES

A wonderful feature of a layer-based slice is that it changes automatically if you change the layer's content. But if you want to move or reshape a layer-based slice *without* changing the layer content, first select the slice with the Slice Select tool ✄ and then choose Slices > Promote to User Slice.

4a

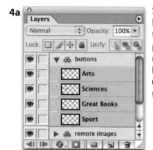

Selecting all the layers in the "buttons" layer group in preparation for making layer-based slices and Over states for the text buttons.

4b

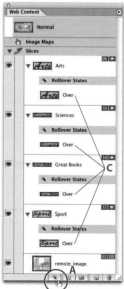

Clicking the "Create layer-based rollover" button ✳ at the bottom of the Web Content palette **A** creates a slice around the content of each selected layer **B** and also adds an "Over" state for each slice, as shown in the Web Content palette **C**.

---

for them **3c**, as you did in step 2. In the Layers palette, Kabili clicked the 👁 for each layer in the "remote arrows" layer group to make those layers invisible again.

4 Slicing the buttons and making them into rollovers. In this step you'll take layer-based slicing one step farther, automatically slicing each button *and* making it into a rollover in one easy step. First, customize ImageReady's default slice-naming rules, if you like, for more efficient slice naming (see "Better Slice Names" below). Each layer in the "buttons" layer group contains a single text button. In the Layers palette, select all four layers by clicking on the "Arts" layer and Shift-clicking on the "Sport" layer **4a**. Now click the "Create layer-based rollover" button ✳ at the bottom of the Web Content palette **4b**. This automatically creates a slice around each of the text buttons, along with an Over state for each of those slices, as reflected in the Web Content palette. Slicing is now complete.

CHANGING DEFAULT SLICE NAMES

To generate short slice names for layer-based slices, you can change ImageReady's slice-naming convention: Choose File > Output Settings > Slices. In the Output Settings dialog box, click in the first of the Default Slice Naming fields and choose "layer name or no." Choose "none" for the other fields. (To shortcut the slice-naming process even more, when you build a web-page layout file in Photoshop, name your *layers* using the underscore instead of the space character, and the underscore will automatically carry over to the slice name, saving you the trouble of substituting it manually.)

5 Confirming the Normal state. The rollovers you're about to program have a Normal state and an Over state. The **Normal** state represents the appearance of the page when it first loads into a web browser, before any of the rollovers is triggered. Click

5

Target the "Normal" state in the Web Content palette, and in the Layers palette make sure visibility is set as shown in figure **1b** (page 722). The image in the working window (shown above) now reflects the way the page will look when it first loads in a viewer's web browser (except the slice boundaries won't be visible).

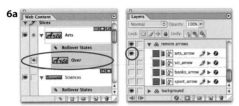

6a

To make the first remote rollover effect for the "Arts" button, select the "Over" state of the "Arts" slice in the Web Content palette. In the Layers palette, make the "arts arrow" layer visible.

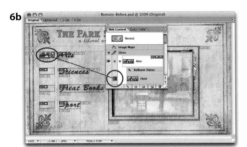

6b

Dragging a target line from the "Over" state of the "Arts" slice in the Web content palette to the "arts_arrow" slice in the working window makes this remote rollover effect functional.

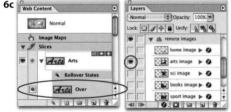

6c

To make the second remote rollover effect for the "Arts" button, select the "Over" state of the "Arts" slice in the Web Content palette. In the Layers palette turn on the 👁 icon for the "arts image" layer and make all other layers in the "remote images" group invisible.

6d

Dragging a target line from the "Over" state of the "Arts" slice in the Web Content palette to the "remote_image" slice in the working window turns on the change of photos, making the second rollover effect functional.

on the "Normal" state at the top of the Web Content palette, and then double-check that layer visibility is set as follows **5**: For the Normal state, make sure **visibility is off** (no 👁 icons) **for all the layers in the "remote arrows" group; visibility is off for all the "remote images" layers except "home image,"** and **visibility is on for all the "buttons" layers**. You should see in the working window all four of the text buttons, no arrows, and an image with white highlights (the "home image").

6 Programming the Over state of a button with remote rollover events. Because of the way the four text buttons were sliced in step 4, each one has an **Over** state, representing the way the page will look when a viewer moves the cursor over that button in a web browser. Now we'll program the remote events for the Over state for the first of the text buttons.

We want two remote events to occur when a viewer mouses over the "Arts" button — we want an arrow to appear next to the "Arts" button and we want the photo to change. Start by programming the "arts_arrow" slice to appear when the "Arts" button is in the Over state: In the Web Content palette, click on the "Over" state indented beneath the "Arts" slice. Go to the Layers palette, and click in the visibility field of the "arts arrow" layer to add an 👁 there **6a**. You'll see an arrow to the left of the "Arts" button in the working window. Now you'll connect the "Arts" button slice that triggers this rollover to the "arts_arrow" slice where this remote event occurs. In the Web Content palette, click on the spiral icon 🌀 to the left of the "Over" state for the "Arts" slice, and drag a target line to the "arts_arrow" slice in the working window **6b**.

Now program the second remote rollover event for the "Arts" button — the change of photographs. With the "Over" state of the "Arts" slice still selected in the Web Content palette, turn your attention to the Layers palette. In the "remote images" layer group, click in the visibility column for the "arts image" layer to add an 👁 icon, and also click to remove the 👁 from the "home image" layer **6c**. In the Web Content palette, click on the 🌀 for the "Over" state of the "Arts" slice again, and this time drag a target line to the "remote_images" slice in the working window **6d**.

7 Previewing the remote effects. Now preview the remote rollover effects in ImageReady to make sure they're working. Click the "Toggle Slices Visibility" button 🔲 near the bottom of the Tools palette to hide the slice outlines so you can get a

Moving the cursor over the "Arts" button brings up the arrow and the "arts image" photo.

Previewing the rollovers for the "Sciences," "Great Books," and "Sport" buttons

All the slices selected at once for optimizing

better look at the image. Next click the "Preview Document" button 🖑 (also near the bottom of the palette), and move your mouse over the "Arts" button. An arrow will appear to the left of the button and a different, larger and darker photo will replace the "home image" **7**. Be sure to click the "Preview Document" button 🖑 again to exit preview mode. If either of the rollover effects didn't work, choose Slices > Delete All, and go back to step 2. This may seem daunting, but it's often faster to start over than to try to guess where the mistake was.

8 Programming the other buttons. Repeat steps 6 and 7 on the "Sciences" button. In brief:

A In the Web Content palette, select the "Over" state of the "Sciences" slice.

B In the Layers palette, make the "sci arrow" layer visible and all other layers in the "remote arrow" layer group invisible.

C Drag a target line from the ⊚ for the "Over" state of the "Sciences" slice in the Web Content palette to the "sci_arrow" slice in the working window.

D In the Layers palette, make the "sci image" layer visible and all other layers in the "remote images" group invisible.

E Drag a target line from the ⊚ for the "Over" state of the "Sciences" slice in the Web Content palette to the "sci_image" slice in the working window.

F If necessary, click the "Toggle Slices Visibility" button 🔲 to turn off the slice outlines. Click the "Preview Document" button 🖑 in the Tools palette.

G Move your mouse over the "Sciences" text button to preview. An arrow will appear next to the "Sciences" button and a new photo will appear. Click the "Preview Document" button 🖑 again to exit preview mode.

Repeat the process for the "Great Books" and "Sport" buttons **8**.

9 Optimizing the slices. The next step is to optimize the slices to make them as small in file size as possible (for quick downloading) while keeping them looking good. JPEG is an appropriate format for the slices of this image-based page.▼ We want all of the photo, arrow, and button slices to blend seamlessly with the book cover photo, so they look like a single image rather than a subtle mosaic. To ensure seamless blending, all the slices are optimized to the same settings, in case different JPEG settings would create a different appearance from slice to slice.

FIND OUT MORE

▼ Choosing a format for web graphics
page 682

9b

The Optimize settings for The Park School web page; compare file size before and after optimizing in the lower left corner of each window in **9a**.

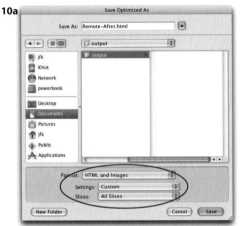

10a

Saving the HTML and image files needed for the page to work in a browser

10b

The image files created from the slices. Each file name, with the exception of the numbered files made from Auto slices, is a combination of slice name, trigger name, and rollover state.

Start by clicking on the 2-up or 4-up tab in the working window. Choose the Slice Selection tool ⌐ in the Tools palette. To begin optimizing, you could choose any of the following options, depending on the layout you were working with. Read all three choices to understand the selection options, and then carry out the third option as the most practical for this file:

- **To choose one slice to optimize**, select the slice by clicking it in the working window or the Web Content palette.

- To save time and **to provide the same optimization for similar slices**, you can select them together for optimizing by Shift-clicking them in the working window or the Web Content palette and choosing **Select > Link Slices for Optimizing** from the menu bar. (The gray Auto slices are automatically linked, so optimizing one of them applies the same settings to all.)

- **To optimize all the slices** together **9a**, choose Select > All Slices from the menu bar.

Next, in the Optimize palette **9b** set the Format to JPEG and experiment with Quality settings; Kabili chose Medium Quality, leaving Amount set at 30. In the Options section of the panel, she turned off the Progressive option to save file size. She turned off Preserve ICC Profile because including the profile adds to file size, and because most web browsers can't read an ICC Profile anyway. She turned off Add Metadata, another option for minimizing file size when including this data isn't important.

10 Saving. Choose File > Save Optimized As. In the Save Optimized As dialog box **10a**, click the "New Folder" button. Near the bottom of the dialog box, choose **HTML and Images** from the "Save as type" menu (Windows) or the Format menu (Mac); leave Slices set to **All Slices**; and click the "Save" button. ImageReady saves JPEG files from your slices, including multiple rollover graphics from the slices involved in the rollovers **10b**. It also produces an HTML file that contains JavaScript to make the rollovers function. You can bring any or all of these files into a site-building program for inclusion in a web site.

The last step is to choose File > Save to save the PSD source file with all of the slicing information you added to it. You'll be able to return to this source file if you ever want to make changes to your page layout or use it as a starting point for a related page.

The he thumbnails produced by Photoshop's Web Photo Gallery▼ are miniature versions of the artwork files themselves. But you can customize them by opening the files in the Thumbnails folder that's generated by the Web Photo Gallery command and making changes. When **Jack Davis** used Web Photo Gallery to make his interactive ***Digital Paintings Gallery***, the original thumbnails varied in proportions (as shown at the right), but by default all had either a height or a width of 75 pixels.

To make square thumbnails, Davis opened each of the files in the Thumbnails folder and changed its canvas size to 75 x 75 pixels (Image > Canvas Size). Then he made a new close-up square image for each painting by Shift-dragging with the Rectangular Marquee to select from the original (large) image and copying (Ctrl/⌘-C). Finally he pasted the copied square into the associated thumbnail file (Ctrl/⌘-V) and reduced its size if necessary to fit the Canvas (one way is to type Ctrl/⌘-T and Shift-drag a corner handle inward). Then he flattened the file (Ctrl/⌘-E) and saved it (Ctrl/⌘-S)

AUTOMATING

To automate a process that you have to repeat for many files (such as changing the Canvas Size of the thumbnails in a Web Photo Gallery), record an Action▼ as you operate on the first file. Then apply the Action to the entire folder of files by using the File > Automate > Batch command.▼

FIND OUT MORE

▼ Web Photo Gallery **page 691**
▼ Recording an Action **page 112**
▼ The Batch command **page 114**

Awakened at two o'clock in the morning with an inspiration for the *animated logo for the Freedom Fries Art Collective*, **Sharon Steuer** raided the refrigerator and took a Claymation-like approach. Like Claymation, her process involved setting up the elements of the scene, then rearranging them to make each new frame. But instead of photographing the scene anew for each frame, she made only one photo and did the rest of the arranging in Photoshop CS2 using the Animation palette and Smart objects.

Steuer started by placing the three french fries to make the "F" logo on a white background and photograph-

ing them with a digital camera. In Photoshop she opened a new document (File > New) in RGB color at 640 by 480 pixels with a black *Background*.

After saving a copy of her intact photo (File > Save As, choosing the "As a Copy" option), she used the Magic Wand ✴ with Contiguous turned off in the Options bar to click on the background and thus select all the white in the image. Switching to Quick Mask mode (using the ◙ button near the bottom of the Tools palette) she tidied up the selection with the Brush and black and white paint; then she switched back to Standard mode ◙ and pressed the Backspace/Delete key. This left the three fries on a transparent layer. She selected all (Ctrl/⌘-A),

copied (Ctrl/⌘-C), then clicked in the working window of the black document, and pasted (Ctrl/⌘-V). To scale the pasted-in "F" to the size she wanted **A**, she used the Free Transform command (Ctrl/⌘-T), Shift-dragging on a corner of the Transform frame.

Steuer then made a loose selection of one of the fries with the Lasso tool ⟲ and copied it to a separate layer (Ctrl/⌘-J). She repeated the selecting and copying process for a second french fry **B**.

She turned each of the three fries layers into a Smart Object by clicking its thumbnail in the Layers palette to target the layer and choosing Layer >

Smart Objects > Group Into New Smart Object. This Smart Object "packaging" would protect the fries from deteriorating as she repeatedly rotated them into new positions to make the frames of the animation.

Steuer turned off visibility for the "F" layer, by clicking its 👁 icon in the Layers palette. Now it was time for the Claymation-like process: With the Auto Select Layer and Show Transform Controls options turned on in the Options bar **C**, she dragged inside the Transform frame with the Move tool ▶⊕ to change the position of each french fry and dragged the double-headed curved-arrow cursor outside the frame to rotate it as needed **D**, pressing the Enter key to complete the transformation. When she had lined up all the fries in the starting position for the first frame of the animation, she opened the Animation palette (Window > Animation), and the starting image appeared in Frame 1. She added another frame by clicking the "Duplicates selected frame" button 🔲 at the bottom of the palette, and moved and transformed each of the Smart Objects again to make the arrangement she wanted for the second frame.

She continued adding frames and re-arranging fries. To add the web site address to the last frame, she first opened the Animation palette's menu by clicking the palette's ⊙ button, and turned off the "New Layer Visible in All Frames" option **E**, so the text she was about to add would appear only in the currently targeted last frame. Then she chose the Type tool **T**, added the address, and converted the type to pixels (Layer > Rasterize >Type).

Steuer had designed the animation assuming the same uniform timing for all the frames. After setting the Animation palette's looping options to Once (in the lower left corner) she previewed the animation by clicking the palette's Play button ▶. To set the timing, she selected all the frames by clicking the starting frame and then Shift-clicking the end frame. She clicked the tiny triangle to the right of the frame delay value at the bottom of one of the frames, chose Other from the pop-out menu, and entered a value of 0.15 sec in the Set Delay field.

To export the animation in Quick-Time format, Steuer had to move the file to ImageReady, so she again saved a copy of her file to preserve its Smart Objects, which wouldn't translate to ImageReady; then she clicked the "Edit in ImageReady" button at the very bottom of Photoshop's Tools palette. In ImageReady she previewed the animation in a browser by clicking the "Preview in [browser]" button near the bottom of the Tools palette, to make sure the timing was right. Then she chose File > Export > Original Document, chose QuickTime from the Format menu at the bottom of the Export Original dialog box, and clicked the "Save" button. In the Compression Settings dialog box **F** she left the format at the default Photo-JPEG, accepted the default Best Depth and Medium Quality settings, and clicked "OK."

Jeff Jacoby used Apple Final Cut Pro to incorporate the QuickTime animation with voice-over, music, and other video, into a QuickTime video trailer for *The Opening Act,* the first event of the FFAC in October of 2005. The final video can be seen at www.freedomfriesart.org if you click on The Opening Act and then choose to view the trailer (or go directly to www.freedomfriesart.org/pages/viewtrailer.html).

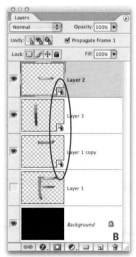

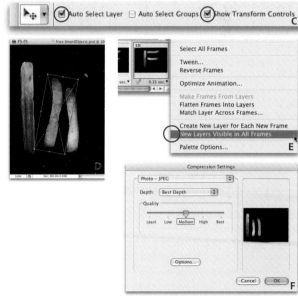

Steve Conley began the artwork for these two episodes of his *Astounding Space Thrills* comic with a hand-drawn sketch that he scanned. He traced the sketch to make black-on-transparent "linework," then added a new layer — his first color layer — by clicking the "Create a new layer" button at the bottom of the Layers palette. Adding more layers — a separate layer for each main color — Conley dragged the linework above them all in the Layers palette. Then with the linework layer active, he selected each area to color, using either the Magic Wand (if the area he wanted to select was completely enclosed by black linework) or the Polygonal Lasso. When using the Polygonal Lasso, he held down the Alt/Option key so he could switch back and forth between Polygonal and normal Lasso operation. He drew the selection boundary so that it overlapped the black, to make sure there would be no gaps between the black lines and

the color fill, thus "trapping" the color. When using the Magic Wand, he turned on Contiguous in the Options bar (to select only the enclosed area he clicked on). He turned off Anti-aliased (to make a selection that would fill solidly with color) and also turned off Use All Layers (to make the selection based on the visible linework layer only). He expanded each Magic Wand selection by 1 pixel (Select > Modify > Expand) before filling it with color, again to trap the color fill under the linework.

When a selection had been made, Conley activated a color layer by clicking its name in the Layers palette, and filled the selection with the Edit > Fill command, or simply painted inside the selection with the Brush and a hard-edged brush tip.

Once the main color fills were in place, Conley added details, first locking transparency (the button at the top of the Layers palette) to create a "frisket" to keep his painting

"inside the lines." He then painted with the Brush, occasionally with the Airbrush option turned on in the Options bar.

The asteroids and landscape texture in the artwork for Episode 229 were created in Bryce, then opened in Photoshop, and dragged into the

main comic file. Conley made the Bryce image in each of these layers a little larger than the area he wanted it to fill, and used the color and linework layers higher in the stack to mask the edges.

Conley created his comic strip artwork large enough to reproduce in print, and then reduced its size for display on the web, scaling the artwork (this can be done with the Image > Image Size command or in the Image Size panel in Photoshop CS2's Save for Web dialog box). He used 468 pixels, a standard banner width on the web, since many websites are designed to accommodate artwork of that size. Reducing the Width to 468 pixels also automatically scaled the Height of the artwork to 190 pixels. He designed the strip to be 250 pixels tall, including the title and ad above the artwork and the buttons below, because at that size it could be seen without scrolling, even on small screens.

Speech balloons were then added. (In Photoshop you can save frequently used shapes as Custom Shape presets, which can then be applied with the Custom Shape tool 🎨.) The balloon layer's Opacity was reduced to 80% to allow the artwork to show through. Conley then added the lettering, using a separate layer for the type in each balloon. He used fonts of his own design as well as others designed especially for comics. Conley did his lettering after the artwork had been reduced to its final dimensions. This meant lettering twice, once for print and once for the web, but he felt the increase in quality made the extra effort worthwhile.

The buttons at the bottom of the comic strip were mapped to URLs using ImageReady's image map function.

COMIC FONTS

A good source for professionally designed comic book fonts is **www.comicbookfonts.com**.

Before posting his comic strip on the web, Conley reduced each strip to 45K or less for quick downloading. When he got the file size well under 45K by reducing the number of colors for one of the optimized views, he used another of the four views to experiment with Diffusion Dither, moving the Dither slider to see if he could improve the color without making the file bigger than 45K.

TARGETING A FILE SIZE

The Optimize to File Size command from the ▶ menu in the Optimize panel of Photoshop's Save for Web dialog or Image-Ready's Optimize palette allows you to choose a target file size. If you work in the 4-Up window, choosing the same target file size for each of the optimized versions, you can compare three combinations of Optimize and Color Table settings to see which produces the best results at your target size.

Appendixes

Appendix A: Filter Demos

YOU'LL FIND THE FILE
in (wow) > Wow Project Files > Appendixes
> Filter Demo-Before.psd (to start)

The filters shown on these pages can be chosen from the list in the lower part of Photoshop CS/CS2's Filter menu.

Many of the filters shown on these pages can also be chosen from the combined alphabetical list that pops up when you choose Filter > Filter Gallery and click on the filter name under the "OK" and "Cancel" buttons on the right-hand side of the Filter Gallery.

Note: If you find that this list isn't available in the Filter Gallery, you can make it accessible by clicking the "New effect Layer" button 🔲 in the bottom right corner of the dialog box.

THIS "CATALOG" demonstrates most of the filters that Adobe supplies with Photoshop. (Not included are the "megafilters" from the top of the Filter menu.) The filters shown are applied to the photo and drawing above. The drawing was made by creating paths with the Pen tool, stroking them with the Brush on a transparent layer, and adding a Layer Style consisting of a white Outer Glow. This drawing layer was stacked over a scan of wood in the layer below and the file was flattened.

The filters in this catalog follow the grouping and order of the Filter menu. Many of the filters are also available by choosing Filter > Filter Gallery and selecting from the alphabetical list (shown lower left) in the Filter Gallery dialog box.

When settings were altered from the default for effect, they are listed in the order they appear in the filter's dialog box. If the default settings were used, no values are shown.

The sample image on which the filters were run is 408 pixels square. Many of the filter settings are in pixel units, so to evaluate the effect of a setting, you have to relate the setting (not exactly but generally) to the size of the image. For an image whose dimensions are approximately twice as big as our sample (800 by 800 pixels, for instance), you might need a setting of 40 pixels to get the same effect that a 20-pixel setting produces in the sample.

Artistic

The Artistic filters are available through Photoshop's Filter Gallery (indicated here by "FG"). Most of the Artistic filters simulate traditional art media. But the Plastic Wrap filter provides highlights and shadows that can add dimension and a slick surface texture.

8 Bits/Channel mode only

Colored Pencil   FG

Cutout   FG

Dry Brush   FG

Film Grain   FG

Fresco   FG

Neon Glow   FG

Paint Daubs   FG

Palette Knife   FG

Plastic Wrap   FG

Poster Edges   FG

Rough Pastels   FG

Artistic (continued)

Smudge Stick   FG

Sponge   FG

Underpainting   FG

Watercolor   FG

NOT ALL FILTERS WORK IN ALL COLOR MODES

If you need to produce your Photoshop file in CMYK, Grayscale, or In-dexed Color for the output process you'll use to publish it, it's still a good idea to do your creative work in RGB mode and then make the color mode conversion afterwards. One reason is that all of Photoshop's filters can be run in RGB mode, but in other color modes the choice narrows dramatically. For instance, Lens Flare and Lighting Effects work only in RGB mode. **In CMYK mode you lose the Filter Gallery** and all the individual filters in it! And in CS2 you also lose the Vanishing Point "superfilter."

Blur

New to CS and CS2 are Average, for filling a selected area with a single "average" color; Lens Blur, for camera depth-of-field effects; Box Blur and Shape Blur, for special effects; and Surface Blur, for smoothing out small differences in tone or color without blurring the image overall.

8 & 16 Bits/Channel, except as noted

Average (32 Bits also)

Blur

Blur More

Box Blur (20) (Photoshop only; 32 Bits also)

Gaussian Blur (10)

Blur (continued)

Lens Blur (Photoshop only)

Motion Blur (45/30) (32 Bits/Channel also)

Radial Blur (Spin/10) (32 Bits/Channel also)

TESTING A BLUR

For the Radial Blur filter use a Quality setting of Draft (quick but rough) to experiment with the Amount and the blur center; then undo (Ctrl/⌘-Z) and use Good (or on a very large image, Best) for the final effect.

Equivalent settings for Smart Blur are Low, Medium, and High.

SHAPE BLUR "STARS"

The Shape Blur filter makes (and blurs) a pattern in areas of high contrast; the pattern depends on the shape you choose in the Shape Blur dialog box. We started each of the five examples below with a white dot (made with the Brush tool 🖌 and Adobe's "Hard Round 19 pixels" brush tip) on a black back-ground. We individually selected and blurred each dot (Filter > Blur > Shape Blur), then added a Levels Adjustment layer to brighten the results.

Stars were made with the following shapes: Top row — Waves (from Nature, Radius 15), Sun 2 (from Nature, Radius 20), Snowflake 3 (from Nature, Radius 20); bottom row — Grid (from Tiles, Radius 15), Tile 3 (from Tiles, Radius 15).

Radial Blur (Zoom/20) (32 Bits/Channel also)

Shape Blur (10/ Tiles: Tile 3) (32 Bits/Ch. also)

Smart Blur (3/25/Normal) (8 Bits only)

Smart Blur (3/25 Edge Only) (8 Bits only)

Surface Blur (15/15) (Photoshop only;
32 Bits/Channel also)

Surface Blur (15/35) (Photoshop only;
32 Bits/Channel also)

Brush Strokes

The Brush Strokes filters are all available through the Filter Gallery (indicated here by "FG"), where their effects can be combined with other filters. The Brush Strokes filters simulate different ways of applying paint.

8 Bits/Channel mode only

Accented Edges   FG

Angled Strokes   FG

Crosshatch   FG

Dark Strokes   FG

Ink Outlines   FG

Spatter   FG

Sprayed Strokes   FG

Sumi-e   FG

RECORDING FILTER SETTINGS

Coming up with the right filter settings or the right combination of filters for a special effect can involve a lot of trial and error, and the steps and settings are easily forgotten. To avoid having to do the work over:

• Some of Photoshop's filters, especially newer ones, have "Save" buttons in their dialog boxes, so you can save your settings. Giving the settings file a descriptive name will help you find it later.

• If you used the Filter Gallery, you can save your settings in an Action after the fact and play it back on other files (see page 260).

• For filters outside the Filter Gallery and without a "Save" button, keeping the Edit History log turned on will at least record the settings with the file (in the Preferences > General panel, check the History Log box, and choose Detailed from the Edit Log Items menu, to record as many of the filter settings as possible). Reading the Log for a file (choose File > File Info and click on History) can help you construct an Action for the effect so you can create that effect again. ▼

FIND OUT MORE

▼ Creating Actions **page 110**

Distort

With the exception of Lens Correction, the Distort filters are designed to add special effects and textures to an image. The Displace filter "bends" the image based on the light and dark areas in a *displacement map* (a separate image that acts like the texture of a surface to which the image is applied). When the displacement occurs, some edge pixels may be pulled inward from an edge, leaving a gap, and others may be pushed off the opposite edge. You can specify that the filter should fill the gap with the pixels pushed off the opposite side (Wrap), or that the pixels closest to the edge should be stretched to fill the gap (Repeat Edge Pixels). A few of the Distort filters (marked here with "FG") appear in the Filter Gallery.

CS2's Lens Correction filter (found in Photoshop only, not Image-Ready) typically removes distortion but can also be used to add it for special effects.

8 Bits/Channel mode, except as noted

Diffuse Glow   FG

Displace (Honeycomb 10/Repeat Edge Pixels)

Displace (Random Strokes 25/Wrap)

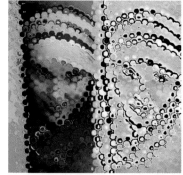

Displace (Snake Skin /Repeat Edge Pixels)

Glass (Frosted)   FG

Glass (Blocks)   FG

Lens Correction (Chromatic Aberration –100/+100; Scale 70; Edge Extension) (Photoshop only; 16 Bits/Channel also)

Lens Correction (Vertical Perspective +50) (Photoshop only; 16 Bits/Channel also)

Distort (continued)

Ocean Ripple   FG

Pinch (100%)

Pinch (–100%)

Polar Coordinates (Polar to Rectangular)

Polar Coordinates (Rectangular to Polar)

Ripple

Shear

Spherize (100%/Normal)

Spherize (–100%/Normal)

Twirl

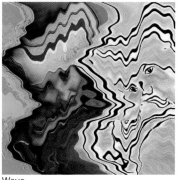

Wave

Zigzag (Pond Ripples)

Noise

The Add Noise filter can be used to "roughen" the texture of an image, and the other four Noise filters (Despeckle, Dust & Scratches, Median, and Reduce Noise) are used for smoothing, or eliminating irregularities. Reduce Noise is useful for eliminating digital camera noise, as well as film grain and JPEG artifact.   8 & 16 Bits/Channel

Add Noise (Gaussian/50%/Monochromatic)

Add Noise (Uniform/50%)

Despeckle

Dust & Scratches (5/25)

Median (5)

Reduce Noise (10/0)

REMOVING CHANNEL NOISE

The Reduce Noise filter can operate on individual color channels. So, for instance, if the Blue channel is noisy and the Green channel shows most of the contrast for fine detail, the noise can be reduced by filtering the Blue channel without blurring the details in the Green channel. This can improve the color image overall or improve the Blue channel as a source for converting color to black-and-white.▼

Clicking the "Advanced" button and choosing the Per Channel panel in the Reduce Noise dialog box allows you to reduce noise in individual channels, as shown here for the Blue channel. A detail of the Blue channel before reducing noise is shown at the right for comparison.

FIND OUT MORE

▼ Converting from color to black & white **page 212**

Pixelate

Most of the Pixelate filters turn an image into a pattern consisting of spots of flat color. For all but Facet and Fragment, you can control the size of the spots, producing very different effects depending on the size settings.

8 Bits/Channel only

Color Halftone

Crystallize (10)

Facet

Fragment

Mezzotint (Coarse Dots)

Mezzotint (Medium Lines)

Mosaic

Pointillize (white Background color)

NAVIGATING FILTER DIALOGS

A typical Photoshop filter interface includes a preview box with enlarged previews, one or more sliders and number fields for setting the filter's parameters, zooming buttons (the "+" and "−" under the preview), and the ability to move a different part of the image into the preview by simply dragging in the preview window (the Hand tool cursor appears automatically) or by clicking a particular place in the working window.

REAPPLYING A FILTER

To repeat the last filter you used, with exactly the same settings as before, type **Ctrl/⌘-F**.

To choose the last filter applied, but with the dialog box open so you can change the settings if you like, press **Ctrl-Alt-F** (Windows) or ⌘-**Option-F** (Mac).

These shortcuts work for individual filters and for combinations set up in the Filter Gallery.

Render

The Render filters create texture or "atmosphere." Two of them act independently of the color in the image: Clouds creates a sky, and Fibers can create a range of fibrous textures.

In addition to the filters that automatically appear in the Render menu, there are two more — 3D Transform and Texture Fill — that you can install: Find the filters in the Plug-Ins folder on the Adobe Photoshop CD-ROM by looking inside the Optional Plug-Ins folder, and within that in the Filters folder. Copy the two files into the Filters folder that was set up when you installed Photoshop (it's inside the Plug-Ins folder).

Texture Fill can be used to fill an alpha channel with a pattern; the channel can then be used with the Lighting Effects filter to create a texture.

The 3D Transform filter can be useful for applying graphics or images to cylindrical shapes in Photoshop CS. A step-by-step tutorial for using 3D Transform, "Applying a Logo with 3D Transform," appears as a printable PDF in Wow Project Files > Appendix on the Wow DVD-ROM. (wow)

8 Bits/Channel, except as noted

Clouds

Difference Clouds

Lens Flare (16 & 32 Bits/Channel also)

Lighting Effects (Soft Direct Lights: both white)

Lighting Effects (Flashlight)

BLUE SKY

When you run the Clouds filter, it produces clouds in the Background color and "sky" in the Foreground color. Using blue as Foreground and white as Background creates a realistic-looking sky.

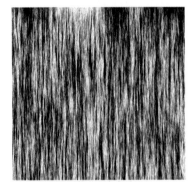

Fibers (16 Bits/Channel also)

Lighting Effects (Default)

Lighting Effects (Flashlight: Texture Ch. Green)

Sharpen

Although there are four Sharpen filters (five in CS2), the ones you'll use most are Unsharp Mask and in CS2 Smart Sharpen, because they are the only ones that let you vary the parameters of the effect. Smart Sharpen can be more complicated to apply than Unsharp Mask, but it lets you control the amount of sharpening in the highlights and shadows. See page 327 for a comparison of Unsharp Mask and Smart Sharpen.

8 & 16 Bits/Channel, except as noted

SPECIAL-EFFECTS SHARPENING

Oversharpening can produce artistic effects. For example, convert to Lab mode (Image > Mode > Lab Color), click the Lightness

channel's name in the Channels palette, and run Unsharp Mask (Amount 500, Radius 20, threshold 0).

Sketch

The Sketch filters, available through the Filter Gallery, include a number of artistic effects. Some of them imitate drawing methods, while others simulate various dimensional media. The Sketch filters use the current Foreground and Background colors. The effects shown here were produced using black and white.

8 Bits/Channel mode only

Sharpen

Sharpen More

Unsharp Mask (32 Bits/Channel also)

Bas Relief   FG

Sharpen Edges

Smart Sharpen (Sharpen 50, 1.0)

OTHER FILTERS FOR SHARPENING

With Sharpen filters it's sometimes difficult to sharpen just the edges without also sharpening areas that you want left smooth, such as the fine texture of skin. Two other filters that can be used for sharpening edges without sharpening texture details are Filter > Other > High Pass (see page 328) and Filter > Stylize > Emboss (page 379).

Chalk & Charcoal   FG

Charcoal FG	Chrome FG	Conté Crayon FG
Graphic Pen FG	Halftone Pattern (Dot) FG	Note Paper FG
Photocopy FG	Plaster FG	Reticulation FG
Stamp FG	Torn Edges FG	Water Paper FG

Stylize

Among the Stylize filters you'll find a diverse collection of edge treatments and other special effects. One of the Stylize filters (Glowing Edges) appears in the Filter Gallery.

8 Bits/Channel, except as noted

Diffuse

Emboss (16 Bits/Channel also)

Extrude (Blocks)

Extrude (Pyramids)

Find Edges (16 Bits/Channel also)

Glowing Edges   FG

Solarize (16 Bits/Channel also)

Tiles

Trace Contour (50/Upper)

Wind (Wind)

NEUTRAL EMBOSSING

To eliminate the color from an image that has been treated with the Emboss filter, keeping

only the highlights and shadows, use Image > Adjustments > Desaturate.

Texture

Most of the Texture filters create the illusion that the image has been applied to an uneven surface. But Stained Glass remakes the image into polygons, each filled with a single color. All of the Texture filters can be found in the Filter Gallery (FG).

8 Bits/Channel mode only

Craquelure   FG

Grain (Sprinkles)   FG

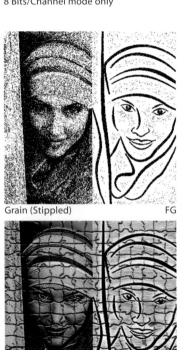
Grain (Stippled)   FG

Grain (Vertical)   FG

Grain (Speckle)   FG

Mosaic Tiles (25/2/4)   FG

Patchwork   FG

Stained Glass (3/1/1)   FG

Texturizer (Brick)   FG

Texturizer (Canvas)   FG

Texturizer (Sandstone)   FG

Video

The De-Interlace filter (not shown here but see page 140) "repairs" images captured on video, replacing either the odd or the even interlaced lines in a way that smooths the image. The other Video filter, NTSC Colors, prevents color "bleed" by restricting colors in the image to those acceptable for television.

8, 16 & 32 Bits/Channel

NTSC Colors

Other

The Other submenu houses the eclectic collection of filters shown here. The Maximum and Minimum filters can be used to thin and thicken line art, respectively.

8 & 16 Bits/Channel, except as noted

Custom (see below)

High Pass (10) (also 32 Bits/Channel)

Maximum (1)

Minimum (1)

Offset (100/100/Wrap Around) (also 32 Bits/Channel)

CUSTOM-MADE FILTERS

It's possible to design your own filters with the Custom interface. When you get an effect you like, you can save it so you can load it later and use it again.

Digimarc

Choosing Filter > Digimarc > Embed Watermark opens a dialog box that lets you embed a recognizable noise pattern in your image, to deter unauthorized use of your work.

8 Bits/Channel mode only

Embed Watermark (4)

Bert Monroy Inserts His Own "Watermark"

WITH THE DIGIMARC FILTER you can embed a registered noise pattern designed to be recognizable, even after changes are made to the file. The filter also identifies the file as watermarked in this way. The watermarking delivers two messages to someone who might consider using your image without checking with you first: (1) you don't want that to happen and (2) if it does happen, you will be able to detect and prove it. But some artists, Bert Monroy among them, feel that a watermark durable enough to survive changes made to the file by an unauthorized user is also strong enough to interfere with the integrity of the image. Bert often includes a copyright notice in the body of his work. But he also inserts a "type ID" in a different spot in each published copy of an image. If he later sees the image used without permission, he can tell where the file came from. The mark is small and unobtrusive — Bert designs it to fit right into the image in a way that makes it virtually invisible unless you're searching for it.

Shown here in a detail enlarged to 200% of the original document size, is Bert Monroy's "type ID" for the *Spenger's* painting that appears in the "Gallery" on page 404 of this book.

Appendix B:
Wow Layer Styles

PHOTO: BEVERLY GOWARD

The **Wow Styles** for photos were designed with print images in mind, at 225 pixels/inch. In our catalog we've applied them to images that are 1000 pixels in their greater dimension (height or width). If you want to see the Drop Shadow that's built into several of the Wow-Edges-Frames Styles (such as **Wow-Edge Color**, shown here), there has to be some empty, transparent space around the image for the shadow to extend into. To add empty space at the edges, choose Image > Canvas Size and increase the Width and Height.

The **Wow Styles** for type and graphics, also designed at 225 pixels/inch, can be applied through the Styles palette or copied from the **Wow-Sampler** files.▼

The **Wow-Button Styles** were designed at 72 pixels/inch, to look good when applied to small on-screen navigational elements.

STYLING A *BACKGROUND*

If you try to apply a Style to a *Background*, nothing will happen. Double-click *"Background"* in the Layers palette to turn the layer into one that can accept a Style.

FIND OUT MORE

▼ Installing the Wow Layer Styles **page 5**

▼ Applying Styles to files at resolutions other than 225 or 72 pixels/inch **page 47**

▼ Copying & pasting a Style **page 46**

THIS APPENDIX IS A "CATALOG" of examples of the **Wow Layer Styles**, those instant solutions that you'll find on the Wow DVD-ROM that comes with this book. Once you install the Wow Styles,▼ you can apply them through Photoshop's Styles palette. The Wow Layer Styles include:

- Styles for photos and other images such as paintings (pages 752–758), for framing them, adding surface texture, or enhancing their color and tone

- Styles that work magic on flat graphics and type, adding color, dimension, and light (pages 759–766)

- Interactive rollover Styles to add appeal to small navigational elements (page 767), enticing website visitors to click the buttons and assuring them that their click has been noticed

You'll also find pointers on how some of the effects work and how you can start with a Wow Style and develop your own — you may want to change a color, substitute a pattern, or scale down a glow without changing the relative size of a bevel effect. Learn more about using, modifying, and developing Styles in "Exercising Layer Styles" on page 44 and in the techniques and "Anatomy" sections in Chapter 8.

Whether you apply a Wow Style to a file that matches the Style's "design resolution" (225 pixels/inch for the photo and graphics Styles, and 72 pixels/inch for the button styles) or to a file at some other resolution,▼ we suggest that you open the Scale Effects dialog box as soon as you apply it. (One way to do that is to choose Layer > Layer Style > Scale Effects.) Experiment with the Scale to see if you want to adjust it for the size of your image or the "weight" of your graphics.

Any Wow Style whose name includes the * symbol uses a built-in pattern. In a file whose resolution is 225 pixels/inch (or 72 pixels/inch for the Wow-Button Styles), the Scale factors 25%, 50%, 100%, and 200% will scale the Style without degrading the pattern. If you scale to some other percentage, or if you use the Style on a file at some other resolution, you may want to zoom in and monitor the quality of the pattern as you scale.

Edges & Frames

The **Wow-Edges-Frames Styles**▼ provide a great start for making your own Styles for framing images on the page.

In **Wow-Soft White** a soft white Inner Shadow makes the edges of the image disappear. The Distance for the Inner Shadow is set to 0 so the fade is even all the way around the image. A white Inner Glow in Saturation mode fades the color at the edges. If you don't want to lose the color, click the Inner Glow effect's 👁 icon in the Layers palette to turn it off.

Wow-Soft White

Wow-Edge Color also uses a white Inner Shadow and Inner Glow, but the Inner Glow is applied in Difference mode, so it turns the colors at the edges to their opposites. In addition, this Style includes a Drop Shadow, which you'll be able to see if there's extra (transparent) space beyond the edges of your image.

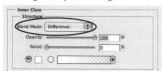

Wow-Edge Color

Wow-Modern creates a darkened stippled edge. The stippling comes from the black Inner Shadow's Noise setting (100%), and its sharp edge comes from the 100% Choke setting, which "hardens" the shadow. A black Inner Glow adds shading at the outer edges.

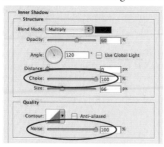

Wow-Modern

Three "traditional" framing Styles — **Wow-Wood Frame**, **Wow-Wood&Mat**, and **Wow-Fabric&Mat** — use the Stroke effect and Bevel and Emboss to make the **frame** itself. For the Bevel and Emboss, the Style is set to Stroke Emboss. The Contour helps shape the molding of the wooden frame. For the Stroke, the Fill Type is set to Pattern. You can change the material by clicking the pattern swatch and choosing a different pattern.

Wow-Wood Frame*

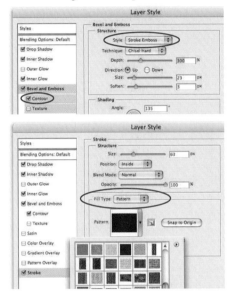

Wow-Wood&Mat*

The **mat** in **Wow-Wood&Mat** and **Wow-Fabric&Mat** is an Inner Glow. The Choke is set at 100% and 90% respectively, to harden the "glow" into a solid stripe. You can remove the mat by turning the Inner Glow effect off (click its 👁 icon in the Layers palette). Or change its color by clicking the color swatch and choosing a new color (for a mat that matches the image, click in the image to sample a color).

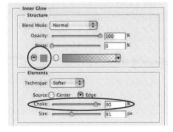

Wow-Fabric&Mat*

Vignettes

The **Wow-Vignette Styles** simulate effects traditionally achieved with lenses and filters, either on the camera or in the darkroom. They focus attention on the center of the image by darkening the edges and in some cases brightening, warming, or cooling the center.

Wow-Top&Bottom creates its effect with a Gradient Overlay. A Reflected black-to-transparent gradient is used, and the Reverse option is checked, to put the clear part in the center with the black on the outside. The Angle for the gradient is set at 90° (vertical), which puts the two dark edges at the top and bottom. The gradient is applied in Overlay mode, and the intensity of the effect can be adjusted by changing the Gradient Overlay's Opacity.

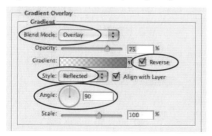

The **Wow-Vignette 1** and **Wow-Vignette 2** series of Styles all include a black Inner Shadow in Soft Light mode, with Distance set at 0 so the darkening is even all around. One difference between the Vignette 1 and Vignette 2 series is the Opacity of the Inner Shadow — it's 75% in the Vignette 1 Styles and 100% in the Vignette 2 series, so the Vignette 2 Styles darken more.

The other component of the **Wow-Vignette 1** and **Wow-Vignette 2** Styles is a light Inner Glow in Overlay mode (Overlay brightens the highlights more than Soft Light would). With Center (instead of

Wow-Top&Bottom

Wow-Vignette 1

Wow-Vignette 1 Warm

Edge) chosen for the Source, the Inner Glow brightens most at the center.

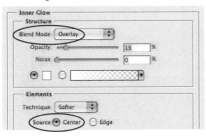

The Size for both the Inner Shadow and Inner Glow is set at the maximum 250 px and Choke at 0, to make both effects as soft and diffuse as possible. So the light spreads out from the center, and the dark spreads in from the edges.

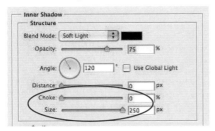

To change the balance between the lightening from the center and the darkening from the edges, you can simply change the Opacity of the Inner Shadow and Inner Glow.

The **Wow-Vignette 1** and **Wow-Vignette 2** Styles vary in the color and Opacity of the Inner Glow. **Wow-Vignette 1 Warm** (its settings are shown below) and the two **Wow-Vignette 2** Styles use a light yellow-to-orange color, so these Styles combine the effects of vignetting and a warming filter. **Wow-Vignette 1 Cool** uses a light blue for the Inner Glow.

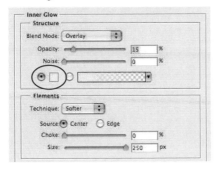

Wow-Vignette 1 Cool

Wow-Vignette 2 Warm

Wow-Vignette 2 Warmer

Tints

The **Wow-Tint FX Styles** apply or remove color, some with edge treatments and overall textures. Edge treatments are created by the Inner Shadow and Inner Glow effects.

Wow-Sepia 1 uses a Color Overlay to apply a warm brown in Color mode. The Opacity of the Color Overlay is reduced to 60% to allow some of the original color to show through.

In **Wow-Sepia 2** the Opacity for the Color Overlay is set higher (at 95%). But another important difference from Wow-Sepia 1 is that the brown used here is a more neutral color and so produces a cooler sepia tint. Built into **Wow-Sepia 2** is an overall surface texture, applied with the Texture feature of Bevel and Emboss. To allow the Texture to show up over the entire image, the Style for Bevel and Emboss is set to Inner Bevel, but an unusual Contour prevents beveling of the edges (for another way to emboss texture without creating a bevel, see the "Pattern, Texture & Bevel" tip on page 764).

For variations on the two **Wow-Sepia** Styles, try adjusting the Opacity to show more or less of the original color, and try changing the Blend Mode for the Color Overlay to Hue to protect neutral colors in the original from being tinted.

Wow-Black&White applies a black Color Overlay in Hue mode (Color or Saturation mode would have worked equally well).

Wow-Subdue applies a white Color Overlay in Normal mode at 80% Opacity, so the image can be used as a background for text or other elements.

Wow-Gradient Tint applies its gradient in Color mode. This Style can be useful for landscapes, since it intensifies the color of sky at the top of the photo and grass below. By choosing a different gradient, you can modify the Style to enhance sunset colors.

Original photo

Wow-Sepia 1

Wow-Sepia 2*

Wow-Black&White

Wow-Subdue

Wow-Gradient Tint

PHOTOSPIN.COM

Grains & Textures

Most of the **Wow-Grain & Texture Styles** use a Pattern Overlay effect to apply a grayscale pattern in Overlay or Soft Light mode. Since medium gray is "invisible" in these two "contrast" modes, only the highlights and shadows affect the image, adding surface texture. **Wow-Texture 05**, **06**, **07**, and **10** use the Texture component of Bevel and Emboss rather than a Pattern Overlay to add "bump" to the surface texture.

Wow-G&T 01*

Wow-G&T 02*

Wow-G&T 03*

Wow-Texture 01*

Wow-Texture 02*

Wow-Texture 03*

Wow-Texture 04*

Wow-Texture 05*

Wow-Texture 06*

Wow-Texture 07*

Wow-Texture 08*

Wow-Texture 09*

Wow-Texture 10*

Chrome

The **Wow-Chrome Styles**▼ were designed to simulate various kinds of shiny, reflective surfaces. Although many of these Styles have built-in reflections, all of them are set up so that you can reflect an image using the method described step-by-step in "Custom Chrome" on page 525.

 Here the **Wow-Chrome Styles** are applied to one of Photoshop's Custom Shapes.▼ The crown shows how the Styles look on relatively thick and thin components, and on sharp and round corners. Notice also what happens to the weight of the elements and the space between them when the bevel in the Style extends outward (as in **05**, **07**, **15**, **17**, and **19**) rather than inward from the edge.

Most of the **Wow-Chrome Styles** completely replace the original color of the graphic or type. **Wow-Chrome 11** is the only one that allows some of the original color to come through. So if you start with a colorful symbol (as shown bottom right) instead of the black one used here, your chrome will show a slight color tint.

ROUND CORNERS

Chrome Styles with rounded rather than sharp bevels (such as **Wow-Chrome 11**) look especially good on graphics or type with rounded corners. You may want to choose artwork or typefaces with that in mind, or adjust some corners after applying the Style.▼

Changing corner points to curve points, and adjusting their positions, rounds the corners.

 Wow-Chrome Samples.psd

FIND OUT MORE

▼ Installing the Wow Styles **page 5**

▼ Applying Layer Styles **page 44**

▼ Custom Shapes **page 434**

▼ Editing paths **page 437**

Wow-Chrome 01*

Wow-Chrome 02*

Wow-Chrome 03

Wow-Chrome 04

Wow-Chrome 05

Wow-Chrome 06

Wow-Chrome 07

Wow-Chrome 08

Wow-Chrome 09

Wow-Chrome 10*

Wow-Chrome 11*

Wow-Chrome 12

Wow-Chrome 13

Wow-Chrome 14*

Wow-Chrome 15

Wow-Chrome 16*

Wow-Chrome 17*

Wow-Chrome 18

Wow-Chrome 19

Wow-Chrome 20

Wow-Chrome 11*
applied to a red graphic

Metal

Some of the **Wow-Metal Styles**▼ have textured surfaces and others have surfaces that are patterned but smooth. "Anatomy of 'Bumpy'" on page 522 tells how a Layer Style that applies a textured surface is constructed. Another important variable is the Size of the bevel in the Bevel and Emboss effect. A large Size, as in **Wow-Cast Metal**, "consumes" more of the shape you apply it to, leaving less top surface than the other **Wow-Metal Styles**, which have lower Size settings.

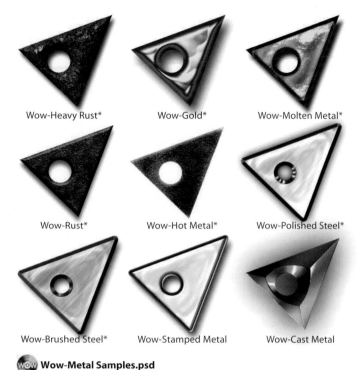

Wow-Heavy Rust*   Wow-Gold*   Wow-Molten Metal*

Wow-Rust*   Wow-Hot Metal*   Wow-Polished Steel*

Wow-Brushed Steel*   Wow-Stamped Metal   Wow-Cast Metal

Wow-Metal Samples.psd

ADJUSTING BLEND MODES

If the shadow or glow in a Layer Style doesn't show up against a white or black background, try changing the Blend Mode for these effects. For instance, **Wow-Hot Metal** shows a hot glow over gray (below) but not over white (right). For a similar glow over white or black, change the Drop Shadow's mode to Multiply and the Outer Glow's to Screen.

Glass, Ice & Crystal

The **Wow-Glass Styles**▼ are clear, allowing an image below in the layer stack to show through. The transparency is achieved with a reduced Fill Opacity, and the background image is brightened by effects applied in Overlay mode. The bright surface reflections in **Wow-Ice** and **Wow-Clear Ice** are created by settings in the Bevel and Emboss effect. The Pattern Overlay effect provides the "inclusions" in **Wow-Crystal** and **Wow-Smoky Glass**.

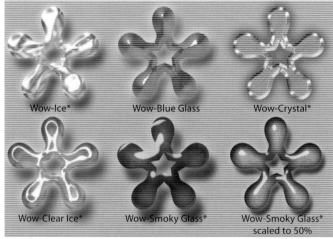

Wow-Ice*   Wow-Blue Glass   Wow-Crystal*

Wow-Clear Ice*   Wow-Smoky Glass*   Wow-Smoky Glass* scaled to 50%

Wow-Glass Samples.psd

SCALING TO FIT

Whenever you apply a Layer Style, especially a dimensional one, experiment by right/Ctrl-clicking the 🗲 icon for the styled layer and choosing Scale Effects to adjust the fit.▼

FIND OUT MORE

▼ Installing Wow Styles **page 5**

▼ Scaling Styles **page 45**

Gems & Polished Stones

Some of the **Wow-Gem Styles**▼ are opaque, while others are transparent or translucent. The illusion of light traveling through and being magnified by the gem (in the **Wow-Gibson Opal**, **Wow-Amber**, **Wow-Tortoise Shell**, and **Wow-Clear Opal**, for instance) is created by a color Drop Shadow effect in Multiply mode and a lighter-color Outer Glow effect, either in Screen mode or Overlay mode.

Here the **Wow-Gem Styles** are applied to a Shape created with the Polygon tool ⬠, which shares a space in the Tools palette with the Rectangle ▭ and other Shape tools. In the Options bar the Polygon was set for 3 Sides and for Smooth Corners (in the Polygon Options panel that appears when you click the tiny Geometry Options triangle to the left of the Sides field).

 Wow-Gem Samples.psd

Wow-Turquoise* Wow-Red Amber* Wow-Gibson Opal*

Wow-Amber* Wow-Jasper* Wow-Abalone*

Wow-Light Marble* Wow-Dark Marble* Wow-Tortoise Shell*

Wow-Clear Opal*

SCALING PATTERNED STYLES

In a Layer Style, a surface pattern applied with a Pattern Overlay effect (such as the surfaces of the **Wow-Wood Styles** and **Wow-Gem Styles**) is pixel-based. If you enlarge the pattern by scaling the Style too much, the pattern may "soften."▼

Woods

Some of the **Wow-Wood Styles**▼ have raised grain, while others are polished and smooth. All of the Styles include a surface pattern, applied with a Pattern Overlay.▼

 Wow-Wood Samples.psd

Wow-Blonde Wood* Wow-Fine Wood* Wow-Bocote*

Wow-Rustic Wood* Wow-Oak* Wow-Birdseye*

FIND OUT MORE
▼ Installing Wow Styles **page 5**
▼ Scaling Styles **page 45**
▼ Pattern & texture in Styles **page 504**

Plastics

The **Wow-Plastic Styles**▼ show different degrees of translucency or transparency. "Anatomy of Clear Color" on page 513 tells how to build these qualities into a Layer Style, and how they interact with the color and dimensional effects that are also part of these Styles.

 Wow-Plastic Samples.psd

Wow-Mottled Purple   Wow-Red   Wow-Edged Swirl*

Wow-Clear Blue   Wow-Clear Orange   Wow-Clear Red

Wow-Textured Swirl*   Wow-Sign Base   Wow-Sign Emboss*

Wow-Rainbow

MORE CLEAR, COLORFUL WOW STYLES

Many of the 150 **Wow-Button Styles** (see page 767) are "plastic-like." These Styles are not restricted to web elements — you can use them for other type and graphics as well. To greatly expand your clear, colorful options, just load the **Wow-Button Styles** into the Styles palette and click one of the thumbnails to apply the Style. Be sure to scale the Style after you apply it, to get exactly the color, clarity, and dimensional look that you want.

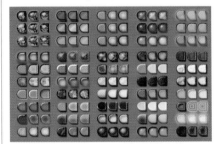

For a closer look at the **Wow-Button Styles**, complete with their ID numbers, see page 767. Most of them have color, surface reflections, and translucency similar to the **Wow-Plastic** Styles.

SIGNS & LICENSE PLATES

Two of the **Wow-Plastic Styles** (**Wow-Sign Base** and **Wow-Sign Emboss**) are designed to be used on stacked layers to create the look of a stamped and painted metal sign or plate. The **Wow-Emboss Bevel.psd** file shows how to structure a sign in two layers using these Layer Styles. This stacking of styled layers works because the **Wow-Sign Emboss** Style uses the Emboss option to build the bevel partly inward and partly outward.▼ The part of the bevel that extends out beyond the edge of the element it's applied to (the sign graphics in this case) is clear, so the color from the layer below can show through.

 **Wow-Emboss Bevel.psd**

FIND OUT MORE

▼ Installing Wow Styles **page 5**

▼ Scaling Styles **page 45**

▼ Bevel structure **page 501 & 537**

Organic Materials

The **Wow-Organic Styles** ▼ take their character from seamlessly tiling patterns made from photos of natural textures. Most of the patterns used in these Styles, along with 17 other natural-materials patterns, can be found in the **Wow-Organic Patterns.pat** file of Pattern presets on the Wow DVD-ROM. The patterns are included in the Styles via the Pattern Overlay effect. In some cases the same pattern is used as the Texture component of the Bevel and Emboss effect to add dimension to the surface texture.

 Wow-Organic Samples.psd

ADJUSTING PATTERN PLACEMENT

If you apply a Layer Style with a fairly large-scale Pattern Overlay (such as those in the **Wow-Seed Pod** Styles) to a relatively small element, you may want to adjust what part of the pattern shows in the element. (This works well for Styles *without* "embossed" surface texture.) To reposition the pattern, open the Pattern Overlay section of the Layer Style dialog box (one way is to double-click the 𝑓 that appears to the right of the name of the layer in the Layers palette, and then click on "Pattern Overlay" in the list of effects). Now move the cursor into the main Photoshop window and drag to reposition the pattern.

Wow-Seed Pod 1**   Wow-Seed Pod 2*   Wow-Water*

Wow-Green Mat*   Wow-Green Mezzo Paper*   Wow-Brown Paper*

Wow-Rice Paper*   Wow-Bamboo*   Wow-Green Weave*

Wow-Brown Weave*

** The **Wow-Seed Pod 1** Style includes a light Outer Glow that doesn't show up against white. See the "Adjusting Blend Modes" tip on page 760.

FIND OUT MORE

▼ Installing Wow Styles **page 5**

Fabrics

The **Wow-Fabric Styles** ▼ are seamlessly repeating patterns that include subtle embossing on the surface. The edges are beveled, but the bevel can be turned off, as described in the "Pattern, Texture & Bevel" tip on page 764 if you simply want to use the pattern as a background. The 6 patterns used in the **Wow-Fabric Styles** and 39 more fabric patterns can be found in the **Wow-Fabric Patterns** presets, shown on page 769.

 Wow-Fabric Samples.psd

Wow-Butterfly*   Wow-Violet*   Wow-Black Geometric*

Wow-Pineapple*   Wow-Yellow Ikat*   Wow-Flowing Triangles*

Rock & Masonry

The **Wow-Rock Styles**▼ have patterned, textured surfaces and beveled edges. For many of these Styles, the same pattern is used as a Pattern Overlay for the surface pattern and as the Texture component of the Bevel and Emboss effect for the surface texture. In **Wow-Veined Stone** the pattern has been inverted in the Texture component, so the dark veins appear to be carved *into* the rock instead of raised from the surface.

Wow-Bricks*

Wow-Green Rock*

Wow-Brown Rock*

Wow-Purple Rock*

Wow-Granite*

Wow-Iron Rock*

Wow-Veined Stone*

Wow-Weathered Wall*

Wow-Stucco*

Wow-Rock Samples.psd

FIND OUT MORE

▼ Installing the Wow Styles **page 5**

PATTERN, TEXTURE & BEVEL

In a Layer Style with a textured surface, such as the **Wow-Veined Stone** Style (shown above), the surface texture is usually applied through the Texture component of the Bevel and Emboss effect. But you can turn off the texture while keeping the bevel in place, or vice versa. Start by opening the Layer Style dialog box (you can do this by double-clicking the 🅕 icon to the right of the "styled" layer's name in the Layers palette. Then work with the list of effects on the left side of the dialog box, clicking "OK" when you've made the changes you want:

- To eliminate the embossed texture but keep the beveled edge, simply click the check box for Texture (under Bevel and Emboss) to remove the check mark **A**.

- To eliminate the bevel but keep the surface texture, it won't work to just turn off Bevel and Emboss, since the Texture is part of it and will disappear along with the bevel. Instead, in the list of effects in the Layer Style dialog box, click the name "Bevel and Emboss" (the name, not the check mark) to open the Bevel and Emboss panel of the dialog box. Note the Size setting in the Structure section. Drag the Size slider all the way to the left to set the Size at 0. The bevel will be gone, but since Bevel and Emboss is still turned on, the Texture effect can be restored. Click the name "Texture" in the list of effects and increase the Depth setting to bring back the surface texture **B**.

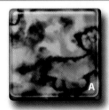

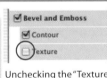

Unchecking the "Texture" effect eliminates texture but keeps the bevel.

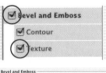

With both "Bevel and Emboss" and "Texture" checked, reducing the bevel's Size to 0 and raising the Texture's Depth to the Depth of the bevel plus the original Depth of the Texture (here 481 + 6), eliminates the bevel but keeps the texture.

Halos & Embossing

Like some of the Styles in "Glows & Neons" on the next page, the **Wow-Halo** Styles▼ create dark or light edge effects, both inside and outside the graphics you apply them to. Here we've applied the Styles to a red graphic. Some Styles include a Color Overlay of black or gray, and some include reduced Fill opacity. In the two "Carved" Styles, a black Color Overlay combined with reducing the Fill opacity, (but not all the way to 0) creates a shaded effect for the recessed surface.

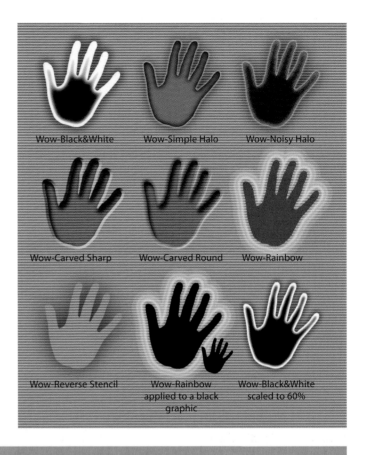

Wow-Black&White   Wow-Simple Halo   Wow-Noisy Halo

Wow-Carved Sharp   Wow-Carved Round   Wow-Rainbow

Wow-Reverse Stencil   Wow-Rainbow applied to a black graphic   Wow-Black&White scaled to 60%

FIND OUT MORE

▼ Installing Wow Styles **page 5**

 **Wow-Halo Samples.psd**

COPYING A SINGLE EFFECT

If one Style includes an effect that you like to "borrow," such as the Outer Glow in the **Wow-Rainbow** Style, you can make it part of another Style, such as **Wow-Black&White**, as follows:

1 In the Layers palette, target the layer you want to "style" by clicking its thumbnail.

2 Add the main Style (**Wow-Black&White** in this case) by clicking its thumbnail in the Styles palette.

3 Duplicate the layer (press Ctrl/⌘-J) and apply to this new layer the Style with the effect you want to copy (in this case **Wow-Rainbow**). Then in the Layers palette, expand the list of effects, if it isn't expanded already, by clicking the tiny arrow next to the 🅕 for the layer.

4 The next step is a little different in Photoshop CS than in CS2:

In CS, in the Layers palette simply drag the effect you want to add to the other layer's Style down to the entry for that layer until a "double border" appears below the entry; then release the mouse button to drop the dragged effect.

In CS2, simply dragging the effect does add it to the "recipient" layer's Style, but it also *removes* it from the "donor" layer's Style; in other words, it *moves* the effect rather than copying it. To *copy* it instead, Alt/Option-drag. In CS2 the signal that you're in the right place to drop the effect is a heavy border around the entire entry for the layer.

The Outer Glow effect from Wow-Rainbow was added to the Wow-Black&White Style, and the Style was then scaled to 60%.

Strokes & Fills

Most of the **Wow-Stroke** Styles▼ include a Stroke effect. You can replace a Stroke or other effect with one from another Style by dragging as described in "Copying a Single Effect" on page 765. The Position of the Stroke determines whether the Style will "fatten" the type or graphic you add it to (by adding thickness at the edges) or "thin" it by encroaching inside the edge.

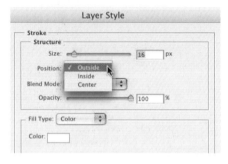

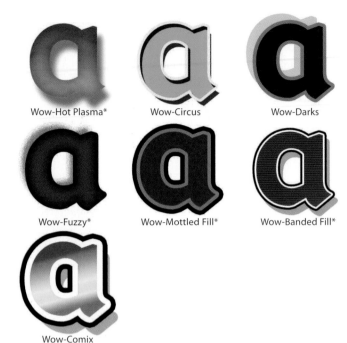

Wow-Hot Plasma*   Wow-Circus   Wow-Darks

Wow-Fuzzy*   Wow-Mottled Fill*   Wow-Banded Fill*

Wow-Comix

 **Wow-Stroke Samples.psd**

Glows & Neon

Most of the **Wow-Glow** Styles use a Fill opacity of 0% to make the type or graphic disappear, and a Gradient-based Stroke effect to add a glow that follows its outline. Some of the **Wow-Glow** Styles▼ work best when you apply them to type or graphics used against dark or middle-tone backgrounds that contrast with their glowing light. Others look like neon tubes in the "off" state or aglow in the daytime. You can change the color of a **Wow-Glow** Style by opening the Layer Style dialog for a layer to which the Style has been applied and adjusting the colors used in the individual layer effects, as described in step 5 of "Crafting a Neon Glow" (page 549).

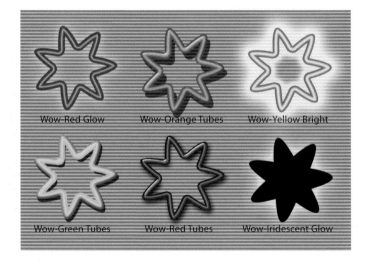

Wow-Red Glow   Wow-Orange Tubes   Wow-Yellow Bright

Wow-Green Tubes   Wow-Red Tubes   Wow-Iridescent Glow

 Wow-Glow Samples.psd

FIND OUT MORE

▼ Installing Wow Styles **page 5**

Button Styles

Shown on this page are 200 Wow Button Styles, designed to work with 72-dpi files, especially for use in turning graphics into on-screen buttons.▼ The **Wow-Button Styles.psd** file (shown at the right) includes 150 individual button layers with Layer Styles — 50 sets with three Styles in each set. The top three rows of each column are different color variations of five Styles.

In the **Wow-Button Rollovers.psd** file (shown below right) there are 50 layers, each with a combined rollover Style▼ made from three related Button Styles, one for each of the Normal, Over, and Down states of the buttons.

Wow Button Styles

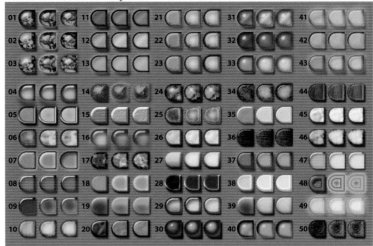

The 150 Wow Button Styles shown above can be loaded into the Styles palette of Photoshop by choosing from the Styles palette's pop-out menu ⊙ and selecting the Wow-Button Styles. Then the Styles can be applied to a 72-dpi file by targeting a layer and clicking the Style's thumbnail in the Styles palette. Or you can copy and paste the individual styles from the Wow Button Styles.psd file, shown above.

Wow Button Rollover Styles

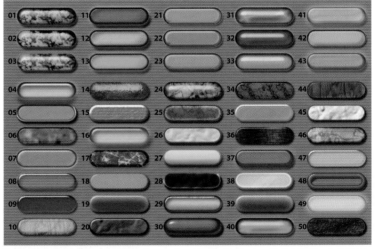

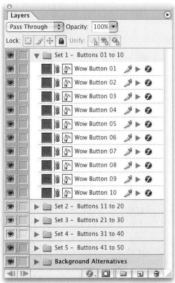

This is the Layers palette for the **Wow Button Rollovers.psd** file shown at the right. You can view the buttons against a light, medium, or dark background by opening the Background Alternatives layer set/group and turning on visibility (the 👁) for the background you want. The same background options are available in the **Wow Button Styles.psd** file shown at the top of the page.

Each of the Wow Rollover Styles shown above includes the JavaScript for Normal, Over, and Down interactivity. You can add the 50 combined Wow Rollover Styles and also the 150 single-state Styles at the top of the page (a total of 200 Styles) to your current ImageReady Styles palette by going to the Styles palette's pop-out menu ⊙ and selecting the Wow-Button Styles. Then the Styles can be applied to a 72-dpi file by targeting a layer and clicking the Style's thumbnail in the Styles palette. To see all the rollovers in operation in a single array like that shown above, you can open the Wow-Button Rollovers.html file (from the Wow Button Sampler HTML page folder) in a Web browser and operate the buttons by moving the cursor over them and clicking.

FIND OUT MORE

▼ Installing Wow Layer Styles **page 5**

▼ Using Layer Styles **page 44**

▼ Rollover Styles **page 716**

Appendix C:
Wow Patterns

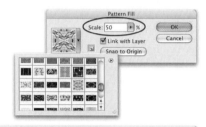

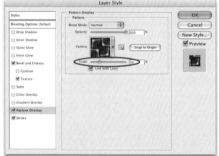

When you apply a pattern in a **Pattern Fill layer** (top) or a **Layer Style**, you can scale it (as shown here) and also adjust its position by dragging in the working window.

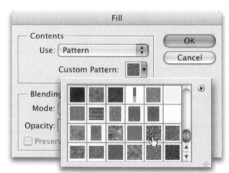

Using the **Edit > Fill** command to apply a pattern doesn't offer the scaling, positioning, and substitution options of a Fill layer or Layer Style. But it provides a way to use a pattern in a layer mask or alpha channel.

FIND OUT MORE

▼ Installing the Wow
  Patterns **page 5**

ON THE NEXT FIVE PAGES are printed swatches of the **Wow Patterns** supplied on the DVD-ROM that comes with this book. Some of these patterns started with a rectangular selection in a scan or digital photo. The **Wow-Marble** and **Wow-Media** patterns were started this way, for example. The rectangle was then turned into a seamlessly repeating pattern using one of the methods described in "Quick Seamless Patterns" on page 562. "Quick Backgrounds & Textures" on page 555 suggests several ways to come up with the original rectangular tile. The **Wow-Fabric** patterns were made using the Terrazzo plug-in from Xaos Tools (www.xaostools.com).

Photoshop has several ways to apply patterns:

- A Pattern Fill layer
- One or more effects in a Layer Style, where patterns can be used as a Pattern Overlay (for surface pattern), the Texture component of the Bevel and Emboss effect (for adding "bump" to the surface), or as a Stroke (for adding pattern around the edges of the layer's content)
- The Edit > Fill command
- The Pattern Stamp tool 🏭

Wherever patterns can be used in Photoshop, you'll find a palette with a menu that lists all the patterns currently in Photoshop's Presets > Patterns folder. ▼ You can also load patterns stored outside this folder by choosing Load Patterns from the palette's menu, opened by clicking the ⊙ button.

PHOTO: DAVID RUDIE

In Terrazzo 2, a plug-in from Xaos Tools, you choose one of 18 Symmetries (ways to arrange the repeats of a pattern element) and designate the area that will be the basis of your pattern. With the Continuous Preview option turned on, Terrazzo shows you new seamless geometric patterns instantly as you change the size or position of the selection or choose a new Symmetry.

Fabric

The **Wow-Fabric** patterns are ideal for backgrounds and fills. Used as the Pattern Overlay effect in a Layer Style, the same pattern can also be applied as the Texture component of the Bevel and Emboss effect to slightly emboss the surface pattern. The **Wow-Fabric Styles** (page 763) are constructed this way. Change the pattern in any of these Styles by substituting one of these **Wow-Fabric** patterns for the Pattern Overlay and Texture in the Style. As shown here, many of the Wow-Fabric patterns have been scaled to 50% to better show the repeating pattern.

Wow-Fabric 01 (50%)

Wow-Fabric 02 (50%)

Wow-Fabric 03 (50%)

Wow-Fabric 04 (50%)

Wow-Fabric 05 (50%)

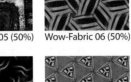
Wow-Fabric 06 (50%)

Wow-Fabric 07 (50%)

Wow-Fabric 08 (50%)

Wow-Fabric 09 (50%)

Wow-Fabric 10 (50%)

Wow-Fabric 11 (50%)

Wow-Fabric 12 (50%)

Wow-Fabric 13 (50%)
Wow-Fabric 14 (50%)
Wow-Fabric 15 (50%)
Wow-Fabric 16
Wow-Fabric 17
Wow-Fabric 18

Wow-Fabric 19 (50%)
Wow-Fabric 20 (50%)
Wow-Fabric 21
Wow-Fabric 22
Wow-Fabric 23 (50%)
Wow-Fabric 24 (50%)

Wow-Fabric 25
Wow-Fabric 26 (50%)
Wow-Fabric 27 (50%)
Wow-Fabric 28 (50%)
Wow-Fabric 29 (50%)
Wow-Fabric 30 (50%)

Wow-Fabric 31
Wow-Fabric 32
Wow-Fabric 33 (50%)
Wow-Fabric 34 (50%)
Wow-Fabric 35
Wow-Fabric 36 (50%)

Wow-Fabric 37

Wow-Fabric 38 (50%)

Wow-Fabric 39 (50%)

Wow-Fabric 40

Wow-Fabric 41 (50%)

Wow-Fabric 42 (50%)

Wow-Fabric 43 (50%)

Wow-Fabric 44 (50%)

Wow-Fabric 45 (50%)

FIND OUT MORE

▼ Working with gradients **page 160**

▼ Adding texture with Layer Styles **page 504**

Marble

The **Wow-Marble** patterns make fine backgrounds "as is," or alter them with an Adjustment layer, added by clicking the ◑ button at the bottom of the Layers palette. Use a Hue/Saturation layer with Colorize turned on; set the Adjustment layer's blend mode to Color in the Layers palette to maintain any black and white in the pattern but tint the grays. Or use a Gradient Map layer; click the gradient sample bar to open the Gradient Editor and move the color Stops or change their colors to get just the effect you want.▼ To generate your own marble-like backgrounds, try the Clouds filter (see page 744).

Wow-Marble B&W 01

Wow-Marble B&W 02

Wow-Marble B&W 03

Wow-Marble B&W 04

Wow-Marble B&W 05

Wow-Marble Purple

Wow-Marble Brown

Wow-Marble Green 01

Wow-Marble Green 02

Wow-Marble Gold 01

Wow-Marble Gold 02

Misc Surface

The **Wow-Misc Surface** patterns are great for creating either smooth and polished or textured surfaces. Some of them are used in the **Wow-Rock Styles** (page 764), and you can make similar Styles of your own by applying one of those Styles to a layer and then substituting a **Wow-Misc Surface** pattern for the Pattern Overlay effect and the Texture component of the Bevel and Emboss effect.▼

Wow-Abstract 01

Wow-Abstract 02

Wow-Abstract 03

Wow-Abstract 04

Wow-Abstract 05

Wow-Abstract 06

Wow-Abstract 07

Wow-Abstract 08

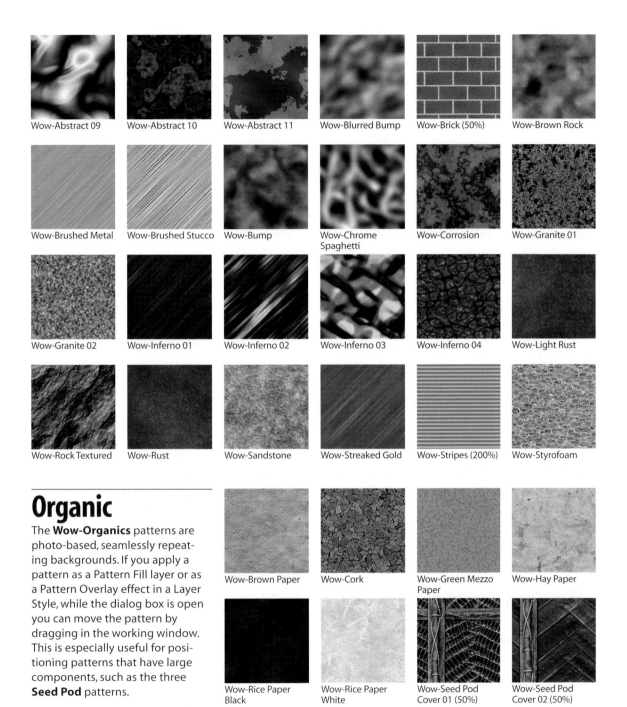

Wow-Abstract 09

Wow-Abstract 10

Wow-Abstract 11

Wow-Blurred Bump

Wow-Brick (50%)

Wow-Brown Rock

Wow-Brushed Metal

Wow-Brushed Stucco

Wow-Bump

Wow-Chrome Spaghetti

Wow-Corrosion

Wow-Granite 01

Wow-Granite 02

Wow-Inferno 01

Wow-Inferno 02

Wow-Inferno 03

Wow-Inferno 04

Wow-Light Rust

Wow-Rock Textured

Wow-Rust

Wow-Sandstone

Wow-Streaked Gold

Wow-Stripes (200%)

Wow-Styrofoam

Organic

The **Wow-Organics** patterns are photo-based, seamlessly repeating backgrounds. If you apply a pattern as a Pattern Fill layer or as a Pattern Overlay effect in a Layer Style, while the dialog box is open you can move the pattern by dragging in the working window. This is especially useful for positioning patterns that have large components, such as the three **Seed Pod** patterns.

Wow-Brown Paper

Wow-Cork

Wow-Green Mezzo Paper

Wow-Hay Paper

Wow-Rice Paper Black

Wow-Rice Paper White

Wow-Seed Pod Cover 01 (50%)

Wow-Seed Pod Cover 02 (50%)

Wow-Seed Pod Spine

Wow-Weave 01 (50%)

Wow-Weave 02 (50%)

Wow-Weave 03

Wow-Weave 04 (50%)

Wow-Weave 05

Wow-Weave 06

Wow-Bamboo Wall

Wow-Tortoise Shell

Wow-Abalone 01

Wow-Abalone 02

Wow-Wood 01 (50%)

Wow-Wood 02 (50%)

Wow-Wood 03

Wow-Wood 04 (50%)

Wow-Wood 05 (50%)

Wow-Wood 06

Noise

Most of the **Wow-Noise** patterns were designed to simulate film grain or digital noise, either overall for artistic effect, or in specific areas that have been blurred and now look "too smooth" to match the rest of the image, as shown in "Focusing Attention on the Subject" on page 288. They can be effective when applied to a layer as a Pattern Overlay effect in a Layer Style, or as a Pattern Fill layer, targeted with a layer mask if needed. The **Wow-Noise** patterns are gray in order to be applied in Overlay or other "contrast" blend modes (see "Media" on page 773).

Wow-Noise Big Soft Color

Wow-Noise Big Soft Gray

Wow-Noise Big Hard Color

Wow-Noise Big Hard Gray

Wow-Noise Small Strong Color

Wow-Noise Small Strong Gray

Wow-Noise Small Subtle Gray

Wow-Noise Small Subtle Color

Media

The **Wow-Media** patterns imitate painting surfaces and paint. Many are gray because they were designed to be applied in one of the "contrast" blend modes — those grouped with Overlay in the blend mode menus found in the Layers palette, the Layer Style dialog, and elsewhere in Photoshop's interface. In these modes 50% gray is invisible, and the darker and lighter tones create highlights and shadows to "texturize" your image, whether you apply the pattern alone or emboss it (one way is with Filter > Stylize > Emboss).

Wow-Canvas Background

Wow-Canvas Texture 01

Wow-Canvas Texture 02

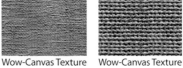
Wow-Canvas Brush + Overlay-Large

Wow-Canvas + Brush Overlay-Medium

Wow-Canvas + Brush Overlay-Small

Wow-Watercolor Background

Wow-Watercolor Texture

Wow-Watercolor Overlay

Wow-Watercolor Salt Overlay

Wow-Cracked Paint

Wow-Coquille Board 01

Wow-Coquille Board 02

Wow-Pebble Board 01

Wow-Pebble Board 02

Wow-Reticulation

Wow-Reticulation Blotched

Wow-Reticulation Rough

Appendix D: Artists & Photographers

Anants 159
www.istockphoto.com

Anderson Photo-Graphics
Richard Anderson 240, 615
(Models, Jennifer Luttrell
and Latisha Tolbert)
4793 N.E. 11th Avenue
Fort Lauderdale, FL 33334
954-772-4210
andersonphotographic@mac.com
www.andersonphotographics.com

Geno Andrews 686, 700
www.genoandrews.com

Daren Bader 401, 408, 409
daren@darenbader.com
www.darenbader.com

Darryl Baird 660
dbaird@umflint.edu
http://spruce.flint.umich.edu/~dbaird
www.re-picture.info

Lucy Bartholomay 148

Lisa Baskin 148

Alicia Buelow 51, 80, 566
415-522-5902
Fax: 415-522-5910
Alicia@aliciabuelow.com
www.aliciabuelow.com

Stanley Breedon 83

Marie Brown 357, 666, 668

Peter Carlisle 7, 110, 556

Garen Checkley 293, 301
GarenCheckley@gmail.com
GarenCheckley.com

Chip Coakley 148

Steve Conley 367, 732

Jack Davis, JHDavis 94, 164, 167, 189,
190, 191, 196, 216, 217, 240, 255, 267,
268, 272,302, 307, 311, 314, 317, 329,
347, 360, 376, 384, 388, 395, 400, 402,
460, 527, 539, 604, 610, 615, 627, 670,
682, 692, 699, 701, 729
www.software-cinema.com/htw

Jill Davis 153

Anaika Dayton 128, 208, 328, 330, 643

Gage Dayton 315

Lily Dayton 357

Mona Dayton 271, 317

Paul Dayton 192, 610

Paul K. Dayton, Jr. 270, 272, 273

Alexis Marie Deutschmann 101, 350

Rod Deutschmann 100, 320, 610
www.infocuslearningcenter.com

Deeanne Edwards 275, 410
info@marinelifephoto.com
www.marinelifephoto.com

Katrin Eismann 96, 207, 284, 348, 349,
595, 651, 652
Katrin@photoshopdiva.com
www.photoshopdiva.com

Frankie Frey 370

Carla Gilbert 285
Carla Gilbert Photography
858-755-3804

Cristen Gillespie 84, 344, 572

Ian Gillespie 37, 596
ian_gillespie@mac.com

Steven Gordon 238, 486, 509
Cartagram, LLC
136 Mill Creek Crossing
Madison, AL 35758
www.cartagram.com

Beverly Goward 32, 200, 209, 245, 666,
668, 752
bgoward@cox.net

Laurie Grace 86, 211, 414
lgrace@gmail.com
860-659-0748

Wendy Grossman 145

Francois Guérin 256

Loren Haury 352

Susan Heller 188, 643, 682, 716
hellersd@yahoo.com

Lance Hidy 7, 52, 148, 367, 412
2 Summer Street
Merrimac, MA 01860
lance@lancehidy.com

Lance Jackson 447
San Francisco Chronicle
900 Mission Street
San Francisco, CA 94103
415-777-8944
ljackson@sfchronicle.com
www.lancejackson.net

Jeff Jacoby 730
Broadcast and Electronic Arts Department
San Francisco State University
info@freedomfriesart.org
www.jeffjacoby.net

Donal Jolley Cover, 15, 18, 50, 57, 121,
146, 211, 452, 474, 517, 537, 570, 588,
611, 614, 620, 655, 664, 672
10505 Wren Ridge Road
Johns Creek, GA 30022
don@s30d.com

K & L Designs 246, 441, 471, 467
Kelly Williamson & Lisa Schornak
619-987-8662
kelly@knldesigns.com
lisa@knldesigns.com
www.knldesigns.com

Jan Kabili 721
jkabili@gmail.com
http://photoshoponline.tv

Michal Koralewski ii
www.sxc.hu

Scott Kosofski 148

Julianne Kost 615

Michael L. Kungl, Mike Kungl 48, 484,
485
M. Kungl Studios
Costa Mesa, CA 92627
info@mkunglstudios.com
www.mkunglstudios.com

Jeff Lancaster 246, 662
Lancaster Photographics
619-234-4325
www.lancasterphoto.com

Aleksejs Lapkovskis 721
www.istockphoto.com

Marv Lyons 671
619-884-8420
lyons@gaialink.com
www.dij-wiz.com

Rob Magiera 81, 568
9636 Ruskin Circle
Sandy, UT 84092
801-943-365
Fax: 801-943-6693
www.studionoumena.com

Martino Mardersteig 148

Alberto Marinho 666
www.istockphoto.com

Chaz Maviyane-Davies 148

John McIntosh 656, 657
209 East 23rd Street
NYC, NY 10010
212-592-2526
www.svacomputerart.com

Bert Monroy 365, 397, 404, 454, 546,
750
11 Latham Lane
Berkeley, CA 94708
510-524-9412
bert@bertmonroy.com

John Odam 134, 138, 482
jodam@san.rr.com

Paul Parisi 148

Chris Pullman 148

Wayne Rankin 82, 658
Rankin Design Group Pty Ltd.
P. O. Box 221
Warrandyte, Victoria 3113
Australia
613-9844-1138
Fax: 613-9844-1138
wayne.@rankindesign.com.au
www.rankindesign.com.au

Robin Radcliffe 643

Lloyd Reynolds 148

David Rudie 26, 768
dave@catalinaop.com

Betsy Sarles 148

Betsy Schulz 662
A Design Garden
www.adesigngarden.com

Sharon Steuer 107, 144, 186, 586, 730
studio@ssteuer.com
www.ssteuer.com

Susan Thompson 234, 356
160 North Elmwood Avenue
Lindsay, CA 93247
559-562-5155
susan@sx70.com
www.sx70.com

Matt Tilghman 643, 716
www.istockphoto.com

Cher Threinen-Pendarvis 106, 375, 394
cher@pendarvis-studios.com
www.pendarvis-studios.com

Anthony Velonis 467, 471

E. A. M. Visser 169, 249, 278, 295, 332,
333, 530, 643
LilVisser@gmail.com

Mark Wainer 49, 117, 406, 650
831-447-2344
mark@markwainer.com
www.markwainer.com

Gay Walker 148

Duncan Walker 721
www.istockphoto.com

Peter Walton 83

William White 93
info@marketplace-creative.com

Rick Worthington 142, 279, 316, 321,
326, 327, 329, 330, 332, 346
rickworthington@sbcglobal.net

Tommy Yune 91

Christine Zalewski 201, 207, 236, 333,
354
www.zalewskiphotography.com

Index

Note: Entries in blue are specific to Photoshop CS2 only and do not apply to version CS

A

EPS (Photoshop) file format, 119
Equalize command, 171
Eraser tool ⟍, 359, 360, 363–364
   Erase To History, 363, 366
Every-line Composer, 422
Exclusion blend mode, 177
Expand command, 65
Export commands (File menu)
   Data Sets as Files, 648
   Original Document, 137
   Paths to Illustrator, 443
   Send Video Preview to Device, 123
   Video Preview, 120
Export commands (File menu,
   ImageReady)
   Animation Frames As Files, 687
   Layers as Files, 681
   Macromedia Flash SWF, 676, 681, 685
Export Transparency command (Help
   menu), 120
exposure, 249–252. *See also* Exposure
   command; Shadow/Highlight
   command
   adjusting
      in Camera Raw, 252, 653
      overall, 249–251
      over limited tonal range, 251–252
   balancing, 657
   overexposed background
      correcting, 12
      preventing with neutral-density filter,
         350
   multiple, combining, 13, 98, 352
   for panoramas, 604, 657
   time, long, 284, 349, 659
   underexposed foreground, correcting,
      12, 169, 267, 275
Exposure command (CS2), 11, 171
Extract command/filter, 13, 62, 63–65,
   629–632
   versus Corel KnockOut 2, 64
   highlighting edges, 629
Extras command, 622
Extrude filter, 747
Eyedropper tool ⟋, sampling color, 158,
   372, 717
eyes
   enhancing, 240, 312
   fixing "eyeshine," 314
   fixing red-eye, 313
   removing puffiness under, 316
"eyeshine" correction, 314

F

Facet filter, 743
Fade command, 31, 178, 220, 634
Fade Match Color command, 634
Fade option, Brushes palette controls,
   363
feathering edges, 56, 59, 80
Fibers filter, 744
   carpet, simulating, 559
   surface texture, 473
   wood, simulating, 559
   woven fabric, simulating, 560
File Browser, 7, 24
   Camera Raw and, 103
   Keywords panel, 129
   metadata, 109
   orientation of files, 109
   Scripts command, 25, 110, 116
   working with multiple files, 25,
      128–133
file compression. *See* compression
File Handling Preferences, 118
   Enable Large Document Format, 119
   Image Previews, 121
   Maximize Compatibility, 118
File Info panel
   descriptions for Web Photo Gallery
      photos, 692
   metadata, 8
file management
   Bridge (CS2), 109–110
   File Browser, 109
   Version Cue, 108
files
   batches, 25
   finding, 132
   renaming
      Bridge (CS2), 130
      File Browser, 129
   resizing, 73–74, 466
   sorting, 130, 131
Fill command, 368, 768
   Color, 210
   patterns, 162
   Use Pattern, 558
Fill layers, 18, 38, 577
   applying color, 158
   versus coloring in regular layers, 413
   file sizes, 385
   fill types, 158–159
   patterns, 162
Fill Opacity, 37, 397, 405, 504–505, 506
   to make element disappear but retain
      Layer Style effects, 405, 455, 500,
      501, 511, 514, 673, 718, 760
filling tools, 367–369

film cameras *versus* digital cameras,
   94–95
Film Grain filter, 736
Filmstrip (view), Bridge (CS2), 128
Filter Gallery, 14, 735
   CMYK mode, 737
   New effect layers, 411
   painting with filters, 369
   recording/saving Actions, 411, 739
   saving filter combinations, 262
Filters
   Adobe, 735–750
   "layering" effects of two or more, 261–
      263, 264–265
   for patterns, 555–560
   Terrazzo 2, 768
Find command (Bridge, CS2), 132
Find Edges filter, 747
   darkening paint edges, 369, 403
   for outlining, 473
flash, 99. *See also* "eyeshine"; red-eye,
   avoiding
   softening shadows caused by, 99, 310,
      325
Flash options, Web Photo Gallery (CS2),
   13
Flash (Macromedia) SWF file format
   animation, 684–685
   exporting, 676, 681, 685
   web graphics, 682–683
Flatten Image command, 20
Flip Horizontal command, 87, 457, 567
Flip Vertical command, 452, 623
focusing attention
   with a dark glow, 295, 300
   Channel Mixer Adjustment layers, 299
   with color, 297, 298, 299, 301
   cropping, 294
   framing with focus, 295
   ghosting
      and tinting, 300
      vignetted ghosting and painting, 296
   Radial Blur masks, 295
   using red, 301
   on selected subjects, 285–290
   spotlighting subjects, 301
folders. *See* groups (CS2); layer sets
Folders panel (Bridge, CS2), 129
Forward Warp tool (Liquify), 617
Fragment filter, 743
frames (animation, ImageReady,
   Photoshop CS2)
   copying/pasting, 700
   creating, 685–686
      by hand, 685, 710–715
      with layer comps, 705–709
      from layers, 685
      with tweening, 685–686, 696–699

K

Kaleidoscope Tile filter, 563
kerning
  Character palette, 423, 450
  type-on-a-path, 426
keyboard shortcuts, 24, 26. *See also* Wow
    Shortcuts.pdf on the Wow DVD-
    ROM
  Actions, 135
  creating/saving (CS2), 8
  Keyboard Shortcuts command, 21, 26
keywords, 131–132
Keywords panel (Bridge (CS2) and File
    Browser), 129
KnockOut 2 (Corel) *versus* Photoshop's
    Extract command, 64
knockouts, 505–506
  for spot color, 230, 232, 233

L

Lab Color mode, 151, 153, 195
  coloring/recoloring images, 224–228
  matching colors, 228
Labeled files (Bridge; CS2), 131
language, spell checking, 422
Large Document Format. *See* PSB file
    format
Lasso tool ⌇, 60–61
  feathering, 56, 304
  selecting irregular shapes, 60
  toggling to Polygonal or Magnetic, 61
layer comps/Layer Comps palette, 10, 21,
    289–290, 335–337, 585–586
  animation using, 705–709
  to compare alternative versions of an
      image, 289–290, 335–337
  slide shows from, 290
Layer Comps To Files command, 10
layer masks, 18, 38, 68, 75–79, 577
  with Adjustment layers, 165, 201, 333
  Blending Options, Blend If, 76, 77, 331
  in building layouts, 635–642
  cleaning up, 66
  contracting, 76, 80
  copying by dragging (CS2), 9
  "double masking" (layer sets/groups)
      79, 584, 670
  editing, 66, 68
  on filtered layers, 78, 328
  framing images, 260–264
  gradients in, 75, 85, 191, 607
  on layer sets/groups, 79, 584, 670
  with Layer Styles, 69
  layering two materials, 543
  linking/unlinking, 68, 80, 543
  in merging, 587

painting, 75, 76, 600,
Paste Into, 68
patterns in, 78
from selections, 68
on sets (CS)/groups (CS2), 79, 577,
    584, 670
shortcuts, 69
softening edges of, 79
with vector masks, 519
Layer Properties dialog box, 113
Layer Set From Linked command,
    583–586
layer sets, 8, 18, 577, 583–584. *See also*
    groups (CS2)
  blend mode, 584. *See also* Pass Through
      blend mode
  creating from layers, 583
  deleting or disbanding, 584–585
  masking, 584
  moving, 584
Layer Style dialog box, 493, 503, 505. *See
    also* Layer Styles
  setting Blending Options, 490–491,
      504–507
    Advanced Blending options, 504–
        505, 523
    "Blend If," 70–71, 76, 331, 333, 505,
        506–507
Layer Styles, 18, 29, 38, 44–47, 490–508.
    See also Layer Styles dialog box;
    Rollover Styles (ImageReady); Styles
    palette; Wow Layer Styles
  applying, 44, 492
  Blending Options, 490–491, 504–507
  bevel, separating from texture, 764
  clipping groups, 79
  color, applying with, 160, 369
  copying, 45, 46
    single effects, 765
  creating layers from, 494
  dragging and dropping, 46
  drawing with, 459
  effects, 494–504
  gradient, applying with, 161, 189, 369
  in ImageReady, 5, 677
  in layer comps, 336, 706–707
  pasting, 45, 46, 492
    to several layers (CS2), 550
  patterns in 162
    placement adjustments, 763
    scaling, 45
  rasterizing for video, 125–126
  resolution, importance of, 47
  in rollover buttons, 718–720
  saving, 47, 490
  scaling, 9, 45, 466, 490, 492, 751, 761
  selections, 69
  texture, 45, 504, 522–524, 764

tweening (animation), 697, 698
  with video, 126
Layer Via Copy command, 286
layer-based slices, 688–689, 724–725
layers, 18, 37–38, 575, 577. *See also*
    Adjustment layers; blend modes; Fill
    layers; layer masks; layer sets/groups;
    Layer Styles; Shape layers; type layers;
    vector masks
  aligning, 82, 575
    linked layers, 27
  animation frames from, 685, 686
  Background, 17
  changing content, 413
  color coding, 577, 585
  converting type to Shape layers, 429, 549
  creating from Layer Styles, 494
  distributing, 27, 716
  duplicating, 20, 30
    layers by copying, 286, 461
    "lightweight copies," 330
    merged layers, 83
  flattening into a *Background,* 20, 564,
      587
  grouping, 18, 79, 341–342, 465, 552, 583
  instruction-based *versus* pixel-based
      elements, 18–20
  layer-based slices, 688–689
  linking, 582
  locking, 360, 577
  merged copies, 30, 409
  merging, 587
  moving, 82
  multiple, 142
  "multitargeting"/ selecting multiple
      layers (CS2), 10, 24, 55, 582, 583
  naming in Actions, 135
  opacity, 37, 82, 577
  rasterizing, 413
  regular layers, 17, 37
  reordering, 586
  "repairs" layers, 30
  transparent, 37
  variables and templates, 10, 11,
      643–649
Layers palette
  blend modes, 173–178, 415
  changes from previous version, 24
  Linked Layers, 582
  Lock icons, 360, 577
  selection, loading as, 67
  styling multiple layers (CS2), 45
  Unify buttons, 684, 686
layout, designing, 636–638. *See also*
    composition
Lens Blur filter, 13, 14, 291–293, 738
  depth of field, reducing, 287–288,
      291–293

N

Natural Media brushes, 378
Natural Scene Designer software, 239
neon effects, 397, 404, 546–550, 766
  animated, 705–709,
  with type, 454–455
Neon Glow filter, 472, 473, 736
nested Actions, 112
nested tables, 689
New Layer Based Slice command, 688
Noise filters, 742
  for restoring film grain, 318–319
  with Healing Brush, 318–319
  for patterns and textures, 556, 557
Noise gradients, 161, 189
  Wow Gradients, 19–26, 187
noise, reducing, 12, 255, 323–324. *See also*
  Reduce Noise filter (CS2)
Normal blend mode, 87, 174
Note Paper filter, 472, 746
NTSC Colors filter, 125, 749
NTSC DV 720 x 480 video format, 141
NTSC (North American) video standard,
  124

O

Ocean Ripple filter, 265, 741
Offset filter, 749
  for finding "seams" in pattern tiles, 562
  for staggering pattern elements, 565
Omnidirectional lighting, 259, 344
onion-skinning technique, 712
Opacity, controlling, 516
opaque ink previews, 233
Open File Browser (CS) or Bridge (CS2)
  command, 128
Open Type fonts, 418, 423
  Creative Suite/Creative Suite 2, 6
Open With Adobe Photoshop CS2
  command (Bridge), 107
Optimize panel/palette, 679, 680, 695,
  720
Optimize To File Size command, 681, 733
Other filters, 745, 749. *See also* High Pass
  filter; Offset filter
Outer Glow effect, 80, 495, 516
  as shadow, 533
out-of-gamut warning, 185, 608–609,
  164–165
Output Settings command (Optimize
  panel), 709, 725
Overlay blend mode, 147, 176, 254
Overlay effects (Layer Styles), 494–497,
  533
Overprint Colors dialog box, 154

P

page layout programs, 441–444. *See also*
  Adobe InDesign
  file formats required, 119
Paint Bucket ♦, 367, 368
Paint Daubs filter, 736
Painter. *See* Corel Painter
painting, 144
  photos for reference, 394
  "post-processing," 369
  with tablet and stylus, 365
  techniques, 359–360
  troubleshooting inability to paint, 360
  watercolor techniques, 370–375
    with Pattern Stamp, 384–387
  wet on wet, 376–380
  with Wow Actions, 398–400
PAL video standard, 124
Palette Knife filter, 736
palettes, docking/nesting, 22
Paragraph palette
  toggling on and off, 422
  type specifications, 419–420, 422
paragraph type, 419–421, 600–602. *See*
  also type
Pass Through blend mode, 178, 512
Paste commands
  Paste As: Paths, 405
  Paste As: Pixels, 526
  Paste As: Shape Layer, 461, 522
  Paste As: Smart Object, 547
  Paste Behind, 68
  Paste Frames, 700
  Paste Into, 68, 144
  Paste Layer Style, 492
  Paste Layer Style to Linked, 45, 46
Patch tool ♦, 13, 253–254
  copying/pasting, 575
  selections, 317
  tint effects, 210
Patchwork filter, 748
Path Selection tool ♦, 438–439, 457
paths, 19, 20, 21, 432–433, 439
  in Adobe Illustrator, 441–444
  aligning, 439, 442
  anchor points, 432, 433, 435, 437–438
  clipping paths, 445–446
  combining, 432, 459
  converting to Shape layers, 438
  editing, 435, 437–439
  filling, 439–440
  hand-drawn with Pen tool, 424
  pasting, 405
  preset paths or shapes, 424
  reshaping, 458
  selection, loading as, 67
  stroking, 439–440
  stroking and filling, 439–440
  subpaths, 438
  transforming, 439
  type-on-a-path, 417–418, 424–426, 428
  warping, 442
  Work Path, 21, 433, 438
Paths palette, 433
  Work Path, 21
Pattern brushes (Illustrator), 442
Pattern metering (digital camera), 97
Pattern Fill layers, 41, 469, 470, 480
  for backgrounds, 288–289
  layer masks, 78
Pattern Maker filter, 560
Pattern Overlay effect, 198, 199, 369, 483,
  495, 496–497, 498
Pattern Stamp ♣, 366
  versus Art History Brush, 384–387
  patterns, 162
  watercolors, 384–387
patterns. *See also* Wow Patterns
  adding to Patterns palette, 565
  applying, 162, 565, 768
  applying color, 162
  blending edges, 563
  defining, 41, 210, 318, 565
  in layer masks, 78
  scaling, 761
  seamless, 562
  Tile Maker filter, 563
  viewing, 497
Patterns palette, 469
PBM (portable bitmap) file format,
  32-Bits/Channel mode (CS2), 122
PDF from Layer Comps command, 10
PDF Image command, 107
PDF (Portable Document Format) file
  format
  Automate > Multipage PDF to PSD
    command, 107
  file transfer and storage, 120
  files readable outside Photoshop users,
    119–120
  Import > PDF Image command, 107
  Open With > Adobe Photoshop CS2
    command (CS2), 107
Pen tool ♦, 424, 434, 435, 437, 458. *See*
  also Magnetic Pen tool
  calligraphic outlines, 80
  combining options, 432
  modes of operation, 431
  style and color options, 432
Pencil tool ✏, 359, 360, 363, 364
Photo Filter Adjustment layer or
  command (CS2), 12, 78, 169, 272
  tint effects, 204–205

remote rollovers, 688, 691, 721–728

Remove Black/White Matte commands, 66, 67

Remove Distortion tool (Lens Correction), 276, 278, 282

Render filters, 737, 744. *See also* Fibers filter; Lens Flare filter; Lighting Effects filters

Replace Color command, 168

Resample Image, Bicubic Sharper command, 142, 466

resampling, 9, 73, 74, 140, 689
- Bicubic Sharper, 142, 255, 466
- Bicubic Smoother, 95, 148, 474
- Image Size dialog box, 73, 74
- printing images, 74
- Resize Image Wizard/Assistant, 73
- resizing up or down, 73–74
- in saving for web, 689

Reset Character/Paragraph commands, 422

Resize Image Wizard/Assistant, 73

Reticulation filter, 472, 746

Reveal in Bridge command (CS2), 7, 22

Reverse Frames command, 700

Revert command, 31, 551

RGB Color mode, 151–152, 525
- applying filters, 737
- converting to CMYK, 184–185, 221
- in ImageReady, 647

RGB color space, 179

right-clicking, 25

Ripple filter, 264, 603, 741

rock surface, simulating, 555, 564, 764

Rollover Styles. *See also* Wow Rollover Styles
- combined Rollover Styles (ImageReady), 677, 678
- Layer Styles, 677, 678
- Wow Button Styles, 676

rollovers, 688, 690–691
- modifying existing rollovers, 720
- remote rollovers, 688, 691, 721–728
- states, 716–720, 725–726

Rotate Canvas command, 378

Rotate Image tool (Photomerge), 580

Rough Pastels filter, 471, 736

round corners, 759

Rounded Rectangle tool ⬜, 433, 434, 637–638

Rubber Band mode (Pen tool), 434

rulers, 27, 456

S

sampling color
- Color Sampler tool 🎯, 162–163, 253
  - Lab numbers, 226
- Eyedropper tool 🖊, 158, 371
- from gradient preview bar, 190

Satin effect, 500–501, 516, 524

saturation, increasing/decreasing, 254–255

Saturation blend mode, 178

Save As commands
- Alternate (CS2), 108
- Embed Color Profile option, 180
- JPEG, 120–121
- Photoshop PDF, 119–120

Save for Web dialog box, 675, 679
- Preview in Browser option, 691

Save for Web Eyedropper (CS2), 709

Save Optimized As command, 681, 687, 728

Save Workspace command (CS2), 109–110

scalable designs, 460–466

Scale command, 71

Scale Effects dialog box, 751

Scale Styles option, 9, 466, 490, 751

scanning
- color depth, 89
- color mode, 90, 91
- 3D, rainbow glare, 90
- film scanners, 90
- flatbed scanners, 89
- image dimensions, 90–91
- multiple images, 92
- PDF images, 107
- pepper grain elimination, 93
- prescanning, 90
- printed material, 92
- resolution, 90, 91–92
- stock photography, 106

Screen blend mode, 31, 175, 532, 548
- layer masks, 77

screen-captures as comps, 232–233

Script Events Manager (CS2), 118
- Actions, 112
- Display Camera Maker.jsx, 116
- new feature, 9

scripts, layer comps, 10

Scripts command, 25, 110, 116
- Image Processor (CS2), 112, 116, 278

scrubbing, 3

Search command (File Browser), 132

SECAM (French) video standard, 124

Select All Frames command, 704

Select Image tool (Photomerge), 580

selections
- antialiased edges, 56
- Blending Options, 70–71
- by color, 56–58
- by color range, 616
- dragging, keys/options, 87
- erasers, 61
- feathered edges, 56, 59, 80, 296
- by hand or procedural methods, 55
- linking slices for optimizing, 728
- loading, 67
- modifying, 65–66
  - contracting, 476, 706
  - expanding, 706
- recovering lost selections, 56
- reversing, 297, 298
- saving, 67
  - as clipping groups, 70
  - as layer masks, 68
  - Layer Styles, 69
  - as vector masks, 68, 69
- by shape, 59–60
- stairstepped edges, 56
- targeting multiple layers (CS2), 10, 24, 55
- transforming, 478, 479
  - Free Transform, Options bar, 71–72
  - Warp option, 71

Selective Color Adjustment layer or command, 84–85, 168–169, 235, 237

sepiatone photos, 196–199, 201

service bureaus, 119

Set Gray Point eyedropper, 270, 306

Shadow effects, 498–499, 498–500

Shadow/Highlight command, 12, 84, 169–171, 267, 275, 321, 324–325, 329, 576, 578

shape and color selections
- Background Eraser tool, 62–63, 65
- Cleanup tool (Extract), 63, 64
- Edge Touchup tool (Extract), 64
- Extract command, 55, 63–65
- Magnetic Lasso tool, 61–62
- Smart Highlighting (Extract), 63, 64

Shape Blur filter (CS2), 14, 737–738

Shape Burst Gradient Stroke effect, 190, 501